THE END OF EMPIRE

Napoleon's 1814 Campaign

George Nafziger

Helion & Company

Helion & Company Limited
Unit 8 Amherst Business Centre
Budbrooke Road
Warwick
CV34 5WE
England
Tel. 01926 499 619
Fax 0121 711 4075
Email: info@helion.co.uk
Website: www.helion.co.uk
Twitter: @helionbooks
Printed by Lightning Source Limited, Milton Keynes, Buckinghamshire

Published by Helion & Company 2015. Reprinted in paperback 2019
Designed and typeset by Mach 3 Solutions Ltd (www.mach3solutions.co.uk)
Cover designed by Paul Hewitt, Battlefield Design (www.battlefield-design.co.uk)
Printed by Hobbs the Printers, Totton, Hampshire

Front cover: 'Le Marin de la Garde pendant la campagne de France en 1814' by 'Peintre des armées' Louis Frégier. Rear cover: Charge of the Württemberg Dragoons at La Rothière, by Richard Knötel.

ISBN 978-1-911628-38-5

British Library Cataloguing-in-Publication Data.
A catalogue record for this book is available from the British Library.

Contents

List of Illustrations

List of Maps

Maps drawn by Bill Russ

Terrain and Military Symbology Key For Tactical (Battlefield) Maps

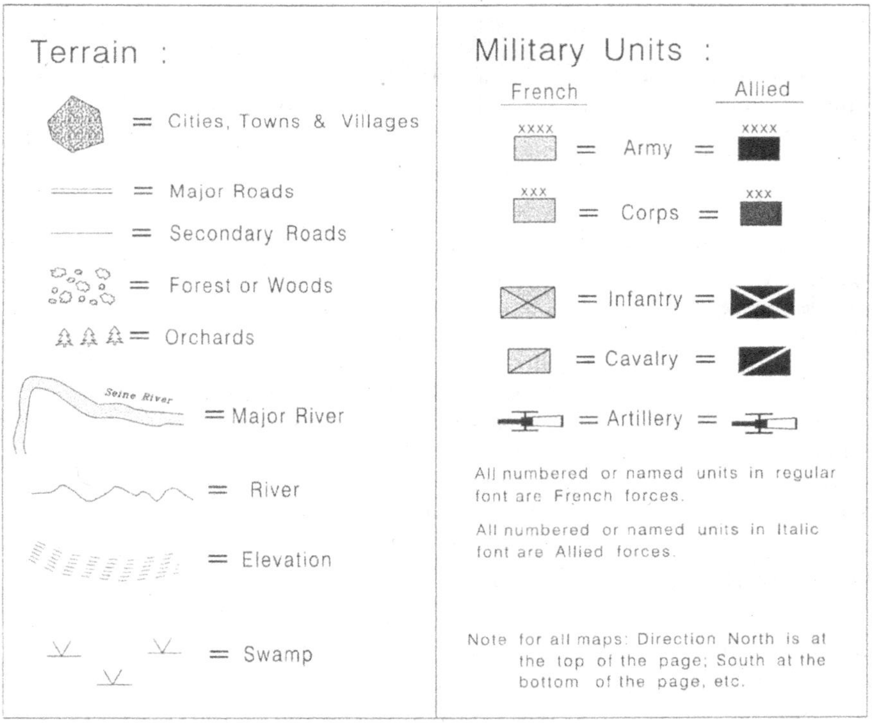

Terrain and Military Symbology Key For Strategic Maps

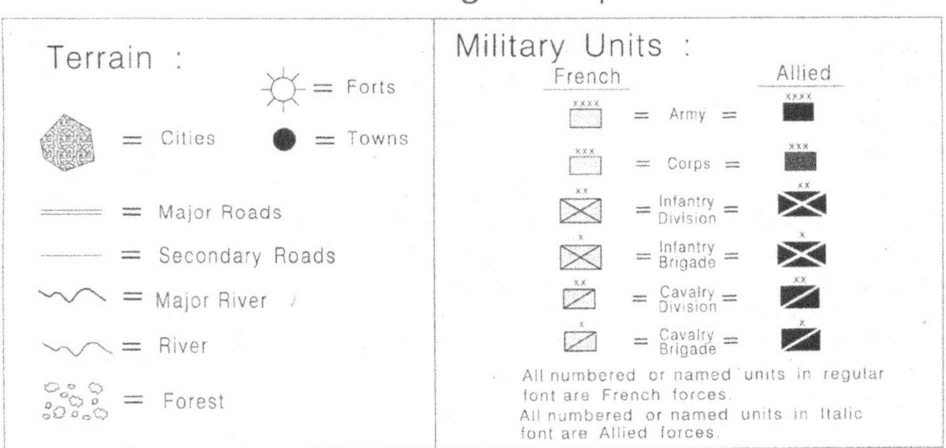

Abbreviations and Terminology

For simplicity's sake, some abbreviations are used for many officers' ranks. In some instances, the full title is used where it is not particularly long. The ranks and their equivalents in current ranks are:

French

Maréchal	Field Marshal
Général de division	Major General (GD)
Général de brigade	Brigadier General (GB)
Colonel	Colonel
Major	Lt. Colonel
Chef d'escadron	Major (cavalry and horse artillery)
Chef de bataillon	Major (infantry and foot artillery)
Capitaine	Captain
Lieutenant	1st Lieutenant
Sous-lieutenant	2nd Lieutenant

Prussian, Russian and most German states

Feldmarschall	Field Marshal (FM)
General der Kavallerie	Lieutenant General (GdK)
General der Infanterie	Lieutenant General (GdI)
Generallieutenant	Major General
Generalmajor	Brigadier General (GM)
Oberst	Colonel
Oberstleutnant	Lt. Colonel (OBL)
Major	Major
Rittmeister	Captain (cavalry)
Hauptmann, Kapitän	Captain (infantry)
Leutnant	1st Lieutenant
Unterleutnant	2nd Lieutenant

Austrian

Feldmarschall	Field Marshal (FM)
General der Kavallerie	General "of Cavalry" (GdK)
General der Infanterie	General "of Infantry" (GdI)
Feldzeugmeister	Lieutenant General (FZM)
Feldmarschal-lieutenant	Major General (FML)
Generalmajor	Brigadier General (GM)
Oberst	Colonel
Oberstleutnant	Lt. Colonel

Rittmeister	Captain (cavalry)
Hauptmann, Kapitän	Captain (infantry)
Leutnant	1st Lieutenant
Unterleutnant	2nd Lieutenant

Note: The term used for an infantry captain in German has changed over the years and varies from source to source. All of the following terms are common forms of the German for 'captain': Hauptmann, Kapitain, Kapitän and Capitain.

Introduction

The 1814 campaign is probably one of the most interesting of all of Napoleon's campaigns. Despite the handicaps under which he operated, Napoleon was like a cornered lion fighting for his very existence as, indeed, he was. The campaign is filled with brilliant maneuvers and stunning victories. It also contains a few blunders that could have cost Napoleon dearly had the Allies been quicker or more aggressive. It is also one of the least known of Napoleon's campaigns – being examined by very few English-language works. For that matter, there are very few detailed works in any language and the entire campaign is relatively under-documented.

The remains of the Grande Armée fell back from its disaster at Leipzig and across the Rhine in December 1813. The disaster that had befallen Napoleon in 1813 was only marginally less than what had befallen him in 1812. In contrast, however, the war was now on the borders of France. In addition, he did not have the reserves to call upon as he had in 1813. Furthermore, though he did have some reserves of manpower and equipment upon which to draw, he did not have time to train them. His situation was, in fact, worse in 1814 than it had been in January 1813.

It is very easy to criticize many of Napoleon's maneuvers and his eagerness to accept battle on every count. He plunged headlong at his enemies time and time again. His aggressive attacks resulted in the total destruction of two Allied corps and the near-destruction of two more. This same aggressive behavior more than once put him in the unenviable position of having bitten off far more than he could ever hope to chew. Any aggressive move on the part of the Allies should have resulted in his total destruction, but time and again they missed these opportunities. Napoleon had no choice and the Allies played a very, very cautious game.

It is necessary that the reader understand this single fact: Napoleon had no choice but to engage the Allies at every opportunity if he had the slightest chance of inflicting significant damage on the Allies. His army was little more than a shadow of what it had been in past years and he was fighting on his own territory. Any gain the Allies made cut into the muscle and bone of his empire and kicked more of the supports away from his throne.

On the other hand, any blow he could strike against the Allies would cause them to hesitate more and more to engage him. If he were able to inflict enough damage on the Allies, Napoleon had a chance of convincing them to withdraw and come to an armistice that would permit him to retain his throne.

If Napoleon lost a decisive battle, the outcome of the campaign would not be significantly different than if he fought only those that he was assured to win. On the other hand, passing up a battle that he might win was a victory for the Allies. If he engaged in a battle and it turned against him but he escaped, Napoleon lost nothing. If he engaged in a risky battle and won, then he increased the chances of holding his throne. What the reader must realize is that in any given battle Napoleon really had very little to lose and everything to win. As Napoleon no longer had his reputation of invincibility to protect, if the battle turned against him Napoleon had nothing whatsoever to lose by withdrawing.

Napoleon's army was a mere shadow of its former self. In order to hold as many men as possible in the ranks, a larger number of conscripts were placed in the Imperial Guard. The hope was that the honor of being a guardsman – even Young Guard – would hold them in the ranks. Solid veterans were drawn from as many places as possible and placed in the Old Guard as well. Though the guard formations were short of their full strength, the strength of the line formations was often minimal. Divisions frequently had strengths of 3-4,000 men – the equivalent of a regiment in 1813. Entire regiments were reduced to the strength of a battalion. Battalions frequently were reduced to the strength of 100 men – a single company. In previous works it was frequently possible to identify the positions and actions of individual regiments. In 1814 this becomes nearly impossible. All the maps and most of the discussions speak only of French divisions and brigades. It is very possible that all the fragmented regiments and battalions in a division were consolidated into battalion-sized formation – permitting them to operate effectively on the battlefield – but no comments to this effect were found.

French records from the Section historique de l'armée du terre at Château Vincennes and the Archives Nationales are very incomplete. Unlike the records for 1813, there are great holes in the army returns for 1814. Battle accounts speak of various formations that cannot be found in the bi-monthly army states. It is, as a result, very difficult to determine the structure of the forces that were present for the French at the various battles fought in 1814.

Of course, the German records were destroyed in the bombings of the Second World War so it became necessary to rely on reputable, but nonetheless secondary, published sources. As a result, though the accounts of the battles are reasonably well documented, identifying the forces that were there has proven exceptionally difficult (and in some cases, impossible).

It is appropriate, at this point, to mention a number of individuals without whose help this work could not have been prepared. As with any history, this one is dependent on the sources with which one has to work. The accumulation of those works frequently becomes – as a result of problems of geography – a collective effort. In some instances languages add yet another barrier. This work is no different.

I am greatly indebted to Nick Semibratov, who graciously translated parts of a number of Russian works – including Bogdanovich's account – and allowed me to work into the manuscript details from the Russian perspective.

The Archives Nationales in Paris was also most helpful – though part of their regular operations (the microfilming of the army returns that they hold) contributed greatly to the development of the picture of the French army throughout the 1814 campaign.

Peter Hofschröer and Geert van Uythoven provided me with copies of a number of invaluable works from personal archives and other sources to which they had access.

I also wish to acknowledge a few close friends who functioned as readers. Their comments and criticisms were both helpful and appreciated: CDR Chris Janiec and Warren Worley.

1

The 1814 Campaign Begins

France was stripped of its last Allies. They had fallen away one after the other. Mecklenburg, Austria, Bavaria, Saxony, Hesse-Darmstadt, Württemberg and Baden had all defected to the Allies – and with their departure, Napoleon's newly-created states of Westphalia and Cleves-Berg had also collapsed… their lands reverting to their former rulers.

The face of Europe had changed. Napoleon's federated empire had collapsed and France was faced with invasion and destruction for the first time since 1793.

The Allies recognized that in order to end the threat of Napoleon to their dream of Europe it was necessary not only to invade France, but to take Paris. It is difficult to determine if they recognized that France was fatigued from so many years of war – and would cease to support Napoleon once Paris was captured – or if they were continuing the traditional style of where victory was determined by the capture of the enemy's capitol. They had not – and did not – fight a war with the idea of destroying the enemy's armies as the key to victory. It was, therefore, necessary in their eyes to invade France and capture Paris.

Any advance by the Allies was faced with the defensive system the French had established on their eastern frontier. France was defended by a belt of 140 fortresses. In the past they had been key in her defense, but now with the reduced state of French military readiness, France was utterly unable to garrison and provision them fully. Should the Allies act quickly, the road to Paris was open.[1]

Between Coblentz and Nijmegen along the Rhine, the French frontier was defended by the two great fortresses of Mainz and Wesel. However, behind them stood three far stronger lines of fortifications. These lines extended from the North Sea at Dunkirk and Ostend, along the course of the Meuse to Givet and Mézières. From there it moved along the river via Montmédy, Longwy and Luxemburg. Between the old-line defensive line and the Rhine there were the fortresses of Juliers, Maëstricht, Venlo, Grave, Gorkum, Bergen-op-Zoom, Flushing and Antwerp. Though these fortresses were structured for the defense of Holland and not the French frontier, they provided a strong bastion against which the left of the French defenses of the Rhine could rest – and made any quick advance through the Lowlands into France next to impossible.

To the south of this heavily-fortified region along the French-Belgian border, another line of French fortresses ran along the course of the Meuse and the Rhine. There were strong fortresses in Landau, Luxemburg, Montmédy, Maubeuge, Lille and Dunkirk.

Facing the Allied center, the course of the Rhine was not defended by any fortresses between Huningue and Fort-Louis. The lines of communication between the fortresses on the Rhine and those of the Meuse were established through Metz, Thionville, Sarrelouis, Bitche, Phalsbourg, and Landau – all of which were fortified. Once clear of these, the Allies would advance further into France and they would encounter still further fortresses along the main roads running between Paris and the German frontier.

---

1 Burghersh, pp. 63-4.

To the Allied left was a neutral Switzerland and whose frontier was covered in France only by Belfort and Besançon. However, Switzerland's mountains made it a difficult passage. In addition, to the west of the Rhine – stretching south from Kaiserslautern to Belfort – were the Vosges Mountains. Belfort effectively plugged the gap and the roads running from Basel, Switzerland (the last passage over the Rhine before entering the Swiss Alps). Then, screening any advance out of neutral Switzerland was screened by the Jura Mountains that stretched south towards Geneva.

Any significant Allied advance would have to pass north of the Vosges Mountains. It would have to pass through Metz, Thionville, Luxemburg or Liège.

Once clear of the Rhine and its fortresses, the Allies would face a number of river lines that were militarily significant and would funnel their advance along a limited number of lines – all of which crossed a number of rivers that formed natural barriers and all the major passages over these rivers were protected by significant fortresses.

The Moselle River runs from Coblentz south through Thionville, Metz, Nancy and into the foothills of the Vosges Mountains. It was fordable only south of Nancy in its uppermost reaches. The other two principal rivers in this region are the Seine and the Marne. They were rarely fordable in the winter (and then only in their upper regions). The Aube is the most important tributary joining the Seine. It is only fordable in the driest of weather. Other tributaries of the Seine are the Yonne and the Loing, which also form significant military barriers.

The Marne has three major tributaries: the Grand-Morin, Petit-Morin and the Ourcq. The first two are minor streams, but their marshy banks turned them into major obstacles. The Ourcq was a more significant river, but it was lined with marshes that were even heavier than those along the Grand and Petit-Morin.

The Aisne flows east to west through Béry-au-Bac and Soissons. It was a significant stream and generally unfordable. It was joined by the Vesle, a minor stream, which ran through Rheims and joined the Aisne above Soissons. The Lette, or Ailette, was to the north and flowed parallel to the Aisne. Both it and the Aisne were tributaries of the Oise.

An Allied advance south from Liège would have to move through Mons, Avesnes, Laon, Soissons and to Paris. South of Laon was the Aisne River, running east and west. Both Laon and Soissons were heavily fortified. As an alternative route from Liège, the Allies could advance south to Mézières – a strong fortress which protected a crossing over the Lower Meuse. Once the Meuse was crossed, the line ran south across the Aisne to Rheims, which was also fortified. From there the main road to Paris moved along the course of the Marne – often re-crossing it as it meanders across plains outside Paris.

Moving from either Coblentz or Mainz required a crossing of the Moselle. This required passage at Tréves – a fortress – and then to the massive fortress at Luxemburg (or moving south to Thionville or Metz – also significant fortresses). Both Thionville and Metz stood on the Moselle and would have to be taken before any further advance into France was possible.

From either Thionville or Metz both roads to Paris moved through the fortress of Verdun, which guarded the passage over the Meuse. From Verdun the line of advance crossed the Upper Aisne and moved to Châlons – another major fortress. Once again the road to Paris moved down the Marne.

To the south of the Metz-Paris road there were a number of options. Crossing the Moselle at Nancy, a major road ran due west across the Meuse to St.-Dizier or Vitry – both on the Marne. From there either line of advance to Paris ran through the plain between the Aube and the Marne rivers.

Moving south of that line – crossing the Marne at Joinville – the roads west ran through Brienne, crossing the Aube River to Troyes, where it crossed the Seine River. From there the road followed course of the Seine to Nogent and Montereau where it crossed the Seine and moved on to Paris.

These rivers formed a strong line of defense and nearly every passage over them was blocked by a significant fortress. If properly manned and equipped, these fortresses promised to make any Allied advance into France a long and difficult process.

Mainz.

During the first days of November 1813, Napoleon brought the remains of the Grande Armée back across the Rhine into metropolitan France. It now contained only about 60,000 men. The French army was then deployed along the left bank of the Rhine in order to defend against the coming invasion. The urgency of the danger and the enormous disparity in military forces remaining to the two belligerents required that Napoleon act promptly.[2]

The French army

The French army – after it had withdrawn across the Rhine – was unable to place sufficient force in place to defend the river should the Allies decide that they wished to force a passage. The losses the French had suffered in Leipzig and the withdrawal back to France were such that a reorganization was absolutely necessary.

The I and XIV Corps remained in Dresden; the IX and X Corps were in Danzig; the XIII Corps was in Hamburg. The IV Corps had been reduced to Morand's 12th Division after the departure of the Fontanelli's 15th (Italian) Division and the defection of Württemberg, which removed Franquemont's 38th Division.

2 de Vauconcourt, Vol. I, p. 49.

The VIII Corps had been dissolved during the Battle of Leipzig and the XII Corps had been dissolved after the Battle of Gross-Beeren. So too were the Armée d'Observation de Bavaria and the IV Cavalry Corps. All that remained were the shattered remains of the II, III, V, VI, VIII and XI Corps and the I, II, III and V Cavalry Corps. Many of these so-called corps consisted of a single division. In early December the French army was deployed as follows:

Unit	Commander	Location
II Corps	Victor	around Worms
III Corps	Ricard	at Bechtheim
IV Corps	Morand	in the Netherlands
V Corps	Sébastiani	at Ingelheim
VI Corps	Marmont	at Oppenheim
VII Corps	Durutte	at Cassel, before Mainz
XI Corps	Macdonald	at Nijmegen
I Cavalry Corps	Bordesoulle	at Simmern
II Cavalry Corps	Excelmans	in Cologne
III Cavalry Corps	Arrighi	in Andernach
V Cavalry Corps	Milhaud	on the Upper Rhine

As of 1 December 1813 the strength of the Grande Armée was as follows:[3]

		Officers & Men Under Arms
1st Old Guard Division	Friant	5,075
2nd Old Guard Division	Curial	1,486
1st Young Guard Division	Dumoustier	1,602
2nd Young Guard Division	Decouz	1,246
2nd Guard Corps		
3rd Young Guard Division	Boyer de Rebeval	2,588
4th Young Guard Division		4,199
3rd Young Guard Corps		
5th Young Guard Division	Rottembourg	908
6th Young Guard Division	Roguet	8,700
Guard Cavalry Division	Duke of Trévise	
1st Guard Cavalry Division		10,785
Guard Park		5,880
I Corps	Maison	4,910
II Corps	Victor	10,436
IV Corps	Morand	24,523
V Corps	Sébastiani	6,539
VI Corps	Marmont	18,506
XI Corps	Macdonald	9,831
I Cavalry Corps	Bordesoulle	3,215
II Cavalry Corps	Excelmans	2,683
III Cavalry Corps	Arrighi	2,021
V Cavalry Corps	Milhaud	3,973
	Total:	129,106

3 French National Archives, Carton AF^{IV} 1346.

On 15 December there were 11,654 officers and men of the National Guards under arms in the 5th Military Division. Finally, there was a force of about 50,000 disorganized stragglers, sick and wounded who flowed back from Germany.

The V Corps was soon reduced to a single division under the command of Albert and passed to the command of Macdonald. It then moved towards Cologne. The II Corps moved to the Upper Rhine under the command of Victor. The III and VI Corps were reduced to a single division. The VII Corps had only contained Durutte's division since Leipzig.

The left wing, under Macdonald, contained the XI Corps – now joined by Albert's division – and the II and III Cavalry Corps. Its right wing stood on Cologne and its left on Nijmegen, Holland.

A new corps was being organized by Nancy under the orders of Maréchal Ney. The Imperial Guard was in Paris, with part in Châlons and in Troyes.[4] These forces totaled only about 45,000 men.

The Duke of Castiglione, Maréchal Augereau, was assigned the duties of organizing the French forces around Lyon. In Belgium stood a scratch force organized by Molitor. It contained only a few French battalions plus a number of foreign battalions whose loyalty was doubtful. Napoleon directed large numbers of his new conscripts into Antwerp in order to provide the fortress with as strong a garrison as he could. He also ordered Vice-Admiral Decrès, Minister of the Navy, to dispatch every gunboat he could to Holland. Later, Napoleon would send Roguet's Young Guard Division to join Molitor and this force would eventually be renamed the I Corps.

Napoleon still held onto Italy and he directed Eugène Beauharnais to organize a force of six divisions to defend that region from the pending Austrian invasion. Eugène was married to a Bavarian Princess. His father-in-law had offered to him, in the name of the Allies, that if he should abandon Napoleon the Allies would give him a principality in Italy for his own. Eugène chose to reject the offer – stating that it was better for his father-in-law to receive in Munich a son-in-law without a crown than a son-in-law without honor.[5]

Initially, Eugène found himself with about 30,000 men facing an Austrian force of 60,000 men. Napoleon would soon adjust this by sending 40,000 conscripts raised in the 7th, 8th and 19th Military Divisions to Armée de reserve d'Italie.[6] In addition, a further 15,000 men were dispatched to Alexandria to complete the battalions already there.[7] If given the time to organize them, Napoleon hoped to have a force of 100,000 men organized for the defense of Italy.

Napoleon's brother-in-law – Joachim Murat, King of Naples – had abandoned Napoleon in October 1813 and returned to his kingdom. In November 1813 he had marched north from Naples – leading an army of 30,000 men and giving Napoleon the impression that he was going to join Eugène in fighting the Austrians. However, Napoleon's faith in Murat was understandably low. The French position in Italy depended heavily on the actions of Murat. Napoleon stated that: "If the King of Naples enters the country of Rome with his army, crosses the departments of Tuscany, to move to the Po River, he is to be well-received and his troops treated as well as is possible."[8]

The third major force available to Napoleon was his army in Spain. These were, without a doubt, his best and most seasoned troops. On 1 December 1813 forces were assigned as follows:

4 de Vauconcourt, Vol. I, pp. 73-4.
5 Thiry, p. 6.
6 Napoleon's Correspondence, No. 20908.
7 Napoleon's Correspondence, No. 20909.
8 Napoleon's Correspondence, No. 20933.

	Officers & Men Under Arms
Garrison of Bayonne	9,204
Army of Spain	85,439[1]
Combined Armies of Aragon and Catalonia	36,216[2]
Total:	130,859

Notes:
1 This figure includes a large number of forces in various garrisons and some Italian forces, but all the Spanish and German units have been deleted. French National Archives, AF^{IV} 1578.
2 This figure includes a large number of troops in various garrisons. French National Archives, AF^{IV} 1579.

The Army of Spain defended the Pyrenees against Allied incursions by the 45,000 English under Wellington, 15,000 Portuguese and 40,000 Spanish that, after the loss of San Sebastian and Pampaluna, stood in the Hendaye region.

The Combined Armies of Aragon and Catalonia faced another force of 70,000 English, Sicilians and Catalans in the eastern Pyrenees.

To supplement this force, in mid-November Napoleon ordered the formation of a Reserve Army of the Pyrenees. It was to be organized with 20 regiments – each with two battalions. On 20 December 1813 this army had four divisions. The battalions of the 1st Division arrived in Bordeaux between 14 and 20 December. Half of its 1,260 men were conscripts. Half of the 2nd Division had not arrived and what was present contained only 464 men. The 3rd and 4th Divisions were present, but contained only 932 and 925 men respectively. Almost all of the battalions present were little more than officer and NCO cadres waiting to be filled out with new conscripts.[9]

Napoleon had another force of veteran troops, but they were beyond his recall. These forces were trapped in the various garrisons in Germany and Poland. Their numbers were significant and they did serve him by holding large numbers of Allied troops in Germany. However, he might well have made better use of their forces if they had been with him in France instead of locked up in Germany.

Danzig held the X Corps and had been under siege since 21 January 1813. Its ordeal was to last until 2 January 1814 when it surrendered to the Allies with an agreement that the garrison would be given the 'honors of war'. However, the agreement was treacherously repudiated by the Tsar. Of the 35,934 in the initial garrison, only about 10,000 remained on 2 January and they were taken prisoner.[10]

Dresden and Torgau were to suffer similar fates and Allied treachery. Dresden had a large garrison of 35,000 men formed of the reorganized I and XIV Corps. Against it the Allies deployed a force of about 40,000 men. On 17 November 1813 the French surrendered to the Allies, who promptly broke their agreement with the French relating to the 'honors of war' and took them all prisoner.

Torgau was a small fortress of the first order on the Elbe. When besieged by the Allies its garrison consisted of 24,650 men. It held out until 10 January 1814. Once again the Allies repudiated their agreement in the armistice and took the French garrison prisoner.

In Hamburg Davout had the 42,000-man XIII Corps, with which he contained 60,000 Allied soldiers. He did not surrender his command until after Napoleon capitulated in April 1814.

Glogau had started the 1813 fall campaign with a garrison of 6,492. The siege was to last until 17 April 1814 when 1,700 French marched back to France. Magdeburg was another major fortress.

9 The strength figures are officers and men under arms. French National Archives, AF^{IV} 1578.
10 D'Artois, p. 454.

Alexander I of Russia, by F. Kruger.

Frederick Wilhelm III of Prussia.

It held out until 16 May 1814 when its 4,000-man-strong garrison of Magdeburg marched out of the fortress. Erfurt had a garrison of 5,000 men when it was besieged by the Allies. It too was to hold out until the end of the 1814 campaign. It surrendered on 6 May. The siege of Marienberg began after the Battle of Leipzig. It had a garrison of 2,000 men. It held out until 21 May 1814 when orders arrived from Paris directing that it surrender.

There were a number of other garrisons. Wesel had a garrison of 10,000 men. It surrendered on 10 May 1814. The Fortress of Kastel had a small garrison and was only blockaded. It surrendered on 19 April 1814. Modlin – a fortress in Poland – capitulated on 2 November and on 1 December 1813 the garrison surrendered. Zamosc – another fortress in Poland – capitulated on 23 November and on 25 November 1813.

With his forces deployed in this manner, Napoleon awaited the opening of the 1814 campaign and the invasion of France. He busied himself with the raising of new drafts for his army; replacing lost equipment in the standing divisions; and in preparing the French fortresses to resist the advance of the Allied armies.

The rebuilding of the Grande Armée

Once the remains of the Grande Armée were across the Rhine, Napoleon moved without delay to Paris and occupied himself with the reorganization of his army. The last conscription order had been issued on 7 October 1813. It was ordered by a Sénatus-Consulte vote in the presence of Marie-Louise and placed 280,000 conscripts at the disposal of the Minister of War. This was not, however, sufficient as Napoleon felt he needed 500,000 men. The Sénatus-Consulte of 12 November 1813 was issued after the defection of Saxony and Bavaria. It ordered the raising of 300,000 men drawn from the classes of the Draft Years 11, 13, 14, 1806 through 1814. Of these, 150,000 men were to report for processing without delay in order to be placed in the field to face the Allied advance. The remaining 150,000 were to be held in reserve and called to arms if France was invaded. This conscription was drawn from all men aged 20 to 35 – or about 2,300,000 men.

However, as Napoleon returned to his capitol, circumstances became more pressing. He published a number of decrees to work in conjunction with the Sénatus-Consulte. The first, of 20 November 1813, raised the initial conscription of 120,000 men authorized by the Sénatus-Consulte of 9 October to 160,000 men.[11]

He then issued the Imperial Decree of 17 November, which ordered the formation of 457 cohorts of National Guard and 54 companies of artillery. This included 127 cohorts of grenadiers (each with 500 men), 260 cohorts with 300 men each and 70 cohorts of fusiliers or mixed cohorts (each with 500 men). Napoleon intended that these cohorts would be used to guard the various fortresses and to police the open towns.[12]

Then Napoleon issued the Imperial Decrees of 30 December 1813 and 6 January 1814 which ordered the raising of 140,000 new National Guards to form active legions that would be called upon according to military needs.

Napoleon now directed that all men aged 20 to 40 be reorganized into two bans. The first ban contained 11,702,800 men – of whom 644,400 men were unmarried. The second ban contained 2,783,000 men – with 1,113,200 unmarried men.[13]

A total of more than 900,000 men were called to the flag, but this number was an illusion. The actual numbers fell short because of a growing rate of draft evasion; the lack of weapons and uniforms; and also the events of the campaign.

To provide these new drafts with officers Napoleon directed that only the 1st Battalion and the 1st Squadron of each regiment were to remain in the field with the army. All officers and non-commissioned officers exceeding the normal compliment were to return to the depots and to become cadres for the new conscripts that were to arrive in the depots.

The conscription that started in the fall of 1813 began quietly enough, but without enthusiasm. A total of 184,000 men were raised. However, the second draft – calling up 150,000 men from the class of 1815 – encountered considerable resistance in the southern and western provinces. In order to meet the draft requirements, the prefects found themselves having to call upon married and family men. Of those who evaded the draft, many joined bands which withdrew into the forests. Finally, at the end of December, several tens of thousands of conscripts were dispatched to the processing centers.[14]

The formation of the National Guard was critical. It was to be formed of married men destined to serve as garrisons for the cities in the interior of France. They were only rarely to be used in battle. These men were able to purchase replacements, but those were both rare and very expensive. The National Guard, organized or reduced to its original organization, offered Napoleon considerable resources. Seemingly, they offered enough to resist the pending invasion even though Napoleon could no longer count on the French departments in northern Italy – nor on the Kingdom of Northern Italy.

11 Thiry, p. 9.
12 de Vauconcourt, Vol. I, p. 50.
13 de Vauconcourt, Vol. I, p. 60.
14 Thiry, p. 10.

The procurement of manpower was only part of the process. After the men were gathered it was necessary to train them, to equip them and to arm them. Napoleon ordered the formation of additional uniform and equipment manufacturing facilities for the necessary equipment in the major cities of Paris, Bordeaux, Lyon, Toulouse, Montpellier and Metz. These were to provide the uniforms and other equipment necessary for his new armies.

The question of horses remained as serious as it had in 1813. Napoleon ordered the replacement of 5,000 useless horses and the procurement of another 5,000 immediately. He then directed the procurement of another 10,000 horses. These 20,000 horses would be enough for the immediate needs of the army, but not more.

The question of muskets was significant. The Grande Armée had lost 700,000 muskets in Russia and Germany. Further significant numbers of weapons were maintained in the various besieged garrisons in Germany. There was a critical shortage of firearms in the Empire. At the end of December in the 1st Military Division – that of Paris – there were 9,195 men and only 6,530 muskets. The depots of the 16th Division had 15,789 men and only 9,470 muskets. To the west – in the Midi and central France – the situation was even worse. The 153rd Line Regiment had 1,088 men and only 142 muskets while the 115th Line had 2,344 men and 289 muskets.[15]

Napoleon reacted by withdrawing the carbines from the dragoons and having them issued to the infantry. He then directed Clarke to disarm the colonial and foreign regiments and pass their weapons to the French line infantry. This effort in disarming foreign regiments excluded the Swiss and the Poles, who were highly unlikely to desert. This, he felt, would provide him with 50,000 muskets. The situation with artillery was equally bad.

In an effort to resolve this problem, Napoleon had the artisans of the various provinces brought to Versailles and to Paris. There and in the various fortresses, weapons works were hastily established and efforts were made to produce as many weapons as fast as possible. However, the lack of weapons was to remain a major problem for Napoleon.

Napoleon then turned his attention to the various fortresses throughout France. They had not been threatened in many years and, as a result, their condition was often badly decayed. Napoleon dispatched engineers to these fortresses with directions to repair the old walls; to trace out redoubts on the heights; to fortify defiles; and to prepare to cut the various dikes and bridges should the Allies approach. He also directed the prefects to work on provisioning these fortifications.

Napoleon also drew troops from his two armies in Spain and Catalonia. They were trained, equipped, combat-hardened and available immediately. The only delay would be the time it took them to march from Spain to the Rhine. At the end of January orders would reach Spain that would detach 13,435 men from the Army of Spain. These forces were the divisions of Leval, Boyer, Treillhard and the dragoon brigade of Sparre.

Napoleon also ordered the formation of a number of new regiments. The first were eight regiments of éclaireurs – a light cavalry regiment. He then ordered the formation of eight new regiments of guard and ordered the existing guard battalions to form two new companies each.[16]

With these resources, Napoleon hoped to organize a formidable army and defend France. His existing army in France had about 130,000 men. When combined with troops drawn from Spain, by the end of December Napoleon would have an army of about 300,000 men; a first reserve army of 300,000 men; and a second reserve army of about 600,000 men.[17]

15 Thiry, p. 12.
16 *Victoires, conquêtes, désastres* Vol. 23, p. 9.
17 de Vauconcourt, Vol. I, pp. 61-2.

The Decree of 4 January 1814 had ordered a levée en masse in several departments.[18] However, as the campaign had progressed by this point, this effort was to have little or no effect on the war. It was possible to raise forces only in the Departments of l'Isère and Mont-Blanc, which were not invaded and occupied. They did begin sending recruits to the various depots where they were equipped and trained.

Two divisions of infantry and one of cavalry were withdrawn from the Army of Spain and marched in haste on Paris. Another infantry division and a cavalry division were detached from the Army of Catalonia and sent to Lyon. The Young Guard was augmented by the formation of six regiments of Voltigeurs and six regiments of Tirailleurs. The National Guard of the departments to the west of Paris were fully mobilized and set in motion. The city of Paris was brought to a state of defense and its National Guard were organized.[19]

The Allies

The Allied army was organized into three armies: the Army of Bohemia, the Army of Silesia and the Army of the North. The Army of Bohemia was deployed as follows:

1st Corps (Colloredo) between Krotzingen and Lohr
Austro-Bavarian Army was between Lohr, Achern and Bischofsheim blockading Kehl
3rd Corps (Giulay) was between Achern and Weingarten
2nd Corps (Meerfeld) between Weingarten and Mannheim
1st Grenadier Division in Heidelberg
2nd Grenadier Division in Wisloch
1st and 2nd Light Divisions between the mouth of the Necker and Gernsheim
Austrian Reserve Cavalry between Heilbronn and Tubingen
1st Russian Guard Infantry Division in Frankfurt
2nd Russian Guard Infantry Division in Offenbach
Prussian Guard Infantry in Sachsenhausen
Russian Grenadier Corps in Michelstadt and Miltenberg
Russian Cuirassiers around Seligenstadt
Platov's Cossacks around Zwingenberg, between Darmstadt and Heidelberg
Wittgenstein's corps, second line, to the left of Neuenstädt on the Kocher, near Heilbronn, with its left on the Mein River

The Army of Silesia was deployed with its advanced posts along the Rhine between the Mein and the Lahn River. The remainder of the army was deployed as follows:

Advanced Guard in Weisbaden and Hocheim
Sacken's corps between Schwarzbach and Wickert, blockading Mainz
Langeron's corps, forming a second line, between the Schwarzbach and the Nidda rivers
Yorck's corps at Langen-Schwalbach and Nastedten extending to the Lahn River
Blücher's corps in Höchst

18 The levée was called in the Departments of Haut-Rhin, Bas Rhin, Vosges, Mont-Blanc, Isre, Cte d'Or, Jura, Doubs and Haut-Sane.
19 Vaudoncourt, Vol. II, pp. 177-8.

Blücher.

At the beginning of December 1813 the Allies had found themselves obliged to detach Bülow's corps from Bernadotte's Army of the North into Holland. The Orangists, who had been working with emissaries from England, were working to liberate Amsterdam. A small force of English troops were landed and met with cries of: "Long Live the House of Orange!" The prospects of fomenting a popular revolution among the Dutch against the French caused the dispatch of further troops and demands for the Prussians and Russians to march on Antwerp.

The remainder of Bernadotte's Army of the North, however, was not to get involved in the immediate campaign as it was assigned the duties of investing Hamburg and keeping Napoleon's Maréchal Davout away from the main theater of the campaign.

The force that the Allies mustered was significant, though not as great as it had been the previous August when they had renewed the fight against Napoleon. On 1 January 1814 – as they crossed the Rhine – their strength was as follows:

Bülow's 3rd Corps (men)	30,000
Winzingerode's corps	36,000
Army of Silesia (Blücher)	
Yorck's 1st Corps	21,447
Sacken's corps	21,550
Langeron's corps	34,103
Total Army of Silesia:	77,100

Main army (Schwarzenberg)	
1st Light Division (Bubna)	6,389
2nd Light Division (Liechtenstein)	3,900
1st Army Corps (Colloredo)	15,536
2nd Army Corps (Liechtenstein)	14,336
3rd Army Corps (Gyulai)	15,261
4th Army Corps (Württemberg)	14,421
5th Army Corps (Wrede)	47,435
6th Army Corps (Wittgenstein)	19,460
Reserve (Hessen-Homburg)	20,130
Total main army:	156,868
Total Allied armies:	299,968

By all appearances, the campaign should be simple. With a force of 300,000 Allied soldiers at their command, the Allied generals saw Napoleon's puny army of 130,000 an insignificant obstacle to their plans. Indeed, the campaign should have been a leisurely stroll from the Rhine to Paris.

Yorck's passage over the Rhine

The movement of the Allies over the Rhine was relatively uneventful and does not merit a great deal of discussion. However, von Plotho does provide an interesting discussion of the movement of Yorck and Langeron's forces over the Rhine. Yorck's crossing was typical of the passage of the Allied armies over the Rhine.

The Prussian passage began after midnight when GL von Hünerbein organized his forces for the passage across the Rhine at the city of Kaub. The infantry was on the riverbank, with the cavalry and artillery arrayed behind the city. The advanced guard – under GM von Katzler – consisted of the Fus/Brandenburg Infantry Regiment, Fus/12th Reserve Infantry Regiment, a battalion of the 14th Silesian Landwehr, two companies of East Prussian Jägers, five squadrons of the Leib Hussar Regiment, a squadron of the Mecklenburg Hussars, a squadron of the Brandenburg Hussars, a squadron of the East Prussian National Cavalry Regiment and Horse Battery #3.

Behind von Katzler came the main body. Oberstleutnant von Hiller commanded the 1/,2/Brandenburg Infantry Regiment, the 1/,2/12th Reserve Infantry Regiment, two battalions of the 14th Silesian Landwehr Regiment and 6pdr Foot Battery #15. Behind von Hiller came Oberstleutnant von Stutterheim with four squadrons of both the Brandenburg Uhlans and the 10th Silesian Landwehr Cavalry Regiment.

The Russian pontoons arrived at midnight and construction began on the bridge almost immediately. The bridge connected Kaub with Pfalz – using parts of an old bridge on an island in the middle of the Rhine.

Yorck issued the following orders for the passage of his army:

> A 12pdr battery shall move from Weisel to the right bank of the Kaub Brook and a half 12pdr battery shall be positioned by the ruins of Gutenfels. These batteries shall fire on the left bank of the Rhine and hinder any French batteries. Two 12pdr guns shall, as soon as the bridge is erected, cross and deploy by the corner of the road by the foot of the plain. The company of jägers, now in Rüdesheim, shall occupy the road from Asmannshaufen (along the Rhine) and fire on the road running from Bingen to Bacharach. The infantry of the 8th Brigade shall move from Kähnen and when it has crossed the Rhine, take possession of

The Prussians crossing the Rhine at Kaub, 1 January 1814, by Richard Knötel.

> the gullies and heights along the road (the village of Hänschhausen) and push to a position between Bacharach and Breitscheid. The 8th Brigade shall push forward two companies of the East Prussian Jägers, the 2nd Leib Hussars, the Brandenburg Uhlans, a squadron of the Brandenburg Hussars, one of the Mecklenburg Hussars and one of the East Prussian National Cavalry Regiment with a horse battery.
>
> Once the bridge is in place the cavalry and artillery for the advanced guard shall cross first, then shall follow the 1st, 2nd and 7th Brigades, the reserve cavalry, the reserve artillery and the East Prussian National Cavalry Regiment (which belongs to the 1st Brigade). The troops shall concentrate by Weisel and move, by and by, to Kaub. No wagons shall cross the bridge until all the troops have passed over the river. Once the advanced guard has crossed it shall move on Stromberg. Generalmajor von Katzler shall command the cavalry of the advanced guard, but the overall command of the advanced guard is with Generalleutnant von Hünerbein. The passage over the Rhine shall begin at midnight, but the infantry of the 1st Brigade shall cross at 7:00 a.m. if the bridge is not ready.[20]

The advanced guard passed over the Rhine by boat or by swimming their horses. The bridge was not in place until 9:00 a.m. Because of this delay, the movement of the 1st Brigade began at 7:00 a.m. in boats. The passage was unopposed and the only French infantry – some 300-400 men – was reported to be some distance away from the crossing.

20 von Plotho, Vol. III, pp. 49-50.

Allied plans

The line of fortresses defending France presented the Allies with a potential problem. A quick rush against them – the positioning of the major Allied army in the middle of them – would oblige the French to abandon them and give the Allies a strong footing in metropolitan France, or oblige Napoleon to sacrifice what remained of his army to drive the Allies back behind the Rhine. This plan was proposed and rejected. Instead, a plan was proposed in which Prince Schwarzenberg would move against Basel (and from there through Switzerland), enter France and move along the line of Belfort, Vesoul and Langres. The Army of Silesia, under Blücher, was to occupy the main Allied positions by Frankfurt and then cross the Rhine at Mannheim and Coblentz. From there he was to operate in the direction of Nancy.

This plan, strongly opposed initially, would delay the invasion of France until January 1814 – giving Napoleon time to prepare for their advance. It was also pointed out that Switzerland was a barrier to the movement of troops and the supplies necessary to support them. Bad weather could spell disaster to any troops with a snow-bound Switzerland to their rear.

At the same time it was pointed out that the division of the Allied army would permit Napoleon to concentrate his army, though to contain 60,000 to 65,000 men against Blücher. If Blücher were forced back Napoleon could collect his garrisons as far as the Elbe and with these reinforcements, fall on the flank and rear of the army engaged in Switzerland.

Opposing these arguments, it was urged that the weakest point in the French defenses had always been through Switzerland. Once strongly occupied, Switzerland would provide a strong base from which to launch an offensive. This line of advance was a natural one for the Austrians, who had learned about the difficulties of an advance across the Lower Rhine during the French Revolution. This line of advance would permit Austria to receive supplies from its own provinces by the most direct route. Furthermore, its southern flank would be covered by a parallel advance by the Austrian Army of Italy.

Once this advance had captured Langres it would hold a commanding position facing the plains of Champagne and Burgundy, which would permit them to dictate a peace on terms they would propose.

Should the Austrians wish, from this position, they could also move against Italy, crush the resistance of the French there and re-establish their hegemony over Italy.[21]

The first major obstacle to this plan was presented by Tsar Alexander II. He was opposed to any violation of Swiss neutrality. However, Austrian troops which were already marching southwards – and Schwarzenberg's persuasiveness – caused the Tsar to listen to some proposals on the subject. He soon consented to communications with the Swiss government to facilitate the passage of Allied troops through their territories.

The Swiss Diet did not agree to the proposals, but was not in a position to oppose their passage – nor was it apparently inclined to oppose their passage through Swiss

Prince Schwarzenberg.

21 Burghersh, p. 66.

territory. In order to insure the best possible reception of the Allies' proposals, severe orders were issued to all Allied commanders near the Swiss border against the infringement of Swiss territory.

On 9 December Schwarzenberg left Frankfurt and moved to Freyburg. The Swiss Diet had placed a corps of 12,000 men under the orders of General de Watteville with orders to defend Swiss neutrality. De Watteville placed his troops along the left bank of the Rhine between Basel and Schaffhausen.

There were, despite the supposed neutrality of Switzerland, some official actions that were anything but neutral. Reports of 300 conscripts being sent to France arrived in the Allied camps. Palisades were furnished from Basel for the Huningue Fortress. An Austrian officer, escaping from French captivity as a prisoner of war, was taken captive by the Swiss and returned to the French. And, as early as August, General Boudet had been permitted to pass through Basel on his way into Germany.

During this period the city of Berne laid blame, via its provincial Diet, on the conduct of its deputies at the Swiss general assembly for having consented to maintain the government as it was then established (and for having established a system of neutrality for which they had no authority to establish).

The Berne provincial Diet refused to publish the neutrality act and separated itself from the general confederation. Von Freudenreich, head of the government, offered to abdicate in favor of a commission of 10 persons established in 1802, but upon the condition the Allies would guarantee the reestablishment of the former limits of the Berne Canton. Count Senft Pilsach was sent by Prince Metternich from Freyburg to Berne on 14 December to negotiate on this basis. If possible, Pilsach was to contact de Watteville and get him to agree to bring his troops over to the Allied cause or to withdraw them from their position on the Rhine. The general sentiment in Switzerland favored no military involvement and withdrawal of their troops. Only the Vaude region, where significant pro-French sentiment remained and which held a strong desire to remain free of the domination of a resurgent Berne, opposed this.

Count Senft Pilsach was successful in persuading de Watteville to retire, but was accused of exceeding his instructions in his dealings with the government of Berne.[22] With his path clear of Swiss interference, Schwarzenberg moved his headquarters to Löchrach While there he received a note from de Watteville announcing his corps' withdrawal behind the Aar River. The Swiss forces withdrew that evening and on the following morning – 21 December – Austrian troops began to march over the Rhine River in four columns. The first crossed at Basel; the second at Crenknach; the third at Lauffenburg; and the fourth at Schaffhausen. On the same day the Allies issued a proclamation to the Swiss announcing the cause of their passage through Swiss territory – guaranteeing Swiss independence and assuring them that on the termination of hostilities the rights and interests of Switzerland would be fixed and guaranteed by all of the powers of Europe.

Early actions on the frontier

To cover their frontier the French placed a garrison of 3,000 men into Landau, 4,900 into Strasbourg, 3,000 into Brisach, 2,600 into Schelestadt, 3,000 into Huningue and 2,000 into Belfort. This was a total of 18,500 conscripts or National Guardsmen – all of whom had arrived with the army in late December.

To defend the gorges of the Vosges, Maréchal Victor concentrated on Saverne and intended to hold this position until he was joined by Marmont, Duke of Ragusa. He was particularly concerned that Allied movements might force him into Strasbourg where he could be cut off and

22 Burghersh, pp. 65-70.

surrounded. However, his plans fell apart on 7 January when the Army of Silesia arrived on the Sarre and prevented the junction of the two French forces.

GD Milhaud's cavalry and a force of infantry established themselves in Baccarat – with their lead elements in Raon-l'Etape. The advanced forces consisted of Duhésme's division – with five battalions – and GD Piré's light cavalry division (and a horse battery).

The French withdrawal left the Allies the masters of the passages from Colmar to Nancy and permitted them access to the basin of the Moselle as well as a line of march through the Vosges and Hundsruck towards Belfort and Landau. This movement however was covered by Maréchal Ney, who commanded a force consisting of a Young Guard division which consisted of four voltigeur regiments (which had only been organized 15 days earlier in Saarlouis), two batteries and 400 cavalry from the general remount depot.

Around the same time, the Crown Prince of Württemberg was ordered to concentrate his army corps on the Army of Silesia. His advanced guard, covered by Platov's Cossacks, encountered a 4,000-man French Young Guard infantry brigade – under the command of General Rousseau – and 200 cavalry under General Duvigneau, who Ney had sent from Nancy to Epinal.

On 11 January the Crown Prince of Württemberg organized his forces into three attack columns. The first column, under GM von Stockmayer, contained the 2/9th and the 7th Infantry Regiment and organized itself by the village of Docelles on the right bank of the Moselle. The second (main) column was under FZM Graf von Franquemont. It organized itself on the left bank of the Moselle by the village of Poucheux. The third column – under GM von Jett – consisted of the 4th Cavalry Regiment, one squadron of the 2nd Cavalry Regiment, five cannon, and the 1/10th Infantry Regiment and organized itself on the left of the Moselle by Xertigny. Supporting the third column was the Kronprinz Dragoon Regiment and three horse guns under GL Prince Adam von Württemberg.[23]

GM von Jett advanced on Saint-Laurent – pushing back the French advanced posts while the main column engaged a strong infantry post by the Char d'Argent farm. The French infantry, however, was unable to hold its ground against the 9th Infantry Regiment and its supporting artillery withdrew into the suburbs of Epinal. GM Döring, commanding the 2nd Infantry Regiment (main column), pushed through Garmenil and over the Moselle and into the suburbs of Epinal.

Unable to hold his ground, Rousseau evacuated the city and moved down the road to Nancy so quickly that generals von Jett and von Stockmayer were unable to catch him. Rousseau was withdrew – pursued by the 2nd and 3rd Cavalry Regiments and seven horse artillery guns to the heights beyond Epinal. As the French arrived by the village of Thaon the Russian General Greckov engaged the head of their column with his Cossacks, threw back the French cavalry and took six officers and about 500 men prisoner. After cutting their way through the Cossacks, the French marched relatively unmolested to Charmes.

The engagement at Epinal had cost the Württembergers minimal casualties, while they claim to have inflicted 1,000 casualties on the French.[24]

Victor sought to occupy Epinal, Remberville and St.-Diéy. He thought that Epinal was occupied only by light troops and sent General Cassagne against it with a force of infantry and 300 cavalry. Cassagne found Epinal strongly held and beat a hasty withdrawal – losing almost all of his cavalry to the sabers of the Württemberg cavalry in the effort.

General Briche's dragoon division did succeed in establishing itself in Remberville after throwing out the 200 Cossacks that occupied it. General Duhèsme, who had occupied St.-Diéy, soon found himself confronted by the corps of General Wrede. Wrede had left Beckers' division

23 Rössler, pp. 395-6.
24 Rössler, pp. 397-9.

in Schelestadt, Brisach and Huningue and then had marched on Langres. His advanced posts – established before St.-Diéy – were pushed back to Sainte-Marguerite by l'Heritier's dragoons, while Duhésme launched a futile attack against Deroy's brigade which blocked his passage. Duhésme pushed back Deroy across the bridge over the Meurthe, but the Allied artillery prevented him from advancing further and he fell back to St.-Diéy. Once there he was struck by an overwhelming Allied force and withdrew yet again – retiring via Saint-Michel on Remberville with heavy losses.[25]

Despite this setback Victor moved to the right into the Haute-Marne in an effort not to abandon the Vosges to the Allies without a fight. However, upon learning that the Army of Silesia had moved past Château-Salins in an effort to cut him off, Victor withdrew to Saint-Nicolas and joined Ney in Nancy.

Wrede – seeing his front clear of French troops – marched on Neuf Château, where he arrived on the 20th and opened communications with the Army of Silesa. As a result of these maneuvers he had nothing in front of him except the forces of the Duke of Trévise, which were moving from Langres to Chaumont.

Schwarzenberg ordered Graf Giulay and the Crown Prince of Württemberg to march on Chaumont. Giulay was to march directly on the city while Württemberg was to move via Bourbonne and Montagny – clearing the French out of Ville-aux-Bois as well as take Choignes and the bridge before the village. However, when he arrived his forces encountered 400 veteran grenadiers who threw the two attacking Württemberg battalions back across the Marne.

The Duke of Trévise found himself attacked frontally and on the right by two army corps, while he was menaced on his left by Graf Wrede's corps. The Duke of Trévise had only the single infantry division of Italians and a division of cavalry which had been with him at Langres. He decided to withdraw on Bar-sur-Aube where he was joined by Michel's 2nd Old Guard Infantry Division. On the way he surprised two Württemberg battalions and thrashed them. Joining the 2nd Old Guard Division brought his forces up to 8,000 infantry and 2,000 cavalry.

On the 24th the two Allied corps advanced on Bar, but the Duke of Trévise had occupied the heights on the right and left with part of his troops and pushed Michel's Old Guard Division from Fontaines to a position between Fontaines and the Aube River. Giulay's advanced guard marched against the French and soon found the French artillery shredding its ranks as it passed out of Clairvaux. As the Austrian columns were thrown into disorder they were charged by Michel's first brigade, which had rushed across the Aube. The Austrians were thrown back and Major Keck fell in the melee – pierced by several bayonet thrusts. The first Austrian line withdrew in disorder behind second – reorganizing itself behind GM Trenck's brigade and a formidable force of artillery. The French attack was stopped short when threatened by a Württemberg brigade that appeared on their right – driving back the French brigade in Colombé and forcing the French to withdraw back across the Aube. The Austrians – now rallied – advanced, pursued the French across the Aube and penetrated into Fontaines. However, a counterattack by the Fusiliers and the Vélites of Turin and Florence – commanded by GD Christiani – chased the offending Austrians back across the Aube.

The Duke of Trévise had placed 2,000 infantry and 400 cavalry – under GD Letort – in the village of Colombé-les-deux-Eglises to watch the Austrians on the road to Chaumont. They soon found themselves in a fight with the Austrian forces under Schwarzenberg and after a lengthy defense, withdrew to Troyes. The following date, 25 January, Giulay entered Bar.

25 *Victoires, conquêtes, désastres*, Vol. 21, pp. 25-6.

2

Negotiations and Politics

In an effort to free his armies in Spain, Napoleon had begun negotiations with Fernando VII – the Crown Prince of Spain. He hoped to end the war with Spain by releasing Fernando VII to send the Spanish armies back to their barracks and to oblige the English to withdraw from Spain. Napoleon placed his proposal of peace via Count Laforêt – the former French ambassador to Spain – before Fernando VII. The proposed terms included that the pension paid to Charles IV, Fernando VII's father, be continued; that a total amnesty be accorded to the Spanish who had served with Spain; and that Spain retain all its possessions – both continental and colonial – and that none of them be ceded to England. Count Laforêt was also empowered to offer, as a last measure, a marriage between Fernando VII and the daughter of Joseph Bonaparte – now the former Bonaparte King of Spain.[1]

However, Fernando VII responded that he would agree to nothing without the consent of the Spanish Regency. The French then set Fernando VII and his brother Carlos free to accompany San Carlos to Spain. Between 8 and 11 December the Duke de San Carlos and the Count Laforêt concluded a peace treaty and re-established the relations of the two nations on the basis that had existed in 1792. The question of a marriage between Fernando VII and a Bonaparte princess would be taken up later. Once the negotiations for what would become the Treaty of Valencay were completed, Fernando VII, his brother and San Carlos departed to place this agreement before the Spanish Regency – the goal being to demonstrate that this treaty had been freely negotiated with a sovereign and not a prisoner.

This effort, unfortunately, resulted in nothing. Napoleon released Fernando VII to return to his states without obtaining anything from either him or the regency.

At the same time there was little sincerity on Napoleon's side of these negotiations. He held Fernando VII in little esteem – knowing how low his popularity was in Spain, as well as how incapable Fernando VII was of ruling Spain.

There remained however, for Napoleon, the problem of his brother Joseph, King of Spain. Joseph was advised of the Treaty of Valencay and that he would receive compensation in the form of Naples or territories in northern Italy. It would appear that Napoleon was as quick to trade away the kingdom of his brother-in-law Murat as he was those of his brother Joseph. Of course, Joseph was not pleased with the Treaty of Valencay or with Napoleon's accusations that he had lost Spain by his own actions.

Family difficulties aside, if peace with Spain was the price of ridding him of the English armies that were slowly bleeding his armies in Spain into ruin, the price was well worth it. A military disengagement with Spain would free up 130,000 trained and equipped soldiers for the coming battles with the Russian, Prussian and Austrian armies – and there was still hope that the Austrian Emperor, his father-in-law, might withdraw from the coalition now that the French armies were back across the Rhine.

1 Thiry, p. 38.

Francis I of Austria, by L. Kupelwiser.

Napoleon's brother Louis, King of Holland, had long since fallen out of favor. In 1810 Napoleon had absorbed the Netherlands into metropolitan France and stripped Louis of his rank and titles. Jérôme had abdicated the throne of Westphalia and had returned to France.

Then there was his brother-in-law Murat, King of Naples. He had abandoned Napoleon in October 1813 – convinced of Napoleon's defeat – and had begun negotiations with Austria to retain his throne. His treason extended beyond that and he proposed to the Austrians that he lead his army north in coordination with theirs to destroy the Kingdom of Northern Italy under Eugène. Murat had dreams of a united Italy under his rule.

Napoleon, suspecting Murat's treachery, charged Fouché on 15 November 1813 with communicating to Murat the necessity of sending an army of 25,000 men north to join Eugène's army on the Po for the defense of Italy. Murat's response was sent on 23 November and stated that he would "put his troops in movement." His letter was insincere, but Napoleon appears to have believed it, in that he wrote Eugène on 3 December stating that Murat "writes me that he shall soon be in Bologna with 30,000 men."

On 1 December Fouché had an audience with Murat, who again reaffirmed his intention to serve Napoleon, but stated that he must "assure the security of his states" before he acted. "The 25,000 men, which I promised the Emperor are en route; the continuous rains, the swollen rivers are the sole cause of the slowness of their march."

Despite further written protestations of his fidelity and willingness to serve Napoleon, the truth came out on 25 December when Murat laid before Napoleon the price of his loyalty. He said: "The proclamation of the independence of Italy – forming a single state or two states having the Po as their borders – will save Italy. Without this it is lost without resources. It will be dismembered again and the goal of Your Majesty wishing to deliver Italy, after having covered it with glory, is destroyed. Place the provinces up to the Po at my disposition and I guarantee to Your Majesty that the Austrians will not cross the Adige River. You shall be, in the negotiations of a general peace, the arbitrator of Italy and you will create in me a powerful and loyal ally." He stated that the Allies offered the Italians independence, but that Napoleon could seize the initiative by creating an independent Italian state under Murat that would both guard his southern border and provide him with a strong new ally.[2] Murat went on to ask that Napoleon give him control of the Catholic Church, Tuscany – which belonged to Napoleon's sister – and the Legations, which were dependencies of the States of Prince Eugène.

The wool drawn from his eyes vis-a-vis Murat, Napoleon exploded. He was unable to do much, but he immediately dispatched a force of his newly-raised soldiers to the Army of Italy and directed Eugène to watch his southern border. He also ordered General Miollis, who commanded Rome, not to issue muskets to Neapolitan troops or to allow them into the fortresses of Rome.

Then came the question of Bernadotte. A former French marshal, now King of Sweden, he had led the Army of the North against the French armies in Germany during the 1813 campaign. Despite this, Bernadotte still held considerable influence in Paris and many thought to replace Napoleon with him.

Bernadotte had become a rallying point for those who wished to overthrow Napoleon in the name of French patriotism and democracy. Bernadotte sought to wrap himself in that mantel by repeatedly stating that he fought not against the French nation, but against Napoleon. Madame de Staël saw him as a hero and wanted him crowned William III of France.[3]

Bernadotte had secretly sent some emissaries to Paris at the end of 1813 carrying a proclamation and authorized to negotiate with the French. However, their reception was cold and they returned as secretly as they had come.[4]

This effort repulsed, Bernadotte then hoped to push his way into the role of negotiator by having the Allies put him forward as the sole suitable conduit for such negotiations with the French. In late December 1813 he stated to the English Emissary, Thornton: "I wish to be the intermediary of the French nation to Europe to permit them to choose the sovereign they might choose, be it Paul, or Peter, or any other, in order to assure to my son the succession of the Crown of Sweden."

A Congress between the Allied leaders was convened at Frankfurt. The first objective of the Allied sovereigns on their arrival at Frankfurt was to impress on Napoleon with conviction that they were ready to make peace with him – and upon terms such that the state of the military resources remaining to him would not seem to justify. Prince Metternich and Count Nesselrode were instructed to communicate to the French government through Baron de St. Aignan.[5]

While the Spanish negotiations were under way, Baron de St. Aignan – minister plenipotentiary of France assigned to the Saxon Court – had been taken prisoner by the advancing Allies. He had complained of this infraction of diplomatic law to Metternich as a violation of the rights of men. Metternich had him released. Later, received by Metternich in Frankfurt, they held discussions that included the ministers of Russia and England. In these discussions they laid forth the basis of a peace: the return of France to its natural limits – the Rhine, the Alps and the Pyrenees. They established that Spain must return to its former rulers – the Bourbons – and that Italy, Holland and Germany were to be re-established as states independent from France and all of the major powers.

Though there was hope for peace in the Allied camp, they all had conflicting goals. The Tsar Alexander proposed Bernadotte as a candidate for the French throne. However, Austria feared a Russian candidate on the French throne would surround them with enemies. Instead the

2 Thiry, pp. 43-5.
3 Scott, p. 155.
4 Thiry, p. 48.
5 Burghersh, p. 55.

Prince Bernadotte, Crown Prince of Sweden.

Metternich.

Austrian court preferred Napoleon to remain on the French throne, but with limited powers and guarantees against his further ambitions. No doubt, Napoleon's marriage to the Emperor of Austria's daughter had no little influence on this decision.

English diplomacy had taken a dominant position. Whether it was skill at the negotiation table or the promise of continued English subsidies matters little. Russia was in England's sway. Prussia, being the weaker power, followed the Russian lead – leaving Austria no choice but to join the general agreement.

England's principal goal was to ensure that a balance of power was established on the continent that would not permit any one nation to challenge her position as the power broker of Europe or her dominance of European markets. To this end England could not afford to have France totally destroyed. France must be retained with sufficient power to act as a counter-balance to the growing power of the east. Austria and Russia must be played off against each other and the Prussian Junkers were to be allowed to return to their agricultural pursuits.

France was to be permitted a fleet, but its numbers were to be closely regulated. England wished to detach the lowlands from France's control – specifically Antwerp and Flushing – which gave them control of the mouth of the Rhine. The English wished France to return to the frontiers of 1790. To garner support of her continental Allies, England proposed to send a fleet to Antwerp. Lord Aberdeen also proposed to Metternich that the Kingdom of Holland be re-established under a single constitution that extended from Texel to Antwerp. The proposal was accepted and transmitted via Baron de St. Aignan to Napoleon.

France was to return to her natural limits – the Rhine, the Alps and the Pyrenees. Spain was to be re-established to independence under the Bourbon dynasty. Italy, Germany and Holland were to be re-established as states independent of France or any other power. Questions as to the establishment of Louis Bonaparte as King of Holland and of Eugène Beauharnais in Northern Italy were not clarified. There were those in Frankfurt who would have accepted Louis and Eugène. There were others who would not. The latter were to win out.

The Duke of Vicenza wrote on 2 December that Napoleon agreed with these basic principles, and on 10 December Metternich announced to the Tsar of Russia, Emperor of Austria and the King of Prussia that: "The French Emperor has adopted the essential basis for the re-establishment of a state of equilibrium and the future tranquillity of Europe."[6] Metternich then wrote back to the Duke of Vicenza that he had laid his proposal before the three sovereigns. He went on to say: "They have resolved that this paper should without delay be communicated to their Allies. Their Majesties do not doubt, but that the negotiations may be opened as soon as the answer shall have been received."[7]

The Duke of Bassano, in a letter dated 16 November, invited the Allies to open a congress in Mannheim to treat for peace on the basis of the independence of all nations with a view to both their continental and maritime relations. However, the Allies rejected this proposal as an evasive response. On 2 December de Caulincourt declared France's acceptance of the general conditions demanded by the Allies. This answer was immediately sent to London by Count Pozzo di Borgo. Pozzo di Borgo was to explain to the British cabinet sentiments of the Allies and to obtain from it a statement of its views.[8]

After discussions with Pozzo di Borgo, the British cabinet sent Lord Castlereagh to the Allied headquarters in Basel. He left England with instructions to negotiate for a peace upon conditions honorable to France, but differing from those proposed at Frankfurt.

It appeared that Napoleon's acceptance of the conditions of Frankfurt were too late. Napoleon broke off discussions with the Allied plenipotentiary. The Allies now no longer felt obliged to acknowledge him as ruler of France.

England now actively supported the reconstitution of the House of Orange. Prussia sought to grab further territories in Germany and Blücher sought only the revenge of marching on Paris. The Tsar Alexander, pushed by Pozzo di Borgo, shared Blücher's dream while Austria sought to grab all of Italy.

The final decision was made when England decided to provide the coalition and the funds necessary for the new campaign – and Count Pozzo di Borgo left for London to negotiate the budget.[9]

During November the congress of the Allied ministers assembled in Frankfurt established the manpower that each of their nations was to provide for the armies destined to invade France. The treaties were concluded on the basis of twice the contingent supplied by each of the German states while they were part of the Confederation of the Rhine. A total of 145,560 line troops and another 145,560 Landwehr were to be provided by the former members of the Confederation of the Rhine. In addition, they were to provide 84,970,000 francs to support the military operations. This sum was raised by each sovereign or governing authority, which renounced the Confederation of the Rhine, committing a year's revenue to the alliance.[10]

These funds were to be handled by a staff of Allied Commissioners – of which Baron Stein was appointed president. A six-year payment schedule was established and each of the new Allies was to liquidate the amount of the obligation by paying 1/24th of the whole every three months. These funds, when received, were to be divided into bills signed by the Allied Commissioners and, bearing five percent interest, were issued as paper currency. The contributions were then

6 *Victoires, conquêtes, désastres*, Vol. 23, p. 5.
7 Philippart, Vol. II, p. 340.
8 Burghersh, p. 60.
9 Thiry, p. 50.
10 Burghersh, p. 42.

divided into sixteenths. Five were to be given to each Austria, Russia and Prussia while one was to be given to Sweden. The financial commitments of Bavaria, Württemberg and Hanover – in consideration of the military exertions they were making – were to be returned to them.

The invasion of France was to occur and there was nothing that Napoleon or the French people could do, but surrender... or fight.

3

Operations in the Lowlands, December 1813-March 1814

Revolt in Holland

The news of the disaster reached the lowlands and showered sparks in Napoleon's rear. Bernadotte had been given the task of occupying the region between Hamburg and Bremen and of then marching on Amsterdam. He lingered outside Hamburg on the pretext of Davout's strength, but in fact he was working on his goal of seizing Norway – and possibly Holstein – from the Danes. In order to pursue his orders to conquer the lowlands he detached two corps – one under Bülow and the other under Winzingerode.

In early November generals Winzingerode and Bülow sent their advanced guard to Düsseldorf. On 12 November it crossed the Rhine. General Benkendorff, commanding a detached corps belonging to General Winzingerode, repulsed GD Carra-St.-Cyr's 3rd Division as he attempted to push into Bremen. Having the initiative, Winzingerode pushed his light troops into Holland – taking Zwolle, Zoltkampt, Kampen, Deventer, Gröningen, Amersfoort and Harderwyk. General Oppen was detached by Bülow from Münster and he promptly took Doesburg and Zutphen.[1]

The Dutch had become increasingly hostile against the French – even before the Allies pushed into Holland. Sensing this, generals Arrighi and Le Brun began withdrawing the elements of French government and authority from Holland. On 15 November – as they abandoned Amsterdam – the city's population rose in revolt. They proclaimed a provisional government in the name of the House of Orange and declared the Prince of Orange Stadtholder ruling until his arrival. Within hours similar revolts occurred in Dordrecht, Delft, Leyden and Haarlem. These were the first of many revolts that would continue throughout the lowlands until Napoleon abdicated in April.

On 1 December General Benkendorff crossed the Zuiderzee from Harderwyk and entered Amsterdam. He immediately took possession of the forts of Muiden and Halfweg. On 2 December the Prince of Orange arrived from England and entered his capital amidst the universal joy of its inhabitants.[2]

Bülow detached Borstell's 5th Brigade to blockade Wesel and moved the rest of his troops in support of Oppen at Doesburg. Deventer was found empty of French troops so the Prussians moved on to Arnheim.

Arnheim was covered by a series of entrenchments which Bülow decided to carry by direct assault. He moved Krafft's and von Thümen's Brigades forward – covering them with cavalry and Prince Louis von Hesse-Homburg's brigade in reserve. He then formed five assault columns that stormed the city successfully.

The two columns on the right were commanded by Oberst von Zastrow, the two on the left were commanded by General Krafft and the central column was under Major Colombé.

1 Burghersh, p. 46.
2 Burghersh, p. 47.

The French garrison suffered considerable loss and fled down-road to Nijmegen pursued by General Oppen's cavalry.[3]

After clearing Arnheim, General Krafft's brigade and the cavalry pushed forward to the Waal to observe and mask the fortresses of Nijmegen and Bommel. General Benkendorff then established blockades of Gorkum and Dordrecht.

General von Thümen and Prince von Hessen then advanced on Utrecht, which quickly capitulated to them. On 17 December General Bülow established his headquarters in Bommel. The forts of Heusden, Lövenstein and Workum fell to General Krafft. St.-André and Crévecoeur were taken by General Oppen. Bülow then sent forward a detachment to relieve Benkendorff of the duties of investing Gorkum. Once relieved, Benkendorff pushed his corps towards Gertruydenberg and Breda, which he quickly occupied. On 6 December a British force of 6,000 men under General Sir Thomas Graham landed at Schevelings, occupied most of the Zeeland and advanced on Bergen-op-Zoom.[4]

Initial organization
Graham's corps
Netherlands 1813

Commanding General: Lieutenant General Sir T. Graham
Guards Brigade: Major General Cooke
- Det. 1st Guard Regiment
- Det. 3rd Guard Regiment

1st Brigade: Major General Skerret
- 2/37th Foot Regiment
- 44th Foot Regiment
- 55th Foot Regiment
- 2/69th Foot Regiment

Veteran Battalion

2nd Brigade: Major General Mackenzie
- 2/35th Foot Regiment
- Det. 52nd Foot Regiment
- 73rd Foot Regiment
- Det. 3/95th Foot Regiment

3rd Brigade: Major General Gibbs
- 2/25th Foot Regiment
- 33rd Foot Regiment
- 54th Foot Regiment
- 3/56th Foot Regiment

Cavalry:
- 2nd KGL Hussar Regiment

Artillery: (Data not available)

On 14 December Bülow pushed von Thümen's 4th Brigade to Leerdam to observe Gorkum. On 16 December he put his corps in motion – moving to invest Gorkum and occupy the banks of the Meuse in order to support the British and to assure the defense of Breda and Gertruydenberg. Zielinski and von Thümen's 3rd and 4th Brigades – under the orders of Oppen – rejoined at Thiel on 17 December before Bommel and crossed the Waal.

General Molitor defended Bommel and the passage over the Waal with his guns, but was unable to do more than inconvenience Bülow. He was obliged to abandon his position, move on Crévecoeur (where he crossed the Meuse) and then to Grave where he joined his small force with that of Maréchal Macdonald. Krafft's Prussian 6th Brigade then crossed the Meuse near Gorkum and occupied Workum and Heusden. Gorkum was invested by Zielinski's 3rd Brigade while Krafft's division remained in Heusden. Von Thümen's 4th Brigade occupied Buren and Thiel, where they observed Niemegen.[5]

The news of the Prussian advance into Holland was well-received, but caused some complaints against Bernadotte to be lodged. It was contended that Sweden was intent only on pursuing its

3 Burghersh, p. 48.
4 Burghersh, p. 49.
5 de Vaudoncourt, Vol. I, p. 200.

own interests in Holstein and, as a result, was preventing the immediate advance of the Allies into the Netherlands – rendering them unable to take full advantage of the Dutch revolt.

One faction urged that the Russian, Prussian and Hanoverian Corps under Bernadotte should be taken from him and sent into Holland, but its counsel was not heeded. However, on 17 December the King of Prussia wrote to Bernadotte – congratulating him on his success against the Danes, who he had forced into an armistice. He then notified him that he had assigned the corps of General Publitz and Oberst Marwitz to his command so that he might deal with Davout in Hamburg. With these reinforcements, the King of Prussia urged him to take his main body into Holland and support both the revolt and the successes of Bülow .

The King of Prussia urged that he should direct General Winzingerode to advance up the Rhine to the neighbourhood of Düsseldorf and relieve General Borstell. Once relieved, Borstell could rejoin Bülow . The King of Prussia then recommended that the Saxon troops be directed to Arnheim.

The Tsar of Russia wrote to Bernadotte from Karlsruhe on 21 December with the same advice. He also wrote to the Duke of Weimar that the Saxon corps – under the orders of General Thielemann – should move to support this movement.

When he received these two letters, Bernadotte directed Winzingerode to advance – stating that if the French should press against his left once in his assigned position, he should join his forces with those of General Bülow.

Winzingerode received these orders on 22 December while in Bremen. He had already detached General Orouch to relieve Borstell. The remainder of his forces arrived in Münster on 30 December and arrived in Düsseldorf on 6 January. The Saxons, under the Duke of Weimar, departed Querfort on 2 January and arrived on the Rhine at Arnheim on 2 February. They relieved General Bülow's corps at Breda on 6 February.[6]

The French in Holland

Lebrun, governor of Holland, withdrew to Utrecht where General Molitor, the military commander of the lowlands, was headquartered. Unfortunately, Molitor commanded only a few foreign regiments of questionable reliability and a few weak French battalions. His force was far too small to re-establish the French domination of the lowlands and resist the advance of the Army of the North. Fortunately for Molitor, Bernadotte did not advance very quickly and he was given time to organize his forces between Naarden and Gorkum where General Rampon had a garrison of 2,000 National Guardsmen raised in French Flanders.[7]

After his defeat at Leipzig, Napoleon began to make preparations to hold the Rhine. He abandoned Davout and 170,000 men in Hamburg and various other fortresses in Germany. With the remains of the Grande Armée Napoleon constituted four groups destined to guard the Rhine along the line from Basel to Arnheim. On the right stood Maréchal Victor with 5,000 men between Basel and Strasbourg. In the center was Maréchal Marmont with 8,000 men between Mannheim and Coblentz. On the left stood Maréchal Macdonald with 9,000 men between Coblentz and Arnheim. Finally, there were 12,000 men under Général de division Morand charged with defending Mainz. This punty force was facing 220,000 men under Schwarzenberg and Blücher.

Napoleon was also keenly aware of the threat to the lowlands. He detached Léfèbvre-Desnoëttes with 2,000 Guard light cavalry and the divisions of Barrois (4th Young Guard) and Roguet (6th Young Guard) into the Barbant. He sent Maréchal Mortier to Namur with the Old Guard.

6 Burghersh, p. 52.
7 Calmon-Maison, p. 2.

Bülow.

Borstell.

Maréchal Victor.

Molitor.

The lack of troops obliged Molitor to evacuate Utrecht on 28 November. He faced 20,000 Prussians and Russians – plus 6,000 English landed under the orders of General Graham. In order to not be cut off from Belgium Molitor found himself obliged to fall back to the Waal and Holland was evacuated.[8]

In Holland there remained garrisons in Naarden and Texel under Admiral Verhuel. He also commanded the Dutch fleet in Texel and acted to save what remained of the Dutch fleet. He took the steps of defending the works at Niewe-Deep, Helder and Texel. He placed the French of the 63rd Equipage – the French who were aboard the Dutch ships – into Fort LaSalle and began the defense with those Dutch that remained loyal. He also released 1,600 Spanish prisoners of war. Admiral Verhuel would not surrender those fortresses until peace had returned to Europe.

Napoleon began to organize a force of 40,000 men destined to operate between Utrecht, Breda, Bergen-op-Zoom and Antwerp using conscripts, National Guardsmen, customs officers

8 Calmon-Maison, p. 13.

and sailors from the fleet in the Scheldt. They were not to be an active field force, but were to occupy strong positions behind inundated lands. General Decaen was recalled from Cataluna and given command of this force.

In Belgium, the Duke Charles de Plaisance was charged with the provisional organization of the I Corps. He directed that the various depots organized new battalions as quickly as possible, but he was plagued by a continual desertion of the Belgians who had had enough of Napoleon. As if their desertion wasn't enough, most of them took their arms and equipment with them when they deserted.

Napoleon then ordered General Decaen to form the cadre of an army with the troops in the 17th and 31st Military Divisions under the orders of General Molitor and Ambert – using them to prepare a defensive line on the Meuse so that its right was covered by Maréchal Macdonald.[9]

On 4 December General Decaen arrived in Antwerp and on 6 December he took command of the forces in Antwerp, but found his command consisted solely of a disorganized mass of sailors who had neither been equipped or trained. That same day 1,300 men of the 46th and 108th Line Regiments, a brigade formed by the 12th and 13th Tirailleurs (3,076 men), a battery, 183 men of the 2nd Guard Lancers and 114 men of the 2nd Guard Chasseurs arrived in Brussels. These men were destined to form the I (bis) Corps. With a body of trained troops around which to mold the disorganized mass of manpower, Decaen began to organize the city's defenses.

One of the two Young Guard Divisions that Napoleon had sent into the Barbant – Roguet's 6th Young Guard Division – occupied Brussels. Decaen ordered Roguet to move to Louvain and a few days later ordered him to move to Antwerp. Decaen was terribly concerned with defending the massive magazines in Antwerp and established his forces there. He then sent Roguet's 6th Young Guard Division on a reconnaissance towards Lierre.

Several detachments of sailors and naval artisans were sent to reinforce the garrisons of Bergen-op-Zoom and Breda. General Ambert was placed at the head of a mobile column – formed from troops drawn from the depots and given the mission of defending the lines of communication. Roguet's 6th Young Guard Division was ordered to organize itself in Louvain.

Decaen's situation was extremely weak. The coast guard had deserted – leaving the islands in the mouth of the Scheldt unguarded. Breda and Willemsted were unoccupied. When he learned that the Allies had sent forces over the Meuse he ordered the evacuation of Breda, Gertruydenberg and Willemsted. On 9 December General Benkendorff arrived before Breda with three Cossack regiments. General Ambert – having orders to abandon Breda – withdrew his 2nd Division. The following day Benkendorff sent a Cossack regiment against Willemsted and Colonel Legrand, its garrison commander, abandoned the city according to his orders. At the same time General Stahl arrived before Gertruydenberg with three other Cossack regiments and General Lorcet, its garrison commander, withdrew with his 300-man garrison after arranging a convention with Stahl.[10] On 14 December Cossacks appeared 15 miles from Antwerp on the road to Breda.

Napoleon, discontent with Decaen's evacuation of Willemsted and other actions, relieved Decaen on 21 December and sent Général de division Maison to assume command of this vital region. He arrived in Antwerp on 25 December.[11] Meanwhile, the divisions of Barrois (4th Young Guard) and Léfèbvre-Desnoëttes were ordered to march to Brussels. Similar orders were given to General Boyer, who was forming his division in Lille.[12]

At the same time Mortier was ordered to move north with Friant's 1st Old Guard Division and Laferrière's 1st (Old) Guard Cavalry Division. To cover their movement and to give the I Corps

9 de Vaudoncourt, Vol. I, pp. 198-9.
10 de Vaudoncourt, Vol. I, p. 200.
11 Calmon-Maison, pp. 38-9.
12 de Vaudoncourt, Vol. I, p. 201.

time to arrive in Antwerp, Napoleon ordered General Roguet to retake Breda and Macdonald to move on 's-Hertogenbosch.

Maison was to command the fortresses of Flushing, Zeeland, Antwerp, Breda, Bergen-op-Zoom, 's-Hertogenbosch, Gorkum, Willemsted, Naarden and all of the posts in Holland occupied by French troops. In addition he commanded the 24th Military Division, the Guard Cavalry Division under Léfèbvre-Desnoëttes and the two 4th and 6th Young Guard Divisions under Barrois and Roguet.

His instructions were first of all to insure French control of Flushing and Zeeland. His second goal was to retain control of Antwerp and his third goal was to hold Bergen-op-Zoom. He was told that he was subordinated to Maréchal Macdonald, who was operating between the Coblentz on the Rhine and Arnheim with the XI Corps and the II Cavalry Corps.

Antwerp was designated as the assembly point for the newly-forming I Corps. It was to be organized with three divisions under the commands of General Ledru-des-Essarts, Ambert and Carra-St.-Cyr (1st, 2nd and 3rd Divisions). Counting on the receipt of the promised troops, Maison directed the forming of those three divisions simultaneously in Lierre, Antwerp and Kessel. While he awaited the arrival of the promised forces he directed the few forces arriving, his foreign troops and the sailors to form a fixed garrison in Antwerp.[13] Maison was to receive only seven-and-a-half of the promised 55 battalions. The others were diverted into the Champagne where they joined the main French army under Napoleon.

Engagement at Breda – 20 December

On 19 December General Roguet moved his division and that of Castex to West-Wesel, where he drove back the Cossacks of General Stahl. On 20 December he arrived before Breda and sent his cavalry to 's-Hertogenbosch – putting a post in Terheyde, on the Gertruydenberg Canal, to give him advanced warning of the approach of an Allied relief force.

Breda was a walled city with 13 bastions, several ravelins and cavaliers, and five horn works. The city's defenses were further strengthened by a palisade. The main strength was the city's position on swampy ground. The city had a population of from 9,000 to 10,000 souls and was held by Benkendorff's tiny force of 1,500 men and eight light cannon. His infantry consisted of 400 Russian jagers and the infantry of the Colombé Streifkorps under Premier-lieutenant von Bockelmann. In addition to some cavalry the Colombé Streifkorps was formed with a detachment of the Fus/Colberg Infantry Regiment, some 40 volunteer jägers and 60 fusiliers.

Benkendorff deployed 250 Russian jagers to defend the Antwerp Gate and sent the 100 Prussian infantry, 150 Russian infantry, 20 Cossacks and three guns to defend the Ginneck Gates. The remaining force – consisting almost entirely of Cossacks – was held as a reserve.[14]

Roguet began a bombardment of Breda between 10:00 p.m. and midnight. General Benkendorff was able to make little response. During the night a detachment of Cossacks returning from Turnhout overran the post at Terheyde. They were attempting to bring with them 18 heavy cannon and ammunition from Willemsted down the Merck Canal to Breda. They were accompanied by 500 Dutch reinforcements and were to be followed by another 2,000.

The day of 21 December passed with useless attacks by the French on Breda's three gates. On the same day the Prussian division of General Krafft moved from Heusden to Dongen, and General Graham – with 8,000 English – arrived at Oudenbosch.

During the evening of 21 December Roguet resumed his bombardment of Breda, but with no particular result. The following day General Léfèbvre-Desnoëttes arrived and assumed

13 Calmon-Maison, p. 41.
14 von Damitz, Vol. I, pp. 147-150.

command. However, upon hearing that the British and Prussians had joined forces he felt the French situation before Breda was jeopardized and withdrew to Antwerp. On 23 December the two French divisions were at Hoogstraeten and Braschaet.[15]

Maison.

The French perspective of the Lowlands

The English were established in North and South Beveland. They had armed the population, provided mounts for a number of the inhabitants and constructed on South Beveland a number of batteries designed to cut the communications between Antwerp and Flushing. They had also made a serious attempt against Fort Bath on the eastern point of South Beveland (there the Scheldt divides into two large branches below Antwerp).

It was urgent for the French to chase the British from this island, where they captured large amounts of foodstuffs. Maison's first action was to reinforce Fort Bath to a strength of 1,000 men. He intended to sally out of the fortress and recapture South Beveland.

Napoleon had also directed Maison's attention to Bergen-op-Zoom, which commanded the right bank of the eastern branch of the Scheldt. Here too the British had intercepted large quantities of provisions vital to the French effort.

On 1 January the garrison forces under Maison stood as follows: Antwerp, 7,625 men; Bergen-op-Zoom, 3,048 men; Bath 1,060 men; and Lillo, 291 men. Another 91 were distributed in various other small garrisons. Of the 12,115 men the only field forces that Maison had were the 4th and 6th Young Guard Divisions of Barrois and Roguet and the light cavalry of Léfèbvre-Desnoëttes.[16]

The divisions of Roguet and Léfèbvre-Desnoëttes stood in Hoogstraeten and in the surrounding villages. Hoogstraeten stood almost equal distance between Antwerp and Breda, but it was not a good defensive position because it did not have good communications. It did however offer a good position for watching Breda, which had already been occupied by the Allies, as well as providing a French presence in the region to suppress any revolutionary tendencies on the part of the Belgian people.

Maison directed that Léfèbvre-Desnoëttes hold his position in Hoogstraeten and that he push strong forces down the roads to Breda and Bergen-op-Zoom in order to contain the Allied advance. He also directed that reconnaissance parties be sent towards Turnhout in order to detect any Allied movement towards Louvain. The French had been able only to provide a small garrison for Brussels of about 200 men of the 72nd Line Regiment and a move through Louvain would threaten Brussels.

At the same time as these instructions were issued, General Ambert – detached to Bergen-op-Zoom with a convoy escort – was directed to move to Lierre and establish his headquarters there. Initially, General Barrois was directed to sweep the countryside along the Dyle and the Néthes and clear any enemy out of the territory between Antwerp and the Meuse. He was to post garrisons on the bridges. However, he was directed to draw his division into Brussels before this sweep was to be started.

15 de Vaudoncourt, Vol. I, p. 202.
16 Calmon-Maison, p. 43.

In order to garrison other cities and depots, Maison was forced to siphon off another 7,000 men destined for the I Corps. The depots in Calais, Dunkirk, Gravelines, Saint-Omer and Lille – which were supposed to see 8,309 conscripts from the first call for 120,000 men – had by 28 December received only 6,020 men. The second call for 300,000 men had allocated to these cities 7,487 men, but only 308 had appeared. While waiting for the rest to arrive from these two drafts, 1,625 had deserted.

Each day deserters and draft dodgers were appearing in Breda where they were incorporated into the Russian formations or assisted the Allied operations. The Belgian people were hostile and encouraged the French soldiers to desert – offering them money. In Holland, a force of 600 French were being formed to capture the Barbant in favor of Louis XVIII. In the departments of Scheldt and Lys, armed bands roamed the countryside – attacking customs houses and small garrisons. In contrast, in the Department of Deux-Néthes – where Antwerp stood – the public sentiment had been dampened by the predations of the Allied forces – mostly Cossacks – that had penetrated into their homeland.

Maison's first aggressive action was to plan a strike at the British on South Beveland. The lack of seasoned and trained troops obliged him to use the escort for the Bergen-op-Zoom convoy. He planned to send 50 horsemen across the ford while General Gilly, who commanded Flushing, debarked 500 men near Borssele.

However, Napoleon intervened and directed Maison to recapture Gorkum. To do this Maison began to gather all available troops in Antwerp. However, contrary winds prevented the orders from reaching Gilly, who landed his forces on 4 January on South Beveland. The English batteries were surprised and the English were pursued into the village of Borssele, which they soon abandoned. Prior to returning to Flushing, Chef de bataillon Joyeux of the 131st Line – who led the operation – spiked the English guns, broke their carriages and destroyed the magazines.[17]

The Allies consolidate

After his failure at Breda, Roguet moved his forces back to a position before Antwerp – extending from Turnhout and Hoogstraeten on the right to Wustwesel and Braaschaat on the left.

Krafft's 6th Brigade occupied Breda and made no further efforts other than sending a reconnaissance towards Nijmegen, where Macdonald supported his left wing. The English established their siege forces around Bergen-op-Zoom and occupied Helvoetsluys, Zierikzee and Steenbergen. They were also charged with observing or blockading Delfzil at the mount of the Ems, Naarden, Texel, Nijmegen, Gorkum, 's-Hertogenbosch, Flushing, Terwere and Walachern.

Bülow moved his headquarters to Bommen, where he awaited Borstell's 5th Brigade. Borstell had begun his march towards Breda on 26 December when his brigade was relieved of its observation duties before Wesel by the cavalry of General Orurk (part of Winzingerode's corps).[18]

Roguet's 6th Young Guard Division remained in its camps at Hoogstraeten, with Ambert's 2nd Division covering his left. That same day GD Maison was designated as commander of the I Corps and arrived in Antwerp. His first orders was to put the fortresses still remaining in French power into a state where they could resist the Allied advance. Bergen-op-Zoom was provisioned for nine months while Flushing and Terwere – as well as the Forts of Batz, Lille and Liftenshoek – were provisioned for a full year.

On 1 January General Bülow drew together von Thümen's, Borstell's, Krafft's and Oppen's brigades together around Breda – preparing for his advance into Belgium and giving the French

17 Koch, Vol. II, p. 119; Calmon-Maison, p. 50; Vaudoncourt, Vol. I, p. 201.
18 de Vaudoncourt, Vol. I, p. 203.

cause to fear an attack on Antwerp.[19] Winzingerode's Corps and the 3rd German Corps had already crossed the Rhine. If the garrison of Antwerp had been sufficiently strong and if the I Corps was organized, Maison should have moved the I Corps and Roguet's division to the Nèthes and the Demer. By allowing these two positions to pass unopposed into the Allies' hands, he had effectively surrendered Belgium to them. After these two points there was no line suitable for the defense. Unfortunately for the French, Maison had no choice. He simply did not have the forces to defend Belgium.

Maison did what he could. He sent a few battalions to reinforce the Antwerp garrison and maintained the bulk of Roguet's division at Hoogstraeten. He had decided to watch events and act accordingly. Should Bülow advance from Breda or Tilburg, Maison would advance to block him. If the English were to move into the vicinity of Bergen-op-Zoom or Rosendael, he would move to place himself between the British and Antwerp.

Maison also dispatched four battalions, two squadrons and four guns – under GD Ambert – to Donck and Braschaet. At the same time, in order to maintain contact with Macdonald, he detached Castex's cavalry and two Young Guard battalions – under General Aymar – to Turnhout.

Ambert's force would only be able to cover the interval between Capellen and Westmalle and had to maintain his communications through Turnhout. As a result, Maison requested Barrois to move his division to the heights of Saint-Job-int-Goor. Fate should have, however, intervened and Barrois was forbidden to leave Brussels except on the order of Napoleon himself. Fortunately for Maison, Barrois was a competent officer and recognized that he could better serve his Emperor's cause by joining his troops with Maison and marched as Maison had requested.[20]

Fifteen days were sufficient for Maison to assure the defenses of Antwerp and the adjacent fortifications. He was now as ready as he could be to meet the Allies' advance.

Maréchal Macdonald – upon seeing his flank menaced by the Allied movements and with Bülow and Graham almost standing in his rear, commanding the left bank of the Meuse – found himself obliged to withdraw his left. On 4 January he evacuated Nijmegen and withdrew his corps to a position between Guelders and Cologne. The XI Corps and II Cavalry Corps were posted between Guelders and Venlo, occupying Xanten. The V Corps (Albert's 1st Division) and the II Cavalry Corps stood between Cologne and the Neuss.[21]

On 9 January Bülow learned that the ice in the Meuse and Rhine had damaged the bridges over those rivers. This meant that Winzingerode would be unable to join him immediately. This meant that his position would become critical if Macdonald moved through Grave and advanced to strike his flank, while Maison stood before him. His only alternative was to take the offensive against the French I Corps. If Bülow were able to defeat Maison, Macdonald would be obliged to withdraw as far as the Maëstricht heights, which would assure his lines of communication with Winzingerode. If his proposed attack failed, the British positions would prevent Maison from pursuing him and would probably cause Macdonald's potential offensive movement to stop. Bülow decided to attack.[22]

Maréchal Macdonald.

19 Calmon-Maison, p. 56.
20 Calmon-Maison, p. 58.
21 de Vaudoncourt, Vol. I, p. 204.
22 de Vaudoncourt, Vol. I, p. 205.

The I Corps continued to remain before Antwerp. Roguet occupied Hoogstraeten with Flament's brigade. Two battalions stood in West-Wesel and Leenhout. Aymar's brigade stood in Turnhout and Léfèbvre-Desnoëttes' cavalry stood between Thruhout and Brecht. General Ambert, with four battalion and 200 cavalry, stood in Donck and Braschaet. Castex's 1st Guard Cavalry Division was in Lierre while Barrois' 4th Young Guard Division was in Brussels.

General Bülow established his headquarters in Breda – establishing liaison with the English under General Graham – and began making plans for an attack on the French. On 9 January Bülow – having resolved himself to the offensive – sent his cavalry in the directions of Turnhout, Ruemonde and Venlo. Venlo was to be attacked by the Colombé Partisans – reinforced by a large force of cavalry and some infantry with the goal of cutting Macdonald's communications with Turnhout and Maëstricht. Two Cossack pulks were sent via Tilburg and Eindhoven towards Turnhout with the goal of scouting General Léfèbvre-Desnoëttes.[23]

On 10 January Bülow sent his own corps forward in three columns. Borstell's 5th Brigade – supported by a force of Russian artillery forming the left column – moved down the road to take Hoogstraeten. After uniting his forces in Gros-Zundert, von Thümen moved his 4th Brigade – the center column – down the high road towards Loenhout and West-Wesel. General Oppen – commanding the right column formed by Krafft's 6th Brigade, the rest of the Russian artillery and part of the reserve cavalry – was ordered to turn Roguet's left and move against the road from Wustwesel to Antwerp. This attack was combined with General Graham's movement of a strong mixed arms column from Rosendael towards Merxhem.

Bülow 's light cavalry superiority prevented Maison from learning the goals of his movements. The appearance of the Allied cavalry on his flank and false reports caused Maison to believe Bülow was marching on Campine sur Diest and Louvain. On 11 January he ordered Barrois and Castex to unite their divisions at Lierre. That same day – at 8:00 a.m. – Borstell's 5th Brigade moved out of Meer in two columns and marched on Hoogstraeten and Vortel.

As Bülow 's forces advanced in three columns, they encountered Maison's forces as they prepared a major reconnaissance effort. His first column – Borstell – marched directly on Hoogstraeten via Meer. The second threatened the Allied left near Loenhout and Brecht. The third column, coming from Meerle, moved against the French left near Merxplas and Turnhout. Borstell, who executed the attack on Hoogstraeten, organized his forces as noted overleaf:

Flament's brigade was already under arms as Borstell's first column – the 5th Brigade reinforced by Oberst von Sydow's detachment[24] – threw back the French advanced posts and moved from Meer and Wertel. GD Roguet had placed his forces on alert because of the appearance of Allied light infantry on his flank and moved a battalion of the 12th Tirailleurs into the Mynderhout cemetery, flanked the road from Meer with another, placed two battalions and four guns in reserve before Hoogstraeten and held two battalions and his park in reserve on the road to Oost-Malle. His dispositions permitted the two battalions between Loenhout and Wustwesel to form as necessary.

However, when the 4,000 British appeared on the road to Rosendael these two French battalions were ordered to cover the French left and moved via Brecht to Wyneghem – that is to say, towards Donck and Braschaet. Maison had foreseen such a move and had already posted Ambert's four battalions there. Roguet then sent an order to Aymar to evacuate and move to Lierre.

At 8:00 a.m. the Allied infantry attacked the 12th Tirailleurs, who delayed and stalled their assault on Hoogstraeten.[25] The Prussian attack consisted of the Fus/1st Pomeranian Infantry

23 Koch, Vol. II, p. 121.
24 Sydow's detachment consisted of an infantry battalion, ten cavalry squadrons and 16 cannon. von Plotho, Vol. III, p. 198.
25 de Vaudoncourt, Vol. I, p. 206 & Calmon-Maison, pp. 61-3.

Borstell's attack on Hoogstraeten

Advanced Guard: Oberstleutnant von Thümen
Jäger Company, Major von Heidenreich
Fus/1st Pomeranian Infantry Regiment
Pomeranian Hussar Regiment (two squadrons)
½ Horse Battery

Main column: Oberstleutnant von Knobloch
1/, 2/1st Pomeranian Infantry Regiment
Dietrich's Russian 12pdr Foot Battery
1/2nd Reserve Infantry Regiment
Pomeranian Hussar Regiment (one squadron)
Jäger Detachment, Pomeranian Hussar Regiment
Pomeranian National Cavalry Regiment

Reserve: Oberstleutnant von Sandrart
Leib Hussar Regiment (three squadrons)
Jäger Detachment, Leib Hussar Regiment (one squadron)
½ Horse Battery
Jäger Detachment, 1st Pomeranian Infantry Regiment
Jäger Detachment, Pomeranian Grenadier Battalion
½ 6pdr Foot Battery #10
Pomeranian Grenadier Battalion

Column: Oberst von Sydow
East Prussian Jäger Battalion (one company)
von Reiche Jäger Battalion
Fus/2nd Reserve Infantry Regiment
Leib Hussar Regiment (one squadron)
Kurmärk Landwehr Cavalry Regiment
½ Horse Battery

Regiment – supported by the skirmishers of the 1/, 2/1st Pomeranian Infantry Regiment and four horse guns – which moved down the road before Hoogstraeten.[26] The 1/1st Pomeranian Regiment and the 1/2nd Reserve Infantry Regiment struck the French rear on the Ostmalle road. On the road to Meer, yet another battalion attacked. After a tenacious defense an order from GB Aymar ordered the evacuation of Turnhout and a withdrawal on Antwerp.[27]

Von Thümen's 4th Brigade advanced in two columns against West-Wesel and Leenhout. General Roguet – attacked frontally by 14,000 men – found himself under attack by a third Prussian column turning his left and the British under General Graham advancing with 4,000 men from Rosendael towards Antwerp. Fearing he would be enveloped, he ordered a withdrawal. The French withdrawal was executed in good order – disputing each ditch. The French troops that withdrew from Hoogstraeten took up positions in Ostmalle that evening while those that evacuated West-Wesel moved to Westmalle. Aymar's brigade – cut off from Hoogstraeten by a Prussian column moving via Vortel – withdrew to Lierre. Koch states that the Prussians report losing 18 officers and 465 men dead and wounded, while the French reported losses of about 300. Sporschil gives the Prussian losses at 15 officers and 400 soldiers dead and wounded, including General Borstell, who was wounded by musket shot and had a horse killed under him.[28]

On 12 January the Allies resumed their offensive with the English moving into Capellen and the Prussians into Braschaet, Groeven-Wesel and Olgehem. Roguet resumed his withdrawal – moving on Antwerp. Flament's brigade occupied Deurne. Two battalions were posted to Weyneghem. Ambert's division occupied Merxhem. Deurne and Merxhem were covered with light entrenchments. Maison presumed that the two divisions in these positions could hold the Allies in check and resolved to put himself at the head of Castex's cavalry and Barrois' division – which were en route from Brussels to Lierre with a forced march – and strike on the Allied left flank and throw them into the sea.

26 von Damitz, Vol. I, p. 360.
27 Koch, Vol. II, p. 122.
28 Sporschil, Vol. II, Band 1, p. 268.

To this end he left Antwerp on 13 January with 1,000 infantry, a horse battery, two foot batteries and marched to Lierre where he joined Castex's division and the 3,600 conscripts which had been sent to him by GD Barrois.[29]

Bülow 's maneuver was met by success and the French withdrew to Wyneghem, Deurne and Merxhem. General Bülow advanced against this position on 12 January. Von Thümen's column moved against Braschaet. Borstell's column moved against Saint-Antoine and Oppen's center column moved against Gravenwesel. The English forces, under Graham, were in Erkeren.

Maison, once again fooled by the appearance of Allied light cavalry on his flank by Heerensthal, assumed that this movement was only a demonstration and united Barrois' 4th Young Guard Division and Castex's 1st Guard Cavalry Divisions near Lierre. In addition he joined several thousand men with them drawn from Antwerp. It was his intention to move this force against Diest, where he believed he would encounter an Allied column marching on Louvain.[30]

Engagement by Merxhem

On 13 January Bülow resolved to renew his attack on the French. Von Thümen's 4th Brigade and Oppen's column were to form his first line. Borstell marched in reserve. At 8:00 a.m. General von Thümen deployed before Merxhem, which General Avy defended with five battalions. That same day General Graham – with a division of 3,000 British under Major General Mackenzie – moved from Rosendael to Calmhout to join the attack on the French at Donck and Merxhem.[31] Two Prussian battalions stood in the interval between the main English and Prussian columns. As von Thümen attacked it frontally, it was attacked in the flank by 3,500 English under General Gibbs.[32]

General Oppen directed an attack against Duerne, which was defended by GB Flament's brigade. This force, under Major Zglinitzki, consisted of two battalions of the 9th Reserve Regiment and the Jäger Detachment of the Königin Dragoons. A second force – two squadrons and a battalion – attacked Schotten and served to link Oppen with von Thümen's brigade.

The Allies made great efforts to cut off the French defending Wyneghem. The village of Wyneghem was attacked by part of Oppen's troops – as well as Borstell's column under Oberst von Zastrow. This force consisted of the Fus/3rd East Prussian Regiment, the Fus/Colberg Regiment, one squadron of the Königin Dragoons, two squadrons of the 2nd West Prussian Dragoons and half of Baumgerten's battery.[33] After a very heavy cannonade, the two Young Guard battalions occupying the village were forced to abandon the village – abandoning one gun to the Prussians.

The Duke of Plaisance – seeing the weakness of the position – sent Ambert reinforcements in the form of a battalion of armed naval artisans. GB Flament moved to assist them – attacking Wyneghem, retaking both the village and the lost gun. On the left, General Avis fell – killed at the head of the 4th Légère Regiment. Merxhem was lost despite the support the battalion sent to assist them. The French troops withdrew and rallied in the Dame suburb of Antwerp. The Allies made themselves masters of Merxhem and began throwing howitzer shells into Antwerp.

Roguet ordered GB Flament, in Duerne, to support the French in Wyneghem. Bülow found his attacks on Wyneghem and Duerne futile and, fearing an attack in his rear by French troops near Lierre, decided to withdraw. Flament reoccupied Duerne. Bülow directed Krafft and his cavalry on Breda while von Thümen marched on Ruysbergen and the two Sunderts. Borstell

29 Koch, Vol. II, p. 123.
30 de Vaudoncourt, Vol. I, p. 207.
31 Burghersh, p. 81.
32 Sporschil, Vol. II, 1st Band, p. 269.
33 von Damitz, Vol. I, p. 369.

moved to Hoogstraeten, West-Wesel and Leenhout. His withdrawal obliged the English to abandon the fruits of their victory and they withdrew to their cantonments.[34] Graham left a rearguard at Rosendael. This inconclusive movement might have come out differently if Maison had not been deceived and detached Barrois' 4th Young Guard Division and Castex's 1st Guard Cavalry Divisions to Lierre. There are some disagreements as to the causalities. Von Damitz gives no French losses, but states the Allies lost five officers and 220 men dead and wounded.[35] Vaudoncourt states the engagement cost the French about 500 casualties and the Allies 800 casualties.[36] Koch gives the French losses at 300 dead, 694 wounded and 15-20 prisoners. He states that the English did not make their losses known, but the Prussians appear to have lost about 620 men.[37] Von Plotho stakes out the high ground for French casualties – claiming they lost over 600 prisoners plus many dead and wounded. He goes on to say that the Prussian 4th Brigade lost two officers and four men dead, three officers and 68 men wounded, while Oppen's column lost about 150 dead and wounded.[38] Roguet wrote Napoleon a complete report on the engagement – stating that the victory was due to the valor of his troops – but gives no casualty figures.

Though it was doubted that the Allies would make a second attack in the near future, Napoleon directed the assembly of the material necessary to defend the city. He ordered Macdonald to leave the banks of the Meuse and to move towards the Ardennes – charging Roguet and Ambert with covering Antwerp. And, after placing 1,000 infantry and 100 Gardes d'honneur in Malines and two other battalions and 100 mixed cavalry in Brussels, he directed Barrois' division and 400 horse from Castex's division move to Louvain (Louvain as it was the junction of four major roads and provided the best position for covering Brussels and Antwerp). From that position Maison could operate with Macdonald, who still stood between Liège and Maëstricht. Despite the advantages of positioning his forces there, the Minister of War ordered him to concentrate his forces before Antwerp. Only when Macdonald informed Maison that he was abandoning Hasselt and Liège did Maison replace his rearguard with a detachment of 1,800 infantry and 800 cavalry under GD Castex and marched to Antwerp only with Barrois' division.[39]

Macdonald's position becomes untenable

During the first days of January Czernichev brought his forces forward to the Rhine (near Düsseldorf). His advanced guard was formed by all of Winzingerode's cavalry. On 6 January Winzingerode's infantry arrived. They remained on the Rhine for a few days – delayed by the ice which clogged the Rhine. During this time, Macdonald – threatened on his right by the Army of Silesia – withdrew towards Trèves. His position was also threatened by St. Priest's corps, which moved against Bonn, and Bülow 's offensive in Holland. He found himself with little choice but to withdraw before the superior Allied force. On 24 January he moved to a position before Maëstricht and Aix-la-Chapelle (Aachen). He had Neuss occupied by a brigade and held his cavalry in Cologne. General Maison, after the battle at Wyneghem, left the divisions of Roguet and Ambert before Antwerp – re-establishing Barrois and Castex in Louvain. Barrois detached two battalions and Castex 100 cavalry, which were sent to Malines. Macdonald then received orders to withdraw to the Marne and join the other corps that Napoleon was concentrating. On

34 Burghersh, pp. 81-2.
35 von Damitz, Vol. I, p. 372.
36 de Vaudoncourt, Vol. I, p. 209.
37 Koch, Vol. II, p. 126.
38 von Plotho, Vol. III, p. 200.
39 Calmon-Maison, p. 84.

12 January the II Cavalry Corps and the troops in Neuss withdrew. On 16 January he began his movement through Liège and Huy. On 18 January Macdonald was in Namur. On 23 January he was in Rhétel and his cavalry was in Mézières. He continued his march on Châlons, where he arrived on 2 February.

On 13 January Winzingerode's Corps began crossing the Rhine. On 15 January Winzingerode's advanced guard was organized and standing in Neuss. On 22 January this advanced guard arrived in Aix-la-Chapelle (Aachen) and on 24 January it was in Liège, where it joined Benkendorff (who had been there since 18 January). On 24 January Winzingerode, who marched behind his advanced guard, arrived in Aix-la-Chapelle (Aachen).

Engagement at St.-Trond

GD Maison established his headquarters in Louvain on 16 January. On 24 January GD Maison sent GD Castex to St.-Trond at the head of 3,400 infantry, 600 Guard cavalry and two guns with orders to make contact with Maréchal Macdonald, who was reported to be moving on Liège.[40]

On 24 January Castex found himself in contact with 300 Cossacks and drove them back. Castex pushed on to the north-west of Liège – encountering 2,000 Allied infantry and cavalry supported by two guns – near the village of Hognoul. Castex sought to force passage.

General Czernichev had sent Benkendorff on a reconnaissance towards Brussels with two Cossack regiments – the Girova and Susoev III Cossack Regiments. The French cavalry charged twice – supported by the infantry of the 72nd Line Regiment – in squares. The seven squadrons of the 1st Guard Lancer Regiment totally outclassed Benkendorff's Cossacks – driving them back in great disorder. Czernichev responded to the sound of the battle by sending two squadrons of hussars and two guns at the trot to Lüttich to support Benkendorff. Colonel Lopuchin responded by sending another Cossack regiment down the road from Namur towards Lüttich and the Prussian Major von Lützow sent his two uhlan squadrons to join the fight.[41] Once Benkendorff was supported by all of Czernichev's cavalry, the tables were turned and Castex was forced to withdraw to Oraye and then to St.-Trond. Though there was no significant pursuit, Castex was wounded – losing his arm.[42] Von Plotho states that the Russians lost two officers and 30 men.[43]

The Allied threat coalesces

From Aix-la-Chapelle, Winzingerode resumed his movement – sending Czernichev via Namur and Philippeville and his infantry marched through Givet and Mézières. The roads before him were clear of any significant French forces.

Maison's situation was difficult, but he was an aggressive man of faith. He constantly thought of the offensive and sent orders to GD Brenier, commandant of the 16th Military Division, to send to Brussels all the troops destined for the I Corps that were present. However, this order was to produce few results as the troops simply were not to be had. Brenier sent a few stray companies north[44], but did not feel he could part with the 300 men from the 17th Line that were searching the local villages for deserters or those companies of the 27th Légère which were charged with

40 de Vaudoncourt, Vol. I, p. 210; Calmon-Maison, p. 76; & von Damitz, Vol. I, p. 351. Oddly, Sporschil states that Castex had 1,200 infantry, 800 cavalry and two guns. Sporschil, Vol. II, 1st Band, p. 279.

41 von Damitz, Vol. I, p. 352.

42 Calmon-Maison, p. 90.

43 von Plotho, Vol. III, p. 202.

44 Brenier sent 125 men of the 51st and 175 of the 75th Line Regiments to Brussels.

surveillance of the Lys Department and with gathering up supplies.[45] Maison had ruthlessly stripped Brussels of what was available and left it with a garrison of about 60 conscripts and a battalion of 400 customs officers.

The Allies had organized a tremendous force in Breda and its surrounding area. They deployed across the countryside to forage and levy contributions upon the population. While Bülow prepared for the invasion of Flanders, Winzingerode's forces pushed into the Walloon provinces. Prince Lapoukin, with 800 Cossacks, occupied Liège as Macdonald's rearguard evacuated the village. Lapoukin's forces then pushed as far as Namur, where they were joined by 5,000 Cossacks under Czernichev. At the same time, Blücher – far to the south – detached several columns of cavalry which moved through Luxemburg and into Belgium.

On 26 January – during the night – a combination of treachery by the city's inhabitants (who opened the gates) and an attack by a Prussian reserve regiment resulted in the fall of 's-Hertogenbosch. The 600-650-man garrison, under Colonel Laraitrie, withdrew to the citadel and surrendered the following day because of a lack of food. On 27 January General Maison found himself surrounded by Winzingerode's corps. He prepared to evacuate his positions between Lierre and Louvain and withdraw to Brussels.

On 27 January the Allies had about 50 squadrons at Namur which were to either operate against Brussels or to pursue Macdonald. The fate of Belgium was compromised by the union of Winzingerode and Bülow 's forces at Namur.

As Bülow prepared to advance into Belgium, Maison began sending out small reconnaissance detachments. One of these detachments encountered Major Helwig's streifkorps. On 28 January Helwig arrived before Louvain and attacked the advanced posts of Meuziau with 1,000 cavalry and 600 infantry. Two companies of voltigeurs from the 72nd Line and a company of the 12th Voltigeurs stopped his attack, pushed Helwig back to Tirlemont and inflicted heavy losses on him.[46] Further French columns were sent towards Aerschot, Diest, Tirlemont and Wavre. All of them were driven back to the gates of Louvain.

During the evening of 30 January Barrois' division departed Malines and marched on Brussels. His plans soon changed as he was ordered to march on Louvain and placed his cavalry and some infantry on the Etterbeek heights, where they watched the roads to Wavre and Louvain. Maison occupied Waterloo with 50 cavalry and 150 infantry. Castex's cavalry and battalion of customs officers were sent to Nivelles. Maison was deploying in an effort to delay the Allied advance into Belgium and give himself time to continue the preparation of the fortresses of Flanders.

Helwig.

On 30 January General Bülow , who had remained around Breda, once again began his advance into Belgium. Having concentrated his forces at West-Wesel and Hoogstraeten, on 31 January he moved to Westmalle. Skirting the city, he once again decided to move against Antwerp. The British had actively solicited such a move – hoping that such action would result in the capture of the French fleet located there (or at least its destruction).[47]

45 Calmon-Maison, p. 87.
46 Calmon-Maison, p. 103.
47 de Vaudoncourt, Vol. I, p. 211.

Second assault on Antwerp

The Duke of Plaisance, stimulated by Maison and seconded by Admiral Missiessy, made every effort to prepare the city for attack. The works at Merxhem were armed and prepared. In order to prolong the defense, Ambert's division was posted in Braschaet and Schotten with instructions not to withdraw until the last extremity. GD Roguet was ordered to evacuate Wyneghem, whose entrenchments were incomplete, and to place advanced posts that would advise of the Allies' attack on the heights around Château Arcul on the road to Deurne. The bridge at Heerensthal was strongly occupied by Colonel Vautrin, whose regiment and four guns stood in Berghem. Flament formed a reserve at the Borgerhout suburb and the rest of the troops of the garrison were deployed within the city.

On 1 February General Bülow – now reassured about his position – advanced against the French positions before Antwerp. The attack began at 8:00 a.m. as von Thümen moved down the Helmont road and engaged Aimer's brigade, which straddled the road supported by 10 guns. The terrain to the left of the road was very broken and difficult as far as Deurne, which was von Thümen's target. Von Thümen's target was protected by the terrain – which prevented maneuver – and the French placed in strong entrenchments.

Two battalions of the 5th East Prussian Regiment, a half battery and two squadrons of Landwehr cavalry – supported by the 2/4th East Prussian Infantry Regiment – made the first Allied attack. The French resisted their assault so ferociously that not only the supporting forces, but the Fus/4th East Prussian, the 2nd East Prussian Grenadiers and another half battery from the reserve were fed into the battle. The French were eventually driven back – losing 300 prisoners. The Prussians then attacked out of the village of Duerne – striking the French by the bridge – but the engagement stalled and night fell – bringing it to an end, or so the Prussians thought.

Unable to hold their positions in the burning village, the Prussians began to withdraw. Seeing a mass of Prussian skirmishers covering the withdrawal of the Prussian troops, GD Roguet ordered Chef d'escadron Briqueville to lead 100 lancers – supported by a battalion of the 12th Tirailleurs and the 13th Voltigeurs – and attack the Prussians. This attack was a complete surprise and quite successful. The Prussians were chased back to their morning positions and the French recovered most of the lost ground. The Prussian skirmishers were cut off and sought to escape through the partially-frozen swamp. However, about 100 were swallowed up by the swamp and another 60 were taken prisoner.[48] The Prussians had launched three frontal assaults over a period of six hours and suffered heavy losses in the attempt.

The 2nd East Prussian Grenadier Battalion, however, remained in the last houses of Duerne. To the right and left of their position 100 men were posted as flank security and the 4th East Prussian Regiment stood 100 paces behind them – acting as a support. General von Bülow posted two further battalions of the Colberg Regiment half-way between Wyneghem and Duerne. The remaining three battalions of the brigade were pulled back to Wyneghem.[49]

General Krafft's column stood in Schotten with the Fus/5th East Prussian Regiment and two squadrons detached from von Thümen's 4th Brigade. The French that had been posted there had withdrawn to Merxhem.

On the Allied right an English artillery train was moving forward. Before Braschaet it was engaged by three French battalions, which were also driven back to Merxhem.

The left column, under General von Oppen, had advanced down the road from Herenthals and crossed the Heerensthal Canal. That evening von Treskow's cavalry brigade arrived in Wommelgen, which was adjacent to Duerne.

48 Koch, Vol. II, pp. 133-4.
49 von Damitz, Vol. II, pp. 207-9.

Second day

That night, it was decided to renew the attack and advance in parallel with the English as they pushed forward. Von Thümen planned to move against the Schin bridge, which he perceived was not defended.

The next morning the two battalions of the Colberg Infantry Regiment were ordered to attack from a position to the right of Duerne and push over the small stream towards Merxhem, while on the left the Fus/4th East Prussian Regiment struck at the same target.

As they advanced, a battalion of the 9th Reserve – formed in a column – marched directly down the road and into the village of Merxhem.

Though the French resisted this advance, the 9th Reserve Regiment cleared the bridge and the two Colberg battalions and the Fus/4th East Prussians pushed over the stream. The assaults for the day appear to have ended there. The 2nd East Prussian Grenadiers moved to a position in Castellen and occupied a few houses in Posto. A gun supported by two squadrons of Landwehr was attached to support them.

The total losses suffered by the Prussians during the fights of 1 and 2 February were two officers, two NCOs and 65 men dead, and 15 officers, 38 NCOs, eight musicians and 565 men wounded. The French losses are not known.[50]

A few Prussian battalions extended to the right so that contact could be maintained with the British, who had struck the French in Merxhem that morning at 10:00 a.m. Graham's 4,800 British and Hanoverian troops – supported by a small Dutch artillery train and under the orders of major generals Gibbs and Taylor[51] – carried Braaschaat and Merxhem – driving the three French battalions before them. The British march had been slow because of the artillery train they carried with them.

Krafft's advance, aided by the evacuation of Wyneghem, attached Schotten – throwing back the three French battalions defending it. General Oppen was unable to cross the Herenthals Canal because of a small French post and, as a result, Oppen did not get his forces into the battle. However, the attack was successful overall and General Graham advanced to the walls of Antwerp.

During the night von Thümen was reinforced by a few of Krafft's battalions and after a conference between the principal Allied generals, it was decided that the English would attack Merxhem and the Prussians would attack the bridges at Schin and the Heerensthal Canal.

At daybreak the Allied assault renewed – with General Ambert pushed back by the first assault. Around 10:00 a.m. the English drove the French back into Antwerp. In Deurne, Roguet was far more successful and held the Prussians back throughout the day. Now that the Allies held Merxhem, the Allies spent the night of 2-3 February preparing batteries behind the Saint-Ferdinand dike and began their bombardment the following morning.[52]

The French fleet in Antwerp, however, had nothing to fear from the bombardment because of the precautions taken by Admiral Missiessy and his staff. The fortress artillery defending Antwerp responded with vigour to the Allied attack.

It was at this time that General Carnot came to relieve the Duke of Plaisance as governor of the city. Carnot had served in 1793 and offered his services to Napoleon in a letter dated 24 January 1814. Carnot's relationship with Napoleon had not been strong. Berthier had proposed Carnot for promotion to général de division in 1800 and Napoleon had rejected the proposal after Carnot had objected to his elevation to Emperor. However, Carnot was motivated by patriotism and Napoleon needed his talents. Clarke (Minister for War) responded

50 von Damitz, Vol. II, pp. 209-11.
51 Koch, Vol. II, p. 130.
52 Koch, Vol. II, p. 135.

to Carnot's request to serve, promoted him to général de division and made him govenor of Antwerp – giving him "the keys of the Empire, our naval arsenal and our gateway to the northern frontiers."[53]

Carnot was well-suited to assume the command of Antwerp as it was a major fortress and it would most assuredly be the target of attack by the Allies as they attempted to move into northern France. His greatest claim to fame was his work *Défense des Places fortes* (*The Defense of Fortresses*) and its publication had given him a unique position in the halls of French military practitioners alongside the vaunted Vauban.

Once in Antwerp he called together a defense committee consisting of himself and his predecessor, General Lebrun;[54] Admiral Missiessy, commanding the Scheldt flotilla; Kersaint, the Admiral Superintendent; Savoye-Rollin, the civil administrator; and the three senior generals (Roguet commanding the Imperial Guard, Ambert the infantry commander and Fauconnet the commander of the fortress). After discussing how to defend the city he inspected the 12,000-man garrison and toured the city's defenses.

Antwerp was well-protected. To the west was the River Scheldt, to the north the land was flooded, to the east were the suburbs of Saint-Willebrord and Borgerhout (which were covered by the River Schyn) and the south was covered by the fortress. To the north of the city were the naval installations. They contained 23 vessels in the main basin and another 17 in the dockyards.

Carnot had recalled Roguet's division to Antwerp – abandoning all but Berghem and Borgerhout as advanced posts. Bülow responded by advancing as far as he could into the abandoned territory and erected a battery at Merxhem. The battery began to fire on the fortress and fired 1,500 shells and 800 incendiary missiles in three days of bombardment.[55]

However, it soon became apparent that this bombardment was not going to be successful and the Allies lacked the means to implement a formal siege. On 6 January – after expending all their ammunition to no effect – the Allies withdrew to their positions before the attacks on Deurne, Braaschaat and Merxhem. Seeking an easier target, on 13 January General Bülow moved his forces south towards Laon, where he planned to join other Allied forces.

In preparing his defense Carnot made many unusual moves. He did not demolish the suburbs, as was the general practice. He saw them as strongpoints to be defended that would help keep the enemy at bay just that much longer. He took other steps to ensure that the garrison did not impose undue hardships on the civilian residents of Antwerp so when the Allies attempted to subvert the Belgians with a propaganda campaign, it failed to arouse much support.

The evacuation of Brussels

As the British and Prussians broke their teeth on the walls of Antwerp, General Maison established himself between Louvain and Malines – resolving to stop the Allied advance and to force them to deploy before allowing them to pass. However, when Major Helwig appeared before Louvain with 700 to 800 cavalry, Maison recognized that he would have to withdraw to Brussels.

During the day of 31 January he made the necessary preparations to abandon Brussels and the following day Barrois' division and part of Castex's division moved to Hall. Their advanced guard was in Elbeck, Ombeck and Henrypont. His reserve was in Tubize.

53 Watson, p. 181.

54 Lebrun had been relieved, but the arrival of the Allies prevented his rejoining Napoleon in France.

55 Watson, p. 183.

General Chambarlhac, commander of the 16th Military Division, was ordered to send 1,200 men from the various infantry depots[56] and 150 men from the 1st Gardes d'honneur Regiment to Tournai and to hold his position until the arrival of General Ledru, who was to withdraw from the fortresses on the Lys all the men capable of undertaking a field campaign. Finally, General Penne was sent to Mons to take command of the few troops that were already united there.[57]

At most, GD Maison could hold Brussels for a few days – and because of political considerations he considered holding Brussels as long as he could. However, the occupation of the city by foreigners was inevitable and he feared that the population would revolt. He quickly decided that holding the city for 48 hours was not worth the sacrifice of his tiny army. GD Maison had evacuated Brussels on 1 February and withdrew to Tournai. Facing Bülow 's 10,000 men, Maison had only 5,500 men – not including the customs battalion blockaded in Maubeuge. His situation was not good.

4th Young Guard Division	104,553
72nd Line Regiment	20,580
Cavalry Division	48,790
Castex's artillery	8,118
Barrois' artillery	9,250
Total:	189,291[58]

Storming of Lierre

Word had arrived in the Allied camp that Lierre contained a small garrison of 1,500 men and a few cannon. Borstell organized his advanced guard the morning of 31 January by Massenhoven and gave Oberstleutnant von Knobloch command of two battalions of the 2nd Reserve Regiment and a Jäger Company – supporting them with three battalions and a battery. Oberst von Sydow remained in reserve with the cavalry and two battalions of infantry. Borstell ordered von Knobloch to attack the Antwerp and Lisper gates if possible and von Knobloch advanced his forces to within 200 paces of the city before the first French post raised the alarm. Borstell quickly deployed his forces to block any relieving force coming from Antwerp – sending his two Cossack regiments and three squadrons of the Leib Hussar Regiment to assume positions on the main road between the two cities.

Meanwhile, Oberstleutnant von Knobloch – at the head of the Fus/2nd Reserve Regiment – assaulted Lierre's Antwerp Gate. His assault was repulsed with heavy losses. In order to not give the French time to react, von Knobloch then sent the 1/2nd Reserve forward – covered by the skirmishers of the Fus/2nd under the command of Hauptmann von Keller. The Prussian skirmishers gained the wall adjacent to the gate and opened it to the attacking Prussians. The moment it opened the 1/2nd Reserve Regiment charged forward at the *Sturmschritt* with von Knobloch at its head on his horse. As they charged towards the gate, von Knobloch was shot and killed. The battalion commander, Major von Massow, fell wounded as well. However, Major von Mirbach, commander of the Fusiliers, led the Fus/,1/2nd Reserve forward and through the gate. They were followed the Fus/1st Pomeranian Infantry Regiment, led by Oberst von Schon. The city passed into Prussian hands.

56 Detachments came from the 51st, 65th and 75th Line Regiments.

57 Koch, Vol. II, pp. 138-9; Calmon-Maison, p.106.

58 Calmon-Maison, p. 122.

A relieving force under Colonel Bautrin was sent towards Lierre from Antwerp. It contained the 11th Tirailleur Regiment and about 60 cavalry. However, it was repulsed and withdrew back to Antwerp.[59]

Engagement at Mons

On 3 February General Penne stood in Mons with 700 infantry of the 25th, 45th and 72nd Line Regiments drawn from their depots. That morning he found himself attacked by a thousand-man detachment of Winzingerode's advanced guard outside Mons. He executed a fighting withdrawal to Valenciennes. Maison sent the 12th Voltigeurs, four guns, 100 of Castex's cavalry and 200 customs guards to his assistance – sensing the threat to the old frontiers. Penne was to attack the Allied forces before Mons and was authorized to withdraw on Valenciennes and Condé if confronted by superior forces. Penne, however, was able to drive the Allies away.

On 4 February Maison transferred his headquarters to Ath and on 10 February he moved to Tournai. From there he could concentrate his forces and scout the roads to Valenciennes, Audenarde, Courtrai and Menin. He sent another detachment to Lannoy.

During the morning of 8 February General Meuziau learned that a force of Allied infantry and cavalry were marching on Lessines. He sent a detachment of the 2nd Guard Lancers, under Capitaine Brack, on a reconnaissance to observe the Allied movement. Brack encountered the Allies near Ollignies, charged them and drove them back – only stopping when coming under infantry fire by Lessines.

Later, in the same direction, a column of French soldiers who had been taken prisoner with the fall of 's-Hertogenbosch – and who had been paroled – were found marching under an escort of a few Allied cavalry. The Allies were using the movement of this column to mask an attempt to surprise the French advanced posts. The ruse being exposed, the Prussians deployed their infantry and Barrois' troops in Ath leapt to their arms. However, nothing came of this as after a few skirmish shots, the Prussians withdrew towards Enghien.

Leaving a small rearguard in Ath, the I Corps concentrated in Tournai on 9 February. As the movements continued, Napoleon sent a request to Maison asking if it was his intention to gather up all the garrisons and detachments in Flanders, join them to his army and draw an equal force from the garrison of Antwerp so as to assume the offensive. At that time these garrisons were disposed as follows:

In and around Lille[60]	5,628
Valenciennes	1,530
Condé	580
Maubeuge	1,108
Landrecies	629
Les Quesnoy	530
Bouchain	172
Douai	811
Ypres	629
Total:	11,617

59 von Damitz, Vol. II, pp. 201-3.
60 Calmon-Maison, p. 152.

Napoleon hoped that Maison could, with this force, throw the Allies out of Belgium rather than allow himself to be shut up in the various Belgium fortresses. Unfortunately, Napoleon did not have as complete a grasp on the situation as Maison did, who wisely declined the invitation to assume the offensive.

The arrival of the 1st Saxon Division

The Prussians occupied Brussels on 3 February and concentrated their forces slowly. Ghent was occupied on 4 February. The Duke of Saxe-Weimar, commanding the 1st Saxon Division, relieved them in Brussels on 6-7 February and the Duke assumed the task of governor of the Low Countries.

During this interval the Prussians sought to engage in a war of skirmishes. On 8 February a column of 150 men drawn from the garrison of 's-Hertogenbosch – moving under parole – arrived before the Allied advanced posts under a cavalry escort. The Prussians sought to take advantage of this and prepared and executed an ambush – violating the general agreements on the conduct of war in this period, much to their shame.[61]

Other actions were undertaken by the Allies. The Prince of Saxe-Weimar and Bülow continued their efforts to take Deventer and Antwerp. These efforts included outright bribery and apparently the price set by the governor of Deventer was too high and their efforts to buy Antwerp were rebuffed outright.

Bülow leaves for France

Bülow , seeing his progress checked, recalled all his detachments except for Zielinski's brigade, which remained blockading Gorkum. On 13 February Bülow marched via Soignies, Jemappes, Mons and Pont-sur-Sambre towards Laon, where he arrived on 24 February. He had left the forces of the Duke of Weimar – about 15,000 infantry, 2,200 cavalry and 32 guns – to continue the campaign in Belgium.[62]

Bülow 's march to Laon was incredibly leisurely and has caused considerable controversy. Some have suggested that it was his goal to push Count Maison's forces into locking themselves into Lille, but this has little justification. It is also possible that he was moving slowly so that he might turn and return to the lowlands should the French do something foolish and give him an opportunity to come storming back in – taking objectives that had evaded him earlier.

As the Prussians marched into the interior of France there was no significant diminishment in the numbers of Allied troops in Belgium. Saxe-Weimar's forces were there and Borstell's brigade was soon relieved by the 2nd Saxon Division. With the arrival of the 2nd Saxon Division, the 3rd German Corps was complete. It was an unusual collection of forces, with the bulk of it being the remains of the old Saxon army and a number of newly-raised Landwehr infantry regiments. In addition it contained the Russo-German Legion, Borstell's Prussian 5th Brigade and von Helwig's Freikorps. One could argue that the Saxons were not likely to be aggressive in their pursuit of the Allies' goals as their hearts had not been in the war since they defected at Leipzig.

As he operated across the Flanders plain, Graham quickly found that he did not have sufficient forces to compete the investment of Bergen-op-Zoom and the other French strongpoints. As a result the 2nd Saxon Division, under General Gablentz, was ordered to move from Sier and join General Sir T. Graham, who was assigned the duties of blockading Antwerp and

61 Koch, Vol. II, p. 141.
62 Calmon-Maison, p. 145.

Prussian dragoons, by Krüger.

Bergen-op-Zoom.[63] Five battalions and four squadrons were placed before Bergen-op-Zoom. A further four battalions and two squadrons – under General Lecoq – masked Condé to Peruvels and Leutze. Five squadrons under General Ryssel were sent to Mons and a Prussian brigade with 6,600 infantry and 1,400 cavalry was sent towards Tournai to cover any movement by Maison.

The 2/2nd Light Infantry Regiment, the Weimar Jäger Corps and the 1st Saxon Horse Battery were dispatched to join Graham in observing Antwerp. Borstell's 5th Brigade – with half of the 1st Saxon 12pdr Foot Battery and the Saxon sapper detachment – formed his right flank near Tournai. General von Ryssel, with the Saxon troops (2nd Provisional Line Regiment, 2/2nd Light Infantry Regiment, three squadrons of cuirassiers and a horse battery), stood by Mons on the left flank. The reserve (the rest of the corps with two Pomeranian Hussar squadrons) stood under General Lecoq near Leutze. Weimar's headquarters was in Ath and covered by the 1/Saxon Guard Regiment and two hussar squadrons – and the Weimar Fusilier Battalion became the garrison of Brussels.[64]

By this method, Saxe-Weimar sought to address his three goals: 1) interdict the garrison of Antwerp along the length of the right bank of the Scheldt, 2) guarantee the lowlands from sorties

63 Burghersh, pp. 82-3; Koch, Vol. II, p. 143.
64 Schuster & Francke, Vol. II, p. 378.

from Ypres, Lille, Valenciennes, Condé, Quesnoy and Maubeuge, and 3) to cover the line from Mons to Avesnes and the operations of the corps of Winzingerode and Bülow .

The French position in Tournai was well-chosen and favored an offensive on both Ghent and Brussels – as well as the various Allied positions along the coast. It also assured communications with Condé and Valenciennes – as well as covering Lille and Douai, which had no garrisons, only depots.

Nonetheless Maison had some fears for his right flank and these fears caused him to abandon his position on 17 February and move to a new position in Marque, which guarded Wambrechies and Quesnoy on the Deule and Armentières further to the left, where General Penne had established himself with a battalion of infantry and 50 cavalry. About 1,000 infantry – drawn from the depots in Lille – joined those drawn from Lys to form a small division under General Ledru. General Saulnier also moved a force of about 100 gendarmes into the defensive line.

Borstell had Major Helwig occupy Tournai and on 22 February sent some infantry on Ypres.[65] Once there, Oberst Geismar attempted to incite a revolution amongst the city's inhabitants. Maison assumed that it was Helwig's intention to move below Lille and cut his communications with the coastal region, so he dispatched Castex's cavalry to the Marque and sent Barrois' 1st Brigade to Armentières with orders to follow the Allied movement. He was positioned on the second road to Menin so as to be able to cover Castex's withdrawal on Lille or, as needs by, to cut the Allied lines of communication from Menin. The success of this small combination appeared assured, however, but Major Helwig took flight and hastily redeployed on Courtrai. General Maison, after reuniting his troops in Menin, chose not to push him further.

As Bülow marched south the Duke of Saxe-Weimar was reinforced by the Anhalt-Thüringian Brigade and awaited the pending arrival of Zielinski's Prussian brigade from Gorkum. He ordered Lecoq and Ryssel to execute a reconnaissance against Condé and Maubeuge with an eye towards establishing communications with the Army of Silesia and determining the French strength in that region. The demonstration against Condé was executed by the 2/,3/Saxon Guard Regiment, the 1st Saxon Provisional Line Regiment, 1st Saxon 6pdr Foot Battery and one squadron of the Pomeranian Hussar Regiment. Their attack was to cost them 10 dead and 23 wounded.[66]

---

65 On 20 February 1813 Borstell's brigade was as follows:
Pomeranian Grenadier Battalion (1/15/48/15/575/0)
1/1st Pomeranian Infantry Regiment (2/17/45/21/663/0)
2/1st Pomeranian Infantry Regiment (2/13/51/8/701/0)
Fus/1st Pomeranian Infantry Regiment (1/12/46/12/550/0)
1/2nd Reserve Infantry Regiment (0/13/42/19/402/0)
2/2nd Reserve Infantry Regiment (1/12/49/9/464/0)
Fus/2nd Reserve Infantry Regiment (0/10/38/9/563/0)
Freiwilliger Fussjäger Det, Pomeranian Grenadiers (0/4/11/3/110/0)
Freiwilliger Fussjäger Det, 1/1st Pomeranian Regt (0/3/3/2/106/0)
Freiwilliger Fussjäger Det, Fus/1st Pomeranian Regt (0/1/6/0/60/0)
1/,2/,3/,4/West Prussian Uhlan Regiment (2/20/50/13/444/507)
Freiwilliger Jäger Sqn, West Prussian Uhlans (0/1/5/1/34/40)
1/,2/,3/,4/Pomeranian Hussar Regiment (4/16/41/9/387/437)
Freiwilliger Jäger Sqn, Pomeranian Hussars (0/3/8/2/69/79)
1/,2/,3/,4/Pomeranian National Cavalry Regiment (1/14/30/8/285/359)
6pdr Foot Battery #10 (eight guns)(0/3/25/1/98)
6pdr Horse Battery #11 (eight guns)(0/4/22/2/105/133)
Numbers are staff officers, senior officers, company officers, trumpeters and musicians, NCOs and soldiers and horses. Bucher, L.F., Beilage III.

66 Schuster & Francke. Vol. II, p. 379.

Altenberg-Gotha Regiment
Line Battalion: Oberst von Munch
Landwehr Battalion: Major von Kirchbach
Anhalt-Dessau-Köthen Regiment
Line Battalion: Oberst Hoppe
Landwehr Battalion: Hauptmann Moebes
Anhalt-Dessau-Köthen Jäger Detachment:
Oberleutnant Harsleben
Anhalt-Bernburg Jäger Battalion:
Major von Sonnenberg
Schwarzberg Line Battalion:
Major von Blumroeder
Schwarzberg Landwehr Battalion:
Major von Munch

Weimar Infantry Regiment
Line Battalion: Major Freiherrn von Lincker
Landwehr Battalion: Major Freiherrn von Wolfsteel
Thüringian Freiwilliger Jäger Battalion:
Major Freiherrn von Seebach
1st Co. (Altenberg-Gotha)
2nd Co. (Weimar)
3rd Co. (Schwarzberg)
Altenberg-Gotha-Weimar Freiwilliger Jäger
Squadron: Rittmeister von Werthern
½ 6pdr Foot Battery formed with captured French
equipment: Premierleutnant Hirschfeld

At the same moment, GD Maison ordered Roguet's division to converge on Ghent – feeling it was no longer necessary at Antwerp because of the inability of the English to establish a siege. He also ordered Castex to throw back all the Prussian posts observing the right bank of the Marque and General Carra-St.-Cyr – commander of Valenciennes, Bouchain and Condé – to advance with their garrisons (about 1,800 men and three guns) down the road to Tournai.

General Lecoq's column encountered Carra-St.-Cyr's column and was thrown back to Vieux-Cond – below Peruvels – and inflicted 100 casualties on the Saxons. Ryssel, unsettled by the cannonade on his right, did not advance to within cannon shot of Maubeuge and bravely reported that it would take a regular, formal siege to reduce this city, which was practically without garrison.

The Duke of Saxe-Weimar, responding to the news from his reconnaissance forces, detached the Thüringian Brigade to Alost and Termonde while GD Maison moved the French divisions of Barrois and Ledru to Courtrai and moved back behind the Marque with the rest of his troops. He did, however, dispatch the 12th Voltigeur Regiment with 100 cavalry across the Marque near Bouvines. This force threw back all the Allied positions along the river once again.

General Borstell, under directions from the Duke, sought to revenge himself by a *coup de main* against Courtrai, but the effort under Oberst Hobe failed.

This war of skirmishes continued, with the French generally maintaining the upper hand. Maison, acting on orders from Berthier, concentrated his forces near Courtrai and moved toward Audenarde on 5 March with about 6,000 infantry and 1,000 cavalry. At the same time General Carnot was ordered to make a sortie on the left of the Scheldt in the direction of Ghent in order to link up with Maison.

The reason for this movement was to threaten the Allied hold on Brussels. General Penne, who flanked the road from Courtrai to Deynze with 500 to 600 men, moved from Saint-Eloyswifwe on Ghent in a manner so as to strike at Ghent at the break of dawn and hold it until the arrival of the main force that evening.

The city of Audenarde still retained its fortifications and very deep moat – flooded with the waters of the Scheldt. The Allies had repaired what damage existed and garrisoned it with five battalions, 400 cavalry and 1½ guard batteries under the orders of Oberst Hobe. [67]

The Duke of Weimar reacts

Suspecting that Maison was to either reinforce the garrison of Antwerp or operate against Brussels, the Duke of Weimar decided to occupy Courtrai and to push troops onto the left bank of the Lys.

67 von Damitz, Vol. III, 1st Part, p. 225.

That same day he sent Oberst Hobe – with five battalions, three squadrons and 10 guns – towards Warcoing. Major Helwig, who was then in Audenarde, was sent towards Courtrai. The following day Hobe and Helwig simultaneously attacked the French posts in Belleghem and Sweveghem and pushed them back on Courtrai.

Barrois responded by sending a column towards Sweveghem to counter Helwig and two battalions – supported by artillery – down the road to Tournai to stop Hobe's advance down that road. Hobe responded to this by moving across the Sweveghem fields to support Helwig. After a short, but sharp, engagement Hobe and Helwig withdrew towards Harlebeke where they re-crossed the Lys and moved on Menin. Hobe thought that Barrois might be evacuating Courtrai, but when he arrived at Menin he found it solidly defended. He then moved to Audenarde and Helwig moved to Deynze.

Maison had thrown a number of battalions – drawn from various garrisons – into Menin. They had been designated to join his small army before it moved against Ghent. In order to effect this movement, Maison now waited only for the organization of his artillery park. Prior to this, Maison's army had lacked any reserve batteries. However, Helwig's presence in Deynze – on the road to Ghent – obliged Maison to modify his projects and suggested to him that the Duke of Weimar intended to march on Brussels and not Antwerp.[68]

Engagement at Audenarde – 5 March

Maison had united all available forces in Courtrai and on 5 March marched on Audenarde with 5,400 infantry, 930 cavalry and 19 guns.

Barrois' division	3,100
Solignac's division	2,300
Chasseurs	500
Lancers	270
Gardes d'honneur[69]	160

Barrois' division formed the head of Maison's column and Solignac's division formed in the rear – covering the park and followed by the bulk of the French cavalry. GB Penne was dispatched with a force of 500-600 men to Vive-Saint-Eloi to watch for Allied movements around Deynze and to watch the road from Ghent – over which Helwig might move to threaten Maison's communications.

Maison's immediate goal was to throw Hobe – who commanded five battalions and 400 cavalry[70] – out of Audenarde, to cross the Scheldt and to push Hobe back to Renaix. Having crossed the Allies' right and pushing Penne from Vive-Saint-Eloi towards Ghent, Maison intended to march on Ghent and effect a junction with Penne.

Maison attacked Hobe's advanced posts in Avelghem and Peterghem. When Hobe saw his advanced posts thrown back, he recognized that he was about to be attacked by major French forces and called on Borstell to send him reinforcements. Borstell sent him 400 cavalry. This force of cavalry apparently consisted of two squadrons of the Pomeranian National Cavalry Regiment and a squadron of the West Prussian Uhlans.

68 Calmon-Maison, pp. 165-6.
69 Calmon-Maison, p.169.
70 Sporschil, Vol. II, Band 2, p. 239.

The Prussian cavalry attacked the head of the French column, but was pushed back to Peterghem, which Hobe had garrisoned with a significant force of infantry and artillery. Maison formed a column with three battalions of Barrois' division on the right and left of the road. The road itself was left for the movement of the French cavalry and two horse guns. The Prussians waited for them on the heights between Peterghem and Audenarde.

Maison advanced a battery of six guns in the intervals of the three battalions and marched this formation forward – at the interval necessary for them to deploy into line – down the two sides of the road. The French drummers pounded their drums – sounding the charge. Cries of: "*Vive l'Empereur!*" arose from the three battalions of Young Guard and they surged forward – bayonets lowered and glistening in the sunlight. It was too much for the Prussians, who without waiting for the arrival of the French infantry, took to their heels and withdrew into Audenarde.

Audenarde was defended by a wall and surrounded with a deep ditch that connected with the Scheldt. When the French arrived before Audenarde, they could not penetrate into the fortification except over a single bridge. At about 4:00 p.m. Maison arrived before Audenarde. He ordered his troops to form two columns and supported them with his artillery. Though Maison did not know it, Hobe had a force of 5,000 men in the city and behind it.

The French began a cannonade and exploded a mine to force the city's gate on the right bank of the Scheldt. Maison then learned that two columns of 2,500 men had been sent that morning against Ghent. One column had marched from Audenarde and the other from Brussels.[71]

GD Maison judged that the capture of the city would cost him more casualties than the city was worth. When he learned that the Allies had been able to keep Penne out of Ghent, he abandoned his project and withdrew back to Courtrai, where he arrived on 6 March after the loss of about a dozen men. In contrast, von Sporschil indicates that the Allies lost 60 men in the exchange and that the French losses were greater – including some 40 prisoners left behind.[72]

The Prussians occupied Tournai, Audenarde and Ghent – as well as held a bridgehead on the Scheldt, which would permit them to move against Courtrai. To present this, Maison deployed his forces as follows: Penne was sent to Belleghem with a battalion, 100 cavalry and 1½ guard batteries; General d'Audenarde – who commanded the 2nd Guard Lancers – marched with one of his squadrons, two battalions and a guard battery on Sweveghem; Colonel de Latour marched on Harlebeke with a battalion, 100 cavalry and two guns; GD Castex marched on Cuerne and Heule with a battalion, two guns and the rest of the cavalry; Barrois and Solignac moved to Courtrai with the remainder of their divisions, 400 cavalry and 12 guns.

Weimar was anxious to learn where Maison was marching and Oberst Hobe detached Oberst von Zastrow with a reconnaissance force of two squadrons, two battalions and two cannon marching from Audenarde. He then ordered Colonel Bihaloff and his Cossacks and Major von Helwig's streifkorps to move from Deinze through Harlebeke.[73]

Weimar then threw a bridge over the Scheldt at Hérine with the intention of attacking Maison's rear with the bulk of his forces, while Oberst Hobe held him in check with his forces. However, Maison's retreat checked Weimar's plan and even resulted in a check being suffered by Weimar. As Oberst von Schon – leading Weimar's advanced guard of three battalions, a hussar squadron and half of a 6pdr battery – moved into Tournai, it encountered Maison's forces and was nearly totally obliterated.[74]

71 Calmon-Maison, pp. 170-172.
72 Sporschil, Vol. II, Band 2, p. 240.
73 Sporschil, Vol. II, Band 2, p. 240.
74 von Damitz, Vol. III, 1st Part, p. 227.

First engagement by Courtrai – 7 March

The Duke of Weimar, harassed without a moment's rest, finally resolved to act and stop Maison's actions. Weimar ordered Hobe to march to Sweveghem while the bulk of the 3rd German Corps marched against Belleghem. At noon on 7 March the Allies attacked the French posts in Belleghem, Sweveghem and Harlebeke. Belleghem was occupied by General Penne with an infantry battalion, a detachment of about 100 cavalry and three guns. Sweveghem was occupied by General d'Audenarde with two battalions, 400 lancers and a half battery. Colonel Latour occupied Harlebeke, Kuerne and Hülfte with two battalions and a few-hundred cavalry. Borstell presented himself with 15,000 men before Belleghem, where Penne stood.

Faced by an Allied column of six battalions and two squadrons, General Penne did not consider it prudent to attempt to hold Belleghem with his tiny force and withdrew to the heights behind the village. Maison learned of the Allied attacks and sent three battalions from Solignac's division, 200 cavalry and a horse battery to support Penne.

The Allied advance was soon stopped by the French artillery, whose fire tore great holes in their ranks as they advanced down the main road. Night fell without a decision being reached and both sides awaited the arrival of dawn to resume the battle.

As Borstell's forces marched past Penne's now reinforced force – in column – they were pounded by the French artillery. The Prussians stopped and deployed along both sides of the road. As they deployed, a few more battalions from Solignac's division and a brigade from Barrois' division arrived from Courtrai. Maison formed his troops in a defensive position and prepared to engage Borstell. However, at 4:30 p.m., Borstell withdrew on Belleghem. Maison left Penne to watch that front and withdrew the bulk of his forces to Courtrai.

While Borstell was being stopped, Hobe – leading 3,000 men – attacked Sweveghem, which was defended by General d'Audenarde with two battalions of Young Guard, two guns and a squadron of guard lancers. Hobe attacked with four Saxon battalions and four Saxon squadrons under the command of Oberst Ziegler. Ziegler advanced his grenadiers – some of which were deployed in a skirmish screen – against the village of Sweveghem. Colonel von Hobe advanced two squadrons and two horse guns to face the village, while the main body of the column marched to the left against Coighem in order to take up positions behind Borstell's main body.

As night fell the Allies launched a new attack against Sweveghem. Three companies of the 1st Pomeranian Infantry Regiment advanced down the highway against Sweveghem, while a fourth company covered the left wing. As the Saxon grenadiers on the right wing began their advance, the three Pomeranian companies advanced at the *Sturmschritt*. The French waited for them behind the church wall and when the Prussians were within a pistol shot of their position, they unleashed a tremendous volley – laying low three Pomeranian officers and 80 men. The Saxon grenadiers then struck with more success.[75]

Numbers began to tell and d'Audenarde was pushed out of Sweveghem – encountering Barrois' division about a half-mile (one kilometer) from the city.[76] As Maison was facing Borstell's massive column, he was unable to send d'Audenarde the reinforcements he requested.

The third Allied column with 1,200 men struck Deynze, but it was turned back by Colonel de Latour without much effort. These three engagements cost the French about 180 casualties.[77]

75 von Damitz, Vol. III, 1st Part, p. 230.
76 Koch, Vol. II, pp. 142-9.
77 Calmon-Maison, pp. 178-181.

Maison retires on Lille

GD Maison realized that his situation was not good and one hour before dawn he evacuated Courtrai. He initially intended to march down the road to Turcoing – a distance of three to four miles (five to six kilometers) – then move to the left against the flank and rear of the Allied forces encamped before Courtrai. The lay of the land appeared to favor such a bold move, but Maison decided against such a move because of the fatigue of his troops. Instead he chose to move to a new position in Mont-Halluin, before Lille, and to put advanced posts in Roncq and Turcoing.

During the morning of 8 March the French headquarters moved to Roncq – accompanied by the bulk of Barrois' division. Barrois occupied Halluin and the cavalry deployed in echelons along the road to Menin. Solignac's division moved to Comines to watch the Lys. However, the following day Solignac discovered that Menin was occupied by a large force of Allied cavalry and Cossacks which Weimar had sent in great haste after learning of the evacuation of Courtrai. Maison responded by moving his headquarters and Barrois to Roubaix.

The Duke of Weimar passed part of the night of 7/8 March contemplating his attack and he had all his forces preparing for the attack at 4:00 a.m. that morning only to discover that the French had escaped him. As a result, his forces put on their dress uniforms and marched on parade through the city to impress on its citizens with their conquest. He then issued a pompous proclamation that the French had lost 2,000 men in the previous day's engagement, when in fact they had lost only 180 men *hors de combat* and prisoner.

4

The Invasion of Switzerland, January 1814

Army of Bohemia

In early January the Allied main army began to move. Bubna's corps, which had crossed the Rhine at Crenknach, was ordered to march through Bearn to Lausanne. From there it was to advance on Geneva. It was followed by the 2nd Corps, under Prince A. Liechtenstein, which marched via Neuchâtel and Pontarlier to Besançon – on which it quickly invested. General Giulay moved his 3rd Corps from Soleure to Biel, Porentruy and Montbelliard. His corps entered Vesoul on 7 January. Colloredo's 1st Corps, M. Liechtenstein's 2nd Light Division and the Austrian Reserves were ordered to march through Bearn, Pontarlier, Dôle and on to Auxonne.

At the same time Bavarian General Wrede, commanding the 5th Corps, and the Crown Prince of Württemberg, commanding the 4th Corps, organized their forces in the vicinity of Basel and bombarded Hunningen. Count Wittgenstein had his 6th Corps blockading the Kehl Fortress and blockading Strasbourg. The Russian and Prussian reserves were to arrive in Basel on 5 January.

The goal of the Allies was to establish themselves in Langres, which was five days' march from Basel. Their march was cautious, despite the fact that since the end of December there was barely a French soldier present to oppose their advance.[1]

In late December 1813 the main army, under Schwarzenberg, contained 190,672 infantry and 29,571 cavalry.[2] These forces were assigned as follows:

	Bns	Sqns	Infantry	Cavalry
Austrian Light Division (Bubna)	5	30	6,573	2,988
Austrian Light Division (M. Liechtenstein)	3	18	4,119	1,668
Austrian Army Detachment (Colloredo)	24	12	15,363	1,127
Austrian Army Detachment (A. Liechtenstein)	20	12	13,521	1,466
Austrian Army Detachment (Gyulai)	24	13	14,193	935
4th (Württemberg) Corps (Crown Prince)	13	16	13,829	1,824
5th (Austrian & Bavarian) Corps (Wrede)	38	54	36,442	6,064
6th (Russian) Corps (Wittgenstein)	39	27	19,350	2,500
Austrian Reserve (von Hessen-Homburg)	26	40	20,371	3,730
Russian & Prussian Guard (Barclay de Tolly)	43	80	32,200	7,200
Army Police Service	[8]	–	4,377	–
Austrian Artillery & Pioneers	–	–	10,334	69
Total			190,672	29,571

1 Burghersh, pp. 71-3.
2 von Bernhardi, Vol. 4, 7th Book, pp. 66-8.

The headquarters of the Allied main army had moved from Basel. On 3 January it was in Altkirch; on 6 January it was in Montbelliard; on the 9th it was in Arcy; the 10th in Villersexel; 11th in Vesoul; and on the 17th it was in Langres. Once in Langres, Prince Schwarzenberg decided to rest his army there for a period – allowing it to recover from the rigors of its advance into France. At the same time he opened negotiations with de Caulincourt, the French Plenipotentiary, who was requested to treat with the Allied ministers at Châtillon.

While the Allied ministers opened negotiations, their generals discussed how to pursue their campaign. One faction actively advocated an aggressive advance deeper into France with the goal of taking Paris. Others argued that to do so would jeopardize their armies to no avail. They argued that the purpose of the Allies was the liberation of Europe by the reduction of French power. As the Allies had already occupied the provinces they intended to liberate, they felt the French government ought to be allowed to decide if it would accept the loss of these provinces. If it did, the war would cease. If not, the war would be continued with the target of that war being the government and person of Napoleon Bonaparte – not the French people. Burghersh noted:

> In a military point of view it should be recollected that every day's advance would reduce the strength of the Allied army by sickness; by losses in actions; and by the extension of the line of operations that once beyond Troyes and Châlons there would be no stopping. The enemy must be pursued to the walls of Paris, or even beyond the capital. Hence, there would be no means of calculating on the arrival of reinforcements to the Allied army – nor would it be possible to fix upon any attainable object as the limit of its operations. Beyond Langres all the roads run towards Paris – non-passable in the winter season for any army which crossed that direction. The communication between the different corps of the Allies would, therefore, be extremely difficult – and all flank movements nearly impossible. On the side of the enemy all operations on the flanks of the Allies would be along the chaussées (roads) and, consequently, easy. He might, therefore, turn the Allied Armies while it would be impossible for them to out-manoeuver him – being unable to operate but in advance, or in retreat. It was also to be remembered that no army could be maintained for any length of time near Châlons and Troyes on account of the poverty of that country; that if the Allies proceeded from Langres to Paris, they would have upon there left the most fertile country in France, which would be occupied by the enemy and from whence he would draw his reserves while the French fortresses in Flanders would be on their right and those on the Rhine, in Lorraine and France Comté on their rear. Thus the Allies would have every disadvantage on their side; the enemy every advantage. If therefore the Allies had not considerable reserves at Dijon, Langres and Joinville, the enemy would annoy them wheresoever he chose and this danger would be augmented if the force of the Allies did not allow them sufficiently to blockade the fortresses left in their rear – in which case the garrisons by joining together might produce the most fatal consequences. Such were the risks the Allies would have to encounter; those of the enemy might, perhaps, be considerable, but it should be remembered that Bonaparte would fight to the last and that this war would become a war of extermination.[3]

Others stated that the French armies, as reduced as they were, could not hope to oppose the Allied armies. They advocated reaping the results of the Battle of Leipzig as soon as possible. These men, seeing that Napoleon had failed to occupy the Swiss frontier with the forces necessary to close that door to France, advocated taking advantage of the existing conditions and pushing hard and fast against the French. They advocated pushing forward before Napoleon was able to

3 Burghersh, pp. 93-4.

rebuild his armies. They recognized the difficulties and advantages of continuing offensive operations were not insignificant, but they also realized that every day they delayed their advance, the inevitability of their victory faded.

French preparations in Langres

The French forces in Langres were limited at best. However, the French Minister of War announced that an army of 100,000 was to be formed in Langres. The city blocked the road to Paris and was the best place to establish a defense to block the Allied advance through Switzerland. The city stood on a steep plateau and was surrounded by old fortifications that were 30 to 40 feet high. The wall was crenulated and flanked with towers – four of which could handle six or eight cannon. However, years of peace had allowed not only the city to encroach on the military terrain, but the condition of the defenses had generally decayed. The city was not in a condition to withstand a major assault or siege.

The formation of the 100,000-man army would not occur. The decree ordering its formation wasn't published in the region until 1 January. The only regular forces in the city were a detachment of the 153rd Line Regiment and a few guardsmen.[4] The villages of Langres, Chaumont and St.-Dizier would form a cohort of second class grenadiers – four companies totalling 300 men each. This, coupled with the badly-armed and almost untrained urban cohort in Langres, gave little to no hope for a defense of Langres.[5]

On 5 January the French withdrew their forces from Combeaufontaine to Fayl-Billot – heavily pressed by large Allied patrols. However, the Allied advance was not especially aggressive. The Allies had, for some reason, reverted to the style of warfare known in the 18th century – executing scientific maneuvers, complicated marches, turning the flanks of positions and a multitude of other archaic military processes that delayed their occupation of Langres until 17 January. With their arrival in Langres, the entire Austrian army had finally passed through Switzerland.[6]

Whether spontaneously generated by fear of the great Napoleon, or if it was a deliberately planted sliver of misinformation, word reached Schwarzenberg that Napoleon had organized a considerable army at Strasbourg with the intention of crossing the Rhine and attacking the Allied troops assembled near Basel. This rumor received a credit and caused a reaction far beyond what Napoleon's meager means could have justified – even if he were even near Strasbourg. The Allies obviously feared that they would encounter the same furious armies of the French Revolution that had greeted their invasion of France in 1792.

Despite those fears they pressed forward in their plans to cross the Rhine and invade France. To this end, Schwarzenberg divided his army into seven columns. The first, under Bubna with some forces from A. Liechtensten's 2nd Army Corps, was to advance with Bubna's forces – marching on Crenzach while the detachment from Liechtenstein's army corps was to march on Basel. From there it would cross the Rhine, march through Hauenstein and Solothurn and arrive in Berne on 24 December. The following day it was to reach Freiburg.

The second column, consisting of Bianchi's division (from the reserve) and Crenneville (from Gyulai's army detachment), was to cross by Basel and march through Münsterthal – arriving in Biel on 24 December.

The third column – under Colloredo – was to go left of the first by Laussenberg, cross the Rhine, move through Aar and on 24 December arrive in Aarwangen.

4 von Damitz, Vol. I, p. 181.
5 Lefebvre de Béhaine, Vol. IV, pp. 88-9.
6 Burghersh, pp. 71-3.

The fourth column – Gyulai – was to go via Laussenberg, over the Strom, then turn right and intercept the main road by Liestal. From there it would march on Solothurn, then move to the right and arrive in Aarburg on 26 December.

The fifth column – under von Hessen-Homburg and containing the light division of M. Liechtenstein, Trautenberg and Weissenwolf's grenadiers and Nostitz's Austrian cuirassiers – was to move through Schaffhausen, cross the Rhine, move to Lenzburg on the Aar and from Aarburg march on Berne, where it was to arrive on 29 December.

Barclay de Tolly.

The three army groups of Wrede, Wittgenstein and Barclay de Tolly – which formed the right wing of the army – would then march on Basel and cross to the right side of the Rhine to cover the advance of the army into Switzerland. They would take Bergschloss Landskron, blockade Hüningen and send a division against Belfort. This force would be the strategic pivot on which the entire army would swing to the right.

The seventh column was formed by the Württembergers under the Crown Prince of Württemberg. It was to follow the main army and pass through Lörrach.[7]

Geneva falls

The first column – consisting of Bubna's light division (about 20,000 men) and the 2nd Army Corps (A. Liechtenstein) – stood before Blasthal on 22 December. On 23 December General Bubna's light corps arrived in Berne. Bubna entered the city at 2:00 p.m. with his staff, a battalion of Peterwardeiner Grenz, a battalion the Gradiscaner Grenz and two hussar regiments to the acclamation of the Bernese citizens.[8]

On the 27th Bubna was in Lausanne and on 30 December it stood before Geneva. Bubna summoned the city to surrender. General Jordy, the garrison commander, refused the summons so Bubna advanced his infantry in three columns to assault the city. Geneva's garrison consisted of 1,800 men supported by 117 guns in its fortifications and 30 field guns. A reinforcement of 1,500-1,800 men had been sent from Grenoble and was already in Annecy, but Jordy did not know of its presence. He had, however, received an order from Napoleon on 26 December to hold the city as long as possible.[9]

On the morning of 29 December Bubna sent Oberst Weiland to the right – along the lake from Nyon to Geneva – with a squadron of the Blankenstein Hussars, a battalion of the Warasdiner Kreuzer Grenz and a battalion of the Wenzel Colloredo Infantry Regiment. The boats necessary to cross the lake were gathered at Versoix. Oberst Zichy, with the 6th Jäger Battalion, a battalion of the Gradiscaner Grenz and six pelotons of the Liechtenstein Hussars, moved on Versoix along the road to Paris – seizing the high ground that dominated the village – and then moved towards the Rhône River. Each column was accompanied by a force of pioneers and was supported by artillery. Klopfstein's column advanced on the Petit-Saçonnex hill with the Reuss-Greitz, Vogelsang, Kaunitz and Wenzel Colloredo Infantry Regiments. The Kaiser Hussars and the remainder of the Blankenstein Hussars were in Ferney. The Austrian forces pushed to within

7 von Bernhardi, Vol. 4, 7th Book, pp. 89-90.
8 Oechsli, pp. 37 & 41.
9 Oechsli, p. 56.

canister range of Geneva's walls and Bubna sent Major Comte Saint-Quentin to summon the city to surrender.[10] Jordy – apparently losing his nerve – surrendered the city and Bubna occupied it that day.[11]

The French garrison had lost its will to resist and feared the city's inhabitants more than Napoleon's wrath for abandoning the city. The terms of capitulation allowed Jordy to withdraw his garrison towards Rumilly, France. Upon their liberation, the citizens of Geneva immediately re-established their ancient form of government.[12]

Bubna.

General Bubna detached a force of troops to occupy Valais and to take up positions on the Simplon and Saint-Bernard passes. He also occupied Fort l'Ecluse. Oberst Simbschen had earlier been detached from Lausanne with 600 men and some cavalry to occupy the Upper Valais and the passes at Saint-Bernard and Simplon. On 28 December he arrived in Saint-Maurice. Once in the Upper Valais he was received with open arms by the inhabitants, who quickly formed a battalion of light infantry – totalling about 1,000 men. Simbschen established posts at the Simplon and Saint-Bernard passes and then destroyed the road to the Simplon to seal it to any potential of French military action.

Bubna did not linger in Geneva but chose to detach General Zechmeister with his brigade, three battalions and a quarter of a cavalry squadron – about 3,000 men – to serve as its garrison. Bubna then marched on Saint-Claude.[13]

Prince A. Liechtenstein invested Besançon 9 January and blockaded the fortresses of Joux and Salims. With these maneuvers the Allied army secured its left flank as it prepared to march on Paris. On 9 January he blockaded Besançon, which stood on the left bank of the Doubs. On 9 January Wimpffen – with six battalions, three squadrons and a battery from Colloredo's army corps – moved through Baume-les-Dames to establish an Allied presence on that flank of Besançon. Erbprinz von Hesse-Homburg arrived on 7 January with the Austrian Reserve from Pontarlier.[14]

On 5 January Bubna moved to Poligny and Salims – from where he dispatched a force of cavalry to establish communications with the Austrians moving through Pontarlier. On 6 January he attacked Dôle, which was defended by General Lambert with a few National Guardsmen. Dôle quickly fell and he moved against Châlons, which was defended by General Legrand with some National Guardsmen from Châlons, Charolles and Autun and a few troops drawn from the depots of the Departments of Saône and Loire. The Austrians were repulsed.

While at Poligny Bubna was reinforced by Longueville's brigade – from A. Liechtenstein's Austrian corps – then standing before Besançon. The arrival of these six battalions brought Bubna's force to around 10,000 infantry and 6,000 cavalry. Bubna's next move was to establish communications with Schwarzenberg's army, which was marching on Lyon.

10 Oechsli, pp. 59-60.
11 de Vaudoncourt, Vol. I, pp. 211-12.
12 Burghersh, p. 74.
13 von Bernhardi, Vol. 4, 7th Book, p. 145. de Vaudoncourt, Vol. I, p. 213 suggests that Zechmeister retained a full six-squadron regiment, but this is unlikely.
14 von Bernhardi, Vol. 4, 7th Book, p. 172.

The city of Lyon was unfortified and relatively ungarrisoned. Its defenders consisted of 800-900 men including 32 from the 4th Gardes d'honneur Regiment, 30 gendarmes, 60 men from the 1st Hussar Regiment, the depot of the 24th Line consisting of a small veteran cadre – and the remainder being new inductees uniforms – and a departmental company of about 100 men. The entire city did not contain a single cannon; a single caisson – and the arsenal was bare without so much as a cartridge in it.[15]

The city was soon reinforced by the arrival of a small force of some 300 to 400 men, which moved down the road to Moulins. A further 14,000 French infantry was reported moving into Grenoble. An Urban Guard was hurriedly raised and equipped with 1,200 muskets.

On 12 January Bubna stood before Bourg, which was now defended by General Musnier. Musnier had deployed his 1,200 men – drawn from the depots of the Department of the Ain – before the city, but upon seeing Bubna's forces he wisely withdrew his tiny force to Pont-d'Ain and then on to Lyon. In the suburbs of Lyon, however, the French National Guardsmen stood and faced the Austrians. They repulsed the first Austrian assault and, despite their efforts, the suburbs soon fell to the Austrians. The Austrians purportedly sacked their conquest for several hours.

On 14 January Bubna issued a proclamation to the inhabitants of the Department of the Ain. It announced a general amnesty to those inhabitants of the department who forswore their right to defend their country. Bubna invoked the "laws of war" – declaring that those who took arms against them would be treated as criminals. This is somewhat ironic in view of the German use of the Landwehr and Landsturm to fight the French the previous year.[16]

Earlier – on 8 January – Schwarzenberg had announced that armed citizens of France, taken captive, would be executed and that the cities and villages which resisted them would be put to the torch. Both decrees had no basis in any of the existing law of the time and appear to have been issued more as a threat without any serious intent of implementation. Certainly, no cities were burned to the ground for such prohibited resistance.

While Bubna was moving on Poligny and Bourg, General Zechmeister established his base of operations in Geneva. The Fort l'Ecluse capitulated on 4 January and the Fort de Joux surrendered on 16 January. The Geneva fortifications were augmented with new exterior works, and a force of light infantry – totaling two battalions – was organized. Once this was done Zechmeister crossed the Rhône River with 3,000 infantry and 1,000 cavalry and moved deeper into France.

Zechmeister's force encountered the former French garrison of Geneva – men augmented with conscripts drawn from the depots of the 7th Military Division and totaling about 1,600 men – near Rumilly. He easily dislodged them and pushed them back towards Chambéry. General Laroche, who commanded this force, then pulled them back – sending part to Echelles and the other part to Montmélian and Fort Barreaux. On 20 January Zechmeister occupied Chambéry.

Bubna resumed his movement from Bourg on 16 January – arriving in Montluel on 18 January with 7,000 infantry and 4,000 cavalry.

Facing Bubna's advance, Augereau – the Duke of Castiglione – arrived in Lyon on 14 January. Once there he found only Musnier's 1,200 men and greatly feared being able to hold Lyon. He moved quickly to Valence where he planned to stop and redirect French troops moving north from the Midi and Cataluna. General Musnier was left in charge of the defense of Lyon, whose garrison slowly rose to 1,700 men by stripping the local regimental depots. Musnier took 1,000 men of his tiny force and positioned them in the Croix-Rousse suburb and the rest were posted in Grange-Blanche and Oulins on the roads to Tarare and Châlons.[17]

15 Guerre, pp. 25-6.
16 de Vaudoncourt, Vol. I, p. 215.
17 de Vaudoncourt, Vol. I, p. 218.

On 17 January General Bubna appeared before Lyon on the road from Amberieux. Musnier responded by leaving only a few pickets in Croix-Rousse, crossed the Saône and established himself to the west of Lyon. That same day Bubna summoned Lyon to surrender. The Austrian officer delivering the summons was greeted by a sharp rebuff by the patriotic citizens of Lyon. Despite the French expressions of defiance he reported to Bubna that their garrison was weak. That night an Austrian patrol penetrated to the quay on the Rhône. Bubna felt that he could take the city with a frontal assault.

Musnier, during the preceding night, received a reinforcement of 700 men and moved between Lyon and Bubna. A large force of National Guardsmen was posted on the Pape and Montessui heights and covered with a screen of skirmishers. General Musnier supported them with a small force of regular infantry. These French forces then proceeded to entrench their positions to face the pending Austrian advance. Meanwhile, a small detachment of Austrian foragers was caught and destroyed in Saint-Jean-de-Thurigneux.

Bubna responded by sending a force of about 500 infantry that pushed back the French skirmishers and approached the barricade at Croix-Rousse, which was guarded by 30 men of the 20th National Guard Company. The Austrian detachment commander exchanged a few quiet words with the French officer in charge of the barricade and then withdrew. The next day a force of 300 men from the 24th Line Regiment were sent to reinforce the advanced posts at St.-Clair and Croix-Rousse. Following their arrival, the Austrian advanced posts were pushed back.[18]

The Austrians pulled back to Miribel. That same night (and the following night) another 1,200 men and a number of field guns sent by Augereau from Valence arrived at Lyon – giving it the means of its defense just in time.

Meanwhile, back in Lyon, efforts to reinforce and build up the garrison continued. When Augereau arrived in Valence he found six companies of the 16th and 140th Line Regiments – about 700 newly-raised men – had just arrived. He immediately sent them on to Lyon, where they arrived on the 19th. They were soon followed by 400 men of the 32nd Lègére and 95 men from the 1st Hussars. The hussars had been destined for the Army of Italy, but Augereau redirected them to Lyon. On the 21st a further 90 men from the depots of the 4th and 31st Chasseur Regiments and two companies of "garde-chasses" were sent on to Lyon.[19]

On 21 January Augereau arrived in the front lines personally – leading a number of squadrons of cavalry. He immediately set about organizing the mobile National Guard and raising a number of volunteer battalions.[20]

That same day General Bubna withdrew his forces – taking up a position at Pont-d'Ain on the left bank of the Ain – where he was to remain until the end of January.

General Zechmeister established his forces in Chambéry on 20 January – occupying himself with supporting the Count de Sonnaz, who was organizing a body of troops amongst the Savoyans. On their side, the French were actively raising other troops. In the 7th Military Division, General Marchand was organizing the Isère National Guard. The Isère responded with zeal and patriotism – forming and equipping not only their National Guards and a free corps, but 100 cavalry. General Barral, who had been retired for some time, was recalled to duty and took command of 1,500 men organizing at Fort l'Ecluse. General Marchand withdrew the troops below Fort Barreaux and placed them on the left of the Isère, facing Montmélian.

On 31 January Zechmeister executed a false attack against Fort Barreaux and moved against Echelles. General Barral – attacked by superior forces and, at the same, being turned – withdrew to

18 Guerre, pp. 47-8.

19 Guerre, pp. 51-2.

20 de Vaudoncourt, Vol. I, p. 219.

Voiron and Saint-Laurent. The false attack against Barreaux was repulsed by a company of the 8th Légère (aided by a few citizens of Barreaux, who carried ammunition to them during the fight).[21]

Other Allied Corps

Bergschloss Landskron, which sat on the Swiss border, did not delay the Allies very long. It had only two days' supply of bread and on 25 December it surrendered. Its garrison of one captain and 65 men were made prisoner and its walls were found to be defended by nine cannon and two mortars. A Bavarian battalion under Oberst Treuberg occupied the fortress to hold it for the Allies.

The Blamont Fortress, which stood on the road to Porentruy to Besançon, fell to the Bavarians the same day as Bergschloss Landskron. Its artillery consisted of 12 cannon and one mortar. The Bavarians garrisoned it with a company and a quarter of a cavalry squadron.[22]

The fate of Hunningen was different. During the night of 25-26 December General Beckers moved his Bavarian division outside Hunningen and began its blockade. The first parallel was dug and batteries equipped with 26 12pdrs, 12 howitzers and six mortars were erected during the night of 29-30 December 1813. Morning and the rising sun were greeted by the explosion of those angry cannon as they directed their fire against the city's defenses. However, this siege was to be a more protracted affair…

Colloredo-Mansfeld.

On 30 December Schwarzenberg ordered that a bombardment begin on Hüningen and concentrated his corps by Cernay on 1-2 January. The offensive against Colmar began on 3 January. That same day Prince von Württemberg blockaded Neubreisach with an infantry brigade and one cavalry regiment and marched with the rest of his corps on Colmar.

The 1st Bavarian Division, under Count Rechberg, moved to attack the Belfort Fortress during the night of 29-30 December. That attack began with a bombardment directed against the fort's northern defenses. Wrede posted his third division, under General de Lamotte, behind the lines as a reserve and Frimont's corps to the north-west of Hunningen to cover any attack by a relieving force from that direction.[23]

The Allies began a process of blockading a fortress and, as successive waves of troops arrived, the original blockading turned the observation of the surrounded fortress over to the succeeding wave.

Thus, when relieved at Mümpelgard, General Bianchi moved his division to blockade Belfort. He was soon relieved and joined the 1st and 3rd Corps (under Prince Colloredo and General Giulay, respectively). This combined force advanced to the west and on 15 January stood before Vesoul – preparing to attack Langres.

The commandant of Hunningen refused to capitulate and responded as vigorously as he could. Wrede responded by discontinuing the siege and reverting to a blockade. The Allied experience at

21 de Vaudoncourt, Vol. I, p. 220.
22 von Bernhardi, Vol. 4, 7th Book, p. 145.
23 von Damitz, Vol. I, pp. 176-7.

Neubrisack was the same. The 4th and 5th Corps were then directed to advance against Colmar, where General Milhaud stood with a force of French cavalry. Milhaud had caught and driven back a force of Austrians under Oberst Scheibler.

As the 4th and 5th Corps appeared on 3 January, Milhaud abandoned Colmar. Wrede pushed to Schlettstadt and blockaded the city. He was now in communication with the Allied 6th Corps, under General Wittgenstein, which had crossed the Rhine on 3 January and occupied Fort Louis. The 6th Corps left 120,000 men to observe Strasbourg and marched the rest towards Saverne, where it would link the Allied main army with the Army of Silesia.[24]

On 9 January the Olviopol Hussars and the 3rd and 34th Jager Regiments were sent towards Pfalzbourg to reinforce the Allied advanced posts on that flank. Pfalzbourg was a well-fortified city with a covered way without pallisade, ravelins between bastions, dry ditch and counterscarp. The city had only 300 horses and the fortress had only two gates – those of Saverne and Saarburg. The garrison consisted of 600-800 men of the 138th and 142nd Line Regiments manning some 30 guns. The city and fortress were important because they sat astride the main road. Pahlen found the fortress too strong to seize by *coup de main* and contented himself with bombarding it with his howitzers – hoping that the lack of water in the city would cause it to burn and be easily taken. He was greatly disappointed when this effort failed and he found himself forced to settle down into a blockade of the fortress and city. These duties were passed on as further Allied troops moved up and by 17 January, Pahlen – with his cavalry and the 4th and 34th Jagers – had moved on to Saarberg via Saverne.[25]

Baron Toll relates that by 10 January Wittgenstein had been joined by the Baden von Freystedt and von Geusau Dragoon Regiments and five infantry batalions.[26]

Gorchakov stood with the 1st Corps before Strasbourg and Kehl. Prince Schachovsky was detached with his division from the 2nd Corps to blockade Landau. The bulk of Puschnitzky's division was encamped by Reschwog, while one brigade – under Duke Eugen von Württemberg – was by Hagenau under the command of Count Pahlen. Pfalzburg, Bitsch and Lützelstein were also blockaded in early January.

By late January the Allied forces watching Strasbourg contained 17,000 men including eight Baden battalions, three Austrian Battalions and 17 Russian battalions, six Baden squadrons, six Russian squadrons and two 1/2 Cossack regiments.[27]

Army of Silesia

During late December 1813 the Army of Silesia received a number of reinforcements and consisted of:

Langeron's corps	35,000	men[28]
Sacken's corps	25,000	
Yorck's corps	25,000	
Kleist's corps	15,000	
Kurprinz von Hessen	24,000	
Herzog von Sachsen-Coburg	18,000	
Total:	142,000	men

24 Burghersh, p. 75.
25 von Plotho, Vol. III, pp. 32-4.
26 von Bernhardi, Vol. 4, 7th Book, p. 166.
27 von Bernhardi, Vol. 4, 7th Book, p. 242.
28 C von W., p. 121.

However the 10,000 Hessians were detached – as were the troops under Herzog von Sachsen-Coburg and Kleist. This left Blücher with the three corps of Langeron, Sacken and Yorck – and a total strength of about 85,000 men.

Blücher directed the Army of Silesia across the Rhine at four locations on 1 January. His right, under General St. Priest, crossed and surprised a French redoubt opposite Lahn. Durutte's division, at Coblentz, was taken by surprise and driven back – losing a number of prisoners and seven guns.

Yorck's corps crossed the Rhine at Kaub and advanced on Creutznach, which was occupied by General Ricard. Ricard, hearing of Durutte's withdrawal, moved to Simmern – on the Hundsruck – to support him. As a result Yorck was able to occupy Creutznach without opposition, while Durutte and Ricard joined at Halzenbach and withdrew on Laubach.

From Creutznach, Yorck moved on the Sarre – arriving in Sarrebrücke, Saarlouis and Mertzig on 9 January. He occupied Trèves with a force commanded by Oberst von Henckel.

General Count Langeron crossed the Rhine at Bingen – moving through the pass in the mountainous, vine-covered banks of the Rhine into the open plains to the west. Because of the terrain the French had a garrison at Bingen – General Charoz's brigade – but it was inadequate to hold Langeron's advance. From Bingen, Langeron marched on Mainz and blockaded that great fortress on 3 January. He then detached General Olsufiev to follow the Army of Silesia.

Maréchal Marmont.

Baron Sacken crossed the Rhine at Mannheim and carried, with some losses, a redoubt that blocked their advance. Once the way was clear the entire corps crossed and moved against Maréchal Marmont, who was posted between Durkheim and Ellerstadt. Marmont was unable to link with Durutte and Ricard before he was engaged by Sacken. His forces being greatly inferior, he was forced to withdraw towards Sarrebrücke – arriving at Kaiserslautern on 5 January and in Sarrebrücke on the 6th. Sacken pushed forward – crossing the Sarre at Sarreguemine. As he pushed past Landau he detached three battalions to blockade it and Oberst Graf Henckel was detached with a few battalions and a few squadrons to observe Trier.[29]

Marmont, finding himself in danger of being attacked by both Sacken and Yorck, had no choice but to withdraw via St.-Avold and arriving in Metz on 12 January. Sacken then marched on Nancy – establishing his headquarters there on 15 January. He immediately detached a division against Toul, which was occupied without resistance. Pont-à-Mousson was captured by GL Vassil'shikov on 13 January.[30]

General Yorck established a bridge at Beking and crossed the Sarre on 10 January. On 13 January his corps stood before the great fortress of Metz, which Blücher directed he blockade. Yorck detached a brigade to this service and then advanced against the fortresses of Saarlouis, Luxemburg and Thionville with the rest of his force. Saarlouis was blockaded by four battalions and four squadrons on the 13th.[31] On the same day, General von Röder – with six squadrons from Kleist's corps – arrived in Trèves and continued westwards to join the Army of Silesia.

On 17 January the Army of Silesia stood on the Moselle. Marmont withdrew across the Meuse – passing through Verdun on 18 January. He rested his army there for two days – standing in

29 C. von W., p. 131.
30 Burghersh, pp. 76-7.
31 von Bernhardi, Vol. 4, 7th Book, p. 196.

line with Victor's corps, which was still in its positions between Vaucouleurs and Commercy. However, on 20 January, Victor – seeing himself menaced on the right by Wrede's corps – withdrew. Unfortunately, he forgot to destroy the bridge at Vaucouleurs. Marmont, finding his wing in the air, was forced to withdraw his right wing. Decouz's 2nd Young Guard Division broke down the Saint-Mihiel bridge and took up positions at Naives, behind the Bar. Lagrange's 2nd Division (VI Corps) moved behind the Aire at Erize. Ricard's 1st Division (VI Corps) and the cavalry remained in Verdun.

On 18 January Yorck's advanced guard occupied Pont-à-Mousson and the investment of Metz – on the left bank of the Moselle – was effected by a battalion and four squadrons. The remainder of Yorck's corps remained stationary.

Sacken's corps, however, moved around Nancy and Olsufiev's corps advanced to Château-Salins.

During the night of 20-21 January an assault was mounted against Metz with a force of 30 jägers from each of the 18 battalions. These 540 men were to attack all six gates; to chop their way in with axes and to lower the drawbridges. The assault was a failure, so the following night 48 6pdrs and 12pdrs began to bombard the city.[32]

During the night of 19 January Luxemburg was invested by Horn's 7th Brigade (Prussian 1st Corps) and Sarrelouis was bombarded by eight howitzers. Yorck's reserve cavalry moved towards Manheule, where it skirmished with Marmont's rearguard. Piquet's brigade – pressed by superior numbers – was thrown into Manheule, where it was supported by the fire of its accompanying infantry. The Prussians withdrew – only to be charged in the rear by the 10th Hussar Regiment. They withdrew to Thiaucourt.

Blücher decided that it was best to leave Yorck's corps stationary before the various French fortresses for a few days – hoping that a few might decide to capitulate. However, he sent Sacken and Olsufiev forward towards Schwarzenberg's army. Barasdin's cavalry division, destined to remain before Metz, assumed its duties on 20 January. On the same day, Sass' 10th Division (11th Corps) – part of Sacken's corps – marched on Toul. Toul was garrisoned by 400 men, who surrendered without a fight. Olsufiev's corps then advanced on Nancy.

Engagement at Saint-Aubin

On 22 January GL Vassil'shikov's cavalry and Scherbatov's corps marched on Ligny. Victor was, at that time, withdrawing to St.-Dizier when he was ordered to assume a position along the Ornain. General Milhaud, as a result, was sent forward with his cavalry. He encountered GL Vassil'shikov's cavalry at Saint-Aubin and found himself in a lively engagement. Unfortunately for Milhaud, his lack of infantry support – facing Vassil'shikov, who had infantry support – obliged him to withdraw on Ligny. After the engagement, GL Vassil'shikov rested his cavalry at Saint-Aubin. The remainder of Sacken's corps was in Void and Vaucouleurs; Olsufiev was in Toul; and Yorck continued to remain stationary – except to replace Horn's division – before Luxemburg with part of Röder's cavalry.[33]

On 23 January Scherbatov's corps attacked the city of Ligny, which was garrisoned by a French brigade (part of their rearguard). His attack was led by the Pskof and Sophia Infantry Regiments, which marched down the main road from Saint-Aubin. The 11th and 36th Jager Regiments – a total of two battalions – moved against the right side of Ligny. The French rearguard fought bravely, but was pushed back to the city's market at the point of the Russian bayonets. The Russians reported leaving 200 casualties in the streets of Ligny.[34]

32 de Vaudoncourt, Vol. I, p. 172.
33 de Vaudoncourt, Vol. I, p. 173.
34 von Damitz, Vol. I, p. 318.

Victor withdrew that same day to St.-Dizier, where Ney stood, after withdrawing from Bar-sur-Ornain. After a heavy engagement the French brigade was forced to withdraw on St.-Dizier as well. The Allies lost about 300 men in this attack. Sacken's corps occupied Ligny and Gondrecourt, while Olsufiev occupied Faucouleurs.

Yorck, feeling he would not be able to take Thionville or any of the other fortresses, began making arrangements to concentrate his corps. On 24 January Sacken occupied Joinville with a division. Scherbatov's two divisions and the cavalry were in Bar-sur-Ornain. Olsufiev was in Gondrecourt. The same day, Marmont – who had departed Verdun on 22 January – reunited his corps at St.-Dizier with the exception of Ricard's (1st Division, VI Corps) and Piquet's brigade, which were posted at Islettes. A rearguard was also posted at Clermont with instructions to cover the road to Châlons.

On 25 January GL Vassil'shikov directed his cavalry against St.-Dizier. That same day the three marshals departed St.-Dizier. Ney marched on Vitry-le-Brûlé, Marmont marched with Decouz's 2nd Young Guard Division and Daumère's cavlary on Vitry-le-Francaise, Lagrange's 1st Division (VI Corps) marched on Vitry-le-Brûlé and Piquet's brigade marched on Outrepont. Victor marched on Perthé, with Duhésme's division leading the march. A single brigade remained in St.-Dizier.[35]

That same day Scherbatov's corps attacked St.-Dizier and forced the French brigade to abandon its post. It quickly marched down the road to Vitry, while the remainder of Sacken's corps and that of Olsufiev joined around Joinville. These moves effectively brought about the junction of the Army of Silesia with the Allied main army.

Kleist's advance westwards

Kleist, having departed the siege of the fortress at Erfurt, had rejoined General Tauenzien and had begun crossing the Rhine on 18 January. Once across the Rhine he marched to join the Army of Silesia with the other troops that had already crossed. These forces included Ziethen's division (five 1/2 battalions and eight squadrons), Pirch's division (six battalions) and Prince August von Preussen's division (six battalions and four squadrons). In total, this force amounted to 14,000 infantry and 1,800 cavalry.[36]

At the end of January Blücher had deployed his forces as follows: A weak Prussian Landwehr cavalry regiment blockaded Saarlouis. General Yusseffovich blockaded Metz. He was later relieved by General Borosdin and followed the army. General von Kleist left 1,000 cavalry blockading Luxemburg and, observing Thionville, then resumed his march. The Kurprinz von Hessen was preparing to follow Blücher. The Mainz blockade corps was rotating as more troops moved up. On 9 January it was General Olsufiev's corps; on 17 January it was a division of Kapsevich's 10th Corps; on 1 February it would be Korff's cavalry (consisting of five cavalry regiments and Rudsevich with one-and-a-half divisions); and on 15 February it would be General Count St. Priest with half of his corps.

By the beginning of March the corps of the Kurprinz von Hessen would be at full strength and would assume the blockading of Trier.[37]

35 de Vaudoncourt, Vol. I, p. 174.
36 de Vaudoncourt, Vol. I, p. 176.
37 C. von W., pp. 135-6.

The Allied 4th Corps

On 31 December the Allied 4th Corps, under the Crown Prince of Württemberg, departed Märkt and crossed the Rhine on a pontoon bridge between St.-Colombé and Enfisheim. Their advance was led by Platov's Cossack corps, which had crossed the Rhine in Basel.

Platov was ordered by Schwarzenberg to advance on the right wing of the main army in order to maintain contact with the Army of Silesia. Their advance was without incident and on 7 January GM Scherbatov stood before Epinal, which was garrisoned by 500 cavalry, 4,000 infantry and a battery of six guns. The cavalry was commanded by General Duvigneau and the infantry by GB Rousseau. They had been detached by Maréchal Ney to garrison the city.

On 10 January the Allied 4th Corps arrived in Remiremont. On hearing that Ney had posted a force in Epinal – consisting of infantry under General Rousseau and cavalry under General Davigneau – the Crown Prince decided to launch an attack on them. The 4th Corps moved forward on 12 January. General Count Platov – marching in support – moved against the French left towards Charmes, which was in the French rear.[38]

Unable to attack Epinal, the Cossacks swept the surrounding region and waited for the arrival of Württemberg on 11 January. Once on the field, the Crown Prince of Württemberg prepared to attack the city with several columns.

The first column – formed of the 2/9th (König) Jäger Regiment and the 7th Line Regiment – was commanded by GM von Stockmayer. It was sent through La Basse (on the right bank of the Moselle) and into the Epinal woods. Stockmayer placed a company in the Epinal woods to secure them as his column moved forward. From there they marched to the junction of the roads from Xertigny and Remiremont – in closed column – through the valley on the right side of the road from Epinal to Bruyères. As he marched, his right flank was covered by General Kaisarov and Scherbatov's Cossack regiments.

The second (or main) column was under the command of FZM Count von Franquemont. It advanced through the village of Poucheux (on the left bank of the Moselle) and contained a squadron of the 2nd Chevauxleger Regiment, four horse guns, the 1/9th (König) Jäger Regiment, the 3rd Infantry Regiment, a foot battery and the 2/6th Infantry Regiment.[39] As a liaison between the first column and the second (or main) column, Generalmajor Döring marched with the 2nd Infantry Regiment through Jarmenil and over the Moselle and Archettes.

The third column – under GM von Jett – moved to Xertigny and contained the 4th Jäger Regiment, the 1/10th Light Infantry Regiment, a squadron of the 2nd Chevauxleger Regiment and five horse guns. Platov supported the attack by concentrating his Cossacks to cover any possible movement from the direction of Nancy. GM Döring held a force by Chenimenil to serve as a link between the main column and Stockmayer's column.

The main column moved down the main road to Epinal – the third column advancing on its left wing down the road from Dompaire to Epinal. As the third column (GM von Jett's) reached Saint-Laurent, it encountered the French advanced posts. The main column encountered them at the Char d'Argent crossroads, where the roads to Remiremont and Plombières met the main road. This position was also occupied by French posts that were quickly cleared. As they moved forward, the fields and houses before Epinal were strongly defended by the French and a heavy engagement of light troops developed. GM Döring, the liaison between the Allied columns, found himself in a sharp fight. The second column marched down the road on the left bank of the Moselle towards Epinal, where it too became engaged in the fight.

38 Burghersh, pp. 85-6.
39 Sporschil, Vol. II, p. 149.

Stockmayer moved against the right as von Jett moved against their left and the French were soon driven down the road to the Haute-Reine mill.[40]

The French had insufficient strength to deal with the Allied advance and withdrew towards Nancy – pursued by the 2nd Chevauxleger Regiment, the 3rd Dragoon Regiment and seven horse guns. When the French arrived at a rise behind Epinal they attempted to take up positions, but the presence of the Kaisarov and Scherbatov Cossacks made that an unwise decision so they resumed their withdrawal.

The Russian General Greckov had occupied the village of Thaon with two Cossack pulks, which lay on the French line of retreat to Nancy. The French attacked with a combined force of infantry and cavalry – repelling a Russian attack, but having to sidestep the position.

This sidewards movement pushed the French towards where Platov stood in a swampy woods with 12 guns. Platov took advantage of his situation to strike the French flank and rear. The French rearguard was formed by their cavalry, which Platov engaged heavily. Despite Platov's efforts, however, the French effected their retreat.

After clearing Epinal the Crown Prince of Württemberg's corps moved through Bains, Vauvillers, Jonvelle, Bourbonne-les-Bains and on to Montigny-le-Roi, where it rejoined the main army.[41]

These maneuvers forced Ney and Victor to abandon Nancy. As the French withdrew from the region to Schwarzenberg's right, Schwarzenberg found himself able to deploy his entire force for the assault on Langres. The Crown Prince of Württemberg was then ordered to advance on Bourbonne-les-Bains. Count Platov was directed to Neuf Château and General Wrede – already in Luneville – was ordered to move against Mirecourt.

Maréchal Mortier.

To assure the success of the attack on Langres, the Austrian reserves were assembled at Gray. The Russian reserves, which had been delayed near Basel for several days and did not cross the Rhine until 13 January, were ordered forward by forced marches so that they might participate in the battle anticipated for 17 January. These maneuvers permitted Schwarzenberg to concentrate 97,000 men against Langres.

Mortier's forces – the garrison of Langres – had originally been destined for the defense of France's northern frontier. They were assembled in Namur and were redirected to Langres when the Allies were seen to be marching on that city. They arrived in Langres on 10 January.

However, Maréchal Mortier was not willing to stand still while this overwhelming force was concentrated against him and withdrew from Langres during the night of 16 January. The Austrian General Giulay entered Langres in the morning of 17 January and was shocked to learn that Mortier had a force of only 10,000 men. Admittedly they were mostly Old Guard, but they would have been woefully inadequate to defend Langres against the forces arrayed against them.

40 Sporschil, Vol. II, p. 150.
41 von Damitz, Vol. I, pp. 188-192.

Skirmish at Chaumont

Mortier withdrew to Chaumont, with Giulay and the Crown Prince of Württemberg in pursuit. They had orders from Schwarzenberg to engage Mortier. Stockmayer, who had been sent towards Langres, was recalled and directed to follow GM von Jett down the road to Chaumont. Behind them marched the Crown Prince's main column. At 7:00 a.m. the main column arrived in Montigny-le-Haut.

Oberstleutnant Rohrig, commanding two hussar squadrons, was sent to the right towards Riaucourt – on the road form Chaumont towards Joinville – to block the movement of any French in that area.[42]

The first French posts were encountered on 18 January at Ville-aux-Bois and quickly driven back to the Marne. However, once they arrived before Choignes they found themselves faced by Mortier's corps. To Rohrig's great surprise he found himself facing the Guard Cavalry as it moved from Ville-aux-Bois towards Choignes.[43]

On 18 January Maréchal Mortier stood with the Old Guard on the Veseignes heights on the left bank of the Marne (behind Choignes and before Chaumont). With Duka's cuirassier division leading their advance, the Allies encountered Mortier's advanced posts on the heights. The French had posted some heavy batteries to cover the crossings on the Marne. The Crown Prince's forces marched forward and encountered this force. After exchanging some artillery shots, the French withdrew across the Marne and broke down the bridge.

The 1/9th Jäger Regiment was ordered to move up the Marne Valley to Choignes and take the bridge over the Marne that was known to be there. The Bavarians arrived in Choignes, chased out the tiny garrison of the village and seized the bridge. Once in possession of the bridge, however, they were immediately faced by Maréchal Mortier leading a battalion of Old Guard Grenadiers. The Grenadiers attacked with gleaming steel bayonets and quickly drove the Württembergers out of the village. French cavalry then crossed over the Marne and attempted to move out of the village, but encountered Württemberg cavalry, which prevented their proposed movement.

The aggressive movement by Mortier, however, drew the attention of the Allied army. Soon Giulay's corps and parts of the Allied reserve began arriving to engage him. Having only one infantry and one cavalry division he withdrew hastily – breaking down the bridges as he went. He hoped to link up with Michel's 2nd Old Guard Division, which was moving down from Luxemburg to Brienne, as well as to pick up the 113th Line Regiment, which was moving forward towards Troyes. Once joined with Christiani, Mortier would have about 16,000 men and 50 cannon.

On the morning of 19 January Mortier moved to Bar-sur-Aube and left a rearguard under General Letort – 2,000 infantry and 400 cavalry – in Colombé-les-deux-Eglises.[44] Letort took up a position on a rise behind the stream flowing from Rouvre. His left flank was in the village of Voigny and a strong battery was posted on his right flank. This battery had a clear field of fire to the road to Colombé and the bridge at Fontaine.

The remainder of the French army – some 4,000 infantry, 10 cannon and four howitzers – stood on the heights on the left bank of the Aube and in the village of Fontaine.

42 Sporschil, Vol. II, p. 153.
43 de Vaudoncourt, Vol. I, pp. 166-7.
44 The strength figures are from Koch. Toll identifies this force as containing four battalions, four squadrons and six guns. If it was, then indeed the battalions and squadrons are surprisingly large in comparison to the other battalions and squadrons in the French army at this time. Toll, Vol. 4, 7th Book, p. 239.

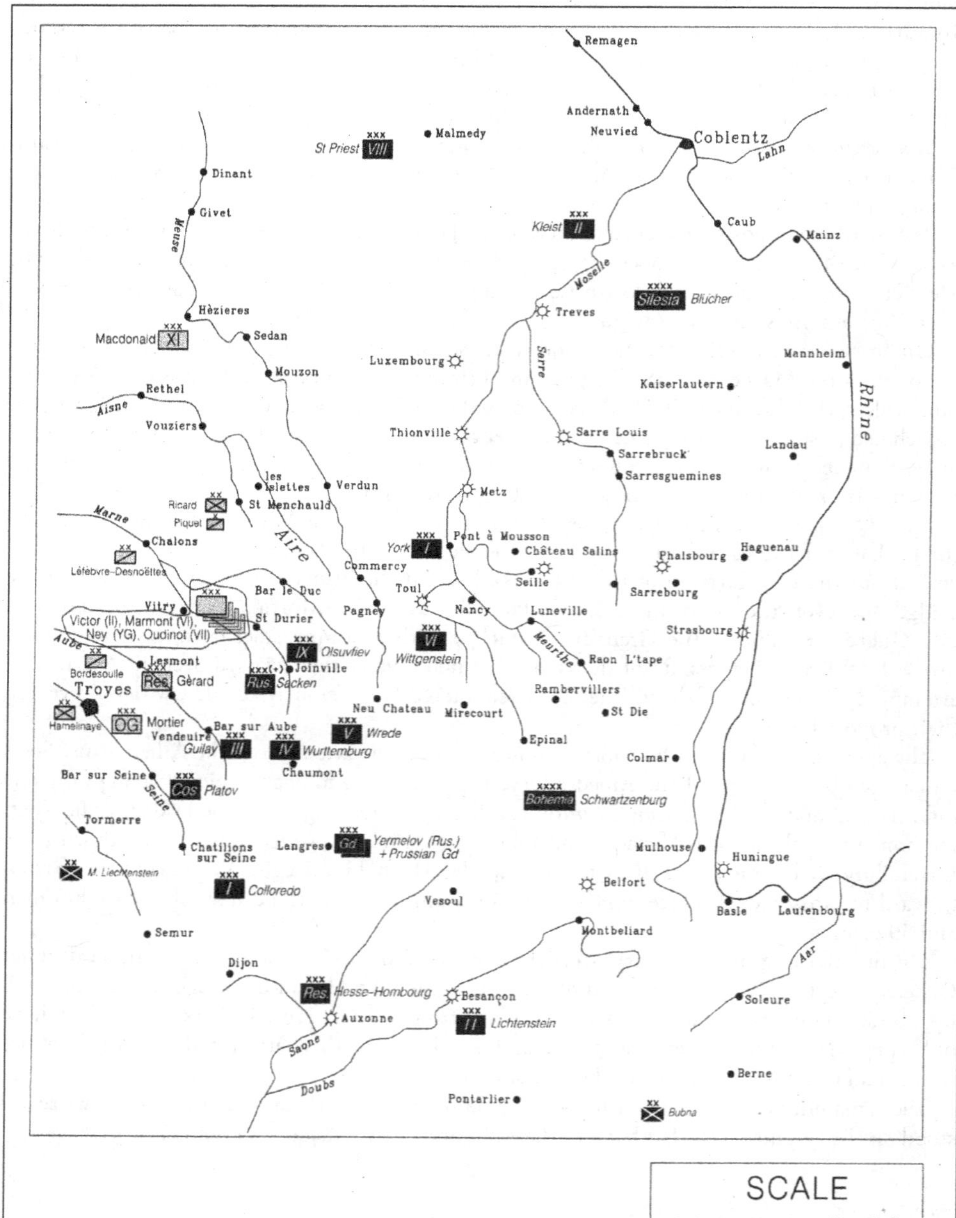

Map 1 Strategic Situation, January 26 1814.

After clearing Chaumont, the Crown Prince of Württemberg marched his corps down the road to Bar-sur-Aube. However, this movement was soon countermanded by an order from Schwarzenberg that directed him to remain in Chaumont. He did not resume his advance on Bar-sur-Aube until 24 January – and then in conjunction with the 3rd Corps.

The Austrian Reserves, under Prince von Hessen; the 1st Corps, under Prince Colloredo; and Bianchi's division, moved from Langres to Dijon – which they occupied on 20 January. He blockaded the Hautebourgogne Fortress with Schäffer's brigade – five battalions in 3,536 men – which had just arrived from Saxony.[45]

Wrede occupied Neuf Château the same day. With the Allies deployed between Dijon and Nancy, the natural defenses of the French border were passed. The Allied armies were now in the heart of France. The corps of Marmont, Ney, Victor and Mortier had been unable to put up any serious resistance to the Allied advance – and the citizens of that region had shown themselves totally indifferent to the presence of the Allied armies.[46]

The Allies had not pursued their invasion of France with any significant vigor to this point. Their objective had been to take Langres and then dictate conditions of peace to the French. There was no plan for any advance beyond Langres. As the campaign was to advance in the following months, the lack of Allied success was frequently attributed to the Allied advance beyond Langres.

The engagement at Bar-sur-Aube

While the Allies debated what actions to take now that Langres was occupied, the French did not remain idle. Maréchal Mortier, reinforced by GD Christiani's brigade,[47] stood unsupported by any other forces at Bar-sur-Aube. Mortier occupied a position in front of Bar-sur-Aube with Fontaine on his right and the village of Fouvré on his left. He placed the 113th Regiment – 1,200 men – and two guns to defend the bridge at Dolencourt, and a regiment of two battalions from the 1st Old Guard Division and three guns on the plateau between Pouervil and Spoy. The village of Fontaine was occupied by the Guard Chasseurs à cheval, a battalion of Old Guard and 400 men of the 2nd Division.[48] A detachment of éclaireurs was in Armentières watching the roads to Doulevant and Soulaines. Letort's brigade[49] and four battalions of the 1st Division – supported by six guns – occupied the village of Colombé-les-deux-Eglises. General Friant had his grenadier brigade and Laferrière's 3rd Guard Cavalry Division before Bar (behind the Voigny stream). Michel's 2nd Old Guard Division occupied the heights between Fontaine and Baroville to the left of the Aube.[50] They straddled the road to Chaumont. The French divided their artillery into three groups. One force faced down the road to Chaumont and the second was by the Boudelin bridge. The third group – seven guns – stood as a reserve behind Bar and deployed to move to the bridge over the Aube or move down the road to Spoy. All told, Mortier had about 14,200 men.[51]

45 von Bernhardi, Vol. 4, 7th Book, pp. 242-3.

46 Burghersh, pp. 87-9.

47 Christiani commanded the 2nd Brigade, the 2nd Old Guard Division and contained the Fusilier Chasseurs and Fusilier Grenadiers.

48 French National Archives, Carton AF^{IV} 1669A.

49 Letort commanded the 2nd Brigade and the 3rd Guard Cavalry Division, which contained the Grenadier à cheval Regiment. As of 1 February this brigade had 45 officers and 842 men.

50 de Vaudoncourt, Vol. I, p. 169.

51 Lefebvre de Béhaine, Vol. IV, pp. 179-180.

The Crown Prince of Württemberg, having joined Giulay's forces, made preparations to attack them. On 24 January the Allied 3rd Corps advanced through La Ferté-sur-Aube, Clairvaux and Fontaine while the 4th Corps moved down the main road from Chaumont.

Schwarzenberg had not wished to subordinate an Austrian to the Württembergers and, as a result, the two corps that moved on Bar-sur-Aube moved independently of one another.

The Württemberg advanced guard – under GM von Stockmayer – consisted of three battalions of light infantry, four cavalry squadrons and a horse battery. At 9:00 a.m. it arrived in Villeneuve. From there it marched on Roi and Montherie and sometime before noon it passed through Villeneuve-aux-Fraines.[52]

GM von Jett – at 10:00 a.m. – stood in Bessy with a detachment of four squadrons of Jäger zu Pferd, a hussar squadron, a horse battery and the 7th Infantry Regiment. Supporting him was the 3rd Dragoon Regiment, a foot battery and a battalion of the 6th Infantry Regiment. The remainder of the Württemberg Corps remained in Chaumont under the command of GL von Koch. This force – eight battalions and a battery – were, for no apparent reason, left idle in Chaumont.[53]

Shortly after noon – as Giulay's attack began – the Württembergers attacked Letort's brigade of French in Colombé. Von Jett attacked Colombé frontally and while Stockmayer moved to turn the flank of the French in Colombé, von Jett was followed by a reserve of four squadrons, two battalions and a battery. However, Stockmayer experienced serious problems. As he tried to move from Montherie to Villeneuve-aux-Fraines he was unable to find a route capable of handling his forces. He turned further to the right through the Beauregard woods – delaying his arrival and mitigating the effect of his movement.

Despite Stockmayer's delay, the enveloping attack and the superiority in numbers of the Allied forces forced Letort to withdraw his brigade to Lignol. Stockmayer's forces did not disturb his withdrawal as they were delayed by the bad roads through the woods (and did not arrive south of Colombé until after the French had withdrawn). Here, Letort deployed his brigade in line of battle before the village of Lignol. Württemberg responded by deploying his advanced guard once it had passed through Colombé and moved forward – supported by the rest of his corps, which was formed in columns. A single brigade facing 12,000 to 13,000 men had little hope of standing long, and once again Letort withdrew back towards the protection of Mortier's main body.

Württemberg passed through Lignol and deployed his corps yet again. His right was towards Voigny and his left on the Aube. Once deployed, the French began a lively cannonade with 20 guns which lasted until dark. Württemberg did not risk an attack.[54]

On his flank, General Giulay's advanced guard had pushed the French advanced posts between Bayel and Baroville. Hohenlohe-Bartenstein's division formed the head of the Allied column. When that was completed – at about 11:00 a.m. – he deployed to attack Fontaine. His first line, Hohenlohe's division, was supported by Mariassy's division and the fire of a battery of 10 cannon and four howitzers.[55] The five battalions of Trenk's brigade opened the attack – led by the Mariassy Ignatz Giulay Infantry Regiments and supported by Czollich's brigade.

General Michel's brigade stopped the Austrian attack and permitted Christiani's brigade to counterattack the stalled Austrians. Christiani's assault was successful and forced the Austrians back towards the rear in disorder. The route would have been complete if Giulay had not promptly sent forward the six battalions of Czollich's brigade. Czollich's forces stopped the French advance

52 Sporschil, Vol. II, p. 169.
53 von Damitz, Vol. I, pp. 234-5.
54 Lefebvre de Béhaine, Vol. IV, p. 180.
55 Sporschil, Vol. II, p. 168.

and stabilized the situation once again.[56] The Austrians assaulted the position a total of three times, but each time the garrison – reinforced by elements of the 2nd Division (notably the Vélites of Turin and Florence) – threw them back. The two sides then settled down into a cannonade which lasted until dusk. The French losses from the engagement were about 400 or 500 men. The Vélites of Florence and those of Turin were reported by the Allies to have fought with great bravery in this engagement.

After dark the French withdrew to Vandoeuvres and on 25 January General Giulay entered Bar-sur-Aube and took the bridge at Bondelaine. The Crown Prince of Württemberg had, in the meantime, driven back the French advanced corps from Colombé-les-deux-Eglises by Lignol to the heights between Voigny and Rouvre. Joining the Allied 3rd Corps, he prepared to make a general attack the following morning. However, Mortier withdrew during the night – retiring to Vandoeuvres.

The engagement had cost the Allies (1,500 dead and wounded, plus about 100 prisoners). Nearly all of the captured Austrian officers expressed their exasperation for the inactivity of the Württembergers.[57] However, Toll indicates that the Württembergers lost 900 men – dead and wounded – and cites Austrian sources as listing 647 Austrians *hors de combat* and 190 lost as prisoners. He also lists the French casualties as 1,200 – including 200 prisoners.[58]

General Sacken, after the capture of Toul on 20 January, crossed the Meuse in two columns. Generals Scherbatov and Vassil'shikov advanced on the right towards Ligny, which fell on 23 January. On the left Blücher marched on Joinville, which he occupied on 25 January. The same day Prince Scherbatov drove Maréchal Victor from St.-Dizier. As a result of these movements, Schwarzenberg was able to advance his army up to a line parallel to Blücher. His left – under Prince Colloredo, moved from Dijon to Châtillon – where it arrived on 28 January. On the same day the Russian and Prussian reserves assembled in Châtillon and General Wrede's corps arrived in Andelot. General Count Wittgenstein, who had attempted and failed in a *coup de main* on the fortress of Phalsbourg, had moved to Nancy and was now moving towards Neuf Château.

The Allied 5th Corps

As the Allies had crossed the Rhine, Wrede's 5th Corps had blocked the fortresses of Hunningen, Neubreisach, Schlettstadt and Strasbourg. When relieved of these duties he sent Habermann's brigade and Dietz's cavalry towards Saint-Marie-aux-Mines and Deroy's infantry brigade towards St.-Diéy.

The Bavarian forces, under GL Wrede, advanced on Schlettstadt and forced GD Milhaud to retire via Saint Marie-aux-Mines towards St.-Diéy. Maréchal Victor, threatened by both Wrede and Wittgenstein, found himself obliged to abandon Strasbourg. He withdrew via Mutzig and merged with GD Milhaud's corps at Baccarat.

Maréchal Ney was ordered by Napoleon to move from Saarlouis towards Nancy with a force of 5,000 infantry and 400 cavalry. He was to join Victor, and combined, the two marshals were to retake the abandoned defiles of the Vosges into the Rhine Valley.

Victor had sent General Milhaud, who had been by Colmar, to move to Saint-Marie-aux-Mines. Victor left Count Ségurin Savern with the 3rd and 4th Gardes d'honneur to observe Wittgenstein's advanced guard and to cover the provisioning of Pfalzburg. Victor then marched his main body around Strasbourg on 5 January – crossing through Mutzig and Framont and moving on to Baccarat, where he joined Milhaud.

56 de Vaudoncourt, Vol. I, p. 170.
57 Lefebvre de Béhaine, Vol. IV, p. 181.
58 von Bernhardi, Vol. 4, 7th Book, p. 241.

From Baccarat Victor moved towards Luneville – which was occupied by Duhèsme's division – with five battalions, a light cavalry brigade and a battery of horse artillery. Duhèsme's forces were watching Wrede's Bavarians.

Outside of this force, the French had few troops with which to oppose the Allied advance down the Moselle and Meurthe towards Nancy and Toul. Responding to this Napoleon ordered Maréchal Kellermann to concentrate at Saarlouis a force drawn from up and down the Rhine, a voltigeur division with 5,200 men – including 400 cavalry drawn from the depots – and two batteries to come from Maréchal Ney.

Maréchal Ney.

Victor, believing Napoleon intended an offensive movement against the Allied advance, ordered Duhèsme (supported by l'Héritier's dragoons) to move from Raon to St.-Dièy and another column – under General Briche – to move down the road to Rembervilliers. A third column, under General Rousseau, was directed from Nancy to Epinal to cover the right flank of the proposed offensive. General Rousseau's column, however, was engaged and driven back by Württemberg at Epinal.

Of the other columns, Briche's advance had been successful and scattered the 200 Cossacks it encountered in the valley between St.-Dièy and Rembervilliers. The French attack was led by General Montélegier at the head of the 6th Dragoon Regiment.[59]

Engagement by St.-Dièy

As Duhèsme's 3rd Division (II Corps) advanced on St.- Dièy it ran headlong into the advanced guard of Deroy's Bavarian Infantry Brigade as the Bavarians pushed out of St.- Dièy. It was about 11:00 a.m. Deroy's column was led by a half squadron of the 5th Chevauxlegers, 30 Cossacks and the sharpshooter company of the 5th Line Regiment.[60] By noon the Bavarians had been driven back through St.-Diéy by the superior numbers of French as far as Raon-l'Etape.

l'Héritier's dragoons led the French pursuit and quickly occupied Ste-Marguérite with skirmishers. They were followed by two infantry battalions, six cavalry squadrons and two guns.

Deroy rushed forward the skirmishers of the 8th and 9th Line Regiments and began organizing his attack column when he was badly wounded by a musket shot. Command passed to Oberst Treuberg.

Covered by their skirmishers, Oberst Treuberg led the 8th and 9th Line Regiments forward in a bayonet attack – supported by two cannon. They marched forward at the *Sturmschritt* towards Ste-Marguérite, where they were met by canister fire from the two French guns posted on the far bank of the Meurthe. The artillery fire was too much and the assault failed. Treuberg launched a second attack that also failed. He then brought forward a gun and a howitzer and supported

59 von Damitz, Vol. I, pp. 192-5.
60 Sporschil, Vol. II, p. 144.

his first line with the Isar Kreise National Feld-Bataillon. The remainder of the brigade served as a reserve.

Launching a third attack, Treuberg directed the grenadier and the schützen companies of the 9th Line Regiment to move against the French right flank while the remainder of the Bavarian attack force drove forward once again. This attack proved successful and the French pulled back to St.- Dièy. The engagement then broke off and the French withdrew. The Bavarians lost one officer and 11 men killed, and four officers and 76 men wounded, while claiming to have inflicted heavy casualties on the French and taking 224 prisoners.[61]

The remainder of the movement of the Allied 5th Corps was uneventful and on 16 January the corps stood between Bruyères, Rembervilliers and St.- Dièy.

Colloredo's Corps

On 14 January Victor began a movement towards Nancy with hopes of linking up with the forces of Ney and Marmont.

Colloredo's corps was in Baigneux between Dijon and Châtillon-sur-Seine. He had detached Wimpffen's division – placing it before Auxonne – and had been reinforced by Liechtenstein's light division, Bianchi's division, Trautenberg's grenadier division and Klebelsberg's cuirassier division. As a result, his force was increased by 37 battalions and 54 squadrons (or about 33,000 infantry and 10,000 cavalry). Giulay's corps was in Bar-sur-Aube, while that of Württemberg was at Colombé; that of Wrede was in Neuf Château; that of Wittgenstein was in Vaucouleurs – with its cavalry at Donjeux between Vignory and Joinville. The Russo-Prussian reserves were in Langres, Platov's corps was around Bar-sur-Aube, and Sacken's corps – and that of Olsufiev – were also around Joinville. Lanskoi had departed St.-Dizier that day. Yorck's corps was united at Pont-à-Mousson except for General Barasdin's forces blockading Metz, detachments from Röder's cavalry watching Thionville and Luxemburg, and a few squadrons before Saarlouis. Behind the Allied line stood Wimpffen's division before Auxonne, Prince Liechtenstein's corps before Besançon, and the remainder of the Austrian reserve at Dijon.

Other Allied Corps

General St. Priest, a French émigré, advanced with his corps through Malmedy and by the end of January arrived at Dinant and Givet (on the Meuse). Once there he established liaison with Winzingerode's army operating in the lowlands.

Winzingerode had arrived on the Rhine, opposite Düsseldorf, on 6 January. Faced by the forces of Bülow and Winzingerode, Maréchal Macdonald – who commanded the French forces on that part of the French frontier – abandoned Cleves and Nijmegen, placed a garrison in Greve and retired to Gelders and Venlo. Macdonald placed a garrison in Juliers and then established his right on Cologne and Neuss. On 13 January Winzingerode's corps crossed the Rhine – led by the cavalry of Czernichev and Benkendorff. On 16 January they entered Aachen and entered Liège on 18 January. Maréchal Macdonald withdrew to Namur where he received orders from Napoleon to march immediately to Châlons-sur-Marne, where Napoleon wished to assemble his army.

Maréchal Macdonald responded immediately – leaving GD Sébastiani with his cavalry to cover his march. Sébastiani abandoned Namur on 24 January and arrived in Mézières on 27 January.

Benkendorff, advancing down the road from Liège to St.-Trond, encountered a force of French Imperial Guard cavalry under GD Castex. Castex has been detached from Antwerp

61 von Damitz, Vol. I, pp. 195-7.

by GD Maison with orders to establish contact with Macdonald. Castex's cavalry held its own against Benkendorff until Czernichev arrived at the head of his cavalry. Castex, overwhelmed by numbers, was obliged to withdraw.

Winzingerode then occupied the fortress of Namur – establishing his headquarters there on 2 February. On 6 February he marched towards Avesnes via Sombref, Binche and Beaumont. Avesnes was occupied on 9 February and Laon on 12 February.[62]

In late January, a raiding party under the Prussian Guard Captain Bergman executed a raid on Montargis. When it arrived it encountered a transport of Spanish prisoners of war being moved from Epernay to Bourges, which it liberated. The column consisted of 405 officers – including 43 lieutenants over 50 years old – 15 cadets, 28 common soldiers, 49 women and four children. The Spaniards related to their liberators that between Epernay and Montargis the French conscripts were gathering in large numbers and that they had seen a substantial force of French marching on Châlons.[63]

The French army

In order to deal with the various maneuvers of the Allied armies, Napoleon established the center of action of the French army on Châlons. On 25 January the French army was deployed as follows: The II and VI Infantry Corps and the I and V Cavalry Corps were in and around Vitry. The Guard Reserve had two divisions in Vitry – one infantry division and a cavalry division in Châlons – which were moving at a leisurely rate towards Vitry under the orders of Oudinot. The I Corps and II and III Cavalry Corps were near Mézières. Macdonald was ordered to relieve Dufour (1st Division, Paris Reserve) and Ricard (1st Division, VI Corps), then in Islettes. Mortier was in Vandoeuvres with the Old Guard. The French extreme right was held by General Allix, who was organizing a weak brigade from the depots of the 18th Military Division in Auxerre. The Grande Armée stood as follows:

62 Burghersh, pp. 78-9.
63 von Bernhardi, Vol. 4, 7th Book, p. 337.

Under Mortier[64]			
Imperial Guard:			
Friant	8 bns	4,600	infantry
Michel	8 bns	3,878	infantry
Laferrière	12 sqdns	2,228	cavalry
Paris Reserve:			
Dufour	14 bns	7,991	infantry
Under Victor			
II Corps (Victor):			
Duhésme	8 bns	2,723	infantry
Gérard	7 bns	3,347	infantry
unassigned	5 bns	2,662	infantry
V Cavalry Corps (Milhaud):			
Piré	12 sqdns	1,050	cavalry
Briche	18 sqdns	1,500	cavalry
l'Héritier	14 sqdns	1,164	cavalry
VI Corps (Marmont):			
Ricard	14 bns	2,917	infantry
Lagrange	15 infantry	4,868	infantry
I Cavalry Corps:			
Piquet	7 sqdns	915	cavalry
Doumerc	16 sqdns	1,900	cavalry
Army of the Lower Rhine			
XI Corps (Macdonald):			
Molitor	10 bns	1,515	infantry
Brayer	6 bns	1,225	infantry
V Corps (Sébastiani):			
Albert	6 bns	1,246	infantry
II Cavalry Corps (Excelmans):			
Dommanget	10 sqdns	1,367	cavalry
Thierry	8 sqdns	775	cavalry
III Cavalry Corps (Arrighi):			
Ameil	6 sqdns	1,043	cavalry
Jacquinot	7 sqdns	812	cavalry
Under Ney			
Guard Reserve (Ney):			
Meunier	8 bns	4,106	infantry
Decouz	8 bns	2,700	infantry
Under Oudinot			
Rottembourg	11 bns	4,605	infantry
Léfèbvre-Desnoëttes	17 sqdns	2,285	cavalry

Total for all four armies: 48,383 infantry, 15,039 cavalry

64 de Vaudoncourt, Vol. I, p. 179.

5

A Battle Won and a Battle Lost: The Battles of Brienne and La Rothière, 31 January-1 February 1814

Napoleon rejoins the army

With the main Allied army concentrating in the heart of France, Napoleon was unable to continue his absence from his armies. He left Paris on 25 January – arriving in Châlons the following day. He took command of his army. This army consisted of the corps of Maréchal Mortier – now joined by the 20,000-man reserve under GD Dufour – stood at Troyes. The corps of Maréchaux Victor and Marmont – 28,000 men – stood near Vitry. Maréchal Macdonald had 10,000 men in Mézières and Ney had another 16,000 men at Châlons. The entire army consisted of 74,000 men.

Napoleon ordered the concentration of the corps of Victor, Marmont and Ney – plus Dufour's division – and immediately led them forward. His first attack was on St.-Dizier, which fell on 27 January. Milhaud's cavalry, supported by Duhèsme's infantry division, struck Lanskoi's cavalry as it was in its bivouacs.[1]

Duhèsme's division struck the Russian advanced guard so hard that they were unable to destroy the bridge. Lanskoi was driven from St.-Dizier back upon Joinville and Eclaron – nearer Blücher's main body, which was assembling in Brienne. Napoleon had positioned his newly-formed army on Blücher's flank and, hoping to find it unsupported by Schwarzenberg, moved to attack it – passing through Montièrender and Vassey on 28 January.

Army of Silesia occupies Brienne

On 26 January Blücher advanced Sacken and Olsufiev's corps towards Vassy and Montièrender. Lanskoi was in St.-Dizier to maintain communications with Yorck's corps. Yorck was concentrating his divisions around Pont-à-Mousson. His cavalry reserve, however, still remained in Verdun. General Pahlen, with Wittgenstein's cavalry (less the Cossacks), was marching on Doulevant. Schwarzenberg's main army remained stationary. Blücher had learned on 26 January of Napoleon's movements and assembled his forces to meet him. The Army of Silesia consisted of the corps of General Sacken and Olsufiev's division – plus part of Wittgenstein's cavalry under the command of Count Pahlen.

On 27 January Blücher occupied Brienne. He deployed Sacken behind the city on the road to Vieux-Brienne in column. Vassil'shikov's cavalry corps was placed on his right. Pahlen followed

1 von Damitz, Vol. I, p. 398.

Sacken through the city and was sent to a position near Eclance between Brienne and Bar-sur-Aube.[2] Olsufiev was posted in the town, Yorck's Prussian corps occupied Saint-Mihiel and his cavalry was in Croix-sur-Meuse. That same day Napoleon departed Châlons for Vitry, where he met the II and VI Corps, the Guard Reserve and the cavalry. Milhaud's cavalry – followed by Duhèsme's 3rd Division, II Corps – moved towards St.-Dizier.

Sacken, by G. Dawe.

Blücher occupied a position along the high road leading from Brienne to Paris – occupying the town of Brienne with General Olsufiev's division.[3] Lanskoi's division, serving as Blücher's advanced guard, was surprised by Milhaud's cavalry and driven back on Joinville. They moved so quickly that they were unable to destroy the bridge at St.-Dizier. The French army quickly took up positions at St.-Dizier.

Dufour's 1st Division (Paris Reserve), which had failed to destroy the bridge at Lesmont because of a lack of sappers, withdrew to Arcis on 25 January and arrived in St.-Dizier on 27 January. Ricard's 8th Division arrived in Erize from Islettes. Brayer's 35th Division, XI Corps, arrived in Vatry-sur-l'Aisen – leading the way for Macdonald's march from Mézières. Mortier departed Vandoeuvres and withdrew to Troyes – occupying everything but the bridge at Guillotière.[4]

Napoleon's goal was marching on St.-Dizier to trap Blücher's army with a rapid movement before it was able to reunite itself. Alone, Blücher's army was unable to resist Napoleon's combined army. Once crushed and the debris thrown back, Napoleon would roll up and crush Wittgenstein at Vaucouleurs and then force Wrede – whose flank he would be threatening – to withdraw. Wrede's movement would permit Napoleon to threaten Schwarzenberg's lines of communication and would oblige him to change his plan of operations.[5]

Blücher pulled his army together and resumed his march. However, he soon received word of Lanskoi's withdrawal from Joinville via Doulevant and Soulaines. He chose to remain in Brienne and to await the next French move. He chose to hold Pahlen's cavalry with him – sending it to Piney. Vassil'shikov's cavalry was sent to Lesmont. Yorck – preceded by Katzler – pushed his advanced guard of two battalions and eight squadrons into Bar-sur-Ornain. However, discovering the village was held by the French, he redirected his march. He then marched up the Meuse to Commercy, where he crossed. Katzler's advanced guard remained before Bar. Prince Wilhelm von Preussen's division moved to Ligny and the remainder of the corps took up positions at Commercy. The city had been occupied by the French VI Corps, but they departed that afternoon and the Prussians entered Bar-sur-Ornain a little later.

The movement of the French army on St.-Dizier and Joinville disturbed Schwarzenberg, who found them threatening. His army was not concentrated, but was deployed over a substantial territory – as was the Army of Silesia. Schwarzenberg feared that Napoleon would move from Joinville against his line of communications between Langres and Vesoul. As a result, he moved to cover his right with the goal of at least protecting the line from Dijon to Dôle. On 29 January he drew up his army in line of battle between the Aube and the Marne.

2 C. von W., p. 139.
3 Burghersh, pp. 109-10.
4 de Vauconcourt, Vol. I, p. 182.
5 de Vauconcourt, Vol. I, p. 185.

The head of Colloredo's Corps occupied Bar-sur-Aube, a brigade was in Spoy and another was at the Dolencourt bridge. The Crown Prince of Württemberg moved from Colombé , past Bar to Maisons. The Russian Grenadiers were in Château-Vilain and the cuirassier divisions of Duka and Kretov were at La Ferté-sur-Aube and Clairvaux. The Russian and Prussian Guard were between Chaumont and Langres. The corps of Wrede and Wittgenstein were ordered to march on Joinville from their positions in Andelot and Gondrecourt. Once there, they were to attack whatever French force they encountered. Blücher deployed his corps between Brienne and Lesmont. Pahlen's cavalry was positioned in Lassicourt, from where it sent reconnaissance forces out towards Braux and Chavanges. Prince Schwarzenberg had directed General Scherbatov – with three Cossack regiments and the four battalions of the 4th and 34th Jager Regiments – to march on Châlons, but now directed him to Mézières (on the road to Montiérender).

During the morning Blücher learned, from Scherbatov's Cossacks, that the French had occupied Boulancourt. He responded by ordering Sacken to concentrate his corps at Lesmont and Olsufiev to take position in Brienne. He was ignorant, however, of the actual French movements and looked upon the occupation of Boulancourt as a demonstration. New Cossacks brought a captured French staff officer to him. Captured between Montièrender and Lesmont, he carried dispatches from Napoleon – announcing his intention to march from St.-Dizier. There was a second order directing Mortier to leave Troyes and close to the right wing of the French army. Blücher, fearing his position was compromised by a retrograde movement by Schwarzenberg, immediately ordered a withdrawal positions by Bar-sur-Aube. He ordered Sacken to move to Brienne and to destroy the bridge at Lesmont.[6]

During the morning of the 29th, Napoleon began his movement from Montièrender with Victor and Ney's corps. Marmont was marching to Vassy with his cavalry – leaving Lagrange's 3rd Division (VI Corps) in St.-Dizier.

Advance on Brienne

Between 10:00 a.m. and noon on 30 January, Piré's 9th Light Cavalry Division departed Boulancourt, where it had been since the previous day. Pahlen's cavalry – 2,500 men – was to the right of the main road by Perthé. Scherbatov's Cossacks stood on the road to Maizières and four Russian Jager regiments, under Scherbatov, were in a position behind Mézières. Piré engaged them both and pushed the Russian infantry back to the heights by Parthes. Scherbatov, reinforced by the Tchougouiev Uhlan Regiment (six squadrons) and four horse guns, stopped his withdrawal and positioned himself on the road that runs from Mézières to Brienne.[7] The weather had made the terrain impassable and the Russian cavalry and artillery had only been able to advance along the road. Piré's 9th Light Cavalry Division was soon joined by the rest of the cavalry under General Grouchy. They deployed in the plains before Mézières with the V Cavalry Corps to the left. As Scherbatov and the French exchanged artillery fire, the first troops of General Sacken – withdrawing from Lesmont – arrived in column behind Brienne on the road from Vitry to Bar-sur-Aube. The 4th and 34th Jager Regiments took up positions before Brienne on the road to Lassicourt. Pahlen moved from Lassicourt and, to cover Sacken's flank during his march, moved to Perthé before the line of French cavalry. Scherbatov was pushed back from his position by Parthes to a new one by Lassicourt.

General Grouchy ordered the V Cavalry Corps to advance against Pahlen under the cover of three batteries. Grouchy's cavalry attacked the Russians and, after several charges and

6 de Vauconcourt, Vol. I, pp. 186-7.
7 *Victoires conquêtes, désastres*, Vol. 23, p. 63.

Grouchy.

counter-charges, drove the Russians back.[8] During this engagement, General Léfèbvre-Desnoëttes was wounded. Pahlen's 2,500 men fell back towards Brienne and sought shelter under three of Scherbatov's battalions (4th and 34th Jager Regiments) and formed squares with the divisions of Briche and l'Héritier in pursuit.[9] The fire of these three squares stopped the French pursuit.

Pahlen passed through Brienne around 3:00 p.m. The Army of Silesia stood in position behind Brienne as a reserve with GM Pantschichscheff's cavalry. Pantschichscheff commanded Sacken's advanced guard. Olsufiev occupied Brienne itself with his 9th Corps – totaling no more than 5,000 men and 24 guns. Sacken's corps, which had been slowed down by its pontoon train, had only just arrived and was still arrayed in columns. Sacken deployed his cavalry on his right.

On the French side, Napoleon decided not to press the cavalry engagement as the Allies had deployed a strong skirmish line in the edge of the city and the ditch along the main road into the city. Instead, he chose to wait for his infantry to arrive on the battlefield. At 3:30 p.m. the head of Victor's (duc de Bellune) column arrived with Duhèsme's division – forming the head of the column. When Duhèsme's division had reached the cavalry, Napoleon ordered a general advance.

The Battle of Brienne – 29 January

As soon as Napoleon's forces arrived they were formed into three large columns. The right column, under GD Château, was to attack the castle of Brienne. The central column, under GD Decouz, was to attack Brienne itself and the left column, under GD Duhèsme, was to turn the right of the Allied position.

Before Brienne the Russians stood with Vassil'shikov, and Pahlen's cavalry was on the left of the main road before Brienne-la-Vieille. The eight Cossack regiments of General Karpov were in Chaumenil, La Chaise and Soulaines. Scherbatov's 4th and 34th Jagers – detached from the Russian 4th Division (von Württemberg's 2nd Infantry Corps) – occupied the part of Brienne that adjoins the road to Lassicourt. Olsufiev's 9th Corps, with the 9th and 15th Divisions, stood southeast of Brienne by the road to Bar-sur-Aube and Montier-en-Der. Sacken's corps was en route from Lesmont.

The French cavalry had been massed since 1:00 p.m. Between 2:00 p.m. and 3:00 p.m. the French cavalry on the left wing was reinforced by the arrival of Milhaud's V Cavalry Corps and

8 von Plotho claims that the Tchougouiev Uhlans captured three cannon, but this claim is not noted in any other sources. It is, therefore, probable that this did not occur, or if it did, the guns were temporarily overrun and not retained – especially in view of the Russian retreat at the end of this battle. von Plotho, Vol. III, p. 198.

9 *Victoires conquêtes, désastres*, Vol. 23, p. 63 indicates that Pahlen's withdrawal was not as a result of combat, but occurred when Pahlen saw himself faced with overwhelming force and chose to withdraw in column. However, this does not seem reasonable in light of Lefebvre-Desnoettes' reported wound. People are not generally wounded in unopposed withdrawals.

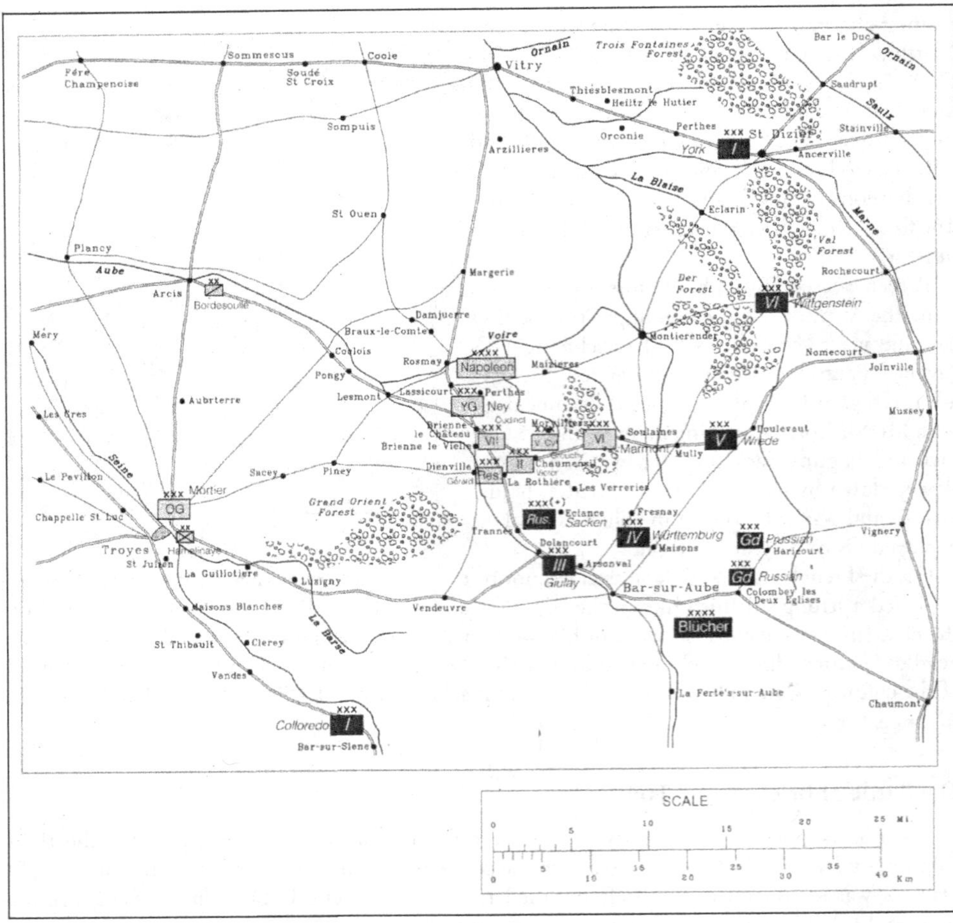

Map 2 Strategic Situation, January 31 1814.

the right wing was reinforced by the arrival of Léfèbvre-Desnoëttes' Guard Cavalry. It then moved forward from the Perthé heights and began its march against Brienne. The three horse batteries with the V Cavalry Corps took both Pahlen's and Vassil'shikov's under cannon fire. Meanwhile, Sacken's corps began appearing as it pushed through Brienne and formed itself in closed columns to the left and right of the road to Bar-sur-Aube. Only the rearguard – the 3rd Dragoon Division, under Pantschichscheff – remained behind Brienne.[10]

Napoleon sent orders to Ney ordering him to press his march harder and come to the battlefield as soon as humanly possible – via to the road to Maizières – with one of the Young Guard brigades of Decouz's division. Napoleon also ordered General Château – chief of staff to Victor – to take command of a second column, turn the city's right and attack the Château.

10 von Damitz, Vol. I, pp. 425-6.

The Battle of Brienne, by Jean Antoine Siméon Fort. Napoleon is in center foreground, accompanied by Chasseurs à cheval of the Guard; Maréchal Victor's infantry move towards Brienne on the right.

GD Grouchy sent forward Briche and l'Héritier's dragoons to engage the Russian cavalry, but their attack was repulsed and the Tchougouiev Uhlans overran the three French horse batteries – capturing them and carrying off their guns. Meanwhile, as this engagement was in progress, French howitzer shells fell amongst the Russian infantry passing through Lesmont and Brienne – and Pantschichscheff's dragoons moved into Brienne.

The French launched yet another attack; this one aimed at Olsufiev's 9th Corps on the right flank. It came close to cutting off part of the Allied army, but still it failed.

About 3:30 p.m. the head of the French II Corps arrived on the field and Duhèsme's 3rd Division, leading the advance, was pushed forward. Duhèsme marched out of the Ajou woods directly against Brienne under the cover of heavy artillery fire. Duhèsme pushed his forces forward and captured part of the outskirts of Brienne. Olsufiev's forces were steadily driven back until they received support in the form of the 4th and 34th Jager Regiments. Duhèsme engaged the Allies for an hour with no advantage going to either side.

During the fight between Olsufiev and Duhèsme, Blücher noted that Duhèsme's troops were only supported by artillery so he ordered Vassil'shikov and Pahlen's 40 squadrons to attack. The attack was very successful.[11] This flanking movement was completely successful, with eight guns being captured and Duhèsme's 3rd Division (II Corps) was broken and thrown into complete confusion.[12]

As Duhèsme launched his attack, Ney arrived on the field. While Duhèsme was engaged – around 4:00 p.m. or 5:00 p.m. – Napoleon sent forward six battalions of Decouz's 2nd Voltigeur (Young Guard) Division in closed columns to the right of Duhèsme's attack.[13] Ney led this force

11 *Victoires conquêtes, désastres*, Vol. 23, p. 65; C von W., p. 140; von Damitz, Vol. I, p. 428.
12 de Vauconcourt, Vol. I, p. 189; Burghersh, p.110.
13 von Plotho, Vol. III, p. 105.

personally down the road to Maizières . Two batteries posted on the right and two more on the left of his advancing infantry pounded Olsufiev's troops in preparation for the final assault. The attack was successful – penetrating into Brienne and capturing two guns from the 12pdr Position Battery #15 (part of Olsufiev's corps) despite the desperate fight of the 4th and 34th Jager Regiments.

However, Duhèsme's collapse obliged Ney to suspend his attack against General Olsufiev's infantry in the village of Brienne and withdraw. From this position Decouz's six battalions of Young Guard continued the fight, despite the fall of night.

The French right column – containing a strong force of cavalry – was able to approach the castle concealed by the terrain. Blücher – not suspecting their advance – had placed a small garrison in that position. The castle was stormed and carried by 400 men of the 37th and 56th Line Regiments led by Colonel Henders. Blücher himself was almost captured in this attack.[14]

During this assault the French also overran and captured four guns. However, a bayonet attack by the Kolyvan Infantry Regiment recaptured them.[15]

With the castle in French hands, they then turned and advanced on Brienne. The Allies, however, were able to repel the French assault, but were not able to recapture the castle despite repeated assaults. GM Udom, with the Russian 9th Division, supported the retreat of the 15th Division. The Russian corps withdrew into Brienne, where it remained the rest of the battle.

Holding a flanking position, Napoleon ordered the guard cavalry under General Léfèbvre-Desnoëttes and the 1st and 2nd Voltigeur (Young Guard) Divisions – GD Decouz and Meunier – to strike at the Allied center in the town of Brienne. Their assault was repulsed with no gain, but many houses of the city were set afire. Decouz attempted to rally his troops, but was mortally wounded – turning command over to Rear Admiral Baste, one of his brigade commanders.[16] Baste would soon have two horses shot from under himself before he too received a fatal wound. As the Young Guard recoiled, they became entangled with Duhèsme's troops.

In one last effort, Grouchy sent forward l'Héritier's division into the city. They were engaged by the Russian light troops and accomplished nothing – though the 22nd Dragoons performed valiantly. As night fell, the battle ended.[17] Brienne remained in the Allies' hands and the castle in the hands of the French.

Blücher, thinking the battle was over, withdrew to the Château after ordering Olsufiev to abandon Brienne at midnight and Sacken to begin his withdrawal at 2:00 a.m. the following morning. However, he left his cavalry on the ground it held the day before. It did have orders to fall back, if necessary, to the plain in front of his new position. The Russian cavalry was pushed back to La Rothière. The French II Cavalry Corps occupied La Rothière.[18] After deploying in front of La Rothière, Grouchy sent a detachment to Chaumenil, where it cleared the village of Cossacks. The divisions of Ricard and Dufour joined Piquet's light cavalry brigade in Rosnay. General Gérard took command of them and directed them to Dienville.

The battle had been hotly contested, but the casualties were light by the standards of the previous year. Indeed, the total casualties suffered by each side were about 6,000 killed, wounded and missing.

The following afternoon the French remained in their lagers behind Brienne while General Vassil'shikov moved through Dienville and GM Karpov II occupied the villages of Soulaines, La Chaise and Chaumenil with his Cossacks. At noon the French formed a column of cavalry

---

14 von Damitz, Vol. I, p. 430.
15 Langeron, p. 385.
16 Decouz died in Paris on 18 February 1814. *Victoires conquêtes, désastres*, Vol. 23, p. 66.
17 Sunset on 29 January occurred at 4:21 p.m. according to Sporschil, Vol. II, p. 219.
18 de Vauconcourt, Vol. I, pp. 193-4.

Napoleon at Brienne, by Jean-Baptiste Madou.

behind the Brienne castle and brought their artillery and infantry forward out of the city – forming a battery of 16 guns and beginning a slow withdrawal. The infantry followed the French reserve artillery in closed columns. The French cavalry moved behind the infantry – screening their withdrawal.

GL Count Pahlen III, who commanded all the cavalry of the Army of Silesia's advanced guard, moved Vassil'shikov to the right of the highway and brought forward seven guns that began a desultory fire on the French. They lacked the ammunition to do much more than annoy the French as they withdrew.

Gérard.

Gérard's column moved into Dienville and occupied it. Victor's II Corps moved into La Rothière and Grouchy deployed the I Cavalry Corps to cover the French positions. That evening a French force of cavalry occupied Chaumenil – driving out GM Karpov II's Cossacks – despite their support by GM Prince Biron von Courland's force.[19] Marmont's VI Corps occupied Soulaines.

19 Prince von Courland's force consisted of two squadrons of the Silesian National Hussar Regiment, its volunteer Jäger detachments and the Jäger Squadron of the Neumark Dragoon Regiment.

On the Allied side of the field, General Pahlen occupied Trannes with his main body – pushing his advanced posts towards Dienville and La Rothière. The corps of Sacken and Olsufiev took up positions by Trannes. Von Blücher set up his headquarters in Arçonval.

Yorck, by Ernst Gebauer.

Engagement by St.-Dizier – 31 January

Fifteen-hundred paces from Major von Schierstädt's position in the woods (along the main road) ran stood the suburbs of St.-Dizier. The woods sheltered a number of Prussian guns. Not waiting for Prince Wilhelm von Preussen's brigade to arrive, General von Yorck ordered the Prussians to attack the French. Oberst von Warburg was ordered to lead the Prussian 2nd Brigade down the main road.

General von Pirch followed the 2nd Brigade with his 1st Brigade and ordered two squadrons of the East Prussian National Cavalry Regiment and the 1st East Prussian and Silesian Grenadier Battalions to move left from Ancerville through the ice houses along the Marne and against St.-Dizier. The 7th Brigade, under General Horn, remained behind the reserve cavalry near Ancerville.

The Fus/1st and Fus/2nd East Prussian Infantry Regiments moved through the woods and over the Weinberg on the right and left of the main road. Kapitain Heute's 6pdr Battery moved to a position where it had a clear field of fire on the city and began lobbing howitzer shells into it.

The French had only weakly garrisoned St.-Dizier and most of the 4,000-5,000 infantry and 700-800 cavalry, under GD Lagrange, stood on the far side of the Marne.

As the two Prussian grenadier battalions closed on the ice houses, the French engaged them with a light skirmish fire and with some artillery fire from the Gigny suburb. However, the French quickly withdrew back across the city's stone bridge. The French cavalry rearguard was the last to withdraw across the bridge. As it did so, the Prussian 1st Foot Battery unlimbered and took the bridge under fire. The musketry of the East Prussian Fusiliers joined the artillery fire to encourage the French on their way. There was apparently more sound and fury in this engagement than bloody combat, as the Prussians lost one dead and a few wounded and the French casualties were about the same.[20]

After the skirmish Yorck moved his army into St.-Dizier – placing the 1st Brigade in Perthé on the road to Vitry. The 2nd Brigade and the reserve cavalry stood before Vassy. The 7th and 8th Brigades, the reserve cavalry and the artillery were posted in and by St.-Dizier. Oberst von Henckel's detachment was in Sermaiz, with his advanced posts pushing towards Vitry.

The advanced guard no longer was under von Katzler and now consisted solely of the Brandenburg Hussars and Brandenburg Uhlans. Command of the 3rd Brigade was assumed by Prince Wilhelm von Preussen and now consisted of the Brandenburg and 2nd Reserve Infantry Regiments, the 14th Silesian Landwehr Infantry Regiment, four squadrons of the 10th Silesian Landwehr Cavalry Regiment, five squadrons of the 2nd Leib Hussars and 6pdr Foot Battery #16.

20 von Damitz, Vol. I, pp. 457-8.

After Brienne, towards La Rothière

Napoleon deployed his army on the ground between La Rothière to Dienville. Maréchal Marmont arrived at Vassy later in the day, where he was attacked by Wrede's advanced guard – fighting with them until Lagrange's 3rd Division (II Corps) arrived. After breaking off that engagement he marched on Montièrender as ordered by Napoleon. General Defrance, with 800 Gardes d'honneur, moved to Lesmont to cover the reconstruction of the bridge. Blücher remained in Trannes – covered by Pahlen's cavalry and supported on his right by von Württemberg's 4th Corps in Maisons and Fresnoy. To his left stood Giulay in Spoy.

Yorck's corps had arrived before St.-Dizier and attacked Lagrange's 3rd Division, VI Corps – advancing down along the two banks of the Marne. Lagrange was obliged to fall back on Vassy, where he rejoined Marmont. Yorck then pushed Pirch's 1st Brigade towards Perthé, on the road to Vitry. He sent Katzler, with nine battalions and 12 squadrons, towards Humbecourt on the road to Vassy.

The French had failed in their effort to cut the Army of Silesia away from the main army and destroy it before the main army could intervene. Despite this, the French remained at La Rothière. During the morning of 31 January the VI Corps marched from Montièrender towards Boulancourt. Its advanced guard encountered Pahlen's cavalry at Soulaines, which were being held at bay by the village's inhabitants. The Russians were chased away. General Van Merlen, who stood as a rearguard in Montièrender with a force of 800 infantry, was surprised by Illowaisky's Cossacks and taken prisoner along with 100 men. The remainder succeeded in rejoining the army. The bridge at Lesmont was, despite Napoleon's order, not rebuilt because of the immediate lack of materials. It would not be repaired until the following day.

Marmont moved up from Vassy and deployed his corps in Chaumenil and Morvilliers, with its advanced guard in La Chaise. The French army was deployed in front of Brienne in the following order: On the right, occupying Dienville, stood GD Gérard with Ricard's 8th Division and Dufour's 1st Division (Paris Reserve) plus Piquet's light cavalry brigade. The center was under Victor, with the II Corps now reduced to two divisions. It occupied La Rothière, Mesnil and Chaumenil with a few battalions deployed before Giberie. Six cavalry divisions, under generals Nansouty and Milhaud, covered his flanks. The French left was under Marmont with a single infantry division and a cavalry division. They occupied Morvilliers and La Chaise.[21] In reserve stood Ney with three divisions of Guard. Mortier, who had departed Troyes on the 30th and marched on Arcis, learned that Colloredo was in Bar-sur-Seine. He stopped his march and immediately returned to Troyes – occupying it with Friant's 1st Old Guard Division and Hamélinaye's 2nd Division (Paris Reserve), and GD Laferrière's 1st (Old Guard) Cavalry Division. Michel's 2nd Old Guard Division was sent back to the bridge at Guillotière.

That same day, Prince Schwarzenberg – assured that the bulk of the French army was at Brienne – resolved to attack them. To this effect he placed Giulay and Württemberg – plus the Russian Grenadiers and Cuirassiers – at Blücher's disposition. The Russian and Prussian Guard were moved before Bar-sur-Aube in reserve. Wrede and Wittgenstein's corps were advancing on Vassy and St.-Dizier, where they were to join Yorck and attack the French XI Corps standing towards Vitry. Pahlen's cavalry was ordered to rejoin its corps and moved on Soulaines, where it encountered a force of French that stopped its march. The Austrian Reserves and the 1st Corps, with Bianchi's division, were placed under Prince Colloredo and ordered to march on Vandoeuvres with the intention of operating against Troyes. The Russian reserves were advanced to Colombé-les-deux-Eglises.

Wittgenstein's 6th Corps marched on Vassy, which it found empty. While there it was ordered to march on St.-Dizier. He ordered Illowaiski XII to occupy Montièrender with five Cossack

21 de Vauconcourt, Vol. I, pp.194-5.

regiments. Wrede advanced to Nom court, near Joinville, where he learned that the French had evacuated Vassy so that they might participate in the upcoming battle. Wrede then decided to march back to Bar-sur-Aube so he could take up a position on von Württemberg's right.

Giulay, in executing Schwarzenberg's orders, marched to Arçonval and Bossancourt in the evening of 31 January. The Russian Grenadiers and the 2nd and 3rd Russian Cuirassiers Divisions marched through the night – arriving at daybreak at Trannes. At the same hour the Russian and Prussian Guard arrived in Ailleville. Blücher did not move his army and Yorck remained in St.-Dizier.[22]

On 1 February the French army stood on the plain of Brienne, where it had been since 1 January. Napoleon deployed his army – from right to left – from Dienville, La Rothière, Petit-Mesnil, La Giberie and La Chaise. His lines extended to the right and rear of this last village to Morvilliers. He recognized that his forces were over-extended. He wanted to push forward and occupy the ground between Trannes and Eclance in order to shorten his lines, but the Allies already occupied that position. The only way he could take that position was through a general attack, but that was too risky in view of the numerical disparity between his army and that of the Allies. Instead, he chose to stay where he was and ordered Marmont to entrench himself in La Chaise and Morvilliers.[23]

Blücher had remained stationary in his positions around Trannes during the day of 31 January. He was awaiting reinforcements from the Allied army. Napoleon understood this and knew that Schwarzenberg was advancing on the road from Auxerre. Despite the pending arrival of even more Allies, he waited quietly in the presence of the Army of Silesia – hoping that Blücher would make some move that would compromise his army and give Napoleon the opportunity to attack.

On the other hand, Blücher knew this and also knew that he would have overwhelming numbers before too long. He had decided to give battle where he stood and awaited the arrival of the corps of Giulay and Crown Prince of Württemberg, with Barclay de Tolly's reserve. In addition, the corps of Wrede and Wittgenstein were maneuvering on his right flank.

Allied battle plan

With his reinforcements scheduled to arrive during the morning of 1 February, Blücher set the time for the attack at noon. The forces on and near the battlefield were as follows:

Allied forces present		
Army of Silesia	27,000	
3rd Corps (Giulay)		12,000
4th Corps (Württemberg)		14,000
Total:		53,000
Due to arrive		
5th Corps (Wrede)		25,000
En route, not to be counted on		
Colloredo's Corps		25,000
Allied Reserve		15,000
		40,000

Total of Allied forces to be engaged in the battle: 78,000 men
Total of all Allied forces approaching battlefield: 118,000 men[24]

22 de Vauconcourt, Vol. I, pp. 196-7.
23 Koch, Vol. I, 169.
24 von Damitz, Vol. I, p. 476.

The figures on the French forces present are not subject to debate. In the following chart, the separate figures for infantry and cavalry are from Sporschil's account of the battle and, apparently, do not include the artillery and train personnel that may be included in the column labelled 'total' (drawn from von Damitz). Von Damitz indicates that the French had 50,460 men, while Sporschil indicates they had 36,140 – and what information is available from the French archives indicates that they had 36,540 men.[25]

French forces on the field

	Sporschil		Sporschil	von Damitz
	Infantry	Cavalry	Total	Total
Right wing:				
Gérard's corps				11,208 men
Brigade Piquet		500		
Division Dufour	3,400			
Division Ricard	3,500		7,400	
Center:				
Victor's corps				14,747
Division Desnoëttes		850		
Division Colbert		880		
Division Guyot		750		
Division Duhèsme	6,100			
Division Piré		870		
Division Briche		1,250		
Division l'Héritier		1,000		11,700
Left wing:				
Marmont's corps				10,000
Division Doumerc		1,800		
Division Lagrange	4,600			6,400
Ney's Reserve				14,505
Division Rottembourg	4,900			
Division Decouz	1,800			
Division Meunier	3,000			
Division Defrance	800	10,500		
Total:			36,140	50,460 men

25 Sporschil, Vol. II, 1st Band, p. 232. (Sporschil cites Koch as his source of these figures.); von Damitz, Vol. I, p. 476; French Archives, Carton C^2 712; French Archives C^2 555. An explanation of the difference in these figures for the French is difficult. The French archives are very sparse of details for this period, though it does appear that Koch consulted what records were available. The veracity of these records, because of their incompleteness, is questionable. Von Damitz's figures may well come from estimates made on the field or sources other than French records. Irrespective of how these figures are looked at, they are all estimates because of the general 'roundness' of them. They are too imprecise to be actual head-counts. Both sets of figures are provided because the truth probably lies somewhere between them.

Blücher's orders to his commanders was as follows:

> At 12:00 noon the corps of General Sacken, formed in two columns, shall move against the village of La Rothière. The first column shall march down the high road, which runs from Trannes to La Rothière. The second column shall march from its position between Trannes and the edge of the woods in the direction of Brienne. GL Olsufiev shall support the second column with his corps."[26] (This was the second, or left center column, which consisted of Count Lieven III's 11th Russian Corps. Lieven was to occupy La Rothière with his 8,000 men. The third (right center) column, under GL Scherbatov (8,000 men), was to move down the main road and take up a position on the right of Lieven. Behind the second and third columns, Olsufiev's 11th Corps (5,000 men) and Vassil'shikov's cavalry corps (4,000 men) formed a second line. Karpov II's Cossacks (2,000 men) and the light cavalry of General Prince Biron von Courland served to link the third and fourth columns.)[27]
>
> The 3rd Army Detachment, under FZM Count Giulay (commanding the first, or 'left' column, with 12,000 men), shall support the advance of the first column."[28] (He was to deploy on the left – in the plain – and to attack the village of Dienville with his left, while his right would support Sacken's corps.)
>
> The Imperial Russian Grenadier Corps and the two cuirassier divisions (Raevsky) shall march from their position by Trannes and take up a position between that village and the wooded heights to serve as a reserve. The 4th Army Detachment – under the command of His Royal Majesty the Crown Prince von Württemberg – shall leave the village of Eclance at noon, advance into and purge the woods adjacent to Chaumenil of French troops and seek to link with the army detachment of Graf Wrede. If the French cannot be cleared form these woods, a battalion from the reserve column of GM Olsufiev shall be deployed to screen the main forces from their musketry. I shall be on the heights between Trannes and the wooded corner.[29]

The terrible mud caused Blücher to direct Sacken to detach the horses from half of his 120 guns and double them up on the remaining 60 guns so that they could maneuver. The 60 unhorsed guns were left in the rear.[30]

The fourth (right) wing column was formed by the 14,000 men of 4th Corps and was commanded by the Crown Prince of Württemberg. It would advance through the Eclance woods against La Giberie and Chaumenil.

The fifth, or right independent wing column, was formed by the 25,000 men of GdC Wrede's V Army Corps. Wrede was directed to advance from Soulaines and demonstrate before La Chaise – and to act, according to circumstances, against the French left flank and rear. When the battle began, the Reserve – consisting of the Russian Grenadier Corps and the 2nd and 3rd Cuirassier Divisions, under the command of GdC Raevsky – stood behind the center right by Bossancourt. The Russian and Prussian Guard, under Grand Duke Constantine and GdI Count Miloradovich, stood by Arçonval and Ailleville. This reserve force totaled about 20,000 men.

Count Colloredo was ordered to move against Vandoeuvres – where he was to be by 2:00 p.m. – and take a position on the road from Dienville that ran through Troyes via Piney. Blücher

26 von Plotho, Vol. III, p. 113.
27 Sporschil, Vol. II, pp. 235-6.
28 von Plotho, Vol. III, p. 113.
29 von Plotho, Vol. III, p. 113.
30 C. von W., p. 148.

Miloradovich.

Bavarian troops at Brienne.

held his reserve in Trannes, which consisted of the Russian Grenadier Corps – and two divisions of cuirassiers echeloned by the rest of the troops of Barclay de Tolly – along the road to Bar-sur-Aube.[31]

In the event that the battle was successful, the Army of Silesia was to march on Vitry; Count Giulay was to occupy Dienville; the Crown Prince of Württemberg was to occupy Brienne; Wrede was to occupy Montiérender; and Count Wittgenstein was to march on St.-Dizier to join with Yorck.

Because of the various nationalities present and the chance for confusion, it was decided that the Allied troops would all wear a white band on their right arm. Though an odd thing, it was necessary to prevent any accidental firing on friendly troops (i.e. the Württemberg or Bavarian troops, who had only a few months before been the enemies of the Allies).[32]

The battlefield

Between the villages of Trannes and Ronay there is a plain that extends about 12 miles and is about three miles wide. It is bordered on the north by the Voire, which runs from the east to the west, in a valley that is generally flooded in the winter. To the east is the swampy woods of Valentigny, the woods of Ajou and the back of the Morvilliers plateau. In the middle of this plain it is bordered by the Beaulieu woods – which extends to the right of Trannes in front of the plateau – and stops on the Aube River. It then runs along the river to Brienne and from there to the castle park and to the ridge of the Lesmont hills. The road from Vitry to Bar runs along this plain – in a straight line – and passes through La Rothière, which lies three miles from Trannes and about six miles from Brienne. The plain is generally low – rising a bit as it moves towards Perthé – then dropping again as it approaches the Bar road. This plain was intensively cultivated, though there are some wooded spots.

The left bank of the Aube is high and dominates the plain on the opposite bank. Nonetheless, an army on the plain would have no concerns if it held the bridges at Lesmont, Radonvilliers, Dienville and Unienville.

31 Koch, Vol. I, p. 171.
32 Koch, Vol. I, p. 172.

The Morvilliers plateau – whose slopes dominate two thirds of this plain on the east side – is covered on its front and sides with woods and swamps, which make movement there by an army almost impossible. Its height makes it the dominant terrain feature of the battlefield.[33]

The French positions

The preliminary maneuvers of the Allies lasted throughout the morning of 1 February. Watching the movement of all these Allied formations gave Napoleon considerable cause for concern. He had hoped that Blücher would attack in the morning before his supporting corps were in position, or that he would decide to withdraw and unite with Schwarzenberg. Blücher's failure to move caused Napoleon to begin to believe that he had been tricked and that Schwarzenberg may be maneuvering on his rear to strike at Troyes. Napoleon decided that perhaps he should retrace his steps towards Troyes. He recalled Ney and ordered Rottembourg's 2nd Tirailleur (5th Young Guard) Division, bivouaced on the heights by Brienne, to prepare to withdraw.[34]

Napoleon's army was deployed with Gérard's corps – posted with it on the right bank of the Aube, occupying Dienville, and its left wing reaching towards La Rothière. Piquet's cavalry brigade (eight squadrons) occupied the position between Gérard's left wing and the main road from Brienne and Trannes. In the French center stood Victor's corps, with Duhèsme's division occupying La Rothière. On the right and left of the city stood one of Duhèsme's regiments. The defense of Petit-Mesnil, Chaumenil and La Giberie was given to a force of 1,900 infantry. The wooded hill in the interval between Les Verreries and the source of the Froide was occupied by four battalions deployed into skirmish order. In the Beaulieu woods stood an advanced post of a single infantry battalion.

In the critical center of the battlefield, between La Rothière and Petit-Mesnil, stood the 23 squadrons of Guard cavalry under GD Nansouty. Nansouty had deployed his horse artillery before his squadrons.

Grouchy's 36 squadrons stood behind the left wing between Petit-Mesnil and the Ajou woods (behind the Froide stream). In front of him stood Marmont's VI Corps. Marmont deployed Lagrange's division on the left wing, with this 1st Brigade in the village of Morvilliers and his second pushed forward facing the exit from the Soulaines forest. His forces also occupied the Beauvoir farm.

Doumerc's I Cavalry Corps stood to the right and left of the road that ran from Doulevant through Morvilliers and on to Brienne (between the Ajou forest and the Beauvoir farm). The three guard divisions of Rottembourg, Meunier and Decouz stood as a reserve behind La Rothière. Defrance's light cavalry – 800 men – stood by the Lesmont bridge.[35]

If any observation can be made of Napoleon's dispositions, it is that he was trying to hold too much ground with too few troops. His infantry force was so small that he was holding large portions of his line with cavalry – exposing it to Allied fire when it would better be held behind a line of infantry or on sheltered ground. The position held by his cavalry behind the Froide stream was strong, but better suited to a close defense by infantry than by cavalry. The occupation of Petit-Mesnil, Chaumenil and La Giberie by French infantry might serve as strongpoints with which to break up any Allied advance between them – permitting the French cavalry to counterattack – but the French cavalry was too far back to support them and would have to cross the Froide before it could move to their support. Yet Napoleon had to occupy those villages because

33 Koch, Vol. I, pp. 172-3.
34 Koch, Vol. I, p. 174.
35 von Damitz, Vol. I, pp. 484-5.

he did not have the infantry to spare and he needed strong defensive positions in which to shelter what he had.

Perhaps a better position, more suited to a defense by his weak infantry arm, could have been found back by Brienne. Napoleon, however, chose to hold what he had captured during the battle for Brienne and stuck his chin out where it was sure to be struck – and struck hard.

The Battle of La Rothière – 1 February

Between noon and 1:00 p.m. Allied columns appeared before the French advanced posts in the plain by La Rothière and in the Beaulieu woods. It was the sound of the bugles in Wrede's corps that told Napoleon that the Allies were advancing.[36] Von Württemberg's corps moved into positions by Eclance – facing Chaumenil – and the other Allied formations moved into line. The battle began shortly later on the left and in the center with a heavy cannonade by the Allies, and on the right by a large volume of musketry.

In the center, Sacken's corps advanced against La Rothière with his left column – consisting of the 8,000 men of Lieven's 11th Corps (10th, 27th and part of the 16th Divisions). The Russian 6th Corps, under Scherbatov (8,000 men), marched to the right of Lieven and in the same direction. Behind them marched Olsufiev's 5,000-man Russian 9th Corps and Vassil'shikov's cavalry corps.

To Sacken's left, FZM Giulay's infantry advanced in battalionsmasse[37] between the high road to La Rothière and the Aube against Dienville, which was occupied by Gérard's Paris Reserve. Giulay's corps contained 20 battalions, 12 squadrons and 56 guns. The interval between Giulay and Sacken was filled by Cossack detachments (and later, Austrian cavalry).

On Sacken's right advanced the 4th Corps under the Crown Prince of Württemberg. It marched from Eclance, through the Beaulieu forest and against La Giberie. Von Württemberg's attack consisted of 21 battalions, 16 squadrons and 24 guns (or about 14,000 men). In the interval between his attack and Sacken's attack it was occupied by 2,000 Prussian cavalry under Prince Biron von Courland and Karpov II's Cossacks.

On the Allied extreme right, attacking Morvilliers, was the Allied 5th (Bavarian) Corps under Wrede. This column contained 29 battalions and 30 squadrons (or about 25,000 men).[38]

The center

At the beginning of the battle Tsar Alexander arrived on Thrann heights and ordered Blücher to send Russian cavalry in an attack on some French batteries. General Vassil'shikov I – with Lanskoi's division – moved ahead, but could not cross the marshy terrain under heavy fire of French guns. In addition, he was attacked by cavalry of Piré, Colbert and Guyot and retreated. Alexander, observing the cavalry's inability to advance, ordered Sacken to deploy all his artillery against the French position.[39]

General Sacken made little progress. The ground over which he had to advance was a sodden quagmire, which required him to double the teams on his artillery. General Nikitin – commanding the artillery – had increased the teams such that the 12pdrs were drawn by 10 horses, the 6pdrs by six horses and the caissons by five horses. He had, as a result, only 36 guns that he was able

36 C. von W., p. 149.

37 Bogdanovich indicates that Giulay advanced in 'battalion columns' – not 'battalionsmasse'. Bogdanovich, p. 120.

38 von Damitz, Vol. I, pp. 487-8.

39 Bogdanovich, p. 121.

Russian infantry at La Rothière, by Richard Knötel.

to bring forward to support Sacken's attack.[40] He also reinforced the artillery crews and some of the excess crew men were sent forward to make the marshy ground and ditches passable for the artillery. General Nikitin had his crews ride the guns and galloped them forward and deployed his batteries on both sides of the main La Rothière road and began firing.

Nikitin's artillery moved against La Rothière and began a rolling fire directed at the gardens and houses of the village defended by Duhèsme's infantry. Sacken's corps advanced in two columns. The right-hand column, supported by Olsufiev, moved against La Rothière. The left column, with the 3rd Corps in reserve, moved against Dienville. This column later would be redirected to join the main attack on La Rothière – leaving the 3rd Corps to attack Dienville alone. An Austrian Brigade, under General Grimmer, was later detached from this force and also directed against La Rothière. The French discovered that Russian artillery had moved ahead of its supporting troops and decided to use this situation.

The initial French attack against Sacken was by either Briche or l'Héritier's dragoons. Their attack was greeted by shot and canister fire at a range of 900 to 1,000 paces. The fire continued until the French cavalry was within 400 paces, when their charge was finally broken. Much of the failure of the French cavalry charge was attributable to the fact that they were obliged to cross a very marshy area that greatly slowed their advance and increased the time they were under fire.

The French cavalry renewed its attack with charges by Piré , Colbert and Guyot's cavalry as a heavy snow began to fall with a strong wind blowing in the direction of the French. Their visibility was greatly limited and the Russian infantry sought to take advantage of this. The Russian infantry moved forward with music and drums beating. The men of the Dnieper Infantry Regiment sang as they advanced. Count Lieven III advanced with his 11th Corps and Lanskoi's 2nd Hussar Division (Akhtyrsk, Marioupol and Alexandria Hussars) attacked La Rothière. Prince Scherbatov's 7th Division attacked on the right. At first Olsufiev's troops – with the rest of the 2nd Hussar Division – were in reserve, but soon were deployed to the right of Scherbatov. The 3rd Dragoon Division, under GM Pantschichscheff, and GM Prince Biron's Prussian detachment[41] advanced more to the right.[42]

40 von Damitz, Vol. I, pp. 488-9.
41 Biron commanded the 2nd Silesian Hussar Regiment and the Silesian National Hussar Regiment.
42 Bogdanovich, p. 122.

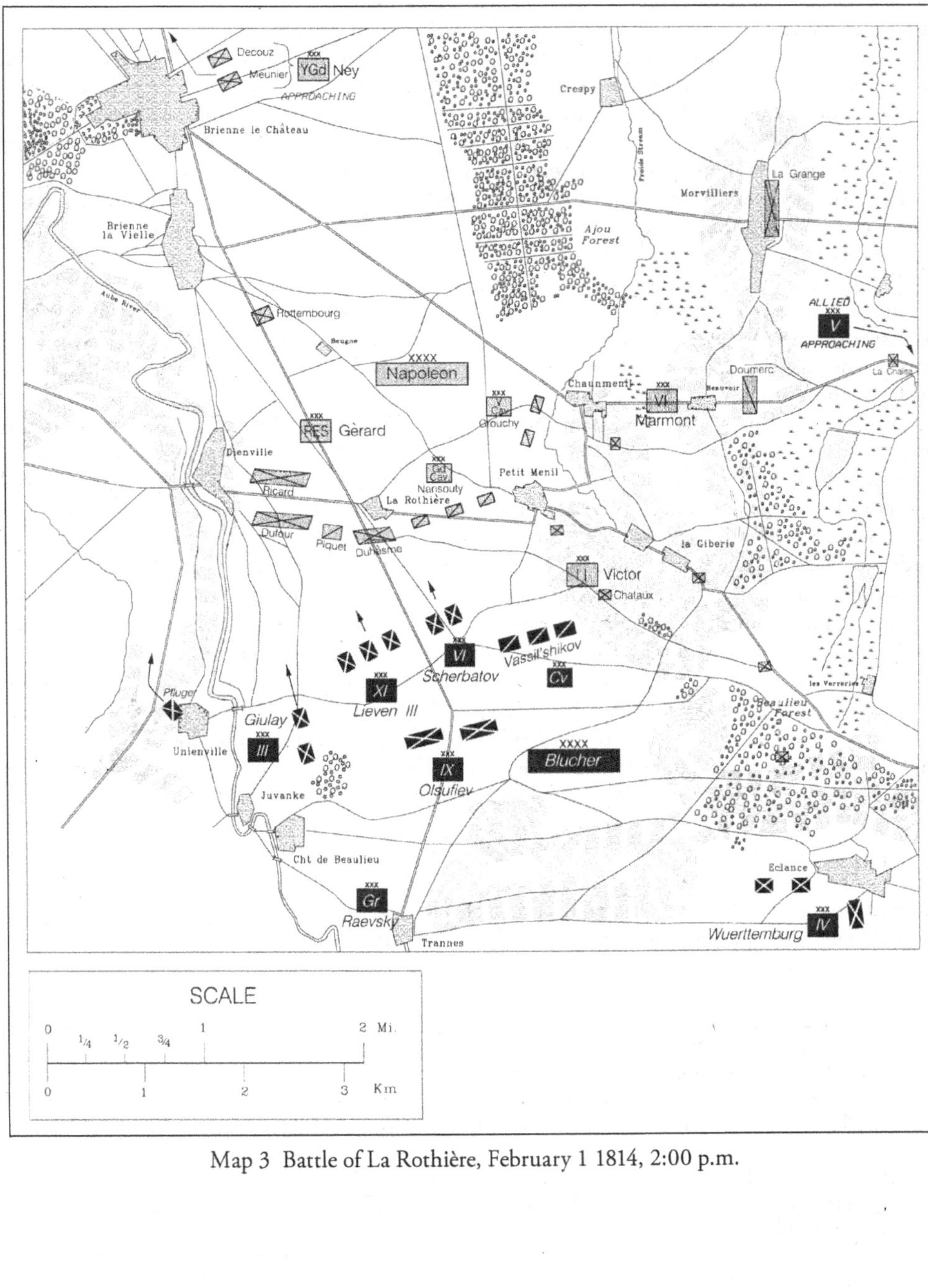

Map 3 Battle of La Rothière, February 1 1814, 2:00 p.m.

The Russian hussars were overwhelmed by the French cavalry and were driven back. The French cavalry's thundering advance continued to close on the masses of Russian infantry. Sacken responded by sending Vassil'shikov – with 12 squadrons of dragoons – against them. Pantschichscheff's 3rd Dragoon Division struck the French cavalry in the front and flank with such force that the French attack stalled. The Russian cavalry drove the French back to Brienne-la-Vieille.[43]

Despite French attacks on Vassil'shikov's right flank by the cavalry of Léfèbvre-Desnoëttes, Pacz and Briche, the Russians broke through French lines and captured a 24-gun battery in conjunction with a battalion of infantry from Count Scherbatov's 7th Division. The capture of the battery obliged the French troops attached to it to retreat to Brienne-la-Vieille. The Marioupol Hussar and Courland Dragoon Regiments greatly distinguished themselves in this engagement.[44] A battalion from Scherbatov's 7th Division quickly occupied the ground and assured Russian control of the captured French guns. Lieven and Olsufiev continued their advance without Scherbatov.

Encouraged by the success of their cavalry, the Russian 18th Infantry Division joined Lieven's Corps as it renewed its attack on La Rothière. As Sacken's troops closed, they were taken under canister fire by Duhèsme's artillery. The weather prevented much use of muskets so Sacken's troops advanced in closed columns with their bayonets. Sacken's troops had pushed into Brienne as far as the church.

Napoleon observed the retreat of Victor's troops and directed Maréchal Oudinot to support them with Rottembourg's 5th Young Guard Division. Also he directed Meunier's 1st Voltigeur Division to his left flank. On the other side, Blücher – with his chief of staff, Gneisenau – moved closer to La Rothière to observe the fighting. Blücher repeatedly encouraged the Russian troops with bellows of: "Vorwärds, Kinder!" ("Forward, children!"). At the same time Barclay de Tolly ordered the 2nd Grenadier Division to join the Russian troops fighting near La Rothière.[45]

Sacken's infantry – then consisting of the 18th Division, Olsufiev's corps, 2nd Grenadier Division and an Austrian brigade of Grimmer (which were detached to La Rothière by Giulay at 7:00 p.m.) – closed on the church as the French cavalry that had been thrown back by Vassil'shikov's cavalry were pushed into old Brienne.[46] In only a few minutes Duhèsme's 3rd Division (II Corps) was broken – abandoning eight cannon[47] – and its refugees fled to Petit-Mesnil, where a number of veteran soldiers turned about and took up positions to continue the fight. However, most of Duhésme's division was taken prisoner or fled the field. It is at this point that the attacks by Sacken and Wrede forced Napoleon to begin his withdrawal.

The left

Gérard stopped Giulay's attack with his artillery – forcing Giulay to attempt a diversion. Giulay sent Pflüger[48] – supported by four guns and two squadrons of the Klenau Chevauxleger (200

43 von Damitz, Vol. I, 490.

44 Koch, Vol. 2, p. 66; von Damitz, Vol. I, p. 490; Bogdanovich, p. 123. von Damitz states that 28 guns were lost, but it is unlikely that there were more than three guard horse batteries present on this flank. Three batteries would have a total of 24 guns.

45 Bogdanovich, p. 123.

46 Sporschil, Vol. II, p. 242.

47 Bogdanovich indicates that only three guns were captured – not the eight indicated by Damitz and Sporschil.

48 Pflüger's brigade was assigned to FML Fresnel's division and contained the Archduke Louis Infantry Regiment #8 (four battalions), Würzburg Infantry Regiment #7 (three battalions) and a brigade battery with 8-6pdr guns. However, at this time the Würzburg Infantry Regiment

cavalry) supported by the Erzherzog Ludwig and Würzburg Infantry Regiments – to force the bridge at Dienville, which was held by a small detachment. It was his goal to occupy the left bank of the Aube and the bridge at Dienville, where the French supported their extreme right.[49] The Austrians successfully stormed the bridge and pushed the defending French back to a ridge that ran between Dienville and the left bank of the Strom.

However, Napoleon saw this and ordered Gérard to maneuver so as to oppose this maneuver. Gérard responded by detaching Boudin's brigade to recapture the bridge and Pelleport's brigade was ordered to close with the village. Two battalions supported by three squadrons took up positions on the crest of a hill overlooking the left bank of the Aube, two further battalions were posted on the right bank near the church, and the rest of the French troops stood in reserve behind the village (and in a right angle with other infantry of the right wing).

The bridge stood at the edge of the village by a ridge which dominated both banks of the Aube and was occupied by the French. The bridge itself was barricaded with wagons, barrels and logs. The terrain did not permit the use of artillery for its defense so the French posted skirmishers in the houses near the bridge and placed a supporting detachment about 300 paces to the rear.

At the same time Dufour's 1st Division (Paris Reserve) was moved into a supporting position slightly to the rear.[50] Pflüger was pushed back and the position recovered by the French. The Mariassy and Ignaz Giulay Regiments (Spleny's brigade, Hohenlohe-Bartenstein's division) launched a bayonet attack supported by Grimmer's brigade – but all attempts of Austrians were without success for a long time.

Seeing his plan for an easy victory was thwarted, Giulay reinforced his attack against the bridge by sending the remainder of Fresnel's division, Czollich's brigade, six guns and some squadrons. GL Fresnel directed the attack personally. The Austrians covered their advance with 10 guns and repeatedly assaulted the bridge to no avail. On the right bank of the river, GM Spleny's brigade advanced against Dienville.

On the left bank of the Aube, Count Giulay contented himself with firing 24 12pdrs against Dienville and the masses of Dufour's division that stood before him. He supported these guns with Grimmer's brigade from the reserves. Later – around 7:00 p.m. – Grimmer's brigade would be ordered back to La Rothière.

Though a murderous fight ranged on the far bank of the Aube, Giulay did not attempt to become involved until twilight. At that time he once again ordered the bridge stormed.[51]

In the twilight – barely knowing where they were going – the Austrians drove forward into the edge of Dienville and pushed to the bridge, where they were greeted by the murderous fire of the French infantry waiting for them. Unable to pass over the barricaded bridge, the Austrians contented themselves with exchanging musketry across the river. Giulay then brought forward his howitzers and began to bombard Dienville – setting it afire. The city became untenable for both and was abandoned at around 11:00 p.m.

The right

On the right, the Crown Prince of Württemberg moved out of Eclance and found the Beauvais woods – in front of La Giberie – occupied by French skirmishers. The Crown Prince detached Stockmayer's brigade, which led the advance, to clean them out of the woods. He detached the

appears to have been detached. R. Friederich indicates that he had only four battalions during this movement. R. Frederich, p. 104.

49 von Plotho, Vol. III, p. 117.

50 Koch, Vol. I, 177 & von Damitz, Vol. I, p. 493.

51 Sporschil, Vol. II, p. 238.

Württemberg 2/10th Light Infantry Regiment into the brush before the Beaulieu forest to serve to secure his left flank.

The attack was led by GM von Stockmayer.[52] It was led by the Württemberg 1/10th Light Infantry Regiment and supported by the Württemberg 9th Jäger Regiment. They quickly threw the French skirmishers back to their main line, but a vicious fire fight soon erupted. After considerable French resistance they were able to occupy and hold those woods, but not after Victor had thrown them out at least once. Victor's persistent resistance obliged the Allies to detach part of their forces against Petit-Mesnil[53]

As the French withdrew, the Württemberg 2nd Jäger zu Pferd Regiment charged out of the woods – hurrying them on their way and reducing their numbers by inflicting several casualties and prisoners.[54] The Erzherzog Ferdinand Hussar Regiment, which normally was assigned to this corps, had been reassigned to the 3rd Corps this day – and so was no longer available to the Prince – so the Prince had to depend on his own cavalry this day.

The Württemberg cavalry and the horse artillery then moved down the road, which the Austrian pioneers were widening to facilitate their passage. The corps 12pdr battery were left in the rear (by Bar-sur-Aube) because the mud prevented it being moved forward into the battle.[55]

The main body of the corps advanced with the Crown Prince of Württemberg at the head of the advanced guard. When they arrived at the La Giberie hill they found a small force of French infantry before them. The Crown Prince ordered an attack by two of his battalions and his cavalry. The French, having no cavalry, withdrew to a stronger position in the village of La Giberie. The Crown Prince of Württemberg, seeing this, sent his infantry forward yet again. This attack by four Württemberg battalions – protected on the left by the demonstration against Victor's II Corps by the Erzherzog Ludwig Hussars and the Erzherzog Wilhelm Infantry Regiment maneuvering before Eclance – succeeded in throwing the French out of the village at around 3:00 p.m.

However, Victor understood the significance of this position and responded immediately – not giving the Allies time to establish their control on the position. He dispatched a divisional infantry attack supported by two batteries. This attack pushed the Württembergers out of half of the village.

The Crown Prince hurried forward the 2nd Infantry Regiment under General Döring, the 2/10th Light Infantry Regiment and two companies of the 8th Regiment supported by the 1st Horse Battery. Further reinforcements in the form of the 7th Infantry Regiment were sent forward. Despite the reinforcements, the French attack was successful and cleared the Crown Prince of Württemberg's troops from the position.[56]

The French defended their position and brought forward a substantial force of artillery that pounded the Württembergers. The Württembergers had only the fire of the single horse battery to respond. The Crown Prince of Württemberg did not feel he had the forces necessary to recapture the position and sent General Toll with a dispatch to Blücher requesting assistance, while he withdrew his forces to Petit-Mesnil. He felt that possession of this village would facilitate the renewal of his attack on Giberie.[57] General Toll was to ask Blücher for reinforcements. In Toll's opinion, the occupation of Giberie heights (the key of the French positions) by the Crown Prince of Württemberg would result in an Allied victory. In contrast, Blücher and Gneisenau thought

52 Rössler, p. 405.
53 *Victoires conquêtes, désastres*, Vol. 23, p. 73.
54 von Damitz, Vol. I, p. 494.
55 Rössler, p. 405.
56 Rössler, p. 406; Sporschil, Vol. II, p. 244.
57 Koch, Vol. I, p. 179.

that only capture of La Rothière and breaking through the French line would decide the battle. In reality, if Giberie had been held by the Allies, all the Allied reserves could have been sent in the direction of Brienne and most of the French army would have been cut off.

Prince von Württemberg's troops were in great danger. General Toll, after Blücher's refusal, went to Tsar Alexander. At 5:00 p.m. the Tsar issued a personal order and the 1st Grenadier Division was sent to aid the Crown Prince of Württemberg.[58]

Württemberg strikes La Giberie again

The Crown Prince of Württemberg's 4th Corps, standing before Maréchal Victor, was reinforced by the 1st Russian Grenadier Division and two divisions of cuirassiers.

He launched an attack against La Giberie with Döring's Bavarian brigade, with the 7th Infantry Regiment leading the attack at the *Sturmschritt* with bayonets lowered.[59] Though bravely defending La Giberie, numbers began to tell and Victor withdrew his forces to Petit-Mesnil and Chaumenil – followed closely by the Württembergers. Meanwhile, the Württemberg 2nd Jäger zu Pferd Regiment pushed to the right of La Giberie and swept the plain on that side of the village clean of French. Three other Württemberg cavalry regiments formed on the right of Wrede's corps, while five Prussian squadrons formed the link between the center. The right wing was supported by Prince Biron von Courland, supported by more guns.[60]

Milhaud's cavalry, with its left wing on the Ajou woods, covered the withdrawal of the French infantry. The Crown Prince of Württemberg then pushed his cavalry between Petit-Mesnil and La Rothière so it could attack the French cavalry under Milhaud. This cavalry force consisted of the 2nd, 3rd and 4th Württemberg Regiments; the Prussian cavalry under Prince Biron;[61] and the Cossacks of General Karpov. From this position they attacked the French cavalry just before nightfall – striking them in the flank and routing them back to Beguné farm – capturing six horse guns and taking a number of prisoners.[62]

A French Guard battery at the wooded point by Chaumenil fired on the Allied 5th Corps – inflicting heavy casualties on them and embarrassing their maneuvers. The Crown Prince of Württemberg ordered the Württemberg Kronprinz Chevauxleger Regiment, then on the right and serving as a liaison between the two corps, to attack this battery.[63] Nansouty had, however, already ordered a force of Polish Guard Lancers to move to the defense of the battery. Zaluski led forward the companies of Dobiecki and Roman and moved to take up positions near the battery. However, Zaluski saw a force of cavalry moving to strike them in the flank, so Captaine Dobiecki's company was detached to drive them off while the remaining squadron proceeded to support Colonel Marin's battery. By the time the Polish lancers had arrived, night had fallen and the only light to be seen was the flash of the cannon.

58 Bogdanovich, p. 125.

59 Generalmajor Döring's brigade consisted of the 1/,2/Duke Wilhelm Infantry Regiment #2, 1/,2/ Infantry Regiment #3, 1/,2/Infantry Regiment #7 and the 1st Foot Battery.

60 Sporschil, Vol. II, 1st Band, p. 245.

61 Biron's force consisted of two squadrons of the 2nd Silesian Hussar Regiment, the Silesian National Cavalry Regiment, the Freiwilliger Jäger squadrons of those two regiments, a Cossack detachment and four horse guns. The force totaled about 2,000 men.

62 von Plotho indicates that six guns were taken by the Kronprinz Regiment and five were taken by the Prince Adam Regiment. von Plotho, Vol. III, p.120.

63 von Damitz, Vol. I, p. 509 indicates that this was the Württemberg 3rd Dragoon Regiment supported by a Bavarian chevauxleger regiment.

Charge of the Württemberg Dragoons at La Rothière, by Richard Knötel.

Oberst Wagner led his Württemberg Dragoons forward – supported by a Bavarian chevaux-leger regiment. As they approached the French in the dark, being familiar with French military methods they cried out – deceptively indicating that they were French.[64] Zaluski and his lancers were completely deceived and the subsequent charge was successful, with the Württembergers taking three guns and the Bavarians the other five. Zaluski and many of his men were taken prisoner.

Wrede's attack

While the struggle for La Giberie went on, the Allied 5th Corps – under Wrede – marched up from Doulevant led by Hardegg's division (with those of Lamotte and Rechberg behind it and the Bavarian 12pdr batteries bringing up the rear).[65] As the 5th Corps moved through the Soulaines woods, it did so in two columns. Wrede's attack began at about noon. The right column, under General Hardegg, was directed against Morvilliers and the left moved against Chaumenil. However, it was decided that each of these two columns was too weak to achieve its assigned objective, so they were recombined about one-and-a-half miles to the right of Morvilliers and before Chaumenil. The attack was led by the Schwarzenberg Uhlan Regiment and an Austrian 2nd Jäger Battalion.

64 Zaluski, pp. 104-5.
65 von Damitz, Vol. I, p. 497.

This attack was not detected by the French in time. When it was observed, the ground greatly delayed the movement of the artillery and there was only time to get Joubert's brigade into position.

The French skirmishers vainly struggled to hold the defenses they had erected during the night. A French battery in front of Morvilliers supported their defense and drew the attention of the Schwarzenberg Uhlans, commanded by Oberst Mengen. Two squadrons of the Schwarzenberg Uhlans[66] charged the French battery and captured all six guns.[67] The casualties suffered by the uhlans were minimal.

The successful charge permitted Wrede to deploy his corps, despite the French artillery fire and the attacks by General Doumerc's cavalry. As soon as the line was formed, Wrede ordered Spleny to turn the village of Chaumenil on the right while General Rechberg attacked it frontally. Hardegg's division, with support by a Bavarian infantry and cavalry brigade, attacked it down the road to Brienne.[68]

Marmont saw the success of the Allied attack and moved to consolidate his position to reduce the danger by repositioning to the right of Morvilliers and forward of Chaumenil. It was too late, however, to do much and only Joubert's brigade was in a position to do anything.

Wrede's attack bore down on the French position. Habermann's brigade, supported by Dietz's 3rd Cavalry Brigade[69] led the attack as several French batteries opened fire and Doumerc's cavalry maneuvered threateningly. The French fought vainly against the advancing Austro-Bavarian columns. Hardegg's Austrian division, supported by Habermann's Bavarian infantry, attacked frontally while Spleny's cavalry division and Deroy's infantry brigade turned right and moved into the woods – moving around Morvilliers.

Joubert's brigade[70] was established in the Beauvoir farm – a central position by the village of Chaumenil. Four battalions from Rechberg's Bavarian division took Bouillenroupt. The 1/ Szeckler Infantry Regiment and the 1/7th Bavarian Infantry Regiment launched a bayonet attack against Joubert's position, supported by Habermann's brigade. Frimont, who directed the attack, also sent two batteries to fire on Chaumenil and divided up the remainder of his Austrian corps between Lamotte and Rechberg's columns. About this time – around 4:00 p.m. – Stockmayer's brigade attacked and carried Petit-Mesnil.[71] Petit-Mesnil, having fallen, put the Württembergers in communication with the Bavarian 5th Corps.

Joubert's position became completely untenable with the frontal assault and the fall of Bouillenroupt so he withdrew, but not before Oberst von Rodt – leading the 1/7th Bavarian Infantry Regiment – was mortally wounded.[72] Joubert's evacuation of the farm collapsed into a rout as General Spleny's cavalry charged, captured three guns and a few hundred prisoners and chased the rest of his brigade into the Ajou woods. Seeing the situation was crumbling, Marmont used a heavy snowfall to send part of his artillery and his personal baggage off to Brienne. This convoy was pursued by Austro-Bavarian cavalry (the 3rd and 4th Bavarian Chevauxlegers and Erzherzog Joseph Hussars) – losing many casualties and three guns.

Marmont's right was also uncovered by the Austrian capture of Chaumenil and he was obliged to abandon Morvilliers – joining the remains of Joubert's 1st Brigade in the Ajou woods. Here he

66 Koch, Vol. I, p. 180 identifies these as Bavarian cavalry, which is probably incorrect as Hardegg commanded an Austrian division. von Damitz, Vol. I, p. 499 clearly states that it was two squadrons of the Schwarzenberg Uhlans.

67 Burghersh, p. 116.

68 Koch, Vol. I, p. 181.

69 Dietz commanded the 4th and 5th Bavarian Chevauxlegers during the Battle of La Rothière.

70 Joubert's brigade was part of Lagrange's 3rd Division, VI Corps.

71 Generalmajor von Stockmayer's brigade contained the 1/,2/König Jäger Regiment #9 and one battalion of the Light Infantry Regiment #10.

72 Sporschil, Vol. II, p. 248.

took up new positions covered by his artillery – establishing himself at the point where the roads from Brienne and Doulevant crossed. Once there he re-established contact with Victor and the rest of the French army. Napoleon observed this and, in order to prevent the Allies from turning his left flank, sent Meunier's 1st Voltigeur Division and 18 guns towards Morvilliers.[73]

The battle from 4:00-7:00 p.m.

On the Allied left, Generalleutnant Fresnel marched forward and drove the French from their positions on the left bank of the Aube and strove to take the bridge at Dienville. The Austrians brought forward a battery of 10 guns and opened a murderous fire on the French – following it up with an infantry attack. However, the French position was too strong and the Austrian attack failed.

Napoleon saw Marmont abandon Morvilliers and, perceiving Chaumenil as being important to his battle, directed Guyot's detachment of Guard service squadrons, an artillery battery of 16 guns and a brigade of Meunier's 1st Voltigeur Division to assist Marmont in holding Chaumenil. Guyot and his troops were not, however, sufficient and their attacks were resisted by the Szeckler and Löwenstern-Wertheim Infantry Regiments.[74] Frimont brought forward 12 guns, which engaged the French artillery, and then charged them with Dietz's 4th and 5th Bavarian Chevauxlegers – supported by the Austrian Erzherzog Hussar Regiment – in the plain between Morvilliers and the Ajou woods. The Allied cavalry came under heavy artillery fire and the sweeping volleys of the French infantry were forced into squares by the charges of the Erzherzog Hussar Regiment. Lamotte's division took advantage of the French loss of momentum and pushed forward. Despite their strong defensive positions and formations, the French were driven back and lost seven guns.[75] The rapidly fading daylight brought the battle in this part of the field to an end.

With the collapse of Marmont's line and the success of Sacken's attack in the center, Napoleon judged the battle as lost and made preparations to cover his means of retreat. He ordered Grouchy to delay the Allied advance as much as he could with Milhaud's cavalry (Piré, Briche and l'Héritier) near the Ajou woods and to support Victor. He ordered Nansouty to take the Guard cavalry and make a demonstration against La Rothière. He also ordered Oudinot to attempt to penetrate into La Rothière with Rottembourg's 2nd Tirailleur (5th Young Guard) Division – 4,900 men).

Rottembourg's division arrived before La Rothière at sunset, just as General Colbert's 3rd Guard Cavalry Division was throwing back the Russians with a successful charge. Oudinot immediately ordered Rottembourg to push his 1st Brigade into the city, but to hold his 2nd Brigade in reserve. Rottembourg divided the 1st Brigade into three columns. General Marguet commanded the right-hand column, which marched down the main road. The center column was under Colonel Trapier and Rottembourg personally commanded the left column.[76]

Rottembourg's columns were greeted by a hail of shot and shell. As they pushed into the city, initially they encountered only the remains of Olsufiev's Russian corps – now effectively reduced to the strength of an infantry regiment. Once inside the city, as they approached the church they were charged by the Astrakhan and Little Russia Grenadier Regiments (Russian 2nd Grenadier Division) and supported by Olsufiev's infantry and Grimmer's Austrian

73 Bogdanovich, p. 127.
74 Sporschil, Vol. II, p. 248.
75 Koch, Vol. I, p. 184 indicates only seven guns were lost, but von Damitz, Vol. I, p. 507 and Sporschil, Vol. II, p. 249 indicate that the French lost 16 fully-equipped and limbered guns. The truth probably lies somewhere in between.
76 Sporschil, Vol. II, p. 242.

Russian cuirassiers charging at La Rothière, by Parchaev.

brigade. The Young Guard were thrown back beyond the edge of the village. Rottembourg's guardsmen stopped, fired a badly-directed volley and then began milling about – unable to advance or withdraw. The Russian column commander, seeing this, thought they were seeking to surrender, advanced and asked them to lay down their arms. Rottembourg, thinking that he wished to talk about a Russian detachment that was cut off by two French columns, advanced to speak to him. Recognizing his error, Rottembourg sought to make the Russian a prisoner. In an exchange that was probably unique in the war, the two officers began a personal fight – each seeking to capture the other. The Russian, however, escaped.[77] Rottembourg then had a battery of four guns fire on the advancing Russians – stopping their advance. At about 10:00 p.m. he then rallied the debris of Marguet and Trapier's columns – about 400 paces from La Rothière – and awaited new orders. Meanwhile, Oudinot's withdrawal forced Napoleon to abandon Dienville.

The Allies then launched a second attack on La Rothière with the Russian 2nd Grenadier Division (with the Astrakhan and Little Russia Grenadier Regiments leading the attack). This attack pushed into the village and then stalled after taking possession of it.

Napoleon, learning of this Marmont's repulse, directed General Drouot to burn the village with the goal of delaying the Allied advance while he withdrew his forces – by echelon from the left flank – to Brienne. Ney and the Guard cavalry were already advancing down the road to Lesmont. Marmont crossed through the Ajou woods and reformed his corps on the far two roads. Doumerc reorganized his cavalry on Marmont's left while Victor bivouaced behind the Beguné farm. Oudinot withdrew from before La Rothière and later saw it in flames. He returned to his

77 von Damitz, Vol. I, pp. 502-3.

bivouacs of the previous night. Gérard, who had refused to be thrown out of Dienville, finally gave way around midnight and withdrew. Milhaud's cavalry covered their retreat across the plain.[78] When the French left Dienville, a battalion of the Austrian Erzherzog Ludwig Regiment crossed the bridge and took 230 French stragglers prisoner.

On the morning of 2 February, Napoleon withdrew. Burghersh says that in doing so the French abandoned 3,600-4,000 prisoners and 73 guns to the Allies.[79] Koch gives the French losses at 54 guns and 6,000 casualties – including 2,400 prisoners.[80] Bogdanovich lists 6,000 casualties and 63 guns lost.[81] Von Damitz echoes Koch's figures for the French casualties and gives the Allied losses at about 6,000 men. He breaks it down showing 16 officers and 452 men lost from the 4th Corps, 200 to 300 from the 5th Corps, 1,000 from the Austrian 3rd Corps and the Russian losses at 3,000 to 4,000 men. The French also lost General Marguet (killed), generals Forrestier and Léfèbvre-Desnoëttes (wounded) and General Merlin (captured). The Russians' casualties included the regimental commander of the Gluchov Cuirassiers, Major Krivonosov (lost), and the commander of 28th Light Artillery Battery, Lt. Colonel Bendersky (killed). Their wounded officers included GL Count Lieven, GM Stavitsky, GM Kologrivov, Nikitin and GM Prince Vadbolsky.[82]

La Rothière caused many problems for Napoleon. First was the loss of men and equipment. The second major problem was the damage to his reputation. Heavily damaged at Leipzig, there was still faith in his skill as a general. Now, a second major defeat began to shake the faith of the French army in his skills. The miserable conditions in the field and the inadequate supplies and support provided to the army had already caused a considerable desertion problem. Now the defeat at La Rothière would compound that problem.

In reviewing the battle, Blücher most assuredly played the field and Napoleon to his maximum advantage. After the Battle of Brienne he drew in his scattered resources and established a situation where he might have inflicted a catastrophic defeat on the French, yet somehow he failed to bring this to pass.

The French army stood in a field too large for its forces. Though its right flank was supported on the Aube, its left wing hung in the air – fully exposed to maneuvers by Blücher's 60-plus cavalry regiments, plus several Cossack regiments. If Wrede had attacked Marmont from Morvilliers and moved his reserves through Morvilliers – attacking simultaneously Giberie, Petit-Mesnil and Chaumenil, pushing through to the Ajou woods – there is little doubt that the French army would have been broken. Its flanks would be turned and it would have no choice but to have fled the field or face utter destruction. As it was, Blücher chose to break up his attack and piecemeal it. The attack on the bridge at Dienville was weak – at best – and easily defeated if detected early. And having failed, it left Blücher faced with a dangerous and risky assault across a river. Blücher was then left with a series of hammer-blows spread across the front of the French line until superiority in numbers finally brought about a resolution to the battle. There was no finesse, little

78 Koch, Vol. I, p. 185.

79 There are two conflicting breakdowns of who captured what in this battle:

	von Plotho	von Damitz
Sacken's corps	25 guns	34
von Württemberg's corps	14	6
Giulay's corps	8	4
General Prince Biron	7	7
Wrede's corps	19	22

von Plotho, Vol. III, p. 126; von Damitz, Vol. I, p. 505; Burghersh, p. 119; Frederich, p. 108.

80 Koch, Vol. I, p. 186; *Victoires conquêtes, désastres*, Vol. 23, p. 66.

81 Bogdanovich, p. 127.

82 Bogdanovich, p. 127.

strategy, and it could be argued that Blücher had so little respect for what he perceived of the French army's military prowess that his maxim was "a few good kicks on the door and the whole rotten structure will fall down."

On the other hand it is inexplicable that Napoleon sat still before Blücher, waiting for him to move, while his own army was in such a vulnerable position. Certainly, he might have profited by a withdrawal calculated to draw Blücher onto ground more suited to the capabilities of Napoleon's army. A withdrawal – coupled with a detachment of a maneuvering force that might position itself in ambush to strike at Blücher's flank or rear – might well have worked. Blücher's actions are certainly contemptuous enough to suggest that he could have been misled to believe that Napoleon would withdraw before the victor of Möckern, the avenger of Jena-Auerstädt.

In addition it is incomprehensible why Napoleon did not order Marmont to entrench himself in La Chaise or Morvilliers, or why he did not think of doing it himself. Why the bridge over the Aube at Dienville was allowed to pass into the hands of the Allies undamaged is inexcusable. For that matter, there is no reason why the bridge at Dienville was not more strongly garrisoned or destroyed. Certainly, its destruction would have released more forces to the main lines and not diverted them to holding a flank that would have been quite secure if the Dienville bridge was destroyed.

The French lost 4,600 killed and wounded, 1,000 prisoners and 67 guns[83] in the two days of Brienne and La Rothière. The Allies lost 6-7,000 killed, wounded and missing.

The French retreat

The French withdrew through Piney, with Maréchal Ney commanding the rearguard at Lesmont and with orders to destroy the bridge. After the bridge was destroyed, he was to withdraw to Troyes. Mortier and the I Cavalry Corps were to move to Ronay. The greater part of the French wounded were abandoned at Brienne because of the lack of transport. The losses from the battle continued.

At daybreak, the French cavalry formed a rearguard – standing in line on the road from Doulevant and supported by a large force of light artillery. At around 8:00 a.m. the Allies advanced their right and moved into Brienne after a short cannonade, but it was too late for them to have any impact on the French withdrawal. The French withdrawal continued in good order.

Ney moved towards Troyes with Milhaud's cavalry covering his rear. The Allies did not pursue him aggressively. Ney stopped before Lesmont and established several heavy batteries of heavy guns to defend the approaches.

Despite their victory at La Rothière, the Allies remained idle and did not pursue the French. They apparently believed that the French would resume the fight the next day and spent the evening bringing further forces onto the battlefield for a renewed fight. The reserves, under the Grand Duke Constantine, arrived at Bossancourt from Colombé-les-deux-Eglises. They were quickly moved forward to Trannes. Prince Colloredo's corps was ordered to stop its movement from Vandoeuvres to Troyes and to assemble at Dienville in support of General Giulay. By acting with such prudence they gave away any of the fruits of their victory that might have gathered in the pursuit.

When Brienne was occupied, the Allied sovereigns assembled in the Château to discuss their next actions. It was decided that the Army of Silesia would march on Châlons, where it would be joined by the corps of Yorck, Kleist and Langeron. Once there it would advance down the Marne and move against Paris.

83 Smith, p. 491; Langeron, p. 388.

It was decided that the main Allied army would move against Troyes and then advance down both banks of the Seine towards Paris. Contact between the two armies would be assured by General Seslavin – who was to occupy Sézanne with 2,000 Cossacks[84] – while 2,500 cavalry under Pahlen would sweep the countryside between Sézanne and the Aube. In addition, Wittgenstein would move along the left bank of the Aube.

This decision reflected the growing sense of over-confidence and self-assuredness that filled the Allied camp. They felt that each of these armies would withstand an attack by the French army by itself – and in the case of Schwarzenberg's main army, they had decided to advance with their army split by a major military obstacle (the Seine River).

Colloredo's corps began its march on Troyes, while those of the Crown Prince of Württemberg and Count Giulay followed Napoleon's main army towards Lesmont. Count von Wrede moved on Ronay. The Allied Guard and reserves marched in two columns: the former via Dienville and Piney on Troyes and the latter marched back to Coulevent on Vandoeuvres.

That evening, Giulay's and the Crown Prince of Württemberg's forces arrived before Lesmont. As they arrived between St.-Christophe and Lesmont, the Austrian Erzherzog Ferdinand Hussar Regiment – which led the advance – encountered a French lancer regiment, which it attacked and threw back. With the lancers cleared away, the Württemberg horse artillery pulled up and began to deploy along the riverbank.[85]

Skirmish at Lesmont

Giulay and the Crown Prince of Württemberg found themselves facing Maréchal Ney, who had deployed his forces – supported by 24 guns – and appeared in no mood to withdraw. They deployed their forces and prepared for action.[86] The two horse batteries of the Allied 4th Corps pulled up and unlimbered and took the French under fire – only to suffer two guns dismounted. This was Ney's signal to cross the bridge.

Ney left one brigade (about 400-500 men) to destroy – and then to prevent the Allies from repairing – the bridge. He then marched with his two divisions towards Piney, where he took up a position on the left of the Aube.

Leading the Allied attack was Stockmayer's light brigade. A battalion of the 9th Württemberg Infantry Regiment led the attack, followed by the three remaining battalions of the brigade. After a short and sharp exchange of fire, the Württemberg Jägers drove into the village and chased the French back down the main street. A squadron of the 3rd Cavalry Regiment charged forward in an effort to seize the bridge, but was savaged by French musketry and forced to withdraw.

At that moment the French set the wooden bridge afire – trapping about 200 of their own men on the far side of the bridge. Once on the far bank – and with the bridge safely burning – the French continued to harry the Württembergers with musketry until about midnight. The Württembergers lost one officer, 71 men and 36 horses from the 9th and 10th Infantry Regiments; the 2nd, 3rd and 4th Cavalry Regiments; and a few artillerists.[87]

84 These are the four Cossack regiments that had earlier been commanded by GM Prince Sherbatov.
85 von Hiller, p. 93.
86 Koch, Vol. I, p. 192.
87 von Hiller, pp. 95-6.

The skirmish at Ronay

Marmont, who had retired on Ronay, was pursued by General Wrede. The 3rd Austrian Jäger Battalion – marching at the head of the 5th Corps – arrived south of Ronay and encountered the French rearguard. Bavarian artillery quickly took the French under the fire. As Marmont's engineers (about 200 men) attempted to destroy the bridge over the Voire, General Curto – leading the Austrian 3rd Jäger Battalion (500 to 600 men) and the Erzherzog Joseph Hussar Regiment – engaged and destroyed them all – seizing the foot of the first bridge. The Jägers, however, suffered heavy losses in this engagement.[88] The Voire was frozen, but several of the Austrian infantry found the ice was too thin to hold them as they fell through and drowned.

Marmont withdrew his troops – lifting the planks on the bridge – and established a battery of four guns and his infantry facing the bridge. More Allied troops arrived as the 1st Brigade of Rechberg's 1st Bavarian Division arrived. Wrede organized his forces and determined to force passage over the bridge. Oberstleutnant Cronegg's battalion[89] – formed in Angriff-Colonnen and supported by the 1/1st Bavarian Line Regiment[90] and the Augsburg Feldbataillon[91] – charged across the first bridge and came under musketry from the buildings on the far bank. The 2/1st Bavarian Line Regiment took up positions on the bank and supported the assault with their fire. General Lagrange ordered the two defending battalions to withdraw behind the second bridge, where they had established a stronger defensive position. The remainder of the 5th Corps stayed in column, out of artillery range.

The Bavarians – seeing the French withdrawing – renewed their advance, but were struck down by a thunderous blast of musketry from the church and surrounding buildings. Cronegg's battalion was trapped and could neither advance or retreat. Seeing this, Rechberg sent forward Merz and Brückner's battalions to support them.[92]

After two hours of unequal fighting, the Bavarians were about to surrender when a force of the Austrian Schwarzenberg Uhlans crossed the Voire at a ford below Rancée and moved against the left of Ronay.[93] The Bavarians' spirit rose and Marmont – seeing his flank threatened – withdrew on Rameau, where he once again established himself.[94] The Bavarians lost 600 to 700 men dead and wounded in this engagement.

Action by Lesmont

As Wrede engaged Marmont by Ronay, the Crown Prince of Württemberg pursued the French cavalry down the main road from Brienne to the Lesmont heights. The Erzherzog Ferdinand Hussar Regiment encountered a French lancer regiment between St.-Christophe and Lesmont, attacked and threw it back – taking a number of prisoners.[95]

As the Württembergers closed on Lesmont, the masses of withdrawing French infantry came into view. It was the guard divisions of Decouz and Meunier under Maréchal Ney.

The cavalry of the 4th Corps advanced in two lines – supported by the fire of a battery of 12pdr guns and the two Württemberg horse batteries, which advanced with them. Leaving the artillery

88 Sporschil, Vol. II, p. 258.
89 Though not identified in any document reviewed, this is probably the Bavarian 3rd Light Battalion.
90 Commanded by Oberst Hertling.
91 The Augsburg Feldbataillon was commanded by Major Brückner.
92 von Damitz, Vol. I, pp. 523-4.
93 von Hiller, p. 94.
94 Koch, Vol. I, p. 194; Burghersh, p. 121.
95 Sporschil, Vol. II, p. 260.

behind and protected by a small cavalry detachment, the remainder of the Württemberg cavalry advanced to engage the French rearguard. They quickly moved to the left of Précy-Saint-Martin and began their attack. GM von Stockmayer moved to capture a bridge. A battalion of the 9th Jäger Regiment, supported by three other battalions of the light brigade, moved down the main road towards the bridge over the Aube.

The French had about 400 to 500 men facing this attack. They were unable to stop the Württembergers and fell back – burning the wooden bridge as they went. They took up positions in the houses adjacent to the bridge and kept it under fire as the Württembergers attempted to cross. With the bridge destroyed, the 4th Corps settled down into its evening bivouac and was soon joined by Giulay's 3rd Austrian Corps.

On 3 February Ney organized his corps before Troyes. Michel's 2nd Old Guard Division was at the bridge at La Guillotière. He had another detachment at La Maison Blanche, on the road to Bar-sur-Seine. Maréchal Marmont, who had retired from Brienne via Ronay and Arcis, arrived in Méry that same day. Napoleon then deployed his army as follows: The Old Guard foot and horse stood by Troyes; the Young Guard was positioned at Pont-St.-Hubert; Victor's corps stood at Pont-Sainte-Marine; the Paris Reserve – reinforced by the 2nd Division – was in Saint-Parre-aux-Tertres; Milhaud's dragoons were in Bouranton, Laubressel, Saint-Maur and Pont-Sainte-Marie; the light cavalry was in Creney; and the Gardes d'honneur of Count Defrance were in Tennelière – covering the road to Bar-sur-Aube.

6

The Aftermath of La Rothière

On 3 February the French army arrived by Troyes, where it found the 2nd Old Guard Division – under GD Michel – holding the Guillotière bridge. Mortier, who had occupied Troyes since 27 January, had departed on the 30th to move on Arcis. However, on learning that it was occupied by the Allies, he had returned to Troyes on 31 January – unaware that Napoleon had wished to link up with him.

On 5 February the French army deployed as follows: The Old Guard infantry and cavalry were in Troyes; the Young Guard was at Pont-Hubert; Victor was in Pont-Sainte-Marie; the Paris Reserve – reinforced by its second division – was in Saint-Parre-aux-Tertes; Milhaud's dragoons were in Bouranton, Laubressel, Saint-Maur and Pont-Sainte-Marie; the light cavalry was in Creney; and Defrance's Gardes d'honneur were in Tenelière – watching the road to Bar-sur-Aube.

Marmont arrived the same day in Arcis and organized a provisional division of 1,500 cuirassiers, dragoons, chasseurs and lancers under GD Bordesoulle. Ricard's division was moved to Aubeterre.[1]

The French army stood temporarily without any orders. Graf Wrede declined to pursue Marmont after La Rothière and returned to Brienne – then moving on to Lesmont, where he paused for 24 hours with Giulay and Württemberg while the bridge was rebuilt. Schwarzenberg (Generalissimo), uncertain of Napoleon's intentions, detached the Russian Guard Light Cavalry Division to see if he was moving on Troyes or Châlons. Their reports resulted in Colloredo moving his forces to a position before Troyes on 3 February. The Allied Guard and reserves stood by Lusigny and Graf Giulay and the Crown Prince of Württemberg pursued the French towards Troyes. Wrede and Wittgenstein moved on Arcis, but Wittgenstein had only moved his advanced guard as far as Plancy. At the same time he was rejoined by Colloredo and Prince Maurice von Liechtenstein to move from Bar-sur-Seine on Troyes. The corps of Platov and Kaisarov moved on Sens, and that of Seslavin was called back to Piney.

At this time the Army of Silesia began to operate independently and broke its communications with the main Allied army. Blücher began moving from Braux-le-Comte and La Fère-Champenoise and moving to take up a position on the left bank of the Marne.[2]

As Napoleon entered Troyes he was greeted by the silence of a distressed population. The citizens feared the probability of a siege and/or the impact of enemy occupation on their limited resources. The stores were nearly empty after the issuance of a bread ration to the French army and the situation appeared very bleak.

The French army consisted, for the large part, of newly-raised solders who lacked the physical endurance to handle the hunger and hardships of a campaign. In the period of eight days after La Rothière, more than 6,000 of them were to desert. The hole in the ranks left by their departure was

1 Koch, Vol. I, p. 195.
2 Koch, Vol. I, p. 196.

The French cavalry under Dommanget and Thiry attacked by the Prussians, 3 February, by Richard Knötel.

filled by the arrival of Hamelinaye's division,[3] but as he arrived, so too did word of the defection of Murat. Morale in the French army was low and rapidly declining.

Though the French arrived in Troyes without any interference from the Allies, M. Liechtenstein's advanced guard soon encountered and drove back the French advanced guards at Maisons-Blanches. Michel's division was sent to push the Austrians back and occupied the positions that evening.

Napoleon intended to hold himself before Troyes until the Allies committed themselves to an offensive move. Troyes stands on the confluence of the Barce and Seine rivers in a vast plain across which an army could maneuver with ease. Troyes proper contained 22,000 inhabitants, factories and magazines of all types – making it able to support the army (as well as making it too important to pass to the Allies without a fight).

On 4 February GD Michel's 2nd Old Guard Division, supported by Briche's dragoons, moved down the road to Bar-sur-Seine to seek contact with Colloredo and Liechtenstein. He encountered them on the heights of Saint-Thiébault. The Austrians were surprised by the offensive nature of this move and quickly deployed. Michel pushed them back and spent the night in Saint-Thiébault – leaving a post of grenadiers-flanqueurs at the Clerey bridge. At 10:00 p.m. this post was attacked, but held. Briche's dragoons reacted quickly and attacked the Austrians – killing about 100 and capturing 150.[4, 5]

The main body of the Austrian army moved to Lusigny and pushed reconnaissance forces towards the Guillotière bridge, occupied by Gérard's advanced guard. The Crown Prince of Württemberg and Giulay established themselves in Piney, while the Army of Silesia moved into

3 The organization of Hamelinaye's division is not known. It does not appear at any time after this period in any of the army returns. It was probably a collection of march units that were immediately distributed amongst the other divisions.

4 Koch, Vol. I, p. 199.

5 Koch, Vol. I, p. 202.

the outskirts of Arcis. This city had been evacuated by Marmont who, after having destroyed the bridges, moved his corps to Droup-Sainte-Marie (down the road from Arcis to Méry). Once there he was rejoined by Ricard's 1st Division, which came from Aubeterre. Though this movement uncovered Troyes on the side facing Arcis, it could be effected without hazard because they were facing few Allied troops at this time.

The day of 5 February passed with little significant movement in the French army, but the Allies were very active. Schwarzenberg, convinced that Napoleon was determined to defend Troyes, decided to turn that position by moving down the road to Bar-sur-Seine – hoping that this would menace his line of retreat and oblige him to withdraw. To accomplish this, Colloredo's corps and M. Liechtenstein's division were ordered to move down that road. The Crown Prince of Württemberg was to support their left by moving on Moutier-Amey and taking Bar-sur-Aube. At the same time, Giulay was to march between the roads to Vandoeuvres and Piney in the direction of Troyes. Wrede was to leave Arcis and move to Vandoeuvres to support these last two corps. The Guard, grenadiers and Russian cuirassiers were to take up cantonments between Chaource, Bar-sur-Seine and Ricey. The Austrian cuirassiers – under Nostitz – were in Pragues, Praslain and Lanteuze. Salins' division, of Giulay's corps, was in Bar-sur-Seine.

These movements by the Allies were not done in any hurry – and they were not what would be considered aggressive moves. Napoleon grew impatient with this lack of action and ordered a false attack against the Allies to provoke them into action. The French army was ordered to hold itself ready to march. Mortier was sent forward with Friant's 1st Old Guard Division to join the 2nd Old Guard Division under Michel, which stood at Maisons-Blanches. The Austrians redeployed in great haste – allowing Mortier to occupy Etroy and take control of its bridge. Napoleon then ordered Mortier to stop wherever he might find himself.

That evening, the Allies – emboldened by the French withdrawal – attacked the Guillotière bridge. Gérard defended this bridge from a heavy attack by the Austrian 1st Corps under Colloredo – inflicting 300 to 400 casualties on them before driving them back.

That evening, dispatches arrived from Macdonald advising Napoleon of the situation on the Marne and the occupation of Châlons by Yorck. The fall of Châlons changed the situation for Napoleon – causing him to abandon his idea of standing before Troyes and committed him to the idea of a second major battle. Macdonald advised Napoleon that the Army of Silesia was marching down the Marne Valley. Napoleon saw that it offered him an opportunity that would permit him to easily draw reinforcements from Paris and the troops coming from Spain, while at the same time falling on Blücher's left flank.

On 6 February the entire French army set out. Oudinot, with Doumerc and Bordesoulle's cavalry – which had crossed the Seine on the 5th and occupied Romilly and Méry – moved to Nogent and was followed by the rest of the army.

Mortier remained in Troyes with the 2nd Old Guard Division, the Paris Reserve and Briche's dragoons to cover the rear of the army.

Schwarzenberg, however, had decided to order an attack. This attack began at 2:00 p.m. on 7 February when Wittgenstein's corps marched to take Piney. Count Pahlen detached a small force to Arcis, where it was to watch the crossings over the Aube. He then marched the rest of his forces through Chaumont to Méry, which he found occupied by Ney. He deployed his cavalry before Méry – facing Ney. The entire Allied army then began its movement on Troyes with the Crown Prince of Württemberg charged with sending a strong reconnaissance towards Laubressel. It found nothing.

While the two armies made these maneuvers, Marmont sent patrols of light towards Lusigny and attacked the Allied advanced posts along the road to Bar-sur-Seine – near Courgerenne – with the 2nd Old Guard Division supported by Briche's dragoons. The French patrols were repulsed, but the Allies reacted as if they were about to be attacked – deploying and losing considerable time while the French army moved on Nogent. The 2nd Old Guard Division withdrew during the night to Maisons-Blanches.

During the day of 7 February, Marmont broke camp and moved in silence towards Troyes and then on to Nogent. The Allies chose to pursue him with a weak detachment of cavalry and infantry detached by the Crown Prince of Württemberg. That evening, the Allied pursuit was in Châtres. However, the French had evacuated everything of value and the Allies found only a few wounded too weak to transport.

The entire Allied army moved into Troyes at 2:00 p.m. on 7 February. Prince von Hohenlohe-Bartenstein was named governor of the city and given four battalions of Russian and Austrian grenadiers to form the city's garrison. The remainder of the Allied army established its bivouacs around the city. General Seslavin was assigned the duty of assuring communications between the main army and the Army of Silesia. He was sent to the extreme left of the main army to join Platov – and their combined Cossacks covered the roads from Sens and Auxerre. The Tsar, the King of Prussia and Schwarzenberg did not move their headquarters to Troyes until the next day.

The rather leisurely movements of the Allies permitted Napoleon to withdraw from any danger of attack and gave him time to do some reorganization of his tattered army. His entire army was soon in and around Nogent.[6]

Hamelinaye's division pulled back to a position before and to the right of the village of Vallant – straddling the main road. It was protected by strong positions on its front and right flank. Defrance, with his gardes d'honneur, moved to Orvilliers. Two battalions of Gérard's 1st Division relieved the detachment left by Ricard's 1st Division (VI Corps) before Méry. General Bélair moved to Mesgrigny with 300 men and Gérard moved two battalions into La Belle-Etoile. The V Cavalry Corps moved into Saint-Martin-de-Bossenay and Romilly.

The remainder of the French army moved into the positions ordered by Napoleon. Victory was in Crancey and Pont-sur-Seine. Mortier was in Chƒtres, Oudinot in Romilly, Ney stood before Nogent and Marmont was on the road to Villenaune.[7]

Despite the confusion of the retreat, Napoleon still had a war to pursue. He directed that Marmont send a strong advanced guard down the road to Vitry to reconnoiter Montmirail. Six-thousand cavalry of the guard marched down the road to Sézanne and, if it was necessary, on 8 February it would be escorted by the Old Guard Infantry (6,000 cavalry) and as many guns as were necessary to complete the mission.[8]

Napoleon reorganizes his army

The first necessity of the Emperor – when he arrived in Nogent – was the reorganization of his cavalry, which had suffered extensively, and to put cadres from the army into the reinforcements which were being organized before Paris. The cavalry, which was to be joined by the provisional corps (under Bordesoulle) and by the regiments which were organized by Pajol, were formed into 10 divisions in four corps. The I Cavalry Corps was formed of the divisions of Merlin and Bordesoulle and commanded by Bordesoulle. The II Cavalry Corps was commanded by Saint-Germain and consisted of his division and that of Maurin. The V Cavalry Corps was placed under Milhaud and consisted of the divisions of Piré, Briche and l'Héritier. The VI Cavalry Corps was placed under the Count de Valmy and was to be formed from the regiments coming from the Army of the Pyrenees with Treilhard and some of those formed by Pajol. Outside of

6 Koch, Vol. I, p. 207.
7 Jacomet, p. 28.
8 Napoleon's Correspondence, No. 21202.

Cossacks marauding, after Peter Hess.

these four corps, the guard cavalry was formed of the divisions of Laferrière, Desnoëttes, Colbert, Guyot and that of Defrance, which consisted of the 4 Gardes d'honneur and the 10th Hussars. However, this latter organization was not fully formed until a bit later.[9] Overall command of the 12,000 French cavalry, not including the guard, was given to GD Grouchy.

Bordesoulle.

During 8 February Napoleon decided to form a distinct corps, with the troops coming from Spain. The divisions of Leval and Boyer – two strong divisions of troops from Spain – were expected momentarily. Napoleon formed them into the VII Corps and assigned them to Oudinot. Leval's division had organized itself in Provins and Boyer's in Nangis. Two foot batteries were attached to each of the divisions and a horse battery was assigned as the corps reserve.

9 de Vauconcourt, Vol. I, pp. 294-5.

The troops that had been under Oudinot were reassigned to Mortier. These forces consisted of Rottembourg's 5th Young Guard Division and the 2nd Old Guard Division.[10]

When the VII Corps was constituted, Oudinot was ordered to move to Provins. Only Leval's division had arrived. Boyer's division would not arrive until 8 February. Both divisions, however, were not in a condition for immediate operations because of their long marches.

Napoleon then committed himself to march on the Marne. He left the II and VII Corps to watch the Seine while the V Cavalry Corps, the Paris Reserve and the VI Cavalry Corps were ordered to March from Bayonne to Orléans. Allix's Flanqueur Division was ordered to Sens and the cavalry depots – under Pajol – and several battalions of National Guards from the west were organized in Montereau by GD Pacthod and destined to move to defend the Yonne and Loing.

The total of these forces did not exceed 30,000 men. Prior to the arrival of the VII Corps, there were only about 24,000 men and the VI Cavalry Corps was not to join them for quite a while.[11]

Unfortunately, Napoleon did not appoint a separate commander to oversee all these operations, but left each corps – under its marshal – reporting directly to him. He did, however, authorize Victor and Oudinot to determine the extent of their command along the Seine and GD Pajol was given command of the defense of the bridges along the Yonne and Loing. Napoleon then left these three independent and uncoordinated commands to face the main Allied army.

Convinced that the Allies would not march from Sens on Fontainebleau until after they captured the Nogent bridge, he ordered Victor to hold that bridge to the last extremity. Unfortunately for Napoleon, the Allies moved on Sens and Fontainebleau without attacking Nogent. Oudinot was to establish himself in Montereau at the confluence of the Yonne and the Seine. He called Victor to join him in the defense of this position.

From his position, Oudinot could support either Napoleon or Pajol as he moved on the Yonne. Pajol left 3,500 National Guards in Montereau and ordered Pacthod to send a battalion to Fossard and another to Moret. With his cavalry, a horse battery and 1,000 infantry he then occupied Saint-Denis, Soucy, Fleurigny and Gisy-les-Nobles – on the roads from Pont-sur-Yonne to Villeneuve- l'Archevêque – at Nogent. He sent a force of cavalry to assure the courier service and to provide liaison with Nogent and Sens. In addition, learning that the Allies had 2,000 cavalry supported by artillery in Villeneuve-sur-Yonne; that Courtenay was occupied; and that Allied detachments were pushing towards Neamours and Montargis, Pajol sent 200 cavalry to Chéroy and Dollot. His cavalry covered and scouted the entire area between Vanne and the Seine.[12]

The Army of Silesia

After the capitulation of Erfurt, General Kleist left the siege of the two citadels to General Jagov and began his march west on January. He commanded about 14,000 men – forming 17 battalions and 12 squadrons. By 2 February his corps stood by Metz. The Russian corps of Kapsevich was relieved by Prussian forces in the blockade of Mainz and marched west – arriving before Nancy on 2 February. Kleist and Kapsevich would soon join hands (to be joined shortly later by Yorck's corps).

Yorck's corps had left the banks of the Moselle on 25 January and marched into France with little opposition. On 30 January GD Lagrange engaged them in a light skirmish, but quickly fell back when ordered to rejoin the main body of the French army. Yorck then found his way open to march on the important city of Vitry. The only force positioned to oppose Yorck was

10 Jacomet, p. 34.
11 Koch, Vol. I, pp. 208-9.
12 Jacomet, pp. 35-6.

that of Macdonald, who was ordered forward. Macdonald marched to defend Vitry in three columns. His march, however, was not very aggressive and he was soon forced to change his line of march and march on Châlons, where he arrived on 30 January. This retrograde movement left the passes through the Argonne without defense other than the local inhabitants, who organized five companies under the command of Duplessis. They were also given two field guns.

The fight for Châlons

On 21 January Macdonald arrived in Châlons as Yorck's advanced guard arrived before Vitry. Vitry, based on its position, was considered as the key to the plains of Champagne. It sat on the main road from Strasbourg to Paris. It stood 35 kilometers from Châlons and 30 kilometers from St.-Dizier. If this road were blocked, the Allies would be forced to move to the right of the main road – trying to march along roads that were nearly impractical.

Vitry was a walled city – defended by six bastions – and stood on the Marne. At the beginning of the campaign all that remained was a terraced enceinte and the moat, which could be filled with water with little effort. Napoleon had left General Montmarie as commander of the garrison of 500 to 600 men and the urban guard. However, the garrison was insufficient to do more than protect the city from a *coup de main*.

By a fortunate accident, the Duke of Danzig had abandoned his senatorial robes and, taking up his sword once again, headed for Châlons. When he arrived there he found the 9th Voltigeur Regiment and a detachment of 80 cavalry. He took command of this force and led them towards Brienne to join Napoleon – marching across the Marne past Vitry. He encountered the lead elements of the Allies and found himself obliged to fall back on Vitry.

His arrival in Vitry energized the inhabitants of Vitry. When Katzler arrived before Vitry a few hours later his reception was so hot he found it wiser to withdraw. This delay gave Macdonald the time he needed to defend the approaches to Châlons. In the city he found about 300 vehicles of the general park – guarded by 100 customs guards – a number of gendarmes from companies displaced by the invasion of the Allies, and a few detachments of infantry under the command of General Simmer. He immediately dispatched the park to the rear. Then on 31 January he pushed an infantry division down the road to Vitry. GD Excelmans' cavalry was sent down the main and back roads in an effort to locate the Allies. Arrighi's cavalry was placed in Nuisement and Méry on the left bank of the Marne.[13]

Yorck, seeing his advanced guard pushed back, feared an offensive movement by the French and stopped his advance. The stopping of his advance gave Macdonald the time to put Excelmans' cavalry in Aulnay and Ablancourt, while the heavy cavalry was in Montigny and Omey. Molitor's 31st Division moved into Aulnay and Chaussée. Albert's 10th Division was in Pogny and Omey. Arrighi's cavalry stood in echelon in Dampierre, Francheville and Sary. General Simmer – with his gendarmes – covered Châlons on the left bank of the Marne.

Skirmish at La Chaussée – 3 February

Yorck remained stationary until 3 February, when he resumed his march at dawn. He marched past Vitry – leaving a brigade to watch the city – and marched on Aulnay. Dommanget's brigade and Molitor's 31st Division executed a fighting withdrawal to Chaussée, where they made a stand.

At 3:00 a.m. the Brandenburg Hussar Regiment moved east of Vitry and reached the main road that led to Châlons. Here it united with General Katzler and the Mecklenburg Hussars, two

13 Koch, Vol. I, p. 220.

squadrons of the Brandenburg Uhlans and the East Prussian National Cavalry Regiment. This force was shortly joined by the eight squadrons of the West Prussian and Lithuanian Dragoons under General Jürgass.[14] Katzler's cavalry formed on the right side of the road, with Jürgass forming his forces on the left. Jürgass arranged his troops with the 1st West Prussian Dragoons in the first line and the Lithuanian Dragoons and their Freiwilliger Jägers formed the second line. Katzler formed his forces in two lines, with the four squadrons of the Brandenburg Hussars in the first line and the two squadrons of the Brandenburg Uhlans in the second line. On his left flank formed Major von Zastrow, with one squadron of the Brandenburg Hussars and a squadron of the East Prussian National Cavalry Regiment. Behind him were the four squadrons of the Mecklenburg Hussars.[15] Between these two cavalry forces stood a force of East Prussian infantry formed in line.

In the distance – in the early glow of a February morning – seven French cavalry regiments and a horse battery (between 2,000 and 3,000 men), under generals Sébastiani and Excelmans, could be seen formed in two limes. It crossed a small stream and moved against the Prussians. Dawn had just begun to break on that cold February morning as the French bugles sounded the attack and all seven French cavalry regiments advanced. The Prussian cavalry had not yet completed its preparatory maneuvers and galloped forward to take up positions on a small hill. As the Brandenburg Hussar Regiment reached this hill they found before them two cuirassier regiments – with a chasseur regiment between them – and the French artillery deployed, but not yet ready to fire. The cry: "*Gewehr auf!*" ("Draw sabers!") echoed through the Prussian ranks and the Prussians advanced to strike the first blow. Major von Zastrow maneuvered to strike the French flank, while Jürgass and Katzler struck them frontally.

The French cavalry drew their carbines and fired on the Prussians at a distance of six paces before closing with swords. The Prussians, however, won the first round – pushing the French first line back. Only the West Prussian Dragoons were repulsed in the initial rush. In their panic to withdraw, the French cavalry screened their battery, which fell into the Prussians' hands. Then the second French line came into the battle and a swirling clash of French cuirassiers, carabiniers and other cavalry erupted as the provisional cavalry regiments of the French II Cavalry Corps engaged the Prussian dragoons.

Things were not completely in the Prussians' favor, as the West Prussian Dragoons were broken by a French cuirassier regiment, which then swung and struck the Brandenburg Hussars in the flank. As a result, much of the recently captured battery escaped. Only one howitzer, three cannon and two caissons were carried off by the Brandenburgers.[16]

A detachment of French lancers faced the Landwehr cavalry, under Graf von Henckel, across the Frion stream. Von Henckel advanced his forces – pushing the French lancers back – and took up a position behind Chaussée, where it encountered Molitor's 31st Division.[17] The Prussian Horse Battery #3 advanced with it and when they encountered the infantry, it unlimbered and took the infantry under fire. Oberst von Warburg then advanced with the Fus/1st and Fus/2nd East Prussian Infantry Regiments and joined the Leib Fusilier Battalion in an exchange of musketry with the French infantry by Chaussée.

Five squadrons of Landwehr cavalry, under Graf von Henckel, then took up a position on the Allied right wing. The French infantry responded by withdrawing to a ridge, but the Prussian

14 Freiherr von Ardenne, p.257.

15 von Damitz, Vol. II, p. 24.

16 von Ardenne, pp. 257-8. According to Sporschil, four guns and three caissons were captured. Sporschil, Vol. 2, 1st Band, p. 319.

17 According to Sporschil, these were Polish lancers and they lost a standard to the Prussians. Sporschil, Vol. 2, 1st Band, p. 367.

cavalry continued to threaten to turn their left flank. They then withdrew to Pogny, where they had to cross over a bridge on the Moivre. Their supporting cavalry turned about and faced the pursuing Prussians once again to give the French sufficient time to withdraw. General Jürgass and Graf von Henckel organized the Lithuanian Dragoons, three squadrons of the 5th Landwehr Cavalry Regiment and two squadrons of the 3rd Landwehr Cavalry Regiment, and drove them forward to attack the French rearguard. In this last engagement the Landwehr purportedly captured a standard from a French lancer regiment.[18]

The engagement broke off and the Prussian advanced guard established itself in the village with the rest of the corps behind it. Once on the far bank, the French were reinforced by a force of infantry and artillery. The artillery – including a 12pdr battery – then took the Prussian cavalry on the far bank under fire and prevented any serious pursuit.

Von Damitz lists the French losses at five cannon, three caissons, one standard and several hundred prisoners and casualties. The Prussians, he says, lost about 100 casualties.

Macdonald did not feel himself strong enough to engage Yorck and ordered a withdrawal to Châlons – the march beginning at 6:00 a.m. in complete silence. Simmer's infantry returned to Châlons and Excelmans' cavalry moved across the Marne. When Yorck realized that the French had withdrawn, he began a vigorous pursuit. Jürgass' cavalry sought a ford near Francheville – hoping to turn the left flank of the French rearguard.

Engagement at Châlons

Macdonald had decided to defend Châlons, but the city was not well-prepared for a strong defense. Its wall and moat were in poor shape. Despite this, General Molitor was ordered to defend the Sainte-Croix Gate and the Jard False Gate. This position was protected by two 12pdr batteries – placed on the heights above the left bank. The Saint-Jean Gate was defended by General Brayer, who placed two howitzers and one cannon in the adjacent bastion that could fire on the road to Vitry. Sébastiani, with Albert's 10th Division, defended the Rheims Gate. Strong batteries were established on the left bank by the bridge to defend its approaches. Kellermann withdrew with the park to Epernay and destroyed the bridges and boats that would permit the Allies' passage over the Marne.[19]

The French light cavalry standing in front of Châlons began a skirmish fight with the advancing Allies until about 9:00 a.m., when they were threatened with being enveloped. They then withdrew to the left bank of the Marne. The Allies discovered a hole in the walls of Châlons between the Rheims and Verdun gates and planned to attack it. They organized an infantry brigade to attack down the Sainte-Ménéhould road – supporting it with a battery.

A cannonade began and General Katzler engaged the French infantry in the Sainte-Memmie suburb in a lively firefight. The Prussian line extended its right towards the Saint-Jacques Gate and at 11:00 a.m. the fight became general. Yorck deployed 40 guns, whose fire ignited several of the houses in the city. Katzler was steadily pushing the French out of the Sainte-Memmie suburb

18 von Damitz, Vol. II, p. 27. Von Damitz clearly identifies these lancers as being 'Polish', but no portion of either the Imperial Guard Polish Lancers or the 7th (Polish) Lancer Regiment could have been present. However, from the description of the French having both cuirassiers and carabiniers present in this engagement, the II Cavalry Corps – which was under Sébastiani – must have been present. This division did contain the 5/2nd, 6/4th and 6/6th Chevauléger-Lancers Regiments and the standard taken may well have belonged to one of those regiments.

19 Koch, Vol. I, p. 222.

and his cavalry advanced in the plains to the right of Compertrix. Two strong forces of infantry – supported by two batteries – threatened the Saint-Jean Gate.

About 1,000 paces from the first houses of Châlons (on the road to Vitry) were two Allies, which ran through the suburb towards the city. The Fus/1st East Prussian Infantry Regiment and a company of the East Prussian Jägers pushed down the right-hand alley and the Fus/2nd East Prussian Infantry Regiment and the second company of the East Prussian Jägers pushed down the left-hand alley. The Fus/2nd East Prussians found themselves more heavily engaged than the Fus/1st East Prussians. The 1/, 2/2nd East Prussian Infantry Regiment advanced in support behind the Fus/2nd. As they advanced, they were taken under fire by a heavy French battery on a hill on the far side of the Marne. As they came under fire, the Fus/2nd became embroiled in a heavy skirmish fight. Soon all the Prussian infantry was engaged in a murderous firefight with the French.

Outside the city, the Prussian reserve cavalry moved up from Sainte-Ménéhould. The 1st West Prussian Regiment moved to face the Rheims suburb. At around 4:00 p.m. the 8th Brigade, under Prince Wilhelm von Preussen, arrived and took up positions by Sainte-Ménéhould. Behind him, the 7th Brigade – under General von Horn – took up a supporting position. Yorck and Prince Wilhelm began examining the walls around the Rheims suburb with the thought of launching an assault.[20]

Prince Wilhelm of Prussia.

Prince Wilhelm directed four howitzers and a 12pdr foot battery to a position on a hill on the road to Sainte-Ménéhould, and another four howitzers, two horse batteries and some foot artillery from the advanced guard on the road from Vitry. These guns were to open a breach in the wall and to bombard the city. They began firing at 8:00 p.m. and fired until 11:00 p.m.

The city fathers – fearing the destruction of their city – pleaded with Macdonald and convinced him not to risk the destruction of the city with a protracted defense. He accepted and a deputation was sent to Yorck to negotiate an armistice and the evacuation of the city. The truce was negotiated and Macdonald was to evacuate Châlons at 6:00 a.m. the following day (and that he would leave the magazines in the condition in which he had found them).

On 5 February – conforming to the terms of the armistice – Macdonald evacuated the city, broke down the bridge over the Marne and marched towards Epernay. His rearguard, commanded by GD Sébastiani, took up a position by Fagnières and Saint-Gibrien. Yorck's corps occupied Châlons at noon and quickly ordered the repair of the bridge.

In their hasty withdrawal the French had failed to block the road to La Ferté (via Montmirail) – leaving the shortest road to La Ferté open to the Allies. Yorck was to take advantage of this, while Blücher continued his march on Saint-Ouen – moving his advanced guard into Fére-Champenoise and his headquarters to Sommepuis.

The loss of Châlons left Vitry encircled. Macdonald ordered its garrison commander to evacuate the city and move his forces over the Marne – marching down the left bank of the Marne until it rejoined Macdonald. Macdonald then directed GD Excelmans' cavalry to Bussy-l'Estree.

This movement was not without danger. It required General Montmarie to move between the Marne and Blücher's army. This march was complicated by the fact that Vitry was filled with military equipment and munitions that had to be saved (if possible). Montmarie began his

20 von Damitz, Vol. II, pp. 32-3.

march at 5:00 a.m., broke down the bridge and marched down the road to Vitry. His advanced guard threw several hundred enemy cavalry out of Vésigneux and would have successfully made his escape had he not stopped to change the horses on his convoy. This delay let Yorck's pursuing cavalry catch up with the convoy. The French fought desperately to save the convoy. The Prussians discharged their cannon into the confused mass of vehicles – driving them forward in panic. However, despite that, the French cavalry and infantry held firm. They marched behind the convoy in good order and that evening reached the city of Bergères, where they rejoined the army.

The following day, Yorck crossed over the Marne below the Châlons bridge. Macdonald continued his retreat on Epernay, where he established his headquarters. Albert's 10th Division formed the rearguard and took up a position in Jalons.

During the day of 5 February Blücher remained in Sommepuis – evaluating the advantages of operating along the roads from Châlons to La Ferté-sous-Jouarre. He realized that even if he failed to cut off Macdonald, he might well catch part of the train that Macdonald had with him. He resolved to pursue the French on the main road with Yorck's corps and to push Sacken's corps down the smaller road through Bergères and Montmirail. Marching a day behind Sacken would be Olsufiev's 9th Corps. The corps of Kleist and Kapsevich would arrive in Châlons on 8 February.

Blücher directed Yorck to march on Château-Thierry. If he encountered significant resistance, he was to cross the Marne and join Sacken's corps. Sacken had instructions to March on Montmirail. Blücher then directed his cavalry towards Sézanne to scour the countryside between the Aube and the Seine. Kleist and Kapsevich were then ordered to execute a force march and arrive in Montmirail on 10 February. As a result, on 6 February Yorck found himself between Châlons and Epernay; Sacken was in Vertus; and Blücher was with Olsufiev's 9th Corps in Soudron. Though he sought to catch Macdonald, his march was leisurely and dangerous.

On 7 February Macdonald continued his retreat – occupying Dormans and Crézancy. Aware of some of Blücher's goals he detached Molitor's 31st Division, Simmer's brigade and Excelmans' cavalry that evening – ordering the latter to leave a brigade in Château-Thierry. The remainder was to take up positions at La Ferté-sous-Jouarre, where the road to Montmirail branched.[21]

On 8 February Macdonald withdrew to Château-Thierry. General Brayer's 35th Division formed the rearguard and took up positions on the heights behind Dormans. Yorck's advanced guard attacked them early in the morning, but the French held firm and executed an orderly fighting withdrawal – moving from position to position. When they arrived in Crézancy they were relieved by Montmarie's brigade[22] (supported by Arrighi's cavalry). Montmarie continued the well-executed fighting withdrawal to Château-Thierry, where they established themselves behind the Marne – breaking down the bridge behind them.

The next day, both belligerents faced one another across the Marne – firing heavily – while the Allies threw a pontoon bridge over the Marne below the broken bridge. The Allies then fought their way across the river – driving the French rearguard towards La Ferté.

The French army, reinforced by the arrival of 2,000 conscripts, formed around the cadres of three battalions under the command of General Minot. Sacken's advanced guard pushed forward and caught Brayer and Molitor's divisions – driving them back in disorder. Their withdrawal was stabilized by the arrival of Albert's 10th Division. The brigades of Bigarré, Schoefer and Beauvais withstood several assaults by the Russian cavalry – pushing them back and taking about 400 prisoners.

21 Koch, Vol. I, p. 228.

22 This brigade consisted of five battalions (two of the 9th Voltigeur Regiment, one from the 46th, one from the 50th and one of the 139th Line – about 2,400 men).

On the 8th, Blücher continued his movement at a casual rate. Sacken left the fighting to his advanced guard and established the rest of his corps in Montmirail. General Olsufiev took up positions at Champaubert – having contact with only a few Cossack squadrons. Kleist and Kapsevich would spend the night in Châlons.

On 10 February Macdonald broke down the bridges at La Ferté and Trilport and withdrew to Meaux, where he encountered 8,000 French National Guardsmen. His retreat was totally undisturbed by the Allies.

The cavalry – under Count Pahlen – moved through the countryside between the two Allied armies and advised Blücher that Napoleon, with his main forces, had crossed from the Seine to the Marne. This news was disturbing to Blücher because of the scattered dispositions of his army. His five corps were spread along a line 50 kilometers long – exposed to defeat in detail. On 10 February he sent out orders to correct this situation – ordering Sacken to pull back to Montmirail, Yorck to move to Château-Thierry and then he ordered his cavalry to move to Sézanne and seek news of Napoleon's location.

Sacken recalled his advanced guard, which might have cut off Macdonald's rearguard, but contented itself with seizing a few caissons and guns. On his side, Yorck crossed the Marne at Château-Thierry.[23]

23 Koch, Vol. I, p. 231.

7

Six Marvellous Days: The Battles of Champaubert, Château-Thierry, Montmirail and Vauchamps

After organizing the defense of the Seine River and leaving 20,000 men under Oudinot and Victor, Napoleon began his movement against the left flank of the Army of Silesia.

Events after February 7

On 8 February Macdonald reported to Napoleon that Yorck's 1st Prussian Corps stood near Epernay with about 18,000 men. The implication was that if only 18,000 men of Blücher's 45,000 men were advancing on the northern route, the rest had to be south of the Marne River. In fact, Yorck was in pursuit of Macdonald down the main road and General Sacken was advancing down the side roads – paralleling Yorck's advance – and intent on cutting him off by La Ferté should he move in that direction.

The location of the remainder of Blücher's forces became clear at 9:00 a.m. on 9 February when Marmont reported from Champaubert that General Sacken and at least 15,000 troops were at Montmirail, 15 miles to the west. Napoleon realized that while Yorck chased Macdonald up the Marne River toward Epernay, Blücher was advancing along the shortest route to Paris (via Montmirail and La Ferté-sous-Jouarre). Sacken was, apparently, the van of the Army of Silesia – with Olsufiev's 9th Corps a day's march behind. Blücher was further in the rear at Vertus – waiting for Kleist and Kapsevich. The Army of Silesia was scattered in four groups – none close enough to support the others. Here was Napoleon's chance to catch his nemesis, Blücher, scattered across the French countryside and destroy him in detail.

On 9 February the Army of Silesia stood as follows:

von Sacken in Montmirail	20,000 men[1]
Olsufiev in Champaubert	3,000
Kleist in Châlons	8,000
Kapsevich in Vitry & Vertus	7,000
Yorck in Dormans	18,000
Total:	56,000

1 C. von W., p. 159.

The surveys of the *ingénieurs-géographers*[2] showed the roads from Nogent via Villenoxe and Barbonne – then on to Sézanne – were not impassable. His roads open, Napoleon chose this route to strike at Blücher.[3] He ordered Oudinot and Ney to march on Sézanne and then marched there himself with his Foot and Horse Guard.

Napoleon wrote his brother Joseph, saying: "I am going to Sézanne with whatever is necessary to beat between La Ferté-sous-Jouarre and Sézanne." He then instructed Macdonald "not to retreat so precipitately." He immediately left Nogent escorted by the service squadrons and slept in Sézanne. It had been raining steadily for five days and the roads from Nogent to Sézanne had become quagmires. So too were the roads on which Blücher travelled between Vertus to Montmirail. The poor condition of the roads and deep mud were to be formidable obstacles for both the French and Allies. This was nothing new, as the road from Sézanne to Champaubert was considered impassable by large formations at that time of the year.

Ney crossed the Seine River at Nogent the previous evening and advanced on Sézanne. He had with him the 1st Voltigeur Division (Meunier), the 2nd Young Guard Division (Decouz), the 1st Old Guard Division (Friant) and Nansouty's three cavalry divisions. The entire French force destined for Champaubert consisted of:

1st Old Guard Division: Général de division Friant (4,796)
- 1st Brigade: Général de division Michel
  - Staff/, 1/, 2/1st Chasseur à Pied Regiment
  - Staff/, 1/, 2/2nd Chasseur à Pied Regiment
- 2nd Brigade: Général de division Cambronne
  - Staff/, 1/, 2/1st Grenadier à Pied Regiment
  - Staff/, 1/, 2/2nd Grenadier à Pied Regiment
- Attached:
  - 1/, 2/, 3/Guard Sapper Battalion
  - 3/Guard Marine Battalion
  - Guard Engineering Train

1st Voltigeur Division: Général de division Meunier (4,133)
- 1st Voltigeur Regiment
- 2nd Voltigeur Regiment
- 3rd Voltigeur Regiment
- 4th Voltigeur Regiment

2nd Voltigeur Division: Général de division Decouz (2,840)
- 5th Voltigeur Regiment
- 6th Voltigeur Regiment
- 7th Voltigeur Regiment
- 8th Voltigeur Regiment

1st Guard Cavalry Division: Général de division Colbert (2,582)
- 2nd Éclaireur Regiment
- 1st Chevauléger-lancier Regiment (Polish)
- Chasseurs à cheval de la Garde
- Grenadiers à cheval de la Garde
- Empress Dragoon Regiment
- Horse Artillery

2 Geographical engineers charged with map-making.
3 Koch, Vol. I, p. 232.

3rd Guard Cavalry Division: Général de division Laferrière
- 1st Brigade: Général de brigade Lyon
  - Chasseurs à cheval Regiment (34/508)
  - Empress Dragoon Regiment (44/691)
- 2nd Brigade: Général de brigade Letort
  - Grenadier à cheval Regiment (45/842)

Guard Artillery: (1,464)
- 7 Foot Batteries
- 4 Horse Batteries
- Train
- Pontooneers

VI Corps: Maréchal Marmont
- Division: Général de division Lagrange (4,868)
  - 1st Line Regiment
  - 15th Line Regiment
  - 16th Line Regiment
  - 62nd Line Regiment
  - 70th Line Regiment
  - 121st Line Regiment
  - 1st Marine Regiment
  - 1/, 2/, 3/, 4/2nd Marine Regiment
  - 1/, 2/, 3/3rd Marine Regiment
  - 1/, 2/, 3/4th Marine Regiment
  - 3/23rd Line Regiment
  - 1/, 3/37th Line Regiment
- 8th Division: Général de division Ricard (2,917)
  - 2/2nd Légère Regiment
  - 7/4th Légère Regiment
  - 2/6th Légère Regiment
  - 9th Légère Regiment
  - 16th Légère Regiment
  - 22nd Line Regiment
  - 2/40th Line Regiment
  - 1/50th Line Regiment
  - 69th Line Regiment
  - 1/136th Line Regiment
  - 1/138th Line Regiment
  - 1/142nd Line Regiment
  - 1/144th Line Regiment
  - 1/145th Line Regiment

I Cavalry Corps: Général de division Doumerc
- Brigade: Général de division Doumerc (1,900)
  - 1st Provisional Hussar Regiment
  - 2nd Chasseurs à cheval Regiment
  - 3rd Chasseurs à cheval Regiment
  - 4th Chasseurs à cheval Regiment
- Brigade: Général de brigade Piquet (915)
  - 10th Hussar Regiment
  - 1st Gardes d'honneur

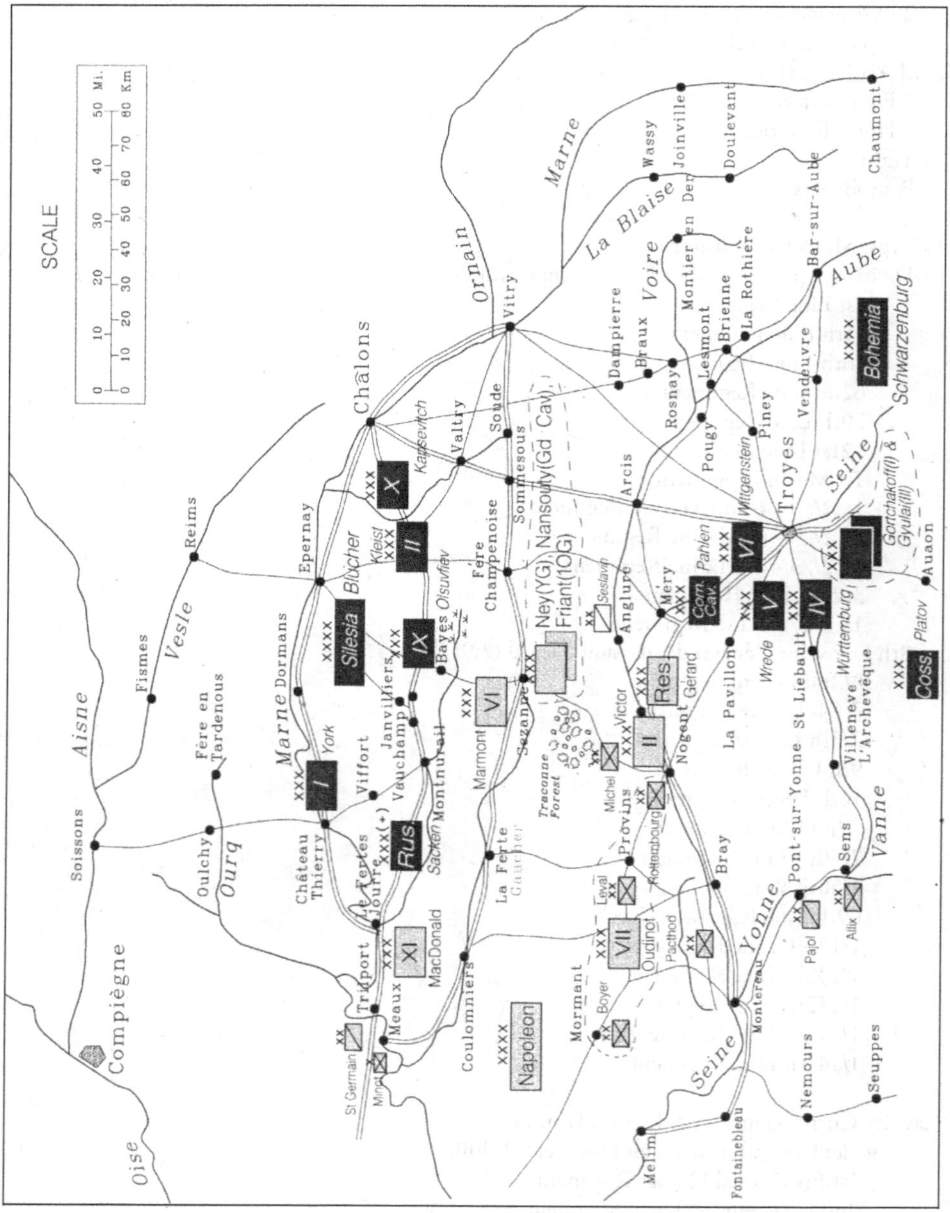

Map 4 Strategic Situation, February 9 1814.

Marmont had already passed down the road from Villauxe to Sézanne. Their passage had left it a foot deep in mud. As they advanced through the mire, Ney's troops lost shoes at every step. The cavalry was forced to march on foot because the horses could not advance through the mud with a man on their back. The limbers and guns of Dulauloy, Griois and Leroy had to be dragged forward with doubled teams formed with peasants' horses and enthusiastic peasants who themselves drew the guns like draft animals. That evening, when the horse and foot guard finally reached Sézanne, all that greeted them were miserable soaked bivouacs. Some of the Guard artillery was still bogged down in the Saint-Gond marshes.[4]

That evening, another dispatch arrived from Marmont reporting that Sacken had left Champaubert at 8:30 a.m. that morning. Sacken's escape was irrelevant. Napoleon had other plans, but unfortunately Marmont, Ney, Macdonald and Victor did not understand his strategy either.

Blücher in Vertus

While Napoleon marched, Blücher remained immobile in Vertus – awaiting the effect of his orders to concentrate his army. In vain, Pahlen attempted to advise him of Napoleon's march on his left flank, but despite the warnings Blücher took no measures to escape the looming disaster. There was time – at this point – to send Kleist and Kapsevich forward, have them link up with Olsufiev and catch Napoleon. However, he did nothing.

Instead, he left Olsufiev hanging in the open and directed Kleist and Kapsevich to march on La Fère-Champenoise with the intention of making contact with the main Allied army and checking Napoleon if he had not yet passed Sézanne. Blücher continued making dispositions, but was acting with complete ignorance of Napoleon's position or his strength.

Olsufiev's command

Olsufiev had orders from Blücher to take up quarters in or around Champaubert to give his troops time to recover from the fatigues and losses suffered at Brienne. Olsufiev's command consisted of:

11th Corps: Generallieutenant Olsufiev
- 9th Infantry Division: Major-General Udom
  - Brigade: Generalmajor Poltarachi
    - Apcheron Regiment (486)
    - Nachebourg Regiment (563)
  - Brigade: Generalmajor Juschkov II
    - Riajsk Regiment (620)
    - Iakoutsk Regiment (533)
  - Brigade: Major Melnik
    - 10th Jager Regiment (335)
    - 38th Jager Regiment (472)
- 15th Infantry Division: Major-General Kornilov
  - Brigade: Lt. Colonel Anensur
    - Vitebsk Regiment (372)
    - Kozlov Regiment (504)

4 Mikhailofsky, p. 99.

Brigade: Generalmajor Mussin-Pushkin
- Kolyvan Regiment (417)
- Kourin Regiment (417)

Brigade: Colonel Tuchanowski
- 12th Jager Regiment (447)
- 22nd Jager Regiment (?)

Artillery:
- Position Battery #15 (probably not present)
- Light Batteries #13 & #29

Olsufiev's Infantry corps contained 3,690 men and was supported by two batteries with 24 guns. Olsufiev had no cavalry attached to his force except for a small staff of 21 mounted orderly officers.[5] On the eve of February 8, Bayés had been occupied by 150 lancers of Marmont's command. The next morning, the French lancers were thrown from Bayés and pushed back to Sézanne by Sacken's cavalry. The ease of this gave the Russians a false sense of security and Olsufiev neglected the most elementary measures, which would have been to destroy or garrison both the bridge and the defile at St.-Prix.

Olsufiev, by G. Dawe.

The Battle of Champaubert – 10 February

On the 9th, the Emperor arrived at Sézanne where, to his great disappointment, he found Marmont.[6] Marmont declared that it was impossible to advance down the rain-soaked roads. He also told Napoleon that his troops were under-strength, exhausted, hungry, discouraged and that the mud clung to the guns and horses – making them unable to move.

Furious, Napoleon ordered him to advance on at any price. He had expected Marmont to be in control of the bridge and defile at St.-Prix. This was the only point where the French army could cross the Petit-Morin River and clear the Saint-Gond marshes to attack the Allies. Once clear of the marshes, Napoleon had expected to launch his troops through Bayés towards Champaubert.

During the evening of 8 February Marmont had sent 150 lancers to occupy Bayés, but on the morning of the 9th, the Russians had reoccupied that position. In addition, Marmont had allowed his forces to be pushed back to Sézanne. It appears that Olsufiev perceived the ease with which Sacken had pushed back Marmont's lancers to Sézanne as an indication that they were only a small reconnaissance cavalry party.

The following day – at about 9:00 a.m. – Napoleon was with Marmont in front of the defile of Saint-Gond. Before them – as they stood on the heights that dominate St.-Prix – they saw the swampy valley of the Petit-Morin, the bridge over it and the opposite slope. A Russian battery and two battalions would have been sufficient to hold the bridge and ruin Napoleon's maneuver.

5 Mikhailofsky, p. 100; von Hiller, p. 120
6 de Ségur, p. 173.

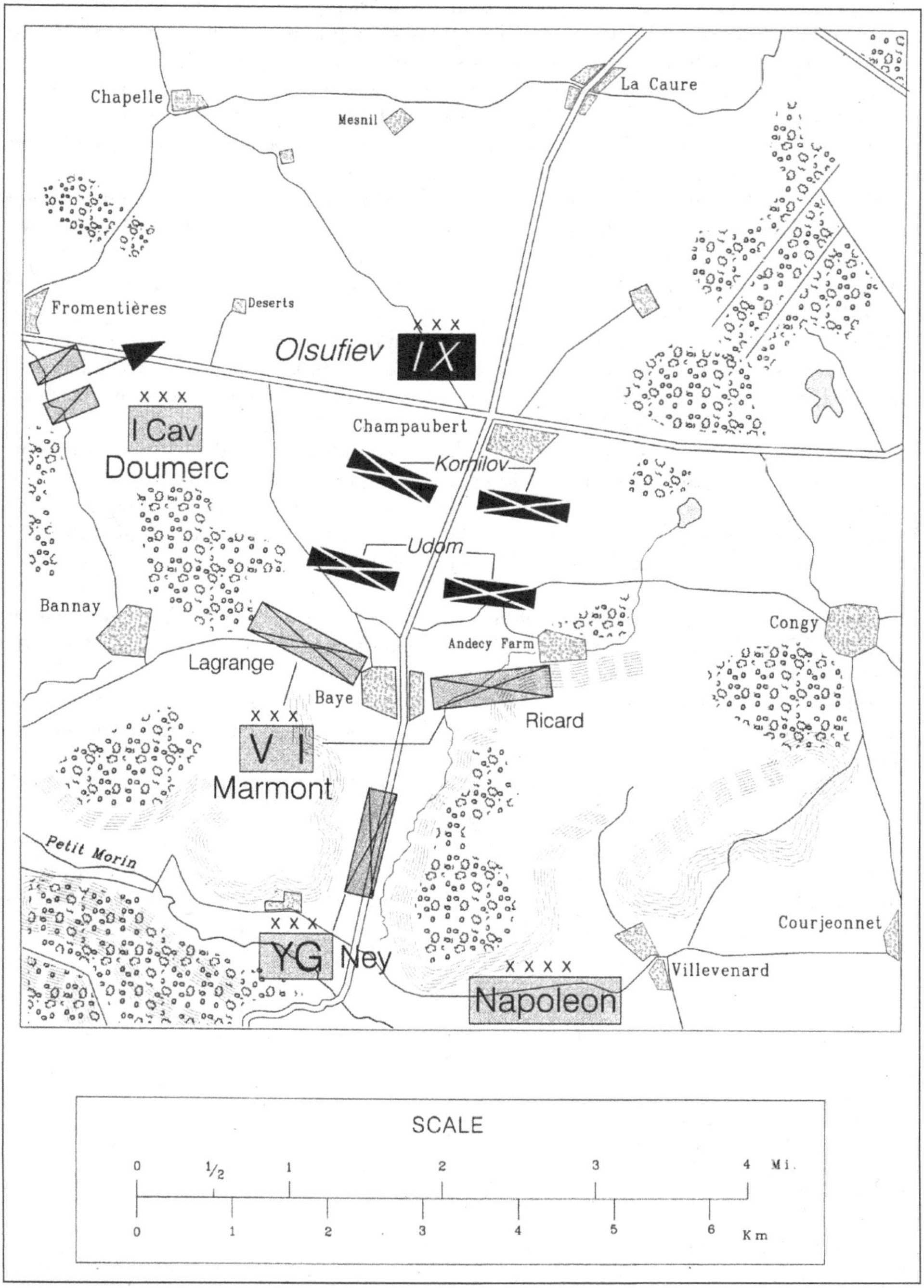

Map 5 Battle of Champaubert, February 10 1814, 1:30 p.m.

Lagrange's 3rd Division led the French advance, followed by Ricard's 8th Division. They crossed the Saint-Gond swamp and pushed forward into St.-Prix.[7] Fortunately for them, the bridge at St.-Prix was intact and the opposite bank free of enemy troops. Napoleon ordered Major Sachon to take 100 Imperial Guard Dragoons to take some prisoners. Galloping into the village of Bannay, they immediately surprised 500 Russians and took them prisoner.

Lagrange's division quickly crossed over the bridge and began moving towards Bannay. A Marine Battalion and the 2nd Légère Regiment marched down the road to the left, which moved into the woods to the left of Bannay.[8] Ricard's division then moved in the direction of Bayés while Pelleport's brigade of Lagrange's division attacked Bannay.

By 10:00 a.m. French cavalry elements were probing the Allied positions at Champaubert and drove back Olsufiev's pickets. This was Olsufiev's first indication that significant French forces were coming up from Sézanne. Recognizing his error in not occupying St.-Prix, he immediately sent Major-General Udom with two jager battalions. The Russian light infantry drove the French skirmishers out of Bayés, but the heads of the French columns quickly showed themselves. Udom called for reinforcements to face the steadily increasing numbers of French. The second brigade of jagers and six guns were dispatched.[9] Udom now had the 10th, 38th, 12th and 22nd Jagers – supported by six guns – to hold Bayés. This was still not enough, and before long the remainder of the corps was brought forward.[10]

Marmont's soldiers had already passed the defile and quickly pushed back these battalions some 500 yards from Bayés and deployed 12 guns. The French forces increased steadily. At about 1:00 p.m. Olsufiev responded by bringing up the rest of his command and deploying between Bayés and Bannay. He placed a second brigade on his right and supported them with a half battery of six guns.[11] The French deployed before Bayés under the cover of the artillery of the I Cavalry Corps.

A lancer squadron, under the orders of General Piquet, charged the left and threw them out of Bayés.[12] While Ricard's 8th Division and Bordesoulle's cavalry quickly occupied Bayés, the Imperial Guard occupied Bannay.

Olsufiev chose to fight it out and deployed his troops 500 yards before Bayés.[13] His left was in a small valley that was almost impassable. To his front he held a very defensible position in a small wood.

Marmont immediately realized that the wood was the key to the Russian position. He sent ahead of Ricard's 8th Division the 113th Line Regiment[14] – completely deployed in skirmish order and supported by two brigades in columns. Then he directed Lagrange's 3rd Division against the plateau that ran between Bayés and Bannay and supported Lagrange with a Marine Battalion, which was in turn supported by the 2/2nd Légère. The Marines and the 2/2nd Légère moved to the right of the woods, where the Russians would have to pass to cut them off.[15]

7 Koch, Vol. I, p. 235.
8 von Damitz, Vol. II, p. 107.
9 Sporschil, Vol. 2, 1st Band, p. 389.
10 Mikhailofsky, p. 101.
11 von Hiller, p. 121.
12 Rothwiller, p. 579.
13 Houssaye says 15 guns, Chandler 24 guns and Lachouque 40 guns.
14 The 113th had just joined Marmont's Corps and was entirely composed of recruits. Their uniform only consisted of a gray greatcoat and a forage cap. They had hardly any cadre at all, which means that they would not be very steady in battle and their maneuvers would be poorly executed.
15 Koch, Vol. I, pp. 235-6.

Champaubert: The cuirassiers of Doumerc are in the foreground; Marmont and Ney's infantry in the background.

The order given, the French advanced – sweeping the Russians from the wood. Olsufiev tried to rally his troops in Bayés, but that village was too open. He had to withdraw while fighting and redeploy his rallied troops on a line extending from the Andecy farm to the Bannay wood. By doing so, Olsufiev still held the road from Sézanne to Epernay that crossed the road from Châlons to Paris at Champaubert.

Olsufiev then received word that the French were closing on Champaubert by both flanks. With both flanks threatened, he formed his corps in mass and slowly withdrew toward Champaubert with the intention of moving from there to Etoges. He also sent 12 guns to Champaubert.[16] The 7/4th Légère swept into Bayés – chasing the retreating Russians before it.[17] At the same time, Pelleport's brigade occupied Bannay.

Olsufiev had only 12 under-strength regiments – all of which were to the strength of a single battalion – and 24 guns. Olsufiev was informed that the French movement through a wood had cut him off from the highway to Châlons. By now, Olsufiev had brought back most of his troops toward the main highway – and after ordering Major-General Poltoratzki to hold Champaubert with the Nachebourg and Apcheron Regiments supported by nine guns,[18] he decided to reopen the road to Etoges by attacking the French that were holding it. He failed in that attempt to break through. The French brought up several artillery batteries against the Russians, while the French cavalry continued its outflanking maneuvers.

Ricard followed the road and Lagrange advanced on the left. The Russian position was the most accessible on that side and the first French attack took place. However, the Russians had deployed there 24 guns, which crushed Lagrange. The bad roads had exhausted the teams so the French artillery had yet to arrive. Lacking artillery support, Lagrange's 3rd Division, VI Corps broke off in disorder. Napoleon and Ney appeared with the numerous Guard artillery, rallied Lagrange and stopped the Russians.

At that time, the 2,000 cavalry that Napoleon sent through Fromentières suddenly appeared on the Russians' rear and at the right of their line. That last event worried Olsufiev.

16 Mikhailofsky, p. 101.
17 Koch, Vol. I, p. 236.
18 Bogdanovich, p. 181.

Napoleon then ordered Count Girardin, aide-de-camp to Berthier, to take two service squadrons – and the head of Doumerc's cavalry – and march around Olsufiev's forces and seize the road to Paris and wait for the Russians to arrive. Marmont, with Ney's help, had unleashed his columns toward Champaubert and collided with the Russian infantry on the plateau, while the Young Guard tied them down between Bannay and the forest as the Guard cavalry surrounded them.

At that time in turn, Ricard attacked Champaubert, took it and lost it again and finally could only secure the first houses. That combat was a bloody one, with an unusual amount of bayonet fighting. Poltoratzki placed his artillery at the crossroad and successfully repulsed several cavalry charges. In Champaubert, a squadron of lancers – under Bordesoulle – charged the Russian left and drove them out of the village.[19]

Then, Lagrange – who had rallied his troops – renewed his attack. He was wounded, but only after he had the pleasure to see the Russians, a brigade and nine guns – under Major General Poltoratzki – forming squares and slowly withdrawing toward Champaubert. While retreating, the Russians kept the French at bay by their regular fire.[20] As Poltoratzki's troops withdrew, they were separated into two groups.

By 3:00 p.m. Poltoratzki's situation was desperate and he was considering retreat toward Etoges, but the direct route toward Etoges was cut off by the French infantry and cavalry and he was unable to break through. Then, the Russian infantry – now short of ammunition – was pushed back from position to position behind Champaubert toward the village of La Caure using their bayonets. Poltoratzki was now cut off from the rest of Olsufiev's command. He withdrew in square towards a wood slightly over two miles from Champaubert. His force was badly disordered, and the French – seeing this – summoned him to surrender. When he refused, the French brought up a horse battery which showered the Russians with canister. The situation went from bad to worse when Poltoratzki found the woods – in which he hoped to find shelter – were already occupied by French skirmishers. Hope gone – and his ranks steadily being carved apart by canister and skirmish fire – he surrendered his two regiments and 10 guns.[21]

Olsufiev's situation was equally grave. He had hoped to withdraw to Etoges, but even after an aggressive bayonet attack he could not cut a path to safety. He then struck off to the left in an effort to gain safety in the village of La Caure.[22] Near the village of La Caure, Olsufiev made a disastrous mistake. In the presence of Marmont, he ordered what was left of his divisions to shift front to the left, and in doing so opened his right flank as he entered that swampy wood. Marmont took advantage of this mistake by ordering a brigade of Bordesoulle's cuirassiers to attack that open flank.[23] The shock was violent and the Russian column, cut off in two, routed and several thousand men were scattered – throwing away their weapons and backpacks. During that 'run for your life' panic, most of the fugitives entered the wood, but all the outlets had already been blocked on Marmont's order. Generals Kornilov and Udom were not taken prisoner and decided to surrender. They collected the remnants of the corps: 1,500 to 2,000 troops, 15 guns and all colors, broke through and retreated by the forest to Port-a-Binson on the road from Eperne to Château-Thierry.[24]

19 Koch, Vol. I, p. 237.
20 Mikhailofsky, p. 102.
21 Bogdanovich, p. 182.
22 Mikhailofsky, p. 103.
23 Rothwiller, p. 579; Koch, Vol. I, p. 237.
24 Bogdanovich, p. 182.

The Russians were routed. Rothwiller states that 3,000 Russians were killed and captured/taken, some drowned in the pond of that wood and 1,500 to 2,000 more were taken prisoners by the peasants. By nightfall, Olsufiev and Poltoratzki were captured – as were 21 guns and their caissons (as well as 200 wagons).[25] Koch gives the Russian losses at 21 guns and their caissons, Olsufiev, two other generals, 47 officers, 1,837 prisoners, 1,200 dead on the field and 200 drowned.[26] Only 1,900 men and nine guns from Olsufiev's command escaped.[27] This meager remainder of the command – now under the command of Kornilov and Udom – withdrew through the forest and reached Port-à-Brisson late at night.[28] Major-General Kornilov took command of what was left of the 9th Infantry Corps.

The French losses appear to have been very light (between 200 and 600 casualties). It appeared to the French that the Napoleon of old had returned and that their star might rise once again.

Blücher, although he heard the sound of gunfire to the west, did not make the least attempt to move to Olsufiev's assistance. Mikhailofsky reports that Olsufiev sent several couriers to Blücher – advising him of the French attack upon his command and of the presence of Napoleon – but the field marshal always answered that: "his apprehensions were groundless; that Napoleon could not be present; and that the detachment acting against our troops could not amount to more than 2,000 men commanded by some partisan. He farther confirmed his previous order to keep possession of Champaubert." At 1:00 p.m. Olsufiev had called a council of his generals. Though this council recommended an immediate retreat to Etoges, Olsufiev answered he could not consent "having been ordered to maintain himself in the position of Champaubert."

The Guard marches to the next battle

On 11 February – at around 5:00 a.m. – Napoleon detached Marmont with Grouchy's cavalry and Lagrange's 3rd Division to Etoges to observe the Allied forces in Vertus. He then set the rest of his army in motion – marching on Montmirail. The Grenadiers à cheval, which had advanced only with the greatest difficulty over the terrible roads, joined Nansouty in his position on the heights by Montcoupeau. The Guard Infantry and the 2nd Brigade of Ricard's 8th Division began their march an hour before dawn and marched in front of the chasseur division under the orders of General Lefebvre-Desnoëttes. Napoleon arrived in Montmirail at 10:00 a.m. and found Nansouty moving to delay Sacken's retreat. Sacken had departed La Ferté the previous evening at 9:00 p.m. and his columns had just begun to appear before La Renaudière.[29]

Battle of Montmirail – 11 February

During the night of 10-11 February General Sacken marched his forces towards Montmirail. His advanced guard and reserve were marching on Sézanne and due to arrive that morning. Yorck, with his battle corps, departed Château-Thierry the day before and took up cantonments on the left bank of the Marne. Only Prince Wilhelm von Preussen was left with a reserve of infantry and two squadrons to guard the bridge and to send reconnaissance detachments to Epernay and La Ferté,

25 Rothwiller, p. 579.
26 Koch, Vol. I, pp. 237-8.
27 von Bernhardi, Vol. 4, 7th Book, p. 382.
28 The high figure of 1,800 is provided by C. von W., C., p. 168 and von Damitz, Vol. II, p. 179. The low figure is from Koch, Vol. I, p. 239.
29 Koch, Vol. I, p. 239.

Prisoners taken at Champaubert; Olsufiev is to the right.

Lefebvre-Desnoëttes.

At Vieux-Maison, Sacken learned that this district was filled with French troops. Sacken commanded a substantial force and stood within relatively easy reinforcing distance of General Yorck's corps. Sacken commanded two infantry and one cavalry corps. The first was the 11th Corps – under Generalmajor von Lieven III – and consisting of the 10th and 27th Divisions, plus a brigade of the 16th Division. The second infantry corps was the 6th Corps (Generallieutenant Tallisin II) and consisted of the 7th and 18th Divisions. The Cavalry Corps, under Generallieutenant Tallisin II, consisted of the 2nd Hussar Division (Generalmajor Lanskoi) and the 3rd Dragoon Division (Generalmajor Pantschichscheff). His assigned reserve artillery, under Generalmajor Nikitin, contained three 12pdr batteries and four 6pdr batteries. The daily returns for the Russian corps indicate that it had about 14,000 men and 80 guns. The Prussians that would be engaged in the day's battle totaled about 5,000 men.

On 11 February Napoleon ordered Maréchal Marmont – commanding Lagrange's 3rd Division, VI Corps, and the Grande Armée's line cavalry (under Général de division Grouchy) – to move on Etoges. With this force he was to observe the roads from Châlons and Vertus. Napoleon's main army did not begin its movement on Montmirail until 5:00 a.m. The 1st Guard Cavalry Division (Général de division Laferrière Levéque), which had remained behind because of the bad roads, joined by the Guard cavalry under Nansouty. The 1st Guard Division and the 2nd Brigade of Ricard's 8th Division, VI Corps, began their march with the Guard Chasseur Brigade, 1st Old Guard Division, leading the way and starting its march one hour before dawn. This column marched until 10:00 a.m., when it arrived on the battlefield. Nansouty was already maneuvering around Sacken's forces when the head of the guard column arrived at La Renaudière.[30]

30 Sporschil, Vol. II, 1st Band, pp. 395-6.

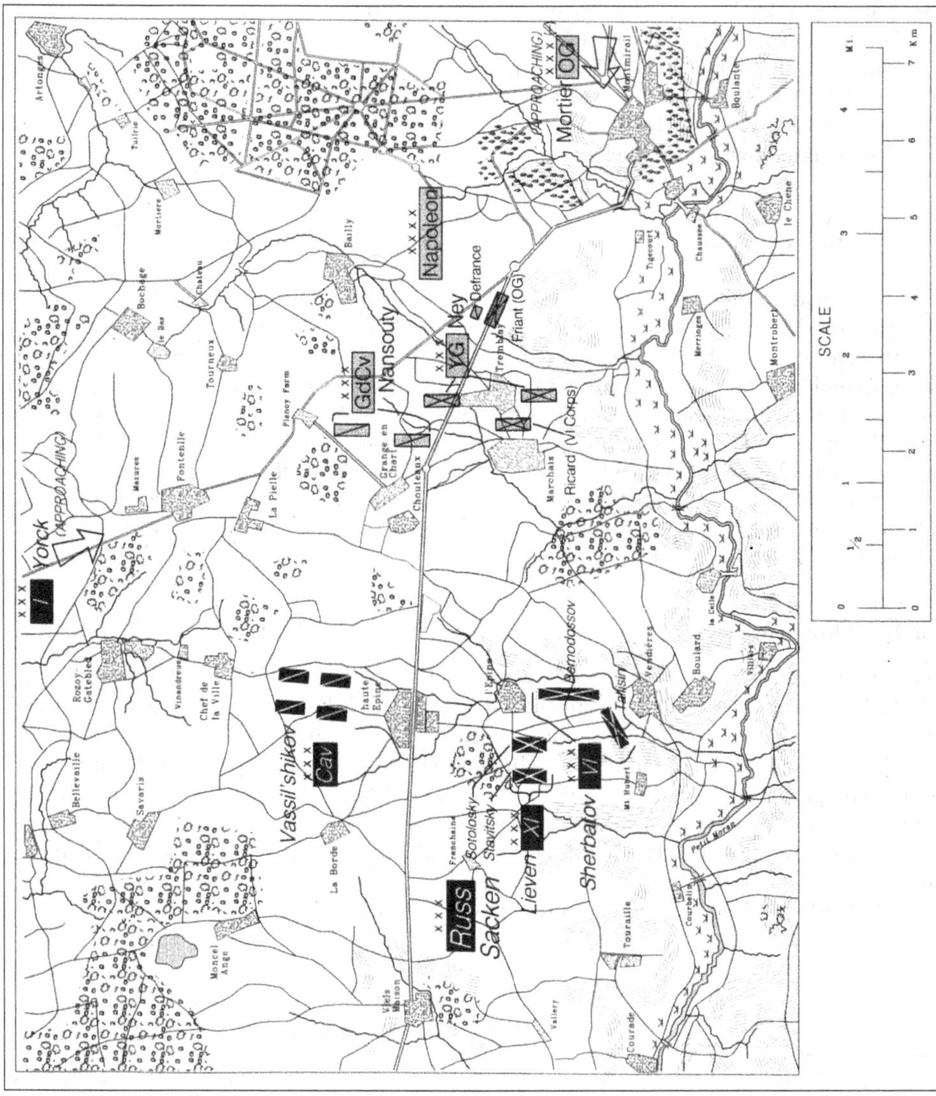

Map 6 Battle of Montmirail, February 11 1814

The French army, under Napoleon on 11 February, appears to have contained:[31]

Young Guard (Ney)	
1st Voltigeur Division (Meunier)	4,133
2nd Voltigeur Division (Decouz)	2,840
1st Division, VI Corps (Ricard)	2,917
3rd Guard Cavalry Division (Laferrière)	2,164
1st Guard Cavalry Division (Colbert)	2,582
3rd Voltigeur Division (Lefebvre-Desnoëttes)[32]	4,947
Gardes d'honneur (Defrance)	896
1st Old Guard Division (Friant)	4,796
2nd Old Guard Division (Michel)	3,878
Total:	27,153

Prussian sources estimated the French as having about 24,000 men present.[33]

The battlefield was bordered in the south by a valley in which the Petit-Morin flows – running westward from Montmirail to La Celle. A tributary of the Petit-Morin flows northwards, across the battlefield, in front of Marchais to La Motte. This steam would form the basis of the French line. A second tributary of the Petit-Morin flows northward further to the west behind Les Meulièrs. Though the Prussians would deploy forces forward of it, their principal lines were to be behind this stream. The land is rolling, with a number of large woods scattered across the battlefield. One significant wood covered what would be the French left flank, where it secured itself on the valley of the Petit-Morin. Marchais stood on the northern edge of this wood. The main road from Montmirail ran roughly east-west – passing to the north of Marchais and running to Les-Yeux-Blois-Haut-Epine.

French deployment

Napoleon deployed his troops in the following order: Ricard's 8th Division (VI Corps) stood behind Marchais, in Pomesson, in regimental columns. The 2/2nd and 7/4th Légère – detached from Ricard's division – took up positions in the small Bailly woods to the right of the Haute-Epine farm.[34] Maréchal Ney, with his two divisions (1st Voltigeur Division under Meunier and the 2nd Voltigeur Division under Curial), stood behind Ricard's 8th Division right and left from Le Tremblay. Nansouty's cavalry stood on the right between the road to Vieux-Maison and Château-Thierry. Friant's 1st Old Guard Division stood in battalion column on the road running from Montmirail to Vieux-Maison in reserve. The battalions stood at 100-pace intervals.[35] On their right flank stood the seven squadrons of Defrance's Gardes d'honneur.

31 Strength figures are from the French Army Archives, Section historique de l'armée de terre (SHAT), Chateau Vincennes, C^2 555 for 1 February 1814.

32 von Damitz identifies a cavalry division present under the command of Lefebvre-Desnoëttes. Based on material in the French archives records for 1 February, the only division that can be identified under Lefebvre-Desnoëttes is the 3rd Voltigeur Division. It is probable that Lefebvre-Desnoëttes had been reassigned to a cavalry division sometime between 1 and 10 February.

33 von Damitz, Vol. II, p. 121.

34 Koch, Vol. I, p. 240.

35 de Beauchamp, Vol. I. p. 271.

Sacken arrives on the field

When Sacken arrived on the battlefield, he saw the French before him and deployed his forces to attack them. He decided to attack through the Petit-Morin Valley and deployed to the right of Haute-Epine – and on both sides of l'Epine-aux-Bois – the most part of his infantry: the 7th and 18th Divisions (which were commanded by GM Talizin because of the illness of Count Scherbatov). The 10th Division stood to the left of them and farther to the left and north stood the 27th Division and General-adjutant Vassil'shikov's cavalry. All infantry was deployed in columns in two lines and, apparently, covered by a triple line of skirmishers.[36] The light artillery was situated in front of the first line on the flanks of infantry. Some of this artillery was deployed in a battery of 36 guns behind the ravine, which ran from Haute-Epine through l'Epine-aux-Bois and Vendières towards the Petit-Morin. This battery was designed to support his attack on Marchais. Heavy Battery #18 (12pdrs) stood to the right of the main road between the 18th and 10th Divisions. To the left of this battery, on a brushy knoll in the direction of Plenoy, stood a second battery. Two other heavy (12pdr) batteries were in reserve.[37] Sacken's command consisted of 14.000 men with 84 guns.

The Russian 11th Corps, under Lieven II, remained in reserve on the main road behind l'Epine-aux-Bois. Apparently the Prussian reserve cavalry, under General Jürgass, stood further to the rear in the direction of Tourneux. However, it was not in a position to intervene in the battle and did not appear on the field.[38]

Sacken began the battle. To capture the village of Marchais, which was the key to Petit-Morin Valley detachment, was created under the command of GM Heidenreich: the Pskov, Vladimir, Tambov and Kostroma Infantry Regiments and two companies from the 11th Jagers.[39] It consisted of 2,360 men with six light guns and the Lukovkin Cossack Regiment.[40]

The Russian infantry quickly crossed the ravine and occupied Marchais. Their right wing was near the grove and their left near a deep ravine. The Lukovkin Cossacks stood on the hill behind the right wing of infantry. The battery could not cross the ravine and was deployed behind the left flank, but at such a distance that it could not take part in battle. Both the villages of Le-Bois-Jean and Courmont – plus the Courmont woods – were overrun.

Friant.

Sacken sent a third column to attack the village of Marchais. This column – under General Heidenreich – consisted of 2,360 men, a Cossack regiment and six guns. This column was Scherbatov's 7th Division. Seeing Scherbatov advance, Ney sent forward Friant's four Old Guard battalions – which were standing by Meulière – to throw the Russians out of Haute-Epine. The Old Guard scattered the Russian skirmishers before them and threw the Russians back.

36 de Beauchamp, Vol. I, p. 271.
37 Bogdanovich, Vol. 1, p. 188; von Damitz, Vol. II, p. 122.
38 Sporschil, Vol. II, 1st Band, p. 397.
39 Bogdanovich, Vol. 1, p. 190.
40 Bogdanovich, Vol. 1, p. 190.

Montmirail, by Vernet.

Napoleon sought to stall Sacken's attack with a cannonade, while GD Michel marched his 2nd Old Guard Division forward from Montmirail. At 2:00 p.m. Napoleon ordered his forces to attack Sacken's left wing. The main attack could come only from the Haute-Epine dairy farm, which would cut off Sacken's infantry from Yorck's 1st Corps (Army of Silesia), which was advancing from Fontenelles. However, Sacken had deployed so much of his corps to defend this point that a French attack was unlikely to succeed.[41]

Count Nansouty was ordered to deploy his cavalry between the roads to Vieux-Maison and Fontenelles to threaten Sacken's left flank, while General Ricard – with 3,000 men – stood before Marchais defending against Sacken's attacks. At the same time, Friant came forward with four battalions of the Old Guard – two of grenadiers and two of chasseurs – down the main road to support the Haute-Epine dairy farm.[42] Seven squadrons of Gardes d'honneur covered the right flank of Friant's infantry. Maréchal Ney, with Decouz and Meunier's divisions, stood behind and to the right of Ricard near Le Tremblay. Farther to the right of Nansouty's cavalry, two regiments of light infantry occupied the grove near the village of Plenoy.

At the same time, Napoleon sent General Guyot forward with four service squadrons[43] from a position on the main road against Haute-Epine. They passed behind this farm – turning the Russian left wing to strike the Russian wing in the direction of l'Epine-aux-Bois.[44] Meanwhile, with the help of Friant's infantry, Ney broke through Sacken's extended first line near Haute-Epine.

41 Sporschil, Vol. II, 1st Band, p. 397.
42 Koch, Vol. I, p. 242.
43 These service squadrons consisted of one squadron of Grenadiers à cheval, one of Dragoons, one of Chasseurs à cheval and one of Lancers.
44 von Damitz, Vol. II, p. 124 & von Hiller, p. 127.

These attacks broke the Russian line and pushed them back to the woods occupied by part of Lieven's 11th Corps.

Sacken sent his second line forward and extended the cavalry on his left towards Fontenelles in order to establish contact with Yorck's advancing Prussians. The leading Prussian formations were in Fontenelles at that point. The Russian cavalry maneuvered to reach the advancing Prussians.

Napoleon perceived Sacken's intentions and ordered General Nansouty forward with the divisions of Laferrière, Colbert and Desnoëttes – plus that of General Guyot with the four guard service squadrons down the main road to strike the Russian center. The attack was very successful. The brigades of Dietrich and Blagovenzenko were broken and fled to reach the safety of the Vieux-Maison woods.[45] However, a counterattack by Vassil'shikov repulsed Nansouty and established communication with Prussian troops. General Guyot, with four Guard service squadrons, was ordered to attack infantry along the main road. Guyot's attack was successful.

The situation was somewhat restored by the arrival of the Prussian brigades of Pirch (1st Brigade) and Horn (7th Brigade) near Fontenelles. The Prussian reserve artillery was not present as the muddy roads had prevented its advance. Instead, it had been sent back to join the Prussian 8th Brigade.[46] Only the little artillery assigned to the Prussian brigades was able to reach the battlefield.[47] As there was only one battery of light guns per one Prussian brigade, Sacken ordered his two reserve heavy batteries to assist the Prussians.[48] Pirch's 1st Brigade passed through Fontenelles at 3:00 p.m. and from there marched on Tourneux. He stopped and organized his brigade into two lines while waiting for the 7th Brigade to close behind him and support his attack. The Reserve Cavalry, which had also left its guns behind because of the roads, observed the French cavalry on the right wing from a position near Château-Thierry.[49]

Generalmajor Pirch began preparing for a strike against the French right flank. The French occupied the Plenoy woods and they were attacked by the freiwilliger jägers of the 1st East Prussian and Leib-Grenadier Battalions. The Prussians sought to capture a bridge over a small stream near the Plenoy woods, which fell quickly as it was lightly defended. The 12 guns of 6pdr Batteries #2 and #3 were drawn forward with considerable effort – joining two Russian guns that were engaging the French flank.[50] At about this time a French officer was captured by the Russians, who reported to them that Napoleon was present on the field and told them of his victory over Olsufiev.

In the meantime, the Russian right wing continued fighting around the village of Pomesson and Marchais. The latter was overrun and lost twice when General Bernodessov (18th Division) drove forward yet again – driving Meunier's 1st Voltigeur (Young Guard) Division out of the village. Napoleon ordered Ricard and Meunier's fatigued divisions forward to recapture the village. Napoleon then ordered the seven squadrons of Defrance's Gardes d'honneur – standing on the road from La Ferté – to advance against the l'Epine-aux-Bois heights. Napoleon also directed Maréchal Lefebvre to bring forward two Old Guard Chasseurs à Pied battalions down the La Chaise-Les Grenots road and strike Marchais and cut off the retreat of the Russians near Marchais. Ricard sent four battalions up the Pomesson Valley to bring the Russians in Marchais under a crossfire. It was at this time that Napoleon dispatched Michel's 2nd Old Guard Division north (against the arriving Prussians).[51]

45 Koch, Vol. I, p. 243.
46 von Plotho, Vol. III, p. 180.
47 Sporschil, Vol. II, 1st Band, p. 398.
48 Bogdanovich, Vol. 1, p. 191.
49 von Damitz, Vol. II, p. 124.
50 von Plotho, Vol. III, p. 180; von Damitz, Vol. II, p. 125.
51 von Damitz, Vol. II, p. 127.

The French cavalry at Montmirail, by Wojciech Kossak.

Simultaneously, Maréchal Lefebvre and General Bertrand – leading two battalions of Old Guard Chasseurs à pied – burst into l'Epine-aux-Bois and Ricard began his attack from the direction of Pomesson. One of the participants remembered: "Our skirmishers were mixed with Frenchmen and were thrown back upon our position… Then we heard the fatal cry: 'La bayonets!' We cried: 'Hurrah!' and crushed the Frenchmen…" Despite the French superiority in artillery (all fields around Marchais had been ploughed with solid shot), the remnants of four Russian regiments – under the command of field officers Zigrot and Lopuchin – defended their post steadfastly. The Russian position in Marchais was hopeless and they were forced to withdraw. It was 5:00 p.m.

When the order for retreat was received the Russian troops crossed the deep ravine, but when they reached the opposite slope they were attacked. Standing on the crossroads to La Ferté, Dietrich and Blagovenzenko's brigades were struck by Defrance's dragoons and suffered huge casualties. The Russians deployed into several small squares and continued their retreat. The French pursued them, but not resolutely. Several hundred skirmishers who had been deployed in front of Marchais were cut off and only 30 of them broke through. Near the road to Château-Thierry, Russian squares were attacked heavily by cavalry – but with the help of two squadrons of Achtir Hussars, under the command of Rottmister Gorstkin, they repulsed their attack. The French also cut off the Sophia Infantry Regiment, but it too broke through.[52]

Sacken, seeing that he could not take Marchais (which he perceived as the key to the battlefield), ordered a withdrawal. He directed the guns on his right wing to withdraw and move under

52 Bogdanovich, p. 193.

the protection of Lieven's guns. He directed his cavalry, under General Vassil'shikov, to join with Yorck's corps.

Night ended the fighting. When the Russian corps arrived on the road to Château-Thierry, Sacken ordered General-adjutant Vasil'chikov and his cavalry to cover the retreat and to make the arrangements to move artillery through marsh and forest on the road to Viffort. In order to make the way easy in deep night – and under heavy rain along the unknown road – campfires were lit to illuminate the road. Each escaping Russian gun was moved by 50 cavalrymen with the help of ropes. At daybreak, the troops arrived in Viffort. Despite all efforts of Vassil'shikov and his troops, the Russians were obliged to leave eight disabled guns. The infantry continued the retreat by the road to Château-Thierry, where Sacken HQ was established. Yorck stayed between Fontenelles and Viffort.[53]

The Prussians arrive

As Marchais was falling, Yorck sent his forces forward – seeking with all his force to reach the road to Montmirail and stop the French advance.[54]

The French, at this time, overran Bailly and advanced. The Prussian 1st Brigade was ordered forward to engage the French and retake the village. Their attack was led by Generalmajor von Pirch II. The 1st East Prussian and West Prussian Grenadier Battalions – supported by two battalions of the 5th Silesian Landwehr Regiment – advanced in the first line with the remainder of the brigade. The Silesian and Leib Grenadier Battalions and the 13th Landwehr Regiment advanced behind them in support. Pirch stood at the head of the two grenadier battalions – screened by a swarm of Prussian skirmishers.[55]

Unfortunately for Pirch, the Prussian attack did not come soon enough and the French began reinforcing their right flank. Maréchal Mortier moved right of the road from Château-Thierry – behind the Bailly woods – and established himself. Four Old Guard battalions occupied the Bailly woods[56] and supported the French 2/2nd and 7/4th Légère Regiments that faced the advancing Prussians. The Prussian attack was greeted by the French with a heavy canister fire – supported by intense musketry – as they arrived a few hundred paces from the village of Bailly. As the Prussians continued advancing against Bailly, they were taken in the flank by French skirmishers. To their right, a Russian battery fired in support of their advance. However, the French defensive fire was too much and the Prussians began to withdraw. Captain von Wunck, commander of the 2/5th Silesian Landwehr Regiment, ordered his battalion forward in a bayonet attack against the French skirmishers on his flank to support his brigade's withdrawal.[57] It is reputed that Yorck personally ran up to the Prussian skirmish line to lend his moral authority to their fight. Rebutting the cries of his staff, warning of the danger, he reputedly said: "Do not disturb me. I want die if you cannot stop the enemy."[58]

Many Prussian officers and men were left lying in the field before Bailly. Pirch himself was wounded in this attack and Oberst von Losthin took over command of the brigade.[59]

53 Bogdanovich, Vol. 1, p. 194.
54 Sporschil, Vol. II, 1st Band, p. 399.
55 von Damitż, Vol. II, p. 128.
56 Sporschil identifies these woods as the Plenoy woods. Sporschil, Vol. 2, 1st Band, p. 400.
57 von Damitz, Vol. II, p. 129.
58 Bogdanovich, Vol. 1, p. 192.
59 von Plotho, Vol. III, p. 181.

As the Prussians fell back, General Michel led his four battalions forward. They were quickly supported by six others from the Bailly woods, which drove into the Prussian right flank. The Leib Grenadier Battalion and the 1/5th Silesian Landwehr Regiment advanced to meet the French attack. The Leib Fusilier Battalion – under the command of Capitain von Holleben, which had just passed through the defile by Tourneux – and the two battalions of the Leib Infantry Regiment arrived on the field and moved to the right of the woods. The 13th Silesian Landwehr Regiment moved behind them. The remainder of the 1st Brigade formed on the left wing of the Leib Regiment. The situation was becoming dangerous and Pirch led a bayonet attack that stabilized the front, though he was seriously wounded in the attack. This done, the Prussians once again began withdrawing.

As they withdrew, the 13th Silesian Landwehr Regiment and the Silesian Grenadier Battalion found themselves attacked by the French as they withdrew through the woods. Though they suffered a number of casualties, they succeeded in throwing the French back and resuming their withdrawal.

The casualties of this battle are, of course, subject to many interpretations. German sources give varying numbers for the Allied and French losses in the battle. Sporschil and von Hiller state the French lost 2,000 dead and wounded. Sources vary on the Allied losses. Sporschil states that the Russians lost nine guns and 1,500 dead and wounded, while the Prussian 1st Brigade lost 33 officers and 844 men. He gives no return for the Prussian 7th Brigade. Von Hiller gives the Allied losses at 3,000 men, 13 guns and the Prussians at 900.[60] Toll reports that the Russians lost 2,800 men – including 800 prisoners – and the Prussians lost 30 officers and 860 men.[61]

Von Plotho states that the Russians lost nine guns and 1,000 prisoners – plus 1,500 dead and wounded. He lists the 1st Prussian Brigade as losing 33 officers and 844 men. Unfortunately, he also provides no returns for any losses by the 7th Brigade.[62]

Von Damitz gives the Russian losses at 2,000 dead and wounded, and 700-800 prisoners and 13 guns taken. He states that the Prussian losses were 33 officers and 844 men. He also gives the French losses at about 2,000 men.[63]

Koch gives the Allied losses at 26 guns, 200 wagons, 708 prisoners and 3,000 killed and wounded (with General Pirch being wounded). He gives the French losses at 2,000 men with generals Nansouty, Michel and Boudin de Roville wounded (as were nearly all the senior officers of Ricard's 8th Division).[64] There is enough consensus to conclude that the French did lose about 2,000 men, while the Allies lost about 3,000 dead and wounded and 700-plus prisoners. As for the numbers of guns lost, the numbers vary too much to reach a definitive conclusion.

The pursuit

Napoleon was deeply involved in his gamble to destroy Blücher's army and had every intention to reap the maximum advantage from his success at Montmirail and Champaubert. He again sent orders to Macdonald directing him to recapture Château-Thierry and deny the enemy the use of its bridge over the Marne. On the 12th, he planned to pursue Sacken and Yorck with as much of his army as was available. If things worked out he would completely destroy these two corps, but everything depended on Macdonald capturing the bridge at Château-Thierry.

60 Sporschil, Vol. 2, 1st Band, p. 400; von Hiller, p. 120.
61 von Bernhardi, Vol. 4, 7th Book, p. 392.
62 von Plotho, Vol. III, p. 182.
63 von Damitz, Vol. II, p. 132.
64 Koch, Vol. I, pp. 245-6.

Wounded following Montmirail, by Delécluze.

In spite of his second victory at Montmirail, Napoleon still felt his position as critical. Olsufiev had been destroyed and Sacken had been heavily engaged and was seriously shaken. Even Yorck had been repulsed. Napoleon estimated that he had eliminated a total of about 11,000 Prussians and Russians and captured 47 guns captured between Champaubert and Montmirail. However, the Marne Valley was still under Allied control. The commands of Sacken and Yorck still contained some 30,000 versus about 15,000 French. In addition, Blücher stood in his rear and would most likely come to the aid of his subordinates with his 20,000 fresh troops and 80 guns.

Napoleon had little doubt that Blücher would brush aside Marmont's 4,000 recruits if he chose to. Finally, for the last three days, Napoleon had ignored Schwarzenberg and his large army. Poor Victor, charged with watching Schwarzenberg's overwhelming force, was already calling for Napoleon's help. Despite all the problems, Napoleon's critical genius saw an opportunity and he seized it. Schwarzenberg was still the old, unaggressive man he had been in 1813 and would not do anything sudden or surprising. Blücher was the aggressive threat, not Schwarzenberg, so it was Blücher that had to be dealt with first.

Napoleon was taking substantial risks in his effort to destroy Blücher's army, but the potential benefits were huge and he wanted to maximize the fruits from his success at Montmirail. On 12 February he planned to pursue Sacken and Yorck with everything he had at his disposal. Once again he ordered Macdonald to recapture Château-Thierry and deny the Allies the use of its bridge over the Marne. Macdonald would close the only line of retreat for these two corps. If things went well he would completely destroy these two corps, but everything depended on Macdonald capturing the bridge at Château-Thierry.

The problem facing Napoleon was: was it possible to continue pushing the Army of Silesia further north – and further away from Schwarzenberg – without jeopardizing Paris. Napoleon had to destroy Sacken and Yorck quickly if he was to restore his situation.

The Battle of Château-Thierry – 12 February

At the break of dawn on 12 February, Sacken's corps passed through the Prussian lines at Montfaucon. Sacken placed a brigade containing the Tambov and Kostroma Regiments, under General Heidenreich, on the left bank of the Marne. Prussian General Katzler occupied the heights by Montfaucon with the Prussian advanced guard. Behind him stood the 1st and 7th Prussian Brigades and the Prussian Reserve Cavalry of General Jürgass.

At around 8:00 a.m.[65] Napoleon sent Saint-Germain's cavalry division and Friant's 1st Old Guard Division, less 1st Brigade, to Vieux-Maison in case Feldmarschal Blücher sought to move through Montmirail. Mortier moved with the Young Guard and the Gardes d'honneur to Fontenelles. Napoleon then took his staff, the reserve artillery and Christiani's 2nd Old Guard Division and marched on Vieux-Maison, where he had left his reserve. What remained of Ricard's exhausted 8th Division was left in Montmirail.

Earlier that morning, Napoleon had rallied General Saint-Germain with a column of 2,400 cavalry – forming the I, II and V Cavalry Corps at Vieux-Maison.[66] These men were recently remounted. Acting on Napoleon's orders, Macdonald had dispatched them in pursuit of Sacken's rearguard. Napoleon had detached Friant's 1st Old Guard Division and posted them in Vieux-Maison, except for four battalions of Old Guard Grenadiers, which he was to take with him.

Once joined with the reserve, Napoleon advanced down the road through Rozoy towards Château-Thierry. General Christiani – now commanding the 2nd Old Guard Division in Michel's place – and Colbert led the advance under the command of Maréchal Mortier.[67] Meunier's 1st Voltigeur Division and four battalions of Friant's 1st Old Guard Division moved along the side roads at the *pas de course*[68] – seeking the Allies. Napoleon's éclaireurs, which preceded his advance, found the road littered with abandoned vehicles and caissons.

Two miles beyond Fontenelles, the vanguard came in contact with the Prussian outposts, which fell back upon their reserves. Around 1:00 p.m., the Gardes d'honneur encountered the lead elements of Horn's 7th Brigade on the slopes of the Caquerets hills. As Christiani arrived before Caquerets he saw General Katzler's forces deployed in battle order across the heights behind a stream. The stream was crossed by a single bridge and stood between two wooded hills. Katzler was positioned to contest Napoleon's march down the road to Château-Thierry. The 1/,2/2nd East Prussian Infantry Regiment stood in the first line with the skirmishers of the four musketeer battalions of the 1st and 2nd East Prussian Infantry Regiments – under Major von Stockhausen – posted in the village of Viffort and covering the ground before it.

Though the Gardes d'honneur led the approach to the Prussian position,[69] Katzler was promptly attacked by the duty squadrons – supported by two Old Guard Chasseurs à Pied battalions and a battery. Katzler's troops delayed the advancing French in this position for a while. However, when the French began turning their flanks, they were obliged to withdraw. From their initial position they pulled back to a second defile defended by General von Horn's 7th Brigade.

The Prussians saw French infantry advancing down both sides of the road from Viffort, while Maréchal Mortier's cavalry marched on the right and another force of cavalry (accompanying Napoleon) advanced up the left from the Caquerets heights.[70]

The French advance was covered by a skirmish line that quickly engaged the Prussian skirmishers. The right flank of the Prussian line was covered by the skirmishers of the 2nd Silesian and the Leib-Grenadier Battalions. The left flank was covered by the skirmishers of the Fus/,1/ Leib Infantry Regiment. The left flank was fixed on the Petite-Noue farm and a small woods.

65 de Vaudoncourt, Vol. I, p. 183.
66 von Damitz, Vol. II, p. 136; Koch, Vol. I, p. 248.
67 von Damitz, Vol. II, p. 135.
68 The *pas de course* is a cadenced run of 250 paces per minute. de Beauchamp, Vol. I. p. 278.
69 Koch, Vol. I, p. 248.
70 von Damitz is probably referring to the service squadrons that operated as Napoleon's guard and were commanded by Guyot. Von Damitz, Vol. II, p. 136.

The French brought two cannon forward and began to bombard the Prussian lines, but made no effort to advance against the Allied flank. Their action was more to hold it in place while a major force of cavalry turned their left flank in an effort to get to the Marne bridge. The remainder of the French force began to deploy before the Allied lines.

With a major fight about to occur with their backs to the river, Yorck ordered the immediate withdrawal of the baggage and equipment over the Marne.

As the French cavalry maneuvered against the Allied left, on the battle line a cannonade ensued. Napoleon sent 200 grenadiers to seize the only breach the Prussian gunners had neglected to cover (near the village of Petite-Noue).[71] They slipped across the stream and into Petite-Noue, chased out the Prussian sharpshooters and took control of the village. At the same time, Mortier sent an attack up the hills by the six battalions of the Guard – under Christiani – supported by the rest of the infantry. The elite cavalry then moved through the narrow defile. The four divisions of Laferrière, Lefebvre-Desnoëttes, Colbert and Defrance – advancing with Ney – maneuvered to the left flank of the Prussian 7th Brigade in the direction of the Grande-Baloy farm. The Russian cavalry standing before Petite-Baloy drew back and joined the dragoon regiment standing behind it. With a major cavalry force moving on their left, Yorck directed Jürgass to take the Prussian Reserve Cavalry and move to intercept the French. Jürgass moved from his position on the right of the road to intercept the French.

The sequence is unclear, but it appears that before Jürgass arrived, the French cavalry – consisting of about 20 weak squadrons – charged and broke three squares. The Prussian cavalry did eventually arrive and it appears to have stabilized the situation long enough to permit a reasonably orderly withdrawal, but was unable to recover the initiative for the Prussians.

The first cavalry versus cavalry charge occurred when the French 10th Hussars attacked the force of Prussian Landwehr cavalry standing on the Allied left flank. Oberstleutnant von Sohr, with the Brandenburg Hussars of Horn's 7th Brigade, had attached itself to the Reserve Cavalry as it marched past. As the French 10th Hussars appeared to be driving back the Landwehr cavalry, Oberstleutenant von Sohr led the Brandenburg Hussars forward – driving them back and forcing them to leave the field.[72]

When Jürgass' cavalry arrived, it formed in two ranks. They totaled about 3,000 cavalry; however a large portion of the Prussian cavalry was Landwehr or militia. Facing them was the cream of the French cavalry arm.[73]

The French cavalry – under Laferrière and Defrance[74] – was formed in a thick mass, with the Guard Dragoons in the front rank and cuirassiers, carabiniers and Grenadiers à cheval in the second. When they collided, a tremendous melee resulted. General Jürgass advanced with the Lithuanian and 1st West Prussian Dragoon Regiments. Some French dragoons stopped at the range of half a musket shot and attempted to stop the advancing Prussian cavalry with a salvo of carbine fire.[75] Despite the fire, the two regimental colonels – von Below and von Unruh – ordered their regiments forward. A furious melee ensued. Adjacent to them, the Brandenburg Hussars engaged the French 10th Hussar Regiment in an inconclusive engagement.[76] Other French dragoons (recently drawn from Spain) struck the Russian dragoon regiment – crushing it under their weight of their charge. These two formations fought between the farms of Petite-Baloy and

71 Koch, Vol. I, p. 249.
72 von Damitz, Vol. II, p. 138.
73 Koch, Vol. I, p. 249.
74 de Vaudoncourt, Vol. I, p. 182.
75 von Damitz, Vol. II, p. 139.
76 von Ardenne, p. 261.

de la Motte, to the right of the main road from Montmirail to Château-Thierry. The Prussian first line was crushed and thrown back on the second line – breaking it and throwing both back in confusion. In a second's time, both lines were destroyed and scattered.[77] Among the trophies left behind were two cannon and a howitzer.[78]

Their flank threatened by the French cavalry, General Yorck then ordered the Prussian 1st and 7th Brigades to pull back and link up with the Russians standing by the La Trinit farm. A strong skirmish line was deployed before both Prussian brigades formed with the skirmishes of the Leib Fusilier Battalion and supported by the 15th Silesian Landwehr Regiment. Behind this position stood the Prussian reserve cavalry on the right of the road. The Russians stood on the left by the Petite-Baloy farm. Further to the rear stood a Russian jager battalion. The Prussian 1st and 7th Brigades began to withdraw. The sharpshooters of Horn's 7th Brigade returned to their battalions and, with great calm and control, marched from their hill position across the open ground by Château-Thierry – the greatest portion of the 1st Brigade down the right of the road. This force consisted of the 1st East Prussian Regiment, the Silesian and Leib Grenadier Battalions and the weakened 5th and 13th Silesian Landwehr Regiments. Rearranging his force once it reached the main road, Horn joined them to the 1/, 2/Leib Infantry Regiment, the Leib-Fusilier Battalion, the West Prussian Grenadier Battalion and the Brandenburg Hussars, which served as a rearguard. The 15th Silesian Landwehr was then detached to the left flank to hold the La Trinit farm. Few of these men were able to rejoin the brigade, as they were caught and cut down that evening by French cavalry.[79]

As the rest of the rearguard withdrew, the Leib Regiment formed the rear of the column. They were surrounded by French cavalry, which attacked repeatedly the infantry around them. As the Leib Regiment moved towards their escape, a French dragoon regiment swung onto the road – blocking its retreat. The Leib Regiment lowered its bayonets and charged the cavalry – driving them away and clearing the path of their advance.[80]

While the French cavalry attack was starting, two battalions of Old Guard grenadiers – under General Petit, supported by the service squadrons – moved along the left of the main highway and drove the Prussians, under Prince Wilhelm von Preussen, back to the Nesle plateau and into Château-Thierry. A Russian brigade under General Heidenreich[81] – consisting of the Tambov and Kostroma Infantry Regiments – stood on the right wing of the Allied line between the main road and a small woods. It was supported by three cannon. Napoleon ordered General Belliard, with the service squadrons, to strike them. General Heidenreich saw the advancing danger and put both of his regiments into square, covered them with skirmishers and sought to withdraw.[82]

The Russian skirmishers were ridden down and scattered by the French cavalry. After firing most of its ammunition, the Russian square was crushed and General Heidenreich was taken prisoner along with three cannon. Those Russians not taken prisoner or killed fled into the Marne Valley or the city of Château-Thierry.

As the Prussian 7th Brigade moved through the open ground before Château-Thierry, they were threatened by the cavalry of General Letort. Letort had moved his forces around the Nogentel woods and appeared suddenly behind the village of Nogentel. The 1st Prussian Brigade appeared before them as they stood by Nogentel. They charged – catching the 5th Silesian Landwehr

77 Sporschil, Vol. 2, 1st Band, p. 402; Koch, Vol. I, p. 250.
78 de Vaudoncourt, Vol. I, p. 182.
79 von Damitz, Vol. II, p. 141.
80 von Ardenne, p. 261.
81 Heidenreich was a brigade commander in the Russian 18th Division.
82 Sporschil, Vol. 2, 1st Band, p. 403.

Regiment and the Silesian and Leib Grenadier Battalions as they cleared the village – inflicting numerous casualties on them. Two guns and a howitzer from the 6pdr Foot Battery #2 were lost to the French.[83] Supported by the freiwilliger jägers of the Brandenburg Hussars, Horn's sharpshooters covered the rear of the Prussian column.

While the 1st Brigade was covering the Allied rear, the 7th Brigade took up positions in the defile by the pontoon bridge over the Marne. The 2/2nd East Prussian and the 2/1st East Prussian Regiments brought up the rear under the command of Major von Stockhausen.[84] As Horn then drew his battalion masses into the suburbs of Château-Thierry, he encountered the two battalions under Major Stockhausen, which had positioned themselves in a ditch and waited for the advancing French.

As more and more of the Allies cleared through Château-Thierry, Stockhausen pulled his troops back. A rearguard was established with the Leib Fusilier Battalion under the command of Captain von Holleben. They were to hold the pontoon bridge until Stockhausen's two battalions had crossed.

However, Stockhausen found himself having to hold off an attack by the Grenadiers à cheval service squadron under General Guyot. Their action permitted the passage of the Allied troops, their artillery and baggage over the Marne, but time was running out for them to make their escape. French skirmishers were already firing on the pontoon bridge as Stockhausen's men fought their way back through the streets of Château-Thierry towards the bridge. The Prussian rearguard – supported by a 12pdr battery – began a heavy supporting fire in an effort to keep the bridge clear of French. It was not enough and the bridge was destroyed – stranding Stockhausen and his men. The destruction of the bridge caused 400 Prussians to fall into French hands.

On the far bank of the Marne, the Allied rearguard – supported by the 12pdr battery – maintained a heavy fire (preventing any immediate pursuit) and gave Yorck and Sacken time to get their withdrawal towards Soissons well under way.

With the escape of the Allies over the Marne bridge, the battle effectively ended. According to Sporschil, the Allies lost about 2,000 men and the French lost about 400 men.[85] Von Damitz gives the Prussian losses at 22 officers and 1,229 other ranks dead and wounded. He also states that three guns were lost. He puts the Russian losses at from 1,200 to 1,500 men.[86] Toll states that Yorck lost 22 officers and 1,229 men, plus three dismounted cannon that were abandoned. He gives the Russian losses at 1,500 men and French losses at 600.[87]

Houssaye gives the Allied losses at 3,000 prisoners, plus 1,500 Russian and 1,250 Prussians *hors de combat* (in addition to 20 guns and a large number of wagons). He lists the French losses at 600. Koch lists the French losses at 400 and gives the Allied losses at three guns, 1,200 dead and wounded and 1,800 prisoners – including General Heidenreich.[88]

The consensus indicates that the French lost about 500 men. The Prussians lost exactly 22 officers and 1,229 men, while the Russian losses seem to have been pretty consistently estimated at 1,500 men.

Sacken and Yorck marched to Qulchy-la-Ville. Around midnight, Prince Wilhelm von Preussen brought his 8th Brigade into Qulchy-le-Chatel and Katzler stood in the rear of the Allied column

83 von Damitz, Vol. II, p. 143.
84 These were units drawn from the Prussian 2nd Brigade.
85 Sporschil, Vol. 2, 1st Band, p. 404.
86 von Damitz, Vol. II, p. 46.
87 von Bernhardi, Vol. 4, 7th Book, p. 396.
88 Koch, Vol. I, p. 253.

as the rearguard. Further back, on the Marne, the Allies watched the French with a contingent of Karpov's Cossacks.

After the battle

In the hours that followed, Napoleon's sappers – helped by the Sailors of the Guard – repaired the bridge as Napoleon had no bridging train. As a result, it was 24 hours before Mortier and the cavalry could resume their pursuit. By that time, the Allies had placed another river (the Ourcq) between themselves and the pursuing French.

Mortier pursued the defeated Allies as they retreated toward Soissons – taking with him Christiani, Colbert, the Gardes d'honneur, artillery and sappers while the Emperor returned to Montmirail.

In spite of his third success against Blücher forces, Napoleon was bitterly disappointed. The results fell short of his goal as he had hoped to completely destroy Yorck and Sacken's corps. Macdonald had scarcely advanced eastward and failed to grasp the importance of retaking Château-Thierry and this invaluable bridge over the Marne. If Macdonald had captured the Château-Thierry bridge, with their retreat route to Epernay cut off by the Guard cavalry, Yorck and Sacken's defeated corps would have been forced to surrender or to fight another battle under very unfavorable conditions. Instead, they were able to escape.

The Battle of Château-Thierry, like that of Montmirail, had been won by the Guards' outstanding performances. In a dispatch to Savary, Napoleon wrote: "My Foot and Horse Guard covered themselves with glory. The dragoons distinguished themselves with a performance comparable to those romances of the Age of Chivalry in which a single knight would take three or four hundred adversaries at once. The enemy seemed struck by a singular terror."[89]

The Allied withdrawal after Château-Thierry

During the night of 12-13 February, generals Yorck and Sacken dragged their battle-weary corps to the heights overlooking the right bank of the Marne. While the battle raged in Château-Thierry, Prince Wilhelm von Preussen had marched his brigade forward towards Soissons and placed the road to La Ferté, below Jouarre, under observation with the Leib Hussar Regiment. His goal was to capture Soissons and to march over the road from Rheims and Châlons and reunite with Blücher.

Yorck was in Fismes and Sacken had withdrawn to Rheims by crossing through La Fire and Tardenois. All the while Blücher had remained immobile at Vertus – awaiting news from his lieutenants. He soon received word that they had been engaged by Napoleon himself and that they were withdrawing on Sézanne. Rather foolishly, Blücher deluded himself into thinking that Marmont's corps – then in Etoges – had no goal other than to cover a withdrawal, so he judged it time to advance and attack Marmont as he marched against Montmirail.

On 13 February he sent his 3,000-man advanced guard forward to march to La Ferté, followed by Kleist and Kapsevich's corps. Kleist's advanced guard had been reinforced by the 7th and 37th Jager Regiments and the horse battery of Colonel Schindschin from Kapsevich's corps.[90] The remains of Olsufiev's corps was ordered to march to Champaubert in order to cover the southern flank of the Army of Silesia.

Marmont was in position at Etoges, with his right supported by the city of Etoges and his left on a plateau occupied by Grouchy's cavalry.

89 Lachouque, p. 356.
90 Langeron, p. 397.

The head of the Russian advanced guard – under the orders of Oberst von Blücher – marched directly against Etoges, while Ziethen moved along the heights to the right of the village and sent his columns forward under the cover of his artillery. Their flank turned, the French cavalry maneuvered to cover the withdrawal of the French infantry on Montmirail – abandoning Etoges to the Allies.

Oberst von Blücher entered Etoges – pushing the French rearguard vigorously towards Champaubert – and positioned himself and Ziethen's 11th Brigade between that village and Fromentières. The two Allied army corps established themselves behind Champaubert, while at the same time sending scouting parties out to clear their flanks and to search for French forces in the directions of Sézanne and Corrobert.[91]

Marmont drew his forces together and established himself in a new blocking position by Vauchamps. He covered his infantry with Grouchy's cavalry.

Ziethen.

The French advance after Château-Thierry

At the break of day on 13 February, the French army began rebuilding the bridge at Château-Thierry. This work was not easy, as the Cossacks constantly fired at the engineers building the bridge. Efforts to locate a boat to cross the river failed until a non-combatant brought a boat and braved the hail of fire – taking a dozen soldiers to the far side. Once across the river, they held the Cossacks at bay long enough for more and more to cross. Soon, work on the bridge was well under way. A first bridge was quickly erected, and soon a second was in place. This second bridge was built by the citizens of Château-Thierry, not by the army.

The Young Guard quickly crossed at the *pas de course* and took positions on the far bank. The cavalry followed behind them to support them should Allied cavalry be nearby. Within six hours, the entire French army had crossed the Marne and was marching in pursuit of Yorck and Sacken.[92]

Maréchal Mortier – commanding the divisions of Christiani, Colbert and Defrance – pursued Yorck and Sacken as far as Rocourt. Their pursuit was sufficiently rigorous so as to capture 300-400 prisoners and to force the destruction of a large number of caissons.

The refugees from the Allied army that had thrown themselves into the woods to escape the French bayonets now found themselves at the mercy of the French citizens, who were exasperated by the treatment they had received from the conquering Allied armies. More than 2,000 such refugees were rounded up – as well as large numbers of arms and munitions.

Napoleon, learning of Blücher's push against Marmont, did not hesitate for a moment to march to the new opportunity. He left Mortier with the divisions of Christiani, Colbert and Defrance to watch the beaten corps of Yorck and Sacken, while he wheeled Friant's 1st Old Guard Division and the Cavalry of General Saint-Germain to move from Vieux-Maison to Montmirail. They joined Ney's Corps and the rest of the Guard Cavalry en route and arrived in Montmirail at 8:00 a.m. – joining Marmont as he continued to withdraw before Blücher's Prussians. Once united, the French army abandoned their defensive and assumed the offense.

91 Koch, Vol. I, p. 257.
92 Koch, Vol. I, p. 256.

As Napoleon advanced on Vauchamps, he ordered Ricard's 8th Division to march down the right of the road while Lagrange's 3rd Division, VI Corps, marched down the left of the road. Saint-Germain's cavalry united with that of General Grouchy and stood on the left of the French position between l'Echelle and Haute-Feuille. On the road marched the Old Guard divisions and Ney's corps – serving as a reserve for Marmont's corps. On the French right wing stood the Guard Cavalry divisions of Laferrière, Desnoëttes and Guyot under the command of General Nansouty. Leval's 7th Division, veterans recalled from Spain, was approaching from the direction of Sézanne.[93]

The French army, standing before Vauchamps, contained about 15,000 infantry and 7,000 cavalry. Before them stood 21,000 Allied infantry and 8,400 cavalry. It was almost 9:00 a.m. when Napoleon arrived to the cheers of his troops. The French, who had executed a forced march that evening, prepared for battle.

The Battle of Vauchamps – 14 February

The Prussians had already occupied Vauchamps when Marmont received the order to attack the village frontally. Grouchy – who had also assumed command of Saint-Germain's cavalry division – was ordered to turn the position by the right and to move through the woods by l'Echelle, Haute-Feuille and Serrechamp. The foot guard and the horse guard formed the reserve on the main road. Blücher was quickly advised by his scouting parties that large masses of French cavalry had arrived on the heights to his right and were maneuvering to turn his flank, while a large force of infantry had appeared on his left – marching from Sézanne to Montmirail.[94] Blücher was greatly disturbed by the appearance of the infantry as he knew it was probably Napoleon that was about to arrive on his left. He quickly shifted two cavalry regiments from his reserve to his left flank to support them against this attack.

In fact, it was not Napoleon, but Leval's 7th Division (VII Corps). Leval commanded 13 battalions – two foot and one horse battery – with a total of about 4,500 men. This was not an insignificant force, however, as they were veterans of Spain. Oudinot had detached Leval, but they were too far from Montmirail to take part in the action.

Vauchamps was defended by Prussian infantry. The 11th and 12th Fusilier Companies of the Fus/2nd Silesian Infantry Regiment – under Major von Watzdorf – were posted in the small woods on the French left flank[95] (and more was in a small woods before the village). General von Ziethen had covered the 11th Brigade with skirmishers from the 10th Infantry Regiment and had supported them with the 10th Reserve Infantry Regiment. He retained a reserve consisting of three battalions and two companies of Silesian Schützen – under the command of Major von Lettow – behind the village of Vauchamps. On the edge of the village stood the 2/1st Silesian and 2/10th Reserve (22nd) Infantry Regiment.[96]

Behind the Prussian left wing stood the advanced guard, 3,000 Russian infantry and two cavalry regiments.

At 10:00 a.m. Ricard's 8th Division was ordered to take the village. At the same time, as he began his advance, a French cavalry column with three regiments had already taken up position on the Prussian right flank. His artillery began firing on the skirmishers hiding in the woods – inflicting heavy casualties on them. To support the skirmishers, the 1/1st Silesian Infantry Regiment was

93 von Damitz, Vol. II, p. 159.
94 Koch, Vol. I, p. 258.
95 von Ebertz, p. 151.
96 von Damitz, Vol. II, p. 161.

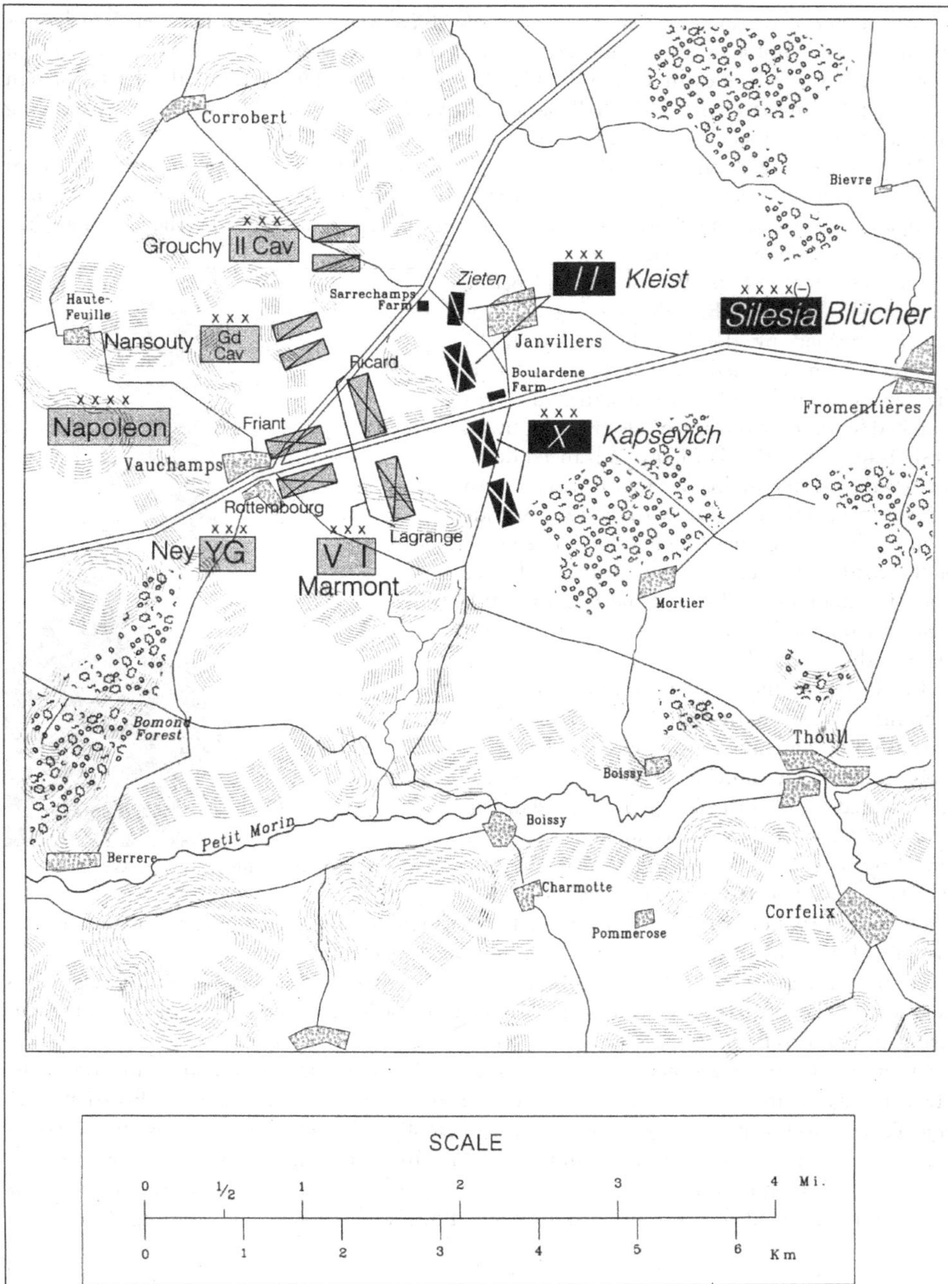

Map 7 Battle of Vauchamps, February 14 1814, 11:00 a.m.

shifted to the right of Vauchamps – supported by half of 6pdr Battery #9 and the 160 men of the 7th Silesian Landwehr Cavalry Regiment. A squadron of the 1st Silesian Hussars, under the command of Rittmeister von Hertel, was sent forward to a position between Vauchamps and the woods to protect the skirmishers should French cavalry be sent forward. As the French approached, the 7th Silesian Landwehr Cavalry, 1st Silesian Hussars and the East Prussian Cuirassier Regiment escorted the half battery forward and began to bombard the advancing French. When the French continued to advance, this force quickly withdrew.[97]

Ricard's 1st Brigade approached on the right – covered by the Beaumont woods. Ricard moved against the Prussian right – striking the Prussian skirmishers, the 11th and 12th Fusilier Companies of Major von Watzdorf – on their right. Despite their efforts, the Prussian skirmishers were soon overpowered.

Prince August of Prussia.

The main body of the Prussians stood before Fromentières. When the advanced guard was heavily engaged by the French cavalry, Kleist and Kapsevich marched their forces to support the advanced guard. Kleist's Prussian 2nd Corps marched forward on the north side of the highway, while Kapsevich's Russian Corps advanced down the south of the highway. The Prussian 10th Brigade formed the first line, with the 12th Brigade forming the second line. About 1,000 paces north of the road, a Russian battery advanced. Prince August von Preussen directed the 9th and 10th Fusilier Companies, Fus/2nd Silesian Regiment, to cover this battery.[98]

The Prussian 2nd Brigade, formed in closed columns,[99] attacked frontally – covered with a skirmish line and moving along the left of the main road. They quickly overran the woods and cleared it of Prussians. The Prussians in Vauchamps prepared for the assault and were reinforced by portions of the rearguard, under Graf Haacke, and supported by a horse battery. Their combined efforts stopped Ricard's advance. The Prussians, encouraged by the repulse of Ricard's two brigades, pushed out of Vauchamps to chase the defeated French columns.

At about the same time, the Brandenburg Cuirassier and 8th Silesian Landwehr Regiments were sent to the left flank to reinforce it. A large force of French cavalry was observed maneuvering around this flank.[100]

Marmont, having no other cavalry available, ordered his escort squadron to attack the advancing Prussians. They succeeded in doing little more than alarming the Prussians and causing them to break stride for a few moments. Napoleon, however, upon seeing the Prussians pause to deal with this feeble attack, sent General Lion forward with his four service squadrons.[101]

Two French cavalry squadrons, which had moved between Sarrechamp and the small woods to the right, charged forward and struck at the Prussian reinforcements coming down from

97 von Plotho, Vol. III, p. 186.
98 von Ebertz, p. 153.
99 Sporschil, Vol. II, 1st Band, p. 411.
100 von Plotho, Vol. III, p. 187.
101 von Damitz, Vol. II, p. 165; Sporschil, Vol. II, 1st Band, p. 411; von Plotho, Vol. III, p. 187.

Janvilliers. Only the squadron of Rittmeister von Hertel stood between them and von Haacke's horse battery standing on the right of the road. Von Hertel's tiny force was swept aside and the French cavalry rushed forward – seizing a battery. Seeing the danger, the chief of staff of the 2nd Army Corps – Oberst von Grolmann – ordered the 7th Silesian Landwehr Cavalry Regiment (160 men under Major von Schmidt) forward.[102] The Landwehr cavalry succeeded in stopping the French and saving the battery momentarily. At this point, Lion's service squadrons rushed forward, chased back the 7th Silesian Landwehr, captured the battery and moved against the Prussian infantry standing before them. One Prussian battalion succeeded in throwing itself into a farm on the left of the village, but the rest were sabered under the eyes of the main Prussian army – formed 600 or 700 meters to the rear.

A force of French hussars then pulled onto the field. Facing them, Oberst Graf Haacke drew forward two squadrons of the East Prussian Cuirassiers and the 8th Landwehr Cavalry Regiment. They formed a line, with the cuirassiers on the right, the Landwehr in the middle and the 1st Silesian Hussars on the left. Facing them was an overwhelming force of French cavalry under GD Grouchy.

Meanwhile, two companies of Old Guard Chasseurs à pied moved up to the farm – on the left of the village – where the Prussian battalion had taken refuge, broke into the courtyard and took the Prussians prisoner. As this occurred along the road, on the right of the road the Guard cavalry and the French cuirassiers engaged the force of Prussian cuirassiers and hussars von Haacke had organized. After several charges, the Prussian cavalry was thrown back by the divisions of Lefebvre-Desnoëttes and Laferrière. They fell back towards the extreme left of the Prussian line of infantry. The infantry, fearing attack, responded by forming itself into square. Two Russian jager battalions on the left flank also formed in square and fought off the French attacks with great bravery.[103]

About this time, Kleist's 2nd Corps and Kapsevich's 10th Corps reached Janvilliers and the Boularderie farm. The 10th Brigade, under General von Pirch, formed itself on the right of the road with its left flank on the road and its right flank in a small wood occupied by the 3/7th Reserve (19th) Infantry Regiment.[104] The Fus/2nd West Prussian Infantry Regiment was ordered into Janvilliers, which was already occupied by a force of Prussian cavalry.

The 12th Brigade of Prince August von Preussen stood behind the 10th Brigade and detached the Fus/,2/11th Reserve (23rd) Infantry Regiment towards Janvilliers. The fusiliers detached their skirmishers into the village and the musketeer battalion took up a position in the church courtyard. Both battalions remained formed. The Russians placed a battery on the heights to the right of the village and fired on the French cavalry as it approached.[105]

The entire French army was in motion. Lagrange's 3rd Division, VI Corps, was marched in column by regiment along the right of the road. A little to the left, and in the same order, followed Ricard's 8th Division. Following the line infantry came the Young Guard under the orders of Ney – to the right of which marched the Old Guard. Three kilometers to the rear, Leval's 7th Division, VII Corps, scrambled to catch up – eager to come to grips with France's enemies. On the flank, with all the line cavalry, Grouchy completed his movement to turn the Allied right flank.[106]

Kleist sent the 3/7th Reserve (19th) Infantry Regiment to his right flank to occupy the Sarrechamp farm, and the Russian 10th Corps – under Kapsevich – formed itself in battalion masses to the left of the road.

102 von Damitz, Vol. II, p. 164.
103 Sporschil, Vol. II, 1st Band, p. 411.
104 von Damitz, Vol. II, p. 166.
105 von Damitz, Vol. II, p. 166.
106 Koch, Vol. I, p. 261.

The Brandenburg Cuirassiers and 8th Silesian Landwehr Regiment – standing before Grouchy's cavalry – were quickly overrun and driven back. In another attack against the Allied flank, 12 French cavalry regiments – organized in four ranks – faced Oberst von Haacke's three half regiments. The Prussians had little hope. They were engaged frontally by the first ranks and, as a rear rank of cuirassiers swung out and struck their flank, their fate was sealed. They fled back to Janvilliers – pursued by the French cavalry – until the French cavalry was turned back by the skirmishers hidden in the scrub and the 2/11th Reserve Regiment. As the French pushed forward, they tried to overrun 6pdr Foot Battery #9. They also penetrated into the edge of the village and a ferocious house-to-house fight erupted.

The position totally compromised, Blücher ordered an immediate withdrawal of his forces. Unfortunately, he did not have enough cavalry to cover his retreat, so he formed his infantry into squares and placed a few batteries between those squares. His wings were covered by five cavalry regiments and the remainder of his artillery was sent to the rear in great haste. He then began withdrawing his squares *en échiquier* and covered them with a screen of skirmishers.[107]

Those formations, in close combat with the French, were ordered to break and scatter "*en débandade*." They were to fall in behind the formed units. One of the more unusual incidents of the Napoleonic Wars occurred at this time when the two companies of the Silesian Schützen found themselves with a squadron of French cavalry sitting on their line of escape from the disaster that was befalling their brigade. The two companies – totaling about 230 men – formed a column at the order of Kapitän von Neumann, fixed their bayonets[108] and charged forward against their antagonists with a scream of anger and fear on their lips. Though some of the French cavalry turned to strike them, the fire from the ranks of the Schützen and their savage attack was more than the French cavalry cared to counter. The French swung away and withdrew – leaving behind them many riderless horses. Surprisingly, as the Schützen found the safety of the woods, they discovered that they had suffered no casualties and only a few men had lost their shakos or bayonets in the attack.[109]

However, Grouchy's I Cavalry Corps pushed through the village and around the right flank. The French cavalry caught the withdrawing Prussians and cut them down in droves. The 1/, 2/, Fus/1st Silesian Infantry Regiment and the 1/,2/10th Reserve Infantry Regiment were destroyed in this action.[110] French accounts state that around 1,000 Prussians were cut down in this charge. The two battalions which sought shelter in the village were taken prisoner and four guns and five caissons were captured. Von Damitz states that of the five battalions forming the advanced guard, Major von Bessel – the commander of the 10th Reserve Regiment – was later only able to organize a single converged battalion of 532 men.

Blücher's withdrawal began about 2:00 p.m.[111] The 12th Brigade led the withdrawal. The mass of the Allied artillery went down the main road as fast as the thick mud would permit. All of the various detached battalions were ordered to rejoin the main body, but the 3/7th Reserve (19th) Regiment – holding the edge of Sarrechamp – could not execute the order. It was trapped, but fate did not catch up with it until after dark. The remainder of the infantry formed in squares and two horse batteries formed on the highway.

The terrain over which he had to retire was opened as far as Champaubert (except for a few woods where he quickly posted small groups of skirmishers with the idea of harassing the attacking

107 Langeron, p. 397; de Beauchamp, Vol. I. p. 285.
108 The bayonets used by the Silesian Schützen were a particularly long blade known as a 'Hirschfänger'.
109 von Otto, p. 65.
110 von Damitz, Vol. II, p. 167.
111 von Ebertz, p. 153.

French cavalry). Blücher's withdrawal was effected in good order as far as Champaubert, but his squares were unable to move through the village so they moved into the large field to the right of the village. Kapsevich's 10th Corps withdrew alongside the Prussians down the southern side of the road.

The two companies of the Silesian Schützen – 230-men-strong – formed column and fixed their bayonets. Not waiting to be caught in the open, they began to withdraw until the French cavalry caught up with them. Safe in their dense formation, they waited until the French were within 50 paces of them and let loose with a terrific volley that emptied many saddles. Because they were marksmen armed with better weapons, every time a cavalryman came close he was a dead man. The Silesian Schützen quickly made their way to the rear.

Profiting from the disorder in the Prussian ranks, Napoleon's service squadrons and two squadrons of Laferrière's 1st Old Guard Cavalry Division charged several other squares, broke one square and captured about 500 prisoners.[112] The Prussian squares held fast except for the 1/7th Reserve (19th) Infantry Regiment. This battalion had been held behind Champaubert. It was equipped with English muskets, but though they were superior arms, they were not enough. As they were attacked frontally by one group of French cavalry, a force of lancers struck their flank and broke their square. 160 men were taken prisoners; four officers and 16 men escaped. The rest of the 459-man battalion were cut down.[113]

The French infantry chased after their cavalry at the *pas de charge* – advancing into Fromentières.[114] Undaunted by this check, Blücher organized his forces and continued to withdraw *en échiquier*. Napoleon, seeing this new disposition, ordered General Drouot to advance all the Guard artillery.[115] Thirty guns advanced and showered the Prussian squares with canister. The Prussians were only able to respond with six guns.

The pursuit was murderous, but it was only an effort to slow the withdrawal of the Army of Silesia. General Grouchy was preparing an even greater disaster for them. The Prussians moved towards Etoges, but as they stood astride the main road before Champaubert, Grouchy gave the order to General Coin – his artillery commander – to close on them with two horse batteries. Unfortunately, the terrible condition of the roads delayed their advance and night fell before they could be brought to bear.

Oberst von Haacke and his tiny force – now reorganized and standing in two lines – once again stood before Grouchy and the I Cavalry Corps only to be driven back again. It fell behind the 11th Reserve Regiment and a string of skirmishers from the 9th and 10th Fusilier Companies, Fus/2nd Silesian Regiment. At this time the 10th and 12th Brigades switched positions and the three battalions of the 2nd Silesian Regiment found themselves in the tail of the retreating Allied army.[116]

As the 10th and 12th Brigades approached Champaubert, Kleist ordered Prince August to send the Fus/2nd Silesian Regiment into the edge of a woods to the north of the main road in an effort to delay any French move along this flank.

At one point the French cavalry pushed between the 10th and 12th Prussian Brigades – almost capturing Blücher and his staff. At this critical moment, Prince August von Preussen – at the head of the 2/2nd West Prussian Infantry Regiment – fired on the French and drove them off.[117]

112 Rothwiller, p. 582.
113 von Damitz, Vol. II, p. 178.
114 Koch, Vol. I, pp. 261-2.
115 Sporschil, Vol. II, 1st Band, p. 413.
116 von Ebertz, p. 154.
117 von Damitz, Vol. II, p. 178.

The 2nd Silesian Infantry charge French cavalry at Vauchamps, by Richard Knötel.

In the dark, Blücher continued his withdrawal when at Grouchy's command, Doumerc, Bordesoulle and Saint-Germain fell upon Blücher's harried forces like a bolt of thunder. They struck from three sides. Prince August von Preussen rode from battalion to battalion ordering them to hold their fire until the French were 30 paces distant.[118]

The Prussians pushed to the east in a desperate effort to reach the woods just to the east of Champaubert. Once there, relative safety would be found. Apparently the 2nd Silesian Infantry Regiment executed a bayonet attack against the French cavalry as it pushed to reach the Etoges woods. Behind them came the Russian 8th Division, under Prince Urusov, serving as the rearguard.[119]

Blücher's lines were pierced and several squares were scattered. The French cannonade ceased and the Guard cavalry arrived at the trot to spread terror through the Prussian ranks. There was truly a great chance that both corps would be cut off and destroyed. On the left flank, Kapsevich's troops, the East Prussian Cuirassier Regiment and part of Ziethen's troops faced off against the French cavalry. Kapsevich's troops marched in échiquier as if on the parade ground.[120]

The French cavalry once again rolled in to waiting masses of Allied infantry. Prince August von Preussen, Feldmarschal Blücher and generals Kleist and Kapsevich were knocked from their horses or swept away by the crush of the fugitives.[121] Crying that he would rather "die than be taken prisoner", Prince August von Preussen drew his saber – as did his escort – and faced about to engage the French cavalry. Gniesenau, however, convinced him to seek shelter with the retreating

118 von Ebertz, p. 155.
119 von Ebertz, p. 156.
120 C. von W., p. 171.
121 Rothwiller, p. 582.

infantry just as a withdrawing Russian battalion turned about and discharged a crashing volley into the pursuing French.[122] Prince August, seeing the wisdom in his words and the opportunity afforded by the firm mass of Russian infantry, joined them and withdrew from the battlefield to fight another day.

The French cuirassiers flew into the midst of the screaming crowd of panicked Prussians – sabering them at will and without resistance. At least part of the Army of Silesia had totally routed. However, the butchery was short-lived as Ney had the recall sounded – fearing that the French cavalry would become too widely dispersed and entangled in the woods.[123] Despite that, two Prussian brigades which brought up the rear of the withdrawal were overrun and lost. They had not given enough attention and while they were threatened defending their right flank, the French cavalry drove in their left.[124]

The withdrawal of the French cavalry gave Blücher a respite and the chance to reorganize his army behind Etoges. A Prussian cuirassier regiment, Ziethen's 11th Brigade and a few Russian battalions remained organized and continued their march on Bergères. Prince Urusov formed a rearguard with the Russian 8th Division[125] and ordered Udom, with the remains of Olsufiev's corps, to hold the exit from the Etoges forest. Udòm had 1,800 men and 15 guns.

Marmont pushed his pursuit with the VI Corps and Doumerc's cavalry relentlessly, except for a short rest in Champaubert. He caught Udom's 9th Division by surprise at the edge of the Etoges park (near the entrance of the city). A single charge by the French cuirassiers put them to flight – abandoning 800 prisoners and seven guns.[126] Marmont profited by this to push Lagrange's 3rd Division, VI Corps, into Etoges – driving the Russians back into the last three Prussian battalions of the 12th Brigade. A Marine Regiment entered the city with bayonets leveled – crushing the Russian resistance – capturing Prince Urusov and 600 Russians, plus eight guns. As the Prussians withdrew, they left the 1st Silesian Hussar Regiment on the outskirts of Etoges to warn of any French advance.

It was at this point that one last tragedy occurred. The 3/7th Reserve (19th) Reserve Regiment, with 290 men, had been cut off in the edge of Sarrechamp. Its commander, Major von Weinskowski, screened it with skirmishers and made the best of his position. Fate proved unkind and this brave battalion was caught by a force of the 1st (Polish) Guard Lancers supported by some horse artillery. Canister drove the skirmishers back to the main body of the battalion, but in its position behind the ditches and walls of Sarrechamp it was secure. However, as the sun began to fall, two battalions of Old Guard marched up. Their sappers cut through the gates and the Old Guard poured into the defensive perimeter followed by the Polish lancers. After a ferocious fight, only 150 men remained alive and all were prisoners. In addition, Etoges yielded a number of prisoners. A French report cites 1,200 prisoners being taken, including: "One colonel, two majors and a large number of officers from the 8th (Russian) Division; all the prisoners having bayonet or bullet wounds."[127]

Koch says that for a loss of 600 men, the French army took 15 guns, 10 flags and 2,000 Prussian prisoners – plus inflicting 3,500 casualties on the Prussians and around 3,500 casualties on the Russians.[128] According to von Damitz, the Prussian losses at Vauchamps were eight officers and 3,908 men dead, wounded and prisoners – plus six guns and one howitzer lost. He

122 de Beauchamp, Vol. I, p. 289.
123 Koch, Vol. I, p. 263.
124 C. von W., p. 172.
125 von Damitz, Vol. II, p. 179.
126 Rothwiller states that 600 prisoners and eight guns were taken.
127 French National Archives, Carton AF^{IV} 1669B.
128 Koch, Vol. I, p. 264.

gives the Russian losses at 2,000 men and nine guns.[129] C. von W. gives Kleist's losses at 3,000 to 4,000 men and Kapsevich's at 2,000 men killed, wounded and prisoners. He also cites Kleist as losing seven guns.[130] Von Toll lists the total Allied losses at 6,000 men and 16 guns. He specifies Prussian losses at 83 officers, 3,944 men and seven guns; the Russian losses at 2,000 men and nine guns. He also lists the French losses at 600 men.[131] Von Plotho gives the total Allied losses at 5,000 to 6,000 men and 15 guns. For the 2nd Prussian Corps he says that 15 officers and 1,487 other ranks were killed; that 11 officers and 447 other ranks were captured; and that 54 officers and 1,970 men were wounded. He also lists six guns and one 7pdr howitzer as being lost. This is a total of 3,904 officers and men *hors de combat* or prisoner.[132]

It is probable that the total Allied losses were around 6,000 men and nine guns. The French losses seem to be consistently stated at 600 men.

Napoleon and Ney returned with the guard to spend the night in Montmirail. Marmont, with the VI Corps and Doumerc's cavalry, spend the night near Etoges. Grouchy, with the cavalry of Saint-Germain and Bordesoulle completely exhausted, bivouaced near Champaubert. Leval's 7th Division, which arrived too late to participate in the battle, was equally fatigued from its forced march and collapsed for the night.

The shattered debris of the Army of Silesia continued its flight to Châlons that night – littering the road with its dead and wounded, plus a multitude of broken and abandoned vehicles. The cavalry, under General Ziethen, formed a rearguard which was followed only by the French. During the next day, Kleist and Kapsevich led their corps over the Marne and moved into cantonments behind Châlons under the cover of a weak division at Etoges, which was badly handled by Marmont. The entire corps reunited itself on the 16th – weakened by a loss of 18,000 to 20,000 men over this week. However, it is possible that this is a substantial overestimate. Von Ebertz claims that "the loss of the Army of Silesia between 10 and 14 February totaled 14,304 men – including 136 Prussian officers and 52 guns."[133] Von Toll cites the total losses at 16,000 and 60 guns.[134]

Things for the Army of Silesia were put right by the arrival of Winzingerode's 30,000-man corps. Covered by these fresh troops, Blücher reorganized his army (principally Sacken and Yorck's commands) and was able to repair much of the effects of his four defeats. In doing so, however, he converged many of the shattered regiments – converting and merging some into single battalions. The converging of whole regiments into single battalions provides tremendous testimony to the beating that the Army of Silesia had taken. The Army of Silesia was soon operational. Nevertheless, Blücher had been taught a serious lesson.

Napoleon's dilemma

Napoleon's intention was to pursue Blücher to Châlons and finish him up. Once that was done, he intended to march via Vitry and fall the rear of the Allied main army, the Army of Bohemia. However, the most recent dispatches he had received informed him that the Army of Bohemia had renewed its offensive and pushed back both Victor and Oudinot. The Allied vanguards had reached Provins, Nangis, Montereau and Fontainebleau. Paris was threatened or, more exactly,

129 von Damitz, Vol. II, p. 181.
130 C. von W., p. 173.
131 von Bernhardi, Vol. 4, 7th Book, p. 405.
132 von Plotho, Vol. III, p. 190.
133 von Ebertz, p. 158.
134 von Bernhardi, Vol. 4, 7th Book, p. 405.

Paris appeared to be threatened. What Napoleon did not know was that Schwarzenberg was equally shaken by the news of Blücher's four defeats. Schwarzenberg reverted to character and once more become very hesitant.

Faced with this, Napoleon had few options based on his imperfect knowledge. What Napoleon did not know was that the Allies' forward march was interrupted. These forces received the orders from a panicked Schwarzenberg to remain on their position and await the development of Napoleon's maneuvers.

Acting on what he did know, Napoleon made his choices. In order to cover Paris, he had to abandon the pursuit of Blücher and turn south to face Schwarzenberg. To Marmont went the honors of the pursuit.

That evening, the all Guard – minus Mortier's detachment – slept at Montmirail and the next day moved to Meaux. On 16 February Napoleon was at Guignes with the Old Guard and his army ready to deal with Schwarzenberg's army.

Results of the battles

With Blücher's escape, what is known as "The Six Days' Campaign of 1814" ended. During these six days, Napoleon had once again shown his skill as a field commander. Earlier in the campaign, Napoleon had suffered a defeat at La Rothière and his record at the end of the 1813 campaign overshadowed his victories in the campaign. In the prelude to Leipzig he had been unable to make things work, but that malaise was gone. In February he handled his small army numbering less than 30,000 with the skill of a surgeon. His subordinates may have failed him again, but not to the extent they had in 1813. In these five days the French army had marched about 80 miles through muddy quagmires, won four victories and inflicted a cumulative total of at least 30,000 casualties at an almost minimal cost. The question of casualties is, however, an interesting one.

As is typical of the victor, subsequent German historians have attempted to hide the failures of the Allies by adjusting the numbers of troops present, reducing casualties and justify their defeats.

A tabulation of Allied reported strengths before and after the battle follows:

	Yorck's Prussian 1st Corps	Kleist's Prussian 2nd Corps	Olsufiev's Russian 9th Corps	Kapsevich's Russian 10th Corps	Sacken's Russian Corps	Korff's Russian Corps
Date						
1/1	21,447		5,595	7,282*	21,550	6,947
2/6		16,000		6,300		
2/16	13,857	9,800	1,500	7,987	14,125	
2/22						3,754
Losses	7,590	6,200	4,095	?	7,425	3,193
Apparent total losses: 28,503 men						
* Does not include officers.						
1/1						
Bns	37½	31	12	16	26	0
Sqns*	42	24	0	0	28	32
Guns	82	96	36?	36?	94	24?

	Yorck's Prussian 1st Corps	Kleist's Prussian 2nd Corps	Olsufiev's Russian 9th Corps	Kapsevich's Russian 10th Corps	Sacken's Russian Corps	Korff's Russian Corps
2/16						
Bns	16½	13	3**	?	?	?
Sqns*	33	40	0	?	?	?
Guns	86	72	12	?	?	?

* Does not include Cossacks.

** 1,500 men, or approximately three battalions.

Between them, the two Prussian corps lost 39 battalions. The annihilation of Olsufiev cost the Russians approximately nine battalions. The average Prussian 1st Corps battalion had 571.92 men. If it indeed lost 21 battalions, that would equate to a loss of 12,010 casualties. The average strength of a Prussian 2nd Corps battalion was 516.13 men. If the corps did lose 18 battalions, that would suggest a loss of 9,290 men. Olsufiev, according to all accounts, lost 4,095 men. This analysis of data suggests that these three corps lost as many as 25,395 men. Russian losses cannot be calculated on an average battalion strength before and after, but the review of strength figures show that Sacken and Korff lost 7,425 and 3,193 men respectively and Kapsevich is reputed to have lost 2,000 at Vauchamps. This would suggest a total Allied loss of between 28,503 and 38,013 men. From this the losses at Brienne and La Rothière should be subtracted, but only Yorck, Kapsevich and Olsufiev were engaged there. Yorck's losses appear to have been insignificant and the Russian total reported losses were 3,000-4,000, which gives us a probable Allied loss for these four battles of 34,000.

Houssaye, working with many sources now unavailable, provides an insight into the process:

> German historians have tried to belittle the credit of these tidy victories by saying that the French fought two against one. To substantiate their claim, they arbitrarily decrease the Allies' effectives and inflate those of the Emperor. However, in taking into account the official returns (from the French archives) and the numbers reported by foreign reports concerning the Allies' units as they crossed the Rhine, we were able to come up with the following numbers (it is well-understood that we reduce by 20 percent for the losses of Olsufiev and Sacken for the Battle of Brienne and La Rothière and 10 percent for that of Yorck, Kleist and Kapsevich):
>
> At Champaubert: Olsufiev's corps – 4,700. Divisions Ricard and Lagrange – 3,200. 1st Cavalry Corps – 1,500. Two squadrons of the Imperial Guard – 150. Total: 4,700 Russians against 4,850 French.
>
> At Montmirail: Sacken's corps – 15,700. Pirch and Horn's brigades (part of Yorck's corps), 16 battalions – 7,000. Ricard's division – 1,200. Guard (10 battalions) – 4,000. Guard Cavalry – 4200. Guards of Honor – 900. Ney's divisions – 2,500. Total: 22,700 Russians and Prussians against 12,800 French.
>
> At Vauchamps: Kleist's corps (less Klüx's brigade) – 13,500. Olsufiev's survivors – 1,500. Kapsevich – 6,500. Ricard and Lagrange's divisions – 3,000. 1st and 3rd Cavalry Corps – 3,600. Guard Cavalry (less Colbert's division) – 3,300. One Old Guard battalion – 400. Total: 21,500 Prussians and Russians against 10,300 French.[135]

135 Houssaye, p. 69.

Those who would serve as Blücher's apologists forget that though Napoleon did have the cream of his army, he had only about 24,000 men facing the 57,000 men of the Army of Silesia. It is also necessary to point out that Houssaye is not without some chauvinistic distortion in his figures. In every battle where he cites strength figures, he cites only those engaged – not those also on the field and within engagement distance.

In his figures for troops present at Vauchamps, he lists only those forces that were actually engaged. This is easily observed in his identification of only a single battalion of Old Guard being involved in the battle. He omits the 1st Old Guard Division (4,000 men), 2nd Old Guard Division (3,000 men), 1st Voltigeur Division (4,000 men), the 2nd Voltigeur Division (2,500 men) and Leval's Division (4,500 men) – 18,000 men – all of whom were marching behind the French cavalry that was actually engaging the Army of Silesia.[136] This would change the ratio quoted by Houssaye at Vauchamps from 21,500 Allies facing 10,300 French to 21,500 against 28,300 French. In Napoleon's defense, though this is a superiority, it is not an overwhelming numerical superiority. It is difficult to evaluate the impact of the superiority of the French forces over those of the Allies in this action. Certainly, elements of the French cavalry were far superior (i.e. Imperial Guard). There were 3,600 French line cavalry and 3,300 Imperial Guard cavalry. The line cavalry did as much of the fighting as the Guard. They were not, however, the cavalry of the pre-1812 French army. Instead, they were the remains of 48 cavalry regiments whose full organizational strength should have been about 48,000 men – not the 3,600 men present. They were cobbled together and formed into ad hoc formations. Full regiments were reduced to the strength of half squadrons and mounted with the last horses available for such service to be found in France. It needs to be remembered that after the disaster in Russia, Napoleon had a terrible time finding enough horses to reequip his army in 1813. There was even less horseflesh available in 1814.

The only analysis that can be made of the total strength figures is that the French actually had more troops on the field than the Allies. On the other hand, when one examines the cavalry strengths, a different story comes to the surface. The Allies, in contrast to their usual situation, had a remarkable inferiority of cavalry on the field at Vauchamps. They had only seven cavalry regiments – two of which were Landwehr. Though the theoretical strength of these regiments would have been around 7,000 men, these regiments probably had a total strength of 2,000 to 2,500 men – certainly no more than 3,000. Since Vauchamps is really a cavalry battle, here is where the key to Vauchamps lies. Not only did the French have twice the cavalry strength of the Allies, half of their cavalry was amongst the best cavalry in the world. In the preceding account, in almost every instance the Allied cavalry was defeated when it engaged the French cavalry.

So, where did this leave Blücher? He was faced in an open plain – ideal cavalry terrain – by an army a third larger than his that had a cavalry superiority that ranged from two to three times larger than his. He could not protect his flanks – as was amply demonstrated by Grouchy's continual movement around them – and if he let his army get caught by the French infantry with French cavalry in his rear, the destruction of his army was a virtual certainty. He recognized this and immediately ordered his army to retreat.

Though Napoleon deserves considerable credit for his strategic genius in bringing off this engagement and catching Blücher's fragmented army in a situation that promised a tremendous Allied defeat, Blücher requires an equal credit for getting his army away at all.

However, even with Blücher's escape at Vauchamps, if Napoleon had been better served by his marshals it is certain that he would have totally destroyed Blücher in a subsequent battle after Vauchamps. Fortunately for Blücher, Napoleon was compelled to turn southward against the Army of Bohemia.

136 These strength figures are estimates based on returns from 1 February and obtained from the SHAT.

Victor failed Napoleon with his inability to hold line of the Seine against Schwarzenberg. Victor's morale had been destroyed by the disaster at Leipzig and the subsequent retreat to France. Victor had become too lethargic for independent command, and a few days after his failure to hold Schwarzenberg, Napoleon removed him from the command.

Victor's was not the only failure. Macdonald's failure to secure the bridge on the Marne at Château-Thierry had spared Sacken and Yorck. If this had been done as ordered, with Yorck and Sacken's line of retreat cut off, they would have either been forced to surrender or totally destroyed. The loss of 41 infantry battalions, 18 artillery batteries, 10 line cavalry regiments and eight Cossack regiments – approximately 30,000 men – would have been a disaster of major proportions to the Allies.

Thus, in two instances where Napoleon stood a chance of destroying a combined total of 70,000 Allied troops, the failures of his marshals reduced the fruits of Napoleon's strategic genius to between 28,000 and 34,000!

8

Actions to the North and South, 6-16 February 1814

After his string of victories over the Army of Silesia, Napoleon immediately sent bulletins announcing his victories to Paris, which had been greatly alarmed at the withdrawal of Macdonald's XI Corps and the advance of the Army of Silesia. New recruits were sent to refill Napoleon's depleted ranks and passed in review at the Carrousel before they were sent to the various army corps. The Parisian Guard began to organize itself at the defenses of Paris.

The news of the victory at Champaubert arrived on 11 February as King Joseph, Napoleon's brother and former King of Spain, held the first review of the Parisian Guard. Joseph feared that Champaubert, like Brienne, would be followed by a defeat. Despite his fears, organization continued on the Parisian Guard.

Napoleon sent orders to Paris directing that detachments be sent from the Parisian Guard to escort the prisoners of war that he wished to ship to the Loire. This brought with it a major problem, as the Parisian Guard was a sedentary force – not intended for operations in the field – and they were greatly afraid that once in the field Napoleon would absorb them into the army. It was only with the greatest difficulty and political machinations that a number of detachments were convinced that it was appropriate and necessary for them to execute this order.

This political trauma, however, was followed quickly by the news of the victories at Montmirail, Château-Thierry and Vauchamps. The morale of Paris soared. Reinforced by the stream of Russian and Prussian prisoners and trophies into Paris, the French people renewed their faith in their Emperor's ability.

Winzingerode's march

General Winzingerode – after occupying Namur – chose not to pursue Macdonald, but permitted his corps to rest until 6 February. At that time, he resumed his march via Sombref on Binche. When there, he marched via Beaumont and Solre on Avesnes.

Vainly, the Defense Council had called attention to Avesnes. However, it had not appeared to be on a likely line of the Allied advance and its defenses were limited to a weak company of veterans. The city's population was alarmed by the appearance of the Russians and, considering the tiny garrison and poor state of the city's defenses, it gave no resistance to Winzingerode's advanced guard. The city was occupied on 9 February without a shot fired in its defense. With the fall of Avesnes, the way to Soissons lay open.

Standing on the Aisne River, Soissons had been converted into a field post. It stood on the crossroads of the roads from Compiègne and Château-Thierry. By a stroke of misfortune, Winzingerode's movement and the retreat of Yorck and Sacken from Château-Thierry put this critical city between two major Allied forces. Winzingerode's attention was drawn to Soissons for many reasons – and when his advanced guard easily drove back part of its garrison, he felt that it was open to a *coup de main*.

Soissons stood on both sides of the Aisne, with the suburb of Saint-Waast connected to it by a stone bridge. It still retained its heavy, though decayed, walls. There were many breaches and places where the defensive capability of the wall was greatly limited. The gates were without defense, though they could be covered with hasty barricades. Soissons had been designated as a gathering point for the French National Guard and, as a result, contained the cadres of six battalions

This included the Vistula Legion, a Polish formation in French service, a depot of 200 Italians and a few hundred gendarmes. The garrison did not lack for leadership, as GD Rusca was the garrison commander – and under him were GB Berruyer, Dauloup-Verdun and Longchamps.[1]

The fall of Soissons

As things stood in Soissons, its capture did not appear to be difficult and Winzingerode felt it would little retard his junction with the Army of Silesia. As a result, he departed Laon on 14 February and joined General Czernichev's forces above Soissons. From there he moved down the road to Laon's Saint-Waast suburb, which he planned to take with an escalade.

General Rusca quickly deployed his forces – positioning two batteries at the Laon Gate – and moved there himself only to be mortally wounded by a bullet. His death broke the already-failing morale of the National Guards. The various other senior officers were engaged at other points and no one took command. The existing measures proved insufficient and Saint-Waast was virtually undefended.

Winzingerode's troops quickly climbed over the suburb's wall. The battalion guarding the Laon Gate was taken in the rear and the gate opened to the Russians, who quickly marched through the suburb to the bridge over the Aisne. General Longchamps stood there with his forces. He attempted to hold the Russians for about 20 minutes, but the Russians soon forced the bridge and the city was invaded. The Russians poured into the city. The French battalions in the city fought more to escape, than to defend, the city as they moved through the city's streets. They left 800 casualties lying in the streets as they withdrew.

Generals Dauloup-Verdun and Berruyer gathered up a few gendarmes and escaped down the road to Compiègne. General Longchamps, withdrawing with the cadres of three battalions, was surrounded by Czernichev's cavalry and forced to surrender. The Russians also captured his artillery.[2]

With the fall of Soissons, Compiègne was threatened. The Russians began to advance down the road from Soissons to Senlis when Winzingerode found himself forced to abandon his conquest because of orders to join the shattered Army of Silesia.

Freed by the withdrawals of Yorck and Sacken, Mortier advanced his forces into the now-vacated Soissons and covered Paris from that direction.

Oudinot and Victor to the south

Prior to embarking on his attack on the Army of Silesia, Napoleon detached Oudinot and Victor to the south with orders to hold the advance of the main Allied army. They were to guard the Seine between Nogent and Montereau. He detached generals Allix and Pajol to support them by defending the area between the Yonne – from Montereau to Auxerre – and to cover Paris along the Fontainebleau road.

---

1 Koch, Vol. I, pp. 270-6.
2 Koch, Vol. I, pp. 227-8.

Advancing from Troyes, the main Allied army had many choices as to how to march against Paris. Along the left bank of the Seine it could move via Sens, Montargis, Nemours and Fontainebleau or via Auxerre, Briare and Orléans. If it wished to advance along the right bank, it would move through Nogent, Bray or Montereau.

There were a number of major terrain obstacles along this route. First, there was the Yonne from Auxerre to its juncture with the Seine; then the Briare Canal, which ran from the Loire to Montargis. There was the Loing Canal, which ran from Loing to Saint-Mamert, and finally, there was the Seine as it ran from Troyes to Loing.

The Yonne was crossed by the bridges at Montereau, Auxerre, Joigny, Villeneuve, Seins and Pont. However, only the roads from Troyes to Auxerre and Sens were capable of handling the movement of an army corps. If those two cities were held – and if the other bridges were destroyed and the few fords were watched – any Allied movement through this region would be extremely difficult.

Maréchal Oudinot.

The Briare Canal was a significant obstacle. It was 16 meters (52 feet) wide with high banks. It was not an insurmountable obstacle because it was crossed by many bridges and locks which, though they could easily be broken, their replacement would not have been difficult.

The Loing Canal, however, was a more significant obstacle as it was crossed by far fewer bridges and its dimensions were larger than those of the Briare Canal.

In the region between the Seine and the Yonne (towards the east) the countryside was used principally for the growing of grapes and not open – eliminating easy movement of troops off the roads. To the left of the Yonne – to the canals between the Loire and the Seine – the countryside was broken by many dry hills, woods and ponds. It was a harsh region – providing poor communications and little sustenance for an army. On the other side of the canals stood the Orléans forest. During winter, this region – extending to Châtenay – was the most difficult region in France to traverse. From there, the Fontainebleau forest – which stood on the Seine and stretched to Moret, Ubis, Chailly and towards Paris – compounded the problems of an army moving in this region.

Between the Yonne and these canals, movements by an army were not possible except if it remained on the road from Auxerre to Briare and Orléans; or the road from Sens to Montargis; or the road from Montereau to Fontainebleau. The first two were terrible roads. On the left of the canals there were three roads to Paris: that from Noyers to Vernisson, Montargis and Nemours to Fontainebleau, or that from Orléans via Pithiviers.

The Seine, from Saint-Mamert to Troyes, is not fordable in the winter. Between Troyes and Nogent there were many wooden bridges, but they are all on minor and insignificant routes. Between the Aube and the Loing, the Seine was crossed by stone bridges only at Montereau, Bray and Nogent. The roads to Paris from Auxerre ran through Montereau and Sens; those from Nangis and Provins passed via Bray and Sens. The roads from Troyes to Paris ran through Nogent or through Langres through Nogent, Méry and Arcis.

In addition, Nogent and Montereau were the pivots of the line of the Seine. Bray had only a secondary importance.

The French army of the Seine

Before reviewing the operations of Oudinot and Victor, it is appropriate to review the forces at their disposal. They were, in effect, left to contain the main Allied army – and the forces at their disposal were to determine what options remained open to them. On 8 February Victor commanded a force consisting of:

II Corps[3]
- Chateau's 1st Division:
  - 1st Brigade 61 officers 822 men
  - 2nd Brigade 63 officers 588 men
- Duhèsme's 2nd Division (10 February):
  - 1st Brigade 110 officers 1,564 men
  - 2nd Brigade 49 officers 709 men
- Corps Artillery 20 officers 55 men

Total: 303 officers 4,238 men

Paris Reserve Corps: Gérard
- Dufour's 1st Division:
  - 1st Brigade 68 officers 945 men
  - 2nd Brigade 29 officers 461 men
- Hamelinaye's Division:
  - 1st Brigade 39 officers 1,172 men
  - 2nd Brigade 32 officers 944 men
- Corps Artillery 14 officers 542 men

V Cavalry Corps
- 9th Light Division (Piré)
- 5th Heavy Division (Briche)
- 6th Heavy Division (l'Héritier)
- Total Strength: 3,500

No details are available for the V Cavalry Corps on 8 February, but Briche's 5th Heavy Cavalry Division consisted of the 2nd, 6th, 11th, 13th, and 15th Dragoons and had 102 officers and 1,008 men on the 8th. The total strength of the forces under Victor came to about 12,700 men on 8 February. The organization of the II Corps was slightly increased on 12 February to a total strength of 5,000 men.

On 8 February Oudinot's corps consisted of:[4]

VII Corps
- 1st Division (Leval) 3,522 effectives
- 2nd Division (Boyer) 171 officers 5,628 men
- 5th Young Guard Division (Rottembourg):
  - Det/Flanqueurs 1 officer 90 men
  - 1st Tirailleur Regiment 10 officers 330 men
  - 5th Tirailleur Regiment 23 officers 698 men
  - 6th Tirailleur Regiment 19 officers 629 men
  - 7th Tirailleur Regiment 28 officers 672 men
  - 8th Tirailleur Regiment 23 officers 578 men

3 Jacomet, pp. 41-6.
4 Jacomet, pp. 46-52.

Escort to Grand Park: Major Salomon
- 7th Tirailleur Battalion 520 effectives
- 8th Tirailleur Battalion 500 men
- Det/29th Légère Regiment 180 men
- Det/19th Line Regiment 150 men
- Det/43rd Line Regiment 150 men
- Det/Chasseurs à cheval 190 men

Total: 1,702 effectives

Blancard's column
- Mixed cavalry force 600 effectives

Pajol's corps
- Delort's brigade 460 cavalry
- 1,800 infantry
- Ducoëtlosquet's brigade 358
- Grouvel's brigade 476
- Horse Battery with six guns

Pacthod's National Guard 2,000 effectives
Troops assigned to defend the Yonne 38 officers 746 men
Customs guards
- 4/15th Line Regiment
- Det/153rd Line Regiment
- Det/121st Line Regiment
- Jura Departmental Companies
- Doubs Departmental Companies

Côte-d'Or Departmental Companies
Det/Vendée National Guards Detachment
Det/Gendarmerie à cheval
Det/23rd Dragoon Regiment

A 500-man detachment, under Major Salomon, was administratively assigned to Rottembourg's 2nd Tirailleur Division. Rottembourg's division had an effective strength of 3,500 men, but when Salomon's forces were added, it rose to about 4,000 men. Pajol's provisional cavalry corps was unusual in that it was attached to Delort, who commanded an infantry brigade containing the 2nd Cherbourg Infantry Regiment and a force of 1,000 National Guardsmen from Pacthod's force. Pacthod was organizing a larger force, but at this time had only about 2,000 of them equipped and ready for operations.

Of the two, Oudinot's corps was significantly larger than Victor's II Corps and fielded about 20,000 men on 10 February. However, Boyer's 9th Division did not arrive until the evening of 12 February. Combined, these two marshals could field about 33,000 troops.

Pacthod.

Immediately after Napoleon departed for Sézanne, the Army of the Seine – under Oudinot and Victor – occupied the following positions: Victor – with the II Corps, the Paris Reserve and Milhaud's cavalry – stood on the left bank of the Seine, Romilly, Gellanes, Saint-Martin-de-Bossenay and Pont watching the three roads from Troyes to Nogent. Oudinot occupied Provins with Rottembourg's 2nd Tirailleur Division – reinforced by 1,200 men from Paris, two companies of National Guards guarded the Bray bridge (which had one arch broken down) and 400-500 cavalry under the orders of General Pajol – watched the right bank of the Seine from Bray to Montereau. Here, General Pacthod was in the process of organizing his National Guards Division. Though he had about 6,000 men he lacked uniforms, muskets and equipment, which rendered his force largely useless. Finally, General Delort covered Montereau with 600-800 cavalry cantoned in Fossard. Though an incredibly weak force, it greatly surpassed that assigned to guard the Yonne.

General Allix guarded Sens with 2,400 men. There were another 1,000 National Guards in Pont under General Montbrun, plus about 600 cavalry under General Ducoëtlosquet. On the extreme right, General Moreau was charged with defending Auxerre. He sought to gather in as many troops as he could, but despite his efforts this force consisted solely of a departmental company and about 20 gendarmes.

The French stood in these positions for four days before the Allied main army began an offensive movement from Troyes. As a result of their victory over Napoleon at La Rothière, the Allied sovereigns felt a sense of invincible superiority over Napoleon. This inflation of ego slowly roused the Allies – propelling them into advancing once again against Paris.[5] Ironically, it was on 10 February – just as Napoleon eradicated Olsufiev's 11th Corps at Champaubert – that Schwarzenberg put his forces in movement towards Nogent, Sens and Auxerre with the idea of marching on Paris down the two banks of the Seine.

Schwarzenberg's plans

During the days after Troyes was occupied, Schwarzenberg was once again struck with a bout of indecisiveness. He was faced with two alternatives: He could march on Paris via Sens – ignoring or masking Nogent – or he could launch an aggressive offensive against Napoleon's rear and attempt to paralyze his pending attack on Blücher. As was his way, however, instead of pursuing either alternative he chose a middle ground and decided to push the bulk of his forces via Sens on Fontainebleau in the hope of obliging the French to divide themselves in response.

In the meantime, Schwarzenberg directed two corps to march on the Seine to "amuse" and to occupy the French by Nogent – holding them on the Seine. His plans laid, Wrede's 5th Corps and Wittgenstein's 6th Corps marched on Nogent-sur-Seine, while on 10 February the 4th Corps (Crown Prince of Württemberg) marched on Sens; the 1st Corps (Bianchi) marched on Villeneuve-au-Chemin via Auxerre and Troyes; and the 3rd Corps (Giulay) marched on Auxerre. The Allied reserve held itself in Bouilly and the Russian and Prussian Guard were in Troyes.

His offensive was to begin on 9 February, but the operations on the Seine were totally distinct and not related to those on the Yonne around Nogent-sur-Seine and Sens.[6]

Engagement at Sens

By the 9th, Wrede and Wittgenstein's 5th and 6th Corps – which had chased Victor's troops across the Ardusson – were ordered to fall back on Nogent. The Crown Prince of Württemberg marched his corps down the road to Sens – arriving on 12 February with the Austrian Reserve in support.

5 Koch, Vol. I, pp. 280-3.
6 Jacomet, p. 58.

He directed Bianchi, who had replaced Colloredo in command of the I (Austrian) Corps, to move via Arce and Cerissiers and join the Württembergers (4th Corps). These two corps were to be supported by Giulay's corps, the Austrian Reserve and M. Liechtenstein's 2nd Light Division.

Bianchi.

Prior to this, the Württemberg advanced guard had arrived before Sens around noon on the 8th. At about 3:00 p.m. 800 Cossacks arrived and pushed into the Saint-Savinien suburb. They were, however, driven back. The city had 8,000 to 9,000 citizens and was surrounded by a high and strong wall supposedly constructed by the Romans. Before the wall was a large moat. Though he commanded only a tiny garrison, General Allix was determined to defend the city to the last extremity.

In making his defensive preparations, Allix thought to break the bridge at Villeneuve-le-Roi. He wrote Pajol of this idea – requesting that a force of 300 men be dispatched to do the job – but Pajol rejected the plan. Allix did not have the forces to do it either, so he abandoned the idea. With the arrival of the Cossacks, he knew he would soon be attacked. By noon on the 9th, Allix knew that the Allies were in the Vanne Valley and knew of Platov's march on Courtenay. He responded by moving the bulk of his forces to Fleurigny to discommode the Allies on their right flank and rear should they move against Sens. Other forces were deployed in echelons on the road to Sens – ready to move wherever the Allies might threaten. Finally, he sent 200 cavalry to Dollot and Chéroy to watch Platov. Pajol was advised of these developments and moved to cover Fontainebleau.[7]

Pajol moved his forces to an offensive position in Fleurigny that considerably cramped the march of the Crown Prince of Württemberg. The terrain over which he had to pass was swampy and required that he move in a march column down the road from Troyes to Sens. A flank attack by the French, in his formation, would be an utter disaster. In addition, if Württemberg was slow in his march, Pajol could operate against his lines of communication.

Attack on Sens

The Crown Prince of Württemberg had two options: The first was to divide his forces and mask Pajol with part of them. The second option was to attack him and drive him away. Either effort would cost the Allies precious time. In addition to occupying this position, Pajol promised Allix that he would come to his assistance if he was attacked.

The main body of the Württemberg 4th Corps arrived in Villeneuve-l'Archevêque on 10 February and stopped there. A reconnaissance force was sent forward to Sens. Allix had sent out his own reconnaissance forces, but they saw nothing. Barely had they returned when Allied cavalry appeared before the Notre-Dame suburb. They were followed, around noon, by the 4th Corps advanced guard – some 4,000 men.

An Allied brigade turned to the right and established itself in the Saint-Antoine suburb and the lead elements of the advanced guard established themselves in the Notre-Dame suburb and

7 Jacomet, p. 70.

sent forward an officer to summon Allix to surrender. Allix responded with a counterattack that drove back the Allied advanced guard and reoccupied the suburb.[8]

The Crown Prince of Württemberg united his corps before the Fontvannes suburb on 11 February. His advanced guard consisted of the Württemberg Light Infantry Brigade (9th and 10th Infantry Regiments), the Württemberg 2nd Horse Battery, 5th Württemberg Cavalry Regiment and an Austrian hussar regiment.[9]

General von Stockmayer deployed his forces in the Notre-Dame suburb. He ordered the 1/9th Jäger König Regiment to move into the Saint-Antoine suburb along the road from Troyes. The 1/10th Light Infantry Regiment moved down the road from Bray. They were supported by the 2nd Horse Artillery Battery. They soon found themselves in a grinding fight with the French troops defending those suburbs.

The cavalry of the advanced guard stood on the road from Bray and on the road to Pont-sur-Seine to screen that flank. The two battalions in the Notre-Dame and Saint-Antoine suburbs spent the entire night in a firefight with the French. At 3:00 a.m. – and again at 6:00 a.m. – the French made major attacks in an effort to recapture the suburbs, but both attacks failed.[10]

The Crown Prince attempted to enter Sens by pounding down its gates with his cannon. He had moved a 12pdr battery to within 200 paces of the city walls. This effort failed, so he attempted to burn the city with howitzer shells. He drew together eight howitzers from four Württemberg batteries and organized them into two batteries. They were then placed on heights to the north of the city and for two hours they threw bombs into the city. The remaining four guns of the 2nd Württemberg Horse Battery were then sent to the main gate leading to Troyes, where they began to fire. The fires started by the Württemberg artillery were immediately extinguished by a panicked citizenry desperate to save their homes and the effort failed. The Crown Prince then called forward a 12pdr battery to knock a breech in the wall.

Again the 12pdr guns were not sufficient for the job and the Crown Prince abandoned the effort, but soon learned that it might be possible to slip a force into the city through a small gate in the wall by the college. This door had been discovered by the Austrian pioneer company of Captain Wonjatschek. The Austrian pioneers led the attack – followed by the 4th and 6th Infantry Regiments.[11]

The gate was soon forced open, but a wall had been built by the French to prevent just such an act. They withdrew under a tremendous hail of musketry from the French soldiers guarding this route. The Allies then sought another passage, but this was not simple because the college was garrisoned by more infantry who also took them under fire.

The 4th (Württemberg) Infantry Regiment, led by the Austrian pioneers,[12] succeeded in penetrating into the court of the building because of a breech in a wall and they continued seeking a passage into the city only to discover that the only passage from the college into the city was barred by another gate that was closed with a portcullis. Covered by this double barrier, the French garrison stood firm behind a steady barrage of musketry. The Württembergers, however, decided that the only way to resolve the issue was by forcing their passage.

Braving the hail of musketry, the Württemberg 1/9th Regiment (Fussjäger) forced open the Troyes Gate and pushed into the city. The 1/10th Infantry Regiment and two companies of the 2/9th (Fussjäger) Regiment broke through the Pont Gate. They were followed by the 2/10th

8 Jacomet, p. 72.
9 von Hiller, p. 145.
10 von Hiller, p. 146.
11 von Damitz, Vol. II, p. 231;Rössler, pp. 416-7.
12 von Hiller, p. 147.

Regiment. The remaining two companies of the 2/9th Regiment and two guns of the 2nd Horse Battery moved along the Yonne from the north and pushed towards the bridge.[13]

Assailed on all sides, the garrison withdrew across the bridge to the island of Saint-Maurice. The Württemberg 4th, 9th and 10th Infantry Regiments pushed across the first bridge onto an island in the Yonne. General Stockmayer advanced at the head of the 9th Regiment. The French held the houses and gardens, and from the windows and behind the stone walls they poured heavy fire into the Württembergers. The French then withdrew across the last bridge and destroyed it in a last defiant act. The Württembergers had not pursued them and gave the French the time to destroy the bridge.

Von Hiller and the Württemberg *Tagebuch* provide very precise details of Allied casualties – listing six officers, 192 men and two horses as being lost. Because the French were fighting and defending behind cover, the *Tagebuch* lists their casualties at around 40-50 men.[14]

The French casualties of 300 men reported by Koch are surprisingly high and most assuredly inaccurate, unless it includes a number of deserters that were presumed lost in the battle.[15]

The French also suffered General Allix severely wounded.

Pajol's actions

Von Württemberg's march appears to have completely escaped Pajol. He had feared being cut off from the road to Montereau and had thought he should maintain the bridge at all costs – and ignored the immediate danger threatening Allix.

Pajol had united all of his infantry and cavalry to move behind Loing – leaving only Montbrun and 900 men at Pont-sur-Yonne to defend the bridge and support Allix in case he found himself obliged to beat a retreat. Pajol planned to be in Fossard that night and in Moret the following day. He hoped that Nemours would hold out long enough to give him the opportunity to move behind the Loing. He wrote GD Pacthod in Montereau to dispatch all available forces to him in Moret.

Pajol.

Pajol's retreat proved disastrous because it left the Sens garrison isolated and sealed its fate. His failure to support Sens minimized its ability to delay the Allied advance and left the road to Paris open.

Allix's withdrawal

On the 12th, after rallying the brigades of Montbrun and Ducoëtlosquet, General Allix took up a position behind Pont-sur-Yonne – using that village as an advanced post. The three generals felt that Pont-sur-Yonne was untenable because of the presence of the Allies around Nemours. They decided, as a result, to abandon their position at 3:00 a.m. the following morning and march on Montereau.[16]

13 von Hiller, p. 149.
14 Rössler, p. 417; von Hiller, p. 150.
15 Koch, Vol. I, p. 286.
16 Jacomet, p. 74.

As the French began withdrawing, the Württemberg advanced guard soon overran their pickets and, after a vigorous skirmish, pursued the French to Montereau. Once in Montereau, Allix found support in the form of Delort's cavalry, which had been driven back by Platov's Cossacks.

Count Pajol stopped his withdrawal and took up new positions to stop the Allied pursuit of Allix. GD Pacthod moved into position between the Yonne and the Seine with about 4,000 National Guardsmen. General Allix was positioned before Montereau – guarding Fossard with a battalion and two 4pdr guns. The cavalry, reunified under the orders of Delort, encamped on the right bank of the Seine between Montereau and Egligny. All of the unarmed National Guardsmen were sent back to Melun and the defense of Moret was confided in General Montbrun.

On 14 February Württemberg moved against Bray, and Bianchi, who followed him, turned to the left and took up positions before Montereau. General Hardegg was sent forward to throw the French advance post out of Fossard. Pajol saw the advancing Allies moving to envelope his two divisions. Upon learning that not only were the bridges on his left in Allied hands and that Oudinot and Victor were retreating to Nangis, he judged it foolish to remain in Montereau any longer so he moved over the bridge and took up new positions at Châtelet.

The Allied advance suddenly stopped because of orders from Schwarzenberg. However, General I. Hardegg – judging it desirable – pushed a reconnaissance force through Montereau and on to Moret. The Austrians entered Moret without opposition as it too had been evacuated. Moret taken, Fontainebleau stood in jeopardy. Its only garrison, the Guard Instruction School, had earlier been sent from Fontainebleau to defend Nemours when that city was threatened by Cossacks.

As a result, the Yonne-Loing line – upon which Napoleon had counted to delay the Allies – held them up no more than 24 hours. It would be the same with the Seine River line.

Engagement at Saint-Aubin

During the morning of 9 February Victor's forces were deployed such that the II Corps was at Pont-sur-Seine. The Paris Reserve Corps was in Saint-Hilaire and the V Cavalry Corps had its advanced posts between Seine and Ardusson.

Cavalry reconnaissance forces had been sent out the previous evening towards Marcilly-le-Hayer, Traînel and towards Sens. The Cossacks were also busy that evening with a force of them standing before Granges. Despite the presence of the Cossacks, Victor learned that the Allies were in Troyes and that they had built a bridge at Méry. Knowing this, Victor sent reconnaissance forces towards Saint-Martin-de-Bossenay where large enemy cavalry detachments were observed.

Victor's fears were justified. Hardegg's 1st Division (5th Corps) had moved to the Granges heights. Wittgenstein's advanced guard (6th Corps), under Pahlen, was marching from Méry to Nogent that morning. Hardegg – joining Pahlen's advanced elements – advanced against Piré's 9th Light Cavalry Division, which was supported by Hamelinaye's division.

The two French divisions were attacked vigorously and thrown back. They took up new positions behind the Gellanes stream on the southern Saint-Hilaire heights. About the same time, Milhaud informed Victor of the presence of an enemy column of seven squadrons, 12 battalions and some artillery in Saint-Martin-de-Bossenay.

Victor believed that he had important Allied forces before him. He feared being turned on the right and cut off from Nogent. Under the pretext of supporting Milhaud's withdrawal, immediately he moved the II Corps to Nogent and ordered Gérard to move to the heights to the east of the Château of Pont-sur-Seine. Piré remained watching the region before Saint-Hilaire until the arrival of new orders.

That evening, Victor arrived in Nogent and received further confirmation of the Allied movement. He responded by ordering the Paris Reserve Corps to join him in Nogent.

Though in moving the II Corps to Nogent Victor was following the letter of Napoleon's orders, he exceeded those orders by withdrawing Gérard and abandoning the heights by Pont-sur-Seine, which he should have retained if he was to delay the Allied advance. Furthermore, he was very distracted by the preparations for the defense of Nogent.

Napoleon had ordered General Blein to take two companies supported by an engineering train company and construct three redoubts and to barricade the city. However, Victor redirected Blein – ordering him to stop work on the redoubts and to devote his efforts to the preparation of interior and exterior barricades for the city. In addition, the second bridge over the Seine was cut.

To make matters worse, when the Allied advanced guard first appeared, Victor immediately withdrew all of his forces to Nogent and left only a weak picket deployed before him. He deployed his forces defensively and appears to have renounced any thought of defending the southern exit from Nogent.[17]

First engagement at Nogent-sur-Seine

On the morning of 10 February Victor's II Corps was assembled a few hundred meters from Nogent at the crossroads of the roads to Pont and Saint-Aubin. The Paris Reserve stood in a position behind Chapelle-Godefroy with its right supported on Tournebride and its left on Bernières. Milhaud's cavalry formed the first line and the II Corps stood in Nogent. Gérard stood in Chapelle with two battalions and two guns at the Ardusson bridge. The V Cavalry Corps was in Ardusson. Piré's brigade stood to the east of Ardusson on the road to Pont-sur-Seine and served as Gérard's advanced guard. This maneuver was well-executed, but it might have been better done if Hamelinaye's division, which formed the right, had occupied Saint-Aubin and if the front had been covered with all of the available artillery.

Nogent contained only about 3,000 citizens and was an open city – lacking walls or other defenses that had existed before the campaign. Victor inspected Nogent's defensive capacity and estimated that it was insufficient – especially to the west. He ordered batteries established on the principal roads and, if time permitted, he intended to defend that part of the city which was south of the Seine. If insufficient time remained, he intended to defend the bridge and the defile at Mériot. Victor perceived that it would be a useless sacrifice of his troops to try to defend Nogent in view of its poor defensive preparations. He resolved that if the city was attacked during the 10th he would withdraw to the right bank of the Seine, defend the bridge as long as possible – destroying it when he was no longer able to defend his position.

At around 2:00 p.m. two Allied columns appeared at Pont-sur-Seine and Saint-Martin-de-Bossenay. They were the divisions of Pahlen and Hardegg who had, the previous day, pushed Gérard out of Romilly. Milhaud, who was in Saint-Martin-de-Bossenay with the cavalry brigades of Briche and l'Héritier, withdrew to the Chapelle heights. Hardegg followed his withdrawal. Pahlen's column moved through the wooded park at Pont and established his infantry in a strong position. Schwarzenberg, however, arrived and ordered Hardegg to move against Saint-Aubin and ordered Pahlen to support his movement towards the right.

Victor responded by moving Duhèsme's 1st Division to a position before the southern exit of Nogent so he could support Gérard, and placed the 1st Division (II Corps) in reserve in the city. He had, in essence, changed his front to the rear and right so that his right wing was now supported on Mâcon.

Hardegg marched against Saint-Aubin in column by battalions – his artillery leading the advance and the Rebrikov and Illowaiski Cossacks and Olviopol Hussars deployed on both

17 Jacomet, pp. 60-1.

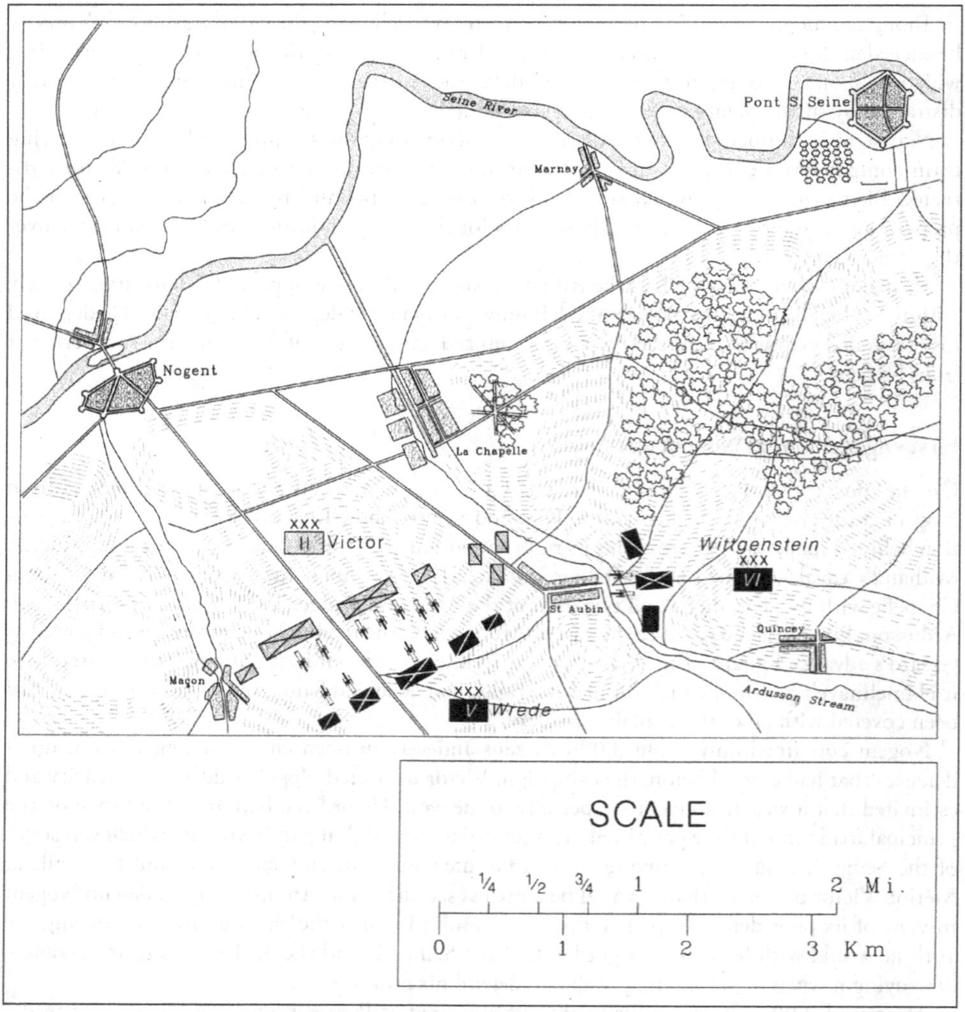

Map 8 Battle of Nogent, February 10 1814, First Phase.

wings. Supporting his move, Pahlen launched a vigorous attack on Chapelle with the 4th Jager Regiment, which carried the position.[18] Gérard, however, sent forward reinforcements to retake the position. The French then launched a successful counterattack and threw Pahlen's troops back. Hardegg was similarly checked by the French at Saint-Aubin and was unable to cross the Ardusson.

18 von Damitz, Vol. II, p. 225.

Night fell shortly after 5:00 p.m. Pahlen and Hardegg's troops bivouaced in their positions with the Austrian cavalry in Mâcon, Hardegg's infantry before Saint-Aubin, Pahlen's division standing before Chapelle and their advanced posts in contact with those of the French.[19]

Though he had checked the Allied advance, Victor decided to cross to the right bank of the Seine and left only 1,000 men – detached elite companies from the 11th and 29th Légère and the 18th Line Regiments – to defend the Nogent bridge. He felt that these defenses would cost the Allies enough casualties if they wished to persist. As the city of Nogent covered nearly the entire left bank of the Seine, it could be considered to have formed a bridgehead of sufficient strength to permit him to defend it with this force.

There were no hills on the far bank to permit the Allies to dominate the position, and if the Allies attempted to cross elsewhere, they would find the position too strongly held – or so Victor believed. At the last moment, he decided not to destroy the bridge upon which Napoleon had attached such importance. The troops assigned to the defense of Nogent were established in the city during the night and the remainder moved to take up positions on the far bank. In addition, they also made efforts to feed and resupply themselves as rations had been very short in the previous few days.

During the night of 10-11 February Victor directed his troops across the bridge and moved them to new positions. The II Corps, the Paris Reserve and the V Cavalry Corps took up positions at Melz, Mériot and Plessis- Mériot. He confided the defense of Nogent to General de Bourmont.

As things stood, Victor had definitively abandoned the defense of the Nogent passage. The weak garrison of Nogent could not hold sufficient space to permit Napoleon, upon his arrival, to deploy his forces and strike at the Allies who otherwise completely dominated the far bank of the Seine. In addition, his choice of positions at Mériot was bad in that it was too close to the potential combat and would not permit him to maneuver to counter any threat to cross the river.

General de Bourmont was ordered to defend Nogent to the last extremity. His brigade consisted of 16 elite companies, 200 dragoons and an unknown number of guns. He deployed 250 men of the 18th Line Regiment in the barricades to the southwest of the city and 250 men of the 11th Line Regiment in the barricades to the east. He established a reserve of 400 grenadiers and voltigeurs, which he intended to direct to the point of the Allied attack. He had epaulements raised to cover his cannon and detached some officers to the clock tower of the city's principal church to watch the terrain.

The Allies were not idle either. Schwarzenberg had decided to pursue his movement on Sens. He ordered Wrede's 5th Corps and Wittgenstein's 6th Corps to take Nogent. The advanced guards of the two corps had bivouaced before Nogent – straddling the road from Saint-Aubin to Troyes – with Pahlen on the right and Hardegg on the left.

At around 9:00 a.m. Pahlen, supported by Hardegg, launched an attack against Nogent. He advanced with his infantry and artillery – leaving his cavalry behind as a reserve. Towards 10:00 a.m. he launched a jager regiment against the city the along the Seine and an infantry regiment down the road from Troyes. Both regiments deployed facing the city, with their right being on the Seine. In addition, Pahlen placed a few guns on the road to Troyes to fire on the bridges.

General de Bourmont responded to the artillery by sending about 100 voltigeurs up the bank of the Seine to a position where they could fire on these guns. Their fire soon obliged the gunners to withdraw.

Pahlen's infantry attack pushed slowly forward – obliging de Bourmont's voltigeurs to pull back into the gardens on the edge of the city. Profiting from this movement, the Russian infantry accelerated its attack and moved against the eastern edge of the city at a run. Jacomet states that

19 Jacomet, pp. 62-4.

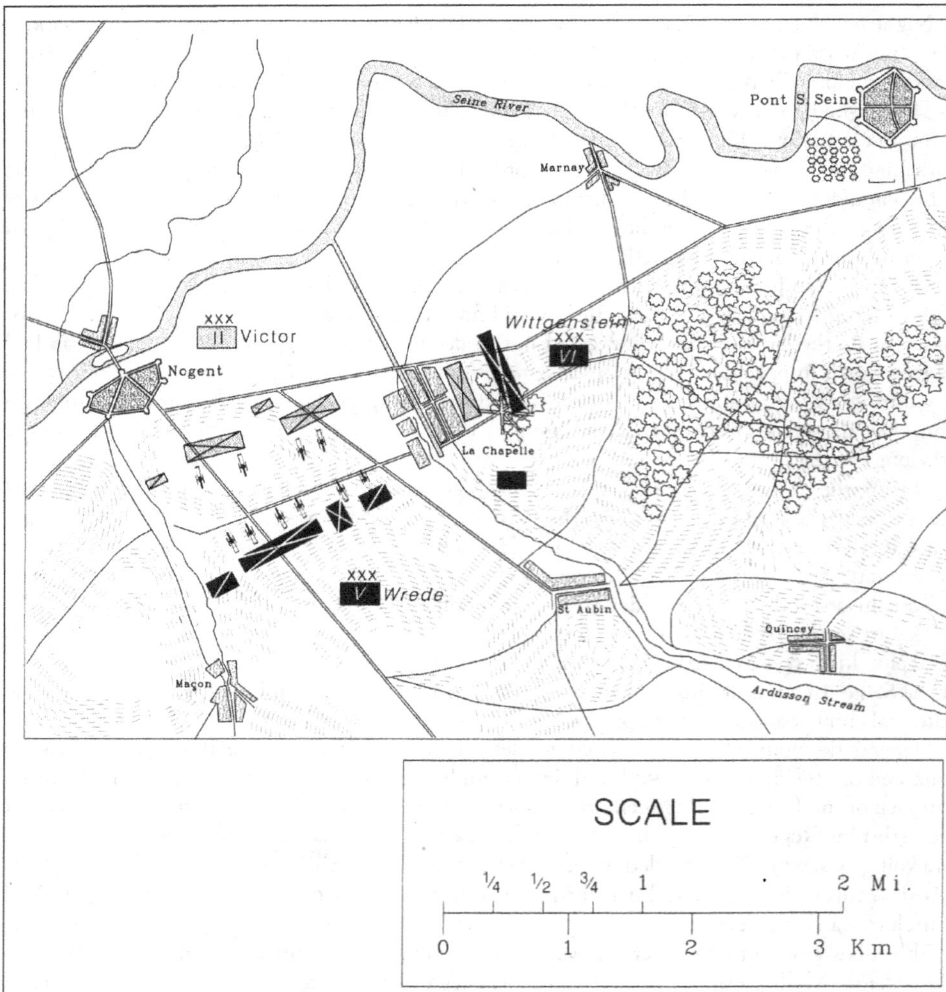

Map 9 Battle of Nogent, February 11 1814, Second Phase.

this movement was executed at the *pas de course*, or, according to French regulations, 250 paces per minute. The only regulated Russian cadence close to this was the UdwonyiSzag, which was 140-160 paces per minute.

General de Bourmont responded by moving a force of voltigeurs into the houses on an island in the Seine where they could fire into the flank of the advancing Russian column. He also placed one 8pdr gun between the two bridges where it could fire canister on the advancing Russians. This was too much for the Russians, and though they had pushed very close to the French defensive positions, they broke and fled back to their lines with significant casualties.

The Russian cavalry chose this moment to support the withdrawing infantry with an audacious charge against the barricade on the road to Troyes. Their charge was greeted by a cannon firing canister enfilading the road and by 80 skirmishers filling the houses and behind crenelated walls. Many saddles were emptied and the decimated Russian cavalry withdrew in disorder.

Pahlen, shaken by this failure, requested that Hardegg move against Nogent and attack it from the west. Hardegg put his troops into motion and moved from Saint-Aubin down the road from Mâcon.

Bourmont was greatly concerned about this new attack, as the city's defenses were incomplete to the west. He hoped the flanking fire from the 100 voltigeurs he had posted in two coal barges tied up to the banks of the Seine would be sufficient to stop this attack. To ensure the effectiveness of their fire, he had the barges moved 150 paces downriver from the city's first barricade. Safe from the bayonets of the attacking Austrians in the middle of the Seine, their fire – plus that from the barricades – was more than the Austrians could handle. Hardegg's assault was also broken.

Pahlen renewed his assault around noon, but Bourmont's dispositions and the courage of the French troops repulsed him yet again. Bourmont, however, was wounded in the knee and passed command to Colonel Voirol of the 18th Line Regiment. The Allies never detected his loss and the fusillade continued the remainder of the night. Despite the change of command and the continued Allied assaults, Nogent was held.[20]

The Yonne-Loing line is abandoned

During the night of 11 February the line on the Yonne River was forced at several points, and Victor – who stood in Mériot – was facing the prospect of being turned on both flanks by an overwhelming Allied force. This was an occurrence which Napoleon had not foreseen. He had anticipated that Schwarzenberg might march to support Blücher's Army of Silesia as he battered it, or that he might continue his march on Paris. However, he never dreamt that Schwarzenberg would divide his forces as Blücher had – opening himself up to the possibility of being defeated one piece at a time. Fortunately for Schwarzenberg, he was facing Victor and Oudinot – not Napoleon. And his fortune continued in that the combined French forces were far from sufficient to give the two marshals any hope of defeating either half of his army should they bring it to battle.

Victor stood immobile before Nogent and Pajol stood at Montereau, where he held the bridge. Both had lost their liberty to maneuver. Their only hope was Oudinot.

Oudinot's situation was difficult. His new corps had yet to be fully formed. That is, the two divisions assigned to the newly-forming VII Corps had yet to rendezvous. Leval's 7th Division was still en route from Spain and had stopped in Provins to allow its stragglers to catch up. It had been reduced by its march to 3,900 effectives.

On 11 February Boyer's 9th Division stood with its 1st Brigade in Melun and the 2nd Brigade in Etampes. Two battalions of the division did not arrive in Nangis until the evening of 10 February. Oudinot also commanded Rottembourg's 2nd Tirialleur Division, but it was burdened with guarding the army's grand park. In addition, Oudinot also commanded Blancard's cavalry column.

Further complicating the situation, since 9 February Oudinot had known that Napoleon might require one of his divisions to cooperate with him in his march on Montmirail. This possibility would, and eventually did, strip him of Leval's 7th Division – his only maneuvering force. Indeed, around noon on 11 February Oudinot received orders from Napoleon to move not only Leval, but Rottembourg's 2nd Tirailleur Division to La Ferté-Gaucher. Napoleon had spent the night in Montmirail and prepared to fall on Sacken between Veilmaisons and La Ferté-sous-Jouarre. He would have no line of retreat but that through Château-Thierry. Napoleon would

20 Jacomet, pp. 65-8.

have only 20,000 infantry and he wished to have numerical superiority on the battlefield. Leval and the two divisions were sent in the direction of Montmirail and Veilmaisons when they began hearing the sounds of cannon.[21]

In case Boyer's 9th Division had not arrived in Melun and Nangis – and if the Allies had already begun an offensive movement and were threatening Montereau – then, and only then, was Oudinot authorized to send only one of his divisions to Montmirail. Oudinot, it is fair to say, was required to make the greatest sacrifices necessary to permit Napoleon to accomplish the destruction of Sacken's corps.

However, Napoleon's orders put Oudinot in a most embarrassing situation. That morning he received dispatches from Pajol announcing that Platov's Cossacks were about to cut him off from Montereau and that he had withdrawn to Fossard. It is true that at the same time he learned that Allix still held Sens, but he did not know how long Allix would resist the Allied assaults. Oudinot was being encircled and his line of retreat was being compromised. No one would be between the Allies and Fontainebleau. Pajol had only 1,200 cavalry and some National Guards – far from enough to stop their advance. Should he cover Montereau and assure Napoleon's assault on Sacken, or should he move to protect the French positions at Nogent-sur-Seine? Oudinot, however, found his decision easy and he followed orders. He directed General Leval to move his division and two batteries to march on La Ferté-Gaucher escorted by Blancard's 400-man cavalry column.

This left Oudinot with Rottembourg's 2nd Tirailleur Division and the baggage train that embarrassed his every movement. As for Boyer's 9th Division, Oudinot awaited news of its location with great anxiety on 11 February. That evening, he was to learn that the 1st Brigade was in Melun and that it would arrive in Nangis on the 12th. The 2nd Brigade, he learned, was some distance to the rear.[22]

During the evening of 11 February Schwarzenberg received word of Napoleon's assault on Blücher's scattered army. He waited impatiently for news of Nogent's capture. He wished to push Wrede and Wittgenstein's 5th and 6th Corps over the Seine as soon as possible. As he waited, Count Witte – who had been dispatched at 10:00 p.m. the previous evening by Blücher – arrived in Troyes and informed Schwarzenberg of the destruction of Olsufiev's 11th Corps at Champaubert (10 February) and of the critical situation of the Army of Silesia.

Estimating the strength of the French army (based on the terror it inspired by this last operation), Witte told Schwarzenberg that Napoleon had established himself with a force of 50,000 men between the 2nd (Prussian) Corps (Kleist) and 10th Corps (Kapsevich) on one hand and the 1st (Prussian) Corps (Yorck) and Sacken's corps on the other. Schwarzenberg found his plans dashed and began to react. He resolved to concentrate the Allied guard and Russian reserve at Méry which, by fortunate accident, he had directed the previous day on this point in order to be able to send them against either Plancy or Nogent. He then ordered General Diebitsch – sent to Plancy by Barclay de Tolly with the Russian Guard Light Cavalry Division and a brigade of grenadiers – to move forward to establish, as soon as possible, communications with the two armies. He directed that Wittgenstein, if Nogent should not fall, to prepare to cross the Seine higher up in order to link up with Diebitsch. If Nogent were to fall, Wittgenstein was to march on Villenoxe. He then ordered Wrede to support this movement by moving his forces to Provins.[23]

During the morning of 12 February Wittgenstein and Wrede moved the bulk of their forces into position by Nogent. At that time they also learned of Olsufiev's destruction. Wrede moved

21 Jacomet, pp. 80-1.
22 Jacomet, pp. 82-3.
23 Koch, Vol. I, p. 294.

his force before Nogent with the intention of striking the French in the city – then he settled down with Wittgenstein to discuss the problems of the pending assault.

Wrede decided that it would be best to detach Lamotte's 3rd Bavarian Division to Bray-sur-Seine to re-establish the bridge, to then cross the Seine and fall on Victor's flank. He then moved a division to Traînel so it could move against either Nogent or Bray depending on how the operations progressed.

On his side, Wittgenstein detached General Rüdinger with a mixed column of infantry, cavalry and artillery to Pont-sur-Seine with the goal of crossing the Seine and falling on Victor's left flank. The forces which remained before Nogent were not to attack the city. The fire from the city was too intense and the troops before the city were more concerned with maintaining their position than making any gains. However, if the French remained in the city by nightfall, they would execute a general attack against the city.

During the morning of 12 February Lamotte's 3rd Bavarian Division occupied Bray-sur-Seine. He established his artillery on the riverbank and quickly drove off the tiny force of French National Guardsmen trying to hold the far bank. Lamotte then sent his troops across in boats and took control of the far bank, occupied the village of Mouy-sur-Seine and made preparations to throw a bridge over the river.

Oudinot, despite the appearance of Allied cavalry in Bray the previous night, did not believe that the Allies would attempt to cross the Seine that morning and persisted in the opinion that they were intent on marching on Paris. During the morning, on Berthier's orders, he moved Napoleon's equipment, the grand artillery park and the Grand General Headquarters – under the escort of Rottembourg's 2nd Tirailleur Division, 200 cavalry and some gendarmes – to the city of Nangis.

Oudinot's misconceptions, however, were soon dispelled when he heard artillery fire coming from Bray-sur-Seine and reports arrived of the Bavarian attack. Oudinot's martial instincts sent him marching to the sound of the guns with all the troops he could muster, despite the gravity of his situation. He judged it more serious that the Allies might force the Seine than that they might be marching on Paris, and he advised Victor of the situation.

Oudinot judged that Victor's situation would become untenable if the Allies crossed at Bray. He also recommended to Victor that he immediately break the bridge at Nogent and leave only those troops necessary to deny the Allies a quick crossing at Nogent. Then he should, with the rest of his forces, move as quickly as possible to Provins.

Oudinot also advised Pajol of the situation and asked him to send word of what was happening at Montereau. If the Allies re-established a bridge at Bray, he feared that Pajol would not be able to hold Montereau.[24]

Oudinot had at his disposal a force of about 1,500 men left from Rottembourg's 2nd Tirailleur Division after the 500 had been sent off to escort the grand park. He also had a detachment of some 300 men from Leval's 7th Division. This latter force was a collection of stragglers that had not arrived in time to join Leval as he marched to Vauchamps.

Oudinot directed Rottembourg to send two battalions immediately and to link up with Leval's 300 stragglers and half of a horse battery. This force was placed under the command of a général de brigade and sent as quickly as possible to the Bray bridge to dispute an Allied passage "to the death" and to prevent the Bavarians from rebuilding the broken arch of the bridge. He still hoped that some of Boyer's troops would arrive that evening in Nangis.

Prior to departing from Provins, Oudinot sent an aide de camp – Colonel Jacqueminot – with an order to General Boyer or to whoever was the senior officer of the 9th Division that was in

24 Jacomet, pp. 87-9.

Nangis to take what forces were available to him and march to Donnemarie with all diligence. They were to take from the two batteries then in Nangis the appropriate number of guns suitable to their total strength.

Unfortunately, Oudinot's luck failed him yet again and there were no troops to be found in Nangis. Nonetheless, he moved personally to Donnemarie – arriving at 4:00 p.m. that afternoon with the intention of rallying whoever appeared for an attack on Bray the following day.

Oudinot asked Victor to move on Provins and to send a strong detachment directly against the right flank of the Allied forces crossing at Bray – and to put at his disposition, if not all, the major part of his cavalry. Oudinot hoped, under these conditions, to have gathered up sufficient forces to successfully repulse the Allies as they moved out of the Bray bridgehead. Oudinot understood that the Allies had to be stopped before they could push a significant force across the Seine. Bray was the weak point in the French line. Victor was at Nogent and Pajol was at Montereau, and if the Allies took possession of a crossing at Bray, they would have to withdraw – abandoning the best defensive position for miles.[25]

During the day of 12 February the Bavarians of Lamotte's 3rd Bavarian Division repaired the bridge, and during the night the entire division crossed to the right bank of the Seine. Rüdinger – at Wittgenstein's orders – crossed the Seine with eight squadrons, two battalions and two 6pdr guns and moved on Pont-sur-Seine. He was ordered to throw a bridge over the Seine and to advance on Nogent via the right bank, but Nogent's fall would render the move on Nogent pointless. Rüdinger crossed the Seine without difficulty and was then ordered to Villenoxe, where he found himself in a light skirmish with part of Milhaud's cavalry.

The fall of Nogent

When Victor learned that Bray had fallen – at about 6:00 a.m. – he ordered Nogent evacuated. As the French withdrew, a violent attack was launched by the Russians. The Russian column on the main road was counterattacked and the Russians were stopped. Colonel Voirol capped his defense of Nogent with a smooth evacuation and the destruction of the bridge over the Seine with an explosive charge.[26]

When the bridge was destroyed, it had on it a Russian officer and about 50 Russian soldiers who had advanced with more ardour than sense.

The French defense of Nogent had cost the Allies 1,800 casualties, while the French had lost only about 400. The destruction of the bridge delayed the Allies, but not for long as Wrede made its reconstruction his major concern. Meanwhile, Rechberg's Bavarian 1st Division marched to Nogent with the goal of crossing the Seine and operating on the far bank the following morning. The bulk of the Allied army then bivouaced around Nogent – using the city as a post for its advanced guard. The following morning, a pontoon bridge was erected at Nogent to permit their easy passage over the Seine.

Victor was shortly rejoined by the defenders of Nogent, and together they departed Mériot at 3:00 a.m. during the morning of 13 February and moved on Provins, where they joined Oudinot. To the west, Pajol held Montereau and Fossard. General Allix had joined General Montbrun in Pont-sur-Yonne on 11 February and then moved on Montereau without having destroyed the bridge at Pont-sur-Yonne. On 12 February the two generals arrived in Fossard-le-Grand and sent orders to Pajol, who had just moved forward to cover their retreat. Pajol had the intention of holding Fossard as long as possible so as to assure the French movement from Montereau and to not withdraw until

25 Jacomet, pp. 90-1.
26 Jacomet, p. 92.

the last possible moment. He estimated that the corps, which had attacked General Allix at Sens, was moving on the Loing. It was his belief that the Allies would content themselves with occupying Montereau and not continue to advance down the road to Paris because of the chance of an attack on their flank (should they do so).

Word was shortly to arrive in the French camp of Napoleon's victory at Montmirail; of the pending arrival of reinforcements; and of Napoleon's intention to march to the support of his southern armies. The Minister of War also announced that strong reserves would be marching on Fontainebleau, Essonne and Corbeil. Pajol was also to receive orders from Oudinot to defend Montereau to the death. All of this gave Pajol confidence in the future and he set about preparing to deal with the Allied advance. He caused the city's defenses to be improved and took up positions on the heights behind the city.

In front of Pajol, the Württemberg 4th Corps stood in the village of Sens and pushed its advanced posts to Pont-sur-Yonne. The length of the Yonne was in Allied hands. Cossacks attacked Montargis, whose garrison withdrew to Gen. Parties of Allied cavalry were seen at many points between Montigny and Ury and in Nemours, where they exchanged shots with the French garrison. Fontainebleau appeared to be at the Allies' mercy.

However, of all of these occurrences, the capture of Bray by the Allies made Pajol's situation most difficult. That evening, Oudinot wrote him saying that he had a small force in Donnemarie and if he was unable to hold the Allies at Bray, Pajol's situation in Montereau would become untenable. Oudinot also directed the headquarters and convoys under the orders of General Sorbier to withdraw to Guignes.

Sorbier had two battalions of Young Guard, a battalion of the 155th Line Regiment and a detachment of 100 men from the 26th Chasseurs à cheval Regiment to guard the convoy. During the course of this movement, he picked up the 6/116th Line Regiment – part of Leval's division.

The fall of Bray had very grave consequences for Oudinot and Victor. Victor was threatened with attacks on both flanks and abandoned Nogent. The choke points had been lost and the Allies were once again free to march on Paris.[27]

Engagement at Luisetaines and Cuterelles

During the morning of 13 February Wittgenstein crossed the Seine at Pont and marched on Villenoxe. His advanced guard marched to Saint-Martin-de-Chennetron and l'Echelle. Rüdinger's force moved through Mont-le-Potier, Mériot and Sordun, where he encountered the French rearguard after it had evacuated Provins and moved down the road to Nangis.

During the night of 12 February Count Wittgenstein rebuilt the bridge at Bray and sent his troops over it at 5:00 a.m. the next morning. Lamotte's Bavarian 3rd Division led the passage over the bridge forming the column's head – his 1st Brigade leading and the 2nd close behind, supported by the 1st and 3rd Bavarian Cavalry Brigades and finally, the Austrian Szeckler Hussar and Knesevich Dragoon Regiments.

Barely had Lamotte's division crossed the Seine when a French column was observed in St.-Sauveur. This was the scratch force that Oudinot had pulled together – part of Rottembourg's 2nd Tirailleur Division – on learning of the capture of Bray. This force was reinforced at 6:00 a.m. on 13 February with Gauthier's brigade – part of Boyer's 9th Division drawn from the Army of the Pyrenees.[28] It was Oudinot's intention to dispute the Allied crossing of the Seine or engaging what had already crossed.

27 Jacomet, pp. 93-5.
28 Jacomet, p. 103.

Wrede had ordered Lamotte to move his division down the road to Donnemarie. Wrede then ordered the two cavalry regiments (Austrian Szeckler Hussar and Knesevich Dragoon Regiments) to move on Everly to cover the road to Provins. General Frimont – with Hardegg and Rechberg's divisions – would not arrive before noon, but they were ordered to take up positions (Rechberg on the road to Donnemarie and Hardegg near Ormes).[29]

Lamotte's advanced guard – led by the squadrons of Rittmeister Lodron and Madroux, 4th Bavarian Chevauxleger – attacked the village of St.-Sauveur, which was occupied by the forward posts of Oudinot's advanced guard (two battalions from Rottembourg's division, 300 men from Leval's division and half a horse battery). The French pickets were driven back to the main French position on the heights to the north of the small villages of Cuterelles and Lusietaines. As they withdrew, the French lost a few prisoners to the Allied cavalry.

Oudinot deployed three brigades of infantry on the Cuterelles heights – in a very strong position – and strongly garrisoned Cuterelles. Count von Wrede – having formed his advanced guard on Vimpelles – pushed the skirmishers of Lamotte's Bavarian 3rd Division to just below the village of Cuterelles, which was strongly engaged by the French. Lamotte's division advanced behind them in line. Wrede, seeing that Oudinot's position could not be taken by a frontal assault, attempted to turn this position on the left. He ordered his chief of staff to occupy the village of Luisetaines with a battalion of the 8th Bavarian Line Regiment (800 men) and six squadrons under Oberst Kracht (700 men) – resolving to take a plateau which extended from Cuterelles to Luisetaines. Once on this plateau, he felt he could place his forces behind the French left.[30] As soon as Oudinot saw this, he sent three battalions.

It needs to be remembered that, at this time, a French line infantry battalion – theoretically 840 men – would be very lucky to have as many as 200 men and three guns to Luisetaines, which had previously been abandoned by the French.[31] A very hot engagement resulted and the French succeeded in establishing themselves in the major portion of the town – pushing back the three Bavarian companies, commanded by Major Massenhausen, that occupied Luisetaines. However, the Bavarians were reinforced by the 800 infantry of the Isar Kreise Legion and the four guns of the Rüdesheimer Half-Battery, which gave them the edge. Count Wrede positioned the half-battery himself, and two companies of the Isar Kreise Legion – supported by the grenadier company of the 8th Line Regiment – attacked and pushed back the French. A battalion of the Bavarian 9th Line Regiment – under Oberst Treuberg, supported by a half-battery – then struck the French in the flank and broke their resistance. The French were pursued as far as the Donnemarie heights.[32]

Oudinot maintained his position, except for Cuterelles, until 4:00 p.m. when Rechberg's 1st Bavarian Division arrived on the field. At the same time, General Frimont appeared with Hardegg's infantry division and Spleny's cavalry on the road from Provins. Wrede then felt he could successfully attack the French.

Rechberg moved to a position parallel to Lamotte and several batteries began firing on Cuterelles, which Wrede proposed to attack with the 11th Bavarian Line. This attack, however, was stopped when it was learned that a strong French column had engaged Hardegg's 1st Division (5th Corps) on the Paroy heights. This new French force was part of Victor's II Corps as it withdrew from Provins in two columns. One of these two columns had come down the road to Nangis and the other on the road to Donnemarie. Both were intent on supporting Oudinot. As night fell, Count Wrede would risk nothing on his left when his right was threatened and

29 Koch, Vol. I, p. 295.
30 Sporschil, Vol. 2, 1st Band, p. 319.
31 Jacomet, p. 104.
32 von Damitz, Vol. II, pp. 246-7.

renounced the effort on Cuterelles. However, he did reinforce his position in Luisetaines with two battalions, a few squadrons of cavalry and three guns. He then let his army go into bivouac. Lamotte's troops settled in between Vimpelles and Luisetaines; Rechberg's Bavarian 1st Division, now in the second line, stood behind the Vieille-Seine stream; Frimont's corps was in Everly, and the artillery remained on the heights between the two lines of infantry.[33]

Oudinot's forces had suffered about 600 casualties – including Gauthier, who was wounded – in the day's actions. Even though Victor was joining him, Oudinot did not feel his position adequately strong and ordered a withdrawal during the night to Nangis. Victor's troops moved first – quickly followed by those of Oudinot. At 3:00 a.m. the two corps were in position before Nangis. The Allies were either not aware of the retreat, or consciously chose not to interfere with it, as the French were not disturbed as they withdrew.

Oudinot sent a report of the actions to both Napoleon and his brother, King Joseph – then serving as Napoleon's representative in Paris. He advised them of the Allied crossing of the Seine and called for reinforcements. Napoleon now began to regret calling Leval's 7th Division north to support his operations. Though Leval's division had arrived on the field at Vauchamps, it was too late to intervene and its usefulness was lost to both armies. As it was impossible to send Leval south to Oudinot, Napoleon ordered Macdonald to draw what he could of his half-organized corps – be they line or National Guard – and march to the support of Oudinot and Victor. Macdonald's XI Corps would contain 12,000 men when it arrived in Guignes.

On 14 February the two marshals were marching on Nangis. They detached a few small pickets on the roads to Provins and Donnemarie. At 3:00 a.m. Oudinot's troops were on the road to Donnemarie and those of Victor were on the road to Provins.

On 15 February the French and Allied armies stood as follows: the Allies held Moret and Fontainebleau and had crossed the Loing. However, Trelliard's 5th Heavy Cavalry Division – drawn from the Army of Spain – and a brigade of Young Guard under General Lagrange had departed Melun and were marching to liberate Fontainebleau. GD Charpentier was organizing a force in Essonne to serve as a reserve and to march, via Corbeil, to support the movements of Victor and Oudinot.

	Infantry	Cavalry
Old Guard, Friant's division	4,500	
Ney:		
Meunier and Curial's divisions	3,000	
II Corps: Victor		
Duhèsme & Château's divisions	5,000	
Reserve: Gérard		
Dufour & Hamelinaye's divisions	4,500	
VII Corps: Oudinot		
Rottembourg's division & Gauthier's brigade	7,500	
XI Corps: Duke of Tarente		
Albert, Brayer & Amey's divisions	8,000	
Guard Cavalry:		
Laferrière, Excelmans & Pacz		3,000
V Cavalry Corps: Milhaud,		
Piré, Briche & l'Héritier's divisions		4,400
VI Cavalry Corps: Kellermann		

33 Koch, Vol. I, pp. 295-8.

Jacquinot, Treillard & Roussel's divisions		4,200
On the right flank:		
General Pajol:		
Pacthod's infantry division	5,000	
Pajol's cavalry division		1,400
By Fontainebleau:		
Allix's division	2,000	500
Charpentier's division	3,500	
Arriving later:		
Leval's infantry division	4,500	
Saint-Germain's cavalry division		1,300
Boyer de Rebeval's division	3,300	500
Total:	50,800	15,300[34]

The main body of Bianchi's corps occupied Montereau. Count Giulay's forces were between Pont-sur-Yonne and Villeneuve-la-Guyard. The main Allied army stood on the right of the Seine, though not concentrated; it was concentrating its forces into major blocks.

Giulay.

Barclay de Tolly had advanced from Méry to Pont-sur-Seine where the Tsar and King of Prussia had established their headquarters. The headquarters of Schwarzenberg was in Nogent with the Russian reserves. The Crown Prince of Württemberg arrived in Bray with the bulk of his 4th Corps. The Austrian reserves were bivouaced between Pont and Seins. M. Liechtenstein's 1st Light Division stood between Bray and Joigny. Forward, on the Seine, Count Wittgenstein occupied Villenoxe and Barbonne. A detachment under Prince Lubomirski observed the Meilleray, in the valley of the Grand-Morin. General Diebitsch was charged with re-establishing communications between the main army and the Army of Silesia and his forces were centered on Montmirail. He had earlier cleared Montmirail and Sézanne of their French garrisons. Finally, Wrede was engaged against Victor and Oudinot – standing with Rechberg's Bavarian 1st Division in Donnemarie, Frimont's corps in Magneux and Lamotte's Bavarian 3rd Division in Villeneuve-le-Comte. A few squadrons were detached to observe the French II and VII Corps in Nangis.[35] Victor, Macdonald, Oudinot, Allix, Pacthod and Pajol concentrated their forces around Nangis. Pajol, Allix and Pacthod occupied the heights of Châlet, with Pajol's cavalry held in the Valence forest and scouting in the direction of Montereau.

King Joseph intervenes

Victor, Macdonald and Oudinot – separated from Napoleon because of his march against the Army of Silesia – found themselves without direction and sent a request to King Joseph, Napoleon's brother and his first lieutenant, requesting that he provide guidance for their operations.

34 von Damitz, Vol. II, pp. 264-5.
35 Koch, Vol. I, pp. 298-300.

Joseph, after receiving the advice of soldiers who knew the region where the three marshals fought, judged that it would be dangerous to leave the army under three marshals of equal rank and authority. This army stood in an open countryside, in the Brie plains – which were favorable to cavalry actions – and cavalry was something the Allies had in significant numbers. He decided that it would be preferable to pull the French line behind the Yères River, which would give them some sort of a barrier to defend. Though not as formidable a barrier as the Marne, it did provide some bottlenecks and limited the terrain that the French would need to protect. One of these positions, Villeneuve-Saint-Georges, had been regarded by the great French Marshal Turenne as an excellent defensive position for a small army – and a small army was exactly what the French had.

This position had the advantage of having its right naturally refused and that the position of Villeneuve could be retained for the retreat. In addition, the left moved obliquely towards the point where Napoleon intended to affect his junction with the three marshals. If the Allies were to advance against this position, they would be moving into a broken terrain occupied by forces unknown to them. This, it was assumed, would give Napoleon sufficient time to affect his movement, merge with the French forces in the region and move to the offensive.

These instructions issued, the three marshals took up the following positions: Victor stood in Chaulmes on the 15th with his left in Fontenay and his right in the Sénart forest on a plateau covered with vineyards and its foot covered by a steeply-banked brook. Oudinot took up positions at Guignes on the main road from Paris to Provins – having his advanced posts in Mormant and his headquarters in Ouzouer-le-Vougis. Macdonald stood on Oudinot's right and had his headquarters in Solers. Pajol departed Châtelet and withdrew to Cramayel, with communications with Macdonald running through Sognolle and with Charpentier through Lieursaint and Corbeil.[36]

Charpentier had been ordered to withdraw to Essonne and to concentrate the Young Guard Corps in a defensive position. He was to occupy Corbeil and tie his movements to those of the three marshals. His corps contained 7,300 men, 650 cavalry and 12 guns.[37]

The French artillery prepared several pontoon bridges over the Seine above the junction with the Marne to permit the French army to withdraw to the left bank of the Seine with the least potential problems should they be pushed from their line on the Yères and the positions of Villeneuve-Saint-Georges.

These measures were executed in good order, but a misunderstanding resulted in an increase in the level of alarm in Paris. King Joseph had ordered that the army's baggage be withdrawn across the Yères. However, this order was either misunderstood or deliberately disobeyed. The train withdrew not only across the Yères, but across the Marne, and established itself below Paris in the Bercy park. With the appearance of the army so near Paris, the capital feared the worst – and those fears were calmed only with the greatest difficulty. The Allies did not follow this movement, and as news arrived in Paris of the defeats inflicted on Yorck and Sacken, a nervous calm returned to Paris.

A council of war was called as a result of the defeats inflicted on Blücher. It was decided that the Army of Silesia would probably be obliged to withdraw on Châlons. They felt that the main Allied army would be obliged to follow Napoleon's movements, while the forces of Wrede and Wittgenstein moved with all haste to Sézanne with the goal of attacking Napoleon's rear, attract his attention and to permit the Army of Silesia to disengage. It was also hoped that this would permit the main Allied army to withdraw to Arcis or Troyes.

Everything was ready to implement this plan when General Haacke arrived at midnight on the 15th with news of the Battle of Vauchamps and Blücher's defeat.

36 Koch, Vol. I, pp. 301-2.

37 Reports 13 and 15 February, French National Archives, Carton AF^{IV} 1669B.

The immediate result is that the Allies abandoned their plan to strike at Napoleon's rear. It was no longer a question of withdrawing to their old positions on the Seine and the Yonne. The corps of Bianchi, Wittgenstein, and the Crown Prince of Württemberg now moved to screen the main army from any aggressive movement by Napoleon.

As the Allies reacted to their defeat at Vauchamps, Chef d'escadron d'ordonnance Gourgaud arrived in Paris to announce to King Joseph that Napoleon was about to arrive. He brought with him news of the great French victory at Vauchamps and took back to Napoleon word of Joseph's actions and those of the three marshals. Napoleon was pleased with Joseph's decisions vis-a-vis the Paris Guard. He also approved the retreat. Indeed, far from dismayed with their retreat, he was pleased to find their armies in good shape and capable of assuming the offensive.[38]

38 Koch, Vol. I, pp. 303-4.

9

The Allies Withdraw: The Engagements at Mormant, Valjouan, Montereau and Méry, 15-23 February 1814

After chasing Blücher from the field at Vauchamps, Napoleon's attention was drawn south to support his marshals facing the main Allied army under Schwarzenberg. Barraged by their panic-filled dispatches, Napoleon had become alarmed and turned south to protect his capital.

Napoleon covered his movement and assured his left by detaching Marmont with the VI Corps and the I Cavalry Corps to hold a position around Etoges, where he was to observe Blücher. Grouchy was sent with 800 cavalry of the II Cavalry Corps and Leval's 7th Division to La Ferté-sous-Jouarre, from where he could support either Marmont or Mortier as he watched Winzingerode's corps at Villers-Cotterets. He also placed General Vincent in Château-Thierry with a flying corps to cover the main road from Châlons to Paris.

Napoleon and his Guard departed Montmirail on 15 February and marched south. The infantry made some of the march on foot and partly on wagons, while the cavalry marched day and night. In 36 hours, they covered 150 kilometers (92 miles).

Arriving in Guignes, Napoleon quickly drew to him General Trelliard's 5th Heavy Cavalry (Dragoon) Division – coming from Spain – and about 1,100 veteran guard grenadiers and chasseurs à Pied, drawn from the Army of the Pyrenees and from the Guard depots. He then issued the following orders:

> Victor is to move before Mormant with his corps, Milhaud's cavalry and that of the Count of Valmy (GD Kellermann), which arrived yesterday.
>
> Duke of Reggio (Oudinot) shall move his corps before Guignes; his headquarters on the side of L'Etage.
>
> The Guard Cavalry shall be in column; the tail in Fontenay and its head in Chaulmes. The Old Guard infantry shall be in Chaulmes.
>
> The Duke of Tarente (Macdonald) shall unite his corps in Etars and Ouzouer-le-Vougis and shall cross the Seigneurs bridge with a division, which he shall place in Yèbles.
>
> Prince of Moscow (Ney) and his two Young Guard divisions shall take a position in Lahoussaye. General Pajol shall move to St.-Germain-de-Laxis.
>
> All of the parks which have been evacuated to Brie and Charenton shall march all night to arrive in Ouzouer-le-Vougis. The engineering park and sappers shall cross only the Seigneurs bridge to come to Guignes.
>
> They shall have their artillery with them – carrying two or three days' bread – and be ready to march and fight at the break of day on the 17th.

The French army, with about 50,000 men, sprang to life with Napoleon's arrival. The strategic situation presented Napoleon with interesting possibilities as only the corps of Wittgenstein, Wrede and Württemberg stood before him on the right bank of the Seine.

After learning of Napoleon's victories over the Army of Silesia, Schwarzenberg had determined to retreat. He ordered Wittgenstein, Wrede and Württemberg to stop their offensive movements, but Wittgenstein chose to ignore these instructions and moved from Provins towards Nangis – pushing Count Pahlen's cavalry before him. General Rüdinger stood at the head of Pahlen's advanced guard on the road to Rosoy – and on that to Brie-Comte-Robert – when he found himself under attack by the French rearguard on the heights at Beauvoir. He was thrown back on the main body of the advanced guard, which then fell back to Bailly, where it found protection under a large force of Allied artillery and Rosen's brigade.

Wittgenstein, by G. Dawe.

Württemberg pushed a reconnaissance force towards Melun, which GB Montbrun had abandoned as he withdrew on Vielleneuve-Saint-Georges. However, when Württemberg arrived, he found that it was now occupied by General Allix, whom Pajol had posted there. He judged it prudent to withdraw to the Surville heights and to occupy Châtelet, Sivry, Vraines and Vulaines with advanced posts.

Reports of strong columns of French infantry passing through Rosoy to Guignes flowed into Schwarzenberg. He wrote Count Wittgenstein – advising him that it was his intention to push his corps and those of Wrede and Württemberg to the right (back of the Seine) not with the goal of marching on Paris, but to establish them in a position by Montereau, Donnemarie and Provins in such a manner as to face the right flank of the French army. He continued by saying that the following day, it was his intention to withdraw his forces to Provins – leaving only his advanced guard facing Nangis. He intended to occupy Villenoxe with two battalions and some cavalry; to send a reconnaissance force towards Ferté-Gaucher and Coulommiers; and, in case the French advanced in force, to concentrate the main army by Bray.

On 16 February the Allied army was deployed as follows: The Russian reserves were at Nogent with orders to destroy the bridge at Pont. Count Wittgenstein was in Nangis, his advanced guard in Mormant; the Bavarians (Wrede) were in Donnemarie, with Hardegg's division in Nangis; the Württembergers were in Montereau – scouting the roads to Melun and Nangis; Count Bianchi stood between Villeneuve-la-Guyard and Moret, with his advanced guard in Fontainebleau; Count Giulay was in Pont-sur-Yonne; the Austrian reserve and M. Liechtenstein's 1st Light Division were in Sens.[1]

On the wings of the army, smaller independent forces operated. General Diebitsch continued to operate in Marmont's rear and Prince Lubomirski watched the countryside from Grand-Morin to Meilleray. To the left, Platov stood in Nemours. General Seslavin's Cossacks spread alarm through the French countryside as far as the gates of Orléans.

On 16 February Napoleon, present at Guignes, gave his orders for his offensive movement for the next day. The positions and strengths of the French army was:

1 Koch, Vol. I, p. 309.

II Corps (Victor) at Chaulmes; had its advance posts toward Verneuil and Beauvoir (464 officers, 6,085 men and 40 cannon)
VII Corps (Oudinot) at Guignes and Ouzouer-le-Vougis; his advance posts towards l'Estang (293 officers, 7,223 men and 34 cannon)
XI Corps (Macdonald) at Solers (358 officers, 8,439 men and 37 cannon)
V Cavalry Crops (Milhaud) – containing the divisions of Piré, Briche and l'Héritier – were at Arcis, observing Beauvoir and Courtomer (4,700 sabers). The dragoon division of Treilhard, coming from Spain, arrived at Guignes on the 16th. It formed part of the VI Cavalry Corps, not yet constituted, under Kellermann (2,788 sabers).

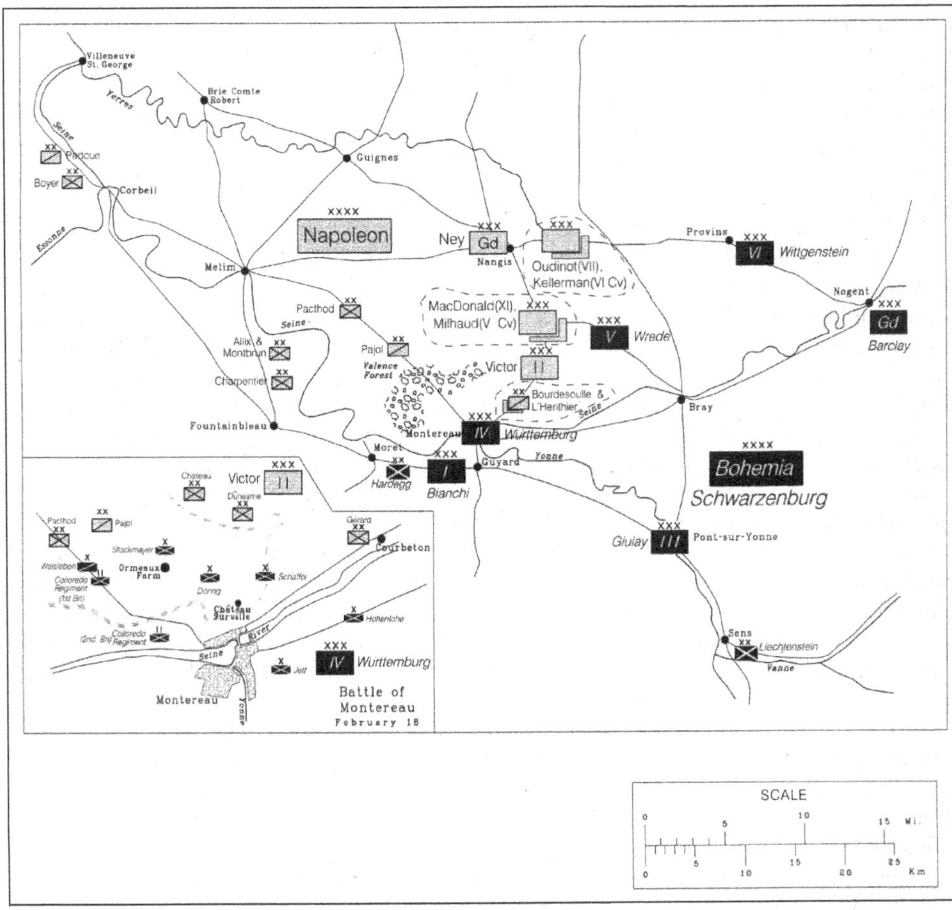

Map 10 Strategic Situation, February 17 1814.

The Old Guard arrived at Fontenay. The cavalry and artillery – plus the two divisions of Young Guard (Ney) – reached La Houssaye. All the corps of the Guard came from Montmirail in the suite of the Emperor by La Ferté-sous-Jouarre and Meaux.

Napoleon's Grand General Headquarters was at Guignes. The baggage of the Grand General Headquarters, the parks and the convoys had withdrawn to Charenton by the orders of King Joseph. On the right, Pajol – with his cavalry – was at Lisy, Fourches, Limoges and Moissy. His 1st Division (Allix) was at Réau; occupied Melun with a detachment of 400 men. His 2nd Division (Pacthod) was at Everly. The total of Pajol's corps was 6,255 infantry and 1,800 to 2,000 cavalry. General Bordesoulle installed at Guignes 581 horsemen of all arms – recruited from Paris on the 15th and organized into three squadrons: one of light cavalry and two of cuirassiers.

To the rear, the 1st Guard Reserve Division (Charpentier) was at Corbeil and Essonne; the 2nd Guard Reserve Division (Boyer de Rebeval) was in formation at the same points. The 1st Reserve Division (Duke of Padua) was in formation at Villeneuve-Saint-Georges.

One should not consider these corps having a regular or uniform organization. The infantry was formed by brigades and not by regiment. Each brigade consisted of five to seven battalions from various units and whose strength varied greatly.

In addition, though the corps of Victor and Oudinot contained only young soldiers brought into the ranks of the regular army, the XI Corps and Pacthod's division were organized almost exclusively of National Guards. This force contained the divisions of Allix, Charpentier, Boyer de Rebeval and the Duke of Padua. The cavalry, in contrast – with the exception of Bordesoulle's conscripts – was formed of excellent elements, which were battle-hardened by many engagements. The dragoons that came from Spain under Treillhard would bring more shine to their reputation for valor.[2]

Facing the French, the Allies occupied the following positions: The Russian reserves were at Nogent-sur-Seine and Bray with the Tsar, the King of Prussia and Schwarzenberg. The Austrian reserves and Liechtenstein's cavalry were at Sens. Wittgenstein was at Nangis with his advance guard at Mormant, under Count Pahlen (10 battalions, four regiments of Cossacks and 14 squadrons of Rüdinger's division). The Bavarian Corps of Wrede was at Donnemarie – pushing on Nangis the divisions of Antoine Hardegg and Spleny (forming with Lamotte's division, Frémont's corps, under the order of Wrede). Giulay's corps was at Pont-sur-Yonne. Ignace Hardegg's division was at Moret and Fontainebleau; Bianchi's division was at Fossard; von Württemberg's corps was at Fossard; Platov and Seslavin's Cossacks were in the Gatinaise and the Orléanaise; Diebitsch and Lubmirski's were at Montmirail and Meilleray.[3]

It was on the 16th that Schwarzenberg learned simultaneously of Blücher's disastrous defeat, Napoleon's march on Meaux with his Guard, and his presence at Guignes at the head of a new army. Upon learning this he issued orders directing all the corps engaged on the right bank of the Seine to withdraw towards Troyes and destroy the bridges over the Seine. He ordered Blücher to join him at Troyes. He planned on concentrating the two armies and marching in concert on Paris.

During the afternoon of the 16th, Napoleon issued his orders. His plan was to drive back the heads of the Allied columns engaged on the road to Paris and to seize, as quickly as possible, the bridges at Montereau and Bray in order to oblige Schwarzenberg to accept combat with his forces dispersed before the Army of Silesia could reconstitute itself and come to Schwarzenberg's aide.

Napoleon's orders were for Victor to take the head and, on the 17th at daybreak, attack Mormant. Count Milhaud, with the divisions of Piré (light cavalry) and Briche (dragoons); the Count de Valmy (Kellermann), with the divisions of Treilhard and l'Héritier (the latter just

2 *Les combats de Mormant, de Villeneuve-le-Comte, et de Montereau (17 et 18 février 1814)*, pp. 1-3.
3 Ibid, p. 3.

coming under his orders that day) were to support Victor. Oudinot was at l'Étang, having Bordesoulle on his right. The Guard, the convoys, the parks and the XI Corps were brought towards Guignes ready to march out – and orders were given to the Minister of War to expedite there, under the command of General Boutard, all the available artillery in Paris. Pajol – with his cavalry and Pacthod's division – was to move to Le Châtelet, then Montereau, while his other division (Allix) was to join Charpentier's division and Montbrun's 200 horse operating on the left bank and marching on Fontainebleau and Moret.

During the evening of the 16th, Oudinot established himself at l'Étang after having driven the Allied advance posts back on Pecqueux. Victor, who was to prepare to march the next day, bivouaced before Pecqueux. Milhaud, sweeping the ground before him, established himself at Aubepierre and Beauvoir.[4]

On the morning of 17 February General Allix – with his force of infantry and cavalry – joined GB Montbrun, who held Charpentier's infantry as a reserve. This force then moved from Melun on Fontainebleau and chased Hardegg's Austrians out of the city. Pajol left St.-Germain-de-Laxis and pushed the Württembergers out of Châtelet and Ecrennes and into Ecluse. Once in Ecluse, Prince Adam von Württemberg – commanding a force of 1,000 infantry and cavalry – stopped the advancing French until Pacthod's National Guard Division arrived at Petit-Châtelet.

Engagement at Mormant – 17 February

At 5:00 a.m. on the 17th, the II Corps formed in three columns. Gérard was in the center on the grand route with the Paris Reserve – having Mormant as its objective. Huguet-Chataux's division was on the right, Duhésme's on the left, and the artillery was between the columns.

To the right of Huguet-Chataux stood Kellermann's corps – his divisions in echelons – the left (Treilhard's division) was pushed forward. Each division was in two lines formed in echelons – the left forward. On Duhésme's left, Milhaud's corps took a symmetrical formation – with Piré's light division formed in echelon on the right – and was the most advanced.

At the same time, the VII Corps deployed behind the II Corps ready to support it. Boyer's division was in two lines – its brigades one behind the other to the north of the grand route at the level of l'Étang. Rottembourg's division, 200 meters to the rear, was separated from it by a small wood. Other portions of the army occupied their assigned positions. The Guard artillery, in column on the road, was at the entrance to Guignes.

During the night, Wittgenstein had received orders to retreat. At daybreak he withdrew on Provins and Nogent and sent word to Pahlen to retire by the same road. That order did not reach Pahlen until he found Napoleon before him. He had been warned by his cavalry that large masses of French were between Fontenay and Chaulmes – moving from the village on Guignes and l'Étang. Skirmishes between advance posts the night before had assured him that a large force of infantry was present between Guignes and Pecqueux. As a result, he had already taken steps to either engage in battle or retreat on the 17th. His advance posts were reinforced during the night and two battalions occupied Mormant. The rest of his infantry was massed behind the village on the right and left of the road. His artillery was in the center and his cavalry was on the two wings.

At 5:00 a.m. Pahlen saw the French movement and realized it was impossible for him to hold them. He sent an officer to advise Wittgenstein that he was preparing to withdraw on Nangis.

Pahlen formed his infantry into battalion masses on the right and left of the road – supporting them with artillery. On his right flank (to the south of the road) were two Cossack regiments

4 *Les combats de Mormant, de Villeneuve-le-Comte, et de Montereau (17 et 18 février 1814)*, p.4.

Mormant, by Jean Antoine Siméon Fort. The infantry of the Guard are in the foreground.

supported by the Illowaiski and Rebrikov Cossack Regiments. On his flank was Rüdinger's cavalry division – formed into two lines of nine and five squadrons.[5]

The Russian movement began in this order masked by the village. The two battalions that occupied Mormant received orders to contain the attack, at any cost, long enough to permit the main body to escape.

Napoleon, at the head of the II Corps, marched on Mormant. His artillery moved down the road while the infantry marched along either side in battalion masses. As the French advanced on Mormant, they encountered Pahlen's forces withdrawing along the l'Étang heights. Pahlen had the Illowaiski and Rebrikov Cossack Regiments covering his right flank. To his left were two squadrons of the Soumy Hussars and four squadrons of the Tchougouiev Uhlan Regiment. He supported them with a weak reserve formed with a few more squadrons. His force contained 2,000 to 2,500 infantry from the 2nd Corps (4th and 34th Jager Regiments and the Selenginsk and Revel Infantry Regiments) and the 14th Division (Tenguinsk and Estonia Infantry Regiments) supported by 1,500 to 1,800 cavalry, nine squadrons of the Soumy and Olviopol Hussar Regiments and the Tchougouiev Uhlan Regiment – plus the weak Illowaiski XII and Rebrikov III Cossack Regiments. Rosen's infantry brigade – serving as a support – stood by Bailly, where the roads to Mormant and Rozoy met.[6]

Victor deployed the II Corps before the village of Pecqueux. The Paris Reserve stood in the center of the II Corps, with Huguet-Chataux's 1st Division on the right and Duhésme's 2nd Division on his left. On the French right was Kellermann with Trelliard's 5th Heavy Cavalry Division and l'Héritier's 6th Heavy Cavalry Division, while Milhaud stood on the left with Piré's 9th Light Cavalry Division and Briche's 3rd Heavy Cavalry Division. The XI and VIII Corps – which were to arrive shortly – formed the second line, while the Guard served as a reserve in Guignes.

Napoleon, seeing the weakness of the Allied forces in front of him, issued orders for his army to redouble its march. Victor marched on Mormant at the *pas accéléré*.[7] Milhaud and Kellermann

5 This division, which contained 20 squadrons, had detached four on Rozoy and two on Mellun. These six squadrons did not take part in the actions of the 17th.

6 von Damitz, Vol. II, p. 268.

7 The *pas accéléré* is a marching rate of 250 paces per minute. It is a cadenced run.

Kellermann.

moved past the village's flanks. At the same time, Subervie's brigade made a quarter conversion to the right and sabered the Allied skirmishers before it, while General Piré – supported by Briche's 3rd Heavy Cavalry Division – marched against the Russian cavalry. On his side, Kellermann was giving the same order to the dragoons of Trelliard and l'Héritier.

The French attack was moulded by the terrain over which it passed. The terrain between Guignes and Nangis was a vast agricultural plain, but broken up and enclosed between the Yvron and the Ancoeur. Mormant was defended by a force of Russians.

Chef de bataillon Gérard, with the 5/32nd Line, attacked Mormant at the *pas de charge*[8] – forcing the Russian infantry out of Mormant and onto the plain. As they reformed and moved to the offensive they were observed by General Ismert,[9] who, conforming to the movement of the infantry, passed the village at this moment. Profiting from surprise, Ismert charged the 4th Dragoons forward – catching the Russians that were still in disorder, broke them and forced them to surrender.[10]

Napoleon, who had arrived at Mormant, took command of the battle and observed Pahlen retiring with his artillery – protected by his cavalry and numerous skirmishers spread across the plain. The tail of the column was about to disappear into the Bisseaux woods – situated two kilometers to the east of Mormant.

Napoleon immediately ordered his two cavalry corps to move down the two sides of the road and to maneuver to stop it, while Gérard's 5/32nd Line followed the road and moved to attack the tail of the Russian column. The Guard artillery received orders to rapidly move before Mormant to cooperate with the attack.

The French cavalry moved at full speed. Kellermann directed l'Héritier to disperse the Russian cavalry and Treilhard to attack the infantry, whose flank was thus uncovered. l'Héritier moved directly against the two Cossack regiments of the first line, which were crushed by the shock of Lamotte's brigade. The Rebrikov and Ilowaiski Cossack Regiments, who came up, were in their turn broken by Collaert's brigade. After a wild melee, the four Cossack regiments – reduced to total confusion – fled in the direction of Nangis aggressively chased by l'Héritier.

Treilhard now moved against the infantry. The rearmost Russian battalion formed square. It was charged by the 16th Dragoons, who broke it, nearly destroyed it and sent its survivors in disorder into the neighbouring battalions.

On the north side of the road, Milhaud maneuvered with equal success. Subervie's brigade of Piré's division overran the Russian skirmishers – covering the infantry and turned to the right – sobering and throwing them into the Bisseaux woods, where they were obliged to surrender. Piré's other brigade moved against Rüdinger's cavalry. Briche's division, which followed it, formed in two lines in echelon such that in turning the Russians (Milhaud's corps) – now reduced to three

8 The *pas de charge* is a marching rate of 120 paces per minute.
9 Commander of the 1st Brigade of Treilhard's division.
10 *Les combats de Mormant, de Villeneuve-le-Comte, et de Montereau (17 et 18 février 1814)*, p. 6.

brigades – found itself in the regulated formation for combat of a cavalry division: 1st Line – Piré's brigade; 2nd Line – Montélégier's brigade; 3rd Line – Ludot's brigade.

The nine squadrons of the first line of Rüdinger's division were broken by Piré; the five squadrons of the second line by Montélégier's brigade; and then the Russian cavalry fled towards Bailly-Carrois. Piré, joined by Subervie's brigade, were ordered to hotly pursue the fugitives. Milhaud, without losing time, now threw Montélégier's brigade into the flank of the Russian infantry and gave orders to Ludot to move to the head of the column so as to prevent it from reaching Grand-Puits.[11]

The Russian cavalry, pressed on all sides, were in a difficult position. General Drouot advanced with all of the Guard artillery. Decimated by the fire of 36 guns manned by the best gunners in the French army, the Russian cavalry broke – fleeing the thundering death before them. The Russian cavalry abandoned the infantry to its fate and fled across the plain.

The position of the Russian infantry was unenviable. It had little choice but to form square and stoically march to the rear as the artillery steadily thinned its ranks. Pahlen, seeing the tail of his infantry stopped and engaged, hastened his march – hoping to reach Grand-Puits and Bailly. He hoped to be able to take a stand in the villages until Hardegg and Spleny's divisions could come up from Nangis and relieve him.

Grand-Puits was a small village and its direct access was barred to cavalry by a line of swamps where the Encoure takes its source. To the east of the line that runs perpendicular to the grand route, in front of the village, was an ancient fortified farm flanked by towers at the corners and surrounded on three sides by a deep wet ditch.

Bailly-Carrois, less important as a population center, consisted of four well-built farms and a church. These were two solid defensive positions that would shelter Pahlen's troops from the French cavalry.

The charges of Montélégier against the left flank of the Russian column delayed its movement. Pahlen, sacrificing a segment of his infantry, pushed to gain Grand-Puits. However, before he could reach it (that line of swamps mentioned earlier – site of the current Yvernois bridge), the head of his column was charged by Ludot and obliged to stop to receive the charge. Napoleon's orders were well-executed and Pahlen was stopped.

Pahlen sent desperate messages for help to Hardegg. When Pahlen's plea for help reached Nangis, only Hardegg's division remained. Spleny had already, in conformance with Schwarzenberg's orders, moved down the road to Montereau. Hardegg had two regiments of cavalry in Bailly and his infantry in Nangis. He realized responding to Pahlen's pleas for help was his own death warrant and refused to advance to his fellow's support. Instead, he retreated. However, not fast enough, as his rearguard – formed of the Schwarzenberg Uhlans and the Ferdinand Hussars[12] – was caught by GD Piré's cavalry and roughly handled. Piré then resumed his pursuit of Rüdinger. Piré then threw a few French squadrons down the road to Provins and rode hell-bent-for-leather as far as Maison-Rouge.[13]

Between Bailly and Nangis, Hardegg's two Austrian cavalry regiments found their path barred by a flood of disbanded cavalry. These were the Cossacks that l'Héritier had chased off earlier. The Austrians were caught up in this mass and fled with them – only 600 horse reaching Nangis pursued by Lamotte's brigade. Their arrival threw panic into Hardegg's infantry – causing several battalion to disband and the rest retired precipitously on Montereau.

11 Ibid, pp. 7-8.
12 Koch identifies these as the Ferdinand Hussars.
13 Koch, Vol. I, p. 312.

Pahlen's infantry was surrounded by the dragoons of generals Milhaud and Kellermann, and completely abandoned. On its two flanks, Treilhard and Montélégier broke one square after another. Drouot's artillery – attached to the 40 guns of Victor's corps – swept the grand route.

Under the pressure of Ludot's brigade, the head of the column was pushed to the south and attempted to cross the Encoeur swamp to reach Fontenailles and the woods. It was destroyed, square by square. The last, formed with two battalions, was broken at the same time in the rear of the column by the 4th and 16th Dragoons (Ismert's brigade) and in the head by the 6th and 13th Dragoons (Ludot's brigade).[14]

The French captured nine to 12 guns and 40 caissons. Their prisoners included the bulk of the Selenginsk, Revel, Tenguinsk and Estonia Regiments. Pahlen lost 2,114 infantry and about a third of his cavalry in this engagement. The Revel and Selenginsk Regiments were so badly handled that they had to be sent back to Plock to be reformed.[15] Milhaud and Kellermann reported only 150 men *hors de combat*. Gérard lost about 30 in his attack on Mormant. The Russians were only able to save two guns.

The Russian survivors fled towards Provins and Villeneuve-le-Comte. Napoleon ordered a pursuit in all directions. Oudinot, with Trelliard's dragoons and the VII Corps, marched on Provins. Macdonald, commanding the XI Corps and the cavalry divisions of Piré and Briche, marched on Donnemarie. Victor – with the II Corps, Paris Reserve, l'Héritier's 6th Heavy Cavalry Division and 500 cavalry drawn from the remount depot by Bordesoulle – marched on Villeneuve-le-Comte. The Imperial Guard rested in Nangis to await the outcome of the pursuits.

Oudinot's left column so startled Wittgenstein's corps that he pulled up and withdrew precipitously a distance of about 10 kilometers (6.25 miles). Macdonald, with the center column, encountered Hardegg – pushing him so hard that the French collected a number of stragglers. By the end of the day, Macdonald's infantry was in Magneux; his cavalry in Jaulney, Villenaux and Montigué; and – as in all stories of successful pursuits – they found freshly-abandoned dinner tables set with sumptuous meals.[16]

Engagement at Valjouan and Villeneuve-le-Comte

Gérard, forming the head of Victor's column, let Nangis at 1:30 p.m. Behind him marched Huguet-Chataux's division, then Duhésme's division. l'Héritier, with his cavalry, preceded the head of this column a bit and marched into the plain to the west of the grand route from Montereau. Bordesoulle stayed next to Gérard on the east of the road.

Around 3:00 p.m. – as the Paris Reserve reached Valjouan – l'Héritier informed Gérard that a large force of infantry blocked the road and occupied the Grande-Maison farm and the village of Villeneuve-le-Comte. Lamotte's 3rd Bavarian Division (Wrede's corps) was on the Valjouan heights. Lamotte knew what was coming, as a number of Hardegg's fugitives had already arrived. Lamotte held a position on the main road with a battalion of the 11th Line Regiment in Grande-Maison and Villeneuve, while the Bavarian cavalry stood on the right facing in the direction of Mazures. The Bavarians also had a force of cavalry massed to the west of the infantry between Villeneuve and the woods.

After a short reconnaissance, Gérard decided to attack immediately. He reported this to Victor – asking him to push the march of the divisions of Huguet-Chataux and Duhésme so that they could support his attack.

14 *Les combats de Mormant, de Villeneuve-le-Comte, et de Montereau (17 et 18 février 1814)*, pp. 9-10.

15 von Damitz, Vol. II, pp. 270-1; Sporschil, Vol. II, 1st Band, p. 330.

16 Koch, Vol. I, p. 313.

Wrede had been in Nangis during the morning of the 17th, while Lamotte encamped at Villeneuve and the rest of the Bavarian corps was at Donnemarie. Upon receiving orders from Schwarzenberg, Wrede had issued orders for a retreat on Bray. The main body of the corps set out immediately. Lamotte was to follow this movement when the cannonade at Morant caused him concern for the divisions posted at Nangis. By Wrede's orders, Lamotte took up a position to receive them.

Almost immediately, Spleny's division and his cavalry – the Sedler Hussars and the Groşevitz Dragoons – debouched from Valjouan. Shortly later, the 600 horse that had escaped from the rout of the Schwarzenberg Uhlans and the Archduke Joseph Hussars arrived. They were reformed into six squadrons and placed to the left of Villeneuve with the eight squadrons of Antoine Hardegg's division.

Lamotte had a few defensive works prepared in Villeneuve and Grande-Maison by the two battalions that occupied them and deployed his division in two lines a little to the rear of the villages – supporting his right on the Malvoisine woods and covered his left with the 14 squadrons mentioned above.

Behind him, with his back on a wood that formed a vast arc, the divisions of Spleny and Antoine Hardegg formed up and rested before moving on Bray.

At the moment the French appeared, Hardegg's division began its movement on Donnemarie. Spleny was to follow him under the protection of Lamotte's division.

Gérard designated Villeneuve and Grande-Maison as objectives for La Hamelinaye's brigade. It deployed before those two villages and advanced under the cover of skirmishers and 12 cannon. Bordesoulle, at the head of his three squadrons, marched with them and was to act in the best circumstances. l'Héritier, on the extreme right, had orders to attack the Allied cavalry.

Dufour's brigade was held as a reserve to deal with any eventualities, while Gérard waited for the arrival of Huguet-Chataux and Duhésme. The battle began at 3:30 p.m. as a battalion of the 86th Line – turning Villeneuve by the west – rapidly carried it and threw out the Bavarian battalion that had occupied it. Bordesoulle – who following this movement had turned the village by the east – charged this disordered troop with his two squadrons of cuirassiers,[17] which sabered it and threw it back on an hussar squadron and a peloton of uhlans that had come to support them. Those two Allied cavalry units were thrown back and pursued hotly to the edge of the wood occupied by a battalion of the Iller Mobile Legion. This battalion sought to defend save the fugitives, but was charged in its turn. It broke and fled into the woods – throwing away its muskets.

This attack had thrown the Bavarian left into great disorder. This was an opportunity to transform, by a vigorous charge, the movement into a rout and chase the Allied cavalry from the battlefield. However, Bordesoulle did nothing and contented himself with some demonstrations before the retreating enemy.

General Lamotte, judging his force as being too small to sustain a serious battle, formed his division into square and began a slow withdrawal from the battlefield. Bordesoulle followed them with his light squadron. The six squadrons reconstituted from the Archduke Ferdinand Hussars and the Schwarzenberg Uhlans saw them and hastened their movement to put themselves in security near the Bavarian infantry at the east of the road from Montereau.[18]

Over 300 were sabered by a force of French conscripts who had only been in the army for eight days and were seeing the enemy for the first time. Apparently, these young men were so aroused by

17 *Les combats de Mormant, de Villeneuve-le-Comte, et de Montereau (17 et 18 février 1814)*, p. 12 suggests it was a light squadron, but with the subsequent attack and results, it seems unlikely that this was only a single light squadron.

18 *Les combats de Mormant, de Villeneuve-le-Comte, et de Montereau (17 et 18 février 1814)*, p. 13.

this action that they took no prisoners. Only one already-wounded Austrian officer was spared by the intervention of Bordesoulle personally. The Schwarzenberg Uhlans and the Archduke Joseph Hussars were then attacked by the French cavalry in overwhelming numbers and lost 200 men.

Lamotte marched his division towards Donnemarie, but before he had gone two kilometers (about a mile) General Gérard's infantry (the Paris Reserve) broke out of the woods and attacked his square with bayonets. The Bavarian square was badly disordered and would have succumbed to the French if they had any cavalry with them. Alas, it was not so. Though badly shaken, the Bavarians continued their withdrawal and made good their escape.[19]

The results of these two engagements were substantial. Over 3,000 casualties and prisoners inflicted and 14 guns captured for a cost of about 800 French casualties, but retrospect suggests it could have been more. And though it could have been a worse defeat for the Allies, it was not magnified or mitigated by any particular errors on either side. Of course, the Allies were overextended once again and Napoleon took advantage of that to bring a superior force against smaller Allied detachments that were either unable or unwilling to support one another.

Though many of the Allied troops escaped him, Napoleon was delighted with the results. He had bloodied the nose of the main Allied army and Marmont reported that he had driven Diebitsch's flying corps back on that of Prince Lubomirski.[20]

On 16 February GD Count Grouchy advised Napoleon that an Allied corps coming from Sézanne had overrun Montmirail and chased out the French garrison of the city. Grouchy was marching from Etoges towards Orbais. Being close at hand, Grouchy bivouaced his troops in Corrobert. From there (the following morning) he marched on Fontenelles and from there to Montmirail.

Another engagement at Montmirail – 17 February

The French attack began with a heavy artillery bombardment – to which the Russians responded only with their skirmishers. This caused Grouchy to believe that the Russians were retreating. He ordered Pelleport's brigade to take the nearest suburb of Montmirail. Pelleport's men advanced into the suburb at the *pas de charge* and captured about 100 grenadiers. At the same time, Colonel Ghéneser – who had pierced the city from the left – pushed his troops to the rear of the Allied barricades. General Diebitsch withdrew his forces in great haste towards Pont-St.-Prix – harassed all the way by GD Doumerc's cavalry.

Marmont – reassured by the outcome of the engagement – established his headquarters in Montmirail, where he was joined by Grouchy when the sound of the gunfire had dissipated. Not a major engagement, it was however, one in a continuing string of victories being chalked up by the French column. Things on the Allied side of the front lines were becoming more and more agitated as a reinvigorated French army began expressing itself on the battlefield.

The Allies withdraw towards Troyes

As soon as Schwarzenberg learned of Pahlen's destruction and Lamotte's battering, he decided to withdraw his army to the left bank of the Seine and to wait for Napoleon's next maneuvers behind this barrier. He had orders sent to Württemberg to hold his corps in Montereau on the right bank to cover the left flank of the army and to protect the concentration of his forces. Wrede was ordered back across the Seine at Bray and was to take up positions on the left bank to guard

19 Koch, Vol. I, p. 315.
20 Koch, Vol. I, p. 317.

the bridge. Wittgenstein was to recross the Seine at Nogent and to establish a bridgehead on the right bank, while holding his forces on the left and to guard a few advanced posts in the wood line at Sordun. The Allied reserves in Traînel and Nogent were designated as rallying points and the headquarters of the sovereigns and Prince Schwarzenberg were moved from Bray to Traînel.

On the French side, Napoleon – upon learning that Victor was not in Montereau – ordered the French army to prepare for an attack on that city the following morning. Pajol was ordered to push everything he found before him and to attack the city from the left at around 7:00 a.m. while the II Corps and Gérard's Paris Reserve were to move against it from the right.

Engagement at Montereau – 18 February

At around 6:00 a.m. Châtelet engaged a few hundred Allied cavalry, which withdrew behind their infantry holding positions in the Valence woods. Pajol charged the Allied infantry successfully and obliged them to withdraw as well. Now master of the defile, Pajol pushed his forces forward again, but found himself threatened by the cavalry under Prince Adam von Württemberg. He responded by organizing a battery of 24 guns on the edge of the woods and deploying Pacthod's National Guard Division under the protection of their fire. The Württembergers, favored by their position, responded with their artillery – and by noon had dismounted 12 of the French guns.

Victor, eager to regain the time he had been accused of losing earlier, found himself at the foot of the Surville heights at around 9:00 a.m. but the Württembergers were too strongly established to cede the position without a fight.

Montereau.

The city of Montereau stood 100 kilometers (62-and-a-half miles) from Paris by the confluence of the Yonne and the Seine and stood on both banks of both rivers. It had two considerable suburbs. The Saint-Maurice suburb was to the east, while the Saint-Nicolas suburb was on the north and along the right bank of the Seine. The former was covered at a distance of half a cannon shot (about 1,000 yards) with the Surville ridge, which was wooded and planted with vines. The Saint-Nicolas suburb, however, faced the Bray plain, which was a large open plain ideal for cavalry.

There were two bridges in the city – one over the Yonne and the other over the Seine – connecting both suburbs with the main city. The city had few defenses – its wall being old and of little value. However, the Surville heights were positioned to dominate both bridges and it was here that Württemberg established his forces.[21]

This position was not a good place to accept battle. It was strong if approached by an enemy coming from the left bank, but it had little to cover its rear and could not prevent a movement from Melun or Nangis by an enemy force. Unfortunately for the Crown Prince of Württemberg, he did not see the weakness of his rear and faced forward to meet the anticipated French advance.

At 9:00 a.m. Huguet-Chataux's division, at the head of the II Corps, debouched onto the Surville plain situated on the right bank of the Seine at its confluence with the Yonne.

Prince von Württemberg defended the position with his army corps of 24 battalions and 16 squadrons. He had a total of 20,000 muskets and 1,900 sabers – plus a strong force of artillery. He had formed his infantry into two lines on the Surville plateau between Villaron and Saint-Martin – towns that were strongly entrenched. Hohenlohe's brigade, as well as Schäffer's (which had arrived the night before), were in the city as a reserve. Schäffer's Austrian Brigade consisted of the Zach Infantry Regiment (three battalions) and the Colloredo Infantry Regiment (two battalions) – plus a foot battery.

Prince Adam von Württemberg's infantry division and the cavalry, under Alvensleben, were opposed to Pajol and occupied a position at Valence seven kilometers to the northwest of Montereau – blocking the road to Paris.

Huguet-Chataux captured the heights, entered Villaron and chased out the defenders (three battalions) and then maintained himself there for a half-hour. After a stubborn resistance, however, he was obliged to evacuate the village and withdraw with heavy loses.

Duhésme's division, arriving in its turn, deployed to renew the frontal attack – leaving a brigade as a reserve – while with Huguet-Chataux's other brigade he moved to turn the plateau by the right and slip towards the bridge so as to gain the road to Paris.

Duhésme's attack against Villaron was repulsed after a bloody fight, but while the Allies were exclusively preoccupied with defending their front, Huguet-Chataux succeeded in gaining the first houses of the suburb of Paris. Driving before him all that opposed his advance, as he threatened the bridge a musket ball struck him – wounding him mortally. His brigade stopped and then withdrew in disorder.

It was 1:00 p.m. and the Allied position remained intact when Gérard debouched onto the battlefield with the Paris Reserve. It was at that moment that he was met by a courier from Napoleon bearing his orders to take command of the II Corps.

Gérard accurately appraised the situation. He began to pull back Duhésme's divisions that had been unfortunately pushed into the low ground to the left of Saint-Martin. He then withdrew the engaged infantry to reorganize it with an eye towards a general and rational attack. To prepare this attack, he put his battery in front of his 40 cannon, which knocked down and mastered the Allied artillery.

Prince von Württemberg – not seeing the infantry carefully concealed in the folds in the ground and judging this deployment of artillery had as its goal to mask the retreat of the French – wished to attack them. On his order, General Döring attacked them aggressively with two battalions and captured one piece, but taken in the flank by a battalion that charged with bayonets he was obliged to fall precipitously – leaving many dead on the ground behind him.

At around 2:00 p.m. Napoleon, coming from Nangis with two squadrons of Gendarmes d'Elite of the Old Guard,[22] took command of the battle and the attack resumed. Before this new

21 Koch, Vol. I, pp. 320-1.

22 *Les combats de Mormant, de Villeneuve-le-Comte, et de Montereau (17 et 18 février 1814)*, p.18 says that there were two battalions of gendarmes, but the only gendarmes in Napoleon's guard were mounted horsemen and they were frequently used as his 'service' (escort) squadrons. This is probably an error on the part of the author calling them 'battalions'.

effort – well-organized and as energetic as the previous – Prince von Württemberg now looked to retreat. However, his escape path was a narrow bridge so he resolved to withdraw little by little – containing the French on his front and precede his withdrawal by his dismounted artillery and the most distant parts of his troops.

Prince Adam von Württemberg, who had held Pajol in check at Valence since the morning, had been advised of the fight before Montereau. The movement that had cost the life of General Huguet-Chataux had produced the fear in him that his army corps might be cut off, and slowly he withdrew without allowing himself to be stopped when he received orders to move as quickly as possible to the left bank. As a result, he hastened his march and some disorder fell into his troops.

Pajol seized this opportunity and, seizing the moment when the Allies were in retreat and no longer master of retracing their steps, he fell on him at the exit from the woods with the cavalry of generals Coëlosquet and Grouvel supporting them with Delort's brigade (and giving these three generals the order to reach the bridge, if it was possible, before the Allies).

La Tombe

Two battalions of Stockmayer's brigade were positioned in Villaron and its surrounding gardens.

The 9th 'König' Jägers were also known as the 'Schwarzen' (or 'Black') Jägers because of the black lapels and trim on their green uniforms. A force under Oberst Graf zur Lippe occupied Villaron. An Austrian battalion supported by four guns occupied the vineyard between Villaron and Surville. A battalion of the Colloredo Infantry Regiment occupied the vineyard to the left of Montereau, on the road to Valance and Melun, near some woods. On the road that ran from there – forming the Allied left – stood four squadrons of the Austrian Erzherzog Ferdinand Hussar Regiment and the Württemberg 5th Chevauxleger Regiment. A four-gun half-battery stood on the road to Valance and its other half supported the Austrian battalion between Villaron and Surville. The 2nd, 3rd and 4th Württemberg Light Cavalry Regiments and Hohenlohe's brigade were behind Montereau in reserve.

The three battalions of the Austrian Zach Infantry Regiment, Schäffer's brigade, stood on the right bank of the Seine in the suburbs of Montereau. Another battalion, from the Colloredo Regiment, was to the right of Villaron and its skirmish screen linked it to Stockmayer's brigade standing in front of Villaron.

Two guns from the foot battery of Schäffer's brigade stood on the corner of the Surville park and covered the road running through that area. The remaining four guns of this battery were posted to support the Zach Infantry Regiment. A 12pdr and 6pdr foot battery were posted the middle of the Allied position.

By Surville, on the side facing Salins, stood a battalion of the Württemberg 9th Jäger Regiment supported by a squadron of the Erzherzog Ferdinand Hussars. For the day's battle, this battalion had been temporarily placed under Austrian General Schäffer's command. A Württemberg 6pdr battery and an Austrian 12pdr position battery – drawn from the reserve – were posted behind Villaron forming the center of the Allied position. Döring's brigade, supported by a 6pdr battery, was posted behind Villaron. The Allied position contained 15 battalions, nine squadrons and 30 guns – or a total of 8,540 infantry and 1,000 cavalry. In addition, should the French seek to cross the Seine, von Jett's brigade stood behind Montereau on the road to Bray and Hohenlohe's Austrian brigade stood by Montereau – each of which was supported by a battery of 6pdr guns.[23]

23 Sporschil, Vol. II, 1st Band, pp. 336-7.

At daybreak, GD Pajol had driven back the Allied advanced posts and taken control of the Valance forest. Shortly afterwards, the Prince of Württemberg received orders from Schwarzenberg to hold the Montereau defile until that evening. Orders in hand, he watched as the French prepared to attack his position.

The French started their assault with a feinted attack down the Salins road towards Courbeton and Saint-Jean. Then came the main attack as GB Huguet-Chataux drove his forces forward – being repulsed by the fire of the 9th 'König' Jägers which was defending Villaron.

Huguet-Chataux was the former chief of staff to the French II Corps and the son-in-law of Maréchal Victor. Huguet-Chataux's troops fell back and regrouped. One of Huguet-Chataux's brigades was held in reserve and tried to turn Stockmayer's left flank.[24] The new target was the bridge over the Seine and the road to Paris. Meanwhile, Duhèsme launched his attack directly into Villaron – and specifically on the Ormeaux farm – only to be repulsed as well.

The turning movement of Huguet-Chataux's one brigade quickly encountered GM Döring and the Württemberg 3rd Infantry Regiment. A counterattack by Döring's brigade drove forward and a vicious bayonet fight erupted. The Württemberger counterattack pushed the French back – momentarily capturing a cannon and caisson, a colonel of the French Guard Artillery, an adjutant to Prince Berthier, four officers and 60-70 Young Guardsmen.[25] GB Huguet-Chataux was struck and killed by a musket shot. His death was the last straw and his brigade evaporated – fleeing to the rear as the Paris Reserve arrived on the field.

As Napoleon arrived in Villeneuve-les-Bordes, he exploded when he learned of the battle. He relieved General Guyot of his command and replaced him with Excelmans at the head of the heavy cavalry of the Old Guard. His furor grew hotter, if it was possible, when he learned of Victor's premature stop the previous day and his slowness to attack that morning. Victor was also relieved of his command and Gérard placed at the head of the French II Corps. Boiling with rage, and not hearing the sound of his guns pulverizing his enemies, he mounted his horse and headed for Montereau.[26]

Gérard, commanding the Paris Reserve, withdrew the skirmishers that were badly deployed in unfavorable terrain on the left of the position and sent them to the right to support the II Corps. At that time, GB Déjean – aide-de-camp to Napoleon – arrived and advised Gérard that Napoleon was on the field and that it was his will that Gérard take command of all the French troops present.[27]

As Gérard reviewed the Württemberg position, he noted the superiority of their artillery was the principal reason for the successful defense of the position. He quickly deployed the 40 guns of the Paris Reserve to silence them and to give the French infantry the opportunity to come to grips with their enemies. Bienvenu indicates that Gérard had 60 guns.[28]

The Württemberg General Döring, seeing only the advance of the guns from the Paris Reserve, thought that he could disrupt their movement and sent the 2/3rd Württemberg Line Regiment – supported by the 1/3rd Line – to attack them. Though this attack momentarily seized one gun, the attacking Württembergers were showered with canister and attacked by 500 men under General Gérard. They were driven back to their original position with substantial losses.

24 Koch, Vol. I, p. 321.
25 Rössler, p. 420.
26 Bienvenu, p. 15.
27 Sporschil, Vol. II, 1st Band, p. 338.
28 Bienvenu, p. 15.

Delort's cavalry advanced – their attack facilitated by Gérard's. Delort was followed by the Breton National Guard and the foot gendarmes that had, until recently, been fighting in Spain. This force moved south of Ormeaux, but provoked a strong reaction from the Austrians.

Between 2:00 and 3:00 p.m. Napoleon arrived at Nangis at a gallop – preceded by the Guard Cavalry. As the army saw him, cries of: "*Vive l'Empereur!*" echoed across the battlefield. The Austrians heard these cries and many turned and fled. He directed the two battalions of gendarmes, which were attached to the Old Guard, to support the attack against the Surville heights. He saw that a withdrawal by the Württembergers through the defile would be difficult and ordered the 4th and 5th Chasseurs à cheval Regiments – followed later by all the artillery – to take the defile.[29]

Napoleon ordered the formation of four attack columns with the objective of taking the Surville plateau and Montereau. Pajol's column was to clear the terrain with his cavalry. A column was to occupy Ormeaux, another was to move against the Surville Château and the fourth was to move down the road to Salins and into the Seine Valley, where it would attack the right wing of the Württemberg 4th Corps.[30]

The Guard was held in reserve before Laval on the Forges heights. The Austrians faced them with Schäffer's brigade – supported by Württemberg forces on his wings.

The French lines erupted with the sound of drums sounding the *pas de charge* and the French infantry rolled forward in a massive attack. The Paris Reserve and the II Corps advanced in two detachments against Villaron and the Surville heights. Minutes later, the third column moved through Courbeton and against the Württemberg right flank and the suburbs of Montereau on the right bank of the Seine.

GD Pajol ordered his artillery to unlimber and prepare the way for his pending cavalry attack. The Allied artillery responded, but had already fired off much of its ammunition. At least one Württemberg gun under Corporal Herre had already fired off 80 rounds. Though a second battery moved up to support the artillery facing Pajol's guns, it was steadily overwhelmed by the four to one superiority and forced to withdraw after suffering heavy casualties.

Relieved by the infantry attack, General Pajol directed his cavalry to charge the infantry on the road to Melun and threw them back into the defile behind the back of the Surville heights and the Seine. This attack cleared the Württembergers from Correaux and the Plat-Buisson farm. They withdrew and set up a hasty defense in the Ormeaux park.[31]

The Austrian battalion in the vineyards by Villaron now stood exposed by the withdrawal of the Württemberg cavalry. Pajol's cavalry overran them and pushed into the Allied (now defenseless) left wing.

Duhésme's 2nd Division (II Corps) – preceded by Pajol's two cavalry brigades under the direct command of General Ducoëtlosquet – pursued the Allied troops down the road to Sens. Capitaine Biot, an aide-de-camp to Pajol, saw the Allies crossing Montereau at a run so as to escape to Fossard. The captain reported this to GD Pajol, who immediately recognized this as a retreat and gave orders for Delort to immediately attack the bridges with his cavalry. Pajol followed with two other brigades under GB Ducoëtlosquet and Grouvel.

This French cavalry, however, was a very fragile weapon. Only 15 days earlier, they had been receiving their initial training at the Versailles cavalry depot. Delort reputedly was afraid that any effort to launch a charge would result in these green troops losing their heads and running off out of control. However, the attack was launched, with Delort leading the attack from the head of the first platoon in the attack. The attack was very successful and Delort held his troops

29 Koch, Vol. I, p. 323
30 Bienvenu, p. 16.
31 Bienvenu, p. 16

together. Pajol, however, received yet another wound. His last had been received at Wachau on 16 October 1813 during the Battle of Leipzig. The French cavalry crashed into the fleeing Allied troops as they pushed over the Seine bridge. Pajol's horse was then shot out from under him as the Württembergers turned to defend themselves. Grouvel then led his brigade against the Allies and moved down the road to Bray, while Pajol and Ducoëtlosquet rejoined Delort in Montereau. Napoleon's service squadrons and the rest of the cavalry pursued the main body of the Allied force across the Seine and the Yonne.

Schäffer's brigade moved to and occupied the Surville Château. The Allied troops could not move back fast enough towards the bridges. Hohenlohe's brigade moved to cover the Allied retreat. In vain the Crown Prince of Württemberg ordered his Württemberg reserve brigade to cover the retreat of his corps, but there was not enough time. The 6th Württemberg Line Regiment, commanded by Oberst Misani, lowered bayonets and charged forward – struggling in vain to open a passage over the Seine bridge and clear the French from the suburb on the far side. Prince Hohenlohe was struck down by a musket shot and the 6th Line scattered as fugitives. Schäffer's brigade was unable to even move out of the city and found itself trapped without being able to take part in the combat.

At the same time, GB Digeon showered the bridges with canister from two Guard batteries – spreading death and disorder among the Württemberg infantry. The Allies struggled to get across the Seine, but General Ducoëtlosquet – at the head of the 7th Chasseurs à cheval – moved in at a gallop, charging into the fugitives struggling to force their way into the city and make their escape.[32]

Duhèsme's 2nd Division (II Corps) followed at the *pas de charge* – capturing or killing every Allied soldier they encountered.

The citizens of Montereau, upon seeing French troops pouring into the struggling masses of Württembergers and Austrians, joined the fray – exacting a vengeance for the treatment they had received at the hands of the Allied troops. They barricaded the streets and sniped at the Allied troops from their houses. The city was transformed into a field of carnage, where the prisoners and wounded found little security or comfort.

From his position on the Surville heights, Napoleon applauded the brilliant charge of his cavalry and its success in capturing the bridges intact. He said: "Among my generals, only Pajol knows how to manage cavalry!"

The Allied troops pushed across the bridges over the Yonne – pursued by French hussars. An Austrian senior officer and 16 pontooneers, acting to stop the French pursuit, cut the cables holding the Yonne bridge in place – dumping a mass of fleeing Allied soldiers into the river.

Gérard's forces cut up and threw back the Austrian infantry under Zach and Colloredo defending Surville, while the Chasseurs à cheval de la Garde crashed down upon them – slicing them to ribbons and taking many prisoners.[33]

That night, Napoleon established his headquarters in the Surville Château; the Guard bivouaced in Montereau; the Paris Reserve, II Corps, and a brigade of Pajol's cavalry were in Fossard; two other cavalry brigades were in Varennes; and Pacthod's National Guard Division was on the right bank of the Seine.

The Crown Prince of Württemberg rallied the remains of his corps behind Marolles and moved to Bazoches, near Bray. He left a rearguard in La Tombe.

32 von Damitz, Vol. II, p. 289.

33 Bienvenu, p. 17.

The honors of the day went to generals Pajol and Gérard. Von Damitz states that the Allies lost 3,000 to 4,000[34] men killed and wounded – and as many prisoners. Sporschil and the *Württemberg Tagebuch* give the Württemberg losses at seven officers and 85 men dead, 26 officers and 688 men wounded, and 2,000 prisoners lost. The *Tagebuch* states that major parts of the 1/9th and 10th Infantry Regiments were dead, wounded or taken prisoner in the struggle to get over the bridges. It goes on to say that the 2nd, 3rd, 6th and 7th Regiments also lost very heavily. Sporschil states that the Austrians lost about 2,000 men.[35] Strength figures for the 4th Corps for 1 February indicate the corps had 14,000 men and those of 23 February – before the arrival of von Laland's brigade – indicate that it was reduced to 10,000. The reported Württemberg casualties of 2,844 officers and men for this battle are not unreasonable, though perhaps a bit understated.

Von Damitz states that the French also captured four standards and six guns, though Sporschil claims only two were lost. Among the dead was Prince Hohenlohe, while General Schäffer was taken prisoner. The French losses were around 2,500 men – including GB Huguet-Chataux dead and Delort wounded.[36]

If anything can be said about this battle, it is that the chaos that occurred as the Allied troops attempted to clear the bridges was horrible and thousands were definitely taken prisoner. The losses in a battle are never so bad as those suffered during a chaotic retreat across a bridge or through a chokepoint – and this is what Napoleon achieved at Montereau. The Württemberg 4th Corps had been savaged and returns for 1 February and 23 February show that it lost 4,000 men – about a third of its strength. Schäffer's brigade of Austrians was apparently destroyed and vanishes from the Allied order of battle. These five battalions, even at half-strength, would have totaled 2,500 men. The estimates of the Allied casualties range from 6,000 to 8,000 and not only are highly possible, but may even be understated.

In view of the process of the battle, the reported French casualties of 2,500 seems high, but may well include a number of new conscripts that decided one battle was quite enough military experience to suit their tastes. Nonetheless, Montereau was a stunning victory for Napoleon and a serious reverse for the Allies.

Engagement at Mouy – 18 February

While Napoleon was engaged at Montereau, the center – under Macdonald – caught up with Wrede's rearguard as it was escorting the Bavarian park across the Seine at Bray. Unfortunately, Macdonald's maneuvers around the swamp delayed his advance and Wrede was able to establish himself on the left bank. He also occupied both halves of the city with a battalion and some heavy batteries were deployed to fire on the far bank. In addition there were 400 to 500 men occupying the village of Mouy, which made a French advance on the bridge impractical. Macdonald remained checked before Bray the entire day.

The Allied withdrawal to Troyes continues

On the left, Oudinot crossed through Provins and took up a position by Sordun. His cavalry pushed to Mériot, which it cleared of Rebrikov's Cossacks. Wittgenstein, however, crossed the Seine successfully and without interference at Nogent.

34 von Damitz, Vol. II, p. 290 .
35 Sporschil, Vol. II, 1st Band, p. 341; Rössler, p. 422.
36 Koch, Vol. I, p. 325; Sporschil, Vol. II, 1st Band, p. 341.

Though the French had missed another opportunity for a decisive victory as the Allies fled before their rapid advance, they did have the advantage of control of the bridge at Montereau. In addition, they were in a position to force both Wrede and Wittgenstein to abandon the line of the Seine because they were in a position to operate against their lines of communications.

To counter the unfortunate check of the Crown Prince of Württemberg, Schwarzenberg resolved to concentrate his forces around Troyes – and from there to reinforce himself with forces drawn from along the Rhine before Napoleon could strike at him a second time or move between his army and that of Blücher. He expedited the issuance of an order directing Blücher to march from Châlons via Arcis and on to Méry so that they might join forces. To support this, Wittgenstein was ordered to hold Nogent for as long as possible and position the bulk of his forces where they could support either Wrede or Württemberg if they were too heavily engaged by the French.

The French army continued its operations, but made some changes in its organizations. The Paris Reserve – weakened by recent battles – was amalgamated into the II Corps, which was now under the command of GD Gérard. Victor, furious at being relieved of command of the II Corps at Montereau, sent to Napoleon his resignation and asked to be permitted to retire to his home. Instead, Napoleon had Berthier transmit to him an order that he take command of a corps of Young Guard consisting of GD Charpentier's 7th Young Guard Division and GD Boyer de Rebeval's 9th Young Guard Division – as they came up from Fontainebleau – and Melun Boyer de Rebeval's division arrived eight days later. It was only partially provided with uniforms and equipment.

Pajol's provisional cavalry corps was dissolved. A combination of his wounds and a fall from his horse on 18 February resulted in his being authorized to withdraw to Paris to recover his health. His cavalry, which consisted of provisional regiments, was broken up and sent back to their parent formations. Pacthod's division was ordered to join Oudinot. Allix's small division, weakened by several engagements, was broken up and its constituent parts were sent to their parent regiments.

The command of the 2nd Reserve Division – which was organized from the cadres of units assigned to the V Corps – was passed to the Maréchal Arrighi (Duke of Padua), who was to complete its organization and send its first brigade as soon as possible to Melun.

In the pursuit after Montereau, General Allix had marched to the Loing and caught Bianchi's rearguard. After suffering 150 casualties and losing 80 prisoners, the Austrians withdrew to Ormesson and Onferville. GD Gérard, marching down the road to Sens, stopped in Pont-sur-Yonne to re-establish the bridge that Hardegg had destroyed.

Macdonald – struggling to cross the Seine at Bray – decided to march down the Seine via Vimpelles, Egligny and Châtenay to cross at Montereau and then move to Marolles – leaving Jacquinot's cavalry with orders to mask this movement from the Bavarians.

On his side, Oudinot – finding it impossible to cross at Nogent – marched via Donnemarie to Bray in the hope of finding an easier passage. The Foot and Horse Guard, under Ney, arrived in Montereau.

As the French marched about blindly in several different directions, the Allies were able to effect their escape. The Austrian reserves and the corps of Giulay and Bianchi moved into Villeneuve-l'Archevêque. M. Liechtenstein's 2nd Light Division was in Grez. Württemberg, after spending the entire night in reorganizing his corps, marched out at dawn and established himself by Nogent between Chapelle and Saint-Aubin. Count von Wrede marched with his infantry on Mâcon. He covered his march with a rearguard under Frimont and supported by a division of the Kretov Cuirassier Regiment.[37]

37 Koch, Vol. I, p. 329.

When Wittgenstein was advised that Napoleon had left Montereau, he reacted by destroying the bridge at Nogent and moved to a position between Pont-sur-Seine and Saint-Hilaire where he could be reinforced by the forces of Prince Gorchakov, who was advancing from the blockade of Strasbourg.

This withdrawal was not disturbed. Macdonald's movement to Montereau and that of Oudinot on Bray had removed the French threat to Wittgenstein's corps.

The French and Allied armies continued their movement through the 20th and 21st without any serious engagements. However, Schwarzenberg – curious if Napoleon's main army had followed him or only an advanced guard – ordered Wrede and Wittgenstein to send reconnaissance forces from Saint-Martin-de-Bossenay to Saint-Aubin and from Romilly to Pont-sur-Seine. The former was under the Austrian Fresnel, who encountered Macdonald's advanced guard and was thrown back harshly onto Frimont's rearguard by Milhaud. The second reconnaissance – under Pahlen – consisted of his cavalry and that of General Diebitsch, which had joined it in Méry. Despite this reinforcement, Pahlen's forces were hotly handled by Oudinot's advanced guard. They were driven back to Châtres – leaving posts at Mesgrigny to guard the entrance to the defile of the Seine near Méry.

Schwarzenberg was convinced by this reconnaissance that he was being pursued by Napoleon's entire army and decided to withdraw behind the Seine River and guard its passages. That day, he ordered von Württemberg's 4th Corps moved to Ruvigny – near Troyes – and the reserves to the Saint-Parre-aux-Tertres heights. The remainder of his forces were to remain stationary with the exception of M. Liechtenstein, who was disturbed in his positions in Villeneuve by a reconnaissance force sent by Macdonald (400 cavalry under General Ameil). Liechtenstein withdrew during the night and moved to Saint-Liébault. Wittgenstein's rearguard crossed the Seine and marched on Villacerf after being relieved in Mesgrigny by the advanced guard of the Army of Silesia.[38]

The Army of Silesia arrives in Méry

The Army of Silesia had slowly reorganized itself by Châlons after the poundings it had taken at Champaubert, Montmirail, Château-Thierry and Vauchamps. This process was still ongoing when Schwarzenberg's order to march to the Seine arrived. Blücher had received four battalions from the 22nd Division and two from the 8th Corps[39] – plus 6,000 infantry and 4,000 cavalry, under the orders of generals Rudsevich and Korff, which had been called down from the blockade of Mainz. On 19 February – when the Army of Silesia began its march to the Seine – it contained about 48,000 men.

According to the latest designs of the Allied sovereigns, it was to act on the left flank and rear of the French. Schwarzenberg hoped this would cause Napoleon to break off his pursuit of the main Allied army. As a beginning of its operations, the Army of Silesia occupied Méry. Sacken's corps physically occupied the city while the advanced guard stood on the left bank of the Seine and the remainder of the army stood on the right bank.

Calmed by his junction with Blücher, Schwarzenberg directed that a general reconnaissance be executed the following day. The Army of Silesia was to cooperate – sending out at least 6,000 cavalry.

38 Koch, Vol. I, p, 330.
39 Langeron, p. 400.

Engagement at Méry – 22 February 1814

However, this reconnaissance would prove unnecessary as Napoleon had already decided to push the Allies as hard as possible and could not do this securely so long as the Army of Silesia held a bridgehead that would permit it to move against his flank and rear. As a result, he ordered Oudinot to seize the Mesgrigny defile and to carry Méry while the other French corps marched on Troyes. Conforming with these orders, P. Boyer's 9th Division advanced, engaged in a hot skirmish with Sacken's advanced guard, dislodged them and resumed its march to Méry.

Méry is a small village standing on both banks of the Seine, united by a bridge. Its houses were in the Tudor style – frame houses with mud and wattle filling in the framework. Their roofs were generally thatch. Only the better houses were of stone.

Gruyèr's brigade

Replacing GB Gauthier – wounded on 17 February 1814 – the brigade formed the head of the French column and advanced against the Allied positions in Méry with their bayonets lowered. Their impetuous advance threw the Allies back across the bridge, but once across the Allies rallied and held the French off with musketry. *Victoires, conquêtes, désastres*[40] indicates that the Russians withdrew from the city – firing the bridge and leaving the half-burnt bridge undefended. French skirmishers took advantage of this to bridge the gaps with planks and push into the burning city after the Russians. However, this story seems rather apocryphal and Koch's account far more reasonable. German sources claim that when the French arrived, the eastern end of the village was on fire – burning because of the fires abandoned by the Russian soldiers of the 6th Corps. On the other hand, French sources indicate the fire was the result of the musketry. Whatever the cause, Scherbatov's troops occupied the houses along the Seine and defended the bridge, but as the day progressed and the fires grew closer, their position became less and less tenable.[41]

The flames and smoke soon drove the Russians from their positions and obliged them to evacuate the houses around the end of the bridge. French skirmishers, taking advantage of the Russian withdrawal, pushed across the bridge. General Gruyèr organized the rest of his brigade – the lead elements of P. Boyer's 9th Division – and charged across the bridge with the intention of encouraging the Russians to continue their flight with the points of their bayonets.[42]

However, once across, Gruyèr discovered the entire Army of Silesia deployed before him. It was organized in two lines of battle – straddling the road to Arcis. Making the best of a bad situation – with a river and burning village behind him – Gruyèr deployed his brigade before the village and began an exchange of musketry.

Yorck then ordered Katzler's advanced guard to attack the French position. Katzler moved down the left of the main road to Méry and two Russian battalions moved down the other side of the road. The Fus/1st and Fus/2nd East Prussian Infantry Regiments struck the French without firing a single shot. They were supported by the Fus/Brandenburg Regiment, the 12th Reserve Regiment and the von Leslie Grenadier Battalion. The French were driven back into the burning village. Gruyèr was wounded in the action. When he fell, his troops withdrew across the Seine and bivouaced on the left bank.

The advance of the other French corps was more successful. Macdonald's cavalry captured a post of 200 Allied cavalry in Pavillon. A complete company of jägers, separated from

40 *ires, conquêtes, désastres* Vol. 23, p. 123
41 Sporschil, Vol. 2, 1st Band, p. 350.
42 Koch, Vol. I, p. 333.

M. Liechtenstein's 2nd Light Division, fell captive as well. Five couriers were also taken. The cavalry squadron of the French advanced guard put to flight a number of Cossacks from Platov's force near the village of Villeneuve – taking about 50 prisoners.

Platov, by G. Dawe.

At noon, the French army advanced onto the Troyes plain in three columns and found it covered with Allied troops. The corps of Wrede, Bianchi, Giulay and the Austrian reserve were deployed with their right supported by the Seine and their left extending through Mongueux to St.-Germain. Their cavalry stood in the first line and their infantry in the second line. The reserve was formed by three divisions of Russian cuirassiers, the Russian Guard Light Cavalry Division and the Prussian Guard Cavalry Brigade – all under the command of Grand Duke Constantine.

Seeing this mighty force deployed and ready for battle, Napoleon chose not to accept battle without all of his forces united. As a result he ordered Gérard to press his march and to move to Villemaur that evening, where he could move by Prunay with Macdonald, who was then in Echemines and Pavillon. Oudinot was to form with Grez on the left of the line. The Imperial Guard was to be in reserve at Châtres. Finally, Grouchy – who after the Battle of Montmirail had been ordered to move through Flambouin on Provins in the hope of cutting off Prince Lubomirski – was ordered to accelerate his march and move to Nogent.

The anticipation of major events excited the French army. Napoleon had no hope other than to give battle and was pleased that Schwarzenberg appeared ready to oblige him. He felt that having the Allies with a river to their back offset their numerical advantage. Adding to this, he recognized that they were no doubt demoralized because of his recent series of victories and the irresolution of their command. He also knew that he had nothing to fear from the Army of Silesia, as it would take Blücher at least 24 hours to put a bridge in place and cross the river. In that time, Napoleon was convinced that the battle would be decided.[43]

Engagement at Therouanne – 23 February

Meanwhile, General Katzler moved across the bridge over the Ourcq at Lisy and continued to serve as the advanced guard of Kleist's Prussian 2nd Corps as it moved on Meaux and on to Therouanne. Behind him came General Ziethen with the reserve cavalry of the Prussian 2nd Corps. Once in Lisy, he learned that large forces of French under Mortier were before him and those of Marmont were coming up fast.

Katzler sent the Prussian Leib Hussar Regiment to Vareddes and the infantry of the advanced guard occupied Gué-à-Treme. Ziethen moved his reserve cavalry behind Gué-à-Treme to support them. Word came that the French had stopped their advance and that the bulk of their forces were by Beauval – a half-hour from Gué-à-Treme. Kleist dispatched an uhlan regiment and three battalions of infantry to the left to occupy Congis. Oberst von Blücher, with two light cavalry regiments, was sent to the right to Marcilly to both cover the flank and to watch the French movements. However, as Oberst von Blücher moved down the road to Bareddes, he encountered

43 Koch, Vol. I, pp. 335-6.

Mortier's corps marching on Gué-à-Treme. Cut off from Gué-à-Treme, he withdrew through Estrepilly to a position behind Therouanne.[44]

At around 4:00 p.m. Christiani's 2nd Old Guard Division – from Mortier's corps, supported by a force of artillery – advanced on Throuanne and Gué-à-Treme. The Prussian artillery engaged the advancing French with their fire, but the French were not to be stopped and deployed 24 guns of their own. The French began to bombard Gué-à-Treme, but the Prussian infantry held fast. After two hours, however, Kleist realized his flanks were exposed to being turned and issued the order to withdraw. As the winter night came early, the falling light allowed the Prussians to slip away, but the French pursued them aggressively down the road to La Ferté-Milon. The French caught the Prussian infantry in the village of Le Plessis and brought them to bay. A skirmish fight, supported by some artillery, erupted. Then the Prussian cavalry struck the French advanced guard – causing it to recoil and breaking the pursuit. The Prussian advanced guard then occupied the gap at Neufchelles and an infantry brigade stood in support in Mareuil. The bulk of the Prussian 2nd Corps withdrew over the stone bridge near Foulaines and lagered on the left bank of the Ourcq near the village.

The two French marshals had hurried the remains of the Army of Silesia on its way towards Meaux – driving it away from union with what Napoleon had decided would be his next target: the main Allied army. The Allies, however, realized that Blücher's Army of Silesia was in sad need of support. Sacken's corps broke its camp on the Marne and moved towards Lisy, but arrived after Kleist had been driven from that position. Sacken encamped his troops for the night and planned to link up with Kleist as soon as possible thereafter.

The next day, orders were issued from the Royal Headquarters that the corps of Bülow, Winzingerode and the Duke of Weimar were to be under the command of Feldmarschal Blücher. It was at 9:00 p.m. on 28 February that Blücher learned of the engagement at Therouanne.[45]

44 Sporschil, Vol. II, 1st Band, pp. 548-9.
45 Sporschil, Vol. II, 1st Band, pp. 549-550.

10

The Allies Withdraw Beyond the Aube

Schwarzenberg chose not to wait for Napoleon and his army – ordering the Allies to continue their retreat during the night of 22-23 February. Volkman's brigade – of Wrede's 5th Corps – was detached to serve as the garrison of Troyes, while M. Liechtenstein's Austrian 2nd Light Division was deployed to cover the withdrawal along the road to Sens. Schwarzenberg did this despite the fact that his army was approximately twice the size of the army facing him![1]

Strength of main Allied army and Army of Silesia before Troyes on 23 February 1814:[2]

Liechtenstein's 2nd Light Division	4,000
Bianchi's 1st Corps	13,000
Giulay's 3rd Corps	11,000
Crown Prince of Württemberg's 4th Corps	10,000
Wrede's 5th Corps	21,000
Wittgenstein's 6th Corps	15,000
Combined Russian/Prussian Guard Corps and Platov's Cossacks under de Tolly	30,000
Army of Silesia	53,000
Total:	157,000

The figures for the 4th Corps do not include the presence of GM von Lalance's Württemberg brigade, which arrived on 23 February. This brigade contained 5,000 men and consisted of the 5th Infantry Regiment "Prinz Friedrich" and the 3rd, 4th, 5th and 6th Land Regiments. In addition – because of the extensive casualties suffered by the 4th Corps at Montereau – it was reinforced with four Austrian cuirassier regiments, four Austrian grenadier battalions and two 6pdr foot batteries under the command of FML von Nostitz and four Russian cuirassier regiments under General Prince von Gallizin.

At the break of day, the French army resumed its advance. The French left and center moved down the two roads to Nogent – maneuvering on the Troyes plain under the protection of a heavy cannonade – while the dragoons of General Roussel, forming the advanced guard of Count Gérard, pushed Liechtenstein's cavalry back before Fontvannes. Liechtenstein commanded 18 squadrons and 16 guns. His actions did not indicate confidence in his position to Roussel, who determined to attack him even though he was far weaker. The first charge by the French, even though not particularly impressive, convinced Liechtenstein to withdraw. Squadrons of the 22nd Dragoons, supported by Ameil's light cavalry, attacked and threw the Austrians back – capturing

1 C. von W., p. 183.
2 von Damitz, Vol. II, p. 330.

six guns and taking 280 prisoners. The Austrian fugitives were pursued vigorously until they took up a position behind their line by the Saint-Savine suburb of Troyes.

Around noon, the investment of Troyes was completed on the left bank of the Seine. The Allies promptly withdrew down the roads to Bar-sur-Seine and Bar-sur-Aube. Only the Bavarian corps remained in Saint-Parre-Aux-Tertres in order to recover the garrison of Troyes and to act as the rearguard for the Allied army. Wittgenstein withdrew on Lesmont – advancing two regiments of light infantry down the right bank of the Seine as far as Villacerf.

Questions of armistice

Schwarzenberg convened a council of war in which he related to his staff the contents of dispatches from Count Bubna. These dispatches advised Schwarzenberg that Maréchal Augereau had received large reinforcements in the form of numerous conscripts and about 12,000 to 14,000 veteran troops drawn from Spain. Bubna went on to relate that these forces had permitted the French to take the offensive and chase the Austrian troops from Chambéry, Mâcon and Bourg. This resulted in a threat against the Allied position in Geneva.

Count Metternich recognized that the Allied situation had changed. It was greatly weakened by its recent defeats – as well as by the rigors of the season. Furthermore, as the main Allied army had depleted the French countryside between it and the Swiss border, so it would have only limited abilities to sustain itself in this region. When the hostility of the population and the growing partisan actions were considered, this ability was further diminished. Metternich felt that losing a battle under these circumstances would spell disaster for the Allied army. It would be cut off from its base and obliged to withdraw between the various fortresses on the Moselle and Vosges. Such a retreat would certainly strip the army of its baggage and heavy equipment, scatter its troops and cripple the Allied effort to subdue France.

In view of this situation, the Allies sought to request an armistice and sent Prince Vinceslas von Liechtenstein to the French lines with this proposition. When he heard of their proposal, Napoleon was quick to accept it. Fifteen days would be enough for him to organize an army of 100,000 men. He immediately directed Berthier to respond to the Allied offer and ask for a site between Troyes and Vandoeuvres where the commissioners could meet. Even though negotiations would soon be under way, Napoleon continued making dispositions for the capture of Troyes.[3]

The Allies found the city of Troyes untenable. Though it was surrounded by walls and deep moats, the city offered no security. Extensive suburbs stood around the city and the walls were breached in two spots for the projected Châtillon Méry Canal project. The Allies had erected numbers of redans and barricades in the village, but they would not withstand the assault of an army. Volkman, the Allied garrison commander, recognized that his job was to hold the city as long as he could so as to permit the main army to escape. He placed guns on the ramparts, closed the gates and prepared to resist any French attack.

Around 4:00 a.m. the French light cavalry of the II and V Corps had thrown back the Allied advanced posts and executed several attacks against the Allied forces in the city. GD Piré summoned Volkman – requesting that he abandon the city. The garrison, however, responded by firing howitzer shells and other incendiaries which ignited the Saint-Martin and Saint-Savine suburbs.

The French responded by dragging a 12pdr battery up to the walls and quickly punched open the "de la Preze" Gate. As the French light infantry prepared for the assault, Austrian plenipotentiaries appeared – announcing that the city would be evacuated that night, but that Volkman

3 Koch, Vol. I, pp. 338-341.

would burn it down if the assault and cannonade continued. Napoleon responded by ordering the assault to stop.

The French army encamped for the night – establishing their bivouacs in their field dispositions. The VII and XI Corps stood before the suburbs of St.-Martin and Noës. The II Corps stood before Saint-Savine between St.-André and Chartreuse; the Young Guard stood by the St.-Luc Chapel; the V and VI Corps stood in the villages near St.-Julien; and the Guard was near Mesgrigny. The Imperial Headquarters were in Châtres Troyes Falls.

On 24 February – at around 3:00 a.m. – the French army awoke. At daybreak, the advanced guard entered Troyes, where they found 600 wounded Allied soldiers who could not be moved and a few hundred marauders who were made prisoner. The Szekler Hussars and Archduke Rudolph Infantry Regiment remained at the Maiguelet Gate to delay any French advance. However, they were engaged and thrown back by the Guard cavalry – under Count Nansouty – as it moved through the city at the trot. The French cavalry moved quickly enough that it was soon able to catch Wrede's rearguard at the Moutier-Amey defile and put them to rout – capturing 180 prisoners. The Bavarian 1/7th Infantry Regiment lost one badly wounded officer, 57 dead and 33 wounded. The French cavalry moved to Villeneuve-Mesgrigny that night.

The French II Corps, in positions by the Guillotière bridge, was ordered to push to the Barce bridge to support Gérard and Marmont in case of need. That evening, it established itself by Saint-Parre-aux-Tertres.

Kellermann, moving down the road to Bar-sur-Seine, moved from St.-Julien to Sarce where he charged Giulay's rearguard – capturing part of his park and 500 men near Saint-Parre-les-Vaudes – then pursuing the rest of Giulay's forces to Bar. Maréchal Macdonald advanced with his XI Corps and the V Cavalry Corps to Saint-Parre-les-Vaudes – linking with Roussel d'Hurbal's 6th Heavy Cavalry Division, which stood in reserve by Maisons-Blanches.

Napoleon preceded the 1st Old Guard Division – making his entry into Troyes at 11:00 a.m. – greeted by a cheering populace.[4] Their joy at his return was spiced more than a bit by the behaviour of the Allied troops – and particularly the Austrian troops – during their occupation.

Shortly after his arrival in Troyes, Napoleon received word that the Allied ministers to the armistice commission had moved to Lusigny. Napoleon responded by sending his aide-de-camp – Count Flahaut – to Lusigny, where he met Count Schuvalov (aide-de-camp to the Tsar), Count Duca (aide-de-camp to the Austrian Emperor) and General Rasch (the Prussian engineer commander).

Ignoring the armistice talks, Napoleon then pondered his next step. He could either continue pressing Schwarzenberg in hopes of bring him to battle, or he could leave a couple of army corps to pursue him and turn the rest of his army north to once again engage Blücher and the Army of Silesia. The Army of Silesia had absorbed six battalions and a dozen squadrons that had left the siege forces at Luxemburg and Thionville – and by 24 February had crossed the Aube at Baudemont. Near there, they engaged Marmont and threw him back to the Marne.

Napoleon's plans

Of Napoleon's options, the continued pressure against Schwarzenberg was the superior if Napoleon was assured that he could force a battle on Schwarzenberg. If Schwarzenberg was defeated, it would compromise Blücher's position even if he were to take advantage of Marmont's feeble corps. However, the chance of a battle with Schwarzenberg was not great.

4 Koch, Vol. I, pp. 342-4.

On the other hand, Blücher's character guaranteed a battle. Weighing against that was the probability of Schwarzenberg once again advancing and threatening both his rear and capital. Ever eager to engage the enemy, Napoleon chose this latter option and detached Macdonald and Marmont to pursue Schwarzenberg down the roads from Châtillon and Bar, while directing General Allix to flank their march from Auxerre. At the same time, he ordered Ney and Mortier – supported by 1,000 cavalry – to observe the Army of Silesia and held in reserve at Troyes the Guard divisions of Excelmans and Friant. This reserve was made ready to march towards the Aube and the Marne as circumstances demanded. After these dispositions were made – on 25 February – the entire Young Guard and Roussel's dragoons moved on Arcis. Marmont had orders to march on Sézanne and GD Laferrisre-Levesque was recalled from Vandoeuvres to Troyes to join the reserve.

Allied plans

Unable to make a decision, Schwarzenberg called his staff together to discuss their options with the King of Prussia at Vandoeuvres at 8:00 a.m. on 24 February.

The council decided that the main Allied army should withdraw to Langres and join the Austria reserves with them there – be it to accept battle or to develop a new offensive plan. They also decided that the Army of Silesia – already separated from the main army – should advance on the Marne with the goal of joining the corps of Winzingerode, Bülow and Voronzov and organizing a force of 100,000 men. Once organized, this force was to march on Paris.[5]

Count Voronzov, by G. Dawe.

The organization of the Army of the Middle was completed in late February. It contained Bianchi's I (Austrian) Corps, the 1st Reserve Division, the VI (Confederation) Corps and the Austrian troops in Dijon – giving it 45,000 to 50,000 men. It was under the orders of the Crown Prince of Hesse-Homburg and directed against Mâcon with the goal of driving back Maréchal Augereau from the Allied lines of communication to Geneva and the Rhine. In addition, it was decided that the Prince of Saxe-Weimar would remain in the lowlands. Bernadotte would remain in Liége because of the various French garrisons still in those areas. However, they would provide support for the Army of Silesia in case of a reverse.

The main army, still under Schwarzenberg, would serve as the hub around which Allied movements would be centered. On its wings, the Army of Silesia and Midi would operate offensively – each actively on the offensive against the opposition before them and the success of the other. Nonetheless, it was also decided that the main army would withdraw to the Aube along the roads to Bar and La Ferté.

On 25 February in the afternoon, Count Gérard marched at the head of Marmont's corps and arrived at the Dolencourt bridge. Hardegg's Austrian division faced him. Duhèsme moved his troops forward with lowered bayonets at the *pas de charge* and drove the Austrians pell-mell into Bar and pressed their pursuit despite the crossfire of the Austrian artillery.

5 Koch, Vol. I, pp. 342-8.

Maréchal Marmont followed with the remainder of his troops and placed Gérard's second division on the Filles-Dieu heights, while he placed Pacthod's National Guard Division on the left bank of the Aube to guard the bridge. The VII Corps was placed on the right with the II Cavalry Corps.[6]

Count Wrede was withdrawing and had left a small rearguard consisting of Vlastov's brigade of light infantry (Russian 5th Division) and Hardegg's 1st Division (5th Corps) in the vineyards on the right of the main road. At around 6:00 p.m. he heard that Bar was lightly held and planned to seize it with a *coup de main*. Bar was situated between the Filles-Dieu heights and the Spoy heights – at the foot of which flowed the Aube River.

Wrede pushed two battalions forward in dense columns through the Chaumont suburb to the city gate, which they quickly seized. They then pushed confidently into the interior of the city – encountering no obstacle until they reached the city square – where they encountered a French battalion. The French fired a volley, which disordered the Bavarians, and followed it up with a bayonet charge that chased both Bavarian battalions back to the far edge of the suburb. The action caused 300 Bavarian and 50 French casualties.

Wrede.

Macdonald advanced his forces down an unguarded road – pushing as far as Essoye, Landreville and Loches – and then posted a cavalry picket in Fontette. An infantry division and a dragoon division were sent to Mussy-l'Evêque, where they scouted the roads to Langres and Châtillon. The French park remained in Bar-sur-Seine.

The close of 26 February found the bulk of the main Allied army that had been between Bar and La Ferté thrown behind the Aube and retreating towards the east. This caused the Vandoeuvres plan to be abandoned.

The Army of Silesia

On 22 February the Army of Silesia, which had been pushed back to Méry by General P. Boyer, established itself on the right bank of the Seine. On 23 February Blücher learned that Schwarzenberg had abandoned the idea of a battle with Napoleon and had evacuated Troyes. Believing himself abandoned, he judged it appropriate to cross the Aube and attack Marmont's corps in an effort to oblige Napoleon to react and send a large detachment north, while the rest of his army went on the defensive.

After deciding to attack, Blücher destroyed the bridges at Arcis and Plancy. On 24 February he launched his forces forward very early in the morning. That evening, he received an order from Schwarzenberg stating that he was to move via Piney to Lesmont and Dienville behind the Aube in order to take up a position on the right of the main Allied army. In its present position, this ordered movement would be most inconvenient. It obliged Blücher to remount the right bank of the Aube – leaving his rearguard vulnerable to the tender ministrations of the French forces under GD P. Boyer.

6 Koch, Vol. I, pp. 348-350.

Blücher had three alternative plans of operation that he might consider. The first was to cross the Aube at Plancy or Arcis – having not received a reinforcement that would raise his army from its strength of 80,000 men.

The second alternative was to move through Epernay and unite with Winzingerode's 30,000-man corps that was en route from Rheims. He could then gather in Bülow's 20,000 men that were in Laon. Once this was done, he could move along the Oise River or the Marne and operate against Paris with a force of 130,000 men.

His third alternative was to use the 50 Russian pontoons that he had and throw them across the river obstacles as necessary in a direct drive on Paris.

In considering the first alternative, it was necessary to consider the source of necessary foodstuffs to support his army. However, this would not be a significant problem. The second alternative was a solid plan of operation based on all the rules of warfare. This would force Napoleon to follow him, but made him too strong for Napoleon to handle with the forces he had available if Blücher did not let his forces get too strung-out. The third alternative required that Napoleon be totally drawn to the main Allied army. It would permit Blücher to join Bülow and Winzingerode near Meaux or La Ferté-sous-Jouarre. By thrusting on Paris, Blücher would then draw Napoleon to him and could bring about the decisive battle.[7]

Of the three choices, the choice to cross at Plancy or Arcis – in the presence of Napoleon, who was moving from Troyes towards those very cities – was least desirable. This movement promised great problems for Blücher. As a result, he chose to excuse himself from executing Schwarzenberg's orders and continued executing his original plans – marching in two columns via Barbonne and Chichey towards Sézanne.

Marmont's retreat

As Marmont stood watching the miserable roads before him, he was startled to see the Allied columns suddenly appear and move in his direction. His first reaction was that this was an enemy column seeking to escape Napoleon's recent attacks. He responded by detaching 800 cavalry to the Pleurs heights to stop the Allied columns if he found himself obliged to move towards Châlons or to harass them if he found himself moving on Château-Thierry. He then posted his forces such that they would support this reconnaissance force should they be driven back by Korff's cavalry.

Marmont's forces were very weak and he greatly feared getting involved with a superior Allied force. Before him, more and more Allied troops appeared – more troops than Marmont could hope to handle. He wisely decided to withdraw to the Vindey heights – one kilometer behind Sézanne – send messengers to Napoleon advising him of the Allied movement and await developments.

While this occurred on the banks of the Aube, Mortier stood observing Villers-Cotterets and Winzingerode's corps. Mortier made preparations to move on the Marne and left GB Moreau in command of a strong garrison in Soissons. He then began marching on Château-Thierry, where he rendezvoused with General Vincent's "flying corps".

On 25 February Marmont – still uncertain of his opponent's plans – withdrew on La Ferté-Gaucher. From there, he marched on Rebais the following day. His rearguard was pressed by the Allies from the banks of the Morin River to La Ferté-Gaucher, but the French light artillery convinced the Allies to maintain themselves at a respectful distance.

Blücher also had his reconnaissance forces out and learned that Montmirail was lightly held by a force of National Guard. He detached a force of 500 cavalry and directed them into the region between Epernay, Château-Thierry and La Ferté-sous-Jouarre. These patrols captured one

7 C. von W., pp. 184-186.

of Mortier's staff officers carrying dispatches to Marmont. These dispatches led Blücher to believe that he faced only 8,000 to 10,000 men. Despite the weak appearance of the French forces, he doubted his ability to cross the Marne in the presence of these two French marshals and decided instead to turn their right and to cross without engaging in a battle. In consequence, at the break of day on 27 February the Prussians advanced via Rebais on Jouarre and La Ferté, while the Russians moved from the vicinity of Coulommiers – where they had camped that night to Jean-les-deux-Jumeaux and on to Trilport. General Korff, with 4,000 cavalry, was directed to observe the French in La Ferté-Gaucher and their movements along the Aube and the Seine.

Mortier, however, had more information than Blücher suspected and moved his forces to La Ferté – ordering General Vincent to form a rearguard with 200 dragoons, 100 Gardes d'honneur and 500 infantry.[8]

Neither of the French marshals wished to run the risk of being cut off from Paris and crossed the Marne at La Ferté – burning the bridge and moving on Meaux. Ricard's 8th Division was sent to a position between Trilport and Monceaux to cover their withdrawal – which was, by necessity, a hasty one. Despite precautions, the fates intervened to make these maneuvers most difficult. At Trilport, there stood only a wretched pontoon bridge – over which Doumerc's cuirassiers struggled with the greatest difficulties. The slow passage of the cavalry delayed the infantry and almost gave the Russians time to intervene. However, the French did succeed in crossing and moved on to Meaux without a disaster being visited upon them.

Engagement at Meaux

Meaux is divided into three parts by the Marne and its branches. The largest portion of the city is on the right bank. It is crossed by the main road from Châlons to Paris. The second part of the city stood on an island. The third part stood on an isthmus formed by the windings of the river and was crossed by the road to Coulommiers and dominated by the Cornillon hill – over which the road passed from the Cornillon suburbs. The three parts of the city were joined by stone bridges. The city's wall had been flanked by towers and covered by a deep moat, but now these defenses had almost ceased to exist. Some minimal effort had been made to defend the gates, but the city was not, otherwise, defensible against a siege or major assault.

As the French army entered Meaux from the direction of La Ferté, Sacken's forces occupied the Cornillon suburbs and the first bridge over the Marne. The garrison of Meaux – formed with 1,600 National Guardsmen – met the Russians at the bridge, but was badly led and dispersed at the first musket shots. After a few minutes, the Russians occupied the city and the island. They quickly spread down the streets of the city – establishing themselves strongly. The Russians also established a battery of four guns on a hill that overlooked the city and took both the market and the city's streets under fire.

Marmont was surprised by their move, but not discouraged. He leapt to the head of his staff and led them forward – with a few other French soldiers – against the Cornillon Gate. His audacious attack was successful despite the hail of Russian musketry and canister. The Russians, however, continued to hold the bridge. At the same time, the French artillery moved through the city at a gallop and on to the Venice heights. Once there, they unlimbered and began a bombardment that silenced the Russian artillery, but did not dislodge the Russians from the city. A hundred or so French casualties were suffered – including GB Pelleport, who was wounded.

8 Koch, Vol. I, pp. 351-7.

As the head of the French columns under Marmont and Mortier found itself entangled at Trilport and at blows with the Russians at Meaux, its rearguard had been caught and was at the point of being cut off.

General Vincent did not leave Château-Thierry until the night of 26-27 February. The Prussian advanced guard had already occupied La Ferté and soon arrived on Montreuil-aux-Lions. Vincent was obliged to shift his line of march to the right and moved through Lizy as he sought to reach Meaux – leaving the roads and cutting cross-country in order to escape Katzler's advanced guard. Katzler had built a bridge across the Marne between Sameron and La Ferté and marched on La Ferté, where he linked his forces with those of Sacken.

At this time, Katzler's advanced guard consisted of the Brandenburg and 2nd Leib Hussar Regiments, the Brandenburg Uhlans, a half-horse battery, the Fus/1st East Prussian Regiment, the Fus/2nd East Prussian Regiment, the Fus/Brandenburg Regiment, the Combined Silesian Grenadier Battalion, the 1st East Prussian Grenadier Battalion and two companies of East Prussian Jägers.[9]

At the same time, General Tettenborn pushed a reconnaissance force from La Fère-Champenoise only to discover that Napoleon was in Blücher's rear. The fastest Cossack in Tettenborn's command carried this news to Blücher, who immediately recognized that the game was lost and it was time to withdraw before Napoleon caught him again. He withdrew in great haste on the two bridges over the Marne and moved all of his army to the right bank except for Yorck's corps, which he left in Jouarre to cover those bridges and permit Korff's cavalry to withdraw from La Ferté-Gaucher. Kleist was ordered to form the head of his column and took up a position in Lizy to cross the Ourcq and move on Thürouanne and Meaux.

Marmont and Mortier

The forces under the two marshals did not exceed 10,000 men. Together they faced the 80,000 men of the reinvigorated Army of Silesia and had no news of Napoleon's whereabouts. They were justifiably fearful of their position and felt obliged to inform the regency of their situation. Colonel Fabvier, one of Marmont's aides, was sent to King Joseph. The news of this new threat to Paris arrived amidst the display of captured flags and cannon from the previous string of victories. The response was immediate and a new 2nd Paris Reserve Division was ordered and formed – using conscripts from the line depots and the small numbers which were reserved for the Guard. A total of 5,000 infantry and 1,000 cavalry were actually present in the depots. The dilemma was if they should be sent to Marmont and Mortier, or if Napoleon would claim them. Where to send the few troops available? Not always a man of decisiveness, King Joseph rose to the situation and dispatched 1,300 infantry and 106 lancers to Mortier and sent another 300 men to the bridges of Saint-Maur and Charenton. Fortunately, Napoleon learned of the critical situation of his marshals and sent orders to Paris to send all troops and artillery available to their assistance. The remainder of the 3rd Provisional Guard Division – 3,600 infantry, 800 cavalry and 48 guns under the command of GB Poret de Morvan – were dispatched immediately.

While awaiting these reinforcements, Mortier and Marmont assumed that Blücher had withdrawn the Russian corps up the Marne with the goal of crossing the Marne without opposition at La Ferté-sous-Jouarre and then move on the Ourcq with the intention of taking up a position on the right bank.

On 28 February General Vincent's forces – forming the extreme advanced guard of Mortier's corps – pushed forward to catch Blücher's Army of Silesia. As he probed forward, his forces encountered

9 Prussian General Staff, Vol. III, p. 65.

Kleist.

Kleist's troops between Parrin and Vareddes – occupying Gué-à-Treme at around 4:00 p.m. The Prussian main forces lay slightly over two miles (five kilometers) behind Thürouanne. The forward posts of Katzler's advanced guard were driven back across the river at Estrepilly by a vigorous charge by Vincent's cavalry. Christiani's 2nd Old Guard Division – preceded by his artillery, 24 guns – then moved against the village of Gué-à-Treme, which he began to bombard.

The left of the Prussian advanced guard was formed by the von Hasse Combined Fusilier Battalion, the Fus/2nd West Prussian Regiment and the von Hüllesheim Combined Musketeer Battalion.[10]

Kleist detached the 10th Brigade to push forward – covered by the Brandenburg Uhlans – against the left while the light cavalry brigade of Oberst von Blücher was sent to the right against Marcilly to cover the two flanks of Katzler's advanced guard.[11]

The Prussian artillery responded to the French guns and an artillery duel lasted for some time. The rest of the 9th and 10th Prussian Brigades deployed in battle order on both sides of the highway. The village was attacked frontally by the 1st Brigade of Christiani's 2nd Guard Division and turned on the right by the Flanqueur-Chasseur Regiment. The four Prussian battalions holding the village – including the von Linsingen Combined Battalion and the combined battalions of the 2nd Silesian Regiment – were chased out of the village, falling back to the cover of their cavalry. The pursuit stopped by the Neufchelles defile.

General Kleist established the bulk of his corps at Fulaines, destroyed the bridge at Lizy and established patrols on the roads to La Ferté-Milon and Nanteuil to guard them. The 9th Brigade occupied the village of Leplessis. The French pursued the Prussians aggressively and a squadron of the Silesian Uhlans attacked and threw back two battalions formed in mass. The pursuit continued until 1:00 a.m. with the 9th Brigade moving to Neufchelles and the 10th Brigade moving to Mareuil.[12] Von Toll indicates that the Prussians lost 11 officers and 934 men in this engagement.[13]

Mortier remained before Lizy. Marmont, who had followed the road to La Ferté-Milon as far as the village of May-en-Mulcien, took up positions behind the village of May-en-Mulcien. Once in place, a heavy cannonade – supported by musketry – erupted and lasted for 12 hours during the night. That night, a heavy, deep snow fell. When dawn broke and the exchange was finished, Kapsevich's Russian Corps had lost about 400 men,[14] the Prussians had lost 150-200 men *hors de combat* and the French had lost about 80.

That evening, Blücher learned of the results of this engagement and that Napoleon was advancing – driving Korff's cavalry before him. Korff reported that the French were advancing in two columns from La Ferté-Gaucher – one marching against Villenoxe and the other against Sézanne. Korff reported he had moved to Rebais. Blücher ordered Korff to cross the Marne at Sameron.

Blücher ordered Yorck, who was still in Jouarre, to cross to the right bank of the Marne and destroy the bridges as soon as he could. Two combined Landwehr regiments (Combined 4th

10 von Ebertz, p. 161.
11 Prussian General Staff, Vol. III, pp. 65-6.
12 Prussian General Staff, Vol. III, p. 66.
13 von Bernhardi, Vol. 4, Book 7, p. 152.
14 Langeron, p. 402.

and 15th Regiments and Combined 5th and 13th Regiments) were left in Ferté-sous-Jouarre to destroy the bridges as soon as the rest of the corps was over the bridge.[15]

Blücher believed that the local obstacles would slow Napoleon enough to cause him no danger and resolved that he would, on the following day (1 March), cross the Ourcq at Crouy – with Yorck and Kapsevich's corps – with the goal of crossing Marmont and Mortier on their left and to take them in the rear, while Sacken distracted them with demonstrations to their front near Lizy.

Korff was then ordered to withdraw to support the raising of a bridge over the Marne. He was to leave two battalions and a half-battery to support this effort. At 10:00 a.m. all of Korff's forces had crossed the Marne and he was ready to resume operations with the rest of the army.[16]

Blücher's plan, however, was doomed from the beginning. Sacken's corps was locked in place by heavy musketry from Mortier's corps. Yorck found the bridge at Crouy to be broken and was obliged to move upstream to Fulaines, where he could cross the Ourcq. At about 6:00 p.m. Blücher, realizing that his plan was not being executed, sent Kapsevich the order to cross the river at Gesvres after erecting a bridge there.

Kapsevich's movement began well enough. The Russian Advanced Guard crossed the river, despite Doumerc's cavalry standing before it. However, Marmont brought forward his infantry to meet them and the engagement soon became hot. Marmont's forces soon took 280-300 prisoners and threw the rest back across the Ourcq.

That evening, both armies bivouaced close enough to maintain a constant vigil. Despite their numerical superiority, it was the Allies who were most uneasy. The cries of greeting by GB Poret de Morvan's Young Guard Division and the clatter of an artillery train with 48 guns as they joined Moriter's corps may have been music to the French, but they sounded like another army arriving and brought gloom and despair to the Allies.

Despite the weakness of their combined forces, the presence of Mortier and Marmont facing the Army of Silesia was a risk well-taken, for significant events were happening elsewhere and their actions supported those events.

The fall of La Fère

Bülow's 3rd (Prussian) Corps had left Belgium after being relieved by the Allied VIII (German) Corps. On 24 February it stood by Laon, with its right flank covered by Geismar's partisan corps. Once here, Bülow thought that La Fère was ripe to fall to a *coup de main*. It had a garrison of only 400 men – mostly National Guards – under General Pomereul, and its earthworks had been erected in 1793.

Winzingerode, by G. Dawe.

A Prussian infantry brigade invested the city on 26 February and began probing attacks into the suburbs, while bombarding it with howitzer shells. Pomereul, feeling himself unable to resist, negotiated an evacuation of the city and withdrew to Noyon under the condition that he would not act in any further capacity for the remainder of the war. His actions allowed 100 guns, a large number of caissons and magazines filled with 20,000,000

15 Prussian General Staff, Vol. III, p. 66.

16 C. von W., p. 197.

francs worth of military equipment to fall into the Prussians' hands. This would have been a major disaster had not Blücher ordered Bülow to move to Laon and then move on the Aisne to operate in conjunction with Winzingerode's corps.

Winzingerode's corps had recently moved from Châlons through Epernay and on Rheims, where it was reinforced by Voronzov's corps (detached from the Army of the North). Once that was accomplished, it marched on Soissons.

Napoleon marches on Blücher's rear

Napoleon stood in Troyes with his eyes fixed on the movements of the two main Allied armies – watching for an opportunity to isolate the Army of Silesia a second time in the Marne Valley and inflict his will upon it. On 27 February he departed Troyes – arriving in Herbisse with all of the Guard cavalry and Friant's 1st Old Guard Division. Ney, who was in Arcis, had Roussel d'Hurbal's 6th Heavy Cavalry Division, a cavalry march regiment under the command of Colonel Ghigny and the brigade of P. Boyer's 9th Division that had been guarding Méry. He drew his forces together in Semoine and Gourganson. Victor had his divisions and a cavalry march brigade under General Wathiez in Salon. GD Arrighi, with the 2nd Paris Reserve Division and a detachment of the I Cavalry Corps under Bordesoulle, was in Villenoxe.

On 28 February the Guard stood between La Ferté-Gaucher and Esternay, and Arrighi was in Bircot-la-Ville and Châtillon. That same day, a force of Guard chasseurs and lancers near La Fère-Champenoise encountered some of Tettenborn's light troops and chased them towards Vertus.

The march from Esternay to Jouarre was frightful. The weather was horrible and the roads barely passable. Despite this, Napoleon was still able to reach Jouarre that night with the Guard cavalry and the head of the Guard infantry column. The roads were so bad, however, that the artillery remained behind – between Rebais and Jouarre – and could not be pulled free from the mud until the following morning. Unfortunately, Napoleon realized that if he was to save his two marshals, he did not have a moment to spare and pressed on as hard as he could. However, first the bridge at Jouarre had to be repaired and this gave his scattered command time to regroup.

Blücher had become aware of Napoleon's movements and, fearful for his rear, wisely withdrew across the Marne at La Ferté and Château-Thierry – abandoning his thrust on Paris. He now pushed to move on the Aisne and link up with Winzingerode and Bülow. By 2 March he had begun his march north towards Soissons. Yorck's 1st (Prussian) Corps led the march – moving to Château-Thierry that night. He was followed by Kapsevich and Sacken, who established themselves in Milon and Ancienville. Kleist was designated to form the rearguard and received orders to send a reconnaissance force towards May and to mask the movement of the rest of the corps.

This reconnaissance force consisted of the Neumark Dragoons, Silesian Uhlans, Silesian Hussars, 6pdr Horse Batteries #8 and #9 and two battalions of the 9th Brigade. The three other battalions of the 9th Brigade followed behind at some distance as a support.[17]

As Ziethen's cavalry marched out of Neufchelles, it was attacked by Merlin's 1st Light Cavalry Division. The Prussians countered with canister from Horse Battery #8, while the Neumark Dragoons, Silesian Hussars and Silesian Uhlans charged the French. Merlin was thrown back on Ricard's 8th Division, which had moved forward in good order supported by Lagrange's 3rd Division and the protection of a battery of 12 heavy guns. An artillery duel soon erupted, which resulted in six Prussian guns being dismounted. By 5:00 p.m. Ziethen was forced to withdraw. Kleist then withdrew his entire force and slowly moved to the Ourcq. Once there, however, he was forced to stop as the other corps had not yet completed its passage of the river.

17 Prussian General Staff, Vol. III, p. 68.

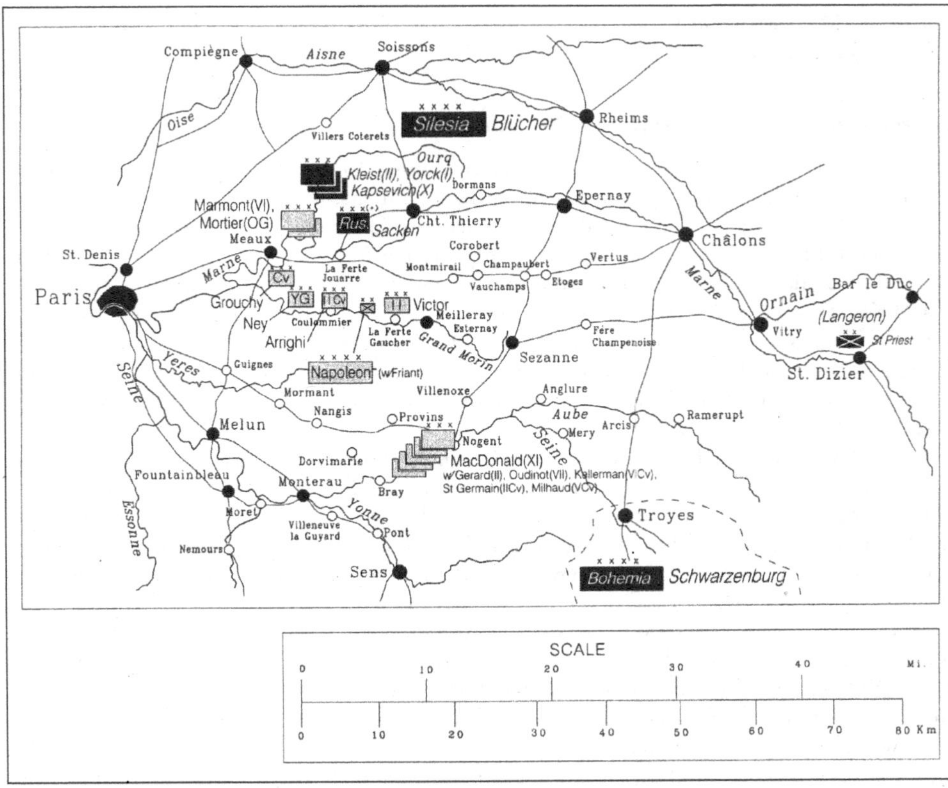

Map 11 Strategic Situation, March 1 1814.

Marmont encountered Kapsevich's 10th Corps in the Mareuil defile and forced it to face about. Kleist moved two battalions, a hussar regiment and a battery of six guns to a position in front of Mareuil – giving them orders to hold their position until everyone had crossed the bridge.

Marmont, not knowing the confusion in the Allied ranks, did not press an attack and contented himself with bombarding the village. Once on the far side of the river, Kleist formed his troops and again resumed his march – happy to have escaped relatively unscathed. He then sent a courier to Kapsevich to advise him of his movements.

Blücher's blunder had almost cost him a corps, but he did not escape without suffering a personal loss because of his errors. His son, Oberst von Blücher, had been charged with commanding the troops defending the Mareuil defile and died as a result of his father's error.

With the Army of Silesia withdrawing, the two French marshals moved their forces to Neufchelles and Vaurinfroy. Napoleon, however, had completed the bridge and crossed the Marne with his army on 3 March at about 2:00 a.m. Friant's 1st Old Guard Division, the Guard cavalry, Grouchy's cavalry and Ney's corps moved into Blücher's rear. At the same time, Victor and Arrighi were ordered to move via Vieux-Maison and Bussières to Château-Thierry. There they were to pick up four Guard horse batteries and two 12pdr Guard batteries and move up the right bank of the Marne. Mortier and Marmont crossed the Ourcq at La Ferté-Milon and the plain on the left bank. Napoleon intended to push the Allies towards Oulchy-la-Ville while he moved via

Braisnes to Micy, where he wished to cross the Aisne on their left flank and while Count Grouchy cut the road from Château-Thierry to Soissons.

Engagement at Neuilly-St.-Front – 3 March

At around 10:00 a.m. Mortier and Marmont encountered the Allied rearguard on the Passy heights. As the infantry was too spread-out on the road to attack, GD Doumerc moved to turn the Allied left with part of his cavalry, while his horse artillery bombarded their front. This maneuver did not succeed, as the French cavalry did not find the shortest road to their objective and the Allies had sufficient time to prepare themselves for the turning movement. Blücher placed Kleist's reserve cavalry on the right of the line. He placed Count Langeron's corps on the left and directed that they take up a position 500 feet to the rear of the brigades of Klüx and Pirch. Kapsevich deployed 24 guns along the right bank of the Ourcq to defend the bridge and deployed skirmishers along the river to prevent any French cavalry from crossing the river at any fords.[18]

Between Klüx and Pirch, there stood a woods. Finally, Blücher threw a battalion into the farm on the right of this small woods and placed 16 cannon before them.

In this position Blücher could only sit and wait as the Ourcq defile was blocked with infantry, artillery and the baggage of the other army corps. If Doumerc's cavalry had been able to maneuver as intended, Blücher's position would have been gravely compromised, but it did not move vigorously enough and arrived too late to do more than grab a few prisoners.

Marmont's infantry also arrived too late to act simultaneously and the Allies escaped its attack as well. As a result, it engaged solely in some musketry and a cannonade between the two banks. The French advance was met by Kapsevich's skirmishers and 24 heavy guns, which kept the French away from the Allied crossings. The Allies finally withdrew after losing 500-600 men – losses which were regarded as very light under the circumstances. As they withdrew, Kapsevich withdrew his heavy guns and deployed a few horse guns to cover the withdrawal. Korff was also obliged to withdraw his guns when the French deployed 30 guns before the bridge and threatened to overwhelm his guns with their fire.

Despite this escape, the situation of the Army of Silesia was still not a happy one. It continued its movement on the Aisne in two columns – moving via Blancy and Parcey as well as down the main route to Soissons. The Allied rearguard was formed with all of their horse artillery and cavalry. Though Blücher was closing on the corps of Bülow and Winzingerode, the latter, however, was on the right bank of the Aisne and there was no place for Blücher to cross over and join with him.

Mortier and Marmont pressed Blücher from behind and established themselves in Neuilly-St.-Front, while threatening his left flank, Napoleon's advanced guard closed on Rocourt. One of his baggage columns had already been captured by the French and Blücher still stood the chance of being pinned against the Aisne.[19]

Soissons falls again – 5 March

While executing Blücher's orders, generals Bülow and Voronzov moved from Laon and Rheims to Soissons on 1 March. The capture of Soissons had depended, in part, on their juncture with the Army of Silesia.

Soissons was in the same condition it had been in when the Russians captured it. Its garrison was not quite as large, but they were veteran and hardened soldiers. There was more and

18 Langeron, p. 403.
19 Koch, Vol. I, pp. 370-4.

better-served artillery than before as well. When the city was invested on 2 March the French artillery responded vigorously to the Allied bombardment.

Knowing the importance of taking Soissons, Bülow sent an emissary to General Moreau – the garrison commander – telling him that no help was coming. Moreau had no idea of the importance of holding Soissons and thought only of saving his troops and sought to make an honorable stand and escape, if possible, so he could rejoin the main French army. As a result, he capitulated. According to the terms of the capitulation, he could take his field guns, but a dispute arose and the Allies wished only to let him take two. The situation brought the Polish troops in French service to a furor. Further excited by the sound of the French guns announcing their approach, they revolted against General Moreau and began to plan a defense of the place without him or his consent. Voronzov, however – sensing the imminent relief of the French garrison – broke the impasse. He said: "Give them all the guns that they claim – and mine as well if they ask for them – but if they leave as a result, we have made a good deal!"[20] The argument over the guns settled, the French withdrew – abandoning Soissons to the Allies. The French garrison then marched on Villers-Cotterets.

The Russian general was right. As a result of the garrison's actions, the Army of Silesia's columns were entering the city in the greatest confusion and disorder. What would Blücher have done, with Napoleon closing in behind him and the Vistula Regiment still holding the city gates in front of him?

The Army of Silesia spent the rest of the day and all of the night of 3-4 March crossing the Aisne. The rearguard, formed by General Kapsevich, withdrew in good order and stopped six hours later in Busancy. Moreau's craven surrender of Soissons had permitted Blücher to escape and establish himself in a position where Napoleon could not hope to strike with any hope of success.

Their quarry having escaped, the French marshals arrived in Hartennes – from where they detached to their rear General Vincent with a small force to Château-Thierry with orders to raise the regional force of National Guard and to prepare an entrenched bridgehead. In addition, he was to gather up the stragglers and the detachments of reinforcements being sent from Paris for the army.

Grouchy's light cavalry moved across the fields and took up a position at Rocourt, with the troops of the Guard in echelon behind him. The Imperial Headquarters was transferred to Montreuil-aux-Lions.

Napoleon now sought to turn the Allied left and ordered GD Grouchy to move to Fismes by way of Fère-en-Tardenois. He then ordered the Imperial Guard to follow Grouchy. At the same time, Mortier and Marmont were ordered to move quickly against the Allied front. Arrighi was ordered to accelerate his march and support the attacks of Mortier and Marmont.

While Napoleon was fresh from his victories to the south, Blücher was scrambling to escape yet another disaster. However, he had been fortunate enough to join Bülow and Winzingerode and directed the Prussians to take up positions on the right and the Russians were sent to the left. He compressed the Army of Silesia and the Army of the North into the region between the Lette and the Aisne. Covered by the rivers and with the crossings strongly guarded as far as Béry-au-Bac, he supported his right on Fontenay and extended his left to Craone.

Winzingerode was to take up positions between Cernay and Bray-en-Laonnaise to watch the Aisne. Sacken's corps was on the right between Bray and Ostel, with a force in Vailly. In Soissons there remained only Rudsevich's 10th Corps with about 8,000 men – more than sufficient to prevent Napoleon's seizing it. Czernichev stood with his cavalry between the Aisne and the Vesle.

20 Koch, Vol. I, p. 376.

At the break of dawn on 4 March the French army marched on Soissons and Fismes. Their march was not difficult and they were faced only by Kapsevich's Cossacks. The French cavalry moved from Fère to Fismes, but Czernichev withdrew steadily before them – offering little resistance. The advancing French were able to capture a number of vehicles abandoned by the Allies along the crossroads.

Napoleon was impatient to come to grips with the main body of the Army of Silesia and ordered General Guyot to push a reconnaissance force – formed from his Guard service squadrons – to Fismes.

General Czernichev, who occupied the village in force, threw the advancing French cavalry back. At that moment, Grouchy arrived with Roussel d'Hurbal's 6th Heavy Cavalry (Dragoon) Division on the Saint-Martin heights. The 5th Dragoons, forming the head of the column, fell on the Allies – supported by the rest of the division – and drove them back to Courcelles.

At around 3:00 p.m. Gros' brigade of the two Flanqueur Regiments (2nd Old Guard Division) pushed into the Paris suburb of Soissons – which was occupied by four Russian jager regiments and some infantry battalions – and engaged them in a lively fight. Another French attack moved against the Rheims Gate. Here, not only was the wall broken in a few places, but the ditch was collapsed. Ricard's division attached the Rheims Gate, which was defended by two Russian regiments under General Kern. Though the French raised some batteries that could fire on the road to Laon, they were unable to effect the Russians. By the time night fell, the French had lost 900 men and the Russians had lost about 1,000.[21]

It was only when Napoleon arrived in Fismes that he learned of Moreau's cowardly abandonment of Soissons. He went into a rage and accused Moreau of having robbed him the fruit of eight days of marching, for Moreau's abandonment of Soissons had permitted the Allies to escape his blow. Moreau was court-martialled, but the revolution of 31 March would open his prison cell and set him free.

There is no doubt that the fall of Soissons saved Blücher's army, but Blücher's defeat may well have not been as decisive as Napoleon had hoped. Blücher's army may have been fatigued by its marches as well as its earlier defeats, but Bülow and Winzingerode's troops were fresh. Also, the bridge over the Aisne at Mincy and the bridges in Vesle were open and held by the Allies.

The blame was not entirely Moreau's because the French army had not made a particularly rapid march. Its pace had been more leisurely than it might have been, and if Napoleon was truly anxious to come to grips with Blücher, he could certainly have pressed his troops to march harder.

What is surprising about this portion of the campaign is the Allies' blundering about the French countryside without adequate reconnaissance, no plan and no coordination. The Allies had a tremendous cavalry advantage and certainly could have sent out more than adequate reconnaissance forces to locate and monitor the French army's movements. Yet despite that capability, Napoleon succeeded in surprising Blücher and his army repeatedly. Though the countryside was hostile, the movement of a large force of cavalry – be it a regiment or brigade – would have been relatively unopposed by the local inhabitants.

21 Sporschil, Vol. II, 1st Band, pp. 556-7.

11

The Battles of Craone, Laon and Rheims, 5-15 March 1814

The fall of Soissons changed everything for the French. Instead of marching to a sure victory against an Allied force trapped against an unfordable river, it found itself faced with the dilemma of attempting to cross a river in the face of an enemy that outnumbered them by threefold.

Having to recalculate his campaign, Napoleon once again began reviewing the situation of his army and those of his enemies. He detached GD Corbineau with Laferrière's 3rd Guard Cavalry Division and sent him towards Rheims, which he presumed to be weakly occupied. He also ordered Grouchy to surprise Braisnes, while Mortier and Marmont looked to recapture Soissons.

The first two missions were to prove successful. On 5 March at around 4:00 a.m. GD Corbineau arrived before Rheims and quickly overran and captured four Allied battalions that were guarding the city. This movement entirely cut all communications by the combined Armies of Silesia and the North with Schwarzenberg.[1]

In the center, GD Roussel moved from Courcelles to Braisnes and threw out at around 2:00 a.m. the 1,000 Cossacks who occupied the village – capturing 100 horses and liberating the French prisoners the Russians had taken during the previous day's reconnaissance.

The tasks required of Mortier and Marmont were more difficult. They moved from St.-Germain with their columns undergoing a heavy cannonade by the Allies on the far bank of the river. They were not able to deploy in the plain or use their artillery until after noon. They brought 30 guns to bear on the Allied positions, but with no results. Rudsevich gave as good as he got.

Around 3:00 p.m. the skirmishers of Christiani's 2nd Old Guard Division advanced into the Paris suburb and took the Allies under fire until night. The suburb was occupied by Colonel Durnov, with the 7th, 29th, 37th and 45th Jager Regiments and a battalion of the Staroskol Infantry Regiment. A Russian battery of 18 guns was joined by 24 more from Kapsevich's 10th Corps and combined, this battery lashed out at the French.[2]

Marmont saw he had little chance of success as things stood and attempted an assault on the Rheims Gate with Ricard's division. The gate was defended by GM Kern, the Belosersk Infantry and the 48th Jager Regiment.[3] By 3:00 p.m. the French assault became very heavy and was covered by the fire of 40 guns. However, this assault proved equally fruitless. The Russian 6th Corps – supported by a brigade of the 8th Corps – held them out of the city, while the 9th Corps remained in the streets of the city serving as a reserve. The city was beyond the French grasp and at 6:00 p.m. they admitted their inability to take the city and withdrew. Rudsevich reportedly lost 1,056 men in the day's engagement.[4]

1 Koch, Vol. I, p. 383.
2 Langeron, p. 412; Prussian General Staff, Vol. III, p. 73.
3 von Damitz, Vol. III, 1st Part, pp. 13-4.
4 Prussian General Staff, Vol. III, p. 74.

While this effort was under way, the French organized some artillery on the ridge near the old Celestin Convent with the intention of firing on the road to Laon. An effort was also undertaken to erect a pontoon bridge facing St.-Germain, but it proved fruitless as well. As night fell, the fighting stopped and the French withdrew to St.-Germain – having lost 800-900 dead and wounded.

If Rheims, which was occupied by the Allies, were retaken, it would renew Napoleon's access to the 2nd Military Division. Napoleon sent an order to General Janssens, the 2nd Military Division's commander, to gather 6,000 or 8,000 men from his depots and to send them to him. However, even though Janssens did not waste a minute addressing his orders, the depots – which on paper were filled with recruits – were found to be bare. Janssens gathered up what he could find and ran them about the rear of the Allied lines – spreading alarm in the rear of the Army of Silesia.

Napoleon felt certain that he would be joined by this division and did not believe that General St. Priest, who occupied Vitry and Châlons, would be in a state to harass his lines of communication – and he now thought of the possibilities of cutting Blücher off from his bases in Belgium by turning his left. There was also the possibility of retaking Laon, but this was made more difficult by the only bridge over the Aisne being at Béry-au-Bac and that the roads between his present position and Laon were miserable. However, the recapture of Laon was worth so much that it was worth fighting the natural obstacles to make the attempt.

GD Nansouty was ordered to leave Fismes – with the Polish Brigade of Count Pacz and Excelmans' cavalry division – and take Béry. This movement was to be supported by all of the troops then in Fismes on the following day. The orders were sent to Mortier and Marmont to abandon the attempt to retake Soissons and to move via Braisnes and Fismes towards Béry.

GD Nansouty's advance met its first obstacle at the defile on the road to Rheims, where he encountered and threw back the lead elements of a Russian cavalry brigade. His troops pushed through the defile at the gallop and struck down all that they encountered. A mixture of fleeing Russians and pursuing French cavalry pushed across the bridge, leaving it in French hands, but continuing to push the Russians as far as Ville-aux-Bois – taking two guns and 200 prisoners.

During this engagement, GD Friant and Meunier's 1st Old Guard and 1st Voltigeur Divisions moved down the left bank of the Aisne and established themselves on the heights between Béry-au-Bac and Corbeny. The French army was deployed as follows:[5]

By Corbeny:
- 2nd Old Guard Brigade
- Guard Reserve Artillery

By Ville-aux-Bois:
- Boyer de Rebeval's division

By Béry-au-Bac:
- d'Hurbal's dragoon division
- 1st & 3rd Guard Cavalry Divisions (Colbert & Laferrière)

By Cormicy:
- Mortier's corps
- 2nd Old Guard Division (Christiani)
- Provisional Young Guard Division (Poret de Morvan)
- Gardes d'honneur (de France)

By Rouey:
- Arrighi's division

5 Hulot, p. 107.

By Braisnes:

Marmont's corps
Ricard's division
Lagrange's division
Bordesoulle's cavalry corps

The Prussian plans – 6 March

Feldmarschal Blücher assumed, after the recent maneuvers, that Napoleon would march on his left flank and directed his baggage towards Laon. He then ordered all of his corps to move to the Craone plateau with the goal of stopping Napoleon's march on Laon. However, Napoleon did not give Blücher the time necessary to act. He directed Grouchy's cavalry to regroup, Laferrière's 3rd Guard Cavalry Division was recalled from Rheims and the brigade of Boyer's 9th Division marched on Corbeny – chasing Czernichev's cavalry before him. Boyer's brigade was in position on the Craone plateau for three hours when the heads of the Allied columns began to appear before him.

Blücher, however, on seeing the French deployed before him, chose not to move out into the plain view of his adversary and decided that the Craone plateau was too narrow for him to deploy his 90,000 men. Upon hearing that a French cavalry division had moved against Laon, he quickly changed his line of march and directed a force of 10,000 cavalry and 60 horse guns under Winzingerode.

This force was organized by drawing units from the corps of Winzingerode, Langeron and Yorck via Chevrigny to the main road from Rheims. They had orders to secure that road from the French advance and give Bülow time to arrive in Laon. If necessary, Bülow could also turn Napoleon's right flank if Napoleon were to choose to attack the Allied positions on the Craone heights the next day.

At the same time the corps of Kleist, Langeron and Yorck were ordered to move on Fétieux to support the march of this cavalry force. Only Winzingerode's corps remained on the Craone plateau. Count Voronzov, established in the villages of Ailles and Vasognes, was supported by Sacken's forces – serving as a reserve and posted in Bray.

These two forces were posted so that they could serve as a pivot for a changing of face by the Allies between the Aisne and Lette rivers, while the combined cavalry would turn the French flanks and strike them in the rear.

Napoleon learned of the Allied troops on the Craone heights and directed Capitaine d'Ordonnance Caraman to lead a reconnaissance force – supported by an Old Guard battalion – in that direction. The French battalion moved up the Pontois mill stream. The woods to the left of Heurtebise were occupied by the 14th Jager Regiment. The 13th Jagers were posted before the farm and executed 10 bayonet attacks against the advancing French – losing 16 officers and 400 men *hors de combat*.[6]

Despite their defense, the French drove back the Russian 13th and 14th Jager Regiments from the crest of the Craone plateau.[7]

The Old Guard battalion was so hotly engaged that Napoleon felt obliged to support them with an entire brigade and directed Ney to execute a diversion on the right. P. Boyer's brigade moved across the Corbeny woods and moved on Saint-Martin, which was occupied by the Navaguinsk and Tula Regiments. They were engaged by Meunier's 1st Voltigeur Division and thrown out

6 von Damitz, Vol. III, 1st Part, p, 25.
7 Prussian General Staff, Vol. III, p. 76.

of the Vaucler Abbey and pushed to the Heurtebise farm. This farm was captured and recaptured several times, but was to eventually remain in the Russians' hands. At 7:00 p.m. Napoleon ordered the engagement to stop and the Old Guard was sent to its bivouacs by Corbeny. Meunier's 1st Voltigeur Division was posted between Heurtebise and Vaucler, while Boyer's was in by the Bouconville mill and stretched to the right by the Bove farm road.[8]

The Battle of Craone – 7 March

During the morning of 7 March Napoleon reviewed the Allied position. The battlefield was limited to the north by the Lette, which flowed in a straight and marshy valley. In the middle of its course, its banks were sharp and deep. The stream ran between 10 and 11 miles (16-17 kilometers) in a bed that varied from one to three miles (two to four kilometers) wide. It flowed gently between the Craone plateau as far as Paissy and Troyon. Between Malmaison and Ange-Gardien, it widened towards Vailly and was enclosed by gardens and hedges. Between Saint-Martin and Ailles, a heavy woods covered the back of the plateau that overlooked the Lette. The front of this position was covered by a ravine.

The Allied army extended from the ravines of the Foulon and Ailles with the Heurtebise farm – and at the village of Saint-Martin to their front was Count Voronzov's corps formed in battalion columns. As Napoleon surveyed the Allied line he saw their first line, straddling the "Route des Dames", which runs from Craone to Vorin – standing around 1,000 meters (1,100 yards) to the west of (behind) the Heurtebise farm with its left supported on a crest that dominated the position and spread across a front of two to three kilometers (1.25-1.9 miles). It consisted of the 13th Jager Regiment, the 24th Division of GM Vuitsch and Pouncet's brigade of the 14th Division (Tula and Navaguinsk Regiments). It totaled 14 battalions and was under the command of General Vutisch. On the right flank of the first line near Vassogne stood GM Benkendorff with the Pavlograd Hussars and four Cossack regiments. The farms of Heurtebise and Roches were occupied by the 14th Jager Regiment – deployed as skirmishers – to act as advanced posts. On its right flank stood two squadrons of hussars. GM Krasovsky commanded this advanced detachment. The left wing – in Ailles – was covered by light troops, with their supporting formed infantry in the village and behind the heights. To the left of this ridge stood a jager regiment and to its right were two further battalions of the first line. The edge of the Foulon ravine was covered by a long skirmish line that was ordered to fall back on Benkendorff's cavalry if it became necessary to withdraw.[9]

The second line stood 600 paces behind the first line and contained the 21st Division (seven battalions) commanded by GL Laptiev. Laptiev also commanded the whole infantry of both lines. The third line was under GL Count Stroganov and stood 800 paces behind the second line deployed between Bovel and Paissy. It contained Jeltovsky's brigade of the 13th Division and Chovansky's 12th Division – nine battalions in all.

The Russian artillery was under the overall command of GM Miakinin and was deployed as follows: 12 heavy and 24 light guns under Colonel Vinspar stood in front of the center of the first line to cover the front of the position and the passage to Heurtebise . Twelve guns from Horse Battery #11 stood in front of the Russian right wing to cover the road from Craone, 12 guns of Horse Battery #9 stood in front of the Russian left wing and dominated the Foulon ravine and six guns of Heavy Battery #28 were to the left of the second line overlooking the Vaucler ravine. These two ravines were the only practical approaches to his position. Six more heavy guns and 24

8 Koch, Vol. I, pp. 384-8.
9 von Damitz, Vol. III, 1st Part, pp. 33-4.

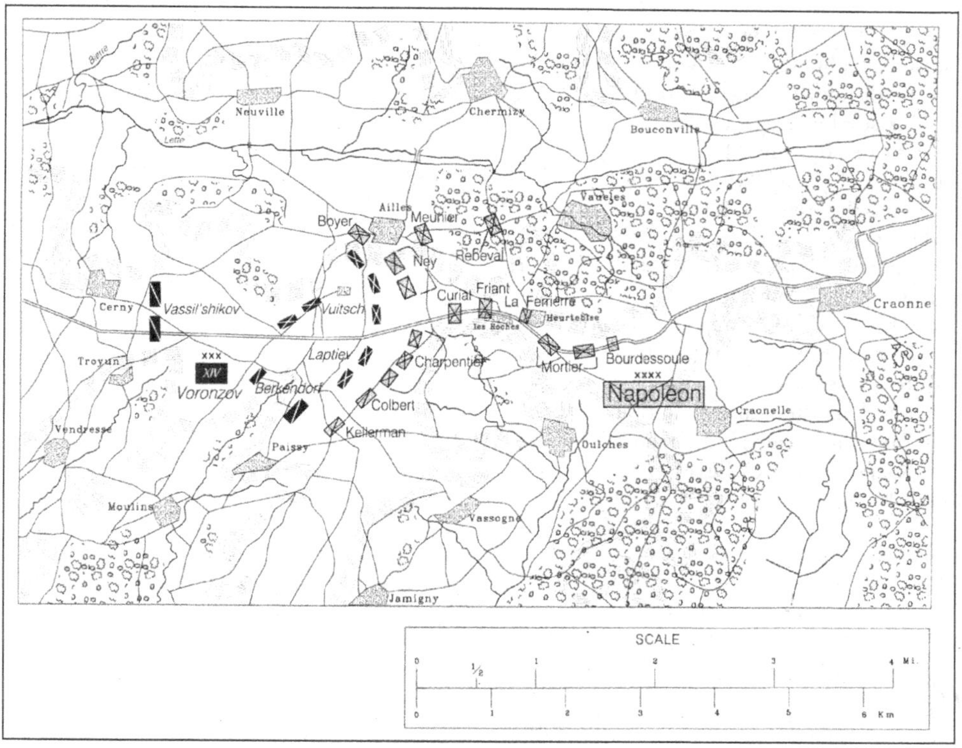

Map 12 Battle of Craone, March 7 1814, 3:00 p.m.

light guns were held in reserve. Of these, 18 rotated forward to replace disabled artillery during the battle and 12 more came into action during the retreat.[10]

Voronzov's forces came to a total of 30-33 battalions (or about 16,300 infantry), eight squadrons (or about 1,000 of regular cavalry) and an equal number of Cossacks. He had a total of 18,000 men supported by 96 guns. Between the villages of Cernay and Troyon – to the southwest of Vassogne (on the plateau) – stood Vassil'shikov's cavalry (about 32 squadrons totalling 4,000 dragoons and hussars) and Karpov's Cossack detachment (a further 1,500 men).[11]

Winzingerode's corps was formed in three lines of dense battalion columns. Sacken's corps stood between Bray and Ange-Gardien. The corps of Langeron, Kleist and Yorck were maneuvering between the Lette and the Bruyères road in an effort to reach the Rheims road and support Winzingerode's cavalry. The total force of the Army of Silesia at this point was about 100,000 men. However, none of the units on the right bank of the Lette would be able to take part of the battle on the Craone plateau.

Langeron's corps stood by Froidemont. However, it would be mostly Voronzov who would bear the brunt of the battle. The forces in the battle were as follows:

10 Bogdanovich, pp. 315-6.

11 Bogdanovich, pp. 315-6; Hulot, p. 114.

Allies:
1st Line, Right Wing: GL Voronzov
Benkendorff's brigade 1,000
Krasovsky's brigade 1,250
Harpe's brigade 2,154
1st Line, Left Wing: GL Voronzov
Vuitsch's division 4,300[12]
2nd Line: GL Voronzov
Leptev's 21st Division 3,500
3rd Line: GL Voronzov
Chovansky's 12th Division 1,800[13]
Scheltuchin's brigade 3,300
Cavalry: Vassil'shikov
Lanskoi's 2nd Hussar Division 1,500
Pantschulischev's 3rd Dragoon Division 1,200
Karpov's Cossack Division 1,200
Total: 16,304 infantry, 4,900 cavalry

French:
Right wing: Maréchal Ney
Boyer's brigade 1,886
Meunier's division 865
Curial's division 1,022
Maréchal Victor:
Boyer de Rebeval's division 3,800
Charpentier's division 3,600

Général de division Grouchy
Roussel's division 2,200
Laferrière's division 1,205
Reserve/Center: Maréchal Mortier
Friant's division 3,800
Christiani's division 3,800
Poret de Morvan's division 3,400
Colbert's division 1,100

Left wing: Général de division Nansouty
Excelmans' division 1,350
Pacz's division 450
Total: 23,573 infantry, 6,350 cavalry

Napoleon knew of the obstacles which an attack on the Allied right would encounter, but did not hesitate to order such an attack because once he was through the defiles, he would be able to

12 Vuitsch's division contained only Krassovsky and Swarikin's brigades. Harpe was detached to the 1st Line.

13 Von Damitz cites this as being Chervansky's brigade, but Chervansky was the 12th Division commander. This division had seen considerable combat and may have been reduced to this strength – or it may be one of his brigades and von Damitz's citation is incorrect.

bring all of his forces into action on the extremity of the Allied line and this maneuver would give him the opportunity to destroy the Allies before they could be supported.

His dispositions were simple and demanded nothing but force and energy. If Napoleon was leading the powerful infantry he had led in the past, he could have driven dense columns up the ravines at the *pas de charge* to strike at the Allies while other French forces demonstrated on his front and left. However, with the exception of Friant and Christiani's divisions, his forces consisted of newly-raised levies that were greatly fatigued and poorly trained. In contrast, the Russian infantry facing him was the cream of the Allied army. They were veteran soldiers hardened to life in the field and long marches. As a result, Napoleon felt obliged to take another approach to the problem before him.

At 9:00 a.m. the Guard batteries had arrived on the plateau to the north of Oulchy and opened fire on the Russian center. The Russians responded in kind, but the antagonists were about 1,500 meters (1,625 yards) apart and the results of this exchange were minimal. Meanwhile, Victor – at the head of Boyer de Rebeval's 9th Division – massed his corps near the small Vauclerc mill alongside the Old Guard Division and the reserve artillery. At 11:00 a.m. Boyer's division had arrived on the battlefield, but Charpentier's division had been delayed because of the sleet-covered roads and was not yet on the battlefield.

The fury of the artillery exchange continued as the French moved into their positions. Meanwhile, the Allied artillery that had been masked from Napoleon's view by the Marion woods revealed its presence by opening fire.

Meanwhile, Count Voronzov ordered General Krasovsky to withdraw to the first line. Two squadrons of the Pavlograd hussars were ordered to cover the horse battery on the left flank. The 2nd Jager Regiment was moved from the second line to the first, and occupied Ailles village.

French infantry at Craone, by Sergent.

Victor deployed Boyer de Rebeval's 9th Division behind a ruined redoubt to protect them from the fire of the battery on the Russian right flank and deployed 12 guns to return the fire. Krasovsky was immediately wounded in the leg and left the battlefield.

Maréchal Ney was ordered to lead the principal attack on the right, which was not to move up to the left of the Lette Valley. He was ordered to converge his corps – that of Victor and Roussel's dragoons – while Nansouty sought to turn the right of the enemy line through the Vassogne Valley with Pacz's Polish brigade and Excelmans' division. In order to give the action the desired unity, it was necessary to delay the attack two hours because Victor and Mortier were still six miles (10 kilometers) from the battlefield.

Napoleon had begun the battle with a cannonade with the first Guard batteries that arrived on the plateau – and their fire played cruelly on the masses of Russian infantry exposed to their fire. However, Ney – upon hearing the gunfire (and for reasons never fully explained) – broke camp, organized his forces into two columns and moved out of Saint-Martin. The right-hand column, under GD Boyer and consisting of his brigade, moved along the edge of the woods and presented itself before the village of Ailles. The left division, organized with Meunier and Curial's divisions, moved to the plateau to the left.

Their march was protected for some time by the edge of the plateau, but when they arrived in view of Ailles and were about to move over the ridge they were greeted by the Allied artillery and musketry, which stopped them cold.

Napoleon, seeing that the battle was already under way, ordered Victor – who had only Boyer de Rebeval's 9th Division near the Vaucler Abbey – to move his artillery forward and engage the Russians by the Marion woods. Boyer would lose several guns to counter battery and the fire of his infantry was not particularly effective because they were all recent conscripts.

Napoleon also sent orders to Grouchy's cavalry and the 3rd Guard Cavalry Division – which he had earlier that morning directed to Corbeny and Nansouty with Pacz's brigade, which was also in Corbeny – to join Excelmans' division on the Vassogne heights and attack the Russian right.[14]

Napoleon supported Boyer with all six of the Guard's batteries. Victor then pushed a column forward by Heurtebise. The French had three columns marching on Voronzov's forces. The first was Pierre Boyer's brigade, the second consisted of the Guard divisions of Meunier and Curial, and the third column was formed by GD Boyer de Rebeval's 9th Division. Unsettled by the French artillery, the Russians pulled back from the Marion woods, set the farm they had occupied afire and withdrew to their first line. A bit later, Victor sent forward the 1st Division in a dense column along the southern edge of the plateau and its artillery deployed to the left of the Guard artillery on the edge of the Voulon Valley.

Victor had pushed his troops forward to a position behind an old redoubt and dragged forward 12 guns, which began to fire on the Russians. Just as these positions were established, Victor was struck in the thigh with a bullet and became *hors de combat*.[15]

Seeing himself struck simultaneously from three points, Voronzov decided to refuse his left wing a little. Ney profited from this to push forward two Young Guard divisions from the woods on the plateau. Boyer de Rebeval linked up with them and advanced his division about 3,250 feet (1,000 meters) and established Bigarré's brigade en masse par divisions on the edge of the woods, which had just been evacuated by the Russian 19th Jager and the Shirvan Regiments. Boyer de Rebeval's division was formed of new recruits – the most senior of which had no more than 20 days of service. Flankers and fusiliers were deployed in skirmish line with Le Capitaine's brigade held in reserve in the woods. The French divisional artillery attempted to protect this movement,

14 Bogdanovich, p. 317; Hulot, p. 116.
15 von Damitz, Vol. III, 1st Part, pp. 38-9.

but the train soldiers and the gunners were badly trained and many guns were dismounted before they were put into battery.

The French guns had two positions on the carriage. When travelling, they were placed with the trunions of the barrel in the rearmost position to shift the balance of the piece to a position more suitable to movement. When they were to be fired, the barrels were shifted forward. If this process was mishandled, the barrel would literally fall off of the carriage. As it weighed many hundred pounds, it was almost impossible to pick it up and put it back on the carriage.

The infantry fire had little effect because the oldest soldier in this division had only 20 days of service. With the two divisions so positioned, the French and Allies began a cannonade at short canister range.

GD Nansouty, with Excelmans' and Pacz's forces, moved via Vassogne on the extreme right of the Allied line. A local citizen named Bussy lived nearby. He had served with Napoleon in the La Fère Regiment during the Revolution and served as a guide for these troops. Unfortunately, the roads were terrible and the supporting horse artillery was unable to follow and remained exposed to the fire of the Russian guns without being able to respond. As the French broke the crest of the plateau, Benkendorff charged them with three Cossack regiments – supported by four squadrons of the Pavlograd Hussars – and the fire of Russian Horse Battery #11 commanded by Colonel Apushkin. The Russian attack was crudely executed and did not slow the advance of the French cavalry.[16]

Unfortunately for Ney, these actions were not sufficient to distract Voronzov from the principal French attack. Ney's corps – reduced by the loss of about 3,000 men – was locked in combat with the 2nd Jager Regiment and Horse Battery #9 under Colonel Parkinson, which were holding positions in the village of Ailles. Ney's force resembled a skirmish force far more than a column of formed infantry.

On his side, Boyer de Rebeval's forces were swept with canister and he feared that attempting to move them to the cover of some woods would cause them to dissolve. The Russian General Swarikin, seeing the condition of the French, swept forward at the head of a battalion of the 19th Jagers (under Lt. Colonel Zariev) supported by the Shirvan Infantry Regiment and two squadrons of the Pavlograd Hussars.[17]

General Boyer ordered General Le Capitaine to form his brigade on the left of Bigarré's threatened brigade. Colonel Parkinson fell amongst his gunners as Voronzov sent GM Glebov's brigade (6th and 41st Jager Regiments) forward from the third line to reinforce the fight.[18]

Le Capitaine's movement was made by the third rank, but as the four battalions of Young Guard broke from the woods they were attacked by the 19th Jagers and Shirvan Infantry supported by two squadrons of the Pavlograd Hussars. General Drouot rushed forward two batteries of Guard artillery and pounded the 19th Jagers in the flank. Drouot, not content with their performance, dismounted and directed the fire of his gunners himself. The fire of Drouot's guns saved the day for the French.

Napoleon was impatient that the main attack was making no progress and ordered GD Grouchy to support it with the available cavalry and operate on his left flank. At 1:30 p.m. Grouchy took Sparre's 11th Cavalry Brigade (5th and 12th Dragoons) and moved across the Vaucler ravine, where he formed the cavalry into line on the angle of the small Saint-Martin woods. He then led them forward – moving across the Heurtebise pass in an attack on the right flank of the Pavlograd Hussars as they were driving back Boyer de Rebeval's 9th Division and breaking them.

16 Koch, Vol. I, pp. 389-394; Bogdanovich, p. 318.
17 Sporschil, Vol. II, 1st Band, p. 579; Bogdanovich, p. 319.
18 Bogdanovich, p. 319.

The French dragoons, veterans of Spain, then charged forward into the middle of the Russian battery they had been ordered to attack – hacking down the gunners of Horse Battery #9 who had the temerity to resist them. The dragoons quickly rallied and moved to relieve the pressure on Boyer de Rebeval's beleaguered division. The Russians rallied forces and sent them against the French dragoons. Both Grouchy and Sparre were struck down – Grouchy grievously wounded by a bullet in the thigh and Sparre with a wound in the knee. Grouchy was forced to withdraw from the battlefield. The dragoons did not remain long without him, were pushed back by heavy Russian pressure and sought refuge behind the Marion woods.[19]

Ney and Boyer de Rebeval sent Napoleon couriers to advise him that they were in danger of being thrown back if they were not sent reinforcements. They reported that the effectiveness of their artillery fire was greatly diminished by the numbers of guns that were dismounted and that their musketry was steadily weakened by the stream of wounded from the ranks. Indeed, despite the blows of their officers – including the omnipresent Ney – panic was beginning to penetrate into the French ranks and they were beginning to break ranks and flee. Though the sources are not clear, it is probable that Boyer's 9th Division collapsed in panic and fled back into the Marion woods, where General Bigarré held a few battalions. Behind the line of the skirmish screen along the woods, Boyer quickly reorganized his division and called them back into the ranks. Though serious, the panic proved to not be irreversible. The Russians, however, were not slow to take advantage of the collapse of Boyer's 9th Division and resumed their advance.

The French cavalry charges

The news of the pending failure of the French army provoked Napoleon to send orders to Mortier and Charpentier's 7th Young Guard Division to expedite their march on Craone. He also ordered GD Laferrière to move across the ravine to support Boyer's division. However, while he was executing this movement, Voronzov saw it was the time to execute a decisive blow against the French and sent General Swarikin forward with the 19th Jagers and the Shirvan Infantry to strike Meunier, Curial and Boyer de Rebeval. The French were driven back into the woods and then pounded by Allied artillery until they withdrew into the Vaucler ravine.

As the Russians advanced, other French forces threatened to overrun and capture a Russian horse battery. The Russians responded with a bayonet attack supported by a brigade drawn from their reserve.

At 1:45 p.m. GD Laferrière led forward the 3rd Guard Cavalry Division – some 2,000 cavaliers of the chasseurs and grenadiers à cheval – and the Empress Dragoons in an effort to stabilize the situation. The French Guard cavalry overran the Russian guns, but were repulsed by their infantry (now formed in square). Laferrière fell – grievously wounded – and the Guard cavalry withdrew behind Heurtebise. Their attack, however, was not in vain since they bought the time necessary for Charpentier's division to arrive and deploy.[20]

Blücher orders a retreat

Though the Russians were having little trouble containing the French attacks, Blücher learned that his orders to Winzingerode had not been executed and began to fear that this would compromise the position of Sacken and Voronzov if they were left to deal with the French alone. As a result, he ordered both Sacken and Voronzov to withdraw immediately.

19 Hulot, p. 122.
20 Bogdanovich, p. 320; Hulot, p. 123.

Upon receiving this order – at about 3:00 p.m. – Sacken moved his infantry down the road to Laon and detached his cavalry to support Voronzov. Despite this, he knew the strength of his position and felt it more dangerous to stand than to withdraw and, subsequently, sent orders for the withdrawal. Vassil'shikov's cavalry was to cover his withdrawal and Sacken began his movement down the road from Soissons to Laon.

With Sacken's withdrawal, Voronzov took the precaution of dispatching all of his damaged guns – 22 in all – and the accumulated wounded to the rear. He then ordered his infantry into a checkerboard of squares to begin an orderly withdrawal.

Despite the disorder in his ranks, Napoleon ordered GD Colbert to rally his lancers on the small Craone plateau and to attempt to move from Craonelle to the Rochers farm. Napoleon also sent orders to press Mortier to expedite the march of his troops. At the same time he ordered GD Charpentier, a native of the region, to assume command of Victor's entire corps and resume the battle – promising to support him with the infantry of the Old Guard.

The French executed a double attack. GD Colbert formed his forces before the Rochers farm despite the Russian artillery and musketry directed at them by the Navaguinsk and Tula Infantry Regiments. GM Ponset, who had been wounded in the 1813 campaign and walked on crutches, stood before these two regiments. He received orders to retreat, but said that he would die, but would not retreat. GM Vuitsch approached him and said: "You can die, but regiments must retreat."[21]

On the other side, Charpentier deployed his forces into dense columns and pushed through the Vaucler ravine and moved along the edge of the woods to the foot of the plateau – protecting himself from the Russian artillery. By 2:30 p.m. Charpentier's division had advanced from its position between the Marion and Quatre Heures woods, where Boyer was renewing his attack. Nansouty's cavalry stood on his left as he advanced to turn the Russian right. Meanwhile, Curial's 2nd Young Guard Division – which had followed Charpentier's division – moved into position by Mutte-aux-Vents.

As soon as the head of Charpentier's first column appeared over the edge of the plateau, the 19th and 44th Jager Regiments – which formed the extremity of the first and second lines – turned to the left and began a heavy musketry. At the same time, Voronzov ordered General Sanders – commanding the reserve brigade – to delay the French advance. The Narva and New Ingermanland Regiments placed themselves oblique to the flank of the first two regiments at a distance of 300 to 400 paces. However, Charpentier was supported by an Old Guard artillery battery and Friant's 1st Old Guard Division, which had finally crossed the ravine.

At the same time, Voronzov ordered one of the brigade commanders of the 12th Division. The 12th Division was reorganized between January and the time of the battle. The actual brigade commander is not known, but it was either Generalmajor Sanders or Schwetschin – who commanded the Narva and New Ingermanland Regiments – to move against the French. These regiments were deployed 300 or 400 paces behind the left flank of the 44th Line Regiment, but when Charpentier was reinforced by Friant's Old Guard and a Guard battery, these two Russian regiments withdrew. The Shirvan Regiment was taken under heavy canister fire. When GL Laptiev arrived near the regiment and tried to encourage the troops, grenadiers of both battalions asked for permission to attack the battery. "With God!" said Laptiev and moved at the head of the attack, but was wounded and left the field. The Shirvan Regiment continued the attack under the command of its commander, Colonel Zvarykin, but he too was soon wounded. The Shirvan Regiment was then surrounded by French cavalry, but despite being low on ammunition, three times it forced its way clear with bayonets and rejoined other troops.

21 Bogdanovich, p. 321.

At 3:00 p.m. the Russian jagers from the 2nd and 6th Jager Regiments retreated from Ailles. GD Boyer's 9th Division, with divisions of Meunier and Curial in support, occupied it. These three divisions occupied the plateau and Mortier's corps deployed in the second line.[22]

In the meantime, Boyer – supported by Meunier and Curial's divisions – threw the 2nd and 6th Jagers out of their positions. This retreat – and the presence of Nansouty's cavalry – convinced Voronzov it was time to retreat and he promptly issued the appropriate orders. As his troops pulled back, the French moved forward and occupied the entire plateau.

Napoleon then ordered Count Drouot to bring into action the six Guard batteries that were held in reserve by placing them in front of the French army, and then ordered all of the cavalry under Count Belliard to move to the left under the orders of Ney and to seek to link up with Nansouty's cavalry in an effort to turn the Russian right flank.[23]

Napoleon prepares the decisive blow

Between noon and 1:00 p.m. Nansouty led his cavalry and the two battalions that had become attached to his force onto the Vassogne plateau and pushed the Allies before him to the ravine north of Paissy. However, the sudden fire from a Russian battery caused him to turn about and withdraw to the south. Reorganizing his forces, he moved to Paissy, where he watched the Russian forces facing him.

At around 2:00 p.m. he was joined by Colbert's 1st Guard Cavalry Division. Colbert had been very hesitant in his actions that morning and this had not escaped Napoleon's attention. Around 2:00 p.m. he ordered d'Hurbal's division to move to the Vassogne plateau and placed GD Belliard in command of all the French squadrons then on the left wing of the French army.

Between 2:00 and 3:00 p.m. – as Charpentier and Nansouty moved onto the Vassogne heights – Ney was not inactive. Though pushed back into the Vauclerc woods he rallied Meunier's 1st Voltigeur Division and pushed them back onto the plateau, where they maintained their position with renewed energy.

At the same time, the French Guard Éclaireurs moved into Chamouille and Martigny – reporting back to Ney on the Allied troops that they could see. Ney, having no reserves, invited Pierre Boyer to send what troops he still had towards Neuville and sent a request for reinforcements to Napoleon.

By this time, the advance of the Russians had been stopped before the Marion woods and they had abandoned the crest of the Ailles ridge to Ney. They were barely holding their positions under the attacks by Charpentier and Nansouty's forces. Napoleon judged it was the time to launch the decisive blow.

Even though an Allied column suddenly appeared by Chamouille, it did not change the situation. The decisive blow would be delivered by Curial's 2nd Young Guard Division – in reserve by Mutte-aux-Vents – and Mortier's corps (1st and 2nd Old Guard Divisions and the 4th Tirailleur Division).

The French cavalry strikes again

Voronzov had no fear for his right and stopped his retreat on the Creney heights – behind a ravine where the plateau formed a new chokepoint – in order to give Sacken's cavalry time to support Benkendorff's brigade. The stop was necessary because the terrain opened up and was ideal for

22 Bogdanovich, p. 322.
23 Sporschil, Vol. II, 1st Band, p. 582.

the use of cavalry – and the Russian cavalry generals took advantage of the terrain to slow the French pursuit.

In one of the narrower places in the plateau, Voronzov ordered the 6th Jager Regiment to occupy a stone wall and to cover the retreat with its fire. When the French approached, they were met with a musket volley and the pursuit stalled. Meanwhile, Sacken ordered GM Nikitin to place his artillery in position behind the retreating Russian troops and fire on the French after the Russian infantry had passed. General Nikitin placed 36 guns in front of the road to Chevrigny and greeted the French pursuit with a destructive cannonade.

Benkendorff's brigade, then the rearguard, found itself engaged with the bulk of the French cavalry and needed its support. This support was most timely, for shortly after it arrived the Pavlograd Hussars were charged by the divisions of Excelmans, Laferrière and the Polish brigade. The Pavlograd Hussars would have been exterminated had they not been able to shelter behind Vassil'shikov's hussars and dragoons.

The Pavlograd Hussars had apparently been detached from Winzingerode's corps and assigned to Sacken's corps cavalry.[24] Vassil'shikov had organized his cavalry in two lines. The first line had 16 squadrons and the second had 32. All of his regiments were organized in columns of squadrons.[25] Vassil'shikov counter-charged and stopped the French attack.

The Russian retreat continued in good order – the regiments moving *en échiquier* under the protection of the formidable Russian artillery. Benkendorff covered the Russian right with his small brigade consisting of the Pavlograd Hussars, the 1st Bug Cossack Regiment and the jagers of GM Krasovsky's brigade.[26]

Belliard moved his forces towards the left with Colbert and Roussel's divisions and soon took the head of the column and maneuvered in vain to try to turn the Russian right. On the Ouarmont heights – his right heavily pressed by Maréchal Ney – Voronzov marched his troops down the road to Chevrigny in order to escape the French as he marched on his crossings over the Lette.

Charpentier saw this movement and moved four guns to a position where they could fire down the straight and narrow road that formed Voronzov's escape route. These four guns caused tremendous damage to the retreating Russians. Charpentier then received orders to march down this road against Roches and engage the Russians and those of Boyer de Rebeval. The Old Guard divisions were also ordered to support this attack.

On the right, the Russians withdrew down the road from Craone to Ange-Gardien. Ney attacked Ailles with his three divisions and Nansouty was sent around the Allied left to try to strike their flank and rear. Colbert formed his cavalry under the fire of the Navaguinsk and Tula Infantry Regiments. At the same time, Charpentier moved between Roches and Ailles. Voronzov sent General Sanders with his brigade forward to drive Charpentier back, but was himself taken under fire by a French Guard battery.

Somewhat later, Ney overran the village of Ailles despite the brave resistance of the 19th and 44th Jager Regiments. At that time, Colbert pushed past Roches and Nansouty and reached the heights over Vassogne.[27]

Colbert attacked the Russians repeatedly – inflicting great disorder in their ranks – but Belliard's hands were full. Under his immediate control he had only his small force of lancers and dragoons with which to face Benkendorff's light brigade and Vassil'shikov's dragoons and hussars. The remainder of the French cavalry was on the right under Nansouty.

24 Langeron, p. 416.
25 von Damitz, Vol. III, 1st Part, p. 44.
26 Bogdanovich, p. 323.
27 von Damitz, Vol. III, 1st Part, p. 46.

At about 2:30 p.m. Napoleon directed the reserve artillery – which had to that point remained behind Heurtebise – to cross the pass to Heurtebise and join the batteries of the Guard and Victor.

At the same time he directed Curial's 2nd Young Guard Division, Friant's 1st Old Guard Division and Laferrière-Lévèque's 3rd Guard Cavalry Division to prepare to advance. As they prepared for the assault, the Imperial Guard artillery redoubled its efforts – throwing shot and shell into the dense masses of Russian troops arrayed before them.

Fifteen minutes after the bombardment increased in its tempo, the reserve artillery pulled into position alongside it at a gallop – doubling the number of guns between the Marion and Quatre Heures woods – and added the roar of their guns to the now almost seamless roar of cannon. A grand battery of 88 guns formed under Drouot's command. A violent canister fire began a few hundred paces from the Russian center. Curial's 2nd Young Guard Division and the Old Guard in its bearskin bonnets – followed by the 3rd Guard Cavalry Division – advanced by successive brigades in lines of attack columns down the road to Dames.

The Russians continued to withdraw in square. Voronzov rode from square to square encouraging his men to hold fast as they marched off the field. Pierre Boyer's division surged forward against Ailles – taking the village. The remains of Boyer de Rebeval's 9th Division and Meunier's 1st Voltigeur Division pushed out of the Marion woods and their position on the nearby ridge. Charpentier's 7th Young Guard Division and Count Belliard's cavalry thrust against the Allied right wing.

The Russian garrison of Ailles fled from the plateau while their center buckled and was thrown back to the edge of the battlefield – 800 meters south-southeast of Ailles. The Russian right fell back to the southern edge of the Paissy ravine.

Just as Napoleon was assured of his success, reports arrived of an enemy column moving from Chamouille and Martigny. These late arrivals did not stop the destruction of the few battalions that remained in the Russian center. Amidst the concentrated musketry and cannon fire these few Russians were torn to pieces, then ridden down by the 3rd Guard Cavalry Division that thrust out between the lines of advancing infantry.

Benkendorff's cavalry brigade was covering the retreat and was caught by the combined divisions of Excelmans, Laferrière and Pacz. He was, however, saved from a nasty fate by the timely intervention of Vassil'shikov's cavalry.

Just as Colbert was attacking a number of Russian squares, Vassil'shikov ordered Lanskoi to lead forward the Marioupol and Alexandria Hussars and drive the French back while the Pavlograd and Elisabethgrad Hussars supported Benkendorff directly. The combined effects of this attack were successful and the French were driven back – losing one cannon.

However, Vassil'shikov's cavalry was counterattacked by Nansouty's cavalry. Being hard-pressed, the three dragoon regiments held in reserve by the Russians – supported by the fire of a large battery – were sent forward to oppose Nansouty. The French cavalry stopped its advance and the Russian hussars reformed under the shelter of their dragoons.[28]

Night caught the French army between Filain and Ostel, where they bivouaced. General Colbert formed the point of the advanced guard and stood in Aisy – extending from the Lette to the Aisne from Pargny to Celle – and pushing his advanced posts to Ange-Gardien.

Voronzov stopped his march after four hours when his forces stood in Chavignon. Here he rallied the garrison of Soissons – which was withdrawing to a position before Laon – and was reinforced by two regiments of jagers, which Benkendorff had directed to form the rearguard.

Winzingerode's cavalry and the corps of Kleist, Yorck and Langeron had departed the previous day to move via Fétieux and attack the French right flank. They had not arrived in that town until

28 von Damitz, Vol. III, 1st Part, p. 48.

that evening, which resulted in their inability to participate in Blücher's plan. Langeron stopped his forces in Troucy and from positions on the far bank, supported Voronzov's crossing of the Lette with a heavy cannonade.[29]

Voronzov's passage over the Lette effectively ended the battle of Craone. The French lost about 8,000 men *hors de combat.* Boyer de Rebeval's division lost about 66 percent of its effectives. The 14th Voltigeur Regiment had 30 of 33 officers *hors de combat.* Among the generals wounded were Victor, Grouchy, Laferrière, Boyer, Bigarré and Le Capitaine. The last two were only lightly wounded.

Von Toll, von Damitz, Koch and the Prussian staff state that the Russians lost 1,529 dead and 3,256 wounded.[30] Bogdanovich and Langeron essentially support these figures.[31] GM Ushakov, commanding officer of the Kourland Regiment, was killed while rallying his men and Colonel Parkinson was killed during the attack of the French cavalry on his battery. The sole son of Count Stroganov was also killed. The wounded included: GL Laptiev, GM Lanskoi (died from his wounds), Count Chovansky, Zvarykin, Maslov and Glebov. The Pavlograd Hussar Regiment lost 22 officers; the 13th Jagers lost 16 officers and 400 other ranks; and the Shirvan Infantry Regiment lost half of its men. No guns or caissons were lost during the retreat.[32]

Bogdanovich, von Toll, von Damitz and Koch all state that the French lost about 8,000 dead and wounded including Victor, Grouchy, Laferrière, GB P. Boyer, Bigarré and Le Capitaine. Boyer de Rebeval's 9th Division lost two-thirds of its men. The 14th Voltigeur Regiment lost 30 officers killed or wounded out of 33.[33] The casualties indicated for the 14th Voltigeur Regiment are not supported by Martinien. This does not, however, mean that this claim is inaccurate. Neither side lost a prisoner and neither side lost a gun or standard, but the field was covered with bodies and broken carriages. It was a Pyrrhic victory for the French as they held the field when the battle was through, but the other hopes of the battle had escaped them.

The campaign continues

Clear of the field, Napoleon now sought to deny Blücher the time necessary to establish himself in Laon and to then seize the city with a brisk attack. He ordered Ney to the Allied right the next day with his infantry and all the cavalry. Marmont had brought Arrighi's division to Roucy and was ordered to move from Béry-au-Bac with that division and the I Cavalry Corps and march on Laon along the main road to Rheims. He was then to establish communications through Bruyères with the main body of the French army.

Blücher, on the other hand – unable to disguise the partial check his plan had suffered – made the necessary dispositions to reunite his army and to prepare for a second battle below Laon. The corps of Langeron, Sacken and Winzingerode were ordered to mass behind the road to Crespy – facing Lanicourt – with all of their cavalry massed in Loisy. The corps of Yorck and Kleist took up positions on the heights between Laon and Vaux, with their cavalry forming a second line on the road to Chambéry. Bülow's corps occupied Chambéry.

At the break of dawn on 8 March Ney, at the head of the Guard and line cavalry, moved through Ange-Gardien and Chavignon in pursuit of Benkendorff. Benkendorff had arrived at

29 Koch, Vol. I, pp. 395-401.
30 von Bernhardi, Vol. 4, Book 7, p. 185.
31 Langeron, p. 417; Bogdanovich, p. 324.
32 Koch, Vol. I, p. 402; Prussian General Staff, Vol. III, p. 78; von Damitz, Vol. III, 1st Part, p. 53; Bogdanovich, p. 325.
33 Bogdanovich, p. 325.

4:00 p.m. in Urcel and had rejoined Winzingerode's advanced guard. Near this village, the road from Soissons to Laon ran on a causeway through an impenetrable marsh. General Czernichev occupied Touvelle with a jager regiment and a second was placed in Chivy. A strong battery enfiladed the road. This should have been more than sufficient to stop the French columns as they appeared before them. The French cavalry deployed to the right and left of the road along the length of the swamp supported by artillery. The French infantry arrived later and, having tried in vain to cross the swamp, took up positions by Urcel. The French cavalry occupied Nouvion, Mailly and Grandchamps – pushing patrols towards Bruyères on the road from Craone to Laon.

General Friant bivouaced that night in Chavignon. Charpentier and Boyer's divisions were near Malmaison. Meanwhile, Marmont – leading Arrighi's division – moved that evening from Roucy to Corbeny. The I Cavalry Corps sent out strong reconnaissance forces down the road from Rheims towards Aiselle and down the road from Laon to Soissons in order to assure that the French rear was clear of the enemy. However, all movement was slowed by the destruction and scattering of the French equipage park by a band of Cossacks near Corbeny.

Soissons proper was entered at 10:00 a.m. on 8 March by the 13th Chasseurs à cheval Regiment (Colbert's division) and no Allied soldiers were encountered. Word was sent back to the army quickly for a garrison to be dispatched to reoccupy and hold the city. Meanwhile, the French cavalry left before Soissons spent its time recovering the artillery and bridging train that Rudsevich had abandoned in the mud as a result of his lack of horses.

On the Aube, Belliard arrived on Chavignon with his cavalry after having swept the countryside from the Lette clear of Allied soldiers. Belliard encountered a few Allied squadrons in Chavignon and threw then back on the Urcel, where they were reinforced. Czernichev, who commanded them, did not stand but chose to withdraw to Touvelle and Chivy, followed by Colbert's cavalry.

At the Aube, near Mailly, Belliard found himself fired on by a battery defending the Oger bridge. Belliard took another route around the battery and by 9:00 a.m. his forces stood before Touvelle facing a combined force of Allied infantry and cavalry.

That evening, local peasants informed Napoleon of the possibility of turning the Touvelle defile by a back road and Napoleon thought it might be possible to launch a *coup de main* against Laon. He ordered Chef d'escadron d'ordonnance Gourgaud to turn the Touvelle position with two battalions of Old Guard Chasseurs à pied, 300 Poles, two squadrons of Old Guard Chasseurs à cheval and two cannon. Ney was then directed to open a hole in the Allied position with his infantry and permit the French cavalry, under Belliard, to move through it and pursue the anticipated fugitives from the attack.[34]

The attack on Touvelle

At 1:00 a.m. Ney's corps – led by a force of volunteers from P. Boyer's brigade and all of the artillery – marched in line except for a pair of cannon with each division, moved down the main road from Soissons, moved through the Mailly and Urcel woods and prepared to attack Touvelle.

At the same time, Belliard's three cavalry divisions stood to the west near Laval – waiting for Ney to secure Chivy and the woods to the north (and to assure them that it was time to advance on Laon).

At 1:30 a.m. Ney issued the order for a simultaneous attack on Touvelle and Chivy by Boyer's volunteers and Gourgaud's detachment. In order to assure his surprise attack, Ney chose not to wait for the arrival of the Guard infantry and marched on Touvelle and Chivy.

34 Prussian General Staff, Vol. III, p. 85.

Boyer's volunteers, guided by local residents, crossed the bridge to the south of Touvelle and turned the village – enveloping its east and north – while driving into Chivy from the south. Simultaneously, Boyer's two cannon took up positions on the highway and opened fire on the southern exit from Touvelle.

The advanced Russian posts were thrown back at bayonet point by the 2nd Légère with cries of: "*Vive l'Empereur!*" ringing in their ears before they were able to get to their own arms. A large number of Russians were taken prisoner long before they were able to put up a defense.

Baron Gourgaud had departed Chavignon at 11:00 p.m. the night before with his small column and moved via the Cléry mill and Chavellois to Chivy, where he was to arrive at about 1:00 a.m. However, the terrain and darkness had delayed his march and he encountered an enemy patrol. As a result, his attack did not produce the anticipated results. Chivy turned into a four-hour battle before the garrison finally surrendered. Ney supported Gourgaud's attack with the rest of his infantry – penetrating to Chivy without effort.

A half-hour before dawn, Count Belliard passed Roussel's 6th Heavy Cavalry Division through the village of Chivy with 300 Old Guard Chasseurs à cheval leading the charge. This force pushed to Laon Mountain, where they were stopped by an explosion of canister from 12 guns.

In the deep darkness it was impossible to continue the attack – and the French stopped to reorganize and prepare for the dawn (when they would renew the attack). The Allied right was supported on the hills between Thierret and Neuville. His center stood at the foot of the Laon Mountain with a large force of artillery. The Allied left stood on the Athies heights. A total of 80,000 men stood in a line of battle, whose advanced posts were in Clacy, Semilly, Ardon and Athies.

When night fell, the French were deployed as follows: Ney was in Urcel, with Meunier's division; Curial's division was in Chavignon; Victor was at La Malmaison with Friant's division, Boyer de Rebeval's division, and Charpentier's division around the city; Mortier was at Filain with Christiani's and Poret de Morvan's division, and Roulnois' cavalry.

The French cavalry was deployed in Mailly, Laval, Nouvion-le-Vineux and pushing towards Presles, Bruyères and Veslud to make contact with Marmont.

Napoleon moved from the Malval farm to Ange-Gardien and finally to Chavignon. He had a total of 26,800 men under his immediate control.

Topography around Laon

At this time, Laon was a very old city of about 7,000 souls. It was situated on a hill of 120 to 130 feet (26-40 meters) in height. The city's defenses extended a distance of about three miles (4,500 meters) and consisted of a wall with 46 towers. The city also had a large number of counter-forts that stood 16 to 19 feet (five to six meters) above the surrounding ground level. Under Henry VI, the eastern part of the city was separated from the rest of the city by a bastioned front that occupied the space between the northern and southern walls.

Laon stood 100 miles (155 kilometers) from Paris and 37 miles (60 kilometers) from Rheims on the main road to Mons and Ghent, which gave it a tremendous importance in this campaign. Because of its excellent position, the Allies had made it a major depot. However, they had erected no works to make it secure from a *coup de main*. Several breaches existed in the walls. The city had 11 gates which were open and unbarricaded. Koch indicates that the only precaution they had taken was to place a force of heavy artillery on the hills of Classon and Saint-Vincent, which only partially dominated the city. How significant this force of artillery was is questionable. Oyon indicates that there were only four cannon available to defend the city.[35]

The region around the city was a lowland. It was a plain broken by several woods, low swampy areas, willow groves and several enclosed paddocks. This plain was crossed from the west to the southwest by a major stream that joined the Lette below the village of Chavignon. The stream was not locked in its bed and formed a large swampy area along its length – crossed in its middle by the road from Soissons to Laon. This marsh covered a distance of two miles (five kilometers) between Touvelle and Chivy.

The city had been occupied for several days by the Allies. The Cossacks had been the first to enter the city and the reaction of the citizens was one of sullen anger. Sixty to 80 soldiers were billeted in each house in the city, which resulted in the usual series of conflicts and outrages, rapes and thefts.[36] The Allied soldiers were surely no different in their behaviour, however, than had been the French soldiers over the years where they had been billeted on the Germans and other occupied nations – or the behaviour of any other European army since the beginning of time.

The Battle of Laon – 9-10 March

Blücher was inclined to take the initiative and ordered his corps commanders to each form their own separate reserve and to deploy their artillery across their front. During the night, there was a heavy frost and the roads became difficult and covered with snow.

The defense of Laon was given to the 3rd Army Corps. Bülow deployed his forces as follows: Six Russian 12pdrs of Dietrich's battery were by the Soissons Gate, Prussian 6pdr Foot Battery #5 stood on a heights to the left of the Soissons road, half of 12pdr Battery #5 stood to the left of the road to Ardon and the remaining six of Dietrich's Russian 12pdrs were near Ardon by the large and small roads to Rheims on a small height. Prussian 6pdr Foot Battery #6 stood to the right of the high road to Rheims, half of 6pdr Foot Battery #19 was on a hill near and slightly to the right of the highway and to its right stood half of 12pdr Foot Battery #4. The Russian battery of Colonel Magdenke and half of a Prussian battery stood in reserve by Marcel. All of Bülow's artillery was under Oberst Holzendorf.

The 2nd East Prussian Battalion (3rd Brigade) and 1/1st Neumark Landwehr Regiment (6th Brigade) remained in Laon. Oberstleutnant von Clausewitz commanded the Semilly garrison consisting of the 1/4th East Prussian Regiment, a detachment of the 1st Battalion and the entire 2/4th Reserve Regiment. The 3rd East Prussian Regiment occupied the Saint-Vincent Abbey with its 2nd Battalion in the garden, the 3rd Battalion in the mill and the 1st Battalion to the rear in reserve.

The 1/4th Reserve Regiment stood to the left of the main road between Laon and Semilly, the 3/4th Reserve stood on the nearby slope and the 9th Company stood a bit further to the left. A detachment of 100 men was pushed down the road to Soissons. The 1/5th Reserve Regiment was placed on the windmill hill to the right of Laon and the 3/5th Reserve Regiment stood to the left of the 1/5th on the city walls. Later, two companies were detached from the 3/5th to Semilly.

The 1/Colberg Regiment stood in the gorge at the foot of the Citadel, the 2/Colberg stood to the left on the Rheims street and the 3/Colberg stood with two companies covering a half Russian battery and the other two in the Berges gorge. The 1/,3/9th Reserve Regiment were in Ardon and the 3/9th stood to the left of the village. The 3/1st Neumark Landwehr was on the

35 Oyon, p. 217.
36 Oyon, pp. 223-4.

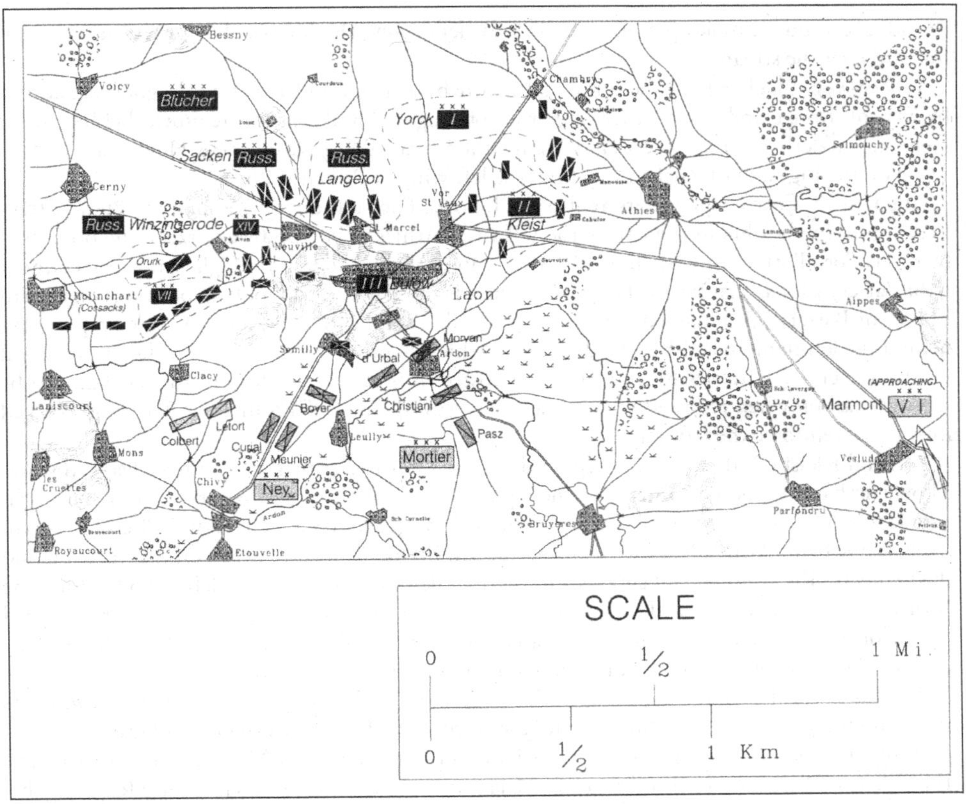

Map 13 Battle of Laon, March 9 1814, 11:00 a.m.

right of the village. The 2/1st Neumark Landwehr Regiment was in La Fère as its garrison. The 6pdr Foot Battery #16 stood on the road to Rheims.[37]

The 1st Pomeranian Landwehr Cavalry Regiment was to the right of Laon on the road to La Fère. The 2nd Pomeranian Landwehr Cavalry Regiment was in the village of Ardon. The 2nd Kurmärk Landwehr Regiment was on the promenade by the Soissons Gate. The 4th Landwehr Regiment and the 1st Leib Hussar Regiment had been dispatched to La Fère.

The III Army Corps reserve cavalry and 6pdr Batteries #5 and #6 were by the Vaux suburb in Lager – later forming up in squadron column and moving before the city. The entire Berges slope was covered with a chain of skirmishers and East Prussian Jägers.

The left wing of the Allied army was formed by the 1st and 2nd Corps. The 1st Corps stood to the left of the 2nd Corps. General von Yorck posted Prince Wilhelm's Combined 2nd and 8th Brigade in the first line with its left wing on the Meierhof Manousse, which was occupied by the Combined Battalion of the 12th and Brandenburg Regiment. Two battalions stood behind the left wing and the two East Prussian fusilier battalions occupied the village of Athies. Horn's brigade stood in the second line and the reserve cavalry – supported by Horse Battery #2 – and

37 Prussian General Staff, Vol. III, p. 80; von Damitz, Vol. III, 1st Part, pp. 73-6.

the advanced guard took up a place behind the left wing. The Mecklenburg Hussars were sent forward over the stream.[38]

Oberst von Blücher held the advanced guard by Fétieux and had two dragoon squadrons by Maison-Rouge and two further squadrons of dragoons and a hussar regiment behind them. General Katzler – with the 2nd Leib Hussars, the Brandenburg Hussars and Horse Battery #2 – stood on the highway to Rheims watching the left wing of Prince Wilhelm.

The I Army Corps deployed its artillery as follows: Foot Battery #2 and half of 12pdr Battery #1 were on the heights to the left by the village of Athies. Two 10pdr howitzers, the other half of 12pdr Foot Battery #1 and all of 12pdr Foot Battery #2 stood on the right wing. Six Pounder Foot Battery #1 was sent forward to support the advanced guard and took up positions on a small hill. Foot Battery #3 remained between the two divisions. Horse Battery #3 took up positions behind the left flank to assist in the defense of Athies. Foot Battery #15 and four howitzers stood in reserve. Horse Batteries #1 and #15 were posted 400 to 500 paces from the left flank to be ready to call on when required. When the fire began, the half of 12pdr Foot Battery #1 moved forward to reinforce the left wing.

General Kleist's 2nd Corps was deployed with three batteries by the Cahufor advanced work, a howitzer battery stood on and below the highway – with 12pdr Foot Battery #3 posted below it – and to its left was 6pdr Foot Battery #8. The 10th Brigade, under General von Pirch I, stood in the first line behind this advanced work and the 9th Brigade, under Klüx, stood in reserve behind the highway. The Neumark Dragoons and the 1st Silesian Hussars (to the left) stood behind the 10th Brigade. The very weak Landwehr squadrons and the 2nd Silesian Hussars were assigned to support the cavalry, and the reserve cavalry and reserve artillery remained behind the II Army Corps[39] (probably of the 7th and 8th Silesian Landwehr Cavalry Regiments).

The woods to the right were occupied by the Fus/1st and Fus/2nd West Prussian Regiments and a company of Silesian Schützen under the command of Oberstleutnant von Lettow.

Winzingerode deployed his forces with Laon on their right and Moulinchart on their left. The village of Aven stood behind them and Clacy was immediately to their front. He formed his infantry in two lines. The first line contained the 12th, 21st, 14th and 24th Divisions. The 13th and 15th Divisions formed the second line and reserve. They were posted behind the left wing of the main line. Orurk's cavalry stood behind the right wing. Winzingerode deployed his artillery across his front.[40]

Langeron and Sacken's corps, organized in division columns, remained behind Laon as the grand reserve. Langeron had detached seven infantry and five cavalry regiments and left them in Mainz. The VI Russian Corps, however, was completely present. The Allied forces stood as follows:

I Prussian Corps (Yorck)	13,500	men
II Prussian Corps (Kleist)	10,600	
III Prussian Corps (Bülow)	16,900	
Langeron's corps	24,900	
Sacken's corps	12,700	
Winzingerode's corps	25,200	
Total:	103,800	

38 Prussian General Staff, Vol. III, p. 81; von Damitz, Vol. III, 1st Part, p. 77.
39 Prussian General Staff, Vol. III, p. 82; von Damitz, Vol. III, 1st Part, p. 78.
40 von Damitz, Vol. III, 1st Part, p. 73.

St. Priest's forces detached to Rheims	
Prussians	2,400
Russians	3,000
Total on field at Laon:	98,400

The French army before Laon probably consisted of 56,000 men – including about 14,000 under Marmont.[41]

Ney was convinced that Laon could not be attacked frontally and chose not to wait until Marmont arrived to make an attack. He renewed the fights around Ardon and Semilly. He did, however, dispatch messenger after messenger every half-hour to Marmont seeking news and asking him to hasten his march. Unfortunately, these men all fell into the hands of Cossacks or were lost. Marmont was – and would remain – isolated.

The night before the battle, the main French forces arrived before the defile at Touvelle. Napoleon decided to attack the defile with a flank maneuver. A road ran through Chavignon via the fields around Ailette, the bridge at Ailes, Chaillevois, Chailvet and crossed through the woods – coming out directly to the west of Chivy. From this position the Touvelle defile could be turned with little effort.[42]

Chef d'escadron Gourgaud was ordered to leave at 9:00 p.m. on the 8th with two battalions and two squadrons of the Old Guard Chasseurs à cheval. Boyer de Rebeval was ordered to lead 400 men in an attack at 1:00 a.m. – about the time Gourgaud was expected to be in Chivy. Boyer's 400 men were to be accompanied by a force of sappers charged with rebuilding any broken bridges that might be encountered.

The attack came off as anticipated and was successful in clearing the defile of Russian soldiers. A cannon from the Mailly park fired on Touvelle repeatedly – drawing the defender's attention in that direction, but causing more noise than harm. The Russians were cleared out of Touvelle with little effort.

All of Ney's infantry (P. Boyer's brigade and Meunier's division) immediately moved through Touvelle and on to Chivy. From Chivy they deployed to the left of the main road and allowed the French cavalry to pass them, with an eye towards a *coup de main* on Laon. Ney's divisions each brought two guns with them. The remainder of their artillery passed through after the cavalry had cleared the defile and the Russian retreat on Laon was assured.

At the same time, General Belliard sent his cavalry towards Chivy to scout out their left and to occupy the villages of Leuilly and Ardon. Both villages were occupied and the French were greeted by their sharp and accurate musketry. At Ardon the French skirmishers led the French advance, but were driven back by the Fus/3rd East Prussian Regiment and the Schützen of the 4th Reserve Regiments working in conjunction with the 9th Reserve Regiment. Seeing that it would be impossible to occupy Laon, Belliard directed d'Hurbal's division towards Leuilly to hold that village – from where it could observe Ardon. He then moved, along with the divisions of Colbert and Letort (formerly Laferrière's division), to Chivy to prevent an Allied movement from that direction.

Napoleon decided that it was desirable to attack Chivy, where the Russian forces were covered by the Saint-Vincent Abbey. Boyer de Rebeval broke up his 400 elite soldiers into small groups – each of which was led by a local peasant.[43] These men attacked with bayonets only – penetrating into the Russian position. The forces under P. Boyer and Meunier launched

41 Prussian General Staff, Vol. III, pp. 83-4.

42 Foch, pp. 15-6.

43 Foch, p. 17. von Damitz, Vol. III, 1 st Part, p.91. Von Damitz says this was only 100 skirmishers.

a violent attack on Chivy. Chivy was occupied by Stroganov's brigade of Chovansky's 12th Division. This brigade had been detached to the village at the same time as the Prussians abandoned Ardon and Semilly.

With Boyer de Rebeval's forces in Stroganov's rear, three Russian regiments succumbed. Montmarie's brigade pierced into the village and established itself there despite a strong fight from the Russians. When Montmarie had complete control of the village, it had taken seven Russian officers and 250 men prisoners.

The bridges and barricades were forced and the infantry cleared the road. It was about 5:30 a.m. as Belliard's cavalry passed through Chivy – preceded by Gourgaud, who had finally arrived.

The French dragoons rushed down the road to Laon – pursuing a cloud of refugees that scattered pell-mell into Semilly, which was defended by von Clausewitz. The hopes of reaching Laon were crushed by a volley of canister fired by the batteries established near Semilly. The French cavalry turned about and disappeared into the morning fog unpursued. Pierre Boyer's brigade, followed by the divisions of Curial and Meunier, marched on Semilly and the Soissons Gate – a village situated at the foot of the Laon plateau. Mortier's corps moved on Ardon and the Ardon Gate. He had orders to move through Corbeny and on to Laon down the road from Rheims. At 7:00 a.m. Ney moved his infantry from Chivy and was followed by the rest of the army.[44]

Ney's advance profited from a thick fog, which broke at dawn just as the snow ceased to fall. With the end of the snow, Boyer's forces arrived before Semilly and began to try to turn it on the east.

Around 7:00 a.m. Ney departed his positions on the road from Chivy to Mons and moved on Laon. At the same time, Mortier sent Poret de Morvan's division through Leuilly to attack Ardon. A heavy fog had fallen upon the plain.

In Ney's corps, P. Boyer's brigade was ordered to attack Semilly. It formed into two attack columns – each of about 700 men. The left-hand column formed to the right of the road and the other was further to the right. Their first attack was greeted by heavy musketry and repelled. During the second attack, the right-hand column entered and took Semilly.

Semilly was occupied by the 1/4th East Prussian Regiment, a detachment of the 1st Battalion and the entire 2/4th Reserve Regiment under the command of Oberstleutnant von Clausewitz. Boyer's movement to the east was observed and engaged by the Prussian garrison. At 9:00 a.m. the French began a heavy cannonade. The heavy smoke from this fire obscured vision and two French 700-man-strong columns, from P. Boyer's brigade emerged from it suddenly at a distance of 60 paces from the village of Semilly.

The 2nd Company, 1/4th East Prussian Regiment, fired a general salvo against the left-hand column, which drove it back. Another Prussian volley drove back the French center, but Boyer's right penetrated into the village and dislodged the Prussians. As the French attempted to consolidate their gains, Blücher dispatched two fresh battalions to support von Clausewitz and von Thümen's brigade moved to support them. GM von Thümen counterattacked with two companies of the 3/5th Reserve Regiment and the French were driven out.[45]

Boyer's troops fell back down the road and rallied behind their artillery, which stood on the right and left sides of the mail road.[46] French skirmishers moved into a ditch and a depression about 200 paces from the village and began a strong skirmish fire against the village. Von Clausewitz's troops were expelled, but when reinforced by the arrival of two companies of the 5th Reserve Regiment sent by von Thümen, they launched a counterattack and recaptured Semilly, but were unable to completely clear them. The French held on tenuously to the gardens around

44 von Damitz, Vol. III, 1st Part, p. 83.
45 Prussian General Staff, Vol. III, p. 87; von Damitz, Vol. III, 1st Part, pp. 84-5
46 Hulot, p. 141.

the village. A steady musketry developed between the French and Prussians as both were steadily reinforced. Bülow reinforced the village by sending the 2/,Fus/4th Reserve Regiment into the village.

Poret de Morvan was able to quickly occupy Ardon because of fire before the walls of Saint-Vincent. An unsupported company of Guard infantry attempted to break through a grill in the walls of the Saint-Vincent gardens, but was forced to withdraw.[47]

At 8:30 a.m. the fighting at Ardon renewed when Poret de Morvan moved out of Leuilly against Ardon by along both banks of the stream – enveloping the village on the west and south. He quickly overran Ardon and those Prussian jägers who were not killed or captured escaped into the morning. By 11:00 a.m. the fog had completely lifted and Poret de Morvan was the undisputed master of Ardon. However, he was soon engaged by the Prussian infantry which lined the ditches and the hedgerows along the road from Bousson to Vaux. He was able to maintain his position only with difficulty.[48]

Meanwhile, Napoleon remained at Chavignon – thinking that he had encountered the Allied rearguard. He had not realized that he was actually engaging 90,000 Allied troops with a force of only 35,000 men.

The divisions of Christiani, d'Hurbal and Pacz moved up behind Poret de Morvan's division. They sent scouts to reconnoitre Breuil, Bruyères and Vorges. The taking of these two villages assured Napoleon that the Allies intended to fight for possession of Laon. The French army then deployed straddling the main road – its right on Leuilly and its left on Clacy hillock. Belliard sent cavalry patrols to the left wing to watch Clacy, as well as in other directions. Behind them, facing Clacy, the French deployed a skirmish line and supported it with 30 guns.

Boyer's brigade stood immobile before Semilly. Meunier and Curial's divisions – plus Gourgaud's detachment – were designated as reserves and deployed as such. The divisions of Colbert and Letort stood southeast of Clacy – watching the locality for any enemy movements. They covered the left flank of Ney and Mortier's corps, as well as the Chivy defile.[49]

The Allied forces were by Ardon and Semilly and were deployed as follows:

Firing towards Semilly:[50]

> Six Russian guns at the exit to the village, to the right of the road to Soissons, at the foot of Madame-Eve and below the tour Pechée.
>
> Six guns to the left of the main road on a small sand ridge 400 meters northwest of Semilly.
>
> Ten guns covering the entrance to Semilly at the entrance and below Creuttes and two half batteries on the high ground before Blanc-Mont flanking Semilly and covering the ground between Semilly and Clacy.

Firing towards Ardon:

> Four 12pdrs and two howitzers by the Morlot mill at the beginning of the walls of the Saint-Vincent Abbey.

Firing towards the road to Rheims:

> Six Russian guns before the Sauvoire woods.

47 Foch, p. 19.
48 Prussian General Staff, Vol. III, p. 86.
49 Hulot, p. 142.
50 Foch, pp. 21-3.

In reserve – at Saint-Marcel – one Russian and a half Prussian Battery.
Infantry
In Laon:

East Prussian Grenadier Battalion
? Neumark Landwehr Regiment

By the Soissons Gate in the barracks on the promenade:

Two Battalions of a Neumark Landwehr Regiment
One Battalion of a Neumark Landwehr Regiment in the gardens

In Saint-Vincent:

One Battalion of the East Prussian Infantry Regiment
One Battalion of the East Prussian Infantry Regiment at Morlot
One Battalion of the East Prussian Infantry Regiment

In reserve at the Calvaire, at the Classon ridge and the old wall of Château Herbert:

Two Battalions, 5th Reserve Regiment.

Along the edge of the mountain:

East Prussian Jägers deployed in skirmish order

In Semilly – under von Clausewitz:

One Battalion, 4th East Prussian Regiment
One 1/2 Battalion, 4th Reserve Regiment
One Battalion, 4th Reserve Regiment in reserve by crossroads near the road to Soissons

By Morlot mill:

One Battalion, 4th Reserve Regiment in reserve by cross

On slope before Ardon:

2 cos – Colberg Regiment – vineyards of La Couloire
2 cos – Colberg Regiment – supporting battery by Sauvoire
2 cos – 9th Infantry Regiment – reserve

Behind Ardon:

1/, ?/9th Reserve Regiment
Fusilier Battalion, 1st Neumark Landwehr Regiment
2nd Pomeranian Landwehr Cavalry Regiment (two squadrons)

Between Ardon and Vaux:
One Battalion, 9th Reserve Regiment

In reserve at the junction of the roads to Marle and Rheims:

One Battalion, Colberg Regiment
Two light batteries
3rd Corps Cavalry

The total strength of Bülow's 3rd Corps was around 16,900 men.

Allied right wing:

Winzingerode had his infantry in two lines between the Thierret farm and the Blanc-Mont woods facing Clacy. Before this infantry stood two batteries. Its left flank was covered by 12 guns placed 400 meters to the northwest of Semilly that were able to fire on Clacy and Semilly. His right was protected by Czernichev, who had posted his cavalry between the Thierret farm and Molinchart, behind 12 guns. The main body of the Russian cavalry was east of the Avin farm. He had deployed a total of 25,000 men and 62 guns.

Allied left wing:

The Allied left was formed by the Prussian 2nd Corps under Kleist and the 1st Corps under Yorck – giving it a total strength of around 24,000 men. These two corps were deployed in two lines. The first line was under Yorck and encompassed the Manoises farm and extended towards the Chambéry stream – the north of which were three hussar regiments. Prince Wilhelm's division (two battalions were in Athies) was covering the artillery of the 1st Corps between Manoises-le-Chauffour. The Silesian Hussars stood on the high road. Pirch's division stood on the road to Rheims with three battalions in the Sauvoire woods and a brigade held to the rear in reserve.

Kleist's 2nd Corps formed the second line, with its left covered by part of the reserve cavalry and 24 guns. It had its reserve posted behind the road to Marle. This reserve consisted of two cavalry regiments – the reserve cavalry and reserve artillery – and the horse artillery.

General reserve:

The general reserve consisted of Sacken's Russian corps – some 13,000 cavalry – on the road to La Fère behind La Neuville, and Langeron's infantry – some 25,000 men – behind that same road on the right and left of Saint-Marcel.[51]

Langeron, by G. Dawe.

At around 11:00 a.m. the fog lifted and Blücher – standing before Madame-Eve near the Pencée Tower – saw the weakness of the army before him. At first, Blücher thought this was a ruse. The forces before him were too small to be the main French army. In addition, the day before, a French spy – the Hanoverian Palm – had been captured and he had announced that Napoleon was coming down the road from Rheims with 90,000 men. The forces before him might be there simply to lure him out of his positions.

At noon Blücher received from his son, Oberst von Blücher, further word that a strong French column

51 Foche, pp. 23-5.

was closing on Festieux. Perhaps the spy was right, perhaps not, but it was too dangerous to risk that he was not telling the truth. Instead, Blücher sent orders to Winzingerode to threaten the French left flank. Winzingerode detached Vassil'shikov with the 2nd Hussar Division.

The 2nd Hussar Division contained the Akhtyrsk, Marioupol, White Russia and Alexandria Hussar Regiments. Sacken's Cossacks – and a number of horse batteries to his right – were given orders that they move around Napoleon's flank by Neuville and Saint-Marcel. Vassil'shikov, in executing this order, also sent Cossack detachments to Mons en Laonnais and Vaucelle.

Winzingerode also ordered Chovansky's 12th Division to advance – supported by a cavalry brigade – against Anizy. The 1st Brigade of the 12th Division, now commanded by Stroganov, followed Sacken's Cossacks as they pushed the French out of Clacy. Chovansky, supported by a cavalry brigade, then pushed through Clacy and advanced against the French left in Mons. However, when Chovansky attempted to push against Mons, he was driven back to Clacy and onto their infantry as he attempted a sortie. Chovansky had been struck by a force of Guard cavalry supported by Grouvel's light cavalry. Having won this engagement, the French installed their artillery on a hill overlooking the field and Grouvel's cavalry pursued the beaten Russians to the walls of the Thierret farm. The pursuing French reined back, however, when they found that Thierret was strongly occupied.

By this time GD Poret de Morvan's 4th Young Guard Division had occupied Ardon and Roussel's dragoons rode to the right towards Sauvoire. Having disposed their forces, the French then struck against the Saint-Vincent Abbey.

Roussel's dragoons stood in support of Poret de Morvan's infantry column advancing on the road towards the abbey. Another column moved from Semilly against Laon's Soissons Gate. Prussian 6pdr Foot Battery #5 directed its fire against the French attacking the abbey – pushing them back to Leuilly. The battery then sent two guns forward to support the Fus/4th Reserve Regiment, which was engaging French skirmishers.

Count Stroganov.

Blücher ordered Bülow's corps to march against Semilly. Around noon, GM Krafft led the 1/9th Reserve Regiment and the Fus/1st Neumark Landwehr – supported by the 2nd Pomeranian Landwehr Cavalry Regiment – against Ardon, while Voronzov's Russians moved into a woods to the southwest of Semilly. A single cannon by the Prussians fired on the French, but the broken nature of the ground prevented the cavalry from operating successfully – though the village still fell to the Prussians. The French lost General Poret de Morvan and Colonel Leclerc in the attack.[52]

The double attack of Voronzov and Bülow's corps against Boyer's brigade succeeded – driving the French out of both Semilly and Ardon. Boyer's troops fell back in disorder and Ney responded by sending Curial's division between Semilly and the Tuileries (800 meters southwest of Semilly). Supported by his artillery and the charges of Gourgaud's Guard cavalry, the Russians were driven back. Gourgaud's charge was supported by another by Count Belliard, which struck the Russians on the left of the road with the light cavalry of General Grouvel. Boyer rallied his troops and moved against Semilly yet again, only to be stopped by the fire of the Prussian artillery to the

52 Prussian General Staff, Vol. III, p. 89.

north and east of the village. Meanwhile, Roussel's division moved against the Prussian forces in Ardon.

These vigorous efforts forced the Prussians to withdraw to Laon. Roussel's dragoons facilitated the re-entry of Poret de Morvan's 4th Young Guard Division into Ardon and then moved down the road to the Lavergny Château and the Sauvoire farm. Poret de Morvan was nominally a brigade commander of this division, but indications are that he had temporarily risen to command the division in the absence of Count Barrois. He seems to have commanded this division until late April. By 1 May he was once again a brigade commander.

A small force of French dragoons was sent down the road to the Sauvoire farm to link up with Marmont's forces, whose arrival was expected any moment along the road to Rheims. Unfortunately, the French found that the Sauvoire farm was strongly held by a force of Prussians and more Prussians were encountered on the road from Vaux to Fétieux, which obliged the dragoons to return.

About this time, Napoleon arrived on the battlefield. Around 1:00 p.m. he established himself at the Chivy crossroads and pondered the situation. Before him was obviously not a demoralized enemy. In fact, he had a numerous and solidly established enemy before him that was taking the offensive and who Ney and Mortier could only contain with great difficulty.

Napoleon faced a situation where he had to engage a more numerous enemy and his forces were divided into two groups completely separated from one another by a forest and a swamp. Marmont's column was weak and isolated on the Athies plain, while the bulk of the army was in broken terrain where it could deploy neither its cavalry or artillery. It was going to be a straight-up infantry fight and numbers would count.

His error apparent, Napoleon ordered Friant's Guard infantry division, Excelmans' Guard cavalry division and the artillery reserve to follow Charpentier and move in all haste to the battlefield.[53]

When they arrived, Clacy and Thierret were held by the Russians; the Prussians were masters of Semilly and were about to be dislodged from Ardon. To the north of Clacy, on the Laon plateau and at the foot of the city, stood masses of Allied infantry supported by strong batteries.

Blücher did not consider his attacks on the center and right as simple demonstrations because he did not believe that Napoleon truly considered striking down the Soissons road. As a result, he was able to act against that French flank in a turning maneuver. Once the corps of Yorck and Kleist were established, their left – supported by the heights that dominated the principal and secondary routes to Rheims – they took up a position with their advanced posts 500 meters (540 yards) from Athies. They were quickly reinforced with a large force from the Allied reserves consisting of the III Army Corps Reserve Cavalry under GM von Oppen.

Bülow once again attacked Poret de Morvan in Ardon. At 4:00 p.m. Krafft led the 1/9th Reserve and Fus/1st Infantry Regiments – supported by the 2nd Pomeranian Landwehr Cavalry Regiment – against Ardon. Their attack was supported by strong artillery and cavalry forces. Poret de Morvan had occupied Ardon with only two battalions. The Prussian attack was more than the French could stop and they withdrew towards Leuilly. Both GB Poret de Morvan and Colonel Leclerc were wounded in this attack.

The engagement on the Allied left wing

The Allied 2nd Corps stood below the village of Athies with the 10th Brigade in the front line and the 9th Brigade behind it in reserve. To its left stood the 1st Corps. The von Hasse Fusilier Battalion and two other fusilier battalions, under the command of Oberstleutnant von Lettow,

53 Hulot, pp. 144-5.

were posted in a woods to the south of the Rheims highway.[54] An advanced guard – consisting of two squadrons of the Neumark Dragoons under Major von Dossow – stood by the Maison-Rouge, near Fétieux, on the road to Rheims. The remainder of the regiment's squadrons and the 1st Silesian Hussars, under Oberst von Blücher (son of the Feldmarschal), were behind Fétieux – supporting the advanced posts. General Katzler stood with the Brandenburg and 2nd Leib Hussars as a reserve slightly further back.[55]

Marmont had begun his march in conformance with his orders and, at about 1:00 p.m. his lead elements – about three cavalry regiments and some infantry – passed through the Fétieux defile. Bordesoulle's I Cavalry Corps pushed Oberst von Blücher's advanced guard aside, then driving back Katzler's brigade,[56] Marmont moved towards Aippes with an eye towards turning Ziethen's left flank. Ziethen, however, moved his cavalry reserve between the village of Athies and the Salmouchy woods and engaged the French – contenting himself with an exchange of carbine shots,[57] redeploying his infantry and reinforcing his position with Benkendorff's Russian light cavalry brigade. Foot Battery #1 took up a position on the heights by Athies supporting Oberst von Blücher and Katzler. Marmont advanced his corps to a distance of about 1,200 meters from the Prussians – facing Vaux and Athies.

The 6th Corps' von Damitz cites this force as having about 1,000 men and 10-12 guns,[58] left the road by Chauffour and moved towards the wooded height facing the village. The Prussians were favored by the terrain and steadily increased their resistance to the French advance. The French advance stalled until 24 guns were brought forward and drove the Prussians back into Athies. The village was soon afire – containing only two defending battalions. It was soon 5:00 p.m.

As if to encourage Marmont to attack, the Prussians established their first line at the bottom of the Butte-aux-Vignes and the Mouillée farm. Von Ziethen pulled his cavalry behind a ridge and formed it in two lines. The cavalry of the 1st Corps stood on the left wing – with the Lithuanian Dragoons in the first rank – and supported on both flanks by the Brandenburg Uhlan Regiment. The second rank was formed by the West Prussian Dragoon and the Combined Landwehr Cavalry Regiments – both under Oberst Count Henkel. The three cuirassier regiments and the uhlan regiment of the 2nd Corps were organized in a similar formation. The 2nd Horse Battery was pushed forward to bombard the French cavalry, while the 7th, 8th and 9th Horse Batteries were held in reserve behind the woods.

Marmont formed with Bordesoulle's cavalry on the right and his infantry in the center between the Roman road and the road to Rheims. The French artillery also stood between the two roads. The Prussians chose not to hold their position and withdrew on Athies. Marmont established two batteries: one on Butte-aux-Vignes with 24 guns that bombarded Athies and the other on a knoll to the left of Butte-aux-Vignes with about 15 guns, which engaged in a gun duel with the Prussian artillery by the Chauffour mill.

Marmont then ordered Arrighi to push into Athies – easily expelling the two Prussian battalions that held the position. The evacuating Prussians set Athies on fire – burning 40 of the 180 buildings in the village. Prussian batteries of the 1st and 2nd Corps swept the road between Athies and the Rheims road. The Prussian guns were on a ridge that provided a clear field of fire – as well as dominated the field before it. The fire of these guns and, especially that of the 1st Corps 12pdr battery, inflicted heavy casualties on Lucotte's French brigade as it advanced against

54 von Ebertz, p. 164.
55 Prussian General Staff, Vol. III, p. 90.
56 Foch, p. 26.
57 von Damitz, Vol. III, 1st Part, p. 94.
58 von Damitz, Vol. III, 1st Part, p. 94.

Prince Wilhelm's 2nd Division, which held Athies. Lucotte's advance – which began at about 3:00 p.m. – was supported by 18 French guns, which stood on the Butte-aux-Vignes heights between the village and the road. Meanwhile, a horse battery of six guns moved to the corner of the Sauvoire woods to bring the Prussian batteries under a crossfire.[59] Lucotte's brigade advanced in two columns. One marched against the southeast of the village and the other turned Athies by the east. After a heated engagement, Lucotte's brigade seized a farm on the edge of the village and secured a lodgement just inside the village just as night began to fall. Facing them was a force of East Prussian fusiliers. This attack on von Lettow's fusiliers obliged the 9th Brigade to move to the right over the highway so as to permit the 10th Brigade to better support von Lettow. They were supported by about 30 Prussian guns.

Marmont had received no news and decided to stop his offensive movements. He placed the VI Corps infantry on the Chauffour heights and the I Cavalry Corps at the foot of the hill on the right. He then sent Colonel Fabvier to a position on his left with 400 cavalry and two guns.[60]

Athies was soon in Marmont's hands, with the Prussians in definite retreat by 6:00 p.m. Marmont thought the day was done and ordered his troops to prepare the night's bivouac. Arrighi's division bivouaced with part on the southeast exit from Athies and part on the slopes of the Butte-des-Moulins. Their advanced posts were in Athies and before the Maison-Bleue. The VI Corps, I Cavalry Corps and the artillery park bivouaced on the western slopes of the Butte-aux-Vignes with part facing west between the road to Athies and Mouillée farm and the Lavergny woods; part stood facing to the north between the VI Corps and the Mouillée farm; and part stood behind the VI Corps in the angle formed by the Athies-Veslud road and the Vaux-Eppes road to the west of the intersection.

Blücher's response

Marmont's attack on his left convinced Blücher that Napoleon was intent on moving down the road to Rheims and decided to cut him off at Marle. In order to execute this maneuver, he moved Winzingerode to the Laon plateau and detached (via Chambéry down the road to Guise) Langeron's infantry and Sacken's infantry in the second line of Prussians and directed them to assume the offensive as soon as Winzingerode was in a position to support them.

The French bivouac for the evening

On his side, Napoleon believed that Blücher would accept battle the following day and awaited news from Marmont. He ordered his infantry to bivouac where it had fought. Friant's 1st Old Guard Division and all of the cavalry – with the exception of Pacz's Polish Brigade – were sent back across the Chivy stream and moved to establish themselves in Touvelle, Chavignon, Mons and Laval.

Napoleon moved to Chavignon at 7:00 p.m. – taking with him Excelmans' cavalry division and Grouvel's light cavalry brigade. Grouvel's brigade had, during the day, not stopped scouting the French left flank – going as far as Lanicourt. The following day, it was ordered to operate on the plateau of the Laffaux windmill with an eye towards assuring communications with Soissons.

While the French established themselves for the night, General Yorck prepared his forces to strike at Marmont. Prince Wilhelm von Preussen, supported by the brigades of Horn and Klüx, was charged to attack the village of Athies from the right. GL Ziethen was to take all of the

59 Sporschil, Vol. II, 1st Band, p. 603.
60 Koch, Vol. I, pp. 403-14.

Meissonier's iconic impression of Napoleon during the Campaign of 1814, following the Battle of Laon.

Prussian cavalry and attack that which opposed him and attempt to turn the French right flank and fall on the French infantry. Kleist was ordered to combine his attack on the French left such that his advance guard, supported by Pirch's brigade, would skirt the woods facing them and link with Yorck on the high road.

The unsuspecting victims were unprepared for their attack. Their advanced posts were insufficient and consisted of two weak battalions on the northern edge of Athies and the eastern roads out of the village. The men were exhausted and without instruction. They did not take the necessary precautions.[61]

Marmont's Corps is crushed

At 7:00 p.m. Yorck and Kleist's two corps marched forward. Oberst von Borck organized four battalions of the 8th Brigade to lead the advance of his division. Oberst von Warburg, with the 2nd Brigade, followed two battalions to the right of the line of advance and two on the right. General von Katzler, with his two cavalry regiments, marched on the left so the he could link up with the reserve cavalry as necessary. General von Yorck remained to the right of Athies by Horn's division and von Kleist marched his corps down the highway.[62]

Prince August ordered that the 9th and 10th Brigades remain concentrated. The battalions formed in attack column with the skirmishers only 50 paces in front of them. Oberstleutnant von Lettow led his three fusilier battalions from the woods and advanced along both sides of the highway as the first line of Kleist's corps. The von Hasse Fusiliers marched down the highway as

61 Hulot, p. 156.
62 von Damitz, Vol. III, 1st Part, p. 99.

the fusiliers of the 1st and 2nd West Prussian Infantry Regiments marched on their left and right respectively. Prince Wilhelm's brigade reached Athies first.[63]

Three horse batteries – #7, #8 and #9 – remained in the woods by Chambéry, while only 6pdr Horse Battery #2 advanced to where it could take the French cavalry in the flank and rear.

The French suspected nothing in their bivouacs when Prince Wilhelm von Preussen's brigade burst from the dark in dense columns on the right and left of Athies and fell on Lucotte's brigade. Oberst von Borck led the four battalions of Wilhelm's 8th Brigade. In a second line behind him came Oberst von Warburg, with the four battalions of Warburg's 2nd Brigade. Horn's 7th Brigade marched on their right in support and Katzler's advanced guard moved on the left to encircle the French, if possible. Von Lettow's advanced guard was supported by the Neumark Dragoons and the 1st Silesian Hussars, under Oberst von Blücher, which advanced down both sides of the highway in column by squadron.[64]

Athies was occupied by Lucotte's brigade. Oberst von Borck led the Combined Battalion of the 12th Reserve Regiment down the main road against the village. The two battalions of the Brandenburg Regiment marched behind it as support and the Combined Battalion of the 14th Landwehr Regiment followed as a reserve. The two fusilier battalions, which had earlier defended the village, reunited with these troops.

As the Prussians advanced, suddenly – when they were close enough to strike – their regimental musicians played and the drums thundered out the *Sturmmarsch* (assault march). The two – and the 12th Reserve on their left in support – attacked the village.[65]

At the same moment, Ziethen's cavalry moved between Salmouchy and a small pond, slammed into Bordesoulle's cavalry and threw them back to the road. Only the Brandenburg Cuirassiers were detached to cover the Prussian artillery. The attack was made by the Lithuanian Dragoons and the Brandenburg Uhlans with two squadrons of uhlans on either flank of the dragoons. The second line of the attack consisted of the West Prussian Dragoons and five squadrons of Landwehr cavalry under Oberst Graf Henckel. The second line was pulled to the right in order to support the attacking infantry. The 2nd Corps Cavalry Reserve, under the command of von Röder, followed at some distance – formed in mass and acting as a general reserve.

Ziethen ordered the second line to move to the right and ordered the Silesian Uhlans to move in that direction as well. A massive cavalry battle erupted. General von Röder ordered his reserve forward. The battle was so confused that the East Prussian Cuirassiers formed themselves to the rear in order to attack and the Silesian Cuirassiers formed themselves in two lines – one facing forward and one to the rear in order to attack. However, the Prussian numbers quickly told and the French resistance collapsed. All of their artillery and baggage was captured. Apparently, some French cavalry chose to receive the Prussian charge standing and sought to fire a volley at them.[66]

The French fled before the victorious Prussians – moving towards the hill where the French VI Corps stood. The VI Corps leapt up to defend itself – grabbing what was readily at hand. Few of the guns were in position to fire, so there was time for only one or two discharges of canister before they were overrun by the von Haase Fusilier and von Heine Battalions.[67]

The gunners tried to drag their guns away with their prolongues, but several became stuck in the ditch along the road. The Neumark Dragoons broke two infantry masses – taking many

63 von Ebertz, p. 166.
64 Prussian General Staff, Vol. III, p. 93.
65 Prussian General Staff, Vol. III, p. 94.
66 von Ardenne, p. 268.
67 von Ebertz, p. 166.

Blücher enters Laon, by Eichstädt.

prisoners and capturing 10 guns. The 2nd Leib Hussars, supported by the Brandenburg Hussars, took 200 prisoners. Some French cuirassiers, however, were organized enough to counterattack and strike at the Prussian infantry. However, they were repulsed with a loss of 60 horses. Their panic was such, however, that they also fired on Bordesoulle's cavalry – thinking them the enemy.

Then all of Langeron's cavalry, under the command of General Korff, moved forward to support the Prussian attack.

The French had begun to rally and began to restore order to their ranks when Kleist's advanced guard crossed the Sauvoire stream and fell on their rear. After a few shots, the French ranks were once again swept with terror and Marmont's corps disbanded – fleeing to Fétieux in a panicked flight. The VI Corps artillery limbered up and began moving down the road to Rheims, but it drew the attention of the Prussian cavalry. The Prussians raced ahead of the withdrawing column and turned to attack its head. They cut its retreat and began slaughtering the teamsters and their horses – immobilizing and capturing Marmont's entire train. The destruction of Marmont's force would have been complete had not Colonel Fabvier's small force arrived and acted as a rearguard – allowing Marmont to retain some semblance of order.

Not only did Marmont lose all of his artillery, but he also lost much of the reserve park which had been marching with him because of its fear of Cossacks. The combined musketeer battalions of the 2nd Silesian Regiment claimed capturing five guns and a howitzer.

Korff's Russian light cavalry pursued the French – herding them along with their cries as far as Corbeny and Craone. From there, the French withdrew to Béry-au-Bac.

Marmont's forces lost a large number of dead and wounded – plus 2,000-2,500 prisoners, 41-46 guns and 131 caissons. They had lost all their artillery and 4,000 men *hors de combat.*[68]

The Prussian 1st Corps lost seven officers and 159 men *hors de combat* and the 2nd Corps lost 26 officers and 526 men *hors de combat.*[69]

Winzingerode spent the night in Semilly and Ardon. Bülow's corps stayed in Laon. Those of Langeron and Sacken were in Chambéry, while Yorck's and Kleist's infantry remained on the field of battle at Athies. All of the Allied cavalry stood before Fétieux.

The Allied pursuit

After delivering a tremendous check to the French, Blücher was certain that they would flee towards Soissons and ordered the corps of Yorck, Kleist and Sacken to march down the high road to Béry-au-Bac in order to open communications with St. Priest's corps, which was moving up. He directed that Langeron move on the Lette by Bruyères and send his pontoon bridge to Micy-Sainte-Adine in order to be able to fall on the French rear. Korff's cavalry was already in Bruyères, where it captured several hundred wounded and refugees from Marmont's corps. However, he was soon sent towards Laon.

Napoleon's reaction

As Marmont was being destroyed on the French left, Napoleon acted on the assumption that Marmont was still en route to support his earlier plans. He issued the following orders:

> The divisions of Charpentier and Boyer de Rebeval – forming the head of the column and supported by the corps of the Prince of Moscow (Ney), Friant's division, the three cavalry divisions and the artillery reserves – shall move from Clacy at 6:00 a.m. and push against the Allied right in the direction of Neuville.
>
> Maréchal the Duke of Ragusa (Marmont) – with the VI Corps, the 2nd Paris Reserve Division and Bordesoulle's cavalry – shall continue to maneuver from the point where they find themselves so as to cut the communications of Laon to Vervins.
>
> Maréchal the Duke of Trévise (Mortier) in the center – with the infantry divisions of Poret de Morvan and Christiani, Roussel's dragoons and the Polish Lancers of Count Pacz – shall form on the left of the main road to Soissons, behind Ardon, in order to support the main attack.
>
> By these dispositions, the Laon plateau shall be turned by the right and by the left – observed and contained on the road to Soissons – that is to say, on its front.

As it stood, Napoleon stood ready with 30,000 troops to attack 100,000 Allied troops in a very strong position. Fortunately for Napoleon, fugitives from Marmont's disaster arrived at his headquarters and advised him of the magnitude of that event. Again reviewing the situation, Napoleon decided that Blücher intended to maintain his main forces in and around Laon while detaching a corps or two to engage the French.

68 Prussian General Staff, Vol. III, p. 96; Sporschil, Vol. II, 1st Band, p. 606.

69 von Damitz, Vol. III, 1st Part, pp. 105-6.

10 March – the action begins

The infantry of Winzingerode's corps, under the command of Voronzov, held only a small knoll outside Semilly and Bülow's troops still held the Laon plateau. The Imperial army took up its weapons, while Blücher looked down on them from the ramparts of Laon. There stood 17,000 French infantry in the middle of a swamp with a narrow defile three miles (five kilometers) behind them – preparing to attack 40,000 Allies in a strong position and 60,000 further Allied troops on their right flank.

Before the French could begin their attack, three Russian divisions under Voronzov attacked Clacy. GM Prince Chovansky, 12th Division, led the Russian infantry while Balck's dragoons moved down the Mons road. Chovansky's attack was supported by Glebov's brigade. Glebov's brigade consisted of the 6th and 41st Jager Regiments.

Fortunately for the French, they had barricaded the approaches to their position and posted artillery to defend them. Three guns stood on the road to Laon, three more enfiladed the road to Sainte-Face, while a full battery stood on the Chapelle hill in the center of the village that commanded the plain for some distance around Clacy.

Charpentier permitted the 12th Russian Division to approach within half-range of his artillery before it thundered its anger – crushing the Russian attack and driving them back to a small woods to the left of Clacy. That attack broken. A second was executed by Prince Glebov's light brigade, 12th Division. This attack was also pushed back by the poorly-trained and inexperienced French soldiers – held together only by the willpower of their officers and NCOs. This attack was crushed and a second major assault was ordered to be executed by part of General Laptiev's 21st Division. Laptiev's assault was checked – as were five further Russian attacks made by the troops of the 12th, 21st and Vuitsch's Divisions. Facing them stood only Charpentier's battered 7th Young Guard Division and the remains of Boyer de Rebeval's 9th Division.

Napoleon moved his headquarters to Clacy and established his headquarters on a small knoll to the right of the village. His orders began flowing from here.

At around 2:00 p.m. the Allied reserves along the crest of the Laon ridge withdrew. Napoleon thought that Blücher was withdrawing his forces and ordered an attack. Curial and Meunier's divisions were ordered to attack. Both divisions advanced in dense (serrée) battalion columns under the protection of a heavy French artillery fire. When they stood at the base of the ridge – by Semilly – two French battalions were sent forward in skirmish formation, with a third battalion advancing behind them in column. They found themselves faced by Oberstleutnant von Clausewitz with the 9th, 10th and 11th Companies, Fus/4th Reserve Regiment, which attacked both of their flanks. The confrontation was one of purely skirmishers and the French slowly gained the upper hand. In response, the Prussian 1/Colberg, 1/9th Reserve and light troops of the 1st Neumark Landwehr Regiments were sent forward to support them.[70] Despite this, the French continued to push forward. As they broke over the crest of the ridge, the Prussians unmasked a battery and its fire broke the French attack. The French attack was over and the soldiers moved to the rear.

The chances of taking Laon by a *coup de main* gone, Napoleon wondered if it might not be possible to skirt the Allied forces along the road to La Fère. Duorot was sent to examine this possibility and soon returned with a clear understanding that it was impossible. Unsatisfied, Napoleon sent Count Belliard with a small party of cavalry to push between the woods and the Molinchard

70 Prussian General Staff, Vol. III, p. 100.

mills as far as possible and see what troops lay in that direction. The presence of enemy forces proved Duorot was right. Napoleon, however, was not to be shaken from his belief for some time. About four hours later, he realized the truth of the situation and decided to withdraw. He ordered the artillery fire to continue until dark, but began making plans to move his forces.

Napoleon directed that preparations be made to withdraw to Soissons with the army – leaving only a few advanced posts on the front lines until dawn. The Imperial Guard marched to Chavignon.

The Allies lost a total of 4,000 men dead, wounded and prisoner that day, while the French – not counting Marmont's losses – lost about 3,500 men.

During the night, the grand park, the equipage park, the wounded and prisoners were dispatched out of harm's way – or so it was thought. As they withdrew, between Ange-Gardien and La Malmaison, a group of Allied light troops attacked the column and liberated the Allied prisoners – as well as capturing about 50 vehicles.[71]

The French retreat to Soissons

At the break of dawn on 11 March the Imperial army began its movement towards Soissons down the road to Anizy and the main road. The Allies did not follow General Charpentier, who formed the rearguard of the right with his divisions and the lancers of General Colbert. The Adjutant-commandant Semery commanded the rearguard of the French column moving down the main road. His force consisted of a brigade from Ney's corps and part of Roussel's dragoons. They were attacked near Touvelle with 1,500 Russian troops at around 9:00 a.m. However, the Russians were ambushed and held back all morning.

The two columns reunited by the Laffaux mill and at 3:00 p.m. the French army stood in position before Soissons. The French cavalry sent parties towards Vailly down the roads to Couchy, Noyon and Fontenay, along the bank of the Aisne and towards Braisnes and Châtelet. Poret de Morvan's 4th Young Guard Division was startled by the cries of Cossacks near the Crécy heights, but soon recovered its composure and regained its positions from those Cossacks with the assistance of Semery's brigade.

Marmont, and the shattered remains of his corps, could no longer remain at the confluence of the Suippe now that Napoleon had withdrawn. He withdrew his forces to the left bank of the Vesle, near Fismes, where he established his headquarters.

For some unknown reason, Blücher chose not to pursue the French aggressively. It was certainly a chance to crush what remained of the Imperial army and end the wars, but Blücher did not avail himself of the opportunity. It is suggested that perhaps he deliberately left open a "golden bridge" so that he would be able to inflict damage, but not trap Napoleon and force a bloody fight to the death. Instead of pursuing, he chose to advance only as far as Béry-au-Bac and cantoned his right on the banks of the Lette. Blücher did not record his reasons and his lassitude remains a mystery.

Blücher's record in these few days of the campaign is mixed. Once thrown back, he wisely recognized that Laon was the single most important position to hold and moved to defend it. His selection of Craone as a blocking position and his proposed maneuver were well-conceived, if less well-executed.

Blücher's actions before Laon were not, however, as inspired. Once Marmont's corps was destroyed, he had the perfect opportunity to send his forces around to cut Napoleon's line of escape and crush – with a frontal assault – the Grande Armée. His actions are an interesting mixture of well-considered moves and missed opportunities.

71 Koch, Vol. I, pp. 415-24.

What provoked Napoleon's actions is less well-documented. The loss of Soissons provoked much of his actions, but all of the movements below the Aisne did nothing to resolve this problem. His attempt to cut Blücher off from Belgium was almost pointless as Blücher's communications had, prior to his movement north, been through eastern France. He had linked up with Bülow and Winzingerode – whose communications were through Belgium – and was probably making use of them. He was in a situation where he had two lines upon which to rely. Being cut off from Belgium would simply have pushed him south towards the main Allied army – achieving a concentration of the Allied armies which Napoleon was anxious to avoid.

Napoleon's engagement at Craone was saved from disaster by the failure of Blücher's pivoting movement on Fétieux and the separation of other parts of the Army of Silesia by the Lette.

Having survived Craone, Napoleon's choice of moving still further north does not reflect his having a comprehension of the forces that faced him under those circumstances. Once at Touvelle, he divided his meager forces and permitted his defeat piecemeal. Admittedly, the main body escaped. However, Marmont's corps was so isolated that it suffered near total destruction.

Napoleon's actions, however, can be justified since he was playing with a short hand in a desperate game of poker. If he played for anything less than the maximum victory, he was destined to lose. He needed victories; he needed the moral ascendancy; he needed to recover lost territory and resources; he needed to impose his will on the Allies. To do less was to lose his throne and, if he lost his army in a desperate gamble, his only personal loss would be his throne. There was nothing to lose and everything to gain.

The French reorganize

The losses of the last several days were disastrous for the French army and Napoleon spent his time at Soissons reorganizing it. The Young Guard Corps, under Ney, and Victor's corps were disbanded – as was the provisional division of GD Poret de Morvan. The remains were used to form two small divisions under generals Curial and Charpentier. The excess cadres, officers and non-commissioned officers were sent to Paris to recruit.

The Minister of War sent three cavalry march regiments to Soissons – about 1,700 new men – assigned to the I, II and V Corps. They were absorbed into the Guard cavalry. Napoleon formed a new division – as part of the line, with the name of "Converged Squadrons" Division – and gave command of it to GD Berckheim. The army was reinforced by the arrival of the Vistula Regiment (with the strength of a single battalion), a horse battery, a regiment of 600 Polish lancers, two companies of sappers, two companies of "cannoniers-guarde-côtes" (coast guard gunners) and about 1,000 conscripts escorting a park. Mortier's corps had 10,609 men and was made up of Christiani's division (2,034 men), Curial (2,796), Charpentier (2,755), 2,062 cavalry and 962 artillerists. Meanwhile, Napoleon led Marmont (7,200 men), Friant's division (3,600), Boyer de Rebeval (3,000), the I Cavalry Corps (2,400), Berckheim's division (1,700) and Sébastiani's Guard cavalry (4,400).[72]

Though Napoleon wished to drive to the Aube as quickly as possible, he also needed to establish Soissons in a state where it could resist any enemy attack. In his correspondence with the Duke of Feltre, Minister of War, the choice for this command fell on Chef de bataillon Gérard. Napoleon spent some time with Gérard in Soissons – explaining his duties and giving him instructions. Napoleon had wished to hold his troops near Soissons for a couple of days – resting them before their next adventure – but events forced him to march yet again.

72 von Bernhardi, Vol. 4, Book 7, pp. 203-4.

The march against St. Priest

Count St. Priest, a French emigré in Russian service, had marched to Vitry via the Ardennes and was reinforced by General Jagow's Prussian brigade – drawn from the blockade of Erfurt. He saw before him the opportunity of seizing Rheims and reopening communications between the Army of Silesia and the main Allied army under Schwarzenberg. On 7 March he stood before Rheims. He knew of the city's small garrison and of the destruction of Mortier's corps, so he felt compelled to quickly seize the city.

The garrison commander – General Corbineau – had only 100 Guard cavalry, about 50 gendarmes and the cadres of three battalions. Upon learning of St. Priest's approach, Corbineau had advised Napoleon of the threat to Rheims and the weakness of the garrison. Napoleon was unable to send him more than the division of the Garde d'honneur.

A division of cavalry was two squadrons – or at most 500 men under normal circumstances. This, however, apparently totaled 400 men.[73] GD Defrance was charged with holding the road from Béry to Rheims and watching the banks of the Aisne. He had 300 to 400 horsemen in Pont-Thierry and at Châlons-sur-Vesle. Napoleon presumed that Rheims would probably fall before he could relieve it.

The city of Rheims had a population of 30,000 and was one of the most significant cities of France both for its industry and for its commerce. It stood on the edge of the Vesle and was enclosed by a wall – part of which ran along the river. The Soissons suburb stood on an island to the southwest.

The city's position, however, made it difficult to defend. Its location put it on a major crossroads. It was close to the exits from the Ardennes, 38 miles (60 kilometers) north of Châlons, 31 miles (50 kilometers) east of Soissons and 78 miles (125 kilometers) from Troyes. Because of this, it was doomed to Allied occupation when the opportunity arose.

The fall of Rheims

St. Priest fixed the time of his attack for the break of dawn on 12 March. His forces were to advance in three columns. The first column was formed of Russian troops under the command of General Emmanuel – commanding the Kiev Dragoons, the Riazan Infantry and the 33rd Jagers supported by two Prussian battalions and supported by a battery of two cannon and two howitzers. The second column consisted of the remainder of the Russian infantry, two Prussian battalions, 50 cavalry and two howitzers under General Pilar. It was to advance along the right bank of the Vesle. General Jagow was to lead the third column with six Prussian battalions, 150 cavalry and 10 guns. Jagow was to attack between the roads of Epernay and Soissons.

The garrison of Rheims consisted of a detachment of infantry, about 4,000 National Guards and eight guns.[74]

The three Allied columns organized themselves at Cormontreuil at 3:00 a.m. and acted so swiftly that Rheims was taken by surprise. The Riazan, Polotsk and Jeletz Infantry Regiments – with the 1st and 33rd Jager Regiments – made the attack down the Réthel road, while the Kiev Dragoon Regiment and Tchernigov Chasseurs à cheval Regiment attacked down the Laon road.

General Jagow, leading the 3/1st Pomeranian Infantry Regiment supported by the 1/1st Pomeranian Infantry Regiment, forced the Paris Gate under the cover of two 12pdr guns and chased the gate's garrison into the city. General Emmanuel encountered more resistance in the Réthel suburb, where he encountered the cadre of the 5th Voltigeur Regiment (Young Guard).

73 *Victoires, conquêtes, désastres* Vol. 23, p. 440.

74 Langeron, p. 427.

They held him at the Cérès Gate briefly, but they soon withdrew because of the cannon fire their colonel heard in the Soissons suburb. As the 5th Voltigeurs withdrew, they encountered an Allied column on the main street (Rue de Vesle) and were obliged to withdraw to the Place des Arcades, where they encountered General Pilar's column, which had moved from the Châlons Gate by way of a small road which ran along the edge of the rampart with the idea of cutting off the retreat of any French units in the city. A sharp bayonet fight resulted and the French were quickly overwhelmed.

A force of 500 French cavalry and 200 or 300 infantry attempted to push down the road to Béry-au-Bac. They were ridden down by the cavalry of Emmanuel and Pantschulischev. They took a colonel, 13 officers and 200 soldiers prisoner. The rest were cut down.[75]

The city was completely in the Allied hands and that portion of the garrison that survived withdrew down the right bank of the Vesle via Saint-Brice. As they withdrew, they were harassed by about 1,000 Allied cavalry, which destroyed the entire cavalry detachment. The infantry escaped as a result of General Defrance's timely arrival. Defrance had come at the gallop at the first sounds of gunfire from Rheims with six squadrons of Gardes d'honneur and hussars.

The Allies, now masters of Rheims, appeared to be in no danger. They had captured 2,500 infantry and 11 guns from the French in their successful assault on the city.[76]

General Emmanuel, however, posted the Kiev Dragoons on the Neuvillette heights and they were attacked by Defrance's cavalry. Though driven back, the Kiev Dragoons kept Defrance's cavalry busy for the rest of the day.

GD Corbineau, however, had not escaped the city and was trapped in it – unable to give orders. General Lacoste, commanding 1,200 men from the recent levée en masse, was also in the city. He was less fortunate and was captured along with part of his men lodged with the city's inhabitants. As the Russians took inventory of their prize, they found nine guns. The losses of the garrison were considerable; those of the Allies were not significant.[77]

After securing Rheims, St. Priest's first goal was to re-establish communications with Blücher via Béry-au-Bac. Knowing of Napoleon's defeat before Laon, his attitude was overly confident. He camped the Russian troops in the city of Rheims and the Prussian troops were posted in the villages to the right and left of the road to Soissons. He sent out patrols as far as Fismes, but was not otherwise very active.

Napoleon, on the other hand, redoubled his activities and, recognizing that holding Rheims was vital to his interests (i.e. organizing the Ardennes forces), acted immediately. Marmont, with the I Cavalry Corps, was ordered to depart the following day from the environment of Fismes and to move on Rheims. All of the Guard cavalry, Friant's division and Boyer's brigade – now reinforced with the Vistula Regiment – were to follow later in the morning.

In order to cover his left and now leave Soissons once again at the mercy of the Allies, Mortier remained in Soissons with Christiani's Old Guard Division and the two Young Guard Divisions of generals Curial and Charpentier. The force in Soissons contained about 8,000 infantry. In addition, there were about 4,000 cavalry under Count Belliard – formed from the dragoons of Roussel, Pacz's lancers and a brigade from the Converged Squadron.

75 Langeron, p. 429.
76 von Damitz, Vol. III, 1st Part, p. 139.
77 Koch, Vol. I, pp. 428-34.

Division under General Curely

Napoleon directed that Mortier send scouts along the length of the Aisne as far as Compiègne, but that he was to avoid any engagements. Mortier was also to establish batteries of heavy guns above and below the city to barricade the village of Saint-Paul – occupying it as an advanced post – and in case he was pressed by very superior Allied forces, he was to withdraw behind the ox-bow in the Aisne with his right and left supported by the river and his center on Saint-Médard.

In order to keep the Allies off-balance, Napoleon recommended that he place a large advanced guard and a large number of guns in Bucy-le-Long with an idea to menace Vailly by the right bank. Napoleon also recommended that Mortier place a battalion and 200 or 300 cavalry under a good officer in Sermoise, with orders to deflect Allied probes and to prevent an enemy effort to cut the Soissons-Rheims road.

The fall of Rheims – or Laon avenged

After making his defensive dispositions on the Lower Aisne, Napoleon moved towards Rheims in the company of his service squadrons.

The cavalry of the I Corps (Bordesoulle) forced the advanced guard of the French army. After leaving Jonchery, it was guided through the woods by local inhabitants encountered by Lieutenant Péan of the 11th Hussars. They served as guides and directed Bordesoulle through Sapicourt on Rosnay. In Rosnay they encountered two battalions of Pomeranian Landwehr and a few squadrons of cavalry from Jagow's force. The arrival of the French was a complete surprise. The Prussian cavalry panicked and fled in chaos from the village – abandoning the infantry.

Marmont's infantry followed Bordesoulle's cavalry and encountered a battalion of the Prussian 5th Kurmärk Landwehr Regiment by Gueux and another at Thillois, a battalion of the 3rd Pomeranian Landwehr Regiment near Rosny on the Ormes plateau, and a second battalion of the 3rd Pomeranian Landwehr (Major Stempel's) by Muizon. After the Prussian cavalry had fled, the Prussian battalions in Gueux, Rosny and Muizon were in grave danger. Upon seeing the advancing French army, the battalion near Rosny choose not to withdraw the five miles (eight kilometers) to Rheims, but instead – pursued by Pelleport's brigade – withdrew through Gueux and established themselves in the Ormes cemetery. Like a cornered animal, the Prussians had backed themselves into a strong, but ultimately indefensible position. Pelleport surrounded the Prussians and began a heavy musketry against their position. Their situation hopeless, the Prussians surrendered, but not before two companies escaped down the road to Thillois. Once in the open, they were caught by General Piquet's brigade, the 10th Hussars and 1st Gardes d'honneur who cut down the Prussians with their sabers.[78]

Major Stempel's battalion in Muizon and the battalion in Thillois were equally surprised. The French arrived before them as they were preparing their dinner. Many of the Prussians fled barefooted and dressed only in shirt. Not only were three battalions shattered and their survivors taken prisoner, but General Jagow was encountered by the French near Gueux as he held an inspection of the cantonments of his men. He was forced to leap on an unsaddled horse and flee St.-Priest – still believing the Grande Armée had been destroyed, paid little attention to the reports of French activity and ignored the sound of their cannon.

The 1/, 3/1st Pomeranian Landwehr Regiment were supported by four cannon and eight howitzers. They stood by Bézannes, where General von Jagow had established his headquarters.

78 Dry, p. 202.

The Gardes d'honneur at Rheims.

The 2/1st Pomeranian stood by Ormes. The 1/Neumark Landwehr stood by Cormontreuil and the 3/Neumark occupied the Sillery bridge.[79]

St. Priest's entire corps – 22 Prussian and Russian battalions, 1,200 Prussian and Russian cavalry and 24 guns – were formed in a double line of battle on the Tinqueux heights. The strength of Allied cavalry is stated as being only 700 by General Langeron [p. 430].

Their right was supported on the Vesle and their left extended towards the Lower Muire. Their reserves were in the Soissons suburb of Rheims and St. Priest had placed a battery on the Sainte-Geneviève plateau supported by the 1st and 33rd Jagers, Riazan Infantry Regiment and two cavalry regiments under General Bistrom – probably General Emmanuel's Kharkov and Kiev Dragoon Regiments. The rest of the Russian cavalry stood on the right wing while the Prussian stood on the left. St. Priest had prepared his position for a vigorous defense. However, he did not anticipate having to push back anything more than a simple reconnaissance.

Bordesoulle's cavalry attacked Bistrom's infantry and cavalry – driving them back. Pleased with the developments so far, Napoleon joined Marmont on the Mont-Saint-Pierre heights. He arrived alone. Ney and the Old Guard, under Friant, had not yet arrived and would be unable to join the battle until later. Napoleon decided not to fully engage his forces and ordered Defrance and Bordesoulle to pull back a bit and stop the fire of their artillery.[80]

Whether intentional or a happy accident, this resulted in a lull on the battlefield which further reinforced St. Priest's belief that this was simply a small and insignificant attack.

79 von Damitz, Vol. III, 1st Part, p. 140.
80 Dry, p. 205.

Rheims.

St. Priest had no thought of strongly occupying the road to Béry or withdrawing his baggage that clogged the streets of Rheims. He peacefully deployed his forces to the west of the city, which he had decided to hold.

The Allied army deployed for battle with Jagow's forces occupying the crest to the west of the small Muire ravine – supporting its wing on Bézannes. In the center were 24 guns on the Sainte-Geneviève in front of the Epernay suburbs. The Russians formed the right – extending to the Vesle by Tinqueux. The Allied reserves massed by the Vesle suburb gate. The bulk of the Russian cavalry was sent to Tinqueux and a Prussian battalion was sent to Sillery to guard the bridge and protect the Prussian parks in Beaumont-sur-Vesle.[81]

Napoleon arrived on the field around 4:00 p.m. and ordered the attack only after having seen that it was impossible to turn the position because there were no bridges over the Vesle. Ney and Friant had finally arrived. Napoleon's intention was to turn the Allied position to the north in order to cut their probable line of retreat on Laon. However, the bridges at Saint-Brice were cut and the Prussian lines extended to the Vesle towards Tinqueux. St. Priest's deployment played into Napoleon's plans perfectly. It was designed to defend against a force of partisans – not a defense against a major military force.

With only two hours of sunlight left, all the infantry of the VI Corps drove forward down the two sides of the main road from Soissons to Rheims – in battalion column – separated by the distances necessary for them to deploy into line. General Defrance's cavalry led the advance while Sébastiani, with the divisions of Colbert and Excelmans, flanked Marmont. Sébastiani assumed command of the Guard cavalry after the evacuation of Troyes – replacing Nansouty – and moved

81 Dry, p. 206.

on Tinqueux. Bordesoulle protected the right flank of the VI Corps to the south of the main road towards Bézannes.

Napoleon marched on the same flank with Merlin's division – supported by a regiment of cuirassiers. Merlin's force was to stop the Prussian forces on their left from pushing towards Sillery. Merlin caught the Prussian battalions, encircled them and forced them to surrender between Trois-Puits and Cormontreuil.

The French artillery was posted to the north of the road – before Croix-Saint-Pierre – while the Old Guard (Friant) and P. Boyer's brigade stood by the artillery ready to support Marmont's attack.[82]

Ricard's division, leading the attack, pushed the Russians back across the Muire ravine – reaching the Sainte-Geneviève heights – while the Russians withdrew back to the Epernay suburb of Rheims. The Allied line was broken in half by the fury of Ricard's attack.

General Ricard attacked and pushed the Allies back into the suburb. St. Priest was suddenly aware that he was being engaged by Napoleon himself, recognized that his position was unmaintainable, abandoned any thought of defending Rheims and ordered his second line to withdraw through Rheims as soon as possible – moving in the direction of Laon. St. Priest ordered Bistrom to cover his withdrawal by establishing the Riazan Infantry Regiment and the 1st and 33rd Jager Regiments in a strong position in the Vesle suburb.[83, 84]

His equipage was ordered to move on Châlons – and only six battalions and his cavalry were between Tinqueux and Sainte-Geneviève.

His withdrawal did not go smoothly, and his right – which was obliged to cross through the Soissons suburb – became tangled beyond Jagow's ability to resolve. St. Priest moved his staff to a position between the main road and the village of Tinqueux. This group, however, attracted the attention of the guard batteries standing by Croix-Saint-Pierre. St. Priest had his shoulder broken by a howitzer shell, fell from his horse and lost consciousness. His aide – Captain Volkoff – carried his body to the Riazan Infantry Regiment, which immediately began to withdraw. St. Priest's command began to fall apart. GL Pantschulischev was unable to mount his horse because of an accident earlier in the day and had been forced to remain in Rheims that day. GM Emmanuel – who was near St. Priest when he was wounded – lost his head and, instead of taking command, ran to Pantschulischev seeking directions. The troops were left without command. The Russian infantry, having no command, would continue its withdrawal for about an hour. They stopped firing and withdrew towards the suburb of Vesle – the only exit from the battlefield. The withdrawal would become a rout as men abandoned their cannon and threw away their equipment to hasten their escape.[85]

Meanwhile, Napoleon had left his position at Croix-Saint-Pierre and joined GD Ricard. The situation on the Sainte-Geneviève had stalled. Napoleon ordered him to launch a bayonet attack. To support this attack, part of Defrance's division moved from its position on the road to Epernay.

General Ségur, leading a force of cuirassiers and the 3rd Gardes d'honneur and followed by the 14th Young Guard Battery, penetrated into the suburbs – falling upon the Russian dragoons at the crossroads to Epernay and Fismes, sabering them, threw a large number into the left branch of the Vesle and captured 14 guns.[86] Unfortunately for the French, at that moment the Riazan Regiment – under Colonel Skobeleff – appeared on the road to Tinqueux as it sought to escape

82 Dry, p. 208.
83 Langeron, p. 431.
84 Dry, p. 210
85 Dry, p, 212.
86 *Victoires, conquetes, desastres, reveres et guerres civiles des françaises 1792 a 1815*, Vol. 23, p. 440.

over the Vesle bridge. Ségur found his force trapped between the fire of the Riazan Regiment and the six battalions of the 1st and 33rd Jagers that had already withdrawn to man the city walls and edges of the Vesle.

The moment of victory for the French cavalry quickly turned to one of disaster. Raked by musketry, it was cut down. Almost all of their horses were killed, their artillery equipment lost, Colonel Belmont fell mortally wounded and Ségur's arm was broken. It was only with the greatest difficulty that Ségur was able to escape capture. By the time supporting French cavalry arrived, Skobeleff had effected the passage of his regiment.

Ségur's charge and Defrance's movement cut the retreat of that part of St. Priest's corps that remained on the left bank of the Vesle. The Riazan Infantry Regiment advanced in a bayonet assault supported by the musketry of a second battalion and canister fired from two guns placed on the Soissons Gate. They carried with them their dying general and brought him to safety. The 1/Riazan occupied the village of Tinqueux and protected the Allied right flank during the withdrawal. Command of the Russian forces now passed to GL Pantschulischev, who placed two battalions in the Soissons Gate and lined up four more on the ramparts of the city.

Marmont's infantry had penetrated into the suburb and formed into dense (serrée) columns. Allied musketry poured from the city's ramparts and inflicted heavy casualties on Marmont's advancing infantry. Because of the nature of the terrain, the strength of the Allied position on the walls and the heavy fire, Marmont sent a battalion of the 20th Line Regiment into the houses closest to the walls, where they maintained a heavy skirmish fire on the Russians until 11:00 p.m. The gate of the city was covered only by a grate covered by a redan six feet high. Artillery was brought forward to pound the gate, despite the heavy musketry that killed many brave gunners, including Captain Guérict of the Imperial Guard.

While the Russians disputed the French efforts to penetrate into the city, Napoleon swept the Allies from the banks of the Vesle. Excelmans re-established the bridge at the Saint-Brice mill with a bridging train that had come forward. Count Kraczinski, at the head of his Polish light horse, passed over the bridge and pushed to the road to Béry-au-Bac followed by Excelmans' division. Once there, they drove back the large force of Allied troops (Emmanuel and Jagow) that had withdrawn to Béry-au-Bac. At this point the Allied rout was complete – and those Allied troops that could, fled in a mob down the three roads to Neufchâtel, Réthel and Châlons. When Jagow arrived in Béry at 5:00 a.m. the next morning, all that remained to him were two small battalions.[87]

Koch and other French sources set the French casualties at 700 or 800 men – including Count Ségur grievously wounded. The Allies lost 700-800 dead, 1,500-1,600 wounded, 2,500-3,500 prisoners, 11-14 guns, 100 caissons and vehicles from the Russian bridging train.[88]

A letter from Macdonald dated 15 March 1814 states the French had taken 4,000 prisoners, 18 cannon and 15 caissons.[89]

In his official report, Napoleon stated that the same battery that had killed General Moreau at Leipzig had also killed General St. Priest, "who had led the Tartars into his beautiful homeland." Von Damitz says that the eight Prussian battalions in the fight lost 1,300 men, the cavalry lost 85 and the artillery lost six howitzers and four cannon.[90]

Napoleon entered Rheims at 1:00 a.m. on 14 March. The village was immediately illuminated and the city's population filled the streets to greet their Emperor and liberator.

87 Dry, p. 217.
88 *Victoires, conquetes, desastres, reveres et guerres civiles des françaises 1792 a 1815*, Vol. 23, p. 440.
89 French Archives, Château Vincennes, C^2-183.
90 von Damitz, Vol. III, 1st Part, p. 150.

French infantry after the Battle of Rheims, by Job.

As St. Priest's corps met its destruction, Blücher decided to rest a few days in his cantonments on the Aisne. Bülow's corps continued its march on Compiègne; Langeron's was in Couchy-le-Château; Sacken sought to dislodge Christiani's division from the Crouy heights; Kleist's corps marched down the Lette; Yorck's corps moved into Corbeny; and Winzingerode's corps moved into Laon – replacing Bülow – and pushed his cavalry towards the Aisne.

Yorck sent a reconnaissance force to Béry-au-Bac. It engaged in a light reconnaissance with the dragoons of General Roussel and suffered around 50 casualties.

The pursuit

During the morning of 14 March Napoleon ordered Marmont to take Merlin's cavalry division and pursue the refuse of St. Priest's corps down the road to Béry-au-Bac. Ney was to advance with Boyer's infantry and Defrance's cavalry and move on Châlons. The remainder of the army took up positions around Rheims.

General Merlin, who commanded Marmont's advanced guard, encountered the Allies near Courcy and thought it was the cavalry that had been beaten the previous day. However, it was General Katzler's fresh cavalry, and the French were driven back – losing about 100 casualties. Fortunately, a brigade of Ricard's division arrived to stop the pursuit.

The French – in order to prevent being taken by surprise – then established themselves on the heights below Béry-au-Bac, barricaded the bridge and mined it. Marmont's remaining troops camped in the vicinity of Cormicy that night, and the cavalry was in Sapigneulle.

When Blücher learned of St. Priest's destruction, he presumed Napoleon had received substantial reinforcements and assumed that he would move a second time from Béry-au-Bac on his left

Rheims, 'The Last Victory', by Maurice Orange.

flank. Dispersed between Noyon and Corbeny, he had every reason to fear this movement. He ordered his forces to concentrate again on Laon and prepared to engage in another general battle. Generals Yorck and Kleist were to reunite at Craone that day. The troops escaping from Rheims were assigned to Yorck and Langeron's corps.

However, Napoleon had already learned that Blücher and his forces in Laon was more than he could handle. He would not venture into that trap again and directed his troops towards the Aube (and part of his troops were already on the Marne). Generals Vincent and Colbert departed Château-Thierry and Rheims and chased Tettenborn's Cossacks from Epernay. Ney, with Defrance and Boyer's divisions marched into Châlons.

Calls for peace

While these minor maneuvers were under way, the bulk of Napoleon's army reorganized and refitted in and around Rheims. It was concluded with a review, which was a sad shadow of earlier reviews, held at Maria-Hilf and Chammartin in that it showed his troops in their nudity and their weakness. It was the shattered remains of a once-powerful army. Many of the battalions had officer cadres that outnumbered the soldiers in the ranks.

Still too proud to accept the Allied terms, Napoleon determined to rebuild his army. He hoped to absorb 6,000 National Guardsmen from the Aisne – requisitioned by the Decree of 5 March – and use them to fill the depleted ranks of Marmont's corps. A further 3,000 were to come from the Department of the Marne to fill out the ranks of Mortier. These recruits were, however, never to be used. They responded to the draft and moved to Rheims, but were sent back to their homes because of the lack of arms with which to equip them.

Napoleon was beginning to be flooded with calls for peace. In order to calm those voices, two decrees were issued on 5 March in Fismes. The first related to the French defensive dispositions and retaliation against the enemy. The other dealt with public functions and French citizens who acted so as to impede the defense of France. These two decrees established that the war would not end until the hope of victory met with a catastrophic end. They declared a war to the death, and declared it the duty of all citizens to rise against the invaders.[91]

Extract from the 1st Decree

Napoleon, in consideration that the enemy generals have declared that they shall shoot any citizen who takes up arms, decrees the following:

1 Not only are all French citizens authorized to carry arms, but required to sound the alarm as soon as they hear the guns of our troops approaching them. They are to assemble, evacuate to the forests, to cut bridges, to block roads and to fall on the flanks and rear of the enemy.
2 All French citizens taken by the enemy – and who are put to death – shall be avenged by the execution of an enemy prisoner of war...

Extract from the 2nd Decree

Napoleon, in consideration that the people of the cities and the countryside are distressed by the atrocities committed against them by the enemy – and especially the Russians and Cossacks – have taken up arms out of a just sentiment of national honor to stop enemy parties; to seize convoys; and to do as much harm to the enemy as possible. He recognizes, however, that in many places they have been turned back by mayors and other officials; decrees:

1 All mayors, public functionaries and inhabitants – who instead of supporting the patriotic spirit of the people and who dissuade citizens from their legitimate defense – shall be considered as traitors and treated as such...

91 Koch, Vol. I, pp. 435-445.

12

Schwarzenberg Resumes the Offensive: The Engagements at Bar and La Ferté, 26 February-18 March 1814

The main Allied army had re-crossed the Aube as a result of Napoleon's threatened attack, and on 26 February it found itself between Bar and La Ferté. Its reserves stood to the rear near Langres. On that day, a dispatch from Blücher arrived at the camp of the King of Prussia, which caused the main army to stop its withdrawal. Blücher announced that the Army of Silesia, after having crossed the Aube and Baudemont, moved on the Marne and was pursued by Napoleon with a major portion of his forces. This news aroused great joy in the Allied camp and Schwarzenberg decided to abandon the plan arrived at in the Vandoeuvres Conference and to resume the offensive the following day.

Wrede's corps and Wittgenstein's corps, which had recently been reinforced by 4,000 men drawn from the siege of Danzig, stood on the Arentières heights – before Voigny – and on the Lignol plateau. The forces of the Crown Prince of Württemberg and Count Giulay stood on the Clairvaux heights.

The French positions facing the Allies were risky in case the Allies chose to attack. To the right of the Aube stood the II Corps under Count Gérard. Gérard had deployed his corps both in front of and behind Bar. Leval's division, VII Corps, stood in the Aube Valley with its left supported on Vernonfait. In a second line was Rottembourg's 5th Young Guard Division. Saint-Germain's cavalry was in Moutiers-en-Ile and Val-des-Vignes. On the left bank of the Aube stood the Count de Valmy's (Kellermann) cavalry division, which was encamped in and around Spoy with orders to move on Bar on 27 February. Pacthod's National Guard division held the Dolencourt bridge and the French artillery park was in Magny-le-Fouchard – protected by a single battalion.

Macdonald's corps stood near Mussy-l'Evêque and Essoye – with its cavalry pushed forward to Fontette – and being ignorant of recent events, stood poised to march on La Ferté.

Schwarzenberg had at hand his two original army corps – which had been joined a few days earlier by a division of Russian cuirassiers – the Austro-Bavarian Corps and the Württemberg Corps. He had more than enough to act.

Napoleon, on the other hand, knew that as soon as Schwarzenberg knew that he was no longer threatening the main Allied army, Schwarzenberg would once again resume his march on Paris. To this end he ordered his lieutenants to withdraw behind the Aube, to guard the defiles and to use what means they could to disguise his departure. They were to do this by announcing his arrival at various places on that front and to move about a headquarters equipped to appear to be the Imperial Headquarters.

However, even considering Blücher's dispatch, these ruses would not work for very long because the two French generals were separated from one another without direct communication

– and this isolation and their weakness would have eventually revealed the truth of the situation to Schwarzenberg.[1]

Persuaded by the King of Prussia, on 27 February Schwarzenberg ordered a general advance by the main Allied army. Wrede, whose corps stopped between Lignol and Bar, was to attack the village of Bar. Wittgenstein was to attack and seize the Vernonfait heights to the right, and on the left, the Crown Prince of Württemberg was to carry La Ferté-sur-Aube and to push his troops down the roads to Vandoeuvres and Troyes.

Engagement at Bar-sur-Aube – 27 February

At 7:00 a.m. the Russians began their march on Bar. Prince Schwarzenberg rode to the Allied advanced posts with the King of Prussia and his sons to review the terrain and to modify, if necessary, his plan of attack. As he reviewed the land before him, he saw that in order to defeat Oudinot it would be necessary to hold the ravines that run into the Aube. He ordered Wittgenstein to turn the French left by Arentières and to move on Arsonval, while Wrede was to distract their right as long as possible until Wittgenstein arrived near Dolencourt and gave him the opportunity to move against Bar and attack the forces of GD Duhèsme.

The city of Bar sat on the right bank of the Aube. The surrounding hills were planted with vineyards and a small stream ran past Arentières to the Aube within the boundaries of the city of Bar. A road ran down the same valley – connecting Arentières with Bar. A crossroad ran from Arentières to Vernonfait and to Lévigny – running parallel to the Aube across the high ground above Bar.

The valley floor was relatively flat and two main roads ran into Bar to Vandoeuvres. One ran down the left bank of the Aube – through the Jocourt woods to Spoy – and then off to Vandoeuvres. The principal road, however, ran down the right bank of the Aube, past Arsonval and the bridge over the Aube to Dolencourt, and continued along the Aube River Valley.

At around 7:00 a.m. Wittgenstein's corps marched from Colombé towards Bar-sur-Aube, arriving late, but taking up positions facing Vernonfait. Wrede's 5th Corps stood between Bar and Lignol in two lines – running between Bar and Arentières. The Austrians were deployed to the right and the Bavarians to the left. At 10:00 am. the Bavarian skirmishers began threatening the city, and Wittgenstein's corps – which had left the main road – began its attack in three columns. The first – under Count Pahlen – consisted of Schachovsky's 3rd Division; the Soumy, Grodno and Olviopol Hussars; the Tschuiugev Uhlans; three Cossack pulks; and a horse battery of 12 guns; and moved against Arentières, the Vernonfait ridge and the Lévigny hills. From there, they moved on Arsonval. Prince Eugene von Württemberg led the second column – containing Pitschnitzki's division – and moved via the heights before the Lévigny forest (his right wing towards Vernonfait, facing the Aube) to support the first column. The advance of this column was led by Stephanov's brigade, containing the 4th and 34th Jager Regiments.

Stephanov's brigade was torn up by the French in the engagement at Mormant on 17 February and was probably quite under-strength by this time. The third column – under Gorchakov – consisted of the divisions of Mezenzov and Helfreich (the Russian 5th and 14th Divisions) supported by the Pskov Cuirassiers and the Loubny Hussars, and moved against Lignol. General Vlassov – commanding Eugene's advanced guard consisting of the 23rd and 24th Jagers – was ordered to occupy the vineyards to the right of the Arentières stream, while the columns attacked the lower Vernonfait heights to prevent the French from occupying them. Stephanov's brigade, 4th Division, moved forward to scout the Lévigny woods (which were on

1 Koch, Vol. II, pp. 1-3.

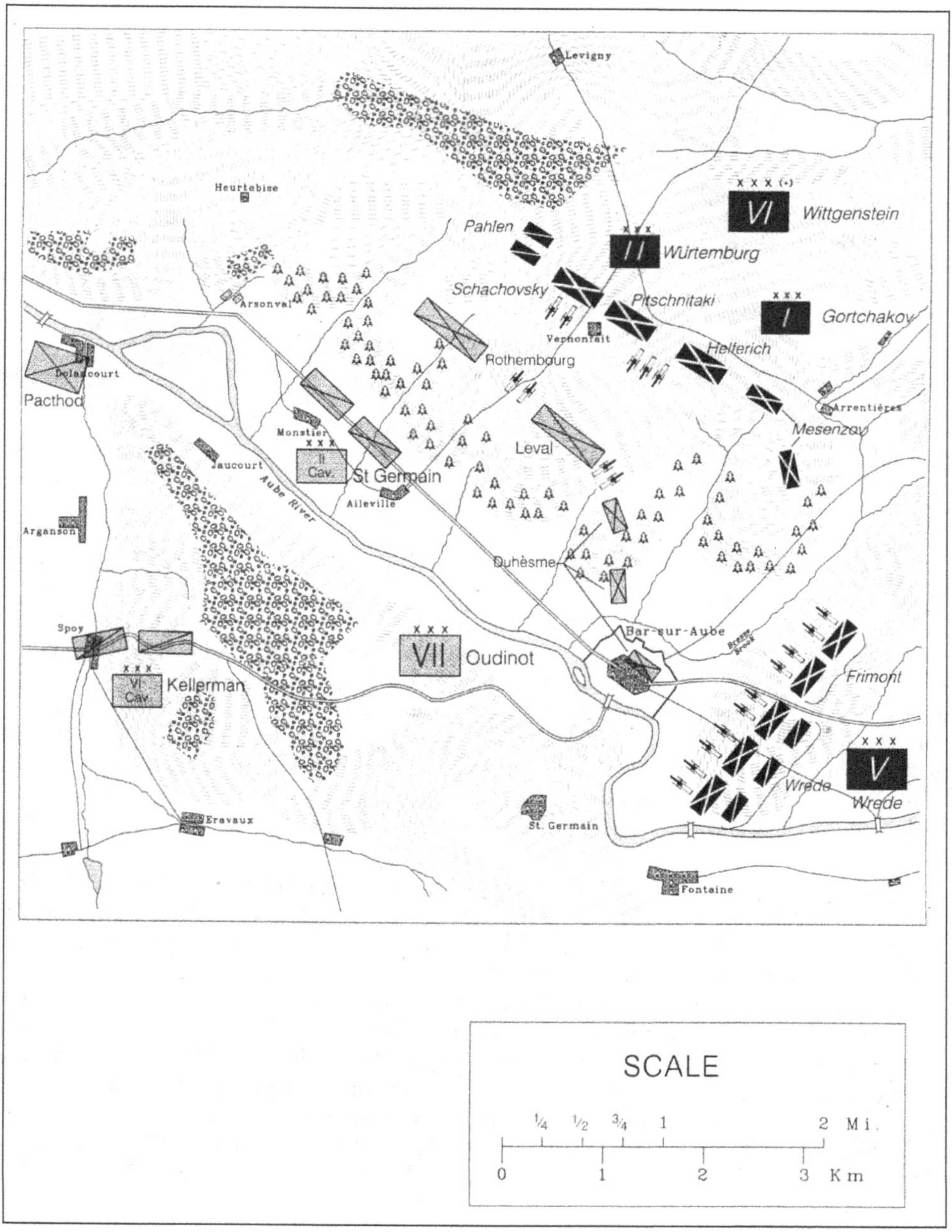

Map 14 Battle of Bar-sur-Aube, February 27 1814.

Bar-sur-Aube.

the Russian right) and Count Pahlen moved his cavalry to the side of Lévigny to surprise the French by Arsonval and Dolemont.[2]

On Wrede's left, an Austrian jäger battalion and two hussar squadrons watched that flank – observing the French cavalry by Spoy. A grenz battalion was posted by the Fontaine bridge.

Though Oudinot had learned of the Allied movements the previous day from the local inhabitants, he had given them little credence. Indeed, even after seeing the Allied movement on his left through the morning fog, he remained unconvinced and judged it useless to recall the VII Corps artillery, which he had cautiously withdrawn the previous night to Magny-le-Fouchard.

It was not until a light cavalry detachment – foraging near the Lévigny woods – was thrown back by the lead elements of Pahlen's cavalry that Oudinot decided it was time to take defensive measures.

Duhèsme's division, supported by eight guns, occupied Bar-sur-Aube.[3] Jarry's brigade stood on the side of Filles-Dieu, while Bélair's brigade moved to the heights of the Malépin plateau, where its skirmishers were quickly engaged. They had encountered the lead elements of the Russian 2nd Division – the Kalouga and Mohilev Regiments.

Leval's division executed a change of front by brigade – with its right wing in advance – and marched by massed battalions ("en masse") towards the summit of the Vernonfait hill. Rottembourg's 5th Young Guard Division took up positions in the second line behind Chassé's brigade, which formed the left of the first line. Saint-Germain's cavalry formed line near Moutiers. Pacthod's division – about 4,500 National Guardsmen – took up positions in front of its bivouacs in the Jocourt woods, with orders to guard the bridge at Dolencourt. The artillery park was in Magny-le-Fouchard – protected by a single battalion of infantry.[4]

2 Fabry, p. 171.
3 von Damitz, Vol. II, p. 448.
4 Sporschil, Vol. II, 1st Band, pp. 437-8.

Charge of the Russian cuirassiers at Bar-sur-Aube, by Parchaev.

These dispositions were completed as the Russian 23rd and 24th Jager Regiments – Sporschil indicates this was the 31st Jager Regiment[5] (Vlassov's brigade, 4th Division) – moved over the ridge by Vernonfait. They were promptly attacked by the 1/101st and 1/,2/105th Line Regiments under General Montfort. The Russians were thrown back into the ravine that runs along the Saint-Jacques woods to the Lévigny woods – losing a number of prisoners to the French.

The appearance of Gorchakov's column, however, stopped the French advance. The Pskov Cuirassiers – supported by a battalion of the Kalouga and Mohilev Regiments (Russian 5th Division) – charged the French without success because of the broken terrain. Nonetheless, their attack gave time for the Allies to deploy a large battery of artillery that began to fire on the French – inflicting substantial casualties.

Under heavy canister fire, the brigades of Montfort and Bélair – which was to Montfort's right – were shaken. Gorchakov saw this and executed a second attack, while Prince Eugene von Württemberg – whose column stood on the Lévigny heights – engaged Chassé's brigade. Gorchakov's attack might have been a disaster for the French had not Pinoteau's brigade arrived in time to support Montfort. The Russians pushed back the French skirmishers until the 10th Légère Regiment and the 3rd Line Regiment successfully counterattacked in time to stabilize the French line. Oudinot felt that this stabilization would not last without artillery and sent Gérard a battery under the command of Chef de bataillon Normand. This proved to be insufficient support and the battery was quickly locked in an engagement with the Russian artillery facing it from the heights. Soon 18-20 French guns began exchanging fire with 47 Russian guns.[6]

5 Sporschil, Vol. II, 1st Band, p. 440.
6 Fabry, p. 172.

Bar-sur-Aube.

Despite the cannon fire, which cut down hundreds of French soldiers, the French troops remained steady in their positions. This caused the Russians to judge that they were, in fact, retreating – and covering their retreat with this brave front.

Eugene von Württemberg was joined by the jager brigade of the 3rd Division as he pushed through the Lévigny woods and Wolff's brigade, same division, marched towards Arsonval. Württemberg maneuvered the four jager regiments of the 2nd Corps through the woods and ravines on the French left, while the French began to withdraw. He then launched an attack with a battalion of the Kalouga Regiment and the 23rd and 24th Jagers under Vlassov.

Meanwhile, Kellermann's cavalry crossed the Aube at the St.-Esprit ford. Kellermann led his cavalry up the road from Bar to Ailleville and quickly engaged them in battle with the Allies. Jacquinot's light cavalry attacked the Loubny Hussars – tearing them to pieces – and drove the Pskov Cuirassiers back in disorder. Supported by the veteran dragoons that had recently been withdrawn from Spain, the action was a clear French victory. Wittgenstein responded by concentrating his artillery in the center and recalled Eugene von Württemberg and Pahlen, whose column stood before Arsonval.

Seeing the Allied artillery, the French General Ismert fell on it with the 4th and 16th Dragoon Regiments. The Russian artillery stood firm and greeted them at a distance of 100 paces with canister fire – driving the French cavalry back three times. In 15 minutes, these two regiments lost more than 400 men.

Despite the failure of these charges, which were unsupported by infantry because of its heavy losses, Prince Schwarzenberg was shaken by the vigour of these attacks and judged it appropriate to reinforce Wittgenstein. He ordered Vieregg's Bavarian cavalry brigade, the Knesevich Dragoons and Szeckler Hussars, and Volkman's Austrian infantry brigade – from Wrede's corps – to move in all haste to support Gorchakov.[7]

7 Sporschil, Vol. II, 1st Band, p. 442.

General Volkman moved to the hill and over the lower crests by Malépin at the moment that Pahlen's forces reached the corner of the Lévigny woods. The arrival of these powerful reinforcements caused Oudinot to abandon any hope of holding his position and he ordered his forces to retreat. Pahlen's column consisted of the Soumy, Grodno and Olviopol Hussars, and the Tschuiugev Uhlan Regiment; a horse battery; Schachovsky's 3rd Division; and three Cossack regiments.

On his side, Schwarzenberg felt that Pahlen's cavalry could not be favorably employed to turn the French left – as originally ordered – and directed them to rejoin Tschuiugev's Cossacks and uhlans standing on the Arsonval heights. His orders to Pahlen would later be countermanded, but Pahlen would arrive in his initially-ordered position too late to act against the French.[8]

At this point, Schwarzenberg ordered a general attack by the 6th Corps on the left and center of the French line, with the 5th Corps ordered to strike the French right wing. Seeing this assault forming up, Oudinot ordered his army to begin its withdrawal.

As the withdrawal of the brigade in the French first line facing him became apparent, Wittgenstein formed a column of eight battalions on the Vernonfait heights. A battalion of the Kalouga Regiment formed the head of the column and led it towards the Filles-Dieu heights. The Kalouga Battalion was followed by the 23rd and 24th Russian Jager Regiments and three Austrian battalions from Volkman's brigade. Meanwhile, Gorchakov began a general assault with his troops. Supporting this attack was a force of Russian artillery. The King of Prussia became so excited about the attack that he rode over to these guns and personally fired several of them.[9]

General Bélair fought desperately to stall their attack – using the terrain to its best effect. However, the canister fire supporting this column forced him to disperse his troops and operate them in skirmish formation. In the middle, General Volkman – with the infantry of Spleny's division – attacked the French II Corps which occupied the vineyards between Arentières and Ailleville, while Wrede attacked Bar-sur-Aube frontally.

Wrede's frontal attack on Bar-sur-Aube consisted of five battalions, with four others attempting to turn its flank along the heights and take its garrison in the rear. Oberst Theobald led a battalion of the Bavarian 10th Regiment – supported by the Kronprinz Regiment – led personally by General Maillot. Two other Bavarian battalions (the Unterdonau National Field Battalion and an unidentified Iller Kreise Battalion) and two battalions of the Szeckler Grenz charged forward – bayonets lowered – against the city as Finkenauer's Bavarian battery, supported by a battalion of the Prinz Karl von Bayern Regiment, fired in support.[10]

Wrede's turning movement – under Oberst Hertling and consisted of the 3rd Light Battalion, 1/, 2/König Regiment and the 10th Augsburg National Field Battalion – moved rapidly across the ridge and closed on the French rear.

Duhèsme had barricaded all entrances to the city and placed batteries on the heights behind the city. He would have held the village for a considerable period had not the withdrawal of the French center and left not rendered such resistance pointless. His troops quickly began an orderly retreat under the cover of his artillery. One of his brigades, formed in square, moved from Bar and into the valley – marching to Ailleville. The other withdrew to the artillery – down the road to Spoy.

Oberst Hertling, who had earlier moved to strike Bar-sur-Aube in the rear, now struck the masses of GD Gérard. The combined Austrian and Bavarian forces struck the French as they made a brief stand by Ailleville. Dietz's cavalry brigade and Rechberg's division took positions by Ailleville, which was then garrisoned by only a single brigade of Duhèsme's division. The remainder had withdrawn to Spoy and joined the French light cavalry.

8 Fabry, p. 172.
9 Sporschil, Vol. II, 1st Band, p. 443.
10 Sporschil, Vol. II, 1st Band, p. 443.

The bulk of the French artillery and part of the II and VII Corps had already crossed the Dolencourt bridge when Pahlen's cavalry appeared on the heights above the village with a battery of 12 guns. The Russian artillery took up a position 325 feet (100 meters) from the road, behind a deep ravine, and began firing on Kellermann's cavalry. The artillery fire instantly caused disorder in the French ranks and the infantry of the rearguard, fearing it would be cut off, threw itself in panic across these forces – sweeping the dragoons with them. Order was only re-established when General Montfort arrived with the 1/105th Line Regiment, some companies of the 1/101st Line Regiment and some Young Guard. Montfort pushed against the right of the Russian battery and forced it to change its position. Order restored, the French rearguard moved behind the wooded hill – facing the Dolencourt bridge – covered the rest of the retreat and then fell back across the bridge to safety.

The French losses were about 2,600 dead and wounded and 460 prisoners. General Pinoteau was wounded. The Allies lost about 2,400 men, with Schwarzenberg and Wittgenstein wounded – though Schwarzenberg's wound was very, very slight.

A total of 40,000 Allies had attacked and surprised 15,000 French – unsupported by artillery and with their backs to a river. Oudinot had fought a more than credible battle – quickly taking up a strong position and holding it far longer than might have been expected. His first failure was to recognize the threat earlier and leaving the VII Corps artillery in the rear. The lack of artillery prevented him from taking full advantage of Montfort's successful attack. He can also be criticized for not supporting Rottembourg and Saint-Germain with the three brigades of Leval's division and for leaving Pacthod's division on the left bank of the Aube (completely out of the action).

However, these criticisms – other than the lack of artillery – are weak, as the ultimate outcome of the battle was never in doubt. The overwhelming numbers of the Allies would certainly have begun to tell before the battle had gone too far. If Pacthod's troops had been brought across the river and a heavy engagement joined – once the inevitable French retreat began – the congestion at the Dolencourt bridge, it might have resulted in the entire corps being destroyed (and the engagement of Leval's troops would have exposed them to fire and casualties that would not be offset by a compensating loss on the part of the Allies). Only the gallant, but foolish, repeated charges of the 4th and 16th Dragoon Regiments against the Russian artillery can truly be subjected to harsh criticism, as they never had more than the most meager chance of success – and cost the French 400 irreplaceable cavalry.[11]

It is sad that Oudinot, in his report to Napoleon, attributed the sad outcome of this action to the lack of firmness in a few regiments. Certainly, history will give them greater justice for their actions in this unequal engagement.

On 28 February the French army posted itself in Vandoeuvres, with its rearguard in Magny-le-Fouchard and advanced posts on the road to Bar and Spoy. There was no pursuit by the Allies other than a few light cavalry.

Schwarzenberg's own announcement of the engagement was equally fallacious – announcing the precipitous march of Napoleon and Augereau towards Dijon and suspended his offensive movement. As the Crown Prince of Württemberg had failed to push Macdonald from his position, Schwarzenberg feared his lines of communication might be cut off should he advance against Oudinot. It was for this reason that Oudinot experienced no significant pursuit, which allowed him to make appropriate defensive dispositions.

As the Allies took advantage of their position in Bar, Napoleon began to fear that his marshals would not be able to execute his plan before his departure from Troyes. As a result, he gave

11 Koch, Vol. II, pp. 4-12.

Macdonald command of the forces moving towards the Aube with the order to take La Ferté and to throw the Allies back to the right bank of the Aube.

In conformance with these instructions, Macdonald directed Milhaud to march on Fontette with the cavalry divisions of Piré and Briche supported by Simmer's infantry brigade. Brayer and Amey's divisions were ordered to move against Essoye and Landreville. l'Héritier, after pushing reconnaissance from Mussy-l'Evêque down the roads to Langres and Châtillon, was to move in the same direction – preceding Albert's division, which was to have supported this operation.

Engagement at La Ferté-sur-Aube – 28 February

The Allied 3rd (Giulay) and 4th Corps (Württemberg) had united and the combined corps were under the command of the Crown Prince of Württemberg. The two corps advanced from Clairvaux to La Ferté, marched through the village and sent its advanced guard across to the far bank of the Aube.

When Milhaud's cavalry arrived on the Villars heights, it encountered Austrian light cavalry. GD Brayer's 12 cannon deployed and began bombarding the Württembergers as the French squadrons deployed on the plateau that commanded La Ferté. The Württemberg cavalry – supported by Klenau's Austrian division – deployed as well, but pounded by the French artillery, it quickly withdrew behind the Allied infantry without trying to attack. The divisions of Brayer and Amey arrived, in the meantime, and the Crown Prince decided that it was appropriate to withdraw back across the river. As the Allies withdrew, they broke down the bridge. The two armies spent the night glaring at each other across the river.

Macdonald's position was very advantageous with regards to the small force at his disposal. The plateau was enclosed between La Ferté, Clairvaux and the Aube. It was not attackable from the front as it commanded La Ferté – as well as that portion of the Aube that ran past it. To completely assure his front, all that was required was the destruction of the bridges at Silvarouvre and La Ferté – and the latter was already gone.

Klenau.

Not knowing of Oudinot's withdrawal – and planning to use the bridges for his own purposes – Macdonald cannot be held at fault for the attack that would hit him the following day. His only action was to barricade the Silvarouvre bridge.

At the break of dawn on 28 February Amey's division and 500 horse of the V Corps were recalled to Troyes by an order from Napoleon. Once there, they were to guard the various parks and equipment. Macdonald, weakened by their withdrawal, felt no urgency other than a reestablishment of communications with Oudinot. To effect this link, he left Milhaud's two cavalry divisions and Brayer's division before La Ferté and concentrated l'Héritier and Albert's divisions – plus some other forces – at Fontette. He intended to lead these forces against Bar, re-establish communications with Oudinot and prepare the defense of the Aube.

In order to open the march for his infantry, he sent forward a force of dragoons on a reconnaissance to Bar and Clairvaux. Allied forces were encountered everywhere – indicating the evacuation of Bar – so Macdonald felt safe marching on Vitry-le-Crois in order to re-establish contact with Oudinot in Vandoeuvres. However, 2,000 Württemberg cavalry had also moved in that direction and stood between Fontille and Fosses. Encountering them, Macdonald withdrew to Fontette surrounded by enemy cavalry. He sent requests to Milhaud to come to his assistance, feared he was about to be attacked by superior forces, and thought all was lost.

The Crown Prince of Württemberg, with his forces standing on the right bank of the Aube between Clairvaux and La Ferté, was in a good position where he waited for the advance of the French. When he saw that the French were making no effort to cross the river – and seeing the barricades on the Silvarouvre bridge – he presumed that they were assuming a defensive posture, but was unwilling to go over to the offensive until ordered to do so by Schwarzenberg.

The Crown Prince ordered Giulay to fire his cannon on the village of La Ferté and to seek to cross over the Aube at Silvarouvre, to strike the right flank of Brayer's division while he sought to cross at Clairvaux, and move via Saint-Usage and Fontette – against what he presumed would be Macdonald's rear.

At about 8:00 a.m. Fresnel's division began to fire its guns against the divisions of Milhaud and Brayer, who responded. Giulay left Pflüger's brigade before La-Ferté-sur-Aube as a reserve. During this false attack – at around 2:00 p.m. – Count Giulay led three brigades of infantry (Czollich, Grimmer and F. Spleny)[12] and Seslavin's cavalry towards Silvarouvre to strike the French flank. General Seslavin's cavalry, which was assigned to him, moved against the Silvarouvre bridge via a discrete detour.

As they arrived before the Silvarouvre bridge, the Austrian artillery began to fire on the French defenders. GD Brayer responded to their fire with a battery of 12 guns. After an hour of cannonade, Giulay came to believe it was unlikely he would hear the fire of the battery that would indicate that Seslavin had arrived and ordered Czollich's brigade to charge the bridge.[13] The French battalion defending the bridge provided so little resistance to the advancing Austrians of the Kottulinsky Infantry Regiment that they barely broke stride as they advanced over the barricades and made themselves masters of the bridge.

Brayer sought in vain to stop this movement with his 12 guns for about 45 minutes, but the effort failed. The time to have retaken the bridge was as the Austrians moved through the barricades – and it needed to be done with bayonets.

On the left, Count Fresnel remained in a strong position on a ridge on the right bank – and after several attempts, forced the French artillery to direct its fire away from the Austrian infantry. Fresnel profited from this by slipping a number of skirmishers into La Ferté and eventually forced the French battalion garrisoning the village to evacuate. He then re-established the bridge and began sending his troops back over it.

Despite the disadvantages of their situation, the French were determined to dispute the battlefield with the Austrians. After a long resistance, however, Milhaud was obliged to order a retreat, which was executed in the best of order down the road to Bar-sur-Seine through the Clairvaux forest. Macdonald's forces stopped the Württemberg cavalry before Fontette and drove it back. The Crown Prince of Württemberg was obliged to take a long detour before he succeeded in reaching Saint-Usage and Fontette. The result was that Macdonald was pursued only by a few Cossacks of Seslavin's brigade.

The French lost about 600 men *hors de combat* and the Allies lost about the same number, plus 150 prisoners.

Reconnaissance on Vandoeuvres

As Count Milhaud rejoined Macdonald, the officers that Macdonald had sent to Oudinot returned from Vandoeuvres and advised him of the French loss at Bar-sur-Aube. From there, the hopes of maintaining control of the left bank of the Aube ended and the XI Corps, despite the fatigue

12 Sporschil, Vol. II, 1st Band, p. 450.
13 von Damitz, Vol. II, p. 471.

of its troops, was obliged to march through the night on Bar-sur-Seine. The Crown Prince of Württemberg followed Macdonald as far as Noës, Viviers and Equilly – sending his advanced posts to Gié and Celle. Count Giulay's forces moved into Loches, Essoye and Landreville. However, Prince Schwarzenberg – still concerned about the news he had received the previous day – still had no desire to make any aggressive movement and limited the actions of his army to ordering Wrede and Wittgenstein to send forward a strong reconnaissance against Vandoeuvres. The cavalry and horse artillery of the two corps were combined and placed under the orders of Baron Frimont, who divided them into two columns. The first column, under Count Pahlen, moved via Amanze towards Val-Suzenay and Vauchonvilliers against Oudinot's left flank. The second column, under General Frimont, advanced via Spoy. Their reserve consisted of a brigade of Russian infantry and two squadrons of hussars, which marched down the main road.

Count Gérard's forces stood before Vandoeuvres. He occupied the Val-Suzenay woods with infantry and pushed Saint-Germain's cavalry forward to warn of the advancing Allies. A heavy cannonade began the engagement, but had no result as Pahlen had left his infantry in Vauchonvilliers – directing that it move across the Barce near Villeneuve-Mesgrigny. This maneuver was very disquieting to Oudinot and he decided to withdraw. His rearguard disputed the Allied advance foot by foot – finally camping in Moutier-Amey. General Frimont occupied Vandoeuvres. Count Pahlen occupied Villeneuve-Mesgrigny, Wrede's corps was in Bar-sur-Aube, Wittgenstein's was in Dienville and Barclay de Tolly's corps moved from Langres to Chaumont.

Reassured by this reconnaissance, and calmed about Napoleon's operations, Schwarzenberg decided to begin a march against Troyes on 2 March.

Oudinot had begun his withdrawal before dawn and his rearguard, under Gérard, was reinforced by Rottembourg's 5th Young Guard Division. Gérard had arrayed his forces near the Guillotière bridge.

Pahlen – who formed the Allied advanced guard – was not ready to force a bridge which he presumed to be well-guarded so he moved through Mesgnil-St.-Père and Gérodot towards Doches, where he had established himself during the night. From here he pushed forces towards Mesgnil-Sellières and Assencières – and from Gérodot he sent a further detachment towards Laubressel. However, these forces were pushed back by French forces. Wrede's infantry arrived in Vandoeuvres and Wittgenstein's infantry spent the night in Piney.

Inasmuch as the Crown Prince of Württemberg was aggressively pursuing him, Macdonald did not hear of the battle on his left and assumed that Oudinot was no longer moving towards Troyes and that nothing would prevent their junction. He deployed his forces to dispute the Allied advance and posted guards at the fords and destroyed the bridges over the Ourcq from the Seine to Fouchères. He placed his heavy guns along the river and behind the Barce – establishing Brayer's division and part of his on some hills – and echeloning the rest of his troops on the left bank of the Seine as far as Fouchères.[14]

The engagement at Bar-sur-Seine

The Crown Prince of Württemberg moved during the morning to attack Macdonald's left flank, while Giulay – who rebuilt the bridge at Ourcq during the night – sent Fresnel's division through Celle to attack Bar frontally and Weiss' brigade moved through Polizot to take the heights that it dominated.

Brayer opposed this movement as instructed – using his artillery to hold off the Allies until the last moment – when the Austrians forced the bridge at the paper mill in Polizot.

14 Koch, Vol. II, pp. 13-21.

Bar was enveloped by a masonry wall that could withstand a few hours' bombardment. Brayer pulled a few battalions into the city, barricaded the gates and awaited the Allied attack with firm resolve. As the various Allied columns reunited by Châtillon, they began a bombardment of the city. Brayer – not desiring to subject the citizens and their homes to an enemy bombardment and attack – abandoned the city and withdrew to Virey, which was occupied by a brigade from Albert's division, and then withdrew across the Barce – destroying the bridge in the face of pursuing Württemberg cavalry.

The engagement cost the French about 100 men, while the Allies lost about 500 men during the engagement. The XI Corps withdrew into the night – arriving in Saint-Parre-les-Vaudes, where Macdonald established his headquarters. Brayer's division moved into the second line near Maisons-Blanches, where General Foucher had already stationed his reserves. Milhaud's cavalry spent the night in Vaux, Fouchères and Romilly so as to support the infantry brigade that observed the Barce.

The French army had achieved its principal goal. All of its divisions were now in contact and Macdonald assumed command of the combined forces.

The attack on the Barce bridges – Laubressel and La Guillotière – 3 March

Schwarzenberg hoped to crush the French before him and stopped on 3 March to plan a combined assault from his present position. Wrede was directed to attack frontally down the road from Vandoeuvres towards La Rivour and to occupy the Courteranges woods. Wittgenstein was to move from Piney and seek to move his forces between Rouilly and Mesgnil-Sellières in order to join the Bavarians near Laubressel. In order to increase the chances of this, the Crown Prince of Württemberg and Count Giulay were ordered to move on Troyes via Bar-sur-Seine. The result of these maneuvers would mean that the French army would be assaulted from three sides at around 1:00 p.m.

The position on the Barce, which was inaccessible from the front and on the right bank because of the water and marshes in the area, offered nonetheless little security because the Laubressel plateau – which held the key to the position – could be turned by the Bouranton Valley, which opened into the Argentolle swamps from the Mesgnil-Sellières plain. This plain and valley were accessible to all arms.

General Gérard was charged by Oudinot to defend this position and he had posted Duhèsme's 1st Division before Folie between the river's edge and the main road – covering the bridge at La Guillotière. Jarry's 1st Brigade, 2nd Division, stood to his left – extending from Courteranges to the Laubressel plateau, where Rottembourg's 5th Young Guard Division had established its bivouacs. They were supported by Saint-Germain's cavalry, which was posted in Saint-Parre-aux-Tertres. The VII Corps infantry and Kellermann's cavalry were placed in front of Pont-St.-Hubert on the left bank of the Seine. Molitor's XI Corps and Milhaud's cavalry were not assigned to a specific position. GD Sébastiani occupied Troyes with Amey's division. Molitor had replaced Macdonald as the commander of the XI Corps by this time. After the dissolution of Macdonald's first army in Meaux on 10 February Sébastiani had remained with the Imperial Headquarters until the capture of Troyes, when Napoleon named him governor of Troyes.

On 2 March the French army, under Macdonald, was as follows:[15]

15 Sporschil, Vol. II, 1st Band, pp. 464-5.

	Bns	Sqns	Men
II Corps – GD Gérard			
Division Duhèsme	17		1,970
Division Hamelinaye	13		1,800
VII Corps – Maréchal Oudinot			
Division Rottembourg	10		2,628
Division Leval	12		4,365
Brigade Chassé		6	2,515
Division Pacthod	10		4,027
XI Corps – GD Molitor			
Division Albert	5		1,520
Division Brayer	5		1,370
Division Amey	14		2,681
Flank Corps			
Division Allix	4	1	1,450
II Cavalry Corps – GD Saint-Germain			
Division Maurin		18	1,325
Division Saint-Germain		10	1,270
V Cavalry Corps – GD Milhaud			
Division Piré		12	1,421
Division Briche		15	1,700
Division l'Héritier		13	1,269
VI Cavalry Corps – GD Kellermann			
Division Jacquinot		15	1,258
Division Trelliard		18	1,747
Total:	96	102	32,316

During the evening of 2 March Gérard commented to Oudinot that their position was not very secure in case of a thaw. A dispatch had arrived from Napoleon during the night which contained the same observation. Oudinot accepted the wisdom of these observations and proposed sending one or two battalions from the VII Corps to a post in Laubressel, but unfortunately, he did not act on his proposal.

The Allied attack began on the morning of 3 March. GL Count Pahlen – the advanced guard of the Allied 6th Corps – was moving at the break of dawn and quickly came into contact with Rottembourg's infantry. Pahlen sought to turn the French left wing, seize the Laubressel heights and send a detachment against Troyes. Meanwhile, the main body of the 6th Corps marched from Piney through Rouilly, Mesgnil-Sellières and Laubressel, where it linked with the 5th Corps. The 5th Corps moved down the main road from Vandoeuvres to the right of La Rivour with the intention of crossing the Barce and occupying the Courteranges woods. A Russian column moved to the left to take the bridge at La Guillotière.

Wrede had concentrated his forces by 10:00 a.m. – linking Rechberg's Bavarian division with three battalions of Hardegg's Austrian division and having all his cavalry in hand. The remainder of the 5th Corps stood by Vandoeuvres, with orders to move through Moutier-Amey and strike the French if they should remain behind the Barce. However, earlier – around 7:00 a.m. – two

French battalions, four squadrons and some guns had crossed the bridge at La Guillotière and had opened fire on the Allied cavalry pickets posted by the bridge.[16]

Pahlen's Russian infantry, the Tchougouiev Uhlan Regiment and the Olviopol Hussar Regiment stood in a position to observe the French, while four horse guns supported by a cuirassier regiment took up posts on the flank while the rest of the cavalry moved behind the Laubressel heights to strike at the French rear via Bouranton and Saint-Parre-Aux-Tertres. The infantry soon got into a heavy firefight with the French.

The village of Bouranton was undefended and the Russian cavalry arrived via Tennelière, which also was not guarded and stood three miles (five kilometers) in the French rear. Once there, General Rüdinger, leading the Rebrikov Cossack Regiment, caught a small French park moving from Tennelière to Troyes with a weak escort and attacked – causing incredible confusion. The French escort and drivers fled – taking the horses – but abandoning the guns and caissons.

Meanwhile, the battle began with Saint-Germain's cuirassiers coming to the defense of the park – executing several charges – and throwing Pahlen's cavalry back behind Bouranton. The result was that only part of the park and 200 prisoners were lost. However, Pahlen's attack announced the beginning of what would be more serious Allied attacks.

Around 1:00 p.m. Wittgenstein's infantry appeared on the heights of Rouilly and Mesgnil-Sellières. They remained there stationary until 3:00 p.m. when the Bavarians began a cannonade. The Russians attacked in two columns. The right-hand column consisted of the corps of Prince Eugene von Württemberg and moved against the left of Bouranton. The left-hand column, Gorchakov's corps, marched against the Laubressel heights – covering its left flank with eight squadrons of uhlans. The two columns advanced in echelons, in masses by battalion – preceded by a large force of artillery, which was covered by a cloud of skirmishers. The right-hand column – the 4th Division – marched to take Laubressel in the flank, while the left column – the 3rd Division – marched against the Bouranton heights. The French had, on this important post, only six guns. The Russians advanced 32 guns at the trot, deployed and began to pound Rottembourg's division with canister. Prince Eugene directed the 4th Jager Regiment to strike the French left flank and rear. The French withdrew and were pursued by a force of Russian cuirassiers, which decided the affair quickly.[17]

It was around 4:00 p.m. and Austrian troops were beginning to arrive and reinforce the Russian corps. The situation was becoming critical for the French.

The Russian 4th Division had great difficulty scaling the Laubressel heights because they were covered with vineyards. Once over the heights, the Russian 4th Division was attacked by Saint-Germain's cavalry, which stood in line to the left of the village. In contrast, Prince Eugene von Württemberg, who led the 3rd Division, moved easily through Bouranton and sought to gain the main road moving via Tennelière – following in Pahlen's footsteps. This movement resulted in several charges by Kellermann's cavalry, who had moved quickly from Saint-Parre-aux-Tertres, where they had moved to replace Saint-Germain.

While this occurred on the left, Wrede sent four or five battalions of Bavarian infantry from Courteranges

Prince Eugene von Württemberg.

16 Sporschil, Vol. II, 1st Band, p. 460.

17 Fabry, p. 173.

– slipping through the icy woods on the right of the Barce – to link up with the Russians, whose progress on the left had been stopped by the presence of about 20 French cavalry squadrons that were already blown as a result of their charges against the more numerous Russian cavalry.

Oudinot had already given the order to retreat as the 1/Kalouga Infantry Regiment, without orders and under the eyes of the King of Prussia, attacked Filles-Dieu. The 2/Kalouga followed as the right wing echelon and the two battalions stormed the heights and struck the right flank of Bélair's French brigade. The Perm and Mohilev Regiments struck Bélair frontally, while Vlassov's jagers and two Austrian battalions under General Volkman marched in support of the attack. Bélair's brigade collapsed and moved rapidly to the rear – encouraged in its flight by the fire of a 12pdr battery.

Fearing that the Allies would turn his flank, Gérard gave the order to retreat. Laubressel was evacuated in good order. Jarry's division supported Rottembourg's division and the two divisions moved to Saint-Parre under the cover of French cavalry and artillery.

At this time, however, Wrede – who had previously contented himself with a cannonade – decided to launch a general assault to force the Barce bridges. He ordered two Bavarian battalions, under Oberst Theobald, to attack Bar down the road from Chaumont. He ordered two battalions from the reserve to follow him in support of this attack. Four Bavarian battalions, under Oberst Hertling, were to attack between Bar and the Aube riverbed. One company of the Szeckler Hussars and two Bavarian battalions, under Major Schönermark, were ordered to move to the right of the city and move against the Aube bridges. They were to be supported by a Bavarian battery posted to the right of the city.[18]

If General Duhèsme had received the order to retreat in time, his troops would have escaped easily. However, not having received the word, Duhèsme assumed that the rest of the French army remained in line and stood fast – bayonets fixed – to fight Wrede's attack. Gérard, not seeing Duhèsme's troops withdrawing, sent forward the word again – ordering Duhèsme to withdraw. Duhèsme finally began his withdrawal, but assaulted by the entire Bavarian army, he could not move down the main road and threw his forces towards the Lower Barce and Saint-Parre-aux-Tertres. Once there Duhèsme found himself assailed by the Allied infantry, as well as the Knesevich Dragoons and the Szeckler Hussars, who aggressively pursued him as he withdrew. Duhèsme's handling of the engagement and withdrawal were excellent – losing only 400 men and two guns.[19]

The withdrawing French infantry was surrounded by enemy infantry and they were in danger of being cut off. On the left of the Seine, the Crown Prince of Württemberg remained very passive – permitting the XI Corps and V Cavalry Corps to move with little interference. A division of infantry guarded Maisons-Blanches – echeloned by cavalry as far as the suburbs of Troyes. On the extreme left, the VII Corps faced a demonstration by Allied cavalry throughout the day.

Koch states that the French lost seven guns and 1,500 prisoners – of whom 600 were wounded. The Allies lost about 1,000 casualties. Von Damitz, however, states that the French lost 2,600 dead and wounded – including General Pinoteau wounded – and 460 prisoners. He gives the Allied losses as 1,200 Russians and 300 Bavarians *hors de combat*.[20]

The Allies occupied Creney, Tennelière and Bouranton on the right bank of the Seine. Platov's Cossacks pushed to Arcis-sur-Aube and Sézanne, whose small garrisons were quickly defeated. The advanced posts of the Crown Prince of Württemberg stood in Aumont-en-île and Moussy – facing Maisons-Blanches.

18 von Damitz, Vol. II, p. 456.
19 Sporschil, Vol. II, 1st Band, p. 463.
20 von Damitz, Vol. II, p. 459.

Macdonald resumes command

These two parts of the French army found themselves reunited before Troyes, where Macdonald rested – still sick. No matter; Macdonald still assumed command of a force of 21,000 infantry and 4,000 cavalry. Seeing his tiny force and the overwhelming forces arrayed against it, Macdonald realized the foolishness of accepting battle on the right bank of the Seine. Even if he were to win the engagement, he had no means to exploit the victory – and the slightest check meant total defeat. He resolved to withdraw to Nogent in a leisurely manner so as to permit his wheeled traffic sufficient time to withdraw.

He ordered Oudinot to watch for the Allies and to be ready to act without compromising the troops moving from Saint-Parre to Troyes. The various corps were obliged to withdraw successively in a manner so as to not be forced to become engaged. To this end, the bridges were barricaded and all the fords were ruined.

After the evacuation of Troyes, the II and VII Corps withdrew down the road to Châtres, while General Pacthod moved with one of his brigades to occupy Bray. The XI Corps and the cavalry of Kellermann and Milhaud were ordered to move down the road to Pavillon. Finally, Oudinot was to establish a rearguard with Saint-Germain's cavalry and the infantry and artillery he judged necessary.[21]

On the Allied side, Schwarzenberg – less fearful of the two marshals than of Napoleon – feared that remaining stationary before Troyes would bring Napoleon back to recover the French position before the Allies could consolidate it, and so ordered Wrede and Wittgenstein to attack the city quickly. The Crown Prince of Württemberg was asked to be ready to assist their attack should it become necessary. The sole goal of this attack was to take Troyes – the key to the Aube Valley. Only the cavalry of Wrede and Wittgenstein's corps were detached to pursue the two marshals.

During the night, the two French marshals stopped and took tally of their situation. Three times during the night, the Allied cavalry attempted to provoke the French into resuming their withdrawal, but failed.

At 8:00 a.m. on 4 March Saint-Parre was attacked by Prince Eugene von Württemberg's corps, four Bavarian battalions and two Austrian battalions. Count Gérard resisted Wittgenstein's attack until about 11:00 a.m. and then he withdrew across the Seine and into the Saint-Jacques suburb. From there, he sent an envoy to Wrede offering to evacuate the city in six hours. However, fearing Napoleon's arrival, Wrede offered only one hour.

Oudinot's withdrawal continued as ordered. Milhaud – upon hearing the gunfire around Troyes – moved past the city and took up positions on the Pavillon road alongside Kellermann, who stood on the main road to Paris. The XI Corps infantry stood in the edge of the suburbs.

Prince Eugene von Württemberg saw that the French did not intend to defend the city, but were intent on covering the withdrawal of their army. He advanced his infantry down the main road as if he wished to push into the eastern side of the city. General Gérard perceived his intentions and crossed the second bridge on the Seine and withdrew after barricading the Saint-Martin suburb. At the same time, Molitor turned past Troyes and formed into a march column on the road to Pavillon.

Eugene von Württemberg deployed his forces and Wrede moved his along the left side and prepared to support his attack. The 2nd Corps organized itself in attack columns in two lines. Colonel Rosen's brigade pushed forward and carried Saint-Parre and followed the French to the gates of Troyes, which were closed in their faces.[22]

21 Koch, Vol. II, pp. 22-30.
22 Fabry, p. 174.

The Allies closed around Troyes and began showering howitzer shells into the city. Once again, they summoned the city. Sébastiani recognized that Troyes was untenable and took advantage of a momentary cessation in the bombardment to withdraw from the city. The various barricades in the city slowed the Allied advance into the city – as did the continual fear of an attack in the heart of the city.

In contrast to his directions, Oudinot neglected to leave a strong rearguard before Chappelle-St.-Luc. He did not perceive it as being necessary. As the French marched down the old and new routes to Paris, suddenly Bavarian cavalry appeared on the Malmaison plains behind Kellermann's cavalry, which was in march column. Surprised by the appearance of the Bavarians and fearing the rearguard had been destroyed, Kellermann's cavalry disbanded and fled – its generals being unable to rally any part of it until it reached Grez. If the French infantry had not held firm, Frimont would have entered into Nogent like the wind.

This last engagement cost the French 400 men, but the firmness of the infantry stopped the disorder and assured the security of the French army. The Allies, however, once again occupied Troyes and began to reorganize themselves after five days of combat and maneuvers.[23]

As Schwarzenberg entered Troyes, the conferences in Lusigny treating for an armistice broke up and the commissioners returned to their respective headquarters.

For 48 hours after taking Troyes, the Allies sacked Troyes – committing all sorts of atrocities and using as a pretext that the inhabitants had mistreated their rearguard during their earlier evacuation and that they had greeted the returning French army with excessive joy.

The following day, the Allies resumed their advance. Wittgenstein marched his corps down the old road to Paris, while Wrede advanced on the new. The Crown Prince of Württemberg and Count Giulay marched on Sens.

Macdonald arrived in Nogent during the morning of 5 March and deployed his troops around the city and along the road to Troyes. Pacthod was detached to Bray with one of his brigades and the XI Corps supported his movement. The ambulances and parks moved on Provins.

Macdonald fully expected to be attacked the following day and spent the night preparing his position. However, during the morning of 6 March the Allies did not appear. He resolved to put the Seine between him and the Allies and to establish his line of defense on the right bank of the Seine. To this end, he moved the bulk of his infantry to Mériot and Plessis-Mériot. Gérard's corps and the cavalry of Saint-Germain formed the rearguard – occupying the Nogent suburbs on the right bank – while the bridge was destroyed. General Pacthod left his second brigade in Bray and detached his 3rd Brigade to escort the parks to Nangis.

The retreat of General Allix on Auxerre

The retreat of the army from the Aube to Troyes obliged General Allix to withdraw on Auxerre down the road from Châtillon. The light division of Prince Maurice von Liechtenstein followed his withdrawal.

The French general hoped to have time to organize the contingent of the levée en masse from the Departments of the Yonne, Aube and Seine-et-Marne, which resulted from the Imperial Decree of 26 February. These efforts, however, were greatly diminished by the Cossacks who roamed the territory between the Seine, Armançon and the Yonne. During the night of 6-7 March alarms were sounded in many places. When sounded, the population of the Yonne moved on the Sens, but this levée – whose formation would have been a great assistance to Macdonald – were unable to organize properly. The cadres of six line battalions which they were to receive had not been sent by

23 Koch, Vol. I, pp. 31-3.

the Minister of War. On the other hand, Prince M. von Liechtenstein had already passed through Noyers, Prince Eugene von Württemberg stood before Sens and the Seslavin Cossacks were spread along both banks of the Bourgogne Canal. General Allix was obliged to withdraw on Auxerre with 2,000 regular infantry and 300 regular cavalry, while dispersing 3,000 to 4,000 French citizens that had been gathered at Sens in response to the call to arms.

Prince Eugene von Württemberg was able to take Sens without a fight and its citizens acted in as conciliatory a manner as possible – hoping to avoid the treatment received by the citizens of Troyes.

At the same time as Sens fell, Macdonald was making his preparations for the defense of the Seine. His movements had been sufficient to break contact with the Allies and Schwarzenberg was obliged to order a reconnaissance.

When the new French position was clear, Schwarzenberg ordered Wittgenstein to attack the French position frontally, while Wrede turned the right flank near Mâcon and sought to move on Nogent. This maneuver began with little difficulty – the only post encountered being one on an island that resisted with heavy musketry the advance of Pahlen's cavalry as Nogent fell. The Cossacks also exchanged carbine shots with the garrison at Bray. Wrede's advanced guard moved into Grisy.

Schwarzenberg believed that the lines of communication with the Army of Silesia had been broken and remained watching the French from his side of the Seine – allowing the French to rest their army.

While sojourning in Troyes, Schwarzenberg learned of and responded to Napoleon's decrees from Fismes. His response was that: "the Allies had never sought to conquer France, but sought only to make a peace with conditions that would assure both France and Europe a durable peace. However, all that resist our arms expose themselves to inevitable destruction." This proclamation, however, was restricted in its circulation to the few French provinces held by the Allies and did little more than irritate the French citizens who already suffered the presence of the invading Allied armies.

It was around this time that the Allied 4th Corps reorganized itself to account for the losses suffered at Montereau. The 3rd, 4th and 5th Land Regiments were disbanded and their troops absorbed into the line regiments.[24] The Württemberg portion of the corps was organized as follows:

1st Division: Generalleutnant von Koch
1st Infantry Brigade: Generalmajor Prince von Hohenlohe
    2nd Infantry Regiment "Herzog Wilhelm" (2)
    3rd Infantry Regiment (2)
    1st Foot Battery, Major von Ehrenfeld (four to six pdrs & two how)
2nd Infantry Brigade: Generalmajor von Misani
    4th Infantry Regiment (2)
    5th Infantry Regiment "Prinz Friedrich" (2)
    2nd Foot Battery, Cpt. von Diskau (four to six pdrs & two how)
3rd Infantry Brigade: Generalmajor von Lalance
    6th Infantry Regiment "Kronprinz" (2)
    Landregiment #6 Heilbronn (1)

24 Rössler, p. 433.

2nd Division: Generalleutnant Döring
4th Infantry Brigade: Generalmajor von Stockmayer
- 9th Jäger Regiment "König" (1)
- 10th Light Regiment (2)
- 7th Infantry Regiment (2)
- Austrian Pioneer Company (Cpt. Wonjatschek) (1 co)

New Allied plans

Discussions in the Allied headquarters concentrated on the proposal that they move with all of their forces on the Marne via Arcis, Sézanne and Montmirail – or via La Ferté-Gaucher to Château-Thierry – where they could cross the Marne and move against Napoleon's line of retreat (as well as re-establish contact with the Army of Silesia). Some voices argued that it was preferable to avoid a major battle and that they should destroy the bridges across the Marne and await the results of Blücher's engagement with Napoleon before linking with the Army of Silesia and moving directly on Paris in concert with the Army of Silesia.

This second proposal recognized that the movement on the Marne had little risk, as Augereau was sufficiently occupied by the 50,000-man-strong Army of the South. However, if Augereau were to march so as to threaten the main army, it was possible to leave the corps of the Crown Prince of Württemberg and Giulay along the Aube and Seine. These two corps, 60,000-men-strong, could move towards Dijon and punish such temerity.

A third group – recognizing the tremendous numerical superiority that the main army had over Macdonald – argued that they should march directly on their goal, force the Seine at Nogent and move on Paris via the right bank of the Seine.

Unfortunately for Schwarzenberg, he could not act only on the military dictates of the situation. There were divergences in the political goals of Austria and the other Allied nations, which had to be considered. As a result, Schwarzenberg decided to remain in Troyes a few days and rest the army.

The arrival of Tettenborn

Tettenborn, commanding a brigade of light cavalry in the Army of the North, had been detached immediately after the conclusion of peace with the Danes and moved from Schleswig on the Rhine. He crossed the Rhine at Cologne in mid-February and was ordered to operate so that he could maintain communications between the Army of the North and the Army of Silesia. His march took him through Trèves and Luxemburg to Montmédy, which he invested with part of his troops, while the rest rebuilt the Stenay bridge. He crossed the Meuse on 23 February – marching on Rheims through Grandpré. Three free companies of French volunteers engaged him in the Argonne forest and delayed his movement until he was forced to engage his entire force to destroy them.

Arriving on the Champagne plains in the first days of March, by 9 March he was in contact with both Blücher and Schwarzenberg – advising Schwarzenberg of Napoleon's probable movement on the Aube. This news provoked Schwarzenberg to fear an attack on his rear and he resolved to concentrate his forces between the Seine and the Aube. As a result, he ordered Wittgenstein to push forward a reconnaissance and to build a bridge at Pont-sur-Seine to attract Macdonald's attention. He directed the remaining corps commanders to leave their advanced troops and to shift to the right, towards Arcis.

Otherwise, the main army remained relatively inactive because of the lack of information on the Army of Silesia and of the Center. The Army of Silesia – after its junction with the corps of Bülow,

Winzingerode and Stroganov – had a tremendous numerical superiority and was in a good position. The Army of the South had received all of its reinforcements and seized Mâcon. Everything was such that a vigorous offensive was possible, but Schwarzenberg constantly feared exceeding the wishes of his sovereign and instead of assuming the offensive, chose to study a series of hypothetical plans of defense.[25]

French reconnaissance

While Schwarzenberg fought with his fears, Macdonald repaired his artillery equipment, rested his cavalry and directed the preparation of his dispositions. On 13 March Wittgenstein built his bridge at Pont-sur-Seine and Wrede's advanced guard concentrated and cannonaded Bray. Macdonald responded by ordering Oudinot to concentrate the VII Corps between the Nogent and Bray roads. Kellermann was ordered to move before Rouilly and Cucharmois in order to cover Provins and Nangis. Milhaud was ordered to send a division to Herm to watch the Seine as far as Bray, while the two others were sent to Echelles to scout the roads to Sézanne and Villenoxe.

Skirmish at Sézanne

The following day – 14 March – Macdonald ordered yet another reconnaissance on Sézanne and Villenoxe. The first was led by General Trelliard and contained 2,400 cavalry from the corps of Kellermann and Milhaud supported by a brigade from Leval's division. It moved via Monceaux and Tourneloup on Sézanne – chasing Kaisarov's Cossacks before them. However, Trelliard's movements drew various Allied detachments towards him and as the French reconnaissance forces moved through Villenoxe and Barbonne, they pushed the French cavalry through the Esternay defile with some losses.[26]

General Saint-Germain commanded the second reconnaissance and led his cuirassiers forward. He encountered Raevsky's advanced guard, commanded by Rüdinger. This force consisted of 12 hussar squadrons, eight cuirassier squadrons and two pulks of Cossacks. The French overwhelmed and drove the Allied cavalry back.

Skirmish by Villenoxe – 14 March

As the French engaged Kaisarov's Cossacks by Sézanne, Count Pahlen sent Lissanovich's brigade towards Nogent with the advanced guard of the 6th Corps to Pont-sur-Seine. The Russian cavalry crossed over the bridge, but the Württembergers remained on the right bank.

At around 4:00 p.m. Count Pahlen moved through Villenoxe and Plessis-Mériot – encountering French infantry in the outskirts of Nogent. French cuirassiers from Saint-Germain's II Cavalry Corps suddenly appeared and chased Pahlen's cavalry back to Villenoxe. They stopped their flight, however, when they encountered Prince Eugene's infantry. The cuirassiers withdrew and Count Pahlen organized a force to pursue them in turn. This force consisted of the Vlassov and Rebrikov Cossack Regiments and the Grodno, Soumy and Loubno Hussar Regiments – with two hussar squadrons leading the pursuit – followed by Stahl's cuirassier brigade.[27]

The Russians moved towards Provins – stopping on the heights by Chalantré-le-Grande and Saint-Martin. The French posts stood on that side of Léchelle. General Illowaiski XII advanced

25 Koch, Vol. II, pp. 31-44.
26 von Damitz, Vol. III, 1st Part, p. 283.
27 Sporschil, Vol. II, 1st Band, p. 497.

with his two Cossack pulks – the Olviopol Hussar Regiment – supported by Leontiev's cuirassier brigade. He advanced to Haussaie, cut off two companies of French tirailleurs and took them prisoner.

This Allied movement alarmed the French and GD Gérard advanced the French II Corps through Mériot and Le Port – placing a division on the Saint-Nicolas heights in front of the road from Nogent to Provins. Bélair's brigade was then directed to attack the Russians in the village immediately to their front. The village was quickly cleared and Bélair moved a battery to the flank of the enemy column – forcing them with its fire to withdraw on Saint-Féréol. However, Saint-Germain's cuirassiers made no effort to engage or delay the Allied withdrawal.

Prince Eugene von Württemberg moved his corps to the heights behind Saint-Féréol and Mont-les-Potiers – extending to his left towards Mériot in an effort to link up with the forces in Nogent and Provins. The 1st Russian Corps – under Prince Gorchakov – had crossed the Seine and took up positions by the Courtavant Canal near Villenoxe.[28]

The main Allied army moves on Arcis

While the Allied advanced guard cavalry repulsed Macdonald's reconnaissance forces, Schwarzenberg had no serious intention of marching on Paris, but wished to draw Napoleon towards him as he moved on Arcis. During the night, one of Blücher's aides arrived with news of Blücher's victory at Laon. Schwarzenberg's distress and irresolution dissipated and he once again began to consider a more direct action on Paris. He resolved to concentrate on Arcis and accept battle if Napoleon offered it.

On his side, Macdonald still anticipated an attack and made all of the necessary dispositions. Bray was evacuated and its bridge destroyed. Macdonald concentrated his infantry below Provins and his cavalry in Echelles. Pacthod was authorized to withdraw from Montereau to Melun or Brie-Comte-Robert in case he was attacked by superior forces. Allix, already redeployed on Nemours, was authorized to withdraw through Moret or Fontainebleau – as he judged best – in order to maintain himself on the left bank of the Loing.

The general park of the Grande Armée and that of Macdonald's forces were evacuated from Guignes and moved on Charenton. However, these prudent measures proved pointless as Schwarzenberg had abandoned his pursuit of Macdonald and concentrated his efforts in deploying his forces before Napoleon's assumed line of march.

The engagement at Cormeron – 16 March

On 16 March – after Schwarzenberg had sufficient time to complete his concentration and his movement behind the Aube – he judged it time to push Macdonald back in order to gain access to the region where he wished to place his left wing. He ordered Wrede to establish a camp between Villenoxe and Chalantré, to occupy the Traconne forest and to push parties on Sézanne. Raevsky was ordered to advance on Provins and to occupy the Sordun forest. The Crown Prince of Württemberg was ordered to erect a bridge at Nogent as soon as the defile was abandoned by the French (and to push his advanced guard to Bray to relieve Hardegg's division), to seize the passage and to occupy the Mériot heights. The Bavarians were divided into two columns and presented the heads of their columns before Villegruie and Villenoxe by noon. Raevsky received orders at 6:00 a.m. to attack the French with Schachovsky's 3rd Division organized in three columns – the first of which was to move against Saint-Martin-de-Chennetron, the second via Saint-Féréol and

28 von Damitz, Vol. III, 1st Part, pp. 284-6.

the third via Pouchères. The Württembergers were charged with making demonstrations that would assist Raevsky's attacks.

Raevsky, by G. Dawe.

Pahlen stood with the advanced guard before Saint-Martin-de-Chennetron. Prince Eugene von Württemberg, with the bulk of the II Infantry Corps, stood behind Saint-Martin-de-Chennetron. Schachovsky's 3rd Division stood on the Chalantré-le-Grande heights. Gorchakov and the I Infantry Corps stood on the Mont-le-Potier heights. The French, consisting of Duhèsme and Leval's infantry divisions and Milhaud's cavalry – some 8,000 men – were deployed before them on the plain between Lugrand and Luboin. The French left was in a small wood by l'Echelle and Cormeron. On the right, they occupied the Sordun woods.[29]

In executing his orders, Prince Eugene von Württemberg marched with his 2nd Corps, Leontiev's cuirassier brigade, the Tchougouiev Uhlan Regiment and the Rebrikov Cossacks against Leval's division bivouaced on the plains behind Echelles; while Prince Schachovsky's (Russian 3rd Division, 2nd Corps) marched against Leval's division (French II Corps) located in the Sordun forest.

At around 8:00 a.m. Prince Eugene attempted to turn the Houssaye park with the Tchougouiev Uhlans and the Rebrikov Cossacks. This Russian cavalry passed in front of Milhaud's cavalry, which passed up the chance to attack it in the flank. Eugene sent his infantry – supported by Leontiev's cuirassier brigade (Gluchov and Pskov Cuirassier Regiments) – and moved between the woods and the village of Echelles, which it occupied. The village of Cormeron was occupied by French skirmishers. At around 6:00 a.m. the French skirmishers were pushed out of Cormeron and Leval pushed forward Maulmond's brigade to support them.

Leval prepared his attack in echelons – the 130th Line Regiment supported by the 3rd Line Regiment – while the skirmishers deployed to dispute the passage of the Richebourg ravine. The village was retaken and the 130th Line remained in it for an hour – protected by the musketry of the 3rd Line Regiment, which deployed behind the ravine.

Prince Eugene von Württemberg reorganized his attack and launched a second attack at 7:00 a.m. The 130th Line Regiment expended its ammunition and was obliged to withdraw until supported by the 6/10th Légère, placed to the left of a grove of trees. The fire of the 6/10th Légère and canister fire from a battery of six French guns stopped the Russian pursuit.

During the course of his attacks, Eugene had bombarded the French infantry in Lunay with his artillery. This continued as he awaited the arrival of the 2nd Corps artillery – supported by an infantry brigade and the 3rd Cuirassier Division – to reengage the French center.[30]

As Eugene was engaged, Schachovsky's 3rd Division – supported by the Grodno Hussars and Stahl's cuirassier brigade – attacked the Sordun forest, but was vigorously repulsed by the French. Heavy musketry – supported by the fire of 20 cannon – was more than the Russians could take.

When these attacks failed, Eugene pushed a force of infantry through the woods to strike at the French left. This maneuver succeeded. The Krementsoug Infantry Regiment pushed the French skirmishers out of the woods; then pushed into a small village and captured nearly an

29 Sporschil, Vol. II, 1st Band, p. 510.
30 Fabry, p. 175.

entire battalion of the French 130th Infantry Regiment. The French did not await the arrival of the rest of the Russians and withdrew.

Engagement at Nogent – 15 March

Leval had engaged only Maulmond's brigade and formed the brigades of Montfort and Chassé on his left. Eugene von Württemberg, however, was not receiving the ordered support from Wrede's Bavarians because the difficult roads had delayed their advance. On the Allied extreme left, the Crown Prince of Württemberg – in making his ordered diversion – prepared to throw a force across the Seine below Nogent.

The advanced guard of Raevsky's corps sealed off part of the Nogent suburbs and the Crown Prince of Württemberg organized a large battery on the right bank of the Seine, which began to bombard the French positions. He then ordered Misani's Württemberg brigade to advance across the Seine and clear out the French. Two companies of the 4th Württemberg Infantry Regiment were sent over on pontoons and the remainder of the attacking force quickly followed. Three companies of the 4th Infantry Regiment pushed into the houses of the suburbs and down the streets towards the broken bridge. The attack of the 4th Infantry Regiment was supported by the von Ehrenfeld Foot Battery and a company of the 5th Infantry Regiment. They made steady progress against Materre's brigade of French infantry – eventually pushing him back over the Seine. The Allied losses were 10 dead and 94 wounded.[31] The French left about 100 dead and wounded behind them.

Despite his successes so far, Macdonald was threatened on the left and was unable to cover his right. He ordered GD Gérard to abandon Nogent immediately and withdraw on Provins. The Crown Prince of Württemberg took advantage of Gérard's withdrawal to begin erecting a bridge, while Schachovsky – finding no one before him – pushed into the Sordun forest and sent his Cossacks into the village of Sordun.

During the night, the Allies occupied the following positions: The Crown Prince of Württemberg was in Nogent, Raevsky was in Mont-le-Potier, the Bavarians were in Plancy and Villenoxe, Barclay de Tolly was in Arcis-sur-Aube and Count Giulay was recalled from Sens to Troyes.[32]

The French evacuate Provins

The Allied positions threatened the front and flanks of Macdonald's forces. Having no direct communications with Napoleon and ignorant of his movement on the Aube, Macdonald was obliged to assume that the main Allied army was still before him and feared that remaining in Provins would subject him to an overwhelming attack. On 17 March he decided to evacuate and began his movement between 2:00 and 3:00 a.m. – moving to a position on the Maison-Rouge heights with his right on Donnemarie and his left on Cucharmois – with his cavalry united at Rouilly to prevent being flanked during his retreat. Gérard formed the extreme rearguard and bivouaced behind Provins in order to contain any enemy advance – be it via the upper city or down the main road. His position on the open plain offered little opportunity to resist a superior enemy with numerous cavalry. Fortunately for Gérard, Napoleon was marching to the field, while Schwarzenberg had accomplished his goal of establishing a position for his left with his minimal efforts and had no intention of engaging Macdonald.

31 Sporschil, Vol. II, 1st Band, pp. 499-500; Rössler, pp. 434-5.

32 Koch, Vol. II, pp. 44-50.

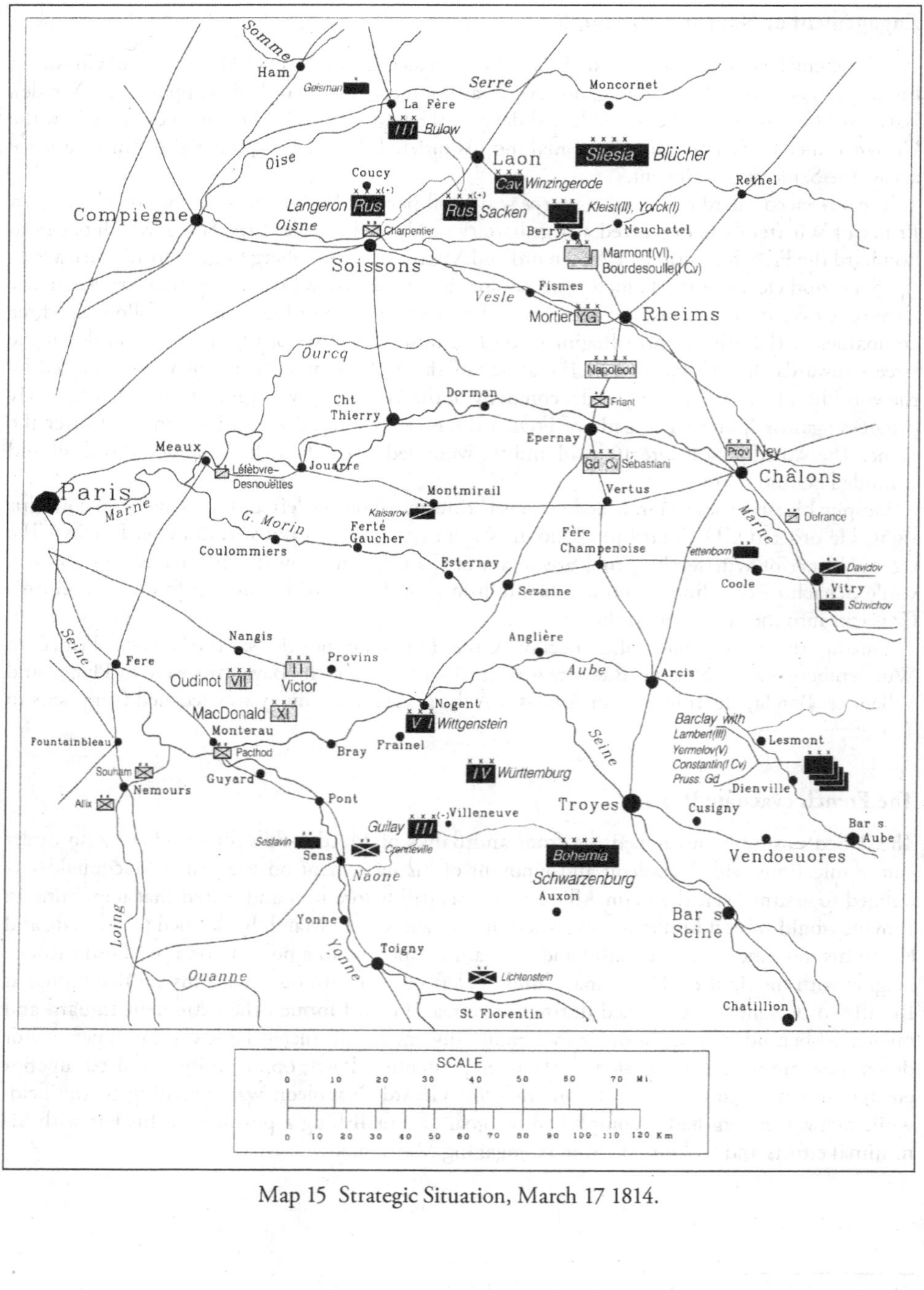

Map 15 Strategic Situation, March 17 1814.

The Grande Armée moves on Arcis

The French army prepared to receive an attack which never came. Schwarzenberg sent orders to the Crown Prince of Württemberg, Raevsky and Kaisarov which cancelled earlier orders because of Napoleon's march on the Aube. Informed that Blücher had not yet begun his pursuit, he believed it was appropriate to take an offensive attitude on the right bank of the Seine – and in case Napoleon moved against his right flank, to remount the Marne. Schwarzenberg thought to execute a concentration on the Trannes, which brought to mind his victory at La Rothière and caused him to hope for renewed success. As a result he directed Raevsky to not occupy his position until after nightfall, to leave Pahlen in Saint-Martin-de-Chennetron and to hold Prince Eugene von Württemberg in Méry, Pont, Nogent and the Sordun forest. The Crown Prince of Württemberg was ordered to withdraw to Grez – with the exception of a single brigade, which continued to hold Nogent. He directed the Bavarians to move from Villenoxe towards Arcis-sur-Aube and to take up a position on the left bank. Count Giulay was arriving in Troyes. Barclay de Tolly concentrated the Russian Guard and reserves in Brienne, and Prince Maurice von Liechtenstein was to remain in Joigny with Seslavin in Pont-sur-Yonne. Before the front of the main army, Tettenborn stood in Cosel. General Davidov – recently arrived from the Rhine – occupied Vitry with the Moscow Dragoons, two infantry regiments and a battery, while Kaisarov held Plancy with his Cossacks.

With his forces so deployed, Schwarzenberg could think of nothing better to do than to take Châlons in order to attempt to reopen communications with the Army of Silesia. GL Lambert pulled together a force for this enterprise by drawing part of the garrison of Vitry and attaching it to the corps of Davidov and Tettenborn. However, they launched their enterprise too late. Napoleon was already there and this Allied force encountered the Imperial Guard cavalry, which thrashed it soundly and sent it scurrying home.

During the morning of 18 March Macdonald was surprised by the simultaneous disappearance of all of the Allied forces before him and realized that it was probably the result of an offensive movement by the Imperial army. He directed that several reconnaissance forces be dispatched in an attempt to contact Napoleon – as well as to determine what the Allies were about.

Macdonald had done a credible job. He had held off an army of 100,000 with a force of 25,000 and defended his Emperor's capitol.[33]

33 Koch, Vol. II, pp. 51-4.

13

Napoleon's March on the Aube: The Skirmishes at La Fère-Champenoise, Plancy and Méry

The Battle at Arcis-sur-Aube – 19-23 March

The sojourn of the Grande Armée in Rheims was indispensable or rebuilding it. A detachment of 3,600 new men were absorbed into the army, which General Janssens had drawn from the various strongholds in the 2nd Military Division.

Janssens' successful march through enemy-held territory caused Napoleon to realize that he could reinforce himself from his garrisons caught behind enemy lines on the Moselle River. Ney had opened the way to Châlons via Sainte-Ménéhould – and with that, communications with General Duvigneau, who commanded the Argonne. Messages were sent to his subordinate, General Cassagne – govenor of Verdun – to send strong detachments against the Allies' rear and attempt to disrupt the movement of their baggage from Nancy. In Metz, Count Durutte was ordered to send 10,000 to 12,000 men from the fortifications of the 3rd Military Division to join the Grande Armée in Châlons.

Napoleon decided that the public spirit in the Moselle, Meurthe and Vosge Departments was such that a call to arms to raise an insurrection against the Allies would be successful – and directed Ney to instigate it. Convinced that proclamations had less effect than examples, Ney demanded a carte-blanche and proposed to send a partisan force of 500 to 600 cavalry into the Vosges to gather up the major portion of the garrisons in that region and to throw them against the Allied supply lines. However, Napoleon was unwilling to permit him to strip the various fortresses and did not wish to deprive himself of Ney's services, so the proposal was rejected.

Soissons, Rheims and Châlons were occupied by the French. The Army of Silesia had been forced away from its original line of operations and Schwarzenberg vainly moved his forces to the Marne to attempt to re-establish contact with Blücher. Unfortunately for Schwarzenberg, his lack of communications with Blücher was less dangerous than his attempt to re-establish those communications. Wittgenstein's corps – which had crossed the Seine at Pont – was well-covered by the Cossacks that Platov had posted in Sézanne, La Fère-Champenoise and Vertus, and the weak detachment of Tettenborn's in Epernay. However, the countryside between the Marne and Aisne remained in the hands of the French, and this movement succeeded only in stretching his front even further – with his right in Epernay and his left in Sens.

The opportunities of this disposition did not escape Napoleon, who resolved to take advantage of it. He decided to execute a maneuver on the Allied rear and, using a few forced marches, put himself in a situation parallel to that which he had found at Mormant, Villeneuve and Montereau.

The organization of the Aisne defense

Before moving away from the Aisne, Napoleon had to establish a defensive line to protect the region. The three divisions of Guard infantry, Roussel's cavalry division and the brigade of converged cavalry squadrons would not give Mortier the strength to fight the Army of Silesia or to observe it. Napoleon decided to detach Mortier's corps, Oudinot with the VI Corps and the I Cavalry Corps, 13,000 infantry and 5,000 cavalry – with a train of 60 guns – and assign them the task of protecting the Aisne line. Belliard – one of Napoleon's aides – strongly encouraged Napoleon to name a commander-in-chief for these operations, but Napoleon refused – again stating that the success of these operations would rest on the harmonious cooperation of the two marshals. The cavalry, which should have been given orders by Belliard, was to receive orders from whichever of the marshals to which they were attached. Otherwise, Napoleon gave no orders to the two marshals other than to watch Blücher, to prevent him from moving to join Schwarzenberg, and to cover Paris.

Napoleon retained the three infantry divisions of Friant, Boyer and Janssens; the cavalry divisions of Excelmans, Colbert, Letort, Defrance and Berckheim; 10,000 infantry; and about 6,000 cavalry. In addition, he awaited the arrival of 4,500 Guard infantry and 1,500 Guard cavalry, which Lefebvre-Desnoëttes had dispatched on 16 March from Paris. He could also hope to be joined by Macdonald's forces when he arrived – that being another 22,000 infantry and 9,000 cavalry. The juncture of these forces would give him an army of 55,000 men – including 17,000 cavalry – which should have been enough to deal with Schwarzenberg's estimated 79,000 men.

Mortier's forces:[1]
- Christiani's division – 2,100 infantry
- Curial's division – 2,800 infantry
- Charpentier's division – 2,800 infantry
- Belliard's cavalry
- Roussel's division – 1,750 cavalry
- Grouvel's brigade – 350 cavalry

Oudinot's forces:
- Ricard's division – 1,000 infantry
- Arrighi's division – 2,100 infantry
- Lagrange's division – 2,100 infantry
- Bordesoulle's detachment
- Merlin's division – 1,150 cavalry
- Bordesoulle's division – 1,250 cavalry

Napoleon began his march on 17 March – with all of the Guard troops – and marched on Epernay. Janssens' division marched on Châlons. Ney moved from Châlons – dispatching Defrance to pursue Davidov's cavalry down the road to Vitry. Defrance was then recalled and sent via Mailly on Vitry – ready to follow Ney's infantry. General Duvigneau was ordered to replace the Châlons garrison with forces drawn from Verdun.

The following day, the right column – consisting of all of the Guard troops – marched on La Fère-Champenoise, where it stopped. Sébastiani chased Kaisarov's Cossacks from the city and pursued them with a "sword in their back" for a distance of nine miles (15 kilometers). He then

1 Vaudoncourt, Vol. II, p. 210.

took up positions in Gourganson, Semoine and Herbisse. The left column occupied Sommesous, which had been abandoned by Wrede's Austro-Bavarian 5th Corps.[2]

The skirmish at La Fère-Champenoise – 18 March

On 18 March Kaisarov – leading 1,500 Cossacks and six guns – encountered 5,000 cavalry, under Sébastiani, near La Fère-Champenoise. Kaisarov's first message to Schwarzenberg – sent at 11:00 a.m. – spoke of being attacked by an overwhelming force, and said that if "not supported" and forced to withdraw, he would move on Arcis. A second message sent a half-hour later stated that Napoleon was with the French cavalry and that he would be in Epernay that night. In addition, Kaisarov reported being attacked by the ubiquitous "Guard."[3] He was driven back towards the Plancy bridge, where he took up new positions.

La Fère-Champenoise.

Schwarzenberg's fear of Napoleon had caused him to expedite orders for a concentration of his forces on Arcis. However, fate intervened and prevented this concentration from happening as he wished. Raevsky was obliged to wait for the Crown Prince of Württemberg to relieve him and could not move to Charny, but stopped in Méry, which resulted in a hole opening in the Allied lines. Schwarzenberg thought that Wrede was acting under his own recognisances and ordered him to re-cross the Aube between Coclois and Arcis to occupy the city of Arcis with Hardegg and Spleny's divisions – and to order them to hold the city to the last extremity. They were to move to Vaupoisson, or on Rechberg's Bavarian division, in case they were forced to abandon the city. Kaisarov – with 1,200 cavalry and six guns – was charged with linking the Bavarian corps with Raevsky's corps, but few of these orders were executed. Schwarzenberg faced the morning with the prospect of dealing with Macdonald – as well as Napoleon – on the right bank of the Marne, with his isolated detachments stretching from Meaux to Châlons. Reacting to this situation, Schwarzenberg directed the Bavarians to defend the Aube as soon as they crossed it. They were to echelon themselves to Pougy.

On 20 March – after leaving a simple rearguard in Lesmont and Ronay – he withdrew on Brienne. The Württembergers and the corps of Giulay and Raevsky were ordered to move on 19

2 Koch, Vol. II, pp. 55-60.
3 von Damitz, Vol. III, 1st Part, p. 337.

March to Troyes, and the following day to Vandoeuvres – leaving General Seslavin to guard the roads from Nogent and Bray during the 19th. Count Barclay de Tolly was to move to Trannes on 20 March.

Napoleon was convinced that the Allies were withdrawing in disorder on Troyes, and on 19 March directed Sébastiani to pursue them, to cross the Aube at Plancy and to not abandon the pursuit. Ney was ordered to move on Arcis.

The skirmish at Plancy – 19 March

On 19 March Sébastiani again encountered Kaisarov's 1,200 Cossacks. Von Damitz indicates that on 18 March Kaisarov had 1,500 troops and Sporschil indicates that on the 19th he had only 1,200. He apparently lost about 300 men the previous day to all causes.[4]

This time, on the Coursemain heights, he gave them a lesson in cavalry tactics – in addition to taking the Plancy bridge. Sébastiani placed 12 guns so as to fire on the six Russian guns on the left bank of the Aube. His Cossacks were outmatched and outnumbered by the French, so Kaisarov pulled his squadrons back under the protection of his battery. This was not sufficient, and the French occupied the position and took possession of the bridge.[5]

Though broken, the bridge was re-established with the assistance of the city's inhabitants – despite the cannon fire directed at the effort. The French infantry arrived shortly afterwards and began crossing the second arm of the Aube at the Charny bridge under the protection of a battalion thrown into the village of Charny. Once they passed over the river, the cavalry was formed into two columns. A column, formed with the divisions of Excelmans and Colbert – and led by Sébastiani – set out in pursuit of the Cossacks, who had occupied and burned Pouan. At 5:00 p.m. Friant's 1st Old Guard Division began moving over the bridge. Napoleon, at the head of Letort's division and his service squadrons, moved down the road to Méry.

With the French in pursuit, Kaisarov withdrew to Pouan and established himself behind the creek – deploying his guns. The Cossacks burned the village to cover their withdrawal. The French pursuit ended with nightfall and Sébastiani was obliged to spend the night in Bessy – awaiting the passage of the French artillery over the marshy Barbuisse stream.

When Wrede learned of the engagement at Plancy, he ordered Baron Frimont to dispatch a mixed force of infantry and cavalry help to Kaisarov. The Knesevich Dragoons and Schwarzenberg Uhlans were sent via Villette – about an hour's march from Pouan – where they deployed with their right on the Aube. The Erzherzog Joseph and Szeckler Hussars deployed to the left of the road. Two battalions of the 1st Szeckler Grenz Regiment occupied Arcis and the Austrian 3rd Jäger Battalion occupied Grand-Torcy and Petit-Torcy. Volkman's infantry brigade stood in reserve behind the cavalry. The Bavarian troops also changed their front. By nightfall, Frimont had withdrawn the Knesevich Dragoons and the Schwarzenberg Uhlans to the left of Saint-Remy-sous-Barbuisse. Kaisarov's Cossacks stood to the left of the cavalry between Remy and Voué. The two hussar regiments put advanced posts by Villette and Erzherzog Joseph pushed elements into Pouan. The 5th Corps spent the night deployed in this manner.[6]

4 Sporschil, Vol. II, p. 535.
5 von Damitz, Vol. III, 1st Part, p. 350.
6 Sporschil, Vol. II, pp. 545-6.

The skirmish at Méry – 20 March

By the time the advanced guard of Napoleon's column arrived at Méry, Raevsky's corps had already evacuated it and moved to Troyes along with Giulay's corps. The Crown Prince of Württemberg had sent his rearguard to occupy the village – ordering it to watch the roads to Arcis and Plancy in an effort to ensure that the French would not move against his flank. Upon seeing the Guard cavalry before their position, the Württemberg rearguard withdrew to the left bank, burnt the bridge and began firing their muskets on the French. Without wasting time responding to their fire, Napoleon ordered Letort to take the service squadrons across the ford below Méry. This bold maneuver caused the Württembergers to evacuate, and would have been a complete success two hours earlier when it would have caught the corps in march column down the new road to Troyes. Despite his diligence, General Letort was unable to do much when he arrived in Châtres other than take a pontoon train with 13 pontoons. He established his division in Grez.

Napoleon returned with his service squadrons from Méry to Plancy, where he spent the night. The Guard infantry spent the night on both banks of the Aube. Ney's march was without incident – no Allied troops being encountered – and he took up position with his infantry in two lines behind the Riverelle farm and his cavalry in Viaspre.

Macdonald departed his positions in Provins – assured by reconnaissance of the previous day that the Allies had withdrawn. At daybreak, he reunited all of his cavalry and moved down the right bank of the Seine – throwing out strong parties towards La Ferté-Gaucher and Sézanne in an effort to obtain news. His infantry was echeloned between Villenoxe to Provins.

Schwarzenberg's irresolution

While the French army maneuvered, the various detached corps of the main Allied army floundered with little direction. Lambert feared encountering the French columns and withdrew to Vitry with Davidov's corps. Tettenborn, who had advanced from Cosel towards Isson the previous day, moved to the right bank of the Marne – hoping to surprise Châlons or to establish communications with the Army of Silesia. Schwarzenberg was disconcerted by Napoleon's rapid movements and did not know where to act. He repeated his intention to concentrate and give battle, but his dispositions and the orders given to the three army corps to concentrate at Vandoeuvres the next day did not indicate he wished to dispute Napoleon's passage of the Aube.

Schwarzenberg's irresolution redoubled Napoleon's confidence – and he was certain that Macdonald would join him the next day. He believed that the Allies were withdrawing in disorder and resolved to give them no respite, so on the morning of 20 March he ordered Sébastiani to move against Arcis.

Sébastiani desperately tried to convince Napoleon that Schwarzenberg had stopped the retreat of the corps of the Crown Prince of Württemberg, Giulay and Raevsky and that they were marching from Troyes to Charmont. Napoleon gave no credence to this report and reiterated his order to move on Arcis. At 10:00 a.m. the Guard cavalry and Ney's infantry arrived. The bridge was reconstructed and the post abandoned by the now-evacuated Bavarian guard were reoccupied, but by French soldiers. The local inhabitants repeatedly advised the French that most of Schwarzenberg's army was no more than 12 miles (20 kilometers) away. Ney and Sébastiani sent word to Napoleon, but continued the implementation of his orders.

Janssens' division was placed astride the road to Lesmont – supported on the left by Grand-Torcy and having P. Boyer's brigade in reserve. Sébastiani organized two divisions astride the road to Troyes – pushing out a reconnaissance force to warn of an Allied advance.

At the same time, Napoleon began his march on Plancy – recalling his cavalry which had crossed to the left bank of the Seine the previous day. Unfortunately, Letort misunderstood the order and returned only with the dragoons – leaving the Guard Grenadiers à cheval and Guard Chasseurs à cheval in their bivouacs. The infantry moved down the length of the right bank of the Aube. Napoleon stopped in Arcis around 1:00 p.m., and called Ney and Sébastiani to him for a conference. He continued to doubt that Schwarzenberg intended to oppose him and sent an ordnance captain to the advanced posts with orders to observe the enemy's movement. This young officer reported seeing nothing but about 1,000 Cossacks, which convinced Napoleon of his security. Though Sébastiani doubted the validity of this reconnaissance, he returned to his post without saying a word. Upon arriving at his posts, however, he immediately sent word back to Napoleon that the Allies had formed attack columns and were marching on Arcis.

French army – 20 March 1814
Ney's command:
  Friant & Henrion's Guard divisions – 8,000 infantry
  Janssens & P. Boyer's divisions – 5,500 infantry
Sébastiani's command:
  Excelmans, Colbert, Letort, Defrance
  Berckheim & Lefebvre-Desnoëttes – 7,300 cavalry
Oudinot's command:
  Saint-Germain & Maurin – 2,500 cavalry
  VII Corps – Leval – 6,500 infantry
Total: 29,800

Allied army – 20 March 1814
Giulay's corps:
  Crenneville, Fresnel & Nostitz – 10,800 infantry, 3,200 cavalry
von Württemberg's corps:
  Prince Adam, Franquemont & Duca – 10,200 infantry, 3,600 cavalry
Wrede's corps:
  Hardegg, Spleny, Rechberg,
  Lamotte & Czoglokov – 22,100 infantry, 4,800 cavalry
Raevsky's corps:
  Prince Eugene, Gorchakov & Pahlen – 16,500 infantry, 3,500 cavalry
Reserve:
  Austrian Grenadiers, Paskevich's grenadiers & Kretov's cuirassiers – 3,000 infantry, 1,600 cavalry
  Russian & Prussian Guard – 15,800 infantry, 4,800 cavalry
  Cossack Corps
  Kaisarov & Seslavin – 3,000 cavalry
Total: 83,400 infantry – 24,500 cavalry[7, 8]

The Allied attack on Arcis-sur-Aube – 20 March

The entire Allied army was on the march. Schwarzenberg had been informed during the morning that Napoleon had only moved his cavalry to the left bank of the Aube – concluding that Napoleon wished to move to Troyes via Méry and Plancy. This settled Schwarzenberg's

7 Vaudoncourt, Vol. II, p. 227.
8 von Damitz, K., Vol. III, 1st Part, pp. 398-9.

irresolution and he decided to march forward. He directed the Crown Prince of Württemberg, Giulay and Raevsky to take their corps towards Plancy and to strike the French as soon as they found them. Meanwhile, Wrede was to create a diversion by attacking Arcis and the Allied Guards and reserves were to unite in Onjon.

The Crown Prince of Württemberg marched in two columns. The first consisted of his Württembergers and Giulay's Austrians. This column marched down the road from Troyes to Plancy. Raevsky's corps formed the second column and followed the road to Arcis. Raevsky was linked to Wrede's 5th Corps by General Kaisarov's cavalry. Another light force – under Spleny and consisting of 1,000 jägers (3rd Jäger Battalion), the Knesevich Dragoons and the Schwarzenberg Uhlans – watched the right bank of the Aube between Pougy and Rameru.

Around 2:00 p.m. – as the head of the French Guard infantry columns arrived in Arcis – Wrede's masses began their march on the village. They were three miles (five kilometers) from the village when General Kaisarov saw before him a superior number of French cavalry supported by a battery. Colbert's division formed the first line, and a second line stood behind them formed from Excelmans' cavalry division.

As the French had no infantry support, Kaisarov ordered a cannonade – then an attack. The two-piece attack captured four French guns and threw back Colbert's division. The successful attack was reinforced by the commitment of the Erzherzog Joseph Hussars and the Szeckler Hussars and the rest of Geramb's light brigade. Their combined assault drove Colbert's 1st Guard Cavalry Division back.[9] Excelmans' division was also pushed back, and both French divisions found themselves so outclassed that it was obvious that their only hope lay in escaping across the river by passing through Arcis.

Charge of the Austrian 2nd Hussars at Arcis-sur-Aube, by Trentsensky.

9 von Damitz, Vol. III, 1st Part, p. 373.

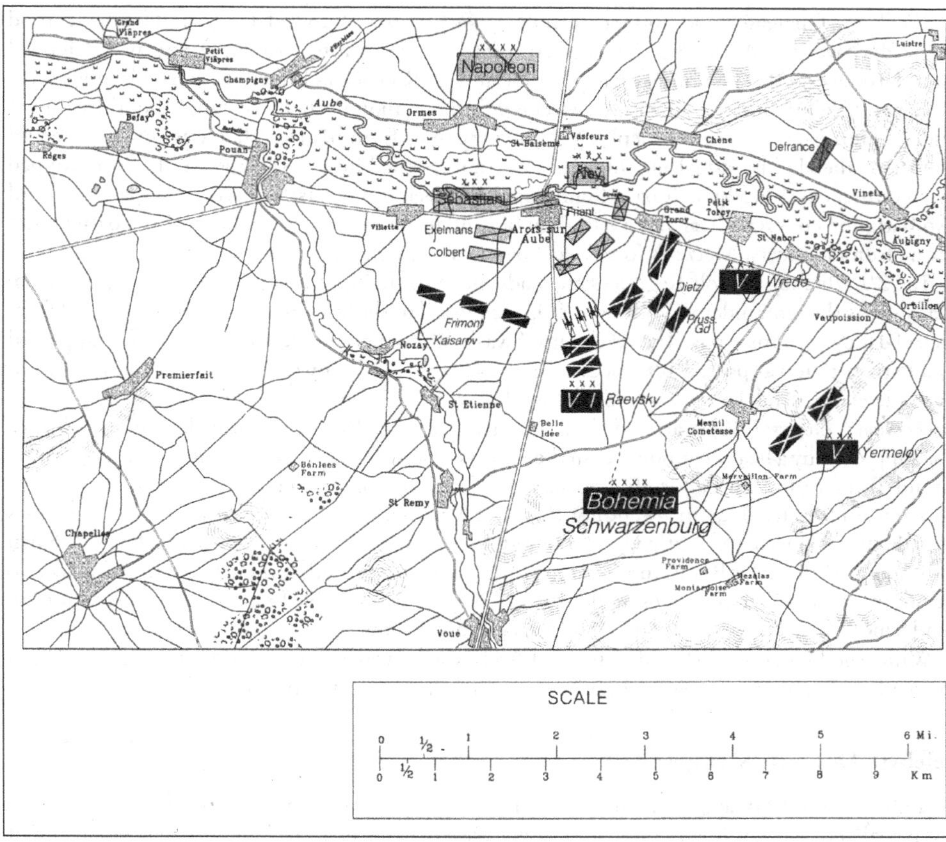

Map 16 Battle of Arcis-sur-Aube, March 20 1814, 2:00 p.m.

Wrede – hearing of this success – reinforced Kaisarov with Frimont's cavalry and three batteries and ordered General Volkman to take the village of Grand-Torcy, march on Arcis and take the bridge to prevent the arrival of the French infantry (and prevent the French cavalry from escaping).

The French cavalry was, at this time, fleeing for the bridge at Arcis as a crowd of fugitives. Napoleon, seeing this, moved forward – sword in hand – throwing himself before them, crying: "See who will re-cross the bridge before me!" The routed French cavalry stopped and they began reorganizing. However, at the same moment, Friant's infantry arrived – crossing the bridge at the *pas accéléré*[10] – and formed outside Arcis. The arrival of this steady infantry rebuilt the confidence of the French cavalry.

On the Allied left flank, General Volkman's brigade pushed through Petit-Torcy and launched an attack on the village of Grand-Torcy. Ney stood before the attack of the Austro-Bavarian forces and the village of Grand-Torcy became the central point of their attacks.[11]

10 The *pas accéléré* is a march cadence of 250 paces per minute. It is a cadenced run.

11 von Damitz, Vol. III, 1st Part, p. 374.

The Torcy Château stood 500 paces from the last houses of Grand-Torcy, and below it stood the bridge over the Aube. Ney had posted himself there to direct the fight and had defended Grand-Torcy and the area immediately behind it with Rousseau's brigade of Janssens' division.

General Volkman's first attack was executed by a battalion of the Erzherzog Rudolf Regiment under Major Metzen. Metzen deployed two companies from his right flank as skirmishers and sent them ahead of his attacking line. The Austrians pushed into the village – only to be stopped by a counterattacking French battalion. Napoleon, seeing the Austrian attack, ordered forward two battalions of grenadiers and a battalion of gendarmes – supporting them with a battery and a squadron of lancers. Metzen's forces were overwhelmed and driven back.

The 2/Erzherzog Rudolf Regiment then advanced to the right so as to strike the French from that side, as the remainder of Volkman's brigade moved to the left – moving against the road from Grand-Torcy towards Arcis. The village itself was again struck by Metzen's battalion – supported by a battery that was posted 100 paces from the village – and showered the French with canister. The village of Grand-Torcy was finally cleared of its French garrison and in Allied hands.[12]

However, General Boyer arrived about that time to assist Rousseau's brigade, and his advance was supported by a heavy cannonade, so the Austrians were pushed back a second time – returning Grand-Torcy to French hands. The possession of this village was the key to Wrede's movement on Arcis and he tried again – sending the 2/1st Bavarian Line supported by all of Rechberg's brigade and Habermann's brigade of Lamotte's (Bavarian) division against the French. Koch indicates only the 2/1st Bavarian Line, but von Damitz indicates that the attack was made by two battalions under Oberstleutnant Willemanns.[13] Ney's only available forces were two battalions of gendarmerie detached from Friant's 1st Old Guard Division.

While the French held Grand-Torcy and Arcis, their cavalry redeployed on the plain between the roads to Plancy and Troyes – heavily engaged with the Austro-Bavarian cavalry.[14]

Lefebvre-Desnoëttes' corps arrives

At nightfall, a column appeared on the road from Plancy to Arcis and caused a disturbance until it was realized that it was the corps of Lefebvre-Desnoëttes – expected since the day before – and consisting of 4,500 newly-organized Young Guard infantry and 2,000 newly-organized cavalry. Though fatigued, they took a position near Plancy under the orders of General Henrion, while the cavalry formed a second line to the right of Arcis.[15]

Night was already beginning to fall when the corps of Lefebvre-Desnoëttes arrived. Sébastiani immediately decided to renew his attacks on the Allies with Lefebvre-Desnoëttes' 2,000 fresh cavalry – and began his movements around 9:00 p.m. His immediate target was an Allied battery on the left flank. He organized a column with the Guard Lancers and Éclaireurs on the point and supported by a force of French cuirassiers. They advanced and immediately crushed Kaisarov's Cossacks, which stood in the way. They then moved against the Russian batteries, which stood on the left wing of the Allied 5th Corps.

A brigade of Russian grenadiers, under Colonel Timrot, had been assigned to cover this artillery. It immediately formed square and blunted the French attack. The Allies sent the 2nd and 7th Bavarian Chevauxleger Regiments forward to counter it. They were supported by the rest of the Austro-Bavarian cavalry under Prince Gallitzin, three divisions of Russian cuirassiers and

12 von Damitz, Vol. III, 1st Part, pp. 375-6.
13 von Damitz, Vol. III, 1st Part, p. 350.
14 Koch, Vol. II, pp. 60-9.
15 von Bernhardi, Vol. 4, Book 7, p. 281.

Wrede and his staff at Arcis-sur-Aube, by Peter Hess.

a squadron of Prussian Guard Cavalry. The presence of such an overwhelming cavalry force caused Sébastiani to abandon any further effort that night. The battle ended and both parties bivouaced for the night – leaving the village of Nozay between them without either side occupying it.[16] They withdrew to their lines and the day's battles quickly died as the night settled in.

Both Napoleon and Schwarzenberg watched the engagement by Arcis as the Crown Prince of Württemberg arrived at Plancy. However, he was 10 miles from the battle and circumstances would not permit him to take part in the day's engagement. The French Guard Grenadiers à cheval, Chasseurs à cheval and Mamlukes had, as mentioned earlier, been left in Grez. They began their march to Arcis at 2:00 p.m. with the captured bridging train. As the Guard Cavalry arrived on the Premierfait heights – between the villages of Reges and Bessy – they encountered

Russian infantryman on campaign, 1814, by Finart.

16 von Damitz, Vol. III, 1st Part, pp. 384-5.

the Allied cavalry under Nostitz and Prince Adam von Württemberg and Pahlen, which were leading the march of Raevsky's corps.[17]

Pahlen detached the Olviopol and Grodno Hussars and the Tchougouiev Uhlans to attack the left flank of the French Guard cavalry near Moulin, while Nostitz's Austrian cuirassiers and Cretov's 2nd Russian Cuirassier Division attacked them frontally. The Württemberg cavalry, under Prince Adam, attacked their right flank. Oberst von Bismark led the attack of the Herzog Louis and Prince Adam Jäger zu Pferd Regiments personally.[18]

The French Guard cavalry taught the Allies why they were Guard, but despite their valor, they were on the verge of being overwhelmed until Curley's brigade of converged squadrons – supported by some horse artillery – arrived to tip the scale.

The Guard cavalry withdrew – with the loss of 120 men and three pontoons to the village of Méry. Von Damitz indicates 120 French casualties, while Rössler states that for 100 Allied casualties, the French lost 12 officers, 300 prisoners and 81 horses.[19]

Méry was occupied by a force of French infantry and the Allied cavalry declined the opportunity to engage them. When night fell, the Guard cavalry once again resumed its march to Arcis via Plancy – leaving the bridging train with General Berckheim.

The result of the first day's battle had been entirely to the French advantage. They had remained in control of Arcis and the battlefield.

Junction with Macdonald

Macdonald had received orders to press his march. On the same day – 20 March – he had detached Oudinot's infantry and Saint-Germain's cavalry early in the morning with orders to move from Boulages and arrive in Arcis by 8:00 a.m. The II and XI Corps – and the V and VI Cavalry Corps – would not arrive for 24 hours. The II and XI Corps spent the night in Marsilly, and the cavalry corps camped near Marsagny.

The night of 20-21 March passed quietly. Napoleon unrealistically anticipated that the previous day's battle had been Schwarzenberg's last effort to cover his retreat. He awaited the break of dawn impatiently in order to determine the direction of the Allied withdrawal and for the arrival of Macdonald's forces. He knew that he could not expect much in the way of significant results from the 18,000-man army he commanded.

During the night, Oudinot – with the VII Corps and the II Cavalry Corps under Count Saint-Germain – arrived at Boulages and would arrive on the battlefield by Arcis around 8:00 a.m. General Gérard (with the II Corps) and Molitor (with the XI Corps) spent the night in Marsilly at the junction of the Aube and the Seine, while Milhaud's V Cavalry Corps and Kellermann's VI Cavalry Corps moved from Marsangis past Anglûre.

Berckheim's cavalry division, which watched the region between Méry and Plancy, were pulled back and joined Letort's cavalry by Arcis. Behind them, the French posted their bivouacs.[20]

On the Allied side of the battlefield, Prince Schwarzenberg had gained some confidence and spent much of the night considering his plan of attack. However, he was to make no significant changes in his previous orders for the battle. The Austro-Bavarian force was to continue to form the right on the Chaudrey heights. Raevsky was to form the center – behind the village of

17 Rössler, p. 436. Apparently, at this time, Prince Adam commanded the 2nd, 3rd and 4th Cavalry Regiments and had a single horse battery with him.
18 von Damitz, Vol. III, 1st Part, p. 381.
19 von Damitz, Vol. III, 1st Part, p. 384; Rössler, p. 437.
20 von Damitz, Vol. III, 1st Part, pp. 396-7.

Mesgnil-la-Comtesse – and the Crown Prince of Württemberg's corps and that of Giulay were to form the left – supporting itself on the Barbuisse stream. He had, however, taken the precaution of covering the right bank of the Aube with Oscherovski's light division and the left of the Barbuisse with Kaisarov's cavalry, while he reinforced the Austro-Bavarian 5th Corps with a division of Russian grenadiers.

The Allied reserves and the Russian Guard were given orders to unite at Mesnil-Lettré. General Seslavin was charged with scouting the roads to Troyes – on the side of Méry and Plancy – and to take all measures necessary to defend St.-Hubert and Saint-Parre-aux-Tertres in case the Allies were forced to evacuate Troyes. Schwarzenberg also recommended to his corps commanders that they guard their reserves in the third line and that they make use of all of their artillery before beginning the action. The 72 reserve Russian guns were ordered forward to act in conjunction with them.

Schwarzenberg's plans

That night, Schwarzenberg sent out orders for his attack the following day. He planned an attack in three columns:

> The first column shall consist of the V Army Corps supported by a division of Russian grenadiers and a division of cuirassiers – taking their direction of march from Chaudrey towards Grand-Torcy, seeking to take it in the rear. The cavalry of the first column shall hold itself massed between the first and second (columns) so as to be ready to advance if needed.
>
> The second column – formed with the united III and IV Army Corps – shall march to the left of Mesgnil-la-Comtesse, advance in the direction of Arcis and advance at the same rate in order to link with the V Army Corps. The cavalry of the second column shall hold itself in mass between the second and third (columns) so as to be ready if needed.
>
> The third column, formed from the VI Army Corps, shall direct its march as the others against Arcis – supported on the left flank by the Barbuisse stream. It shall advance at the same rate as the other columns.[21]
>
> The Foot Guard shall occupy the Mesnil-Lettré heights. The Guard Cavalry shall follow the second column in mass in order to support the cavalry of the right or left flanks as necessary.

Around 1:00 p.m. the Allies organized the three attack columns and at 2:00 p.m. began their march on Arcis. Count Pahlen, with the light cavalry of the VI Army Corps, moved across the Barbuisse creek when it encountered the French advancing in the other direction.

The second day at Arcis – 21 March: Grand-Torcy

Early on the morning of 21 March Napoleon recalled the French infantry and cavalry which stood between Méry and Plancy. Oudinot and Saint-Germain crossed the Aube with their corps – as did the divisions of Berckheim and Defrance. After Napoleon assigned them their positions in the line, he sent reconnaissance forces from Grand-Torcy down the road to Lesmont. As Wrede was withdrawing to Chaudrey, this reconnaissance saw nothing more than a few platoons of cavalry, which confirmed Napoleon's opinion that the Allies were withdrawing. As a result, at 10:00 am. Napoleon ordered Sébastiani to attack across the main battlefield. Ney was to support

21 The phrase used is: 'advance at the same height', which does not translate easily. In fact, it means that several columns would advance in a line – keeping abreast with each other.

this movement with his infantry in order to render the shock decisive. After a short cannonade, the heads of the columns appeared at the crest of the plateau, where Ney and Sébastiani discovered the Allied position before them. The Allies awaited them in three lines – stretching from the Aube to the Barbuisse. Their front was covered by a cloud of skirmishers and their massed artillery – something over 100 guns. This apparently included two 12pdr batteries, the artillery of the Allied 6th Corps and two Russian Guard horse batteries.[22]

The shock experienced by Ney and Sébastiani is understandable when one considers that they saw 100,000 men deployed before them – ready to receive their attack.

The French reacted immediately, with Sébastiani's cavalry striking Pahlen's right and throwing it back until it was supported by the Allied second line. This situation could not last long, and any further movement by Ney would open Arcis and the Aube bridge to attack by Wrede.

Pahlen's cavalry recovered and engaged the French on the Nozay heights – pushing them back towards Villette. During their counterattack, Kaisarov's Cossacks attacked Colbert's 1st Guard Cavalry Division – supported by two squadrons of the Erzherzog Joseph Hussars – and captured four guns. Colbert's left wing tried to respond, but was stopped and disordered by canister fire from an Austrian horse battery. Colbert's division was broken and flew back in disorder – breaking Excelmans' division.

At this moment, Friant's 1st Old Guard Division appeared. Napoleon led his grognards through the town and deployed them in line of battle under a hail of bullets and canister. Napoleon placed himself in a most exposed position to inspire and embarrass those of his troops whose morale was failing. A howitzer bomb burst near his feet – covering him with smoke and dust and killing his horse under him. He quickly mounted another and stood facing the Allied batteries. Count Wrede saw the initial success of his left wing and decided to advance his right. In doing so, he ordered five battalions of Volkman's Austrian brigade to seize Grand-Torcy. It was very important to capture this village because some hundred paces behind its last buildings stood the Arcy bridge.[23]

At the same time, Raevsky's infantry (VI Army Corps) arrived and engaged Leval's 7th Division with its skirmishers and musketry.[24] As Raevsky moved against Leval's division, which was supported by Sébastiani's cavalry, it took Leval's infantry under cannon fire.

The Württemberg Light Cavalry Division, under Prince Adam, and Nostitz's Austrian cuirassier division stood in the area between the 3rd and 6th Corps. As the Allies approached Arcis, Prince Adam placed himself at the head of his cavalry and led them forward quickly to a position on Pahlen's right. FZM Graf Giulay detached the Rosenberg Chevauxleger Regiment to join him.

Two battalions of the 1st Szekler Regiment were sent to help Volkman. On the right, Spleny's division covered Wrede's troops from the right. Meanwhile, Bavarian troops in the center were stopped by strong batteries in front of the town. Volkman's troops moved through Petit-Torcy at 3:00 p.m. and rushed towards Grand-Torcy. Grand-Torcy was occupied with two battalions and two cannon of Rysso's brigade (Janssens' division). Maréchal Oudinot saw that the Allies were launching a concentric attack and withdrew his forces to a small height before the village. Only a light screen of French cavalry remained deployed before them.[25]

On the right stood one battalion of the Erzherzog Rudolf Regiment, under Major Metzen, with two companies of skirmishers. They advanced to the right – up the Aube River – and attacked Grand-Torcy, broke Rysso's infantry and pursued it to Arcy. Napoleon saw the danger and reinforced his left with two battalions of Guard grenadiers, a squadron of gendarmes, one

22 Rössler, p. 439.
23 Bogdanovich, p. 400.
24 von Damitz, Vol. III, 1st Part, p. 402.
25 von Damitz, Vol. III, 1st Part, p. 403.

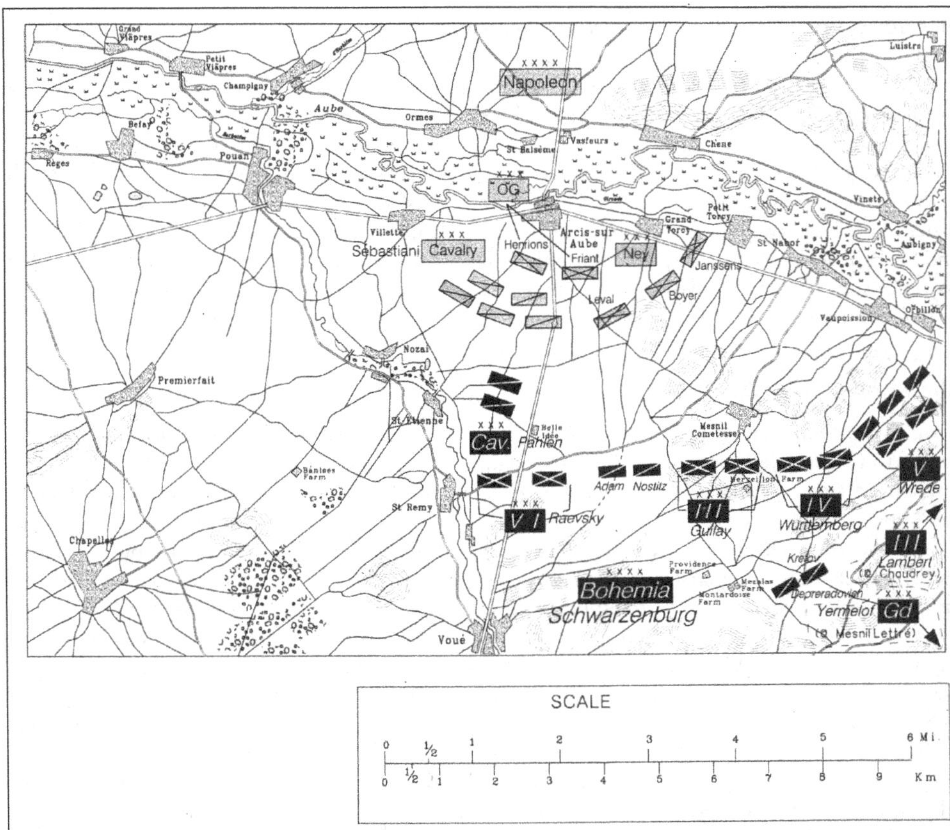

Map 17 Battle of Arcis-sur-Aube, March 21 1814, 10:00 a.m.

of the lancers and a horse battery. But before these troops arrived, P. Boyer's brigade threw the Austrians out of Grand-Torcy. Major Metzen was mortally wounded. General Volkman sent in all remaining battalions and recaptured the village. The situation was not strong, so Volkman sent to General der Kavallerie Wrede for reinforcements. Two battalions of the Szekler Regiment were sent to the left to fill the gap between the center and right wing.[26] General der Kavallerie Wrede wanted to capture the village at all costs and, at first, reinforced Volkman with three battalions of the Prinz Karl von Bayern Regiment.

Then he sent to his aid Habermann's brigade (Lamotte's division). Before these troops arrived, Major Dubois – leading one battalion of the Erzherzog Rudolf Regiment – captured Grand-Torcy for the third time, but Guard battalions supported by troops under Janssens and P. Boyer recaptured it again. For the three hours – between 5:00 and 8:00 p.m. – 15 Allied battalions under Volkman, Habermann and Prince Karl repeatedly attacked and penetrated into Grand-Torcy, but were thrown back every time. Habermann was killed on the Allied side, and Janssens on the

26 Bogdanovich, p. 401.

French. The Erzherzog Rudolf Regiment alone suffered 500 casualties. Some Austrian battalions fired all of their ammunition and were ordered to retreat to Chaudrey.

GM Tschoglikov received orders to reinforce troops in Grand-Torcy. The 1st Grenadier Division, Heavy Battery #30 (under Colonel Nilus), Light Battery #14 (under Colonel Cheremisinov) and GM Lewaschoff's cuirassier brigade (Starodub and Novgorod Regiments) moved under his command. GM Jemilianov, with the Pernov and Kexholm Regiments (each with one weak battalion each), reinforced the Bavarians who stormed Grand-Torcy. At the same time, Light Battery #14 and Heavy Battery #30 – supported by GM Sulima's brigade (Tauride and St. Petersburg Regiments) and Lewaschoff's cuirassier brigade – advanced against the French batteries supporting Grand-Torcy and obliged them to withdraw to the town. Irrespective of all of this, the French successfully defended Grand-Torcy.

The withdrawal to Arcis

Around 1:00 p.m. the situation became untenable and Napoleon, surrendering to the situation, ordered a retreat. Ney began to withdraw – beginning with the two Guard infantry divisions and Janssens' division – with Sébastiani covering their retreat *en échiquier* to give them time to cross the Aube.

The overall situation was such that Napoleon had little choice. He was greatly outnumbered and his back was to a marshy river with a single bridge. To stand and accept battle with his greatly inferior forces would be to embrace disaster. As it was, if Schwarzenberg were an aggressive commander and had launched an aggressive attack, disaster would have embraced Napoleon anyway – but it was not so. As it was, Sébastiani's attack on Schwarzenberg's left had convinced him that Napoleon was maneuvering for a further assault and he lost precious time.

Sébastiani's maneuvers kept the Allies in the dark about Napoleon's movements until about 2:00 p.m. Ney and the Guard effected their withdrawal in good order – as did the bulk of the army. Napoleon, however – fearing being pressed too hard by the Allies – ordered Oudinot to take three brigades of infantry (drawn from Spain) and hold the Aube crossing. They were to establish themselves as solidly as possible in the city of Arcis.

Montfort's brigade occupied the suburb across the roads from Lesmont and Troyes. Maulmond guarded the suburb on the road to Méry and Chassé's brigade was posted in reserve. Rottembourg's 5th Young Guard Division, which had been escorting the park, arrived about this time and took up positions on the right bank of the Aube so as to cover the withdrawal of the three brigades in the town. Meanwhile, the French sappers destroyed the Villette bridge and erected barricades with wagons and other materials on the principal roads into Arcis. It was 3:00 p.m. when the advancing Allied line reached the outskirts of Mesgnil-la-Comtesse.

It was 3:00 p.m. when Schwarzenberg finally realized that the French were withdrawing. He didn't have a moment to waste. However, he had spent all morning fearing a massive attack and had not given a moment's consideration to plans to pursue Napoleon. Not a man to act without a plan, he responded immediately and called a conference of his corps commanders to consider what to do. In a meeting on the Mesgnil-la-Comtesse heights, it was resolved that Wrede would send a cavalry brigade – supported by a horse battery – in pursuit of the French, while the rest of the army crossed the Aube as quickly as possible and moved between Donnement and Dommartin. The Russian Guard Light Cavalry Division, which was already on the right bank, was put under Wrede's orders. One Russian grenadier division was to occupy the Chaudrey heights while the second was to occupy the Mesgnil-la-Comtesse heights. A cuirassier division was assigned to support them and the rest of the reserve was ordered to march to a position behind Voire to support the Bavarians and to cover the line of retreat. As can be seen, the mental attitude of the Allies was one of extreme caution and timidity.

The Crown Prince of Württemberg and Giulay were to attack Arcis in three columns, while the Russian grenadiers marched via Mesgnil-la-Comtesse and Chaudrey – on Napoleon's left – and attacked Grand-Torcy.[27]

The Allies attack Arcis

Pahlen – leading the cavalry from Raevsky's corps – pushed hard on the French squadrons, which continued to withdraw *en échiquier* towards Nozay – intent on crossing the Aube at the Villette bridge. As the Allies pushed forward, they encountered a French cavalry brigade forming part of the rearguard. It may have consisted of two regiments from Letour's brigade (1st Light Cavalry Division). The Allies attacked the French from several sides. They were attacked from the left by the regiments of Count Pahlen (Olviopol and Grodno Hussars and Tchougouiev Uhlans). The 2nd Cuirassier Division attacked frontally, while the Württemberg and Austrian cavalry attacked from the right. Most of the French brigade was captured.[28]

Of the approximately 1,000 French cavalry involved, only a few escaped by the road to Méry. All others were cut down or captured. Pahlen's cavalry captured 160 prisoners – including Lt. Colonel Laffite.

The three attack columns of the Crown Prince of Württemberg were preceded by the Russian and Prussian reserve artillery and supported by the Russian 3rd Cuirassier Division. This force arrived before Arcis around 4:00 p.m. and began a lively cannonade. The Württemberg cavalry and two batteries moved to a height from which they could fire on the French cavalry. Sébastiani refused to be subjected to this fire and quickly withdrew his cavalry across the bridge in Villette to the far bank – breaking the bridge down behind him.

The Allied 6th Corps marched against Oudinot's infantry. The artillery – with the Württemberg cavalry – moved to engage Oudinot and was soon joined by two Austrian 12pdr batteries and the 1st and 2nd Russian Guard Horse Batteries, which took up positions on the road to Chaudrey. Further Allied guns moved up and soon 80 guns began pounding Oudinot's lines.[29]

Oudinot – seeing himself menaced by this massive force – encouraged his troops to stand fast, but made preparations for their withdrawal. The converging fire of the Allied artillery inflicted heavy losses in his ranks – dismounting several guns and throwing the traffic over the bridge into chaos – as the infantry of Rottembourg's 5th Young Guard Division attempted to cross simultaneously with the cavalry. The infantry that didn't cross with the cavalry crossed at five smaller bridges and weirs.

Fortunately for the French, the Allies did not act in a more coordinated manner and the French withdrawal was not turned into the disaster it could have become. Allied skirmishers pushed into the houses of the Méry suburb, but lacking sufficient support, they were chased back by the 10th Légère. This success was only fleeting and the 10th Légère was soon forced back through the city and across the bridge. The withdrawal, however, was violent. General Leval was wounded and General Maulmond had his horse killed under him. The approaches to the bridge were blocked by dead bodies, equipment and abandoned weapons.

The Crown Prince ordered the city stormed. The Allied skirmishers quickly pushed into the edge of the Méry suburb. The French 10th Légère – supported by another unit – were driven back by the Allied skirmishers. As the main Russian column approached, Prince Eugene von

27 Koch, Vol. II, pp. 70-8.
28 Bogdanovich, p. 402.
29 von Damitz, Vol. III, 1st Part, pp. 404-5.

Württemberg pushed his infantry corps into the western side of the city. At the same time, the head of Giulay's corps pushed into the city.

The Crown Prince put General-adjutant Oberst von Wernhardt in command of two battalions of the Würzburg Infantry Regiment and directed him against the eastern side of the city, where the road to Grand-Torcy entered it. Their attack overran the French barricades and effectively broke the French defense of the city.[30]

General Chassé, on the verge of being taken prisoner, seized a drum and beat the charge. At the head of 100 veteran soldiers of the 16th Légère and the 28th Line, he drove back the Allied skirmishers and gave the last few French soldiers time to withdraw across the Aube. It was now about 6:00 p.m.

Oudinot established himself in Chène – at the fork of three roads – and in position to support the retreat of Maulmond's brigade, which had been left in the suburb to oversee the destruction of the bridge.

At around 9:00 p.m. the remainder of Macdonald's troops arrived in Ormes. Lefebvre-Desnoëttes' cavalry – some 2,000 men – arrived in Arcy. Henrion's Young Guard Division (4,500 men) stopped by Plancy. The sound of the artillery had hastened their march. They had marched from St.-Saturnin to Plancy over the dikes – in order to pass through the swamps – and were extremely fatigued. The XI Corps was in Ormes and the II Corps stood in Vaipre.

General Sébastiani, reinforced by Lefebvre-Desnoëttes' cavalry, attacked the Allied left wing near Barbuisse at 10:00 p.m. Kaisarov's Cossacks and the 7th Bavarian Chevauxleger Regiment were broken. Frimont's troops stood in great danger, but Colonel Timrot deployed the Tauride Grenadiers in square and beat off several attacks. Bavarian cavalry stopped the French and bought time for the 3rd Cuirassier Division to arrive to stabilize the situation. Supported by a squadron of the Prussian Guard – under Rittmeister Barner – as well as the Szekler Hussars, they obliged the French cavalry to retreat behind Nozay. The artillery duel lasted between 10:00 and 12:00 p.m.[31]

Napoleon and his Guard moved to Sommepuis, where they camped for the night. They were supported by Saint-Germain's cavalry in Mailly.

The bulk of the Allied army stopped before the Aube – remaining on the battlefield. Wrede crossed the Aube at Lesmont and marched through the night to arrive at Chalette. The Russian Guard Light Cavalry Division crossed the Aube at Rameru and had its advanced posts in Vinet and Luistre.

Both Koch and von Bernhardi list the French losses for the two days of battle as three guns and 4,200 men – including about 800 prisoners.[32] The losses for the Austro-Bavarian 5th Corps were 224 officers and 2,000 men *hors de combat.* Von Damitz states that the Allies lost 1,500 dead and wounded on the 20th, and another 300-400 dead and wounded on the 21st.

Arcis was a very close call for Napoleon. Again, he was playing a high-stakes game – pushing for everything he could – but he demonstrated himself able to recognize when the battle was beyond his grasp and successfully withdrew his army from what could have been a disastrous situation. What else could he do when his total army had only 30,000 to 40,000 men and the Allies currently had about 200,000 men in the field opposing him?

In fact, the French army had shown itself to be as brilliant on the battlefield as ever. The divisions of Janssens and Boyer – plus two battalions of gendarmes, or 7,000 men – had fought against Wrede's corps and a division of grenadiers totaling 22,000 men. The cavalry divisions of

30 von Damitz, Vol. III, 1st Part, p. 407.
31 Bogdanovich, p. 403.
32 von Bernhardi, Vol. 4, Book 7, p. 291.

Excelmans and Colbert – 2,500 men – had fought and stopped 7,000 Allied cavalry drawn from Wrede's 5th Corps and Kaisarov's Cossacks.[33]

The French march on Vitry

After passing the Marne at the Frignicourt ford with his Guard, Napoleon ordered Ney to move on Vitry. Ney marched on Vitry with Lefol's division. Lefol assumed command of the division that had been commanded by Janssens prior to his wounding on 20 March at the Battle of Arcis. He was supported by two of Milhaud's dragoon divisions under Briche and l'Héritier. This force summoned the Allies occupying Vitry while demonstrating against the city. The garrison contained five Russian battalions, three Russian squadrons, two Prussian battalions and two Prussian squadrons – about 5,000 men – supported by 41 guns under the command of Colonel Schvichov. Schvichov, quite intimidated by the presence of significant French forces, asked to be able to send an officer to the Allied General Headquarters.[34]

This request was rejected, and a second summons was sent to the city – accompanied with far more menacing movements by the French troops. This did nothing more than to harden the Allied commander in his resolve to do his duty.

A new French campaign plan

Napoleon had hoped to seize the city with a *coup de main* – not a direct assault. He also did not know that the garrison had 5,000 men and 41 guns. As a result, he encamped his forces outside of cannon shot from the city in Blacy and Vitry-le-Brûlé. Napoleon and the Guard – under Friant, Henrion and Letort – spent the night in Farémont. The II and XI Corps, Trelliard's division, and Sébastiani's cavalry took up positions on the Dosnon heights. Oudinot, with the divisions of Leval and Rottembourg, stood before Arcis and lined the right bank of the Aube with batteries from Ormes to Torcy.

The resistance Napoleon encountered at Vitry opened his eyes to his situation. He had hoped for a brilliant success from his maneuver, but was robbed of it by the weakness of his army. He now decided that in order to hope for a chance of winning the campaign, he would have to risk uncovering Paris and march into the rear of the Allied armies. In addition to cutting the Allied lines of communications, he could gather more veteran troops to his standards from the various garrisons that were cut off. In the Vosges alone, he could hope to gather up 10,000 to 12,000 fresh troops which Durutte had gathered in the 3rd Military Division. A new opportunity opened up and Napoleon resolved to implement it.

The decision made, Napoleon marched his army towards St.-Dizier on 23 March in the company of Friant's 1st Old Guard Division and the cavalry of generals Lefebvre-Desnoëttes, Saint-Germain, Defrance and Piré. Piré's division led the march – supported by Defrance's Gardes d'honneur. In St.-Dizier, they encountered and captured 900 prisoners and a bridging train. They then pushed on to Doulevant, while the infantry and Imperial Headquarters remained in St.-Dizier.

Macdonald's troops broke camp at daybreak. The II Corps formed the advanced guard and were in march column between Grand-Fenu and Custonne when they heard a heavy cannonade in the direction of Sommepuis. General Gérard was curious to know what was happening, and personally rode to Nivelet and learned that the artillery parks belonging to Macdonald had been taken by Allied cavalry.

33 Koch, Vol. II, pp. 79-83.

34 de Vaudoncourt, Vol. II, p. 246.

Macdonald had been ordered to leave Arcis during the night of 23 March – after organizing his troops and sending his staff officers from Plancy to Nogent and from St.-Saturnin to Villenoxe – in order to direct those men moving through the swamps via Sézanne to Sommepuis. The parks which were near Boulagės were ordered to move to Pleurs the following day, where General Amey would accompany them via Cauroy and Gourganson to St.-Saturnin. Unfortunately, these well-laid plans were misunderstood. Amey thought he was to move his forces to Sézanne and lost track of the artillery, which arrived at the assigned rendezvous without escort. It was almost immediately attacked by the Russian Guard Light Cavalry Division, which came down the old Roman road.[35]

The artillery park commander was not intimidated by the appearance of this cavalry and formed his charges into square. He had 400 to 500 gunners and sappers to defend his park. The Russian cavalry apparently executed a couple of unsuccessful charges against this square. Unfortunately for the French, the light cavalry was supported by some horse artillery – and the fear of howitzer shells detonating a caisson caused them to flee. Count Oscherovski – who led the attack – reported capturing 27 guns, but was able to safely bring away only 15 of them. Apparently, their ability to haul off their prizes was limited because the French drivers had cut the traces on their horses and fled – abandoning everything.[36]

Gérard pushed his infantry forward at the double and attacked the Russians and took up a position near Moulin-à-vent. The Russians withdrew – taking with them 300 prisoners, 14-15 fully-equipped guns and some 60 powder wagons. The eight guns they could not take with them were spiked.

The French advanced guard continued moving down the main road from Arcis and arrived at 2:00 p.m. in Blacy, where they encountered Ney's dragoons, which then moved on St.-Dizier.

The main body of Macdonald's troops moved to cross the Marne at Frignicourt and established themselves in Villotte and Bignicourt. Sébastiani's cavalry rejoined the main body in St.-Dizier.[37]

Allied actions – 21-23 March

On 21 March the instant Schwarzenberg was assured that the French columns had crossed the Aube and were marching on Vitry, he decided to deploy his army behind the Puy River. The Crown Prince of Württemberg was ordered – as soon as he could force passage – to take up a position between Dampierre and Corbeil, with his corps and that of Raevsky. Wrede was to place his corps in a second line at Donnement. The Guards and reserves formed a third line behind the Voire. Giulay's corps was to occupy Arcis.

The following morning – 22 March – he changed his dispositions and decided to move his army towards Vitry. His intention was, if the Crown Prince of Württemberg could move through Arcis, he should take up positions on the Dosnon. If he could not, he was to support the Allied right.

In compliance with these orders, the Crown Prince of Württemberg threw a pontoon bridge over the Aube at Rameru and began moving his troops forward. Giulay attempted to push his troops out of Arcis, but was stopped by Maulmond's brigade until nightfall. The advanced guard of Raevsky's corps crossed the Aube and the Crown Prince of Württemberg occupied Luistre with the five Cossack regiments of General Illowaiski.[38]

35 von Damitz, Vol. III, 2nd Part, p. 16.
36 von Bernhardi, Vol. 4, Book 7, p. 301.
37 Koch, Vol. II, pp. 84-90.
38 de Vaudoncourt, Vol. II, p. 247.

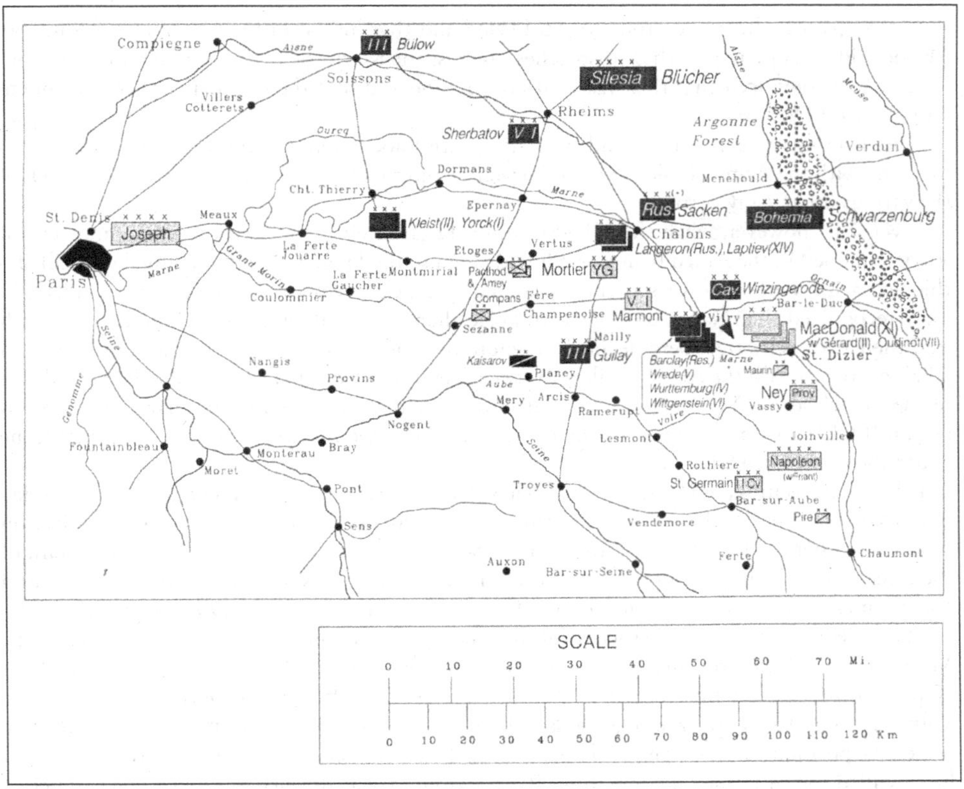

Map 18 Strategic Situation, March 24 1814.

Unfortunately for the Cossacks, they encountered Sébastiani's cavalry, which chased them out of the city. This was countered by an advance by Pahlen with the rest of the advanced guard, which drove back the French cavalry. Pahlen then remained in Luistre to observe Macdonald's forces. That evening, Wrede and Württemberg had their corps deployed on the Corbeil heights – covered by the cavalry of General Frimont. Raevsky stood in Dampierre; the Allied guard and reserves were between Dommartin and Donnement; Giulay was still in Arcis; the Guard Light Cavalry Division, under Ojarovsky, was in Metiercelin (near Sommepuis); and General Kaisarov was between Méry and Plancy, with General Seslavin before him in Sézanne. Liechtenstein's division, which had departed Joigny, now covered Dijon. General Tettenborn (who still occupied Châlons), now informed of the French march, pushed parties towards Cosel and Sommesous. One of these detachments intercepted a French courier with dispatches for the Empress.[39]

Allies resolve to march on Paris

Count Oscherovski advised Barclay de Tolly of his capture of part of Macdonald's train and sent him a number of dispatches – addressed to Macdonald – found on a courier taken in the same engagement. These dispatches informed the Allies that Napoleon had passed the night in

39 de Vaudoncourt, Vol. II, p. 248.

Longchamps, that he was en route to St.-Dizier, and that his cavalry was moving on Joinville. Macdonald was ordered, in these dispatches, to cross the Marne below Vitry and join Napoleon. Barclay was convinced that this was vital information and sent the originals to Schwarzenberg with General Diebitsch.

After reading these dispatches and consulting with Radetsky and Diebitsch, he resolved to join his army with the Army of Silesia along the Marne and to send an order expediting the march of the various other army corps.

It was late, however, when the Allied columns began their march and they were uncertain if Vitry remained in the Allied hands or if it had fallen to the French. Another council was called – this time with the Tsar of Russia. The captured dispatches were reviewed and discussed at length. They recognized that Napoleon hoped to oblige them to withdraw to the Rhine by his march into their rear. Schwarzenberg decided to ignore this movement by Napoleon and to march on Châlons to join with the Army of Silesia. Once joined, they would operate on the flanks and rear of the French army. This decision was put into effect that evening and the march on Châlons began. If Châlons was occupied by the French, the Allies would throw a bridge over the Marne either above or below Châlons.

Later that evening, word came that Vitry had not fallen to the French. Winzingerode's advanced guard, under the orders of Czernichev and Tettenborn, had come into communication with Pahlen behind the sources of the Somme-Soudé. At that time, they were very uncertain of the direction of the French movement as the various French corps occupied a semi-circle around Vitry, which gave no clear indication if the French were marching on St.-Dizier or on Châlons.

The Allied movement was so successful that Schwarzenberg ordered the Bavarians to cross the Marne. It was felt that this movement was useful in that it permitted the Allies to keep an eye on Napoleon. During the morning of 24 March the Russian staff called a conference with Prince Volkonski, Barclay de Tolly and generals Toll and Diebitsch. After examining the map and the respective positions of the army, Tsar Alexander called a conference. Diebitsch, with passion and logic, called for an immediate march on Paris – arguing that the city was Napoleon's principal depot and that public opinion and support would collapse. The other members of the council supported this position.

The Tsar then charged General Toll to transmit to Schwarzenberg the conclusion of this conference and to persuade him to adopt that plan. The Tsar also sent word to the King of Prussia.

As this conference took place, Schwarzenberg was advised that the Army of Silesia had occupied Rheims and Château-Thierry; that it was about to enter Châlons; and that all of its cavalry – under the orders of Winzingerode – was between Somme-Soudé and the Cosel.[40]

40 Koch, Vol. II, pp. 91-5.

14

Operations of the Army of Silesia, 13-30 March 1814

Skirmish at Béry-au-Bac

It was around noon on the 14th when the Prussian 60-man picket – under Lieutenant von Wedell of the Brandenburg Hussar Regiment – on the high road running from Rheims to Béry-au-Bac, spotted the advancing French. The 2nd Leib Hussars and the Brandenburg Hussar Regiment had their bivouacs on that side of the Aisne. The village of Béry-au-Bac had only a few houses on that side of the river and they were occupied by a single company of infantry. Earlier, the French had destroyed the bridge at Béry and the remaining structure was passable by cavalry only if they were tightly packed. Aside from the units already mentioned, the 3/Leib Hussars – under Major von Schenk – were on the right flank near Fismes.

As word of the approaching French spread, General Katzler ordered the 1/Leib Hussars – under Krafft – to support von Wedell's picket. It moved up to the bridge and detached a platoon behind the bridge in order to prevent the French from forcing a crossing. Krafft moved it at a trot to a rise that dominated the approaches to the bridge. The remaining three platoons then moved at a trot to the right of the main road.[1]

As the first platoon arrived before the high ground, it was engaged by French skirmishers and a skirmish fight erupted. This ended abruptly when a squadron of French lancers arrived and drove it off. More French cavalry began arriving, and soon eight to 10 squadrons of lancers, dragoons and Gardes d'honneur stood before the Prussian position.

Katzler drew together his cavalry, the remaining squadrons of the 2nd Leib Hussars, the Brandenburg Hussars and a few squadrons of Russian mounted jagers. The 2nd Leib Hussars and the 4/Brandenburg Hussars formed line – with four more squadrons forming a second line behind them. This formation apparently engaged the French for about an hour, but could not stem the French advance.[2]

The overwhelming French force drove the Prussian and Russian cavalry back. French artillery was posted on the hill that dominated Béry-au-Bac and it began bombarding the Allied positions, while French infantry moved up to the riverbank. The position was soon untenable for the Allies and Katzler withdrew his forces down the road to Corbeny.[3]

1 von Damitz, Vol. III, 1st Part, pp. 151-5.
2 von Ardenne, p. 270.
3 von Damitz, Vol. III, 1st Part, p. 156.

Nansouty and Pacz force a passage at Béry-au-Bac.

Mortier and Oudinot face Blücher

After 13 March Mortier occupied the positions that Napoleon had ordered him to assume below Soissons. Oudinot returned from Fismes on 15 March, as ordered, and took up a position on his right along the Aisne – stretching to Béry-au-Bac. These two corps had a total force of 13,000 infantry and 3,600 cavalry and could not long resist the Army of Silesia, which had a total of 109,000 men under arms if Blücher was to resume the offensive.

The Prussian field marshal remained quiescent until 18 March when he learned that Napoleon had departed Châlons and Epernay for his maneuver on the Aube, and concentrated his forces around Craone and Corbeny – ordering the corps of Kleist and Yorck to march on Béry-au-Bac (to clear it of French) and ordered Winzingerode to push his cavalry across the Aisne at Asfeld-la-Ville and attack their flank.

Oudinot did not believe that he had the means to dispute Blücher's passage and, fearing a movement against his flanks, abandoned Béry-au-Bac and advised Mortier of his intended movement. Mortier responded by moving on Fismes with the divisions of Curial, Christiani and Roussel – leaving only Charpentier's division before Soissons. Grouvel's brigade was detached to Compiègne to watch the Lower Aisne.

On 18 March the Army of Silesia appeared along the Aisne at two points. Kleist and Yorck formed the advanced guard and appeared before Béry-au-Bac and Pontavaire. Oudinot, not having withdrawn, ordered Béry-au-Bac defended and deployed part of his infantry and six guns along the bank of the river. In order to oppose the construction of a bridge, Oudinot dispatched Bordesoulle and a force of cuirassiers – plus part of his infantry – to the Roucy heights. Mortier, however, continued his movement on Rheims and posted Roussel's dragoons in Neuvillette.

The two Prussian corps arrived at their destination and prepared to attack. Ricard's division occupied Béry-au-Bac – defying the numerical superiority of the Allies – while Kleist began to construct his bridge. The construction of this bridge took all morning because of the fire of a battery placed near it and the fire of 300 French skirmishers. However, despite this effort, it was completed by the end of the day and Oudinot was obliged to abandon his defense of the river. With the bulk of his infantry, Oudinot then withdrew on Fismes – leaving a brigade of infantry and another of cavalry in Béry-au-Bac to destroy the bridge.

With the bridge at Béry-au-Bac destroyed, this rearguard withdrew – but it was not a peaceful withdrawal. Czernichev had passed his light cavalry over the Aisne at a ford near Asfeld and attacked the French light cavalry – pushing it in disorder back on the French infantry.

Blücher directed that three regiments of light cavalry and the reserves of the two Prussian corps – under Ziethen – pursue Oudinot, who was in Cormicy. The Army of Silesia then deployed with Kleist's corps in Pontavaire – leaving a brigade on the right bank. Yorck's advanced guard was in Blazy-les-Perles. The main body of the army was in Juvincourt and La Ville-aux-Bois. Baron Sacken's corps was in Corbeny, Winzingerode's was in Amifontaine, and that of Langeron was in Ramecourt.

On 19 March Blücher had two bridges over the Aisne. He ordered Kleist and Yorck to pursue Oudinot via Cormicy and Roucy towards Vesle. He ordered Winzingerode to move on Rheims in two columns – the infantry via Béry-au-Bac and his cavalry via Asfeld-la-Ville. Sacken was ordered to move against Pontavaire, while Langeron was to move to Béry-au-Bac. Bülow was recalled from La Fère and was ordered to march to the Ange-Gardien heights in order to be able to march either on Soissons or Wailly. A single battalion was left to form the garrison of Laon.

The two French marshals were separated by a distance of 19 miles (30 kilometers) and were about to be attacked simultaneously. Their movements were compromised and the situation was serious. Oudinot would have been better advised to withdraw on Rheims instead of Fismes, as it had numerous crossroads and gave him greater opportunities for maneuver. However, his instructions were to cover Paris and he believed that he was obliged to remain between Blücher and the capitol.

Oudinot learned of Winzingerode's march on Rheims, but reports exaggerated his strength to 40,000 men. He contacted Mortier and convinced him to close on his position – noting that if instead they were to join at Rheims, Charpentier's division would be cut off from them in its position on the Lower Aisne.

In response, Mortier began his march at daybreak on 19 March and by 8:00 a.m. his column was already in Jonchery when an erroneous message arrived and convinced him to return to Rheims. His infantry stopped and his rearguard of dragoons turned about and moved back at the gallop. It was about noon when the Russian advanced guard began to appear and there was only a Cossack pulk in the city, which was engaged by what garrison remained in the city. Surprised by the sudden return of the French, Winzingerode formed his columns and made preparations to fight for possession of Rheims. The French dragoons boldly re-entered Rheims, but it was hardly sufficient to hold the city. Count Belliard arrived with Roussel's dragoon division and deployed it along the main road – facing Vesle – and dispatched a battalion of Guard Fusiliers to occupy the Saint-Brice mill. The dragoons then dismounted, barricaded the city's gates and soon a cannonade began along the two banks of the Vesle and near the Laon and Réthel gates.

However, the French infantry did not arrive and Belliard did not know why. He sent an officer to Mortier to advise him of the situation and to ask for orders. Unfortunately, there was no time to wait for the infantry, which was not coming in any circumstances. Belliard's force faced Winzingerode's entire corps and had no hope of standing, so it wisely withdrew after holding its position until the end of the day.

Winzingerode misinterpreted the strength of the French resistance to indicate a large garrison and did not think himself capable of taking it that evening. He stopped his columns and gathered up all the ladders in the surrounding villages to prepare for an assault. However, darkness fell at 7:00 p.m. and he stopped his preparations. Belliard's withdrawal occurred in silence and without incident as he moved to Jonchery. From that same village, Mortier moved that night to the Fismes heights to the left of Oudinot. His position was not quiet, as his advanced posts fired across the Vesle at the Prussian advanced posts throughout the night.

That evening, Yorck's corps encamped at Romain and Vanteley; Kleist in Blazy-les-Perles; Sacken in Pontavaire; Langeron in Béry-au-Bac; and Bülow closed on Soissons. Winzingerode's corps camped outside Rheims – not occupying it until the following morning.[4]

During the afternoon of 20 March the two French corps united on the Saint-Martin hill, with the Ardres stream to their front and Fismes as an advanced post. This position was an excellent one from which to retard – for a while – the Allied advance, but it was a bad field for a battle because in case of a need to withdraw, the only retreat was down bad roads – while it left the main road from Soissons to Paris (and that from Rheims to the Marne) completely open. Oudinot understood Berthier's call for revenge against the Prussians and sought to draw them near Mareuil-en-Dôle, where there was a good battlefield.

Blücher saw the possibility of establishing his communications with the main Allied army via Rheims, which had been ceded to him by the overly strict adherence of the two French marshals to their instructions to stay between him and Paris. Rheims being opened, he resolved to put himself into contact with Schwarzenberg using his light troops and to prepare to operate in concert with Schwarzenberg if the distance was not too great. As a result, Winzingerode was ordered to hold Rheims with his infantry; to establish bridges over the Vesle; and to push his cavalry to Epernay and Vitry. Generals Yorck and Kleist were ordered to continue watching the two French marshals and to hold them in place with demonstrations. He directed Baron Sacken to march on Wailly, to raise a bridge there and to push his advanced guard to Mont-Saint-Martin, where Mortier was rejoined by Charpentier's division.

Charpentier had abandoned Soissons and Compiègne to the protection of their garrisons. However, Soissons was not in a good position to be held against a *coup de main*. It was garrisoned by two sapper companies and about 800 workers who did not have sufficient time to properly repair the city's defenses. Only the work on St.-Wast was in a condition to serve as a citadel. Mortier had left 2,800 men and 39 guns there under the command of Commandant Gérard. The garrison of Compiègne was under Major Ottenin and consisted of about 600 Young Guard.

In the evening, the cavalry of generals Yorck and Kleist joined in Courlandon – under the orders of Ziethen – crossed the Vesle and moved to establish themselves in a position on the French right. General Bülow marched on Soissons and had a sharp engagement with its garrison. Langeron remained in reserve at Béry-au-Bac.

The fall of Châlons to Tettenborn

During the maneuvers of Blücher's corps, Tettenborn reoccupied Châlons when the Gardes d'honneur withdrew – and before General Duvigneau had the time to establish a garrison in the city. This stroke once again opened up communications with the Army of Silesia and resulted in considerable joy at the Allied headquarters. However, the situation was not completely stable as word arrived of a mixed force of French infantry and artillery marching on Châlons from the Ardennes – and word that the population in the countryside had risen in arms. Feldmarschal Blücher ordered Count Langeron to detach Count von Witte – with a flying corps of 1,000 cavalry and 2,000 infantry – to march on Réthel to engage or observe this force. The French force in question was Janssens' division, which after beginning a march on Rheims, disappeared across the countryside without leaving a trace.

On 21 March Mortier and Oudinot received an order from Berthier – carried by General Vincent – to join Napoleon via Châlons or Epernay in the region around Vitry. With this order they realized their error in not reuniting at Rheims, and since the only road from Fismes passed

4 Koch, Vol. II, pp. 95-101.

Prussian horse artillery, by Richard Knötel.

through Epernay, they began their march in that direction – reaching Château-Thierry in two columns via the roads moving from Fère to Tardenois and through Cramaille to Oulchy-le-Châtel.

Cavalry engagement at Oulchy-le-Châtel

At 4:00 a.m. on 21 March word arrived at the headquarters of the Army of Silesia that the forces of Marmont and Mortier stood on the heights by Mont-Saint-Martin and that they were marching on Dôle. The Prussians set out in pursuit – hoping to catch them.

General von Ziethen advanced with the combined reserve cavalry of the Prussian 1st and 2nd Corps – moving between Sapponay and Cramaille. His left-wing column, under Oberst von Blücher, was formed from the advanced guard cavalry and consisted of the Neumark Dragoons and the 1st Silesian Hussar Regiment. It was directed to move around the Cugny heights. The right-wing column, consisting of the Brandenburg Uhlan and Silesian Cuirassier Regiments (and supported by the brigade of Oberst von Wrangle), was sent against Oulchy. General von Jürgass followed them with three more cavalry regiments that served as a reserve.

The right wing of the Prussian cavalry threw the French cavalry that occupied Oulchy back, but the Prussian left column was unable to push back the forces it encountered.

Blücher launched a second attack – this time moving against the bridge over the Ourcq, passing over it and capturing a column of 18 limbered cannon.

At about 2:00 p.m. General Katzler moved against Fère-en-Tardenois. By Coincy, the Brandenburg Hussars encountered a French squadron, which they drove back. The two Prussian hussar regiments then pushed between Coincy and Rocourt – encountering a force of French cavalry and guns (supported by three infantry battalions) in Rocourt.

They skirmished inconclusively until 6:00 p.m. when General von Ziethen moved up his artillery and the French withdrew towards Château-Thierry. Unwilling to continue the pursuit of the French, von Ziethen stopped his advance and held the reserve cavalry by Oulchy-le-Châtel.[5]

5 von Damitz, Vol. III, 1st Part, pp. 196-197.

Prussian infantry charging, by Anton Hoffmann.

and Sacken stood by his right – leaving Bülow to undertake the siege of Soissons alone. A flying cavalry corps was formed and ordered to march on Villers-Cotterets to chase the garrison of Compiègne, which had escaped into the Villers-Cotterets forest.

Mortier and Oudinot knew the country around Montmirail well and paused for 24 hours in the region to collect 10,000 men that were dispersed in the region. Many of these detachments were more than willing to join because of the advance of the Army of Silesia. The detachments absorbed were:

1 Two brigades from Pacthod's division – 4,000 men – left behind by Macdonald on 18 March to guard the three bridges over the Seine and on 22 March directed from Villenoxe on Sézanne, where they had just arrived.
2 Amey's division – around 1,800 men – which had been marching from St.-Saturnin on Sézanne instead of escorting Macdonald's ill-fated artillery park.
3 A column of 800 line and National Guard, a half-battery and 100 troopers from the 13th Hussar Regiment. They had left Meaux on 19 March under orders of Adjudant-commandant Noizet, with a convoy of 80 vehicles and 100,000 rations of bread and brandy. They were ordered to arrive in Sézanne on 21 March.
4 The 8th and 9th Cavalry March Regiments – about 800 men – which had left Versailles on 18 March and found themselves in Coulommiers on 19 March.
5 A provisional division organized in Meaux by General Ledru-des-Essarts, with 1,500 infantry and 450 cavalry.
6 The free corps of Colonel Simon with 400 infantry and 40 lancers, which had been fighting around Coulommiers.

Independent of these troops, Mortier and Oudinot had available to them Allix's division; the nucleus of Souham's 2nd Paris Reserve Division (which was reinforced with the 4th Cavalry March Regiment – plus a force of 4,500 infantry); 500 cavalry; and 16 guns which were deployed uselessly beyond the Yonne – from Auxerre to Montereau – by special order of the Minister of War.

Lacking guidance and information, the two marshals continued their march on Châlons on 23 March. Their advanced guard, formed by General Merlin, encountered an Allied cavalry post near Bergères and chased it off. This was a foraging party which Tettenborn had detached in Vertus. The French light cavalry threw them back, recaptured 16 wagons of pillage and captured about 100 of the Allied troopers.[7]

The French army then established itself in Bergères and Etoges, where General Vincent made his happy reunion after an encounter with the Russians near Orbais.

One of Belliard's staff officers made a fortunate discovery in his lodging in Vertus. It was a number of dispatches addressed to Tettenborn which announced the resolution of the Tsar to march with the two main armies directly on Paris. However, Mortier and Oudinot thought that the papers were a deception and chose to ignore them.

Blücher resolves to join Schwarzenberg

Though Blücher recognized the necessity of preventing the two French marshals from rejoining Napoleon, he also felt an overwhelming need to join Schwarzenberg so that he might strike Napoleon in his flanks and rear while was engaged frontally by Schwarzenberg. He chose to detach the two Prussian corps to pursue Mortier and Oudinot and directed Winzingerode to cross the Aube with 46 horse guns, 10 cavalry regiments and 20 Cossack regiments – a total of 8,000 – and to threaten the French army's path in the Marne plains. His infantry, under Voronzov, was ordered to march on Châlons and to be replaced in Rheims by the corps of Langeron and Sacken. Blücher wished to pass Langeron and Voronzov over the Marne the following day and to then concentrate the three Russian corps between the Marne and the Aube. The corps of Yorck and Kleist were to continue in the direction of Montmirail and pursue Mortier and Oudinot without respite, but only with their cavalry. General Bülow was to continue the siege of Soissons and hold himself ready to march on either Paris or the Marne. In case of a reversal, he was to guard the city with a single brigade.

Everything was put into movement (except for Voronzov) and the three Russian corps were united that evening in Rheims and all of Winzingerode's cavalry moved to the left bank of the Marne.

That evening, Blücher learned of the successes of the main Allied army and word of Napoleon's plans. Schwarzenberg also advised Blücher of the intention of the two armies to march on Paris. Everything was ready for implementation and Blücher had only to send the three Russian corps to Châlons instead of crossing the Marne near Epernay.

During this junction of the two Allied armies – destined to administer the final blow to Napoleon's throne – Mortier and Oudinot marched on Vitry via the road through Vatry and La Fère-Champenoise. Belliard had proposed following this route for several reasons. First, he judged it dangerous to pass the army across the open Marne plains. Secondly, he observed that La Fère-Champenoise was as close to Vitry as Vatry and that in case of a need to march on Paris, a good route was available, which minimized the threat of cavalry as far as Somme-Soudé. Mortier held the same opinion, but Oudinot argued strongly against it and the march on Vatry was finally accepted. To support this, General Vincent was detached towards Montmirail with a force of 200

7 de Vaudoncourt, Vol. II, p. 281

Young Guard, 50 dragoons and 50 Gardes d'honneur to observe the movement of the Prussian corps and to follow the army as far as Château-Thierry should a threat appear from that flank.

The march on Vatry occurred without incident, and during the evening of 24 March Mortier's troops took up a position straddling the roads from Troyes to Châlons and from Vertus to Vitry. Oudinot posted his troops on the road from Fère to Vitry. However, Vincent was delayed in his movement because he encountered detachments from Ziethen's forces and engaged them.

Various detachments seek to join Mortier and Oudinot

Pacthod's division – two brigades with about 4,000 men – arrived in Sézanne on 23 March. General Amey, who had been directed there by accident, arrived the same day with his 1,800 men. In addition, a large convoy – under the command of Adjudant-commandant Noizet and consisting of 80 wagons loaded with bread, cognac and military equipage – was already in the village with an escort of 800 men and a squadron of the 13th Hussar Regiment.

The following day, Pacthod and Amey learned by indirect means that a French army corps was marching down the secondary roads to Châlons in an effort to join Napoleon. They resolved to await it and put themselves and a provisions convoy under Adjudant-commandant Noizet – arriving from Sézanne – under its protection. There remained only 1,000 men in Châlons to guard the line of communication. On their arrival in Etoges that evening, the generals learned that Mortier and Oudinot had been there the previous night and now stood behind Somme-Soudé. Rejoicing in their belief that they were saved, they dispatched staff officers to the marshals requesting orders.

The same day Pacthod departed Sézanne, GD Compans arrived in the city with orders to organize a junction of all the troops in the region and to establish it as a communications center for the army. Shortly behind him arrived two cavalry march regiments – each with about 400 men.[8]

Bülow besieges Soissons

Bülow's 3rd Prussian Corps stood before Soissons – holding the French garrison on the walls. The French commander – Chef de bataillon Gérard – commanded 3,000 to 4,000 infantry (mostly veterans) including the Vistula Legion Regiment, 600 Polish lancers, two companies of sappers and two coast artillery companies. It was a sufficient garrison to force Bülow into a protracted siege. Bülow was more than willing to oblige the French and began siege operations. During the night of 22-23 March Bülow erected a pontoon bridge over the Aisne at Vailly. That day, Bülow sent his reserve artillery and the 3rd Prussian Brigade over the Aisne. He was moving his forces about, but he was proceeding with a siege. During the night of 24-25 March 300 workers moved forward and opened the first trench. By dawn, the trench was 800 paces long and garrisoned with a force of jägers. During the night of 27 March the Prussian artillery opened fire on Soissons from the trenches. That night, the Prussians extended their trench to 1,500 paces in length.

During the night of 29-30 March the Prussians pushed their trenches forward and the French launched a sortie in an effort to delay their operations. The size of the French force is not known – nor is its casualties – but the Prussians reported 12-15 dead and wounded. The damages to the entrenchments were minor, but the siege was destined to be lifted. Orders from Blücher had arrived ordering Bülow to abandon the siege and march on Paris.[9]

8 de Vaudoncourt, Vol. II, pp. 273-4.
9 von Damitz, Vol. III, 2nd Part, pp. 213-5.

15

Peace and Politics: The Congress of Châtillon

The Quadruple Alliance is formed and the situation of the French Empire

Though the 1814 campaign continued to extract its price in blood across the winter plains of France, men of peace and diplomacy continued to attempt to resolve the issues at the negotiations table.

Napoleon had, based on the proposals made to Baron de St. Aignan in November 1813, charged Caulaincourt to undertake the representation of France in the Congress of Châtillon. Granted full, unlimited powers of negotiation, Caulaincourt arrived in Nancy on 6 January and requested that Metternich send passports through the Allied lines so he could either proceed to the Allied headquarters or to Mannheim – the city designated for the next congress. However, Vienna was no longer in charge of the congress and Metternich was unable to send the safe conducts requested. The Allies were waiting for the arrival of Lord Castlereagh.

Caulaincourt waited eight days. During this time, he was forced to withdraw as the Allied armies penetrated into France. On 17 January he sent a dispatch to Napoleon stating: "Our position has significantly changed in the last few days. The rapid march of the enemy on all points, the invasion of a large part of the territory of the Empire and the discouragement of the people makes an armistice indispensable. I have, therefore, need to know the intentions of Your Majesty. It seems, in the present circumstances, that I do nothing if you chose not to send me your orders."

Caulaincourt spoke of the urgency of stopping the Allied advance; of seeking any possible means of detaching the continental Allies from England; of minimizing the influence exercised by England on the negotiations; and to remove England's ability to wreck any negotiations and prolong the fight.

It was Caulaincourt's perception that the Allies' successes gave them the anticipation of obtaining great concessions and anticipated changes in their demands from those of the proposals of Frankfurt once Castlereagh arrived.[1]

Napoleon, recognizing what faced his empire, sent Caulaincourt a letter directing that he seek a private audience with Metternich and attempt to negotiate an armistice.

Conference of Langres

Lord Castlereagh departed London on 27 December and after installing the Prince of Orange as King of Holland in Amsterdam, arrived in Langres on 28 January. In a conference held the next day with Count Stadion – where the ministers and ambassadors of Russia, Austria, Prussia and England met – they established the basis of any negotiations that would be held with France at Châtillon.

1 Koch, Vol. I, pp. 320-1.

The plenipotentiaries of the four powers took it upon themselves to represent all of Europe in these negotiations. It was decided that there would be no discussions relative to maritime law; that France would be required to withdraw to its 1792 borders – with the possibility of some mutually agreeable transfers of land; that Napoleon would have no right to intervene in the distribution of those detached portions of his empire; and that Napoleon would renounce his sovereignty or rights of protectorship over Italy, Germany and Switzerland.

As these decisions were being made in Langres, Caulaincourt finally obtained his passports to proceed to Châtillon. All the while, he continued to demand from Napoleon further instructions and more greatly expanded powers to negotiate in case the Allies chose to abandon their demands from the Frankfurt Congress and demand even further concessions from France.

The situation was not improved by the Allied victory at La Rothière, but Napoleon continued to present a bold front – writing Caulaincourt to press the negotiations and to accelerate a resolution for the sake of the suffering of the French people, but without indicating to Caulaincourt what sacrifices he was willing to inflict on the French people.

Caulaincourt and Berthier

Perplexed by the situation and seeing nothing but the exaggerated Allied pronouncements of their victory at La Rothière, Caulaincourt needed information. However, Napoleon and the Duke of Bassano gave him no information, so he turned to Napoleon's chief of staff – Maréchal Berthier – writing the following:

> I write to Your Highness as the most noble and devoted servants of the Emperor. Once again, there is a battle and the enemy have triumphed! This situation impedes our negotiations does it not? Does it not make all questions more difficult? Does it not augment all demands? The evil genius that has destroyed the great plans of the Emperor continues to do so. Has it not brought us enough misfortune? Tell Napoleon the truth. Show him that the situation is grave; any delay provides only risks without offering any advantage. Speak truly with me, my Prince. Do you still have an army? Can it recover itself in 15 days, or will it accept its fate. If no one has the courage to second me, and to tell me the truth, I must depend on what information I can gather from the gazettes of the Duke of Bassano and I will not know what I must do. With only these stories – that we have lost all our conquests – there remains but to save France. The fault will not be mine, as I have not ceased to demand of the Emperor that he send me instructions – and that to better serve him, he give me the responsibilities to execute them. In the name of our master; in the name of all that you hold most dear; my Prince, speak to him, write me and we will save his throne and the motherland.

The Châtillon Congress opens

As it stood, the Châtillon Congress was opening with Caulaincourt pleading for instructions and information about the conditions of France's armies. Facing him were the representatives of the four other major European powers whose armies had invaded France and taken the first battle. The Allies' representatives were Count Rasumowski, Count Stadion and Baron Humbolt, who were, respectively, the plenipotentiaries of Russia, Austria and Prussia. England – not content with directing the negotiations from afar – sent three emissaries (Lords Aberdeen, Cathcart and General Charles Stewart).

Facing not just four adversaries, but six, Caulaincourt sent yet another dispatch to Napoleon – pleading that he dispatch two or three more plenipotentiaries to assist him in the negotiations.

Though Baron de St. Aignan (who had handled the negotiations at Frankfurt) might have been an excellent choice, Napoleon chose instead to leave Caulaincourt alone at the negotiating table.

The first conference

Caulaincourt did not look forward to this meeting, as he was equipped with only ill-defined powers and he looked forward only to difficulties as the first meeting of the negotiators met. Fortunately for the harried Caulaincourt, as the plenipotentiaries met, Count Rasumowski declared that he had still not received his documents authorizing him to negotiate. Caulaincourt seized upon this opportunity to suggest that though it was normal to exchange their authorization to negotiate at the moment of signature, that it would suffice in this instance to submit certified copies. This proposition was adopted and Count Stadion made two declarations.

In the first, the plenipotentiaries declared that they were authorized to represent not only the courts which sent them, but as well as for all the European powers engaged in the existing war. The second declaration was that the Allied courts regarded any effort by France to open negotiations on the maritime code as contrary to the objective of the calling of the congress and to their efforts to re-establish peace in Europe.

Caulaincourt accepted the first declaration – not wishing to raise difficulties so early in the negotiations – and with regards to the second statement, responded only in the most general of terms, stating that: "it was never the intention of France to ask for any degradation of the rights of man" in the hope of maintaining his ability to return to this issue at a later date.

And with this exchange, the first day of negotiations ended. Caulaincourt, however, had realized by this exchange that the Allies had a single agenda and that their actions had been orchestrated in advance and in concert by their respective courts. It was apparent that any effort for even the most modest and simple amendment to the protocol would lead to substantial debate.

Caulaincourt.

The second conference

As the representatives of the five powers met in the second conference, the Allies laid out their position, which formed the basis of their instructions: "The Allied powers are united in their view that the future security and independence of Europe – with their desire to see France in an equal position to the rank which it has always occupied in the political system, and considering the situation in which Europe finds itself placed vis-a-vis France as a result of the successes of their armies – the plenipotentiaries of the Allied courts are ordered to demand that France return to the borders it had before the Revolution – except for arrangements of convenience that may mutually be agreed upon, and except the restitutions which England is ready to make for the general interest of Europe against the retrocessions demanded below by France, which shall be made against the conquests which England has made during the war; for which, in consequence, shall France abandon all direct influence outside its future limits and that the renunciation of all the titles which imply sovereignty over Italy, Germany or Switzerland, which shall be the immediate result of this agreement."[2]

2 Koch, Vol. I, pp. 322-330.

This declaration resulted in a lively debate. Caulaincourt responded by evoking the basis of negotiation offered in the Frankfurt Congress. The responses of the Allied negotiators varied from ignoring the proposition to providing elusive responses to it. Caulaincourt immediately recognized that as soon as he made one concession, the Allies would demand yet another. He responded by observing that if France were returned to its 1792 borders, that France would not hold the same position in European politics as it had under Louis XVI because of the changes in the face of European politics since that time. He responded that the demands of the Allies were too great for him to give an immediate response. He requested an adjournment of a few hours to consider his position. The Allies consented.

Having retired to his quarters at 8:00 p.m. Caulaincourt wrote a note stating that he had renewed the proposal made by his court to make great sacrifices for the sake of peace. He noted the demand made in that day's session by the Allies was based on the proposals made by them at Frankfurt and was rooted in what the Allies called France's 'natural limits'. He noted that the Allies had accepted France's position in the European power structure. However, the note went on to declare that they were asking that a principle be applied to France that they were unwilling to apply to themselves. He wrote that France was willing to make sacrifices, but that the number and types of these sacrifices to be made by France depended on the sum of those sacrifices and on any compensations for them. He ended his note demanding that the Allies make a positive explanation of previously cited points.

The Allied response was cool at best. The note was taken ad referendum and later used by them as a pretext for suspending the congress. They demanded that Caulaincourt withdraw his note so that they might not be forced to respond to it as the basis for renewed discussions. Caulaincourt resolved after reconsidering his ill-defined powers from the Duke of Bassano to desist in further pretensions. However, Count Rasumowski declared that he was no longer able to negotiate and the session ended.

An armistice is requested

Caulaincourt attempted repeatedly to identify and categorize the views of the various Allies in an effort to separate and to categorize them into manageable groupings. He perceived from the silence from Napoleon and Berthier that everything was lost and took matters into his own hands in an effort to avoid the Allied occupation of Paris. On 9 February he wrote Metternich proposing that if France were to agree to return to its 1792 boundaries, an immediate armistice be signed. He was, however, uncertain if the Allied plenipotentiaries had such authority.

Metternich transmitted Caulaincourt's letter to the council of Allied sovereigns. They decided that a preliminary treaty, which had the effect of an armistice for France, was acceptable to their goals. As a result, a peace treaty – with nine articles – was prepared and sent to the plenipotentiaries, with authorization to conclude this treaty with a few designated variations. The main objective of this treaty was the restoration of a balance of power, which had been proposed by Napoleon at an earlier date.[3]

The fourth conference

The fourth meeting of the negotiators occurred on 17 February – 10 days after the suspension of negotiations. The Allied representatives opened the meeting with a return to the declaration of

3 Philippart, Vol. I, p. 335.

7 February and Caulaincourt insisted that at least the preamble be deleted. However, the Allied representatives remained inflexible and proffered an addition to the protocol.

This addition acknowledged Caulaincourt's reservations, but reiterated the unshakable resolution of the Allies to establish a "just equilibrium in Europe." Of course, this justice was justice as seen in the eye of the victor. Having resolved this issue, the parties settled down to the principal objective: the draft treaty. That draft treaty contained the following stipulations:

Article 1 was related to the re-establishment of peace. According to Article 2 Napoleon was to renounce for himself and his successors all of the conquests made by France since 1792 and at the same time abandon any constitutional influence, direct or indirect, outside of its former borders by consequence of the possession of titles such as 'The King of Italy', 'Protector of the Confederation of the Rhine' or 'Mediator of the Swiss Confederation'.

Article 3 reiterated the principle of the sovereignty, liberty and absolute independence of the various states of Europe.

Article 4 demanded that Napoleon recognize the following reorganization of Europe: Germany was to be composed of independent states – united in a confederation. Italy was to be divided into independent states that were to be in the Austrian and French sphere of influence. Holland was to be established as a kingdom under the House of Orange and its territories were to be expanded. Switzerland was to be a free and independent state under the guarantee of all the great powers – including France – and Spain, under the rule of Fernando VII, was to resume its former borders.

Furthermore, Napoleon was to recognize the Allies' right to determine – according to their existing network of treaties – the limits and scope of the territories ceded by France, with France having no right to intervene.

Article 5 stated that England would restore to France – with the exception of the islands of the Saintes and Tobago – all the conquests they had made since 1792 and that the Allies engaged to employ their good offices to encourage Sweden and Portugal to return Guadeloupe and Cayenne.

England also promised to return to France the establishments and conquests to the east of Cape Bonne-Espérance – with the exception of the islands of Saint-Maurice, Bourbon and their dependencies – under the condition that France would not fortify those regions, nor inject into them garrisons or armed forces larger than necessary to maintain the peace. This article also forbade the importation of slaves and ceded to England all rights to the island of Malta.

Article 6 stipulated that Napoleon would, as soon as this treaty was ratified, abandon all fortresses in the ceded territories – and in Germany – that were still occupied by French troops without exception. Mainz was to be vacated immediately. In six days Luxemburg, Antwerp, Bergen-op-Zoom, Mantua, Palma-Nova, Venice and Peschiera were to be vacated. Those on the Oder and Elbe were to be turned over in 10 days – and everything else was to be vacated in 15 days. The fortresses were to be turned over intact, with all munitions and artillery. The French were to be permitted to depart with their personal weapons and baggage.

In addition, in four days, Napoleon was to surrender to the Allies the French fortresses of Besançon, Belfort and Huningue to serve as depots until the signing of a definitive peace treaty.

The 1st, 7th, 8th and 9th articles contained the methodology relating to peace, the cessation of hostilities, the line of demarcation between the hostile armies, the ratification of the preliminary treaty and the signing of a definitive treaty.

Caulaincourt took issue with the proposed renunciation of the crown of Italy. He also requested that the kingdom of the King of Saxony be restored to its pre-1792 boundaries; that the King of Westphalia be recognized in his territories by the Allied powers; and finally, that Prince Eugene's rights as the heir to the Kingdom of Italy be recognized. The Allied plenipotentiaries responded by directing Caulaincourt's attention to Article 4, which stated that France would have no input into the disposition of territories which it had ceded. Caulaincourt then requested a few days to consider the Allied proposals.[4]

Napoleon rejects the proposed treaty

Caulaincourt immediately dispatched a copy of the draft treaty to Napoleon – also sending him the basis for a counter-offer which he proposed to produce as soon as possible. However, he also attempted to impress on Napoleon that for the sake of peace it would be necessary to cede Holland, Belgium, Piedmont, Mainz and part of Mont-Tonnerre.

Unfortunately, Caulaincourt's proposal and the draft treaty arrived at a most inopportune moment. It arrived in Napoleon's hands immediately after he had won the battles of Champaubert, Montmirail, Château-Thierry and Vauchamps. Smelling the blood of his vanquished enemies on his hands, Napoleon felt that the terms offered were too harsh and that his star was once again in the ascent on the battlefield. Better terms would be won by force of arms and he felt that one major battle would save the Empire. However, fearing that the fruit of such a victory would be thrown away by accident on the negotiating table, Napoleon withdrew Caulaincourt's unlimited powers to negotiate. He also broke his silence about the situation in the field and advised Caulaincourt that he would be providing him more favorable circumstances in which to negotiate. He ended his letter to Caulaincourt with the comment: "The Allies forget that I am closer to Munich than I am to Paris!"

The Treaty of the Quadruple Alliance

Caulaincourt was now in an embarrassing situation vis-a-vis the Allied plenipotentiaries and sought to alleviate the situation. He sought additional instructions endlessly, but Caulaincourt was once again drowned with the silence from Paris except for one letter from Napoleon, which advised Caulaincourt that he had written the Austrian Emperor Francis – his father-in-law – and gloated on the impact this letter would have. The letter was filled with recriminations and propositions. However, it did not have its desired effect and hardened the Allies in their position. It also aroused doubts in the Allied camp of Napoleon's sincerity to negotiate. Though not the principal cause, it encouraged the signing of a renewed defensive and offensive treaty between the Allies that was directed at France and would last for 20 years.

In its first and second articles, the four signing powers contracted to pursue the war against Napoleon with all their means and to not make a separate peace with him. England, by the terms of Article 3, would pay a subsidy of £5,000,000 sterling in 1814 – in instalments of £416,666 – to be divided equally between the remaining three powers. It also stipulated that if the amount was not renegotiated by 1 January the same amount would be again pledged to the war effort.

Articles 7 and 8 were the defensive alliance, in which each party agreed to come to the aid of the other if attacked by France. They were to provide auxiliary corps of 60,000 men within two months to support the attacked party. England, however, was to provide a contingent of foreign troops in its pay or to provide subsidies of £20 sterling per infantry man or £30 sterling per cavalry trooper.

The Quadruple Alliance was signed on 1 March by the plenipotentiaries of the four powers after a conference on 28 February held with Caulaincourt, which had proven fruitless.

4 Koch, Vol. I, pp. 331-340.

General Yorck moved his headquarters to Fère, while Kleist moved to Cramaille. Winzingerode remained in Rheims and pushed a party down the road to Epernay. Langeron marched from Béry-au-Bac to Baslieux and Sacken marched from Vailly to Braisnes, with his advanced guards moving on Soissons (where they arrived the next day).

Engagement at Epernay – 14 March

Earlier, on 14 March – after the French had occupied Ferté-sous-Jouarre and Château-Thierry – General Vincent, who was in Château-Thierry, was ordered to move to Epernay. At the same time, General Colbert was ordered to move there from Rheims. Before noon on 15 March the French troops passed through the forest between Rheims and the Marne. Their advanced troops encountered an Allied cavalry picket and drove it back. At the same time, a French column – under General Vincent and containing 300-500 infantry and 125 cavalry – moved against the bridge over the Marne leading to Epernay. The French had no artillery, but still occupied Epernay with little problem.

Tettenborn learned that the French flying corps occupied Epernay and detached Colonel Pfuhl with two Cossack regiments and two 6pdr guns to clear them out. When Pfuhl arrived, Vincent was unwilling to be chased from his post by such a small force and decided to stand fast – hoping that he would soon be reinforced by Oudinot and Mortier.

Pfuhl's initial attack was rebuffed, but at about 2:00 p.m. Pfuhl learned that Winzingerode's advanced guard was about to arrive. Vincent was cut off and obliged to march on Dormans via the Vancienne forest – abandoning Epernay to the Cossacks – but not before the bridge was destroyed by an explosive charge.

According to von Damitz, the French infantry – abandoned by its cavalry – was surrounded and obliged to surrender. Tettenborn and Falkenhausen remained by the bridge until dusk and then withdrew to rejoin the main Allied forces nearby.[6]

During the morning of 16 March an Allied detachment arrived in Velye from Châlons and reported to Tettenborn that Rheims had fallen to the French. Before marching on Rheims, St. Priest had left two infantry regiments and a dragoon regiment in Châlons under generals Davidov and Vassil'shikov III. This force united itself with the Prussian battalion left to watch the Sillery bridge and the larger part of the Allied survivors fleeing from Rheims. They then established communications with Tettenborn.

Tettenborn also learned that on 14 March – after Napoleon had taken Rheims – Maréchal Ney, with Defrance's cavalry division; P. Boyer's infantry division; and an important artillery park marched on Châlons – chasing Davidov's tiny force from the city.

General von Tettenborn gathered up all this news of French movements and the battle at Rheims and sent a message to Schwarzenberg informing him of the events of the past few days. He then marched to Cosel, where on 16 March he joined the cavalry detachments of the main Allied army.

As Oudinot and Mortier arrived in Château-Thierry, they learned of Vincent's escape. This caused them to believe that the main road was too heavily occupied by the Allies for them to use it – and they turned to the secondary roads. They destroyed the bridges in Château-Thierry and ordered Vincent to rejoin them via Orbais, while they marched towards Montmirail. Ziethen's cavalry reserve continued to pursue them and arrived on the right bank of the Marne. Kleist and Yorck's corps arrived on the Ourcq at Cugny, Oulchy and Billy. Their light cavalry was in Neuillly and La Ferté-Milon. Winzingerode's infantry remained in Rheims, while his cavalry marched on the Marne with the goal of striking Napoleon's rear. Langeron advanced to Fismes

6 von Damitz, Vol. III, 1st Part, pp. 167-9.

The fifth conference

Several days passed from when Caulaincourt was given the peace proposal – and no response was heard from him by the Allied plenipotentiaries; nothing – not even complaints or requests for modifications. It was then decided that it was necessary to demand of Caulaincourt a response to the plan and an explanation of the delays.

The Allies resolved to remain firm in their position on the proposed treaty and steadily became reinforced in their belief that Caulaincourt's silence was tantamount to a rejection of the peace plan. Their thoughts were formally communicated to Caulaincourt in writing – ending with the statement that if no response in substantial accord with the proposed treaty was received, the Allied plenipotentiaries would consider the congress as terminated and would return to their respective headquarters.

In addition to submitting this written declaration to Caulaincourt, Count Stadion added a verbal statement that he and his colleagues stood ready to discuss – in the spirit of conciliation – all modifications which did not vary from the basic principles, but which might be of an essential nature to France.

Caulaincourt responded to the Allies' reproaches by stating that the Allies had had all the time they felt necessary to develop their position and to deliver their proposals and that they should permit him the same opportunity to prepare his response. He went on to point out the difficulties of communications, the weather and various other problems with couriers that made liaison with his Emperor very slow and difficult. He ended by stating that France ardently wished peace and that he was doing as much as possible to bring it about. Caulaincourt also responded in his letter to Prince Metternich that the armistice he had requested had been refused.

The Allies continued to press him for a time for his response or a counter-proposal, and finally he promised that by 10 March they would have it. He then wrote Napoleon of this embarrassing meeting, but he was still unaware of the signing of the Quadruple Alliance Treaty. He told Napoleon that he doubted that military victories by him would "greatly influence the fundamental questions of peace." He felt that they were firmly resolved to their position and that they were less inclined to accept different terms than he had expressed in his last letters. He felt that the terms of the Frankfurt Congress were the best that could be hoped for.

Napoleon received this dispatch on 2 March in La Ferté-sous-Jouarre as he sought to administer the final blow to the Army of Silesia. His response was, as a result, tainted with his hopes and did not accept what Caulaincourt was trying to tell him. He abandoned his earlier conciliatory tone to Caulaincourt – stating that France would not withdraw beyond its 'natural borders' and directed Caulaincourt to use this as a pretext to gain both time and to obtain a clarification on the Allies' intentions for the future constitution of Europe. To Caulaincourt, this note was more designed to cause a rupture of the talks than to procure the desired information.

Caulaincourt wrote back on 6 March stating that he did not feel that Napoleon was in a position sufficiently strong to make such demands – and that sacrifices were necessary if peace was to be obtained. He also warned Napoleon that if action was not taken now, the opportunity for peace might well escape him. He stated that if the French did not produce a counter-proposal on the basis of the Frankfurt Congress, everything was lost.

Caulaincourt stated that the English were there – filled with hate and desirous solely of sating their passions. He perceived that a rupture of the negotiations was what they desired most. He went on to state that once the negotiations were broken off, there would be no further opportunities to reopen them. Any chance at a negotiated peace would vanish.

In his letter, Caulaincourt also advised Napoleon that an Austrian diplomat had come to him – on the orders of Prince Metternich – asking that he stress to Napoleon the necessity of concluding a peace as quickly as possible.

Napoleon received this letter the day after the Battle of Craone. He had also just learned of Macdonald's evacuation of Troyes. Napoleon did not respond, but the Duke of Bassano did – sending some materials for the counter-project. Napoleon proposed the cession of Dutch-Barbant, Wesel, Cassel, Kehl and the Thalweg of the Rhine – plus a few changes in the basis of the Frankfurt proposals regarding Italy. He did not wish to surrender Mainz, but would consent to its fortress being leveled. Cassel would be sufficient. He attached no importance to the lost colonies, and the loss of Ile de France and Ile de Bourbon were no obstacle to the peace. In addition, Caulaincourt was advised that these were his first thoughts – not an ultimatum – but if the first word of the Allies was their ultimatum, then the negotiations should be considered ruptured. Caulaincourt was to receive these communications on 10 March.

The sixth conference

Caulaincourt sent a note to the Allied plenipotentiaries advising them of his receipt of instructions and a counter-proposal from his government. His note provoked a lively discussion and they decided that Napoleon's response was a response to their demands – not a counter-proposal – and were at the point of breaking off the negotiations. To save the situation, Caulaincourt announced verbally that Napoleon would renounce all claims of sovereignty over any territories outside the borders of France; that he recognized the independence of Spain under Fernando VII; that of Italy, of Germany and of Switzerland under the guarantees of the great powers; and of Holland under the Prince of Orange. He then stated that if England and France were to effect a durable peace, France was ready to make concessions to England of overseas possessions. The Allied plenipotentiaries responded that the acceptance of these points did not answer their questions regarding the note – with the outline of Napoleon's demands – but chose to consider it as a point of reference.

The seventh conference

On 13 March a seventh meeting of the plenipotentiaries was convened and the Allies opened with a protocol declaring that they had taken into consideration the note presented by Caulaincourt at the meeting of 10 March and the verbal declaration dictated by him at that same meeting. They stated that the written note could not be taken into consideration without derailing the entire negotiation.

They stated that Caulaincourt's verbal statement was solely the acceptance of a number of the points of their initial proposal, but that it did not respond to the major portion of the proposed treaty. As a result, it could not be considered as a counter-proposal to the points put forward by the Allied plenipotentiaries.

They then called upon Caulaincourt to either accept or reject their proposal or to put forth a counter-proposal that could be discussed. They then permitted a suspension of the conference for a further 24 to 36 hours in which Caulaincourt could prepare his counter-proposal.[5]

Negotiations are resumed

Word of Napoleon's check before Laon on 9-10 March had arrived in the Allied headquarters. The Allied sovereigns were, as a result, determined to bring the negotiations to a conclusion as rapidly as possible.

5 Koch, Vol. I, pp. 341-352.

Caulaincourt – for his part – had withdrawn and, taking the guidance at hand (plus Napoleon's note), prepared a definitive treaty with 29 articles that addressed every point of contention.

The eighth conference

On 15 March Caulaincourt reviewed this proposed treaty with the Allied plenipotentiaries.

Rupture of talks – Declaration of the Allied powers on the breaking off of negotiations

The Allied powers owe it to themselves, to their people and to France – as the negotiations at Châtillon are broken off – publicly to declare the reasons which induced them to enter into negotiations with the French government, as well as the causes of the breaking off of the negotiations.

Military events – to which history can produce no parallel – overthrew in the month of October last, the ill-constructed edifice known under the name of the French Empire; an edifice erected on the ruins of states – lately independent and happy – augmented by conquests from ancient monarchies and held together at the expense of blood, of the fortune, of the welfare of a whole generation.

The Allied sovereigns – led by conquest to the Rhine – thought it their duty to proclaim to Europe anew their principles, their wishes and their object. Far from every wish of domination or conquest – animated solely by the desire to see Europe restored to a just balance of the different powers – resolved not to lay down their arms till they had obtained the noble object of their efforts: they made known the irrevocableness of their resolutions by a public act and they did not hesitate to declare themselves to the enemy's government in a manner conformable to their unalterable determination.

The French government made use of the frank declarations of the Allied powers to express inclinations to peace. It certainly had need of the appearance of this inclination in order to justify in the eyes of its people the next exertions which it did not cease to require. But everything, however, convinced the Allied cabinets that it merely endeavored to take advantage of the appearance of negotiation in order to prejudice public opinion in its favor, but that the peace of Europe was very far from its thoughts.

The powers – penetrating its secret views – resolved to go and conquer in France itself; the long-desired peace. Numerous armies crossed the Rhine; scarcely were they past the first frontier when the French minister for foreign affairs appeared at the outposts.

All the proceedings of the French government had henceforth no other object than to mislead opinion; to blind the French people; and to throw on the Allies the odium of all the miseries attendant on an invasion.

The course of events had given the Allies a proof of the full power of the European league. The principles which, since their first union for the common good had animated the counsels of the Allied sovereigns, were fully developed. Nothing more hindered them from unfolding the conditions of the reconstruction of the common edifice. These conditions must be such as were no hindrance to peace after so many conquests.

The only power calculated to throw into the scale indemnification for France, England could speak openly respecting the sacrifices which it was ready to make for the general peace. The Allied sovereigns were permitted to hope that the experience of the elate events would have had some influence on a conqueror exposed to the observation of a great nation, which was, for the first time, witness – in the capital itself – to the miseries he had brought on France.

This experience might have convinced that the support of thrones is principally dependent on moderation and probity. The Allied powers, however – convinced that the trial which they made must not endanger the military operations – saw that these operations must be continued during the negotiations. The experience of the past – and afflicting recollections – showed them the necessity of this step. Their plenipotentiaries met those of the French government. Meantime, the victorious armies approached the gates of the capitol. The government took every method to prevent it falling into our hands. The plenipotentiary of France received orders to propose an armistice – upon conditions which were similar to those which the Allies themselves judged necessary for the restoration of a general peace. He offered the immediate surrender of the fortresses in the countries which France was to give up, on condition of a suspension of military operations.

The Allied courts – convinced by 20 years' experience that in negotiations with the French cabinet it was necessary carefully to distinguish the apparent from the real intention – proposed, instead of this, immediately to sign preliminaries of peace. This measure would have, for France, all the advantages of an armistice without exposing the Allies to the danger of a suspension of arms. Some partial advantages, however, accompanied the first motions of an army collected under the walls of Paris – composed of the flower of the present generation; the last hope of the nation; and the remainder of a million warriors who, either fallen on the field of battle or left on the way from Lisbon to Moscow, have been sacrificed for interests with which France has no concern. Immediately, the negotiations at Châtillon assumed another appearance. The French plenipotentiary remained without instructions and went away instead of answering the representatives of the Allied courts. They commissioned their plenipotentiaries to give the project of a preliminary treaty – containing all the grounds which they deemed necessary for the restoration of the balance of power – and which a few days before had been presented by the French government itself, at a moment doubtless when it conceived its existence in danger. It contained the groundwork for the restoration of Europe.

France restored to the frontiers, which under the government of its kings had insured to it ages of glory and prosperity, was to have – with the rest of Europe – the blessings of liberty, national independence and peace. It depended absolutely on its government to end, by a single word, the sufferings of the nation; to restore it with peace; its colonies; its trade; and the restitution of its industry. What did it want more? The Allies now offered – with a spirit of pacification – to discuss its wishes on the subject of mutual convenience, which should extend the frontiers of France beyond what they were before the wars of the Revolution.

Fourteen days elapsed without any answer being returned by the French government. The plenipotentiaries of the Allies insisted on fixing a day for the acceptance or rejection of the conditions of peace. They left the French plenipotentiary the liberty to present a contre project on condition that this contre project should agree in spirit – and in its general contents – with the conditions proposed by the Allied courts. The 10th of March was fixed by the mutual consent of both parties. This term being arrived, the French plenipotentiary produced nothing but pieces – the discussion of which, far from advancing the proposed object, could only have caused fruitless negotiations. A delay of a few days was granted at the desire of the French plenipotentiary. On 15 March he had at last delivered a contre project, which left no doubt that the sufferings of France had not yet changed the views of its government. The French government – seceding from what it had itself proposed – demanded, in a new project, that nations which were quite foreign to France, which a domination of many ages would not have amalgamated with the French nation, should now remain part of it; that France should retain frontiers inconsistent with the fundamental principles of equilibrium, and out of all proportion with the other great powers of Europe; that it should remain master of the same positions and points of aggression – by means of which its government – to the misfortune of Europe and that of France – had effected the fall of so many thrones and so many revolutions; that members of the family reigning in France should be placed on foreign thrones; the French government, in short – that government which for so many years has sought to rule no less by discord than by force of arms – was to remain the arbiter of the external concerns of the powers of Europe.

By continuing the negotiations under such circumstances, the Allies would have neglected what they owed themselves. They would, from that moment, have deviated from the glorious goal they had before them; their efforts would have been turned solely against their people. By signing a treaty upon the principles of the French project, the Allies would have laid their arms in the hands of the common enemy; they would have betrayed the expectations of nations and the confidence of their Allies.

It is in a moment so decisive for the welfare of the world that the Allied sovereigns renew this solemn engagement till they have attained the great object of their union.

France has to blame its government alone for all its suffering. Peace alone can heal the wounds which a spirit of universal domination – unexplained in history – has produced. This peace shall be the peace of Europe; no other can be accepted. It is at length time that princes should watch over the welfare of the people without foreign influence; that nations should respect their mutual independence; that social institutions should be protected from daily revolution; property respected, and trade free.

All Europe has absolutely the same wish to make France participate in the blessings of peace: France – whose dismemberment the Allied powers neither can, or will, permit. The confidence in their promises may be found in the principles for which they contend. Then whence shall the sovereigns infer that France will take part in the principles that must fix the happiness of the world, so long as they see that the same ambition – which has brought so many misfortunes on Europe – is still the sole spring that actuates the government; that while French blood is shed in torrents, the general interest is always sacrificed to private. Whence, under such circumstances, should be the guarantee for the future if such a desolating system found no check in the general will of the nation? Then is the peace of Europe insured – and nothing shall in future be able to disturb it.[6]

6 Philippart, Vol. I, pp. 336-344.

16

Operations in the Lowlands: The Assault on Bergen-op-Zoom and The Battle of Courtrai, March-April 1814

In early March, General Carnot – in conformance with his orders – pushed part of his garrison into Lokeren. However, on learning that Maison had withdrawn to Lille and that the English were concentrating on Calmhout, Carnot withdrew back to his original positions in Antwerp.

Though Carnot feared an attack on Antwerp, it was not Graham's intention to attack Antwerp. Instead, he sought to make another attempt on Bergen-op-Zoom. Bergen-op-Zoom stood on the Scheldt, which had always been a region of considerable economic power and was probably (from the English perspective) the most important real estate on the continent. That Graham would seek to take the fortress of Bergen-op-Zoom was quite within keeping with the history of British involvement on the continent and, as a result, very predictable.

Recognizing this threat earlier, Maison and Decaen had built up a garrison in the city of about 4,000 men. However, desertions, sickness, and bad food had reduced the garrison to around 2,700 men. Unfortunately for the French, to fully occupy the city's defenses required a garrison of 12,000 men!

Description of Bergen-op-Zoom and Graham's plans

The fortress of Bergen-op-Zoom was designed by the engineering genius Coëhorn in 1688, who employed all the resources of his art in preparing its defense. As a result, the city's defenses were very strong and the city had survived many sieges since its construction.[1] However, in 1814 its garrison – under the able General Ambert – was small and the moats were frozen, which would facilitate any attack that winter.

The garrison consisted of 2,700 men: one artillery company (79 men), one veteran gunner company (50), 1/2 miner company (42), sailors (400), six companies of veterans (300) and one battalion of the following regiments: 12th Line Regiment (600), 17th Line Regiment (250), 21st Line Regiment (274), 51st Line Regiment (560) and a force of 145 men from various miscellaneous units. They were mostly recruits and, for the most part, Belgians.

The city was divided into two parts: the extensive city proper, which was circular in shape, and the port quarter or the basin, which was shaped like a hatchet – giving the whole the general shape of a violin. The port and the city were almost joined together by ramparts and buildings, with the communications between them being via a gate known as the 'False Gate' in the old

1 Jones, Vol. II, p. 287.

Fausse-Porte castle, which stood in the middle of the buildings. The piers in the port all had rows of houses on them – giving the city a unique flavour.[2]

The city was protected by 16 bastions and its walls had three gates, through which ran the roads to Steenbergen, Breda and Antwerp. The port quarter had only one gate – known as the 'Porte d'Eau' ('Water Gate') – which went only to the 'Fort d'Eau' ('Water Fort') via a dike. There were also 26 sally ports – four of them being large enough for the passage of vehicles. The other sally ports were also quite large.

The Fort d'Eau stood in the middle of a deep and wide ditch filled with water. It had steps leading down to the Scheldt. It was revetted with masonry, but the scarp was not over 12 feet high.

The eastern and southern fronts of the fortress, which faced France, were the strongest. The eastern front was covered by an entrenched camp with four redoubts on its salient angles. These redoubts were so large as to nearly be bastions. The fortress was well-finished except for the scarp, which was not revetted with masonry beyond a height of 16 feet. This defect, though not important to a formal siege, was dangerous in the case of an escalade.[3]

The western (water) front of the fortifications was earthen and the scarp had no counterscarp. The scarp was not particularly steep and suitable for cavalry maneuvers. Behind the scarp stood the real defense of this flank – a broad ditch with six feet of water and a swampy salt flat that was inundated at high tide and wholly unsuitable for the trenches required by siege operations.

To the north of this salt flat was a narrow piece of reclaimed land between the dikes and ditches known as the 'Little Polder'. It ran westwards and ended in the Fort d'Eau. Beyond the polder and parallel to it on the north side flowed the Zoom Canal. This canal led from the port and formed the communication link between the port and the Scheldt. To the north of the canal was another swampy salt flat, which extended to the Tholen dike. The Tholen dike had been thrown up in the latter half of the 18th century in a land reclamation project. It was perpendicular to the canal near the demi-bastion in the northwest angle of the fortress.

The northern face of the fortress was earthen, with water-filled ditches. There were no demi-lunes and the defense of this quarter depended on a large entrenched camp known as the Steenbergen lines. These lines – with the other works – formed a huge, fortified four-sided region defined by Steenbergen, Bergen-op-Zoom, Klundert and Willemstadt.[4] Some of these deficiencies were corrected by the construction of entrenchments and a palisade of the re-entrant angles between the bastions. However, the weakness of the garrison prevented the adequate occupation of these works.

The fortress was well-designed and, being Dutch, it was designed to defend from an attack from the south (i.e. the French). As a result, the French garrison – which faced the potential of attack from any direction, most particularly the north – was not in as comfortable a position as had been earlier Dutch garrisons. The Steenbergen lines required a whole army for their defense and no such French force was available. Willemstadt, another key to the defenses, was actually in Allied hands. Fort d'Eau was prepared to receive reinforcements from the sea – again, not designed to the advantage of the French, who did not control the surrounding seas. As a result, the French moved the entrance for reinforcements around to the gorge of a bastion in the rear. In order to ensure the security of this passage, they spent considerable effort keeping the surrounding flooded ditch flowing and free of ice – lest that ice permit an enemy easy access to it. The ice was broken with axes and saws at a tremendous cost in the form of physical exertion by the garrison. As events would later prove, however, it was an effort well-expended.

2 Koch, Vol. II, pp. 151-2.
3 Fortescue, Vol. X, p. 34.
4 Fortescue, Vol. X, p. 35.

The population of Bergen-op-Zoom was about 5,000-strong and consisted principally of people whose lives were closely tied to the sea. As a result of the blockade, these people were reduced to a state of misery and penury. Graham had excellent intelligence on the status of the citizens of Bergen-op-Zoom and fully expected the cooperation of a significant portion of the population during his planned assault.

Graham was pressed to execute his attack without delay because of bad news coming from other parts of France. He selected 8 March – birthday of the Prince of Orange – as the date for his assault on the fortress. Purportedly, he had the intent of sending the Prince of Orange a bouquet made of the keys to the city as a present. Graham expected reinforcements, under Wallmoden, but they were moving in his direction slowly – not being expected in Bremen until 26 February. Should the French invade Flanders in force, he had only his British soldiers and the Saxons.

The British attack

Graham did not have the facilities or time to begin a formal siege, so he planned a direct assault. In preparation for the assault, the 1st Division moved to Halsteren and Huibergen – northwest and southeast of Bergen-op-Zoom. The 2nd Division was employed to cover the movement should the French attempt to attack it from the direction of Antwerp.

Graham organized his force of 4,000 men into four columns for the assault. The 1st column had 1,000 men of the Guards under Lord Proby. It was assigned to attack between the Antwerp and Port gates and force an entrance by the Orange Bastion in the rear of the entrenched camp on the southern front. It was to then ascend the rampart and advance along it to join the other columns. The assigned engineering officer was Lieutenant Sperling.[5]

The second column – on the left center and consisting of 1,200 men from the 33rd, 55th and 2/69th Regiments of Foot – was to advance from Huibergen under Colonel Morrice. This column was assigned to move to the right of the Breda Gate and escalade the front immediately next to the Steenbergen lines. Captain Michelle, Royal Artillery, volunteered to act as engineer and accompanied this column.

The third column was to attack the right center. The 650 men of the 2/21st, 2/37th and 2/91st Regiments of Foot – under Colonel Henry – were to make a false attack against the Steenbergen Gate and to serve as a reserve for the fourth column. The fourth column was on the extreme right. It consisted of 500 men from the 2/21st, 2/37th and 2/44th Regiments of Foot supported by 600 men of the Royals under Colonel Carleton of the 44th. It was to march from Halsteren under cover of darkness and reach the junction of the Tholen dike and the Scheldt by 9:00 p.m. From there, it was to be guided to its attack position. It was to slip across the tidal flats by the port and into the village – attacking where the dike abuts the fortress. The left-center attack was to be the principal attack, while those of the left and right were to concentrate on it. Henry's column, after its feints were finished and the French were diverted, would act as a reserve.

The assault columns were to be within cannon-shot of the fortress by 9:00 a.m. and the assault was scheduled for 8 March at 10:30 a.m. All of the columns were guided into position by local inhabitants.[6]

Earlier, Graham had written Bunbury, stating that: "There is no hope of taking Bergen-op-Zoom by *coup de main* without an understanding within – which I am trying to arrange." The watchwords were arranged such that they would accommodate the Dutch supporting effort. Unfortunately for Graham, this Dutch effort never occurred.

5 Jones, Vol. II, p. 289.
6 Koch, Vol. II, p. 151; Fortescue, Vol. X, p. 37.

The assault on Bergen-op-Zoom.

The assault begins

Despite Graham's plans and orders, things went wrong from the beginning. Though not scheduled to attack until 9:30 a.m. Henry's column executed their 'false attack' near the Steenbergen Gate at 8:30 a.m. They surprised the French, bayoneted them and broke into the lunette that covered the gate. They lacked the tools necessary to break open the gate and were quickly taken under fire by the city's defenders.[7]

As soon as musketry broke the dawn, the French artillery commander rushed to the spot and discharged the guns that flanked this entrenchment from the east with his own hands. The musketry and artillery fire quickly became general on this flank. Despite the immediate response and heavy fire, a force of 400 men from Henry's column made its way past the palisade,[8] through the entrenchment and used their scaling ladders to connect the two ends of the drawbridge. They crawled over the moat on their ladders, scaled the low revetment of the scarp, clambered over the superior slope and the parapet, and succeeded in reaching the interior of the rampart. Despite the size of this force, they were not united as a single body of men and several were overpowered and bayoneted.

The rear of the column – suffering from heavy fire – was not so fortunate and was driven back in disorder with considerable loss. It is evident that either Colonel Henry or his subordinates entirely ignored Graham's orders. They not only ignored Graham's specified times for the assault, but forgot that their function was not to execute a real attack – but only a feint – and they were then to become the principal reserve. It is probable that Colonel Henry felt he was

7 Jones, Vol. II, p. 291.
8 von Damitz, Vol. III, 1st Part, p. 234.

being denied his right to the glory of being the captor of Bergen-op-Zoom and deliberately ignored Graham's orders.[9]

Despite this total failure to follow orders, its effect was exactly what Graham had ordered in that the entire French garrison rushed to this quarter – leaving the rest of the town almost entirely ungarrisoned.

Upon hearing the sound of Henry's premature attack, Carleton's column – which contained the men of generals Gore and Skerrett – reacted immediately and launched their own assault. Though the tide was not at its lowest, the additional few inches of water in the ditch would make little difference. Moving down the Tholen dike, the British reached the cross-dike, where they turned right and moved along the foot of the glacis. They marched on a front of six to eight men and crossed the Zoom Canal and reached the port's basin almost without resistance. A gunboat positioned to command the passage fired a shot or two and immediately rowed away.[10]

Two emplaced guns were abandoned by the French without any resistance.

The ease of their advance aroused the notorious British 'foxhunt' reaction that had so often brought the British to ruin. Carleton, excited by the thought of an easy capture, cried: "First in Badajoz, first in Bergen-op-Zoom." He then turned south – marching his column along the gorge of the bastions that flanked the Porte d'Eau with about 150-250 men of the 44th Regiment following him. Skerrett, during the advance, had continually cried out: "Remember, men, you are to get out of that ditch to your right." He then led the tail of the column to the left and took the two bastions at the western end of the northern front in the reverse, which he took with little effort. The Royals – a total of 600 men – were left at the Porte d'Eau without orders and under Colonel Müller (an officer purportedly with no initiative and even less military skill).[11]

The French reaction

General Bizanet, commander of the fortress, stood in the central square of the city in the middle of his reserve. Shortly after learning of the repulse of Henry's attack, Bizanet learned that the British (Skerrett and Gore) had forced their way into the port and presumed this to be the main British attack.[12]

He overreacted and ordered the whole of his reserves – consisting of sailors and veterans – to move at the double (with some supporting field guns) to the Porte d'Eau. He had too quickly committed his last available manpower, for loud shouts of: "Oranje Boven" (the Dutch watchword) were heard near Antwerp.

Carleton had left a few men to guard the quays and pushed the rest along the ramparts of the western and southern defenses. He then assailed the whole of the French guards in the flank, killed a few, took many prisoners and chased the remainder away from the Antwerp Gate. He then seized the gate's guardhouse and left a small force to lower the drawbridges and to hold the mouth of the street leading into the city.

Leading the rest of his force, Carleton then moved almost to the Breda Gate, where he encountered part of the French 12th Line Regiment drawn up to receive him. Carleton had dropped so many detachments to hold various positions and guard prisoners that he barely had 100 men left with him. He brazenly marched against the French and called upon the French to

9 Fortescue, Vol. X, p. 38.
10 Jones, Vol. II, p. 292.
11 Fortescue, Vol. X, p. 39.
12 Koch, Vol. II, p. 154.

surrender. Their response was a crushing volley of musketry which cut down Carleton and over half of his remaining men.

Though a seemingly foolish act, by this time Morrice's column should have been near the Breda Gate – and if they had, the situation would have merited such a call for surrender. However, Morrice's men were not where they should have been. There are two explanations to be found for this.

Fortescue states that for an unknown reason, Morrice's men had been seized by a panic during their advance and fled before the first shot was fired at them. Graham and his entire staff reportedly galloped about rounding them up for quite a while until they could be rallied.[13]

Jones, however, has another story and states that they found no obstacle to their approach except a 16-foot-wide lunette in the ice, which they quickly crossed. Once on the glacis, they were discovered and taken under heavy fire. Despite the fire they continued into the ditch, but after several failed attempts – and the loss of 200 men – they withdrew out of the ditch and reformed beyond the glacis.[14]

Whichever is true – and Fortescue's explanation is the more plausible – Morrice's men were not where they should have been. In the meantime, Carleton's column was wrecked and the survivors fell back to the bastion to the east of the Antwerp Gate.

The fourth column, under Lord Proby and General Cooke, came into action shortly afterwards. The Guards, as ordered, had moved up to the foot of the glacis between the entrenched camp and the port. They found the ice in the moat broken and impassable so they returned and crossed between the two westernmost works of the entrenched camp, marched on the Orange Bastion which divided the revetted and unrevetted portions of the southern front, and began their descent into the ditch on 10 ladders. Lightly opposed and losing only a few men, they then advanced up the scarp and took possession of the bastion.

The bastion in hand, Cooke then directed his main body into the houses overlooking the quays of the port. He maintained a heavy musket fire on the French and sent out a strong patrol – some 300 men – under Lieutenant Colonel Clifton, looking to make contact with Skerrett, while another detachment of the 2/1st Guards was sent towards the Antwerp Gate.[15]

It was now slightly after 11:00 a.m. and Bergen-op-Zoom was still neither won nor lost. Of the four attack columns, two and part of the third had successfully entered the city. Skerrett held the arsenal, part of the northern portion of the port and had pushed troops eastward along the northern defenses of the city towards the Steenbergen Gate. Portions of Henry's column were also near the gate. The Royals held the Porte d'Eau. Cooke held all the roads south of the port's basin and was directing heavy musketry into the French in the streets of the city. Gore, now commanding the remains of Carleton's column, still held the bastion immediately to the east of the Antwerp Gate.[16]

The French held only six of the 16 bastions: the one immediately to the west and the five immediately to the east of the Steenbergen Gate. The heavy guns on these bastions poured volcanic fire of canister along their front. French field guns in the city swept the streets and quays with such fire that the British were forced under cover. In addition, Skerrett's men were engaged by the French garrison in a musketry duel of horrendous proportions between small groups of men fighting desperately.

13 Fortescue, Vol. X, p. 40.
14 Jones, Vol. II, p. 295.
15 Jones, Vol. II, p. 297.
16 Fortescue, Vol. X, p. 41.

During the course of the fighting, the French troops came pouring back into the central square – crying that their ammunition was expended. The situation was critical and close to panic, but for the coolness of the French officers. Most of the arsenals and munitions were in British hands. The French officers rallied their men while the chief engineer passed out axes. The locked doors of the three remaining magazines were chopped down and ammunition passed out. Their ability to fight restored, panic quickly passed and the French resumed the fight.

It lay in the hands of Morrice and his now-rallied column to settle the battle. They marched forward again, only to find their path along the northeast corner of the city blocked by the broken ice of the moat and the fire of the bastions on their flanks. They fell back after suffering 200 killed and wounded.

Carleton's detachment by the Antwerp Gate was driven back before it was able to lower the drawbridge. The aggressive French had dragged up a field gun and were threatening to annihilate them and the remains of Gore's force, which had fallen back to that position.

Just as the situation was as its most desperate, Clifton – leading a body of Guardsmen – arrived on the scene. They overran and captured the French field gun, fired a volley and followed up with a charge that scattered the French – driving them back to the Antwerp Gate. The French were pursued by the Guard and the remains of Gore's men into the central square. Had the British succeeded in driving them from the central square, they would have made themselves master of the city – but a party of 50-60 gendarmes (formed in line before the main guard) marched forward and delivered a crushing volley. The advancing British staggered and their fleeing foe quickly rallied behind the gendarmes. Forming themselves into an irregular, dense mass the British were unable to fire. The French, bayonets gleaming, recovered their senses and charged at the struggling mass of British – pursuing them back, recapturing their lost gun and all their lost ground.

The battle swayed back and forth as the British struggled against their more numerous foe, but numbers soon began to tell. At length, Gore, Clifton and Macdonald fell. When Clifton fell, his detachment lost heart, broke and fled to the bastion with the French hot on their heels.[17]

As the British attack collapsed on this front, Skerrett also found himself heavily engaged. The French forces, which he had driven out on the northwestern bastion, had succeeded in rallying on a picket of 300 men in the next bastion to the east. They then established themselves in a building known as the 'new powder-magazine'. However, the British seized a windmill in a more commanding position in the same bastion. The fight resumed with a renewed fury. Despite their lesser numbers, the British gained the upper hand – and the French were beginning to break – when a force of 400 French (supported by three field guns) arrived, began firing canister and allowed them to renew the fight. The battle erupted with a refreshed vigor until both Skerrett and the commander of the French sailors were killed. Lacking their leader, the British morale broke; the French stormed the windmill; and the British were driven back to the northwest bastion. The British took up a position in the gorge of this bastion – behind a barricade of logs – and waited for the assault to run its course.[18]

While the others were engaged within the city's walls, Cooke had remained before the Antwerp Gate, which he had been unable to force because of the French defensive fire. Even if he had been able to force it, his entrance into the city would have been blocked by a demi-lune – still occupied by the French – which commanded the passage.

Having had only one brief message from Clifton, Cooke eventually gave his detachment up for lost. He then sent Lieutenant Colonel Rooke of the 2/3rd Guards with a small party towards the

17 Fortescue, Vol. X, pp. 42-3.
18 Jones, Vol. II, p. 294.

Antwerp Gate. As he advanced, he was startled to find the shattered remains of Clifton and Gore's columns streaming back – hotly pursued by the French.

Rooke's force took the French under fire and, swept by the fire of the rest of the brigade, the French pursuit collapsed into a mad scramble back into the city. Rooke launched his force in pursuit and soon found himself inside the Antwerp Gate facing an occupied demi-lune that stopped further progress in that quarter.

After the failure of the attack on the northeast corner, Graham had withdrawn Morrice's column and sent them around by the route which Proby had taken into the Orange Bastion. Morrice was able to enter the fortress unopposed and quickly joined Cooke. However, Cooke was uncertain of the situation and chose not to weaken his force by attempting to seize more of the fortress than he could hope to control. He was also leery of once again plunging into the streets where he had suffered so cruelly earlier in the attack.

At the same time Graham ordered Henry's column to march to this spot, but Henry had converted his feint attack into a real attack. The reserve had become a storming party and was no longer available. In fact, only about 150 of the 55th Regiment of Foot were left unengaged. Graham, upon learning this, chose to keep them at hand rather than commit his last tiny reserve.

By 1:00 a.m. the fighting died down and the senior British artillery and engineer officers made their official report to Graham that the city was in his possession. Unfortunately, they neglected to consult with the French, who had a different opinion. Graham responded by ordering forward 600 more Guards from Putten and Wow and 350 men of the 2/35th Regiment of Foot – to which he added the remains of Henry's column and a few men from the 55th, which Graham had kept with him. This gave him a force of 1,300 men with which to clean up the remains of the French garrison.

For the following five to six hours, Graham had no doubt that he was master of Bergen-op-Zoom – and with some reason. Cooke had command of about 2,000 men from Proby, Morrice and Carleton's columns – including 600 men of the 4/1st Royals, which had barely been engaged. Though the French had recovered about three-quarters of the ramparts, three of the gates and taken a large number of prisoners, Graham felt that they had suffered equally and were nearly driven from the southern quarter of the port. Some of the French had escaped through the False Gate and unlimbered three field guns to bar the entrance into the town and to enfilade the passage to the northern quarter of the port. Others had raised the drawbridge crossing the basin to stop the British pursuit. Furthermore, though both Cooke and Graham were unaware of it, there was still a large number of British in the two bastions adjoining the arsenal at the northwest corner and many survivors of Henry's column hidden near the Steenbergen Gate. However, these were cut off from Cooke by the rising tide in the basin.

The battle resumed about 3:00 a.m. on a clear moonlit morning. The French were striking Skerrett's column in the two northwest bastions. The British used a huge pile of palisades that had not been emplaced because of the frozen ground as a rampart flanking the gorge of the bastion and turned around the heavy guns so as to command the entrance to the gorge. The French infantry attempted again and again to penetrate into the bastion under the fire of their supporting artillery, but were driven back by a storm of canister and musketry. Only the difficulty in working the heavy guns had prevented the British from annihilating the French.[19]

In the southern quarter of the port, the combatants were similarly deadlocked. Every attempt by the French to penetrate into the Orange Bastion by the ramparts on the east of it was stopped by the flanking fire of the Guards in the houses. Similarly, the British attempts to penetrate into the French portion of the city via the False Gate were stopped by the French field guns in the gate.

19 Fortescue, Vol. X, pp. 44-6.

It was only, however, with the greatest effort that the artillery was able to keep the British from forming on the quays and storming the False Gate.

As if this deadlock weren't enough, six British soldiers cut off from their unit had set themselves up in a house on the street leading to the Antwerp Gate. Here, they fired on everything that marched into view. Similarly, French marksmen were stationed on the ramparts and harassed the Guards with an incessant sniping that was to inflict a substantial number of casualties on them.

The French counterattack

Fatigue began to tell on both sides and the battle now settled down into an unusual pattern. The still of the night would be broken by a half-hour of thunderous firing that would suddenly die away and quiet would return to the city. During the quiet moments – between 2:30 and 3:00 a.m. – a French colonel made a reconnaissance of the front and reported to Ambert that piecemeal attacks would not bring success. He recommended that all the troops be gathered up and thrown into a single attack that would succeed by sheer numbers and élan.

More than half of the French garrison stood on the works on the eastern side of the fortress between the Steenbergen Gate and the Antwerp Gate. They were unengaged and unutilized, but they had been sent there at the beginning of the assault and forgotten.

Ambert, seeing the wisdom of the advice, ordered his troops – some 600 men – organized into three columns. The right column, on the northern side, was to advance first and give the signal for the other two to follow. The 51st Line Regiment formed the head of the right column and was followed by the 17th and 12th Line Regiments. It was agreed that they should move with bayonet only from the vicinity of the windmill into the northwest bastion, while a party of sailors slipped along the edge of the scarp and turned the rear of the British holding the pile of palisades awaiting installation.

The French attack was successful. The British on the northern front – struck in the front and rear – instantly broke and fled to the refuge of the basin of the port or the main ditches. The rear of the French column – supported by three field guns – then turned to the left and drove the British from the arsenal. It quickly moved across the basin of the port on a small swing-bridge little more than a foot wide – despite the fire of the Guards on the south side of the basin – and drove the British before them to the Porte d'Eau. The drawbridge of this gate over the ditch had not been lowered. The fleeing British soldiers were trapped! Some jumped down into the ditch; others reached the glacis – where cannon fire from the western ramparts crushed them into oblivion – but the bulk were taken prisoner by the French, who lowered scaling ladders down to save them.

As he saw the French approach the Porte d'Eau, Colonel Müller of the 4/1st Royals sent a message to Cooke pleading for help. Cooke dispatched the 33rd Regiment to join him – reducing his forces to somewhere around 1,200 men. Müller's performance, however, so far had been more than inadequate. He had remained stationary for six hours – taking no initiative.

Cooke had earlier had some idea of taking the offensive and had sent a message to Graham requesting permission to do so and advice if Graham preferred him to clear the streets or hold the ramparts. However, Müller's call for help arrived before Graham's instructions arrived, so the 33rd Regiment of Foot was lost to Cooke.

Colonel Müller, on the other hand, relates that he found himself struck by the French supported by field guns that inflicted heavy casualties on his force and obliged him to surrender. However, his losses were less than 120 and he allowed 500 men to be taken unhurt. The 33rd, which had joined him by that time and had about 600 men, declined to accept the French offers of hospitality and quickly scrambled back over the ramparts to make their escape. They returned to Graham – leaving 100 dead and wounded and 50 prisoners behind them.

The French attacks on the right were completely successful, but those on the center and left had stalled. The center column had attempted to push out of the False Gate, but the fire of the Guardsmen in their front and flank stopped their attack dead in its tracks. They contented themselves with sweeping the quays and streets with canister fire to keep the British pinned in their positions in the houses.

The left column – led by the 21st Line – consisted mostly of organized sailors, veterans and gunners. They tried to push into the Orange Bastion, but were stopped dead by a furious barrage of canister and musketry. They were driven back with heavy losses. However, they still held the bastion immediately to the east of the Orange Bastion – cutting Cooke's communications to Graham. Seeing the necessity of taking this position, Cooke dispatched the 55th and 2/69th Regiments of Foot. These same regiments, which earlier in the night had broken in panic, took the French position with swift military precision.

Despite this success, Cooke's position was tenuous. His position was slowly decaying as the French brought more and more pressure to bear on him. To the northwest – across the port – the French turned the heavy guns of a bastion and began to pound his position. A French column moved against their left flank while another moved against their right. The remainder of the garrison fired artillery and musketry on the British front. The column attacking their left was greeted with musketry and dispersed. However, the right-hand column began firing on the British with both musketry and field guns and skirmishers fired on the British from every conceivable spot that afforded them any cover. British casualties began to mount seriously.[20] Proby suggested that part of the British troops should withdraw, and a large number made good their escape using the scaling ladders they had used to enter the city.

Seeing the British begin to withdraw, the French launched a second attack – but it was repulsed by the 55th and 2/69th Regiments of Foot. Initially, the French let them withdraw unmolested except for a heavy musketry and canister fire that poured from the demi-lune before the Antwerp Gate and pounded the British as they crossed the glacis. However, the French subsequently made a serious effort to cut off the British communications by taking points along the walls that flanked the British withdrawal. These points were cleared of the French by a charge of the 55th Regiment led by majors Muttlebury and Hogg.

The remainder of Cooke's men – mostly from the 1st Guards – continued to hold their position. A third French attack now came from the direction of the Porte d'Eau, while the central column was gathering combustibles so that they could fire the entire southern quarter of the port.

At this point, Colonel Jones of the Guards – who had been taken prisoner – listened to the reports of other British prisoners from all over the city as to the status of the British assault. Jones felt that further butchery was pointless and volunteered to stop the fighting. Ambert accepted his offer on the condition that all British within the walls should surrender. Jones, taking the arm of Captain Denis of the French artillery, advanced waving a white handkerchief and walked into the fire of the two battling parties. Only with some difficulty did the fighting stop.

Jones was conducted to Cooke and advised him of Müller's surrender and the defeat of the detachments of Clifton, Skerrett and Carleton. At 9:00 a.m. he agreed that his men should lay down their arms – unaware that Graham was preparing to advance to his assistance with reinforcements.[21] Two hours later – when Graham arrived – he found that he had come in vain.

As the French cleaned up the city, they tallied the British losses. They reported 2,077 British prisoners and 800 dead. They estimated the total British losses at 4,000, while theirs were limited

20 Jones, Vol. II, pp. 302-3.
21 Koch, Vol. II, p. 155.

to 160 dead, 300 wounded and about 100 prisoners. The French reported capturing four flags – including that of the 2/1st Guards.[22]

Conclusion of the battle

The failure of the assault on Bergen-op-Zoom is Graham's, but needs to be shared with several of his lieutenants. Henry threw away Graham's reserves by his impulsive urge to attack and his failure to obey orders. Müller's lack of initiative and foolishness cost Graham 500 prisoners when they could have easily escaped with the 33rd Regiment of Foot. Carleton's excitement caused him to charge recklessly forward, but this is not necessarily bad. A sudden thrust – when opportunity presents itself – can win the day. Carleton took a chance and paid with his life. However, his decision to drop so many detachments can be severely criticized, as it so weakened his attacking force that it lost its mass and was no longer able to carry itself forward when it encountered French resistance.

The principal fault, however, lies with Graham. He committed between 4,000 and 4,800 of his men. He had a total of about 7,500 men in his original force and appears to have received reinforcements of at least four battalions from the 21st, 37th, 91st and Royals – probably another 2,000 men. His total force approached the strength of 10,000 men and he committed less than half of it to the operation.

In contrast, the garrison consisted of only 2,700 men – most of whom were not professional soldiers (though Graham may well not have known this). The bottom line is that Graham was attacking one of the best-designed fortresses in Europe. His attack lacked sufficient strength to assure success and he held his reserves too far back to support his attack when it ran into trouble.

Furthermore, there were no significant French forces in the vicinity and, if Graham was concerned, he might be struck by another French force while committed to such an engagement. He should have coordinated with the Duke of Weimar to cover his attack.

Conventional wisdom on attacks requires a 3:1 ratio of the attacker over the defender to give an assurance of success and, with this in mind, Graham should have committed his entire force to the attack. Not only did he commit forces less than twice the strength of the French to the attack – ignoring the impact of the fortifications on the defense – he also appears to have held the remainder of his force (some 5-6,000 men) more than an hour's march from the fortress. It is difficult to find fault with the French actions in this engagement. Certainly, when General Bizanet responded to Carleton's attack, he reacted and sent his entire reserves to counter Carleton. Then again, the strength of this reserve is not known – and if one has three fires and only one bucket, one can fight only one fire. He made a decision and the result was the destruction of Carleton's column – though other portions of the fortress were to fall to the British. If he had not destroyed Carleton and frittered his reserves away in small packets – as did Carleton – it is probable that the British would have captured Bergen-op-Zoom.

Antwerp's garrison marches out

Antwerp's garrison was not passive behind its walls and there were occasional sorties to keep the besiegers off-balance. One such sortie occurred on 17 March when at 6:00 a.m. the garrison launched an attack with five battalions and six guns against Contich. The Allied posts in Waerloos were driven back quickly and support sent forward from Düssel and Waelhem. General Gablentz

22 Koch, Vol. II, p. 156; Calmon-Maison, p. 193. Jones, Vol. II, p. 304 states that the number of British prisoners surrendered the next day was 1,800.

sent forward a battalion and a squadron from Mecheln to engage the French. They were quickly joined by the Saxon 1st Light Infantry Regiment, which stormed into Waerloos. Two companies of Saxon Schützen and a company of the Prussian 4th (Elbe) Reserve Infantry Regiment drove the French forage parties back. Laden with the fruits of their sortie, the French withdrew towards Antwerp with a gun from the Saxon 2nd Horse Battery – adding speed to their footsteps as they moved down the road from Contich. Casualties on both sides were minor.[23] The blockading forces consisted of six infantry battalions and four squadrons of uhlans and dragoons – half Saxon and half Prussian – plus the Saxon 1st Horse Battery. It is unlikely that they exceeded 3,000 men.

In mid-March, Napoleon felt the need for a diversion in the north to distract Bülow and keep him away from France. He ordered Clarke – the Minister of War – to withdraw all army troops from Antwerp and send them as reinforcements to Maison. On 26 March Maison forwarded these orders to Carnot, governor of Antwerp, who was shocked that Napoleon intended to strip his garrison and leave him with only 2,000 able-bodied seamen to man its defenses. He protested to Maison that the city's defenses required 15,000 men to adequately defend them. Maison, on his own initiative, authorized Carnot to retain his garrison. Events justified his decision, and when Paris eventually fell, Antwerp was still firmly in French hands. The Allies were still desperate to take Antwerp, and all efforts – including a proffered million-franc bribe to General Ducos to surrender the citadel – were rebuffed.[24]

The Duke of Weimar marks time

While Graham was suffering his reversal at Bergen-op-Zoom, the Duke of Weimar – despite his superiority over the French – took no action against the French as he waited for Thielemann to arrive with 15,000 men. He contented himself with screening Courtrai, Tournai and Mons. During this time, the blockaded French garrisons, however, did not remain quiescent. General Maran – governor of Ostend – upon learning that an Allied cavalry detachment was in Bruges, gathered up forces from the garrisons of Ostend, Dunkirk and Nieuport and marched on Bruges. On 12 March he overran Bruges, imposed a contribution of 100,000 francs on its citizens, chased off the Allied garrison and threw out the government imposed on the city by the Allies.[25]

Colonel Schouller, the commandant of the Maubeuge garrison, kept his forces active as well despite their small numbers. On 9 March he took the bulk of his garrison and made a sortie in an effort to capture a major Allied artillery convoy. However, the movement of Allied troops from Avesnes forced Schouller to abandon his effort just as he was about to capture the convoy.

Schouller was later to exact his revenge. On 10 March he learned that a column of 500 French prisoners was in Solre-sur-Sambre and en route to Mons. Schouller executed another sortie on 11 March with 400 infantry, 30 cavaliers of the 1st Chasseurs à cheval and two guns under the command of Major Reinhartz. Reinhartz was ordered to march on Vieux-Reng, which stood on the line of march of the column of prisoners. He prepared an ambush – and the moment the head of the column entered his trap, the chasseurs and 100 men from the customs battalion charged it.

As soon as the prisoners, which included a number of Old Guard grenadiers and chasseurs, heard the cries of: "*Vive l'Empereur!*" they threw themselves on their escorts – contributing to their liberation. The escort had consisted of 150 Prussian infantry and 40 Saxon cuirassiers – 30 of which immediately became prisoners.

23 Bucher, pp. 106-8.
24 Watson, p. 187.
25 Calmon-Maison, p. 195.

Despite these little setbacks, the Duke of Weimar finally felt himself secure enough to begin acting. He had accumulated a force of 24,000 infantry and artillery, 3,000 cavalry and 41 guns. He felt the time was now right for an attack on Maubeuge and organized his forces for that attack. Weimar did not have a siege train and decided that he would have to take Maubeuge by surprise. Thielemann was directed to guard Tournai and contain Maison. On 17 March Weimar's forces set out for Maubeuge.

Ryssel's brigade composed of the Provisional Saxon Guard Regiment, 2/2nd Saxon Light Regiment, 3/2nd Saxon Provisional Line Regiment, 2/2nd Saxon Landwehr Regiment, two companies of the Weimar and Gotha Freiwilliger Jägers , two squadrons of Saxon cuirassiers, one squadron of Weimar and Gotha Freiwilliger Jäger zu Pferd, one squadron of the Pomeranian Hussars, 12 heavy field guns (which included half of a Prussian battery) and four English 24pdrs[26] and eight mortars – and was to take up positions at Saint-Ghislain to cover Mons and to watch Valenciennes and Condé.

General Borstell – commanding nine battalions, eight squadrons and eight guns – moved to Bavay to mask Valenciennes and Condé. Lecoq's Saxon division – with seven battalions, three squadrons and 24 heavy guns – was designated to implement the siege of Maubeuge and to observe Philippeville. Finally – to complete his disposition – 10 battalions, four squadrons and 17 light guns were placed under the command of Generalleutnant Thielemann. They were to observe – from positions near Tournai – the French corps organizing below Lille. Thielemann was also given superior command of the forces of Colonel Gihalov, Major Helwig and Major Puckler, who occupied Ghent, Courtrai and Bruges.[27] Once Weimar's forces arrived before Maubeuge, there was a reorganization and redeployment of troops. Around 19 March the Allied forces were allocated as follows:

Main body by Mons: Generalmajor von Ryssel[28]

By Condé – on the right bank of the Haine:
- Weimar Battalion
- Pomeranian Hussar Regiment (two squadrons)
- Two Horse Guns

In Quivrain:
- 2/2nd Saxon Line Regiment
- Pomeranian Hussar Regiment (one squadron)
- Two Horse Guns

In St.-Chislain:
- 1/2nd Saxon Line Regiment
- Pomeranian Hussar Regiment (one squadron)
- Two Horse Guns

Observing Mons:
- 3/2nd Saxon Landwehr Regiment

26 Schuster, O. Francke, F.A., Vol. II, p. 382; von Eggloffstein, p. 76. Schuster and Francke refer to these troops as 'Thüringian', which is technically correct, but very misleading. These troops came from the two states of Saxe-Gotha and Saxe-Weimar, which were located in the Thüringian forest area. As a result, the actual state names have been used in lieu of Schuster and Franke's original terminology.

27 Koch, Vol. II, pp. 157-8.

28 Bucher, pp. 103-5.

Observation forces before Valenciennes, Quesnoy and by Bavay: Generalleutnant von Lecoq

- Pont-sur-Sambre:
  - Pomeranian Hussar Regiment (one squadron)
  - Four Guns
- Watching Landrecies (Russian Colonel Nasakyn):
  - Unknown force – probably Cossacks
- Facing Philippeville:
  - 2nd Landwehr Regiment (one battalion)
  - Pomeranian Hussar Regiment (jäger squadron)
- Blockade of Maubeuge (right bank of the Sambre):
  - 1/, 2/, 3/Saxon Grenadier Regiment
  - 2/2nd Saxon Light Regiment
  - Saxon Cuirassier Regiment (one squadron)
  - 1st 12pdr Foot Battery
  - 1st 6pdr Foot Battery
  - Foot Battery (12 British siege guns)
- Blockade of Maubeuge (left bank of the Sambre):
  - 3/2nd Saxon Line Regiment
  - 2nd Saxon Landwehr Regiment (one battalion)
  - Weimar & Gotha Freiwilliger Fussjäger (two companies)
  - Weimar & Gotha Freiwilliger Jäger zu Pferd (one squadron)
  - Saxon Cuirassier Regiment (one squadron)
- Corps by Tournai (Generalleutnant von Thielemann):
  - 1st Saxon Provisional Line Regiment (three battalions)
  - 1st Saxon Landwehr Regiment (two battalions)
  - Saxon Cuirassier Regiment (two squadrons)
  - Saxon Hussar Regiment (two squadrons)
  - Artillery
  - One 6pdr Battery
  - ½ Battery (French 6pdr guns)
  - One 9pdr Battery (English guns)
- Other:
  - von Helwig's Streifkorps (by Courtrai)
  - Cossack Regiment (Colonel Bychalov, in Ghent)
- Brussels Siege Forces:
  - Weimar Landwehr Battalion
  - Gotha Landwehr Battalion
  - Schwarzberg Landwehr Battalion

Maubeuge was not in a condition to sustain a long siege, but Colonel Schouller had prepared it to resist attack. In addition, his already small garrison was diminished by the recent departure of the customs battalion. What remained was a weak battalion of the 25th Line Regiment, the 1st Pas-de-Calais National Guard Battalion, a battalion of customs officers, the depot of the 1st Chasseurs (which had only 30 mounted men), a company of citizen gunners and the recently-liberated French prisoners. It totaled about 2,000 infantry and 800 cavalry.

When Lecoq arrived before Maubeuge on 18 March Schouller's troops were established before the city. Part of his troops were on the Assevent heights, which dominated the left bank of the Sambre, and part of it was at Rousies at the site of an old entrenched camp between the right bank of the river and the Philippeville road. Lecoq moved his forces to a position along the

Sambre and began preparing batteries between Assevent and Recquignies. That same day, he was reinforced by the arrival of the 1/,2/,3/2nd Kurmärk Landwehr Regiment under Major Graf von Klinkowström. He spent the days of 19 and 20 March examining the place and preparing his plans – the first of which entailed the construction of three batteries with 4-24pdrs, 6-12pdrs and eight mortars.[29]

The French were not passive and a sortie was launched on 21 March. After much excitement and shouting, the results were not particularly significant. The 3/1st Saxon Line Regiment lost two dead, 13 wounded and one missing; the 2/1st (Wittenberg) Saxon Landwehr Regiment lost five dead, 11 wounded and one missing; the Saxon Hussars lost two dead and eight wounded; and the artillery lost two wounded.

At 11:00 p.m. during the night of 22-23 March the Allies began a bombardment of the fortress, where Schouller – pressed by superior forces – had withdrawn his garrison. The citizen gunners, whose wives carried ammunition to the guns, responded vigorously for 24 hours. At about 9:00 p.m. a French howitzer shell fell into the ditch of the Saxon redoubt where the ammunition was stored – igniting 140 howitzer shells with a tremendous explosion.[30] With his ammunition nearly exhausted, the Duke of Weimar summoned Colonel Schouller to surrender. That proposal rejected, he called upon Schouller for an armistice, which was also rejected. Soon the lack of ammunition for their guns had forced the Allies to abandon any thought of a siege and their effort was reduced to a simple blockade. The Saxons then withdrew to their original positions.

During this, Borstell had remained stationary by Bavay – from which he watched Valenciennes. Ryssel was called back from Saint-Ghislain so he could deploy on the left of Lecoq's forces and complete the investment.

Seeking to verify that the Allies had abandoned their siege works, Schouller sent out a sortie on 24 March. Five-hundred infantry and 60 cavalry moved out in the morning – pushing as far as Ferrières-le-Grand, where they finally encountered serious resistance. Though the French withdrew, they completed the destruction of the batteries that the Saxons had raised earlier. Maubeuge then settled down for what would be a long blockade.[31] The Allied numbers, however, would continue to grow. Shortly after the sortie of the 24th, the Allies received a reinforcement of four Westphalian Landwehr battalions and a Fussjäger detachment under the command of Oberstleutnant von Rüchel.

Rüchel's detachment was as follows:

1st Battalion (1st Westphalian Landwehr Regiment) (17 officers / 693 men)
2nd Battalion (1st Westphalian Landwehr Regiment) (15 / 693)
3rd Battalion (1st Westphalian Landwehr Regiment) (16 / 620)
4th Battalion (2nd Westphalian Landwehr Regiment) (16 / 647)
Hauptmann von Wulssen's Fussjäger Company (1st Westphalian Landwehr Regiment) (1 / 143)

Though reinforced, they would do little but watch the fortress walls.

Maison by Lille

Maison had abandoned Courtrai to the Allies and taken his troops to Lille. Here he sought to reinforce his tiny army from the great city. If he conformed with the intentions of Napoleon, the urban militias would be left to guard the cities while the line troops were drawn into Solignac's

29 Koch, Vol. II, p. 159.
30 Schuster, O. Francke, F.A., Vol. II, p. 383.
31 Calmon-Maison, pp. 201-3.

division. However, the National Guards did not appear – for the most part – to be imbued with any significant enthusiasm for undertaking a campaign. Their organization proceeded slowly and the inhabitants of the region seemed resigned to accepting the yoke of their enemies.

Maison believed that the Allies would begin attacking the various cities along the old French frontier. Because of this, he did not wish to completely strip the region of regular troops. He drew his drafts, as a result, principally from the garrisons of Ypres and Ostend. At the same time, he directed General Brenier to dispatch every man possible from the depots to Lille. However, this effort was to produce little result. Funds were lacking and the drafts in the depots lacked almost everything necessary to outfit them as soldiers. Those that were sent to the front came in cloth breeches and white shirts. The basics were completely lacking. Furthermore, there had been a large increase in desertions in the Department du Nord. Up to the date of 20 March the 16th Military Division had provided only 6,600 men for the I Corps, but Maison judged it absolutely necessary to leave 5,500 of those men in various garrisons – leaving only 1,100 reinforcements for his corps.[32]

The I Corps had risen to 7,103 men total – 5,611 infantry, 1,015 cavalry and 477 artillerists – when definitive news arrived that the Duke of Weimar was advancing on France. Maison anticipated that attacks would be made on Maubeuge or Valenciennes and directed his senior commanders to each hold a battalion ready to send as reinforcements to whichever city was attacked. Maison also abandoned his positions in Roubaix and Tourcoing – concentrating his troops around Lille. Solignac's division moved into the Madeleine suburb, Barrois' 4th Young Guard Division moved into the Hellemmes suburb and the cavalry stood in Marque and Fretin. The gendarmerie was recalled from Armentières and posted in Haubourdin.

The I Corps had just finished this redeployment when on 21 March Thielemann – who occupied Tournai – decided to attack Lille with part of his troops. He organized his forces into three columns. The main column (2/1st Saxon Provisional Line Regiment, two battalions of the 1st Saxon Landwehr Regiment, two Saxon cuirassier squadrons and nine guns – including seven from the 1st Saxon 6pdr Battery) marched south against Quesnoy-sur-Deule Pont-à –Marque via Orchies and St.-Amant, where they drove back weak French detachments. It was intended to maintain communications with Ypres.

The second column – under Major François – contained one battalion of the Wittenberg Landwehr, a Saxon cavalry squadron and one gun from the 1st Saxon 6pdr Foot Battery. It marched southwest towards Bouvines and on 21 March arrived on the Marque after some heavy fighting. It crossed the Marque at three points – pushing back the French advanced posts towards Hellemmes and Lezennes – where the main body of Barrois' 4th Young Guard Division was located. The third column – under Oberst Fürst Schönberg – contained the 3/1st Saxon Provisional Line Regiment, one Saxon hussar squadron and three guns from the Hirsch Half-Battery. It followed behind the second column and was obliged to come to its assistance.[33]

As Barrois concentrated his troops to face the advancing Allies, the city's gunners manned their weapons, the bourgeois gunners ran to their pieces and the sedentary National Guards took up their arms.[34]

The garrison joined Solignac's division and the main body of French cavalry and marched on Sainghin, where they threatened the left flank and rear of the advancing Allies. Attacked frontally by Barrois and threatened with an assault in their flank, the Allied forces withdrew behind the Marque – looking for a strong position. In a charge of his Guard cavalry, Castex threw the Allies back to Tressin and Bouvines – capturing about 60 and killing and wounding approximately

32 Calmon-Maison, pp. 208-9.

33 Schuster, O. Francke, F.A., Vol. II, pp. 383-4.

34 Koch, Vol. II, p. 161.

another 100. The French pursued them and pushed them as far as Baisieux and on to Cysoing. By nightfall, they had withdrawn to Tournai – despite the condition of the ground – which was turning into a morass with the thaw.

During the same day, Thielemann sent another column forward with the intention of putting it between Maison and the fortresses along the French frontier. This force marched to Orchies, where it encountered the 75th Line Regiment supported by two cannon and 200 cavalry. The Allied force of 2,000 men and seven guns engaged the French for four hours, but made no progress and eventually withdrew back to Tournai as well.[35]

Despite the successes of his tiny army, as long as he was deprived of Roguet's division Maison had little hope of any major success. Maison had directed Carnot to hold this division by Bevern and Saint-Nicolas – such that it could join the I Corps near Ghent when the opportunity arose.

When Maison learned that the Duke of Weimar had attacked Maubeuge, he found his chance. While Maubeuge held the Allies tightly locked in their blockade effort, Maison took the opportunity to march on Ghent not only to divert Weimar from the siege, but to establish a junction with the Antwerp garrison. He spent the day of 24 March completing the munitions of his troops.

During the morning of 25 March the I Corps marched out of Lille. The I Corps stood as follows:

- 4th Young Guard Division: Barrois (2,971 men)
  - 1/, 2/2nd Tirailleur Regiment
  - 1/, 2/3rd Tirailleur Regiment
  - 1/, 2/4th Tirailleur Regiment
  - 1/, 2/12th Voltigeur Regiment
- Solignac's division: (2,820 men)
  - Det/27th Légère Regiment
  - Det/17th Line Regiment
  - Det/28th Line Regiment
  - Det/51st Line Regiment
  - Det/65th Line Regiment
  - Det/75th Line Regiment
- Castex's cavalry division (990 men)
  - 2nd Guard Lancer Regiment (Young Guard)
  - 2nd Guard Chasseur Regiment (Young Guard)
  - Gardes d'honneur
- Artillery: General Noury (477 men and 21 guns)

Maison's first act was to throw Major Helwig out of Menin. He then marched into Courtrai and sent advanced elements down the road to Ghent as far as Vive-Saint-Eloi. However, in order to cause Helwig to believe that he was marching on Audenarde, Maison detached Penne's brigade from Solignac's division and ordered it to march to Peterghem with some cavalry and a few light guns. They were ordered to march to Pelleghem – a distance of 38 miles (60 kilometers) – in one day.[36]

The following day, Penne's brigade had formed the advanced guard of the I Corps. Maison's forces surprised Deynze and arrived before the walls of Ghent at 2:00 p.m. The 200 Cossacks – under Colonel Bychalov – two guns and a Belgian regiment (forming under the command of Colonel Polis) formed the garrison of Ghent.

35 Calmon-Maison, pp. 210-3.

36 Koch, Vol. II, p. 618.

As the French approached, the Cossacks bravely marched out to meet them and their fate – a swift and terrible fate under the sabers and lances of the Guard cavalry. The survivors fled back to the city. The advancing French found the city's gates closed to them, but Penne's brigade attacked a weakly-held gate and forced entry into the city. A squadron of Cossacks charged again, but were thrown back and almost entirely annihilated by the 2nd Guard Lancers. Bichalov fled the city to Melle; both Colonel Polis and the major portion of his regiment were taken prisoner.[37]

The Belgian officers – technically French citizens – merited execution under French law, but that execution would have significant repercussions amongst the civilian population, which was already greatly disaffected towards France. Choosing the wiser and less risky path, Maison decided to treat them as simple prisoners of war and let the issue end with that. Both Thielemann and the Duke of Weimar, upon learning of Polis' capture, wrote Maison. Thielemann asked that he be treated as a prisoner of war, while the Duke threatened reprisals against the French officers held by them as prisoners of war.

Maison responded to Thielemann stating that Polis and the others were being treated as prisoners of war, but that if he had chosen to enforce the laws of France, Thielemann's letter would have arrived too late to affect his decision. His response, if any, to the Duke is not known.

Contact with Antwerp

Having established himself in Ghent, Maison set about establishing communications with Antwerp. He learned that enemy couriers were seen in the direction of Lokeren, so he dispatched his chief of staff – Colonel Villatte – with a company of voltigeurs riding in wagons and an escort of 50 cavalry to protect him as far as Lokeren.[38]

Villatte carried an order to Carnot directing him to release Roguet with his artillery – as well as the lancers and Gardes d'honneur – which were still in Antwerp. Villatte arrived in Antwerp that night. Less than 40 hours after leaving Lille, Maison had his troops by Antwerp.

Though Carnot would be surrendering a substantial force, it was presumed by Clarke, the Duke de Feltre and the French Minister of War that Admiral Missiessy would surrender 3,000 marines to the governor of Antwerp – making good the loss. This would still leave the admiral with his fleet, the flotilla of gunners and 2,500 support personnel and not seriously threaten the French hold on Antwerp.

Roguet departed Antwerp on 27 March, crossed the Scheldt and marched towards Gontrode and Gyzenzeele, where Maison positioned him to convince the Allies that he was preparing to march on Brussels via Alost. In fact, Maison intended to withdraw once again to Lille and relieve Maubeuge.[39]

The Allied response

Thielemann was an aggressive officer who apparently had a grudge against the French. He had deserted the Saxon army in 1813 – while still technically an ally of the French – and had joined the Prussian army. Since that time, his behaviour towards the French had been one of constantly seeking battle when the opportunity arose. Upon learning that Maison had marched to Ghent, he thought to move to cut him off, but realizing that he would face far superior forces, he was obliged to concentrate his seven Saxon battalions and a few Saxon squadrons – a total of 5,000 men – in

37 Calmon-Maison, pp. 214-7.
38 Koch, Vol. II, p. 619.
39 Calmon-Maison, pp. 218-23.

Audenarde. He recognized that Maison's maneuver was designed to reinforce the French I Corps – not to move against Brussels.

However, the Duke of Weimar was not as insightful as Thielemann and moved to cover Brussels. He called General Wallmoden to move his division from Louvain and join him in Alost. Weimar concentrated 9,000 infantry and 900 cavalry there, while (he hoped) Thielemann would threaten his flank with 15 battalions and 700 cavalry. At the same time, Allied detachments were posted in Courtrai, Harlebeke and Deynze; a detachment was sent to Leutze to support the garrison of Tournai; and Major Helwig was dispatched to reinforce the chain of pickets before Condé and Valenciennes.[40]

Maison's boldness had brought him 4,000 infantry, 260 cavalry and 14 cannon. Roguet's 6th Young Guard Division contained the 9th, 10th, 11th, 12th and 13th Tirailleur Regiments – each of two battalions. This raised the strength of the I Corps to 9,700 infantry, 1,360 cavalry and 35 cannon. Though he remained inferior to the Allied forces arrayed before him, the odds were narrowing.

Maison escapes south

Maison established Roguet's 6th Young Guard Division in Gontrode, pushed reconnaissance forces down the road to Alost and deliberately spread the word among the inhabitants that it was his intention to march on Brussels. He laid the seeds of a deception to encourage the Duke of Weimar to continue marching north, while he turned his attention to how to evade Thielemann's forces in Audenarde.

Should Thielemann, with his 12,000 men (15 battalions and 500 cavalry), position himself on the road to Courtrai between the Lys and the Scheldt rivers; if Wallmoden posted his division between the Scheldt River and Audenarde; and should the British detach some of their siege forces around Antwerp, the situation of the French army would become critical.[41] This would cut off Maison from both Antwerp and Lille and leave him no alternative but to withdraw into the maritime fortifications. The return to Lille was absolutely necessary if he was to continue any serious campaign.

Maison decided to march immediately on Courtrai. To cover his movement, he sent Solignac's division and a squadron of Young Guard Chasseurs à cheval to Peterghem to cover the movement of his troops. On 30 March Maison evacuated Ghent – marching in two columns. Solignac, with his division and a squadron of cavalry, followed the left bank of the Scheldt. The main body of the I Corps marched down the road to Courtrai via the right bank of the Lys. Its advanced guard cleared Deynze of the Allied advanced posts under Major Puckler and threw them back. The few Prussian cavalry cantoned in Courtrai withdrew when the French appeared – allowing Maison to occupy Courtrai with his army.[42]

The Battle of Courtrai – 31 March

As soon as Thielemann learned that Maison had escaped, he called together his dispersed forces and marched from Audenarde to Avelghem with the hope of engaging Solignac's division, which he supposed he would encounter near Avelghem. He also invited Wallmoden to march on Audenarde with his forces and join the operation.

40 Calmon-Maison, p. 224.
41 Koch, Vol. II, p. 620.
42 Calmon-Maison, pp. 225-7.

Thielemann moved his main body to Avelghem, while his advanced guard (1st Brigade) moved from Heestert to Sweveghem. Once there, the 2nd Brigade – under Prince Paul von Württemberg – was to march on Tournai. The Helwig Freikorps was to cover the right flank.

At 6:00 a.m. on 31 March the Allied advanced guard, under GM Brause, surprised the French posts in Sweveghem and pushed them back. Major Helwig covered the left flank facing Belleghem – moving down the road towards Courtrai. GM Brause ordered the 1/1st Saxon Landwehr Regiment to move towards Harlebeke and to advance – maintaining alignment with the advanced guard – until it was at a point where it could overlook Courtrai. The 2/,3/1st Saxon Landwehr Regiment and four guns followed behind the main body as a reserve.

The Allied 2nd Brigade moved into Sweveghem via the main road. They detached the two cuirassier squadrons and two guns behind as a reserve. When Brause's main body arrived at the designated point, it found Maison's entire force deployed before it. Upon learning this, Thielemann left his main body in Sweveghem under Prince Paul von Württemberg and rode forward to observe the French for himself.

After evaluating the French, Thielemann ordered his main body forward. The Saxon 1st Brigade commenced to deploy on the heights – straddling the road. Two-and-a-half battalions and five guns followed Prince Paul forward to a position about 1,500 paces from Sweveghem, where they deployed into three distinct columns. The 3/3rd Landwehr Regiment and the Schwarzberg Battalion – supported by two guns (captured French 6pdrs) – took up a position behind them on the Windmill hill.[43]

Maison responded by sending several guns forward to delay the Allied deployment and subsequent advance. When he realized that the Allies were coming only down the road from Audenarde, he decided to attack them – striking them in both flanks and frontally.[44]

Barrois was ordered to march from Harlebeke to Sweveghem to attack the Allied right and cut off their retreat, while Solignac – marching from Belleghem – was to threaten the Allied left. Roguet's division, forming the French center, stood on the road to Audenarde. He was to lock the Allies in place while the other two divisions marched against Thielemann's forces. Castex held his cavalry in reserve to support Roguet.

The terrain made the extensive use of artillery difficult and soon a heavy exchange of musketry began along the entire front. Maison's soldiers successfully pressed Thielemann's forces wherever they encountered them. The French troops were either depot units or had veteran cadres and the ranks filled with recent conscripts, but many of the Saxons were far worse – especially the Landwehr battalions, which had never been under fire before.

Prince Paul von Württemberg commanded the Allied advanced guard. He drew up the 1/, 2/3rd (Saxon) Landwehr Regiment into closed column, with the Bernberg Battalion behind them as support.[45] Without orders, Prince Paul moved forward – deploying five companies of Saxon Landwehr as skirmishers to attack Courtrai and supporting them with his formed Landwehr.[46] Two companies of Rudolstädters (Schwarzberg Battalion) – under Hauptmann von Schauroth – and one Sonderhausen company – under Hauptmann Schumann – were also sent forward as skirmishers and extended the skirmish line to the left.[47]

GD Maison had deployed his regiments in line and sent a strong skirmish force to hit Thielemann's left wing. Shortly later, four battalions of Roguet's 6th Young Guard Division

43 Bücher, pp. 180-1.
44 Schuster, O. Francke, F.A., Vol. II, p. 384; Koch, Vol. II, p. 622.
45 Bücher, p. 182.
46 Sporschil, Vol. II, 2nd Band, p. 250.
47 Schüler, pp. 64-5.

supported by artillery and cavalry were ordered to strike the Allied center, with the 10th Tirailleur Regiment leading the assault – advancing at the *pas de charge*.[48] The assault of the Young Guard threw back the 1/1st Saxon Landwehr Regiment.

Thielemann moved his artillery and the Saxon cuirassiers by Sweveghem forward to support his leading elements as they became heavily engaged. His advanced guard was now totally deployed as skirmishers.

Before long, Thielemann realized that he had caught more than he had expected – finding himself facing not just Solignac's lone division, but the entire I Corps. He ordered a retreat and his retreat turned into a rout. The 2/,3/1st (Saxon) Landwehr Regiment came under heavy pressure and were saved momentarily by a timely charge of the Saxon Hussar Regiment.

The 2nd Young Guard Chasseurs surged forward under the orders of Castex and Meuziau – sabering the Saxon cuirassiers and rolling over their infantry. Thielemann's lines were crushed and sent back in great disorder. The main body of the Schwarzberg battalion, not engaged, formed part of the covering force of the rearguard.

The remainder of the Saxon forces pushed between the divisions of Barrois and Solignac into Maison's trap. Penne's brigade struck their left, while Darriule's Young Guard brigade (Barrois' division) stood behind them on the road to Audenarde. Thielemann's command collapsed and the terrified Saxons scattered in every direction. The two squadrons of Saxon cuirassiers – under Oberst Thümmel – supported by a squadron of Saxon Hussars, charged the advancing French to little effect. The respite Thielemann gained by their sacrifice was only momentary.

One Saxon Landwehr battalion found itself trapped against a wall and was obliged to surrender, and three limbered guns were captured. Hundreds of Saxons were taken prisoner – many killed on the battlefield – while more were drowned as they attempted to swim the Scheldt. There are, as usual, many conflicting figures on the Saxons' losses. Schuster and Francke state that three officers and 252 men were killed, 17 officers and 423 men were wounded and 19 officers and 493 men were captured[49] (either the 2nd or 3rd Battalion, 3rd Saxon Landwehr Regiment).

A slightly larger number – 1,900 men killed, wounded and prisoner – is reported by von Eggloffstein.[50] Koch states that the Allies lost three 6pdrs and 800-900 men *hors de combat*.[51]

Blücher provides several strength returns. According to those returns, the 2/,3/3rd (Saxon) Landwehr Regiment were badly savaged and apparently combined into a single battalion after the battle. Their total strength on 25 March was 32 officers and 1,416 men. On 20 April (though there may have been reinforcements) the two battalions had a combined strength of 34 officers and 678 men – indicating a loss of 746 men. Over the same period, the 1/3rd (Saxon) Landwehr seems to have lost four officers and 41 men. The 1/,2/,3/1st (Saxon) Landwehr declined in strength by one officer and 298 men. Over the same period, the Schwarzberg Battalion lost one officer and 59 men. The losses of the Bernberg Battalion, the Saxon Cuirassiers, the Saxon Hussars and the artillery cannot be gagged since they all apparently received reinforcements after the battle. The upshot is that Saxon records clearly indicate the loss of around 1,100 men *hors de combat*.[52]

By 2:00 p.m. Thielemann's army was fleeing down the road to Audenarde – pursued by Darriule's brigade as far as Kerkhove. The battle had cost the French about 300 casualties.[53]

48 Koch, Vol. II, p. 622
49 Schuster, O. Francke, F.A., Vol. II, p. 384.
50 von Eggloffstein, p. 93.
51 Koch, Vol. II, p. 623.
52 Bücher, Beilage I.
53 Calmon-Maison, pp. 228-31.

Saxe-Weimar redeploys his forces

Maison deployed his forces to renew his attack, but learned that during the night, the four Allied battalions already in the city had been reinforced by Gablentz's brigade and a detachment from Oberst von Thümen. Maison realized that his hopes of taking Courtrai were lost and decided to withdraw to Lille. Not capturing Courtrai was surely a disappointment, but not enough to offset his pleasure at repaying the perfidious Saxons for their betrayal of the French the year before at Leipzig. The Swedes had relieved Gablentz's Prussian brigade at the Antwerp blockade – allowing it to move south to join Saxe-Weimar. In addition, a brigade of Saxon Landwehr, Wallmoden's Hanoverian division and other newly-arrived detachments brought his available forces to about 40 battalions, 30 squadrons and 56 guns. Maison was greatly outnumbered and he had little alternative but to continue his march south.

Saxe-Weimar directed Thielemann's shattered corps (11 battalions, four squadrons, Helwig's partisans and 16 guns) to march on Tournai. General Lecoq moved to Mons with 14 battalions, four squadrons and 14 guns supported by two Cossack pulks. A reserve of seven battalions, six squadrons and 26 guns was established in Ath. A second (similar) force under General Wallmoden was established in Lessines.[54]

Wallmoden's march

When he received Thielemann's call for help after Courtrai, Wallmoden moved from Alost to Audenarde and reoccupied Ghent with a column under the command of Oberst von Lottum. Lottum arrived before Courtrai that evening and immediately encountered General Audenarde with his lancers, the French gendarmes and a regiment from Barrois' division. Lottum was obliged to withdraw to Harlebeke.

Garrison of Ghent (strength figures as of 1 April 1814):

2nd Guard Lancer Regiment (Young Guard) (832 men / 685 horses)
Gendarmes d'Elite (55 / 57)
1st Gendarme Squadron (70 / 72)
2nd Gendarme Squadron (77 / 77)
Unknown Tirailleur Regiment

Maison's movements after Courtrai

After his victory at Courtrai, Maison sent Solignac's division towards Tournai. Barrois was detached to observe Avelghem and Maison, and then led Roguet's division and the bulk of the cavalry down the road to Tournai. As he moved through Pecq, Maison learned that Solignac had pushed back the enemy posts and stood before Tournai. Maison dispatched a force of cavalry and artillery to join him.

In fact, Maison's goal was to distract the Allied commanders to a new threat and away from his train and baggage. His movement against Tournai was a ruse. He still intended to march his entire army to Lille, but the baggage train was slow and needed time for the march.

The French artillery took up positions to the north of Tournai – on the road to Audenarde and to the west on the road to Lille – and opened fire as night fell. The Allies had left a garrison of 2,100 men and 30 horses in Tournai under the command of Oberst von Eggloffstein. Von Eggloffstein commanded the Gotha Battalion, the two battalions of Anhalt-Dessau-Köthen, 30 men of the 4/ Saxon Hussar Regiment and four English 9pdr cannon.

54 Koch, Vol. II, p. 625.

Solignac's skirmishers pushed up to the ramparts of the city and began shooting down the Allied defenders. Von Eggloffstein responded with the fire of a number of heavy guns on the walls of the city, but with little effect. As the battle began, Maison had only Solignac's division with him as Barrois' 4th Young Guard Division remained watching Avelghem and would join the march on Lille – serving as a rearguard to cover the march of the French gendarmes, the prisoners taken at Courtrai, the grand park and the French baggage train. Roguet's 6th Young Guard Division would not arrive until later. However, as all the troops had been engaged earlier in the day at Courtrai, they were fatigued and Maison decided to stop any action that night and stopped the artillery fire at 10:00 p.m.

During the night, Maison's posts on the left bank of the Scheldt advised him of the arrival of reinforcements into the city. Gablentz's cavalry brigade arrived from Audenarde and took up positions to support the garrison. The following morning, Maison departed the Orcy heights and withdrew to Lille. Later in the morning, he had reunited his entire army at Lille.[55]

Military necessities to the south required Borstell to move south and take up positions before Soissons. As a result, the Duke of Saxe-Weimar found it necessary to lift the siege of Maubeuge. Borstell had also been responsible for blockading Condé, Quesnoy and Valenciennes. Lecoq could not remain before Maubeuge and still assure the communications of the Army of Silesia or to the blockade forces around Mons that ran via Beaumont and Avesnes. On 30 March he was obliged to abandon his blockade of Maubeuge and marched to Givry.

Maison took no action immediately, but soon decided to march on Landrecies and cut the Allied lines of communications. He gathered up his forces and on 4 April at 2:00 a.m. he dispatched Solignac's division – supported by the Young Guard Chasseurs à cheval and their artillery. Solignac was to post his infantry in Orchies and his cavalry in the villages around Pont-à-Marcq. He was to be ready to withdraw, if heavily attacked, in the direction of Béthune.

Later in the day, the rest of the I Corps marched via Pont-à-Marcq on Orchies. The lancers led the march, followed by Barrois' 4th Young Guard Division; the grand park; Roguet's 6th Young Guard Division; and the gendarmes. As this column approached Orchies, Solignac moved his division to Saint-Amand. That night, Maison's advanced guard – the forces under Solignac – was in Saint-Amand and the main body of his corps was in Orchies. The following morning, they marched on Valenciennes.

While in Valenciennes, Maison learned of the Allied occupation of Paris. With the lifting of the siege of Maubeuge, Maison decided it was best that he return to Lille and to reinforce the various garrisons under his command to cover all eventualities. General Penne remained in Valenciennes with his brigade. The army then moved through Bouchain and Douai – leaving detachments – and returned to Lille on 6 April. A few days later, word of the formation of a provisional government and the armistice arrived. Maison and Thielemann exchanged notes. Both felt that further shedding of blood was pointless and agreed to an armistice between them to start on 7 April.[56]

55 Calmon-Maison, pp. 232-8.
56 Calmon-Maison, pp. 239-42.

17

Operations around Lyon: The Battles of Mâcon, Saint-Georges and Limonest, January-March 1814

The quick fall of Geneva to the Allies did not prove advantageous to them. It persuaded Count Bubna that the rest of the campaign would not be particularly taxing and caused him to linger for three days establishing his position. Bubna's 1st Light Division appears to have undergone several changes early in the campaign. Initially, he started out with two mixed brigades: Scheither (two battalions, 12 squadrons and a horse battery) and Zechmeister (three battalions, 18 squadrons and two horse batteries). On 24 December Bubna's command underwent a major reorganization. Scheither's brigade was detached, but the Kaiser Hussars and Warasdiner Grenz from Scheither's brigade remained. Klopfstein and Longueville's brigades were assigned to Bubna's division along with a 12pdr battery from the 2nd Corps. The Gradiscaner Grenz from von Coburg's brigade (2nd Corps) were also assigned to Bubna. Bubna's command now consisted of 15 battalions including one jäger, two grenz and 12 line battalions; 18 squadrons of hussars from the Kaiser, Liechtenstein and Blankestein Hussars; and five batteries – including one 12pdr battery. He commanded a force of approximately 9,000 infantry, 2,160 cavalry and 40 cannon.[1]

It appears to have been reorganized yet again – and according to the Austrian archives, when it entered France it was organized as follows:[2]

- Brigade: Generalmajor Zechmeister
  - 6th Jäger Battalion
  - Broder Grenz (one battalion)
  - Liechtenstein Hussar Regiment (one squadron)
  - 1 Wurst Battery
- Detachment from 1st Division
  - Peterwardeiner Grenz (one battalion)
  - Würzburg Dragoon Regiment (six squadrons)
  - Blankenstein Hussar Regiment (six squadrons)
- Brigade: Generalmajor Klopfstein
  - W. Colloredo Infantry Regiment (three battalions)
  - Kaunitz Colloredo Infantry Regiment (three battalions)
  - 1 Brigade Battery

1 Lefebvre de Béhaine, Vol. IV, p. 332 & p. 340.
2 Austrian War Archives, File 2, No. 1.

Brigade: Longueville (formerly Vogelsang's brigade)
Reuss-Greitz Infantry Regiment (three battalions)
Vogelsang Infantry Regiment (two battalions)
1 Brigade Battery
Detachment from 2nd Army Corps:
Gradiscaner Grenz (one battalion of four companies)
Brigade: Scheither
5th Jäger Battalion
Warasdiner Kreuzer Grenz (one battalion)
Kaiser Hussar Regiment (six squadrons)

Bubna did not send out his first reconnaissance forces until 4 January – and they were sent only to Gex and Lyon. The former, however, was stopped at Saint-Claude and the latter by Fort l'Ecluse, which convinced him that the entire border was denuded of troops. Indeed, Zechmeister invested Fort l'Ecluse, fired a few howitzer shells into it, had the French fire back one cannon shot and the commander – Lecamus de Coëtanferra – immediately surrendered himself and what of his garrison had not escaped.[3] Despite this, rather than marching directly on Lyon, he decided it was wiser to match his movements with that of the right flank of the main army and, instead, marched on Poligny and sent detachments to Arbois, Lons-le-Saulnier and Salins, which he invested. The following day, he forced the bridge at Dôle and pushed General Lambert back to Auxonne. Prince A. Liechtenstein was directed to move to the right bank of the Doubs and to blockade Auxonne – as well as Besançon.

The French situation was difficult, at best. Chef de bataillon Pillioud – commander of the Department of the Ain – upon hearing of the Allied invasion, had begun organizing his defense. He had ordered the gendarmerie brigades to move forward and establish themselves on the main roads. He then moved to Cerdon, where he took command of a column of 625 men drawn from the 24th Line and 32nd Légère under Chef de bataillon Ivaldi. Ivaldi's forces were marching on Geneva under orders from General Poncet – commander of the 19th Military Division. These men had only five cartridges each. Ivaldi's column was redirected to Cluze, where the roads from Saint-Claude and Nantua meet. After dark that evening, a reconnaissance force of a company of voltigeurs from the 24th Line and some gendarmes were sent to investigate Nantua. It was found to be occupied by Austrian hussars, but a premature charge by the French gendarmes was beaten off and the French withdrew. The next morning, 2,000 cartridges arrived in the French camp. Now fully-armed, they marched forward again and found Nantua abandoned.[4]

Bubna was advised that generals Legrand and Musnier had concentrated – respectively, in Châlons and Bourg – all of the available manpower in the departments of Saône-et-Loire and l'Aine; he resolved to march against them. He reinforced Longueville's brigade and sent him against the two French generals, while he left Zechmeister's brigade in Geneva. His goal was to deny Musnier and Legrand the time to organize their forces. He feared that they might attempt to concentrate and take offensive action. He then detached a strong force of cavalry to march against Châlons, and then marched on the Ain with the bulk of his army.[5]

As with the other French detachments at this time, Musnier commanded a tiny force of relatively untrained soldiers and refused to allow himself to be engaged. He withdrew on 12 January

3 Lefebvre de Béhaine, Vol. IV, p. 376.
4 Lefebvre de Béhaine, Vol. IV, p. 376.
5 Koch, Vol. II, pp. 211-2.

to Lyon – leaving the Bourg National Guard to garrison the city of Bourg. Legrand, however, was able to hold his position and rebuff the Allied attempts to pass over the bridge at Saône.

When the Allies arrived before the city of Bourg, the Bourg National Guard refused to even speak to the parliamentarian who presented himself before their gates. However, the National Guards were not up the fight and the city was quickly taken and pillaged. Many of the city's citizens abandoned the city – some fleeing westwards and others joining the army to avenge the rape of their homes.

Immediately after the sacking of Bourg, Count Bubna resumed his march directly against Lyon, which was probably the richest city in the region. He assumed that Musnier's tiny force of conscripts would flee rather than offer any resistance, but he ignored the fact that he would have to pass Mont-Blanc, where General Laroche was organizing a considerable force.

Bubna had no news of Valais, where Colonel Simbschen had been sent from Lausanne to secure the Simplon and Saint-Bernard passes. As a result, he lost several days while he opened communications through Ain and Nantua to Geneva. He contented himself with pushing a weak advanced guard down the road to Lyon. When he learned that Simbschen – supported by a battalion of Swiss from the province of Valais – was in a position to defend the passes to Italy, he felt sufficiently bold to march against Thonon.

Earlier, Bubna had been advised that Laroche had under him only the garrison of Geneva reinforced by a few hundred conscripts. He thought little of any threat from Laroche. Bubna doubted, therefore, that Laroche could undertake an offensive against both Bourg as well as Geneva. As a result, he ordered Zechmeister to turn the garrison of Geneva over to the Geneva Chasseurs, which were forming, and to attack the French corps in Rumilly with his forces. He was to push them as far as Chambéry, while Bubna marched towards Lyon with the bulk of his forces after leaving some detachments to garrison Bourg and Mâcon.[6]

Other Allied actions

In the early part of January – as the Allies advanced into France – there were a number of fortified border cities that presented a threat to the Allied lines of communication and had to be blockaded, so it proved necessary to divide up the rear area commands. FML Graf Klebersberg was given command of all Allied troops on the right bank of the Rhône and General Zechmeister took command of those on the left. FML Fürst A. Liechtenstein blockaded the fortress of Besançon and FML Wimpffen closed Auxonne. The Crown Prince von Hesse-Homburg had overall command of the Austrian troops between the Saône and Doubs – as well as the blockading forces around the various fortresses. He established his headquarters in Dijon, which was garrisoned by two grenadier battalions and the Lothringen Cuirassier Regiment.[7]

French activity along the Swiss border

Napoleon had dispatched Maréchal Augereau from Paris on 11 January. He was to assume command of the region around Lyon and arrived there on 14 January – just as Bubna's advanced guard entered Montluel.

Lyon was not strongly held. There were supposed to be about 6,000 regular combatants in the region, but when Maréchal Augereau arrived, he found only the 1,200 under Musnier and another 250 veterans.

6 Koch, Vol. II, pp. 213-4.
7 Sporschil, Vol. 2, 2nd Band, p. 182.

The political situation in Lyon was not good either. Many of the wealthy manufacturers had fled the city and the call to arms to the citizens for the defense of the city had resulted in a very limited response. Maréchal Augereau found himself having to defend the second city of France with almost nothing.

His first step was to send orders that all levies moving through Valence were to be rerouted to Clermont to accelerate the organization of the Puy-de-Dôme and Cantal National Guard. The marshal then left Lyon and ordered Musnier to hold the city as long as possible, while he organized new troops. Musnier found himself with 1,700 men attempting to defend a very large city whose population was unfriendly, if not openly hostile.

Maréchal Augereau.

The city of Lyon

Lyon sits on the junction of the Rhône and Saône rivers – and on the right bank of the latter river. It was divided into three parts. The first, or Guillotière suburb, was an open suburb along the Rhône and ran only about 250 yards along the river. The second part was between the Rhône and the Saône. It was surrounded by an old wall, studded with bastions, but without a ditch. On the east stood the Croix-Rousse suburb, which ran along the ridge of the same name. To the east was the Serin suburb, which ran for 1,000 yards along the left bank of the Saône. Finally, the last part of the city, which was both the oldest and most densely populated, stood on the Saône surrounded by an old wall flanked with round and square towers – plus a few bastions. It had no moat or ditch and stretched to the bluffs on the eastern side of the of the Fourvière ridge.

This portion of the city was not dominated by – but it was masked to the west – by the village of Saint-Irenée, which was on the western end of the same ridge. Further to the north was the Vaize suburb, which ran along the right bank of the Saône. This entire flank was open to the threat of a few batteries.

The placement of artillery to threaten Lyon was facilitated by the Croix-Rousse heights, which dominated the Croix-Rousse suburbs and the plains by Guillotière, which were criss-crossed by a web of roads which would facilitate the establishment of incendiary batteries.

In addition, the Saône River offered little protection as it was crossed by seven bridges built of stone, wood and pontoons, which provided passage almost the entire length of the city as it ran along the river. There were also two bridges on the Rhône – over which ran the roads to Pont-de-Veauvoisin, Grenoble and Vienne. However, between the Rhône and the Saône there were only the bridges at Trévoux and Lons-le-Saulnier, which passed through Bourg.

General Musnier realized that the citizenry did not have the time to break the numerous dikes and dams which covered their department; his defense problems would be compounded as a result. Musnier recognized that Count Bubna would, of choice, advance down the roads from Bourg. He responded by putting observation posts in Grange-Blanche and at the Oullins bridge to observe the roads to Châlons, Moulins, Clermont and Puy. He also threw 1,000 men into the edge of the Croix-Rousse suburb.[8]

The first contact between Musnier and Bubna's troops occurred on 16 January – some 10 miles (15 kilometers) from Lyon on the roads to Dombes and Amberieux. These were minor skirmishes

8 Koch, Vol. II, pp. 215-9.

because of the deliberate inundations to the east of Lyon. These same inundations obliged Bubna to abandon his intent to march directly via Meximieux and move through Amberieux. The following day, Musnier withdrew his troops across the Saône and established them at the fork in the roads to Châlons, Moulins and Clermont. On the peninsula in the river, he left only a few small pickets. His total force – the 1st Division – consisted of 4,000 men, four guns and 200 men of the 1st Hussars and 31st Chasseurs.[9]

Bubna, not appreciating the weakness of Musnier, lost more time on the 18th with reconnaissance and the dispatch of parliamentarians. Vainly, the few German artisans in the city attempted to convince him that Lyon was deserted. He did, however, permit a patrol to be led by them during the night as far as the piers of the Rhône, where they stopped to refresh themselves – thinking they would seize a position on the Croix-Rousse ridge the next day.

Their timidity convinced Musnier that the Allies intended a *coup de main* and resolved to dislodge them with a night attack – immediately after receiving a reinforcement of 700 men from the 16th and 145th Line Regiments en route from Valence by Augereau.

Bubna, however, learned of their approach and withdrew to the heights where the Château La Pape stood. This Allied withdrawal was to prove decisive for the defense of Lyon, for it reinvigorated the spirit of the Lyonnaise population and they began arming their National Guard.

On 20 January 400 men of the 32nd Légère and the first two guns arrived. The following day, 170 cavalry from the 4th and 31st Chasseurs à cheval Regiments arrived with the third gun. They were assigned to Musnier's division, which on 21 January 1814 was as follows:

Musnier's division[10] as of 21 January 1814
- 16th Line Regiment (9 officers / 320 men)
- 2/24th Line Regiment (22 / 426)
- 5/24th Line Regiment (3 / 91 – all conscripts, no uniforms)
- 145th Line Regiment (12 / 300)
- 32nd Légère Regiment (4 / 209 – all without shoes)
- 32nd Légère Regiment (0 / 400 – all without shakos)
- 2nd Marine Artillery Regiment (5 / 255)
- Various gendarmes (6 / 140)
- 1st Hussar Regiment (9 / 165)
- 4th and 31st Chasseurs à cheval Regiments (around 70 men)
- 2nd Horse Artillery Regiment (1 / 50 – the gunners are not mounted and the guns have no harnesses)

During the following days, the Austrians were pushed back to Montluel, where they took up positions that they held until the end of January. Lyon had a fortunate escape from the predations of the marauding Austrians. On the other hand, Mont-Blanc was not so lucky.

General Zechmeister departed Geneva on 18 January with about 1,800 men and a battery of eight guns. He attacked the French posted at Rumilly and drove them back. General Laroche, commander of the 7th Military Division, had moved his headquarters to Chambéry when he learned of Zechmeister's advance. He immediately withdrew his forces and marched on Echelles and Montmélian. The column that moved down the latter route was closely pressed by Austrian cavalry and was unable to hold the bridge over the Isère. The Austrians pushed them to Pontcharra

9 Zins, p. 53.
10 SHAT, Carton C^2 556.

– and a position under the protection of Fort Barreaux. On 20 January Zechmeister occupied Chambéry.

With the Allies advancing into the eastern provinces of France, Napoleon had sent Count Saint-Vallier as a special commissioner to the 7th Military Division. He was critical of Laroche's handling of the campaign and directed Count Marchand, then occupied with raising the National Guard in Grenoble, to assume command of all the troops in the region and asked Count Dessaix to second him. At the same time, calls went out to organize the National Guard in the menaced provinces. One organized two free companies of veteran soldiers and hunters reputed to be good shots. A third company was organized from customs officers. The department mounted and equipped – at its expense – 100 veteran cavalry, which were drawn from the depots and provided the equipment necessary to field a battery of six guns.[11]

Upon arriving in Barreaux, General Marchand found a mass of nearly-naked and demoralized conscripts suffering from the bureaucratic lack of attention to their needs. His first concern was, after addressing the needs of his men, to occupy a position in Chavanne and a position on the left of the Isère, which dominated the Montmélian bridge.

The position on the Montmélian bridge was occupied by 400 French infantry on 25 January. The wooden floor of the bridge had been removed and two cannon had been placed 200 paces from the bridge, where they could enfilade it. Attacked by Austrian infantry on that day, the French fire proved too much for them – dismounting the supporting Austrian artillery and driving them back.[12]

Once Marchand was certain that his right and center were in a state of defense, he moved to Echelles. Here, Maréchal de camp Bicomte de Barral – a veteran soldier that had been retired 20 years – had voluntarily left his retirement and, despite his great age and many infirmities, assumed command and began organizing a force of 1,500 men for the defense of France.

Zechmeister could have succeeded in occupying Grenoble, but like Bubna, lingered eight days before attempting a *coup de main*. After determining that the French would not cede any further terrain to him without fighting, he turned against the French post at Echelles on 31 January. Echelles stood on and blocked the road from Chambéry to Lyon. In order to distract the French, on the same day he made probes against Barreaux and Chavanne.

General Barral did not have a large force to defend his post in Echelles. His conscripts and National Guards were attacked from many sides – and after a short resistance, withdrew to Voiron and Saint-Laurent-du-Pont, where Count Marchand stopped them with promises of reinforcements en route.

A false attack against the mountain which dominated Fort Barreaux offers an example of devotion that is seldom matched in military history. The company of the 8th Légère that defended this post soon fired off all its cartridges, and children from the village of Barreaux – aged 10 to 12 – fought for the honor to carry ammunition to them. These children moved among the soldiers while under fire – distributing fresh ammunition to them – and continued these perilous trips until the Austrians abandoned their attack. In contrast, the demonstration against Chavanne consisted solely of some artillery fire.

While Zechmeister's troops were in action around Mont-Blanc, Count Bubna came to the conclusion that he could safely occupy all the territory between the Saône and the Ain if he occupied Châlons.

On 6 February another clash occurred near Fort Barreaux and Chapareillan. At 10:00 a.m. several Austrian detachments of infantry and cavalry moved on the hamlet of Bellecombe and

11 Koch, Vol. II, pp. 219-21.

12 Guerre, p. 56.

deployed for battle around the church and the old château. They moved to turn Fort Barreaux and to clear out the French troops that defended its approach. When the fight had run for a while, the French began to run low on ammunition. Bodies of Austrian troops began to move against the village of Chapareillan – driving the 600 French defenders into the center of the village. Yet another Austrian column, under Zechmeister, moved down the main road supported by artillery.

The Austrian pressure was too much for the French in Chapareillan, who withdrew in good order into the Servette forest. Meanwhile, a general engagement began all along the line that eventually proved successful for the French. The Austrians were obliged to abandon Chapareillan and withdraw.[13]

The fall of Châlons

General Legrand had held the bridge on the Saône for 15 days with about 200 men supported by a force of Sedentary National Guard. When the Austrians arrived before his position and began to pound it with artillery, his tiny command was quickly forced to withdraw on Charolles. Châlons was rapidly occupied without further incident. Oberstleutnant Menninger – commanding two squadrons of the Würzburg Dragoons and two companies of infantry – pursued Legrand with the goal of pushing him across the Loire. Major Bailleux – commanding six companies of the Devaux Infantry Regiment and four companies from the Argenteau Infantry Regiment – occupied Châlons and Givry. The remainder of the brigade then moved to Mâcon on 8 February. On 13 February the brigade was joined by two squadrons of Westphalian Hussars. They were used to form the link between Mâcon and Tournus.[14]

Bubna, having taken Châlons so easily, disarmed the inhabitants in the departments of the Ain and Saône-et-Loire and put Scheither's brigade in Villefranche, Mâcon, Tournus and Châlons. Between the Saône and the Ain he retained only the brigades of Klopfstein and Longueville, with Zechmeister assigned to guard Savoy.

Augereau saw the weakness in Bubna's dispositions and was quick to take advantage of it to organize his army. The conscripts destined to form 16 battalions had yet to arrive, so he encouraged the formation of the Damas free corps – formed of veteran soldiers and "men of good will."

A number of veteran officers from the region volunteered their services and asked that they be allowed to raise free companies that would be assigned to the principal valleys such as those of Saint-Martin, Oyonnax, Michaille, Valromey, etc. where the hardy and vigorous mountain folk would be ideally suited to a guerrilla war against the Austrians. However, the marshal felt this effort would be ineffective – and a waste of resources – and declined their offer.

The only services offered that excited his attention was that of the artillery. He raised and organized four companies of artillery train – equipping them with everything they would need for a campaign.

Troops continued to move into the region, with six reserve battalions arriving from Vienne with about 4,000 men. Maréchal Augereau organized them into the garrison of Valence and directed General Bardet to complete their organization. A few days later, the 2nd Toulon Regiment and a battalion of the 145th Line Regiment arrived in the company of General Pouchelon, 80 cavalry and two guns. They were sent to guard the Tarare hill. Finally, on 14 February a column of troops coming from Spain arrived and the Army of the Rhône began its final organization.[15]

13 Guerre, pp. 57-8.
14 Sporschil, Vol. 2, 2nd Band, p. 185.
15 Koch, Vol. II, pp. 222-6.

Organization of the Army of the Rhône

With the constant flow of reinforcements, the composition of these two forces changed considerably and, with the arrival of 4,000 National Guardsmen from the eight surrounding departments, the numerical disparity between the French and Austrian forces were greatly diminished. Before long, Augereau commanded 17,000 men, while Bubna had only 12,000 men of all arms.

As forces flowed into Lyon, Augereau organized them into four divisions. The first was commanded by General Musnier and consisted of much of the infantry coming from Spain and part of the troops that Augereau found in Lyon. It had a total of 5,500 men.

The second division was placed under GB Pannetier and was formed around a core of veteran troops from Spain. The remainder of the division was formed with veteran troops from France. The division contained 4,200 men. The third division – under General Bardet – was formed around the 4th Reserve (or Nîmes) Division, which was formed with six incomplete battalions. They were, for the most part, conscripts that were lacking most of their equipment. To give them some strength, the cadres of two veteran battalions were attached to the division. The division contained a total of 3,500 men. The fourth division, under GD Marchand, was organized from cadres of various regiments fleshed out with ill-trained conscripts and contained about 4,800 men. The National Guards garrisoning the various strongpoints in the Hautes-Alpes were administratively assigned to this division.

Situation of the 4th Reserve Division of the Midi[16] upon its departure from Nîmes
6/67th Line Regiment (19 / 778)
6/79th Line Regiment (19 / 781)
6/20th Line Regiment (19 / 691)
6/23rd Légère Regiment (19 / 707)
6/115th Line Regiment (19 / 682)
6/60th Line Regiment (19 / 698)

Maréchal Augereau established a reserve formed around the depot of the 24th Line Regiment and 3,000 National Guardsmen that were of little use in the field. The cavalry was placed under the command of Lieutenant-Général Digeon and consisted of the 4th and 12th Hussars, the 13th Cuirassier Regiment, a few mounted gendarmes and various detachments of the 1st Hussars, the 4th and 31st Chasseurs and 60 chasseurs of the Légion Lyonnaise. The cavalry division contained around 2,000 men.[17]

In addition, Gustave de Damas led a force of partisans that was assigned to observe the road to Bourbonnaise and to maintain communications between Tarare and Mâcon through the mountains.

With 17,000 men in hand, Augereau felt himself able to consider taking the offensive and resolved to clear the Austrians out of the region between the Saône and the Ain. With his forces organized, Augereau began deploying them to face the advancing Austrian army. Musnier occupied the center of the line, General Bardet stood on the right and Marchand was on the extreme right.[18]

To effect this, General Pannetier was ordered to move via Villefranche towards Mâcon. General Musnier was to march via Montluel on Meximieux and from the south on Pont-d'Ain and Bourg, where the former was to put himself in communication with Maréchal Augereau. Marchand was

16 SHAT, Carton C² 556.
17 Guerre, pp. 64-5.
18 Guerre, pp. 65-6.

informed of this movement and was requested to execute a diversion against Chambéry or some other point of his choosing. A detachment was to move on Bourgoine to maintain communications between Bardet's division and that of Marchand as they moved through the mountains. At the same time, Pouchelon and Bardet's divisions were called to Lyon – with the former being replaced on the Tarare hill by the Damas partisans. Pouchelon is known – on 4 January – to have taken command of a brigade containing 7,000 men (including 1,845 new conscripts) from the 1/,2/18th Légère, 4/5th, 4/14th, 7/79th and 7/81st Line Regiments.

The 13th Cuirassiers arrived in Lyon, on the 17th, and were immediately sent forward to join the main army. When they arrived, they were immediately engaged and lost their colonel.

The French take the offensive

Augereau's plan was to gain terrain – and this plan offered the best chance of success. He intended to move with the divisions of Pannetier and Musnier – moving through Meximieux and Nantua on Geneva. The city of Geneva had been evacuated by the Austrians and could probably be taken without firing a shot. In the worst case, Augereau would be joined outside its walls by General Marchand. The presence of the French before Geneva would force Bubna to march for Switzerland via Lons-le-Saulnier. If he decided to accept battle with the French, he would be obliged to march via Bourg on Lons-le-Saulnier, which would permit the destruction of Bubna's army.

The plan was implemented on 17 February, but Augereau judged that his presence in Lyon was indispensable and turned command over to his lieutenant. At the same time, the 2nd Division – commanded by GB Pannetier – with 4,500 men, six guns and the 13th Cuirassiers struck the Allies. On 18 February – around 6:00 a.m. – Pannetier advanced on Villefranche. On 19 February he contacted 3,000 Austrians – driving them out of Mâcon and taking 300 prisoners. The Allies withdrew to Châlons – harassed all the way by the groups of enraged citizens armed with their personal firearms.[19]

The Austrians offered almost no resistance. Pannetier threw back their advanced posts at Villefranche and took about 100 prisoners. The following day, General Scheither took Mâcon after a hot engagement. On the 18th, Musnier moved on Meximieux, which Klopfstein occupied with 1,000 infantry, 300 cavalry, two cannon and a howitzer. General Musnier threw Klopfstein's posts out of Meximieux. Apparently, these advanced posts were under the command of Oberst Weiland and pursued them to the village of Loye. In Loye, the Austrian force grew to 1,500 infantry, 500 cavalry and six guns, but they still could not stop the French. Loye was cleared. The Austrians lost about 300 prisoners to the approximately 30 casualties suffered by the French. Through the 19th, the French pushed the Austrians back to the east.

Augereau decided that the route followed by this latter column was the best route and sent Pouchelon's division down it to reinforce his attacking army. At the same time, Musnier executed a forced march against Bourg with the goal of cutting off everyone between the two cities. Klopfstein withdrew his forces – evacuating Nantua and marching on Bourg – where he rejoined Bubna. Bubna had no interest in engaging in an unequal battle and the Austrians resumed their withdrawal. On 19 and 20 February the French occupied both abandoned cities. It is reported that these engagements cost the Austrians three officers and 60 men dead and wounded.[20] French sources suggest that they might have been higher since they report having sent 800 prisoners to Avignon.[21]

19 Zins, p. 54.
20 Sporschil, Vol. 2, 2nd Band, p. 186.
21 Zins, p. 55.

As these operations occurred, French reinforcements continued to move towards Lyon. On the 19th, the 2nd Régiment de Toulon, a battalion of the 145th Line, two cannon and approximately 80 cavalry began their march to join Musnier. On 24 February the 4th Hussars and a battery of light artillery marched for Bourg, while the 12th Hussars and the remainder of the artillery coming from Spain moved into Mâcon to reinforce General Pannetier. On the 24th, the Nîmes Reserve Division found itself finally in a condition to join the war. It was placed under General Bardet and ordered to be before Nantua on the 27th.[22]

On his side, Count Marchand correctly judged that his best option was to recapture Echelles, which threatened Lyon. He prepared his corps for the assault and, in case of success, planned to pursue them as far as Chambéry. As a consequence, General Dessaix – who had 1,400 men in Chavanne since the end of January – was ordered to force a passage over the Isère (below Montmélian) on 16 February. He was to throw the Austrians out of Montmélian and to occupy the Marches heights with a column of 800 men under Major Bois – coming from Barreaux. From there he was to move against Chambéry, while Marchand marched down the road from Lyon with 1,600 men.[23]

The attack on this post presented great difficulties, as the Austrians had cut the road to the Echelles pass. This pass was crossed only by a road of rock known as the 'Grotte', which had been barricaded such that only three or four men could pass through it at a time. In order to reach Echelles, this pass had to be opened to the French.

The recapture of Echelles

Major Thilori – of the 18th Légère – was tasked on 15 February with this operation. He was to lead the voltigeurs of the 1st Line Regiment supported by the grenadiers of the 1st Line and the carabiniers of the 18th Légère. The voltigeurs, with their muskets over their shoulders, threw themselves against the barricade on the Grotte – rushing through heavy musketry and through the barricade. They rushed to the Chambéry side and engaged in a half-hour battle. While they were engaged, the carabiniers and grenadiers moved forward at the *pas de charge* against the Austrian lateral positions and threw out their occupants.

The following day, Marchand led his corps through the pass and marched on Chambéry, while General Dessaix forced a passage over the Isère – chasing the Austrians (consisting of a battalion of the Peterwardeiner Grenz and two cannon) from Montmélian – and affected his junction with Major Bois' column.

The Austrian detachments were assailed from all sides and saved themselves by fleeing in disorder to Chambéry. Once there, General Klebelsberg rallied them on the heights behind the city. Rather than assault Chambéry, Marchand chose to maneuver against it and oblige the Austrians to abandon it. During the morning of 19 February a column of 600 men marched against the Lemens heights behind the Allied position, while another attack was executed against the Reclus bridge. The Austrians were pushed back to a position before Aix, which was covered frontally by a swamp, while its flanks were supported on a mountain and the Lake of Bourget.

The Austrians withdrew on Aix – from which they fled on 22 February after a well-executed French cavalry charge. Their total force was approximately 2,200 to 3,000 infantry and 800 cavalry as they withdrew to Annecy. Once there, they were engaged by General Serrant at the head of 2,000 men and chased back from three successively strong positions. During these

22 Zins, p. 55.
23 Koch, Vol. II, pp. 227-30.

clashes, the Austrians lost one cannon and a significant number of casualties.[24] The French apparently lost 70 men killed or wounded.[25]

Augereau – master of Mâcon and Bourg – linked his forces with those of Marchand, then in Chambéry, by way of the roads through Nantua. He was pleased with the initial results of his offensive operation. However, he had truly done little more than push the Austrians a few more miles from Lyon. He had not been able to deliver a decisive blow that would drive them from France. When the news of his success was passed to Napoleon, it was presented that he was marching on Geneva and the Vaude. Napoleon responded that: "Count Bubna has no more than 10,000 miserable troops with which to oppose you, which will disappear like a fog before the sun; before the faces of the veteran troops coming from Spain. France and Switzerland have their eyes on you. The Vaudois and the Argoviens have 16 battalions of militia ready to march at your side; the Cantons of Saint-Gall, of Soleure, and part of Zurich awaits only your presence to declare in favor of the French." To this, Napoleon added: "You should forget that you are 56 years old and think about the beautiful days of Castiglione." Augereau's imperial title was the 'Duke de Castiglione'. However, a few days later, Napoleon's tone changed when he wrote: "I am not at all pleased with your dispositions. You are dispersing your forces in many directions – to the points where the enemy is dispersed rather than striking at his heart."

Napoleon continued by ordering Augereau to put himself at the head of his troops – in a single column – and march into the Vaude or the Jura (wherever the Austrians were to concentrate). This large mass of forces, he stated, would assure success. Despite Napoleon's prompting, the Army of the Rhône remained. Augereau had only conscripts and National Guards – with the exception of 10,000 veterans – coming from Spain. These 7,000 men were badly-equipped and poorly-trained. Time was necessary to bring them into a condition that would permit them to take to the field successfully.

Reserve Brigade: Général de brigade Rémond[26] as of 25 February 1814
- 6/24th Line Regiment (721)
- Rhône National Guard Regiment (408)
- Haute-Loire National Guard Regiment (297)
- Puy-de-Dôme National Guard Regiment (199)
- Cantal National Guard Regiment (171)
- Haute-Vienne National Guard Regiment (993)
- Indre National Guard Regiment (535)
- Nièvre National Guard Regiment (264)

On 1 March Napoleon detached from Suchet's army (in Spain) a division of 10,000 men with orders to march to Lyon, and ordered Prince Borghese to organize another 6,000 to 8,000 in Turin and to send them over the Alps in the first days of April. In addition, he detached – as quickly as they could be sent – 66 officers and 286 NCOs from the general infantry depot in Paris. They were to be placed in the National Guard battalions and used to train them.

Augereau's inaction gave Bubna time to concentrate his dispersed units. Scheither's brigade, which had been pushed to the Loire by Paray-le-Monial and Digoin, was ordered to move to Châlons and to defend it to the last extremity. Bubna then withdrew on Prince A. Liechtenstein, who was blockading Auxonne and Besançon. GL Klebelsberg, along with Klopfstein's brigade,

24 Guerre, p. 68.
25 Zins, p. 56.
26 SHAT, C[2] 426.

was sent via Saint-Claude to Geneva and charged with the command of all Austrian troops assigned to the defense of the city. Count Bubna held himself ready to follow with the rest of his vision, if necessary, to defend Geneva.

At the same time Bubna informed Schwarzenberg of this change in the state of affairs. This dispatch caused considerable problems and tumult in the Allied headquarters. Schwarzenberg wrote Bubna – exhorting him to dispute every foot of terrain until the reinforcements that were being sent could arrive.

Marchand – who was convinced that once you had your enemy on the run, you should pursue him as hard and as long as possible – did not stop at Chambéry any longer than was necessary to improve his artillery train's horses and to retake the lead mines at Moutier. Lead was in critical shortage and these mines were to provide considerable relief to the French effort in the east.

Marchand's corps resumed its march on 23 February and occupied Aix as quickly as the Austrians abandoned it. He then pushed his advanced posts as far as Albens, where the road forked to Geneva. GB Serrant's brigade marched on Annecy and contained 1,200 men and three guns. The entire corps contained 2,300 men and five guns.[27]

That same day, Zechmeister moved his forces to a position by Fier, where they could link up with Klopfstein's brigade under FML Klebelsberg. His advanced guard stood by Albens – the junction – of the roads from Rumilly and Annecy. It consisted of six companies, a squadron and four guns under Oberst Benczeck. Oberst Zichy stood in Rumilly with two battalions, two squadrons and four guns. To the left (by Annecy) stood General Zechmeister himself – with a force of nine companies, two squadrons and six cannon covering the left flank.[28]

It was on 24 February – two miles below the Alby bridge – that GB Serrant encountered the Austrian advanced guard at Albens and drove them back to Annecy. That evening and next morning, Zechmeister pulled his forces behind the Usus stream and took up positions by Frangy and Chable. That same day, FML Graf Klebelsberg moved Klopfstein's brigade to Frangy. He posted Oberstleutnant Derra with two squadrons of the Kaiser Hussar Regiment between this position and Geneva. On the 25th, GB Serrant took the bridges at Broigny and Caille – placing his headquarters in Coursel.

Marchand, on the other hand, encountered the Austrians at Rumilly that day and threw them back on Fier. The following day, he took the bridge at Copet and pushed on to Frangy, where he arrived unopposed on 27 February.

Because of the constant French pressure, the Austrians did not succeed in regrouping their force until they reached the Usus stream. Here they pulled together 10 battalions and eight squadrons – totaling 5,600 men – and 29 guns. GL Klebelsberg was advised by Bubna that he would be constantly supported by reinforcements coming from Switzerland. He also posted Zechmeister's brigade between St.-Julien and Bardonex and that of Klopfstein between Archamp and Landreci. He was resolved to defend the approaches to Geneva. At this time, Bubna's forces were organized as follows:[29]

Brigade: GM Scheither
- Gradiscaner Grenz Regiment (one battalion)
- Warasdiner Kreuzer Grenz Regiment (one battalion)
- 5th Jäger Battalion
- Kaiser Hussar Regiment (four squadrons)

27 Koch, Vol. II, pp. 231-40.
28 Sporschil, Vol. 2, 2nd Band, p. 191.
29 Austrian War Archives, File 2, No. 752.

Brigade: GM Zechmeister
- 2nd Jäger Battlaion
- Broder Grenz Regiment (one battalion)
- Liechtenstein Hussar Regiment (eight squadrons)

Brigade:
- Peterwardeiner Grenz Regiment (one battalion)
- Vincent Chevauxleger Regiment (two squadrons)
- Würzburg Dragoon Regiment (six squadrons)
- German Legion: Graf Bentheim
- 1 Jäger Battalion
- 2 Line Infantry Battalions

Cavalry (two squadrons)
- Oberst von Hammerstein's Westphalian Hussars (four squadrons)[30]

Augereau, informed of this success, learned of the arrival of eight battalions of National Guard in Lyon and decided to operate as Napoleon had directed. He directed Musnier to march from Nantua via Lons-le-Saulnier, Chiette and Moret to Nyon, where Pannetier's division and all the cavalry were united under the orders of GD Digeon. General Bardet – with the reserve brigade – and General Pouchelon – with two battalions from Musnier's division – were ordered to cross the Rhône at the Bellegarde bridge (or the Seyssel bridge) and to unite before Geneva with General Marchand, who would direct them to their final destinations. There remained only a single line battalion and seven National Guard battalions – or 3,600 – in Lyon.

Eight days prior, these movements would have achieved exceptional results. However, they were too late and missed their goal. His march had always operated under the most favorable conditions. Ordonneau's brigade formed the advanced guard and, as it marched into Lons-le-Saulnier, it threw back the Austrians – chasing them to Poligny. The French claim to have inflicted 400 casualties and prisoners (total) on the Austrians.[31] The following day, they were in Petit-Chiette. On 2 March they were in Moret – with the main body of the army strung out to Lons-le-Saulnier, where Augereau had established his headquarters.

Engagement at St.-Julien – 1 March

Marchand advanced Dessaix's brigade to within cannon shot of the Austrian pickets at Luisettes on 28 February with little resistance. Dessaix had been reinforced with a battalion of the 79th Line Regiment and the two battalions of General Pouchelon's force with the goal of throwing the Austrians out of Geneva. Despite the strong position the Austrians had assumed before Geneva, Marchand believed that he could throw them back and liberate that portion of the Empire. He developed his attack with three columns. The first, under General Serrant, was to move along the bottom of the Salève Mountain and turn the left of Zechmeister's brigade by Moissin and Laplace. General Dessaix's column was to march against Tairier and Turens – and from there, against the right of General Klopfstein (on the left of the Aire), while Marchand attacked in the center against the Austrian positions in St.-Julien. Marchand commanded the third – or central – column, and marched directly against St.-Julien.

30 This particular regiment had served with the French army until August 1813 when it deserted to the Allies.

31 Zins, p. 65.

At around 8:00 a.m. Serrant's column struck the Warasdiner Kreuzer Grenz, which formed the left wing of the Austrian position by Chable, and drove them back – clearing the Austrian advanced posts from Chable and Moissin and advancing its guns to pound Laplace.

Closer to 10:00 a.m. the French left column – Dessaix – advanced from the heights by Luisettes in three smaller columns and pushed the Austrians from Viri and Crache. The strongest of Dessaix's three columns pushed through Viri and on to the high plateau by Songy. The middle column moved down the main road from La Cotte and the third advanced between La Cotte and Pressily. The Austrian advanced posts withdrew to Ognon, where Major Osthaus stood with a half battalion of the W. Colloredo Infantry Regiment. The Austrians stalled the French advance until their position was threatened by the arrival of Dessaix's first column by Songy.

Dessaix sought to push the Austrians back by turning their right flank and directed a battalion to move up the Aire Creek Valley and then between Crache and Tairier. Zechmeister, however, had responded to the initial attack by sending a battalion of the W. Colloredo Infantry Regiment to the heights by Tairier to cover the threatened right flank. Despite this, Dessaix's attack on Major Osthaus' three companies was successful and drove the Austrians back – and he occupied both Crache and Tairier as well as the intervening heights. By that evening, General Dessaix had made himself master of Tairier and was advancing down the Turnes ravine.[32]

Meanwhile, Marchand had advanced his forces against St.-Julien and occupied the heights before the village. Moving from the heights through Grassy to Savonay (behind a screen of flankers), Marchand's troops moved against St.-Julien and Ternier. Three companies of the W. Colloredo Infantry Regiment deployed and engaged them, while the Austrian troops in Ternier – three companies of the Peterwardeiner Grenz under Oberstleutnant Wahler – held the defile against their advance.

When the French left column took Tairier, Marchand launched a new assault on St.-Julien. Two-and-a-half companies of the Vogelsang Infantry Regiment, under Major Mylius, counterattacked and threw them back as another attack by the W. Colloredo Infantry Regiment – supported by a detachment of the Vogelsang Infantry Regiment – counterattacked and carried Tairier.

Dessaix responded by sending forward fresh troops against the Austrian flank as Marchand responded with a heavy frontal assault directly against St.-Julien. The flank attack was stopped by five companies of the Kaunitz Infantry Regiment – commanded by Hauptmann Potier of the General Staff. Marchand's frontal attack, however, was not so easily dealt with. Before St.-Julien there developed a heavy artillery fight. Fourteen Austrian guns, with Leutnant Selander commanding four Austrian 12pdr guns, engaged the French artillery and dismounted two or three guns. The cannonade ushered in the night – leaving the battle a tactical Austrian victory. The Austrians appear to have lost about 650 casualties. The French casualties were certainly higher – perhaps running as high as 1,200 to 1,400 men.[33]

The two belligerents camped that night on the battlefield. Klebelsberg stood proud, having retained his position. Marchand, however, was disturbed at his failure and further distressed upon learning that he had fired off most of his ammunition and might have to withdraw to Barreaux – a distance of 60 miles (100 kilometers) from Geneva. Fortunately, General Bardet – after taking Ecluse that day – was rapidly advancing down the road from Lyon, which the Austrians had thought well-defended. This news startled Count Bubna, who began to fear a French attack on the right of the Rhône, where Geneva's wall was open to a *coup de main*. He ordered Klebelsberg to abandon his position, to break the bridges at Arve and to withdraw to Geneva.

32 Sporschil, Vol. II, 2nd Band, pp. 193-4.

33 Sporschil, Vol. II, 2nd Band, p. 195.

Count Marchand was pleased with the Austrians' discomfort. Bardet's brigade passed Farges – on the road from Lyon – and reassured Marchand of his position. However, his lack of munitions caused him to not immediately resume his advance. On 2 March he assembled his force on the Arare plateau and established communications with Bardet, while dispatching orders for a resupply of powder and lead from Fort l'Ecluse.[34]

The following day, Marchand moved to the left bank of the Arve and Bardet's brigade moved to St.-Genix. Marchand thought himself able to summon Geneva to surrender from this position. That day, Count Bubna also learned that General Musnier had, with the aid of the local inhabitants, cleared the snow from the Rouses pass and that his advanced guard – under General Ordonneau – had pushed to Saint-Cergue in the Vaude. Bubna found himself faced with either shutting himself up in Geneva, or continue maneuvering in the field and leaving Geneva open to a *coup de main*.

Bubna had already hastily dispatched his cavalry to Yverdon and sent one of Geneva's principal inhabitants back to the French to act as his representative. Augereau overreacted – thinking Geneva already his – and changed his plans. He believed that Marchand's corps – reinforced by Bardet's brigade – would be sufficient to assure the fall of Geneva. He recalled General Musnier from Saint-Laurent and Champagnolles with the goal of uniting him with the divisions of Pannetier and Digeon – then advancing to engage Liechtenstein in battle under the walls of Besançon.

News of the implementation of Augereau's new plans reached Bubna and caused Bubna to remain in Geneva – certain that Marchand would be unable to take the city by a *coup de main* and knowing that he did not have the means to reduce it by siege.

Bianchi advances in the south

While Augereau and his forces stood engaged on the Swiss border, the inhabitants of the Ain, Saône-et-Loire, Jura and Mont-Blanc found themselves facing their own Allied army without the benefit of an army to counter them. Lacking a formed military, the inhabitants rose from their foyers, picked up their guns and went into the mountains to engage the Austrian Army of the South in a war to the death between small detachments and single men.

On 1 March the forces under Bianchi's command stood as follows:

- 1st Corps:
  - Division: Feldmarschalleutnant Graf I. Hardegg
    - Deutsch-Banat Grenz Regiment (two battalions) (1,075 men)
    - Reisch Dragoon Regiment (six squadrons) (618 men)
    - Hessen-Homburg Hussar Regiment (six) (648)
    - Two Cossack pulks (350)
  - Division: Feldmarschalleutnant Fürst von Wied-Runckel
    - Brigade: Generalmajor Graf Salins
      - de Ligne Infantry Regiment (three) (2,357)
      - Czatorisky Infantry Regiment (two) (1,605)
      - One brigade battery
    - Brigade: Generalmajor Lakardovsky
      - Albert Gyulai Infantry Regiment (two) (1,500)
      - Reuss-Plauen Infantry Regiment (three) (1,176)
      - One brigade battery

34 Koch, Vol. II, pp. 241-4.

Division: Feldmarschalleutnant Baron Bianchi
- Brigade: Generalmajor Hirsch
  - Hiller Infantry Regiment (two) (1,638)
  - H. Colloredo Infantry Regiment (three) (1,222)
  - One brigade battery
- Brigade: Generalmajor Graf Haugwitz
  - Hessen-Homburg Infantry Regiment (two) (958)
  - Davidovich Infantry Regiment (two) (1,049)
  - One brigade battery

Division: Feldmarschalleutnant Baron Lederer
- Brigade: Generalmajor Scheither
  - Gradiscaner Grenz Regiment (one battalion)
  - Warasdiner Kreuzer Grenz Regiment (one battalion)
    - Total infantry: (1,587)
  - Kaiser Hussar Regiment (four squadrons)
    - Total cavalry: (16 squadrons) (1,648)
  - One cavalry battery
- Grenadier Brigade: Generalmajor Fürstenwerther[35]
  - Grenadier Battalion Czarnozi
  - Grenadier Battalion Obermayer
  - Grenadier Battalion Berger
  - Grenadier Battalion Oklopsia
    - Total infantry: (two battalions) (1,360)
  - One brigade battery
- Cuirassier Brigade: Generalmajor Kattalek
  - Erzherzog Albert Cuirassier Regiment
  - Lothringen Cuirassier Regiment
    - Total cuirassiers: (four squadrons) (450)

The Allies had organized 40,000 men into the Army of the South and placed them under the command of Baron Bianchi. On 3 March the Army of the South was in Beaune, and on 4 March it pushed a detachment to Châlons to reinforce General Scheither. A second detachment, under General Wimpffen, marched into Villette and Villers-Robert. A third column was sent – under Prince Philippe von Hesse-Homburg – to occupy Dôle.

Grand Duke Prince Hesse-Homburg.

Augereau ignored the movements occurring around him. He was locked on the destruction of Liechtenstein and freeing Besançon and Auxonne, but directed that Marchand and Bardet return to him as soon as Geneva was taken. When that was done, Augereau intended to march with all his forces towards the Upper Rhine – across the Department of Doubs. The execution of this plan was established

35 Fürstenwerther's brigade was reduced to two grenadier battalions, but it is not known which two were present and which had been detached.

for 5 March, but those plans were abandoned when the Austrians took a post in Louhans from the French and Wimpffen's column attacked Poligny.

In truth, General Gudin took up his position only after losing 300 casualties and taking 100 prisoners as he pushed on to Arbois. However, as Augereau received news of this success and considered a push on Louhans, he learned that Bianchi was maneuvering on the right bank of the Saône so as to cut off Lyon and that a cloud of light troops extended from Mervan to Saint-Trivier. Fearful for his lines of communication, Augereau saw Lyon once again threatened. He had, during his long stay in Lyon, aroused the citizens to re-establish the massive field fortifications that had been erected in 1793. Works were raised on the Fourvière and St.-Just hills; batteries were raised in the Belle-Allemande Tower; in the Cuire cemetery; at the head of the Croix-Rousse suburb – covering the left bank of the Rhône – and at the bridges at Guillotière and Morand. Finally, to arm all these works, 80 guns withdrawn from Spain (and which had been in Avignon) were emplaced. However, despite the strength of the works, Augereau had left only a weak garrison to hold them – a garrison that was in no state to defend them.

He had two options to save Lyon. The first was to march rapidly with the divisions of Musnier, Pannetier and Digeon across the Saône to Tournus or Mâcon and then march directly at the Austrians, or better, march to Lyon by the direct route and take up positions at Limonest.

Though marching to Limonest was the least desirable choice, it was Augereau's choice. He directed Bardet to re-cross the Rhône and conduct a demonstration against Mâcon, while Augereau marched on the right of the Saône with the remainder of his army. Accordingly, the appropriate orders were issued.

The main body united on 5 March at Lons-le-Saulnier – and by 9 March was in Lyon. That same day, Bardet's brigade occupied Bourg; Pouchelon's division occupied Pont-d'Ain; and General Rémond – who had previously occupied the Vaize suburb – marched forward to a position where he could watch the Austrians in Villefranche with a force of two battalions and 50 gendarmes.[36]

However, as usual, the Austrians sauntered forward in no particular rush in their military maneuvers. Bianchi dawdled in Châlons until a number of other columns had advanced to a point parallel to his position. Augereau, somewhat reassured, suspected that he had been the victim of misinformation and resolved to kick the small force of Austrians out of Mâcon.

General Musnier was ordered, as a result, to march on 10 March to Villefranche with his division and the 12th Hussars. He was to assume command of the two battalions of General Rémond that were stationed there and to attack Mâcon the following day. At the same time, generals Bardet and Pouchelon were to demonstrate against the Saint-Laurent bridgehead. Augereau and the rest of the army were to remain on the road to Villefranche. The last information he had received indicated to him that Mâcon was occupied only by about 1,500 men of an advanced guard. However, Bianchi had taken up positions in Mâcon and detached Ignace Hardegg with a force down the left bank of the Saône in the direction of Bourg. His advanced guard, under General Scheither, held Maisons-Blanches after clearing it of armed peasants.

Engagement at Mâcon – 11 March

On 11 March Musnier's advanced guard moved forward, in accordance with orders, led by the 12th Hussars. At 1:00 p.m. it encountered Austrian pickets at Saint-Georges, attacked them and drove them back to Maisons-Blanches. Guerre, p. 82 indicates that the Austrians attacked the French – not vice-versa. I am inclined, however, to believe that the French launched the attack as both Koch and von Damitz state that it was thus. General Scheither was surprised and attempted

36 Koch, Vol. II, pp. 245-8.

to recall and organize his 12 squadrons on the highway. However, Colonel Colbert – at the head of 450 hussars of the 12th Hussar Regiment – gave him no time to deploy and launched a furious charge against the head of his column. The Austrian cavalry was thrown back and sabered. The Austrian artillery was overrun and two guns attempting to unlimber and fire were overrun and captured before they could fire. General Scheither, wounded by Chef d'escadron Plessen of the 12th Hussars, dismounted and only saved himself by fleeing on foot.[37]

Despite their success, the French had bitten off far more than they could chew. Bianchi responded immediately – moving to the south of Mâcon and deploying two divisions between Saint-Clément-les-Mâcon and Charnay. He also called Prince von Wied-Runckel to return immediately with Salins' brigade – from Cluny to Mâcon – which he wanted to hold at any cost. As the French pushed through the column, the Vincent Chevauxleger Regiment and the Westphalian Hussars recovered from their terror, reorganized, faced the 12th Hussars and charged into what would become a murderous saber fight. As the hussars began to fold under the weight of the assault, two companies of voltigeurs arrived at the *pas de course*.[38] The voltigeurs moved along the flanks of the fight and began firing into the Austrian cavalry until the Austrians broke and withdrew. Encouraged by this reinforcement, the audacious Colbert took two squadrons and charged down the road in pursuit of the beaten Austrian cavalry. The remaining squadron charged a light battalion – which flanked his left – and forced it to lay down its arms. It was 11:00 a.m. as Scheither's cavalry withdrew from the fight and moved to Varennes, where it took up positions with two battalions and remained until about 2:00 p.m.[39]

The Westphalian Hussars had served with the French during the 1812 invasion of Russia, but had shown themselves to be "timid" at the Battle of Valoutino-Goro and their refusal to charge had cost the French an opportunity to encircle and destroy a large portion of the Russian army.

In the 1813 campaign, what remained of the hussars had been rebuilt and deployed with Victor's II Corps – only to desert very quickly to the Allies on 23 August.

Though the beginning boded well, Musnier soon learned that an entire Austrian corps lay in Mâcon. Musnier reacted immediately – deploying his force (some 6,000 men). The hussars and artillery followed the main road – flanked on the right by the 20th Line and on the left by the 67th Line. Behind them marched the four battalions of the 32nd Line and the 2nd Toulon National Guard Regiments (in column, by divisions). General Ordonneau, who commanded, was ordered to march via a hidden march against the Chintrè heights on which the city of Mâcon stood. Having these dispositions, Musnier was prepared to evict a small detachment or defend himself in an engagement against a major enemy force. However, if facing a major force, Musnier had no reserve and the column marching on his left risked being cut off if the enemy advanced vigorously along the main road.

Mâcon stood on the Saône River with a single stone bridge passing over the river. Bianchi had concentrated most of his forces in Mâcon, but Prince von Wied-Runckel ordered Salins' brigade to Cluny and Jakordovsky's brigade to move right to Charollois. The remainder of Bianchi's division was in Mâcon. Fürstenwerther's grenadier brigade was on the heights of Saint-Clément-les-Mâcon.[40] To the left and rear of Saint-Clément were posted the Iarossy and Oklopsia Grenadier Battalions. In the center of the Austrian position was a battery of 16 guns. Four further guns were placed in a garden on the heights by Saint-Clément – and to defend them, the Simbschen Infantry Regiment stood to the right of the village. Quallenberg and Hirsch's brigades were

37 von Damitz, Vol. III, 1st Part, p. 432.
38 The *pas de course* was a marching rate of 250 paces per minute or, fundamentally, a cadenced run.
39 Zins, pp. 70-1.
40 von Damitz, Vol. III, 1st Part, p. 433.

posted by Les Carteronnes. Charnay was occupied by an infantry battalion, three squadrons of dragoons and three guns. On the right wing – by Charnay – stood a battalion of the Hiller Infantry Regiment, two squadrons of the Würzburg Chevauxlegers and three guns. To secure the right flank, by the village of St.-Vincelles stood a battalion of the Hessen-Homburg Infantry Regiment and two guns. The critical bridge in Mâcon was defended by a battalion and two guns. Two infantry battalions from Haugwitz's brigade occupied Vinzelles and Loches. The cuirassiers of General Kuttalek stood behind Mâcon. The battlefield was too cut up to permit the use of anymore cavalry, so it was withdrawn to the east.[41]

Musnier was convinced that the Austrians standing before him were limited to an advanced guard – not the main body. Encouraged by the rapid progress of his cavalry, Musnier forgot that he lacked any substantial support and pushed forward. The artillery moved down the road – flanked on each side by battalions of the 20th and 67th Line. The remainder of Ordonneau and Rémond's brigades moved in closed columns down the road.

At 2:00 p.m. Scheither and Haugwitz were thrown out of Varennes and Musnier decided to move on Mâcon in two columns. He sent his artillery and cavalry down the main road – again with the 20th and 67th flanking them as they marched down the road. At the same time, he ordered Ordonneau to turn the Austrian right and take the heights running from Chaintré to Vinzelles, Saint-Léger and Charnay. Rémond was to support this movement.

Musnier counted on Bardet's demonstration against the Saint- Laurent bridgehead – and above all, on Ordonneau's maneuver. However, Bardet's maneuver failed to occur, and as Ordonneau advanced towards Léger and Vinzelles – the Allied right – his brigade was stopped by the Esterhazy and Davidovich Regiments. This was Quallenberg's brigade, which was apparently assigned to Hardegg's division (reinforced by part of Fürstenwerther's grenadier brigade).

Musnier ordered an attack on Saint-Clément. The brave 20th and 67th Line Regiments (Estéve's brigade) were battle-hardened veterans of the Spanish campaign. They marched forward with their drums rolling thunder as they attacked the Simbschen Infantry Regiment holding the Allied flank by Saint-Clément. The roar of their muskets and their impetuous and audacious attack proved too much for the Austrians, who were driven back into the village. Musnier's victorious battalions advanced to within a cannon shot of Austrian lines – securing his right on Vinzelles and his left on the Saône .

The advance of the 20th and 67th Line was pounded to a stop by the fire of the 16 Austrian guns and their supporting grenadiers (Fürstenwerther), but not before they carried Saint-Clément. Despite heavy losses, the two French regiments renewed their assault. The Austrian brigades – under Fürstenwerther and Haugwitz – however, proved more than their élan could overcome and they were driven back.[42]

After an hour of an unequal fight on the French right and center – and several failed charges – Musnier saw five of his nine guns dismounted and his right was rapidly running out of ammunition.

Meanwhile, Ordonneau was grievously contused as his troops carried Vinzelles and pressed his march forward. By around 4:00 p.m. his forces were on the point of carrying Charnay and were threatening the Austrian battery to the west of the village. Bianchi decided it was time to launch his attack. He ordered Hirsch and Quallenberg to advance against the French. He launched a cavalry charge from Charnay by two squadrons of the Würzburg Dragoons, and a squadron of the Kaiser Hussars – under Major Ehrenstein of the General Headquarters Staff – against Musnier's left.

41 Sporschil, Vol. II, 2nd Band, p. 207; Zins, p. 71.
42 Sporschil, Vol. II, 2nd Band, pp. 208-9.

Ordonneau's movement, however, threatened his right and Bianchi responded by ordering a charge by a squadron of the Reisch Dragoons that drove the French back to Loches. Bianchi then ordered a general advance of his entire force. Musnier responded by ordering his forces to retreat – and it was executed in good order and without incident. Bianchi, however, did dispatch a force of grenz and cavalry to follow the retreating French.

Koch states that during the engagement, the French lost 93 dead, 230 wounded, 360 prisoners and two dismounted guns abandoned on the field. Zins substantially agrees with Koch. However, von Damitz gives the French losses at 20 officers, 500 prisoners, two guns and several caissons. He states that the Austrians lost about 500 men.[43] Sporschil gives the Austrian losses as four officers and 81 men dead, and 22 officers and 774 men wounded, captured and missing.[44] He states the Austrians captured 520 prisoners – including 20 officers and two guns.[45]

On 12 March Bianchi concentrated his corps around Mâcon, but made little effort towards a pursuit that might reap the laurels of the previous day's battle. Prince von Hesse-Homburg, it seems, had persuaded him to bring forward his reserves. Perhaps they feared a renewal of the battle. Augereau, however, was in no position to renew the engagement. He concentrated his troops at a position near Georges-de-Reniens and gave Musnier's division a well-deserved day of rest. He established his advanced posts in Belleville, Saint-Jean d'Ardières and Cerci.

Meanwhile, General Bardet – whose division barely numbered 4,000 men – was seriously threatened by the superior forces of Ignace Hardegg and Wimpffen. He was obliged to abandon Bourg and withdrew to Meximieux. During the evening of the 12th, he established his division in positions around Marlieux and Chalamont.

At an Allied conference of war held on the 13th, it was decided that Wimpffen's division and the Austrian reserve corps should move to the right bank of the Saône and rejoin Bianchi's corps. The attack on Lyon would be via Villefranche-sur-Saône . Only Hardegg's division – containing the brigades of H. Hardegg and von Coburg – would remain on the left bank during the march on Lyon. There would be a general advance in three columns – one moving through Bourg to Meximieux and the other to Chalamont via Montluel. The other would move along the Saône via Trévoux and Neuville. In order to cover the rear of the army from the partisans of Damas and the bands of armed peasants that roamed the Allied rear, a detachment of light troops was sent towards the Loire. In addition, a garrison was established in Mâcon that consisted of two battalions and an artillery battery.

Wimpffen.

As the Austrians decided on their strategy, the French occupied positions across their front. A brigade from Pannetier's division and a squadron of the 4th Hussars were in Belleville. Pannetier's other brigade and the rest of the 4th Hussars were posted in Saint-Georges and strongly occupied the village of Layé-Longsard. Musnier's 1st Brigade (Ordonneau) and the 12th Hussars occupied Arnas – watching the road from Beaujeu. Two battalions of Musnier's 2nd Brigade, the 13th Cuirassiers and the artillery

43 von Damitz, Vol. III, 1st Part, p. 434; Koch, Vol. II, pp. 251.
44 Zins, p. 73. However, Zins' source is not known, so he may have used Sporschil.
45 Sporschil, Vol. II, 2nd Band, p. 210.

reserve were in Villefranche. The main body of Musnier's 2nd Brigade (Gudin) stood before Villefranche.[46]

Prince Philippe von Hesse-Homburg rightly suspected that the French were concentrating around Villefranche and moved his forces to the right of the Saône – uniting them around Mâcon on 16 March. On 17 March Prince Philippe divided his forces into two columns – under Bianchi and Wimpffen – and directed Prince von Coburg to guard the left bank of the Saône . He then ordered Count Hardegg to pursue Bardet's French brigade to Bourg.

Allied army, 20 March 1814

	Infantry	Cavalry	Guns
Bianchi's column:			
Bianchi's division	8,000	–	24
von Wied-Runckel's division	8,000	–	16
Grenadier Division	3,000	–	8
Lederer's division	–	3,000	16
Wimpffen's column:			
Wazel's brigade	4,300	–	8
German Legion	2,800	1,000	8
Mumb's brigade	4,800	–	8
On the left bank of the Saône:			
von Coburg's brigade	1,200	750	8
Before Miribel:			
Hardegg's division	2,500	3,000	16
In reserve:			
Austrian troops	9,000	750	16
Hesse-Darmstadt troops	7,000	600	8

Augereau greatly feared an attack on the morning of the 16th and ordered Musnier and Digeon to have their men standing at arms at the break of dawn. He gave orders for Pannetier to withdraw on Villefranche in case of an attack down the road from Beaujeu. On the other bank of the Saône, Bardet still stood in Meximieux. Facing Geneva, Marchand had been obliged to withdraw and take up positions on the passes to the Rhône. Four companies stood in Seyssel with orders to burn the bridge if the Austrians attacked. Four other companies occupied Châtillon-en-Michaille to watch the road from Nantua, and two further companies guarded the stone bridge at Bellegarde. Bellegarde had also been prepared for destruction with demolition charges. General Dessaix remained in Carouge with 4,000 men to contain Bubna's movements.

On the morning of 17 March the bulk of the Austrian Army of the South stood in positions on the right bank of the Saône . It advanced in two columns on Belleville. The first consisted of the 1st Corps and departed Lanci for Belleville – moving through the Cerci defile. The second column, Wimpffen's division, was concentrated behind La Maison Blanche and moved directly on Belleville via the main road. Prince Philippe von Hesse-Homburg formed the general reserve with the German troops and the Austrian troops that had formerly been part of the 6th Corps.

46 Zins, pp. 74-5; Koch, Vol. II, p. 254; von Damitz, Vol. III,1st Part, p. 439.

The Allied forces contained about 47,000 infantry, 5,400 cavalry and 112 guns facing Augereau – who commanded 12,089 men, 1,725 cavalry and 29 guns.[47]

During the evening of 17 March the two armies camped in the presence of each other. Scheither's advanced guard stood before Odenas on the road from Beaujeu to Villefranche. Wimpffen's advanced guard stood around Belleville. The troops of von Hesse-Homburg were at Saint-Jean d'Ardières and an infantry regiment supported by two guns was posted in Pilliers – covering communications with the first and second columns.

In the French cantonments, Pannetier had been reinforced by the 4th Hussars and stood in his original position before Saint-Georges-de-Reneins. His left was supported by Layé, and Longsard – with Musnier's 1st Brigade (Ordonneau) – established with the 12th Hussars in Arnas watching the road to Beaujeu. Musnier's 2nd Brigade (Gudin) and the 13th Cuirassiers were ordered to depart Villefranche at the break of dawn and form a reserve at the crossroads leading to Beaujeu and Villefranche.

Engagement at Saint-Georges

On the morning of the 18th, Estève's brigade and the 4th Hussars stood before Saint-Georges-de-Reneins. Estève and the brigades of Gudin and Ordonneau formed Augereau's first line, which extended from Saint-Georges-de-Reneins on the right (to Layé), which formed the center of the French line – and on to Longsard and Le Chambély, which formed its extreme left. The 12th Hussars stood on the left to protect that flank. Pouchelon's brigade and the 13th Cuirassiers were held in reserve by Arnas, with their right on the road from Mâcon to Villefranche and their left on the road to Beaujeu. The Layè and its château were occupied and put into a state of defense.

On 18 March Prince Philippe von Hesse-Homburg ordered an attack on the French lines. The Austrian generals Bianchi and Wimpffen were to act in concert – attacking the French right – while Prince von Wied-Runckel's division attempted to turn the French left around Beaujeu and occupy the Pouilly heights. A small detachment was ordered to move along the right bank of the Saône with the goal of attracting the French attention in that direction. In addition, von Wied-Runckel was assigned the task of holding General Pannetier in check.

This plan, however, did not promise any type of significant victory in that it would only serve to push the French back down their natural line of retreat.

The double attack on the French right was to be executed with a massive force because its outcome was in question. Attacked at 6:00 a.m. Gudin's brigade ceded its post in Layé-Longsard and was pushed by the head of Bianchi's column, but the pursuit stopped when Gudin was supported by Pannetier's reserve.

Ordonneau's brigade was struck by the Austrians moving from the Odenas heights around 10:00 a.m. and was pushed back on Marsangue and Layé. Bianchi was forced to reinforce his advanced guard with the Hiller Infantry Regiment – and later with Salins' brigade.

Facing Pannetier's division, General Gall ordered an attack and pushed Estève's troops back through Saint-Georges-de-Reneins. The young Hessian troops were carried away with their success and pushed through Saint-Georges without stopping to reorder their ranks. Seizing this opportunity, Pannetier ordered a counterattack and launched the 4th Hussars and Estève's brigade at the disorganized Hessians. Gudin's brigade also shifted over to the offense.

Gall's Hessian brigade was caught by the 4th Hussar Regiment and torn to pieces. The French 20th Line Regiment advanced at the *pas de charge* into Layé-Longsard. The rabble that remained of the Hessian brigade fled through Saint-Georges in panic – fleeing down the slopes and into

47 Zins, pp. 75-6.

the head of Wimpffen's column as it moved onto the battlefield. The *pas de charge* was a march cadence of 120 paces per minute – or about 260 feet per minute.

Wimpffen launched Haugwitz's brigade in an attack in order to slow, if not stop, the French attack and give Gall's shattered brigade time to rally. The Simbschen and Hesse-Homburg Infantry Regiments advanced, bayonets lowered, against Saint-Georges. Haugwitz vainly attempted to stop the French on the heights behind the village, but fell grievously wounded and his brigade was thrown back. Czollich, Wimpffen's chief of staff, took command of Haugwitz's brigade and directed its withdrawal to the heights on the left bank of the Vauxonne. The Simbschen Infantry's strong face and some charges by the Würzburg Dragoons gave Czollich the time necessary to bring order back to the ranks of Haugwitz's brigade as the remainder of Wimpffen's column arrived – marching at the *geschwindschritt*.[48]

Bianchi realized that a frontal assault on Layé and Longsard would cost him a tremendous number of casualties. As a result, he ordered Prince von Wied-Runckel to send Söldenhoffen's brigade to the right of the Beaujeu-Villefranche road and to move towards Rues so as to skirt the French position on the left and push into their rear past Ouilly into Villefranche.

The violence of the battle redoubled and lasted until nightfall along all the line. Augereau decided it was wise to order a general withdrawal to Limonest. Seeing the French withdrawal, Baron Bianchi launched his cavalry in pursuit – under the orders of General Lederer – in the hope of catching the French rearguard as it attempted to pass through the Saint-Georges defile. A squadron of the Würzburg Dragoons pushed through Saint-Georges and attacked a force of French hussars, which they threw back. The French hussars fled back into the French infantry – temporarily throwing it into disorder. At that moment, FML Lederer directed the advanced guard of the two Austrian columns to unite and move to cut off the French troops forming their right and center by arriving at the Saint-Georges-de-Reneins defile before they could escape.

When the Austrian cavalry arrived, they were taken under heavy fire by the grenadiers of the 67th Line Regiment. Chastened, the Austrian cavalry permitted the French to withdraw to Echelles, where they set up their advanced posts. Apparently, this force of cavalry was limited to a half-squadron of the Erzherzog Ferdinand Hussars. The pursuit was not particularly aggressive.[49]

On the French left, Ordonneau – facing von Wied-Runckel's division – was thrown out of Layé-Longsard for a second time. He executed a fighting retreat – contesting every foot of ground as he withdrew. Regular and controlled volleys stopped the Austrian cavalry, though at one point his artillery was seriously threatened with capture. A brilliant charge by the 12th Hussars and 13th Cuirassiers allowed the French artillery and infantry to escape and effectively ended that portion of the battle.

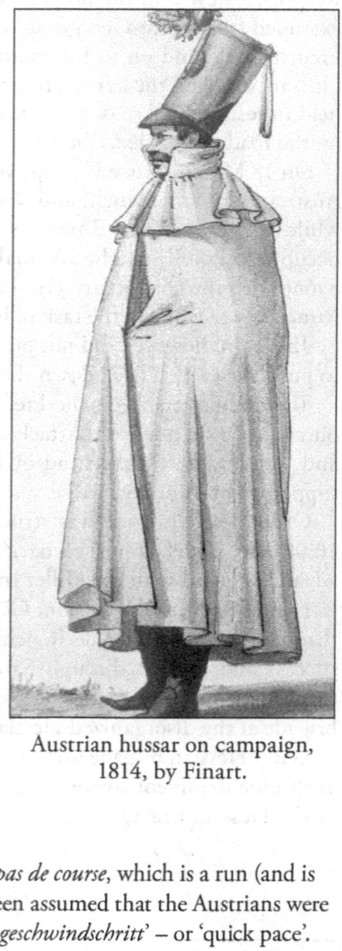

Austrian hussar on campaign, 1814, by Finart.

48 The original source, Zins, p. 78, states that they arrived at the *pas de course*, which is a run (and is also a march) pace – and found only the French army. It has been assumed that the Austrians were actually moving at their fastest marching pace, which was the '*geschwindschritt*' – or 'quick pace'.

49 von Damitz, Vol. III, 1st Part, p. 441.

Söldenhoffen's brigade arrived too late in Rues and was unable to do more than fire a few stray cannon shots at the French rearguard as it withdrew towards Lyon. Unable to catch the withdrawing French, von Wied-Runckel moved his forces to Ouilly and maneuvered in conjunction with Bianchi's column. Together, they took the steps necessary to organize their forces to pursue the French. Meanwhile, Augereau moved his forces in good order to Limonest. The Austrian advanced guard followed them at a respectful distance as far as Chères.[50]

The Battle of Saint-Georges cost the Austrians 23 officers and 1,386 men *hors de combat.* No casualty figures are known for the French.[51]

The French by Limonest

Augereau established Musnier's division, the 13th Cuirassiers, the 4th Hussars and 12 guns in a position straddling the road before the village of Limonest. His 4,003 infantry occupied the line of heights that ran from Couzon to the 'Le Semonet' stream.

Part of Pouchelon's brigade (Bardet's division) was detached to Musnier, who deployed the 2/32nd Légère (558 men), the 1/2nd Toulon Regiment (601 men), 6/24th Line (699 men) and a detachment of the 16th Line (254 men) as the first line before the Limonest position. They were supported by two 8pdrs, two 4pdrs and two 6" howitzers.

Musnier's second line was formed by Ordonneau's brigade and consisted of the 1/,2/20th and 1/,2/67th Line Regiments – about 1,861 men. Small detachments from Ordonneau's brigade were detached to furnish posts on the crest that ran from Verdun to Mont-Ceindre. Musnier was ordered to defend "to the death" the line of hills he occupied and the road to Mâcon and the crests of the Mont-d'Or.

General Pannetier's 2nd Division (5,781 men) stood in the center – defending the Dardilly plateau. Gudin's brigade, with the 1/,2/1st Légère and 1/,2/16th Line Regiments (2,464 men), occupied the Paillet hill. It extended to the right and Musnier's forces touching Ordonneau's brigade by the source of the Semonet stream. The 1/,2/,3/,4/13th Cuirassiers and 1/,2/,3/,4/4th Hussars (1,120 men) formed Pannetier's second line. Pannetier's division was posted between the road to Tour de Salvagny and Vaise and the road from Chère and Vaise. Estève's brigade (1/,2/7th Line and 23rd Légère – 2,197 men) occupied Dardilly and the ridge between the two branches of the Planches stream, with its left overlooking the road to Tour de Salvagny. Gudin's brigade stood to Estève's right and extended towards the road from Chère to Vaize, where it touched Ordonneau's brigade. Pannetier's division was supported by a single battery of six guns. Pannetier's orders directed him to hold the center and threaten the flank of any Austrian troops moving against Digeon down the road from Tour de Salvagny to Vaise.

Digeon – commanding 3,621 infantry – stood the extreme French left by Grange-Blanche, where he observed the road to Tour de Salvagny. Digeon was supported by Colbert's 1/,2/,3/12th Hussars (463 men) and a battery of six guns, two 8pdrs, two 4pdrs and two 6" howitzers. Digeon's orders were to protect the French left and to take Tour de Salvagny – if possible.

General Rémond commanded the Lyon Reserve Brigade and stood in Vaise and the barricades before Lyon with nine cannon and 3,425 National Guardsmen.[52] The total forces deployed by Augereau consisted of 15,247 infantry, 1,583 cavalry and 27 guns – of which nine were held in reserve.

50 Zins, pp. 78-9.
51 Zins, p. 80.
52 Guerre, pp. 84-5; Zins, pp. 83-4.

On the extreme French right – on the far side of Mont-d'Or – stood General Bardet. His command was charged with stopping any Allied advance via Bresse and extended his line via Caluire to the Saône . From there, it could cover the road from Trévoux to Lyon. His six battalions occupied the area around Miribel and consisted of the 6/60th Line, 6/23rd Légère and the 7/67th Line (2,072 men) of the Nîmes Division and two battalions of Pouchelon's brigade (2/24th Line and detachments of the 16th and 145th Line combined into a single battalion – 1,098 men). Supporting this force of 3,170 infantry were 195 men of the 1st Hussars and 64 men of the 4th and 31st Chasseurs supported by a battery of four 4pdrs and two 6" howitzers.

Bardet also commanded General Gay, who occupied positions around Mercières, Vernay, and Caluire and was directed to observe the routes to Trévoux, Bourg and Pont-d'Ain. He commanded two battalions of the 1/,2/79th Line Regiment, 1,800 veterans of the Peninsular War, the 6/115th Line with 569 men, and 24 gendarmes à cheval. The total of Bardet's forces was 5,539 infantry and 283 cavalry – or a total of 5,822 men and six guns with their crews.[53] Augereau had deployed a total of 20,786 infantry, 1,976 cavalry and 1,507 gunners with 33 guns on the hills before Lyon. Facing him on the right bank was an Austrian force of around 43,000 infantry, 5,000 cavalry and 100 guns. On the left bank stood another 8,000 Austrian infantry and 24 guns. The total Austrian forces attacking Lyon consisted of 56,000 men and 124 cannon.

The Limonest position ran along a chain of sharp heights which ran between the Saône and the Azergues Valley, where the roads to Moulins and Châtillon ran. With the exception of the highway to Mâcon, which arrived in Limonest, only small back roads were to be found in the immediate vicinity of Limonest. From their perches on the high crests, the French looked down on a plain which extended between Brévenne and the Saône . Augereau, with his 10,000 men, sought to hold the Allies in this position until a second division – drawn from Spain – could arrive. Augereau lacked the troops necessary to cover the road from Moulins to Arbresle. General Bardet, reinforced with the garrison of Lyon, faced Hardegg's division. Holding its position was critical, for if they were driven back, Lyon would be threatened. Because of this danger, a battalion and 100 cavalry were sent to the Salvagny Tower – part of the Lyon defenses – and General Saint-Sulpice dispatched to Lyon all of the Gardes d'honneur from his regimental depot that were in a condition to march.

This is how things stood on 19 March: The fate of Lyon depended on a battle heavily weighted in the favor of the Allies. Prince Philippe, sensing his advantage, looked to maneuver against Augereau's left flank and gain the road to Moulins. To this end, he left Hardegg's division and von Coburg's brigade on the left bank of the Saône to hold General Bardet in place. He then spent the rest of the day making the preparations necessary to move the major part of his forces to the confluence of the Brévenne and the Azergues, and pushing his advanced guards through the Vavres woods towards Dommartin.

Augereau, doubting that he would be attacked frontally, put only Musnier's division on the heights between the Saône and the road to Châlons. He put a brigade from Pannetier's division – the 4th Hussars – and the 13th Cuirassiers on a plateau that ran from Limonest to Dardilly. Finally, he posted Digeon's division with the 12th Hussars and Beurmann's brigade, which had arrived eight hours earlier from Spain, before Grange-Blanche. To the right of Limonest stood Estève's brigade in Dardilly. Bardet stood between the Saône and the Rhône – observing a column in Miribel marching along the road to Bourg. In addition, two battalions of the 1/,2/79th Line Regiment were detached to Calvire to check any movement along the left bank of the Saône.[54]

53 Zins, p. 85.
54 Koch, Vol. II, pp. 254-6; von Damitz, Vol. III, 1st Part, p. 442.

The Battle of Limonest – 20 March 1814

Prince Philippe, after having reviewed the French positions, called a halt to prepare his plan of attack. Generalleutnant Baron Bianchi, with his column, was to cross the Dorieux defile and form his forces between Dommartin and the Salvagny Tower. Then he was to push directly against Lyon – flanked on the right by 500 or 600 skirmishers led by Major Nageldinger. This force was to move from crest to crest to find either the left or the rear of the French. General Wimpffen was not to engage the French until Bianchi had occupied enough terrain to deploy. Mumb's brigade, directed by a staff officer, was to follow the crest of the heights that ran from Chaselay to Lyon in an effort to turn the French flank and strike the rear of the French position at Limonest. Hardegg and Prince von Coburg were to drive Bardet from his position. Hardegg was also to thrust his cavalry down the right bank of the Rhône in order to cut the road to Vienne. In addition, Weid-Runkel was to send a detachment of 600 to 700 men down the main road to Francheville and push his skirmishers as close to Lyon as possible.[55]

In conformance with this plan, all the Austrian columns began their march at 6:00 a.m. at the break of dawn. Musnier believed his position was in danger of being turned and withdrew on Lyon. Wimpffen encountered the brigades of Pouchelon and Ordonneau and engaged the heads of his columns from Le Semonet as far as Montluisan, but with little vigor, as not only did the French hold strong positions, but he was awaiting the arrival of Mumb's brigade. During these initial engagements, the Austrian reserve closed upon the II Corps from Les Chères to Dommartin while the 2,600 men and eight guns – under Mumb – advanced resolutely into the Mont-d'Or.

Mumb's brigade – part of Wimpffen's division – after several delays, struck and dislodged the French pickets on the heights of Salagon, Couzon and Saint-Romain. He then pursued a weak French force until about 1:00 p.m. His artillery struggled to pass over the Collognes plateau as he took possession of the heights between Thoux and Mont-Ceindre. From there, his soldiers looked down on Lyon and the rear of the French army.[56]

At the same moment, Bianchi – whose advanced guard had already overrun the Salvagny Tower – formed his line before the village and marched against the Dardilly plateau. Von Wied-Runckel's division led the attack against Dardilly – pressing Estève's brigade with the fury of its attack.[57]

Musnier knew that the Austrians had seized a foothold on the Dardilly plateau, but when he saw Mumb's brigade appear behind him, he abandoned his efforts to push the Austrians off the heights and withdrew on Vaize.

Musnier's movement left the flank of Gudin's brigade hanging in the air – unprotected on the Paillet heights – and forced him to withdraw towards Duchère and Ecully. Pannetier's six-gun battery was unable to stop the Austrian masses moving against his front and, when he saw Musnier withdrawing on his flank, directed Estève's brigade to withdraw from Dardilly and Duchère and fall back on Digeon's position.[58] The village and adjoining heights fell to the Austrians, with the French leaving six guns in the Austrians' hands.

As Musnier's division marched to the rear, Pannetier followed with his division. Receiving only a feeble fire on his front, Bianchi set about pursuing his success and directed his attention to his left. Wimpffen – seeing Pouchelon and Ordonneau's brigades abandon their positions – pushed forward aggressively on Limonest and Saint-Fortunat as Bianchi ordered his corps to push forward from Dardilly.

55 Zins, p. 86.
56 Zins, p. 86.
57 von Damitz, Vol. III, 1st Part, p. 443.
58 Guerre, p. 90.

Limonest.

Since 11:00 a.m. General Digeon had watched the Austrians maneuver and had no idea that GB Estève had abandoned his position. He thought to make a probe towards the La Tour-de-Salvagny – under General Beurmann – with three of his four battalions, 300 cavalry and four guns.

The appearance of Beurmann's column obliged Bianchi to abandon his forward movement. Bianchi ordered von Wied-Runckel to stop Beurmann, while Bianchi halted the remainder of his forces to await the outcome. Upon arriving at the Dardilly heights, Prince von Wied-Runckel was detached by Baron Bianchi. He engaged Beurmann and a serious engagement soon occurred as Beurmann executed a fighting withdrawal. This allowed Pannetier and Musnier to withdraw relatively unhindered.

Digeon, despite the fall of the village and knowing of Nageldinger's march against Clermont, withdrew to Grange-Blanche with a firm resolve to hold that point to the last. He placed Adjutant-commandant Ricard, with a battalion of the 1/32nd Légère and another from the 3/116th Line Regiment, on a hillock to the right of the road to Moulins. He posted two battalions of the 1/,2/115th on a ridge to the left, which commanded the branch in the road to Clermont. The 12th Hussar Regiment was held in reserve by Demi-Lune.

Prince von Wied-Runckel's division marched forward and collided with Digeon in his new position. A heated battle erupted that was to last until 5:00 p.m.

At some point during the Austrian advance, the French 12th Hussars advanced up the road from Clermont and struck the Hiller Infantry Regiment – and the 13th Cuirassiers were thrown against Wimpffen's division as it pushed forward. Both attacks were, apparently, repulsed with little effort and resulted in little delay in the Austrian advance. It was probably Mumb's brigade that the 13th Cuirassiers engaged.

Reassured on his right, Feldmarschal-leutnant Bianchi continued to push Pannetier's division to the left – hoping to link his attack with that of General Mumb and to make room for Wimpffen's forces, which were following behind him in dense (*serré*) columns. Around 3:00 p.m. the French right and center were pushed back to the gates of Lyon. Mumb's skirmishers pushed into the Vaize suburb as Augereau met with the city's civil authority. It was then that Augereau learned of the retreat of the French army. He organized the forces in Lyon and directed them to the ridges of Duchère and Rochecardon at the *pas de charge*. Once there, the French found the Austrians in force. The furious battle that erupted would end only with nightfall.

The Austrian attack on the French left

Digeon's right flank was being turned as Augereau sent General Guillemet forward to support him with the 13th Cuirassiers and a half-battery of horse artillery. As the three horse guns came into action by the fork in the road, six guns manned by naval gunners formed in battery on the hill defended by Adjutant-commandant Ricard. Despite these reinforcements, Wimpffen permitted Prince von Wied-Runckel to extend towards the right. GD Digeon, now menaced by von Wied-Runckel's movement, deployed three companies of the 115th Line to engage the Austrian skirmishers with a heavy fusillade.

The Austrian advance was slow. Their light infantry was engaged by the outskirts of the Saint-Just suburb as GD Digeon learned that his artillery and infantry were running short of ammunition. He responded by ordering two charges. The first was by two squadrons of the 13th Cuirassiers, which fell on the right of a six-gun Austrian battery, sabered its gunners and drove back its train. Baron Hammerstein quickly drew together the platoons of the German Legion Hussars and a squadron of the Kaiser Hussars and threw them at the 13th Cuirassiers in an attempt to recover the captured guns. Their effort, however, was futile and the cuirassiers carried away all six guns.

The other French forces consisted of one squadron of the 12th Hussars. The 12th Hussars attacked the Hiller Regiment as it marched down the road to Clermont. This regiment was crushed, its colonel and 360-400 soldiers captured and the remainder fled down the road to the east. The violence of these two assaults was too much for the Austrians and they withdrew for the night.

The Austrian false attack

Between the Saône and the Rhône, Count Hardegg marched against GD Bardet's position at Miribel – wasting most of the day in pointless demonstrations. Prince von Coburg, who marched from Neufville to Calvire, was attacked by the French battalions from Calture under the orders of General Gay. Prince von Coburg responded by sending the Kienmayer Hussars forward in a charge and supporting it with a battalion of the Banat Grenz. This attack was easily repelled by the 79th Line Regiment. On this flank, the Austrians did not gain an inch of terrain.

The casualties caused by the battle were low. The French lost around 1,000 men and the Austrians lost around 3,000. The losses, however, were not sufficient to turn the strategic situation. The French army contained about 23,000 men, while Crown Prince Philippe von Hesse-Homburg had over 53,000 Austrians and Allied troops at his command.[59]

As the battle ended, Augereau returned to Lyon and called a conference with Senator Chaptal and Prefect Count de Bondy, Commissioner General of Police and of the municipal corps. The mayor was called upon to determine if the citizens of Lyon were willing to defend their city, but he thought it unlikely as the National Guard had only 2,500 poor muskets. The troops available in the depots totaled about 1,400 men of the 24th Line – lacking uniforms and weapons – 20 from the 1st Hussars and 42 from the 4th Gardes d'honneur (also unarmed and without uniforms).[60]

2/,5/24th Line Regiment (25 officers / 517 men)
Det/2nd Marine Regiment (5 / 255)
Det/32nd Légère Regiment (4 / 209)
2/145th Line Regiment (12 / 390)
7/16th Line Regiment (9 / 320)

59 Zins, p. 90.
60 Lefebvre de Béhaine, Vol. IV, p. 404.

Gendarmes (6 officers / 140 men / 96 horses)
1st Hussar Regiment (9 / 165 / 174)
4th & 32nd Chasseurs à cheval Regiments (0 / 71 / 71)
Artillery (1 / 50 / 51)

It was noted that the city had only four days of food and no possibility of resupply if the Austrians controlled the roads and rivers. Furthermore, the city did not wish to suffer the horrors of a city taken by assault.

The evacuation of Lyon

Augereau perceived his situation as untenable and resolved to abandon Lyon and withdraw to the Isère with the goal of bringing GD Marchand's corps under his control (and also to be in a position to contest the junction of the Allied Army of the South with Wellington's Peninsular army). His withdrawal was to be effected in great secrecy so the artillery, ambulances, caissons and other wheeled traffic departed during the night in silence. They were followed two hours and 15 minutes later by the army, with Bardet's division forming the rearguard.

During the night, a few hundred hussars from the Hessen-Homburg Regiment crossed the Rhône and moved to the vicinity of Meizieux – cutting the road to Vienne.

As a result of Augereau's withdrawal, the second city of France fell into Allied hands. Austrian reports indicate that they found 22 guns, 2,500 muskets and munitions. They also reported that they had lost 72 officers and 2,803 non-commissioned officers and men killed, wounded and prisoner during the days of 19 and 20 March. The French losses, during the same period, were 530 on the 18th and 416 on the 20th – or a total of 946 men *hors de combat*.[61] The French retreat to Valence was not disturbed by the Austrians and they arrived on 23 March.

Actions around Geneva

While the two main armies engaged one another, Bubna stood in Geneva with 8,000 men – facing Marchand. Between 6 and 23 March the Austrians made no movements other than on 12 March when FML Wimpffen took position of Saint-Claude and posted Klebelsberg's division in Trenex to observe the Jura passes.

Klebelsberg learned that Bardet had left only 100 men in the Fort l'Ecluse and thought he might be able to seize it by a *coup de main*. However, upon his approach, the alarm went out – calling the local male population out to oppose him. Obliged to establish batteries on very unfavorable positions, he began a pointless cannonade through the day. After expending all his ammunition, he withdrew and was pursued by 3,000 armed peasants as far as Péron. His rash effort cost him about 100 men for no gain.

With the Austrians being quite inactive, Count Marchand had covered his right flank with the Rhône – with only two battalions occupying the bridges at Bellegarde and Seyssel. He had just reinforced himself with Vedel's division – which came from the Transalpine departments – when on 23 March he learned of Augereau's withdrawal from Lyon.

Marchand withdraws to Grenoble

GD Marchand was now quite isolated and decided to withdraw to Grenoble. Fort l'Ecluse was evacuated, the Seyssel bridge burned and its garrison sent to Moirans. At the same time, he

61 Koch, Vol. II, pp. 256-62.

dispatched two other battalions to guard the bridge at Pont-Beauvoisin. The remainder of his division marched in two columns. The first – under General Serrant – marched via Annecy and the other – commanded by Marchand – marched towards Rumilly.

Count Bubna wasted no time re-establishing the bridges at Arave and began his pursuit of the French with Klebelsberg's division. General Sarrant's retreat was too closely followed by Zechmeister. At Alby, Sarrant suddenly turned about to deal with this annoyance and drove his forces back into Zechmeister with such a fury that the Austrians scattered before him – driving them into the torrent at the Broigny bridge and pursuing the shattered remnants as far as Caille. The Austrians lost 300 prisoners.

Arriving in Chambéry, Count Marchand continued his withdrawal to the Isère and took up his old positions from January between Montmélian and the Echelles. Here he took up positions on what would be the right of the new French line.

The Allied occupation of Lyon guaranteed their control of Geneva and Mont-Blanc, made them masters of the two gates to Italy and relieved all concerns for their lines of communication.

On 22 March – as he arrived in Valence – Augereau learned of the British capture of Bordeaux and received an order to redirect 6,000 of the 10,000 men about to arrive from Spain to Libourne. Augereau wrote Eugène that all was lost if he could not cross the Alps and return to help defend France. He then took the 16,000 men which remained to him and positioned them at Pont-St.-Esprit, where he could march to oppose a linkup between Prince Philippe and the Duke of Wellington.

Fortunately for Augereau, the Austrians chose instead to send out only a few small detachments from Lyon. Detachments were sent to Roanne, Feurs, St.-Etienne and Bourgoing before the Austrians began their march on Valence – and by the 25th, only their advanced guard had moved on St.-Vallier.[62]

The French reasoned that von Hesse-Homburg would, in his pursuit of the French, direct considerable forces to Grenoble. To prevent this, Colonel Cubières was sent to Voiron with two battalions of the 18th Légère. Once there, he fortified the defile and erected a battery with 21 guns on the left bank of the Isère.

The engagements at Voiron and Voreppe

The Austrians sent a column of 2,500 men against the position held by Colonel Cubières. They caught him 10 kilometers below Voiron in a sharp engagement. Marchand found the position too dangerous and ordered him to withdraw to Voreppe, where the roads to Grenoble and Lyon branched. At the same time, Augereau broke down the Roman bridge and burnt the bridge on the road from Marseille to Lyon.

The post at Voreppe was attacked on 3 April by Wimpffen's division. The engagement lasted several hours, but being outnumbered, Cubières once again withdrew to the position he had fortified earlier.

Facing the French, Count Bubna had organized all his forces for a push against General Dessaix in his post at Chavanne. However, the destruction of the bridge made a frontal assault impossible. The Austrians then moved upstream to Conflans – where the Arc joins the Isère – and crossed the river. Thus flanking the French position, Count Dessaix resisted their assault for a while and then withdrew to Maurienne with two battalions after sending the rest of his forces – under General Serrant – to take up a position at Pontcharra (facing Fort Barreaux).[63]

62 Koch, Vol. II, pp. 263-7.
63 Koch, Vol. II, pp. 636-7.

Marchand's position was very difficult, but the destruction of the various bridges over the Isère provided him with the space to recover his equilibrium. He extended his left towards Grenoble and Augereau sent two battalions upstream to support him.

Expecting an attack, Augereau was stunned when on 12 April an Allied officer appeared requesting an interview. This parliamentary advised him of the fall of Paris and the subsequent revolution in the city. No French courier had arrived with this word, but an agreement was quickly reached that both sides would remain in their present positions until the new French government had time to communicate with Augereau the details of France's position. A few days later, he learned of Napoleon's abdication and his war ended.

Summary

The outcome of the engagements in and around Lyon are not surprising in view of the Allied superiority of numbers. Twenty-thousand men had been thrown back by 50,000. The French had occupied a strong position, and if Augereau had perhaps been more aggressive in his defense, he might have delayed or stopped the Allied advance. In view of the limited aggressiveness displayed by Prince Philippe, it is highly likely that Augereau missed his chance when he failed to take Geneva. The Allies were always very sensitive to their lines of communication and the fall of Geneva would have probably forced them to withdraw rather precipitously.

There was danger in this in that it might have also provoked a major battle, which Augereau's force was ill-equipped to handle. It seriously lacked artillery and the overwhelming numbers might well have resulted in Augereau's being cut off from his own line of retreat.

However, if a major battle before Geneva was avoided, the aggressive thrust to Geneva would have only delayed the inevitable. The Empire had only a few weeks left to it and, in fact, little was to be gained by the sacrifice of French and Allied lives at this point.

18

The House of Cards Collapses: The Battle of La Fère-Champenoise

The engagements at Sézanne, Chatilly, La Ferté-Gaucher, Moutis, Trilport and Meaux – and the march on Paris

While the Army of Silesia stood on the banks of the Marne between Châlons and Château-Thierry, the main Allied army stood on the right bank of the Cosel. The main Allied army was faced by two French armies – one standing before it and a second on its left flank – under the commands of Mortier and Marmont. Marmont, on the left flank, stood in a position to move to the left of the Sommé-Soudé between Vatry and Soudé. The two Allied armies were ready to march against Paris, while the two French armies sought only to rejoin Napoleon.

On 24 March Mortier pushed cavalry reconnaissance forces down the roads from Troyes to Châlons and Saint-Quentin on his right. No enemy troops were found in the direction of Nuisement and reports indicated that Châlons was occupied by only a few hundred Allied cavalry. Marmont's reconnaissance forces marched on Maisons and encountered no Allied troops. They reached the conclusion that Napoleon's actions had pushed the Allies below St.-Dizier and that St.-Dizier could be approached without danger the following day by moving down the road to Sommepuis.

That evening, the horizon was lit by an immense line of campfires between the Cosel and Marne rivers. This failed to pique the curiosity of either marshal who, supported by reports, continued with their illusions and determination to march down the road to Vitry.

Mortier's advanced guard crossed to the left bank of the Sommé-Soudé at 6:00 a.m. on 25 March. At the same time, three divisions of the Guard broke camp and began their march on Soudé-Notre-Dame.

The Allied armies marched in two columns on La Fère-Champenoise. Their guard and reserves moved in the direction of Montepreux. Raevsky's corps and that of the Crown Prince of Württemberg – preceded by their cavalry – marched down the highway from Vitry to La Fère-Champenoise and were followed at a distance by Wrede's Bavarians. Giulay's Austrian corps was to move through Semoine and join the Crown Prince of Württemberg's column.[1]

Engagements at La Fère-Champenoise and Maréch – 25 March

Count Pahlen formed the advanced guard of von Württemberg's column. He was invited by the Crown Prince of Württemberg to scout his front with patrols, which he promptly did at 3:30 a.m. the morning of 25 March. When at Cosel, he assumed a position at the head of the column and

1 de Vaudoncourt, Vol. II, p. 276.

at around 8:00 a.m. he stood in sight of Soudé-Saint-Croix. Pahlen's forces consisted of 3,600 cavalry.[2]

Brigade: Generalmajor von Rüdinger (Delianov?):[3]
- Grodno Hussar Regiment (6)
- Soumy Hussar Regiment (6)

Brigade: Generalmajor Dechterev
- Loubny Hussar Regiment (4)
- Olviopol Hussar Regiment (4)

Brigade: Generalmajor Lissanovich
- Tchougouiev Uhlan Regiment (6)
- Cossacks: Generalmajor Illowaiski XII (about 1,000 men)
- Vlassov II Cossack Regiment
- Illowaiski XII Cossack Regiment
- Rebrikov III Cossack Regiment
- Tschermuschin II Cossack Regiment
- Jaroslav Cossack Regiment

At 6:00 a.m. Mortier's infantry broke camp and, with Roussel's dragoons serving as an advanced guard, advanced from Vatry and moved up the left bank of the Soudé.[4] Meanwhile, Marmont's troops were in their camps – rousing themselves from their night's sleep – when at about 6:00 a.m. Pahlen's cavalry arrived on the ridge on the other side of the Somme-Soudé and began a heavy cannonade. A stunned Marmont made his dispositions – quickly organizing his forces under the Allied gunfire and before the eyes of an ever-expanding force of Allied cavalry. Marmont sent a frantic note to Mortier asking him to join him, but it would take Mortier two hours to move his forces from Vatry to Soudé-Saint-Croix. This was too long for Marmont to hold his position and it was more reasonable to unite their forces at Commercy. Awaiting Mortier's troops, Marmont quickly deployed his troops on the heights of Soudé-Saint-Croix – beginning a cannonade. Count Pahlen and Prince Adam saw Marmont's hesitation and decided to attack immediately. GM Dechterev, commanding the Olviopol and Loubny Hussar Regiments (possibly supported by a Cossack regiment), began a turning movement through Soudé-Notre-Dame around the French left flank. In order to cover the Allied right, General Lissanovich – commanding the Tchougouiev Uhlans and Illowaiski XII with three Cossack regiments and four horse guns – moved further to the right to Dommartin l'Estree.[5]

Prince Adam von Württemberg was ordered to simultaneously attack the French left with his cavalry. General Delajanov – with eight squadrons and a Cossack pulk supported by Kretov's cuirassier division and 12 horse guns – moved against the French center.

2 von Bernhardi, Vol. 4, Book 7, p. 322. Von Toll indicates that the Russians had 1,986 Russian hussars and uhlans in 21 squadrons – plus 513 Cossacks.

3 Bogdanovich, Vol. 2, p. 479; von Damitz, Vol. III, 2nd Part, p. 61. Von Damitz indicates that this brigade was commanded by von Rüdinger, while Bogdanovich indicates that it was commanded by Delianov. Since no other sources have been found to clarify this, both names will be used.

4 Derode, p. 4.

5 Bogdanovich, Vol. 2, p. 479.

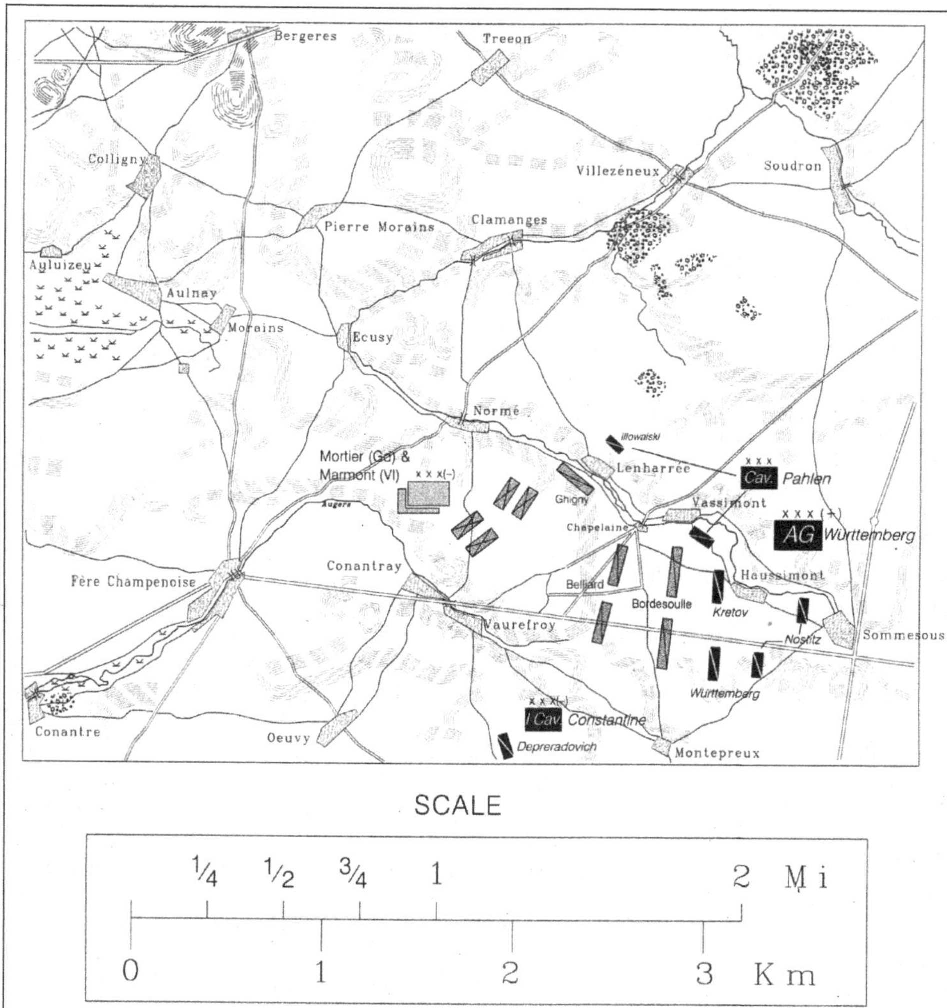

Map 19 Engagement at La Fère-Champenoise, March 25 1814.

Advanced Guard: Generalleutnant Prince Adam von Württemberg (1,566 men total)[6]
- 1st (Württemberg) Cavalry Brigade: Generalmajor von Walseben
  - 5th Cavalry Regiment "Jäger" (4)
  - Erzherzog Ferdinand Hussar Regiment (5) (Austrian)
  - 1st Horse Battery, Cpt. von Breithaupt (4-6pdrs & 2 howitzers)
- 2nd (Württemberg) Cavalry Brigade: Generalmajor von Jett
  - 2nd Cavalry Regiment "Jäger Herzog Louis" (4)
  - 3rd Cavalry Regiment "Dragoner Kronprinz" (3)
  - 4th Cavalry Regiment "Jäger Prince Adam" (4)
  - 2nd Horse Battery, Cpt. von Bürgi (4-6pdrs & 2 howitzers)

Austrian Cuirassier Division: General Graf Nostitz (2,305 men total)
- Cuirassier Brigade: Generalmajor Graf von Desfours
  - Liechtenstein Cuirassier Regiment (6)
  - Kaiser Cuirassier Regiment (6)
- Cuirassier Brigade: Oberst von Seymann
  - Konstantin Cuirassier Regiment (6)
  - Sommariva Cuirassier Regiment (6)

Russian 2nd Cuirassier Division: Generalleutnant Kretov (1,567 men total)
- Brigade: Generalmajor Leontiev
  - Gluchov Cuirassier Regiment (5)
  - Pskov Cuirassier Regiment (5)
- Brigade: Generalmajor Stahl II
  - Ekaterinoslav Cuirassier Regiment (2)
  - Astrakhan Cuirassier Regiment (4)

The Allies had about 10,000 cavalry facing 4,934 cavalry under the commands of Marmont and Mortier. The Allied movements and the size of their forces caused Marmont to recognize that he had to withdraw if he was to give Mortier sufficient time to arrive.

Along the front stood the 12 guns of the 23rd Horse Battery of Colonel Markov. They were covered by the Soumy and Grodno Hussars under GM von Rüdinger (Delianov?). The 2nd Cuirassier Division was held in reserve. The Württemberg cavalry began its turning movement around the right French flank. Threatened with a double envelopment, Marmont could not hold his position and began to retreat to Commercy. Two voltigeur companies were left in Soudé-Saint-Croix to slow down Allied attacks. Like the Prussians at Château-Thierry in February, these brave Frenchmen were soon surrounded and taken prisoner.

Bordesoulle's cavalry advanced to try to save these brave voltigeurs and to stop the aggressive Allied attack, but was driven back with heavy losses by von Rüdinger's brigade, the Grodno and Soumy Hussars, a Cossack pulk, Kretov's cuirassiers and a battery of four 6pdr horse guns.[7]

Count Pahlen immediately began his pursuit of the French along the main road with his hussars, cuirassiers and eight horse guns. The Tchougouiev Uhlans, Illowaiski's Cossacks and four guns were detached to Estree to hold Mortier's troops as they approached Commercy from the direction of Estree as the Württemberg cavalry began its turning movement around Marmont's right.[8]

Mortier's column had begun its march at about 6:00 a.m. Count Belliard arrived before Dommartin with Roussel's division when he encountered Dechterev's cavalry brigade, the

6 Strength figures are from von Bernhardi, Vol. 4, Book 7, p. 322.
7 von Damitz, Vol. 3, 2nd Part, p. 65; Bogdanovich, Vol. 2, p. 479.
8 Bogdanovich, Vol. 2, p. 480.

Olviopol Hussar Regiment, the Tchougouiev Uhlan Regiment and a Cossack pulk supported by some artillery, which immediately took Roussel's dragoons under fire.[9] Belliard attacked them and drove them out of the way of Mortier's advancing columns. After the march resumed, Illowaisky's three Cossack pulks appeared before Dommartin l'Estree on Mortier's flank. Charpentier's division, which was in the tail of the column, found itself cut off and obliged to move to Sommesous, where it arrived with no significant losses.[10]

Marmont was uniting his forces behind Soudé-Saint-Croix, which he defended with several companies of voltigeurs,[11] with his cavalry in the first line and his infantry in the second. His left was covered by Colonel Ghigny's eight 'marche' regiments – facing Illowaiski's Cossacks on his left flank. On his right flank, the Crown Prince of Württemberg's cavalry deployed with Desfours' Austrian cuirassier brigade in support, and Kretov's Russian cuirassier division deployed in the center. An engagement soon erupted the length of the French lines.

Despite these difficulties, the two corps joined and reformed themselves to the left and right of Sommesous. The pursuing Allies were met by the fire of 30 guns and were obliged to stop. The French marshals took advantage of this and deployed their troops on both sides of Commercy. Mortier's corps stood to the left of this village and Colonel Ghigny, with eight 'régiments de marche',[12] stood on the extreme left to observe Illowaiski's Cossacks. The thunder of the guns lasted for two hours. The French amassed more than 60 guns against the Allies' 36 guns. Despite the French strength in the artillery duel, the French position had one fault: a deep stream divided their position in two separate parts and their flanks were uncovered. Charpentier's division joined the line at this point. It had been momentarily cut off and lost some prisoners.[13]

During this period, the French left was constantly threatened by Illowaiski's 1,000 Cossacks. This obliged the French to maneuver this flank to attempt to put a ravine between them and, under the covering fire of their artillery, pulled that wing back to a position between Sommesous and Montepreux. In this new position the infantry was secure, but the French cavalry had lost its ability to act. Throughout this, the French artillery dominated the field, as the Allies had brought forward only a small portion of their artillery.[14]

Colonel Ghigny's marche regiment remained on the left – observing Illowaiski's Cossacks. Von Württemberg's cavalry, Kretov's cuirassiers and Delajanov's light brigade continued to face the French front, while Dechterev's cavalry brigade moved between Lenharrée and Normé.

By noon, the bulk of the Allied cavalry of the left wing had moved through the defile between Soudé and Sommesous, but were not yet able to reform to face the French right. The Württemberg 4th Jäger zu Pferd Regiment and the Austrian Erzherzog Ferdinand Hussars – supported by Desfours' Austrian cuirassier brigade – advanced against the French. The remaining Württemberg cavalry – with its two horse batteries – and Seymann's cuirassier brigade remained behind.[15]

Under these circumstances – and the appearance of the Austrian cuirassiers – the two French marshals were obliged to retreat to the right to fix their flanks on marshy riverbanks. Their troops retreated in *en échiquier* on Conantre – two leagues from Sommesous.

9 Derode, p. 4.
10 de Vaudoncourt, Vol. II, p. 278.
11 Derode, p. 5.
12 A "regiment de marche" is a collection of battalions that are formed from companies drawn from the depots of regular line regiments. They were assembled for the purpose of moving to the front and minimizing desertion. Though used in combat on occasion, this was not their intended purpose.
13 Derode, p. 5.
14 Koch, Vol. II, pp. 381-4.
15 von Damitz, Vol. III, 2nd Part, p. 68.

Austrian cuirassiers charging at La Fère-Champenoise.

The Württemberg 4th Jäger zu Pferd Regiment attacked the French frontally, while the Erzherzog Ferdinand Hussars moved against the French cavalry regiment on the end of the French line. The Austrians, under Desfours, followed this attack in column. The Austrian hussars' attack was immediately successful – driving the French back. The Liechtenstein Cuirassiers moved to exploit the hussars' success, but were taken in the flank by two French lancer regiments and immediately taken under canister fire by French artillery. Overwhelmed by the French response, the Liechtenstein Cuirassiers scurried to the rear and sheltered behind the Erzherzog Ferdinand Hussars and Jäger zu Pferd. Prince Adam saw this, moved forward to reunite his cavalry and prepared them to renew the assault.[16]

The Allied actions on the right were more successful. At the same time as Prince Adam's attack floundered, Count Pahlen moved against the French cavalry that stood somewhat behind Sommesous. Count Nostitz – at the head of the Klenau and Rosenberg Chevauxlegers – and Prince Constantine – leading Depreradovich's 1st (Guard) Cuirassier Division – had moved towards the French extreme left towards Montepreux – forcing the French to again begin withdrawing *en échiquier*, supporting their left, in a movement from Vassimont towards Chapelaine – and with some of their forces moving towards Lenharrée. However, before they could clear the defile at Lenharrée, Pahlen sent Illowaiski's five Cossack pulks to occupy it. General von Rüdinger (Delianov?) moved between Vassimont and Haussimont with the Grodno and Soumy Hussars – covered by four horse guns – to occupy the Soudé stream defile as Kretov's cuirassier division followed in support. Pahlen then moved with his remaining cavalry – the Loubny and Olviopol

16 von Damitz, Vol. III, 2nd Part, p. 69; Bogdanovich, Vol. 2, p. 481.

Hussar Regiments and the Tchougouiev Uhlan Regiment – through the Lenharrée defile and against the French right flank.[17]

Belliard vainly sent Roussel's dragoons around the left – attempting to take the Allied charge in the flank. However, finding themselves facing a second enemy line that stretched beyond their left that threatened to charge them, these dragoons turned about – without orders – and withdrew behind GD Merlin's division. General Latour-Foissac – at the head of the 8th Chasseurs à cheval Regiment – however, advanced his regiment forward in column by squadrons and drove it into the advancing Allied cavalry – checking their impetuous advance for a while.[18] However, the Russian cavalry soon resumed its pursuit – capturing five guns between Commercy and Lenharrée.

It was 2:00 p.m. For six hours, the French had seen in front of them only Allied cavalry and, despite their losses, expected to withdraw in order to La Fère-Champenoise. Suddenly, a strong east wind blew up. At first, the French were blinded by the dust; then with heavy rain and hail. The French infantry defended itself with bayonets against the Allied cavalry, but was obliged to cross a ravine near Conantre village.

Barclay had heard the cannonade from the direction of Pahlen's advanced guard and had ordered Count Ojarovsky with the Guard Dragoons and Guard Uhlans to advance to their assistance. He wanted to send the 3rd Cuirassier Division, but Depreradovich was at hand and said that his four regiments had yet to be engaged with the French since they crossed the Rhine. Barclay granted Depreradovich permission to engage the French. Depreradovich moved at the head of his division supported by one Guard horse battery. The Chevalier Guard led the advance and the entire division moved out at a trot.

When the French marshals retreated to Conantre, their infantry led the withdrawal and the cavalry was deployed as a rearguard. Near Conantre they encountered a ravine that contained a stream three to four feet wide. It was lined by hedges and poplar trees and formed a half-circle about three miles on the La Fère-Champenoise plain before falling further to the south into a tributary of the Aube. This would prove a major obstacle, and as they struggled to cross it, Count Pahlen's cavalry attacked.[19]

At the same time, Grand Duke Constantine appeared on the French right with the Russian 1st Cuirassier Division, the Guard Dragoon Regiment, the Guard Uhlan Regiment and a Guard horse battery.

1st (Guard) Cuirassier Division
- Brigade: Generalmajor Arsenieff
  - Chevalier Guard Regiment (4)
  - Garde à cheval Regiment (4)
- Brigade: Generalmajor Baron Rosen
  - Life Guard Cuirassier Regiment (4)
  - Empress Cuirassier Regiment (4)
- Guard Light Cavalry Brigade: Generalmajor Tschallikov
  - Guard Dragoon Regiment
  - Guard Uhlan Regiment
  - Guard Hussar Regiment
  - Guard Don Cossack Regiment (detached to guard the Tsar)

17 von Damitz, Vol. III, 2nd Part, p. 70.
18 de Vaudoncourt, Vol. II, p. 279; Derode, p. 5.
19 Derode, p. 5.

The Russian Guard cavalry profited from the French as they struggled across the ravine's muddy stream and charged the French cavalry, which had barely reformed, and threw them back on the infantry. The routing French cavalry rushed across the stream and carried away both Marmont and Mortier in their panic.[20]

The Russian Guard Battery took the French near the Conantre ravine under fire. This battery, together with the Horse Guard and Guard Dragoons under Grand Duke Constantine, moved around the ravine on the left. The Guard Uhlan Regiment, led by GM Chalikov, struck the French flank.

Depreradovich's 1st (Guard) Cuirassier Division, supported by the Chevalier Guard and Horse Guard, charged. Favored by the position of the French line, they struck the ill-formed French cuirassiers under Bordesoulle. The shattered French cavalry fell back on the infantry, while the Russians captured two guns. All the Young Guard battalions did not have time to form square and two regiments of Jamin's brigade were cut down, while General Jamin, many of his officers and eight guns were captured.[21] Le Capitaine's Young Guard brigade – 1,000-men-strong – was attacked three times by the Württemberg 4th Jäger zu Pferd without success. A fourth attack – by the Württembergers and supported by the Erzherzog Ferdinand Hussars – however, broke Le Capitaine's square – sabering and hacking at its infantry until many were slain. Two squares of Jamin's brigade, torn by canister, was sobered and Jamin was captured.[22] The French withdrew to the village of Conantre with the cavalry in pursuit. At the same time, the Allies pursued the French army's left wing and center, while the 4th Württemberg Cavalry Regiment attacked the Young Guard squares three times and took two guns. GM von Jett led the 4th Württemberg Cavalry and the Austrian Erzherzog Ferdinand Hussars forward in a fourth attack, broke it and put most of its infantry to the sword.[23]

Again, the skies broke – showering both sides with hail and rain. The French muskets would no longer fire. The French responded with bayonet and a tremendous melee evolved. Twice, both marshals were forced to seek shelter in squares of their infantry.

Eventually, the strong face presented by Ricard and Christiani's divisions on the extreme ends of the line gave the French cavalry the time necessary to cross the Conantre ravine and reorganize. Despite this small victory, the Allies captured 24 guns, more than 60 caissons and a complete train battalion, which were abandoned before the village.

Satisfied with this success, Prince Schwarzenberg contented himself with a leisurely pursuit consisting of horse artillery and cavalry under Pahlen and Prince Adam von Württemberg. They moved with Conantre on their left and extended into the La Fère-Champenoise plain, which was favorable to cavalry actions.

The French last reserve – consisting of the 5th, 6th, 7th and 8th Voltigeurs supported by a battery of eight 12pdrs and a howitzer – stood on a ridge to the right of Conantre on the right bank of the Des Auges stream. They were struck by the Austrian Erzherzog Ferdinand Hussars and threw them back with a heavy musketry fire. Prince Adam brought forward the Constantine Cuirassiers and two squadrons of the Kaiser Cuirassiers, which coupled with the Erzherzog Ferdinand Hussars, renewed the attack. At this point in the battle, Seslavin's detachment appeared from Pleurs and panic spread among Jamin's brigade, which collapsed and fled to the rear.

With the collapse of Jamin's brigade, the last hope of the French collapsed. The rest of the French army was attempting to rally behind the Conantre ravine when a few of Jamin's panic-stricken fugitives ran through their lines. They could normally have been easily stopped, but

20 Derode, p. 5.
21 von Damitz, Vol. III, 2nd Part, p. 74.
22 Derode, p. 5.
23 Bogdanovich, Vol. 2, p. 482.

La Fère-Champenoise.

their panic was infectious and the entire French force panicked – fleeing in the direction of La Fère-Champenoise. During the attacks and pursuit of the French to Conantre, more than 24 guns were captured and found on the field of battle: Chevalier Gardes – six; Horse Guard – six; Emperor Curassiers – three; Leib-Garde Uhlans – six; Leib-Garde Dragoons – two; and Count Pahlen's cavalry – 20.[24]

The French army was threatened with total destruction when the 9th Heavy Cavalry Marche Regiment – with 400 men – arrived. Judging by the sound of the cannonade before him, its colonel – Colonel Leclerc – requested permission from GD Compans to advance. He arrived before La Fère-Champenoise just as the panicked French troops were arriving before the village and were about to disintegrate before the Allied light cavalry. The appearance of this heavy cavalry caused the light cavalry to withdraw and gave the two French marshals time to rally their troops on the Linthes heights.

Despite this, in their rush to move through the defile by Conantre, the French lost 24 guns and 60 munitions wagons – plus an entire train battalion.[25]

Colonel Leclerc's attack bought precious time for Marmont and Mortier's troops to collect their shattered forces on the Linthes heights. The French forces were deployed in two lines: infantry on the left wing in battalion columns; cavalry on the right partly in lines, partly in regimental columns. While the French rallied their forces, the sound arose to their left as a column struck vigorously at the enemy. Word came that Napoleon had arrived to save them. Reddened by their shame, those who had been fleeing before the Allies only minutes before quickly rallied with cries of: "*Vive l'Empereur!*" ringing across the fields. Sadly for the French, Napoleon was not on the battlefield and would not arrive that day.

24 Bogdanovich, Vol. 2, p. 483.
25 von Damitz, Vol. III, 2nd Part, p. 74.

The French cuirassiers of GD Bordesoulle formed the first line, but they were engaged frontally by the Württemberg artillery and struck in the flank by the cavalry of General Seslavin. The French lost nine guns to counterattacking Cossacks and were driven back. The Allied light troops pursued the French to Allement, where they arrived at 9:00 p.m.

Schwarzenberg, the Russian Tsar and the Prussian King arrived on the battlefield at this time with a simple escort and were startled to hear a cannonade growing on their right when they thought the French were routed. They recalled the bulk of their cavalry, which they had detached to pursue the beaten French, and pressed the march of their infantry through Sommesous in order to oppose the French column that was striking them on the right.

The French forces under Mortier and Marmont profited from this to resume their withdrawal and move on Allement, where they arrived at 9:00 p.m. Throughout this march, Allied light troops pressed them closely – capturing several equipment wagons.

The unknown French column that had arrived on the field and saved the French from total disaster was, in fact, the divisions of Pacthod and Amey.

Pacthod's battle

GD Pacthod had been marching to join Mortier and Marmont – and had departed Vatry at daybreak. He was passing through Villesneux at about 10:00 a.m. when he received orders to stop in Bergères and remain there until he received further orders.

Pacthod's National Guard division was escorting a major food convoy consisting of 30 munitions wagons, many personal equipment wagons and several more wagons filled with food and other necessary supplies. He had with him between 6,000 and 8,000 infantry, 100 hussars and 16 cannon. The convoy had marched almost all night and its horses were greatly fatigued. The convoy advanced on a four-wagon front, but moved very slowly.

Though aware of the situation, Pacthod felt he had the time to rest his force in Villesneux. However, as he was stopping, he found himself attacked by Korff's 1,200 line cavalry consisting of the Kargopol, New Russia and Mitau Dragoons; the Tchernigov and Livonia Chasseurs à cheval; and a horse battery of 12 guns moving down the road from Châlons to Etoges. He formed his troops into line – his right supported by the village and his left covered by a very large square formed by Amey's entire division.[26] Von Damitz indicates that the Russians had only four horse guns. However, Langeron indicates that it was a full horse battery with 12 guns.[27]

The precious convoy formed to the rear

When Pacthod bivouaced near Villesneux, he was attacked by GL Korff's cavalry, which formed the advanced guard of Blücher's Army of Silesia and moved along the Châlons-Bergères road. That morning, Korff had received information from Gneisenau about Pacthod's column and train moving to Vatry. General Korff, with his cavalry and Karpov's Cossack detachment and four guns from Horse Battery #8, moved at a trot to Germinon.

Korff crossed the Somme-Soudé River and caught the French between Villesneux and Trecon. The French troops were deployed in battalion columns with two batteries in front. Their right flank was near Villesneux and their left was covered by a large square. The train and parks were behind the line.

26 de Vaudoncourt, Vol. II, p. 282.
27 von Damitz, Vol. III, 2nd Part, p. 80; Langeron, p. 448.

Pacthod took the decision to abandon the wagons and doubled the teams on his artillery. He continued his retreat in squares by regiment, which overlapped and had their corners facing each other so that they could fire from all four faces if attacked.

The Russian cavalry attacks were not particularly serious – nor dangerous – against this strong formation. They were handily repelled in an hour-and-a-half and the French then continued to withdraw towards La Fère-Champenoise.[28]

General Korff ordered GL Pantschulischev to attack the French right with the Tchernigov and Kargopol Dragoons. Other forces were directed to attack the center and left. Pacthod's tiny force of cavalry was routed and most of it was captured by Cossacks. On the other hand, the French infantry – with the help of artillery – successfully defended itself. An attack by the Mitava Dragoons provoked Pacthod to continue his march – retreating *en échiquier*. He withdrew his infantry formed in six masses, with his guns in the intervals and his cavalry in front. The wagons were covered by small detachments of infantry. The convoy advanced with a frontage of four wagons and all soon reached Clamange. Once there, however, it became necessary to abandon the convoy or risk the certain destruction of his troops. The horses were stripped from the wagons and the teams on the guns were doubled. To cover this operation, Major Caille was sent to occupy Clamange with two battalions. Here he fought off numerous attacks by strong cavalry forces. One of these attacks was commanded by GM Pantschulischev and Poll leading the Kargopol and Tchernigov Dragoons.[29] Bogdanovich indicates that Pantschulischev captured an entire battalion, but no French sources indicate this victory.[30] Under the cover of Caille's two battalions, the main body of Pacthod's division deployed its infantry in six chessboard squares, abandoned its train and park and withdrew on Ecury-le-Repos. At this time, the Dorpat and Seversk Regiments arrived. General Korff ordered Captain of Artillery Focht to fire canister on the troops in Clamange and then ordered an attack against them with the Dorpat and Livonia Chasseurs under GM Count Pahlen II and Chrouchev. As Clamange was cleared, Korff received a message that Karpov's Cossack regiments had captured 47 officers, 500 soldiers and a large train near Vatry.

The withdrawal continued in regimental squares. At their wings and across their rear stood 16 cannon. The squares and cannon savagely flailed the Allied cavalry with canister and musketry – teaching them that the French were still to be respected. This French artillery was responded to by the guns commanded by Colonel Souvarov of the Don Cossacks and Captain 2nd Class Focht of the 8th Horse Battery, and a charge by the Dorpat and Livonia Chasseurs. These last two regiments had been sent by Langeron under the command of General Pahlen II to support Korff's assault. This brought Korff's forces to about 2,000 line cavalry and 1,000 Cossacks.[31]

GD Pacthod sought to gain the safety of La Fère-Champenoise in this formation, but Count Pahlen II succeeded in establishing himself behind Pacthod's division with the Dorpat and Livonia Chasseurs à cheval Regiments. Langeron suggests that it was the Seversk – not the Livonia – Chasseurs. He states that Livonia was with Korff.[32] This presented Pacthod with the alternatives of surrendering, or fighting his way through. After a short conference, General Delort proposed charging the Russians while the rest of the French troops contained Korff's forces. This recommendation was adopted. As soon as Delort's brigade was formed in attack columns, it advanced at the *pas de charge* against Pahlen II's Russian cavalry and forced them to withdraw.[33] However,

28 Koch, Vol. II, pp. 385-9.
29 Langeron, p. 448.
30 Bogdanovich, Vol. 2, p. 484.
31 von Damitz, Vol. III, 2nd Part, p. 84.
32 Langeron, p. 448.
33 Derode, p. 5.

the sounds of battle had attracted the cavalry of Sacken's corps, which appeared to replace Pahlen and executed several charges. Delort was obliged to form his brigade into squares and withdraw.[34]

Korff's cavalry was fatigued by their lengthy engagement and paused in their attack. Vassil'shikov's 2nd Hussar Division arrived and extended to the right – towards Petit-Morin and Petit-Aulnay – to turn the French squares. At this moment, the Tsar, the King of Prussia and Prince Schwarzenberg arrived on the field. The remainder of the Russian and Prussian Guard cavalry and the reserves moved through Euvy. Von Württemberg and Raevsky's corps arrived in Conantre, where they stopped to reorder themselves after passing through the swampy defiles by Soudé and Sommesous.

As Tsar Alexander arrived by Commercy, he saw many wounded Frenchmen and ordered two squadrons of Leib-Cossacks of his escort to pick them up. When the sovereigns arrived in La Fère-Champenoise – designated to become their headquarters – the Tsar proposed to the King of Prussia and Prince Schwarzenberg to go to the advanced guard. Only one squadron of Leib-Cossacks remained with the Tsar (4th Squadron was with the headquarters in La Fère-Champenoise). Soon the 23rd Horse Battery passed through La Fère-Champenoise. It was delayed by replenishment of cannon-shots. Some minutes later, an officer arrived from General Kretov to Count Pahlen. Kretov had sent a warning to Pahlen about French movement towards La Fère-Champenoise.[35] At first, Kretov's warning was doubted, but the Tsar ordered a reconnaissance by Volkonski's troops to verify Kretov's report.

The sovereigns watched the approach of Pacthod's troops and directed the Prussian Guard cavalry and the Russian Guard Hussars and Guard Cossacks forward. They called the reserve under the Grand Duke Constantine forward as well – though it still had not passed through La Fère-Champenoise.

The Tsar ordered the 23rd Horse Battery to return and placed it under the command of Prussian General Rauch. Colonel Markov loaded his guns with canister and solid shot in one load and began rapid fire on short range. As Frenchmen were in a ravine, Markov's shots struck Vassil'shikov's cavalry. Vassil'shikov deployed some of his guns and ordered them to reply. Four Russian solid shots fell near the Emperor. Vassil'shikov reported to the Tsar that his division stood behind the French. The Tsar ordered both him and Korff not to press on the French, but to give an opportunity to artillery to break up the French infantry.[36]

After a heavy pounding by the Allied artillery, Pacthod was engaged by the Prussian and Russian Guard cavalry on his right. At the same time, Korff attacked him frontally and Vassil'shikov's 2nd Hussar Division attacked his left and rear.[37] Meanwhile, Raevsky's 6th Russian Corps moved into position by La Fère-Champenoise and the 20th and 21st Russian Jager Regiments from Schachovsky's 3rd Division – supported by Colonel Markov's Russian Horse Battery #23 – moved to the heights occupied by the Allied sovereigns.

Pacthod had already suffered heavy losses and would soon be surrounded on all fronts by overwhelming forces. He resolved, therefore, to march towards the Saint-Gond swamps. Unfortunately, the Allied pursuit was particularly aggressive and Pacthod began to fear that they would not reach the security of the swamps. He began to harangue the National Guardsmen with the shame of capitulation and that their lives were at stake. His words and the gravity of the situation struck home. The French squares became as solid as rocks and erupted into a rolling fire that flailed

34 Koch, Vol. II, pp. 390-1; de Vaudoncourt, Vol. II, p. 283.
35 Bogdanovich, Vol. 2, p. 485.
36 Bogdanovich, Vol. 2, p. 486.
37 de Vaudoncourt, Vol. II, p. 284; von Damitz, Vol. III, 2nd Part, p. 86.

the enemy cavalry with an unexpected fury. The helpless victim once held in their clutches had become a desperate, clawing animal giving better than it took.

Vassil'shikov led forward the Kinburn and Smolensk Dragoons, the Seversk Chasseurs and the Guard Cavalry in a massive cavalry attack, but it was repelled and driven back with losses.[38]

In response, Tsar Alexander directed forward a brigade of Raevsky's corps, but before it could arrive on the field, 78 Russian guns began to rake the French squares with canister and threw them into disorder. General Borosdin, at the head of the New Russia and Kargopol Dragoons, crushed Pacthod's right where GD Pacthod stood – sabering those that resisted, taking seven guns and forcing the rest to surrender. Square after square was crushed and surrendered.

GB Thévenet – leading part of Amey's division – formed into one large square, reached the swamps near Bannes and sought some shelter from the Russian cavalry, despite the fire of 78 cannon. General Depreradovich, with the Chevalier Gardes Regiment and four guns from the 6th Horse Battery, moved at a trot through Petit-Morin and Aulnay-aux-Planches, deployed on the road to Brann and barred the way of retreat to their enemies.[39]

A flag of truce was sent with Flugel-adjudant Rapatel, Captain of General Staff Durnovo, Oberstleutnant von Thile and a trumpeter. General Pacthod, who was wounded in the hand, asked the Prussian officer: "What do you want?" The response was: "Surrender. You are surrounded on all sides." The fire of Russian guns increased. Pacthod listened calmly and said: "No negotiations will be made under the fire" and von Thile was taken prisoner. Flugel-adjudant Rapatel arrived before the French with a white handkerchief, but was killed with a bullet. A French emigre, Rapatel was a former aide-de-camp to General Moreau. His brother was serving as a captain of artillery and was in that square as it was summoned to surrender.

The efforts to cause the French to surrender having failed, the Russians attacked from all sides. First, two Chevalier Gardes squadrons under Colonel Uvarov; the Guard Cossacks; Guard Uhlans; and Seversk Dragoons charged the square. The Kinburn and Smolensk Dragoons – with two squadrons of Lubno Hussars – supported this last decisive attack. The Tsar – with his escort – entered the square and stopped the Chevalier Gardes, who rushed at one of the battalions as the few survivors laid down their arms.

The butchery was terrible, with every square being broken and not a man escaping. The French sold their lives dearly – trading bayonet thrust for saber slash with the mounted eastern hordes. No quarter was asked or given, though the New Russia and Kargopol Regiments did take some prisoners in the charge that broke the first square.[40] In the end, Thévenet was wounded and captured, seven cannon were taken and this last brave attempt crushed.

Thus ended the Battle of La Fère-Champenoise. The French lost 9,000-11,000 men – including 5,000 *hors de combat*, which was most of the men present. The Allies also claim to have captured 80 cannon and 250 munitions wagons.[41] GD Amey and Pacthod, GB Jamin, Delort, Bont and Thévenet were taken prisoner and presented to the Tsar Alexander, who in recognition of their valor, released them on their parole.

The Allies lost 4,000 men killed or wounded. Colonel Efremov, of the Guard Cossacks Regiment, was wounded.

There are several reasons for the disaster at La Fère-Champenoise. First was the bad choice of position. The terrain was open and suitable for the Allied cavalry, which the Allies finally used to overwhelm and cut off a French infantry force, despite two years of massive cavalry superiority.

38 von Damitz, Vol. III, 2nd Part, p. 92.
39 Bogdanovich, Vol. 2, p. 487.
40 Langeron, p. 450.
41 von Damitz, Vol. III, 2nd Part, p. 95.

'Episode of the Campaign of France', by Horace Vernet.

Certainly, Pacthod should not have been directed to wait in Bergères, but directed immediately to march on La Fère-Champenoise to support the left of the two retreating French corps and to cover the Conantre defile. In addition, once Pacthod had diverted the Allies' attention, the two marshals should have marched on Sézanne – not Allement. If they had marched on Sézanne, they could have linked up with the forces under Compans, which were in that vicinity. However, probably the biggest French failure was their failure to adequately reconnoitre the region and the failure of either marshal to wonder about the massive display of campfires that lit the sky of 24-25 March between the Cosel and Marne rivers.

The result of the French failure at La Fère-Champenoise was that the road to Paris was open and there was nothing that the French could do to shut it again. That night, the Allies slept on the battlefield. The three monarchs and Schwarzenberg established their headquarters on the field as well.

The forces engaged were as follows:[42]
French under Mortier

	Infantry	Cavalry	Guns
Imperial Guard			
Divisions	7,400		30
GB Christiani			
GD Curial			
GD Charpentier			
Divisions	2,050		
Roussel			
Col. Ghigny			
Marmont			
Divisions	4,900		38
GD Ricard			
GD Lagrange			
GD Arrighi			

42 de Vaudoncourt, Vol. II, p. 287.

Divisions		2,300	
GD Bordesoulle			
GD Merlin			
Pacthod			
Divisions	5,800		16
GD Pacthod			
GD Amey			
Total:	18,100	4,350	84
Allies			
von Württemberg's corps			
Pahlen's cavalry		3,500	12
von Württemberg's cavalry		2,000	12
Kretov's 2nd Cuirassier Division		1,600	12
General Nostitz		3,700	24
Klenau Chevauxlegers			
Rosenberg Chevauxlegers			
Nostitz's cuirassiers			
Grand Duke Constantine			
Russian Guard Cuirassiers		1,600	12
Russian Guard Light Cavalry Brigade		2,400	12
Prussian Guard Cavalry		800	8
Seslavin's Cossacks		1,500	2
Korff's cavalry corps		5,400	22
Vassil'shikov's 2nd Hussar Division		3,900	12
Total:		26,400	128

The Army of Silesia

The three Russian corps of the Army of Silesia pushed to Etoges, while the bulk of the two Prussian corps remained in Montmirail. Part of the Army of Silesia, under General Vincent, marched through Verdelot and Rebais. General Yorck, upon hearing a violent cannonade around noon, sent a reconnaissance towards Sézanne – under General Ziethen – formed by his cavalry reserve and supported by some infantry. What they heard was the Battle of La Fère-Champenoise.

Several hours after their arrival in Allement, Mortier and Marmont consulted over what actions to take next. They decided to detach a cavalry force and attempt to establish contact with Compans, but they were struck by an apathy that sapped their initiative and sense of urgency. This force did not leave until the next morning – and when it did, it was instructed to invite Compans to join the marshals upon their arrival.

However, Compans was unwilling to remain in his position – having learned of the presence of Kleist and Yorck in Montmirail. Ziethen's approach obliged him to withdraw around midnight so that he could cover a considerable convoy of material. He marched to join the two marshals and left a rearguard in Sézanne, with orders to hold its position until 2:00 a.m.

Marmont and Mortier began their march at 2:00 a.m. on 26 March. Roussel's dragoons led the march – advancing in pairs down a very difficult road. Behind them marched the regiments of colonels Ghigny, Christophe and Leclerc. Behind them came the I Cavalry Corps, the artillery and then the infantry marching by the flank. A division of Marmont's corps formed the rearguard. Mortier and Marmont personally marched with the rearguard.

The night was extremely dark, with only an occasional fire lit at intervals along the road over the summit of the Saint-Pierre Mountain by Sézanne. Not wishing to blunder into Sézanne, a dragoon was sent on foot – slipping and sliding into the city. He returned shortly later to announce that the city was deserted.

However, as the French learned this disagreeable news, the Allies' pickets advanced to examine the French advanced guard. They were part of Ziethen's forces – apparently consisting of the Brandenburg Uhlans and the 1/,2/,Jägers/Lithuanian Dragoon Regiment. They had entered Sézanne and chased GD Compans' rearguard out of the city. The remainder of the Prussian force – consisting of the 3/,4/Lithuanian Dragoons – stood outside of the city while the two squadrons of the combined 3rd, 5th and 10th Silesian Landwehr Cavalry Regiments moved against the road from La Fère-Champenoise.[43]

At this point, Compans commanded about 1,000 infantry and a single cavalry squadron. He had detached his two cavalry regiments to join Mortier and Marmont.[44] As the Prussian pickets cried out their alarm, the French column – formed in mass by pelotons in a small field to the right of the road – turned and bolted away in panic. Near Allement, Count Belliard and GD Roussel called out to them and brought them to a halt. The dragoons were rallied and reformed – and so too was the remainder of the column calmed down.

There was not a moment to lose – and it was decided that the bold approach was best. The French generals decided that they would ram their forces through Sézanne and move to the heights that dominated the Belle-Croix Valley.

The engagement at Sézanne

The Prussians had received word that the French were present – and as the French decided what to do (then prepared to do it), the Prussians busied themselves getting ready to repel the French attack. The break of dawn exposed the 1,000 cavalry that barred the French advance. The French fired on them frontally with a horse battery, while French cavalry struck their left in the Belle-Croix Valley. These French attacks were not pressed home, but they were sufficient to convince the Prussians to withdraw down the road to La Ferté to the right of Morin. Von Damitz indicates that the Prussians received some reinforcements in the form of the East Prussian Cuirassier and the West Prussian Dragoon Regiments. Apparently, the East Prussian Cuirassiers were, at this point, reduced to a strength of 187 men and formed in two squadrons.[45] However, they were not sufficient to prevent the French movement.

During this cavalry engagement, GB Christiani led his 2nd Old Guard Division through the village at the '*pas redoublé*'[46] and established himself on the target heights by the branch of the roads to La Ferté and Coulommiers.

The engagement ended at around 9:00 a.m. The French cavalry, after turning Sézanne from right to left, rejoined the main road by the tile works and formed the rearguard with a horse battery. The Allies reported 23 dead, 59 wounded and 25 prisoners – or a total of 107 men – and claim to have taken 300 prisoners.[47] The French indicate they lost about 200 men – including 60 prisoners.

43 von Damitz, Vol. III, 2nd Part, p. 112.
44 de Vaudoncourt, Vol. II, p. 290.
45 von Damitz, Vol. III, 2nd Part, p. 115.
46 The "*pas redoublé*" is a term being used by the author, not a regulation cadence. That said, I suspect the author is talking of the "*pas de course*," which was a cadenced run of 250 paces per minute.
47 von Damitz, Vol. III, 2nd Part, p. 117.

The French army then resumed its march – moving from Coulommiers to Esternay; then to Réveillon towards La Ferté-Gaucher – with GD Compans bringing up the rear.

The column stopped at Moeure at 4:00 p.m. and soon learned that they were being pursued by an enemy force. The Prussian cavalry did not engage the rearguard and followed the road to La Ferté, which ran to the right of Grand-Morin. The Crown Prince of Württemberg, at the head of the advance of the main Allied army, had arrived in Sézanne three hours after the French left it and immediately turned to pursue them down the road that ran directly to La Ferté-Gaucher.[48]

On the morning of 26 March the Allied army resumed its march. Schwarzenberg's advanced guard consisted of the infantry and cavalry of the corps of Württemberg and Raevsky, Nostitz's cavalry and the reserve grenadiers – all united at 6:00 a.m. by Conantre under the orders of the Crown Prince of Württemberg. About 10:00 a.m. Pahlen – whose artillery had been reinforced by 30 guns from the artillery reserve – began his march on Sézanne, where he arrived at 1:00 p.m. There he found Kleist's advanced guard – under Oberst von Blücher – and united with them. They then pursued the French marshals via Esternay. Blücher – with the corps of Langeron, Sacken and Stroganov – followed the road to Montmirail. Voronzov's corps left Châlons to rejoin the army and the corps of Yorck and Kleist moved on La Ferté-Gaucher. Their advanced guard – consisting of eight squadrons and followed by Horn's brigade – led their advance.[49]

GD Compans had escaped his immediate threats and had arrived in Réveillon without incident. At the break of day on 26 March he resumed his march on La Ferté-Gaucher. He had barely established his forces when they were attacked by Yorck, whose forces sought to cut off the retreat of the corps beaten the day before. General Vincent was obliged to leave Montmirail and moved to Rebais. From there he moved through Coulommiers, where he rallied 1,000 men – most of whom had escaped Pacthod's destruction. This raised Compans' force to 2,200 infantry and 250 cavalry. Combined, Compans and Vincent took up a position on the heights behind Coulommiers and destroyed the bridges on the Morin. Horn's brigade then took up a position before La Ferté-Gaucher and on the left bank of the Morin. The head of Kleist's column was just approaching the village.

The Prussians judged that the bulk of the French army had not yet passed and established themselves solidly in La Ferté-Gaucher – on the two banks of the Grand-Morin – and continued the pursuit of Compans with Horn's infantry brigade and a few squadrons of cavalry.

The engagement at Chatilly

Compans – no longer seeing himself pursued by the Prussian cavalry – ordered his division to stop in Chatilly. It was a good position with many advantages, but his division was already demoralized – and when Horn's Prussian brigade struck it at around 2:00 p.m. it was thrown back with a loss of 300 prisoners. It fell back in disorder to Coulommiers, where General Vincent had gone the night before and had rallied about 1,000 fugitives of all arms from the armies of Mortier and Marmont.

Using these men as a basis, Compans rallied his division and decided to take up a position on the Montanglaust heights below Coulommiers. Here he passed the night after breaking all the bridges over the Grand-Morin.

48 Koch, Vol. II, pp. 392-8.
49 de Vaudoncourt, Vol. II, p. 292.

The engagement at La Ferté-Gaucher and Moutis

Mortier and Marmont knew nothing of Compans' division and resumed their march on La Ferté-Gaucher at 1:00 p.m. At 2:00 p.m. they encountered a picket of the Mecklenburg Hussars under Leutnant von Zülow and drove them back.[50] Mortier moved from Moutis to La Ferté at 4:00 p.m. and found Prince Wilhelm von Preussen's brigade of Prussian infantry standing on the heights on the left bank of the Petit-Morin before the city of La Ferté. Prince Wilhelm's force was too small to cover the terrain and was charged with covering Kleist's reserve artillery on the right side of the Grand-Morin Valley.

A light cannonade broke out. Prince Wilhelm had not yet been joined by the rest of Kleist's corps and the Prussian reserve artillery – and he feared being turned. Mortier deployed his forces before Lécherolles and forced Prince Wilhelm to withdraw his brigade to the right of the Morin – leaving behind only a screen of skirmishers. He then threw three battalions into La Ferté and deployed the rest of his brigade into line – covered by a battery of 16 guns.

La Ferté-Gaucher was the point where the roads from Sézanne ran along the banks of the Morin. Beyond Coulommiers ran the only road which ran towards Paris. This was a critical chokepoint in the road network for both sides.

La Ferté-Gaucher stands in a narrow valley, with the Morin running along the edge of the village – forming a moat. The hills forming the edge of the bank are quite tall – particularly those of the right bank, which command those of the opposite bank. Added to this, at a distance of 600 meters from the village, the high road was cut into the edge of the hill – forming a type of a trench that was defensible its entire length. The Prussians had occupied the village with three battalions under Oberst von Siöholm. On a rise before the village were two guns. The remainder of the division remained in column – in reserve behind the city – except for a number of batteries posted on the right side of the Grand-Morin, where they could fire on the flank of the French as they moved down the main road.

The French Guard infantry – under GB Christiani – marched down the main road as far as Maison-Dieu, where they sought to penetrate into the village. Mortier ordered a second, simultaneous attack down the main road. When the French columns appeared, the Prussians directed the fire of their artillery against the heads of their columns. After reviewing the position, Mortier ordered an immediate assault down the main road while a second division sought to move into the village by advancing along the banks of the river. With both attacks repulsed and the approach of night, Mortier feared being caught in this position and decided to withdraw to the Chartronge plateau by the gorge that separated it from the Lécherolles plateau.

As the French Guard executed this movement, Marmont's corps found Pahlen's cavalry had caught up. Reinforced by Kleist's advanced guard, which had been separated from Ziethen that morning, this force of Allied cavalry opened up a cannonade on the French. The French artillery was badly outnumbered by the Allied artillery, which constantly received more and more guns from Yorck's reserves. Soon it faced 48 Allied guns. In addition, Kleist's corps was beginning to enter the line.

Pahlen ordered his cavalry and most of his artillery to march on Courgivaux in order to turn the French position and occupy the Moutis crest. Oberst von Blücher and Illowaiski's Cossacks were all that remained before the VI Corps. Shortly later, Marmont learned from Mortier that he could not force his way through La Ferté-Gaucher and that he was obliged to withdraw down the road to Provins.[51]

50 von Damitz, Vol. III, 2nd Part, p. 107.
51 de Vaudoncourt, Vol. II, p. 294.

French infantry on the attack, by Sergent.

About this time, the three Landwehr cavalry regiments of Kleist's corps, a company of Silesian Schützen and two guns under Major von Schmidt moved through La Ferté-Gaucher and reoccupied the heights they had held when the French arrived.[52] As they rushed forward, they took 136 prisoners (probably the Silesian National Cavalry Regiment and the 7th and 8th Silesian Landwehr Cavalry Regiments. These three regiments totaled about 200 men at this time).

Cossack carrying despatches, by Vernet.

Covering Mortier's withdrawal, Marmont held a position along a small stream, which ran in front of the Meaux woods. Count Pahlen was turning the small branches of the Morin and moved so that he could interpose himself between the two French marshals to prevent their linking up – as well as to place himself between them and Paris. He marched on Courgivaux in order to

52 von Damitz, Vol. III, 2nd Part, p. 109.

reach Moutis. Oberst von Blücher led his force down the road to Réveillon, while Marmont – seeing that Mortier had not forced the passage at La Ferté-Gaucher – moved Bordesoulle's cavalry to the right and established Joubert's brigade to cover the withdrawal of the rest of the troops onto the Chartronge plateau. Once both corps were on the plateau, the marshals took up positions by the Larnière farm for a few hours to let their troops rest.

In the meantime, the Crown Prince of Württemberg – being advised that the passage from Courgivaux to Moutis was impractical for artillery – called Count Pahlen back and rejoined him on the road to Saint-Martin-du-Bauchet. Only a few Cossacks were to continue the direct march on Moutis. This permitted Joubert to march his brigade to Provins that night without incident.

During this day, the only Allied forces that were active were those of Yorck, Kleist, the Crown Prince of Württemberg and Raevsky. This general inactivity by the Allies was fortunate for the two marshals as it was apparent that their armies were badly outnumbered, out-maneuvered and the morale of their forces was falling apart. It can be argued that Schwarzenberg had reverted to his old methods of the leisurely 18th century war, but perhaps he was confident of the superiority of his position – and his army – and wanted the shattered remains of the corps under the two marshals to reach Paris so he could defeat them before the gates of the city and maximize the impact of their destruction.

Certainly, occupying Paris would be a devastating blow to French morale, but by making the political heart of France witness the destruction of two marshals before their foyers would convince them of the hopelessness of their situation.

That evening, the Allied army was positioned as follows: The corps of the Crown Prince of Württemberg and Raevsky, with their cavalry and grenadiers, were in Villeneuve-de-Lion and Moutis; Wrede's corps was in Meilleray; Giulay's corps – charged with escorting the artillery park – was in Treffaux; the Guard was in Veziers; Seslavin's Cossacks were advancing from Sézanne to Provins; and Kaisarov's Cossacks were near Arcis. Kleist and Yorck bivouaced in La Ferté-Gaucher, where Ziethen's cavalry rejoined them. Horn's brigade was in Rebais; the corps of Langeron, Sacken and Stroganov were in Montmirail; and Voronzov's corps was in Etoges.

The French marshals move to Provins

The two French marshals reunited their corps at Larnière and already began to regret their stop at Moeure. They knew that the road to Paris was open to the Allied main army and that they were obliged to march via Nangis towards Paris in an effort to provide some sort of defense for Paris.

Mortier and Marmont resumed their march at 2:00 a.m. on 27 March – moving via Chartronge, Courtacon and Champcenetz towards Provins, which they reached at 10:00 a.m. They had abandoned all hope of reaching Meaux before the Allies. Even Pahlen had abandoned his pursuit of the French in Courtacon and was recalled from there to Crécy. He left only 1,000 Cossacks under General Illowaiski to follow the French.

These Cossacks arrived before Provins at 3:00 p.m. Though they took no action to threaten the city, from their position on Mont-Jubert their appearance was sufficient to infect the French with panic and send them out of Provins in great disorder. However, the various French reconnaissance forces had returned with word that the Allies were not to be found in any direction – and soon calm returned to the demoralized French. They moved to the Maison-Rouge plateau to spend the night. It was a major error for the Allies to have marched too little that day. During the night, a division – under GD Souham – arrived in Nogent. It had been recalled from the Yonne to support the rapidly deteriorating French situation. Marmont directed it to remain in Nogent and cover the withdrawal of the rest of the French army.

GD Compans – still in the field – withdrew to Meaux, with General Vincent flanking his right and arriving in Trilport as Compans' forces arrived in Meaux. There were 600 infantry and

600 cavalry in Meaux under the orders of GD Ledru-des-Essarts. Koch indicates that Ledru had 1,500 infantry and 600 cavalry. This feeble reinforcement gave Compans the resolution to defend the Marne passage for at least a day and raised his forces to 3,800 infantry and 850 cavalry.[53] He then gave command of all his cavalry to General Vincent and ordered him to move to a position before Trilport.

The engagements at Trilport and Meaux

The Army of Silesia marched on Meaux with its Prussian elements moving through Coulommiers and the Russians passing through La Ferté-sous-Jouarre. Langeron's advanced guard, under the command of General Emmanuel, arrived at 5:00 p.m. before the foot of the Saint-Jean-les-Deux-Jumeaux plateau. General Vincent's cavalry – supported by 500 to 600 National Guardsmen – disputed the position with him, but the Russians were soon supported by the arrival of Yorck's advanced guard, which arrived to the right of the road to Coulommiers. Vincent had no choice but to withdraw across the Marne at Trilport and to pull the pontoon bridge back to the left bank. The Allies sent forward a cloud of skirmishers, a few hundred horse and about 20 guns to cover the construction of their own bridges.

Once the Allies had their own bridges over the Marne, they sent the cavalry of General Katzler and Oberst von Blücher forward supported by Horn's combined (1st and 7th) infantry brigade, which was supported by two battalions of the Leib Infantry Regiment.[54] They quickly engaged the forces under Ledru and drove him back towards Meaux. Part of the Allied infantry pushed along the riverbank – sliding into the Cornillon suburb – and engaged in a musketry exchange with Compans' forces. Meanwhile, the corps of Yorck and Kleist pushed into Trilport; Langeron's forces moved towards Saint-Jean and Sameron; Sacken moved against La Ferté-sous-Jouarre; and Voronzov moved against Bussières.

Having no major blocking force before them, the Allied main army camped that night in Guerard, Mouron, Saint-Pierre-en-Veuve, Chailly and Montaimey.

During the night of 27-28 March both the main Allied and French armies remained undisturbed, though there was minor skirmishing with both musketry and artillery exchanged by the Army of Silesia and GD Compans' corps.

At daybreak on 28 March the Prussian advanced guard began its march on Meaux. Shortly afterward, the main army marched behind them in two right columns. Raevsky's corps, the Guard, the reserves and the Austrian grenadiers marched along the road to Lagny to Rouilly, where they marched to the right down the road to Nanteuil. The Württembergers – followed by Giulay's corps – marched via Crécy and Couilly. Wrede was ordered to keep his corps in Chailly facing to the rear and to push his advanced guard towards La Ferté-Gaucher to observe the roads from Sézanne and Provins in case Napoleon should choose to execute a counter-march into the Allies' rear. The Allied forces present consisted of:[55]

Advanced Guard Infantry: Oberst von Lettow
- From 1st Corps:
  - Fus/1st East Prussian Infantry Regiment (Captain Besserer)
  - Fus/2nd East Prussian Infantry Regiment (Captain Loebell)
  - Leib Fusilier Battalion (Captain Steinäcker)

53 de Vaudoncourt, Vol. II, p. 297.
54 von Damitz, Vol. III, 2nd Part, p. 166.
55 von Damitz, Vol. III, 2nd Part, p. 177.

From 2nd Corps:
- 2/6th Reserve Regiment (Major Koschkull)
- Fus/1st West Prussian Regiment (Major Haine)
- Fus/2nd West Prussian Regiment (Major Hundte)
- Silesian Schützen (two companies) (Captain Neumann)

Advanced Guard Cavalry: Oberst von Blücher

From 1st Corps:
- 1/, 2/, 3/, 4/2nd Leib Hussar Regiment (Oberstleutnant Stöffel)
- 1/, 2/, 3/, 4/Brandenburg Hussar Regiment (Oberstleutnant Sohr)
- Unknown Horse Battery (eight guns)

From 2nd Corps:
- 1/, 2/, 3/, 4/Neumark Dragoon Regiment (Oberst von Borck)
- 1/, 2/, 3/, 4/Silesian Hussar Regiment (Major Engelhardt)
- Unknown Horse Battery (eight guns)

GD Compans judged that it was more important to march on Paris than to linger around Meaux for a few hours, and began his march early in the morning. General Vincent formed his rearguard – evacuating the city after destroying the bridge and a powder magazine. Still in their bivouacs, the explosion of the magazine caused great alarm in the Prussian ranks and they ran to their arms. The Prussian advanced guards began their pursuit immediately and arrived before Claye to find that Compans had established a strong position reinforced by three battalions of Young Guard – under General Guye – supported by about 400 cuirassiers and as many Polish lancers hastily sent forward from Paris. However, the strength of the Prussians grew continually – forcing Compans to withdraw to Villeparisis and then to Montsaigle, where he resolved to make a stand.[56]

The Allied cavalry thought it could push into the village of Montsaigle without resistance, but was stunned and stopped by the heavy musketry coming from houses. They were obliged to pull back and wait for infantry support. GD Compans profited from this momentary relief to order General Vincent to form his cavalry behind the village and to the right of the road.

With the Claye defile open, the Prussian advanced guard moved through and deployed to the left of the main road on the Grosbois heights. Pirch's 10th Brigade followed them and deployed – straddling the main road. Klüx was next and deployed his 9th Brigade to the left behind the rearguard. Ziethen's cavalry then moved forward and moved to the Lepin heights to turn Compans' position.

The Prussians slowly drew forward 6pdr Foot Battery #8 and it began firing on the Montsaigle woods. It was covered on the right by the 2nd Leib and the Brandenburg Hussars and on the left by the von Linsingen Combined Musketeer Battalion. The skirmishers of the von Linsingen Battalion occupied a small woods and were soon taken under fire by the French artillery.

On the right flank were the Fus/2nd and the Fus/1st West Prussian Regiments under Oberst von Lettow.[57] A prolonged engagement began at the head of the Montsaigle and Gorsbois woods. Oberst von Lettow moved his two battalions to the heights to the left of the woods and established himself as the link between the Prussian 9th and 10th Brigades. The Combined Jäger/Schützen Battalion, under Captain von Neumann, was then moved forward to a position behind the woods to serve as a reserve.

56 de Vaudoncourt, Vol. II, p. 297.
57 von Damitz, Vol. III, 2nd Part, p. 183.

The Allies successively brought into the action all of Kleist's corps. Horn's brigade, from Yorck's corps, was moved into line near Souilly and Compans moved to a new position between Villeparisis and the woods. As Compans withdrew, von Lettow's West Prussian fusiliers pressed them closely. The Combined Jäger/Schützen Battalion thrust itself forward and engaged the French at a range of 40 to 60 paces. The Fus/2nd West Prussians advanced – supported by the Leib Fusilier Battalion – and pressed against the French right flank and engaged them with musketry. Two companies of the Leib Fusiliers were sent on a wide sweeping movement to the French rear and a detachment of one captain, three officers and 133 French soldiers were taken prisoner.[58]

The area between the main road and the Montfonde and Montsaigle farms was occupied by the Mulot and Mony woods. Three battalions – the Graf Reichenbach Battalion supported by the East Prussian and Leib Fusilier Battalions – were sent to the left to turn the farm by moving along the Lepin road, while two others – the von Haase and von Hüllesheim Battalions[59] – attacked through a hole in the Grosbois woods on the Villeparisis road. The three Prussian battalions charged with the flank attack suffered greatly from the French fire in the Mulot woods and the vineyards. The battalion defending Montsaigle did not surrender its position until after it had extracted a bloody payment from the Prussians.[60]

Meanwhile, the two West Prussian Fusilier Battalions and the 2/6th Reserve Regiment moved around Montsaigle and attacked the heights in the direction of Le Pin. A large number of French skirmishers occupied the vineyard and the surrounding area. The Fus/2nd West Prussians moved to take Montsaigle in the rear, while the two other battalions struck it in the right flank. Despite the heavy French musketry, the Fus/2nd West Prussians pushed forward. Its commander – Major von Hundt – was shot dead, but his troops pressed on. This attack, soon supported by much of von Klüx's 9th Brigade, threatened the French line of retreat so that Montsaigle was evacuated. The Prussian light troops continued to press them. Two batteries – 6pdr Foot Battery #7 and Horse Battery #2 – moved forward to support their pursuit.[61]

Despite the Prussian skirmishers and supporting artillery, Compans resumed his retreat – moving in good order. Villeparisis was filled with skirmishers and Vincent's cavalry, which stood behind it, moved to the right rear – placing themselves parallel to the road. The Prussian cavalry attempting to turn the village was stopped by the fire of the French skirmishers. The Prussian infantry then advanced and drove back the French skirmishers as they came out of the village to pursue the cavalry. The Prussian infantry cleared the village with little difficulty, but when its columns began to poke their heads out of the village, the French cavalry fell upon them. The cuirassiers of Colonel Dugeon and the Polish Éclaireurs drove into them relentlessly – pushing them back into Villeparisis and taking 240-250 prisoners.[62]

Their rashness chastened, the Prussians meekly watched as the French division resumed its withdrawal to Bondy, where it took up position at 8:00 p.m. – leaving a rearguard in the edge of the forest before Livry. The French lost about 200 men during the day's engagements, while the Prussians lost between 400 and 600.

That night, the Army of Silesia established itself with its Prussian elements in Villeparisis, Montsaigle, Soulier and Messy. The Russian elements were between Trilport and Meaux.

The Allied attempt to rebuild the bridge at Meaux was delaying the main Allied army, so the right column was ordered to march to Trilport and cross the pontoon bridge located there. It

58 von Damitz, Vol. III, 2nd Part, p. 184.
59 von Ebertz, p. 170.
60 de Vaudoncourt, Vol. II, p. 299.
61 von Damitz, Vol. III, 2nd Part, pp. 186-7
62 Koch, Vol. II, pp. 406; von Damitz, Vol. III, 2nd Part, p. 187.

was then to take up a position in Crécy. Raevsky's corps camped that night in Nanteuil and the reserves stood before Meaux. The Württembergers were in St.-Germain and Giulay's Austrians were in Mouron.

The French marshals arrived in Nangis, where they separated. Mortier marched down the main highway to Paris and camped in Guignes. Marmont marched to Melun. Their movement was followed by General Seslavin as far as Provins. Here, Seslavin encountered Illowaiski and turned his observation duties over to him – returning to rejoin Pahlen's forces.

On 29 March Schwarzenberg ordered Blücher to detach an army corps in Meaux – on the right bank of the Marne – and to take the remainder of his forces down the road to Soissons, while the main army crossed at Meaux and Trilport and took up a position on his left.

The Allies march on Paris

The two Allied armies marched in three columns on Paris. The right column consisted of the Army of Silesia – with the exception of Sacken's corps – and marched along the road from Charny, Maury and Aulnay. The center column consisted of the Guard, the reserves and Raevsky's corps. It crossed the Marne at Meaux and Trilport, then marched via Claye on Bondy. The left column consisted of the Württembergers, Giulay's corps and the Austrian grenadiers under the command of the Crown Prince of Württemberg. However, the Crown Prince's column was unable to cross at Langy, as anticipated, because the bridge was down. As a result, it was to cross at Meaux and then march along the Marne via Charmentray and Chelles.

Baron Sacken was ordered to remain in Trilport and Wrede was to march to Meaux and establish his corps on the left of the river – pushing his cavalry to Crécy and his advanced posts to Coulommiers to cover the Allied advance on Paris.

The three columns began their march at dawn on 29 March. The Prussian advanced guard's cavalry skirmished with that of General Vincent as parliamentarians presented themselves at the lines. Vincent received these two senior officers – one an aide of Feldmarschal Blücher and the other a Major of the Russian Guard attached to the staff of the Tsar. They requested to be taken to the government in Paris to discuss peace terms.[63] Vincent, acting under orders from Compans, took their dispatches and returned them to their lines. These documents were addressed to the Duke of Feltre – the Minister of War.

A ceasefire is requested

While the two Allied parliamentarians were making their efforts to communicate with the French government, General Yorck sought a few hours' suspension of arms and his request was dispatched by General Katzler. It was requested that the two armies would remain where they were, but Vincent learned that the Army of Silesia was profiting from this pause to shift its right down the roads to Petits-Ponts and Senlis, so Compans resumed his withdrawal towards Paris.

Count Ornano, after scouting the fields before Pantin, was warned that Compans was withdrawing on him and moved the Guard reserves between the suburb of Chapelle and Pré-Saint-Gervais – presuming that Compans occupied Pantin. However, as a result of a misunderstanding, Compans crossed the Ourcq Canal and took a position on the right of the village on the Beauregard plateau, which dominated Pré-Saint-Gervais. He occupied Belleville as well – leaving the line from Romainville and Bagnolet to Marmont's troops. General Vincent – holding back the Prussian cavalry – crossed the canal by Saint-Denis and placed his bivouacs by Chapelle.

63 de Vaudoncourt, Vol. II, p. 301

The Army of Silesia marched via the roads from Petits-Ponts and Soissons – establishing its advanced guard in Grand-Dracy. The Prussian corps of Yorck and Kleist were in Aulnay, while Langeron was in Le Bourget and Voronzov was near Villepinte.Le Bourget is now one of the two principal airports for Paris and is the field where Charles Lindberg landed in his famous trans-atlantic flight.

The Allied main army arrived from the roads from Allemagne and Lagny. Along this latter road, the corps of the Crown Prince of Württemberg could not advance beyond Anet. However, Barclay de Tolly moved the reserves and Russo-Prussian Guards into Bondy, where the sovereigns had established their headquarters.

Raevsky's corps and Pahlen's cavalry marched to Noisy-le-Sec. Their advanced elements had penetrated as far as Romainville and Pantin without encountering a single French soldier. General Raevsky could have occupied those positions and held them strongly, but let the opportunity slip.

Marmont and Mortier – after joining at Brie-Comte-Robert – arrived in Charenton around noon and established their infantry in Saint-Mandé, Vincennes and Charonne. Their cavalry was in Montreuil, with the villages to the rear being left to Mortier – whose infantry occupied Charenton, Conflans and Bercy – while General Belliard's cavalry occupied the Picpus suburbs of Paris.

The two French corps were deployed on the outskirts of their capital – facing an overwhelming force. However, instead of a burst of frantic defensive activities, they remained idle all afternoon in their bivouacs.[64]

64 Koch, Vol. II, pp. 399-413.

19

The Battle and Occupation of Paris, 30 March 1814

The topography around Paris in 1814

Paris sits in an open plain through which the Seine and Marne rivers meander and join. Paris was one of, if not the largest, city in continental Europe in 1814. It was surely the cultural center of Europe and probably the second-most significant financial center. In March 1814, however, it was also to become a battlefield and the site of the last battle of the 1814 campaign. Today, the battlefield is entirely under pavement and has vanished. The multitude of little villages that once surrounded the city – and were the center of fierce fighting – are little more than stops on the subway filled with sidewalk cafés, tourists and Parisians scurrying about their daily lives in the middle of a massive city. No markers or monuments are to be found of the battle fought on 30 March 1814.

The battle was fought on the north side of Paris. The principal battlefield lay between Saint-Denis and Paris at the mouth of an ox-bow in the Seine. North of Saint-Denis was a chain of hills running east-west, which dominated Claye, Anet and Lagny. Another chain of hills and plateaus ran towards Auteuil and were broken by the Seine at Saint-Denis as it flowed past Lagny and Saint-Cloud. This chain of hills grew smaller in size as it neared the village of Rosny and formed a ridge between the Bondy plain and the Marne Valley below Nogent.

Between Saint-Denis and Paris was an open plain. The first feature of note was a series of entrenchments – just north of La Chapelle – that were left over from the panics of 1792. Immediately south of these trenches was a major ridge (the Montmartre ridge) – now the site of a gleaming white stone church – which ran more or less east and west for a distance of 1,400 yards (1,300 meters). The Montmartre ridge stands at the mouth of the ox-bow of the Seine River to the east of Paris. At a distance of about 1,000 yards (one kilometer) to the east – southeast of Montmartre – stood the village of Batignolles, which was atop a rather sharp hill. To the south, beyond this point, stood the edge of the city of Paris.

Inside the ox-bow – to the west of the Batignolles hill – there was a string of low and unremarkable hills as they closed the external boulevards of Paris near Neuilly, where their crest again rose and remained elevated until they reached Passy – divided by the streams running into the Bois-de-Boulogne (a large forest) and across the Clichy plain – joining those that ran through the Roule and Champs-Elysées suburbs. The hills of Passy and Auteuil ended in the Bois-de-Boulogne and in the Point-du-Jour plain. Much of the ox-bow was filled by the Bois-de-Boulogne, which was a large wooded park. Though not thick woods, the Bois-de-Boulogne effectively prohibited any military movement beyond that point.

To the east of La Chapelle was the village of La Villette. Just to the east of La Villette was the Seine-Ourcq Canal. A second canal ran from Saint-Denis to the Seine-Ourcq Canal and joined that canal just to the east of La Villette. The Seine- Ourcq Canal came from the north-east – running in a straight line across the battlefield until it was within about three miles of La Villette – when it turned due west for a distance of about a mile, then began a broad, sweeping turn until it was running southeast through the eastern suburbs of Paris. It then turned south and linked up with the Seine just beyond the three islands in the Seine that formed the oldest portion of the city of Paris. The canal made this great sweeping turn in order to go around a large plateau.

On this plateau were a number of villages that would play a major part in the battle. The westernmost was Belleville. To the east were Bagnolet and Malassise – and the largest of them, Montreuil. On the easternmost finger of the plateau stood the village of Fontenav. Continuing to the east – at the foot of the plateau – was the village of Nogent-sur-Marne. Romainville stood on the northern edge of the plateau, with Noisy-le-Sec just to the north of it at the bottom of the plateau. To the northeast of Noisy-le-Sec and on the southern bank of the Seine-Ourcq Canal stood the village of Bondy.

To the south of the plateau stood the village of Vincennes and the large Bois-de-Vincennes, which pressed up to the northern bank of the Marne, where it joined the Seine and extended to Nogent-sur-Marne. Situated in the village of Vincennes is the Château Vincennes, with its white stone walls and palace. Once the palace of kings, it would become the headquarters of the French army in the First World War – and in the Second World War was used as a headquarters by the Germans. Spared from Hitler's orders that it be blown up, this fortress still exists today and is the home of the French army archives – housing the records of the Grande Armée and the day in 1814 when it was captured by the Allies.

Situation in Paris

The Regency Council had begun to take measures to respond to the approaching danger from the east. The Empress and King of Rome had departed for Tours. The members of the council, the various grand dignitaries and the ministers began preparing as well. King Joseph, Clarke (the Minister of War) and the Minister Director remained in Paris, but the government was transferred to the Loire. Paris was an important city, but what made it most important to Napoleon was the fact that it was the seat of the Imperial government.

The King of Spain, Joseph Napoleon, was serving as the Lieutenant-Général to Napoleon in the 1st Military Division. As such, he was responsible for the defense of Paris and had the authority to make use of all resources available in and around the city to effect its defense.

There were three different forces available to Joseph. First was the National Guard under Maréchal Moncey, Duc de Conegliano; then there were the line troops under Hulin and Ornano; and the Guard Reserves. Unfortunately for Napoleon, Joseph was not a soldier or administrator cut from the same bolt of cloth as his brother. As a result, the military organization assigned to the defense of Paris suffered under an incoherent organization and administration.

In January, Napoleon had rejected a plan submitted by the Defense Council for the construction of a comprehensive earthwork defense around the city. As a result, the city was covered solely by minor wooden works capable of repulsing a *coup de main* by cavalry, but nothing more. However, with the approach of Schwarzenberg, this plan was resuscitated and its implementation begun. Crenelated wooden works were erected to protect sentinels. The gaps in the city's walls were filled with masonry or strong palisades and a communications road was erected that ran around the city inside the city's wall.

The artillery assigned to the defense of the walls consisted of 40 4pdrs and 20 8pdrs. A further 12 4pdrs and four 8pdrs served as a reserve on each of the banks of the Seine.

A total of 56 barricades or gates were organized and categorized. The first-class barricades – on the left bank of the Seine – were those of Fontainebleau, Orléans and Maine. On the right bank of the Seine they were Passy, Neuilly, Roule, Clichy, Saint-Denis, Pantin and Trône-de-Charenton, where the highways met. Because of their commercial importance, these routes were kept open day and night, which required that they be garrisoned. The minor barricades or gates were those that could be closed with no grave inconvenience. These served only the local secondary roads.

The French concentrated their artillery at the first-class barricades. One of the reserves was placed at Trône, from where it could move to the Charenton, Pantin and Villette barricades to face an enemy arriving along the roads from Melun, Lagny or Meaux, or Soissons. The other was placed at the Fontainebleau barricade so as to be able to respond to an Allied advance along the left bank of the Seine. From there, it could move to the Orléans or Maine barricades – as well as communicate with the right bank artillery reserve via the Pont-d'Austerlitz (one of the main bridges over the Seine in Paris).

Crenelated wooden defensive posts to protect the sentinels were raised at the bridges at Saint-Maur, Charenton and Neuilly, but the Paris heights and its exterior suburbs remained without defense until Blücher's second march on Paris convinced Joseph that the city required such works.

The earlier plan rejected by Napoleon was given to Count Déjean and orders were sent that it be executed. Déjean gathered up the few engineering officers available and began surveying the terrain for the preparation of defenses. A Fortification Council was organized to oversee and coordinate the fortification effort. King Joseph, however, felt uncomfortable executing its plans and sent them to Napoleon for review.

By 22 March Napoleon's response to these proposals had still not arrived in Paris – and it became apparent that Paris would soon be visited by part or all of the Armies of the North or Silesia. The time had come to act. Chevalier Allent, Count Maurice Mathieu and all of the other soldiers available to King Joseph advised that he act immediately, but the fear Napoleon instilled in Joseph caused him to be as conservative as possible in his actions and progress was delayed. As a result, the proposed guard posts were barely finished on the morning of 29 March. As a result, Paris lacked any significant fortifications when the Allies arrived at its gates.[1]

The National Guard

The Paris National Guard was raised by the Decree of 3 January and consisted of 12 legions. Each legion had four battalions of five companies – including one grenadier and four chasseur companies. This was a total of 48 battalions and 240 companies of infantry. The legions corresponded to the 12 municipal arrondissements of the city of Paris. As much as possible, the battalions corresponded to the 48 quarters of the city. Each company was to have 125 men – giving the battalions a total strength of 625 men – and each legion a strength of 2,500 men. The entire force was to have 30,000 men.[2]

Subsequent decrees formed an artillery corps, an engineering corps and a company of guides à cheval. The artillery was organized into two battalions using the 300 students of the École Polytechnique and about 480 gunners drawn from the Veterans' Home. They were to serve the batteries and reserves assigned to the defense of the various barricades. The bridging and road engineers were organized into the engineering corps and charged with the construction of the defensive wooden works of the city. The company of guides was to rise to a strength of three squadrons and, being so small, was never employed.

The Decree of 15 March placed the Paris National Guard under the command of Maréchal Moncey, Duc de Conegliano, but only the guards of Belleville, Bercy, Saint-Denis and the students of the Alfort School actually existed. All of the rest of the rural guards existed only on paper.

1 Koch, Vol. II, pp. 426-30.
2 de Vaudoncourt, Vol. II, p. 310.

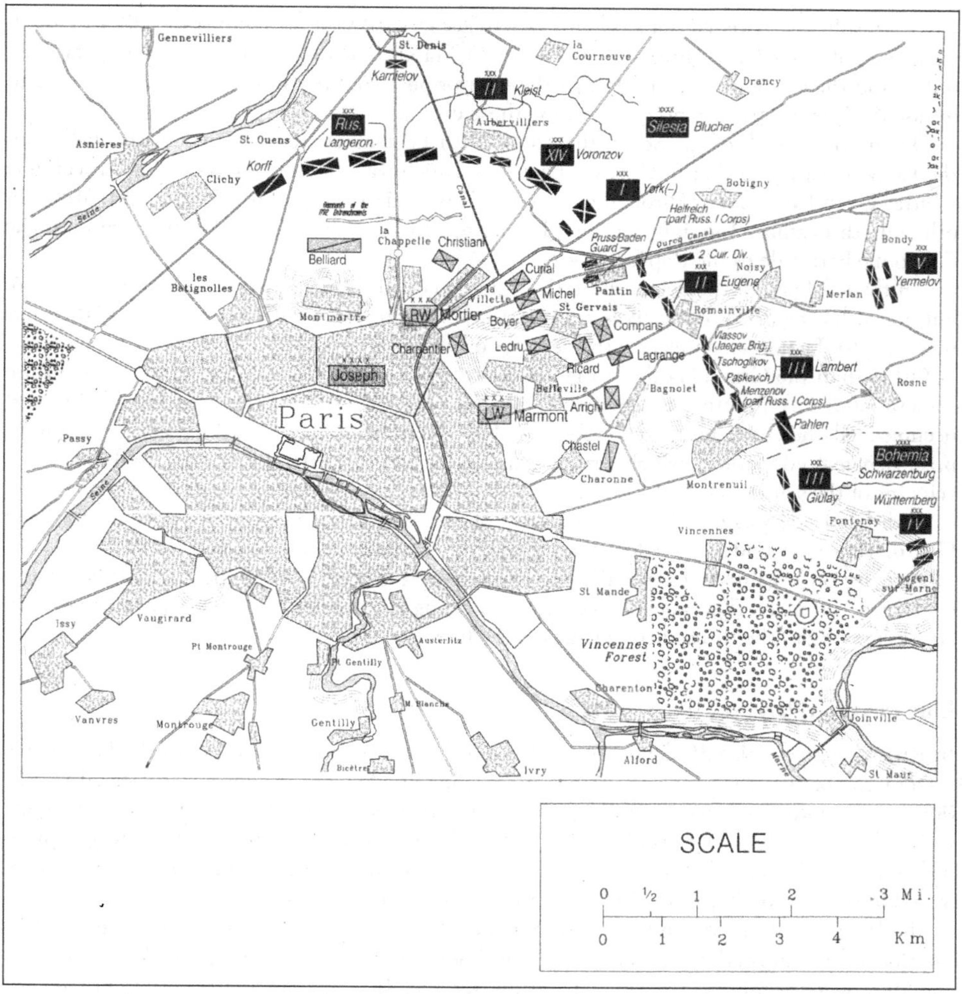

Map 20 Assault on Paris, March 30 1814.

Under the guidance of Maréchal Moncey, the Paris National Guard began to take on some consistency during the first days of March, but this progress was constantly blocked by an endless string of nearly insurmountable obstacles. The grenadiers were only partly-equipped. The arsenals had been stripped of equipment, muskets and munitions – so those who were armed had carbines or other miscellaneous weapons gathered on the various battlefields of the past 20 years. In order to equip the Paris National Guard with some sort of weapon, pikes were ordered fashioned – but they were coolly received. The worst firearm was to be preferred to a pointy stick! The first serious distribution of firearms occurred on 27 March when Ornano released 2,000 muskets from the Imperial Guard under the express condition that they be returned the next day. A further 4,000 muskets were distributed on 29 and 30 March.

As a result, the Paris National Guard never exceeded 12,000 men and only 6,000 to 7,000 were actually armed with firearms. It was on 23 March that they were first given operational orders and they were directed to occupy the interior posts and barricades of the city in order to release the line troops currently performing those duties.

On the right bank of the Seine, the 1st and 4th Legions guarded the left of the wall from the Passy barricade to that in Clichy. The center, which was the most extended and susceptible to attack, ran from Clichy through Charonne. This section was guarded by the 2nd, 3rd, 5th, 6th and 7th Legions. The right was guarded by the 8th and 9th Legions and stretched from the Charonne barricade to the Rapée barricade.

On the left bank of the Seine, the 11th Legion guarded the center – running from Bièvre to, but not including, the Fourneaux barricade. To their right was the 10th Legion and to their left was the 12th Legion – completing the defenses of the south of the city.

Other than the Grand'Garde de l'Hötel-de-Ville (City Hall Guard), the Honor Posts in the Tuileries and Luxemburg – those of the police in each mayorship – the Paris National Guard occupied all the small posts and public establishments with the exceptions of the hospitals, prisons, gates and markets, which remained under the control of the gendarmerie and the retired veterans of the army.

Each barricade was garrisoned by a picket of 50 grenadiers or chasseurs from the National Guard. They were under the orders of a superior officer designated by the governor.

Each legion organized 12 grand'gardes, which were placed around the city's defenses and contained 100 men. They were charged with manning the smaller barricades and, in case of an attack, moving to the threatened portions of the line.

Line forces in Paris

In Paris there were also 30 depots of the various infantry regiments serving in the field, a few veteran companies, the Paris Gendarmerie and the Paris Sapeurs-Pompiers (firemen). In addition, within two days' march of the city were the depots of a further 60 infantry regiments, which as of 25 March contained about 20,000 men. These various depots had a very, very high percentage of NCOs and officers and Napoleon directed the formation of companies from these men. However, as of 29 March this order was yet to be implemented.

The Paris Gendarmerie and the Paris Sapeurs-Pompiers, however, were more important to the city in their normal duties than they would be if they were thrown into the line as soldiers and they were exempted from any frontline service. In addition, the government did not have at its disposition appropriate troops to replace those guarding the prisons and hospitals. Despite these difficulties, enough men were scraped out of the system to put garrisons in Saint-Denis and Vincennes and to send detachments to the bridges at Saint-Maur, Charenton and Neuilly.

The remount depot in Versailles contained only about 1,000 mounted men in any condition to enter the line. They were organized into a marche regiment under Colonel Carignan, which was used to escort the Empress to Rambouillet on 30 March.[3]

The Imperial Guard reserve in Paris

Paris also contained the cadres of 22 battalions of Young Guard in late 1813. The formation of Charpentier and Boyer de Rebeval's divisions had drawn heavily on these men, but as the battalions in the field suffered losses, the cadres returned to Paris to gather in more men. As of

3 Koch, Vol. II, pp. 431-6.

28 March these depots contained 3,600 infantry, 1,500 cavalry and 150 artillery or train soldiers. These troops were available for immediate use – and when the Allies were approaching Meaux, a force of 1,500 infantry and 700 cavalry was drawn from this force, were placed under General Guye and sent to Compans' division. On 29 March a further 1,500 infantry and 300 cavalry formed the escort of the Empress and the King of Rome. As a result, when the Allies appeared before Paris, this force of Young Guard had been so reduced that only 600 infantry and 300 cavalry remained. Out of desperation, 4,000 raw conscripts were thrown together with these men and organized into a division that was placed under the command of GD Michel, who was still recovering from his wounds.

Departure of the regency for Blois

Preparations for the departure of the Empress and the King of Rome were made in secret – as was their departure. They left under heavy escort during the night of 29 March and headed for Blois. At the break of day on 29 March word of the threat to Paris was released. The archives and other government documents were evacuated. The various ministries began burning documents to prevent their capture. For the most part, the public officials remained in Paris and continued to perform their duties, but they had been sending their wives and children out of the city for some time. In their place, Paris had become crowded with French citizens fleeing from the territories occupied by the advancing Allies. As a result, the city was clogged with their carts and wagons; their animals; and their possessions. This collection of material clogged the streets and obstructed the barricades.

King Joseph caused the city to be posted with a proclamation stating that Napoleon had beaten Winzingerode on 26 March at St.-Dizier and had captured 2,000 prisoners and taken his artillery. This caused the citizens of Paris to conclude that Napoleon would arrive before the city at the same time as the Allies. This was wishful thinking, as Napoleon considered the defense of Paris a secondary objective to striking at the Allies' rear.

Defensive preparations

The three military commanders in Paris were ordered to redouble their efforts to prepare their troops for battle. Maréchal Moncey issued a proclamation calling up the National Guard. He advised them that two thirds would be assigned to the line army and that one third would be retained in Paris to occupy key positions. The nine legions defending the right bank of the Seine were organized into grand'gardes and reserves were formed that were destined to support the various posts around the city.

As the Allies were coming from the right bank of the Seine, the three legions on the left bank were stripped to a minimum and a strong reserve was organized that would move to threatened points or deal with civil unrest. Each of the barricades was given over to the command of a chef de bataillon and the main roads of the city were cleared of obstructions to permit the rapid movement of reinforcements.

Military govenor Hulin agreed with these dispositions and deployed his limited forces to best support this. Count Ornano, however, took those measures necessary to put his force into the line and serve with General Compans. He then departed from Paris, moved with part of his cavalry to Pantin and took up positions there.

At around noon, King Joseph began a mounted tour of the city's defenses accompanied by General Maurice Mathieu – his chief of staff – and the chief of staff of the Paris National Guard. He paid special attention to those possible routes of advance of the Allies and the heights that dominated them.

Chevalier Allent commented to Joseph that an Allied column could pass through Villeparisis and seize the point where the small bridges joined the Allemagne bridge by moving over the Ourcq Canal at Mitry. As a result, Joseph moved to Pantin and the heights that formed or ran to the left of the Romainville position. He directed that Ornano post his cavalry at the Folie mill and observe the plain from Noisy-le-Sec to Bondy. He then moved to Rosny – where the Allied troops would appear on the roads from Montfermeil and Lagny – and examined the lay of the land on that front.

Despite having reviewed the terrain, Joseph's understanding of it was incomplete and his only objective was to determine the best distribution of those forces available to him for the defense of Paris. His review of the land complete, Joseph returned to the Tuileries and entered into conference with the three marshals. He then dictated the dispositions of his troops.[4]

French deployment before Paris

On the morning of 30 March Marmont was to occupy positions at Romainville and Compans and Ornano were to defend Pré-Saint-Gervais and Pantin – as well as the area between the heights and the Seine-Ourcq Canal. The Seine-Ourcq Canal was a substantial obstacle – crossable only at the various bridges. It had a depth of from five to six feet and a width of 15 paces. The bridge at Pantin was of iron, while the bridge at La Villette was wooden.[5]

Mortier's corps was ordered to take up positions between the canal and Montmartre and to occupy the lengths of the suburbs of Villette and Chapelle. King Joseph was to establish his headquarters on Montmartre, where Count Hulin was also to place his command post. The remainder of the troops defending Paris were to take up positions in the interior of city – guarding the barricades and defending the city's walls.

The two artillery reserves – as well as 28 useless guns on the left bank of the Seine – were limbered up and positioned by the Trône barricade. Major Evain, of the line artillery, was given command of this force. The guns were served by Imperial Guard Veteran Cannoneers, who were to lay the guns.

No further adjustments to these positions were judged necessary by Joseph in the placement of the National Guards – as had been effected by Maréchal Moncey that morning. The National Guard was directed to take up their arms as soon as they heard the alarm.

There were serious concerns for the administration about the effectiveness of this National Guard force. Though they numbered about 12,000, they were not expected to perform anything more than hold the walls and other fixed defenses – and their ability to do even that was doubtful.

And with this, the defenses of Paris were set. Mortier, Marmont, Ornano and Compans formed the first line of defense extending from Montmartre to Charonne. The defense of the city's walls stood under General Hulin, who served as governor of Paris and commanded 12,000 doubtful and unenthusiastic National Guardsmen. The opposing forces at Paris – on 30 March – numbered as follows:

4 Koch, Vol. II, pp. 437-42.
5 Freiherr von Lüdingshausen, p. 43.

French	Infantry	Cavalry[6]
Right wing: Maréchal Marmont		
Bordesoulle (Thierry & Laville)		895
Chastel (Vincent)		1,600
Merlin (Huber & Latour-Foissac)		850
Arrighi (Lucotte)	1,250	
Ricard (Pelleport & Clavel)	726	
Lagrange (Fournier & Joubert)	1,395	
Compans (Chabert)	2,220	
Ledru (Bongars)	1,600	
Boyer de Rebeval (Guye)	1,850	
Left wing: Maréchal Mortier		
Michel (Sécrétan & Robert)	4,000	
Charpentier (Lagrange & Le Capitaine)	1,500	
Curial (Bigarré)	1,820	
Christiani (Gros)	1,630	
Ornano (Dautancourt)		320
Roussel (Rigaud & Sparre)		1,900
Garrisons:		
Saint-Denis	570	
Vincennes	400	
Neuilly	250	
Charenton	450	
Maur	300	
Total:	19,961	5,565

Allies		
Right column: Feldmarschal Blücher		
Yorck	12,000	3,500
Kleist	11,000	3,000
Langeron	14,000	5,000
Voronzov	15,000	
Center column: Barclay de Tolly		
Raevsky	16,000	3,000
Reserve grenadiers & cuirassiers	6,000	3,000
Guard	15,000	4,000
Left column: Crown Prince of Württemberg		
von Württemberg's corps	10,000	2,000
Giulay's corps	15,000	3,000
Austrian Grenadiers	5,000	
Total:	119,000	26,500

6 The names in parentheses are the names of the brigadier generals. The names of the divisional generals are to the left and the wing commanders are identified as such. Sporschil, Vol. II, 2nd Band, pp. 338-9; de Vaudoncourt, Vol. II, p. 313.

The Allies' plans

On 29 March the Allies stood on the plain before Paris. The Tsar of Russia, the King of Prussia, Schwarzenberg, Blücher, Barclay de Tolly and the Minister Count von Nesselrode met in Bondy to develop their plans for capturing Paris.

It was decided that the attack would occur on the morning of 30 March. Time was not taken to realign the Allied armies' positions or to determine the French dispositions. Word had arrived that Napoleon had begun his march from St.-Dizier to the Marne on 26 March and that the various corps detached to the Yonne and the Loing had been ordered to march to the defense of Paris. Waiting a second day would give Napoleon and his forces time to arrive. The capture of Paris was necessary – before Napoleon and these forces arrived – to bring about the collapse of the Imperial government.

The time of the attack being established, the target was established as the occupation of the heights of Belleville and Montmartre. The control of the attack on Mont-Montmartre was to be given to Feldmarschal Blücher and his army, which was moving through Le Bourget with the goal of either masking or occupying Saint-Denis. The remainder of his dispositions were left to his discretion.

Barclay de Tolly was to move down the Allemagne road with the 6th Corps and the Allied reserves. He was charged with attacking the Belleville heights. The Guard and Russian and Prussian reserves were ordered to guard Pantin, to act along the Allemagne road and to support the principal attacks as necessary. Raevsky – who was at the center of the main Allied army with his corps, the Guard and the reserve – was directed to threaten the village of Pré-Saint-Gervais, to attack the Belleville and Romainville heights, to occupy Montreuil and Bagnolet and to move Pahlen's cavalry corps to the foot of the Vincennes heights to observe that position (as well as to provide a link to the Crown Prince of Württemberg).[7]

Wrede and Sacken's corps were to cover the engagement by Meaux and Trilport and prevent any intervention by Napoleon and his army should he appear on the battlefield.

The corps of the Crown Prince of Württemberg – supported by Giulay's corps – was ordered to march via Lagny to the Rosny heights and Neuilly-sur-Marne, to capture the bridges at Saint-Maur and Charenton, to clean the Bois-de-Vincennes of troops, to invest the Château Vincennes and to support the attacks against the Belleville heights. The principal function of these last corps – like those or Sacken and Wrede, which had been left in Meaux and Coulommiers – was to cover the Allies' decisive action on Paris and to prevent anymore French troops from intruding into their operations.[8]

The Allied plans to take the Montmartre and Belleville heights were based on the actions anticipated by the French when they prepared their plans for the defense of Paris in January. Though the plan of defense against this maneuver had been reinstated in March, its implementation was totally inadequate to defend against the anticipated thrust. To make matters worse, the Montmartre heights were not included in the French line of defense and were abandoned to the events of the day. The strength of the Allied army was, at this time, as follows:[9]

7 von Damitz, Vol. III, 2nd Part, p. 270.
8 von Damitz, Vol. III, 2nd Part, p. 271.
9 von Damitz, Vol. III, 2nd Part, pp. 275-6.

Main army		
Giulay's Austrian corps	10,000	
4th Corps (Württemberg)	15,000	including von Nostitz's Reserve
5th Corps (Wrede)	20,000	
6th Corps (Raevsky)	12,000	
Russian, Prussian & Baden Guard	16,000	
Total:	73,000	
Army of Silesia		
Sacken's corps	10,000	
Langeron's corps	17,000	
Yorck's corps	10,000	
2nd Prussian Corps (Kleist)	8,000	
Russian corps (Voronzov & Stroganov)	12,000	
Total:	57,000	

The Battle of Paris

Before daybreak, drums called the Paris National Guard to arms. The garrison troops formed in their barracks and the various corps drew themselves into formation from their bivouacs. Mortier, Marmont and the various French generals left their quarters in Paris and joined their forces in the field.

At daybreak, King Joseph left the Palais du Luxemburg with his chief of staff and staff – moving to a pavilion situated on Montmartre on the road to Clignancourt where it crossed the Cinq-Moulins knoll. Count Hulin, after moving weak detachments of guard and Paris police into the heights, moved to Joseph's headquarters with the directors of the artillery and engineers. The Minister of War, the Minister Director and the First Inspector General of Engineers – plus a growing mass of general officers, senior officers and others – moved to Joseph's headquarters on Montmartre requesting orders.

Joseph's pavilion was placed so as to permit a clear view of the plain extending towards Saint-Denis, but did not permit a view of the Seine-Ourcq Canal – nor the Romainville heights. In conformance with his orders of the previous day, the chief of staff of the Parisian National Guard moved to the heights to observe the forces, the positions and the movements of the Allied forces.

Maréchal Moncey – who was to command the National Guard – held an inspection of his troops, reinforced the barricades, inspired the troops as best as could be done, sent detachments to the various high-points and sent skirmishers to the line.

The French deployed their forces as follows: On the extreme right stood Marmont's cavalry in line between Charonne and Montreuil. In the first line was Chastel's division and Bordesoulle's I Cavalry Corps. Arrighi formed his forces on the Malassise plateau – covering Bagnolet – and put troops in Montreuil to cover his right. Lagrange's division stood before the Bruyères park – straddling the road from Belleville to Romainville. Chastel's division consisted of the cavalry commanded by General Vincent. However, Vincent had passed command to Chastel at 7:00 a.m. that morning because of wounds.

Ricard's division stood in reserve, in mass, in the interior and on the left of the Bruyères park – straddling the road from Belleville to Romainville and covered by the army corps artillery, which stood on the Tourelles knoll in the middle of the old Saint-Fargeau park.

Ledru's division stood on the heights of Pré-Saint-Gervais – having before it Compans' division deployed in skirmish formation in the Romainville forest. Boyer's division stood behind Pantin to the right of the road. Boyer de Rebeval had apparently taken command of this division at 6:00 a.m. that morning. This division contained the 1/,2/,3/11th Voltigeur Regiment – plus a collection of flanqueuers, grenadiers and tirailleurs swept out of the various depots and hastily

Episode of the Battle of Paris, by Vernet. Moncey is shown center.

organized into two further battalions. It had a total of about 2,000 men organized into a single brigade under GB Guye.[10] Michel's division was deployed with Sécrétan's brigade behind Pantin and Robert's brigade in Aubervilliers. Michel's division contained 4,000 infantry drawn from the Guard Infantry depots – including about 1,000 which had arrived the previous day from the Western Departments and had been armed that morning. As a result, it should not be considered an elite formation.[11]

Charpentier's division stood massed at the foot of the Chaumont heights. Curial's division was behind Pantin in reserve supporting Michel's division. Christiani's division stood in mass between Chapelle and Villette. Belliard's cavalry stood before the 1792 entrenchments between Chapelle and Saint-Ouen. Belliard's cavalry had apparently been reinforced immediately before the battle with a force of 300 men drawn from the Guard depots.[12] Roussel's dragoon division was to the right and Ornano's division was to the left.

Nine position batteries covered the front of the army and the principal avenues. Four guns were on the Fontarabie heights – covering the road from Montreuil. A battery of six guns was on Mont-Louis – covering the flank of the Charonne-Ménilmontant road. Another battery – stood to the left of the Bruyères park – and a second on the Beauregard heights covered the roads of Pré-Saint-Gervais. A battery of 12 12pdrs stood before Pré-Saint-Gervais – defending the gap between Pantin and Romainville. A battery of four guns was established on the Chaumont heights. A 12-gun 12pdr battery was placed in Rouvroy, which covered the Aubervilliers plain and the road from Petits-Ponts. The head of Chapelle was defended by a five-gun battery on Montmartre by the Lancette mill – and the last battery, with two guns, stood at the base of the

10 Sporschil, Vol. II, 2nd Band, p. 345.
11 Sporschil, Vol. II, 2nd Band, p. 344.
12 Sporschil, Vol. II, 2nd Band, p. 347.

Montmartre hill covering the avenues from Clichy and Saint-Ouen. A total of 53 guns were deployed – including 24 12pdrs.[13]

The day started with a positive note for the French, as the Army of Silesia had neglected to occupy Aubervilliers, which was necessary for it to launch its ordered attack on Montmartre, Chapelle and Villette. Its advanced guard was in Grand-Dracy. Langeron, Kleist, Yorck and Voronzov's corps stood between Le Bourget, Aulnay and Villepinte. They were spread over such a great distance that it made the issuance of orders unnecessarily protracted.

On the Allied extreme right stood the corps of the Crown Prince of Württemberg and Count Giulay. They were obliged to march along the Marne and could not arrive in position before the middle of the day. Their goal of taking the Saint-Maur and Charenton bridges would be delayed as well.

The remainder of the army was under the immediate orders of Barclay de Tolly and stood between Livry, Romainville and Pantin. The 6th Corps, under Raevsky, stood in the villages between Romainville and Bondy. It was the only force ready for immediate action, but it did not receive orders to do so.

At about 6:00 a.m. the sun crept over the horizon – announcing the arrival of the fateful day. The still of the morning was broken by the first cannon shot that would become the Battle of Paris.

At 7:00 a.m. Prince Eugene von Württemberg received orders from Raevsky to advance against Pantin. He was to be supported by the two cuirassier divisions under General Kretov. Barclay de Tolly directed part of the Allied Guards and reserves to advance to support this attack.[14] Eugene's 3rd Division, under Schachovsky, moved left of the plateau and marched on Romainville. The 4th Division, under Puschnizky, stood by the Romainville woods. Puschnizky advanced with Helfreich's 14th Division in support and Menzenov's 5th Division supporting it. These reserves were, apparently, the Russian 1st Corps under Gorchakov.

Boyer de Rebeval's Young Guard Division formed before Pantin – facing it as the two Russian divisions passed through the village. Boyer was too weak to withstand the shock of their attack and withdrew to the right of GD Michel's division, which stood on the main road to Allemagne. The two combined divisions began a cannonade at about 7:00 a.m. and their fire stopped the Russian advance. At the same moment, Compans deployed Ledru's division on the heights of Pré-Saint-Gervais and pushed it into the Romainville woods. Marmont arrived with the VI Corps in the Bagnolet Valley. Lagrange's division, which was at the head of the column, deployed on the Romainville plateau when it encountered Menzenov's 5th Division – covered by its skirmishers. Schachovsky's 3rd Division, also covered by its skirmishers, marched towards the Romainville woods. Lagrange's division deployed with Fournier's brigade on the right and Joubert's brigade on the left of the Belleville road. Joubert joined up with Ledru's division. Ricard's division placed itself in reserve by the Bruyèrès park, with its back against the Deux-Tourelles heights and the corps artillery. Arrighi's division established itself on the Malassise plateau before Bagnolet. Vincent's cavalry – now commanded by Chastel – moved to Villette and took a post to the right of the first line of General Bordesoulle. Menzenov did not succeed in taking Bagnolet, but Marmont was cut off from Compans.

Marmont sent the Colonel of Engineers Paris to a high position in the rear of the lines – on which stood a telegraph – so that he could observe the Allied movements. At the same time, Marmont and Compans decided to go to the offensive so as to drive the Russians out of the Romainville woods and to position their forces closer to Romainville.

13 de Vaudoncourt, Vol. II, pp. 327-8.
14 Sporschil, Vol. II, 2nd Band, p. 344.

Compans defending Pantin, by Schommer.

Marmont, however, did not want to disengage his front as he sought to go over to the offensive. In order to do this, he had to occupy Romainville and Pantin. Compans attacked the Russians in the Romainville woods, Lagrange moved against the Russians frontally and Boyer de Rebeval pushed his skirmishers over the back of the slope towards Pantin. Menzenov's column was caught in march column and thrown back to the bottom of the slope by the Romainville park. Compans' division cleaned Schachovsky's division out of the woods – forcing them to the backside of the hill.

Boyer de Rebeval's skirmishers pushed into the first buildings of Pantin – obliging Eugene von Württemberg to deploy behind the village.

The Young Guard skirmishers pushed forward into Pantin. Here, they appear to have engaged Roth's 25th and 26th Jager Regiments in a lively skirmish fight.[15] General Stall led Kretov's two cuirassier regiments against the French Guard tirailleurs. Stall's cuirassiers caused the skirmishers to withdraw, but the terrain was not good for cavalry and they were swept with canister and withdrew behind Pantin.

The battle continued around the two villages with a marked advantage to the French. During this engagement, Mortier – with the divisions of Christiani, Curial, Charpentier and Belliard's cavalry – moved behind the VI Corps and occupied their earlier positions. Langeron was, at this moment, moving through Le Bourget – and his advanced guard attacked Robert's brigade in Aubervilliers.

At about 9:00 a.m. Barclay saw that Raevsky was about to be pushed out of Pantin and Romainville and decided to send in part of his reserves, which were arriving from Bondy. Paskevich's 2nd Grenadier Division was directed against Romainville to support Menzenov's 5th Division. Tschoglikov's 1st Grenadier Division was dispatched to the Romainville woods to support Schachovsky. Kniaschnin's brigade was detached from the 1st Grenadier Division to

15 Sporschil, Vol. II, 2nd Band, p. 344.

support Schachovsky's forces before Romainville and then advanced with the remainder of his division to the right of the woods.

In the plain marched the Prussian Guard and Baden Guard infantry – under von Alvensleben – to a position where they could support the Russian troops in Pantin. The Prussian Foot Guard was to advance to Pantin and support the 4th (Puschnizky) and the 14th (Helfreich) Divisions.[16] The Prussian and Baden troops marched in the following order: Fus/1st Guard Regiment, 1/2nd Guard Regiment, Baden Leib-Garde-Grenadier Battalion, 2/2nd Guard Regiment, 1/1st Guard Regiment, 2/1st Guard Regiment, Guard Jäger Battalion, Guard 6pdr Foot Battery, and Fus/2nd Guard Regiment.[17]

Raevsky, however, did not think it possible to push out of Pantin against the barricades because of the guns on the heights – which dominated the road – so he resolved to march against the guns. Menzenov's 5th Division – supported by GM Kniaschnin with two grenadier battalions – was directed against the village and woods of Romainville. They then pushed towards Montreuil – threatening to turn Marmont's right. They were supported by Pahlen's cavalry, which deployed before the Malassise plateau – occupying Montreuil, which was defended by Arrighi.

GM Tschoglikov led the four other grenadier battalions – supporting the renewed attack of Schachovsky's 3rd Division – on the woods. Puschnizky's 4th Division was directed to advance between Pré-Saint-Gervais and the Romainville woods. Ljalin's brigade of Helfreich's 14th Division was recalled from Romainville, where it joined Roth's brigade – reuniting the division. Here, it was soon reinforced by the arrival of the Prussian Foot Guard.[18]

At the same time, GM Kniaschnin advanced to support the Allied center with a brigade of the 1st Russian Grenadier Division. GM Tschoglikov, with the other brigade of that division, marched to the right against the Bois de Romainville (Romainville woods).

The French troops on the heights behind Romainville, under Marmont, were attacked on the left front by the divisions of Tschoglikov and Kniaschnin – supported by all of Pahlen's cavalry – and were pushed from Montreuil. Pahlen pushed reconnaissance forces towards Vincennes in an effort to contact the Crown Prince of Württemberg and moved against the du Trône barricade to contain Bordesoulle's cavalry. He also prepared to push Arrighi from the Malassise plateau into the Bagnolet Valley – encountering a large number of National Guardsmen deployed in skirmish formation. Pahlen also detached GM Illowaiski XII with a force of three Cossack regiments to Villeneuve-le-Comte to observe the region between the Seine and the Marne.

While this was occurring, GD Compans stood on the heights of Pré-Saint-Gervais and pushed Ledru des Essart's division into the Romainville forest. General Vincent was recalled by Marmont and sent from Chapelle to Belleville with his cavalry.

Prince Eugene von Württemberg was sent with the remainder of Puschnizky's badly shot-up 4th Division to seize a woods that were occupied by the troops of GB Chabert (General Compans' division) – striking Marmont's left flank. Württemberg ordered Schachovsky's 3rd Division – which stood behind Puschnizky's 4th Division and had been reinforced by Vlassov's jager brigade, Menzenov's 5th Division – to advance with the 1st Grenadier Division (Tschoglikov) against the Bruyères park and the village of Pré-Saint-Gervais. The 2nd Russian Curiassier Division (Kretov) was placed in reserve behind them.[19] The Volhynie Regiment and the two jager regiments were detached. What remained was the Tobolsk, Krementsoug and Minsk Infantry Regiments.

16 Sporschil, Vol. II, 2nd Band, pp. 349-50.
17 Freiherr von Lüdingshausen, p. 42.
18 de Vaudoncourt, Vol. II, pp. 332-4.
19 Sporschil, Vol. II, 2nd Band, pp. 350-1.

Prince von Württemberg rallied Puschnizky's 4th Division behind Schachovsky's division at the base of the Romainville heights. He then dispatched it against the village of Pré-Saint-Gervais, which formed Boyer de Rebeval's extreme right and was defended by only two battalions. Helfreich's 14th Division also attacked from Pantin against Maisonettes. Stephanov's jager brigade stood on a ridge to the Russian right and advanced to strike the French left. Prince Eugene von Württemberg's goal was to isolate Compans from Boyer de Rebeval's division – as well as splitting the army of Mortier from that of Marmont.

Marmont pushed his troops up the plateau on the Bagnolet side. They were on the crest of a valley when they saw the second column of Raevsky's corps, under Gorchakov, advancing out of the mouths of the ravines that descend on Pantin and Romainville. The Russians sent four regiments – under Menzenov – against Bagnolet, while General Vlassov led his jager brigade – supported by Schachovsky's 3rd Division – against the Bruyères park. Count Pahlen, who led the united cavalry of the 6th Corps, was on the left wing and marched against Montreuil. The only cavalry supporting Prince Eugene was Kretov's Russian Cuirassier Division, which also moved against Pantin, but was held back as a reserve.[20] The Russian attack pushed the French defenders out of Pantin and the Romainville woods were occupied by the Russians, but only after a ferocious firefight that cost the Russians dearly.

At that moment, Fournier's brigade formed the head of the French column and to the right of the Belleville road, while Joubert's brigade formed behind him and to the left of the Belleville road. Joubert also extended to his left to come into contact with Ledru's troops.

During the first attacks, Mortier deployed his forces in the plain. Charpentier's division remained massed at the foot of the Chaumont knoll. Boyer de Rebeval's division was designated to support the attack against Pantin by Sécrétan's brigade. Christiani's division was to move to a position between Villette and Chapelle – ready to support Robert's brigade. On the extreme left, Belliard's cavalry – augmented by 300 cavalry of General Dautancourt – established itself between Chapelle and Saint-Ouen.

As the Russian attack developed, Marmont was threatened on both his front and flanks and began shifting his positions to counter those threats. He dispatched Fournier's brigade – some 600 men – to engage Kniaschnin's brigade (Russian 1st Grenadier Division). Fournier, however, quickly fell grievously wounded. However, instead of intimidating his brigade, it fired their ardor and morale – allowing them to check Kniaschnin's advance.

Ledru advanced to support Compans, who was under heavy pressure in the Romainville woods. Ledru's division marched forward and engaged Puschnizky's division as it arrived on the heights. Puschnizky's troops were thrown back in disorder on Pantin, and Ledru's division advanced behind them to assist Compans as he tried to stop Tschoglikov's grenadiers and Schachovsky's infantry before the Romainville woods. Schachovsky lightly occupied Romainville with his skirmishers – as well as the plain and ridge overlooking the village. He moved Vlassov's jager brigade to his left wing, where it supported Prince Eugene. The four remaining regiments of the 5th Division (Menzenov) were pushed forward by Gorchakov towards Bagnolet – and he extended towards Pahlen's light cavalry near Montreuil. Apparently, Vlassov's brigade was transferred to Eugene von Württemberg's command during the battle.[21]

Marmont detached Ledru's division to support Compans, who had withdrawn the 11th Voltigeur Regiment from Pré-Saint-Gervais to the plateau to support Chabert's brigade, which was heavily engaged in the Romainville woods by Puschnizky and Schachovsky's columns. Ledru's

20 von Damitz, Vol. III, 2nd Part, p. 287.
21 Sporschil, Vol. II, 2nd Band, p. 348.

division found its line of advance cut by Puschnizky's column – which it threw back to Pantin – and arrived in time to check the advance of Tschoglikov's column.

Marmont, upon hearing from Compans that he was too heavily engaged to dispatch any troops to support Boyer de Rebeval, dispatched Colonel Fabvier with 300 to 400 troops. This reinforcement arrived just as Stephanov's skirmishers began penetrating into the village. Colonel Stephanov – leading the 3rd Jager Regiment – and Colonel Russinov – leading the 4th Jagers – advanced in an attack that was met with heavy canister fire from Boyer de Rebeval's artillery, which included a battery of 12 12pdr guns. Both colonels were killed.

As Prince Eugene von Württemberg's attack proceeded, the French marched against Pantin and Romainville. Helfreich's 14th Division was deployed with Roth's brigade – the 25th and 26th Jager Regiments – in Pantin; and Ljalin's brigade – Tenguinsk and Estonia Musketeers – in Romainville. In the French attack, Roth was wounded. The Russians' attack was stopped and they were thrown back. Prince Eugene von Württemberg's attack was crushed and he forswore renewing his assault against the pugnacious French line.

Reinforcements for both sides streamed towards Pantin – leading to a stalemated situation until Barclay de Tolly decided to dispatch some of his guard and reserve troops to take the village. Barclay recognized that the possession of Pantin and Romainville would be the deciding factor of the day's battle, but none of the other forces, the Army of Silesia – or the corps of Giulay or the Crown Prince of Württemberg – were on the field to support this effort. Though the elite soldiers of the Allied Guard and reserves were seldom committed – and usually only in critical situations – to decide the battle, they were never committed to the fight so early as they were on this day. However, because each hour the French held out increased the possibility that Napoleon would appear with the rest of his army, it was absolutely necessary for Barclay de Tolly to act as he did.

The Allied Guard attacks Pantin

As the battle stood, all of the Allied attacks had been repulsed. On the right, Arrighi had not ceded any ground except for the village of Montreuil – and the possession of that village gave the Allies no advantage.

Because the Allied attacks had not succeeded, Barclay de Tolly came to the conclusion that it was best to hold his positions in Pantin, Romainville and Montreuil and await the arrival of the Army of Silesia. The Allied regiments had lost their cohesion and were effectively operating entirely in skirmish formation because of the terribly broken terrain. In order to give his troops time to reorganize, Barclay de Tolly sent Prince Eugene von Württemberg forward with the 3rd and 4th Divisions of Schachovsky and Puschnizky. Menzenov's 5th Division – supported by Pahlen's cavalry – marched against Romainville.[22]

Mortier had left Curial's division before the Pantin barricade to support Sécrétan's brigade, which was in Rouvroy, and he directed Charpentier's division to occupy Chapelle. Christiani's division remained between Chapelle and Villette. On his front, Mortier had only Robert's brigade engaged – and it was in Aubervilliers.

On the French left, GD Michel attacked Pantin with Sécrétan's brigade. Prince Eugene von Württemberg had withdrawn Puschnizky's division – and only four regiments of Helfreich's 14th Division remained in Pantin. GD Boyer de Rebeval's division supported the attack with a single battalion. The Russian 14th Division – Helfreich – defended the village bravely. The pressure of the French was too great and Helfreich's division would have been driven out of the village had

22 de Vaudoncourt, Vol. II, p. 331.

not the Prussian Guard Brigade arrived to support it. Pantin was occupied by the Tenguinsk and Estonia Infantry Regiments and the 25th and 26th Jager Regiments.[23]

At 12:00 p.m. when it arrived behind Pantin, the Prussian Guard Brigade deployed across the road in three columns as follows:

Right of road:[24]
1st column: Oberstleutnant von Block
 Fus/1st Guard Regiment (approximately 450)
 1/2nd Guard Regiment (40 officers / 6 musicians / 372 men)
2nd column: Oberstleutnant von Müffling
 Baden Leib-Garde-Grenadier Battalion
 2/2nd Guard Regiment (43 / 10 / 448)
 Two cannon & one howitzer – Guard 6pdr Foot Battery
Left of road:
3rd column: Oberstleutnant von Witzleben
 Fus/2nd Guard Regiment (39 / 13 / 387)
 1/, 2/1st Guard Regiment
The three battalions of the 1st Guard Regiment totaled 44 officers and 1,300 men
 Guard Jäger Battalion
 Four cannon & one howitzer – Guard 6pdr Foot Battery

Oberst von Alvensleben, leading the Prussian Foot Guard, arrived behind Pantin at 12:00 p.m. This village was, at that time, occupied by the four weak regiments of Helfreich's Russian 14th Division, which had totally deployed in skirmish formation to defend the village.

This is unusual, in that the Russian infantry regiments were totally deployed in skirmish formation. I know of no other written records of Russian line regiments so dispersed during the entire period of the Napoleonic Wars. Russian General Roth was already wounded and the mass of the wounded filled the alleys of the village.[25] Only two cannon supported them. These guns stood at the edge of the Russian position and fired on the French guns.

Oberst von Alvensleben had gone forward of the village in order to observe the circumstances on the battlefield. In addition to observing the Russian positions, he caught sight of Boyer de Rebeval and Michel's forces marching on the village and that they were about 800 paces from the Russian position. He reacted by ordering the first battalions at the head of his first column. The Prussian first column was screened by Russian skirmishers and supported them directly with the skirmish platoon of the 1/2nd Prussian Guard Regiment – and contained the Fus/1st Guard and 1/2nd Guard Regiments supported by two cannon from the 6pdr Guard Foot Battery – under the command of Oberstleutnant von Block.

This column was to march directly through the village and to support the Russian skirmishers. The Prussian Guard arrived in time to prevent the two Russian guns from falling into the French hands. The skirmishers of the 1/2nd Guard Regiment moved around the right of the village to the causeway, which ran along the canal, and moved to link up with the advanced guard of Katzler's 1st Prussian Corps.

A second column – the 2/2nd Guard Regiment and the Baden Leib-Garde-Grenadier under Oberstleutnant von Müffling – remained to the eastern side of Pantin serving as a reserve. The

23 Sporschil, Vol. II, 2nd Band, p. 352.
24 Freiherr von Lüdingshausen, p. 42.
25 von Damitz, Vol. III, 2nd Part, p. 301.

third column – containing the 1/,2/1st and Fus/2nd Guard Regiments supported by four cannon and a howitzer from the 6pdr Guard Foot Battery under Oberstleutnant von Witzleben – moved from the left of Pantin. To the Prussian's left stood a Russian battery covered by Russian skirmishers and two grenadier battalions.[26]

Bigarré's brigade attacked the Russians – supported by the fire of the French batteries in front of Boyer de Rebeval's division, which showered the Prussians with canister and forced them to seek the shelter of Pantin's narrow streets. Pantin, like many French villages, was formed with massive stone houses and surrounded by a 10-foot-high wall.

Oberstleutnant von Block quickly ordered the skirmishers of his column to close ranks left and right – and by this means, secure his flanks. He then pushed his column into the middle of the French mass. Things were desperate for the Prussians and the Fus/1st Guard Regiment was ordered to execute a bayonet attack to stabilize the situation. Under Oberstleutnant von Block, it quickly reorganized from a section column into an attack column and rolled out of the village streets in a bayonet attack. Its skirmishers were not deployed, so it was closed on the right and left by Russian infantry.[27]

Facing them were three French battalions formed in echelon, with the middle battalion forward. The Prussian Guard Fusiliers marched against them at the *Sturmschritt*. When they were within 50 paces, the French battalions turned about and withdrew. The fusiliers deployed and delivered a volley into their rear as they withdrew. However, the fusiliers were even closer to the French artillery and began to suffer from it. Soon they were swept not only by canister fire from the French heavy battery, but by skirmish fire. The French had advanced a large force of skirmishers to within 300 paces of the fusiliers.

The French had also moved forces to the right – behind the bend of the Ourcq Canal – and poured more heavy fire into the Prussian battalions.[28]

Von Block was struck down by a musket shot and Major von Barnekow was also wounded. The Prussian battalions, however, continued their movement forward. Hauptmann von Ziethen led the Fus/1st Guard Regiment towards the houses along the road in Maisonettes. It took up a position with the 1/2nd Guard Regiment on its left. It quickly began suffering heavy and significant losses. The French began concentrating their fire on the exposed Prussians.

Cannon and musketry fire poured into them from the front, left of the Pré-Saint-Gervais heights, and right of the bend in the Ourcq Canal. In addition to this, a few units of Old Guard Infantry began to move forward as if to attack them. Though in a strong position, the Prussians were forced to withdraw. The fusiliers marched a few hundred paces and stopped. The French sent their skirmishers bounding after them.

At a great interval to the right of Pantin, a battery of Russian guns engaged the advancing French. A half-hour later, this fire was joined by a few guns from the Prussian Guard Foot Battery.

The two Russian Guard Battalions remained by the Prussian guns for an hour-and-a-half in this defensive position.[29] The skirmishers from the Guard Fusiliers, under Capitain von Knobelsdorf, were engaged by Rouvroy with the French and were supported by forces from Prince Wilhelm von Preussen's Combined 2nd and 8th Brigade, Yorck's 1st Corps.

While the Guard Fusiliers advanced, the 1/2nd Guard Regiment moved out of Pantin and moved left along the highway until it joined the Guard Fusiliers. To their left were some troops

26 von Damitz, Vol. III, 2nd Part, p. 302; Sporschil, Vol. II, 2nd Band, p. 353; von Reinhard, p. 397; von Damitz, Vol. III, 2nd Part, pp. 302-3.

27 von Reinhard, p. 398.

28 von Damitz, Vol. III, 2nd Part, p. 303.

29 von Damitz, Vol. III, 2nd Part, p. 304.

from Katzler's advanced guard – about two companies – which had advanced through Rouvroy and along the canal.

To defend itself, the Guard Fusiliers soon deployed themselves entirely into skirmish order. At this time, two battalions of Old Guard advanced and drove them and the 2/1st Guard Regiment back. While this occurred, several Russian guns moved out of Pantin and moved through the intervals of the Prussian battalions. Later, three guns from the Prussian Guard 6pdr Battery moved forward. These guns all engaged the French battery firing on the Prussian infantry. The Fus/1st Guard Regiment was suffering tremendous casualties and shortly would have only 70 of its original 450 men standing unwounded to the colors.[30] This battalion had a theoretical strength of 640 men. The Guard Battalions were generally over-strength at the beginning of the campaign – and this particular battalion probably had a strength of from 350-450 men when the Battle of Paris began.

Oberst von Alvensleben convinced himself that the occupation of Pantin in the battle required the commitment of another battalion. He sent Barclay de Tolly a message requesting authorization to engage the rest of the brigade. Barclay's permission arrived and von Alvensleben ordered the first attack column to march through Pantin.[31]

The Prussian four battalions organized themselves in an area covered from enemy fire near the church courtyard. However, once they moved over the crest of the rise, they immediately came under heavy fire from a battery of French 12pdr cannon and 24pdr howitzers. The Prussian column suffered heavy casualties and inclined to the right to escape the fire from the French guns. The 1/1st Guard Regiment – under Major von Grabow – which formed the right wing, found itself faced with the need to move over the highway, which would expose it to the fire of eight French guns. The road was being swept with bouncing balls and howitzer shells. Von Grabow cleared the hazard by ordering his troops to trot across the road after having them wheel to the right, face left and, in what amounted to a column of threes at an open interval, move across the road.[32]

As the Prussian column moved, it was joined by von Müffling's column – consisting of the 2/2nd Guard Regiment in the first line and the Baden Leib-Garde-Grenadier Battalion in the second. They moved out of Pantin and took up a position about 100 paces from the 1st Guard Regiment. The three guns of the Guard 6pdr Foot Battery had been joined by two more, but two of the original three had already been dismounted. As the two Prussian columns advanced, the three remaining guns in Pantin came out and joined the rest of the battery. Once formed, the battery was covered by the 1st and 4th Skirmisher Platoons of the 1/1st Guard Regiment.

Once deployed, the Prussian Guard began a general attack. They advanced in linear order and in two lines – plus a reserve. The French received the Prussians with a volley at 80 paces and withdrew. Their withdrawal was orderly, but soon became less orderly. The 2/1st Guard suffered heavily from the French artillery placed on the Beauregarde and Cahumont heights. Facing them was a mixture of French line and National Guard troops.[33]

Both attacking forces threw themselves against the French. The French artillery stood on the Pré-Saint-Gervais heights, which on the left wing stood on the left of the Prussian attack. Part of the French artillery fired on the Russian 6th Corps near Romainville. Another portion of the French artillery fired on Pantin and the Pantin plain. At this time, French skirmishers pushed into Pré-Saint-Gervais – driving the Russians back until they held only a few gardens and walls, with their supporting troops pushed to a position between Pré-Saint-Gervais and Pantin.

30 von Reinhard, p. 400.
31 von Damitz, Vol. III, 2nd Part, p. 305.
32 von Reinhard, p. 402.
33 von Reinhard, p. 403.

In the small plain between Pré-Saint-Gervais and the Ourcq Canal there were two masses of French infantry on the right of the highway (Boyer de Rebeval's division) and two more French infantry masses to the left of the road (Sécrétan's brigade). Before them was a mass of French skirmishers. On the highway stood four guns that fired directly down the road. A 10-gun battery by the Ourcq Canal fired on the exits from Pantin – as well as the front of the village. Its fire was joined by that of the batteries on Pré-Saint-Gervais – forming a deadly crossfire. Behind the middle of the French position, the French posted their reserve. It stood on the road in a group of houses so as to cover Maisonettes, which made it impossible for the Prussians to judge their strength.[34]

To the right of the Prussian Guard – on the other side of the canal – stood Curial's infantry division (Mortier's corps) supported by its artillery. The skirmishers of the Guard and Advanced Guard of the Prussian 1st Corps pushed forward from the causeway and over an iron bridge on the canal.

Oberst von Alvensleben led his brigade forward into the crossfire of French artillery. The French infantry held its fire and delivered its first volley at 80 paces. The salvo was badly delivered and the Prussians stormed forward through it.

The Prussian column, under Oberstleutnant von Müffling, struck the French by the Ourcq Canal – pushing them back and overrunning and capturing the French battery of 14 guns and a number of caissons.

At the same time, Oberstleutnant von Witzleben's column struck the French before them. A number of squadrons of French Guard Cavalry charged forward to support their infantry, but were repulsed by the bayonets of the 2/1st Guard Regiment.

After the success of their attack, Oberst von Alvensleben ordered the 1/1st Guard Regiment and the Guard Jäger Battalion to occupy the houses of Maisonettes on the highway so as to be able to strike in the flank any effort by the French infantry on the Pré-Saint-Gervais heights to clear the Prussian Guard from the Pantin plain.[35]

Despite the Prussian casualties, Sécrétan's brigade was heavily pressed on both wings and was being swamped by skirmishers.[36] Sécrétan withdrew and was pursued by the Guard skirmishers and jägers of the 2nd Freiwilliger-Jäger Company as far as Maisonettes. It was 2:00 a.m. when he was obliged to withdraw. Barclay de Tolly, having witnessed the events by Pantin, sent a force of cavalry to support von Alvensleben.

The French guns on the plain were driven back and re-established their crossfire with 24 heavy French guns that now stood behind the canal and on the Pré-Saint-Gervais heights.

Despite the superiority of his forces, Barclay recognized that he needed to reorganize his troops. It was 2:00 p.m. In order to achieve this pause he needed more troops, but all that remained to him were the two divisions of Russian Guard.[37]

Because of his limited resources, Barclay de Tolly decided to await the arrival of Blücher and the Crown Prince of Württemberg. He rallied his skirmishers and his dispersed regiments.

Marmont profited from this pause to reorganize his line and to prepare for the next Allied attacks. Mortier repaired Colonel Sécrétan's position and supported him with Curial's division. He continued disputing possession of Aubervilliers with Langeron. Meanwhile, Blücher began sending forward the corps of Yorck, Kleist and Voronzov.

34 von Damitz, Vol. III, 2nd Part, p. 307.
35 von Damitz, Vol. III, 2nd Part, p. 308.
36 Freiherr von Lüdingshausen, p. 39.
37 de Vaudoncourt, Vol. II, p. 336.

The fight in the Pantin plain occurred between 1:00 and 2:00 p.m. – as did the attack on the Romainville plateau by the Army of Silesia.[38]

The Prussians take Rouvroy

General Michel had been grievously wounded and his right reinforced by Curial's division. They were about to be engaged by the Army of Silesia, as Blücher intended to send a force across the bridge over the Seine-Ourcq Canal where the small bridges join the Allemagne bridge. From there, it was to move between Pantin and the canal to link the right of the main Allied army with the right of the Army of Silesia.

At 11:00 a.m. the advanced guard of Yorck and Kleist's corps arrived on the Seine-Ourcq Canal. This combined force contained seven battalions and 10 squadrons under the command of General Katzler. It passed over the Seine-Ourcq Canal and occupied the Rouvroy farm without any resistance from the French. Katzler is known to have had under his command the Fus/1st West Prussian Infantry Regiment – and at least one Russian jager regiment – and the 1st and 2nd Leib Hussars.

Katzler then looked to advance against Maisonettes while the Prussian Guard moved out of Pantin. However, the Prussians were taken under fire by a French 12-gun battery, which began to sweep the Prussian Guard columns. The Fus/2nd Guard Regiment marched in the lead with the two battalions of the 1st Guard Regiment following behind them at a distance of 150 paces.[39] The artillery fire forced them to move behind the cover of Pantin's houses. Katzler moved behind the Rouvroy farm – seeking shelter as well. They then set up a battery of eight 12pdrs by the farm and a second 12pdr battery – later a third battery – to the right of the road to Senlis (facing the canal). These three batteries engaged the French battery.[40]

Mortier was, however, being heavily pressed on the left of the canal and recalled Curial – leaving only Colonel Sécrétan to cover the village of Maisonettes and the flank of Belleville. The Chaumont hill was not occupied except for weak detachments of the 5th and 6th Paris Guard Legions supported by a four-gun battery manned by students from the École Polytechnique. The valley between the Chaumont and Beauregard hills was weakly occupied and the road which ran from Maisonettes to Belleville offered the Allies a means of turning Marmont's left.

When Raevsky's corps was reorganized, Barclay changed his plan of attack and organized his forces in columns – holding them ready to attack. Gorchakov, with Menzenov's and Helfreich's 5th and 14th Divisions, moved from Montreuil to attack Charonne. General Lambert, commanding Tschoglikov's 1st Grenadier Division and Paskevich's 2nd Grenadier Division, began an attack on Belleville and Ménilmontant. Prince Eugene von Württemberg moved Schachovsky's 3rd Division (about 3,000 men) and Puschnizky's 4th Division (about 4,000 men) to strike Belleville from the other side. The Prussian Guard Brigade – formed in attack column and led by the Fus/1st Guard Regiment and Udom's 2nd Russian Guard Division – moved out of Pantin. Kretov's cuirassiers supported the attack on Belleville, while Pahlen's cavalry covered and protected the attack on Charonne.[41]

38 von Damitz, Vol. III, 2nd Part, p. 309.
39 Freiherr von Lüdingshausen, p. 47.
40 de Vaudoncourt, Vol. II, p. 344.
41 Freiherr von Lüdingshausen, p. 40.

The view from the French command

Such was the situation on the battlefield, at 11:00 a.m. King Joseph – despite the reports of his marshals – refused to believe that the bulk of the Allied force present had been repulsed. It was not until the chief of staff of the Paris Guard brought a map and showed the movements of all the troops that his fears were dissipated. However, the situation was not good, as he had no reserves. His force was entirely committed. The chief of staff was sent back to his post to observe the battle – as well as to request that Mortier send a detachment to support Marmont.

Joseph's concerns were further reduced when General Hulin sent him an engineer of the Sapeurs-Pompiers, who had passed through the Allied lines by Pantin. He was taken by the Cossacks and held until he was taken to the Allied headquarters in Bondy. He took advantage of the opportunity to note as much as he could of the Allied forces and their deployment. He was returned to the French lines with a proclamation from Schwarzenberg to the people of Paris. This proclamation attempted to separate the cause and concerns of the inhabitants of Paris from those of Napoleon. This proclamation, when handed to Joseph, correctly convinced him that he was engaging the heads of two of the Allied armies.[42]

Stunned by this news, Joseph called a council of war. While this council met, it was announced that more Allied troops were pouring onto the plain south of Saint-Denis and that they appeared intent on turning Mortier's left. This was the Army of Silesia maneuvering so as to execute the attacks it had been ordered to make. General Count Voronzov marched from Villepinte and was in the rear when the corps of Kleist and Yorck arrived on the Pantin heights.

Katzler crosses the Seine-Ourcq Canal

Blücher directed that his advanced guard – under Katzler – cross the bridge over the Seine-Ourcq Canal (where the small bridges join the Allemagne bridge) and that they then move between Pantin and the canal to link the right of the main Allied army with the right of the Army of Silesia. It would also provide Blücher with a strongpoint – be it necessary for offensive or defensive operations.

Prince Wilhelm von Preussen was directed to take six battalions and hold the interval between the canal and the road to Senlis. The remainder of Yorck and Kleist's corps were ordered to move down this road and attack Villette, occupy positions before Mortier and to permit Langeron the ability to extend to the right. Langeron's movement required the clearance of Aubervilliers of Colonel Robert's skirmishers. He was to cross the new excavations for the canal and detached General Kapsevich to join Kornilov – then in Saint-Denis. Parallel to the attack by Kapsevich and Kornilov – down the Révolte road against the Bois-de-Boulogne – the remainder of Langeron's attack would attack Montmartre. A detachment was to be posted on the road from Saint-Ouen to Paris to observe the right of Montmartre and the Batignolles suburb.

The overwhelming appearance of the Army of Silesia shook Joseph to the core. He was uncertain of what he should do. He consulted with generals Déjean and Maurice Mathieu, who recommended that he withdraw from the battlefield. Langeron's movement to the right would cut off the Pont de Sevres and prevent Joseph's withdrawal in that direction – though the road to Fontainebleau would still be open. Joseph's nerve failed and he wrote Mortier and Marmont – authorizing them to capitulate both their armies and Paris. Hulin was charged with transmitting

42 de Vaudoncourt, Vol. II, p. 338.

this message and with taking measures to evacuate the garrison from Paris. The various ministers were advised to join the Empress and to expedite the withdrawal of the government from Paris.[43]

As the Army of Silesia deployed on the Saint-Denis plain, the corps of the Crown Prince of Württemberg arrived at Neuilly-sur-Marne. Giulay was detached to watch this position and Württemberg moved his corps to the Nogent heights at 11:00 a.m. – leaving a battalion in Nogent – then moving to the Fontenay heights. Once there, he divided his corps into two columns.

The Württembergers attack

Though the French occupied Nogent-sur-Marne, the Fontenay-aux-Bois and the Vincennes forest, a quick attack led by Oberst Münchingen (leading his Württemberg cavalry regiment) cleared the way for the Württembergers to march on Saint-Maur. A battalion of the 4th Württemberg Regiment was detached to Nogent to prevent any French movements from that direction.

The Crown Prince of Württemberg's first column consisted of Hohenlohe's brigade (four battalions), Misani's brigade (three battalions) and Lalance's brigade (four battalions). The brigades of Misani and Lalance were placed in reserve and the first column moved in the direction of Saint-Maur. The Saint-Maur park was closed, so the walls were breached. A battalion was sent against the Saint-Maur bridge and the main body marched on Charenton.

The second column – consisting of Stockmayer's brigade (four battalions) and supported by four Austrian grenadier battalions – marched down the road from Neuilly to the Bois-de-Vincennes. It easily brushed aside the weak force of line infantry and National Guardsmen. A battalion was detached to watch the village and Château of Vincennes. From there, the column marched on Saint-Maur. Saint-Maur was undefended and the bridge was covered only by a small wooden defensive work on the left bank that was open to the rear. The French forces in the vicinity consisted of 300 conscripts and eight guns. Despite their courage, they were easily ejected and the bridge (and six to seven guns) were captured by the 10th Württemberg Infantry Regiment.[44]

The Crown Prince detached an infantry battalion to maintain what he had captured so far and marched the rest of his forces (three Württemberg light battalions). These three battalions were from the 9th and 10th Regiments. They had suffered heavy casualties – nearly being wiped out at the Battle of Montereau – and around 6 March had been rebuilt using men from the 3rd, 4th, 5th and 6th Land Regiments and four grenadier battalions against the Charenton bridge. Another battalion marched along the edge of the Marne. The battalions were the Puteani, Frisch, Hromada and Lanyi Grenadier Battalions.

Attack on the Charenton bridge

The bridge at Charenton, like that at Saint-Maur, was protected by a minor defensive wooden work on the right bank of the Seine. It was guarded by a company of veterans, the Alfort Students' Battalion and a few gunners. They were hardly enough to stop the massive column marching on their rear. Despite their weakness, when this tiny force thought it was to be struck in the rear, it resolved to sell its position and its honor dearly. They moved into the village and deployed their limited artillery to oppose the advancing Allies.

The main attacking force consisted of the four Austrian grenadier battalions and Hohenlohe's brigade (1/3rd and 1/,2/2nd Württemberg Infantry Regiments) supported by the Austrian Erzherzog Ferdinand Hussar Regiment. The 2/3rd Württemberg Infantry Regiment advanced

43 de Vaudoncourt, Vol. II, p. 339.
44 de Vaudoncourt, Vol. II, p. 341.

down the Marne, while the main force moved through the woods and attacked Charenton from the Paris side.[45] The defenses at the bridge consisted of eight guns manned by conscripts and under the command of a senior gunner.

Two battalions of Württembergers marched through Charenton at the *Sturmschritt* – drums thundering off the village walls and their leather boots pounding in unison – bayonets lowered and their faces set in grim resolve.

The fate of the French forces was inevitable – and the tiny French garrison was quickly pushed back to their defensive position, where they hoped to make a stand. However, the Württembergers pressed them too closely – so closely that they were pushed out of their post before they could set it afire. The fight was quick and sharp. A few shots, the roar of a cannon and the French conscripts took to their heels. Five cannon were captured and only three were saved.

The French then moved away from the bridge and down the roads to Provins and Melun. They were pursued by some light troops, while others moved down the Marne to its confluence with the Seine and stopped before Port-à-l'Anglais. Here, fortunately, the ferry was destroyed and they were unable to cross to the left bank of the Seine.

The moment the Crown Prince's troops took the Charenton bridge in the rear, he directed a light cavalry force down the road to Paris to cover his right flank. They were also to watch if any French troops that might sortie from Paris.

The portion of the walls of Paris facing these cavalry was garrisoned by the 9th Legion of the Paris National Guard. They had, however, been weakened by the dispatch of a number of detachments to various threatened posts. Two strong patrols from this legion and some National Guardsmen from the Bercy suburb were the only French forces encountered by von Württemberg's cavalry. They withdrew quickly and evacuated both Bercy and the Bercy Château. The few barricades erected by the French were unable to even inconvenience the Allied cavalry.

Count Pahlen stood before Montreuil as the Crown Prince of Württemberg arrived in line. He dispatched a few troops to mask Château Vincennes and sent the Tchougouiev Uhlan Regiment to watch the barricade du Trône.

In the French line, General Vincent stood between Montreuil and Charonne. General Laville stood on the extreme right of Count Bordesoulle's corps and observed this movement. The barricade by du Trône now contained only the weak reserve of the 8th Legion. The rest of the legion was in the interior of the city and guarded other barricades. A large percentage of them were deployed in skirmish order between Charonne and Montreuil.

As Württemberg pulled into the Allied line, Major Evain sent forward the Paris Guard Reserve Artillery manned by students from the École Polytechnique. The road to Vincennes was flanked by two terraced walls and was accessible to the Allied light troops only from the front, which gave Major Evain confidence that his gunners could advance without significant risk even though he had no infantry escort. He felt he could stop the Allied light cavalry and also thought that by engaging them he could create a useful diversion on Marmont's flank. He began his movement at about 1:00 p.m. escorted by a few gendarmes.

The 28 pieces were handled by inexperienced gunners and drivers, so the train of limbers and caissons straggled rather badly. When they arrived at the junction of the Charonne-Saint-Mandé road, Major Evain deployed the first guns in battery along the highway. Other guns were deployed on his left facing down the road to Charonne. Soon they were firing – and their fire was directed at the Russian uhlans posted before Montreuil.[46] Count Pahlen directed that the Russian 23rd Horse Battery engage the annoying French guns. He then directed General Kamenev

45 Sporschil, Vol. II, 2nd Band, pp 366-7.
46 de Vaudoncourt, Vol. II, p. 342.

Austrian (Hungarian) grenadiers at Charenton.

to attack them by moving behind the houses and farms of Petit-Vincennes. The Russian artillery began firing canister, but they were too far away and its effect was nil. Switching to ball, they quickly dismounted a number of French guns.

While the gun duel progressed, Kamenev moved past the screening houses, past the park and château, and attacked the French guns. The gendarmes defending the guns were driven back and became entangled in the caissons and limbers. The inexperienced drivers were thrown into disorder. The Tchougouiev Uhlans then fell upon the gunners – killing them and capturing the guns. Kamenev soon found himself in a position where he thought he could threaten General Vincent's flank with a charge, but the 30th Dragoon Regiment appeared and charged them in the flank – crushing them – driving them back and recapturing the French guns.

Major Evain's gunners re-manned their guns and repaid the Russians for their ill manners with a shower of canister. The National Guard detachment at du Trône, despite its weakness, detached a small force under Chef de bataillon Saint-Romain and Captain Calmer and sent it forward to assist in the battle. General Kamenev withdrew – dragging with him several guns and six of the students from the École Polytechnique. Fifteen other students were wounded by the uhlans' lances.[47, 48]

As the Crown Prince of Württemberg made his attack on Charenton, he also sent his cavalry through the Bois-de-Vincennes and Saint-Mandé. The barricades at Bercy and Charenton – as well as those at the Bercy suburb – were guarded only by part of the 9th National Guard Legion and some of the National Guardsmen from the suburb. The Allied cavalry pushed their patrols back and occupied Bercy. However, the Crown Prince did not advance beyond the barricades

47 Koch, Vol. II, pp. 460-74.
48 de Vaudoncourt, Vol. II, p. 343.

Students from the École Polytechnique defending Charenton.

– holding his cavalry before Saint-Mandé and Bercy. Giulay's corps established itself as a reserve on the Fontenay-aux-Bois heights. It was about 3:00 p.m.

Barclay attacks

Barclay had recalled his skirmishers and reorganized his corps after its initial failure. He held the ground before his position by engaging the French in a heavy artillery bombardment, while he waited for the Crown Prince of Württemberg to attack and the Army of Silesia to occupy the ground between the Seine-Ourcq Canal and Montmartre. Mortier had realigned his forces and now had only the Guard Reserves standing before Pantin.

When the Army of Silesia was in place, Barclay decided it was time to renew his attack. Raevsky directed Menzenov's 5th Division to march against Arrighi, who occupied the Malassise plateau. In this position, the French had escarpments and steep slopes to their back. They withdrew and Arrighi shifted his advanced posts to Charonne and Bagnolet. His line moved to the hill to the left of the valley and refused his right behind the valley.

As Russian columns attacked Marmont frontally, Prince Gorchakov directed Menzenov's 5th Division against the village of Bagnolet and personally moved with Helfreich's 14th Division against Charonne. They were taken under heavy musketry, but Marmont was soon obliged to withdraw so as to align himself with Arrighi. Bordesoulle and Chastel's cavalry pulled back into the Charonne Valley. Bagnolet and Charonne fell to the Russians, who then sent their skirmishers against the barricade at Fontarabie and the Mont-Louis cemetery. Fortunately, the Fontarabie hill was occupied with a four-gun French battery supported by a battalion of the 7th National Guard Legion under the command of Colonel de Brévennes. The terrain made its position a strong one and it was supported on its right by the 8th and 9th Legions occupying the small suburb before the Montreuil barricade. The 7th Legion had its skirmishers deployed in the gardens and vineyards between Charonne and Montreuil. The battery's fire slowed Gorchakov's advance, while 50 French skirmishers advanced bravely to fire on Helfreich's infantry. Their fire – and that of the battery – served to stop the Russians and hold their position in Charonne.

The center and left

At about 1:00 p.m. Barclay gave the order for another general attack. Prince Eugene von Württemberg, with his two divisions, advanced towards the Romainville woods. General Lambert, with the Grenadier Corps, marched out of Romainville. Stahl's cuirassier brigade marched between the two columns.

Schachovsky's 3rd Division and Puschnizky's 4th Division led the assault down the road from Romainville to Belleville – flanked on the left by Stahl's Astrakhan and Pskov cuirassier regiments and on the right by the eight grenadier battalions of GM Tschoglikov's 1st (Russian) Grenadier Division. This massive strike force easily brushed aside Chabert's feeble brigade (Compans' division) and marched rapidly down the Belleville road – preceded by a swarm of skirmishers.[49]

Part of Generallieutenant Kretov's 2nd Cuirassier Division

Lagrange's division was entirely deployed in skirmish formation and Ricard's division – 700 men – was massed in reserve on the Bruyères park heights. The terrain favored and permitted the French skirmishers to repel minor attacks, but they were unable to block this massive force (though they clawed at its flanks as it marched forward). Marmont, seeing the Russian advance, resolved to make a major effort to stop it and ordered GB Clavel – one of Ricard's brigade commanders – to form into attack column. Clavel's brigade amounted to a weak battalion. It marched forward – led by Marmont personally – against the head of Puschnizky's division. It advanced bravely, but a Russian battery established in the woods (on a hill where it overlooked the road) took it under fire and threw it into disorder. The Russians immediately took advantage of this. The grenadiers on the left flank and the cuirassiers on the right advanced and threw them back. Marmont's horse was killed under him and his chief of staff and Clavel were wounded. The refugees of the battalion threw themselves back on their reserve, with the Russians in hot pursuit. However, GD Compans brought forward a battalion of Young Guard from the Telegraph hill – and Colonel Ghéneser, who occupied the Bruyères park, fell on their rear with 200 men. The audacious French attack stopped the Russian advance. While the Russians attempted to rally in the park, Marmont rallied the dispersed units of his corps on the Telegraph hill.

Marmont reformed his forces (5,000 exhausted men) in a line that extended from Mont-Louis to Pré-Saint-Gervais – running through the Saint-Fargeau park – and would normally be occupied by 10,000 to 12,000 men. He ordered the cavalry of Bordesoulle and Chastel to cover the right flank by Ménilmontant and the position of Mont-Louis, while Arrighi – recalled from Bagnolet – established himself in the Saint-Fargeau park near Ménilmontant facing the Tourelles ridge. The park was filled with artillery and skirmishers. The divisions of Ricard, Lagrange and Ledru extended from the Telegraph hill to Belleville. Boyer de Rebeval's division stood in Pré-Saint-Gervais and the hills of the Beauregard plateau below the village. The Guard Light Infantry Brigade – under the orders of GD Michel – covered the village of Maisonettes and guarded the bridges over the Seine-Ourcq Canal. On the extreme right stood the cavalry of Bordesoulle and Chastel. This position was such that cavalry posted there was wasted. It should have been moved to the left, where it could operate against the Allies in the Saint-Denis plain.

49 de Vaudoncourt, Vol. II, p. 346.

Having finally occupied the Bruyères park, Charonne and Bagnolet, Barclay de Tolly deployed to chase Marmont from his new position.

Allied attack on Ménilmontant, Belleville and Pré-Saint-Gervais

Barclay prepared to attack Marmont's new position. He directed Gorchakov – with his two divisions – to occupy the Mont-Louis heights. General Lambert was to attack Belleville with Tschoglikov's 1st Grenadier Division and Ménilmontant with Paskevich's 2nd Grenadier Division.

Barclay also realized that it was possible to take Pré-Saint-Gervais in the rear – and at the same time attack it frontally with the forces of Prince Eugene von Württemberg. However, to effect the flank attack, it was necessary to clear Colonel Sécrétan's brigade out of Maisonettes and throw him towards Pantin. Barclay directed Gdl Yorck to send four infantry battalions to his right – under the orders of Prince Wilhelm von Preussen – and to link with Katzler's troops near Rouvroy. Combined, they were to fall on Maisonettes and throw the Chasseurs-Vétérans out of their positions holding the Ourcq bridges.

GL Yermolov advanced with a Guard Grenadier Brigade – consisting of the Leib-Guard and the Pavlov Grenadier Regiments – to take the village of Maisonettes. They were then to move between the Beauregard and Chaumont hills to strike Belleville in the flank and take the Pré-Saint-Gervais position in the rear. Prince Eugene von Württemberg was to hold himself ready with his troops to make a simultaneous assault.

Yermolov, by G. Dawe.

In a simultaneous attack, General Tschoglikov was to strike Belleville; Paskevich was to attack Ménilmontant; and Count Menzenov – supported on his left by Pahlen's cavalry – was to move against the flank of this village and the heights which separated it from the Mont-Louis cemetery.

The Allied attacks rolled forward and were so powerful that only the most desperate defense by the French had any hope of stopping their irresistible advance – and irresistible it was, for numbers told and pushed the French back. GD Chastel launched his cavalry against Menzenov's cavalry in a valiant, but futile attack. The artillery on Mont-Louis showered them with shot and shell to no effect. Soon the French were being steadily pushed back to the walls of Paris. The Russians penetrated into the right flank of Ménilmontant. Pahlen's cavalry cleared the French skirmishers and detachments out of the suburbs of Montreuil and Fontarabie – driving them back towards the city walls and threatening the flank of the French cavalry. The Russian infantry (supported by infantry) quickly occupied the hills of Mont-Louis and Ménilmontant – dominating the exterior boulevards and Amandiers orchards. They positioned their artillery so as to be able to throw howitzer shells into the closest sections of the city of Paris.

Ménilmontant falls

Arrighi – threatened in the rear and attacked frontally by Paskevich – withdrew from Ménilmontant to Belleville with the Allies in hot pursuit.

At nearly the same time, Prince Eugene von Württemberg attacked Pré-Saint-Gervais frontally. As Yermolov moved against Maisonettes, GM Scheltuchin's Russian Guard brigade, the

Russian 1st Guard Division, the Prussian Guard Brigade and General Katzler advanced against Sécrétan's brigade and Curial's division in Maisonettes.

Prince Eugene von Württemberg rallied Puschnizky's division and directed them to attack the village of Pré-Saint-Gervais, which was defended by two battalions from Boyer de Rebeval's division – a total of 1,850 guardsmen.[50] Despite their vigorous resistance, the Russian skirmishers pushed into the village. Marmont responded by sending Colonel Fabvier forward with 300 men from Ricard's division. Again, the Russians were thrown back and showered with canister from the dozen 12pdr guns which stood before Boyer de Rebeval's line.[51]

At about 12:15 p.m. the Prussian Guard took advantage of the withdrawal of Sécrétan's brigade from Pantin to march out of the village in column. The 70 men remaining in the Fus/1st Guard Regiment led the advance, with the 1/1st Guard and Guard Jägers following them. The Fus/,2/2nd Guard and the Baden Leib-Garde-Grenadier Battalion advanced on the right flank.

The Prussians quickly found themselves faced by a line of French Guard wearing bearskins – Boyer de Rebeval's division. Upon seeing the notorious Old Guard, Oberst von Alvensleben cried out to his Guard Fusiliers: "There you see Napoleon's Guard Grenadiers! Show them that the King of Prussia's Guard Fusiliers – the former Leib Fusiliers – do not fear them!"[52]

When the Prussians advanced to a distance of 80 paces from the French, the French line discharged its first volley.

The French position battery, which earlier had held the Allied forces in check, had fired off all its original ammunition. It had just received a supply of ammunition, but it proved useless as it was of too small a caliber. The French were thrown back on the barricades that ran through the village of Maisonettes. Colonel Christophe – who had been sent by Mortier with his regiment to support Sécrétan – attempted a charge, but it failed when he was charged in the flank by Katzler's cavalry. The French battery was abandoned and taken by the Prussians.[53] The Prussian Guard had, by the end of the day, captured 24 French guns and three caissons in bayonet attacks.

In the second line of the Prussian Guard Brigade, the Fus/1st Guard Regiment stood on the right and the 1/,2/1st Guard Regiment stood on the left of the main road. During the engagement, the 1/1st Guard Regiment pushed more to the right as it closed on the Fus/1st Guard Regiment. The 2/1st Guard Regiment, however, remained to the left of Maisonettes. The three battalions stopped in this position because they were now covered by the dike, which protected them from the French artillery firing on Maisonettes from the Belleville heights. Three companies of the Garde Jägers and the Freiwilliger Jägers of the Guard Regiment were posted on the Belleville plateau, where they engaged the French to stop any French attack from the direction of Pré-Saint-Gervais. The 2nd Russian Guard Division was then sent forward to support the Prussians.[54]

General Yermolov occupied the exterior of the suburb in force – and seeing that he was not threatened with a flank attack, moved down the Chaumont and Beauregard heights. He judged that the French battery that stood before him was only covered by skirmishers and directed a force of the Prussian and Russian Guard – protected by batteries and preceded by a large number of skirmishers – into the valley between the Chaumont and Beauregard hills. The 4th Company, Garde Jägers, occupied the Beauregard heights.

The Allies broke into two columns. One moved into Belleville – down the lateral streets – while the other moved behind Boyer de Rebeval's division. A Russian column, with artillery and

50 Freiherr von Lüdingshausen, p. 39
51 de Vaudoncourt, Vol. II, p. 335.
52 Freiherr von Lüdingshausen, p. 43.
53 de Vaudoncourt, Vol. II, p. 351.
54 Freiherr von Lüdingshausen, p. 48.

light infantry support, moved down the road up the Chaumont hill – overrunning the French batteries before them. The National Guardsmen – supported by detachments from the 5th and 6th Legions, and various gunners – fought hard (attempting to stop the pursuit), but their numbers were too few. The Prussians overran their positions and their light infantry penetrated into the lower streets of Belleville and the approaches to the Trois-Moulins hill, while the heavy column of infantry pushed over the Trois-Moulins hill.

As Yermolov took the Chaumont hill and established himself on the approaches to Belleville, part of his troops turned to strike Pré-Saint-Gervais in the rear in support of Prince Eugene von Württemberg's frontal assault on the same village. Six battalions of Richter's brigade and the Russian Guard attacked the rear of Pré-Saint-Gervais.[55]

GD Compans saw this threat approaching and threw Boyer de Rebeval's division and the Polish Éclaireurs – under Captain Zajonczek (all that remained of Chastel's cavalry) – against the advancing Russians. The Poles threw back the Russian skirmishers on their columns – permitting Compans to profit from this delay and withdraw Boyer de Rebeval's division from the threatened position in Pré-Saint-Gervais. Boyer de Rebeval moved to Belleville with the greatest difficulties – pushing over walls and barricades; through narrow alleys and gardens. Unfortunately, the passage was too difficult for his artillery and most of it was abandoned. Zajonczek was a nephew of the famous general of the same name.

Prince Eugene von Württemberg took advantage of this withdrawal to overrun Pré-Saint-Gervais and pushed his skirmishers into Belleville – supported by those of General Yermolov.

The fight for Belleville

Marmont defended Belleville personally. He watched the developments on his flanks and was particularly concerned with his flanks and rear being attacked because of the withdrawals of Arrighi, Chastel and Bordesoulle. His situation was serious and required an immediate solution. Marmont, his chief of staff, and generals Ricard, Boudin and Pelleport assembled the bravest of their troops and together threw themselves against the Russians. Marmont was struck by a musket ball and received a strong contusion. Ricard was wounded in the foot, Pelleport received a bayonet thrust, but the French remained masters of the village and the left brigade of Lagrange's division recovered its first position.

Marmont profited from a momentary pause in the action to re-establish the order in his lines. He strongly garrisoned the high road that ran to Ménilmontant and placed the rest of his infantry in the lower roads to defend them against the Russians occupying the Moulin hill and dominated the main road to the point where it dropped rapidly towards the barricade.

Marmont's position was not strong – nor particularly tenable. The Allies were all around him – holding Charonne and Ménilmontant. They were already throwing howitzer shells into Paris and the Russian cavalry of Pahlen had pushed the French cavalry back to the Paris barricades. All that remained was to fight in the streets of Paris. At this point, Marmont felt it was time to use the authority given to him by King Joseph. However, before so doing, he sent couriers to Mortier to determine his position and his attitude towards such action.

When the courier arrived at Mortier's headquarters, he found the situation no less critical. Though Marmont did not yet know of Mortier's desperate situation, he took it upon himself to send his aide-de-camp to Schwarzenberg, who stood on the heights before Belleville watching Barclay de Tolly's attacks.

55 de Vaudoncourt, Vol. II, p. 350.

Schwarzenberg agreed to a suspension of the conflict on the provision that the French withdraw to the walls of Paris and that both Mortier and Marmont work in concert to prepare a convention stipulating their evacuation of Paris.

The fall of Aubervilliers to the Russians

Earlier, before Marmont began his negotiations for a ceasefire, Langeron's corps had begun its offensive movement. Aubervilliers was quickly overrun, and by 1:00 p.m. Colonel Robert's skirmishers were chased back to La Chapelle. He also threw back the combined infantry and cavalry force under the Polish Major Kozietulsky – attempting to take munitions to Saint-Denis.

Generals Kapsevich and Kornilov had blockaded Saint-Denis and moved the bulk of their forces against Clignancourt and La Chapelle. Count Langeron arrived with the bulk of his corps on the Saint-Ouen heights and directed a detachment of infantry – supported by artillery under the command of Kapsevich – down the road to Batignolles. They were to take up positions where they could observe any movement out of Paris behind the Clichy barricade.[56]

General Rudsevich was, at the same time, ordered to move a force of cavalry supported by infantry and artillery down the Révolte road towards the Bois-de-Boulogne. His column consisted of the remains of St. Priest's Russian 8th Corps and contained the Rilsk, Jeletz, Polotsk, Ekaterinbourg, Riazan and Belozersk Infantry and the 1st, 30th, 33rd and 48th Jagers.[57] It was to sweep the Clichy plain clear of French and to observe any French forces in the barricades to the west of Paris.

Because it was no immediate threat and because he was too heavily occupied by the attack of the Army of Silesia, Mortier paid it little attention. He contented himself with ordering General Belliard to watch his left – moving via Clignancourt towards the Clichy plain to observe Langeron's movement. The only forces allocated to this movement was a small Guard cavalry force under the command of General Dautancourt. This force consisted of 320 horse grenadiers, dragoons, chasseurs, mamelukes and éclaireurs drawn from the various depots.

After taking those measures prudent for the security of his left, Mortier occupied himself with the masses of Allied troops that stood before him. While Katzler marched to the support of the Allies in Pantin, Prince Wilhelm von Preussen advanced against Villette and General Horn – flanked by four regiments of Cossacks – marched against La Chapelle. Voronzov's corps deployed before Aubervilliers and the road to Saint-Denis. Horn's 7th Brigade, Yorck's corps, advanced against the windmill south of the village of Saint-Ouen, with Pirch's 10th Brigade marching to its left against La Chapelle. The 9th Brigade remained in reserve behind them. Six-pounder Foot Battery #7 moved to the heights to the east of the Saint-Denis-Paris highway – covered by the von Haase Fusilier Battalion. The Prussian battery took the French guns before La Chapelle under fire.

Horn's 7th Brigade received the order to attack La Chapelle and a screen of skirmishers was organized on his front using the von Haase Fusilier Battalion and three other schützen platoons under the command of Leutnant von Molitor. As the 9th Brigade advanced, the 10th Brigade formed a second line behind it.[58]

The advance of the 7th, 8th and 10th Brigades quickly overran a fleché standing before La Chapelle. The National Guards defending it fled to La Chapelle.

The situation was critical for the French. At the moment that Yermolov had moved the Russian and Prussian Guard from Pantin to strike Sécrétan, Prince Wilhelm von Preussen had changed

56 de Vaudoncourt, Vol. II, p. 345.
57 Langeron, p. 468.
58 von Ebertz, p. 173.

his front to the right and presented himself before Villette. Voronzov's corps closed on Villette from the other side of the canal. Horn's brigade and Kleist's 2nd Corps had arrived at the edge of La Chapelle.

The first attack on Villette was supported by General Voronzov, who entered the line as the attack occurred. The artillery that Mortier had held in the old 1792 entrenchments and redoubts – and especially those works before the village – opened a thunderous barrage on the advancing Allied troops. The Allied artillery responded – bounding balls down the main streets of Villette and La Chapelle. Mortier ordered Colonel Christophe – placed between the villages – to charge the Allied cavalry, but his French dragoons were taken in the flank by the Brandenburg Hussars and struck frontally by the 2nd Leib Hussars.[59] The French cavalry was thrown back on the French artillery. Horn attacked Charpentier's division aggressively, with the Combined Silesian-East Prussian Grenadier Battalion fighting its way through La Chapelle foot by foot.

Prince Wilhelm von Preussen sent two Prussian Landwehr battalions to attack the bridge over the canal at Saint-Denis (before Villette), while at the same time Krasovsky's Russian brigade (13th and 14th Jager Regiments) struck the village from the left. Mortier called Curial's division forward as the Prussians appeared before Aubervilliers. Sécrétan's brigade stood as the only defense of Maisonettes.

Maisonettes falls

Colonel Sécrétan, who was grievously wounded, still held his position in Maisonettes with 160 to 180 Chasseurs-Vétérans – defending their position by the bridge to the death.[60]

Shortly before 4:00 p.m. the 1/1st Prussian Guard Regiment and the Guard Jäger Battalion pushed their way into the first houses of Maisonettes. French skirmishers lined the canal bank from Villette to the outworks of Rouvroy and engaged the advancing Prussians in the flank. A French battery by Villette supported them, but was soon taken under fire by Lehmann's Guard 6pdr Battery.

Harried by this fire, Oberst von Alvensleben ordered the 1/1st Guard Regiment and the skirmishers of the Guard Jägers to move against the canal and clear off the opposing French skirmishers. The third and fourth skirmish platoon of the 1/1st Guard and two platoons of Guard Jägers soon began a firefight across the 15-pace-wide canal.[61]

The Prussian push into Maisonettes was soon supported by the arrival of most of the 2nd Guard Regiment and the Baden Leib-Garde-Grenadiers. The village was quickly overrun and Sécrétan's brigade was pushed out.

Villette falls

Numbers told – and the Prussians seized the bridge at Saint-Denis – and Prince Wilhelm von Preussen pushed his entire brigade into the village and pushed his skirmishers along the left of the dike. His attack was supported by a Russian Guard brigade, which advanced along the left of the highway. Prince Wilhelm was the brother of the King of Prussia. Apparently, this brigade contained the Pavlov Grenadiers and the Leib-Grenadiers.

59 von Ardenne, p. 273.
60 Koch, Vol. II, pgs 480-90.
61 von Reinhard, p. 405.

Voronzov reinforced his attack with fresh troops and, at the same time, Katzler repulsed an attack by Colonel Christophe. Katzler was then ordered to push his infantry against the bridge over the Seine-Ourcq Canal to take Villette in the rear.

Curial's division was in no position to resist these attacks and was forced to abandon the batteries that defended the village. Katzler seized the bridge over the canal – pushing the 2nd Leib Hussars in the lead – and 14 French guns were captured.[62]

Mortier ordered GD Christiani to retake Villette. His chief of staff, Saint-Charles, was detached with the Flanqueuer-Grenadiers to support the Chasseurs-Vétérans. Despite the reinforcements, the Flanqueuers and Chasseurs-Vétérans were forced to abandon the bridge and crossed over the bridge pressed by a Prussian column. Prussian skirmishers lined the dikes and harassed them as they retreated. However, as the Prussian column crossed the bridge, the Flanqueuer-Grenadiers struck them and threw them back across the bridge. The élan of the Flanqueuer-Grenadiers was too great for the Prussians to resist, and the young French guardsmen pushed 100 paces forward. However, their tiny number was insufficient for them to hold the ground they conquered. As they chased one group of Prussians before them, other Prussians formed behind them. Soon the Flanqueuers were forced to stop. They were surrounded on every side and called upon to surrender. They responded that they would litter the ground before them with the blood and corpses of their enemies, and cut their way to freedom.[63]

The main portion of the division – converged before the Valette – fought with no less valor in the main streets of the village. The oldest French soldiers were aged 30, but they were the victors of many battles and they were fighting before the eyes of their parents, wives and friends. They were defending their home, the honor of the Imperial Guard and the capital of their country.

As the Allies were being repulsed before Villette, Mortier learned that Sécrétan had been forced to abandon Maisonettes and that the Russian and Prussian Guard were in position so as to attack his rear. He immediately ordered a retreat.

A Prussian column advancing down the main road was fired upon by four French guns. They were going to clean the village of the French despite the canister falling on them, while the Prussian Guard – after having forced the bridge – arrived in the rear of the village where it joined Paris. This movement convinced Mortier to recall his troops to the barricades of Paris. The withdrawal was made in good order, with a battalion holding the main street with its fire. La Chapelle was evacuated in the same manner. The troops stationed between Villette and La Chapelle withdrew *en échiquier* under the cover of the French artillery. Between La Chapelle and Montmartre, Colonel Robert's brigade used the favorable terrain of the Cinq-Moulins hill to cover their withdrawal. The withdrawal of General Le Capitaine's brigade – serving as the rearguard – was executed with precision despite being under the enemy fire. Student of Guibert, he was killed at the Battle of Waterloo.

Langeron's movement to the west did not disturb the movement. Only the movement of Rudsevich's cavalry had an effect, as it pushed down the Révolte road and entered the village of Clichy – forcing General Belliard to move back to the foot of Montmartre and leaving his right in the village of Clignancourt and supporting his left on the Batignolles-Saint-Ouen road. In this position, the chasseurs, mamelukes and éclaireurs de la Garde – supported by the grenadiers in reserve – joined about 250 to 280 National Guards of the 2nd Legion as they engaged the Russians in the vineyards to the right of the road.

62 von Ardenne, p. 273.
63 de Vaudoncourt, Vol. II, p. 363.

Langeron's movement was virtually unopposed by Marchand, who deployed only his limited cavalry to face him. Marchand required almost all of his troops to deal with the attacks of Kleist, Yorck and Voronzov.

The situation on the left was like that on the right. However, Marmont's communication regarding the possibility of a ceasefire was the first communication Mortier had received. Indeed, he still had not received his authority to capitulate – if necessary – and would not until about 5:00 p.m. His officers – and those of Count Belliard – had sought King Joseph in vain, so Mortier felt obliged to hold his position as long as possible.

Napoleon sends word to Paris

In the meantime, General Baron Déjean – an aide-de-camp to Napoleon – had been moving as quickly as he could to Paris. He arrived in Dolencourt with verbal instructions for Mortier and Marmont. Napoleon was on his way to save his capital. He directed the marshals to not try to save Paris by force of arms and to attempt to preserve it from occupation by the Allies. He directed them to approach Schwarzenberg with a peace overture directed to the Emperor of Austria.

Though Mortier realized that such a communication after a lost battle under the walls of Paris would not produce the desired effect, he sent General Lapointe – his chief of staff and parliamentary – to Schwarzenberg with a confidential dispatch. Unfortunately, Schwarzenberg was misinformed and responded that his sovereign had not permitted him to negotiate a separate peace and attached a copy of the Declaration of the Allied powers from the now-terminated Châtillon Congress.

In the meantime, the Tsar of Russia and King of Prussia – watching the progress of the Army of Silesia – had come to the conclusion that the French situation was desperate.

The Tsar summons Mortier to surrender

General Lapointe had not yet returned to Mortier's headquarters when Count Orlov – aide-de-camp to Tsar Alexander – arrived at Mortier's headquarters and, in the name of his sovereign, called upon Mortier to surrender. Shocked by this summons, Mortier responded that the Allies were still a long ways from Paris and that before he would accept such a dishonorable surrender, he would fight on in the ruins of the city.

However, in the interval, Marmont had concluded his truce and word reached Mortier of this agreement. Despite his earlier statements, he was now reduced to joining his colleague in the process of negotiating a convention that met their dignity and honor. He moved to Villette, where he encountered Count Nesselrode (Tsar Alexander's minister), Count Orlov, Count Paer (aide-de-camp to Schwarzenberg) and Captain Peterson (representing the English). At the same time, staff officers of both armies – preceded by trumpets – marched down the line and announced the ceasefire to all combatants.

The Montmartre heights were to be surrendered to the Allies – as required by the earlier agreement for the suspension of hostilities – and the French prepared to withdraw behind the walls of Paris. An aide-de-camp of the Tsar was sent to Langeron to advise him of the ceasefire, but this officer deliberately delayed the announcement because of his desire to engage in the battle – and the fighting would continue for some time in front of Montmartre, Batignolles and the Neuilly barricade.[64]

64 Koch, Vol. II, pp. 491-6.

On the French side, as Marmont returned to his forces from the armistice discussions, he arrived in time to find the 30th Dragoons – under Colonel Ordener – had just charged and crushed three Russian squares formed in the vineyards by the Chaumont hills.[65]

Operations before Montmartre

During the morning, Montmartre was reinforced by a few detachments of the Paris National Guard. The 9th and 10th Legions had sent a few pelotons of grenadiers and chasseurs, but by 11:30 a.m. – as Langeron had begun his movements and as Joseph departed – the French generals had ordered these units to move down into the Clichy plain and to Batignolles. On Montmartre, there would remain only a weak detachment of veterans and conscripts drawn from the Paris garrison. Because the position was so poorly-defended (and because there was no other infantry), the Sapeurs-Pompiers de la Garde were sent forward – though weakened by detachments to the Tuileries and their barracks on Rue de Clichy. The artillery placed on the hill consisted of two batteries. One had five 6pdr guns and was posted by the Lancette mill. The other had only two 6pdr guns and was posted by Moulin-Neuf. Nearby, on the Clignancourt heights, stood only Belliard's cavalry and his horse artillery.

The French forces were too weak to stop any concentrated attack on that flank – in particular against the Batignolles suburb or an attack down the Saint-Ouen and Clichy roads to Paris. Already, Emmanuel's cavalry was moving to the Villiers heights from Clichy, and his skirmishers were engaged on the plain with those of the Paris National Guard. They would shortly be pushing into the suburbs of Batignolles and Mouceaux. On the other side, an infantry column – supported by a battery – marched down the road from Saint-Ouen and soon took up a position where the road broke the crest that descended from the Garde's hut towards Clichy. These attacks on the front and flank were supported by a diversion against the western barriers – notably Neuilly. An Allied column appeared on the Révolte road – moving quickly against the Porte Maillot with less than a kilometer to reach its target.

Between Clichy and Neuilly, the city wall and its exterior suburbs were defended only by the Paris National Guard. The extreme left of the army extended just to Montmartre – leaving the defense of this western region to be defended by Maréchal Moncey.

Maréchal Moncey saw Langeron's movement down the Révolte and Clichy roads and moved to the Clichy barricades. Count Regnaud de Saint-Jean d'Angely, chief of the 2nd Legion, was ordered to move to Blois. Chef de bataillon Odiot – provisional commander of the legion and the detachments at Clichy and on the Saint-Ouen road – moved a light battery to fire on the Allied column on the Saint-Ouen road by the Garde's hut and supported its fire with the two guns on the Deux-Moulins heights.

The detachments that had moved down from Montmartre into the plain were, by noon, moving back to Batignolles – pressed by the Russian light troops. Maréchal Moncey ordered them to move into the houses so that they could fight more effectively (and with less peril) to support the light battery – and to cover, in case of need, the withdrawal of Dautancourt's brigade.

This front stabilized, Maréchal Moncey moved to the other positions. His chief of staff then moved to Montmartre to report to King Joseph of the situation and found Joseph's headquarters deserted. From this position, however, he saw Emmanuel's cavalry marching down the Révolte road and quickly returned to the Neuilly and Roule barricades to watch these movements more closely. The barricade commanders, advised of Emmanuel's' approach, prepared their men and prepared the posts on the crests which dominated the Thermes and the plain of the

65 Rapetti, p. 93.

Russian infantry at Montmartre.

Bois-de-Boulogne. They sent out patrols and skirmishers and the artillery was pulled before the Arc de Triomphe, where it could cover the fields before it.

However, the movement of these troops attracted the attention of Langeron's troops moving to the west. Those moving down the Saint-Ouen road stopped their advance, while those on the Révolte road inclined to the left and attempted to push the French skirmishers back behind the barricades. However, as they reached the Maillot Gate, Emmanuel decided he did not wish to move into – and become engaged – in the Bois-de-Boulogne. Instead, he detached a light force – screened by skirmishers and supported by artillery – and sent them towards the l'Etoile barricade, which was supported by a four-gun French battery. It was uncertain if he wished to penetrate into the west of Paris or simply alarm the road from the Arc de Triomphe to the Tuileries, but this action was not enough to draw too much attention from the French because of a more threatening movement on their front.

A force of artillery destined to contain the Batignolles suburb was marching down the Saint-Ouen road and was at the crest by the Garde's hut. In addition, Rudsevich's corps – 20 battalions – moved between the hut and to the left of Clignancourt. Kapsevich marched against the center and right of Clignancourt. The two columns were preceded by a heavy artillery force, which moved to within a short range of the French cavalry and began pounding it. Belliard was soon forced to withdraw his cavalry. Dautancourt charged the Russians with Chef d'escadron Lafitte's chasseurs and GB Sparre – attached with the 5th and 12th Dragoons – but all attacks failed. Soon the entire line was forced to withdraw to the foot of Montmartre. Langeron then brought forward 30 to 36 guns – which resumed pounding the French cavalry – and sent it fleeing at a gallop up the narrow streets of the suburb and to the summit. Included in the mad rush up the hill were the march regiments of colonels Christophe, Ghigny and Leclerc; Roussel's dragoons; and Dautancourt's brigade.

Prussian cavalry approach Montmartre; its windmills can be seen in the distance.

In the middle of the precipitous retreat, General Belliard noted the Guard Sapeur-Pompier Battalion on the left side of the hill and threw himself into them. These 250 men were the only infantry formation that Kapsevich and Rudsevich encountered as they passed over the hill.[66]

Belliard's cavalry withdrew through the barricades held by Mortier. Two squadrons – one of cuirassiers and one of dragoons – moved along the exterior boulevards, where they encountered the chief of staff to the Parisian National Guard. He invited these two squadrons to join them and protect Maréchal Moncey's left, which still occupied Batignolles. These two squadrons advanced to Batignolles and encountered Russian light troops, who by virtue of their numbers, forced them to withdraw back to the Mouceaux barricade.

This withdrawal, the capture of Montmartre and the Allies' menacing march past Batignolles down the Saint-Ouen and Clichy roads was more than the National Guards could handle. They literally abandoned their positions and fell back in terror on the Clichy barricade.

Batignolles is evacuated

Mortier and his chief of staff moved into panic and attempted to rally the troops. Rallied, the grenadiers and chasseurs were posted in the windows and buildings around the defensive position by Clichy. The Cannoniers-Vétérans stood by their guns with lit matches ready to defend their positions. Soon the Russian light troops approached and were greeted with a tremendous volley of fire that drove them into the houses along the streets.

Unfortunately for the French, the Russians had organized a battery on the heights by Batignolles that quickly made the French position untenable. The French withdrew to a barricade formed from overturned wagons and cut lumber. A second such barricade was hastily raised

66 de Vaudoncourt, Vol. II, p. 370.

further down the street by the Sapeurs-Pompiers from their barracks and supported by men, women and children from the neighbourhood who sought to defend their home.

The Allies, however, chose not to assault the barricade, but waited for their artillery to arrive. As their infantry occupied the adjoining buildings and began to take the barricades under fire, the trumpeters arrived – announcing the ceasefire. The fire stopped by the Clichy barricade, but was to continue yet a bit longer further to the west – by Neuilly – where the 1st Legion and Emmanuel's troops were hotly engaged.

The ceasefire was soon in effect all along the line until an incident reignited the firing by the Clichy barricade. The Russian skirmishers were established in the buildings near the barricade when a movement that appeared to be offensive was committed by a force of National Guardsmen posted in an exterior work. Suddenly, they began firing – and did so until Langeron sent an envoy to Maréchal Moncey to stop it.[67]

Convention for the evacuation of Paris

Despite these incidents, Mortier and Marmont were in Villette discussing the clauses of the capitulation. After a lively debate, it was settled that the army would withdraw its equipment and that they would have the entire night to effect this evacuation. The Allied troops would enter Paris at 6:00 a.m. and could not recommence hostilities until 9:00 a.m. These agreements were verbal and Mortier was charged to reducing them to writing and signing them in the name of Mortier with the Counts Orlov and Paer.

The army turned over the barricades it had defended to the Paris National Guard. General Hulin relieved it of the positions it had held inside the city with the National Guard as well. Mortier's troops quickly evacuated the city under the direction of Curial. Curial marched them across the Pont-d'Austerlitz and down the road to Fontainebleau, where they established themselves at midnight behind Villejuif – facing Paris. Belliard's cavalry, after a short stop, marched in the same direction. Marmont moved down the Champs-Elysées to rendezvous with the corps which had fought under his orders. The Polish Cossacks spent the night at Bas-Passy before the Versailles barricade. The following day – at around 4:00 a.m. – various French troops marched across the Pont d'Iéna and the Pont de Concorde – moving on the Orléans and Maine barricades.

As the French abandoned the battlefield that they had defended against overwhelming odds, the Tsar of Russia and the King of Prussia moved to the Saint-Chaumont heights and overlooked Paris as the last rays of the evening sun fell on Paris – their breasts filled with the satisfaction of knowing that their fight was almost over and that they had won an immense political victory.

When they returned to Bondy – to Schwarzenberg's headquarters – the Tsar promoted Barclay de Tolly to the rank of Field Marshal. Barclay's headquarters was established in Romainville, with his army encamped before Pantin and on the Belleville, Ménilmontant and Mont-Louis heights. The Army of Silesia was posted on Montmartre and in its environs. The Crown Prince of Württemberg and Giulay established their corps at Saint-Maur and Charenton. Emmanuel's troops occupied Thermes – the Maillot Gate – with units on the Seine bridges between Auteuil and Boulogne.

Inside Paris, its people were drawn from their homes – with curiosity – to the heights, where they could look over the Allied army encamped before their city. The light of the Allied campfires lit up the sky to the north of their city for the first time in their memory. Indeed, for the first time since the 100 Years' War, Paris had an enemy at their gates – and this was a victorious enemy.[68]

67 Koch, Vol. II, pp. 497-505.
68 Koch, Vol. II, pp. 506-8.

Losses in the battle

The Prussian Guard Brigade, which had been in the thick of the battle, lost 69 officers and 1,286 NCOs and men. The entire Prussian losses for the day were 87 officers and 1,753 NCOs and men.[69] The Russian and French losses are not known.

The capitulation of Paris

The final capitulation was signed at 2:00 a.m. by colonels Fabvier and Denis acting for the marshals who had already departed. Counts Orlov and Paer signed for the Allies. Articles 1, 2, 3, 4 and 7 stated that the French army would evacuate the city by 7:00 a.m. on 31 March and that the Allies would occupy it at 9:00 a.m. as previously agreed. The magazines and military establishments were to be left in the state in which they were found prior to the capitulation. The wounded and unattached soldiers who remained in the city after 9:00 a.m. would be considered prisoners of war.

Articles 5, 6 and 8 addressed civil concerns. The National Guard and Urban Guard were stated to not be part of the army and they were to be either retained, disarmed and / or disbanded at the pleasure of the Allies. The fate of the municipal police force was also to be up to the wishes of the Allies.[70]

The National Guard was retained as the proper instrument for maintaining public order and protecting the public and governmental buildings. This was decided before the Allies actually entered the city. When the Allies did march in, the Tsar Alexander, the King of Prussia, Prince Schwarzenberg, the various generals, the English commissioners and their respective staffs marched at the head of a long column of infantry, cavalry and artillery. The order of entry into Paris of the armies was:[71]

Prussian Guard Cavalry
Russian Guard Light Cavalry Division
Austrian Grenadier Brigade
Russian Grenadier Corps
2nd Russian Guard Infantry Division
Prussian Guard Infantry Brigade
1st Russian Guard Infantry Division
Three Russian Cuirassier Divisions

They marched down the Champs-Elyseés and down the boulevards d'Italiens and de la Madelaine. Their parade was greeted by cries of: "*Vive les Bourbons! Vivent les souverains! Vivent nos libérateurs!*"from the closet Bourbonists who were more interested in not having the city sacked (and recognized that the Bourbons were about to return). Their sense of self-preservation through a period of change was greater than their attachment to the Bourbon cause ("Long live the Bourbons! Long live the sovereigns! Long live our liberators!").

Later, after the victory parade was complete, Caulaincourt arrived to present to the Tsar a new set of peace propositions from Napoleon, but he pled Napoleon's case in vain and left empty-handed.

Paris became a raging torrent of anti-Bonapartism. The people declared him a traitor, the French senate stripped him of the throne and his family of its hereditary rights to the throne. The white Bourbon cockade sprouted everywhere. A new provisional government was established and the end of Bonapartist rule in France was proclaimed.

69 von Reinhard, p. 414.
70 Koch, Vol. II, pp. 514-5.
71 Freiherr von Lüdingshausen, p. 59.

The Allied entry into Paris, by F. de Maleque.

20

The Battles and Sieges on the Eastern Frontier of France

Hamburg

Hamburg stands on the Elbe River, on the northwestern coast of Germany, near Holland. Because it is in western Germany, it did not come under siege by the Allies until long after Napoleon's defeat at Leipzig. The city was a fortress of the first order and connected to it was the adjoining city of Haarburg, which was also fortified.[1] During the 1814 campaign, it was garrisoned by Davout's XIII Corps. Davout had the XIII Corps organized into two parts. The first was a mobile force and the second was a fixed garrison. They were as follows:

Mobile forces:
3rd Division: Général de division Loison (8,842 men)[2]
- Brigade: Général de brigade Rome
  - 1/, 2/, 3/, 4/15th Line Regiment
  - 3/, 4/44th Line Regiment
- Brigade: Général de brigade Leclerc
  - 1/, 2/, 3/, 4/48th Line Regiment
  - 1/, 2/, 3/, 4/108th Line Regiment
- Artillery: Mathis
  - 3/8th Foot Artillery Company
  - 17/8th Foot Artillery Company
  - Unidentified Horse Battery
  - Det. 1/6th Principal Artillery Train
  - Det. 5/7th Principal Artillery Train

40th Division: Général de division Vichery (10,000 men)
- Brigade: Général de brigade Delcambre
  - 1/, 2/, 3/,4/30th Line Regiment
  - 1/, 2/, 3/, 4/61st Line Regiment
- Brigade: Général de brigade Gengoult
  - 1/, 2/, 3/, 4/111th Line Regiment
- Artillery: Grosjean
  - 12/2nd Foot Artillery Company
  - 18/8th Foot Artillery Company
  - Det. 7/2nd (bis) Artillery Train
  - Det. 3/8th (bis) Artillery Train

1 Savary, p. 31
2 French Archives, Carton XP3; Henke, 1813-1814, pp. 172-3.

Garrison of Hamburg:
50th Division (Immobile): Général de brigade Pécheux (9,680 men)
  Brigade: Général de brigade Avril
    1/, 2/, 3/, 4/33rd Légère Regiment
    2/, 3/, 4/29th Line Regiment
  Brigade: Général de brigade Osten
    2/, 5/3rd Line Regiment
    3/, 4/, 5/105th Line Regiment
Cavalry: Général de division watier Saint-Alphonse (5,800 men & 3,800 horses)
  Brigade: Général de brigade Dubois
    1st Provisional Cuirassier Regiment
      4/1st, 4/2nd, 4/3rd, 4/4th Cuirassier Regiments
    2nd Provisional Cuirassier Regiment
      4/5th, 4/6th, 4/7th, 4/8th Cuirassier Regiments
    3rd Provisional Cuirassier Regiment
      4/9th, 4/10th, 4/11th, 4/12th Cuirassier Regiments
    Cuirassier Regiment de marche
      3/, 4/, 5/28th Chasseurs à cheval Regiment (3) (dismounted)
    Depot/17th Polish Uhlan Regiment
    General Cavalry Depot

Other troops:
  13th Veteran Battalion (600 men)
  Isolated Depot Battalion
  Foot and Horse Customs Soldiers
  Foot and Horse Gendarmes (230 men)
  Reserve and Grand Park
  4/5th Horse Artillery Company
  8/4th Sapper Battalion
  Artillery Artisan Det.
  Det. 4/5th (bis) Artillery Train
  Det. 1/6th (bis) Artillery Train
  Det. 3/6th (bis) Artillery Train
  Det. 1/6th Principal Artillery Train
  12th Equipage Train Battalion
  5th Equipage de Flotille (25 gunboats) (1,200 men)
  Naval Artificier Battalion (600 men)
  Fortress Artillery: (3,630 men)
  8th Artillery Regiment (six companies)
  Three Artillery Companies from other Artillery Regiments

On 19 November 1813 Bülow and Winzingerode – commanders of part of the Army of the North – were ordered to clear northwest Germany of the French army. On 1 December an Allied Army of the North, with 45,000 men and 153 guns, stood before Hamburg. Davout responded by withdrawing the bulk of his field army into the city, but Bernadotte had his eyes on Norway and soon departed – leaving only a light screen to blockade Hamburg as he marched north with the rest of his army.

By the middle of November, a Russian corps of about 7,000 men and 36 guns – commanded by Stroganov – stood on the left bank of the Elbe. On 29 November he received orders to blockade

Haarburg. Stroganov began a series of skirmishes and Cossack patrols around the outworks in the villages of Wilftorf, Eisendorf and Heimfeld.

Corps: Generallieutenant Stroganov
- 12th Division: Generalmajor Cherwansky
  - Brigade: Generalmajor Sanders
    - Smolensk Infantry Regiment (2)
    - Narva Infantry Regiment (2)
  - Brigade: Generalmajor Schwetschin
    - Alexopol Infantry Regiment (2)
    - New Ingermannland Infantry Regiment (1)
  - Brigade: Generallieutenant Glebov
    - 6th Jager Regiment (2)
    - 41st Jager Regiment (1)
  - Brigade from 13th Division: Generalmajor Scheltuchin
    - Pensa Infantry Regiment (2)
    - Saratov Infantry Regiment (2)
  - Position Battery #31
  - Light Batteries #53 & #46

On the right bank of the Elbe stood Voronzov with his Russian corps of 7,134 men and 30 guns – supported by von Lützow's Freikorps of 2,322 men and nine guns – and the Hamburg Bürgergarde of 280 men and 30 cavalry (plus a few battalions of Mecklenburg Landwehr that had been left behind).

Infantry: Generallieutenant Count Voronzov
- 21st Division: Generalmajor Leptev
  - Brigade: Colonel Rosen
    - Petrovsk Infantry Regiment (1)
    - Lithuania Infantry Regiment (1)
    - Podolsk Infantry Regiment (1)
  - Brigade: Colonel Rüdinger
    - Neva Infantry Regiment (1)
    - 2nd Jager Regiment (1)
    - 44th Jager Regiment (2)
- Division: Generalmajor Vuitsch
  - Brigade: Generalmajor Swarikin
    - Chirvan Infantry Regiment (2)
    - Bourtirki Infantry Regiment (2)
    - 19th Jager Regiment (2)
  - Brigade: Generalmajor Laharpe
    - Navaguinsk Infantry Regiment (1)
    - Tula Infantry Regiment (1)
    - Converged Grenadier Battalions 9th, 15th & 18th Divisions
  - Brigade: Generalmajor Krassovsky
    - Oumsk Infantry Regiment (2)
    - 13th Jager Regiment (2)
    - 14th Jager Regiment (2)

Artillery:
Horse Batteries #1 (10), #4 (8), #7 (12), #11 (12), #13 (12) & #21 (12 guns)
Light Batteries #42, #48 & #56
Position Batteries #7, #28 & #31

When the French withdrew from Schwarzenbeck to Bergdorf on 3 December Voronzov followed them with his forces. His headquarters were established in Ahrensburg on 6 December and on 9 December they were in Duvenstedt, with his advanced posts on the line running from Wellingsbüttel-Rahlstedt-Bergdorf. On 13 December the lines shrank again – with Voronzov moving his headquarters to Pinneberg – and on the eastern front only part of the von Lützow Freikorps, the Bürgergarde and the Mecklenbergers remained.[3]

The Polish Reserve Army – some 30,000 men under the command of General Count von Bennigsen – had, after completing the capture of Dresden, marched westwards. On 24 December the lead elements of the Polish Reserve Army – under generals Docturov and Tschaplitz – arrived on the Elbe.

During the last days of December, Bennigsen's army moved up and closed off Hamburg from the right bank of the Elbe. On the left bank of the Elbe, General Stroganov took up positions and blockaded Haarburg.

During the last days of December, the occupation of Bille and Ochsenwerder were contested with a number of skirmishes. During the night of 1-2 January the Russians attempted a landing against Ochsenwerder with eight ships loaded with Russian troops. They were, however, so heavily engaged by the French that they withdrew with heavy losses.

On 3 January GL Markov attacked the villages of Winterhude, Eppendorf, Hohenluft and Eimsbüttel and threw the French out of them. The French, under General Delcambre, counterattacked and recovered the lost villages.[4]

On 5 January the French dispatched an 800-man-strong attack against the advanced posts of General Tschaplitz by Eichbaum. The French attack drove the Russians back. However, Russian reinforcements soon arrived and the French withdrew.

Eight days later – on 13 January – a strong French detachment marched against the villages of Winterhude, Uhlenhorst and Eppendorf, which were occupied by the blockading troops of the Russian right wing under GL Markov. The French attacked these villages, but they were repulsed after a vigorous fight.[5]

On 20 January the Allies undertook a double assault. On the left bank, Bennigsen directed Stroganov to attack Haarburg and the Black hill. A small village by Haarburg and a blockhouse to the south of the city were taken. The French withdrew into the fortress and the Russian column followed up the Winsener road. In the fortress, General Pécheux held a small reserve of his best troops – the elite companies of the 48th and 108th Line Regiments and the 5th Naval Equipage Battalion. They attacked the left flank of the Russian column and drove them back.[6]

Bennigsen, by G. Dawe.

3 Henke, pp. 124-5.
4 Henke, p. 127.
5 Sporschil, Vol. I, p. 1,203.
6 Henke, p. 129.

In the engagement, the Russian troops spiked nine heavy guns and captured 150 and killed 30 Frenchmen. In addition to the success of this attack, General Tschemschushnikoff undertook yet another attack against Ochsenwerder on the Island of Wilhelmsburg. The entrenchments of Moorwerder Island were destroyed, the French thrown out, four guns taken and 12 officers and 500 men were taken prisoners.

On 25 January – after General Rossy, with his troops from Magdeburg, had arrived to join the Blockade Corps – Graf Bennigsen ordered him to attack the French and push them into an even smaller region. He launched his attack against the fortified village of Hamm on the right bank – from the so-called Auffschläger Weg – and from Stadtdeich (and at the same time, he launched another attack against the outerworks by Wandsbeck and Altona). GM Tschemschuschnikoff struck from Ochsenwerder aainst the Moorfelt entrenchments and captured them. Colonel Wotoroff struck at the French positions by Auffschlag, which he carried and occupied. General Gogel attacked the fortified suburb of Hamm frontally and in the flank – and captured it after an hour's engagement. The French occupied the church court, but they were also driven from that position. General Rossy attacked with two columns from Wandsbeck and struck the French advanced posts – driving them back – while General Markov attacked from Altona. Despite the deep snow and the intense French fire, all of the Allied attacks of this day succeeded. All of the various positions were taken by bayonet. The French were driven back to within canister range of the city – with heavy casualties – and the loss of eight officers and 300 soldiers taken prisoner.

Around this time, General Stroganov resumed his march to the Rhine and was relieved by the corps of GL Count Wallmoden on the left bank of the Elbe. On 23 and 24 January the Hanoverian line brigade (with the exception of some battalions, which remained in Glückstadt) took up quarters by the city; the light brigade in and around Buxtehude; and the cavalry, the Russo-German Legion and the Hanseatic troops by Winsen and Hittfeld.[7]

On 26 January GL Wallmoden's troops took over the blockade of Haarburg. Four battalions of the Russo-German Legion and their jager companies – the 1st Russo-German Legion Hussar Regiment – and a horse artillery battery took up posts to the right of Hittfeld and stretching on to the Elbe. As support for this group, the other three legion battalions – the 2nd Russo-German Legion Hussar Regiment – and two horse batteries were posted in Winsen. To the left of Hittfeld and extending on to the Elbe stood the light and line brigades of Hanoverian troops, three Hanoverian squadrons, six squadrons of Hanseatic Hussars and two foot batteries. The blockade force on the left bank of the Elbe had 7,000 men – including 1,800 cavalry. The Hanseatic infantry had withdrawn to Bremen to reorganize.

The French troops were, since the attack of 20 January, limited to occupying Haarburg proper and in the entrenchments on the Black, Gromhof and the Krumm forest hills. The villages of Lauenbrook, Ecksdorf and Wilsdorfer lay under the guns of the fortifications of Haarburg. The time of the year made bivouacing very difficult – and it was at this time that only weak posts were placed out, while the support troops stood to the rear. The French remained calm and occupied only their entrenchments outside Neuland, which were necessary for their communications across the Elbe to Ochsenwerder.

The Elbe was Davout's link to Haarburg when flowing, but it was his enemy when frozen – and now it was covered with ice. Bennigsen decided, therefore, to execute an assault on the Island of Wilhelmsburg. On 2 February the Russian Opolochenie Corps of GL Count Tolstoy arrived before Hamburg. The blockading corps on the right bank of the Elbe was now divided into three corps. The left wing was under GdI Docturov; in the center was that of GL Tolstoy; and the right wing was under GL Markov. The purpose of the intended attack on the Island of Wilhelmsburg

7 Sporschil, Vol. I, p. 1,204.

was, if possible, to break the link between Hamburg and Haarburg. General Ahrenschildt was instructed to support this undertaking with an attack on Haarburg. The day set for the attack was 9 February.

Three columns were organized of Russian troops. The first – under GM Emme, who replaced GM Paskevich – was directed to move from Ochsenwerder against the French posts by Busch, and from there against the batteries by Götzerhorst. It contained nine battalions of the 26th Division, four light cannon, 200 Cossacks, two squadrons of regular cavalry and a pioneer company.

The second column, under General Tolstoy, was to march against the Red bridge and the Billwerder in order to link with the first column on Wilhelmsburg Island. The column contained eight battalions, four light cannon, 200 Cossacks, two squadrons of regular cavalry and a pioneer company.

The third column, under General Markov, was to march from Neinstädten below Altona on the frozen Elbe and take the French posts on the Waltershof and Tradenau islands in the rear, while their main force marched over Rossneuhof Island towards Wilhelmsburg to link with the other two columns. Markov's column contained eight battalions, four light cannon, 200 Cossacks, two squadrons of regular cavalry and an engineer company.[8]

General Ahrenschildt was instructed to advance over the Elbe dike by Lauenbrook and strike the French fortifications at Haarburg in support of the Russian attacks on Wilhelmsburg. At the same time, he was ordered to organize his attack column so that when Wilhelmsburg was taken and the Russians were in the French rear striking at Haarburg, he was to launch a heavy attack against the front of the French entrenchments.

The plan was executed on 9 February before daybreak. The first column, under Emme, struck quickly and drove the French back with bayonets – taking their posts. As they moved towards the main bridge, a French support column came forward, but it was repulsed and six heavy cannon were taken. The French General Osten was wounded and captured. The march of the second column, under Tolstoy, was hindered by the ice and it was unable to support the attack of the first column.[9]

The third column, under Markov, fulfilled to that extent their objectives as they had sent a detachment into the rear of the French posts on Waltershof and Tradenau islands – and then, with their main column, marched against Rossneuhof Island, where they overran a battery and marched towards Wilhelmsburg. However, as they closed on the bridge, they were met with heavy artillery fire that drove them back.

The Russian attack captured 12 cannon, 60 powder wagons and 30,000 cartridges – as well as a large quantity of food – and 16 officers and 1,000 men prisoners. The Allies estimated the French losses at 1,000 dead and wounded – including generals Osten and Romè and three colonels. The Russians lost 15 officers and 300-400 men.

The capture of Wilhelmsburg Island had not succeeded, however – but not because of a failure of the diversionary attack against Haarburg. The 4th and 6th Battalions, Russo-German Legion, were on the right wing and marched against Ballenhausen and Neuland; the Hanoverian troops on the left flank marched against Moorburg; while in the center, the remaining troops of the Russo-German Legion marched against the French entrenchments. A heavy fire erupted on the side of Neuland to open the battle. The skirmishers of the 4th RGL Battalion supported by two companies of the 4th RGL Battalion attacked Fünfhusen – and though it was defended by 800 French of the 48th and 61st Line Regiments under General Rome, they carried both Fünfhusen and Neuland. Their attack was successful, but they lost two officers and 89 men dead and wounded.

8 Henke, p. 137.
9 Sporschil, Vol. I, p. 1,205.

The next attack did not occur until 17 February when Bennigsen ordered a new attack on Wilhelmsburg Island. Detachments under Tschaplitz and Schepeleff were to attack Hamburg and Arenschildt was to attack Haarburg, while two columns advancing from Billwerder and Ochsenwerder – under generals Emme and Tolstoy – struck at Wilhelmsburg and a third column (under Markov) marched from Altona to join with them.

Davout was forewarned of the attack. The garrison of Wilhelmsburg was maintained at full alert and met the Russian attack with a vigorous defense. The three Russian columns marched down the main road – striking Hamburg and Haarburg frontally – and threw the French behind the walls of the city. General Ahrenschildt – attacking with the 1st and 6th RGL Battalions – caused the French in Haarburg to destroy the last bridge linking it to Wilhelmsburg. This success finally broke the link between the garrisons of Haarburg and Hamburg. This done, Bennigsen gave the order of the Russian troops to break off their attack. Four cannon, seven officers and 312 French soldiers were captured. The total French losses – as reported by the Allies – were 500 dead and wounded, while the Russians admitted to losing seven officers and 87 men.[10]

On 23 February the Allies launched another attack on Wilhelmsburg. The battle was short and the Russian attack failed. Further attacks were launched on 24 and 28 February – and again on 5, 6 and 12 March. None of them succeeded.

The blockade of the fortress continued uneventfully until the middle of March, when Graf Wallmoden – leading his Hanoverian troops and the Russo-German Legion – departed for the Rhine. His positions were taken over by the English General Lyon, who commanded the Hanseatic troops and a small detachment of Hanoverian troops before Haarburg. Even this force was ordered off on 4 April when it was sent to Bremen. Graf Tolstoy then took over their positions with seven opolochenie battalions, an infantry brigade, four cavalry regiments and three batteries.

1st Hanoverian Division: Major General Lyon[11]
- Light Brigade: Lt. Colonel Martin
  - Lüneburg Battalion
  - Bremen-Verden Battalion
- Line Brigade: Lt. Colonel Hackett
  - Lauenburg Battalion
  - von Bennigsen Battalion
  - von Langwehr Battalion
- Hanseatic Brigade: Oberst von Witzleben
  - 1st Battalion
  - 3rd Battalion

Cavalry:
- Lüneburg Hussar Regiment
- Bremen und Verden Hussar Regiment
- Hanseatic Cavalry Regiment
- Chur-Hannoversche Feldjäger

Russo-German Legion: Generalleutnant von Ahrentschild
- Jager Company
- 1st Russo-German Battalion

10 Sporschil, Vol. I, p. 1,206.
11 Henke, p. 130.

2nd Russo-German Battalion
3rd Russo-German Battalion
4th Russo-German Battalion
5th Russo-German Battalion
6th Russo-German Battalion
7th Russo-German Battalion
1st Russo-German Hussar Regiment
2nd Russo-German Hussar Regiment

General Emme occupied the line between the right bank of the Elbe and Bille with his troops. General Tschaplitz's troops were between Bille and the left bank of the Old Elbe Canal, where stood the two detachments of GdI Docturov. Markov's forces stood between the right bank of the old Elbe Canal and the Elbe.

Orders had arrived in Hamburg for Davout to break out of his fortress and link up with the garrison of Magdeburg. Once united, they were to march through Holland. On 1 April General Pécheux led three battalions against the Moorburger entrenchments and the adjoining dike. The French attack was driven back by Major Klenke – leading the Lüneburg jägers. On 4 April the French again struck at the Moorburger entrenchments. Davout personally led a column against the Damm road and General Vichery led a second column to its right as they marched against the heights by the Moorburger trenches. The Moorburger works were occupied by the French, with the support of guns firing from across the Elbe. The Allies rushed forward reserves and stabilized the situation. The French then withdrew back into the fortress.[12]

No further attempts were made by the French to break the blockade. On 14 April the first news arrived in Hamburg of the events in Paris. Lt. Colonel Aubert, a Danish officer, was sent to Hamburg with a note from Bennigsen. He was authorized to negotiate an armistice and transmitted Bennigsen's note, which stated that the Allies had occupied Paris and that the French senate had recognized Louis XVIII as King of France. In an exchange of notes, Davout requested that a French officer be sent to France to verify the truth of what Bennigsen had told him and to obtain orders from the French government. However, before this could be arranged, on 20 April a note was sent to Davout stating that two French officers had arrived from the French government and requested to enter the city. Word was also sent of Napoleon's abdication. On 26 April negotiations began on an agreement between Davout and Bennigsen which would send a French officer – in the company of a Russian officer – to Paris with dispatches from Davout. Hostilities between the two sides would cease. No further work would continue on the fortress' fortifications; there was a total exchange of all prisoners held; and assurances were made for the maintenance public and private property – and for the delivery of food – by the Russians.

Meanwhile in Paris, General Delcambre had been given orders by Louis XVIII to go to Hamburg with a dispatch requesting that Davout evacuate Hamburg, Haarburg and the surrounding fortifications. On 11 May General Count Gérard arrived in Hamburg with a letter from General Dupont – the new Minister of War – stating that Gérard was to assume command of the XIII Corps, the garrison of Hamburg. Realizing that it was truly finished, on 11 May 1814 Davout turned command over to him. The French finally departed Hamburg on 31 May.[13]

12 Sporschil, Vol. I, p. 1,207.
13 Vigier, pp. 171-88.

Sieges in France

When the Allied army was reorganized for the invasion of France, it consisted of the Army of Bohemia – or the 'Hauptarmee' ('Main army') – under the command of Feldmarschal Fürsten Schwarzenberg. This army was organized with two independent divisions – those of Bubna (1st Light Division) and M. Liechtenstein (2nd Light Division) – and six army corps under Colloredo (1st Corps), A. Liechtenstein (2nd Corps), Giulay (3rd Corps), the Russian corps under Wittgenstein (6th Corps), the Bavarian – or 1st – German Bundescorps (5th Corps) under Wrede, and the Württemberg or – 7th – German Bundescorps (4th Corps). In addition, there was the main army reserve, which included the Austrian Reserve Corps of Erbprinzen von Hesse-Homburg and the Russo-Prussian Guard and Grenadiers under Barclay de Tolly. All told, it had 228,650 men and 684 guns when the invasion began.

In addition to these forces, two other German Bundescorps were raised. The first was the 6th German Bundescorps, which was organized with troops from Austria, Würzburg, Frankfurt, Hessen-Darmstédt, Isenburg and Reuss under the command of Prince Philippe von Hesse-Homburg. The second was the 8th German Bundescorps and was formed with troops from Baden, Hohenzollern and Liechtenstein under the command of General Grafen von Hochberg. This corps was later reinforced by the addition of 10,000 Württemberg troops. These two German Bundescorps were to add 33,000 men to support the Allied main army.

The Army of Silesia, under Blücher, contained 93,391 men and 436 guns. As a reinforcement to the Army of Silesia, two German Bundescorps were organized. The first was the 4th German (Kurhessen) Bundescorps – which was organized under the command of Kurprinz von Hessen – and the other was the 5th German Bundescorps (containing troops from Berg, Waldeck, Lippe, Nassau, von Coburg, Meiningen, Hildburghausen and Mecklenburg-Strelitz organized under the command of the Duke of Saxe-Coburg). They would provide the Army of Silesia with another 44,000 men.

The Army of the North was under the command of Bernadotte, the Crown Prince of Sweden. It was a combined force of Russians, Prussians and Swedes. The Russian Polish Reserve Army was in Hamburg. Tauentzien's Prussian corps was besieging the various French garrisons in fortresses along the Oder and Elbe. Bülow and Winzingerode's corps were to operate in the lowlands and eventually advance into France to join the main Allied armies. Bernadotte's Army of the North commanded some 60,850 men and 258 guns.

As a reinforcement to this army, two further German Bundescorps were organized. The 3rd German Bundescorps was organized with troops from the Kingdom of Saxony and the Saxon Ducal houses of Weimar and Gotha, Schwarzberg, and Anhalt under the Duke of Weimar. The 2nd German Bundescorps was organized with troops from Hanover, Brunswick, Oldenburg, the Hanseatic Cities and Mecklenburg-Schwerin and placed under the command of the Duke of Walmoden. These two corps would have a total of 60,000 men.[14]

Tauentzien.

14 Renouard, pp. 16-7.

However, these new corps were not raised immediately. Parts of them were formed from the remnants of the German contingents that had fought with Napoleon in 1813 (so there were trained cadres), but the bulk of the troops were new drafts. In Hanover, Brunswick and Hesse-Kassel, the armies were organized from the remains of the Westphalian army. The formation of new armies takes time – even if the cadres are solid and well-trained. They take uniforms, weapons, munitions, horses and a multitude of other material in order to be ready to take to the field and engage an enemy. As a result, these Bundescorps did not spring from the ground that Napoleon had sewn with dragons' teeth as fully-armed warriors. Indeed, they began organizing once Napoleon had departed Germany, but they would not arrive in France to join the Allied armies duelling with Napoleon until the campaign was well under way. Once these formations were organized, they dribbled into the field in brigade and divisional strength rather than as a fully-formed corps.

As the Allied armies pushed into France, they bypassed several powerful fortresses where the French had placed garrisons. Historically, it had been the practice to reduce such fortresses before advancing into the enemy's country, but since the French Revolution, it became more and more common for the invading army to bypass fortresses – sealing them in with blockading forces – and pushing their main armies against the enemy.

In 1814, however, the Allies masked the major fortresses of Metz, Thionville, Luxemburg, Saarlouis, Longwy and several other fortress cities as they pushed into France. The blockade and actions of these fortresses are closely interlinked and, as a result, difficult to examine separately. As a result, the actual blockades of Metz, Thionville, Luxemburg and Saarlouis will be discussed first and separately. Where the blockades of these fortresses interlink during GD Durutte's operations, the actions around each of these fortresses will be addressed in chronological sequence. In addition, it is necessary for the reader to understand that sieges are generally months of boredom punctuated by an occasional few moments of battle that quickly subside back into the boredom of intermittent artillery fire and the digging of trenches.

Metz

On 4 January 1814 the Duke of Valmy – Maréchal Kellermann – issued an order of the day concerning these three fortresses. They were to be provisioned to withstand a siege of two months and to prepare for the Allied advance.

Metz was a fortress of the first rank and was one of the strongest fortresses in France. It lay at the junction of the Seille and the Moselle rivers, with the main city and fortress lying on the right bank of the Moselle. On the left bank of the Moselle was a strong bridgehead, which was linked to the city with a stone bridge. The city and bridgehead were surrounded by strong walls and a ditch that could be flooded. In addition, in preparation for the coming campaign, the glacis was cleared of houses for a distance of 1,500 paces. To the east, in the direction of Saarlouis, was the Fort Belle Croix.

The city had a population of 40,000 souls and the garrison – under GD Durutte – consisted of 5,000 infantry, 3,000 National Guards and 200 cavalry from the depots of various regiments. The city's walls were armed with numerous guns and the city's magazines did not lack ammunition.[15]

The blockade of Metz began on 17 January with forces from Yorck's corps – specifically Horn and Pirch's brigades. On 6 February 1814 the fortress of Metz was blockaded by Russian troops of the 1st Dragoon Division under GL Borosdin. These troops were later relieved by those of General Yusseffovich. On 24 March Yusseffovich's forces were relieved by the Kur-Hessian Brigade under

15 Renouard, pp. 59-60.

General Müller.[16] On 26 March Müller's brigade before Metz consisted of the Kurfürst and Kurprinz Regiments, the 2nd "von Lossberg" Grenadier Battalion, two battalions of the 3rd Landwehr Regiment, the 1/,2/,3/,4/Leib Dragoons, the Hussar Regiment, the 3rd Freiwilliger Reitende Jäger Squadron and the Holzapfel Battery. It had a total of about 7,750 men.[17]

On 31 March GM von Müller was ordered to reduce the forces around Metz to an observation force and march with the rest to Luxemburg. He detached the Leib Dragoon Regiment, Kurprinz Regiment, 3rd Reitende Jäger Squadron and the Holzapfel Battery. Of this force, two squadrons of the Leib Dragoons; the Kurprinz Regiment; the Gelernte Jägers; and six guns were left in Luxemburg and the rest returned to Metz.[18]

Thionville

General Hugo – who was named to command Thionville on 10 January – implemented this order by requisitioning supplies from the villages on the left bank of the Moselle in the vicinity for a distance of two or three leagues.

Thionville was no stranger to war. In 1792 it had been bombarded by the Austrians. The city had 6,000 residents and stood on the left bank of the Moselle in a small and terrible plain. It was surrounded by wooded hills – many of which were within cannon-shot of the city. It was closely surrounded by several small villages: Sierck, Rodemack, Hettange, Florange, Cathenon, Manom and Konismaker ('Königsmachern', or 'King Maker') to name a few. The first two – Sierck and Rodemack – contained the Near fortresses, which were military posts. The first stood on the road from Thionville to Trier and the second was positioned to guard the eastern approaches to the city. However, because of the cramped space between the river and the hills, everything was well within the effective range of either muskets or cannon.

In 1814 the city's fortifications consisted of a forward work covered with bastions. The Luxemburg Gate exited the city through a horn work, while the right bank of the Moselle was covered with a crown work and a fortress. These two works covered the roads to Saarlouis and Trier and communicated with the main fortress via a wooden bridge on masonry piers.

The garrison consisted of the Young Guard Division of GD Decouz and the depot of the 96th Line Regiment – reinforced with various conscripts. However, on 14 January the Young Guard was sent to Metz – leaving only 150 men behind in the depots. In the interim, Hugo organized a few companies of National Guard and organized a company from the workers of the city and the Haute-Yutz and Basse-Yutz regions. Further reinforcements arrived on 11 January when a 300-man-strong battalion of the 14th Line Regiment arrived – and on 24 January when 300 armed conscripts assigned to various light regiments were incorporated into the depot of the 96th Line Regiment. Finally, a weak gendarmes battalion was organized.

The garrison was now, however, to remain constant until the Allies arrived and closed it off. There was a constant flow of convoys between Thionville and the other fortresses. One such convoy of 300 men was sent to Luxemburg on 12 January.

Though the garrison of Thionville was small, every effort was made to improve the fortifications of the city. The walls were strengthened, the glacis were cleared and the ditch flooded. The walls mounted 30 guns.[19]

16 Sporschil, p. 437.
17 Renouard, p. 116.
18 "Gelernte jager" were "learned huntsmen." These were men who were experienced huntsmen that entered service and were crack shots.
19 Renouard, pp. 61-3.

The blockade of Thionville began on 17 January with forces from the 2nd Prussian Corps Reserve Cavalry under GM von Röder. The Prussians were shortly relieved by three battalions and a squadron of Jäger zu Pferd of the Kur-Hessian Brigade of General Müller – a total of 2,500 men and a half-battery. This force consisted of the 1st Grenadier Battalion and the 1/,2/Kurfürst Regiment.

On 13 February the garrison launched a major sortie, with further sorties on 18, 19, 26 February and 9 March. On 18 and 19 February there were major sorties and an engagement. On 18 February the French force consisted of 1,500 infantry and 30 cavalry. The sortie of 19 February was much smaller – containing only about 100 infantry and 40 cavalry.[20]

By 21 February Müller's brigade grew to include the 1st Grenadier Battalion, the Fus/,1/,2/ Kurfürst Regiment, two companies of Gelernte Jägers, two companies of Freiwilliger Fussjäger and two squadrons of the Freiwilliger Reitende Jäger. The force came to a total of 3,387 men. Further Hessian reinforcements flowed into Müller's brigade – including the 1st and 3rd Landwehr Regiments and the Holzapfel Foot Battery. These companies were formed from college students.

On 26 February the sortie contained a force of 300 infantry, 20 cavalry and two cannon. The French had with them a force of wagons – and the purpose of their sortie was to gather supplies from the surrounding territory. The resulting engagement with the Hessians was not very serious in that the Hessians lost only two dead, 13 wounded and four missing. On 9 March a force of 300 to 400 French sortied against Manom. This was, however, not quite as serious an engagement as that of 26 February and they withdrew back into the fortress.[21] The blockade of Thionville was re-established on 30 March because of Durutte's march.[22]

Luxemburg

The blockade of Luxemburg began on 17 January with forces from Yorck's corps. The Prussians were relieved by the Hessians under General Dörenberg, who commanded the Fus/Kurfürst and the 1/,2/Kurprinz Regiments. They were later reinforced by the arrival of the Prinz Solms Regiment and the 1st Freiwilliger Fussjäger Company (von Eschwege) and 200 hussars.[23] Command of the blockade forces passed to GM Prince von Solms-Braunfels and Dörenberg assumed overall command of the blockade forces of both Thionville and Luxemburg. By 22 February Solms-Braunfels commanded a force consisting of the Fus/Kurprinz Regiment, the Landgraf Karl and Prinz Solms Regiments, two companies of Gelernte Jägers, one company of Freiwilliger Fussjäger, a detachment of hussars, the "Wille" Battery and a detachment of miners. The force contained 4,876 men.[24]

The garrison executed sorties against their antagonists on 13 and 15 February and on 8, 15 and 18 March. On 13 February an engagement was executed by a force of three French infantry companies – about 50 cavalry – and two guns. The 15 February sortie was executed by a similar force. On 15 February the siege forces, under General von Dörenberg, consisted of:

Kurfürst Grenadier Battalion
Kurprinz Grenadier Battalion
1/, 2/, 3/Kurfürst Infantry Regiment
1/, 2/, 3/Kurprinz Infantry Regiment

---

20 Renouard, pp. 150-1.
21 Renouard, pp. 161-2.
22 Sporschil, p. 438.
23 Renouard, p. 111.
24 Renouard, p. 112.

Landgraf Karl Infantry Regiment
Prinz Solms Infantry Regiment
Gelernte Feldjäger
Freiwilliger Fussjäger
Hussar Detachment
Freiwilliger Reitende Jäger
Detachment of Miners and Sappers
Total: 8,856 men

On 8 March there was a major engagement by Eich and Weimerschkirch. The French attacked at 7:30 a.m. with a force of about 100 men and a gun against Weimerschkirch, which was defended by the Fus/Kurprinz Regiment. Hauptmann von Dalwigk's 4th Company defended the village. The 3rd Company, under Hauptmann Ebert, covered the left flank. The 1st Company (Hauptmann Neuber) defended Eich and the 2nd Company (Hauptmann von Berlepsch) stood as a reserve. The French eventually brought forward a second gun and the engagement lasted until 2:00 p.m. The Hessians lost 12 dead, 37 wounded and seven missing.

The sortie on 15 March was in the same area as that of 8 March, but the 18 March sortie struck at Herl and Hollerich. The forces engaged were small and the casualties were minor.

On 26 March the blockading force was under GM Prince von Solms-Braunfels and consisted of the Landgraf Karl and Prinz Solms Regiments, three companies of Freiwilliger Fussjäger, a detachment of hussars, half of the "Wille" Foot Battery and a detachment of miners. It came to a total of 3,980 men.[25]

The progress of the siege was broken by the appearance of General Durutte's division, which drove off the weak blockading force. On 3 May the French departed the fortress and returned to France.

Saarlouis

The blockade of Saarlouis began on 17 January with forces from Yorck's corps. On 19 January a battery of four 10pdr and four 7pdr howitzers was set up and began bombarding the fortress.[26] Among the blockading forces were the Mitau Dragoons and the 4th Ukranian Cossack Regiment. However, on 23 January the Cossacks were sent to Mézières. The blockade duties were taken over by Major von Bieberstein, who continued its blockade until the end of the campaign. On 26 March Major von Bieberstein commanded two companies of the 2/1st Kur-Hessian Landwehr Regiment, the 1st Silesian Landwehr Uhlan Regiment (240-250 men) and the von Grolmann Prussian Infantry Battalion. His command came to a total of 1,018 men.[27]

Verdun and Longwy

These two fortresses were not blockaded for a long time. It was with the appearance of General Prince Biron von Courland – with his column of replacement battalions and independent squadrons after the Battle of Brienne – that they were finally blockaded. Prince Biron von Courland's orders were to keep these two fortresses masked so that the garrisons could not disrupt the flow of supplies to the Army of Silesia.

25 Renouard, p. 116.
26 Renouard, p. 74.
27 Renouard, p. 117.

General Prince Biron von Courland's problems multiplied when a popular insurrection broke out – instigated and supported by the garrisons of Verdun and Longwy. On 23 March – when ordered to quell the disturbances – he marched out of Nancy with a mixed force of Prussians and Russians consisting of 4,720 infantry, 742 cavalry and 12 guns.

Continuing his effort to suppress the rebellion, Prince Biron von Courland marched to Bar-le-Duc surrounded and harried by the armed peasantry. General Yusseffovich, who commanded the Metz blockading force, detached a force to Toul to support him. On 26 March the greatest portion of his forces were at Naives and his advanced guard was in Bar-le-Duc. Here, he linked up with General Winzingerode after his disastrous battle at St.-Dizier. Winzingerode joined his forces with those of Prince Biron von Courland and then led the combined force to Saint-Mihiel on the Mass, where they covered the city of Nancy. On 27 March, with the threat of an engagement with Napoleon gone, this combined force then marched on Verdun – encountering a force of French in the field.

Verdun's garrison commander was General Duvigneau, who had marched out of Verdun to meet the Allies. He commanded 3,000 men, five cannon and was supported by a large force of armed peasants. Prince Biron von Courland attacked him and threw him back. Prince Biron von Courland then marched on Verdun to attack the city. He detached a force of cavalry to Bar-le-Duc and another in the direction of Chaumont on reconnaissance missions. The French had abandoned both Bar-le-Duc and Ligny. They were now occupied by the Prussians.

In the meantime, General Yusseffovich had been relieved before Metz by General Müller's Kur-Hessians and marched on Estain in order to attack Verdun. The Allied general governor of Lorraine – Alopäus – however, ordered him to suppress the revolution in the countryside. On 1 April General Prince Biron von Courland learned that Durutte was in Thionville and Luxemburg – with a force of 12,000 men and 39 guns – and that he was marching on Verdun. Von Courland retreated towards Bar-le-Duc to escape certain destruction. From there, he marched on Nancy and then on to Bernécourt, where on 1 April he joined with the forces of General Yusseffovich. This combined force then marched on Neuf Château. On 3 April the two generals were at Bernécourt and General Müller's Kur-Hessians were in Pont-à-Mousson. In addition, the Prussian forces – under Oberst von Unruh – were in Pont-à-Mousson.

The combined forces of Prince Biron von Courland and Yusseffovich were as strong as those of Durutte – and the decision was made to engage Durutte in battle. However, Durutte had already withdrawn his division under the guns of Metz. Only the French advanced guard could safely be attacked – and it was engaged and driven back. A combined attack by the forces of Prince Biron von Courland, Yusseffovich and Müller was in the process of being planned when word came of the fall of Paris, Napoleon's abdication and the ascension of Louis XVIII to the throne – ending the campaign.[28]

Durutte's operations

After the Battle of Arcis-sur-Aube, Napoleon had marched to strike the lines of communication of the Allied main army. He sent General Durutte an order to take most of the troops from Metz and draw detachments from the fortresses of Thionville, Saarlouis, Luxemburg, Verdun and Longwy and organize them into a division with which he should either join Napoleon's main army or march against Schwarzenberg's flank (should it be exposed to such a blow). Durutte marched out of Metz with 8,000 men – moving through Bouzenville and to Saarlouis – then to Thionville. The blockading force before Thionville was under Oberst von Haynau and consisted of the 1st Grenadier Battalion, a battalion from the 1st and 2nd Landwehr Regiments, two

28 Sporschil, p. 439.

companies of Gelernte Jägers, two companies of Freiwilliger Fussjägers, three squadrons of the Freiwilliger Reitende Jägers, a detachment of miners and half the "Wille" Foot Battery. It came to a total of 3,300 men.[29]

The first word of Durutte's advance in the Thionville blockade corps came from two Cossacks of the Metz blockade corps when they contacted Major von Haller on 16 March. Haller quickly sent word to GM von Müller that as he had been told by the Cossacks, Durutte's column consisted of three infantry battalions and a cavalry regiment.

At about 3:00 p.m. Durutte's column emerged from the Illange forest and marched directly on Thionville. The next morning, they encountered Hessian entrenchments at La Grange and moved directly to attack them with musketry and cannon fire. The engagement was short and sharp – with the French not pressing the attack home.

That morning at 9:30 a.m. a column of 650 men of the 96th Regiment, about 60 recovering wounded of the Young Guard, three 4pdr cannon and two munitions wagons executed a sortie and marched towards Metz (and were on the right bank of the Moselle). The purpose of this was a diversion intended to distract the Hessian detachment in Metz. General Hugo marched out of Metz – in yet another sortie – and marched towards Saarlouis with a strong column formed from the 14th Line Regiment and two cannon.

General Durutte sent a sortie towards Haute-Yutz. The French accomplished their purpose and Major Haller's force was reduced by the detachment of some of his forces to the right bank of the Moselle. The Hessians not only relaxed their vigil in the Illange woods, but also in its vicinity, which opened up Durutte's proposed line of advance. Major von Haller was quickly engaged in a vicious fight with General Hugo's column. Casualties were not great and the Hessians were driven in the direction of Longwy.

On 19 March the Hessian forces – under von Müller – were deployed as follows: On the left bank of the Moselle, GM von Müller's headquarters stood in Hettange. The 1/Kurfürst was deployed in cantonments in Hettange, Zetrich, Garsch, Koeking and Cathenon. They were supported by an artillery detachment with one howitzer, two cannon; a Freiwilliger Fussjäger and Gelernte Jäger detachment of four officers, 26 NCOs and 282 soldiers; and a mounted detachment of three officers, seven NCOs and 35 Reitende Jägers.

In Guentrange, Weymerange and Betange was a force under Major Brethauer. It consisted of Fus/Kurfürst; a detachment of one officer, 7 NCOs and 74 Freiwilliger Fussjägers; and a detachment of one officer and six Reitende Jägers. In Hebange, Daspich and Florange – under Major Reiss – was the 2/Kurfürst Regiment; two officers, five NCOs and 80 Freiwilliger Fussjägers; one officer, two NCOs and 20 Reitende Jägers.

On the right bank of the Moselle, the 1st Grenadier Battalion was deployed in Illange, Erpelhof, Stuckange, Kenzich and Basse-Ham; four officers, 20 NCOs, 218 Freiwilliger Fussjägers and Gelernte Jägers; one officer, four NCOs and 31 Reitende Jägers; and one officer and four artillerists.

On 21 March the newly-arrived 4th Squadron of Freiwilliger Reitende Jägers were posted to Cathenon and Hettange, with pickets in Maison-Rouge. Furthermore, on 22 and 24 March a battalion of the 1st and another of the 2nd Landwehr Regiments occupied the villages of Hebange, Florange, Daspich and Weymerange on the Hessian left flank.

On 24 March the battalion of the 2nd Landwehr Regiment (mentioned above) moved to Hettange, with its 1st Company posted as an advanced post; the 2nd and 4th Companies in a reserve position; and the 3rd Company – under majors von Barthel and Hanstein – moved to Garsch.[30]

29 Renouard, p. 116.
30 Renouard, pp. 160-70.

On 22 March Oberst von Haynau took command of the forces before Thionville and Müller took command of those before Metz. This change of command had barely occurred when at 3:00 a.m. on 26 March Major von Meiborn marched to Maison-Rouge with a column of 200 men of the 1st Landwehr Regiment to relieve those forces of the 2nd Landwehr Regiment.

On 24 March – at around 3:00 p.m. – the Saarlouis blockade force learned of Durutte's advance with 6,000 to 8,000 men. Von Bieberstein responded by calling in all his detachments and immediately withdrew towards Saarbrücke – sending out some cavalry patrols to observe the French movements.

On the evening of 24 March Major von Haller – part of the Thionville garrison – learned that GD Durutte had departed Metz at 5:00 a.m. on 24 March with a column of 6,000 to 8,000 infantry, 150-200 cavalry, 14-18 field guns and six horse guns. He attacked and threw back General Yusseffovich's forces from all of its positions as he marched through Saarlouis. Durutte entered Saarlouis on 26 March. Haller responded by shifting his forces to face Durutte's advance and stripped his forces such that they would have very serious difficulty handling any sortie from Thionville. On 26 March word came that the Hessian forces on the right bank of the Moselle would be Durutte's target. The Hessians began shifting their forces to deal with the anticipated French attack and a probable supporting sortie by the garrison of Thionville.

On 27 March the French struck the Hessian advanced posts outside Thionville. Guérin and Beurmann's brigades marched against Manom and attacked the entrenchments by La Grange, which they sought to turn. At the same time, they sent a strong detachment – under the command of Major Hubert – against Guentrange and the adjacent heights.

This three-pronged attack engaged the Hessian 1st Grenadier Battalion and the light troops of the advanced posts. The Guentrange heights were taken by the French with a bayonet assault, which killed 10 Hessians and captured 50 others. The Hessians fell back and linked up with two companies of the 1st Landwehr Regiment – under Major von Meibom – which were also part of the Hessian right wing.

Although this withdrawal to Hettange was in no way a hasty withdrawal, the two companies of the 1st Landwehr Regiment – under Oberstleutnant Ronneberg – which stood in Terville and Weymerange, were swept up by the withdrawal and the attack of the three French detachments against Manom, Geutrange and down the road to Luxemburg. They were quickly rejoined to their battalion.

The Hessian position by Hettange was bordered on the east and west by woods and stood on a slight rise that overlooked the main road – over which the French must advance. The Hessians massed five guns – including a captured French 4pdr gun, plus their light troops – on this ridge. Around 10:00 a.m. the French approached this position and were taken under fire by the Hessian guns. They then sought to move around the position.

The Hessians deployed their forces on the hill as follows: The von Haller Grenadier Battalion stood to the west of the road on the edge of the woods; the 2nd Freiwilliger Fussjäger Company stood to the right; and the 3rd Freiwilliger Fussjäger Company stood to the left of the road. The guns stood on the road covered by the mounted jägers. The rest of the position was occupied by the two battalions of the 1st and 2nd Landwehr Regiments and the rest of the Hessian forces.

As their position was not strong – and the French forces outnumbered them – the Hessians began a careful program of retreating from position to position until they had fallen back far enough to link up with the pickets of Lieutenant Echternach standing before Thionville.[31]

The French sought – constantly – to turn the Hessian left flank and to drive them off the road to Luxemburg. After about two hours, the Hessians had withdrawn from Hettange to the

31 Renouard, pp. 185-9.

village of Roussy. Once there, they were joined by the Fus/Landgraf Karl Regiment; the 2/Prinz Solms Regiment; half of the "Wille" Battery; and one squadron of Hussars under GM Prince von Solms-Braunfels. Solms-Braunfels' force had been dispatched from Luxemburg to reinforce the Thionville blockade force.

Durutte's forces, however, were still too strong and the Hessians continued their fighting withdrawal. From Bas-Runtgen, the 2/Prinz Solms and 1st Grenadier Battalion covered the withdrawal, which moved through Preich, Aspelt, Syren and Conteren. This withdrawal was greatly hindered by the bad weather and the movement of the few guns the Hessians held, which required great efforts by both the teams of horses and the men.

The remainder of the blockading force had also been ordered to withdraw, and it moved to avoid the French – as well as to link up with the rest of the blockade force.

Meanwhile, Durutte had not only broken the blockade of Thionville, but he also drew some of the garrison's forces into his command. Now that his force was enlarged, he resumed his march towards Luxemburg.

The Hessians were not idle, and on 28 March General von Dörenberg took command of the combined blockade forces from Luxemburg and Thionville. He deployed them between Grevenmachern and Remich on the road that runs to Luxemburg. Only the Fus/Prinz Solms stood in Weimerschkirch.

The rest of the Hessian troops were deployed as follows: The 1/,2/Landgraf Karl Regiments stood on the road to Grevenscheurhof. To the left was the 2/Prinz Solms Regiment. The 1/Prinz Solms Regiment stood on a ridge by Sandweiler and on the road running to Remich (towards Luxemburg). The Fus/Landgraf Karl Regiment, the jägers and miners – plus a detachment from the 2/Prinz Solms Regiment – stood before the left wing east of Hamm. The Thionville blockade corps was deployed in the second and third lines behind this line.

At 9:00 a.m. the French appeared before the Hessian position and the Hessians engaged them with the fire of two cannon, which stood on the road before Grevenscheurhof. The French responded with their own artillery. As the two forces engaged, the Hessian Hussars attacked a French infantry force and forced them into square as the 2/Prinz Solms and the 2/Landgraf Karl Regiments drove back the French attacking towards Luxemburg. Meanwhile, the 1/Prinz Solms Regiment supported the Hessian battery as it advanced – and the 2/Prinz Solms Regiment marched so as to turn the French left flank. These attacks were beaten back and the French overran the Hessians (by Hamm) and pushed back their left wing. The engagement lasted from 1:00 p.m. to 4:00 p.m. and ended with the Hessians withdrawing. The losses were, overall, very light – and the Hessians reported losing eight dead, 39 wounded and 13 missing.[32]

That evening, the French marched into Luxemburg. They drew some detachments from the garrison and then departed for Longwy. The blockade corps around Thionville returned and once again closed the city after Durutte's French had marched off. On 30 March the Hessians and French broke contact. Word, however, arrived in the Hessian camp suggesting that on 2 April Durutte was in Longuion (southwest of Longwy). During the evening of 3 April – at 10:00 p.m. – GM von Müller organized his forces in the following order and dispatched them to intercept Durutte:

Advanced Guard: Oberst von Marschal
- Leib Dragoon Regiment (one squadron)
- Fus/Kurfürst Regiment
- 50 Gelernte Jäger

32 Renouard, pp. 190-7.

Main body:
- 2/3rd Landwehr Regiment
- 20 Gelernte Jäger
- 1/3rd Landwehr Regiment (three companies)
- Leib Dragoon Regiment (one squadron)
- Reitende Jägers (one squadron)
- 2nd Grenadier Battalion
- 50 Gelernte Jäger
- Two Guns
- 1/Kurfürst Regiment
- 2/Kurfürst Regiment (two companies)

Protecting baggage:
- Remaining Jägers
- 2/Kurfürst Regiment (two companies)
- Hussar Detachment

Von Müller left a company of the 1/3rd Landwehr Regiment at Richemont to cover the magazines – as well as to watch the road to Briey. The advanced guard marched through Woippy and Lorry towards Moulin in order to occupy that region. It deployed its advanced posts towards Ars on the Moselle and a small detachment of dragoons was sent to watch the road to Verdun.

The 2/3rd Landwehr Regiment and 40 jägers marched from Lorry to Platteville; and three companies of the 1/3rd Landwehr Regiment and a squadron of the Leib Dragoons was in Lorry to patrol the road from Saulny to Briey.

The 2nd Grenadier Battalion occupied Woippy, while the two guns, eight companies of the Kurfürst Regiment, the Saxon Hussars and the 3rd Reitende Freiwilliger Squadron occupied Maison-Rouge.[33]

During the morning of 4 April the French, under Durutte, attacked the Hessians and drove them from their position – killing seven, wounding 25 and 182 were missing or taken prisoner.

Between 6 and 8 April the Hessians began shifting their forces. On 8 April General von Müller received the order to march to support General Yusseffovich in his operations against Durutte. He organized a force consisting of the 1/Prinz Solms Regiment, the 1/2nd Landwehr Regiment, the Fus/Landgraf Karl Regiment, two companies of Gelernte Jägers, the "Wille" Battery and the Holzapfel Battery with six guns. This force was then dispatched towards Metz.

On 10 April von Müller's force – as he marched on Metz – was organized in two columns. The second column, on the left, was also known as the main column. It marched towards Richemont under the direct of command of GM von Müller. It contained:

Advanced Guard: Oberst Leutnant Schäffer
- Hussars (one squadron)
- Gelernte Jägers (one company)
- Fus/Landgraf Karl Regiment

Main body: Oberstleutnant von Benning
- Fus/Kurfürst Regiment
- "Wille" Battery
- 1/Kurfürst Regiment
- 2/Kurfürst Regiment (escorting the baggage)

33 Renouard, pp. 215-18.

1/2nd Landwehr Regiment
Hussars (two squadrons)
Rearguard:
3rd Reitende (mounted) Jäger Squadron

The 2/Kurfürst Regiment had detached two companies to cover the baggage – which was in Hebange – where the 1/2nd Landwehr Regiment joined the column in order to rejoin its regiment. The first, or right-hand column, was under the command of Oberst von Marschal and marched on Briey. It contained:

Advanced Guard: Major Boedicker
Leib Dragoon Regiment (one squadron)
Gelernte Jägers (two companies)
Main body: Oberst Zincke
2nd Grenadier Battalion
1/Prinz Solms Regiment
Holzapfel Battery
1/3rd Landwehr Regiment (escorting the baggage)
2/3rd Landwehr Regiment
Rearguard:
Leib Dragoon Regiment (less than one squadron)

The second column marched on Richemont and occupied a position behind the Orne. Its advanced posts were by Mondelange and Haugondange, with patrols moving towards Mézières. The first column moved through Briey to the Orne and took up positions on the Orne, with advanced posts towards Saint-Marie.[34]

On 10 April the first column was ordered to attack. It marched out of Briey at daybreak. The order for a general attack was passed to the second column by the firing of three cannon. On that signal, the first column moved through Lorry and sent its jägers and two battalions to Platteville supported by the rest of the column. The second column attacked Woippy.

However, a Prussian officer – Graf Pinto – arrived with news that Yusseffovich and Durutte had begun verbal negotiations on ending their engagement. Word had arrived of the fall of Paris, Napoleon's abdication and the restoration of the Bourbons. The Hessian attack was stopped. Negotiations were to proceed and the campaign against the fortresses ended.

Morand.

Mainz

Mainz, deep in modern Germany, had a garrison of French soldiers under the governorship of GD Morand – one of Napoleon's finest divisional generals. Cassel was commanded by GD Guilleminot.

34 Renouard, pp. 230-41.

The 5th German Bundescorps, under the command of the reigning Duke of Sachsen-Coburg, arrived before Mainz in early February and began the blockade of the fortress between 16 and 18 February. On the left bank of the Rhine – commanding what was the right wing of the blockade – was the Austrian Oberst Graf Degenfeld-Schomburg. The left wing was under Oberst von Bismarck of the Principality of Nassau. On the right bank of the Rhine stood the forces of Prussian General Hünerbein. Hünerbein was charged with blockading Cassel. Sachsen-Coburg established his headquarters in Oppenheim.

The blockade corps was too weak to attempt an assault or initiate a formal siege. They chose instead to attempt to allow starvation and disease do their work for them – or, at least, to contain the fortress garrison until such time as the field campaign brought about a decisive result.

On 17 April the blockading corps informed the garrison of the armistice that had been signed. Louis XVIII's order arrived to surrender the city, and on 4 May it was turned over to the Germans. Of the city's garrison of 31,000, 19,000 had perished since mid-November because of a typhus epidemic. Only 12,000 returned to France.[35]

Strasbourg

Strasbourg had been blockaded earlier in the campaign by Wittgenstein's corps, but as it marched into France to pursue Napoleon, the blockading duties were passed to the Baden troops (VIII German [Bundes] Corps) under the command of GL Graf Hochberg. Hochberg was charged both with blockading Strasbourg and the fortresses of Kehl, Landau, Pfalzburg, Bitsch, Lichtenberg and Lützelstein.

The garrison of Strasbourg was under the command of GD Broussier. His garrison was far too strong for Hochberg to consider a direct assault or formal siege, so like Mainz, Hochberg settled down to blockade the city. Hochberg's forces appear to have consisted of the following:

1st Brigade: Oberst von Brandt
- 1/, 2/Grossherzog Infantry Regiment Nr. 3
- 2nd Landwehr Battalion
- 3rd Landwehr Battalion
- 4th Landwehr Battalion

2nd Brigade: Generalmajor von Neuenstein
- 1/, 2/Graf Hochberg Infantry Regiment Nr. 2
- 1st Landwehr Battalion
- 5th Landwehr Battalion
- 6th Landwehr Battalion

3rd Brigade:
- 1/, 2/von Stockhorn Infantry Regiment Nr. 1
- Light Infantry Battalion
- 7th Landwehr Battalion
- 8th Landwehr Battalion

Cavalry Brigade: Generalmajor von Schäffer
- 1/, 2/, 3/, 4/, 5/von Freystedt Dragoon Regiment Nr. 1
- 1/, 2/, 3/, 4/, 5/von Geusau Dragoon Regiment Nr. 2
- 1/, 2/, 3/Freiwilliger Jäger zu Pferd Regiment

35 Sporschil, p. 431.

Artillery: Oberst von Losollay
- 2nd Foot Battery (six guns)
- 4th Foot Battery (six guns)
- Horse Battery (two guns)
- Freiwilliger Regimental Horse Battery (two guns)

Total: 15,409 men and 2,504 horses. The Landwehr contained the contingents from Hohenzollern, Liechtenstein and von der Leyen.

Of these, however, before Strasbourg – from the Baden contingent – were three infantry battalions, four Landwehr battalions, a dragoon regiment and a Freiwilliger Jäger squadron (5,575 men and 134 officers). The Russian contingent consisted of a cavalry squadron, 85 Cossacks and 18 12pdr guns with Russian gunners. The total Allied force before Strasbourg was about 6,378 men and 18 guns.

Before Kehl – the fortified bridgehead over the Rhine (by Strasbourg) – there were two Baden infantry battalions, three Landwehr battalions, four companies of artillery and train totaling eight guns, 85 officers and 4,067 men. The remainder of Hochberg's forces were deployed before Landau and Pfalzburg.

There were several sorties by the garrison – on 24 January, 28 March and 5 April – though they were repulsed by the Allies with little loss. When word of the fall of Paris reached Hochberg on 13 April he passed it to GD Broussier and an armistice was arranged. When the campaign ended, Strasbourg was to remain French, but the fortress of Kehl passed to Germany.

Pfalzburg

The garrison of Pfalzburg consisted of 1,500 men under the command of Colonel Brançon. Initially, it was besieged by the Russians, but Hochberg's Baden troops took over the blockade supported by a small force of Russians. The Baden force consisted of an infantry and a Landwehr battalion, and a dragoon regiment. The Russians provided a detachment with four guns. The entire contingent totaled 52 officers, 2,181 men and the four guns.

During the night of 1-2 February a bombardment caused a fire to erupt and an armistice was signed to last until 21 February. A second fire erupted on 29 March as a result of yet another bombardment, which further weakened the garrison. However, the garrison held out until 13 April when a capitulation was negotiated, which allowed for a joint Allied / French tenancy of the fortress. On 20 April – when the campaign ended – the French evacuated the fortress.[36]

Landau

Landau was a fortress occupied by a French garrison of 1,100 men – including 50 cavalry – under the command of General Berrière. In January, Prince Schachovsky blockaded it – and on 17 January a French sortie successfully destroyed five Russian guns. Part of the Russians were replaced by troops from Hochberg's 8th German Bundescorps. The Baden forces appear to have consisted of 20 officers and 790 men – organized in an infantry battalion – and two companies of artillery with two guns. Remaining with them were four battalions and a company of Russian infantry, two cavalry commandos, a kalmuck commando and an artillery detachment with two 12pdr guns. The Russians totaled 63 officers and 2,321 men.

36 Sporschil, p. 432.

On 26 March the French executed a sortie with 400 men supported by guns. However, the sortie was an abject failure, with most of the troops being killed, wounded or captured.

Word of the end of the campaign reached the fortress with General Schramm – and a deputation from France arrived. On 25 April General Berrière recognized Louis as King of France, opened the fortress gates and turned the fortress over to General Schramm.[37]

Hüningen

The garrison of Hüningen consisted of 4,000 men under the command of Colonel Chancel. The engineering troops were under Colonel Pinot and the artillery under Chef de bataillon Lallier. The 5th Army Corps of General Wrede had begun the siege and was replaced by the Bavarian forces under GL Graf Beckers. Beckers also had command of the troops blockading Neubreisach and Schlettstadt. The blockading forces before Hüningen were under the command of General Baron Zoller, who commanded a force of 2,536 men from the Bavarian 6th Line Regiment; the 14th National Feld Bataillon Ansbach; the 1st Light Infantry Battalion; a squadron of the 6th Chevauxleger Regiment; and the Danner 6pdr Foot Battery. In addition, there was a company of Würzburg infantry.

Conditions inside the fortress rapidly declined, so on 22 January the garrison commander launched a major sortie which destroyed a portion of the trenches, but was repulsed by the actions of the Bavarian 1st Light Battalion.

At the beginning of February, the besiegers were reinforced by the arrival of 1,400 infantry – from the Austrian Czatorisky and Argenteau Regiments – and two Bavarian artillery companies under Hornberger and Weishaupt. The Allied artillery began a heavy bombardment of the city during the night of 8 February – but little resulted. During the night of 8-9 March the four batteries now contained 16 Bavarian guns and they began a steady bombardment that by 10 March had fired 1,560 bombs and shells into the city. However, the results were insignificant.

At the end of March the Austrian generals Danno, Dedowich and Fasching arrived with a force of engineer officers, sappers, miners and pioneers to begin a formal siege. In addition, they brought with them 21 howitzers and 21 mortars. Further reinforcements – in the form of 4,400 Austrian infantry under the command of General Baron Taxis – arrived, but General Zoller remained in overall command.

The French made two sorties – one on 30 March and another during the night of 31 March. Neither was particularly successful, though much of the second parallel was destroyed and some equipment was dragged away. Further batteries were then erected along the Rhine by the Allies and during the night of 5 April a heavy bombardment began against a tower – killing 16 of the garrison. The tower was overrun by a battalion of the Argenteau Regiment and the remainder of the French garrison manning that tower was taken.

During the night of 6 April the second parallel was opened only 500 paces from the fortress and during the night of 8-9 April 54 guns were placed in 14 batteries along the parallel.

During the day of 10 April these batteries began firing on Michelfeld and Neudorf, but news of the surrender of Paris and Louis XVIII's ascension arrived. Zoller stopped the fire. A short armistice was arranged, but the garrison commander – Colonel Chancel – was not willing to accept his word. The bombardment and siege activities continued as a result – and on 16 April the siege finally ended as a result of the intervention of the Grand Dukes Nicholas and Michael of Russia.[38]

37 Sporschil, p. 432.
38 Sporschil, pp. 433-4.

Schlettstadt (Schelestadt)

The blockade forces consisted of General Graf Pappenheim with three Bavarian infantry battalions and a squadron of cavalry. Schlettstadt itself was a significant fortress, with 69 guns and a substantial garrison.

The blockade initially consisted of little more than a series of advanced post skirmishes. After 17 January a number of siege guns were brought forward and put into battery. During the night of 30-31 January the guns opened fire on the fortress for the first time. Heavy firing persisted through 5 February but the extravagant use of ammunition soon forced them to stop their bombardment.

On 16 February the garrison executed a strong sortie with infantry, cavalry and artillery down the road to Colmar. It overthrew a Bavarian infantry company – inflicting on it 20 dead and wounded and capturing 12 prisoners. General Pappenheim ordered forward another company and a platoon of cavalry to strike the sortie in the flank, while he personally led another company – supported by a 12pdr gun – against the head of the French column. The French were driven back and the engagement ended as they withdrew back into the fortress.

Another sortie was launched on 6 March and a 45-minute battle was fought – with the French losing heavily before they were driven back into the fortress.

In early April, Graf Pappenheim found himself distracted from his siege efforts by a revolt of the peasantry. In late March, Neuf Château – under the command of Lieutenant Schacht – was attacked and overrun by armed peasants. The Bavarians were driven back to Mirecourt. This followed Napoleon's march into the rear of the Allied armies as he sought to disrupt their lines of communication. The Department of the Meurthe and the border departments of the Haut-Rhin erupted. General Beckers reinforced Epinal with 1,000 men. On 6 April Pappenheim cornered a strong force of peasants in a strong house in the village of Rathau. The house was taken and large numbers of weapons were captured – along with a number of Frenchmen. About this time, Napoleon's abdication became known and the anti-guerrilla campaign ended. On 20 April the commandant of Schlettstadt accepted Louis XVIII as King and the siege ended.[39]

Neubreisach

The garrison of Neubreisach was under the command of General Dermancourt. His garrison contained 3,000 infantry, 150 cavalry and 230 artillerists. Outside the walls of the fortress was the Austrian General Minutillo. His forces relieved the Württemberg forces that initially surrounded the fortress in early January and consisted of three battalions – mostly Landwehr – from the Jordis Infantry Regiment and two squadrons of Bavarian cavalry. Only a single Austrian foot battery was on hand, but this was soon reinforced by the arrival of some Bavarian howitzers.

During the night of 25-26 January Minutillo led forward a force under the guns of Fort Mortier and destroyed the Aloys mill, which was used by the garrison.

The siege of Neubreisach developed according to the normal and historical siege process, with sorties being executed by the French on 10, 11, 14, 24, 25, 26 and 30 January, and on 3, 7, 16 and 26 February. On 11 March there was yet another major sortie. On 1 April there was yet another sortie. However, that was the last such sortie – and on 21 April word of Napoleon's abdication arrived and the siege ended.[40]

39 Sporschil, pp. 435-6.
40 Sporschil, pp. 435-6.

Belfort

At the end of December the city of Belfort was surrounded by a mixed force of Bavarians, Russians and Austrians. Finally – on 28 January – the siege was taken over by Austrian GM Drechsel with a force of 2,700 infantry, 50 cavalry and four guns.

The French garrison totaled 3,000 infantry and 70 chasseurs à cheval under the command of Colonel Legrand. The fortress was not well-prepared for the siege and it suffered from a heavy desertion among the Italian soldiers in the garrison. By the end of March, Colonel Legrand withdrew his garrison into the citadel.

The French were not alone in their misery and disease ravaged the ranks of the besiegers so badly that they required a reinforcement in the form of a new battalion drawn from the siege forces at Hüningen. There were several sorties – the biggest of which were on 29 January and 13 March where the French sought to obtain food. Eventually, the lack of food forced Legrand to capitulate on 16 April. When the citadel was occupied, the Austrians found 77 cannon with more than sufficient shot and powder.[41]

Besançon

The fortress of Besançon was besieged by the forces of Feldmarschal-leutnant Fürst Aloys Liechtenstein. The garrison commander, GD Marulaz, launched a major sortie against Liechtenstein on 3 March – with 1,800 men supported by the heavy guns of the fortress. The Austrian advanced posts were easily thrown back. The Austrian posts in Trois-Chapeloles and Chapelle-des-Puits were attacked as well. The Allies reported 150 French casualties and 82 casualties of their own.

The critical part of the blockade of Besançon came when Napoleon moved through St.-Dizier and everyone thought that he would break the blockades of Auxonne and Besançon and join with the Army of Lyon. The French peasantry took up arms and soon A. Liechtenstein found himself hip-deep in a revolt. The regimental wagons of the blockade corps were sent to Pontarlier and the artillery reserve was sent to Estallons. In addition to having to deal with an armed citizenry, the long wagon train of the main Allied army, which moved past Besançon, could not be hidden from General Marulazand – and Liechtenstein rightly feared a sortie against it.

The sortie came twice – once on 31 March and again on 1 April. Both sorties, however, were driven back into the fortress with heavy losses. However, after the Battle of Paris, Besançon – like so many other fortresses – quickly surrendered. However, Besançon was to remain in French hands.[42]

Auxonne

Auxonne was commanded by GD Anderossy, who commanded 2,500 infantry, 80 cavalry and more than 60 guns. After the departure of Feldmarschal-leutnant Wimpffen's division, which had begun the blockade of Auxonne in January, the blockade effort was taken over by General Baron Rothkirch. The only major sortie occurred on 10 February and was driven back with losses. The blockade was, otherwise, uneventful – and with Napoleon's abdication, Auxonne was to remain in French hands.[43]

41 Sporschil, p. 436.
42 Sporschil, pp. 436-7.
43 Sporschil, p. 437.

Auxerre

At the end of January 1814 Feldmarschal-leutnant Fürst M. Liechtenstein closed up General Allix in the Auxerre fortress. However, the blockade was broken in February because military events drew Liechtenstein off to Armançon. General Allix built his garrison into the Auxerre Volunteer Division and had free reign of the area until Fürsten M. Liechtenstein returned on 9 March. The blockade would remain until after the abdication.[44]

Maëstricht, Venlo and Grave

Maëstricht and Venlo were besieged by the Swedish army at the end of February. Neither siege was eventful. Both fortresses raised white flags on 24 April to recognize the sovereignty of Louis XVIII.

Grave endured a nasty little siege, but held out until 16 May when word arrived of the end of the campaign and the signing of a peace treaty.[45]

Jülich

The commander of this fortress on the Roer was General St. Loup – and his garrison contained 4,000 infantry, 160 cavalry and 120 guns. In the beginning of the campaign, a detachment of Winzingerode's corps observed the fortress and the Illowaiski IV Cossacks were replaced on 17 March by the von Lützow Freikorps. The Illowaiski IV Cossacks detached a small force of 40 Cossacks to continue with the blockade. A series of pickets (feldwachten) were established around the fortress. Each picket contained a force of infantry and cavalry. The main body of the von Lützow Freikorps was deployed with the 1st and 2nd Battalions, 10 Cossacks, three cannon and a howitzer in Hambach. On the left bank of the Roer, in Kirchbach, was a picket containing an infantry company and 30 Cossacks. Another picket, containing a company, was in Meerstein. A reserve consisting of the 3rd Battalion, two squadrons and three 3pdr cannon stood in Aldenhoven (on the road to Aachen).

From 18 to 23 February the von Lützow Freikorps fired on the fortress every night 10 or 12 times just to keep the garrison slightly agitated. On 22 February the French sent some workers out to clear the brush and trees (and to destroy some houses on the glacis) and covered them with a small sortie. No serious fight began with this action. On 24 February a similar sortie was executed to destroy some houses 1,400 paces from the fortress wall – and it engaged one of the blockade force picket of 14 Tyrolean Jägers. The sortie contained 500 infantry, 40 cavalry and one cannon.

The Prussian picket was driven back on the rest of the company and a serious little engagement began. The French deployed a strong skirmish line. The gun was placed in the middle of their formation, with the cavalry on the right. The Prussians responded by sending in more troops and finally broke the French attack with the use of its artillery.

Yet another sortie occurred on 26 February with 300 infantry, 60 cavalry and one horse gun. In this instance, the picket before them contained two companies. A nasty little skirmish fight arose, which lasted from 10:00 a.m. until 5:30 p.m. The losses were insignificant.[46]

On 9 March four batteries were raised in the region of where these sorties had occurred. One stood on the Galgenberg and contained two guns. Two more guns were posted before Steterich, a gun and an howitzer were posted to the right of the Karthause and three cannon were on the left

44 Sporschil, p. 437.
45 Sporschil, p. 440.
46 Schlüster, pp. 186-96.

bank of the Roer. The fire of these guns was responded to by the French on a steady and regular basis.

The strength of these batteries was increased on 12 March. Three guns remained on the left bank of the Roer, but four Swedish guns and two Swedish howitzers were installed on the Galgenberg; two guns and two howitzers of the Freikorps were posted at the foot of the Galgenberg; and one gun and one howitzer from the Freikorps were posted by Karthause. Once in place, the cannonade resumed at a slow, steady pace. From 18 to 23 March a total of 1,628 cannonballs and 158 howitzer shells were fired by the Freikorps on the fortress.[47]

The von Lützow Freikorps was relieved on 24 March by the Mecklenburg-Schwerin troops. On 4 May the French garrison finally surrendered the fortress to the Allies.[48]

47 Schlüster, pp. 197-203.
48 Sporschil, p. 440.

21

The Last Days of the Empire: Marmont's Treachery, Souham's Defection and Napoleon's Abdication

Daybreak of 24 March found Napoleon marching on Joinville with the Guard, and the V and VI Cavalry Corps. Macdonald marched on St.-Dizier with the VII and XI Corps and Counts Gérard and Saint-Germain formed the rearguard of the French army in Perthes and Longchamps.

General Winzingerode, who had orders to follow the French with his 10,000 cavalry, had not moved past Maisons on the 24th. His advanced guard, under Tettenborn, had only reached Thieblemont and his march was undisturbed by the French.

Napoleon, persuaded that the success of his enterprise depended on the speed of his movements and the sensitivities of Schwarzenberg, resumed his march early on the morning of 25 March. The light cavalry of GD Piré and Jacquinot was pushed down the roads to Bar-sur-Aube and Chaumont. Piré moved into the village and established himself on the Allied line of retreat. He captured large amounts of equipment and stopped numerous political agents – amongst whom he found Baron Vitrolles, who had the good fortune of escaping from the Allies by virtue of his title as Inspector of Experimental Farms. The Imperial Guard occupied Brienne and Doulevant, while the XI Corps moved into Vassy – covered to the rear by the VII Corps, which guarded the passes through the forest.[1]

The engagement at Humbecourt

As the French rearguard moved past Humbecourt, it was taken under canister fire by a horse battery that General Tettenborn had placed on the right bank of the Marne. Its fire threw the French columns into disorder. Fortunately, General Trelliard's dragoons, VI Cavalry Corps, found a sheltered road that ran behind the village of Valcourt and it permitted Gérard's infantry to pass in greater security. Two artillery companies – 16 guns – were deployed on a plateau and engaged the Allied battery of eight guns, while about 100 French skirmishers crossed the Marne at a ford and moved against the battery. Though covered by four squadrons of the Isoum Hussars, the battery was forced back. The hussars lost a few casualties to canister and Tettenborn was apparently hit by a canister shot, but not seriously wounded.[2]

The problem of the battery resolved, the French resumed their march, but Tettenborn kept nipping at their heels. A force of Cossacks were found deployed before Humbecourt and in

1 Koch, Vol. II, pp. 547-8.
2 von Damitz, Vol. III, 2nd Part, p. 136.

Eclaron. The main body of the Allied cavalry moved to St.-Dizier and Czernichev's brigade moved from Vitry to Montiérender.

Napoleon, when advised of this news, was delighted. He was certain that the main Allied army was following him as he marched away from Paris.

Upon learning of the march of the French army, the commander of the Allied general park and heavy baggage, which stood in Bar- sur-Aube, evacuated his charges as quickly as he could to Belfort. The movement of this wagon train quickly fell into disorder and promised great results for the French – and Piré's leading elements had already captured a number of cannon and equipment when word came of the Allied advance on Paris. This word came, initially, from prisoners taken to the Imperial Headquarters who announced the junction of the two Allied armies and their march on Paris. Napoleon did not initially believe them and had their reports suppressed while he considered their information.

During the morning of 26 March Napoleon was advised by Macdonald that the rearguard had seen absolutely nothing but light cavalry, which brought dramatic confirmation to what the prisoners had been saying. Napoleon determined that it was necessary to send a strong reconnaissance force to the rear. The Cossacks standing before Humbecourt were thrown back on Valcourt, where General Tettenborn attempted to defend himself in order to give his commanding officer time to assemble the necessary forces. However, he was soundly thrashed and thrown back across the Marne.

Napoleon arrived on the Valcourt plateau and saw the Allies formed in line of battle on the opposite bank. He had two battalions of chasseurs occupy St.-Dizier, where he supported his left. His right extended towards Vitry and his flank was protected by infantry posted in the Perthes woods. He then sent foot and mounted skirmishers to the bank of the Marne. His first line stood before the road – facing the river. His second line stood behind the road. His artillery, intermixed with some cavalry squadrons, stood on the road which dominated the vicinity. The forces facing one another were as follows:

RUSSIANS[3]

Reserve Cavalry: Generallieutenant Count Orurk
- 3rd Hussar Division: Generalmajor Jurkowitz
  - Brigade: Generalmajor Pahlen
    - Isoum Hussar Regiment
    - Elisabethgrad Hussar Regiment
    - Pavlograd Hussar Regiment
- 2nd Dragoon Division: Generalmajor Balk
  - Brigade: Generalmajor Drewitsch
    - St. Petersburg Dragoon Regiment
    - Riga Dragoon Regiment
    - Finland Dragoon Regiment
  - Brigade: Generalmajor Galanthé
    - Polish Uhlan Regiment
    - Volhynie Uhlan Regiment
  - Brigade: Generalmajor Sagrétzky
    - Niejine Chasseurs à cheval Regiment
    - Jaroslav Opolochenie Cossack Regiment

3 von Damitz, Vol. III, 2nd Part, pp. 139-40.

Irregular Cavalry: Generalmajor von Chernichev[4]
Balbin #2 Cossack Regiment
Diaczkin Cossack Regiment
Vlassov #3 Cossack Regiment
Sisaev Cossack Regiment
Chirov Cossack Regiment
Horse Battery #12
Detachment:
Bug Cossacks (one pulk)
Detachment: General Marischkin
Grekov #9 Cossack Regiment
Barbantchikov #2 Cossack Regiment
Lotchilin #1 Cossack Regiment
Detachment: Colonel Melnikov
Melnikov #4 Cossack Regiment
Melnikov #5 Cossack Regiment
Illowaiski #4 Cossack Regiment
Pantilejev Cossack Regiment
Grekov #9 Cossack Regiment
Total: approximately 7,750 men

FRENCH

	Infantry	Cavalry	Total
Ney's corps	4,800	800	5,600
Sébastiani's corps	5,200	5,200	10,400
Lefebvre-Desnoëttes	4,500	1,500	6,000
Macdonald's VI Corps	22,876	9,990	32,866
Total:	37,376	17,490	54,866

Engagement at St.-Dizier

Believing that he faced Schwarzenberg's advanced guard, Napoleon recalled the infantry corps which was near Vassy and ordered his cavalry to cross the Marne at the Hallignicourt ford. Count Sébastiani crossed his cavalry over the Marne in column of platoons and deployed to the right and left of the ford – supported by the cavalry of Saint-Germain, Milhaud and Valmy, who formed on his flanks. The Guard infantry – that of GD Count Gérard and Maréchal Macdonald – followed across the Marne behind the cavalry, but Oudinot moved on St.-Dizier via the road from Joinville. The army then formed with the cavalry in the first line and the infantry in the second line – between Hallignicourt and Hoiricourt – with the French beginning the engagement on the left, advancing by echelons, while the center and right marched in line.

Baron Winzingerode was startled when he realized that he had the entire French army advancing on him – and desperately sought to avoid battle in a terrain so unfavorable to cavalry. However, he feared losing the infantry guarding St.-Dizier and ordered Baron Tettenborn to cover the road to Vitry, while the main body of his forces marched on that village via Bar-sur-Ornain.

4 Von Damitz indicates that there were 19 Cossack pulks present, with a strength of 250 men each. Unfortunately, the precise organization of Chernichev's forces are not known and the 15 Cossack pulks shown are all that were known to be with the Army of Silesia at that time.

The weak Russian advanced guard – consisting of the Isoum Hussars supported by six horse guns – moved back from the edge of the river to rejoin the five Cossack pulks and two horse guns to form a half-crescent line. The French line moved up before him – swelling from 15,000 to 20,000 (and eventually to 30,000 men).[5]

Following his orders, Tettenborn placed himself at the head of the Isoum Hussar Regiment. He deployed two Cossack regiments to the front and held two back as a reserve, then executed several charges – all of which were repulsed with heavy losses – and suffering further losses from the fire of the infantry posted in the Perthes woods. On his side, Winzingerode pushed his forces to move on St.-Dizier. However, the French Guard cavalry threw itself on his column, crushed it and chased the fugitives as far as the Trois-Fontaines woods.

As Winzingerode's column was being destroyed, Oudinot moved into St.-Dizier at the *pas de charge*. The Allied garrison fled before him – marching on Bar at a cadence of 120 paces per minute, which was the fastest cadence used by the French short of a cadenced run.

The Allies were entirely broken and without support. The French cavalry redoubled its activity and audacity. GD Milhaud charged furiously down the road to Vitry and captured six guns. General Letort, leading the Empress Dragoon Regiment, crushed and sabered an infantry square that was seeking shelter in the woods. On the right, GD Kellermann – the Comte de Valmy – (son of Maréchal Kellermann, the Duke of Valmy) pursued at the grand trot the Allied columns that fled down the road to Bar. The French infantry followed the cuirassiers and dragoons at the *pas de course* – bayoneting anyone who escaped the sabers of the French infantry. Oudinot – at the head of Kellermann's cavalry – continued the pursuit of the Russians until they were five kilometers from Saundrupt, where night forced them to take up positions. Macdonald chased Baron Tettenborn as far as Perthes and did not stop shooting at his troops until nightfall. The Imperial Headquarters remained in St.-Dizier that night. The Russians had lost 1,500 to 1,800 men during the course of the day – including 500 prisoners, nine guns, a bridging train and all their baggage. The French lost about 600 men *hors de combat*.

Napoleon marches on Paris

The principal result of the destruction of Winzingerode's column was to convince Napoleon that the main Allied armies were not following him. Despite the trophies at his feet, he knew that the fatal blow was launched at his throne and glory. Finally convinced that the Allies were indeed marching on Paris, he decided to march as fast as possible to the succor of Paris. He intended to march via Châlons, but this required the capture of Vitry, which was to prove difficult. Nonetheless, the entire army (with the exception of the VII Corps and the VI Cavalry Corps) began their march on Vitry at daybreak of 27 March – pushing before them the brigades of Tettenborn and Czernichev.[6]

When the French appeared before Vitry, its governor showed himself firm in his resolve to hold the city against an apparent direct assault. On the other hand, to the French it appeared too strong to hazard a direct assault, and Napoleon called a conference with Berthier and Ney to review the possibility of pushing the army into the Vosges. Oudinot already stood in Bar and Durutte was near Verdun. However, Berthier and Ney argued strongly against the project – arguing that to abandon the Allies' trail was to abandon Paris to them and to pass the initiative to them.

Napoleon responded by suggesting a march on Paris via Sézanne and Coulommiers. Berthier believed it was impractical and addressed the danger of crossing the Marne in the face of the enemy – especially a numerically stronger enemy. For the first time in many years, Napoleon listened to advice. Ney spoke to him, however, of the danger of abandoning Paris to the Allies,

5 von Damitz, Vol. III, 2nd Part, p. 146.
6 Koch, Vol. II, pp. 549-53.

which convinced Napoleon that it was necessary to return to St.-Dizier and march via Bar-sur-Aube and Troyes to reach the Fontainebleau forests.

The decision being made, the march began – but the weather was terrible. The counter-march might otherwise have been the source of considerable complaining, but the troops knew the objective and the urgency of their march, so there was little grumbling. The complaints were only that the troops would have preferred an assault on Vitry to retracing their earlier steps. They moved between Marolles and Valcourt, where Albert's division and Trelliard's dragoons formed the rearguard. Napoleon and his Guard slept that night in St.-Dizier.

At the moment when the main body of the French army began retracing its steps, Oudinot entered Bar and threw scouts across the Meuse to gather word of the division moving from Metz with GD Durutte. However, nothing was learned – and in two days, he found himself between Longwy and Verdun. General Winzingerode – favored by this change in direction – was assured of passage over the Meuse and sent the Prussian division of Prince Siren von Courland (then en route from Nancy) to take up a position in Saint-Mihiel. Von Courland commanded a replacement detachment which contained two Russian battalions, seven Prussian replacement (ersatz) infantry battalions, one Prussian jäger company, 100 Cossacks and seven cavalry replacement companies.

The counter-march of the main army obliged Oudinot to also withdraw. He received orders to rejoin Napoleon in all haste and began the ordered movement that night. He executed this order with some regret, as the approach of his corps to the Department of the Meuse had begun to arouse the spirit of the people. He proposed calling for an insurrection and calling the people of Lorraine to arms. However, Berthier – whose advice prevailed – responded that such an endeavor would not return the advantages it promised because it lacked the cavalry force to support the infantry that it would raise. However, he did forward blank commissions for those who might wish to call up such an insurrection.

On 28 March the army began its movement on Troyes in four columns. The first column consisted of the artillery and the light cavalry of the V and VI Cavalry Corps. The first column marched from Chaumont on Troyes. The second column was formed by the mounted Guard and it marched on Brienne. The third column consisted of the Guard infantry – then standing around St.-Dizier. It was placed under the orders of Ney. The fourth column consisted of the large force – a total of six corps – commanded by Macdonald. This column marched on Vassy. Count Gérard held Valcourt and did not move until Oudinot moved from St.-Dizier on the road to Joinville (and then moved that evening from Huibecourt to Vassy).

The roads were terrible and the march hard for all involved. Those vehicles trapped in the mud were burnt and their horses transferred to the teams drawing the guns.

When Winzingerode found that Napoleon no longer pursued him, he moved to St.-Dizier and called Tettenborn and Czernichev to him.

On 29 March Napoleon placed himself at the head of his cavalry and marched towards Vandoeuvres. At this time, a courier from Paris arrived – sent by King Joseph – announcing the arrival of the combined Allied armies at Meaux. He responded by sending General Déjean to Paris to ask the marshals not to allow Paris to fall to the Allies, and prepared the peace proposals which were presented to Schwarzenberg by Caulaincourt just after Paris had fallen. Napoleon then marched forward at 3:00 p.m. that afternoon – escorted only by two squadrons – as he moved to Troyes.

The two squadrons moved with him to Dolencourt, where they joined Piré's cavalry. The main body of the Guard cavalry pushed on to Troyes – arriving that night. The Guard infantry camped in Lusigny that night.

In Dolencourt – between 3:00 and 4:00 a.m. – Berthier sent out orders to all the corps commanders advising them of the goal of the march. This dispatch announced that Mortier and Marmont were before Paris engaged in battle with the Allies. The requirements of the march were laid out and the rest intervals were to be kept to the minimum necessary. It was to be a forced march.

Macdonald described the situation as follows:

> It is too late to save Paris – at least by the route which we are following. It is 50 leagues from here; supposing that force marches and no obstacles are encountered – and that march would require four days at least. And in what state to engage in a battle would our army arrive?
>
> Yesterday, the Allies were at Meaux – pushing their advanced guard before Paris – and we have sadly learned today that they are behind the barricades. Will the combined corps of Mortier and Marmont be sufficient to hold the Allies in check for us to arrive? This is a gratuitous supposition, assuming the Allies do not notice our approach to the Marne or our passage over it.
>
> It is my recommendation that if Paris falls to the Allies, that Napoleon should march on Sens; call all the detached corps to him via Melun and Fontainebleau; and march with us towards the Duke of Castiglione – Maréchal Augereau – and give the decisive battle on terrain we select after having fully rested our troops. Finally, if Providence should mark our final hour, we shall succumb honorably without ending our days miserable, dispersed, taken and despoiled by the Cossacks.[7]

Meanwhile, Winzingerode advanced very slowly on the 29th – moving only as far as Montiérender. On 30 March the French Foot and Horse Guard marched through Troyes and marched into the night – collapsing with fatigue in Villeneuve-l'Archevêque. Napoleon had preceded them by several hours and departed the city that evening at 6:00 p.m. with his service squadrons, which took him to Villeneuve-la-Guyard. From there, Napoleon moved without escort to Fontainebleau. He still hoped to prevent the fall of Paris and, by his appearance, inspire the inhabitants – giving them the force necessary to delay the Allies for 48 hours and give his army time to arrive on the battlefield.

Napoleon arrived in Fontainebleau in a single carriage followed by Berthier and the Duke of Vicence – preceded by a single rider. At the moment this rider arrived in the "heart of France", he encountered Belliard and his cavalry. He announced Napoleon's approach almost immediately to Belliard and his troops. Napoleon arrived moments later in the midst of his troops. His carriage stopped and he descended from it. He immediately asked: "Belliard, what is this that you are here with your cavalry? Where is the enemy? At the gates of Paris? And the army… Who is guarding the capital? The Paris Guard? Where are my wife and son? Where is Mortier? Marmont? The Empress and the King of Rome… did they depart for Rambouillet – and from there, I suppose, for Orléans? The marshals are doubtlessly still in Paris finishing their arrangements." Belliard finally broke through the barrage of questions and began to explain to Napoleon what had transpired since 19 March when Napoleon had left them on the Aisne and then proceeded to recount the events of the battle for Paris. Berthier and the Duke of Vicence arrived shortly afterward. Napoleon thought to move to Paris and arouse the Paris National Guard. Belliard discouraged him – advising him that the city was occupied by 120,000 Allied troops. Napoleon asked about the convention and Belliard replied that he did not know who had concluded it – only that: "Mortier had told him that it existed and that he was to march on Fontainebleau." The conversation was not a happy one for the interrogated Belliard – and even less happy for Napoleon when he realized that the situation for Paris was hopeless. Napoleon, resigned, decided to return to Fontainebleau. He issued orders for the rest of the troops – arriving from Paris – to take up positions on the Longjumeau heights behind the small Essonne River.

On 31 March the debris of the army that had fought to save Paris was encamped around Napoleon. In two days, they had all gathered by Fontainebleau. Though Paris was lost, there were

7 Koch, Vol. II, pp. 554-60.

still immense resources – and moving south to join the armies there was discussed at length (as was a guerrilla war to be ignited behind the Allied lines). However, Napoleon did not abandon the prospect of a negotiated peace.

While Mortier and Marmont established themselves – according to their orders – on the Essonne, the rest of the army continued marching from the east to join them. Napoleon sent a dispatch in the custody of the Duke of Vicence to Tsar Alexander with propositions which he thought would attract his attention, but when it was received, the Tsar rebuffed it as the Allied sovereigns had agreed not to treat with Napoleon.

Reorganization of the French army

Immediately after his return to Fontainebleau, Napoleon turned to his highest priority – the reorganization of the French army. All of the provisional regiments were dissolved and absorbed into other regiments. Boyer de Rebeval's division rejoined Mortier's corps. Marmont's corps was reinforced by two battalions of veterans – by the divisions of Compans and Ledru – as well as all the troops that had been part of the Paris garrison. As both Mortier and Marmont's corps had lost all their artillery between the battles of La Fère-Champenoise and Paris, each was provided with 30 new, fully-equipped cannon. The Gendarmerie à Pied de la Seine, de Seine-et-Marne and Seine-et-Oise were organized into a single battalion of about 600 men. They were brigaded with the Gendarmerie from Spain and assigned to Friant's division. The horse gendarmerie joined the elite squadron to form a regiment of 500 men and was assigned to Lefebvre-Desnoëttes' division.

General Préval had, on the order of King Joseph, evacuated the general depot of remounts to Mantes. During the night of 31 March he was ordered to continue his operations in Orléans or Samur. Finally, Colonel Vertillac had withdrawn to Versailles with 2,200 men from the various infantry depots. He was ordered to move this force to Milly.

The general staff was also reorganized. GD Ornano became the commander of the Guard cavalry. GD Guyot, who had commanded the service squadrons, was given command of the 1st Guard Division – replacing GD Colbert, who was wounded. GD Count Kraczinski was named general-in-chief of all the Poles in French service and directed to organize them into a division. In addition, Macdonald was ordered to stop his column between Sens and Montereau, where it currently stood.

Plans for a campaign around Paris

Napoleon spent the next day planning a new campaign around Paris. Several of the marshals were called to participate in the discussion – as was the Duke of Bassano. After a lengthy discussion as to if it was more advantageous to maneuver around Paris or to withdraw on the Loire, all of the marshals – with the exception of one – were in favor of moving to the Loire. Despite the near-unanimous preference, Napoleon adopted the plan to operate around Paris.

For the remainder of the day, Napoleon did not show himself except for a review of the Grenadiers and Chasseurs à pied. As they marched past him, they greeted him with their accustomed cries of acclaim as they had at the Tuileries; in Schönbrun; Potsdam; el Prado; and before the Kremlin.

Positions on 3 April

On 3 April the French army began maneuvering around Paris. Macdonald moved via Montereau and took up positions with the II and XI Corps on the Surville heights. Saint-Germain's cavalry and the park of the II and XI Corps was in Cannes. Oudinot – with the VII Corps – and

Kellermann's cavalry was in Villeneuve-la-Guyard and its vicinity. GD Milhaud was in Emans and Noisy and Allix's division was in Auxerre.

Imperial review of the Guard

On 3 April a review was held of all the Imperial Guard troops in the court of Cheval-Blanc. The infantry was massed along the two sides of the court at a depth of 15-20 men. After reviewing their ranks, Napoleon placed himself in the middle of the court and called the most senior officer, non-commissioned officer and soldier of each company to form in a circle around them and read to them a proclamation. It read:

> Soldiers! The enemy has stolen three marches on us and has captured Paris. It is necessary to chase them out. Native Frenchmen, those émigrés who we have pardoned have arrayed themselves with the white cockade and have joined themselves to our enemies. Turn on them! They shall receive the price of this new outrage. We swear to conquer or to die – and to make them respect the tricolor cockade which, after 20 years, we find on the road of glory and honor.

Thousands of throats echoed with cries of: "*Vive l'Empereur!*"

The soldiers returned to their ranks and marched out at the pas accélére to be replaced by the cavalry, which greeted Napoleon as they always had in time of peril or ceremony.

Despite period propaganda, Napoleon apparently did not promise the pillage of Paris to the Young Guard. There was no reason for vengeance or animosity towards the Parisians. It was generally believed that if the army were to penetrate into Paris, that the city would rise in arms and attack the Allies from all sides.

At around 6:00 p.m. all the Imperial Guard began marching on the Essonne River. Obliged to march along a road that passed through the Fontainebleau forest, its march was prolonged into the beautiful, clear and moonlit night. They marched in complete silence. Only the clatter of their equipment and the steady drumbeat of their march betrayed their presence. Their column was interspersed with several howitzer batteries and the elite artillery followed them.[8]

The Imperial Headquarters moved to Moulignon and the infantry took up positions in Boissise-le-Roi, Bordes, Moulignon and Auverneaux. The cavalry of General Defrance moved to Ferté-Aleps.

The right of the French army stood in Melun and its left was in Ferté-Aleps. Corbeil and Essonne were occupied by Marmont. The part of Melun on the left bank of the Seine was occupied by the cavalry depots under General Chanez. The troops under Macdonald took up positions with the infantry in the second line in Villiers, Chailly-en-Bière and Fontainebleau. His cavalry stood on the banks of the Erolle from St.-Germain to Boissise. The entire army did not exceed 36,000 men.

On 2 April the Army of Silesia – which was now commanded by Barclay de Tolly – stood on the road from Orléans to Palaiseau, Chilly and Longjumeau and pushed its advanced posts to Montlhéry and Arpajon. Giulay and the Crown Prince of Württemberg's corps were established between Villeneuve-le-Roi and Atys to the right of Fontainebleau. To the left of the Fontainebleau road stood Raevsky's corps – with the Bavarians in reserve between Paroy and Rongis – while General Kaisarov stood between Donnemarie and Moutereau. Bülow's corps was recalled from Soissons – leaving only von Thümen's brigade before the city. The only Allied forces in Paris were the Russian and Prussian Guard and the Allied reserve divisions.

8 Koch, Vol. II, pp. 561-70.

Allied defensive dispositions

It did not take long for Schwarzenberg to begin to worry that Napoleon would march against his left flank and turn the Allies before Paris. He responded to this fear by ordering the main Allied army to be ready to form up – on the first signal – in two lines between the Morangis park and Juvisy. The Army of Silesia was to hold itself ready to form behind the Longjumeau heights. Versailles was occupied and advanced posts were pushed to the banks of the Yvette between Arsay, Chavreuse and Dampierre. A pontoon bridge was erected in Conflans and covered with strong earthworks. Vassil'shikov's corps, which was still blockading Château Vincennes, occupied the Saint-Maur bridge.

The Russian grenadiers departed Paris and moved to Rongis, where they formed a third line behind the Bavarians. They were replaced on the Montmartre heights by a brigade from Bülow's corps. These arrangements permitted the Allies to shift from the offensive to the defensive as necessitated by any actions Napoleon might take.

Marmont's treachery

Word reached the Allies that Napoleon had concentrated his army and was ready to march on Paris with 50,000 men. That being the case, the Allied commanders decided that they would evacuate Paris and take up a position by Meaux. The orders were ready to be issued to Barclay for this retrograde movement, but Schwarzenberg delayed their issuance in order to speak with his representatives to Marmont. Schwarzenberg was eager to have the pro-Bourbonist Revolution in Paris since 31 March published, with the invitation of the newly-established provisional government to embrace the cause of the nation against Napoleon. Schwarzenberg had these overtures sent to Marmont, who was flattered that such communications were directed to him. Marmont saw himself as a kingmaker and opened negotiations with the provisional government. He quickly concluded an agreement with Schwarzenberg, which neutralized his corps and moved it via Versailles to a point outside of the theater of operations. In signing the agreement, Marmont acted in concert with Count Souham – one of the senior divisional commanders of the army. Chastel and Lucotte were not involved and did not like the terms of the agreement, but the rest of the general officers were slowly and successively let in on the secret.Marmont, the Duke of Ragusa, made his mark on both the history of France and on its language with this act. His title passed into the French lexicon as the word 'raguseré', which means 'to betray'.

Schwarzenberg then advised the Allied sovereigns of his agreement with Marmont and issued orders for his troops to cover Marmont's withdrawal – should Napoleon choose to intervene – and to ensure that the Allies did not attack him as he made his long flank march across the front of the Allied armies. To assist in this movement, two Bavarian cavalry regiments were ordered to march parallel to the French column until they arrived in Fresnes, when two Russian regiments would escort them to Versailles. Versailles was strongly garrisoned by the Allies.

Napoleon at Fontainebleau, 31 March 1814, by Paul Hippolyte Delaroche.

Napoleon abdicates in favor of his son

Not only did Marmont learn of the events in Paris, but so too did the other marshals. They had left their families and their friends there, and those individuals had been able to communicate with the marshals – advising them of the change of government in Paris, its decrees and the sentiment of Paris vis-a-vis Napoleon. This – coupled with the Allied occupation of Paris, Lyon and Bordeaux; with the regency having moved to the Loire; and the establishment of the provisional government in Paris – had begun to cause the glue that held Napoleon's Empire to come unstuck.

In order to save France from the horrors of a foreign war and a civil war, the marshals went to Napoleon at once – accompanied by the Grand Maréchal du Palais and the Duke of Vicence. Ney spoke first – recounting the terrible situation of France and requesting that Napoleon spare France further trauma. Napoleon had no remedy to the situation and the marshals responded by suggesting that he abdicate. Napoleon considered this a few minutes. Realizing that he had no resources left but the army – and that its commanders were no longer his to control – he responded that he would prepare an act renouncing the throne in favor of his son under the regency of the Empress.

In effect, he promised to abdicate the night of the 3rd and asked that Ney, Macdonald, the Duke of Vicence, Caulaincourt and Oudinot carry it to the Allied sovereigns. These four departed with the document to explain to Marmont that Napoleon had abdicated in favor of his son. Unable to keep the details of his negotiations with the Allies from his colleagues, Marmont provided them with all the details. Macdonald asked him had he concluded his arrangements. On his negative response, Macdonald advised him that nothing should preclude him from joining the other commissioners. The Duke of Vicence added that his (Marmont's) joining the group would add even greater weight to their position. However, Marmont excused himself from being a plenipotentiary for Napoleon. The other marshals advised him that the only way to escape his embarrassment was either to go to Fontainebleau and to confess to Napoleon the truth of what had passed, or to accompany them to Paris. Marmont was unwilling to face Napoleon's wrath and chose to go with them to Paris. He joined Macdonald in his carriage and left Souham in charge of his corps with instructions to make no movements until his return.

When they arrived in Chevilly – in search of Schwarzenberg's headquarters to explain their mission – Marmont refused to join them and remained in Macdonald's carriage. In Chevilly, Macdonald met with Prince Eugene von Württemberg – explaining their mission. Prince Eugene advised him that Marmont's corps was abandoning Napoleon and passing over to the Allied side. Macdonald stated that he knew nothing of this, but Prince Eugene gave him his word that the agreement was concluded.

Macdonald returned to his carriage and expected to discuss this with Marmont. Macdonald now understood that Marmont's treachery was far more advanced than he had confessed and decided that it was better to not attempt to bring him along to their meeting with Schwarzenberg. He confronted Marmont with Prince Eugene's words, but Marmont once again denied that anything had been concluded.

Immediately after the commissioners had departed, word ran through the camps that Napoleon had abdicated. Excitement ran high and Napoleon responded by issuing the following statement:

> I have been requested to abdicate in favor of the King of Rome – and I have done as they asked. Except this is not in the interest of France. My son is an infant. My wife is excellent – one could not find better. However, she knows nothing of the affairs of government. You will, as a result, have an Austrian regency which will last 12 to 15 years and you shall see Schwarzenberg serving as Vice-Emperor of the French. You will not agree with this. It logically follows, in the Austrian perspective, that the other powers would never consent to

permit my son to rule if I still live. Certainly not, because they are afraid I would take the reins of government from my wife's hands. As a result, I expect nothing positive from the actions of the marshals.

Souham defects

A few hours after Marmont's departure, Napoleon precipitated the execution of Marmont's agreement with Schwarzenberg by calling Souham to him for discussions. However, the letter gave no indication of the reasons for the conference, and the guilty Souham feared he was being called in so he could be arrested. He called a conference of the conspiring generals of Marmont's corps and, by a unanimous agreement, they resolved to execute the agreement and march on Versailles without waiting for instructions from Marmont. They immediately took precautions to protect the movement. Ricard's division, which was guarding the Essonne, was relieved. Pickets were placed along the main road with orders to stop and conduct to GD Souham any couriers with dispatches from the Imperial Headquarters. The movement orders were sent directly to the forces of GDs Chastel and Lucotte without notifying the two generals.

At 4:00 a.m. the corps arose from its bivouacs and marched out. Bordesoulle's cavalry formed the head of the column, with the artillery following it. The infantry marched on each side by sections. The cavalry of GD Chastel formed the rearguard. All movement was made in complete silence – as if they were acting to surprise the enemy.[9]

Initially, the soldiers and officers of corps – who did not know of the agreement – thought that they were executing a serious flank attack on the Allies' right flank, but the appearance and parallel march of the Bavarian cavalry soon convinced them that something was amiss. At Fresnes, some officers and about 100 Polish éclaireurs recognized the deception and cried that they were being tricked and that they did not wish to be separated from their brothers-in-arms. They immediately turned and quickly marched back towards Fontainebleau. Murmurs quickly riffled through the column – and the efforts of the generals to restore order were useless. Discipline and subordination crumbled, but they also realized that they could not safely turn about and return to Fontainebleau without precipitating an attack by the Allies that would be overwhelming.

With Souham's failure to appear, Napoleon sent a second officer to him around 3:00 a.m. This officer returned to announce to Napoleon that the VI Corps had disappeared. Napoleon immediately directed that Belliard take a few squadrons and immediately scour the roads from Fontainebleau to find it. Confused and awaiting an explanation for these strange orders, Belliard heard Napoleon exclaim: "Who would have expected such a blow from Marmont! A man with whom I have broken bread... who I drew up from obscurity... to whom I gave fortune and reputation!" After a moment of silence, he began again: "There you have the fate of sovereigns, General Belliard; it is the action of ingrates... Ah! Surely Marmont's corps does not know where he leads them. Yesterday, he gave me marks of his strong attachment – for which I can only believe that he had already abandoned me. This is an irreparable disaster. To horse, despite this, to see these things for yourself and return as fast as possible with a report of the actions you have taken."

Departing immediately, Belliard soon arrived on the Essonne, where Mortier was filling the line.

9 Koch, Vol. II, pp. 571-82.

The marshals in Paris

As soon as they arrived in Paris, Ney, Macdonald and the Duke of Vicence communicated the object of their mission to the provisional government, which did not hide that they were not well-disposed towards their mission. That same evening, they obtained an audience with Tsar Alexander. They explained to the Tsar that Napoleon offered his abdication, but that if nothing positive came of the overture, that Napoleon would resume the fight. The Tsar decided to consult with the other sovereigns and made no promises to the marshals – adjourning the meeting for a day. His remarks were taken by the marshals as a positive reception of their overtures and they dispatched a courier to Fontainebleau to advise Napoleon of the apparent favorable reception of his offer.

Though the arrival of this positive news in Fontainebleau brought joy to most, Napoleon did not feel that happiness and remained quietly worried all day.

At the Allied conference – reviewing the proposal – the causes of the regency and the restoration conflicted. Arguments were heated. Those who supported the Napoleonic Regency stated that a Restoration of the Bourbons would bring back all the abuses that had caused the Revolution and would be much as if the English had restored the Stuarts of the throne of England.

Those supporting the restoration spoke more to the rights of kings and justice for those despoiled by the Revolution.

Napoleon's representatives – the marshals – had pointed out that Napoleon still commanded tremendous resources and that the war was far from over. Napoleon still commanded the army of the Rhône; of Italy; and of the Midi – plus innumerable garrison forces. The Allies knew they were also slowly dissipating their army into garrisons to hold what they had conquered in a hostile land.

Abdication conditionally refused

It was refused, conditionally, but still – it was refused. Ney was dumbfounded, then immediately responded with the arguments that had earlier won an apparent conditional acceptance by the Tsar. It was to no avail. As Ney argued his case, an Allied courier arrived with news that Marmont's corps had defected. Though the word was transmitted in Russian, the Duke of Vicence understood the language and whispered: "Bad news!" – at which point, the Tsar began to lecture them – asking them if they knew that Marmont and his corps had defected. The marshals responded that this was impossible – to which the Tsar responded by showing them the dispatch from Schwarzenberg announcing the defection. Napoleon now had no choice but absolute abdication. It was Marmont's action that finally ended Napoleon's hope for any hold on power in France through negotiations.

Dispositions for withdrawal to the Loire

Not waiting for any news from Paris, Napoleon began to act. On 6 April GD Gérard was ordered to take the Malesherbes bridge with the brigade he held in Ury and to defile his corps across it and march on Puiseaux. He was to be followed, successively, by the corps of Macdonald and Oudinot – protected on the flanks by the cavalry of Defrance, Milhaud and Saint-Germain. The Guard divisions of Friant and Henrion and line division of Roll were to depart their bivouacs at 6:00 a.m. and march on Puiseaux under the protection of the three Guard cavalry divisions under Ornano. GD Kellermann – whose cavalry corps stood on the Loing (near Nemours) – was informed of this movement, directed to march the following day on Péthiviers and to rejoin the army if he was obliged to fight. Mortier's corps and the divisions of Roussel and Leval did not leave their positions on the Essonne until 7:00 a.m. When they did, they marched on Fontainebleau – covering the withdrawal of the grand park and the main army.

This movement was not executed without obstacles. The Allied right extended towards the road to Orléans. Péthiviers, which stood on this road, was held by 150 Allied light infantry. Kellermann found it occupied by a considerable force. On one side were the light troops of General Kaisarov – numbering 1,200 to 1,500 cavalry – which had crossed the Loing, pillaged Soupe and were marching on Puiseaux. Rigaud's dragoon brigade – marching from Nemours – drove them back from the road.

In addition, Tettenborn found himself facing General Allix and was also driven back. Though harassed, Napoleon's army was on the road to the Loire – calling in the various detachments as it marched south.

While the march was in progress, news of the failure in Paris arrived. The news of Napoleon's conditional abdication had become common knowledge in the army – and word arrived that Napoleon was now faced with either continuing the war or an absolute abdication. Soldier and officer alike knew that this would mean civil war in France. News of Marmont's defection also spread and was widely blamed for the failure of the marshal's mission to Paris.

Whether it was a desire to spare France further suffering, or if Napoleon was simply tired of war, it will never be known what caused it, but Napoleon had begun seriously considering offering his absolute abdication to the Allies as the means of ending the war. He rewrote his instructions to his plenipotentiaries and gave them authorization to proffer an absolute abdication to the Allies. The marshals and the Duke of Vicence then departed for Paris with the new proposal. This action taken, he began to work out the details for uniting his army with the Army of Italy as it evacuated northern Italy.

As these preparations were made, Napoleon ordered a review of the II and VII Corps. Oudinot received this order with some surprise, as he had heard officially of the absolute abdication. Though it suggested an unusual state of affairs, he chose to comply rather than invite an explosion of temper.

The two corps arrived at noon in the Cheval-Blanc court. They did not occupy much space in their greatly reduced state. Little remained of the army that had been the terror of Europe for 20 years. However, the troops seemed more attentive to their sad state of affairs than to the glories of the past. It turned out to be a serious and somber affair.

Immediately after the parade, Napoleon called Oudinot to him and asked him if he could be certain of the devotion of his corps. Oudinot responded: "No sire, Your Majesty has abdicated. Yes, but under conditions. It is true, sire, but the soldier does not know political restrictions." Napoleon thought momentarily, and responded: "Well, let us await news from Paris." With his world collapsing and in ruins, Napoleon had sought solace and comfort in the affection of his family – the army. Oudinot's response – and the review – had done little to invigorate Napoleon's spirit. It was over.

The ongoing negotiations for an armistice left everyone in a state of uncertainty. When the armistice became public, it was learned that it had divided France into zones occupied by the French army and those of the Allies. The Allies were to occupy France from the mouth of the Seine along the right bank and from the southern borders of the departments of Seine-Inférieure, l'Oise, Seine-et-Oise, Seine-et-Marne, l'Yonne, Côte-d'Or, Saône-et-Loire, Rhône and Isère as far as Mont-Cenis.

The main headquarters returned to Fontainebleau, but the army continued to remain in its positions for a few days. However, all was not said and done. In Versailles, Marmont's troops were in a tumult. After the rupture of the negotiations in favor of a regency, Marmont went to Versailles to learn from Souham the reason for his actions. When he arrived, he called for a review of the corps to be held at noon and issued the following order of the day:

> Soldiers! For the last three months, you have been in constant combat – and in those three months you have been crowned with further glory. Neither the perils, nor the fatigues, nor the privations have diminished your zeal – nor your love for your country. Your country sends you its thanks through me and it appreciates all that you have done for it. However, the time has arrived, soldiers, where the war you have fought has become a war without purpose. It is time for you to rest. You are the soldiers of your country. It is public opinion that you should follow and it is my order that you pull back from the useless dangers in order to conserve your noble blood – that you might pour out again – when the voice of the country and public interest would protest your efforts. Good cantonments are assured you and my paternal concerns for you shall soon be forgotten, I hope, as shall the fatigues which you have endured.

This proclamation achieved the dissipation of the doubts of the officers and men, but it did not find them prepared for the change that was about to occur. Suddenly, a rumor flashed through the ranks that the Russians would be coming to disarm them – then all the officers and men would be made prisoners of war and taken to the depths of Siberia. Panic and anger reigned. Officers tore off their epaulets and broke their swords. Soldiers threw down their arms, while others swore to die before they surrendered them. The cries and confusion in the ranks added to the disorder. The senior officers tried to restore order, but it was impossible. The entire corps disbanded – platoons moving into the city. Large numbers soon gathered at the central square, where many talked of returning to Fontainebleau. Eventually, however, the panic subsided and the men quietly entered their cantonments.

Negotiations in Paris

In Paris, Ney, Macdonald and the Duke of Vicence resumed their negotiations with the Allies on the basis of a total abdication. Principal among the concerns was where Napoleon would go once he abdicated, and the Island of Elba – off the French and Italian coasts – was chosen.

On 7 April in Paris (as well as in Fontainebleau), Napoleon's abdication was considered final – even though it was still conditional and subject to negotiations. The provisional government in Paris declared for Louis XVIII and declared all acts and judgements of Napoleon's regime null and void. On 8 April the provisional government continued the process of dismantling Napoleon's government and its legislation.

Absolute abdication

On 11 April the negotiations over Napoleon's abdication and the fate of his family were signed. Macdonald and the other commissioners ratified it. Napoleon was briefed on the contents of the agreement and then dictated to the Duke of Bassano his abdication in these terms:

> The Allied powers – having proclaimed that the Emperor Napoleon was the sole obstacle to the restoration of peace in Europe – the Emperor Napoleon, faithful to his word, declares that he renounces for himself and his heirs the thrones of France and Italy, since there is no personal sacrifice, including my life, which I am not ready to make for the interest of France.[10]

10 Koch, Vol. II, pp. 583-610.

Napoleon's farewell to the Old Guard in the courtyard of the palace at Fontainebleau, by Antoine-Alphonse Montfort.

It was done. The 1814 campaign was finished and Napoleon was Emperor no more. In a few weeks, he would be taken aboard ship and transported to Elba, where he was to remain for the rest of his days.

His family – the Grande Armée – may have been in a shambles, but the Bourbons would punish it even further. The Bourbon Restoration immediately set about casting it in their image – disbanding numerous regiments, renumbering the rest and renaming others after members of the Royal Family – as had been the tradition in the Royal Army before 1789. The tricolor was abandoned, and the eagles – the sacred eagles for which so many thousands had died – were recalled and destroyed one after the other until only a few, which had been secreted away by diehard Bonapartists, remained.

France was ravaged. Funds were desperately short and thousands of soldiers were thrown out of the only profession they had known. The Bourbons were so eager to expunge anything of the Imperial period from France that they even directed that the eagles be broken off the soldiers' shako plates because the shortage of funds prevented new shako plates being issued. This left a constant reminder on every soldiers' head of what had been and was now gone. A shako was a cylindrical, leather hat that had replaced the bicorne as the authorized headgear for almost all the soldiers of Europe during the previous 15 years. On the front of these shakos, each soldier had a metal plaque that bore the coat of arms or other insignia of his regiment. The plates worn by the French had an imperial eagle as a separate part of this plaque that was relatively easily removed by breaking it off.

Retrospect on the campaign

Though it ended in failure, the 1814 campaign is arguably Napoleon's finest campaign. In fact, there was little hope for any other outcome in the campaign because Napoleon's army had effectively been destroyed at Leipzig six months earlier. The morale of the army never seems to have recovered from that disaster, and the heart had gone out of the French people to support anymore war. Napoleon began raising new armies as he had in 1813, but this army was a very fragile instrument. Before La Rothière, it seemed to be growing in strength, but after Napoleon's failure at La Rothière, desertion became a major problem. Indeed, even the brilliant victories of early February over the Army of Silesia could not restore the aura of invincibility to Napoleon's reputation. Certainly, rebuilding his army required manpower, horses and guns. The French supply of horses had been expended and consumed by the end of 1813, so there were few left to him. Throughout the campaign, Napoleon was able to keep his army fully-equipped and armed – noting how he replaced Marmont and Mortier's at Fontainebleau after the fall of Paris. The problem was manpower. Those recruits that were taken in were exceeded by the wastage due to the horrendous winter conditions in which they fought, by desertion and by combat losses. Of the Allies' independent armies, three of them – the Army of Silesia, the Army of the North and the main army (formerly known as the Army of Bohemia) – were larger than Napoleon could field if his army contained every Frenchman then in a uniform.

It shouldn't have been much of fight, but it was. Incompetence, overconfidence, indecisiveness and timidity on the part of the Allies repeatedly opened windows of opportunity to Napoleon. Napoleon plunged through each of these windows with the desperation of an Emperor with no choice, but to double-down on every play. It was an all or nothing game.

Napoleon's game was not flawless either, but as discussed earlier, he had no choice if he was to survive the campaign. His politics had been foolish and he should have recognized that a throne in a France with its pre-1792 borders was better than no throne at all. He was greedy and overestimated his ability to deal militarily with his adversaries. That having been said, he played his game well and even succeeded in minimizing his losses when he found he had bitten off more than he could chew – as at Laon. The straw that was to do him in was, as it had been in 1813, the failures of his subordinates. Marmont and Mortier were not up to the independent command that he assigned them. Perhaps, one could argue, that having a divided command and expecting them to operate together as peers was a mistake. On the other hand, it may also have been Napoleon's recognition that one overall commander could make a bad judgement and lose everything, but two co-commanders had a chance of being half-right all the time and that he would probably not lose everything if one of them made a major mistake.

As the opposing armies stood, Napoleon would have had to have been seconded by a brilliant marshal to hold the Allied main army at bay with the slender forces available to Mortier and Marmont – and though the two marshals did not show any inspired generalship and frequently cried "wolf" when things were not as bad as they thought, they did not fight an inept campaign.

Augereau's operations on the eastern frontier (near Switzerland) were neither inspired nor inept. He faced overwhelmingly superior forces in the end. Though he failed to provision Lyon for a siege, which eliminated any opportunity of holding the city, it is difficult to suggest with certainty that occupying a besieged fortress was in Napoleon's best interest. Politically, the loss of Lyon was significant, but Augereau preserved a large army and kept it available to Napoleon in the field should he feel fit to draw upon it. Certainly, having preserved that army – and having kept it available for Napoleon – was preferable to having it locked in a fortress to wither slowly into oblivion.

Only Napoleon's northern flank, the lowlands, was the campaign well-played. Here, Maison handled the I Corps in a superb manner. His resources were as limited as those provided to any of Napoleon's generals. Yet, despite this handicap, he outmaneuvered and outfought the Prussians, Russians, Saxons and the English. His only significant losses occurred very early in the campaign when he was struggling to pull together his army. Here, the Allies missed their chance – and if they had been aggressive to any significant degree, they could have scooped up far more of the lowlands than they did. The lowlands campaign is best described as one between a superior French commander and a series of inept Allied commanders.

Of course, it was Marmont's final treachery that ended the campaign. Napoleon had finally accepted that some serious concessions were necessary, but hoped to cling to some vestige of power through a regency. Marmont's treachery obliterated even these last hopes.

As for the Allies' operations, nowhere did they show any inspiration or good generalship until the very end, when Schwarzenberg finally realized that Paris was open if he abandoned his 18th century military mindset. He cut his supply lines and lunged those last miles to Paris to end the war. Though not genius, it was an incredibly bold act for a marshal who had shown himself devoid of any decisiveness for the previous seven months.

On the topic of poor generalship, the Allies did everything possible to explore new regions of ineptness. Blücher had half of his army chewed up and Olsufiev's corps obliterated by his overconfidence. St. Priest was killed and his corps destroyed by a bout of miserable generalship. The Duke of Weimar blundered about Belgium with a force several times larger than Maison – and every time he caught Maison, he came away with burnt fingers. And then there is Graham's blundering, that was magnified by the incompetence and foolishness of his subordinate officers.

All of the Allied army commanders showed a decided lack of enterprise or willingness to use their forces. They were so afraid of Napoleon that they invariably yielded the initiative to him – even though they outnumbered him handily at every turn. It is almost amazing that they finally discovered their advantage in strength and stumbled into Paris. Again, they were too steeped in the 18th century style of warfare – and certainly not a little bit intimidated by the name 'Napoleon'.

Introduction to the Appendices

Sources

The French orders of battle are drawn extensively from the archives at Chateau Vincennes (known as the Section historique de l'armée de Terre, or SHAT) and the Archives Nationales. The Allied orders of battle come from various published archival and non-archival sources.

Formation seniority

The unit closest to the left margin is the senior formation – and all units listed immediately below and indented are part of that command.

Strengths

The strength figures do vary. Generally, they are the 'men under arms' – not the 'effective' strength, which includes various categories of individuals not present – often including those in hospital, etc. If one strength figure is presented, it is the total strength of the unit (and may or may not include officers). If two figures are presented, they are the numbers of officers and men.

The material taken from the SHAT for the French cavalry can provide two different sets of figures. If three figures are present, the numbers are officers, men and total horses. If four figures are present, the numbers are officers, men, officers' horses and men's horses.

Appendix I

Plan proposed at the Allied headquarters at Frankfurt for operations against France against Maréchal Davout[1]

Swedes	10,000
Walmoden	15,000
Total:	25,000

Under Bernadotte – destined to pass the Rhine (near Cologne) and separate Holland from France:

Swedes	15,000
Winzingerode	30,000
Bülow	20,000
Saxons	15,000
Total:	80,000

Under Blücher – destined to cover the country on the two banks of the Main River:

Yorck	12,000
Langeron	30,000
Sacken	10,000
Total:	52,000
Hessians	10,000
Westphalians	20,000
Reinforcements	15,000
Württembergers, Baden and Darmstadt	10,000
Kleist	15,000
Total:	70,000

Destined to act through Switzerland and advance though the Jura into France:

Guards and Reserves	30,000
Wittgenstein	10,000
Reinforcements	15,000
Austrians	120,000
Bavarians	30,000
Total:	205,000

In Italy – destined to march on the Var and establish communications with Wellington:

Austrians	68,000

Corps engaged in sieges on the Elbe:

Bennigsen	20,000
Tauentzien	28,000
Klenau	18,000
Chasteler	9,000
Tolstoy	25,000

1 Burghersh, *Memoir of the Operations of the Allied Operations*, pp. 328-30; p. 331; pp. 332-4.

Total:	100,000

Total forces deployed:

Austrians	215,000
Russians	147,000
Prussians	87,000
Bavarians	30,000
Westphalians	20,000
Hessians	10,000
Saxons	15,000
Swedes	25,000
Walmoden	11,000
Württembergers, Baden and Darmstadt	10,000
Reinforcements	30,000
Total:	600,000

It should be noted that the 10,000 Hessians and the 20,000 Westphalians were yet to be raised. The Russian reinforcements en route are noted as: "being upon their march." The Saxon force shown at 15,000 never exceeded 7,000. Langeron's Corps was considerably weaker than shown; the Austrian force – indicated as 120,000 men – did not exceed 80,000 men. This would indicate that the actual number should more reasonably be estimated at 482,000 men.

Proposal for the operations of the Allied armies

Transmitted to Bernadotte
2 November 1813

> It is proposed that the Army of Bohemia should place its left upon the Mein and its right upon the Sieg; the Army of Silesia – its left on the Sieg and its right towards Düsseldorf; the Army of the North – after destroying that of Davout – should undertake the siege of Wesel and move upon Holland. The whole of these armies – after being allowed the time necessary to recruit – should pass to the left of the Rhine.

Number, disposition, and employment of the Allied armies as proposed by Blücher

Russian Guard and Grenadier Reserves	30,000
Wittgenstein's Corps	10,000
Army of Bohemia	120,000
Army of Silesia	52,000
Bavarian Army	30,000
Total:	242,000

B: Disposable in a few weeks:

Kleist's Corps	15,000
Former Confederation of the Rhine Troops	20,000
Total:	35,000

C: Reinforcements en route:	
Destined for Wittgenstein	15,000
Destined for Langeron and Sacken	15,000
Destined for Yorck and Kleist	12,000
Total:	42,000

D: Troops disposable in near future when Elbe fortresses fall:	
Klenau	18,000
Chasteler	9,000
Tolstoy	25,000
Total:	52,000

Further formations coming from the Princes of the Confederation of the Rhine: 150,000

Further troops offered by Bavaria:
40,000

Total: 190,000

What is anticipated to actually arrive (50 percent): 121,000

1. The 30,000 Bavarians (or an equal number of Austrians) will remain on the right bank of the Rhine to observe Mainz. They will not go too near it, but will take up a strong position some leagues from that fortress and will confine themselves to fording the neighboring villages to evacuate whatever may be useful to the garrison.
2. 212,000 combatants will pass the Rhine on different points – leaving corps of observation before Landau and Strasbourg – and will take the direction of Metz and Nancy.
3. After the reduction of Erfurt (or of Dresden), Kleist's Corps – and all the troops of the ex-Confederation of the Rhine, which will then be disposable – will march towards the Upper Rhine, when (according to circumstances) they will either relieve the corps of observation in Alsace, or invade Franche-Comtéby Switzerland. In the first instance, the corps which will be relieved will form a reserve for the Grande Armée.
4. All troops of the German princes, which shall become disposable at a subsequent period, will form themselves into a grand reserve and will take their position wherever the course of operations may render it advisable.
5. Wallmoden's Corps – a part of Winzingerode and Bülow's corps – will be directed towards the Lower Rhine, will pass that river and try to force their way by Liége and Givet.
6. Thielemann's Corps will pass the Rhine at Ehrenbreitenstein, will take up the strong position of the Chartreuse near Coblentz and will – according to circumstances – either support the operations of the corps directed upon Givet, or those of the main army.
7. The Swedish Army Corps, part of Winzingerode's Corps and all the troops which will be available after the reduction of the fortresses on the Elbe will be opposed to Davout and the Danes.
8. Supposing the main army – while it marches on Metz and Nancy – were to leave behind it 35,000 men to observe the fortresses in Alsace, it still brings 182,000 men into the field – from which (deducting 7,000 sick, etc.) there remains 175,000 effective men. These will be joined by 42,000 from the reinforcements (C) and will form an army of 217,000 men, with a reserve of 100,000:

Near Mainz (30,000); in Alsace (35,000); troops mentioned under B (35,000); and a second reserve of 121,000 troops mentioned in D.

There is nothing to prevent the proposed operations from commencing immediately. They are independent of those in Italy, and of the army of Lord Wellington – and, whatever successes either of these may obtain, must be of advantage to the armies on the Rhine and contribute to their successes (without such being a necessary condition of them).

By this operation, the enemy must place strong garrisons, munitions, artillery and provisions of all kinds in Mainz, Strasbourg, Luxemburg, Metz, Thionville, Landau, Brissac, Saarlouis and all the small fortified towns of the Vosges and on the Rhine. He will, consequently, have but very few troops with which to form an army capable of resisting the Allies – nor could he supply it with artillery and ammunition. If, after the complete formation of the troops of the Germanic Confederation, we should not have dictated peace to France, our immense masses of troops would then give us the means of menacing the capital and reducing it by taking away its subsistence. When the main army shall be arrived before Metz and Nancy, the following will be the disposition of the forces:

Near Metz	212,000
In Alsace	35,000
Near Mainz	30,000
Near Coblentz	15,000
In Alsace and Switzerland	35,000
Near Liége	50,000
Grand Reserve	121,000
Total:	498,000

Appendix II

French garrisons of the Lowlands, November 1813

17th Division: General Molitor

Amsterdam:
Général de brigade Bouvier-des-Eclats
Converged French Light Infantry (840)[1]
Dutch Guard Veterans (101)
Dutch Reserve Company (102)
Civil Guard Cavalry (109)

Gorkum:
Général de brigade Marie
1/, 2/, 3/1st Antwerp Regiment (1,773)
1/, 2/, 3/2nd Antwerp Regiment (1,757)
Veteran Gunners (115)
1st Dutch Colonial Battalion (284)
2nd Amsterdam Civil Guard Battalion (404)
1st Company, Texel Regiment (145)

Utrecht:
Général de brigade Schiner
Det / Converged French Light Infantry (50)
3/, 4/Pupilles de la Garde (1,272)
Foot Artillery (86)
Pioneers (71)
Dutch Reserve Company (103)

Naarden:
Général de brigade Quétard
Veterans (135)
Foot Artillery (80)
Amsterdam Civil Guard (411)
Texel Regiment (439)

Helder:
Général de brigade Mayer
Foot Artillery (63)
Pioneers (54)
Texel Regiment (295)
Colonial Battalion (127)
Dutch Coast Artillery (106)

1 Figure is the number of men present.

La Haye:
Dutch Reserve Company (102)

Breil:
Captain Harchapt
- Foot Artillery (12)
- Trexel Regiment (147)

Helvoetsluys:
Chef de bataillon Bauer
- Foot Artillery (16)
- Trexel Regiment (147)

Rotterdam:
Dutch Civil Guard (197)

Other:
Dutch Coast Artillery (924)
French Gendarmerie (300)

Zeeland islands:
General Ambert

Flessingue (Flushing):
Général de division Gilly
- 131st Line Regiment (one battalion) (510)
- Miners (10)
- Sapper-Veterans (42)
- Foot Artillery (157)
- French Pioneers (unarmed) (931)
- Dutch Pioneers (458)

Middelbourg:
French Deserter Detachment (75)
Dutch Pioneers (unarmed) (113)

Tervuere:
Det / 131st Line Regiment (98)
French Pioneers (141)

Rhittem:
French Veteran Gunners (89)

Zierick-Zee:
Général de brigade Ducos
French Veteran Gunners (97)

On the coast:
Dutch Coastal Gunners (812)

Elsewhere:
French Gendarmerie (138)

Appendix III

Allied Army of the North, November 1813-January 1814

Commanding Officer: Prince Bernadotte, Crown Prince of Sweden
- Prussian 3rd Corps: Generalmajor von Bülow (19,172 infantry and 6,240 cavalry)
  - 3rd Brigade: Generalmajor Zielinski
    - 2nd East Prussian Grenadier Battalion
    - 1/, 2/, Fus/3rd East Prussian Infantry Regiment
    - 1/, 2/, Fus/4th Reserve Infantry Regiment
    - 1/, 2/, 3/3rd East Prussian Landwehr Regiment
    - 1/, 2/, 3/, 4/1st Leib Hussar Regiment
    - 6pdr Foot Battery #6
  - 4th Brigade: Generalmajor von Thümen
    - 1/, 2/, Fus/4th East Prussian Infantry Regiment
    - 1/, 2/, Fus/5th Reserve Infantry Regiment
    - East Prussian Jäger Battalion (two companies)
    - 1/, 2/, 3/2nd Pomeranian Landwehr Regiment
    - 1/, 2/, 3/, 4/1st Pomeranian Landwehr Cavalry Regiment
    - 6pdr Foot Battery #8
  - 5th Brigade: Generalmajor von Borstell
    - Pomeranian Grenadier Battalion
    - 1/, 2/, Fus/1st Pomeranian Infantry Regiment
    - 1/, 2/, Fus/2nd Reserve Infantry Regiment
    - 1/, 2/, Fus/Elbe Infantry Regiment
    - 1/, 2/, 3/2nd Kurmärk Landwehr Regiment
    - 1/, 2/, 3/, 4/Pomeranian Hussar Regiment
    - 6pdr Foot Battery #10
  - 6th Brigade: Oberst von Krafft
    - 1/, 2/, Fus/Colberg Infantry Regiment
    - 1/, 2/, Fus/9th Reserve Infantry Regiment
    - 1/, 2/, 3/1st Neumärk Landwehr Regiment
    - 1/, 2/, 3/, 4/2nd Pomeranian Landwehr Cavalry Regiment
    - 6pdr Foot Battery #16
- Reserve Cavalry: Generalmajor von Oppen
  - Brigade: Oberst von Treskow
    - 1/, 2/, 3/, 4/Königin Dragoon Regiment
    - 1/, 2/, 3/, 4/Brandenburg Dragoon Regiment
    - 1/, 2/, 3/, 4/2nd West Prussian Dragoon Regiment
  - Brigade: Oberst von Hobe
    - 1/, 2/, 3/, 4/Westphalian Uhlan Regiment
    - 1/, 2/, 3/, 4/2nd Silesian Hussar Regiment
    - 1/, 2/, 3/, 4/Pomeranian National Cavalry Regiment
  - Brigade: Oberst von Sydow
    - 1/, 2/, 3/, 4/2nd Kurmärk Landwehr Cavalry Regiment
    - 1/, 2/, 3/, 4/4th Kurmärk Landwehr Cavalry Regiment
  - Artillery:
    - 6pdr Horse Batteries #5 and #6

Reserve Artillery: Generalmajor von Holtzendorff
12pdr Foot Batteries #4 and #5
6pdr Foot Battery #19 and ?
6pdr Horse Battery #11
Park Columns #3, #4 and #6
Pioneer Companies #4 and #5

Freikorps von Lützow:
3 Infantry Battalions
2 Squadrons Hussars
1 Horse Battery (8-6pdrs)
Attached:
1st Freiwilliger Jäger Battalion: Major von Reiche
2nd Raiding Party: Major von Colombé
70 men of the Guard Light Cavalry Regiment
50 men of Brandenburg Cuirassier Jäger Squadron
20 men of Neumärk Dragoon Regiment
20 men of Silesian Uhlan Regiment

Russian Corps: Generallieutenant Winzingerode (19,944 infantry and 11,475 cavalry)
Advanced Guard: Generalmajor Orurk
3rd Hussar Division: Generalmajor von Pahlen
Elisabethgrad Hussar Regiment (7)
Pavlograd Hussar Regiment (6)
Isoum Hussar Regiment (6)
2nd Dragoon Division: Generalmajor Balk
Brigade: Generalmajor Drewitsch
St. Petersburg Dragoon Regiment (4)
Riga Dragoon Regiment (4)
Finland Dragoon Regiment (4)
Brigade: Generalmajor Galanthe
Polish Uhlan Regiment (5)
Volhynie Uhlan Regiment (5)
Brigade: Generalmajor Sagratzky
Nijine Chasseurs à cheval Regiment (2)
Twer Opolochenie Cossack Regiment (2)

Cossack Corps: Generalmajor Czernichev
Brigade: Lapuschin
Illowaisky IV Don Cossack Regiment
Djaschkin Don Cossack Regiment
Brigade: Generalmajor Narischen
Grekov IX Don Cossack Regiment
Bradantdchikov II Don Cossack Regiment
Melnikov V Don Cossack Regiment
Brigade: Stahl I
1st Bashkir Regiment
1st Bug Cossack Regiment
Brigade: Colonel Patelejev II
Popov XII Cossack Regiment
Patelejev II Cossack Regiment
Brigade: Colonel Benkendorff
Sysoev III Cossack Regiment

Girova Cossack Regiment
Grekov XVIII Don Cossack Regiment
Brigade: Generalmajor Ilowaisky IV
Rebrejev II Cossack Regiment
Vlassov III Cossack Regiment
Balbin II Cossack Regiment
Infantry: Generallieutenant Count Voronzov
21st Division: Generalmajor Leptev
Brigade: Colonel Rosen
Petrovsk Infantry Regiment (1)
Lithuania Infantry Regiment (1)
Podolsk Infantry Regiment (1)
Brigade: Colonel Rüdinger
Neva Infantry Regiment (1)
2nd Jager Regiment (1)
44th Jager Regiment (2)
Division: Generalmajor Wuitsch
Brigade: Generalmajor Swarikin
Chirvan Infantry Regiment (2)
Bourtirki Infantry Regiment (2)
19th Jager Regiment (2)
Brigade: Generalmajor Laharpe
Navaguinsk Infantry Regiment (1)
Tula Infantry Regiment (1)
Converged Grenadier Battalions 9th, 15th and 18th Divisions
Brigade: Generalmajor Krassovsky
Oumsk Infantry Regiment (2)
13th Jager Regiment (2)
14th Jager Regiment (2)
Artillery:
Horse Batteries #1 (10), #4 (8), #7 (12), #11 (12) #13 (12) and #21 (12 guns)
Light Batteries #42, #48 and #56
Position Batteries #7, #28 and #31

Assigned from the Polish Reserve Army
Corps: Generallieutenant Stroganov
12th Division: Generalmajor Cherwansky
Brigade: Generalmajor Sanders
Smolensk Infantry Regiment (1)
Narva Infantry Regiment (1)
Brigade: Generalmajor Schwetschin
Alexopol Infantry Regiment (2)
New Ingremannland Infantry Regiment (1)
Brigade: Generallieutenant Glebov
6th Jager Regiment (1)
41st Jager Regiment (1)
Brigade from 13th Division: Generalmajor Scheltuchin
Pensa Infantry Regiment (2)
Saratov Infantry Regiment (2)
Position Battery #31
Light Batteries #53 and #46

2nd German (Saxon) Corps: Duke of Weimar (32,940 infantry and 4,920 cavalry)
- Division: Generalleutnant Lecoq
  - Brigade:
    - Staff Dragoons (1)
    - 1/, 2/, 3/, 4/Saxon Cuirassier Regiment
    - 1/, 2/, 3/, 4/Saxon Uhlan Regiment
    - 1/, 2/, 3/, 4/, 5/Saxon Hussar Regiment
  - Brigade:
    - Jäger Battalion
    - Grenadier Regiment (three battalions)
    - 1st Line Infantry Regiment (three battalions)
- Division: Generalleutnant Ryssel #1
  - Brigade:
    - 2nd Line Infantry Regiment (three battalions)
    - 3rd Line Infantry Regiment (one battalion)
  - Brigade: Generalmajor Gablentz
    - 1st Light Regiment (two battalions)
    - 2nd Light Regiment (two battalions)
- Division: Generalmajor Prince Paul von Württemberg
  - Brigade: Eglofstein
    - Weimar Jäger Battalion
    - Gotha Infantry Battalion
    - Schwarzberg Infantry Battalion
    - Anhalt-Dessau Infantry Battalion
    - Anhalt-Bernberg Infantry Battalion
- Division: Generalleutnant onv Thielman
  - Brigade: Generalmajor Libenau
    - 1st Saxon Landwehr Regiment (three battalions)
    - 2nd Saxon Landwehr Regiment (three battalions)
  - Brigade: Generalmajor Brause
    - 3rd Saxon Landwehr Regiment (three battalions)
    - 4th Saxon Landwehr Regiment (three battalions)
  - Brigade:
    - Cavalry (one squadron)
    - Bialov Cossack Regiment (two squadrons)
- Hanoverian Division:
  - Brigade: Esdorf
    - 1/, 2/, 3/, 4/Bremen and Verden Hussar Regiment
    - 1/, 2/, 3/, 4/Esdorf Hussar Regiment
  - Brigade: Keilmansegg
    - Hanoverian Freiwilliger Jägers (one battalion)
    - Lauenburg Battalion
    - Verden Battalion
    - Light Battalion
    - Luneburg Battalion
  - Brigade: Ahrenschild
    - 1st Russo-German Legion Infantry Battalion
    - 2nd Russo-German Legion Infantry Battalion
    - 3rd Russo-German Legion Infantry Battalion
    - 4th Russo-German Legion Infantry Battalion
    - 5th Russo-German Legion Infantry Battalion
    - 6th Russo-German Legion Infantry Battalion
    - 7th Russo-German Legion Infantry Battalion

1st Russo-German Legion Hussar Regiment
2nd Russo-German Legion Hussar Regiment
Brigade: Tettenborn
4 Cossack Regiments

Swedish Army: Feldmarshal Count Stedingk
1st Division: Generalmajor Posse
Field Artillery, Gotha Regiment
1st Brigade: Generalmajor Schulzenhain
Svea Garde (1)
Andra Gardet (1)
Lifregimentets grenadierer (1)
Lifgrenadierer (2)
Drottingens Infantry Regiment (1)
2nd Brigade: Generalmajor Lagerbring
Upplands Infantry Regiment (2)
Södermanlands Infantry Regiment (2)
Norra Skanes Infantry Regiment (1)
2nd Division: Generalleutnant Saendels
Field Artillery, Svea Regiment
3rd Brigade: Generalmajor Bransdstroem
Westgöta Infantry Regiment (2)
Westmanlands Infantry Regiment (2)
Nerikes Infantry Regiment (2)
4th Brigade: Colonel Reutterskoeld
Skaraborgs Infantry Regiment (2)
Elfsborgs Infantry Regiment (2)
Wermland Field Jägers (1)
3rd Division: Generalleutnant Boye
Field Artillery, Wendes Regiment
5th Brigade:
Jönköpings Infantry Regiment (2)
Södra Skanes Infantry Regiment (1)
von Engelbrechtens Infantry Regiment (1)
Mecklenburg Brigade:
Guard Grenadier Regiment (1)
Mecklenburg Line Infantry Regiment (2)
Foot Jäger Battalion (1)
7th Brigade: Colonel Hederstierna
Kronobergs Infantry Regiment (2)
Calmare Infantry Regiment (2)
Konungens Infantry Regiment (1)
Cavalry Brigade: Generalleutnant Skioeldebrand
Lifgardet till häst (5)
Pomeranian Legion Cavalry (1)
Lifregimentets cuirassier (4)
Smalands Dragon Regiment (6)
Mörners Hussar Regiment (8)
Skanska Karabinierer (4)
Mecklenburg Jäger zu Pferd Regiment
von Schill Hussar Regiment

Other:
- Artillery Park
- Reserve Artillery
- Engineering Corps
- Pontooniers
- Saxon Sappers
- Pomeranian Foot Legion

Saxon Army Artillery:
- 62 guns (distribution unknown)

2nd German Corps: Duke von Braunschweig
- Division: Oberst Olterman
  - Brigade: Westphal
    - Brunswick Hussar Regiment (3)
    - Brunswick Uhlan Squadron (1)
    - Jägers (three companies)
  - Brigade: Oberstleutnant Buttler
    - Jäger Regiment (three battalions)
  - Brigade: Oberstleutnant Specht
    - Line Infantry Regiment (three battalions)
  - Brigade: Major Biers
    - Landwehr Infantry Regiment (three battalions)
  - Mecklenburg-Schwerin Contingent: Generalmajor Fallois
    - Mecklenburg Grenadier Battalion
    - Mecklenburg Infantry Regiment (2)
    - Mecklenburg Freiwilliger Jägers (1)
    - Mecklenburg Freiwilliger Jägers zu Pferd (one squadron)
- Hanseatic Division: Colonel Witzleben
  - Brigade: Oberstleutnant Deluis
    - Hamburg Regiment (two battalions)
    - Bremen Regiment (one battalion)
    - Lubeck Regiment (one battalion)
  - Brigade: Major Arnim
    - Hamburg Cavalry Regiment (six squadrons)
    - Lubeck Cavalry Regiment (two squadrons)
    - Bremen Cavalry Regiment (one squadron)
  - Oldenburg Contingent: Oberstleutnant Werdenberg
    - Oldenburg Infantry Regiment (two battalions)
  - Hanoverian Contingent: Generalmajor Dörenberg
  - Brigade: Kielmansegg
    - Cumberland Hussar Regiment (?)
    - Line Infantry (22 battalions)
  - Brigade: Lyon
    - Landwehr (10 brigades)
  - Corps Artillery:
    - 64 guns

Appendix IV

English forces in the Netherlands, 28 December 1813

Commanding Officer: General Sir Thomas Graham

- Guard Brigade: Major General Cock
  - 1st Foot Guards Regiment
  - 2nd Foot Guards Regiment
  - 3rd Foot Guards Regiment
- 1st Brigade: Major General Sterret
  - 37th Foot Regiment
  - 44th Foot Regiment
  - 55th Foot Regiment
  - 69th Foot Regiment
  - Royal Veterans
- Light Brigade: Major General MacKenzie
  - 35th Foot Regiment
  - 52nd Foot Regiment
  - 73rd Foot Regiment
  - 95th Foot Regiment
- 2nd Brigade: Major General Gibbs
  - 25th Foot Regiment
  - 33rd Foot Regiment
  - 54th Foot Regiment
  - 56th Foot Regiment
- Artillery:
  - 4 Foot Companies

Appendix V

Polish Reserve Army, December 1813

Polish Reserve Army
Corps: General Docturov
  26th Infantry Division: Generalmajor Paskevich (later Emme)
    Brigade: Generalmajor Savonia
      Ladoga Infantry Regiment (2)[1]
      Poltava Infantry Regiment (2)
    Brigade: Generalmajor Schemtschuschnikoff
      Nivegorod Infantry Regiment (2)
      Orel Infantry Regiment (2)
    Brigade: Generalmajor Gogel
      5th Jager Regiment (2)
      42nd Jager Regiment (2)
    Artillery:
      Position Battery #26 (12 guns)
      Light Battery #47 (161 men)
  Cavalry Division: Generallieutenant Tschaplitz
    Brigade: Generalmajor Repninsky
      Combined Dragoon Regiment (5)
      1st Converged Chasseurs à cheval Regiment (4)
      2nd Converged Chasseurs à cheval Regiment (4)
    Brigade: Generalmajor Kreutz
      2nd Converged Uhlan Regiment (4)
      Taganrog Uhlan Regiment (4)
      Siberian Uhlan Regiment (2)
      Jitomir Uhlan Regiment (2)
    Artillery:
      Horse Battery #2 (12-6pdrs)

They were followed shortly by:
  13th Division: Generalleutnant Markov III
    Brigade: Generalmajor Rossy
      Galitz Infantry Regiment (3)
      Veliki-Lotz Infantry Regiment (3)
  16th Division: Generalmajor Bullatov
    Neuschlot Infantry Regiment (3)
    Mingrelia Infantry Regiment (3)
    27th Jager Regiment (3)
    43rd Jager Regiment (3)

1 Figure in parenthesis is the number of battalions or squadrons.

Militia Corps: Generalleutnant Count Tolstoy
1st Militia Corps: Generalmajor Morumzov
- 1st Nichegorod Opolochenie Infantry Regiment (3)
- 2nd Nichegorod Opolochenie Infantry Regiment (3)
- 3rd Nichegorod Opolochenie Infantry Regiment (3)
- 4th Nichegorod Opolochenie Infantry Regiment (3)
- 5th Nichegorod Opolochenie Infantry Regiment (3)
- 1st Kazan Opolochenie Infantry Regiment (3)
- 2nd Kazan Opolochenie Infantry Regiment (3)

2nd Militia Corps: Generalmajor Titov
- 1st Pensa Opolochenie Infantry Regiment (3)
- 2nd Pensa Opolochenie Infantry Regiment (3)
- 3rd Pensa Opolochenie Infantry Regiment (3)
- 3rd Raizan Opolochenie Infantry Regiment (3)
- 1st Raizan Opolochenie Jager Regiment (3)

Light Cavalry Division: Generalleutnant Schepelov
- Brigade: Colonel Graf Bennigsen
  - Converged Hussar Regiment (5)
  - Converged Dragoon Regiment (5)
  - 1st Converged Mounted Jager Regiment (4)
- Brigade: Colonel Klebek
  - 2nd Converged Mounted Jager Regiment (4)
  - 1st Converged Uhlan Regiment (5)
  - 2nd Converged Uhlan Regiment (4)
- Opolochenie (Militia) Cavalry Division: Generalmajor Prince Tenischev
  - Brigade: Colonel Kaslov
    - Pensa Opolochenia Cavalry Regiment (5)
    - Simbrisk Opolochenia Cavalry Regiment (5)
    - Nichegorod Opolochenia Cavalry Regiment (5)
  - Brigade: Colonel Nebolsin
    - Kostroma Opolochenia Cavalry Regiment (5)
    - Riazan Opolochenia Cavalry Regiment (5)
    - Kasan Opolochenia Cavalry Regiment (5)
  - Reinforcements en route:
    - Irkutz Hussar Regiment
    - Perejeslav Mounted Jager Regiment
    - Teraspol Mounted Jager Regiment

Cossack Corps: Generalmajor Prince Bagration
- Platov V Cossack Regiment
- Andrianov III Cossack Regiment
- Schamscheva II Cossack Regiment
- 4th Ural Cossack Regiment
- 5th Ural Cossack Regiment
- 9th Bashkir Regiment
- 11th Bashkir Regiment
- 14th Bashkir Regiment
- 15th Bashkir Regiment
- Assigned Artillery: Generalmajor Resvoy
  - Position Batteries #16, #22, #26, #45 and #52
  - Light Batteries #1, #18, #47 and #64
  - Pensa Opolochenie Battery (4 6pdr guns)

Horse Batteries #2, #10, #22 and #30

Other:

- Afanassiev III Miner Company
- Schavitsch Pioneer Company
  - Schtender Sapper Company
  - 1st Pontooneer Company
  - 2nd Pontooneer Company

Appendix VI

French Army, 1-6 January 1814

Imperial Guard: Maréchal Mortier, Duc de Trevise
- 1st Old Guard Division: Général de division Friant
  - 1st Brigade: Général de brigade Petit
    - 1/1st Chasseur à Pied Regiment (20 / 668)[1]
    - 2/1st Chasseur à Pied Regiment (17 / 612)
    - 1/2nd Chasseur à Pied Regiment (17 / 425)
    - 2/2nd Chasseur à Pied Regiment (12 / 493)
  - 2nd Brigade: Général de brigade Cambronne
    - 1/1st Grenadier à Pied Regiment (22 / 738)
    - 2/1st Grenadier à Pied Regiment (19 / 668)
    - 1/2nd Grenadier à Pied Regiment (22 / 542)
    - 2/2nd Grenadier à Pied Regiment (14 / 549)
  - Attached:
    - 1st Company, Guard Sappers (3 / 104)
    - 2nd Company, Guard Sappers (3 / 156)
    - 3rd Company, Guard Sappers (2 / 55)
    - Guard Engineering Train (1 / 27)
    - 3/Guard Marines (3 / 97)
    - 6/Guard Marines (3 / 180)
    - 7/Guard Marines (3 / 120)
    - Guard Administrative Workers (1 / 24)
- 2nd Old Guard Division: Général de division Michel
  - 1st Brigade: Général de brigade Gros
    - 1/Fusilier Chasseur Regiment (11 / 369)
    - 2/Fusilier Chasseur Regiment (9 / 360)
    - 1/Fusilier Grenadier Regiment (17 / 187)
    - 2/Fusilier Grenadier Regiment (15 / 127)
  - 2nd Brigade: Général de brigade Christiani
    - 1/Flanker-Chasseur Regiment (9 / 64)
    - 2/Flanker-Chasseur Regiment (7 / 60)
    - 1/Flanker-Grenadier Regiment (8 / 60)
    - 2/Flanker-Grenadier Regiment (7 / 62)
    - Vélites of Turin (18 / 202)
    - Vélites of Florence (14 / 129)
  - Artillery: Captain Eggerlé
  - 1st Young Guard Company (2 / 71) (4-6pdrs and 2-24pdr how)
  - Guard Train Detachment (2 / 79)
- 2nd Young Guard (2nd Voltigeur) Division: Général de division Decouz
  - Brigade: Général de brigade Baron Peles
    - 1/5th Voltigeur Regiment (9 / 95)
    - 2/5th Voltigeur Regiment (11 / 90)
    - 1/6th Voltigeur Regiment (10 / 107)

1 Figures are the number of officers and the numbers of men present.

2/6th Voltigeur Regiment (16 / 116)
Brigade: Général de brigade Bigarré
1/7th Voltigeur Regiment (10 / 228)
2/7th Voltigeur Regiment (8 / 257)
1/8th Voltigeur Regiment (7 / 167)
2/8th Voltigeur Regiment (4 / 152)
5th Young Guard (2nd Tirailleur) Division: Général de division Rottembourg
1st Brigade: Général de brigade Marques
1/5th Tirailleur Regiment (16 / 276)
2/5th Tirailleur Regiment (10 / 268)
1/6th Tirailleur Regiment (16 / 257)
2/6th Tirailleur Regiment (12 / 355)
2nd Brigade: Général de brigade Charrière
1/7th Tirailleur Regiment (18 / 248)
2/7th Tirailleur Regiment (9 / 240)
1/8th Tirailleur Regiment (17 / 192)
2/8th Tirailleur Regiment (10 / 185)
1st (Old) Guard Cavalry Division: Général de division Laferière Levéque
1-7/2nd Guard Lancer Regiment (Old Guard) (40 / 590 / 746)[2]
1-6/Guard Chasseurs à cheval Regiment (Old Guard) (47 / 688 / 759)
1-6/Guard Dragoon Regiment (Old Guard) (54 / 806 / 967)
2nd (Old) Guard Cavalry Division:
1-6/Guard Grenadier à cheval Regiment (Old Guard) (52 / 968 / 1,106)
1/, 2/Gendarmes d'Elite (19 / 524 / 505)
Artillery and Park Park: Colonel Major Grioirt
2nd Young Guard Foot Artillery (2 / 57) (6-6pdrs and 2 howitzers)
3rd Young Guard Foot Artillery (3 / 71) (6-6pdrs and 2 howitzers)
4th Young Guard Foot Artillery (2 / 49) (6-6pdrs and 2 howitzers)
5th Young Guard Foot Artillery (1 / 51) (6-6pdrs and 2 howitzers)
6th Young Guard Foot Artillery (1 / 55) (6-6pdrs and 2 howitzers)
8th Young Guard Foot Artillery (2 / 47) (none)
9th Young Guard Foot Artillery (2 / 67) (6-6pdrs and 2 howitzers)
10th Young Guard Foot Artillery (2 / 66) (6-6pdrs and 2 howitzers)
11th Young Guard Foot Artillery (2 / 77) (2 / 66) (6-6pdrs and 2 howitzers)
12th Young Guard Foot Artillery (3 / 57) (none)
13th Young Guard Foot Artillery (2 / 49) (2 / 66) (6-6pdrs and 2 howitzers)
14th Young Guard Foot Artillery (2/57) (2/66) (6-6pdrs and 2 howitzers)
1st Old Guard Foot Artillery (2/80) (6-6pdrs and 2 howitzers)
2nd Old Guard Foot Artillery (3 / 86) (6-12pdrs and 2 howitzers)
3rd Old Guard Foot Artillery (2 / 33) (6-12pdrs and 2 howitzers)
4th Old Guard Foot Artillery (3 / 69) (6-12pdrs and 2 howitzers)
5th Old Guard Foot Artillery (2 / 85) (6-12pdrs and 2 howitzers)
6th Old Guard Foot Artillery (3 / 62) (unknown)
1st Old Guard Horse Artillery (3 / 56) (4-6pdrs and 2 howitzers)
2nd Old Guard Horse Artillery (3 / 59) (4-6pdrs and 2 howitzers)
4th Old Guard Horse Artillery (3 / 73) (4-6pdrs and 2 howitzers)
5th Old Guard Horse Artillery (3 / 79) (4-6pdrs and 2 howitzers)
6th Old Guard Horse Artillery (3 / 76) (4-6pdrs and 2 howitzers)

2 Figures are the number of officers, number of men and number of horses present.

1st-6th Cos, 1/1st Guard Train Regiment
1st-6th Cos, 2/1st Guard Train Regiment
Total Train: (24 / 1, 391 / 1, 375)
1st-6th Cos, 1/2nd Guard Train Regiment
1st-6th Cos, 2/2nd Guard Train Regiment
Total Train: (21 / 1,025 / 721)
1st Artisan Pontooneers Company (2 / 78)
2/3rd Sapper Battalion (2 / 30)
3/7th Sapper Battalion (2 / 55)
3rd Co., Marine Guards (1 / 28)
1st Guard Equipage Company (2 / 122)
2nd Guard Equipage Company (2 / 113)
1/, 2/, 3/Adminsitrative Artisans (14 / 312)
National Guards:
1/, 2/Aisne National Guard Regiment
1/Loiret National Guard Regiment
1/, 2/Seine et Marne National Guard Regiment
1/Seine et Oise National Guard Regiment
1/Eure et Loir National Guard Regiment
1/, 2/l'Oise National Guard Regiment
1/, 2/Seine National Guard Regiment
1/, 2/Chareuse National Guard Regiment
1/Sevres National Guard Regiment
1/Vendé National Guard Regiment
1/, 2/Loire National Guard Regiment
1/, 2/Vienne National Guard Regiment
1/, 2/Ile et Vilaine National Guard Regiment
1/Morbihan National Guard Regiment
1/Finistère National Guard Regiment
1/, 2/Nord National Guard Regiment
1/, 2/de la Manche National Guard Regiment
1/, 2/Orne National Guard Regiment
1/, 2/Eure National Guard Regiment
1/, 2/Seine inferièure National Guard Regiment
1/, 2/Somme National Guard Regiment
1/, 2/Indre et Aisne National Guard Regiment
1/Loire et Cher National Guard Regiment
1/, 2/Maine et Loire National Guard Regiment
1/Mayenne National Guard Regiment
1/, 2/Sarthe National Guard Regiment
Division defending the Saône:
1/, 2/Doubs National Guard Regiment
1/, 2/Haute Saône National Guard Regiment
1/, 2/Jura National Guard Regiment
1/, 2/l'Ain National Guard Regiment
1/, 2/Côte d'Or National Guard Regiment
1/, 2/Aube National Guard Regiment
1/, 2/Marne National Guard Regiment
1/, 2/Yonne National Guard Regiment
1/, 2/Loire National Guard Regiment
Paris Reserve: Général de division Gérard (strength as of 15 January 1814)
1st Division: Général de division Dufour
1st Brigade: Général de brigade Jarry

6/29th Légère Regiment (19 / 758)
7/29th Légère Regiment (17 / 600)
7/12th Line Regiment (19 / 635)
7/15th Line Regiment (18 / 558)
7/2nd Line Regiment (14 / 625)
6/4th Line Regiment (17 / 623)
2nd Brigade: Général de brigade de Bellair
8/32nd Line Regiment (21 / 560)
8/58th Line Regiment (24 / 426)
3/135th Line Regiment (18 / 400)
3/155th Line Regiment (16 / 818)
3rd Brigade: Général de brigade Bourmont
1/113th Line Regiment (20 / 706)
3/113th Line Regiment (15 / 689)
4/113th Line Regiment (16 / 747)
Artillery:
1 Foot Battery (2 /120)
1 Horse Battery (2 / 96)
2/14th Principal Train Batalion (1 / 124)
2nd Division: Général de division Hamélinaye
1st Brigade: Général de brigade Tarayre
2/5th Légère Regiment (15 / 572)
Det. 2/5th Légère Regiment (2 / 248)
4/3rd Marine Regiment (6 / 232)
Det. 4/3rd Marine Regiment (2 / 248)
2/138th Line Regiment (21 / 397)
2/142nd Line Regiment (20 / 2200
2/144th Line Regiment (21 / 542)
2nd Brigade: Général de brigade Donop
3/16th Légère Regiment (17 / 609)
4/23rd Légère Regiment (21 / 594)
4/86th Line Regiment (10 / 221)
4/26th Line Regiment (8 / 285)
4/121st Line Regiment (15 / 400)
3/122nd Line Regiment (16 / 656)
3rd Brigade: unknown
4/66th Line Regiment (15 / 106)
4/15th Line Regiment (15 / 100)
2/70th Line Regiment (15 / 100)
4/82nd Line Regiment (14 / 590)
3/1st Marine Regiment (15 / 370)

Corps des Vosges: Maréchal Ney, Prince de Moscowa
1st Young Guard (1st Voltigeur) Division: Général de division Meunier
Brigade: Général de brigade Lacoste
1/1st Voltigeur Regiment (20 / 499)
2/1st Voltigeur Regiment (9 / 479)
1/2nd Voltigeur Regiment (19 / 530)
2/2nd Voltigeur Regiment (9 / 502)
Brigade: Général de brigade Rousseau
1/3rd Voltigeur Regiment (13 / 671)
2/3rd Voltigeur Regiment (14 / 621)
1/4th Voltigeur Regiment (22 / 693)

2/4th Voltigeur Regiment (12 / 718)
National Guard:
1/, 2/Ardennes National Guard Regiment
1/, 2/Meuse National Guard Regiment
1/, 2/Marne National Guard Regiment
1/, 2/Moselle National Guard Regiment
1/, 2/Meurthe National Guard Regiment
1/, 2/Vosges National Guard Regiment
1/, 2/Bas-RhinNational Guard Regiment
1/, 2/Haut-Rhin National Guard Regiment
Other Imperial Guard:
3rd Young Guard (3rd Voltigeur) Division: Général de division Boyer de Neberal
1/, 2/9th Voltigeur Regiment (23 / 289)
1/, 2/10th Voltigeur Regiment (21 / 171)
1/, 2/11th Voltigeur Regiment (28 / 368)
1/, 2/12th Voltigeur Regiment (33 / 1,655)
1/, 2/13th Voltigeur Regiment (35 / 1,455)
4th Young Guard (1st Tirailleur) Division: Général de division Barrois
1/, 2/1st Tirailleur Regiment (25 / 894)
1/, 2/2nd Tirailleur Regiment (27 / 990)
1/, 2/3rd Tirailleur Regiment (27 / 1,384)
1/, 2/4th Tirailleur Regiment (24 / 828)
6th Young Guard (3rd Tirallleur) Division: Général de division Roguet
1/, 2/9th Tirailleur Regiment (38 / 1,096)
1/, 2/10th Tirailleur Regiment (42 / 1,499)
1/, 2/11th Tirailleur Regiment (30 / 1,501)
1/, 2/12th Tirailleur Regiment (30/1,591)
1/, 2/13th Tirailleur Regiment (28/1,355)
2nd Guard Cavalry Division: Général de division Guyot
Guard Chasseurs à cheval Regiment (6) (47 / 602)
Guard Grenadier à cheval Regiment (6) (55 / 932)
Guard Dragoon Regiment (6) (57 / 665)
Gendarmes d'élite (2) (17 / 494)
Troops à la Suite:
1st Gardes d'honneur (8) (68 /1,443)
2nd Gardes d'honneur (8) (24 / 1,127)
3rd Gardes d'honneur (9) (42 / 1,476)
4th Gardes d'honneur (9) (31 / 796)
Artillery (as of 1/1/14):
3/4th Horse Artillery
7/4th Horse Artillery
8/4th Horse Artillery
Provisional Young Guard Division:
Fusilier Grenadier Regiment (5th and 6th Companies)
Fusilier Chasseur Regiment (5th and 6th Companies)
Flanker Chasseur Regiment (5th and 6th Companies)
Flanker Grenadier Regiment (5th and 6th Companies)
1st Tirailleur Regiment (5th and 6th Companies)
2nd Tirailleur Regiment (5th and 6th Companies)
3rd Tirailleur Regiment (5th and 6th Companies)
4th Tirailleur Regiment (5th and 6th Companies)
9th Tirailleur Regiment (5th and 6th Companies)
10th Tirailleur Regiment (5th and 6th Companies)

11th Tirailleur Regiment (5th and 6th Companies)
12th Tirailleur Regiment (5th and 6th Companies)
13th Tirailleur Regiment (5th and 6th Companies)
12th Voltigeur Regiment (5th and 6th Companies)

Guard Artillery Reserve and Park: Colonel Frion

2/Young Guard Foot Artillery (2 / 57)
3/Young Guard Foot Artillery (3 / 71)
4/Young Guard Foot Artillery (2 / 49)
5/Young Guard Foot Artillery (1 / 51)
6/Young Guard Foot Artillery (1 / 55)
8/Young Guard Foot Artillery (2 / 47)
9/Young Guard Foot Artillery (2 / 67)
10/Young Guard Foot Artillery (2 / 66)
11/Young Guard Foot Artillery (2 / 77)
12/Young Guard Foot Artillery (3 / 57)
13/Young Guard Foot Artillery (2 / 49)
14/Young Guard Foot Artillery (2 / 57)
1/Old Guard Foot Artillery (2 / 80)
2/Old Guard Foot Artillery (3 / 86)
3/Old Guard Foot Artillery (2 / 33)
4/Old Guard Foot Artillery (3 / 69)
5/Old Guard Foot Artillery (2 / 85)
6/Old Guard Foot Artillery (3 / 62)
1/Old Guard Horse Artillery (3 / 56)
2/Old Guard Horse Artillery (3 / 59)
4/Old Guard Horse Artillery (3 / 73)
5/Old Guard Horse Artillery (3 / 79)
6/Old Guard Horse Artillery (3 / 76)
1/, 2/, 3/, 4/, 5/, 6 companies 1/1st Guard Train Regiment
1/, 2/, 3/, 4/, 5/, 6 companies 2/1st Guard Train Battalion
(Train Total: 24 / 1,391)
1/, 2/, 3/, 4/, 5/, 6 companies 1/2nd Guard Train Regiment
1/, 2/, 3/, 4/, 5/, 6 companies 2/2nd Guard Train Battalion
(Train Total: 21 / 1,029)
1st Guard Artisian/Pontooner Company (2 / 78)
1st Guard Sapper Company (3 / 104)
2/5th Sapper Battalion (2 / 30)
3/7th Sapper Battalion (2 / 55)
3/Guard Marine Battalion (1 / 28)
1/Guard Military Equippage (2 / 122)
2/Guard Military Equippage (2 / 113)
1/, 2/, 3/Guard Artisians (14 / 312)

Général Park (as of 1/1/14):

1/4th Foot Artillery
8/4th Foot Artillery
10/4th Foot Artillery
14/4th Foot Artillery
18/4th Foot Artillery
35/4th Foot Artillery
28/5th Foot Artillery
10/6th Foot Artillery
21/7th Foot Artillery
27/7th Foot Artillery

1/8th Foot Artillery
10/8th Foot Artillery
12/8th Foot Artillery
13/8th Foot Artillery
28/8th Foot Artillery
4/9th Foot Artillery
8/9th Foot Artillery
5/10th Foot Artillery
7/10th Foot Artillery
13/10th Foot Artillery
15/10th Foot Artillery
17/10th Foot Artillery
8/1st Horse Artillery
8/2nd Horse Artillery
1/3rd Horse Artillery
5/3rd Horse Artillery
8/3rd Horse Artillery
6/6th Horse Artillery
7/6th Horse Artillery
1/, 2/5th Artisian Battalion
11/1st Pontooneer Battalion
12/1st Pontooneer Battalion
13/1st Pontooneer Battalion
14/1st Pontooneer Battalion
12 – 12pdrs
152 – 6pdrs
57 – 24pdr howitzers
25 – 12pdr caissons
126 – 6pdr caissons

Corps du Haut Rhin: Maréchal Marmont, Duc de Raguse
VI Corps: Maréchal Marmont
1st Division: Général de division Ricard
Brigade: Général de brigade Fournier (267 / 3,994)
3/2nd Légère Regiment (16 / 143)
7/2nd Légère Regiment (forming)
2/4th Légère Regiment (21 / 847)
3/4th Légère Regiment (20 / 206)
6/4th Légère Regiment (forming)
2/6th Légère Regiment (20 / 222)
3/6th Légère Regiment (forming)
3/40th Line Regiment (21 / 287)
4/40th Line Regiment (forming)
3/43rd Line Regiment (18 / 201)
4/43rd Line Regiment (forming)
2/50th Line Regiment (19 / 362)
3/, 4/50th Line Regiment (forming)
Brigade: Général de brigade Boudin
2/65th Line Regiment (22 / 252)
4/65th Line Regiment (forming)
1/136th Line Regiment (24 / 485)
2/136th Line Regiment (forming)
1/138th Line Regiment (28 / 328)

2/138th Line Regiment (forming)
1/142nd Line Regiment (21 / 301)
2/142nd Line Regiment (forming)
1/144th Line Regiment (33 / 700)
2/144th Line Regiment (forming)
1/145th Line Regiment (25 / 507)
2nd Division:Général de division Lefol
Brigade: Général de brigade la Grange
3/9th Légère Regiment (20 / 300)
4/9th Légère Regiment (forming)
2/16th Légère Regiment (18 / 298)
3/16th Légère Regiment (forming)
4/1st Line Regiment (16 / 189)
3/14th Line Regiment (19 / 211)
3/15th Line Regiment (21 / 202)
Brigade: Général de brigade Clavel
4/16th Line Regiment (16 / 183)
2/, 3/62nd Line Regiment (26 / 564)
2/70th Line Regiment (19 / 310)
2/, 4/70th Line Regiment (forming)
3/, 6/121st Line Regiment (33 / 403)
4/121st Line Regiment (forming)
3rd Division: Général de division Lagrange
Brigade: Général de brigade Joubert
3/23rd Line Regiment (20 / 350)
4/23rd Line Regiment (forming)
1/, 2/, 3/, 4/37th Line Regiment (61 / 802)
2/37th Line Regiment (forming)
1/, 2/1st Marine Regiment (42 / 584)
3/, 4/1st Marine Regiment (forming)
Brigade: Général de brigade Pelleport
1/, 2/, 3/, 4/2nd Marine Regiment (68 / 1,194)
1/, 2/, 3/3rd Marine Regiment (42 / 410)
4/3rd Marine Regiment (forming)
1/, 2/, 3/4th Marine Regiment (39 / 472)
4/4th Marine Regiment (forming)
23rd Cavalry Brigade: Général de brigade Beurmann
1-6/10th Hussar Regiment (50 / 695 / 787)
Artillery:
6/, 25/, 26/3rd Artillery (7 / 152)
13/, 16/5th Artillery (6 / 148)
2/1st Horse Artillery (3 / 60)
4/4th Principal Train Battalion (2 / 105)
2/8th (bis) Train Battalion (2 / 122)
1/, 5/9th Principal Train Battalion (3 / 161)
2/4th Sapper Battalion (3 / 50)
1/6th Sapper Battalion (3 / 50)
4/7th Sapper Battalion (3 / 22)
Durutte's Division: Général de division Durutte
Brigade: (1,100 men)
1/, 4/36th Légère Regiment (?)
3/, 4/131st Line Regiment (?)
1/, 3/, 4/132nd Line Regiment (?)

Artillery: (6 guns)

I Cavalry Corps: Général de division Doumerc
1st Brigade: Général de brigade Piquet
1st Provisional Regiment
1/6th Hussar Regiment (3 / 44 / 47)
2/7th Hussar Regiment (3 / 68 / 71)
3/8th Hussar Regiment (5 / 80 / 85)
4/16th Chasseurs à cheval Regiment (7 / 131 / 138)
5/1st Chevauléger-lancier Regiment (10 / 163 / 173)
6/3rd Chevauléger-lancier Regiment (9 / 158 / 167)
7/5th Chevauléger-lancier Regiment (9 / 156 / 163)
8/8th Chevauléger-lancier Regiment (3 / 31 / 34)
2nd Provisional Regiment
1/8th Chasseurs à cheval Regiment (7 / 129 / 136)
2/9th Chasseurs à cheval Regiment (2 / 32 / 34)
3/25th Chasseurs à cheval Regiment (0 / 5 / 5)
4/1st Chasseurs à cheval Regiment (8 / 137 / 144)
5/2nd Chasseurs à cheval Regiment (0 / 5 / 5)
6/3rd Chasseurs à cheval Regiment (0 / 7 / 7)
7/6th Chasseurs à cheval Regiment (4 / 79 / 83)
2nd Brigade: Général de brigade Daudenarde
3rd Provisional Regiment
1/2nd Cuirassier Regiment (8 / 95 / 103)
2/3rd Cuirassier Regiment (10 / 163 / 173)
3/6th Cuirassier Regiment (5 / 66 / 71)
4/9th Cuirassier Regiment (10 / 136 / 146)
5/11th Cuirassier Regiment (6 / 61 / 66)
6/12th Cuirassier Regiment (6 / 84 / 90)
4th Provisional Regiment
1/4th Cuirassier Regiment (10 / 159 / 169)
2/7th Cuirassier Regiment (11 / 135 / 146)
3/14th Cuirassier Regiment (6 / 52 / 58)
4/7th Dragoon Regiment (7 / 52 / 59)
5/23rd Dragoon Regiment (9 / 158 / 167)
6/28th Dragoon Regiment (5 / 90 / 95)
7/30th Dragoon Regiment (3 / 49 / 52)
Artillery: Colonel Lavoye
3/1st Horse Battery
1/6th Horse Battery
Total: 6 guns

V Cavalry Corps: Général de division Milhaud
6th Heavy Division: Général de division l'Heritier
1st Brigade: Général de brigade Lamotte
18th Dragoon Regiment (17 / 201 / 251)
19th Dragoon Regiment (23 / 223 / 283)
20th Dragoon Regiment (14 / 146 / 182)
2nd Brigade: Colonel Mermet
22nd Dragoon Regiment (23 / 260 / 314)
25th Dragoon Regiment (25 / 238 / 295)
Artillery: Colonel Etchegayen
4/2nd Horse Artillery (3 / 75) (4-6pdrs and 2 howitzers)

2/3rd Horse Artillery (3 / 85) (4-6pdrs and 2 howitzers)
1/8th Principal Train Battalion (1 / 71)
1/12th Principal Train Battalion (1 / 81)
9th Light Division: Général de division de Piré
1st Brigade: Général de brigade Subervie
Staff/3rd Hussar Regiment (4 / 8 / 19)
1/3rd Hussar Regiment (8 / 134 / 151)
2/3rd Hussar Regiment (7 / 112 / 128)
Cadre/3rd Hussar Regiment (5 / 0 / 10)
Staff/26th Chasseurs à cheval Regiment (3 / 8 / 27)
1/26th Chasseurs à cheval Regiment (8 / 122 / 133)
3/26th Chasseurs à cheval Regiment (4 / 32 / 41)
4/26th Chasseurs à cheval Regiment (4 / 26 / 34)
2nd Brigade: Général de brigade l'Hermoncourt
Staff/14th Chasseurs à cheval Regiment (5 / 3 / 24)
1/14th Chasseurs à cheval Regiment (4 / 87 / 86)
3/14th Chasseurs à cheval Regiment (2 / 40 / 52)
4/14th Chasseurs à cheval Regiment (5 / 89 / 102)
Staff/27th Chasseurs à cheval Regiment (5 / 3 / 24)
1/27th Chasseurs à cheval Regiment (4 / 140 / 147)
3/27th Chasseurs à cheval Regiment (7 / 55 / 70)
4/27th Chasseurs à cheval Regiment (5 / 37 / 48)
5/27th Chasseurs à cheval Regiment (3 / 72 / 83)
5th Heavy Division: Général de brigade Collaert
Brigade: Général de brigade Montelegier
2nd Dragoon Regiment (25 / 324 / 395)
6th Dragoon Regiment (25 / 296 / 363)
11th Dragoon Regiment (28 / 354 / 429)
Brigade: Général de brigade Ludor
13th Dragoon Regiment (20 / 200 / 260)
15th Dragoon Regiment (18 / 305 / 378)

II Corps: Maréchal Victor, Duc de Bellune
1st Division: Général de division Jamin (95 / 2,628)
1/24th Légère Regiment (25 / 495)
2/, 4/24th Légère Regiment (forming)
1/19th Line Regiment (20 / 620)
2/, 4/19th Line Regiment (forming)
1/37th Line Regiment (19 / 582)
2/, 4/37th Line Regiment (forming)
1/56th Line Regiment (31 / 931)
2/, 4/56th Line Regiment (forming)
6/61st Line Regiment (forming)
6/11lth Line Regiment (forming)
2nd Division: Général de division Forestier (131 / 3,216)
1/26th Line Regiment (30 / 771)
1/, 2/, 4/18th Line Regiment (59 / 1,326)
1/46th Line Regiment (23 / 730)
2/, 4/46th Line Regiment (forming)
4/, 6/, 7/57th Line Regiment (forming)
1/, 2/93rd Line Regiment (18 / 389)
4/, 5/93rd Line Regiment (forming)
3rd Division: Général de division Duhésme (123 / 2,539)

3/7th Line Regiment (9 / 500)
4/, 6/7th Line Regiment (forming)
2/11th Line Regiment (29 / 467)
2/, 4/11th Line Regiment (four companies forming)
2//2nd Line Regiment (21 / 774)
3/, 4/2nd Line Regiment (four companies forming)
1/,2/4th Line Regiment (43 / 1,194)
4/4th Line Regiment (forming)
2/72nd Line Regiment (26 / 498)
4/72nd Line Regiment (forming)

Artillery:
7/2nd Foot Artillery (2 / 63) (6pdrs)
19/2nd Foot Artillery (3 / 36) (6pdrs)
5/, 7/, 11/, 22/9th Foot Artillery (10 / 168) (6pdrs)
17/1st Foot Artillery (2 / 105) (12pdrs)
6/1st Horse Artillery (2 / 50)
4/4th Horse Artillery (4 / 108)
6/4th Horse Artillery (?)
4/, 6/6th (bis) Train Battalion (2 / 142)
3/, 4/8th Principal Train Battalion (4 / 129)
4/1st Principal Train Battalion (1 / 43)
4/11th Principal Train Battalion (0 / 5)
4/12th (bis) Train Battalion (1 / 108)
5th (bis) Train Battalion (assigned, not present)

Engineers:
2/2nd Sapper Battalion (2 / 54)
3/3rd Sapper Battalion (1 / 32)
3/5th Sapper Battalion (3 / 61)

Cavalry Brigade: Général de division Séguo (1,500 before Saverne)
1st Gardes d'honneur
2nd Gardes d'honneur
3rd Gardes d'honneur (nine squadrons) (32 / 1,483 / 1,379)
4th Gardes d'honneur (nine squadrons) (63 / 1,820 / 1,269)

Army of the Lower Rhine: Maréchal Macdonald, Duc de Tarente
IV Corps: Général de division Morand
1st Division: Général de division Damade (169 / 1,748)
Brigade: Général de brigade Schweikert
4/, 6/5th Légère Regiment (23 / 192)
2/5th Légère Regiment (forming)
1/, 2/8th Line Regiment (32 / 299)
1/,2/,4/23rd Line Regiment (29 / 455)
2/23rd Line Regiment (16 / 108)
Brigade: Général de brigade Estève
6/96th Line Regiment (forming)
1/, 2/, 3/, 4/13th Line Regiment (43 / 585)
1/, 2/, 3/137th Line Regiment (28 / 114)
13th Division: Général de division Guilleminot (187 / 2,438)
Brigade: Général de brigade Gruyer (absent)
1st Provisional Regiment
4/1st Line Regiment (24 / 660)
2/95th Line Regiment (39 / 612)
3/82nd Line Regiment (20 / 206)

Brigade: Général de brigade Vergez (absent)
- 1/156th Line Regiment (7 / 232)
- 2/156th Line Regiment (9 / 227)
- 52nd Provisional Line Regiment
- 3/52nd Line Regiment (15 / 247)
- 2/54th Line Regiment (18 / 257)

Brigade: Général de brigade Morio (absent)
- 3/67th Line Regiment (15 / 575)
- Staff/104th Line Regiment (2 / 0)
- 2/104th Line Regiment (18 / 211)
- 3/104th Line Regiment (17 / 300)

32nd Division: Général de division Durutte (170 / 2,580)

Brigade: Général de brigade Choisy
- 35th Provisional Line Regiment
- 1/135th Line Regiment (13 / 402)
- 2/103rd Line Regiment (28 / 450)
- 3/66th Line Regiment (14 / 305)

Brigade: Général de brigade Eromelin
- 3/131st Line Regiment (14 / 171)
- 4/131st Line Regiment (14 / 194)
- 1/36th Légère Regiment (19 / 249)
- 4/36th Légère Regiment (19 / 215)
- 1/132nd Line Regiment (17 / 277)
- 3/132nd Line Regiment (14 / 168)
- 4/132nd Line Regiment (18 / 149)

51st Division: Général de division Semelé

Brigade: Général de brigade Aymard
- 10th Provisional Regiment
  - 3/10th Légère Regiment (17 / 349)
  - 2/21st Légère Regiment (32 / 429)
  - 3/17th Légère Regiment (16 / 217)
- 32nd Provisional Regiment
  - 3/32nd Line Regiment (13 / 183)
  - 2/89th Line Regiment (13 / 263)
  - 4/47th Line Regiment (21 / 322)

Brigade: Général de brigade Lagarde
- 25th Provisional Regiment
  - 1/25th Légère Regiment (18 / 227)
  - 2/29th Légère Regiment (17 / 419)
  - 4/29th Légère Regiment (17 / 190)
  - 3/26th Line Regiment (18 / 101)
- 63rd Provisional Regiment
  - 2/63rd Line Regiment (13 / 197)
  - 2/122nd Line Regiment (38 / 793)
  - 3/86th Line Regiment (13 / 147)

Artillery: Général de division Taviel
- 1/2nd Artillery (2 / 51)
- 3/2nd Artillery (2 / 56)
- 10/2nd Artillery (2 / 33)
- 24/2nd Artillery (3 / 45)
- 26/2nd Artillery (3 / 54)
- 3/5th Artillery (3 / 46)
- 12/5th Artillery (3 / 32)

27/5th Artillery (3 / 67)
7/3rd Horse Artillery (2 / 84)
3/5th Horse Artillery (3 / 75)
6 – 12pdrs
28 – 6pdrs
12 – 24pdr howitzers
3/4th Principal Train Battalion (1 / 82)
4/4th Principal Train Battalion (1 / 74)
2/8th Principal Train Battalion (1 / 68)
1/3rd (bis) Train Battalion (1 / 70)
3/3rd (bis) Train Battalion (2 / 84)
6/3rd (bis) Train Battalion (1 / 52)
1/10th (bis) Train Battalion (2 / 64)
2/, 8/1st Sapper Battalion (3 / 106)
Engineers: Colonel Isoard
2/1st Sapper Battalion (1 / 44)
8/1st Sapper Battalion (2 / 62)
1/4th Sapper Battalion (1 / 57)
4/6th Sapper Battalion (1 / 42)
7/4th Military Equipage Battalion (1 / 114)

Units being detached to XI Corps in Mainz:
2/21st Légère Regiment (16 / 260)
3/54th Line Regiment (18 / 257)
2/95th Line Regiment (22 / 378)
Cavalry Division in Mainz: Général de brigade Merlin
1/, 2/, 3/, 4/2nd Gardes d'honneur Regiment (40 / 560 / 517)
5/, 6/, 7/, 8/, 9/2nd Gardes d'honneur Regiment (174)
10/2nd Gardes d'honneur Regiment (1,033)
18th Dragoon Regiment
11th Cuirassier Regiment
1st Chasseurs à cheval Regiment
6th Chasseurs à cheval Regiment
8th Chasseurs à cheval Regiment
10th Hussar Regiment
14th Hussar Regiment

XI Corps: Maréchal Macdonald, Duc de Tarente
31st Division: Général de division Molitor
1st Brigade: Général de brigade Simmer
1/19th Légère Regiment (19 / 278)
2/19th Légère Regiment (14 / 196)
3/19th Légère Regiment (14 / 282)
2nd Brigade: Général de brigade Bardet
3/5th Line Regiment (16 / 171)
3/11th Line Regiment (11 / 172)
1/107th Line Regiment (11 / 219)
2/107th Line Regiment (16 / 171)
3/107th Line Regiment (15 / 134)
4/107th Line Regiment (9 / 128)
35th Division: Général de division Brayer
1st Brigade: Général de brigade Lauberdière
2/51st Line Regiment (13 / 338)

2/55th Line Regiment (17 / 448)
1/123rd Line Regiment (28 / 323)
3/123rd Line Regiment (17 / 424)
5/123rd Line Regiment (13 / 328)
2nd Brigade: Général de brigade Delors
Staff/124th Line Regiment (12 / 13)
1/124th Line Regiment (18 / 352)
3/124th Line Regiment (18 / 382)
5/124th Line Regiment (12 / 92)
1/127th Line Regiment (27 / 421)
3/127th Line Regiment (17 / 186)
4/127th Line Regiment (13 / 105)
Swiss Demi-Brigade:
1/1st Swiss Line Regiment (19 / 415)
1/2nd Swiss Line Regiment (21 / 400)
1/3rd Swiss Line Regiment (19 / 458)
1/4th Swiss Line Regiment (1 / 36)
36th Division: Général de division Charpentier
1st Brigade: Général de brigade Bigarré
2/21st Légère Regiment (337)
1/28th Légère Regiment (169)
1/22nd Line Regiment (415)
2nd Brigade:
2/54th Line Regiment (591)
2/59th Line Regiment (252)
3/69th Line Regiment (261)
2/95th Line Regiment (405)
Battalions being passed to the XI Corps
2/21st Légère Regiment
2/54th Line Regiment
2/95th Line Regiment
Cavalry:
1/, 2/, 3/Jerome Hussar Regiment (35 / 292 / 374)
Corps Artillery: Général de division Foucher
6/1st Foot Artillery (2 / 41)
26/1st Foot Artillery (3 / 102)
19/2nd Foot Artillery (3 / 62)
20/2nd Foot Artillery (3 / 93)
27/7th Foot Artillery (3 / 69)
Provisional Foot Artillery Company (2 / 82)
4/6th Horse Artillery (3 / 71)
Total: 18 guns
Provisional Pontooneer Company (0 / 112)
6/3rd (bis) Train Battalion (1 / 63)
2/5th (bis) Train Battalion (1 / 71)
Det/6th (bis) Train Battalion (4 / 60)
1/8th Principal Train Battalion (2 / 98)
Det/3rd Principal Train Battalion (1 / 117)
17th Artillery Artisian Co (1 / 91)
Det/Imperial Gendarmes (1 / 59)
4/10th Miliary Equipage Battalion (2 / 123)
Corps Engineers: Général de brigade Valazé
Det/2nd Sapper Battalion (2 / 56)

Det/5th Sapper Battalion (3 / 53)
Det/7th Sapper Battalion (3 / 75)
1/1st Miner Battalion (3 / 102)

V Corps: Général de division Sébastiani
10th Division: Général de division Albert
1st Brigade: Général de brigade Schaeffers (absent)
1/135th Line Regiment (19 / 202)
2/135th Line Regiment (9 / 222)
1/139th Line Regiment (21 / 148)
2/139th Line Regiment (22 / 96)
1/140th Line Regiment (23 / 141)
2/140th Line Regiment (14 / 138)
1/141st Line Regiment (20 / 92)
2/141st Line Regiment (17 / 91)
1/149th Line Regiment (24 / 134)
2/149th Line Regiment (14 / 103)
2nd Brigade: Général de brigade Beauvais
1/150th Line Regiment (12 / 231)
2/150th Line Regiment (6 / 299)
1/152nd Line Regiment (18 / 125)
2/152nd Line Regiment (8 / 129)
1/153rd Line Regiment (23 / 129)
2/153rd Line Regiment (16 / 123)
1/154th Line Regiment (19 / 158)
2/154th Line Regiment (13 / 157)
1/155th Line Regiment (18 / 184)
2/155th Line Regiment (8 / 169)
19th Division: Général de division Amey
1st Brigade: Général de brigade Vandedem
1/150th Line Regiment (12 / 231)
2/150th Line Regiment (7 / 200)
1/152nd Line Regiment (19 / 125)
2/152nd Line Regiment (9 / 120)
2nd Brigade: Général de brigade Thèvenet
1/153rd Line Regiment (23 / 120)
2/153rd Line Regiment (16 / 123)
1/154th Line Regiment (19 / 158)
2/154th Line Regiment (13 / 157)
1/155th Line Regiment (18 / 184)
2/155th Line Regiment (8 / 169)
Corps Artillery:
3/1st Foot Artillery (4 / 34)
16/1st Foot Artillery (2 / 21)
15/4th Foot Artillery (2 / 52)
2/5th Horse Artillery (3 / 71)
1/5th Principal Train Battalion (2 / 116)
3/5th Principal Train Battalion (2 / 90)
2/6th Sapper Battalion (2 / 29)
Imperial Gendarmes (1 / 27 / 32)
Reinforcements en route:
2/152nd Line Regiment (495)
5/149th Line Regiment (500)

5/154th Line Regiment (140)
5/139th Line Regiment (500)
Det. 5/153rd Line Regiment (300)

II Cavalry Corps:
Provisional Division:
1st Provisional Regiment
1/5th Hussar Regiment (7 / 78 / 96)
2/9th Hussar Regiment (6/ 84 / 100)
3/11th Chasseurs à cheval Regiment (6 / 62 / 82)
4/12th Chasseurs à cheval Regiment (10 / 114 / 138)
5/2nd Chevauléger-lancier Regiment (9 / 91 / 123)
6/4th Chevauléger-lancier Regiment (13 / 154 / 194)
2nd Provisional Regiment
1/4th Chasseurs à cheval Regiment (8 / 69 / 88)
2/7th Chasseurs à cheval Regiment (6 / 77 / 93)
3/20th Chasseurs à cheval Regiment (8 / 92 / 116)
4/23rd Chasseurs à cheval Regiment (9 / 155 / 175)
5/24th Chasseurs à cheval Regiment (10 / 175 / 203)
6/6th Chevauléger-lancier Regiment (6 / 85 / 101)
3rd Provisional Regiment
1/1st Carabinier Regiment (9 / 91 / 113)
2/2nd Carabinier Regiment (11 / 179 / 206)
3/1st Cuirassier Regiment (9 / 119 / 143)
4/5th Cuirassier Regiment (6 / 84 / 100)
5/8th Cuirassier Regiment (7 / 52 / 68)
6/10th Cuirassier Regiment (7 / 101 / 118)
Artillery: Lt. Colonel Graillat
1/1st Horse Artillery (3 / 38)
5/5th Horse Artillery (3 / 70)
Total: 4 guns
Det/1st (bis) Train Battalion (1 / 49)

III Cavalry Corps: Général de division Arrighi, Duc de Padoue
Light Division: Général de division Baron de Lorge
1st Brigade: Général de brigade Mouriez
Staff/5th Chasseurs à cheval Regiment (8 / 0 / 52)
3/, 4/5th Chasseurs à cheval Regiment (21 / 173 / 229)
3/10th Chasseurs à cheval Regiment (15 / 146 / 182)
4/15th Chasseurs à cheval Regiment (7 / 85 / 104)
3/21st Chasseurs à cheval Regiment (9 / 66 / 94)
3/22nd Chasseurs à cheval Regiment (8 / 110 / 136)
2nd Brigade: Général de brigade Amiel
5/, 6/13th Chasseurs à cheval Regiment (20 / 283 / 354)
4/29th Chasseurs à cheval Regiment (5 / 35 / 46)
3/2nd Hussar Regiment (13 / 135)
5/4th Hussar Regiment (5 / 11 / 26)
4/12th Hussar Regiment (9 / 65 / 92)
Heavy Division: Général de division Jacquinot
1st Brigade: Général de brigade Wolf
4/4th Dragoon Regiment (9 / 39 / 56)
3/5th Dragoon Regiment (10 / 75 / 100)
3/12th Dragoon Regiment (10 / 102 / 137)

3/14th Dragoon Regiment (11 / 41 / 71)
4/24th Dragoon Regiment (3 / 68 / 74)
2nd Brigade: Général de brigade Quinette
3/16th Dragoon Regiment (4 / 57 / 73)
3/17th Dragoon Regiment (11 / 90 / 128)
3/21st Dragoon Regiment (9 / 60 / 87)
3/26th Dragoon Regiment (4 / 53 / 68)
5/27th Dragoon Regiment (3 / 79 / 81)
5/13th Cuirassier Regiment (6 / 91 / 102)
Artillery:
5/1st Horse Battery (3 / 61) (4-6pdrs and 2 howitzers)
2/1st Principal Train Battalion (1 / 44)
Reserve Cavalry Division forming in Versailles: Général de division Bordessoulle
Brigade: Général de brigade Wathier
8th Cuirassier Regiment (4 / 75 / 84)
5th Dragoon Regiment (4 / 94 / 103)
1st Chasseurs à cheval Regiment (5 / 126 / 137)
2nd Chasseurs à cheval Regiment (4 / 125 / 134)
5th Chasseurs à cheval Regiment (3 / 56 / 63)
9th Chasseurs à cheval Regiment (3 / 41 / 51)
Brigade:
7th Cuirassier Regiment (2 / 51 / 56)
4th Chevauléger-lancier Regiment (3 / 43 / 50)

I (bis) Corps: Général de division Maison
Division: Général de division Fauconnet (in Antwerp)
2/4th Légère Regiment (759)
1/, 2/7th Légère Regiment (346)
3/13th Légère Regiment (794)
3/25th Line Regiment (235)
Det/28th Line Regiment (278)
4/, 7/36th Line Regiment (113)
6/48th Line Regiment (436)
7/57th Line Regiment (284)
3/58th Line Regiment (664)
5/, 6/108th Line Regiment (799)
2nd Antwerp National Gaurd Regiment (72)
3rd Côtes du Nord National Gaurd Regiment (317)
Veterans (791)
Miners (one company) (46)
Veteran Miners/Sappers (one company) (27)
Compagnie de Réserve (88)
3/3rd Foreign Regiment (527)
23/5th Foot Artillery (52)
25/6th Foot Artillery (98)
123rd, 124th, 126th, 127th and 128th Coastal Artillery Companies (333)
Pioneers (88)
Garrison of Antwerp:
5/48th Line Regiment (10 / 172)
6/48th Line Regiment (15 / 483)
5/108th Line Regiment (14 / 164)

6/108th Line Regiment (13 / 618)
5/4th Marine Regiment (20 / 662)
Depot/8th Artillery Regiment (7 / 366)
123rd Coastal Artillery Company (2 / 60)
124th Coastal Artillery Company (2 / 75)
126th Coastal Artillery Company (1 / 5)
127th Coastal Artillery Company (1 / 89)
128th Coastal Artillery Company (2 / 25)
6th Veteran Company (54 / 1,325)

Garrison of Bergen-op-Zoom:
5/4th Marine Regiment (254)
6/4th Marine Regiment (5 / 249)
Sailors (464)
Det/4th Veteran Company (148)
Det/6th Veteran Company (260)
5th French Pioneer Battalion (0 / 0) (assigned, not present)
2nd or 7th Veteran Cannonier Company (35)
Det/12th Line Regiment (360)
Det. 3/17th Line Regiment (320)
Det/21st Line Regiment (315)
3/ or 4/51st Line Regiment (787)
1st Veteran Sapper Company (0 / 0) (assigned, not present)
3/3rd Foreign Regiment (0 / 0) (assigned, not present)
Gendarmes (34)

Garrison of Batz:
6/15th Légère Regiment (674)
Veteran Gunners (77)
Sailors (291)
Gendarmes (24)

Garrison of Lillo:
4/ or 7/36th Line Regiment (247)
Det/1st Foot Artillery (21)
Sailors (74)

Garrison of Liesskenshaek:
4/ or 7/36th Line Regiment (100)
Det/1st Foot Artillery (15)
Sailors (25)

Garrison of the Ile de Cadzand: Général de division Rousseau
5/27th Legere Regiment (3 / 147)
3/13th Legere Regiment (0 / 0) (assigned, not present)
3rd Battalion, Garde Nationale de Cherbourg (7 / 438)
6th Veteran Company (2 / 147)
9/6th Foot Artillery (2 / 83)
13/9th Foot Artillery (2 / 65)
116th Coastal Gunners (2 / 88)
2nd Volunteer Pioneers (117)
Foot Gendarmes (19)
Horse Gendarmes (1 / 9)

Garrison of Ile de Walacheren:
6/131st Line Regiment (13 / 725)
Det. 5/131st Line Regiment (5 / 36)
Miners (0 / 9)
Veteran Miners (0 / 38)

25/1st Foot Artillery (1 / 69)
22/6th Foot Artillery (3 / 88)
23/6th Foot Artillery (1/110)
8/24th Foot Artillery (3 / 73)
117th Coastal Artillery Company (2 / 112)
118th Coastal Artillery Company (1 / 116)
119th Coastal Artillery Company (1 / 109)
Veteran Gunners (3 / 87)
Det/6th Veteran Company (1 / 111)
1st Cohort Garde Nationale de Calais (13 / 300)
23rd Chasseurs à cheval Regiment (2 / 81)
Deserter Processing Depot (0 / 63)
1st Colonial Pioneers (8 / 158)
3rd French Pioneer Company (3 / 140)
5th French Pioneer Company (4 / 80)
7th French Pioneer Company (3 / 118)
8th French Pioneer Company (3 / 80)
10th French Pioneer Company (2 / 87)
3rd Foreign Pioneer Company (2 / 148)
5th Foreign Pioneer Company (2 / 114)
Engineers (8 / 9)
Foot Gendarmes (0 / 42)
Horse Gendarmes (3 / 9)

3rd Young Guard Division: Général de division Boyer de Rebeval (in Lille)
9th Voltigeur Regiment (25 / 402)
10th Voltigeur Battalion (27 / 447)

4th Young Guard (1st Tirailleur) Division: Général de division Barrois (in Brussels)
1st Brigade: Général de brigade Poret de Morvan
1/1st Tirailleur Regiment (18 / 425)
2/1st Tirailleur Regiment (9 / 411)
1/2nd Tirailleur Regiment (9 / 309)
2/2nd Tirailleur Regiment (11 / 376)
2nd Brigade: Général de brigade Dariule
1/3rd Tirailleur Regiment (12 / 337)
2/3rd Tirailleur Regiment (9 / 369)
1/4th Tirailleur Regiment (12 / 432)
2/4th Tirailleur Regiment (7 / 388)

6th Young Guard (3rd Tirailleur) Division: Général de division Roguet
1st Brigade: Général de brigade Flamand
Staff/12th Tirailleur Regiment (9 / 6)
1/12th Tirailleur Regiment (11 / 689)
2/12th Tirailleur Regiment (10 / 764)
Staff/13th Tirailleur Regiment (2 / 6)
1/13th Tirailleur Regiment (11 / 638)
2/13th Tirailleur Regiment (10 / 600)
2nd Brigade: Général de brigade Jamin
Staff/12th Voltigeur Regiment (2 / 3)
1/12th Voltigeur Regiment (11 / 593)
Staff/13th Voltigeur Regiment (5 / 11)
1/13th Voltigeur Regiment (11 / 558)
2/13th Voltigeur Regiment (14 / 617)
3rd Brigade: Général de brigade Aymard

Staff/9th Tirailleur Regiment (6 / 6)
1/9th Tirailleur Regiment (12 / 448)
2/9th Tirailleur Regiment (14 / 454)
Staff/10th Tirailleur Regiment (5 / 7)
1/10th Tirailleur Regiment (17 / 554)
2/10th Tirailleur Regiment (18 / 452)
Artillery:
Gunners (6 / 76)
10 6pdrs and 4 24pdr howitzers
Train (3 / 82)
2nd Guard Cavalry Division: Général de divisoin Baron Castex
1st Guard Lancer Regiment (35 / 555 / 627)
2nd Guard (Red) Lancer Regiment (35 / 459 / 551)
Young Guard Chasseurs à cheval Regiment (40 / 600 / 685)
Det/1st Gardes d'honneur (7 / 117)
Artillery:
3rd Old Guard Horse Battery (3 / 53)
Guard Train Detachment (1 / 56)

Army of Lyon: Maréchal Augereau, Duc de Castiglione
Reserve (Genève) Division: Général de division Meusnier de la Converserie
(division infantry = 1,780 men)
1st Brigade: Général de brigade Pouchelon
1/, 2/18th Légère Regiment
4/5th Line Regiment
4/11th Line Regiment
7/79th Line Regiment
7/81st Line Regiment
2nd Brigade: Général de brigade Bardes
7/64th Line Regiment
3/, 4/8th Légère Regiment
2/23rd Line Regiment
7/60th Line Regiment
2/, 5/24th Line Regiment (23 / 395)
2/32nd Légère Regiment
7/16th Line Regiment
2/145th Line Regiment
2nd Marine Regiment (300)
3/1st Line Regiment
Attached:
Cavalry (60 men)
National Guards (38 battalions) (31,200 men)
Cavalry Brigade:
4th Gardes d'honneur (12 / 251)
1st Hussar Regiment (5 / 199)

Appendix VII

Allied armies, 1 January 1814

Prussian 3rd Corps: Generalmajor von Bülow
- 3rd Brigade: Generalmajor Zielinski
  - 2nd East Prussian Grenadier Battalion
  - 3rd East Prussian Infantry Regiment
  - 4th Reserve Infantry Regiment
  - 3rd East Prussian Landwehr Regiment
  - 1st Leib Hussar Regiment
  - 6pdr Foot Battery #6
- 4th Brigade: Generalmajor von Thümen
  - 4th East Prussian Infantry Regiment
  - 5th Reserve Infantry Regiment
  - East Prussian Jäger Battalion (two companies)
  - 2nd Pomeranian Landwehr Regiment
  - 1st Pomeranian Landwehr Cavalry Regiment
  - 6pdr Foot Battery #8
- 5th Brigade: Generalmajor von Borstell
  - Pomeranian Grenadier Battalion
  - 1st Pomeranian Infantry Regiment
  - 2nd Reserve Infantry Regiment
  - Elbe Infantry Regiment
  - 2nd Kurmärk Landwehr Regiment
  - Pomeranian Hussar Regiment
  - 6pdr Foot Battery #10
- 6th Brigade: Oberst von Krafft
  - Colberg Infantry Regiment
  - 9th Reserve Infantry Regiment
  - 1st Neumark Landwehr Regiment
  - 1/, 2/, 3/, 4/2nd Pomeranian Landwehr Cavalry Regiment (286)
  - 6pdr Foot Battery #16

Reserve Cavalry: Generalmajor von Oppen
- Brigade: Oberst von Treskow
  - Königin Dragoon Regiment
  - Brandenburg Dragoon Regiment
  - 2nd West Prussian Dragoon Regiment
- Brigade: Oberst von Hobe
  - Westphalian Uhlan Regiment
  - 2nd Silesian Hussar Regiment
  - Pomeranian National Cavalry Regiment
- Brigade: Oberst von Sydow
  - 2nd Kurmärk Landwehr Cavalry Regiment
  - 4th Kurmärk Landwehr Cavalry Regiment
- Artillery:
  - 6pdr Horse Batteries #5 and #6
- Reserve Artillery: Generalmajor von Holtzendorff
  - 12pdr Foot Batteries #4 and #5

6pdr Foot Battery #19 and ?
6pdr Horse Battery #11
Park Columns #3, #4 and #6
Pioneer Compànies #4 and #5
Freikorps von Lützow:
3 Infantry Battalions
2 Squadrons Hussars
1 Horse Battery (8-6pdrs)
Attached:
1st Freiwilliger Jäger Battalion: Major von Reiche
2nd Raiding Party: Major von Colombé
70 men of the Guard Light Cavalry Regiment
50 men of Brandenburg Cuirassier Jäger squadron
20 men of Neumark Dragoon Regiment
20 men of Silesian Uhlan Regiment

Russian Corps: Generallieutenant Winzingerode
Advanced Guard: Generalmajor Orurk
3rd Hussar Division: Generalmajor Juckowsky (von Pahlen)
Elisabethgrad Hussar Regiment (6)
Pavlograd Hussar Regiment (6)
Isoum Hussar Regiment (6)
2nd Dragoon Division: Generalmajor Balk
Brigade: Generalmajor Sagratzky
Nijine Chasseurs à cheval Regiment (2)
Twer Opolochenie Cossack Regiment (1)
Brigade: Generalmajor Galanthe
Polish Uhlan Regiment
Volhynie Uhlan Regiment
Brigade: Generalmajor Drewitsch
St. Petersburg Dragoon Regiment
Riga Dragoon Regiment
Finland Dragoon Regiment

Cossack Corps: Generalmajor Tschernischev
Brigade: Lapuschin
Djaschkin Don Cossack Regiment
Illowaisky IV Don Cossack Regiment
Brigade: Generalmajor Narischen
Grekov IX Don Cossack Regiment
Bradantdchikov II Don Cossack Regiment
Melnikov V Don Cossack Regiment
Brigade: Stahl I
Andrejanov II Don Cossack Regiment
1st Bashkir Regiment
1st Bug Cossack Regiment
Brigade: Colonel Patelejev II
Popov XII Cossack Regiment
Patelejev II Cossack Regiment
Brigade: Colonel Benkendorff
Sysoev III Cossack Regiment
Girova Cossack Regiment
Grekov XVIII Don Cossack Regiment

Brigade: Generalmajor Ilowaisky IV
Rebrejev II Cossack Regiment
Vlassov III Cossack Regiment
Balbin II Cossack Regiment
Detachment of 9th Bashkir Regiment
Infantry: Generallieutenant Count Woronzov
21st Division: Generalmajor Leptev
Brigade: Colonel Rosen
Petrovsk Infantry Regiment (1)
Lithuania Infantry Regiment (1)
Podolsk Infantry Regiment (1)
Brigade:
Neva Infantry Regiment (1)
44th Jager Regiment (2)
2nd Jager Regiment (1)
Brigade: (from 14th Division) Generalmajor Harpe
Navaguinsk Infantry Regiment (1)
Tula Infantry Regiment (1)
Converged Grenadier Battalions 9th, 15th and 18th Divisions
Brigade: (from 15th Division) Generalmajor Krassovsky
13th Jager Regiment (2)
14th Jager Regiment (2)
Brigade: (from 24th Division) Generalmajor Wuitsch
Chirvan Infantry Regiment (2)
Bourtirki Infantry Regiment (2)
19th Jager Regiment (2)
Artillery:
Horse Batteries #1 (10), #4 (8), #7 (12), #11 (12) #13 (12) and #21 (12 guns)
Light Batteries #42, #48 and #56
Position Batteries #7, #28 and #31

Assigned from the Polish Reserve Army
Corps: Generallieutenant Stroganov
12th Division: Generalmajor Cherwansky
Brigade: Generalmajor Sanders
Smolensk Infantry Regiment (2)
Narva Infantry Regiment (2)
Brigade: Generalmajor Schwetschin
Alexopol Infantry Regiment (2)
New Ingremannland Infantry Regiment (1)
Brigade: Generallieutenant Glebov
6th Jager Regiment (2)
41st Jager Regiment (1)
Brigade from 13th Division: Generalmajor Scheltuchin
Pensa Infantry Regiment (2)
Saratov Infantry Regiment (2)
12th Jager Regiment
22nd Jager Regiment
Position Battery #3l
Light Batteries #53 and #46

Army of Silesia: General of Cavalry von Blücher
1st Prussian Corps: General of Infantry von Yorck (as of 1/1/14)
- 1st Brigade: Generalmajor von Steinmetz (Generalmajor Pirch II after 1/3/14)
  - 1st East Prussian Grenadier Battalion (1)
  - Silesian Grenadier Battalion (1)
  - Leib Grenadier Battalion (1)
  - West Prussian Grenadier Battalion (1)
  - 1/, 2/, 3/, 4/13th Silesian Landwehr Regiment
  - 1/, 2/, 3/, 4/East Prussian National Cavalry Regiment (with jägers)
  - 6pdr Foot Battery #2
  - Line Infantry (80 / 3,425)
  - Jägers (9 / 330)
  - Landwehr (143 / 4,683)
  - Line Cavalry (25 / 555)
  - Cavalry Jäger (5 / 143)
  - Artillery (3 / 93)
- 2nd Brigade: Oberst von Warburg
  - 1/, 2/, Fus/1st East Prussian Regiment (in Frankfurt until 1/21/14)
  - 1/, 2/, Fus/2nd East Prussian Regiment
  - 1/, 2/, Fus/, 4/Mecklinburg-Strelitz Hussar Regiment
  - 6pdr Foot Battery #1
- Line Infantry (86 / 4,691)
  - Jägers (3 / 194)
  - Landwehr (62 / 2,206)
  - Line Cavalry (19 / 404)
  - Cavalry Jäger (0 / 46)
  - Artillery (4 / 90)
- 7th Brigade: Generalmajor von Horn
  - 1/, 2/, Fus/Leib Infantry Regiment
  - 5th Silesian Landwehr Regiment (2)
  - 15th Silesian Landwehr Regiment (2)
  - Brandenburg Hussar Regiment (with jägers)
  - 6pdr Foot Battery #3
  - Line Infantry (53 / 2,635)
  - Jägers (5 / 273)
  - Landwehr (140 / 4,449)
  - Line Cavalry (13 / 279)
  - Cavalry Jäger (5 / 195)
  - Landwehr Cavalry (10 / 252)
  - Artillery (4 / 110)
- 8th Brigade: Generalmajor Hunerbein
  - 1/, 2/, Fus/Brandenburg Infantry Regiment
  - 12th Silesian Landwehr Regiment (2)
  - 12th Reserve Infantry Regiment (2)
  - 2nd Leib Hussar Regiment (with jägers)
  - 6pdr Foot Battery #15
  - Line Infantry (93 / 4,633)
  - Jägers (0/84)
  - Landwehr (71 / 2,031)
  - Line Cavalry (11 / 287)
  - Landwehr Cavalry (12 / 278)
  - Artillery (3 / 94)

Reserve Cavalry: Oberst von Jürgass
- Brigade: Oberst Henkel Donnersmaker
  - Lithuanian Dragoon Regiment
  - 1st West Prussian Dragoon Regiment
- Brigade: Generalmajor von Katzeler
  - 1st Neumark Landwehr Cavalry Regiment
  - Brandenburg Uhlan Regiment
- Brigade: von Bieberstein
  - 10th Silesian Landwehr Cavalry Regiment
  - 5th Silesian Landwehr Cavalry Regiment
- Artillery:
  - Horse Batteries #1 and #2
  - Line Cavalry (79/1,952)
  - Cavalry Jäger (8 / 310)
  - Landwehr Cavalry (4 / 1,337)
  - Artillery (6 / 321)
- Reserve Artillery:
  - 12pdr Foot Batteries #1 and #2
  - Horse Battery #3 and #12
  - Park Column #13
  - 2 Pioneer Companies
  - Artillery (24 / 498)
  - Pioneers (4 / 129)
- Attached:
  - Raiding Party: Major von Falkenhausen
    - 3rd Silesian Landwehr Cavalry Regiment (two squadrons)
  - Raiding Party: Captain von Boltenstern (Cologne)
    - 1 Company Guard Jäger Battalion (soon dissolved)
  - Raiding Party: Generalmajor Prince Biron von Kurland (500 men)
    - 2nd Silesian Hussar Regiment (2)
    - Silesian National Cavalry Regiment (2)
    - Jäger Detachment from the Neumark Dragoon Regiment (1)
    - Cossack detachment with four light guns

Russian Corps: Generallieutenant von Sacken (21,550 men)

6th Corps: Generallieutenant Por Tallisin II
- 7th Division: Generalmajor Prince Scherbatov
  - Brigade: Colonel Kritschinikov
    - Pskof Infantry Regiment (1)
    - Moscow Infantry Regiment (1)
  - Brigade: Colonel Augustov
    - Sophia Infantry Regiment (1)
    - Libau Infantry Regiment (1)
  - Brigade: Colonel Dieterich
    - 11th Jager Regiment (1)
    - 36th Jager Regiment (1)
- 18th Division: Generalmajor Bernodessov
  - Brigade: Lt. Colonel Blagovenzenko
    - Vladimir Infantry Regiment (1)
    - Dnieper Infantry Regiment (1)
  - Brigade: Generalmajor Heidenreich (brigade destroyed on 2/12)
    - Tambov Infantry Regiment (1)
    - Kostroma Infantry Regiment (1)

Brigade: Generalmajor Metcherinov
28th Jager Regiment (1)
32nd Jager Regiment (1)
Artillery:
Position Battery #10
Light Batteries #19 and #24

11th Corps: Generalmajor von Lieven III
10th Division: Generalmajor Sass
Brigade: Generalmajor Sokolovsky
Jaroslav Infantry Regiment (1)
Kursk Infantry Regiment (1)
Bieloserk Infantry Regiment (2)
Brigade: Colonel Achlestischev
8th Jager Regiment (1)
39th Jager Regiment (1)
From 16th Division:
Brigade: Lt. Colonel Selivanov
Kamtchatka Infantry Regiment (1)
Okhotsk Infantry Regiment (1)
27th Division: Generallieutenant Stawitzky
Brigade: Colonel Lewandowsky
Odessa Infantry Regiment (1)
Vilna Infantry Regiment (1)
Brigade: Colonel Alexejev
Simbrisk Infantry Regiment (1)
Tarnopol Infantry Regiment (1)
Brigade: Colonel Kalogruivoff
49th Jager Regiment (1)
50th Jager Regiment (1)
Artillery:
Position Battery #18
Light Batteries #34 and #35

Cavalry Corps: Generallieutenant Vassilьshikov
2nd Hussar Division: Generalmajor Lanskoi
Brigade: Generalmajor Waddolski
Akhtyrsk Hussar Regiment (6)
Marioupol Hussar Regiment (5)
Brigade: Generalmajor Kaslowsky
White Russia Hussar Regiment (4)
Alexandria Hussar Regiment (5)
3rd Dragoon Division: Generalmajor Pantschichscheff
Brigade: Generalmajor Uschakov
Smolensk Dragoon Regiment
Kurland Dragoon Regiment
Brigade: Generalmajor Umanez
Tver Dragoon Regiment
Kinburn Dragoon Regiment
Horse Artillery Battery #18 (10 guns)
Brigade: Generalmajor Karpov II
Karpov II Don Cossack Regiment
Semintschikov IV Don Cossack Regiment

Lukowken II Don Cossack Regiment
Kuteinikov IV Don Cossack Regiment
Grekov I Don Cossack Regiment
St. Petersburg Opolochenie Cossack Regiment
4th Ukrainian Cossack Regiment
2nd Kalmuck Regiment
Artillery:
Horse Batteries #6 and #7
Reserve Artillery: Generalmajor Nikitin
Position Batteries #10, #13 and #18
Light Batteries #24, #28, #34 and #35
1 Pioneer Company

Russian Corps: General of Infantry Langeron (26,561 men as of 1/1/14)
8th Russian Corps: Generallieutenant St. Priest (11,893 men on 1/1/14)
11th Division: Generalmajor Gurgalov
Brigade: Generalmajor Karpenkov
Polotsk Infantry Regiment (2)
Jeletz Infantry Regiment (2)
Brigade: Lt. Colonel Turganeff
Rilsk Infantry Regiment (2)
Ekaterinburg Infantry Regiment (2)
Brigade: Generalmajor Bistrom
1st Jager Regiment (2)
32nd Jager Regiment (2)
17th Division: Generalmajor Pilas
Brigade: Colonel Kern
Riazan Infantry Regiment (2)
Bieloserk Infantry Regiment (2)
Brigade: Colonel Schertov I (Detached to Metz)
Wilmanstrand Infantry Regiment (2)
Brest Infantry Regiment (2)
Brigade: Major Sabelin
30th Jager Regiment (2)
48th Jager Regiment (2)
Artillery:
Position Battery #33
Light Batteries #32 and #33

9th Corps: Generallieutenant Olsufiev (corps destroyed 2/9/14) (5,594 men on 1/1/14)
9th Division: Generalmajor Udom II
Brigade: Generalmajor Poltarachi
Nacheburg Infantry Regiment (1)
Apcheron Infantry Regiment (1)
Brigade: Generalmajor Juschkov II
Riajsk Infantry Regiment (1)
Iakout Infantry Regiment (1)
Brigade: Major Melnik
10th Jager Regiment (1)
38th Jager Regiment (1)
15th Division: Generalmajor Kornilov
Brigade: Lt. Colonel Anensur
Kolyvan Infantry Regiment

Kourin Infantry Regiment
Brigade: Generalmajor Mussin-Pushkin
Vitebsk Infantry Regiment
Kozlov Infantry Regiment
Brigade: Colonel Tuchanowski
12th Jager Regiment (1)
22nd Jager Regiment (1)
Artillery:
Position Battery #15
Light Batteries #13 and #29

10th Corps: Generallieutenant Kapsevich (total: 7,282 men on 1/1/14)
8th Division: Generalmajor Urusov
Brigade: Colonel Schenschen
Archangle Infantry Regiment (2)
Schusselburg Infantry Regiment (2)
Old Ingremannland Infantry Regiment (2)
Brigade: Colonel Suthof
7th Jager Regiment (2)
37th Jager Regiment (2)
22nd Division: Generalmajor Turtschaninov
Brigade: Generalmajor Schapskoy
Olonetz Infantry Regiment (1)
Viatka Infantry Regiment (2)
Staroskol Infantry Regiment (1)
Brigade: Generalmajor Vassiltschikov
29th Jager Regiment (1)
45th Jager Regiment (1)
Artillery:
Position Battery #39
Light Batteries #3 and #56

Cavalry Corps: Generallieutenant Korff
1st Dragoon Division: Generallieutenant Borosdin II
Brigade: Generalmajor Gengross
Mitau Dragoon Regiment (3)
New Russia Dragoon Regiment (3)
Brigade: Generalmajor Pohl
Kargopol Dragoon Regiment (4)
Moscow Dragoon Regiment (3)
Detached from 4th Dragoon Division: Generalmajor Emmanuel
Kharkov Dragoon Regiment (4)
Kiev Dragoon Regiment (4)
1st Chasseur Division: Generallieutenant Pantschulischev
Brigade: Generalmajor Denissiev
Arasmass Chasseurs à cheval Regiment (1)
Sieversk Chasseurs à cheval Regiment (4)
Tchernigov Chasseurs à cheval Regiment (3)
From 2nd Chasseur Division:
Brigade: Generalmajor Pahlen II
Dorpat Chasseurs à cheval Regiment (2)
Livonia Chasseurs à cheval Regiment (1)
Ukrainian Cossack Division: Generalmajor Witte

Brigade: Generalmajor Scherbatov
1st Ukrainian Cossack Regiment
2nd Ukrainian Cossack Regiment
3rd Ukrainian Cossack Regiment
Artillery:
Horse Battery #8
Don Cossack Battery #2

Cossack Corps: Generalmajor Grekov VIII
Kuteinikov VIII Don Cossack Regiment
Sewassov II Don Cossack Regiment
Isaev II Cossack Regiment
Grekov XXI Don Cossack Regiment
Gegova Cossack Regiment
Rubashkin Cossack Regiment
Stavropol Kalmuk Regiment
Artillery: Generalmajor Vassilitzky
Position Batteries #2 (seven guns), #15(12), #32(11), #34 (12) and #39 (12)
Light Batteries #3, #19, #29, #32 and #33 (12-6pdrs ea)
Pontooneer Companies #4 and #5
Pioneer Companies (3)

Main Allied Army: Field Marshal Prince Schwarzenberg
1st Light Division: Feldmarschal-leutnant von Bubna (6,389 men on 1/1/14)
Brigade: Generalmajor von Scheither
Kaiser Hussar Regiment (6)
Vincent Chevauxleger Regiment (6)
5th Jäger Battalion
Warasdiner Kreuzer Grenz Regiment (1)
Brigade: Generalmajor von Zechmeister
Liechtenstein Hussar Regiment (6)
6th Jäger Battalion
Brod Grenz Regiment (1)
Brigade:
Blankenstein Hussar Regiment (six squadrons)
Laroche Dragoon Regiment (6)
Peterwardeiner Grenz Regiment (one battalion)
Artillery:
3 Wurst Batteries
Total: 6,389 men
1st Light Division: Feldmarschal-leutnant Bubna
Brigade: Generalmajor von Klopfstein
W. Colleredo Infantry Regiment (3)
Kaunitz Infantry Regiment (3)
Brigade Battery (8-6pdrs)
Brigade: Generalmajor von Longueville
Reuss-Greitz Infantry Regiment #18 (3)
Vogelsang Infantry Regiment #47 (3)
Brigade Battery (8-6pdrs)
Brigade: Generalmajor von Zechmeister
6th Jäger Battalion
Liechtenstein Hussar Regiment #7 (6)

1/Gradiscaner Grenz Regiment (1)
Wurst Battery (6-6pdrs)
Brigade:
Warasdiner Grenz Regiment (1)
Kaiser Hussar Regiment (6)
Blankenstein Hussar Regiment (6)
Wurst Battery (6-6pdrs)
Reserve Artillery:
1 Position Battery (6-12pdrs)
2nd Light Division: Feldmarschal-leutnant M. Liechtenstein (3,900 men on 1/1/14)
Brigade: Generalmajor Prince von Hesse-Homberg
7th Jäger Battalion
O'Reilly Chevauxleger Regiment #1 (6)
Wallachian-Illyrian Grenz Regiment (2)
Wurst Battery (6-6pdrs)
Brigade: Generalmajor von Geppert
Grenz Regiment #7
1st Jäger Battalion
2nd Jäger Battalion
Palatinal Hussar Regiment (6)
Kaiser Chevauxleger Regiment (6)
Wurst Battery (6-6pdrs)

1st Corps: FZM Colleredo-Mansfeld (15,636 men on 1/1/14)
1st Division: Generallieutenant Hardegg
Brigade: Generalmajor Raigecourt
Deutsch Banat Grenz Regiment #12 (2)
Hesse-Homburg Hussar Regiment #4 (6)
Riesch Dragoon Regiment #6 (6)
1 Wurst Battery (6-6pdrs)
2nd Division: Feldmarschal-leutnant von Wimpffen
Brigade: Generalmajor von Wumb
Froon Infantry Regiment #54 (3)
de Vaux Infantry Regiment #25 (3)
Brigade Battery (8-6pdrs)
Brigade: Generalmajor von Watzel
Argenteau Infantry Regiment #35 (3) (includes one Landwehr Battalion)
Erbach Infantry Regiment #42 (3)
Brigade Battery (8-6pdrs)
3rd Division: Feldmarschal-leutnant Prince von Wied-Runckel
Brigade: Generalmajor von Salin
de Ligne Infantry Regiment #30 (3)
Czartorski Infantry Regiment #9 (3)
Brigade Battery (8-6pdrs)
Brigade: Generalmajor von Quasdonawich
A. Gyulai Infantry Regiment (3)
Reuss-Plauen Infantry Regiment (3)
Brigade Battery (8-6pdrs)
Artillery Reserve:
1 Foot Battery (6-12pdrs)
2 Foot Batteries (6-6pdrs ea)

2nd Corps: FML Prince A. von Liechtenstein (14,336 men on 1/1/14)
1st Division: FML Prince A. von Liechtenstein
- Brigade: Generalmajor Prince von Coburg
  - Kienmayer Hussar Regiment #8 (6)
  - Gradiscaner Grenz Regiment (1)
  - Wallachian-Illyrian Grenz Regiment (1)
- Brigade: Generalmajor von Hardegg
  - Archduke John Dragoon Regiment (6)
  - Archduke Rainier Infantry Regiment (3)
  - Brigade Battery (8-6pdrs)
- Brigade: Generalmajor von Vogelsang
  - Reuss-Greitz Infantry Regiment (3)
  - Vogelsang Infantry Regiment (3)
  - Brigade Battery (8-6pdrs)
- 2nd Division: Feldmarschal-leutnant von Greth
  - Brigade: Generalmajor von Klopfstein
    - W. Colloredo Infantry Regiment (2)
    - Kaunitz Infantry Regiment (3)
    - Brigade Battery (8-6pdrs)
  - Brigade: Generalmajor von Beck
    - Strauch Infantry Regiment #24 (2)
    - Bellegarde Infantry Regiment #44 (2)
    - Brigade Battery (8-6pdrs)
  - Reserve Artillery:
    - 2 Foot Batteries (6-6pdrs ea)
    - 1 Foot Battery (6-12pdrs)

3rd Corps: FZM I. Giulay (15,261 men on 1/1/14)
1st Division: Feldmarschal-leutnant Crenneville
- Brigade: Generalmajor von Hecht
  - Klenau Chevauxleger Regiment #5 (7)
  - St. George Warasdiner Grenz Regiment (1)
- Brigade: Generalmajor von Trenck
  - Rosenburg Dragoon Regiment (6)
  - St. George Warasdiner Grenz Regiment (1)
  - Wurst Battery (6-6pdrs)

2nd Division: Feldmarschal-leutnant Prince von Hohenlohe-Bartenstein
- Brigade: Generalmajor von Spleny
  - Mariassy Infantry Regiment #37 (2)
  - I. Gyulai Infantry Regiment #60 (2)
  - Brigade Battery (8-6pdrs)
- Brigade: Generalmajor von Grimmer
  - Kollowrath Infantry Regiment #36 (2)
  - Frolich Infantry Regiment #28 (3)
  - Brigade Battery (8-6pdrs)

Division: FML Fresnel
- Brigade: Generalmajor von Pflüger
  - Archduke Ludwig Infantry Regiment #8 (4)
  - Würzburg Infantry Regiment #7 (3)
  - Brigade Battery (8-6pdrs)
- Brigade: Generalmajor von Csollich
  - Kottulinski Infantry Regiment #41 (3)
  - Kaiser Infantry Regiment #1 (2)

Brigade Battery (8-6pdrs)
Reserve Artillery:
1 Foot Battery (6-12pdrs)
2 Foot Batteries (6-6pdrs ea)

4th Corps: Feldmarschal Crown Prince of Württemberg (11,569 men as of 1/1/14)
Cavalry Division: Generalieutenant Prince Adam of Württemberg
Brigade: Generalmajor von Alvensleben
1/, 2/, 3/, 4/Duke Louis Chasseur Regiment #2
1/, 2/, 3/, 4/Crown Prince Dragoon Regiment #3
1st Horse Artillery Battery (6-6pdrs)
Brigade: Generalmajor von Jett
1/, 2/, 3/, 4/Prinz Adam Chasseur Regiment #4
2nd Horse Battery (6-6pdrs)
Infantry: Generallieutenant von Koch
1st Brigade: Generalmajor von Stockmayer
König Jäger Regiment #9 (2)
Light Infantry Regiment #10 (1)
Brigade: Generalmajor Döring
Duke Wilhelm Infantry Regiment #2 (2)
Infantry Regiment #3 (2)
Infantry Regiment #7 (2)
1st Foot Battery
Brigade: Generalmajor Prince of Hohenlohe-Kirchberg
Infantry Regiment #4 (2)
Infantry Regiment #6 (2)
2nd Foot Battery

5th Corps: (Austro-Bavarian forces) Grandduke von Wrede
Austrian Contingent: (17,874 men as of 1/1/14)
1st Division: FML von Hardegg
Brigade: Colonel von Geramb
Archduke Joseph Hussar Regiment (6)
1st Szekler Grenz Regiment (2)
Wurst Battery (6-6pdrs)
Brigade: Colonel von Mengen
Schwartzenburg Uhlan Regiment (6)
3rd Jäger Battalion
2nd Division: FML von Spleny
Brigade:
Jordis Infantry Regiment (4)
Archduke Rudolph Infantry Regiment (4)
Brigade: Generalmajor von Minutillo
Szekler Hussar Regiment (6)
Knesevich Dragoon Regiment (6)
Wurst Battery (6-6pdrs)
Reserve Artillery: Generalmajor von Swertnick
12pdr Brigade Battery (6-12pdrs)
2 6pdr Brigade Battery (6-6pdrs)
Bavarian Contingent:
1st Division: Generallieutenant von Rechberg
1st Brigade: Generalmajor Prince Karl of Bavaria
1st Bavarian Infantry Regiment (2)

- 3rd Bavarian Infantry Regiment (1)
- 1/Oberdonau Landwehr Regiment
- 3rd Light Infantry Battalion

2nd Brigade: Generalmajor von Maillot
- 1st Bavarian Infantry Regiment (1)
- 2nd Bavarian Infantry Regiment (1)
- 2/Oberdonau Landwehr Regiment
- 1/Main Landwehr Regiment
- 2nd (combined) Light Infantry Battalion

1st Light Cavalry Brigade: Generalmajor von Vieregg
- 1/, 2/, 3/, 4/1st Bavarian Chevauxleger Regiment
- 1/, 2/, 3/, 4/2nd Bavarian Chevauxleger Regiment
- 1/, 2/, 3/, 4/7th Bavarian Chevauxleger Regiment

Artillery:
- Wurst Battery (6-6pdrs)
- Light Battery (8-6pdrs)

2nd Division: Generallieutenant von Beckers

Brigade: Generalmajor von Pappenheim
- 4th Bavarian Infantry Regiment (2)
- Combined Battalion of Salzach Landwehr (1)
- 1/Regen Landwehr Battalion (1)
- 4th Light Battalion (1)

Brigade: Generalmajor von Zoller
- 6th Bavarian Infantry Regiment (2)
- 1/Rezat Landwehr
- 1/Inn Landwehr
- 1st Light Battalion

2nd Light Cavalry Brigade: Generalmajor von Elbracht
- 1/, 2/, 3/, 4/3rd Bavarian Chevauxleger Regiment
- 1/, 2/, 3/, 4/6th Bavarian Chevauxleger Regiment

Artillery:
- Wurst Battery (6-6pdrs)
- Light Battery (8-6pdrs)

Division: Generallieutenant Lamotte

Brigade: Generalmajor von Habermann
- 11th Bavarian Infantry Regiment (2)
- 7th Bavarian Infantry Regiment (1)
- 1/Unterdonau Landwehr Battalion
- 1/Iller Landwehr Battalion

Brigade: Generalmajor Deroy
- 5th Bavarian Infantry Regiment (1)
- 8th Bavarian Infantry Regiment (1)
- 9th Bavarian Infantry Regiment (1)
- 2/Iller Landwehr Battalion
- 1/Isar Landwehr Battalion

3rd Light Cavalry Brigade: Generalmajor von Elbracht
- 1/, 2/, 3/, 4/4th Bavarian Chevauxleger Regiment
- 1/, 2/, 3/, 4/5th Bavarian Chevauxleger Regiment

Artillery:
- Wurst Battery (6-6pdrs)
- Light Battery (8-6pdrs)
- Corps Artillery Reserve:
- 4 Heavy Batteries (6-12pdrs ea)

6th Army Corps (Russian): Grandduke Wittgenstein
1st Infantry Corps: Generallieutenant Gorchakov II (5,393 men on 1/1/14)
 5th Division: Generalmajor Menzenzov
  Brigade: Generalmajor Nabokov
   Perm Infantry Regiment (1)
   Sievesk Infantry Regiment (1)
  Brigade: Colonel Milavanov
   Mohilev Infantry Regiment (1)
   Kalouga Infantry Regiment (1)
  Brigade: Generalmajor Vlastov
   23rd Jager Regiment (1)
   24th Jager Regiment (1)
 14th Division: Generalmajor von Helfrich
  Brigade: Generalmajor Ljalin
   Tenguinsk Infantry Regiment (1)
   Estonia Infantry Regiment (1)
  Brigade: Generalmajor Roth
   25th Jager Regiment (1)
   26th Jager Regiment (1)
  Artillery:
   Light Batteries #26 and #27 (12 guns ea)
   Position Battery #14 (12 guns)

2nd Infantry Corps: Generallieutenant Prince Eugene von Württemberg (10,524 men as of 1/1/14)
 3rd Division: Generallieutenant Prince Schachovsky
  Brigade: Colonel von Wolff
   Tchernigov Infantry Regiment (2)
   Mourmonsk Infantry Regiment (2)
  Brigade: Colonel Schelwinsky
   Revel Infantry Regiment (2)
   Seleguinsk Infantry Regiment (1)
  Brigade: Colonel Kapustin
   20th Jager Regiment (1)
   21st Jager Regiment (1)
 4th Division: Generalmajor Puschnizky
  Brigade: Colonel von Rosen
   Tobolsk Infantry Regiment (2)
   Krementchug Infantry Regiment (1)
  Brigade: Colonel Kursonov
   Minsk Infantry Regiment (2)
   Volhynie Infantry Regiment (1)
  Brigade: Colonel Stepanov
   4th Jager Regiment (2)
   34th Jager Regiment (2)
  Artillery:
   Light Batteries #14 and #6 (12 guns ea)
   Position Battery #3 (12 guns)
 3rd Hussar Division: Generallieutenant Pahlen (3,543 men as of 1/1/14)
  Brigade: Generalmajor Delajanov
   Grodno Hussar Regiment (6)
   Soumy Hussar Regiment (5)
  Brigade: Generalmajor Dechterev

Loubny Hussar Regiment (5)
Olviopol Hussar Regiment (4)
Brigade: Generalmajor Lissanewitz
Tchougouiev Uhlan Regiment (8)
Corps Reserve Artillery:
Horse Batteries #11 & #23
Pioneer Company Kanatchikova
Pioneer Company Zetova
Cossacks:
Vlassov II Cossack Regiment
Illowaisky XII Cossack Regiment
Rebrikov III Cossack Regiment
Tschermuschin II Cossack Regiment
Jaroslav Cossack Regiment

Austrian Reserves: Grandduke Prince Hesse-Homburg (20,130 men as of 1/1/14)
Cavalry: Feldmarschal-leutnant von Nostitz
1st Division: Feldmarschal-leutnant von Klebelsberg
Brigade: Generalmajor von Auersberg
Grand Duke Constantine Cuirassier Regiment (5)
Sommervia Cuirassier Regiment #5 (5)
Brigade: Generalmajor Desfours
Liechtenstein Cuirassier Regiment (5)
Kaiser Cuirassier Regiment (5)
2nd Cuirassier Division: Feldmarschal-leutnant von Lederer
Brigade: Generalmajor von Rothkirch
Archduke Albert Cuirassier Regiment #3 (5)
Franz Mayland Cuirassier Regiment (5)
Brigade: Generalmajor von Ruttalek
Lothringen Cuirassier Regiment #7 (5)
Crown Prince Ferdinand Cuirassier Regiment (5)
Division: Feldmarschal-leutnant Bianchi
Brigade: Generalmajor von Hirsch
Hiller Infantry Regiment #2 (2)
H. Colleredo Infantry Regiment #33 (2)
Brigade Battery (8-6pdrs) (?)
Brigade: Generalmajor Haugwitz
Hesse-Homburg Infantry Regiment #19 (2)
Simbschen Infantry Regiment #48 (2)
Brigade Battery (8-6pdrs) (?)
Brigade: Generalmajor von Gutemberg
Esterhazy Infantry Regiment #32 (2)
Davidovich Infantry Regiment #34 (2)
Brigade Battery (8-6pdrs) (?)
Division: Feldmarschal-leutnant Weissenwolf
Brigade: Generalmajor Fürstenwerder
Grenadier Battalion Czarnozi
Grenadier Battalion Obermayer
Grenadier Battalion Berger
Grenadier Battalion Oklopsia
Brigade: Generalmajor von Beigel
Grenadier Battalion Habinay
Grenadier Battalion Portener

Grenadier Battalion Fischer
Grenadier Battalion Ruber
Brigade: Generalmajor von Klenau
Grenadier Battalion Frisch
Grenadier Battalion Mösel
Grenadier Battalion Putheany
Brigade: Generalmajor von Luz
Grenadier Battalion Rosmann
Grenadier Battalion Lany
Grenadier Battalion Hormada
Artillery: FML von Reisner
5 Foot Batteries (8-6pdrs)
26 Companies Field Artillery
27 Companies Artillery Workers
8 Pioneer Companies
400 Pontooneers

Russo-Prussian Reserves and Guards: General of Infantry Barclay de Tolly
Cavalry: Generallieutenant Prince Gallizin V (8,409 men on 1/1/14)
1st Cuirassier Division: Generallieutenant Depreradovich
Brigade: Generalmajor Arsenjeff
Chevalier Guard Regiment (6)
Horse Guard Regiment (6)
Brigade: Generalmajor von Rosen
Emperor Cuirassier Regiment (4)
Empress Cuirassier Regiment (4)
2nd Cuirassier Division: Generallieutenant Kretov
Brigade: Generalmajor Leontiev
Gluchov Cuirassier Regiment (5)
Pskof Cuirassier Regiment (5)
Brigade: Generalmajor Stahl II
Ekaterinoslav Cuirassier Regiment (2)
Astrakhan Cuirassier Regiment (4)
3rd Cuirassier Division: Generallieutenant Duka
Brigade: Generalmajor Protassov
Military Order Cuirassier Regiment (4)
Little Russia Cuirassier Regiment (4)
Brigade: Generalmajor Lewaschoff
Novgorod Cuirassier Regiment (4)
Starodoub Cuirassier Regiment (5)
Guard Light Division: Generalmajor Schevich (later Ojarovski)
Guard Hussar Regiment (6)
Guard Dragoon Regiment (6)
Guard Uhlan Regiment (6)
Guard Horse Battery #1 (8 guns)
Guard Horse Battery #2 (8 guns)
Guards Infantry: Generallieutenant Yermolov (12,950 Russians as of 1/1/14)
1st Guard Division: Generallieutenant Rosen
Brigade: Generalmajor Potemkin
Preobragenski Guard Infantry Regiment (3)
Semenovski Guard Infantry Regiment (3)
Brigade: Generalmajor Chrapowitzky
Ismailov Guard Infantry Regiment (3)

Guard Jager Regiment (2)
Guard Military Equippage Battalion + 2 6pdr guns
2nd Guard Division: Generalmajor Udom I
Brigade: Generalmajor Scheltuchin
Lithuania Guard Infantry Infantry Regiment (3)
Leib-Guard Grenadier Regiment (3)
Brigade:
Finland Guard Infantry (2)
Pavlov Guard Grenadiers (2)
Guard Artillery Brigade:
1st and 2nd Guard Position Batteries
1st and 2nd Guard Light Batteries
1 Pioneer Company
Prussian Guard Cavalry Brigade: Generalmajor von Starkenfels
(1,263 men on 1/1/14)
1/, 2/, 3/, 4/, 5/Garde du Corps Regiment
1/, 2/, 3/, 4/Guard Light Cavalry Regiment
Guard Horse Artillery Battery (8-6pdrs)
Prussian Guard Infantry Brigade: Colonel von Alvensleben
(4,647 men on 1/1/14)
1st Garde Regiment zu Fuss (2)(with three jäger companies)
2nd Garde Regiment zu Fuss (2)(with three jäger companies)
Guard Jäger Regiment (1) (with one jäger company)
Guard Foot Artillery Battery (8-6pdrs)
Attached:
Baden Leibgarde Grenadier Battalion (872)
Baden Horse Artillery Battery (7-6pdrs)

Grenadier or 3rd Corps: Grandduke Raevsky (10,005 men as of 1/1/14)
1st Division: Generalmajor Tschoglikov
Brigade: Generalmajor Kniaschnin II
Count Arakcheyev Grenadier Regiment (2)
Ekaterinoslav Grenadier Regiment (2)
Brigade: Colonel Jemilianov
Tauride Grenadier Regiment (1)
St. Petersburg Grenadier Regiment (2)
Brigade: Generalmajor Sulima
Kexholm Grenadier Regiment (2)
Pernau Grenadier Regiment (2)
2nd Division: Generalmajor Paskevich
Brigade: Generalmajor Pissarev
Kiev Grenadier Regiment (2)
Moscow Grenadier Regiment (2)
Brigade: Generalmajor Damas
Astrakhan Grenadier Regiment (1)
Fangoria Grenadier Regiment (1)
Brigade:
Siberia Grenadier Regiment (2)
Little Russia Grenadier Regiment (2)
Emperor Grenadier Regiment (1)
Artillery:
2 Light Batteries
1 Heavy Battery

(32 guns total)
Reserve Artillery: Generalmajor Schussnet (1,267 men on 1/1/14)
2 Position Batteries
1 Light Battery
1 Horse Position Battery
2 Horse Light Batteries
1 Sapper Company
1 Pioneer Company

Cossack Corps: Ataman Platoff (later Seslavin) (3,143 men on 1/1/14)
Ataman Don Cossack Regiment
Grekov VIII Don Cossack Regiment
Illowaisky X Don Cossack Regiment
Kortin IV Cossack Regiment
Tschernomoren Cossack Regiment
Kortin IV Cossack Regiment
Scheltonoskin I Cossack Regiment
Don Light Battery (12-6pdrs)
Raiding Parties: Generalmajor Scherbatov (1,064 men on 1/1/4)
3rd Orenburg Opolochenie Cossack Regiment
1st Taptjaren Cossack Regiment
4th Ural Cossack Regiment
Jagodin II Cossack Regiment
Austrian Raiding Parties: (632 men on 1/1/14)
Horin I Cossack Regiment
Jelmursin Cossack Regiment

Prussian 2nd Corps: Generalmajor von Kleist (as of 1/6/14)
(total of 16,000 men on 1/6/14)
9th Brigade: Generalmajor von Klüx
1/, 2/, Fus/1st West Prussian Infantry Regiment
6th Reserve Infantry Regiment (2)
1/, 2/, 3/7th Landwehr Infantry Regiment
Silesian Schützen (two companies)
1/, 2/, 3/, 4/Neumark Dragoon Regiment
6pdr Foot Battery #7 (8-6pdrs)
10th Brigade: Generalmajor von Pirch I
1/, 2/, 3/2nd West Prussian Infantry Regiment
1/, 2/, 3/7th Reserve Infantry Regiment (the 3/7th was taken prisoner on 2/14/14)
1/, 2/, 3/, 4/, 5/8th Silesian Landwehr Cavalry Regiment
6pdr Foot Battery #8 (8-6pdrs)
11th Brigade: Generalmajor von Ziethen
1/, 2/, Fus/1st Silesian Infantry Regiment (destroyed 2/14)
1/, 2/10th Reserve Infantry Regiment (destroyed 2/14)
Silesian Schützen Battalion (two companies)
1/, 2/, 3/, 4/1st Silesian Hussar Regiment
6pdr Foot Battery #9l (8-6pdrs)
12th Brigade: Generalmajor Prince August of Prussia
1/, 2/, Fus/2nd Silesian Infantry Regiment
11th Reserve Infantry Regiment (2)
1/, 2/, 3/, 4/7th Silesian Landwehr Cavalry Regiment
6pdr Foot Artillery Battery #21 (8-6pdrs)
Reserve Cavalry: Oberst von Hacke

1/, 2/, 3/, 4/Silesian Cuirassier Regiment
1/, 2/, 3/, 4/Silesian Uhlan Regiment
Horse Artillery Batteries #8 (8-6pdrs)
Artillery: Oberstleutnant von Lehmann
12pdr Foot Batteries #3 and #6 (8-12pdrs ea)
6pdr Foot Batteries #11 and #13 (8-6pdrs ea)
Horse Batteries #9 and #10 (8-6pdrs ea)
Howitzer Battery #1
Detached to the siege of Luxemburg and Thionville:
Brigade: Generalmajor von Roder
1/, 2/, 3/, 4/East Prussian Cuirassier Regiment
1/, 2/, 3/, 4/Brandenburg Cuirassier Regiment
Raiding Party: Generalmajor Prince Biron
2 Reserve Batteries
4 Landwehr Regiments
2 Landwehr Cavalry Regiments
1 Pioneer Company

Appendix VIII

Allied 3rd Army Corps, 3 January 1814

Royal Saxon Army:
- General Staff (19 / 7)
- Cavalry:
  - Staff Dragoons (one squadron) (0 / 69 / 62)
  - 1/, 2/, 3/Cuirassier Regiment (31 / 459 / 469)
  - 1/, 2/, 3/Uhlan Regiment (31 / 398 / 398)
  - 1/, 2/, 3/Hussar Regiment (30 / 428 / 428)
- Line Infantry:
  - Staff/, 1/Grenadier Regiment (18 / 672)
  - 2/Grenadier Regiment (20 / 692)
  - 3/Grenadier Regiment (14 / 657)
  - Staff/, 2/1st Provisional Regiment (14 / 487)
  - 3/1st Provisional Regiment (18 / 665)
  - Staff/, 2/Provisional Regiment (14 / 487)
  - 3/Provisional Regiment (18/665)
  - Jäger Battalion (10 / 396)
  - 1/1st Light Regiment (12 / 436)
  - 2/1st Light Regiment (9 / 435)
  - 2/2nd Light Regiment (12 / 523)
- Artillery:
  - 1st Horse Battery (six guns) (4 / 141)
  - 2nd Horse Battery (six guns) (4 / 141)
  - 1st 12pdr Battery (4 / 200)
  - 1st 6pdr Battery (4 / 170)
  - 1st Reserve Park (4 / 138)
  - Sapper-Pontooneer Detachment (1 / 52)
- Thuringia-Anhalt Division:
  - Weimar Fusilier Battalion (14 / 729)

Appendix IX

Abstract return of French armies, 5 January 1814

Army of Colmar: Maréchal Marmont
II Corps:
1st Division (6,001 men present)
VI Corps:
1st Division (4,070 men present) (1,354 en route)
2nd Division (3,153 men present) (875 en route)
3rd Division (3,463 men present) (726 en route)
Artillery (771 men present)
I Cavalry Corps:
Total: (3,051 men present)
V Cavalry Corps:
Total: (4,255 men present)
Other:
Durutte's Brigade (1,399)
1st Gardes d'honneur (1,000)
23rd Light Cavalry Brigade (900)

Army of Epinal: Maréchal Ney
2nd Old Guard Division (1,735 men present) (6,265 reinforcements in the depots)
1st Voltigeur Division (5,200 men present) (1,200 reinforcements in the depots)
2nd Voltigeur Division (1,132 men present) (5,268 reinforcements in the depots)
Division of 3rd Battalions of 1st and 2nd Voltgeur Divisions (6,400 reinforcements in depots)
National Guard (13,080 men in depots)

Army of Langres: Maréchal Mortier
1st Old Guard Division (5,089 present) (1,315 reinforcements in the depots)
2nd Tirailleur Division (831 present) (8,769 reinforcements in the depots)
Provisional Young Guard Division (11,200 men in the depots)
Reserve Division (2,000 en route, 24,400 men in the depots)
1st Old Guard Cavalry Division (2,567 men present)
1st and 2nd Cavalry Divisions (6,000 men in depots)
National Guard (36,720 men in depots)

Army of Lyon: Maréchal Augereau
Geneva Division (1,600 men en route, 12,800 in depots)
National Guard (31,200 men in depots)

Command: Maréchal Victor
II Corps:
2nd and 3rd Divisions (3,997 men present) (935 en route, 22,400 in depots)
Gardes d'honneur Division (2,000 men present)
National Guard (9,888 men present)
Depots of 5th Division (unknown)

Command: Général de division Morand
IV Corps:
  1st Division (4,592 men present)
  2nd Division (1,766 men present)
  3rd Division (967 men present)
  4th Division (3,882 men present)
  Artillery and Engineers (1,020 men present)
  Total: 3,700 men en route and 6,400 reinforcements in depots
  2nd Gardes d'honneur Regiment (1,000)

Command: Maréchal Macdonald
XI Corps:
  1st Division (2,639 men present)
  2nd Division (4,304 men present)
  Total: 3,988 men en route and 12,000 reinforcements in depots
Molitor's Command (1,750 men present)
Wesel Garrison (1,360 men present)
V Corps (3,600 men present)
II Cavalry Corps (2,241 men present)
III Cavalry Corps (1,972 men present)

Command: Général de division Maison
I Corps (5,470 men present and 28,000 reinforcements in depots)
  3rd Tirailleur Division (7,500 men present)
  1st Tirailleur Division (1,300 men present and 5,100 reinforcements in depots)
  3rd Voltigeur Division (294 men present and 4,506 reinforcements in depots)
  2nd Guard Cavalry Division (2,379 men present)
Arrighi's Command (5,994 men present)

Defense of Saône and Jura:
National Guard (1,590 reinforcements in depots)

Appendix X

French forces drawn from Spain for 1814 campaign in France, January 1814

7th Division: Général de divison Leval
- Brigade: Général de Pinoteau (3,143)
  - 10th Légère Infantry Regiment (1)
  - 3rd Line Infantry Regiment (1)
  - 45th Line Infantry Regiment (1)
- Brigade: Général de Montfort (2,285)
  - 17th Légère Infantry Regiment (1)
  - 101st Line Infantry Regiment (2)
  - 105th Line Infantry Regiment (2)

9th Division: Général de divison Boyer (2,992)
- Brigade: Général de Chassé
  - 16th Légère Infantry Regiment (1)
  - 8th Line Infantry Regiment (1)
  - 28th Line Infantry Regiment (2)
- Brigade: Général de Gauthier (2,595)
  - 120th Line Infantry Regiment (3)
  - 122nd Line Infantry Regiment (2)

Cavalry:
- Brigade: Général de Ismert (1,619)
  - 4th Dragoon Regiment
  - 21st Dragoon Regiment
  - 26th Dragoon Regiment
  - Total: seven squadrons
  - 1 Horse Battery (six guns)
- Brigade: Général de Ormancy (1,247)
  - 14th Dragoon Regiment
  - 16th Dragoon Regiment
  - 17th Dragoon Regiment
  - 27th Dragoon Regiment
  - Total: seven squadrons
  - 1 Horse Battery (six guns)
- Brigade: Général de Sparre (554)
  - 5th Dragoon Regiment (2)
  - 12th Dragoon Regiment (2)
  - 2 Horse Batteries (12 guns)

Appendix XI

Winzingerode's Russian Corps (passing over the Rhine) 6 January 1814

Russian Corps: Generallieutenant Winzingerode
Cossack Corps: Generalmajor Chernichev
- Brigade: Illowaisky IV
  - Grekov XVIII Don Cossack Regiment (9 / 286)
  - Sysoev III Cossack Regiment (14 / 327)
  - Balbin II Cossack Regiment (9 / 363)
  - Vlassov III Cossack Regiment (6 / 317)
  - Girova Cossack Regiment (12 / 306)
- Brigade: Generalmajor Drevitsch
  - Nijine Chasseurs à cheval Regiment (2) (24 / 248)
  - Finland Dragoon Regiment (4) (32 / 465)
- Brigade: Generalmajor Majevski
  - 13th Jager Regiment (2) (35 / 1,178)
  - Unknown Light Battery (12 guns) (5/181)

Cossack Corps: Benkendorff
- Brigade: Stahl I
  - 1st Bashkir Regiment
  - 1st Bug Cossack Regiment
  - Andrejanov Cossack Regiment
- Brigade: Generalmajor Patton
  - Tula Infantry Regiment (2) (34 / 992)
  - 2nd Jager Regiment (1) (16 / 468)
  - Horse Battery #1 (?) (10 guns) (8 / 183)

Main Battle Corps: Generallieutenant Count Voronzov
- 21st Division: Generalmajor Leptev
  - Brigade: Generalmajor Rüdinger
    - Neva Infantry Regiment (1) (25 / 598)
    - Petrovsk Infantry Regiment (1) (32 / 704)
    - Lithuania Infantry Regiment (1) (31 / 581)
  - Brigade: Colonel Rüdinger
    - Podolsk Infantry Regiment (1) (30 / 547)
    - 44th Jager Regiment (2) (28 / 966)
- 24th Division: Generalmajor Wuitsch
  - Brigade: Generalmajor Swarikin
    - Chirvan Infantry Regiment (2) (45 / 1,188)
    - Bourtirki Infantry Regiment (2) (49 / 1,123)
    - Oumsk Infantry Regiment (2) (48 / 1,133)
- 3rd Hussar Division: Generalmajor von Pahlen
    - Elisabethgrad Hussar Regiment (7) (60 / 890)
    - Pavlograd Hussar Regiment (6) (24 / 553)

- Cossacks:
  - Illowaiski IV Don Cossack Regiment (16 / 378)
  - Djaschkin Don Cossack Regiment (16 / 378)
- Artillery: (17 / 675)
  - Light Batteries #42, #48 and #56
  - Position Batteries #7, #28 and #31

Division: Generalmajor Orurk
- Cossacks: Generalmajor Narischkin
  - Grekov IX Don Cossack Regiment (15 / 343)
  - Bradantdchikov II Don Cossack Regiment (12 / 413)
  - Lotschilin I Don Cossack Regiment (8 / 330)
  - Volhynie Uhlan Regiment (5) (40 / 649)
- Brigade: Generalmajor Sanders
  - Smolensk Infantry Regiment (1) (29 / 705)
  - Narva Infantry Regiment (1) (38 / 766)
- Brigade: Generalmajor Schwetschin
  - Alexopol Infantry Regiment (2) (28 / 775)
  - New Ingremannland Infantry Regiment (1) (22 / 689)
- Cossacks: Generalmajor Melnikov
  - Melnikov IV Don Cossack Regiment (17 / 331)
  - Melnikov V Don Cossack Regiment (12 / 286)
  - Rebrejev II Cossack Position Battery (12-12pdrs) (8 / 153)

Division: Generalleutnant Voronzov
- Cossacks: Generalmajor Pantelejev II
  - Pantalejev II Don Cossack Regiment (10 / 238)
  - Popov XIII Don Cossack Regiment (5 / 287)
- Brigade: Generalmajor Drewitsch
  - Isoum Hussar Regiment (6) (49 / 747)
  - Riga Dragoon Regiment (4) (27 / 493)
- Brigade: Generalmajor Harpe
  - Navaguinsk Infantry Regiment (2) (39 / 1,115)
  - Converged Grenadiers, 9th, 15th and 18th Divisions (3) (52 / 1,815)
- Artillery: (17 / 490)
  - Light Battery #42 (12-6pdrs)
  - Position Battery #31 (12-12pdrs)

Division: Generallieutenant Stroganov
- Cossacks:
  - 9th Bashkir Regiment (1 / 130)
  - Jakontov Volunteer Cossacks (10 / 105)
  - Polish Uhlan Regiment (59 / 633)
- Brigade from 13th Division: Generalmajor Scheltuchin
  - Pensa Infantry Regiment (2) (31 / 833)
  - Saratov Infantry Regiment (2) (35 / 802)
- Brigade: Generallieutenant Glebov
  - 6th Jager Regiment (1) (42 / 262)
  - 41st Jager Regiment (1) (24 / 575)
- Artillery: (18 guns and 9 / 354)
  - Position Battery #31 (12 12pdrs)
  - Light Battery #46 (12 6pdrs)
  - Light Battery #53 (12 6pdrs)

Appendix XII

4th German Bundescorps as ordered, 10 January 1814

Commanding Officer: General der Infanterie Kurprinz von Hessen
1st (Kur-Hessian) Brigade: Generalmajor Prince von Slom Braunfels
- 1st Grenadier Battalion
- Landgraf Karl Infantry Regiment
- Prinz Solms Infantry Regiment
- 1st Landwehr Regiment
- 3rd Landwehr Regiment
- Gelernte Jäger (two companies)
- 2 Foot Batteries (eight guns ea)
- Freiwilliger Reitende Jäger (two squadrons)

2nd (Kur-Hessian) Brigade: Generalmajor von Müller
- 2nd Grenadier Battalion
- Kurfürst Infantry Regiment
- Kruprinz Infantry Regiment
- 2nd Landwehr Regiment
- Gelernte Jäger (two companies)
- Freiwilliger Fussjäger (two companies)
- 2 Foot Batteries (eight guns ea)
- Hussar Regiment
- Freiwilliger Reitende Jäger (two squadrons)

Appendix XIII

Marmont's Command, 21 January 1814

VI Corps: Maréchal Marmont
- 8th Division: Général de division Ricard (2,412 men)
  - 2nd Légère Regiment
  - 4th Légère Regiment
  - 6th Légère Regiment
  - 9th Légère Regiment
  - 16th Légère Regiment
  - 136th Line Regiment
  - 138th Line Regiment
  - 142nd Line Regiment
  - 144th Line Regiment
  - 145th Line Regiment
- 20th Division: Général de division Lagrange (3,387 men)
  - 1st Line Regiment
  - 15th Line Regiment
  - 16th Line Regiment
  - 23rd Line Regiment
  - 37th Line Regiment
  - 70th Line Regiment
  - 121st Line Regiment
  - 62nd Line Regiment
  - 1st Marine Regiment
  - 2nd Marine Regiment
  - 3rd Marine Regiment
  - 4th Marine Regiment
- Artillery: (970 men)
  - 5 Foot Companies
  - 2 Horse Companies
  - 52 guns, including 6-12pdrs
  - Other:
    - 3 Engineer Companies (300 men)

V Cavalry Corps: Général de division Doumerc (1,764 men)
- 1st Provisional Light Cavalry Regiment
- 2nd Provisional Light Cavalry Regiment
- 3rd Provisional Heavy Cavalry Regiment
- 4th Provisional Heavy Cavalry Regiment
- 23rd Light Cavalry Brigade: Général de brigade Piquet (856 men)
  - 1st Gardes d'honneur Regiment
  - 10th Hussar Regiment

Appendix XIV

Bordesoulle's Cavalry Division, 24 January 1814

1st Brigade: Général de brigade Morin
 4th Cuirassier Regiment (5 / 92 / 11 / 92)[1]
 7th Cuirassier Regiment (4 / 104 / 9 / 104)
 8th Cuirassier Regiment (4 / 102 / 9 / 102)
2nd Brigade: Général de brigade Guillon
 2nd Dragoon Regiment (2 / 43 / 4 / 43)
 13th Dragoon Regiment (3 / 41 / 6 / 41)
3rd Brigade: Général de brigade Wathier
 1st Chevau-léger Regiment (6 / 139 / 13 / 139)
 2nd Chevau-léger Regiment (6 / 142 / 11 / 142)
 3rd Chevau-léger Regiment (5 / 97 / 11 / 97)
 4th Chevau-léger Regiment (5 / 43 / 7 / 43)
 5th Chevau-léger Regiment (3 / 74 / 5 / 74)
 8th Chevau-léger Regiment (2 / 27 / 4 / 27)
4th Brigade: Général de brigade Losquet
 1st Chasseurs à cheval Regiment (9 / 122 / 19 / 122)
 12th Chasseurs à cheval Regiment (2 / 50 / 5 / 50)
 24th Chasseurs à cheval Regiment (8 / 196 / 18 / 196)
 26th Chasseurs à cheval Regiment (1 / 27 / 2 / 27)
 27th Chasseurs à cheval Regiment (2 / 74 / 5 / 740)
Artillery:
 Horse Battery from Epernay (4 / 125 / 10 / 168)

1 Numbers are officers, men, officers' horses and men's horses.

Appendix XV

Pajol's Cavalry Division, 24 January 1814

1st Brigade: Général de brigade Gronvel
- 4th Dragoon Regiment (3 / 67 / 7 / 67)
- 5th Dragoon Regiment (4 / 93 / 9 / 93)
- 12th Dragoon Regiment (5 / 131 / 10 / 131)
- 14th Dragoon Regiment (2 / 94 / 4 / 94)
- 17th Dragoon Regiment (7 / 184 / 16 / 184)
- 21st Dragoon Regiment (3 / 90 / 7 / 90)

2nd Brigade: Général de brigade Delort
- 10th Chasseurs à cheval Regiment (3 / 87 / 7 / 87)
- 13th Chasseurs à cheval Regiment (4 / 152 / 9 / 152)
- 22nd Chasseurs à cheval Regiment (2 / 118 / 4 / 118)

Artillery:
- Horse Battery from Epernay (unknown)

Appendix XVI

French Army at Châlons, 25 January 1814

Commanding Officer: Emperor Napoleon I
Chief of Staff: Maréchal Berthier

Right wing: Maréchal Mortier
Imperial Guard:
- 1st Old Guard Division: Général de division Friant
  - 1/, 2/1st Chasseur à Pied Regiment (1,265)
  - 1/, 2/2nd Chasseur à Pied Regiment (898)
  - 1/, 2/1st Grenadier à Pied Regiment (1,393)
  - 1/, 2/2nd Grenadier à Pied Regiment (1,044)
  - 1st, 2nd and 3rd Guard Sapper Companies (105)
- 2nd Old Guard Division: Général de division Michel
  - Flanqueuer-Chasseur Regiment (1,042)
  - Flanqueuer-Grenadier Regiment (285)
  - Vélites of Turin (333)
  - Vélites of Florence (164)
  - Fusilier-Chasseur Regiment (1,366)
  - Fusilier-Grenadier Regiment (688)
- 1st (Old) Guard Cavalry Division: Général de division Laferire-Lévéque
  - Guard Chasseurs à cheval Regiment (585)
  - Guard Dragoon Regiment (734)
  - Guard Grenadier à cheval Regiment (909)
- Guard Artillery:
  - 7 Foot Batteries (459)
  - 4 Horse Artillery Batteries (319)
  - Pontoonier-Ouvriers (21)
  - Artillery Train (665)

Paris Reserve:
- Division: Général de division Dufour
  - Brigade: Général de brigade Jarry
    - 8/32nd Line Regiment (673)
    - 12th Légère Regiment (510)
    - 29th Légère Regiment (736)
    - 58th Line Regiment (406)
  - Brigade: Général de brigade de Bellair
    - 7/2nd Légère Regiment (600)
    - 6/4th Légère Regiment (580)
    - 7/15th Légère Regiment (554)
    - 3/135th Line Regiment (554)
    - 139th Line Regiment (369)
    - 155th Line Regiment (836)
  - 3rd Brigade: Général de brigade Bourmont
    - 1/, 3/, 4/113th Line Regiment (2,173)
  - Artillery and Train: (300)

Center:

II Corps: Maréchal Victor, Duc de Bellune

- 1st Division: Général de division Jamin
  - 1/24th Légère Regiment (520)
  - 1/19th Line Regiment (640)
  - 1/37th Line Regiment (601)
  - 1/56th Line Regiment (962)
- 2nd Division: Général de division Forestier
  - 1/26th Line Regiment (801)
  - 1/, 2/, 4/18th Line Regiment (1,385)
  - 1/46th Line Regiment (753)
  - 1/, 2/93rd Line Regiment (408)
- 3rd Division: Général de division Duhèsme
  - 2/11th Line Regiment (496)
  - 2/2nd Line Regiment (405)
  - 1/, 2/4th Line Regiment (1,237)
  - 2/72nd Line Regiment (524)
- Artillery: (989)
  - 7/2nd Foot Artillery (6pdrs)
  - 19/2nd Foot Artillery (6pdrs)
  - 5/, 7/, 11/, 22/9th Foot Artillery (6pdrs)
  - 17/1st Foot Artillery (12pdrs)
  - 6/1st Horse Artillery
  - 4/4th Horse Artillery
  - 6/4th Horse Artillery
  - 4/, 6/6th (bis) Train Battalion
  - 3/, 4/8th Principal Train Battalion
  - 4/1st Principal Train Battalion
  - 4/11th Principal Train Battalion
  - 4/12th (bis) Train Battalion
- Engineers: (153)
  - 2/2nd Sapper Battalion
  - 3/3rd Sapper Battalion
  - 3/5th Sapper Battalion

Cavalry Corps: Général de division Milhaud

- 6th Heavy Division: Général de division L'Heritier
  - 1st Brigade: Général de brigade Lamotte
    - 18th Dragoon Regiment (218)
    - 19th Dragoon Regiment (246)
    - 20th Dragoon Regiment (154)
  - 2nd Brigade: Colonel Mermet
    - 22nd Dragoon Regiment (283)
    - 25th Dragoon Regiment (263)
- 9th Light Division: Général de division de Piré
  - 1st Brigade: Général de brigade Subervie
    - 1/, 2/3rd Hussar Regiment (278)
    - 1/, 3/, 4/26th Chasseurs à cheval Regiment (207)
  - 2nd Brigade: Général de brigade l'Hermoncourt
    - 1/, 3/, 4/14th Chasseurs à cheval Regiment (234)
    - 1/, 3/, 4/, 5/27th Chasseurs à cheval Regiment (331)
- 5th Heavy Division: Général de brigade Collaert
  - Brigade: Général de brigade Montelegier

2nd Dragoon Regiment (349)
6th Dragoon Regiment (321)
11th Dragoon Regiment (367)
Brigade: Général de brigade Ludor
13th Dragoon Regiment (220)
15th Dragoon Regiment (333)
Artillery: Colonel Etchegayen (319)
4/2nd Horse Artillery (4-6pdrs and two howitzers)
2/3rd Horse Artillery (4-6pdrs and two howitzers)
1/8th Principal Train Battalion
1/12th Principal Train Battalion
Cavalry Brigade: Général de division Ségur
3rd Gardes d'honneur (750)
4th Gardes d'honneur (319)

VI Corps: Maréchal Marmont
1st Division: Général de division Ricard
Brigade: Général de brigade Fournier
3/2nd Légère Regiment (112)
3/4th Légère Regiment (136)
2/6th Légère Regiment (197)
3/40th Line Regiment (223)
2/50th Line Regiment (190)
Brigade: Général de brigade Boudin
2/65th Line Regiment (97)
1/136th Line Regiment (582)
1/138th Line Regiment (108)
1/142nd Line Regiment (95)
1/144th Line Regiment (306)
1/145th Line Regiment (261)
2nd Division: Général de division Lefol
Brigade: Général de brigade Lagrange
3/9th Légère Regiment (130)
2/16th Légère Regiment (199)
4/1st Line Regiment (194)
3/15th Line Regiment (340)
Brigade: Général de brigade Clavel
4/16th Line Regiment (120)
2/, 3/62nd Line Regiment (228)
2/70th Line Regiment (339)
3/, 6/121st Line Regiment (400)
3rd Division: Général de division Lagrange
Brigade: Général de brigade Joubert
3/23rd Line Regiment (76)
1/, 2/, 3/, 4/37th Line Regiment (721)
1/, 2/1st Marine Regiment (508)
Brigade: Général de brigade Pelleport
1/, 2/, 3/, 4/2nd Marine Regiment (740)
1/, 2/, 3/3rd Marine Regiment (543)
1/, 2/, 3/4th Marine Regiment (279)
23rd Cavalry Brigade: Général de brigade Beurmann
10th Hussar Regiment (six squadrons) (548)
1st Gardes d'honneur (367)

- Artillery: (539)
    - 6/, 25/, 26/3rd Artillery
    - 13/, 16/5th Artillery
    - 2/1st Horse Artillery
    - 4/4th Principal Train Battalion
    - 2/8th (bis) Train Battalion
    - 1/, 5/9th Principal Train Battalion
- Engineers: (322)
    - 2/4th Sapper Battalion
    - 1/6th Sapper Battalion
    - 4/7th Sapper Battalion

I Cavalry Corps: Général de division Doumerc

- 1st Brigade: Général de brigade Piquet
    - 1st Provisional Regiment (272)
        - 1/6th Hussar Regiment
        - 2/7th Hussar Regiment
        - 3/8th Hussar Regiment
        - 4/16th Chasseurs à cheval Regiment
        - 5/1st Chevauléger-lancier Regiment
        - 6/3rd Chevauléger-lancier Regiment
        - 7/5th Chevauléger-lancier Regiment
        - 8/8th Chevauléger-lancier Regiment
    - 2nd Provisional Regiment (432)
        - 1/8th Chasseurs à cheval Regiment
        - 2/9th Chasseurs à cheval Regiment
        - 3/25th Chasseurs à cheval Regiment
        - 4/1st Chasseurs à cheval Regiment
        - 5/2nd Chasseurs à cheval Regiment
        - 6/3rd Chasseurs à cheval Regiment
        - 7/6th Chasseurs à cheval Regiment
- 2nd Brigade: Général de brigade Daudenarde
    - 3rd Provisional Regiment (614)
        - 1/2nd Cuirassier Regiment
        - 2/3rd Cuirassier Regiment
        - 3/6th Cuirassier Regiment
        - 4/9th Cuirassier Regiment
        - 5/11th Cuirassier Regiment
        - 6/12th Cuirassier Regiment
    - 4th Provisional Regiment (582)
        - 1/4th Cuirassier Regiment
        - 2/7th Cuirassier Regiment
        - 3/14th Cuirassier Regiment
        - 4/7th Dragoon Regiment
        - 5/23rd Dragoon Regiment
        - 6/28th Dragoon Regiment
        - 7/30th Dragoon Regiment
- Artillery: Colonel Lavoye (191)
        - 3/1st Horse Battery
        - 1/6th Horse Battery
        - Total: six guns

Left wing: Maréchal Macdonald
XI Corps: Maréchal Macdonald
31st Division: Général de division Molitor
139th Line Regiment (317)
149th Line Regiment (298)
28th Légère Regiment (312)
70th Line Regiment (260)
46th Line Regiment (328)
Artillery and Train: (243)
35th Division: Général de division Brayer
Swiss Grenadiers (98)
19th Légère Regiment (272)
5th Line Regiment (283)
11th Line Regiment (304)
107th Line Regiment (268)
Artillery and Train: (221)

V Corps: Général de division Sébastiani
Division: Général de division Albert
1/, 2/135th Line Regiment (325)
1/, 2/152nd Line Regiment (279)
1/, 2/154th Line Regiment (142)
1/, 2/140th Line Regiment (280)
1/, 2/141st Line Regiment (220)
Artillery and Train: (198)
3/1st Foot Artillery
16/1st Foot Artillery
15/4th Foot Artillery
2/5th Horse Artillery
1/5th Principal Train Battalion
3/5th Principal Train Battalion
2/6th Sapper Battalion

Cavalry Corps:
Provisional Division:
1st Provisional Regiment (117)
1/5th Hussar Regiment
2/9th Hussar Regiment
3/11th Chasseurs à cheval Regiment
4/12th Chasseurs à cheval Regiment
5/2nd Chevauléger-lancier Regiment
6/4th Chevauléger-lancier Regiment
2nd Provisional Regiment (860)
1/4th Chasseurs à cheval Regiment
2/7th Chasseurs à cheval Regiment
3/20th Chasseurs à cheval Regiment
4/23rd Chasseurs à cheval Regiment
5/24th Chasseurs à cheval Regiment
6/6th Chevauléger-lancier Regiment
3rd Provisional Regiment (390)
1/1st Carabinier Regiment
2/2nd Carabinier Regiment
3/1st Cuirassier Regiment

        4/5th Cuirassier Regiment
        5/8th Cuirassier Regiment
        6/10th Cuirassier Regiment
        4th (Carabinier) Provisional Regiment (250)
        5th (Cuirassier) Provisional Regiment (275)
        Joseph Napoleon Regiment (250)
    Artillery: Lt. Colonel Graillat (270)
        1/1st Horse Artillery
        5/5th Horse Artillery
            Total: four guns
        Det/1st (bis) Train Battalion

III Cavalry Corps: Général de division Arrighi, Duc de Padoua
    Light Division: Général de division Ameil
            1st Provisional Hussar Regiment (201)
            2nd Provisional Chasseur Regiment (842)
    Heavy Division: Général de division Jacquinot
        1st Brigade: Général de brigade Wolf
            3rd Provisional Dragoon Regiment (740)
            4th Provisional Cuirassier Regiment (72)
    Artillery: (228)
            5/1st Horse Battery (4-6pdrs and two howitzers)
            2/1st Principal Train Battalion
Guard reserve: Maréchal Ney, Prince de Moskowa
    1st Young Guard (1st Voltigeur) Division: Général de division Meunier
        Brigade: Général de brigade Lacoste
            1/, 2/1st Voltigeur Regiment (657)
            1/, 2/2nd Voltigeur Regiment (940)
        Brigade: Général de brigade Rousseau
            1/, 2/3rd Voltigeur Regiment (1,263)
            1/, 2/4th Voltigeur Regiment (1,144)
        Artillery and Train: (140)
    2nd Young Guard (2nd Voltigeur) Division: Général de division Decouz
        Brigade: Général de brigade Baron Peles
            1/, 2/5th Voltigeur Regiment (680)
            1/, 2/6th Voltigeur Regiment (633)
        Brigade: Général de brigade Bigarré
            1/, 2/7th Voltigeur Regiment (717)
            1/, 2/8th Voltigeur Regiment (670)
5th Young Guard (2nd Tirailleur) Division: Général de division Rottembourg
            1/, 2/1st Tirailleur Regiment (800)
            1/, 2/5th Tirailleur Regiment (959)
            1/, 2/6th Tirailleur Regiment (733)
            1/, 2/7th Tirailleur Regiment (811)
            1/, 2/8th Tirailleur Regiment (990)
            1/, 2/Flanker-Chasseur Regiment (312)
            2 Foot Artillery Companies (342)
        Cavalry:
            2nd Éclaireur Regiment (313)
            Polish Guard Lancer Regiment (600)
            Guard Chasseurs à cheval Regiment (511)
            Guard Grenadier à cheval Regiment (401)
            Guard Dragoon Regiment (460)
        Horse Artillery and Train: (300)

Appendix XVII

Allied 3rd Army Corps, 25 January 1814

Royal Saxon Army:
- General Staff (21 / 7)
- Cavalry:
  - Staff Dragoons (0 / 62 / 62)
  - 1/, 2/, 3/Cuirassier Regiment (23 / 443)
  - 1/, 2/, 3/Uhlan Regiment (22 / 364)
  - 1/, 2/, 3/Hussar Regiment (30 / 411)
- Line Infantry:
  - Staff/, 1/Grenadier Regiment (17 / 621)
  - 2/Grenadier Regiment (18 / 654)
  - 3/Grenadier Regiment (12 / 647)
  - Staff/, 2/1st Provisional Regiment (13 / 466)
  - 3/1st Provisional Regiment (16 / 633)
  - Staff/, 2/Provisional Regiment (14 / 524)
  - 3/Provisional Regiment (14 / 543)
  - Jäger Battalion (9/357)
  - 1/1st Light Regiment (11 / 474)
  - 2/1st Light Regiment (8 / 474)
  - 2/2nd Light Regiment (12 / 518)
- Artillery:
  - 1st Horse Battery (six guns) (4/127)
  - 2nd Horse Battery (six guns) (4/127)
  - 1st 12pdr Battery (4 / 189)
  - 1st 6pdr Battery (4 / 162)
  - 1st Reserve Park (4 / 122)
  - Sapper-Pontooneer Detachment (2 / 53)
- Thuringia-Anhalt Division:
  - Weimar Fusilier Battalion (13 / 639)

Appendix XVIII

French forces, Battle of La Rothière, 1 February 1814[1]

Commanding Officer: Emperor Napoleon I

Right wing:
1st Brigade: Général de brigade Piquet (640)
- 10th Hussar Regiment (4)
- 1st Gardes d'honneur (4)

Paris Reserve: Général de division Gérard
- 1st Division: Général de division Dufour (3,400)
  - 1st Brigade: Général de brigade Jarry
    - Provisional Regiment
      - 8/32nd Line Regiment
      - 6/58th Line Regiment
    - Provisional Regiment
      - 7/12th Légère Regiment
      - 6/29th Légère Regiment
  - 2nd Brigade: Général de brigade de Bellair
    - Provisional Regiment
      - 7/2nd Légère Regiment
      - 6/4th Légère Regiment
    - Provisional Regiment
      - 3/135th Line Regiment
      - 139th Line Regiment
      - 3/155th Line Regiment
  - 3rd Brigade: Général de brigade Bourmont
    - 1/, 3/, 4/113th Line Regiment
  - Artillery: unknown
  - Artillery and Train: (300)
- 8th Division: Général de division Ricard (3,500)
  - Brigade: under Généraux de brigade Fournier and Boudin
    - 3/2nd Légère Regiment
    - 2/, 3/4th Légère Regiment
    - 2/6th Légère Regiment
    - 3/9th Légère Regiment
    - 2/16th Légère Regiment
    - 3/40th Line Regiment
    - 2/50th Line Regiment
    - 1/136th Line Regiment
    - 1/138th Line Regiment
    - 1/142nd Line Regiment

---

1 Sources: Koch, F., *Memoirs pour servier à l'Histoire*; von Damitz, K., *Geschichte des Feldzuges von 1814*; French Archives, Carton C²712; French Archives, C²555.

1/144th Line Regiment
1/145th Line Regiment
Center: Maréchal Victor
2nd Guard Cavalry Division: Général de division Léfèbvre-Desnoëttes (850)
2nd Éclaireur Regiment
1st (Polish) Guard Lancer Regiment
Guard Chasseurs à cheval Regiment
Empress Dragoon Regiment
Guard Grenadier à cheval Regiment
Horse Artillery and Train
1st Guard Cavalry Division: Général de division Colbert (880)
2nd Éclaireur Regiment
2nd Chevauléger-lancier Regiment
Chasseurs à cheval de la Garde
Grenadiers à cheval de la Garde
Empress Dragoon Regiment
Horse Artillery

Service Squadrons: Général de division Guyot[2]
Grenadier à cheval Regiment (one squadron)
Chasseurs à cheval Regiment (one squadron)
1st Guard (Polish) Lancer Regiment (one squadron)
Empress Dragoon Regiment (one squadron)
1st Division: Général de division Duhèsme (4,200)
1/24th Légère Regiment
1/19th Line Regiment
1/37th Line Regiment
1/56th Line Regiment
By La Gibre:
1,900 unidentified infantry
9th Light Cavalry Division: Général de division Piré (870)
1st Brigade: Général de brigade Subervie
3rd Hussar Regiment
26th Chasseurs à cheval Regiment
2nd Brigade:
14th Chasseurs à cheval Regiment
27th Chasseurs à cheval Regiment
5th Heavy Cavalry Division: Général de division Briche (1,250)
1st Brigade: Général de brigade Montelegier
2nd Dragoon Regiment
6th Dragoon Regiment
11th Dragoon Regiment
2nd Brigade: Général de brigade Gudiot
13th Dragoon Regiment
15th Dragoon Regiment
6th Heavy Cavalry Division: Général de division l'Héritier (1,000)
1st Brigade: Général de brigade Lamotte
18th Dragoon Regiment
19th Dragoon Regiment

2 These squadrons were drawn from the divisions of Laferrière-Lévéque, Lefebvre-Desnoettes and Colbert. However, it is not known from which they were drawn.

20th Dragoon Regiment
2nd Brigade: Général de brigade Collaert
22th Dragoon Regiment
25th Dragoon Regiment
Artillery:
1/2nd Horse Artillery
4/2nd Horse Artillery
2/3rd Horse Artillery
1/8th Principal Train Battalion
1/12th Principal Train Battalion

Left wing:
I Cavalry Corps: Général de division Doumerc
Division: Général de division Doumerc (1,900)
1st Provisional Hussar Regiment
2nd Provisional Chasseur Regiment
3rd Provisional Chasseur Regiment
4th Provisional Chasseur Regiment
Artillery:
Horse Artillery Battery
VI Corps: Maréchal Marmont
3rd Division: Général de division Lagrange (4,600)
Brigade: Généraux de brigade Joubert and Pelleport
3/23rd Line Regiment
1/, 2/, 3/, 4/37th Line Regiment
1st Line Regiment
15th Line Regiment
16th Line Regiment
70th Line Regiment
121st Line Regiment
1/, 2/1st Marine Regiment
1/, 2/, 3/3rd Marine Regiment
62nd Line Regiment
1/, 2/, 3/, 4/2nd Marine Regiment
1/, 2/, 3/4th Marine Regiment
132nd Line Regiment

Reserves:
5th Young Guard (2nd Tirailleur) Division: (4,900) Général de division Rottembourg
1/, 2/1st Tirailleur Regiment
1/, 2/5th Tirailleur Regiment
1/, 2/6th Tirailleur Regiment
1/, 2/7th Tirailleur Regiment
1/, 2/8th Tirailleur Regiment
Det. Flanqueur-Chasseur and Flanqueur-Grenadier Regiments
2 Foot Artillery Companies
1st Young Guard (1st Voltigeur) Division: (3,000) Général de division Meunier
Brigade: Général de brigade Lacoste
1/, 2/1st Voltigeur Regiment
1/, 2/2nd Voltigeur Regiment
Brigade: Général de brigade Rousseau
1/, 2/3rd Voltigeur Regiment
1/, 2/4th Voltigeur Regiment

Artillery and Train: (129)
2nd Young Guard (2nd Voltigeur) Division: Général de division Curial (1,800)
Brigade: Général de brigade Baron Peles
1/, 2/5th Voltigeur Regiment
1/, 2/6th Voltigeur Regiment
Brigade: Général de brigade Bigarré
1/, 2/7th Voltigeur Regiment
1/, 2/8th Voltigeur Regiment
Artillery and Train
Cavalry Division: Général de division Defrance
Brigade: Général de brigade Ségur
3rd and 4th Gardes d'honneur

Appendix XIX

Allied forces, Battle of La Rothière, 1 February 1814

(Information drawn from Koch, Kraft and Bogdanovich)

Commanding Officer: General of Cavalry von Blücher

Left wing: FZM I. Giulay
3rd Corps: FZM I. Giulay (12,000 infantry and 1,500 cavalry)

- Division: FML Crenneville
  - Brigade: Generalmajor von Hecht
    - Klenau Chevauxleger Regiment #5 (7)
    - St. George Warasdiner Grenz Regiment (1)
  - Brigade: Generalmajor von Trenck
    - Rosenburg Dragoon Regiment (6)
    - St. George Warasdiner Grenz Regiment (1)
    - Wurst Battery (6-6pdrs)
- Division: FML Fresnel
  - Brigade: Generalmajor von Pflüger
    - Archduke Louis Infantry Regiment #8 (4)
    - Wurzburg Infantry Regiment #7 (3)
    - Brigade Battery (8-6pdrs)
  - Brigade: Generalmajor von Csollich
    - Kottulinski Infantry Regiment #41 (3) (2,214)
    - Kaiser Infantry Regiment #1 (2) (1,558)
    - Brigade Battery (8-6pdrs)
- Division: FML Prince von Hohenlohe-Bartenstein
  - Brigade: Generalmajor von Spleny
    - Mariassy Infantry Regiment #37 (2)
    - J. Gyulai Infantry Regiment #60 (2)
    - Brigade Battery (8-6pdrs)
  - Brigade: Generalmajor von Grimmer
    - Kollowrath Infantry Regiment #36 (2) (1,602)
    - Frölich Infantry Regiment #28 (3) (2,790)
    - Brigade Battery (8-6pdrs)
  - Reserve Artillery:
    - 1 Foot Battery (6-12pdrs)
    - 2 Foot Batteries (6-6pdrs ea)

Center: General of Infantry Sacken
Army of Silesia:

- Russian Corps: Generallieutenant von Sacken
- 11th Corps: Generalmajor von Lieven III (8,000 infantry)
  - 10th Division: Generalmajor Sass
    - Brigade: Generalmajor Sokolovsky
      - Jaroslav Infantry Regiment (1)
      - Kursk Infantry Regiment (1)
      - Bieloserk Infantry Regiment (2)

Brigade: Colonel Achlestischev
8th Jager Regiment (1)
39th Jager Regiment (1)
From 16th Division:
Brigade: Lt. Colonel Selivanov
Kamtchatka Infantry Regiment (1)
Okhotsk Infantry Regiment (1)
27th Division: Generallieutenant Stawitzky
Brigade: Colonel Lewandowsky
Odessa Infantry Regiment (1)
Vilna Infantry Regiment (1)
Brigade: Colonel Alexejev
Simbrisk Infantry Regiment (1)
Tarnopol Infantry Regiment (1)
Brigade: Colonel Kalogruivoff
49th Jager Regiment (1)
50th Jager Regiment (1)
Artillery:
Position Battery #18
Light Batteries #34 and #35

6th Corps: Generallieutenant Prince Scherbatov (8,000 infantry)
7th Division: Generalmajor Por Tallisin II
Brigade: Colonel Kritschinikov
Pskof Infantry Regiment (1)
Moscow Infantry Regiment (1)
Brigade: Colonel Augustov
Sophia Infantry Regiment (1)
Libau Infantry Regiment (1)
Brigade: Colonel Dieterich
11th Jager Regiment (1)
36th Jager Regiment (1)
18th Division: Generalmajor Bernodessov
Brigade: Lt. Colonel Blagovenzenko
Vladimir Infantry Regiment (1)
Dnieper Infantry Regiment (1)
Brigade: Generalmajor Heidenreich
Tambov Infantry Regiment (1)
Kostroma Infantry Regiment (1)
Brigade: Generalmajor Metcherinov
28th Jager Regiment (1)
32nd Jager Regiment (1)
Artillery:
Position Battery #10
Light Batteries #19 and #24

9th Corps: Generallieutenant Olsufiev (5,000 infantry)
9th Division: Generalmajor Udom II
Brigade: Generalmajor Poltarachi
Nacheburg Infantry Regiment (1)
Apcheron Infantry Regiment (1)
Brigade: Generalmajor Juschkov II
Riajsk Infantry Regiment (1)

Iakout Infantry Regiment (1)
Brigade: Major Melnik
10th Jager Regiment (1)
38th Jager Regiment (1)
15th Division: Generalmajor Kornilov
Brigade: Lt. Colonel Anensur
Kolyvan Infantry Regiment
Kourin Infantry Regiment
Brigade: Generalmajor Mussin-Pushkin
Vitebsk Infantry Regiment
Kozlov Infantry Regiment
Brigade: Colonel Tuchanowski
12th Jager Regiment (1)
22nd Jager Regiment (1)
Artillery:
Position Battery #15
Light Batteries #13 and #29

Cavalry Corps: Generallieutenant Vassil'shikov (3,000 cavalry)
2nd Hussar Division: Generalmajor Lanskoi
Brigade: Generalmajor Waddolski
Akhtyrsk Hussar Regiment (6)
Marioupol Hussar Regiment (5)
Brigade: Colonel Vassil'shikov
White Russia Hussar Regiment (4)
Alexandria Hussar Regiment (5)
3rd Dragoon Division: Generalmajor Pantschulischev
Brigade: Generalmajor Uschakov
Smolensk Dragoon Regiment
Kurland Dragoon Regiment
Brigade: Generalmajor Umanez
Tver Dragoon Regiment
Kinburn Dragoon Regiment
Horse Artillery Battery #18
Artillery:
Horse Batteries #6 and #7
Reserve Artillery: Generalmajor Nikitin
Position Batteries #10, #13 and #18
Light Batteries #24, #28, #34 and #35
1 Pioneer Company
Brigade: Generalmajor Karpov II (3,000)
Karpov II Don Cossack Regiment
Semintschikov IV Don Cossack Regiment
Lukowken II Don Cossack Regiment
Kuteinikov IV Don Cossack Regiment
Grekov I Don Cossack Regiment
St. Petersburg Opolochenie Cossack Regiment
4th Ukrainian Cossack Regiment
2nd Kalmuck Regiment
Brigade: Brien de Courland (1,500 cavalry)

Forces unknown: RightFieldmarshal Crown Prince of Württemberg
4th Corps: Fieldmarshal Crown Prince of Württemberg (12,000 infantry and 2,500 cavalry)
Cavalry Division: Generalieutenant Prince Adam of Württemberg
Brigade: Generalmajor von Alvensleben
1/, 2/, 3/, 4/Duke Louis Chasseur Regiment #2
1/, 2/, 3/, 4/Crown Prince Dragoon Regiment #3
1st Horse Artillery Battery (6-6pdrs)
Brigade: Generalmajor von Jett
1/, 2/, 3/, 4/Prinz Adam Chasseur Regiment #4
2nd Horse Battery (6-6pdrs)
Infantry: Generallieutenant von Koch
Brigade: Generalmajor von Stockmayer
1/, 2/König Jäger Regiment #9
Light Infantry Regiment #10 (1)
Brigade: Generalmajor Döring
1/, 2/Duke Wilhelm Infantry Regiment #2
1/, 2/Infantry Regiment #3
1/, 2/Infantry Regiment #7
1st Foot Battery
Brigade: Generalmajor Prince of Hohenlohe-Kirchberg
1/, 2/Infantry Regiment #4
1/, 2/Infantry Regiment #6
2nd Foot Battery

Extreme right: General der Infanterie von Wrede
5th Corps: (Austro-Bavarian Forces) GdI von Wrede (18,000 infantry and 3,600 cavalry)
1st Division: FML von Hardegg
Brigade: Colonel von Geramb
Archduke Joseph Hussar Regiment (6)
1st Szekler Grenz Regiment (2)
Wurst Battery (6-6pdrs)
Brigade: Colonel von Mengen
Schwarzenberg Uhlan Regiment (6)
Jäger Battalion
2nd Division: FML von Spleny
Brigade:
Jordis Infantry Regiment (4)
Erzherzog Rudolph Infantry Regiment (4)
Brigade: Generalmajor von Linutillo
Szekler Hussar Regiment (6)
Knesevich Dragoon Regiment (6)
Wurst Battery (6-6pdrs)
Reserve Artillery: Generalmajor von Swertnick
12pdr Brigade Battery (6-12pdrs)
2 6pdr Brigade Battery (6-6pdrs)

Bavarian Contingent:
1st Division: Generallieutenant von Rechberg
Brigade: Generalmajor Prince Karl of Bavaria
1/, 2/1st Bavarian Infantry Regiment
3rd Bavarian Infantry Regiment (1)
1/Oberdonau Landwehr Regiment
3rd Light Infantry Battalion

- Brigade: Generalmajor von Maillot
    - 1st Bavarian Infantry Regiment (1)
    - 2nd Bavarian Infantry Regiment (1)
    - 2/Oberdonau Landwehr Regiment
    - 2nd Light Infantry Battalion
- 1st Light Cavalry Brigade: Generalmajor von Vieregg
    - 1/, 2/, 3/, 4/1st Bavarian Chevauxleger Regiment
    - 1/, 2/, 3/, 4/2nd Bavarian Chevauxleger Regiment
    - 1/, 2/, 3/, 4/7th Bavarian Chevauxleger Regiment
- Artillery:
    - Wurst Battery (6-6pdrs)
    - Light Battery (8-6pdrs)

2nd Division: Generallieutenant von Beckers

- Brigade: Generalmajor von Pappenheim
    - 1/, 2/4th Bavarian Infantry Regiment
    - Combined Battalion of Salzach Landwehr
    - 1/Regen Landwehr
    - 4th Light Battalion
- Brigade: Generalmajor von Zoller
    - 1/, 2/6th Bavarian Infantry Regiment
    - 1/Rezat Landwehr
    - 1st Light Battalion
- 2nd Light Cavalry Brigade: Generalmajor von Elbracht
    - 1/, 2/, 3/, 4/3rd Bavarian Chevauxleger Regiment
    - 1/, 2/, 3/, 4/6th Bavarian Chevauxleger Regiment
- Artillery:
    - Wurst Battery (6-6pdrs)
    - Light Battery (8-6pdrs)

3rd Division: Generallieutenant Lamotte

- Brigade: Generalmajor von Habermann
    - 1/, 2/11th Bavarian Infantry Regiment
    - 7th Bavarian Infantry Regiment (1)
    - 1/Unterdonau Landwehr
    - 1/Iller Landwehr
- Brigade: Generalmajor Deroy
    - 5th Bavarian Infantry Regiment (1)
    - 8th Bavarian Infantry Regiment (1)
    - 9th Bavarian Infantry Regiment (1)
    - 2/Iller Landwehr
    - 1/Isar Landwehr
- 3rd Light Cavalry Brigade: Generalmajor von Elbracht
    - 1/, 2/, 3/, 4/4th Bavarian Chevauxleger Regiment
    - 1/, 2/, 3/, 4/5th Bavarian Chevauxleger Regiment
- Artillery:
    - Wurst Battery (6-6pdrs)
    - Light Battery (8-6pdrs)
    - 4 Heavy Batteries (6-12pdrs ea)

Reserves: Grand Duke Constantine

Russo-Prussian Reserves and Guards: Barclay de Tolly

Cavalry: Generallieutenant Prince Gallizin V (4,000 cavalry)

- 1st Cuirassier Division: Generallieutenant Depreradovich
    - Brigade: Generalmajor Arsenjeff

        - Chevalier Guard Regiment (6)
        - Horse Guard Regiment (6)
    - Brigade: Generalmajor von Rosen
        - Emperor Cuirassier Regiment (4)
        - Empress Cuirassier Regiment (4)
- 2nd Cuirassier Division: Generallieutenant Kretov
    - Brigade: Generalmajor Leontiev
        - Gluchov Cuirassier Regiment (5)
        - Pskof Cuirassier Regiment (5)
    - Brigade: Generalmajor Karatheff
        - Ekaterinoslav Cuirassier Regiment (2)
        - Astrakhan Cuirassier Regiment (4)
- 3rd Cuirassier Division: Generallieutenant Duka
    - Brigade: Generalmajor Protassov
        - Military Order Cuirassier Regiment (5)
        - Little Russia Cuirassier Regiment (4)
    - Brigade: Generalmajor Lewaschoff
        - Novgorod Cuirassier Regiment (4)
        - Starodoub Cuirassier Regiment (5)
- Guard Light Division: Generalmajor Schewitsch
        - Guard Hussar Regiment (6)
        - Guard Dragoon Regiment (6)
        - Guard Uhlan Regiment (6)
        - Guard Horse Battery #1 (12-6pdrs)
        - Guard Horse Battery #2 (12-6pdrs)

Guards Infantry: Generallieutenant Yermolov (12,000 infantry and 4,800 cavalry)

- 1st Guard Division: Generallieutenant Rosen
    - Brigade: Generalmajor Potemkin
        - Preobragenski Guard Infantry Regiment (3)
        - Semenovski Guard Infantry Regiment (3)
    - Brigade: Generalmajor Chrapowitzky
        - Ismailov Guard Infantry Regiment (3)
        - Guard Jager Regiment (3)
        - Guard Military Equippage Battalion and 2 6pdr guns
- 2nd Guard Division: Generalmajor Udom I
    - Brigade: Generalmajor Scheltuchin
        - Lithuania Guard Infantry Regiment (3)
        - Leib-Guard Grenadier Regiment (3)
        - Finland Guard Infantry (2)
        - Pavlov Guard Grenadiers (2)
- Guard Artillery Brigade:
        - 1st and 2nd Guard Position Batteries
        - 1st and 2nd Guard Light Batteries
        - 1 Pioneer Company
- Prussian Guard Cavalry Brigade: Generalmajor von Starkenfels
        - 1/, 2/, 3/, 4/, 5/Garde du Corps Regiment
        - 1/, 2/, 3/, 4/Guard Light Cavalry Regiment
        - Guard Horse Artillery Battery (8-6pdrs)
- Prussian Guard Infantry Brigade: Colonel von Alvensleben
        - 1st Garde Regiment zu Fuss (2) (with three jäger companies)
        - 2nd Garde Regiment zu Fuss (2) (with three jäger companies)
        - Guard Jäger Regiment (1) (with one jäger company)
        - Guard Foot Artillery Battery (8-6pdrs)

Attached:
Baden Leibgarde Grenadier Battalion (872)
Baden Horse Artillery Battery (7-6prs)

Grenadier Corps: Generalleutnant Raevsky (8,000 infantry)
1st Grenadier Division: Generalmajor Tschoglikov
Brigade: Generalmajor Kniaschnin II
Count Arakcheyev Grenadier Regiment (2)
Ekaterinoslav Grenadier Regiment (2)
Brigade: Colonel Jemilianov
Kexholm Grenadier Regiment (2)
Pernau Grenadier Regiment (2)
Brigade:
1st Jager Regiment
3rd Jager Regiment
2nd Grenadier Division: Generalmajor Paskevich
Brigade: Generalmajor Pissarev
Kiev Grenadier Regiment (2)
Moscow Grenadier Regiment (2)
Brigade: Colonel Sulima
Tauride Grenadier Regiment (1)
St. Petersburg Grenadier Regiment (2)
Brigade:
8th Jager Regiment
14th Jager Regiment
3rd Grenadier Division:
Brigade: Generalmajor Damas
Astrakhan Grenadier Regiment (1)
Fangoria Grenadier Regiment (1)
Brigade:
Siberia Grenadier Regiment (2)
Little Russia Grenadier Regiment (2)
Grand Duchess Catherine Grenadier Battalion (1)
Brigade:
26th Jager Regiment
29th Jager Regiment
Artillery:
Light Battery #2
Heavy Batteries #1 and #30
Reserve Artillery: Generalmajor Schussnet
(Note: Known to have had 286 guns)
Position Batteries #2, #5, #7, #13, #28, #29 and #34
Horse Batteries l, #2, #10 and #18
1 Sapper Company
1 Pioneer Company

Appendix XX

German 3rd Corps, 8 February 1814[1]

Royal Saxon Army:
- General Staff (24 / 7)

Cavalry:
- Staff Dragoons (1 / 62)
- 1/, 2/, 3/Cuirassier Regiment (24 / 442 / 434)[2]
- 1/, 2/, 3/Uhlan Regiment (21 / 345 / 329)
- 1/, 2/, 3/Hussar Regiment (27 / 380 / 358)

Line Infantry:
- Staff/, 1/Grenadier Regiment (17 / 464)
- 2/Grenadier Regiment (18 / 658)
- 3/Grenadier Regiment (11 / 649)
- 3/1st Provisional Regiment (12 / 461)
- Staff/, 2/1st Provisional Regiment (17 / 628)
- Staff/, 2/2nd Provisional Regiment (14 / 515)
- 3/2nd Provisional Regiment (16 / 555)
- Jäger Battalion (9 / 361)
- 1/1st Light Regiment (10 / 454)
- 2/1st Light Regiment (8 / 450)
- 2/2nd Light Regiment (12 / 535)

Artillery:
- 1st Horse Battery (six guns) (4 / 139)
- 2nd Horse Battery (six guns) (4 / 138)
- 1st 12pdr Battery (4 / 187)
- 1st 6pdr Battery (4 / 166)
- 1st Reserve Park (4 / 128)
- Sapper-Pontooneer Detachment (1 / 51)

Thuringia-Anhalt Division:
- Weimar Fusilier Battalion (13 / 658)

1 Source: Bogdanovich, M.I., *Istorich Voin l8l4 Goda Vo Frantsiii Nizlozhenich Napoleona I.*

2 Numbers are officers, men and horses. The horse figure probably does not include officer's horses.

Appendix XXI

French forces, Battle of Champaubert, 9 February 1814

Commanding General: Napoleon Bonaparte

1st Old Guard Division: Général de division Friant (4,796)
  1st Brigade: Général de brigade Cambronne
    Staff/, 1/, 2/1st Chasseur à Pied Regiment
    Staff/, 1/2/2nd Chasseur à Pied Regiment
  2nd Brigade: Général de brigade Petit
    Staff/, 1/2/1st Grenadier à Pied Regiment
    Staff/, 1/2/2nd Grenadier à Pied Regiment
  Attached:
    1/, 2/, 3/Guard Sapper Battalion
    3/Guard Marine Battalion
    Guard Engineering Train
  1st Young Guard (1st Voltigeur) Division: Général de division Meunier (4,133)
    1st Voltigeur Regiment
    2nd Voltigeur Regiment
    3rd Voltigeur Regiment
    4th Voltigeur Regiment
  2nd Young Guard (2nd Voltigeur) Division: Général de division Curial (2,840)
    5th Voltigeur Regiment
    6th Voltigeur Regiment
    7th Voltigeur Regiment
    8th Voltigeur Regiment
  1st Guard Cavalry Division: Général de division Colbert (2,582)
    2nd Éclaireur Regiment
    2nd Chevauléger-lancier Regiment
    Chasseurs à cheval de la Garde
    Grenadiers à cheval de la Garde
    Empress Dragoon Regiment
  Horse Artillery:
3rd Guard Cavalry Division: Général de division Laferrière-Lévesque
  1st Brigade: Général de brigade Lyon
    Chasseurs à cheval Regiment (34 / 508)
    Empress Dragoon Regiment (44 / 691)
  2nd Brigade: Général de brigade Letort
    Grenadier à cheval Regiment (45 / 842)
  Guard Artillery: (1,464)
    7 Foot Batteries
    4 Horse Batteries
    Train Pontooneers

VI Corps: Maréchal Marmont
  Division: Général de division Lagrange (4,868)
    1st Line Regiment
    15th Line Regiment

16th Line Regiment
62nd Line Regiment
70th Line Regiment
121st Line Regiment
1st Marine Regiment
1/, 2/, 3/, 4/2nd Marine Regiment
1/, 2/, 3/3rd Marine Regiment
1/, 2/, 3/4th Marine Regiment
3/23rd Line Regiment
1/, 3/37th Line Regiment
8th Division: Général de division Ricard (2,917)
2/2nd Légère Regiment
7/4th Légère Regiment
2/6th Légère Regiment
9th Légère Regiment
16th Légère Regiment
22nd Line Regiment
2/40th Line Regiment
1/50th Line Regiment
69th Line Regiment
1/136th Line Regiment
1/138th Line Regiment
1/142nd Line Regiment
1/144th Line Regiment
1/145th Line Regiment
Artillery:
13 Field Guns (6pdrs and howitzers)
8 12pdrs
9 Horse Guns (6pdrs and howitzers)

I Cavalry Corps: Général de division Bordesoulle
1st Light Cavalry Division: Général de division Merlin
1st Brigade: Général de brigade Wathier
6th Hussar Regiment
7th Hussar Regiment
8th Hussar Regiment
1st Chevauléger Regiment
3rd Chevauléger Regiment
5th Chevauléger Regiment
7th Chevauléger Regiment
8th Chevauléger Regiment
2nd Brigade: Général de brigade Guyon
1st Chasseurs à cheval Regiment
2nd Chasseurs à cheval Regiment
3rd Chasseurs à cheval Regiment
6th Chasseurs à cheval Regiment
8th Chasseurs à cheval Regiment
9th Chasseurs à cheval Regiment
16th Chasseurs à cheval Regiment
25th Chasseurs à cheval Regiment
2nd Heavy Cavalry Division: Général de division Bordesoulle
1st Brigade: Général de brigade Thiry
2nd Cuirassier Regiment

3rd Cuirassier Regiment
6th Cuirassier Regiment
9th Cuirassier Regiment
11th Cuirassier Regiment
12th Cuirassier Regiment
2nd Brigade: Général de brigade Laville
4th Cuirassier Regiment
7th Cuirassier Regiment
14th Cuirassier Regiment
7th Dragoon Regiment
23rd Dragoon Regiment
28th Dragoon Regiment
30th Dragoon Regiment
Artillery: (strengths as of 2/15/14)
3/1st Horse Artillery (2 / 75) (six guns)
1/6th Horse Artillery (detached)
2/1st (bis) Train Battalion (1 / 74)
Det/8th (bis) Train Battalion (0 / 18)

Appendix XXII

Allied forces, Battle of Champaubert, 9 February 1814

9th Corps: Generallieutenant Olsufiev
- 9th Infantry Division: Major-General Udom
  - Brigade: Generalmajor Poltarachi
    - Apcheron Regiment (486)
    - Nacheburg Regiment (563)
  - Brigade: Generalmajor Juschkov II
    - Riajsk Regiment (620)
    - Iakout Regiment (533)
  - Brigade: Major Melnik
    - 10th Jager Regiment (335)
    - 38th Jager Regiment (472)
- 15th Infantry Division: Major-General Kornilov
  - Brigade: Lt. Colonel Anensur
    - Vitebsk Regiment (372)
    - Kozlov Regiment (504)
  - Brigade: Generalmajor Mussin-Pushkin
    - Kolyvan Regiment (417)
    - Kourin Regiment (417)
  - Brigade: Colonel Tuchanowski
    - 12th Jager Regiment (447)
    - 22nd Jager Regiment
  - Artillery:
    - Position Battery #15 (probably not present)
    - Light Batteries #13 and #29

Appendix XXIII

French Corps under Victor, 10 February 1814[1]

II Corps: Maréchal Victor
- 1st Division: Général de brigade Château
  - 1st Brigade:
    - 1/24th Légère (22 / 252)
    - 1/19th Line (27 / 450)
    - 1/27th Line Regiment (12 / 120)
  - 2nd Brigade:
    - 1/11th Légère Regiment (22 / 197)
    - 1/2nd Line Regiment (22 / 132)
    - 1/56th Line Regiment (18 / 250)
  - Artillery and Train: (10 / 206)
    - 17/5th Foot Artillery (2 / 57)
    - 10/6th Foot Artillery (3 / 67)
    - 4-12pdrs, 5-6pdrs and 6-4pdrs
    - Unknown Train: (3 / 82)
- 2nd Division: Général de division Duhèsme
  - 1st Brigade:
    - 1/26th Légère Regiment (25 / 225)
    - 1/, 2/, 4/4th Line Regiment (54 / 761)
    - 1/, 2/10th Line Regiment (41 / 538)
  - 2nd Brigade:
    - 1/, 2/6th Line Regiment
    - 1/72nd Line Regiment
    - 1/93rd Line Regiment
  - Artillery and Train: (10 / 249)
    - 8/9th foot Artillery (2 / 32) (4-8pdrs and two 24pdr howitzers)
    - Unknown Train: (7 / 182)

1 Jacomet, *Campagne de 1814*, p. 159.

Appendix XXIV

French forces, Battle of Montmirail, 11 February 1814[1]

Commanding Officer: Emperor Napoleon I
Napoleon's Escort: Général de division Guyot[2]
1st Chevauléger-lancier Regiment (one squadron)

Chasseurs à cheval de la Garde (one squadron)
Grenadiers à cheval de la Garde (one squadron)
Empress Dragoon Regiment (one squadron)

Old Guard: Maréchal Mortier
- 1st Old Guard Division: Général de division Friant (4,796)
  - 1st Brigade: Général de division Cambronne
    - Staff/, 1/, 2/1st Chasseur à Pied Regiment
    - Staff/, 1/, 2/2nd Chasseur à Pied Regiment
  - 2nd Brigade: Général de division Petit
    - Staff/, 1/, 2/1st Grenadier à Pied Regiment
    - Staff/, 1/, 2/2nd Grenadier à Pied Regiment
  - Attached:
    - 1/, 2/, 3/Guard Sapper Battalion
    - 3/Guard Marine Battalion
    - Guard Engineering Train
- 2nd Old Guard Division: Général de division Michel (3,878)
    - 1/, 2/Flanqueur-Chasseur Regiment
    - 1/, 2/Flanqueur-Grenadier Regiment
    - Vélites of Florence
    - Vélites of Turin
    - 1/, 2/Fusilier-Chasseur Regiment
    - 1/, 2/Fusilier-Grenadier Regiment

Young Guard: Maréchal Ney
- 1st Young Guard (1st Voltigeur) Division: Général de division Meunier (4,133)
    - 1st Voltigeur Regiment
    - 2nd Voltigeur Regiment
    - 3rd Voltigeur Regiment
    - 4th Voltigeur Regiment
- 2nd Young Guard (2nd Voltigeur) Division: Général de division Curial (2,840)
    - 5th Voltigeur Regiment
    - 6th Voltigeur Regiment
    - 7th Voltigeur Regiment

---

1 Strength figures are based on Army Archives, Château Vincennes, C^2 555 for 1 February 1814. Sources: Clerc, *Campagne de Marechal Soult*; French Army Archives, Château Vincennes, C^2 555; French National Archives, Carton AF^{IV} 1665B.

2 These four squadrons were detached from the 1st, 2nd and 3rd Guard Cavalry Divisions, but it is not known from which they came.

- 8th Voltigeur Regiment

1st Guard Cavalry Division: Général de division Colbert (2582)

- 2nd Éclaireur Regiment
- 2nd Chevauléger-lancier Regiment
- Chasseurs à cheval de la Garde
- Grenadiers à cheval de la Garde
- Empress Dragoon Regiment
- Horse Artillery

2nd Guard Cavalry Division: Général de division Léfèbvre-Desnoëttes[3]

- 1st Lancer Regiment (7) (40 / 640)
- Old Guard Chasseurs à cheval Regiment (6) (40 / 627)
- Guard Dragoon Regiment (6) (50 / 750)
- Grenadier à cheval Regiment (6) (55 / 899)
- Gendarmes d'élite (2) (23 / 411)

3rd Guard Cavalry Division: Général de division Laferrière-Lévesque

- 1st Brigade: Général de brigade Lion
  - Chasseurs à cheval Regiment (34 / 508)
  - Empress Dragoon Regiment (44 / 691)
- 2nd Brigade: Général de brigade Letort
  - Grenadier à cheval Regiment (45 / 842)
- Guard Artillery: (1,464)
  - 7 Foot Batteries
  - 4 Horse Batteries
  - Train
  - Pontooneers

VI Corps:

8th Division: Général de division Ricard (2,917)

- 2/2nd Légère Regiment
- 7/4th Légère Regiment
- 2/6th Légère Regiment
- 9th Légère Regiment
- 16th Légère Regiment
- 22nd Line Regiment
- 2/40th Line Regiment
- 2/50th Line Regiment
- 3/65th Line Regiment
- 1/136th Line Regiment
- 1/138th Line Regiment
- 1/142nd Line Regiment
- 1/144th Line Regiment
- 1/145th Line Regiment

Cavalry Division: Général de division Defrance (896)

- 1st Gardes d'honneur
- 2nd Gardes d'honneur
- 3rd Gardes d'honneur
- 4th Gardes d'honneur
- 10th Hussar Regiment

3 Strengths are as of 28 January 1814. Numbers are officers and men.

Appendix XXV

Allied forces, Battle of Montmirail, 11 February 1814[1]

Russian Corps: Generallieutenant von Sacken
11th Corps: Generalmajor von Lieven III
- 10th Division: Generalmajor Sass
  - Brigade: Generalmajor Sokolovsky
    - Jaroslav Infantry Regiment (1)
    - Kursk Infantry Regiment (1)
    - Bieloserk Infantry Regiment (2)
  - Brigade: Colonel Achlestischev
    - 8th Jager Regiment (1)
    - 39th Jager Regiment (1)
- From 16th Division:
  - Brigade: Lt. Colonel Selivanov
    - Kamtchatka Infantry Regiment (1)
    - Okhotsk Infantry Regiment (1)
- 27th Division: Generallieutenant Stawitzky
  - Brigade: Colonel Lewandowsky
    - Odessa Infantry Regiment (1)
    - Vilna Infantry Regiment (1)
  - Brigade: Colonel Alexejev
    - Simbrisk Infantry Regiment (1)
    - Tarnopol Infantry Regiment (1)
  - Brigade: Colonel Kalogruivoff
    - 49th Jager Regiment (1)
    - 50th Jager Regiment (1)
  - Artillery:
    - Position Battery #18
    - Light Batteries #34 and #35

6th Corps: Generallieutenant Por Tallisin II
- 7th Division: Generalmajor Prince Scherbatov
  - Brigade: Colonel Kritschinikov
    - Pskof Infantry Regiment (1)
    - Moscow Infantry Regiment (1)
  - Brigade: Colonel Augustov
    - Sophia Infantry Regiment (1)
    - Libau Infantry Regiment (1)
  - Brigade: Colonel Dieterich
    - 11th Jager Regiment (1)
    - 36th Jager Regiment (1)
- 18th Division: Generalmajor Bernodessov
  - Brigade: Lt. Colonel Blagovenzenko

1 Sources: Clerc, *Campagne de Marechal Soult*; Bogdanovich, M.I., *Istorich Voin l8l4 Goda Vo Frantsiii Nizlozhenich Napoleona I.*

Vladimir Infantry Regiment (1)
Dnieper Infantry Regiment (1)
Brigade: Generalmajor Heidenreich
Tambov Infantry Regiment (1)
Kostroma Infantry Regiment (1)
Brigade: Generalmajor Metcherinov
28th Jager Regiment (1)
32nd Jager Regiment (1)
Artillery:
Position Battery #10
Light Batteries #19 and #24

Cavalry Corps: Generallieutenant Vassil'shikov
2nd Hussar Division: Generalmajor Lanskoi
Brigade: Generalmajor Waddolski
Akhtyrsk Hussar Regiment (6)
Marioupol Hussar Regiment (5)
Brigade: Colonel Vassil'shikov
White Russia Hussar Regiment (4)
Alexandria Hussar Regiment (5)
3rd Dragoon Division: Generalmajor Pantschulischev
Brigade: Generalmajor Uschakov
Smolensk Dragoon Regiment
Kurland Dragoon Regiment
Brigade: Generalmajor Umanez
Tver Dragoon Regiment
Kinburn Dragoon Regiment
Horse Artillery Battery #18
Brigade: Generalmajor Karpov II
Karpov II Don Cossack Regiment
Semintschikov IV Don Cossack Regiment
Lukowken II Don Cossack Regiment
Kuteinikov IV Don Cossack Regiment
Grekov I Don Cossack Regiment
St. Petersburg Opolochenie Cossack Regiment
4th Ukrainian Cossack Regiment
2nd Kalmuck Regiment
Artillery:
Horse Batteries #6 and #7
Reserve Artillery: Generalmajor Nikitin
Position Batteries #10, #13 and #18
Light Batteries #24, #28, #34 and #35
1 Pioneer Company

Prussian 1st Corps: General of Infantry von Yorck
1st Brigade: Generalmajor von Pirch II
1st East Prussian Grenadier Battalion (1)
Silesian Grenadier Battalion (1)
Leib Grenadier Battalion (1)
West Prussian Grenadier Battalion (1)
13th Silesian Landwehr Regiment (4)
1/, 2/, 3/, 4/East Prussian National Cavalry Regiment (with jägers)
6pdr Foot Battery #2

7th Brigade: Generalmajor von Horn
- 1/, 2/, Fus/Leib Infantry Regiment
- 4th Silesian Landwehr Regiment (2)
- 15th Silesian Landwehr Regiment (2)
- Brandenburg Hussar Regiment (with jägers)
- 6pdr Foot Battery #3

Appendix XXVI

French forces, Battle of Vauchamps, 14 February 1814

Commanding Officer: Emperor Napoleon I

Old Guard: Maréchal Mortier[1]
- 1st Old Guard Division: Général de division Friant
  - 1st Brigade: Général de division Cambronne
    - 1/, 2/1st Chasseur à Pied Regiment
    - 1/, 2/2nd Chasseur à Pied Regiment
  - 2nd Brigade: Général de division Petit
    - 1/, 2/1st Grenadier à Pied Regiment
    - 1/, 2/2nd Grenadier à Pied Regiment
  - Attached:
    - 1/, 2/, 3/Guard Sapper Battalion
    - 3/Guard Marine Battalion
    - Guard Engineering Train
- 2nd Old Guard Division: Général de brigade Christiani (3,878)
    - 1/, 2/Flanqueur-Chasseur Regiment
    - 1/, 2/Flanqueur-Grenadier Regiment
    - Vélites of Florence
    - Vélites of Turin
    - 1/, 2/Fusilier-Chasseur Regiment
    - 1/, 2/Fusilier-Grenadier Regiment

Young Guard: Maréchal Ney
- 1st Voltigeur Division: Général de division Meunier (4,133)
    - 1st Voltigeur Regiment
    - 2nd Voltigeur Regiment
    - 3rd Voltigeur Regiment
    - 4th Voltigeur Regiment
- 2nd Voltigeur Division: Général de division Curial (2,840)
    - 5th Voltigeur Regiment
    - 6th Voltigeur Regiment
    - 7th Voltigeur Regiment
    - 8th Voltigeur Regiment
- 2nd Guard Cavalry Division: Général de division Léfèbvre-Desnoëttes[2]
    - 1st Lancer Regiment
    - Old Guard Chasseurs à cheval Regiment
    - Guard Dragoon Regiment
    - Grenadier à cheval Regiment
    - Gendarmes d'élite
- 3rd Guard Cavalry Division: Général de division Laferrière-Lévéque
  - 1st Brigade: Général de brigade Lion

1 The Guard infantry was not engaged significantly and served as a reserve.
2 The strength of the two Guard cavalry divisions was about 3,500 men.

Chasseurs à cheval Regiment
Empress Dragoon Regiment
2nd Brigade: Général de brigade Letort
Grenadier à cheval Regiment
Guard Artillery:
7 Foot Batteries
4 Horse Batteries
Train
Pontooneers

VI Corps: Maréchal Marmont[3]
3rd Division: Général de division Lagrange
1st Line Regiment
15th Line Regiment
16th Line Regiment
62nd Line Regiment
70th Line Regiment
121st Line Regiment
1st Marine Regiment
1/, 2/, 3/, 4/2nd Marine Regiment
1/, 2/, 3/3rd Marine Regiment
1/, 2/, 3/4th Marine Regiment
3/23rd Line Regiment
1/, 3/37th Line Regiment
8th Division: Général de division Ricard
2/2nd Légère Regiment
7/4th Légère Regiment
2/6th Légère Regiment
9th Légère Regiment
16th Légère Regiment
22nd Line Regiment
2/40th Line Regiment
2/50th Line Regiment
3/65th Line Regiment
1/136th Line Regiment
1/138th Line Regiment
1/142nd Line Regiment
1/144th Line Regiment
1/145th Line Regiment
Corps Artillery (as of 2/15/14):
13 Field Guns (6pdrs and howitzers)
8 12pdrs
9 Horse Guns (6pdrs and howitzers)
Det. 1/2nd Foot Artillery (0 / 10)
6/3rd Foot Artillery (2 / 32)
23/3rd Foot Artillery (2 / 6)
25/3rd Foot Artillery (2 / 14)
2/4th Foot Artillery (1 / 14)
11/4th Foot Artillery (2 / 36)
13/5th Foot Artillery (2 / 21)

3 The divisions of Ricard and Lagrange contained about 3,000 men.

14/5th Foot Artillery (2 / 29)
15/5th Foot Artillery (2 / 23)
16/5th Foot Artillery (2 / 42)
27/5th Foot Artillery (2 / 20)
2/1st Horse Artillery (2 / 43)
7/3rd Horse Artillery (2 / 60)
8/5th Horse Artillery (2 / 47)
1/3rd (bis) Train Battalion (1 / 50)
1/4th Principal Train Battalion (1 / 40)
4/4th Principal Train Battalion (1 / 76)
2/8th (bis) Train Battalion (1 / 77)
1/9th (bis) Train Battalion (1 / 47)
5/9th (bis) Train Battalion (1 / 32)
2/12th Principal Train Battalion (1 / 12)
2nd Military Equippage Battalion (0 / 12)

Line Cavalry: Général de division Grouchy[4]
I Cavalry Corps: Général de division Bordesoulle
1st Light Cavalry Division: Général de division Merlin
1st Brigade: Général de brigade Wathier
6th Hussar Regiment
7th Hussar Regiment
8th Hussar Regiment
1st Chevauléger Regiment
3rd Chevauléger Regiment
5th Chevauléger Regiment
7th Chevauléger Regiment
8th Chevauléger Regiment
2nd Brigade: Général de brigade Guyon
1st Chasseurs à cheval Regiment
2nd Chasseurs à cheval Regiment
3rd Chasseurs à cheval Regiment
6th Chasseurs à cheval Regiment
8th Chasseurs à cheval Regiment
9th Chasseurs à cheval Regiment
16th Chasseurs à cheval Regiment
25th Chasseurs à cheval Regiment
2nd Heavy Cavalry Division: Général de division Bordesoulle
1st Brigade: Général de brigade Thiry
2nd Cuirassier Regiment
3rd Cuirassier Regiment
6th Cuirassier Regiment
9th Cuirassier Regiment
11th Cuirassier Regiment
12th Cuirassier Regiment
2nd Brigade: Général de brigade Laville
4th Cuirassier Regiment
7th Cuirassier Regiment
14th Cuirassier Regiment
7th Dragoon Regiment

4 The I and II Cavalry Corps contained about 3,600 men.

23rd Dragoon Regiment
28th Dragoon Regiment
30th Dragoon Regiment
Artillery (strengths as of 2/15/14):
3/1st Horse Artillery (2 / 75) (six guns)
1/6th Horse Artillery (detached)
2/1st (bis) Train Battalion (1 / 74)
Det/8th (bis) Train Battalion (0 / 18)

II Cavalry Corps: Général de division Saint-Germain
2nd Light Cavalry Division: Général de division Berckheim
3rd Brigade: Général de brigade Dommanget
5th Hussar Regiment
9th Hussar Regiment
11th Chasseurs à cheval Regiment
12th Chasseurs à cheval Regiment
2nd Chevauléger Regiment
4th Chevauléger Regiment
4th Brigade: Général de brigade Jamin
10th Hussar Regiment
6th Chevauléger Regiment
7th Chasseurs à cheval Regiment
20th Chasseurs à cheval Regiment
23rd Chasseurs à cheval Regiment
24th Chasseurs à cheval Regiment
2nd Heavy Cavalry Division: Général de division Saint-Germain
3rd Brigade: Général de brigade Blancard
1st Carabinier Regiment
2nd Carabinier Regiment
1st Cuirassier Regiment
4th Brigade: Général de brigade Sopranzy
5th Cuirassier Regiment
8th Cuirassier Regiment
10th Cuirassier Regiment
13th Cuirassier Regiment
Artillery:
2 Horse Batteries
7th Division: Général de division Leval (4,500 men)
Brigade: Général de brigade Pinoteau
1/, 2/10th Légère Infantry Regiment
1/3rd Line Infantry Regiment
1/5th Line Infantry Regiment
1/, 4/130th Line Infantry Regiment
Brigade: Général de brigade Montfort
1/17th Légère Infantry Regiment
1/101st Line Infantry Regiment
1/, 2/105th Line Infantry Regiment
Artillery:
2 Foot Batteries
1 Horse Battery

Appendix XXVII

Allied forces, Battle of Vauchamps, 14 February 1814

Commanding Officer: Feldmarschall Blücher

Prussian 2nd Corps: Generalmajor von Kleist (total: 13,500 men)
- 10th Brigade: Generalmajor von Pirch I
  - 1/, 2/, 3/2nd West Prussian Infantry Regiment
  - 1/, 2/, 3/7th Reserve Infantry Regiment (the 3/7th was taken prisoner on 2/14/14)
  - 1/, 2/, 3/, 4/, 5/8th Silesian Landwehr Cavalry Regiment
  - 6pdr Foot Battery #8 (8-6pdrs)
- 11th Brigade: Generalmajor von Ziethen
  - 1/, 2/, Fus/1st Silesian Infantry Regiment
  - 1/, 2/, Fus/10th Reserve Infantry Regiment
  - Silesian Schützen Battalion (two companies)
  - 1/, 2/, 3/, 4/1st Silesian Hussar Regiment
  - 6pdr Foot Battery #9 (8-6pdrs)
- 12th Brigade: Generalmajor Prince August of Prussia
  - 1/, 2/, Fus/2nd Silesian Infantry Regiment
  - 11th Reserve Infantry Regiment (2)
  - 1/, 2/, 3/, 4/7th Silesian Landwehr Cavalry Regiment
  - 6pdr Foot Artillery Battery #21 (8-6pdrs)
- Cavalry Brigade: Oberst von Haackee
  - 1/, 2/, 3/, 4/Silesian Cuirassier Regiment
  - 1/, 2/, 3/, 4/Silesian Uhlan Regiment
  - Horse Battery #8 (8-6pdrs)
- Brigade: Generalmajor von Roder
  - 1/, 2/, 3/, 4/East Prussian Cuirassier Regiment
  - 1/, 2/, 3/, 4/Brandenburg Cuirassier Regiment
- Artillery: Oberst Braun
  - 12pdr Foot Batteries #3 and #6 (8-12pdrs ea)
  - 6pdr Foot Batteries #11 and #13 (8-6pdrs ea)
  - Horse Batteries #9 and #10 (8-6pdrs ea)
  - Howitzer Battery #1

10th Corps: Generallieutenant Kapsevich (6,500 men)
- 8th Division: Generalmajor Urusov
  - Brigade: Colonel Schenschen
    - Archangel Infantry Regiment (2)
    - Schusselburg Infantry Regiment (2)
    - Old Ingremannland Infantry Regiment (2)
  - Brigade: Colonel Suthof
    - 7th Jager Regiment (2)
    - 37th Jager Regiment (1)
- 22nd Division: Generalmajor Turtschaninov
  - Brigade: Generalmajor Schapskoy
    - Olonetz Infantry Regiment (1)

Viatka Infantry Regiment (2)
Staroskol Infantry Regiment (1)
Brigade: Generalmajor Vassil'shikov
29th Jager Regiment (1)
45th Jager Regiment (1)
Artillery:
Position Battery #39
Light Batteries #3 and #56

9th Corps:
8th Division: Generalmajor Udom II

(This corps was destroyed on 2/9/14. The 1,500 survivors were organized into three to four combined battalions and a single battery. Its precise organization is unknown and was quite temporary, as it lost another 600 casualties and all its guns at the end of this battle. Horse Battery #8 is reported to have been present at the battle and may well have been assigned to this division.)

Appendix XXVIII

Württemberg Contingent, 15 February 1814[1]

4th Corps: Fieldmarshal Crown Prince of Württemberg
Advanced Guard: Generalmajor von Alvensleben
5th (Württemberg) Jäger Regiment (4)
Archduke Ferdinand Hussar Regiment (5) (Austrian)
1st Horse Artillery Battery (four 6pdrs and two howitzers)
Brigade: Generalmajor von Stockmayer
König Jäger Regiment #9 (2)
Light Infantry Regiment #10 (2)
Austrian Pioneer Company, Cpt. Wonjatschek

Main body: Feldzeugmeister von Franquemont
Cavalry: Generalmajor von Jett
Prince Adam Jäger zu Pferd Regiment #4 (4)
Duke Louis Chasseur Regiment #2 (4)
Crown Prince Dragoon Regiment #1 (4)
2nd Horse Battery (four 6pdrs and two howitzers)
Infantry: Generallieutenant von Koch
Brigade: Generalmajor Döring
Duke Wilhelm Infantry Regiment #2 (2)
Infantry Regiment #3 (2)
Infantry Regiment #7 (2)
1st Foot Battery (four 6pdrs and two howitzers)
Brigade: Generalmajor Prince of Hohenlohe-Kirchberg
Infantry Regiment #4 (2)
Infantry Regiment #6 (2)
2nd Foot Battery (four 6pdrs and two howitzers)
Austrian Brigade: Generalmajor von Schäffer
Colloredo Infantry Regiment (2)
von Zach Infantry Regiment (3)
6pdr Foot Battery, Oberleutnant Jerasky
12pdr Foot Battery, Oberlieutenant Weigel

1 Source: von Hiller F., *Geschichte des Feldzuges 1814 gegen Frankreich unter besonder Berücksichtigung der Anteilnahme der Königlich Württembergischen Truppen.*

Appendix XXIX

French Army of Lyon, 15-16 February 1814[1]

Commander-in-Chief: Duke of Castiglione, Maréchal Augereau

Chief of Staff: Général de brigade Ducasse
Commander of Artillery: Général de division Desvaux de Saint-Maurice
- Division of Reserve of Lyon: Général de division Baron Musnier
  - Brigade: Général de brigade Ordonneau
    - 1/, 2/1st Légère Regiment (38 / 1,268)
    - 1/, 2/16th Line Regiment (43 / 1,165)
  - Brigade: Général de brigade Gudin
    - 1/, 2/23rd Légère Regiment (44 / 993)
    - 1/, 2/7th Line Regiment (41 / 1,149)
    - 1 six-gun battery attached (120)
- Division of Catalogne: Général de brigade Pannetier
  - Brigade: Général de brigade Estève[2]
    - 1/, 2/20th Line Regiment (44 / 1,077)
    - 1/, 2/67th Line Regiment (38 / 1,160)
  - Brigade: Général de brigade Pouchelon[3]
    - 16th Légère Regiment (three companies) (425)
    - 2/32nd Légère Regiment (465)
    - 62nd Line Regiment (470)
    - 64th Line Regiment (501)
    - 145th Line Regiment (547)
    - 1 six-gun battery attached (133)
- Nismes Reserve Division: Général de brigade Bardet[4]
    - 6/23rd Légère Regiment (730)
    - 6/20th Line Regiment (647)
    - 6/60th Line Regiment (721)
    - 6/67th Line Regiment (665)
    - 6/79th Line Regiment (721)
    - 6/115th Line Regiment (841)
    - Detachment of 2nd Marine Artillery (four guns) (117)
- Cavalry: Général de division Digeon
  - Brigade: Général de brigade Guillemet[5]

1 Sources: Du Chasse, *Les Operations de l'Armée de Lyon 1814*; Koch, F., *Memoirs pour servier à l'Histoire de la Campagne de 1814*. Koch provides figures and organization for 15 February, while du Chasse does the same for 16 February. Koch's figures are single numbers, while those of du Chasse are two. Koch's figures and organization were used in preference to du Chasse, except when they were very close.
2 These are veteran forces withdrawn from Spain.
3 This brigade was formed with conscripts thrown together with the cadres of these battalions.
4 This brigade consisted of conscripts thrown in with the battalion cadres. It had originally been destined to reinforce the Army of Aragon.
5 These units were veteran troops withdrawn from Spain.

1/, 2/, 3/, 4/4th Hussar Regiment (20 / 630)
1/, 2/, 3/12th Hussar Regiment (20 / 525)
1/, 2/, 3/, 4/13th Cuirassier Regiment (35 / 627)

Cavalry of Lyon: Général de division Count St. Sulpice
Detachments of:
4th Gardes d'honneur (1 / 22)
4th Chasseurs à cheval Regiment («squadron) (56) (cadre)
31st Chasseurs à cheval Regiment («squadron) (63) (cadre)
1st Hussar Regiment (1 / 92) (cadre)
179 men detached to Bourg
164 gendarmes detached in Bourg

Artillery:
2nd Horse Artillery (39)
3rd Foot Artillery (2 / 94)
7th Foot Artillery (2 / 80)
Marine Foot Artillery (16 / 498)
Train (2 / 100)
6 – 8pdrs
17 – 6pdrs
4 Howitzers

National Guards Brigade: Général de brigade Redmond (garrison of Lyon)
1/, 2/2nd Toulon Regiment (2) (870)
Rhône National Guard Battalion (1) (408)
Haute-Loire National Guard Battalion (1) (397)
Puy-de-Dôme National Guard Battalion (1) (299)
Cantal National Guard Battalion (1) (271)
Haute-Vienne National Guard Battalion (1) (993)
l'Indre National Guard Battalion (1) (535)
la Nièvre National Guard Battalion (1) (264)
Hautes-Alpes National Guard Battalion (1) (601) (garrison of Brançon)
Naval Gunners and Train (two guns) (53)

Division: Général de division Marchand
Brigade: Général de Serrant
8th Légère Regiment (1) (430)
18th Légère Regiment (2) (718)
26th Légère Regiment (320)
1st Line Regiment (400)
5th Line Regiment (443)
7th Line Regiment (320)
11th Line Regiment (393)
23rd Line Regiment (243)
60th Line Regiment (428)
7/79th Line Regiment (405)
81st Line Regiment (483)
4th and 31st Chasseurs à cheval Regiments (1 squadron ea) (103)
Volunteer Gunners (110)
2 Free Companies (250)
Customs Guards Company (160)

Appendix XXX

Austrian Army advancing on Lyon, 16 February 1814

1st (Austrian) Corps: Feldmarschallieutenant Bianchi
- 1st Division: Generalmajor Scheither
  - 5th Jäger Battalion (1) (393)
  - Broder Grenz Infantry Regiment (1) (620)
  - Kaiser Hussar Regiment (6)
  - Westphalian Hussar Regiment (6)
  - Vincent Chevauxleger Regiment (6)
    - Total cavalry: 1,621
  - Artillery:
    - 1 Battery
- 2nd Division: Generalmajor Bakony
  - 1st Brigade: Oberst Retzey
    - Hiller Infantry Regiment (3)
    - Collorado Infantry Regiment (3)
      - Total: 4,184 men
  - Artillery:
    - 1 Battery
  - 2nd Brigade: Generalmajor Quallenberg
    - Esterhazy Infantry Regiment (3)
    - Davidovich Infantry Regiment (3)
      - Total: 3,728 men
  - Artillery:
    - 1 Battery
- 3rd Division: Prince von Wied-Runckel
  - 1st Brigade: Graf von Salins
    - de Ligne Infantry Regiment (3)
    - Czartorisky Infantry Regiment (3)
      - Total: 4,120 men
  - Artillery:
    - 1 Battery
  - 2nd Brigade: Oberst Soldenhoffen
    - Giulay Infantry Regiment
    - Reuss Infantry Regiment
      - Total: five battalions and 2,319 men
  - Artillery:
    - 1 Battery

2nd (Austrian) Corps: Feldmarschallieutenant Baron Wimpffen
- 1st Brigade: Generalmajor von Gall
  - 1,609 Infantry
  - 464 Cavalry
  - 1 Battery
- 2nd Brigade: Graf Haugwitz
  - Simbschen Infantry Regiment
  - Hessen-Homburg Infantry Regiment

Total: seven battalions and 3,568 men
1 Battery
3rd Brigade: Generalmajor von Mumb
Froon Infantry Regiment
Erbach Infantry Regiment
de Vaux Infantry Regiment
Argenteau Infantry Regiment
Kottulinski Infantry Regiment
Total: eight-and-a-half battalions and 3,689 men
1 Battery

3rd (Austrian) Corps: Erbprinz Hessen-Homburg
Division: Emile von Hesse-Darmstadt
1st Brigade: Generalmajor Folenius
4 battalions – 2,838 men
1 battery
2nd Brigade: Generalmajor Moser
5 battalions – 1,925 men
1 battery
3rd Brigade: Generalmajor Fürstenwerther
5 battalions – 3,412 men
Cavalry Division: Generalmajor Graf Wartensleben
Brigade: Genralmajor Kuttalek
Herzog Albert Cuirassier Regiment
Lothringen Cuirassier Regiment
Prince Ferdinand Cuirassier Regiment
Erzherzog Franz Cuirassier Regiment
Total: 22 squadrons and 2,700 men
1 Battery
Detached on lines of communication:
Erzherzog Ferdinand Hussar Regiment (6) (700)
Detachment on left bank: Feldmarschallieutenant I. Hardegg
1st Brigade: Generalmajor Graf H. Hardegg
Deutsch Banat Grenz Regiment (2) (1,000)
Riesch Hussar Regiment (6)
Hessen-Homburg Hussar Regiment (6)
Cossacks (6)
Total: 1,624 cavalry
1 Battery
2nd Brigade: Prince von Coburg
Gradiscaner Grenz Regiment (1)
Vogelsang Infantry Regiment (1)
Erzherzog Rainer Infantry Regiment (1)
Total infantry: 1,150
Brigade:
Erzherzog Johann Dragoon Regiment (6)
Kienmayer Hussar Regiment (6)
Unknown Cavalry (6 squadrons)
Total: 1,580 cavalry
1 Battery

Appendix XXXI

French forces, Montereau, 17-18 February 1814[1]

Right wing:

- II Corps: Maréchal Victor (as of 2/15/14)
  - 1st Division: Général de brigade Châteaux
    - 1st Brigade:
      - 1/24th Légère Regiment
      - 1/19th Line Regiment
      - 1/37th Line Regiment
    - 2nd Brigade:
      - 1/2nd Line Regiment
      - 1/56th Line Regiment
      - 1/11th Légère Regiment
  - 2nd Division: Général de division Duhèsme
    - 1st Brigade:
      - 1/26th Légère Regiment
      - 1/, 2/4th Line Regiment
      - 1/, 2/18th Line Regiment
    - 2nd Brigade:
      - 1/, 2/46th Line Regiment
      - 1/72nd Line Regiment
      - 1/93rd Line Regiment
- Reserve of Paris: Général de division Gérard
  - 1st Division:
    - 1st Brigade:
      - 3/12th Légère Regiment
      - 6/29th Légère Regiment
      - 8/32nd Line Regiment
      - 6/58th Line Regiment
    - 2nd Brigade:
      - 3/135th Line Regiment
      - 7/15th Légère Regiment
      - 2/5th Légère Regiment
  - 2nd Division:
    - 1st Brigade:
      - 4/26th Line Regiment
      - 86th Line Regiment
      - 82nd Line Regiment
    - 2nd Brigade:
      - 121st Line Regiment
      - 3/122nd Line Regiment
      - 2/142nd Line Regiment

1 Sources: *Spectateur* Militaire; French National Archives, Carton AF^{IV} 1665B.

Artillery:
- 11 6pdrs and howitzers
- 4 12pdrs
- 5/17th Foot Artillery
- 10/6th Foot Artillery
- 8/9th Foot Artillery
- 24/9th Foot Artillery
- 7th (bis) Train Battalion
- 14th Principal Train Battalion
- 7th Principal Train Battalion

V Cavalry Corps: Général de division l'Héritier (as of 2/9/14)
- 3rd Light Cavalry Division: Général de division Piré
  - 5th Brigade: Général de brigade Suzervie
    - 3rd Hussar Regiment
    - 26th Chasseurs à cheval Regiment
  - 6th Brigade: Général de brigade Ducoëtlosquet
    - 14th Chasseurs à cheval Regiment
    - 27th Chasseurs à cheval Regiment
- 3rd Heavy Cavalry Division: Général de division Briche
  - 5th Brigade: Général de brigade Montelegier
    - 2nd Dragoon Regiment
    - 6th Dragoon Regiment
    - 11th Dragoon Regiment
  - 6th Brigade: Général de brigade Ludot
    - 13th Dragoon Regiment
    - 15th Dragoon Regiment
- 4th Heavy Cavalry Division: Général de division l'Héritier
  - 7th Brigade: Général de brigade Lamotte
    - 18th Dragoon Regiment
    - 19th Dragoon Regiment
    - 20th Dragoon Regiment
  - 8th Brigade: Général de brigade Collaert
    - 22nd Dragoon Regiment
    - 25th Dragoon Regiment
  - Artillery:
    - 10 6pdrs and howitzers

I Cavalry Corps: Général de division Bordesoulle[2]
- Organization unknown

Left wing: Maréchal Oudinot
- 5th Division Young Guard: Général de division Rottembourg (as of 2/14/14)
  - Brigades: Charrière and Bauduin
    - 1st Tirailleur Regiment
    - 5th Tirailleur Regiment
    - 6th Tirailleur Regiment
    - 7th Tirailleur Regiment
    - 8th Tirailleur Regiment

2 A detachment of 500 men from depots en route to the main body of the corps, which was attached to Marmont and Mortier.

Detachment of Flanqueurs from the Army of Spain: Général de division P. Boyer
Brigade: Général de brigade Gauthier
1/ and 2/2nd Légère Regiment
1/24th Line Regiment
1/ and 4/122nd Line Regiment
6/33rd Line Regiment (conscripts)

VI Cavalry Corps: Kellermann (as of 2/9/14, but organization not complete until 2/20/14)
III Cavalry Corps:
4th Light Cavalry Division: Général de division Jacquinot
7th Brigade: Général de brigade Ameil
4th Chasseurs à cheval Regiment
5th Chasseurs à cheval Regiment
10th Chasseurs à cheval Regiment
13th Chasseurs à cheval Regiment
15th Chasseurs à cheval Regiment
28th Chasseurs à cheval Regiment
8th Brigade: Général de brigade Wolf
9th Chevauléger Lancier Regiment
21st Chasseurs à cheval Regiment
22nd Chasseurs à cheval Regiment
2nd Hussar Regiment
4th Hussar Regiment
12nd Hussar Regiment
5th Heavy Cavalry Division: Général de division Trelliard (from Spain)
9th Brigade: Général de brigade Ismert
4th Dragoon Regiment
14th Dragoon Regiment
16th Dragoon Regiment
10th Brigade: Général de brigade Ormancy
17th Dragoon Regiment
24th Dragoon Regiment
27th Dragoon Regiment
6th Heavy Cavalry Division: Général de division Roussel d'Hurbal
11th Brigade: Général de brigade Sparre
1/, 2/5th Dragoon Regiment
1/, 2/12th Dragoon Regiment
12th Brigade: Général de brigade Rigaud
21st Dragoon Regiment
26th Dragoon Regiment

Center:
XI Corps: Maréchal Macdonald (as of 3/1/14)
Division: Général de division Albert
Brigade: Général de brigade Beauvais
3/139th Line Regiment
1/ and 2/Régiment de Brest
Brigade: Général de brigade Schäffe
1/140th Line Regiment
1/ and 2/Régiment de Rochefort
Division: Général de division Amey
Brigade: Général de brigade Chevenot
1/ and 2/149th Line Regiment

1/ and 2/Garde Nationale de Calvados
1/Garde Nationale de Manche
Division: Général de division Brayer
Brigade: Général de brigade Simmer
2/ and 6/19th Line Regiment
3/5th Line Regiment
3/11th Line Regiment
Brigade: Général de brigade Quiot
1/107th Line Regiment
1/ and 2/Garde Nationale du Norde

Provisional Cavalry Corps: Général de division Pajol
Brigade: Général de brigade Delort (460 men)
Detachments from:
5th Chasseurs à cheval Regiment
10th Chasseurs à cheval Regiment
11th Chasseurs à cheval Regiment
13th Chasseurs à cheval Regiment
21st Chasseurs à cheval Regiment
29th Chasseurs à cheval Regiment
Brigade: Général de brigade Grouvel (476 men)
Detachments from:
12th Dragoon Regiment
16th Dragoon Regiment
21st Dragoon Regiment
24th Dragoon Regiment
26th Dragoon Regiment
29th Dragoon Regiment
Brigade: Général de brigade Ducoëtlosquet (400 men)
Detachments from:
2nd Hussar Regiment
4th Hussar Regiment
12th Hussar Regiment
Detachment:
2nd Régiment de Cherbourg
Artillery:
1 horse battery (6 guns)

At Montereau:
National Guard Division: Général de division Pacthod (8,000 men)
1st Brigade: Général de brigade Rost
1st Regiment of Sarthe
3rd Regiment of Indre et Loire
2nd Brigade: Général de brigade Bont,
2nd Regiment of Loire et Cher
5th Regiment of Seine et Marne
3rd Brigade: Général de brigade Kozinsky
4th Regiment Maine et Loire
Artillery:
26/6th Foot Artillery (2 8pdrs and 4 4pdrs)
Det/2nd (bis) Train Battalion
Det/4th Principal Train Battalion
Reserve:
24/6th Foot Artillery (4 12pdrs and 2 howitzers)

12/8th Foot Artillery (4-6pdrs and 2 howitzers)
12th (bis) Train Battalion Train
8/3rd Horse Artillery (4 6pdrs and 2 howitzers)

At Pont sur Yonne:
Detachment: Montbrun
200 Customs men
1,000 National Guardsmen

At Sens:
Brigade: Général de brigade Allix (2,400 men)
4/115th Line Regiment
Detachments from:
121st Line Regiment
153rd Line Regiment
Garde Nationale de Vendee
Departmental Companies of Jura, Dour and Côte d'Or
23rd Dragoon Regiment
Gendarmes à cheval

In reserve:
Imperial Guard: Emperor Napoleon I
Old Guard Division: Général de division Friant
Brigade: Général de brigade Petit
1st Grenadier à Pied Regiment
2nd Grenadier à Pied Regiment
Brigade: Général de brigade Cambronne
1st Chasseur à Pied Regiment
2nd Chasseur à Pied Regiment
Young Guard: Maréchal Ney
1st Young Guard Division: Général de division Meunier
Brigade:
1st Voltigeur Regiment
2nd Voltigeur Regiment
3rd Voltigeur Regiment
4th Voltigeur Regiment
2nd Young Guard Division: Général de division Curial
Brigade:
5th Voltigeur Regiment
6th Voltigeur Regiment
7th Voltigeur Regiment
8th Voltigeur Regiment
1st Guard Cavalry Division: Général de division Colbert
Organization unknown

Detached to Marmont and Mortier:
2nd Guard Cavalry Division: Général de division Léfèbvre-Desnoëttes
1st Regiment Chevauléger-lancier de la Garde (Polish)
Empress Dragoon Regiment
3rd Éclaireur Regiment
3rd Guard Cavalry Division: Général de division Laferrière-Lévesque
Grenadier à cheval Regiment
Chasseurs à cheval Regiment
1st Éclaireur Regiment
Attached: Général de brigade Pacz
Polish Line Lancer Regiment

Appendix XXXII

Battle order of the Allied 4th Corps, 15 February 1814

Commanding Officer: Crown Prince of Württemberg

Advanced Guard:
- Brigade: Generalmajor von Alvensleben
  - Jäger zu Pferd Regiment #5 (4 squadrons)
  - (Austrian) Erzherzog Ferdinand Hussar Regiment (5 squadrons)
  - 1 Horse Battery
- Brigade: Generalmajor von Stockmayer
  - 1/, 2/König Jäger Regiment #9
  - 1/, 2/Light Infantry Regiment #10
  - 1 Austrian Pioneer Company

Main body: Feldzeugmeister Graf von Franquemont
- Cavalry: Generalleutnant Prince Adam von Württemberg
  - Brigade: Generalmajor von Jett
    - 1/, 2/, 3/, 4/Duke Louis Chasseur Regiment #2
    - 1/, 2/, 3/, 4/Prinz Adam Chasseur Regiment #4
    - 1st Horse Artillery Battery (6-6pdrs)
    - 2nd Horse Artillery Battery (6-6pdrs)
- Infantry: Generalleutnant von Koch
  - Brigade: Generalmajor Döring
    - 1/, 2/Herzog Wilhelm Infantry Regiment #2
    - 1/, 2/3rd Infantry Regiment
    - 1/, 2/7th Infantry Regiment
    - 1st Foot Battery
  - Brigade: Generalmajor Prince of Hohenlohe-Kirchberg
    - 1/, 2/Infantry Regiment #4
    - 1/, 2/Infantry Regiment #6
    - 2nd Foot Battery
  - Austrian Brigade: Generalmajor von Schäffer
    - Colloredo Infantry Regiment (2)
    - von Zach Infantry Regiment (3)
    - Austrian Foot Battery
  - Reserve Artillery:
    - 1 Austrian 12pdr Position Battery

Appendix XXXIII

Battle order of the Prussian 1st Corps, 16 February 1814

1st (Prussian) Corps: General of Infantry von Yorck (total strength: 13,715 men)
- 1st Division: Generalmajor von Horn
  - 1st Brigade: Oberst von Losthin
    - Combined Grenadier Battalion
    - 1st East Prussian / West Prussian Grenadier Battalion
    - Combined Grenadier Battalion
    - Silesian Grenadier Battalion
    - Leib Grenadier Battalion
    - Combined Landwehr Battalion
    - 5th Silesian Landwehr Regiment
    - 13th Silesian Landwehr Regiment
    - East Prussian Jägers (2 comapnies)
  - 7th Brigade: Oberst von Roedlich
    - Leib Infantry Regiment (3)
    - Combined Landwehr Battalion
    - 4th Silesian Landwehr Regiment
    - 15th Silesian Landwehr Regiment
    - East Prussian National Cavalry Regiment (4)
  - Division Artillery:
    - 6pdr Foot Battery #3 (8 guns)
    - 1/2 12pdr Foot Battery #1 (4 guns)
    - 1/2 Horse Battery #3 (4 6pdr guns)
- 2nd Division: Generallieutenant Prince Wilhelm of Prussia
  - 2nd Brigade: Oberst von Warburg
    - Combined Fusilier Battalion
    - Fus/1st East Prussian Regiment
    - Fus/2nd East Prussian Regiment
    - 1st East Prussian Regiment (2)
    - Combined Battalion
    - 1/, 2/2nd East Prussian Regiment
    - Combined Battalion
    - Remains of the 6th Silesian Landwehr Regiment
  - 8th Brigade: Oberstlieutenant von Hiller
    - Combined Battalion
    - Fus/Brandenburg Infantry Regiment
    - 3/12th Reserve Infantry Regiment
    - Combined Battalion
    - 1/, 2/Brandenburg Infantry Regiment
    - Combined Battalion
    - 1/, 2/12th Reserve Infantry Regiment
    - Combined Battalion
    - 14th Silesian Landwehr Regiment
    - Mecklenburg-Strelitz Regiment (4)

Division Artillery:
- 6pdr Foot Battery #1 (8 guns)
- 1/2 12pdr Foot Battery #1 (4 guns)
- 1/2 Horse Battery #3 (4 6pdr guns)

Reserve Cavalry: Generalmajor von Jürgass

Abteilung: Oberst Count von Henkel
- Lithuanian Dragoon Regiment (5)
- 1st West Prussian Dragoon Regiment (4)
- Combined Landwehr Cavalry Regiment (5)
- 5th Silesian Landwehr Cavalry Regiment
- 10th Silesian Landwehr Cavalry Regiment

Abteilung: Generalmajor Katzeler
- Brandenburg Hussar Regiment (4)
- Brandenburg Uhlan Regiment (4)
- 2nd Leib Hussar Regiment (4)
- Horse Battery #2 (8 6pdrs)
- Horse Battery #12 (8 6pdrs)

Artillery: Oberst von Schmidt
- Howitzers of 12pdr Battery #2 (2 10pdr howitzers)
- 12pdr Foot Batteries #2 (12 12pdrs)
- Horse Battery #1 (8 6pdrs)
- 6pdr Foot Battery #2 (8 6pdrs)
- 6pdr Foot Battery #15 (8 6pdrs)

Park Column:
- Park Column #13
- 1st Pioneer Company, Lt. von Salvigny
- 2nd Pioneer Company, Lt. Rhaden

Total of about 13,715 men

Appendix XXXIV

Battle order of the Prussian 2nd Corps, 16 February 1814

2nd Corps: Generalleutnant von Kleist (total: 9,800 men)
- 9th Brigade: Generalmajor von Klüx
  - 1/, 2/, Fus/1st West Prussian Infantry Regiment
  - 6th Reserve Infantry Regiment (2)
  - Silesian National Cavalry Regiment
  - 7th Silesian Landwehr Cavalry Regiment
  - 6pdr Foot Battery #7 (8-6pdrs)
- 10th Brigade: Generalmajor von Pirch I
  - 1/, 2/, 3/2nd West Prussian Infantry Regiment
  - Combined Battalion
  - 7th Reserve Infantry Regiment
  - Combined Battalion
  - 1/, 2/, Fus/1st Silesian Infantry Regiment
  - 10th Reserve Infantry Regiment (2)
  - Combined Battalion
  - 1/, 2/2nd Silesian Infantry Regiment
  - 11th Reserve Infantry Regiment
  - Combined Fusilier Battalion
  - Silesian Schützen (2 companies)
  - 2nd Silesian Hussar Regiment
  - 8th Silesian Landwehr Cavalry Regiment
  - 6pdr Foot Battery #8 (8-6pdrs)
- Reserve Cavalry: Generalleutnant von Ziethen
  - Brigade: Oberst von Blücher
    - Neumark Dragoon Regiment
    - 1st Silesian Hussar Regiment
  - Brigade: Oberst Graf Haacke
    - Silesian Cuirassier Regiment
    - Silesian Uhlan Regiment
  - Brigade: Oberst von Wrangel
    - East Prussian Cuirassier Regiment "Grand Duke Constantine"
    - Brandenburg Cuirassier Regiment
  - Artillery:
    - Horse Artillery Battery #7 (8-6pdrs)
    - Horse Artillery Battery #8 (8-6pdrs)
  - Reserve Artillery: Oberstleutnant Lehmann
    - Horse Batteries #9 and #10 (8-6pdrs ea)
    - 6pdr Foot Batteries #9 and #11 (8-6pdrs ea)
    - Howitzer Battery #1

Total of about 9,800 men

Sacken's Russian Army Corps, 18 February 1814:
It is not known if this division changed its organization, but on 18 February it had 50 staff officers, 472 senior officers, 1,356 NCOs and 12,297 rank and file.

Appendix XXXV

Battle order of Kapsevich's Russian Army Corps, 17 February 1814

Detached from 8th Corps:
- 17th Infantry Division: Generalmajor Kern
  - Bieloserk Infantry Regiment
  - 48th Jager Regiment

Detached from 9th Corps:
- 1,500 survivors of Olsufiev's 9th Corps and 12 guns

10th Corps: Generallieutenant Rudsevich
- 8th Division: Generalmajor Urusov
  - Brigade: Colonel Schenschen
    - Archangel Infantry Regiment
    - Schusselburg Infantry Regiment
    - Old Ingremannland Infantry Regiment
  - Brigade: Colonel Suthof
    - 7th Jager Regiment
    - 37th Jager Regiment
  - Artillery:
    - 2 Batteries

22nd Division: Generalmajor Turtschaninov
- Brigade: Generalmajor Schapskoy
  - Olonetz Infantry Regiment (1)
  - Staroskol Infantry Regiment (1)
- Brigade: Generalmajor Vassil'shikov
  - 29th Jager Regiment (1)
  - 45th Jager Regiment (1)
- Artillery:
  - Light Battery #34 (12 guns)
  - Light Battery #33 (5 guns)
  - 1 Pioneer Company

Cavalry Corps: Generallieutenant Korff
- 1st Dragoon Division: Generallieutenant Borosdin II
  - Brigade: Generalmajor Gengross
    - Mitau Dragoon Regiment (3)
    - New Russia Dragoon Regiment (3)
  - Brigade: Generalmajor Pohl
    - Kargopol Dragoon Regiment (4)
  - Brigade: Generalmajor Denissiev
    - Sieversk Chasseurs à cheval Regiment (4)
    - Livonia Chasseurs à cheval Regiment (1)
    - Ukrainian Cossack Division: Generalmajor Witte
  - Brigade: Generalmajor Scherbatov
    - 2nd Ukrainian Cossack Regiment
    - 3rd Ukrainian Cossack Regiment
  - Other:
    - Selimonov II Don Cossack Regiment
    - Don Cossack Battery #2 (6 guns)

Total strength: 7,987 rank and file; officers not included.

Appendix XXXVI

French army of Lyon, 20 February 1814

Commanding Officer: Maréchal de Castiglione
Chief of Staff: Général de brigade Ducasse
Artillery Commander: Général de division Desvaux de Saint-Maurice

Lyon Reserve Division: Général de division Musnier
 1st Brigade: Général de brigade Pouchelon
  Troops arriving successively in Lyon (3,100)
 2nd Brigade: Général de Ordonneau
  1/, 2/20th Line Regiment
  1/, 2/67th Line Regiment
   Total: (2,300)
  1/, 2/2nd Toulon Regiment (1,250)
  1/145th Line Regiment (580)
2nd (Catalogne) Division: Général de division Pannetier de Valdotte
 1st Brigade: Général de brigade Gudin (2,400)
  1/, 2/7th Line Regiment
  1/, 2/23rd Légère Regiment
 2nd Brigade: Général de brigade Estève (2,300)
  1/, 2/16th Line Regiment
  1/, 2/1st Légère Regiment
Nismes Reserve Division: Général de brigade Bardet (4,400)
  Organization unknown
Cavalry Division: Général de division Digeon
  1/, 2/, 3/, 4/13th Cuirassier Regiment
  1/, 2/, 3/, 4/4th Hussar Regiment
  1/, 2/, 3/12th Hussar Regiment
   Total: (1,850)
  Gardes d'honneur (350)
 Artillery: (800 men)
  27 guns
 National Guard Reserve Brigade: Général de brigade Rémond
  2 Battalions (1,500)

Corps Francs: (200 foot and 20 mounted)
Corps: Général de Marchand (between Grenoble, Barreaux, Voreppe and La Chavanne)
  8 guns
  3,900 infantry
  110 cavalry

Corps: Major Groslambert (guarding Mont-Cenis)
  600 infantry
  26 cavalry

Appendix XXXVII

Organization of the French Cavalry after reorganization and arrival of Spanish reinforcements, 20 February 1814[1]

Commanding Officer: Colonel-Général of Chasseurs Count Grouchy

I Cavalry Corps: Général de division Bordesoulle
- 1st Light Cavalry Division: Général de division Merlin
  - 1st Brigade: Général de brigade Wathier
    - 6th Hussar Regiment (147)
    - 7th Hussar Regiment (71)
    - 8th Hussar Regiment (84)
    - 1st Chevauléger Regiment (177)
    - 3rd Chevauléger Regiment (167)
    - 5th Chevauléger Regiment (164)
    - 7th Chevauléger Regiment (122)
    - 8th Chevauléger Regiment (131)
  - 2nd Brigade: Général de brigade Guyon
    - 1st Chasseurs à cheval Regiment (145)
    - 2nd Chasseurs à cheval Regiment (95)
    - 3rd Chasseurs à cheval Regiment (107)
    - 6th Chasseurs à cheval Regiment (94)
    - 8th Chasseurs à cheval Regiment (135)
    - 9th Chasseurs à cheval Regiment (134)
    - 16th Chasseurs à cheval Regiment (141)
    - 25th Chasseurs à cheval Regiment (105)
- 1st Heavy Cavalry Division: Général de division Bordesoulle
  - 1st Brigade: Général de brigade Thiry
    - 2nd Cuirassier Regiment (125)
    - 3rd Cuirassier Regiment (175)
    - 6th Cuirassier Regiment (191)
    - 9th Cuirassier Regiment (146)
    - 11th Cuirassier Regiment (166)
    - 12th Cuirassier Regiment (192)
  - 2nd Brigade: Général de brigade Laville
    - 4th Cuirassier Regiment (170)
    - 7th Cuirassier Regiment (148)
    - 14th Cuirassier Regiment (199)
    - 7th Dragoon Regiment (120)
    - 23rd Dragoon Regiment (179)
    - 28th Dragoon Regiment (196)
    - 30th Dragoon Regiment (153)
  - Artillery:
    - 2 Horse Batteries (172)

1 Source: von Damitz, K., *Geschichte des Feldzuges von 1814*, Vol. II, Table VI.

II Cavalry Corps: Général de division Count Saint-Germain
2nd Light Cavalry Division: Général de division Maurin
3rd Brigade: Général de brigade Dommanget
5th Hussar Regiment (185)
9th Hussar Regiment (123)
11th Chasseurs à cheval Regiment (98)
12th Chasseurs à cheval Regiment (124)
2nd Chevauléger Regiment (131)
4th Chevauléger Regiment (177)
4th Brigade: Général de brigade Jamin
6th Chevauléger Regiment (192)
7th Chasseurs à cheval Regiment (182)
20th Chasseurs à cheval Regiment (177)
23rd Chasseurs à cheval Regiment (203)
24th Chasseurs à cheval Regiment (208)
2nd Heavy Cavalry Division: Général de division Saint-Germain
3rd Brigade: Général de brigade Blancard
1st Carabinier Regiment (143)
2nd Carabinier Regiment (196)
1st Cuirassier Regiment (188)
4th Brigade: Général de brigade Sopranzy
5th Cuirassier Regiment (160)
8th Cuirassier Regiment (98)
10th Cuirassier Regiment (108)
13th Cuirassier Regiment (143)
Artillery:
1 Horse Battery (83)

V Cavalry Corps: Général de division Milhaud[2]
3rd Light Cavalry Division: Général de division Piré
5th Brigade: Général de brigade Subervie
3rd Hussar Regiment (12 / 133)[3]
26th Chasseur Cheval Regiment (22 / 274)
6th Brigade:
14th Chasseurs à cheval Regiment (6 / 112)
27th Chasseurs à cheval Regiment (12 / 125)
3rd Heavy Cavalry Division: Général de division Briche
5th Brigade: Général de brigade Montelegier
2nd Dragoon Regiment (25 / 281)
6th Dragoon Regiment (21 / 276)
11th Dragoon Regiment (26 / 383)
6th Brigade: Général de brigade Ludot
13th Dragoon Regiment (15 / 119)
15th Dragoon Regiment (20 / 210)
4th Heavy Cavalry Division: Général de division l'Héritier
7th Brigade: Général de brigade Lamotte
18th Dragoon Regiment (14 / 194)
19th Dragoon Regiment (19 / 158)
20th Dragoon Regiment (12 / 97)

2 French Archives, Carton C[2] 557.
3 Numbers are officers and men.

8th Brigade: Général de brigade Collaert
22nd Dragoon Regiment (17 / 236)
25th Dragoon Regiment (2 / 361)
Artillery:
4/2nd Horse Artillery (2 / 48)
2/3rd Horse Artillery (2 / 42)
8/6th Horse Artillery (2 / 41)
Total guns:
4 – 6pdrs
6 – 4pdrs
4 – 24pdr howitzers
1/8th Principal Train Battalion (1 / 44)
1/12th Principal Train Battalion (1 / 56)
2/14th Principal Train Battalion (0 / 26)

VI Cavalry Corps: Général de division Kellermann, Count de Valmy
4th Light Division: Général de division Jacquinot
7th Brigade: Général de brigade Ameil
5th Chasseurs à cheval Regiment (207)
4th Chasseurs à cheval Regiment (123)
10th Chasseurs à cheval Regiment (170)
13th Chasseurs à cheval Regiment (303)
15th Chasseurs à cheval Regiment (93)
28th Chasseurs à cheval Regiment (83)
8th Brigade: Général de brigade Wolf
9th Chevauléger Regiment (116)
21st Chasseurs à cheval Regiment (95)
22nd Chasseurs à cheval Regiment (117)
2nd Hussar Regiment (178)
4th Hussar Regiment (116)
12th Hussar Regiment (64)
5th Heavy Cavalry Division: Général de division Trelliard
9th Brigade: Général de brigade Ismert
4th Dragoon Regiment (570)
14th Dragoon Regiment (395)
16th Dragoon Regiment (255)
10th Brigade: Général de brigade Ormancy
17th Dragoon Regiment (339)
24th Dragoon Regiment (106)
27th Dragoon Regiment (502)
6th Heavy Cavalry Division: Général de Roussel d'Hurbal
11th Brigade: Général de brigade Sparre
5th Dragoon Regiment (532)
12th Dragoon Regiment (478)
12th Brigade: Général de brigade Rigaud
21st Dragoon Regiment (621)
26th Dragoon Regiment (674)
Division: Général de division Defrance
1st Gardes d'honneur Regiment (139)
2nd Gardes d'honneur Regiment (128)
3rd Gardes d'honneur Regiment (140)
4th Gardes d'honneur Regiment (172)
10th Hussar Regiment (317)

Appendix XXXVIII

French XI Corps, 21 February 1814[1]

XI Corps: Maréchal Macdonald, duc de Tarente
- Division: Général de division Albert
  - 1st Brigade:
    - 28th Légère Regiment (47 / 692)
    - 139th Line Regiment (22 / 405)
    - 1/Régiment de Brest (21 / 314)
    - 2/Régiment de Brest (9 / 335)
    - 3/Régiment de Brest (18 / 418)
  - 2nd Brigade:
    - 7th Line Regiment (27 / 647)
    - 140th Line Regiment (35 / 400)
    - Regiment de Rochefort (17 / 597)
  - Artillery: (strength as of 3/15/14)
    - 15/4th Foot Artillery (44)
    - 18/6th Foot Artillery (36)
    - 2/5th Horse Artillery (60)
    - 2/9th Principal Train Battalion (16)
    - 3/6th Principal Train Battalion (64)
    - 2/11th Principal Train Battalion (101)
- Division: Général de division Amey
  - 2nd Brigade:
    - 46th Line Regiment (17 / 270)
    - 1er Bataillon de Calvados (10 / 177)
    - 1er Bataillon de la Manche (4 / 260)
  - Artillery: (strength as of 3/15/14)
    - 6/4th Horse Artillery (4-8pdrs and 12 howitzers) (31)
    - 1/5th Principal Train Battalion (39)
- Division: Général de division Brayer
  - 1st Brigade:
    - 13th Hussar Regiment (15 / 267)
    - Grenadiers/3rd Swiss Regiment (3 / 39)
    - 19th Légère Regiment (20/360)
    - 5th Line Regiment (11 / 95)
    - 11th Line Regiment (7 / 109)
    - 107th Line Regiment (35 / 400)
  - 2nd Brigade:
    - 86th Line Regiment (10 / 589)
    - Gardes Nationale du Nord (34 / 782)
  - Artillery: (strength as of 3/15/14)
    - 6/1st Foot Artillery (25)
    - 19/2nd Foot Artillery (52)
    - 20/5th Foot Artillery (52)

1 French Archives, Carton C[2] 556.

1/8th Principal Train Battalion (79)
2/5th Principal Train Battalion (56)

Corps Artillery: (strength as of 2/21/14)
Foot Artillery (11 / 397)
Horse Artillery (2 / 50)
Train (11 / 616)
12 12pdrs
4 8pdrs
12 6pdrs
9 24pdr howitzers
28 12pdr caissons
6 8pdr caissons
20 6pdr caissons
19 howitzer caissons
18 infantry caissons

Reserve Artillery: (strength as of 3/15/14)
22/1st Foot Artillery (20)
18/4th Foot Artillery (11)
27/1st Foot Artillery (1)
Artillery Artisans (1)
4/1st (bis) Train Battalion (2)
1/11th Principal Train Battalion (19)
1/13th Principal Train Battalion (23)
3/14th Principal Train Battalion
4/14th Principal Train Battalion (47)
6/3rd (bis) Train Battalion (33)
3/5th Principal Train Battalion (24)
1/11th Principal Train Battalion

Appendix XXXIX

French II and VII Corps, 22 February 1814[1]

II Corps: Maréchal Victor, Duc de Bellune
- 1st Division: Général de division Duhèsme
  - 1st Brigade:
    - 1/24th Légère Regiment (22 / 170)
    - 11th Légère Regiment (34 / 160)
    - 2nd Line Regiment (15 / 49)
    - 1/19th Line Regiment (32 / 295)
    - 1/37th Line Regiment (12 / 100)
    - 56th Line Regiment (12 / 200)
  - 2nd Brigade:
    - 26th Légère Regiment (20 / 175)
    - 4th Line Regiment (23 / 337)
    - 18th Line Regiment (21 / 271)
    - 46th Line Regiment (10 / 239)
    - 7th Line Regiment (15 / 140)
    - 93rd Line Regiment (12 / 120)
  - Artillery: (4 / 100) (8 6pdrs and 2 howitzers)
  - Train: (1 / 83)
- 2nd Division: Général de division Dufour
  - 1st Brigade:
    - 12th Légère Regiment (14 / 134)
    - 29th Légère Regiment (15 / 201)
    - 32nd Line Regiment (10 / 190)
    - 58th Line Regiment (16 / 115)
    - 5th Légère Regiment (12 / 120)
    - 15th Légère Regiment (11 / 70)
    - 135th Line Regiment (15 / 68)
    - 155th Line Regiment (14 / 366)
  - 2nd Brigade:
    - 26th Line Regiment (6 / 115)
    - 82nd Line Regiment (16 / 297)
    - 86th Line Regiment (13 / 157)
    - 122nd Line Regiment (15 / 335)
    - 142nd Line Regiment (13 / 232)
  - Artillery: (4 / 100) (8 6pdrs and 2 howitzers)
  - Train: (1 / 88)
- Corps Artillery Reserve:
    - Artillery: (3 / 84) (4 12pdrs, 4 6pdrs and 4 howitzers)
    - Train: (2 / 150)
    - Park:
    - Artillery: (3 / 84) (1 6pdr and 2 4pdr and 3 howitzers)
    - Train: (1 / 112)

1 Source: French Archives, Cartons C² 555, C² 556.

- Cavalry: Général de division Roussel
    - 21st Dragoon Regiment (42 / 577)
    - 26th Dragoon Regiment (37 / 569)
    - Det/4th Dragoon Regiment (3 / 62)
    - Det/5th Dragoon Regiment (12 / 170)
    - Det/14th Dragoon Regiment (3 / 90)
    - Det/17th Dragoon Regiment (7 / 156)
    - Det/12th Dragoon Regiment (11 / 147)
    - Det/16th Dragoon Regiment (1 / 46)
  - Artillery:
    - 2/2nd Horse Artillery (3 / 105)
    - 2/6th Train Battalion (3 / 55)
    - Det/7th Principal Train Battalion (1 / 48)
    - 3/, 5/10th (bis) Train Battalion (0 / 123)

VII Corps: Maréchal Oudinot, duc de Reggio

- 5th Young Guard Division: Général de division Rottembourg
  - 1st Brigade: Général de brigade Charrière
    - 5th Voltigeur Regiment (20 / 535)
    - 6th Voltigeur Regiment (25 / 560)
  - 2nd Brigade: Général de brigade Bauduin
    - 7th Voltigeur Regiment (42 / 1,108)
    - 8th Voltigeur Regiment (9 / 259)
  - Artillery:
    - 11th Young Guard Artillery Company (6-6pdrs and 2 howitzers) (2 / 94)
    - 9th Guard Train Company (1 / 46)
- 9th Division: Général de division P. Boyer
  - 1st Brigade: Général de brigade Gruyère
    - 1/2nd Line Regiment (16 / 337)
    - 2/2nd Line Regiment (10 / 248)
    - 6/2nd Line Regiment (11 / 335)
    - 1/24th Line Regiment (18 / 448)
    - 6/36th Line Regiment (14 / 510)
    - 1/122nd Line Regiment (24 / 447)
    - 4/122nd Line Regiment (15 / 269)
  - 2nd Brigade: Général de brigade Chassé
    - 1/16th Légère Regiment (14 / 498)
    - 1/8th Line Regiment (10 / 421)
    - 1/28th Line Regiment (19 / 311)
    - 3/28th Line Regiment (14 / 308)
    - 1/54th Line Regiment (17 / 466)
  - Artillery:
    - 22/5th Foot Artillery (2 / 74)
    - 10/8th Foot Artillery (2 / 70) (8-6pdrs and 4 howitzers)
    - 2/4th Principal Train Battalion (1 / 23)
    - 2/9th (bis) Train Battalion (1 / 121)
  - Reserve:
    - 19/1st Foot Regiment (1 / 96) (5 4pdrs, 2 8pdrs and 1 howitzer)
    - 12th (bis) Train Battalion Train (1 / 111)
    - 2nd (bis) Train Battalion (0 / 33)
    - 8/3rd Horse Artillery (2 / 70) (4 6pdrs and two howitzers)
    - Train: (2 / 72)

Appendix XL

6th Heavy Cavalry Division, 22 February 1814[1]

6th Heavy Cavalry Division:
- 11th Brigade: Général de brigade Sparre
  - 5th Dragoon Regiment (25 / 393)
  - 12th Dragoon Regiment (28 / 325)
- 12th Brigade: Général de brigade Rigaud
  - 21st Dragoon Regiment (unknown)
  - 26th Dragoon Regiment (unknown)
- Artillery:
  - 3/3rd Horse Artillery (3 / 84)
  - 3/2nd Horse Artillery (3 / 96)
  - 2/5th Principal Train Battalion (1 / 117)
  - 1/2nd (bis) Train Battalion (0 / 14)
  - 5/6th Principal Train Battalion (1 / 132)

1 French Archives, Carton C^2 557.

Appendix XLI

Prussian 2nd Corps, 24 February 1814

Commanding General: Generallieutenant von Kleist

- 9th Brigade: Generalmajor von Klüx
  - Fus/, 1/, 2/1st West Prussian Infantry Regiment
  - Fus/6th Reserve Infantry Regiment
  - 6th Reserve Infantry Regiment (1)
  - 6pdr Foot Battery #7
  - 7th Silesian Landwehr Cavalry Regiment (4)
  - Silesian National Hussar Regiment (4)
- 10th Brigade: Generalmajor von Pirch I
  - Fus/, 1/, 2/2nd West Prussian Infantry Regiment
  - Combined Fusilier Battalion von Haase
  - 2nd Silesian Infantry Regiment (1)
  - 7th Reserve Infantry Regiment (1)
  - 1st Silesian Infantry Regiment (1)
  - Schützen Battalion (2 companies)
  - 6pdr Foot Battery #8
  - 2nd Silesian Hussar Regiment (4)
  - 8th Silesian Landwehr Cavalry Regiment (4)
- Cavalry Reserve: Generallieutenant von Ziethen
  - Brigade: Oberstlieutenant von Blücher
    - Neumark Dragoon Regiment (4)
    - 1st Silesian Hussar Regiment (4)
  - Brigade: Major von Wrangel
    - Grand Duke Constantine Cuirassier Regiment (4)
    - Brandenburg Cuirassier Regiment (4)
  - Brigade: Oberstlieutenant Count von Haacke
    - Silesian Cuirassier Regiment (4)
    - Silesian Uhlan Regiment (4)
  - Brigade: Generalmajor Prince Biron (detached to the infantry)
    - 2nd Silesian Hussar Regiment (4)
    - Silesian National Hussar Regiment (4)
  - Artillery:
    - Horse Battery #7
    - Horse Battery #8
    - Artillery Reserve: Oberstlieutenant von Lehmann
    - Horse Battery #9
    - Horse Battery #10
    - 6pdr Battery #9
    - 6pdr Battery #11
    - 7pdr Howitzer Battery #1

Appendix XLII

German 3rd Corps, 24 February 1814[1]

Royal Saxon Army:
- General Staff (24 / 7)

Cavalry:
- Staff Dragoons (1 / 59)
- 1/, 2/, 3/Cuirassier Regiment (27 / 442 / 422)
- 1/, 2/, 3/Uhlan Regiment (27 / 367 / 361)
- 1/, 2/, 3/Hussar Regiment (28 / 422 / 419)

Line Infantry:
- Staff/, 1/Grenadier Regiment (15 / 619)
- 2/Grenadier Regiment (18 / 638)
- 3/Grenadier Regiment (14 / 645)
- Staff/, 2/1st Provisional Regiment (13 / 439)
- 3/1st Provisional Regiment (17 / 577)
- Staff/, 2/Provisional Regiment (14 / 506)
- 3/Provisional Regiment (16 / 535)
- Jäger Battalion (10 / 363)
- 1/1st Light Regiment (9 / 436)
- 2/1st Light Regiment (8 / 434)
- 2/2nd Light Regiment (12 / 520)

Artillery:
- 1st Horse Battery (6 guns) (4 / 130)
- 2nd Horse Battery (6 guns) (4 / 129)
- 1st 12pdr Battery (3 / 170)
- 1st 6pdr Battery (4 / 147)
- 3rd 6pdr Battery (1 / 57)
- 1st Reserve Park (3/92)
- Sapper-Pontooneer Detachment (2 / 51)

Thuringia-Anhalt Division:
- Weimar Fusilier Battalion (13 / 609)
- Gotha Battalion (19 / 895)
- Schwarzenberg Battalion (10 / 541)
- Bernberg Battalion (Landwehr) (11 / 459)
- Weimar Landwehr Battalion (6 / 540)
- Gotha Landwehr Battalion (15 / 518)
- Weimar and Gotha Jäger Squadron (5 / 51 / 51)
- Weimar Freiwilliger Jäger zu Fuss Company (3 / 83)
- Gotha Freiwilliger Jäger zu Fuss Company (3 / 83)

1 Source: Bücher, L.F., *Der Feldzug des dritten detuschen Armee-Corps in Flandern.*

Appendix XLIII

Saxon Landwehr regiments, 28 February 1814

1st Landwehr Regiment: Oberstleutnant von Arnsdorf
1st "Dresden" Battalion: Oberstleutnant von der Mosel
2nd "1st Wittenberg" Battalion: Major von François
3rd "1st Niederlausitz" Battalion: Major von Könnitz
2nd Landwehr Regiment: Major von Wolan
1st "1st Thurngian" Battalion: Major von Taucher
2nd "2nd Thurngian" Battalion: Major von Panitz
3rd "1st Voigtl-Neustädt» Battalion: Major von Römer
3rd Landwehr Regiment: Oberst von Dierschen
1st «1st Leipzig» Battalion: Hauptmann von Zimmerman
2nd «Erzgeberg» Battalion: Major von Elterlein
3rd «Schönberg» Battalion: Major von Kommerslaedt
4th Landwehr Regiment: Major von Selmnitz (interum)
1st «Meissner» Battalion: Major von Selmnitz
2nd «2nd Leipzig» Battalion: Major von Bünau
3rd «1st Oberlausitz» Battalion: Major von Buchner
5th Landwehr Regiment: unknown
1st «2nd Meissner» Battalion: Hauptmann von Sahr
2nd «2nd Wittenberg» Battalion: Hauptmann von Roos
3rd «2nd Niederlausitz» Battalion: Major von Köckritz
6th Landwehr Regiment: unknown
1st «2nd Oberlausitz» Battalion: Hauptmann von Unwerth
2nd «2nd Erzgeberg» Battalion: Hauptmann von Einsiedel
3rd «2nd Voigtl.-Neustädt» Battalion: Hauptmann von Lindemann
7th Landwehr Regiment: unknown
1st «3rd Oberlausitz» Battalion: Hauptmann von Steindel
2nd «3rd Leipzig» Battalion: Hauptmann von schreibershofen
3rd «3rd Erzgeberg» Battalion: Major von Borberg

Appendix XLIV

Austrian Army of the South, February 1814[1]

Geneva

Division: General of Cavalry Prince Hessen-Homburg
- Brigade: Generalmajor Baron Zechmeister
  - Jäger Battalion #6
  - Broder Grenz Regiment (1)
  - Liechtenstein Hussar Regiment (6)
  - 6pdr Horse Battery
- Brigade: Generalmajor Klopfstein
  - W. Colloredo Infantry Regiment (3)
  - Kaunitz Infantry Regiment (3)
- Brigade: Feldmarshcall-Lieutenant Klebelsberg
  - Peterwardeiner Grenz Regiment (1)
  - 2 6pdr Brigade Batteries
  - Lewenehr Dragoon Regiment (2)

In Geneva:
- Reuss Greitz Infantry Regiment (3)
- Levenher Dragoon Regiment (4)
- Blankenstein Hussar Regiment (6)
- 6pdr Cavalry Battery

1st Column: Feldmarschall-Lieutenant Baron Bianchi
- Brigade: Generalmajor Raigecourt
  - Deutsch Banat Grenz Regiment (2)
  - Hessen-Homburg Hussar Regiment (6)
  - Riesch Dragoon Regiment (6)
- Brigade: Generalmajor Scheither
  - Jäger Battalion #5
  - Warasdiner Kreutzer Grenz Regiment (1)
  - Kaiser Hussar Regiment (6)
  - Saint-Vincent Chevauxleger Regiment (6)
  - 6pdr Cavalry Battery

Division: Feldmarschall-Lieutenant Wied Runkel
- Brigade:
  - de Ligne Infantry Regiment (3)
  - Czartorisky Infantry Regiment (3)
  - 6pdr Brigade Battery
- Brigade: Generalmajor Quasdanovich
  - Albert Gyulai Infantry Regiment (3)
  - Reuss Plauen Infantry Regiment (3)

Reserve Division: Feldmarschall-Lieutenant Bianchi
- Brigade: Generalmajor Hirsch
  - Hiller Infantry Regiment (2)
  - H. Colloredo Infantry Regiment (2)

1 Source: von Plotho, *Der Krieg in Deutschland und Frankreich*.

Brigade: Generalmajor Count Haugwitz
Hessen-Homburg Infantry Regiment (2)
Simbschen Infantry Regiment (2)
Brigade: Generalmajor Quallenberg
Esterhazy Infantry Regiment (2)
Davidovich Infantry Regiment (2)
Grenadier Brigade: Generalmajor Fürstenwerther
Grenadier Battalion, Iarossy
Grenadier Battalion, Oklopsia
Grenadier Battalion, Berger
Grenadier Battalion, Obermeyer
Cuirassier Division: Feldmarschall-Lieutenant Lederer
Brigade: Generalmajor Rothkirch
Erzherzog Franz Cuirassier Regiment
Kronprinz Ferdinand Cuirassier Regiment
Brigade: Generalmajor Kutalek
Herzog Albert Cuirassier Regiment
Lothringen Cuirassier Regiment
2nd Column: Feldmarschall-Lieutenant Baron Wimpffen
Light Division: Generalmajor von Coburg
Brigade: Generalmajor Mumb
Gradiscaner Grenz Regiment (1)
1st Wallachian Grenz Regiment (1)
Kienmayer Hussar Regiment (6)
6pdr Cavalry Battery
Brigade: Generalmajor Watzel
Argenteau Infantry Regiment (4)
Erbach Infantry Regiment (3)
6pdr Brigade Battery
Austro-German Legion:
Brigade: Generalmajor Count Bentheim
1st Hussar Regiment
2nd Hussar Regiment
4 Infantry Battalions

Reserve or 6th German Confederation Corps: Feldmarschall-Lieutenant Prince Phillip of Hessen-Homburg
Brigade: Generalmajor Metschery
J. Colloredo Infantry Regiment (2)
Zach Infantry Regiment (3)
Brigade: Oberst Moser
Grossherzoglich Würzburg Infantry Regiment (3)
Fürst Reuss Infantry Regiment (1)
Brigade: Oberst Isenburg Buebingen
Frankfurt Infantry Regiment
Fürst Isenburg Infantry Regiment
Fulda Infantry Battalion
Hesse-Darmstadt Division: Generallieutenant Prince Emile of Hesse-Darmstadt
Brigade: Generalmajor von Schaeffer
1/, 2/, 3/Leibgarde Infantry Regiment
1/, 2/, 3/Leib-Infantry Regiment
Brigade: Generalmajor von Gall
1/, 2/, 3/Erbgrossherzog Infantry Regiment
1/, 2/Light Infantry Regiment
Chevauxleger Regiment
Foot Battery (8 guns)

Appendix XLV

Forces under General Marchand, February 1814

Commander-in-chief: General de division Marchand

Brigade: General de brigade Serrant
3/18th Légère Regiment (16 / 352)
1/18th Line Regiment (20 / 550)
4/5th Line Regiment (19 / 407)
4/11th Line Regiment (19 / 560)
3/23rd Line Regiment (15 / 360)
7/79th Line Regiment (15 / 189)
7/81st Line Regiment (12 / 263)
3/1st Line Regiment (20 / 606)
Customs Guards (20 / 159)
4th Chasseurs à cheval Regiment (5 / 38)
31st Chasseurs à cheval Regiment (1 / 22)
Foot Artillery (1 / 23)
Gendarmes (4 / 92)

Detached to Mont-Cenis: Commandant Gros Lambert
7th Line Regiment (2 / 67)
9th Line Regiment (4 / 205)
53rd Line Regiment (0 / 125)
156th Line Regiment (0 / 73)
Sappers (0 / 49)
19th Chasseurs à cheval Regiment (1 / 25)

Joined in March:
Division: General de division Count Vedel
1st Brigade: General de brigade Baron de Lefosse
4/7th Line Regiment (20 / 700)
3/153rd Line Regiment (20 / 820)
2nd Brigade: Major Olivet
7/20th Line Regiment (15 / 625)
10/62nd Line Regiment (20 / 648)
Attached:
14th Hussar Regiment (3 / 80)
1/1st Sapper Battalion (3 / 149)
1/1st Bataillon de Train d'Equippage (2 / 120)
28/4th Foot Artillery Regiment (2 / 120) (8-6pdrs and 2-24pdr howitzers)
Division: General de brigade Pouchain
3/35th Line Regiment (20 / 418)
8/35th Line Regiment (21 / 739)
1/112nd Line Regiment (21 / 684)
4/112nd Line Regiment (20 / 639)
Gendarmes à cheval of 29th and 30th Legion (26 / 268)
Division: General de division Beurmann
1st Brigade: General de brigade Ricard

1/32nd Légère Regiment (15 / 885)
3/116th Line Regiment (16 / 734)

2nd Brigade: Colonel Gay
1/, 2/79th Line Regiment (40 / 1,760)
1/, 2/116th Line Regiment (38 / 1,462)

3rd Brigade: Colonel Grange
1/, 2/102nd Line Regiment (43 / 1,657)
1/, 2/115th Line Regiment (31 / 1,769)

Detachments:
3/102nd Line Regiment (20 / 631)

Artillery:
Artillery (15 / 369)
Gendarmes (1 / 16)
Artisans (0 / 151)

Appendix XLVI

Austrian Army of the South, 1 March 1814[1]

1st Lieutenancy: Feldmarschal-leutnant Count Bubna
- Division: Feldmarschal-leutnant Bubna
  - Brigade: Generalmajor Zechmeister
    - 6th Jäger Battalion
    - Broder Grenz Regiment (1 battalion)
    - Liechtenstein Hussar Regiment (6 squadrons)
  - Brigade: Generalmajor Klopfstein
    - W. Colloredo Infantry Regiment (3 battalions)
    - Kaunitz Infantry Regiment (3 battalions)
  - Artillery:
    - 1 Battery
- Division: Feldmarschal-leutnant Klebelsberg
    - Levenher Dragoon Regiment (2)
    - Peterwardeiner Grenz Regiment (1 battalion)
- Garrison of Geneva:
    - Reuss-Greitz Infantry Regiment (3 battalions)
    - Levenher Dragoon Regiment (4 squadrons)
    - Blanckenstein Hussar Regiment (6 squadrons)
    - 1 Battery

2nd Lieutenancy: Feldmarschal-leutnant Baron Bianchi
- Division: Feldmarshcal-leutnant Ig. Hardegg
  - Brigade: Generalmajor Raigecourt
    - Deutsch-Banat Grenz Regiment (2 battalions)
    - Hessen-Homburg Hussar Regiment (6 squadrons)
    - Reisch Dragoon Regiment (6 squadrons)
  - Brigade: Generalmajor Scheither
    - 5th Jäger Battalion
    - Warasdiner-Kreutzer Grenz Regiment (1 battalion)
    - Kaiser Hussar Regiment (6 squadrons)
    - Vincent Chevauxleger Regiment (6 squadrons)
  - Artillery:
    - 2 Light Batteries
- Division: Generalmajor Prince von Wied-Runckel
  - Brigade:
    - Prince de Ligne Infantry Regiment (3 battalions)
    - Czartorisky Infantry Regiment (3 battalions)
  - Brigade: Generalmajor Quasdanovitch
    - Albert Giulay Infantry Regiment (3 battalions)
    - Reuss-Plauen Infantry Regiment (3 battalions)
  - Artillery:
    - 2 Batteries

1 Source: Koch, F., *Memoirs pour servier à l'Histoire.*

Division: Feldmarschal-leutnant Bianchi
- Brigade: Generalmajor Hirsch
  - Hiller Infantry Regiment (2 battalions)
  - J. Colloredo Infantry Regiment (2 battalions)
- Brigade: Generalmajor Haugwitz
  - Hessen-Homburg Infantry Regiment (2 battalions)
  - Simbschen Infantry Regiment (2 battalions)
- Brigade: Generalmajor Quallenberg
  - Esterhazy Infantry Regiment (2 battalions)
  - Davidovich Infantry Regiment (2 battalions)
- Artillery:
  - 3 batteries

Division: Feldmarschal-leutnant Lederer
- Brigade: Generalmajor Fürstenwerther
  - Grenadier Battalions (5 battalions)
- Brigade: Generalmajor Rothkirch
  - Erzherzog Frederick Cuirassier Regiment (6 squadrons)
  - Prince Ferdinand Cuirassier Regiment (6 squadrons)
- Brigade: Generalmajor Kutalek
  - Erzherzog Albert Cuirassier Regiment (6 squadrons)
  - Lothringen Cuirassier Regiment (6 squadrons)
  - 3rd Lieutenancy: Feldmarschal-leutnant Wimpffen
- Brigade: Generalmajor Prince Colberg
  - Gradiscaner Grenz Regiment (1 battalion)
  - 1st Wallachian Grenz Regiment (1 battalion)
  - Keinmayer Hussar Regiment (6 squadrons)
  - Bentheim German Legion: Generalmajor Bentheim
  - 1st Bentheim German Legion Hussar Regiment (6 squadrons)
  - 2nd Bentheim German Legion Hussar Regiment (6 squadrons)
  - Bentheim German Legion Infantry (4 battalions)

Division: Feldmarschal-leutnant Wimpffen
- Brigade: Generalmajor Mumb
  - Froon Infantry Regiment (3 battalions)
  - Devaux Infantry Regiment (3 battalions)
- Brigade: Unknown
  - Argenteau Infantry Regiment (4 battalions)
  - Erbach Infantry Regiment (3 battalions)
- Artillery:
  - 2 batteries

Division: Unknown
- Brigade: Generalmajor Metschery
  - J. Colloredo Infantry Regiment (2 battalions)
  - Zach Infantry Regiment (3 battalions)
  - Ferdinand Hussar Regiment (6 squadrons)
- Brigade: Oberst Moser
  - Würzburg Infantry Regiment (3 battalions)
  - Reuss Infantry Battalion
- Brigade: Oberst Isenburg Buebingen
  - Frankfurt Infantry Battalion (1 battalion)
  - Isenburg Infantry Battalion (1 battalion)
  - Fulda Infantry Battalion (1 battalion)
- Artillery:
  - 1 Battery

Division: Prince Emil von Hessen
- Brigade: Generalmajor Schäffer
  - Hessian Leib-Garde Regiment (3)
  - Hessian Guard Infantry Regiment (3)
- Brigade: Generalmajor Gall
  - Erbprinz (Hessian) Infantry Regiment (2 battalions)
  - Prince Emil (Hessian) Light Infantry Regiment (2 battalions)
  - Hessian Chevauxleger Regiment (4 squadrons)

Appendix XLVII

French I, VII and XI Corps, 1 March 1814[1]

I Corps: Général de division Maison
- 4th Young Guard Division: Général de division Comte Barrois
  - Brigades: Généraux de brigade Poret de Morvan and Darriule
    - 1/2nd Tirailleur Regiment (13 / 384)
    - 2/2nd Tirailleur Regiment (8 / 357)
    - 1/3rd Tirailleur Regiment (14 / 401)
    - 2/3rd Tirailleur Regiment (11 / 390)
    - 1/4th Tirailleur Regiment (15 / 359)
    - 2/4th Tirailleur Regiment (11 / 329)
    - 1/12th Voltigeur Regiment (18 / 466)
    - 2/12th Voltigeur Regiment (13 / 631)
- Division: Général de division Solignac
    - 17th Line Regiment (not listed)
    - 18th Line Regiment (1 / 40)
    - 51st Line Regiment (7 / 181)
    - 65th Line Regiment (20 / 233)
    - 75th Line Regiment (5 / 130)
- Cavalry: Général de division Castex
    - 2nd Guard Lancer Regiment (Young Guard Squadrons) (22 / 258)
    - 2nd Guard Chasseurs à cheval Regiment (Young Guard Squadrons) (23 / 531)
    - 1st Gardes d'honneur Regiment (6 / 145)
    - Young Guard Artillery
    - 3rd Guard Horse Artillery
    - 3rd Young Guard Foot Artillery
    - 13th Young Guard Foot Artillery
    - 14 6pdrs and 6 5.7" howitzers
  - Young Guard Train: Not listed, but presumed present
    - 7/1st Young Guard Train Regiment
    - 8/1st Young Guard Train Regiment
    - 10/1st Young Guard Train Regiment
    - 8/2nd Young Guard Train Regiment
    - 2/2nd Young Guard Train Regiment
    - Ouvriers-Pionniers

VII Corps: Maréchal Oudinot, Duc de Reggio
- 5th Young Guard Division: Général de division Rottembourg
  - 1st Brigade: Général de brigade Charrière
    - Staff/5th Voltigeur Regiment (6 / 13)
    - 1/5th Voltigeur Regiment (7 / 157)
    - 2/5th Voltigeur Regiment (7 / 149)
    - Staff/6th Voltigeur Regiment (5 / 6)
    - 1/6th Voltigeur Regiment (10 / 154)

1 Source: French Archives, Carton C^2 556.

2/6th Voltigeur Regiment (9 / 159)
2nd Brigade: Général de brigade Bauduin
Staff/7th Voltigeur Regiment (10 / 7)
1/7th Voltigeur Regiment (11 / 186)
2/7th Voltigeur Regiment (9 / 195)
3/7th Voltigeur Regiment (10 / 381)
Staff/8th Voltigeur Regiment (10 / 13)
1/8th Voltigeur Regiment (13 / 219)
2/8th Voltigeur Regiment (8 / 279)
3/8th Voltigeur Regiment (12 / 451)
Artillery:
11th Young Guard Artillery Company (6-6pdrs and 2 howitzers) (4 / 71)
9th Guard Train Company (1 / 53)
7th Division: Général de division Baron Leval
1st Brigade: Général de brigade Pinoteau
Staff/10th Légère Regiment (7 / 7)
1/10th Légère Regiment (12 / 282)
2/10th Légère Regiment (5 / 214)
3/10th Légère Regiment (6 / 225)
Staff/3rd Line Regiment (6 / 12)
1/3rd Line Regiment (13 / 395)
Staff/15th Line Regiment (5 / 13)
1/15th Line Regiment (12 / 346)
1/130th Line Regiment (9 / 199)
4/130th Line Regiment (11 / 217)
2nd Brigade: Général de brigade Montfort
Staff/17th Légère Regiment (4 / 3)
1/17th Légère Regiment (15 / 410)
Staff/101st Line Regiment (5 / 4)
1/101st Line Regiment (13 / 407)
Staff/105th Line Regiment (9 / 21)
1/105th Line Regiment (10 / 330)
2/105th Line Regiment (9 / 279)
Staff/118th Line Regiment (3 / 15)
6/118th Line Regiment (15 / 473)
Artillery:
19/1st Foot Artillery (2 / 103)
2/4th Principal Train Battalion (2 / 50)
5/12th (bis) Train Battalion (1 / 91)
9th Division: Général de division Pierre Boyer
2nd Brigade: Général de brigade Chassé
1/16th Légère Regiment (16 / 337)
1/8th Line Regiment (16 / 373)
1/28th Line Regiment (22 / 262)
2/28th Line Regiment (9 / 259)
3/28th Line Regiment (15 / 378)
1/54th Line Regiment (12 / 516)
Artillery:
23/5th Foot Artillery (2 / 68)
10/8th Foot Artillery (1 / 68)(8-6pdrs and 4 howitzers)
2/4th Principal Train Battalion (0 / 28)
2/9th (bis) Train Battalion (2 / 96)

Reserve:
19/1st Foot Regiment (5 4pdrs, 2 8pdrs and 1 howitzer)
12th (bis) Train Battalion Train
2nd (bis) Train Battalion
8/3rd Horse Artillery (4 6pdrs and 2 howitzers) Train

XI Corps: Maréchal Macdonald, Duc de Tarente
Division: Général de division Albert
1st Brigade: Général de brigade Schaeffer
Staff/139th Line Regiment (6 / 8)
3/139th Line Regiment (12 / 308)
Staff/1st Regiment de Brest (8 / 1)
1/1st Regiment de Brest (35 / 824)
2/1st Regiment de Brest (26 / 717)
2nd Brigade:
Staff/140th Line Regiment (6 / 9)
1/140th Line Regiment (18 / 533)
Staff/Regiment de Rochefort (8 / 4)
1/Regiment de Rochefort (18 / 467)
2/Regiment de Rochefort (15 / 334)
Artillery (strength as of 3/15/14):
15/4th Foot Artillery (44)
18/6th Foot Artillery (36)
2/5th Horse Artillery (60)
2/9th Principal Train Battalion (16)
3/6th Principal Train Battalion (64)
2/1lth Principal Train Battalion (101)
Division: Général de division Amey
2nd Brigade:
Staff/149th Line Regiment (5 / 4)
1/149th Line Regiment (11 / 118)
2/149th Line Regiment (11 / 107)
1er Bataillon de Calvados (16 / 176)
1er Bataillon de la Manche (14 / 310)
Artillery (strength as of 3/15/14):
6/4th Horse Artillery (4-8pdrs and 1 howitzer) (31)
1/5th Principal Train Battalion (39)
Division: Général de division Brayer
1st Brigade:
Staff/19th Légère Regiment (10 / 31)
2/19th Légère Regiment (6 / 380)
6/19th Légère Regiment (14 / 351)
3/5th Line Regiment (14 / 121)
3/1lth Line Regiment (7 / 397)
2nd Brigade:
1/107th Line Regiment (31 / 391)
1/Gardes Nationale du Nord (14 / 175)
2/Gardes Nationale du Nord (12 / 180)
Artillery (strength as of 3/15/14):
6/1st Foot Artillery (25)
19/2nd Foot Artillery (52)
20/5th Foot Artillery (52)
1/8th Principal Train Battalion (79)

- 2/5th Principal Train Battalion (56)

Corps Cavalry:

- Staff/13th Hussar Regiment (7 / 3)
- 1/13th Hussar Regiment (9 / 141)
- 2/13th Hussar Regiment (7 / 134)

Corps Artillery Equipment:

- Foot Artillery strength (19 / 398)
- Horse Artillery strength (8 / 135)
  - 15 12pdrs
  - 4 8pdrs
  - 17 6pdrs
  - 12 24pdr howitzers
- Sappers (7 / 88)
- Artillery Train (15 / 730)
- Equipage Militaire (2 / 94)
- 10th Hospital Company (2 / 92)

Reserve Artillery (strength as of 3/15/14):

- 22/1st Foot Artillery (20)
- 18/4th Foot Artillery (11)
- 27/1st Foot Artillery (1)
- Artillery Artisans (1)
- 4/1st (bis) Train Battalion (2)
- 1/11th Principal Train Battalion (19)
- 1/13th Principal Train Battalion (23)
- 3/14th Principal Train Battalion
- 4/14th Principal Train Battalion (47)
- 6/3rd (bis) Train Battalion (33)
- 3/5th Principal Train Battalion (24)
- 1/11th Principal Train Battalion

Appendix XLVIII

French Army before Troyes under Macdonald, 2 March 1814[1]

II Corps: Général de division Gérard[2]
- 5th Young Guard Division: Général de division Rottembourg
  - 1st Brigade: Général de brigade Charrière
    - Staff/5th Voltigeur Regiment (6 / 13)
    - 1/5th Voltigeur Regiment (7 / 157)
    - 2/5th Voltigeur Regiment (7 / 149)
    - Staff/6th Voltigeur Regiment (5 / 6)
    - 1/6th Voltigeur Regiment (10 / 154)
    - 2/6th Voltigeur Regiment (9 / 159)
  - 2nd Brigade: Général de brigade Bauduin
    - Staff/7th Voltigeur Regiment (10 / 7)
    - 1/7th Voltigeur Regiment (11 / 186)
    - 2/7th Voltigeur Regiment (9 / 195)
    - 3/7th Voltigeur Regiment (10 / 381)
    - Staff/8th Voltigeur Regiment (10 / 13)
    - 1/8th Voltigeur Regiment (13 / 219)
    - 2/8th Voltigeur Regiment (8 / 279)
    - 3/8th Voltigeur Regiment (12 / 451)
  - Artillery:
    - 11th Young Guard Artillery Company (6-6pdrs and 2 howitzers) (4 / 71)
    - 9th Guard Train Company (1 / 53)
- 7th Division: Général de division Baron Leval
  - 1st Brigade: Général de brigade Pinoteau
    - Staff/10th Légère Regiment (7 / 7)
    - 1/10th Légère Regiment (12 / 282)
    - 2/10th Légère Regiment (5 / 214)
    - 3/10th Légère Regiment (6 / 225)
    - Staff/3rd Line Regiment (6 / 12)
    - 1/3rd Line Regiment (13 / 395)
    - Staff/15th Line Regiment (5 / 13)
    - 1/15th Line Regiment (12 / 346)
    - 1/130th Line Regiment (9 / 199)
    - 4/130th Line Regiment (11 / 217)
  - 2nd Brigade: Général de brigade Montfort
    - Staff/17th Légère Regiment (4 / 3)
    - 1/17th Légère Regiment (15 / 410)
    - Staff/101st Line Regiment (5 / 4)
    - 1/101st Line Regiment (13 / 407)
    - Staff/105th Line Regiment (9 / 21)
    - 1/105th Line Regiment (10 / 330)
    - 2/105th Line Regiment (9 / 279)

---

1 Source: French Archives, Carton C[2] 556 and C[2] 557; Koch, F., *Memoirs pour servier à l'Histoire.*
2 Strength figures as of 1 March 1814.

Staff/118th Line Regiment (3 / 15)
6/118th Line Regiment (15 / 473)
Artillery:
19/1st Foot Artillery (2 / 103)
2/4th Principal Train Battalion (2 / 50)
5/12th (bis) Train Battalion (1 / 91)
9th Division: Général de division Pierre Boyer
2nd Brigade: Général de brigade Chassé
1/16th Légère Regiment (16 / 337)
1/8th Line Regiment (16 / 373)
1/28th Line Regiment (22 / 262)
3/28th Line Regiment (9 / 259)
6/28th Line Regiment (15 / 378)
1/54th Line Regiment (12 / 516)
Artillery:
23/5th Foot Artillery (2 / 68)
10/8th Foot Artillery (1 / 68) (8-6pdrs and 4 howitzers)
2/4th Principal Train Battalion (0 / 28)
2/9th (bis) Train Battalion (2 / 96)
Reserve:
19/1st Foot Regiment (5 4pdrs, 2 8pdrs and 1 howitzer)
12th (bis) Train Battalion Train
2nd (bis) Train Battalion
8/3rd Horse Artillery (4 6pdrs and 2 howitzers)
Unknown Train
National Guard Division: Général de division Pacthod[3]
1st Brigade: Général de brigade Rost
1st Regiment of Sarthe (25 / 990)
3rd Regiment of Indre et Loire (29 / 662)
2nd Brigade: Général de brigade Bonté
2nd Regiment of Loire et Cher (44 / 984)
5th Regiment of Seine et Marne (8 / 263)
3rd Brigade: Général de brigade Kozinsky
4th Regiment Maine et Loire (33 / 989)
Artillery:
26/6th Foot Artillery (2 8pdrs and 4 4pdrs) (2 / 68)
Det/2nd (bis) Train Battalion (0 / 22)
Det/4th Principal Train Battalion (2 / 83)
Reserve:
24/6th Foot Artillery (4 12pdrs and 2 howitzers) (3 / 63)
12/8th Foot Artillery (4-6pdrs and 2 howitzers) (3 / 63)
12th (bis) Train Battalion Train (1 / 110)
8/3rd Horse Artillery (4 6pdrs and 2 howitzers) (4 / 57)

VII Corps: Maréchal Oudinot, Duc de Reggio[4]
5th Young Guard Division: Général de division Rottembourg
1st Brigade: Général de brigade Charrière
1/, 2/5th Voltigeur Regiment (13 / 161)
1/, 2/6th Voltigeur Regiment (14 / 112)

3 Strength returns are as of 5 March 1814.
4 Strength returns are as of 5 March 1814.

2nd Brigade: Général de brigade Bauduin
1/, 2/, 3/7th Voltigeur Regiment (31 / 340)
1/, 2/, 3/8th Voltigeur Regiment (7 / 87)
Artillery:
11th Young Guard Artillery Company (5-6pdrs and 2 howitzers) (2 / 71)
9th Guard Train Company (1 / 53)
7th Division: Général de division Baron Leval
1st Brigade: Général de brigade Pinoteau
1/, 2/10th Légère Regiment (26 / 682)
1/3rd Line Regiment (18 / 380)
1/15th Line Regiment (17 / 341)
1/, 4/130th Line Regiment (25 / 455)
2nd Brigade: Général de brigade Montefort
1/17th Légère Regiment (18 / 359)
1/101st Line Regiment (18 / 370)
1/, 2/105th Line Regiment (28 / 594)
6/118th Line Regiment (16 / 520)
3rd Brigade: Général de brigade Chassé
1/16th Légère Regiment (11 / 315)
1/8th Line Regiment (12 / 347)
1/, 3/, 6/28th Line Regiment (42 / 958)
1/54th Line Regiment (8 / 445)
Artillery:
19/1st Foot Artillery (8-6pdrs and 4 howitzers) (2 / 108)
2/4th Principal Train Battalion (2 / 50)
5/12th (bis) Train Battalion (1 / 91)
9th Division: Général de division Pierre Boyer
2nd Brigade: Général de brigade Chassé
1/16th Légère Regiment
1/8th Line Regiment
1/28th Line Regiment
3/28th Line Regiment
6/28th Line Regiment
1/54th Line Regiment
Artillery:
22/5th Foot Artillery (8-6pdrs and 4 howitzers) (2 / 68)
2/4th Principal Train Battalion (0 / 28)

XI Corps: Général de division Molitor[5]
Division: Général de division Albert
1st Brigade: Général de brigade Schaeffer
Staff/139th Line Regiment (6 / 8)
3/139th Line Regiment (12 / 308)
Staff/1st Regiment de Brest (8 / 1)
1/1st Regiment de Brest (35 / 824)
2/1st Regiment de Brest (26 / 717)
2nd Brigade:
Staff/140th Line Regiment (6 / 9)
1/140th Line Regiment (18 / 533)
Staff/Regiment de Rochefort (8 / 4)

5 Strength figures are as of 1 March 1814.

1/Regiment de Rochefort (18 / 467)
2/Regiment de Rochefort (15 / 334)
Artillery (strength as of 3/15/14):
15/4th Foot Artillery (44)
18/6th Foot Artillery (36)
2/5th Horse Artillery (60)
2/9th Principal Train Battalion (16)
3/6th Principal Train Battalion (64)
2/11th Principal Train Battalion (101)
Division: Général de division Amey
2nd Brigade:
Staff/149th Line Regiment (5 / 4)
1/149th Line Regiment (11 / 118)
2/149th Line Regiment (11 / 107)
1er Bataillon de Calvados (16 / 176)
1er Bataillon de la Manche (14 / 310)
Artillery:[6]
6/4th Horse Artillery (4-8pdrs and 1 howitzer) (31)
1/5th Principal Train Battalion (39)
Division: Général de division Brayer
1st Brigade:
Staff/19th Légère Regiment (10 / 31)
2/19th Légère Regiment (6 / 380)
6/19th Légère Regiment (14 / 351)
3/5th Line Regiment (14 / 121)
3/11th Line Regiment (7 / 397)
2nd Brigade:
1/107th Line Regiment (31 / 391)
1/Gardes Nationale du Nord (14 / 175)
2/Gardes Nationale du Nord (12 / 180)
Artillery (strength as of 3/15/14):
6/1st Foot Artillery (25)
19/2nd Foot Artillery (52)
20/5th Foot Artillery (52)
1/8th Principal Train Battalion (79)
2/5th Principal Train Battalion (56)
Corps Cavalry:
Staff/13th Hussar Regiment (7 / 3)
1/13th Hussar Regiment (9 / 141)
2/13th Hussar Regiment (7 / 134)
Corps Artillery Equipment:
Foot Artillery strength (19 / 398)
Horse Artillery strength (8 / 135)
Sappers (7 / 88)
Artillery Train (15 / 730)
Equipage Militaire (2 / 94)
10th Hospital Company (2 / 92)
15 12pdrs
4 8pdrs
17 6pdrs

6 Strength figures are as of 15 March 1814.

12 24pdr howitzers
36 12pdr caissons
5 8pdr caissons
35 6pdr caissons
25 howitzer caissons
32 infantry caissons

Reserve Artillery (strength as of 3/15/14):
22/1st Foot Artillery (20)
18/4th Foot Artillery (11)
27/1st Foot Artillery (1)
Artillery Artisans (1)
4/1st (bis) Train Battalion (2)
1/11th Principal Train Battalion (19)
1/13th Principal Train Battalion (23)
3/14th Principal Train Battalion
4/14th Principal Train Battalion (47)
6/3rd (bis) Train Battalion (33)
3/5th Principal Train Battalion (24)
1/11th Principal Train Battalion

Flanqueur Division: Général Allix (1,450 men)
Fusilier Chasseur Regiment
Fusilier Grenadier Regiment
Flanqueur-Chasseur Regiment
Flanqueur-Grenadier Regiment

II Cavalry Corps:[7]
2nd Light Cavalry Division: Général de division Maurin
1st Brigade: Général de brigade Dommanget
5th Hussar Regiment (5 / 54)
9th Hussar Regiment (4 / 38)
1/, 2/11th Chasseurs à cheval Regiment (18 / 137)
1/, 2/12th Chasseurs à cheval Regiment (20 / 154)
2nd Chevauléger-lancier Regiment (15 / 75)
4th Chevauléger-lancier Regiment (2 / 84)
2nd Brigade: Général de brigade Jamin
6th Chevauléger-lancier Regiment (3 / 33)
7th Chasseurs à cheval Regiment (14 / 86)
20th Chasseurs à cheval Regiment (13 / 58)
23rd Chasseurs à cheval Regiment (5 / 63)
24th Chasseurs à cheval Regiment (9 / 192)
10th Hussar Regiment (detached)
Artillery:
Det/5th Horse Artillery (3-6pdrs and 1 howitzer) (2 / 51)
280 ball and 53 canister
Det/1st (bis) Train Battalion (1 / 34)
Det/2nd Principal Train Battalion (1 / 17)
2nd Cuirassier Division: Général de division Delort
1st Brigade: Général de brigade Blancard
1st Carabinier Regiment (13 / 85)
2nd Carabinier Regiment (11 / 83)

7 Strength figures are as of 10 March 1814.

1st Cuirassier Regiment (9 / 76)
2nd Brigade: Général de brigade Sopranzy
5th Cuirassier Regiment (8 / 94)
8th Cuirassier Regiment (12 / 95)
10th Cuirassier Regiment (10 / 94)
13th Cuirassier Regiment (4 / 110)
Artillery:
Det/6th Horse Artillery (4-6pdrs and 2 howitzers) (2 / 76)
560 ball and 40 canister
Det/10th Principal Train Battalion (1 / 64)

V Cavalry Corps: Général de division Milhaud[8]
3rd Light Cavalry Division: Général de division Piré (strength as of 2 March 1814 – 1,421 men)
5th Brigade: Général de brigade Subervie
3rd Hussar Regiment (12 / 133)
26th Chasseur Cheval Regiment (22 / 274)
6th Brigade:
14th Chasseurs à cheval Regiment (6 / 112)
27th Chasseurs à cheval Regiment (12 / 125)
3rd Heavy Cavalry Division: Général de division Briche (strength as of 2 March 1814 – 1,700 men)
5th Brigade: Général de brigade Montelegier
2nd Dragoon Regiment (25 / 281)
6th Dragoon Regiment (21 / 276)
11th Dragoon Regiment (26 / 383)
6th Brigade: Général de brigade Ludot
13th Dragoon Regiment (15 / 119)
15th Dragoon Regiment (20 / 210)
4th Heavy Cavalry Division: Général de division l'Héritier (strength as of 2 March 1814 – 1,269 men)
7th Brigade: Général de brigade Lamotte
18th Dragoon Regiment (14 / 194)
19th Dragoon Regiment (19 / 158)
20th Dragoon Regiment (12 / 97)
8th Brigade: Général de brigade Collaert
22nd Dragoon Regiment (17 / 236)
25th Dragoon Regiment (2 / 361)
Artillery:
4/2nd Horse Artillery (2 / 48)
2/3rd Horse Artillery (2 / 42)
8/6th Horse Artillery (2 / 41)
Total Guns
4 – 6pdrs
6 – 4pdrs
4 – 24pdr howitzers
1/8th Principal Train Battalion (1 / 44)
1/12th Principal Train Battalion (1 / 56)
2/14th Principal Train Battalion (0 / 26)

8 Regimental strength figures are as of 20 February 1814.

VI Cavalry Corps:[9]

- 5th Heavy Cavalry Division: Général de division Trelliard
  - 9th Brigade: Général de brigade Ismert
    - 1/4th Dragoon Regiment (16 / 114)
    - 2/4th Dragoon Regiment (8 / 79)
    - 3/4th Dragoon Regiment (4 / 84)
    - 4/4th Dragoon Regiment (6 / 84)
    - 1/14th Dragoon Regiment (18 / 174)
    - 2/14th Dragoon Regiment (12 / 155)
    - 1/16th Dragoon Regiment (12 / 152)
    - 2/16th Dragoon Regiment (7 / 123)
  - 10th Brigade: Général de brigade Ormancy
    - 1/17th Dragoon Regiment (15 / 183)
    - 2/17th Dragoon Regiment (9 / 134)
    - 3/17th Dragoon Regiment (5 / 32)
    - 4/17th Dragoon Regiment (8 / 133)
    - 24th Dragoon Regiment (2 / 19)
    - 1/27th Dragoon Regiment (14 / 159)
    - 2/27th Dragoon Regiment (8 / 119)
    - 3/27th Dragoon Regiment (3 / 68)
    - 5/27th Dragoon Regiment (4 / 65)
  - Artillery:
    - 6/2nd Horse Artillery (5-6pdrs and 1 howitzer) (2 / 86)
    - 4/6th Principal Train Battalion (1 / 106)
- 6th Heavy Cavalry Division: Général de division Roussel d'Hurbal
  - 11th Brigade: Général de brigade Sparre
    - 5th Dragoon Regiment
    - 12th Dragoon Regiment
  - 12th Brigade: Général de brigade Rigau
    - 21st Dragoon Regiment
    - 26th Dragoon Regiment
  - Artillery:
    - 3/3rd Horse Artillery
    - 3/2nd Horse Artillery
    - 2/5th Principal Train Battalion
    - 1/2nd (bis) Train Battalion
    - 5/6th Principal Train Battalion

9 Strength figures are as of 7 March 1814.

Appendix XLIX

French VII Corps, 5 March 1814[1]

VII Corps: Maréchal Oudinot, Duc de Reggio
- 5th Young Guard Division: Général de division Rottembourg
  - 1st Brigade: Général de brigade Charrière
    - 1/, 2/5th Voltigeur Regiment (13 / 161)
    - 1/, 2/6th Voltigeur Regiment (14 / 112)
  - 2nd Brigade: Général de brigade Bauduin
    - 1/, 2/, 3/7th Voltigeur Regiment (31 / 340)
    - 1/, 2/, 3/8th Voltigeur Regiment (7 / 87)
  - Artillery:
    - 11th Young Guard Artillery Company (5-6pdrs and 2 howitzers) (2 / 71)
    - 9th Guard Train Company (1 / 53)
- 7th Division: Général de division Baron Leval
  - 1st Brigade: Général de brigade Pinoteau
    - 1/, 6/10th Légère Regiment (26 / 682)
    - 1/3rd Line Regiment (18 / 380)
    - 1/15th Line Regiment (17 / 341)
    - 1/, 4/130th Line Regiment (25 / 455)
  - 2nd Brigade: Général de brigade Montfort
    - 1/17th Légère Regiment (18 / 359)
    - 1/101st Line Regiment (18 / 370)
    - 1/, 2/105th Line Regiment (28 / 594)
    - 6/118th Line Regiment (16 / 520)
  - 3rd Brigade: Général de brigade Chassé
    - 1/16th Légère Regiment (11 / 315)
    - 1/8th Line Regiment (12 / 347)
    - 1/, 3/, 6/28th Line Regiment (42 / 958)
    - 1/54th Line Regiment (8 / 445)
  - Artillery:
    - 19/1st Foot Artillery (8-6pdrs and 4 howitzers) (2 / 108)
    - 2/4th Principal Train Battalion (2 / 50)
    - 5/12th (bis) Train Battalion (1 / 91)
- National Guard Division: Général de division Pacthod
  - 1st Brigade: Général de brigade Rost
    - 1st Regiment of Sarthe (25 / 990)
    - 3rd Regiment of Indre et Loire (29 / 662)
  - 2nd Brigade: Général de brigade Bonté
    - 2nd Regiment of Loire et Cher (44 / 984)
    - 5th Regiment of Seine et Marne (8 / 263)
  - 3rd Brigade: Général de brigade Kozinsky
    - 4th Regiment Maine et Loire (33 / 989)
  - Artillery:
    - 26/6th Foot Artillery (2 8pdrs and 4 4pdrs) (2 / 68)

1 Source: French Archives, Carton C^2 556.

Det/2nd (bis) Train Battalion (0 / 22)
Det/4th Principal Train Battalion (2 / 83)

Reserve:

24/6th Foot Artillery (4 12pdrs and 2 howitzers) (3 / 63)
12/8th Foot Artillery (4-6pdrs and 2 howitzers) (3 / 63)
(8-6pdrs and 4 howitzers)
12th (bis) Train Battalion Train (1 / 110)
8/3rd Horse Artillery (4 6pdrs and 2 howitzers) (4 / 57)

Appendix L

French VI Cavalry Corps, 7 March 1814[1]

VI Cavalry Corps:
- 5th Heavy Cavalry Division: Général de division Trelliard
  - 9th Brigade: Général de brigade Ismert
    - 1/4th Dragoon Regiment (16 / 114)
    - 2/4th Dragoon Regiment (8 / 79)
    - 3/4th Dragoon Regiment (4 / 84)
    - 4/4th Dragoon Regiment (6 / 84)
    - 1/14th Dragoon Regiment (18 / 174)
    - 2/14th Dragoon Regiment (12 / 155)
    - 1/16th Dragoon Regiment (12 / 152)
    - 2/16th Dragoon Regiment (7 / 123)
  - 10th Brigade: Général de brigade Ormancy
    - 1/17th Dragoon Regiment (15 / 183)
    - 2/17th Dragoon Regiment (9 / 134)
    - 3/17th Dragoon Regiment (5 / 32)
    - 4/17th Dragoon Regiment (8 / 133)
    - 24th Dragoon Regiment (2 / 19)
    - 1/27th Dragoon Regiment (14 / 159)
    - 2/27th Dragoon Regiment (8 / 119)
    - 3/27th Dragoon Regiment (3 / 68)
    - 5/27th Dragoon Regiment (4 / 65)
  - Artillery:
    - 6/2nd Horse Artillery (5-6pdrs and 1 howitzer) (2 / 86)
    - 4/6th Principal Train Battalion (1 / 106)
- 6th Heavy Cavalry Division: Général de division Roussel d'Hurbal
  - 11th Brigade: Général de brigade Sparre
    - 5th Dragoon Regiment
    - 12th Dragoon Regiment
  - 12th Brigade: Général de brigade Rigaud
    - 21st Dragoon Regiment
    - 26th Dragoon Regiment
  - Artillery:
    - 3/3rd Horse Artillery
    - 3/2nd Horse Artillery
    - 2/5th Principal Train Battalion
    - 1/2nd (bis) Train Battalion
    - 5/6th Principal Train Battalion

1 French Archives, Carton C² 557.

Appendix LI

French forces, Battle of Craone, 7 March 1814[1]

Commanding Officer: Napoleon Bonaparte
Chief of Staff: Maréchal Berthier
Colonel-Generals: Général de division Count Grouchy (Chasseurs), Général de division Count Belliard (Cuirassiers)
Artillery Commander: Général de division Count Ruty

Right wing: Maréchal Ney

- 2nd Provisional Young Guard Division: Général de division Boyer de Rebeval (1,886 men) (assigned infantry unknown)
  - Artillery:
    - 14/1st Foot Artillery
    - 8/7th Foot Artillery
    - 5/14th Principal Train Battalion
- 1st Young Guard (1st Voltigeur) Division: Général de division Meunier (865 men)
  - 1st Voltigeur Regiment
  - 2nd Voltigeur Regiment
  - 3rd Voltigeur Regiment
  - 4th Voltigeur Regiment
- 2nd Young Guard Division: Général de division Curial (1,022 men)
  - 5th Voltigeur Regiment
  - 6th Voltigeur Regiment
  - 7th Voltigeur Regiment
  - 8th Voltigeur Regiment

Corps: Maréchal Victor

- 9th Division: Général de division P. Boyer (3,800 men)
  - 1st Brigade: Général de brigade Gruyère
    - 1/, 2/, 6/2nd Légère Regiment
    - 1/24th Line Regiment
    - 6/36th Line Regiment
    - 1/, 4/122nd Line Regiment
  - 2nd Brigade: Général de brigade Chassé (detached, not present)
    - 1/16th Légère Regiment
    - 1/8th Line Regiment
    - 1/, 3/28th Line Regiment
    - 1/54th Line Regiment
  - Artillery:
    - 22/5th Foot Artillery
    - 10/8th Foot Artillery (8-6pdrs and 4 howitzers)
    - 2/4th Principal Train Battalion
    - 2/9th (bis) Train Battalion

1 Sources: French Archives, Carton C^2 556; Koch, F., *Memoirs pour servier à l'Histoire.*

7th Young Guard Division: Général de division Charpentier (3,600 men)
3/3rd Tirailleur Regiment
3/3rd Voltigeur Regiment
3/4th Tirailleur Regiment
3/4th Voltigeur Regiment
3/5th Voltigeur Regiment
3/6th Voltigeur Regiment
3/10th Tirailleur Regiment
3/11th Tirailleur Regiment
3/12th Tirailleur Regiment
3/7th Voltigeur Regiment
3/8th Voltigeur Regiment
3/11th Voltigeur Regiment
Cavalry: Général de division Grouchy
6th Heavy Cavalry Division: Général de division Roussel d'Hurbal (2,200 men)
11th Brigade: Général de brigade Sparre
5th Dragoon Regiment
12th Dragoon Regiment
12th Brigade: Général de brigade Rigaud
21st Dragoon Regiment
26th Dragoon Regiment
Artillery:
3/3rd Horse Artillery
3/2nd Horse Artillery
2/5th Principal Train Battalion
1/2nd (bis) Train Battalion
5/6th Principal Train Battalion
3rd Guard Cavalry Division: Général de division Laferrière-Lévésque (1,250 men)
1st Brigade: Général de brigade Lion
Chasseurs à cheval Regiment (34 / 508)
Empress Dragoon Regiment (44 / 691)
2nd Brigade: Général de brigade Letort
Grenadier à cheval Regiment (45 / 842)

Reserve: Maréchal Mortier, Duc de Trevise
1st Old Guard Division: Général de division Friant (3,800 men)
1st Brigade: Général de brigade Cambronne
1/, 2/1st Chasseur à Pied Regiment
1/, 2/2nd Chasseur à Pied Regiment
2nd Brigade: Général de brigade Petit
1/, 2/1st Grenadier à Pied Regiment
1/, 2/2nd Grenadier à Pied Regiment
Attached:
1/, 2/, 3/Guard Sapper Battalion
3/Guard Marine Battalion
Guard Engineering Train
2nd Old Guard Division: Général de brigade Christiani (3,300 men)
Brigade:
Fusilier Chasseur Regiment
Fusilier Grenadier Regiment
Vélites of Turin
Brigade: Général de brigade Gros
Flanqueur-Chasseur Regiment

Flanqueur-Grenadier Regiment
Vélites of Florence
Artillery:
25/3rd Foot Artillery
2/7th Horse Artillery
2/7th bis Train Battalion
2/13th Principal Train Battalion
3/9th (bis) Train Battalion
3rd Provisional Young Guard Division: Général de brigade Poret de Morvan (4,800 men) (organization unknown)
1st Guard Cavalry Division: Général de division Colbert (1,100 cavalry)
2nd Éclaireur Regiment
2nd Chevauléger-lancier Regiment
Chasseurs à cheval de la Garde
Grenadiers à cheval de la Garde
Empress Dragoon Regiment
Horse Artillery

Left wing: Général de division Count Nansouty
Brigade: Général de Brigade Pacz (450)
3rd Hussar Regiment
14th Chasseurs à cheval Regiment
26th Chasseurs à cheval Regiment
27th Chasseurs à cheval Regiment
Division: Général de division Excelmans (1,350 cavalry) (assigned cavalry unknown)

Appendix LII

Russian forces, Battle of Craone, 7 March 1814[1]

Commanding General: Lieutenant General Voronzov

1st Line: Right wing:

Detachment: General von Benkendorff (1,000)
- 1/, 2/, 3/, 4/, 5/, 6/Pavlograd Hussar Regiment
- Bug Cossacks (1 pulk)

Brigade: Krassovsky (1,250)
- 14th Jager Regiment (1)
- 15th Jager Regiment (1)
- Position Battery #31 (12-12pdrs)
- Horse Battery #21 (12-6pdrs)
- Horse Battery #7 (12-6pdrs)

Brigade: Generalmajor Harpe (2,154)
- Navaguinsk Infantry Regiment (2)
- Converged Grenadiers, 9th, 15th and 18th Divisions (3 battalions)

Left wing:

Corps: General Vuitsch (4,300 infantry)

24th Division: General Swarikin
- 1/, 3/Chirvan Infantry Regiment
- 1/, 3/Bourtirki Infantry Regiment
- 1/, 3/19th Jager Regiment

14th Division: General Poncet

Brigade:
- 1/, 3/Toula Infantry Regiment
- 1/, 3/Navajinsk Infantry Regiment

2nd Line:

21st Division: General Laptieff (3,500 infantry)

Brigade: Colonel Rosen
- Lithuania Infantry Regiment (1)
- Podolsk Infantry Regiment (1)
- Petrovsk Infantry Regiment (1)

Brigade: Generalmajor Rüdinger
- Neva Infantry Regiment (1)
- 2nd Jager Regiment (1)
- 44th Jager Regiment (1)

Artillery:
- Position Battery #28 (12-12pdrs)
- Light Battery #42 (12-6pdrs)
- Light Battery #46 (12-6pdrs)

1 Sources: Koch, F., *Memoirs pour servier à l'Histoire*; Bogdanovich, M.I., *Istorich Voin l8l4 Goda Vo Frantsiii Nizlozhenich Napoleona I.*

3rd Line: Lieutenant General Stroganov
12th Division: Generalmajor Count Chovansky (1,800)
Smolensk Infantry Regiment (1)
Narva Infantry Regiment (1)
New Ingremannland Infantry Regiment (1)
Alexopol Infantry Regiment (1)
6th Jager Regiment (1)
41st Jager Regiment (1)
13th Division: General Selutschin (3,300)
1/, 3/Saratov Infantry Regiment
1/, 3/Pensa Infantry Regiment
Position Battery #53 (12-12pdrs)
Horse Battery #11 (12-6pdrs)
Light Battery #56 (12-6pdrs)
2nd Hussar Division: Generalmajor Lanskoi (1,500)
Brigade: Generalmajor Waddolski
Akhtyrsk Hussar Regiment (6)
Marioupol Hussar Regiment (5)
Brigade: Colonel Vassil'shikov
White Russia Hussar Regiment (4)
Alexandria Hussar Regiment (5)
3rd Dragoon Division: Generalmajor Pantschichscheff (1,200)
Brigade: Generalmajor Uschakov
Smolensk Dragoon Regiment
Kurland Dragoon Regiment
Brigade: Generalmajor Umanez
Tver Dragoon Regiment
Kinburn Dragoon Regiment
Horse Artillery Battery #13 (12-6pdrs)
Brigade: Generalmajor Karpov II (1,200)
Karpov II Don Cossack Regiment
3 unknown Cossack Regiments
Horse Artillery
Horse Battery #1 (10-6pdrs) (2 in Altenburg)
Horse Battery #4 (8-6pdrs)
Horse Battery #11 (12-6pdrs)

Appendix LIII

French Army, Battle of Laon, 9-10 March 1814

Corps: Maréchal Ney
9th Division: Général de division P. Boyer
1st Young Guard (1st Voltigeur) Division: Général de division Meunier
2nd Young Guard Division: Général de division Curial

Corps: Maréchal Victor, Duke de Bellune
2nd Provisional Young Guard Division: Général de division Boyer de Rebeval
7th Young Guard Division: Général de division Charpentier

Corps: Général de division Grouchy
6th Heavy Cavalry Division: Général de division Roussel
3rd Guard Cavalry Division: Général de division Laferrière-Lévésque

Corps: Maréchal Mortier
1st Old Guard Division: Général de division Friant
2nd Old Guard Division: Général de brigade Christiani
3rd Provisional Young Guard Division: Général de brigade Poret de Morvan
1st Guard Cavalry Division: Général de division Colbert

Corps: General Nansouty
Cavalry Division: Général de division Excelmans
Cavalry Division: Général de division Pacz

Corps: Maréchal Marmont
8th Division: Général de division Ricard
3rd Division: Général de division Lagrange, Général de division Arrighi (Duc de Padua)

I Cavalry Corps:
2nd Paris Reserve Division:

Total strength French army: 56,000

Appendix LIV

Allied forces, Battle of Laon, 9-10 March 1814[1]

I Army Corps: General von Yorck
Combined 1st and 7th Brigade: General von Horn
East Prussian Jäger Battalion (2 companies)
Combined Force
Leib Grenadier Battalion
West Prussian Grenadier Battalion
Combined Force
Silesian Grenadier Battalion
1st East Prussian Grenadier Battalion
1/, 2/, Fus/Leib Infantry Regiment
Combined Force
5th Silesian Landwehr Infantry Regiment
13th Silesian Landwehr Infantry Regiment
Combined Force
4th Silesian Landwehr Infantry Regiment
15th Silesian Landwehr Infantry Regiment
Combined 2nd and 8th Brigade: Prince Wilhelm von Preussen
1/, 2/, Fus/1st East Prussian Infantry Regiment
2nd East Prussian Infantry Regiment (2)
1/, 2/Brandenburg Infantry Regiment
1/, 2/12th Reserve Infantry Regiment
Combined Force
Fus/12th Reserve Infantry Regiment
Fus/Brandenburg Infantry Regiment
6th Silesian Landwehr Infantry Regiment (1)
14th Silesian Landwehr Infantry Regiment (1)
Reserve Cavalry: General von Jürgass
1/, 2/, 3/, 4/East Prussian National Cavalry Regiment
1/, 2/, 3/, 4/Mecklenburg Strelitz Hussar Regiment
1/, 2/, 3/, 4/Brandenburg Hussar Regiment
1/, 2/, 3/, 4/2nd Leib Hussar Regiment
1/, 2/, 3/, 4/Lithuanian Dragoon Regiment
1/, 2/, 3/, 4/1st West Prussian Dragoon Regiment
1/, 2/, 3/, 4/Brandenburg Uhlan Regiment
3rd, 4th and 5th Silesian Landwehr Cavalry Regiments (5 squadrons)
Artillery: Oberst von Schmidt
6pdr Foot Battery #1
6pdr Foot Battery #2
6pdr Foot Battery #3
6pdr Foot Battery #15
12pdr Foot Battery #1
12pdr Foot Battery #2

1 Source: Prussian General Staff, *Pläne der Schlachten und Treffen.*

6pdr Horse Battery #1
6pdr Horse Battery #2
6pdr Horse Battery #3
6pdr Horse Battery #12

2nd Army Corps: Generalleutnant von Kleist
9th Brigade: General von Klüx
1/, 2/, Fus/1st West Prussian Infantry Regiment
1/, 2/6th Reserve Infantry Regiment (3rd Battalion in Erfurt)
Neumann Combined Light Battalion
Unknown Fusilier Battalion
Silesian Schützen Battalion
10th Brigade: General von Pirch I
1/, 2/, Fus/2nd West Prussian Infantry Regiment
Reichenbach Combined Musketeer Battalion
Linsingen Combined Musketeer Battalion
Haas Combined Musketeer Battalion
Hüllesheim Combined Musketeer Battalion
Cavalry: General von Ziethen
1/, 2/, 3/, 4/East Prussian Cuirassier Regiment
1/, 2/, 3/, 4/Brandenburg Cuirassier Regiment
1/, 2/, 3/, 4/Silesian Cuirassier Regiment
1/, 2/, 3/, 4/Neumark Dragoon Regiment
1/, 2/, 3/, 4/1st Silesian Hussar Regiment
1/, 2/, 3/, 4/2nd Silesian Hussar Regiment
1/, 2/, 3/, 4/Silesian Uhlan Regiment
Silesian National Cavalry Regiment (2)
7th and 8th Silesian Landwehr Cavalry Regiment (2)
Artillery: Oberst von Braun
12pdr Foot Battery #3
12pdr Foot Battery #6
7pdr Howitzer Battery #1
6pdr Foot Battery #7
6pdr Foot Battery #8
6pdr Foot Battery #9
6pdr Horse Battery #7
6pdr Horse Battery #8
6pdr Horse Battery #9

3rd Army Corps: General von Bülow
3rd Brigade: Prince von Hessen-Homburg
2nd East Prussian Grenadier Battalion
1/, 2/, /Fus/3rd East Prussian Infantry Regiment
1/, 2/, /Fus/4th Reserve Infantry Regiment
4th Brigade: General von Thümen
1/, 2/, /Fus/4th East Prussian Infantry Regiment
2/, 3/5th Reserve Infantry Regiment
6th Brigade: General von Krafft
1/, 2/, /Fus/Colberg Infantry Regiment
1/, 2/, /Fus/9th Reserve Infantry Regiment
1/, 3/1st Neumark Landwehr Infantry Regiment
Reserve Cavalry: General von Oppen
Prince Wilhelm Dragoon Regiment (2)

1/, 2/, 3/, 4/, Jäger/Königin Dragoon Regiment
1/, 2/, 3/, 4/2nd West Prussian Dragoon Regiment
1/, 2, 3/, 4/1st Pomeranian Landwehr Regiment
1/, 2, 3/, 4/2nd Pomeranian Landwehr Cavalry Regiment
Artillery: General von Holtzendorff
6pdr Foot Battery #5
6pdr Foot Battery #6
6pdr Foot Battery #19
6pdr Horse Battery #11
12pdr Foot Battery #4
12pdr Foot Battery #5
2 Russian 12pdr Batteries

Russian forces: General Winzingerode
Advanced Guard: General Chernichev
1/, 2/, 3/, 4/Volhynie Uhlan Regiment
Cossack Corps:
Balbin #2 Cossack Regiment
Diaczkin Cossack Regiment
Vlassov #3 Cossack Regiment
Sisaev Cossack Regiment
Chirov Cossack Regiment
Horse Battery #12
Corps: General Vuitsch
24th Division: General Swarikin
1/, 3/Chirvan Infantry Regiment
1/, 3/Bourtirki Infantry Regiment
1/, 3/19th Jager Regiment
14th Division: General Poncet
Brigade:
1/, 3/Toula Infantry Regiment
1/, 3/Navaguinsk Infantry Regiment
15th Division: General Krassovsky
14th Jager Regiment (1)
15th Jager Regiment (1)
Position Battery #31
Light Battery #21
Light Battery #26
Corps: Generallieutenant Count Stroganov
12th Division: Generalmajor Count Chovansky
Smolensk Infantry Regiment (1)
Narva Infantry Regiment (1)
New Ingremannland Infantry Regiment (1)
Alexopol Infantry Regiment (1)
6th Jager Regiment (1)
41st Jager Regiment (1)
13th Division: General Selutschin
1/, 3/Saratov Infantry Regiment
1/, 3/Pensa Infantry Regiment
Position Battery #53
Light Batteries #48 and #56
21st Division: General Laptieff
Lithuania Infantry Regiment (1)

Podolsk Infantry Regiment (1)
Petrovsk Infantry Regiment (1)
Neva Infantry Regiment (1)
2nd Jager Regiment (1)
44th Jager Regiment (1)
Position Battery #28
Light Battery #42
Light Battery #46

Reserve Cavalry: Generallieutenant Count Orurk
1/, 2/, 3/, 4/Isoum Hussar Regiment
1/, 2/, 3/, 4/Elisabethgrad Hussar Regiment
1/, 2/, 3/, 4/St. Petersburg Dragoon Regiment
1/, 2/, 3/, 4/Riga Dragoon Regiment
1/, 2/, 3/, 4/Finland Dragoon Regiment
1/, 2/, 3/, 4/Nijine Chasseurs à cheval Regiment
Jaroslav Opolochenie Cossack Regiment

Detachment: General von Benkendorff
1/, 2/, 3/, 4/, 5/, 6/Pavlograd Hussar Regiment
Bug Cossacks (1 pulk)

Detachment: General Marischkin
Grekov #9 Cossack Regiment
Barbantchikov #2 Cossack Regiment
Lotschilin #1 Cossack Regiment

Detachment: Colonel Menikov
Melnikov #4 Cossack Regiment
Melnikov #5 Cossack Regiment
Illowaisky #4 Cossack Regiment
Pantalejev Cossack Regiment
Grekov #9 Cossack Regiment

Appendix LV

German 3rd Army Corps, 10 March 1814[1]

Royal Saxon Army:
General Staff (27 / 7)

Cavalry:
- Staff Dragoons (1 / 59)
- 1/, 2/, 3/Cuirassier Regiment (30 / 539 / 452)
- 1/, 2/, 3/Uhlan Regiment (23 / 329 / 311)
- 1/, 2/, 3/Hussar Regiment (28 / 356 / 342)

Line Infantry:
- Staff/, 1/Grenadier Regiment (14 / 645)
- 2/Grenadier Regiment (17 / 629)
- 3/Grenadier Regiment (15 / 668)
- Staff/, 2/1st Provisional Regiment (14 / 530)
- 3/1st Provisional Regiment (17 / 640)
- 1/Provisional Regiment (13 / 520)
- Staff/, 2/Provisional Regiment (16 / 513)
- 3/Provisional Regiment (16 / 553)
- Jäger Battalion (13 / 540)
- 1/1st Light Regiment (10 / 580)
- 2/1st Light Regiment (10 / 580)
- 2/2nd Light Regiment (13 / 654)

Landwehr:
- 1/1st Regiment (14 / 756)
- 2/1st Regiment (13 / 710)
- 3/1st Regiment (14 / 750)
- 1/2nd Regiment (11 / 733)
- 2/2nd Regiment (13 / 732)
- 3/2nd Regiment (16 / 746)
- 1/3rd Regiment (20 / 661)
- 2/3rd Regiment (17 / 700)
- 3/3rd Regiment (15 / 716)
- 1/4th Regiment (17 / 768)
- 2/4th Regiment (16 / 766)
- 3/4th Regiment (15 / 676)

Artillery:
- 1st Horse Battery (6 guns) (4 / 134)
- 2nd Horse Battery (6 guns) (4 / 133)
- 1st 12pdr Battery (2 / 168)
- 2nd 12pdr Battery (4 / 200)
- 1st 6pdr Battery (4 / 149)
- 3rd 6pdr Battery (1 / 57)
- 1st Reserve Park (2 / 91)

1 Source: Bucher, L.F., *Der Feldzug des dritten deutschen Armee-Corps in Flandern.*

Grand Park (16 / 396)
Sapper-Pontooneer Detachment (2 / 52)

Thuringia-Anhalt Division:
Weimar Fusilier Battalion (12 / 666)
Gotha Battalion (18 / 856)
Schwarzberg Battalion (10 / 543)
Dessau-Köthen Battalion (16 / 576)
Bernberg Battalion («Landwehr) (11 / 440)
Weimar Landwehr Battalion (5 / 290)
Gotha Landwehr Battalion (16 / 547)
Schwarzberg Landwehr Battalion (12 / 450)
Dessau-Köthen Landwehr Battalion (16 / 576)
Weimar and Gotha Jäger Squadron (5 / 56 / 56)
Weimar Freiwilliger Jäger zu Fuss Company (4 / 85)
Gotha Freiwilliger Jäger zu Fuss Company (4 / 85)
Schwarzberg Freiwilliger Jäger zu Fuss Company (4 / 154)

Appendix LVI

Württemberg 4th Corps, 13 March 1814[1]

Commanding Officer: Feldmarschal Kronprinz von Württemberg

Advanced Guard: Generallieutenant Prince Adam von Württemberg
- 1st Cavalry Brigade: Generalmajor von Walseben
  - 5th Cavalry Regiment "Jäger" (4)
  - Erzherzog Ferdinand Hussar Regiment (5) (Austrian)
  - 1st Horse Battery, Cpt. von Breithaupt (4-6pdrs and 2 howitzers)
- 2nd Cavalry Brigade: Generalmajor von Jett
  - 2nd Cavalry Regiment "Jäger Herzog Louis" (4)
  - 3rd Cavalry Regiment "Dragoner Kronprinz" (4)
  - 4th Cavalry Regiment "Jäger Prince Adam" (4)
  - 2nd Horse Battery, Cpt. von Bürgi (4-6pdrs and 2 howitzers)
- 4th Infantry Brigade: Generalmajor von Stockmayer
  - 9th Jäger Regiment "König" (1)
  - 10th Light Regiment (2)
  - Austrian Pioneer Company (Cpt. Wonjatschek) (1 company)

Main body: Feldzeugmeister Graf von Franquemont
- 1st Division: Generallieutenant von Koch
  - 1st Infantry Brigade: Generalmajor Prince von Hohenlohe
    - 2nd Infantry Regiment "Herzog Wilhelm" (2)
    - 3rd Infantry Regiment (2)
    - 1st Foot Battery, Major von Ehrenfeld (4-6pdrs and 2 howitzers)
  - 2nd Infantry Brigade: Generalmajor von Misani
    - 4th Infantry Regiment (2)
    - 5th Infantry Regiment "Prince Freiderich" (2)
    - 2nd Foot Battery, Cpt. von Diskau (4-6pdrs and 2 howitzers)
  - 3rd Infantry Brigade: Generalmajor von Lalance
    - 6th Infantry Regiment "Kronprinz" (2)
    - Landregiment #6 Heilbronn (1)
- 2nd Division: Generallieutenant Döring
    - 7th Infantry Regiment (2)
  - Grenadier (Austrian) Brigade: Generalmajor von Trenk
    - Putheany Grenadier Battalion (1)
    - Frisch Grenadier Battalion (1)
    - Hromada Grenadier Battalion (1)
    - Lany Grenadier Battalion (1)
    - 2 6pdr Batteries
  - Cuirassier Brigade: Generalmajor Graf von Desfours
    - Liechtenstein Cuirassier Regiment (6)
    - Kaiser Cuirassier Regiment (6)
  - Cuirassier Brigade: Oberst von Seymann

1 Source: von Hiller, F., *Geschichte des Feldzügen*.

Konstantin Cuirassier Regiment (6)
Sommariva Cuirassier Regiment (6)
Reserve Artillery:
Austrian 12pdr Foot Battery, Oberlieutenant Wiegel

Reinforcements: en route from Württemberg for 2nd Division[2]
Leib-Infantry Regiment #1 (2)
3 Land Regiments

Note: In the battle of Montereau on 18 February the 9th and 10th Württemberg Infantry Regiments were nearly totally destroyed or captured. In addition, the 2nd, 3rd, 6th and 7th Württemberg Infantry Regiments had suffered very heavy losses. The Württemberg elements of the corps report losing 2,844 men in this battle. These regiments were rebuilt around 6 March by disbanding the 3rd, 4th and 5th Land Regiments and absorbing their men into the under-strength line regiments.

2 Departed from Württemberg 21 February 1814.

Appendix LVII

French forces, Battle of Rheims, 13 March 1814

I Cavalry Corps: Général de division Bordesoulle
- Gardes d'honneur Division: Général de division Defrance
- 1st Light Cavalry Division: Général de division Merlin
- 2nd Heavy Cavalry Division: Général de division Bordesoulle

Reserve Corps: Maréchal Mortier
- 1st Old Guard Division: Général de division Friant
- 2nd Old Guard Division: Général de brigade Christiani
- 3rd Provisional Young Guard Division: Général de brigade Poret de Morvan
- Guard Cavalry: Général de division Sébastiani
- 1st Guard Cavalry Division: Général de division Colbert
- Division: Général de division Excelmans

Corps: Maréchal Ney
- 9th Division: Général de division P. Boyer
- 1st Young Guard (1st Voltigeur) Division: Général de division Meunier
- 2nd Young Guard Division: Général de division Curial

VI Corps: Marmont
- Division: Général de division Lagrange (232 officers / 1,463 men)
- Division: Général de division Ricard (94 officers / 625 men)
- Division: Général de division Arrighi (145 officers / 621 men)
- Cavalry: (72 officers / 626 men)

Total present: probably about 33,000 men

Appendix LVIII

Allied forces, Battle of Rheims, 13 March 1814

8th Russian Corps: Generalleutnant St. Priest
- 11th Division: Generalmajor Gurgalov
  - Brigade: Generalmajor Karpenkov
    - Polotsk Infantry Regiment (2)
    - Jeletz Infantry Regiment (2)
  - Brigade: Generalmajor Bistrom
    - 1st Jager Regiment (2)
    - 33rd Jager Regiment (2)
- 17th Division: Generalmajor Pilar
  - Brigade: Colonel Kern
    - Riazan Infantry Regiment (2)
    - Bielosersk Infantry Regiment (2)
  - Artillery:
    - Unknown Light Battery (12 guns)
    - Detached from 4th Dragoon Division: Generalmajor Emmanuel
    - Kharkov Dragoon Regiment (4)
    - Kiev Dragoon Regiment (4)
- 1st Chasseur Division: Generalleutnant Pantschulischev
  - Brigade: Generalmajor Denissiev
    - Arasmass Chasseurs à cheval Regiment (1)
    - Seversk Chasseurs à cheval Regiment (4)
    - Tchernigov Chasseurs à cheval Regiment (3)

Prussians: General von Jagow
- 1/1st Pomeranian Landwehr Regiment (7 / 15 / 5 / 202)[1]
- 2/1st Pomeranian Landwehr Regiment (9 / 17 / 1 / 266)
- 3/1st Pomeranian Landwehr Regiment (14 / 32 / 8 / 343)
- 1/5th Kurmärk Landwehr Regiment (11 / 28 / 3 / 265)
- 2/5th Kurmärk Landwehr Regiment (15 / 34 / 8 / 259)
- 3/5th Kurmärk Landwehr Regiment (9 / 23 / 3 / 152)
- 1/3rd Pomeranian Landwehr Regiment (detached before battle)
- 3/3rd Pomeranian Landwehr Regiment (12 / 32 / 9 / 327)
- 1/2nd Neumark Landwehr Regiment (15 / 19 / 8 / 221)
- 3/2nd Neumark Landwehr Regiment (detached before battle)
- 7th Kurmärk Landwehr Cavalry Regiment (9 / 8 / 2 / 58)
- 1st West Prussian Landwehr Cavalry Regiment (4 / 14 / 2 / 21)
- von Oppen Prussian 6pdr Foot Battery (eight guns)
- Prussian 7pdr Howitzer Battery (six guns)

1 Numbers are officers, NCOs, musicians and rank and file.

Appendix LIX

French Army of the Rhône, 15 March 1814[1]

1st Division: Général de division Musnier
 1st Brigade: Général de brigade Ordonneau
  1/, 2/20th Line Regiment (851)
 2nd Brigade: Adjudant-Commandant Passelac
  2/32nd Légère Regiment (588)
  1/2nd Toulon Regiment (601)
  6/24th Line Regiment (699)
  Det/16th Line Regiment (254)
 Artillery:
  2-8pdrs, 2-4pdrs and 2-6" howitzers
2nd Division: Général de division Pannetier
 1st Brigade: Général de brigade Gudin
  1/, 2/1st Légère Regiment (1,280)
  1/, 2/16th Line Regiment (1,184)
 2nd Brigade: Général de brigade Estève
  1/, 2/23rd Légère Regiment (1,078)
  1/, 2/7th Line Regiment (1,119)
 Artillery:
  2-8pdrs and 2-4pdrs
3rd Division: Général de division Bardet
 Detached Brigade: Général de brigade Pouchelon
  2/24th Line Regiment (538)
  Det. 7/16th Line Regiment (247)
  Det. 2/145th Line Regiment (313)
 1st Brigade: Général de brigade Soyez
  6/23rd Légère Regiment (527)
  6/60th Line Regiment (513)
  7/67th Line Regiment (518)
 2nd Brigade: Général de brigade Lachèse
  6/20th Line Regiment (514)
  6/115th Line Regiment (569)
 Cavalry:
  Det/1st Hussar Regiment (140)
  Det/4th Chasseurs à cheval Regiment (16)
  Det/3st Chasseurs à cheval Regiment (48)
  Imperial Gendarmes (24)
 Artillery:
  4-4pdrs and 2-6" howitzers
  4th Division: Général de division Marchand
 Brigades: Généraux Serrant and de Barral
  3/8th Légère Regiment (275)
  1/18th Légère Regiment (527)

1 Zins, pp. 283-8.

3/1st Line Regiment (589)
4/5th Line Regiment (1,013)
4/11th Line Regiment (722)
3/23rd Line Regiment (388)
7/60th Line Regiment (266)
7/79th Line Regiment (271)
7/81st Line Regiment (375)
Corps francs (182)
Customs Guards (201)
4th Chasseurs à cheval (43)
31st Chasseurs à cheval (23)
Simplon Gendarmes (26)
Léman Gendarmes (29)
Gendarmes de Mont-Blanc (41)
8th and 29th Cos/2nd Artillery Regiment (136)
3rd Provisional Train Company (55)
Artillery:
6-12pdrs
Reserve Brigade: Général de brigade Rémond
Rhône National Guard Regiment (595)
Cantal et Haute-Loire National Guard Regiment (585)
Haute-Vienne National Guard Regiment (878)
Indre National Guard Regiment (786)
Nièvre National Guard Regiment (393)
Puy-de-Dôme National Guard Regiment (188)
Cavalry Division: Général de division Digeon
1st Brigade: Général de brigade Guillemet
1/, 2/, 3/, 4/4th Hussar Regiment (583)
1/, 2/, 3/, 4/12th Hussar Regiment (463)
1/, 2/, 3/, 4/13th Cuirassier Regiment (537)
Det/1st Hussar Regiment (55)
Chasseurs Lyonnais (87)
Artillery:
2-8pdrs, 2-4pdrs and 2-6" howitzers
Artillery Division: Général de division Saint-Maurice
28/3rd Foot Artillery Regiment (2-8pdrs and 4-4pdrs) (95)
1st Company, Naval Gunners (120)
2nd Company, Naval Gunners (118)
3rd Company, Naval Gunners (122)
4th Company, Naval Gunners (122)
7/4th Horse Artillery Regiment (59)
9th Artillery Artisan Company (24)
1st Provisional Train Company (128)
2nd Provisional Train Company (113)
3rd Provisional Train Company (55)
2nd Park Division (2-4pdrs)
Lyon artillery depot (2-8pdrs and 3-4pdrs)

En route from Spain:
Division: Général de brigade Beurman
1st Column: Adjudant commandant Ricard
1/32nd Légère Regiment (900)
3/116th Line Regiment (750)

2nd Column: Général de brigade Gay
1/, 2/79th Line Regiment (1,800)
1/, 2/116th Line Regiment (1,500)
3rd Column: Adjudant-Commandant Grange
1/, 2/102nd Line Regiment (1,700)
1/, 2/115th Line Regiment (1,800)
4th Column:
3/102nd Line Regiment (651)
Artillery and Train (384)
Gendarmerie (17)
Military Administration (151)

Appendix LX

Marchand's Division in Grenoble, 15 March 1814

3/8th Légère Regiment (14 / 274)
1/18th Légère Regiment (18 / 636)
3/1st Line Regiment (18 / 598)
4/5th Line Regiment (18 / 774)
4/11th Line Regiment (19 / 722)
3/23rd Line Regiment (16 / 376)
7/60th Line Regiment (4 / 294)
7/79th Line Regiment (14 / 252)
7/81st Line Regiment (13 / 374)
Garrison of Mont-Cenis (? / 504)
Customs Officers (66 / 206)
Corps francs (11 / 291)
4th and 25th Chasseurs à cheval Regiment (66)
Foot Artillery (1 / 22) (7 – 4pdrs and 1 howitzer)
Gendarmes (94)

Appendix LXI

Miscellaneous French forces, 15 March 1814[1]

Polish Corps: Général de division Dombrowski
- Infantry: Général de brigade Sierawski
  - Staff/Vistula Regiment (10 / 10)
  - 1/Vistula Regiment (15 / 345)
  - 2/Vistula Regiment (17 / 374)
  - Staff/Depot Vistula Regiment (7 / 7)
  - Infantry/Depot Vistula Regiment (3 / 349)
  - Cavalry/Depot Vistula Regiment (3 / 111)
  - Veterans/Depot Vistula Regiment (2 / 48)
  - Officers à la suite (372)
  - Garde d'honneur (199)
- Artillery:
  - 1st Foot Battery "Radziwzenski" (5 / 124)
  - 2nd Foot Battery "Pietka" (5 / 124)
  - 3rd Foot Battery "Choynacki" (5 / 124)
  - 4th Foot Battery "Bryalski" (5 / 125)
  - 1st Horse Battery "Orlinski" (5 / 119)
  - Sappers "Miller-Capitz" 4 / 60)

Berckheim's Cavalry Division: Général de division Berckheim
- 1st Brigade: Général de brigade Curely
  - 1st Provisional Regiment (406)
    - 9th Hussar Regiment (62)
    - 11th Chasseurs à cheval Regiment (80)
    - 23rd Chasseurs à cheval Regiment (99)
    - 26th Chasseurs à cheval Regiment (19)
    - 2nd Chevauléger-lancier Regiment (149)
  - 2nd Provisional Regiment (492)
    - 12th Chasseurs à cheval Regiment (85)
    - 4th Chevauléger-lancier Regiment (82)
    - 6th Chevauléger-lancier Regiment (325)
  - 3rd Provisional Regiment (179)
    - 3rd Hussar Regiment (77)
    - 16th Chasseurs à cheval Regiment (13)
    - 26th Chasseurs à cheval Regiment (64)
    - 27th Chasseurs à cheval Regiment (21)
- 2nd Brigade: Général de brigade Mourier
  - 1st Provisional Regiment (501)
    - 1st Carabinier Regiment (92)
    - 2nd Carabinier Regiment (92)
    - 9th Cuirassier Regiment (149)
    - 10th Cuirassier Regiment (86)
    - 13th Cuirassier Regiment (124)

1 French Archives, Carton C^2 555, C^2 556 and C^2 557.

2nd Provisional Regiment (229)
15th Dragoon Regiment (126)
2nd Dragoon Regiment (8)
18th Dragoon Regiment (36)
19th Dragoon Regiment (8)
20th Dragoon Regiment (15)
25th Dragoon Regiment (38)

Appendix LXII

French Guard under Léfèbvre-Desnoëttes, 16 March 1814[1]

Old Guard Chasseurs à pied (101)
9th Voltigeur Regiment (1,225)
Provisional Guard Battalion (772)
Old Guard Grenadiers à Pied (66)
Provisional Guard Battalion (268)
Provisional Battalion (detached) (367)
1st Éclaireur Regiment (150)
2nd Éclaireur Regiment (100)
3rd Éclaireur Regiment (135)
1st Guard Lancer Regiment (120)
2nd Guard Lancer Regiment (200)
Guard Chasseurs à cheval (330)
Guard Dragoons (260)
Guard Grenadiers à cheval (130)
Gendarmes d'élite (60)
Two Artillery Companies (14 guns)

1 French Archives, Carton C^2 556.

Appendix LXIII

French Army under Napoleon on the Aisne, 17 March 1814[1]

Wing: Maréchal Mortier, Duc de Trevise
- 2nd Guard Division: Général de brigade Christiani
  - Brigade: unknown
    - Fusilier Chasseur Regiment (565)
    - Fusilier Grenadier Regiment (551)
    - Vélites of Turin (61)
  - Brigade: Général de brigade Gros
    - Flanqueur Chasseur Regiment (434)
    - Flanqueur Grenadier Regiment (371)
    - Vélites of Florence (52)
- 2nd Young Guard Division: Général de division Curial
  - Brigade: Général de brigade Lagrange
    - 1st Voltigeur Regiment (165)
    - 2nd Voltigeur Regiment (127)
    - 3rd Voltigeur Regiment (286)
    - 4th Voltigeur Regiment (174)
    - Converged 1/14th Tirailleur Regiment (522)
    - 1/, 3/14th Tirailleur Regiment
    - 3/13th Tirailleur Regiment
  - Brigade: Général de brigade Le Capitaine
    - 2/14th Tirailleur Regiment (426)
    - Converged 1/14th Tirailleur Regiment (556)
    - 1/14th Tirailleur Regiment
    - 3/11th Tirailleur Regiment
    - Converged 1/13th Tirailleur Regiment (540)
    - 3/3rd Tirailleur Regiment
    - 4th Tirailleur Regiment
    - 10th Tirailleur Regiment
- 7th Young Guard Division: Général de division Charpentier
  - Brigade: Général de brigade Jamin
    - 5th Voltigeur Regiment (217)
    - 6th Voltigeur Regiment (322)
    - 7th Voltigeur Regiment (468)
    - Converged 8th Voltigeur Regiment (236)
    - 4th Voltigeur Regiment
    - 8th Voltigeur Regiment
  - Brigade: Général de brigade Bigarré
    - 3/3rd Voltigeur Regiment (155)
    - 3/14th Voltigeur Regiment (282)
    - 2/11th Voltigeur Regiment (534)
    - 9th Tirailleur Regiment (1 battalion) (541)

1 Koch, F., *Memoirs pour servier à l'Histoire.*

- Artillery:
    - Artillery and Train (600)
    - Sappers (150)
- 6th Heavy Cavalry Division: Général de division Roussel d'Hurbal
    - Brigade: Général de brigade Sparre
        - 5th Dragoon Regiment (412)
        - 12th Dragoon Regiment (317)
    - Brigade: Général de brigade Rigaud
        - 21st Dragoon Regiment (483)
        - 26th Dragoon Regiment (530)
        - March Regiment (Colonel Guigy) (320)
        - March Regiment (unknown)
        - Horse Artillery (212)

Wing: Maréchal Marmont, Duc de Raguse

- 8th Division: Général de division Ricard (940 men)
    - Brigade: Général de brigade Pelleport
        - 6th Légère Regiment
        - 4th Line Regiment
        - 6th Line Regiment
        - 136th Line Regiment
    - Brigade: Général de brigade Clavel
        - 6th Légère Regiment
        - 19th Légère Regiment
        - 138th Line Regiment
        - 144th Line Regiment
- 3rd Division: Général de division Lagrange (2,060 men)
    - Brigade: Général de brigade Joubert
        - 23rd Légère Regiment
        - 37th Légère Regiment
        - 15th Line Regiment
        - 16th Line Regiment
        - 70th Line Regiment
        - 121st Line Regiment
    - Brigade: Général de brigade Fournier
        - 1st Line Regiment
        - 62nd Line Regiment
        - 132nd Line Regiment
        - 1st Marine Regiment
        - 2nd Marine Regiment
        - 3rd Marine Regiment
        - 4th Marine Regiment
- Division: Général de division Arrighi, Duke of Padua (2,080 men)
    - Brigade: Général de brigade Lucotte
        - 43rd Line Regiment
        - 65th Line Regiment
        - 70th Line Regiment
        - 85th Line Regiment
    - Brigade: unknown
        - 43rd Line Regiment
        - 50th Line Regiment
        - 66th Line Regiment
        - 88th Line Regiment

Artillery and Train

I Cavalry Corps:

1st Light Cavalry Division: Général de division Merlin

Brigade: Général de brigade Huber

6th Hussar Regiment (97)
7th Hussar Regiment (53)
8th Hussar Regiment (49)
1st Chevauléger Regiment (79)
3rd Chevauléger Regiment (85)
5th Chevauléger Regiment (70)
7th Chevauléger Regiment (67)
8th Chevauléger Regiment (75)

Brigade: Général de brigade Latour-Foissac

1st Chasseurs à cheval Regiment (60)
2nd Chasseurs à cheval Regiment (53)
3rd Chasseurs à cheval Regiment (85)
6th Chasseurs à cheval Regiment (47)
8th Chasseurs à cheval Regiment (67)
9th Chasseurs à cheval Regiment (80)
16th Chasseurs à cheval Regiment (83)
25th Chasseurs à cheval Regiment (63)

2nd Heavy Cavalry Division: Général de division Bordesoulle

Brigade: Général de brigade Thiry

2nd Cuirassier Regiment (72)
3rd Cuirassier Regiment (97)
6th Cuirassier Regiment (120)
9th Cuirassier Regiment (83)
11th Cuirassier Regiment (93)
12th Cuirassier Regiment (121)

Brigade: Général de brigade Laville

4th Cuirassier Regiment (95)
7th Cuirassier Regiment (84)
14th Cuirassier Regiment (124)
7th Dragoon Regiment (70)
23rd Dragoon Regiment (98)
28th Dragoon Regiment (123)
30th Dragoon Regiment (86)
Artillery and Train (281)

	Infantry	Cavalry	Artillery	Total:
Mortier:	7,585	2,062	962	10,609
Marmont:	5,080	2,379	757	8,216
Total:	**12,665**	**4,441**	**1,719**	**18,825**

Facing the combined Armies of Silesia and North with:

Prussians:	Infantry	Cavalry	Artillery	Total:
von Yorck:	8,870	3,298	1,651	13,799
Kleist:	7,165	2,581	1,151	10,897
von Bülow:	13,628	2,643	1,091	17,362
Russians:				
Langeron	18,432	5,426	1,827	25,685
von Sacken	8,335	3,903	1,358	13,596
Winzingerode	13,966	11,331	2,432	27,729
Overall total:	**70,396**	**29,182**	**9,490**	**109,068**

Appendix LXIV

Wittgenstein's Corps, 18 March 1814[1]

Cavalry: Generalleutnant Graf Pahlen
- 2nd Cuirassier Division: Generallieutenant Kretov
  - Brigade: Generalmajor Leontiev
    - Gluchov Cuirassier Regiment (6) (1 / 3 / 16 / 55 / 431)[2]
    - Pskof Cuirassier Regiment (6) (0 / 2 / 17 / 54 / 361)
  - Brigade: Generalmajor Stahl II
    - Ekaterinoslav Cuirassier Regiment (3) (1 / 2 / 13 / 39 / 217)
    - Astrakhan Cuirassier Regiment (4) (1 / 3 / 18 / 50 / 283)
- 1st Hussar Division: Generallieutenant Pahlen
  - Brigade: Generalmajor Delajanov
    - Soumy Hussar Regiment (2) (2 / 1 / 14 / 28 / 124)
    - Grodno Hussar Regiment (5) (1 / 2 / 40 / 50 / 315)
  - Brigade: Generalmajor Dechterev
    - Loubny Hussar Regiment (2) (0 / 0 / 2 / 22 / 220)
    - Olviopol Hussar Regiment (4) (2 / 1 / 17 / 27 / 255)
- 3rd Uhlan Division:
  - Brigade: Generalmajor Lissanewitz
    - Tchougouiev Uhlan Regiment (8) (1 / 1 / 44 / 75 / 642)
  - Reserve:
    - Horse Battery #6 (8 guns) (0 / 4 / 12 / 126)
    - Horse Battery #23 (3 guns) (sent to reserve to reorganize)

1st Infantry Corps: Generalleutnant Prince Gorchakov II
- Cavalry:
    - Det/4th Dragoon Division:
    - Ingremannland Dragoon Regiment (3) (0 / 1 / 11 / 11 / 59)
- 3rd Hussar Division: Generalmajor von Pahlen
    - Irkusk Hussar Regiment (1) (0 / 1 / 2 / 7 / 23)
- 5th Division: Generalmajor Menzenzov
  - Brigade: Generalmajor Nabokov
    - Perm Infantry Regiment (2) (0 / 1 / 2 / 21 / 45 / 841)
    - Sieversk Infantry Regiment (2) (1 / 3 / 24 / 68 / 819)
  - Brigade: Colonel Milavanov
    - Mohilev Infantry Regiment (2) (0 / 3 / 23 / 66 / 894)
    - Kalouga Infantry Regiment (2) (0 / 1 / 20 / 68 / 981)
  - Brigade: Generalmajor Vlassov
    - 23rd Jager Regiment (2) (0 / 5 / 27 / 84 / 959)
    - 24th Jager Regiment (2) (1 / 1 / 15 / 67 / 853)
- 14th Division: Generalmajor von Helfrich
  - Brigade: Generalmajor Ljalin

1 von Bernhardi, Vol. 4, Book 8, pp. 423-6.
2 Numbers are: first series – squadrons or battalions; second series – colonels, senior officers, junior officers, NCOs, soldiers/troopers.

- Tenguinsk Infantry Regiment (1) (1 / 1 / 26 / 53 / 320)
- Estonia Infantry Regiment (1) (1 / 1 / 10 / 29 / 490)

Brigade:
- Tula Converged Regiment (1) (0 / 1 / 4 / 26 / 353)
- Navaguinsk Converged Regiment (1) (0 / 0 / 3 / 23 / 365)

Brigade: Generalmajor Roth
- 25th Jager Regiment (1) (0 / 1 / 8 / 45 / 487)
- 26th Jager Regiment (1) (0 / 2 / 25 / 58 / 826)

14th Artillery Brigade:
- Light Battery #27 (10 guns) (0 / 0 / 6 / 16 / 230)
- Position Battery #14 (12 guns) (0 / 1 / 6 / 8 / 117)

2nd Pioneer Brigade:
- Lt. Colonel Kinitschikov Pioneer Company (0 / 1 / 2 / 8 / 94)

2nd Infantry Corps: Generallieutenant Prince Eugene von Württemberg

3rd Division: Generallieutenant Prince Schachovsky

Brigade: Colonel von Wolff
- Tchernigov Infantry Regiment (2) (0 / 3 / 34 / 73 / 804)
- Mourmonsk Infantry Regiment (2) (0 / 3 / 23 / 81 / 982)

Brigade: Colonel Schelwinsky (Brigade was sent to Plock to reorganize)
- Revel Infantry Regiment
- Seleguinsk Infantry Regiment

Brigade: Colonel Kapustin
- 20th Jager Regiment (2) (1 / 3 / 24 / 34 / 809)
- 21st Jager Regiment (1) (0 / 1 / 16 / 43 / 516)

4th Division: Generalmajor Puschnizky

Brigade: Colonel von Rosen
- Tobolsk Infantry Regiment (2) (0 / 2 / 17 / 61 / 713)
- Krementchug Infantry Regiment (2) (1 / 3 / 27 / 72 / 755)

Brigade: Colonel Kursonov
- Minsk Infantry Regiment (1) (0 / 1 / 10 / 20 / 329)
- Volhynie Infantry Regiment (2) (0 / 3 / 18 / 74 / 899)

Brigade: Colonel Stepanov
- 4th Jager Regiment (2) (0 / 1 / 13 / 44 / 680)
- 34th Jager Regiment (1)(0 / 2 / 6 / 29 / 402)

3rd Artillery Brigade:
- Light Batteries #6 (12 guns) (0 / 1 / 9 / 13 / 175)

21st Reserve Brigade:
- Position Battery #33 (12 guns) (0 / 1 / 4 / 17 / 217)

Detached:

1st Hussar Division: Generalmajor Seslavin
- Soumy Hussar Regiment (3) (1 / 2 / 18 / 36 / 203)

1st Hussar Division: (Blockade of Kehl)
- Loubny Hussar Regiment (3) (0 / 1 / 32 / 34 / 300)
- Tschermuschin Don Cossack Regiment (0 / 1 / 7 / 10 / 287)
- 1/2 Bislov II Don Cossack Regiment (0 / 0 / 2 / 2 / 139)

3rd Artillery Brigade:
- Position Battery #3 (12 guns) (0 / 1 / 7 / 15 / 242)

14th Brigade: (Blockade of Landau)
- Jaroslav Cossack Regiment (0 / 4 / 14 / 42 / 278)
- Light Battery #27 (2 guns) (0 / 0 / 1 / 1 / 26)

2nd Reserve Brigade:
- Position Battery #29 (12 guns) (0 / 0 / 5 / 15 / 270)

Headquarters Escort
Cavalry
2nd Bug Cossack Regiment (0 / 2 / 5 / 2 / 30)
Commando, Don Cossack Regiment Solotarev (0 / 0 / 0 / 1 / 3)

Infantry
Olonetz Opolochenie (1) (1 / 0 / 12 / 25 / 196)
Vologda Opolochenie (1) (0 / 2 / 9 / 15 / 188)

Appendix LXV

French I Corps, 20 March 1814[1]

4th Young Guard Division: Général de division Barrois
- 1/, 2/12th Voltigeurs (19 / 581)
- 1/, 2/2nd Tirailleur Regiment (26 / 771)
- 1/, 2/3rd Tirailleur Regiment (24 / 610)
- 1/, 2/4th Tirailleur Regiment (27 / 793)

Solignac's Division: Général de division Solignac
- Brigade: Général de brigade Penne
  - Det/27th Légère Regiment (12 / 465)
  - Det/17th Line Regiment (21 / 618)
  - Det/28th Line Regiment (16 / 346)
- Brigade: Unknown
  - Det/51st Line Regiment (20 / 422)
  - Det/6th Line Regiment (21 / 391)
  - Det/75th Line Regiment (18 / 470)
- Artillery and Train:
  - 3rd Old Guard Horse Artillery Company (4 / 95) (4-6pdrs and 2 5.7" howitzers)
  - 3rd Young Guard Foot Artillery Company (5-6pdrs and 2 5.7" howitzers)
  - 13th Young Guard Foot Artillery Company (5-6pdrs and 2 5.7" howitzers)
    - Total Foot Artillery: (9 / 145)
  - 7/1st Train Battalion
  - 8/1st Train Battalion
  - 10/1st Train Battalion
  - 8/2nd Train Battalion
  - 2/2nd Train Battalion
    - Total Train: (3 / 216)
  - Artisan Pioneers (0 / 5)

Cavalry: Général de division Castex
- Brigade: Général de brigade Meuziau
  - 2nd Guard Chevauléger Regiment (Young Guard Squadrons) (23 / 256 / 66 / 256)
  - 2nd Guard Chasseurs à cheval Regiment (Young Guard Squadrons) (23 / 538 / 65 / 537)
  - 1st Gardes d'honneur (7 / 141 / 20 / 141)
- Other:
  - Gendarmerie (1 / 24 / 2 / 24)

1 Calmon-Maison, J.J.R., *Le General Maison et le ler Corps de la Grande Armée*. Numbers are officers, men, officers' horses and men's horses.

Appendix LXVI

Casualties of Lefol's Division at Arcis-sur-Aube, 20 March 1814[1]

2nd Légère Regiment (0 / 1 / 0 / 2 / 10 / 0)
24th Line Regiment (0 / 1 / 0 / 0 / 7 / 0)
34th Line Regiment (6 / 1 / 0 / 200 / 124 / 0)
Vistula Regiment (0 / 11 / 0 / 11 / 76 / 0)
12th Line Regiment (1 / 10 / 0 / 37 / 167)
36th Line Regiment (0 / 0 / 0 / 12 / 41 / 0)
122nd Line Regiment (1 / 10 / 0 / 29 / 294 / 0)
4th Bataillon de Marche (2 / 0 / 0 / 3 / 115 / 0)

1 French Archives, Carton C[2] 556. Numbers are officers killed, officers wounded, officers captured, enlisted killed, enlisted wounded and enlisted captured.

Appendix LXVII

Bavarian Army Corps, Battle of Arcis-sur-Aube, 20-21 March 1814[1]

Commanding Officer: Général der Kavallerie Graf Wrede
Headquarters:
Feldgendarmerie Squadron
- 1st Division: Generalleutenant von Rechberg und Rothenlöwen
  - 1st Brigade: Generalmajor Prince Karl von Bayern
    - 1/1st Line Infantry Regiment
    - 2/1st Line Infantry Regiment
    - 1/3rd Line Infantry Regiment
    - 3rd Jäger Battalion
    - 10th National Field Battalion
  - 2nd Brigade: Generalmajor Graf Spreti
    - 2/2nd Line Infantry Regiment
    - 1/10th Line Infantry Regiment
    - 11th National Field Battalion
    - 15th National Field Battalion
  - 1st Cavalry Brigade: Generalmajor Freiherr von Vieregg
    - 2/, 3/, 4/, 5/1st Chevauléger Regiment (4)
    - 2/, 3/, 4/, 5/2nd Chevauléger Regiment (4)
    - 1/, 2/, 3/7th Chevauléger Regiment (3)
  - 1st Artillery Commando: Oberst Göschl
    - 5th 6pdr Foot Battery
    - 4th Wurst Battery (6pdrs)
- 3rd Division: Generalleutenant von Freiherr von Lamotte
  - 1st Brigade: Generalmajor Jason von der Stockh
    - 1/11th Line Infantry Regiment
    - 2/11th Line Infantry Regiment
    - 1/7th Line Infantry Regiment
    - 1st Iller Kreis Battalion
    - 1st Under-Donau Kreis Battalion
  - 2nd Brigade: Generalmajor von Deroy
    - 1/5th Line Infantry Regiment
    - 1/8th Line Infantry Regiment
    - 1/9th Line Infantry Regiment
    - 5th National Field Battalion
    - 6th National Field Battalion
  - 1st Cavalry Brigade: Oberst Diez
    - 2/, 4/, 5/4th Chevauléger Regiment
    - 2/, 4/, 5/Chevauléger Regiment
  - 3rd Artillery Commando: Major Wagner
    - 9th 6pdr Foot Battery

1 *Königlich Bayernisch Kriegsarchiv, Darstellungen aus der Bayerischen Kriegs-und Heeresgeschichte.*

1st Wurst Battery (6pdrs)
Artillery Reserve: Hauptmann Ulmer
30pdr Mortar Battery
6pdr Foot Battery
3rd 12pdr Foot Battery
8th 12pdr Foot Battery
11th 12pdr Foot Battery
12th 12pdr Foot Battery
Pontooneer Company
Munition Reserve
Main Munition Reserve:
Field Laboratory
Munition Column

Appendix LXVIII

German 3rd Army Corps, 25 March 1814[1]

Royal Saxon Army:
- General Staff (27 / 7)
  - Cavalry: (1 / 59 / 59)
    - Staff Dragoons (1 / 59 / 59)
    - 1/, 2/, 3/Cuirassier Regiment (32 / 547 / 464)
    - 1/, 2/, 3/Uhlan Regiment (26 / 429 / 411)
    - 1/, 2/, 3/Hussar Regiment (35 / 545 / 525)
  - Line Infantry:
    - Staff/, 1/Grenadier Regiment (11 / 607)
    - 2/Grenadier Regiment (17 / 629)
    - 3/Grenadier Regiment (15 / 688)
    - 1/1st Provisional Regiment (14 / 508)
    - Staff/, 2/1st Provisional Regiment (14 / 503)
    - 3/1st Provisional Regiment (17 / 624)
    - 1/Provisional Regiment (13 / 520)
    - Staff/, 2/Provisional Regiment (16 / 513)
    - 3/Provisional Regiment (16 / 546)
    - Jäger Battalion (13/540)
    - 1/1st Light Regiment (10 / 580)
    - 2/1st Light Regiment (10 / 580)
    - 2/2nd Light Regiment (13 / 654)
  - Landwehr:
    - 1/1st Regiment (14 / 756)
    - 2/1st Regiment (13 / 710)
    - 3/1st Regiment (14 / 750)
    - 1/2nd Regiment (11 / 733)
    - 2/2nd Regiment (13 / 732)
    - 3/2nd Regiment (16 / 746)
    - 1/3rd Regiment (20 / 661)
    - 2/3rd Regiment (17 / 700)
    - 3/3rd Regiment (15 / 716)
    - 1/4th Regiment (17 / 768)
    - 2/4th Regiment (16 / 766)
    - 3/4th Regiment (15/767)
  - Artillery:
    - 1st Horse Battery (6 guns) (4 / 134)
    - 2nd Horse Battery (6 guns) (4 / 133)
    - 1st 12pdr Battery (2 / 168)
    - 2nd 12pdr Battery (1 / 200)
    - 1st 6pdr Battery (1 / 119)
    - 3rd 6pdr Battery (1 / 57)

1 Bucher, L.F., *Der Feldzug des dritten detuschen Armee-Corps in Flandern*. Numbers for cavalry units are officers, men and horses.

1st Reserve Park (2 / 91)
Grand Park (16 / 396)
Sapper-Pontooneer Detachment (2 / 52)
Thuringia-Anhalt Division:
Weimar Fusilier Battalion (12 / 666)
Gotha Battalion (18 / 856)
Schwarzberg Battalion (14 / 492)
Dessau-Köthen Battalion (16 / 576)
Bernberg Battalion («Landwehr) (11 / 429)
Weimar Landwehr Battalion (5 / 290)
Gotha Landwehr Battalion (16 / 547)
Schwarzberg Landwehr Battalion (12 / 450)
Dessau-Köthen Landwehr Battalion (16 / 576)
Weimar and Gotha Jäger Squadron (5 / 56 / 56)
Weimar Freiwilliger Jäger zu Fuss Company (4 / 84)
Gotha Freiwilliger Jäger zu Fuss Company (4 / 85)
Schwarzberg Freiwilliger Jäger zu Fuss Company (4 / 154)
Russo-German Legion:[2]
1/, 2/, 3/, 4/1st Russo-German Hussar Regiment (24 / 600 / 600)
1/, 2/, 3/, 4/2nd Russo-German Hussar Regiment (24 / 600 / 600)
Keilmannsegg Jäger Battalion (13 / 560)
1st Russo-German Legion Battalion (14 / 400)
2nd Russo-German Legion Battalion (14 / 400)
3rd Russo-German Legion Battalion (14 / 400)
4th Russo-German Legion Battalion (14 / 400)
5th Russo-German Legion Battalion (14 / 400)
6th Russo-German Legion Battalion (14 / 400)
1st Horse Battery (8 guns) (5 / 188)
2nd Horse Battery (8 guns) (5 / 188)
Foot Battery (8 guns) (5 / 200)
Park Column (4 / 74)

2 The numbers for the Russo-German Legion do not appear to be actual field returns, but estimates. Normal strength for the hussar regiments was 30 / 615 / 611, Keilmannsegg – 18 / 600; infantry battalions – 20 / 887; and horse artillery – 5 / 188.

Appendix LXIX

French forces, Battle of Paris, 30 March 1814[1]

Commanding Officer: King Joseph, Lieutenant de l'Empereur
Chief of Staff: Général de division Count Mathieu
Minister of War: Général de division Duc de Feltre
Commandant 1st Military Division: Général de division Count Hulin

Right wing: Maréchal Marmont
Provisional Cavalry Corps: Général de division Compans
Division: Général de division Chastel
Brigade: Général de brigade Vincent

I Cavalry Corps: (1,600 cavalry deployed in a line between Charonne and Montreuil)
1st Light Cavalry Division: Général de division Merlin (850 men)[2]
Brigade: Général de brigade Huber
6th Hussar Regiment (0 / 1)
7th Hussar Regiment (7 / 34)
8th Hussar Regiment (3 / 35)
1st Chevauléger-lancier Regiment (1 / 54)
3rd Chevauléger-lancier Regiment (3 / 30)
5th Chevauléger-lancier Regiment (3 / 26)
7th Chevauléger-lancier Regiment (1 / 33)
Brigade: Général de brigade Latour-Foissac
1st Chasseurs à cheval Regiment (10 / 18)
3rd Chasseurs à cheval Regiment (6 / 39)
8th Chasseurs à cheval Regiment (23 / 114)
9th Chasseurs à cheval Regiment (3 / 9)
16th Chasseurs à cheval Regiment (6 / 38)[3]
2nd Heavy Cavalry Division: Général de division Bordesoulle (895 men)[4]
Brigade: Général de brigade Thiry
2nd Cuirassier Regiment (5 / 54)
3rd Cuirassier Regiment (4 / 43)
6th Cuirassier Regiment (8/ 49)
9th Cuirassier Regiment (15 / 118)
11th Cuirassier Regiment (9 / 45)
12th Cuirassier Regiment (12 / 79)
Brigade: Général de brigade Laville[5]
7th Dragoon Regiment (7 / 48)
23rd Dragoon Regiment (10 / 92)

1 Koch, F., *Memoirs pour servier à l'Histoire*; Rapetti, *La Défection de Marmont en 1814;* French Archives, Carton C^2 555, C^2 556 and C^2 557.
2 The regimental strengths for Merlin's division date from 5 April 1814.
3 Deployed in a 2nd line behind the road to Montreuil.
4 The regimental strengths for Bordesoulle's division date from 5 April 1814.
5 Deployed in a 2nd line behind the road to Montreuil.

28th Dragoon Regiment (11 / 80)
30th Dragoon Regiment (11 / 64)
4th Cuirassier Regiment (20 / 210)
7th Cuirassier Regiment (11 / 138)
14th Cuirassier Regiment (1 / 12)

VI Corps:
Division: Général de division Arrighi
Brigade: Général de brigade Lucotte (1,250 men)[6] [7]
1st Veteran Battalion (22 / 631)
2nd Veteran Battalion (24 / 680)
2/45th Line Regiment (29 / 162)
2/50th Line Regiment (25 / 80)
1/65th Line Regiment (12 / 38)
1/66th Line Regiment (9 / 73)
1/72nd Line Regiment (11 / 47)
3/85th Line Regiment (25 / 25)
1/88th Line Regiment (15 / 81)
8th Division: Général de division Ricard (726 men)
Brigade: Général de brigade Pelleport
6th Légère Regiment
4th Line Regiment
6th Line Regiment
136th Line Regiment
Brigade: Général de brigade Clavel[8]
6th Légère Regiment
19th Légère Regiment
138th Line Regiment
144th Line Regiment
3rd Division: Général de division Lagrange (1,395 men)[9]
Brigade: Général de brigade Fournier
1st Line Regiment
62nd Line Regiment
132nd Line Regiment
1st Marine Regiment
2nd Marine Regiment
3rd Marine Regiment
4th Marine Regiment
Brigade: Général de brigade Joubert
23rd Légère Regiment
37th Légère Regiment
15th Line Regiment
16th Line Regiment
70th Line Regiment
121st Line Regiment

6 Regimental strengths of Lucotte's brigade date from 4-5 April.
7 Occupying Montreuil and covering Bagnolet on the Malassie plateau.
8 In reserve – massed by battalion – before the Tourelles ridge.
9 Deployed with the first brigade to the right and the second to the left of the Belleville-Romainville road.

Provisional Corps: Général de division Compans
Division: Général de division Compans
Brigade: Général de brigade Chabert (2,220)[10]
(organization unknown)
Division: Général de division Ledru des Essarts
Brigade: Général de brigade Bongars (1,600)[11]
(organization unknown)
Division: Général de division Boyer de Rebeval[12]
Brigade: Général de brigade Guye (1,850)
Staff/, 2/6/19th Légère Regiment
3/5th Line Regiment
3/11th Line Regiment
2nd Brigade:
11/107th Line Regiment
1/, 2/Gardes Nationale du Nord
Artillery:
6/1st Foot Artillery
19/2nd Foot Artillery
20/5th Foot Artillery
1/8th Principal Train Battalion
2/5th Principal Train Battalion

Left wing: Maréchal Mortier
Guard Depots: Général de division Michel (4,000 men)
Brigade: Colonel Sécrétan
(behind Pantin, organization unknown)
Brigade: Colonel Robert
(before Aubervilliers, organization unknown)

Guard Corps:
7th Young Guard Division: Général de division Charpentier (1,500)[13] [14]
Brigade: Général de brigade Lagrange
1st Voltigeur Regiment (19 / 92)
2nd Voltigeur Regiment (12 / 104)
3rd Voltigeur Regiment (22 / 206)
4th Voltigeur Regiment (26 / 151)
5th Voltigeur Regiment (20 / 101)
7th Voltigeur Regiment (9 / 76)
Brigade: Général de brigade Le Capitaine
10th Voltigeur Regiment (24 / 268)
11th Voltigeur Regiment (17 / 100)
Cadre 12th Voltigeur Regiment (8 / 25)
Cadre 13th Voltigeur Regiment (5 / 24)
14th Voltigeur Regiment (16 / 121)
15th Voltigeur Regiment (20 / 196)

10 In skirmish formation in the Romainville woods.
11 Part deployed and part in mass on the Beauregard ridge.
12 Part deployed and part in mass before the village of Pre-Saint-Gervais.
13 Strengths as of 15 April 1814.
14 In reserve, massed at the foot of the Chaumont ridge.

2nd Young Guard Division: Général de division Curial [15]
Brigade: Général de brigade Bigarré (1,820)
5th Voltigeur Regiment
6th Voltigeur Regiment
7th Voltigeur Regiment
Converged 8th Voltigeur Regiment
4th Voltigeur Regiment
8th Voltigeur Regiment
3/3rd Voltigeur Regiment
3/14th Voltigeur Regiment
2/11th Voltigeur Regiment
9th Tirailleur Regiment (1 battalion)
2nd Old Guard Division: Général de brigade Christiani[16]
Brigade: Général de brigade Gros (1,630)
Fusilier Chasseur Regiment
Fusilier Grenadier Regiment
Flanqueur Chasseur Regiment
Flanqueur Grenadier Regiment
Vélites of Florence
Vélites of Turin

Cavalry Corps: Général de division Belliard
6th Heavy Cavalry Division: Général de division Roussel d'Hurbal (1,900)[17]
Brigade: Général de brigade Rigaud
21st Dragoon Regiment
26th Dragoon Regiment
2 March Regiments
Horse Artillery
Brigade: Général de brigade Sparre
5th Dragoon Regiment
12th Dragoon Regiment
Artillery:
3/3rd Horse Artillery
3/2nd Horse Artillery
2/5th Principal Train Battalion
1/2nd (bis) Train Battalion
5/6th Principal Train Battalion
Brigade: Colonel Ghigny
Unknown Marche Regiment(s)
Brigade: Général de brigade Christophe
Unknown Marche Regiment(s)
Brigade: Général de brigade Leclerc
Unknown Marche Regiment(s)

15 In reserve, massed behind Pantin – ready to support the attack of Secrétan's brigade.
16 In reserve, massed between Lavillette and La Chapelle – ready to support Robert's brigade.
17 Deployed on a line before the entrenchments of 1792 between the road from Saint-Denis and the avenue of the Maillot Gate.

Division: Général de division Ornano[18]
Brigade: Général de brigade Dautancourt (320)
Unknown Chasseurs à cheval
Other units unknown

Commandement: Maréchal Moncey, Duc de Conegliano
Paris Guard: (6,000 men)[19] [20]
1st Paris National Guard Legion
2nd Paris National Guard Legion
3rd Paris National Guard Legion
4th Paris National Guard Legion
5th Paris National Guard Legion
6th Paris National Guard Legion
7th Paris National Guard Legion
8th Paris National Guard Legion
9th Paris National Guard Legion
10th Paris National Guard Legion
12th Paris National Guard Legion
Paris Guard Artillery: (780 men)
Reserve: Major Evain
Combined force with Imperial Guard
Veteran-Cannoneers and students from the Ecole Polytechnique with 28 guns
Detachment: Grosbert
(organization unknown)
Line Artillery: (210)
Naval Gunners serving the batteries at Rouvroy, Pré-Saint Gervais and the Fontarabie ridge
Miscellaneous Garrisons:
Saint Maur (300 men, cadres of line infantry units)
Charenton (450 men, veterans' company and Elèves de l'Ecole de Alfort Battalion)
Vincennes (400 men, Young Guard Battalion and veterans' company)
Saint-Denis (570 men, Young Guard Battalion and the cadres of two line battalions)
Neuilly (250 men, cadre of line infantry battalion and a veteran company)

18 Deployed on the extreme left – standing by the Château Saint-Ouen Avenue.
19 On the extreme right of the extreme left on the heights of Fontarabie, Chaumont, Montmartre, Batignolles, Monceaux and l'Etoile. In skirmish formation in the Bercy, Menilmontan, Charonne and Belleville gardens and in the Clichy plain.
20 Division was composed of various veteran battalions and the Ecole Polytechnique Battalion.

Appendix LXX

Allied forces, Battle of Paris, 30-31 March 1814[1]

Blocking forces:

3rd Corps: FZM I. Giulay (10,000 men)
- Division: FML Crenneville
  - Brigade: Generalmajor von Hecht
    - Klenau Chevauxleger Regiment #5 (7)
    - St. George Warasdiner Grenz Regiment (1)
  - Brigade: Generalmajor von Trenck
    - Rosenburg Dragoon Regiment (6)
    - St. George Warasdiner Grenz Regiment (1)
    - Wurst Battery (6-6pdrs)
- Division: FML Fresnel
  - Brigade: Generalmajor von Pflüger
    - Archduke Louis Infantry Regiment #8 (4)
    - Wurzburg Infantry Regiment #7 (3)
    - Brigade Battery (8-6pdrs)
  - Brigade: Generalmajor von Csollich
    - Kottulinski Infantry Regiment #41 (3) (2,214)
    - Kaiser Infantry Regiment #1 (2) (1,558)
    - Brigade Battery (8-6pdrs)
- Division: FML Prince von Hohenlohe-Bartenstein
  - Brigade: Generalmajor von Spleny
    - Mariassy Infantry Regiment #37 (2)
    - J. Gyulai Infantry Regiment #60 (2)
    - Brigade Battery (8-6pdrs)
  - Brigade: Generalmajor von Grimmer
    - Kollowrath Infantry Regiment #36 (2) (1,602)
    - Frölich Infantry Regiment #28 (3) (2,790)
    - Brigade Battery (8-6pdrs)
  - Reserve Artillery:
    - 1 Foot Battery (6-12pdrs)
    - 2 Foot Batteries (6-6pdrs ea)

1 Sources: Bogdanovich, M., *Istoria voini 1814 goda vo Francii i nizlojenia Napoleona I, po dostovernim istochnikam;* von Hiller, F., *Geschichte des Feldzuges 1814 gegen Frankreich unter besonder Berücksichtigung der Anteilnahme der königlich Württembergischen Truppen.* This is the probable organization of the Allied forces at the Battle of Paris. This order of battle, however, is a construction based on the known organizations of the various Allied corps and divisions and various documents that identified these forces as being present in the battle.

4th Corps: Feldmarschal Kronprinz von Württemberg (15,000 men)[2]
Advanced Guard: Generallieutenant Prince Adam von Württemberg
1st Cavalry Brigade: Generalmajor von Walseben
5th Cavalry Regiment "Jäger" (4)
Erzherzog Ferdinand Hussar Regiment (5) (Austrian)
1st Horse Battery, Cpt. von Breithaupt (4-6pdrs and 2 howitzers)
2nd Cavalry Brigade: Generalmajor von Jett
2nd Cavalry Regiment "Jäger Herzog Louis" (4)
3rd Cavalry Regiment "Dragoner Kronprinz" (4)
4th Cavalry Regiment "Jäger Prince Adam" (4)
2nd Horse Battery, Cpt. von Bürgi (4-6pdrs and 2 howitzers)
4th Infantry Brigade: Generalmajor von Stockmayer
9th Jäger Regiment "König" (1)
10th Light Regiment (2)
Austrian Pioneer Company (Cpt. Wonjatschek) (1 company)

Main body: Feldzeugmeister Graf von Franquemont
1st Division: Generallieutenant von Koch
1st Infantry Brigade: Generalmajor Prince von Hohenlohe
2nd Infantry Regiment "Herzog Wilhelm" (2)
3rd Infantry Regiment (2)
1st Foot Battery, Major von Ehrenfeld (4-6pdrs and 2 howitzers)
2nd Infantry Brigade: Generalmajor von Misani
4th Infantry Regiment (2)
5th Infantry Regiment "Prince Freiderich" (2)
2nd Foot Battery, Cpt. von Diskau (4-6pdrs and 2 howitzers)
3rd Infantry Brigade: Generalmajor von Lalance
6th Infantry Regiment "Kronprinz" (2)
Landregiment #6 Heilbronn (1)
2nd Division: Generallieutenant Döring
7th Infantry Regiment (2)
Grenadier (Austrian) Brigade: Generalmajor von Trenk
Putheany Grenadier Battalion (1)
Frisch Grenadier Battalion (1)
Hromada Grenadier Battalion (1)
Lany Grenadier Battalion (1)
2 6pdr Batteries
Cuirassier Brigade: Generalmajor Graf von Desfours
Liechtenstein Cuirassier Regiment (6)
Kaiser Cuirassier Regiment (6)
Cuirassier Brigade: Oberst von Seymann
Konstantin Cuirassier Regiment (6)
Sommariva Cuirassier Regiment (6)
Reserve Artillery:
Austrian 12pdr Foot Battery, Oberlieutenant Wiegel

2 In the Battle of Montereau on 18 February the 9th and 10th Württemberg Infantry Regiments were nearly totally destroyed or captured. In addition, the 2nd, 3rd, 6th and 7th Württemberg Infantry Regiments had suffered very heavy losses. The Württemberg elements of the corps report losing 2,844 men in this battle.

Right wing:
Army of Silesia: Generalfeldmarschal Blücher
1st Army Corps: General von Yorck
Prussian General Staff, *Plan der Schlachten und Treffen* (about 12,000 men)
Combined 1st and 7th Brigade: General von Horn
East Prussian Jäger Battalion (2 companies)
Combined Force
Leib Grenadier Battalion
West Prussian Grenadier Battalion
Combined Force
Silesian Grenadier Battalion
1st East Prussian Grenadier Battalion
1/, 2/, Fus/Leib Infantry Regiment
Combined Force
5th Silesian Landwehr Infantry Regiment
13th Silesian Landwehr Infantry Regiment
Combined Force
4th Silesian Landwehr Infantry Regiment
15th Silesian Landwehr Infantry Regiment
Combined 2nd and 8th Brigade: Prince Wilhelm von Preussen
1/, 2/, Fus/1st East Prussian Infantry Regiment
2nd East Prussian Infantry Regiment (2)
1/, 2/Brandenburg Infantry Regiment
1/, 2/12th Reserve Infantry Regiment
Combined Force
Fus/12th Reserve Infantry Regiment
Fus/Brandenburg Infantry Regiment
6th Silesian Landwehr Infantry Regiment (1)
14th Silesian Landwehr Infantry Regiment (1)
Reserve Cavalry: General von Jürgass
1/, 2/, 3/, 4/East Prussian National Cavalry Regiment
1/, 2/, 3/, 4/Mecklenburg Strelitz Hussar Regiment
1/, 2/, 3/, 4/Brandenburg Hussar Regiment
1/, 2/, 3/, 4/2nd Leib Hussar Regiment
1/, 2/, 3/, 4/Lithuanian Dragoon Regiment
1/, 2/, 3/, 4/1st West Prussian Dragoon Regiment
1/, 2/, 3/, 4/Brandenburg Uhlan Regiment
3rd, 4th and 5th Silesian Landwehr Cavalry Regiments (5 squadrons)
Artillery: Oberst von Schmidt
6pdr Foot Battery #1
6pdr Foot Battery #2
6pdr Foot Battery #3
6pdr Foot Battery #15
12pdr Foot Battery #1
12pdr Foot Battery #2
6pdr Horse Battery #1
6pdr Horse Battery #2
6pdr Horse Battery #3
6pdr Horse Battery #12

2nd Army Corps: General von Kleist (about 8,000 men)
Infantry: Prince August von Preussen
9th Brigade: Generalmajor von Klüx

1/, 2/, Fus/1st West Prussian Infantry Regiment
6th Reserve Infantry Regiment (2)
Silesian National Cavalry Regiment
7th Silesian Landwehr Cavalry Regiment
6pdr Foot Battery #7 (8-6pdrs)
10th Brigade: Generalmajor von Pirch I
1/, 2/, 3/2nd West Prussian Infantry Regiment
Combined Battalion
7th Reserve Infantry Regiment
Combined Battalion
1/, 2/, Fus/1st Silesian Infantry Regiment
10th Reserve Infantry Regiment (2)
Combined Battalion
1/, 2/2nd Silesian Infantry Regiment
11th Reserve Infantry Regiment
Combined Fusilier Battalion
Silesian Schützen (2 companies)
2nd Silesian Hussar Regiment
8th Silesian Landwehr Cavalry Regiment
6pdr Foot Battery #8 (8-6pdrs)
Reserve Cavalry: Generalleutnant von Ziethen
Brigade: Oberst von Blücher
Neumark Dragoon Regiment
1st Silesian Hussar Regiment
Brigade: Oberst Graf Haacke
Silesian Cuirassier Regiment
Silesian Uhlan Regiment
Brigade: Oberst von Wrangel
East Prussian Cuirassier Regiment "Grand Duke Constantine"
Brandenburg Cuirassier Regiment
Artillery:
Horse Artillery Battery #7 (8-6pdrs)
Horse Artillery Battery #8 (8-6pdrs)
Reserve Artillery: von Braun
Horse Batteries #9 and #10 (8-6pdrs ea)
6pdr Foot Batteries #9 and #11 (8-6pdrs ea)
Howitzer Battery #1

3rd Army Corps: General von Bülow
3rd Brigade: Prince von Hessen-Homburg
2nd East Prussian Grenadier Battalion
1/, 2/, /Fus/3rd East Prussian Infantry Regiment
1/, 2/, /Fus/4th Reserve Infantry Regiment
4th Brigade: General von Thümen
1/, 2/, /Fus/4th East Prussian Infantry Regiment
2/, 3/5th Reserve Infantry Regiment
6th Brigade: General von Krafft
1/, 2/, /Fus/Colberg Infantry Regiment
1/, 2/, /Fus/9th Reserve Infantry Regiment
1/, 3/1st Neumark Landwehr Infantry Regiment
Reserve Cavalry: General von Oppen
Prince Wilhelm Dragoon Regiment (2)
1/, 2/, 3/, 4/, Jäger/Königin Dragoon Regiment

1/, 2/, 3/, 4/2nd West Prussian Dragoon Regiment
1/, 2, 3/, 4/1st Pomeranian Landwehr Regiment
1/, 2, 3/, 4/2nd Pomeranian Landwehr Cavalry Regiment
Artillery: General von Holtzendorff
6pdr Foot Battery #5
6pdr Foot Battery #6
6pdr Foot Battery #19
6pdr Horse Battery #11
12pdr Foot Battery #4
12pdr Foot Battery #5
2 Russian 12pdr Batteries

Russian forces: General of Infantry Langeron (20,000 men)
8th Russian Corps: Generallieutenant Rudsevich
11th Division: Generalmajor Gurgalov
Brigade: Generalmajor Karpenkov
Polotsk Infantry Regiment (2)
Jeletz Infantry Regiment (2)
Brigade: Lt. Colonel Turganeff
Rilsk Infantry Regiment (2)
Ekaterinburg Infantry Regiment (2)
Brigade: Generalmajor Bistrom
1st Jager Regiment (2)
33rd Jager Regiment (2)
17th Division: Generalmajor Pilas
Brigade: Colonel Kern
Riazan Infantry Regiment (2)
Bieloserk Infantry Regiment (2)
Brigade: Major Sabelin
30th Jager Regiment (2)
48th Jager Regiment (2)
Artillery:
Position Battery #33
Light Batteries #32 and #33

9th Corps: Generalmajor Kornilov
1 Combined Battalion (1,500 men and 12 guns)

10th Corps: Generallieutenant Kapsevich
Detached from 8th Corps:
17th Infantry Division: Generalmajor Kern
Bieloserk Infantry Regiment
48th Jager Regiment

Detached from 9th Corps:
1,500 survivors of Olsufiev 9th Corps and 12 guns

10th Corps: Generallieutenant Rudsevich
8th Division: Generalmajor Urusov
Brigade: Colonel Schenschen
Archangel Infantry Regiment
Schusselburg Infantry Regiment
Old Ingremannland Infantry Regiment

- Brigade: Colonel Suthof
    - 7th Jager Regiment
    - 37th Jager Regiment
- Artillery:
    - 2 Batteries

22nd Division: Generalmajor Turtschaninov
- Brigade: Generalmajor Schapskoy
    - Olonetz Infantry Regiment (1)
    - Staroskol Infantry Regiment (1)
- Brigade: Generalmajor Vassil'shikov
    - 29th Jager Regiment (1)
    - 45th Jager Regiment (1)
- Artillery:
    - Light Battery #34 (12 guns)
    - Light Battery #33 (5 guns)
    - 1 Pioneer Company

Cavalry Corps: Generallieutenant Korff
- 1st Dragoon Division: Generallieutenant Borosdin II
    - Brigade: Generalmajor Gengross
        - Mitau Dragoon Regiment (3)
        - New Russia Dragoon Regiment (3)
    - Brigade: Generalmajor Pohl
        - Kargopol Dragoon Regiment (4)
    - Brigade: Generalmajor Denissiev
        - Sieversk Chasseurs à cheval Regiment (4)
        - Livonia Chasseurs à cheval Regiment (1)
- Ukrainian Cossack Division: Generalmajor Witte
    - Brigade: Generalmajor Scherbatov
        - 2nd Ukrainian Cossack Regiment
        - 3rd Ukrainian Cossack Regiment
    - Other:
        - Selimonov II Don Cossack Regiment
        - Don Cossack Battery #2 (6 guns

Corps: Generallieutenant Count Voronzov
- 21st Division: Generalmajor Leptev
    - Brigade: Colonel Rosen
        - Petrovsk Infantry Regiment (1)
        - Lithuania Infantry Regiment (1)
        - Podolsk Infantry Regiment (1)
    - Brigade: Unknown
        - Neva Infantry Regiment (1)
        - 44th Jager Regiment (2)
        - 2nd Jager Regiment (1)
    - Brigade: (from 14th Division) Generalmajor Harpe
        - Navaguinsk Infantry Regiment (1)
        - Tula Infantry Regiment (1)
        - Converged Grenadier Battalions 9th, 15th and 18th Divisions
    - Brigade: (from 15th Division) Generalmajor Krassovsky
        - 13th Jager Regiment (2)
        - 14th Jager Regiment (2)
    - Brigade: (from 24th Division) Generalmajor Wuitsch

Chirvan Infantry Regiment (2)
Bourtirki Infantry Regiment (2)
19th Jager Regiment (2)
Artillery:
Horse Batteries #1 (10), #4 (8), #7 (12), #11 (12), #13 (12) and #21 (12 guns)
Light Batteries #42, #48, & #56
Position Batteries #7, #28 & #31

Main Allied army: Prince Schwarzenberg
6th Army Corps (Russian): Generalleutnant Raevsky (14,000 men)
1st Corps: Generalleutenant Gorchakov II
5th Division: Generalmajor Menzenzov
Brigade: Generalmajor Nabokov
Perm Infantry Regiment (1)
Sieversk Infantry Regiment (1)
Brigade: Colonel Milavanov
Mohilev Infantry Regiment (1)
Kalouga Infantry Regiment (1)
Brigade: Generalmajor Vlassov
23rd Jager Regiment (1)
24th Jager Regiment (1)
14th Division: Generalmajor von Helfrich
Brigade: Generalmajor Roth
25th Jager Regiment (1)
26th Jager Regiment (1)
Artillery:
Light Batteries #26 and #27
Position Battery #14

2nd Corps: Generalleutenant Prince Eugene von Württemberg
3rd Division: Generalleutnant Prince Schachovsky
Brigade: Colonel von Wolff
Tchernigov Infantry Regiment (2)
Mourmonsk Infantry Regiment (2)
Brigade: Colonel Kapustin
20th Jager Regiment (1)
21st Jager Regiment (1)
4th Division: Generalmajor Puschnizky
Brigade: Colonel von Rosen
Tobolsk Infantry Regiment (2)
Krementchug Infantry Regiment (1)
Brigade: Colonel Kursonov
Minsk Infantry Regiment (1)
Volhynie Infantry Regiment (1)
Brigade: Colonel Stepanov
4th Jager Regiment (1)
34th Jager Regiment (1)
Artillery:
Light Batteries #14 and #6
Position Battery #3
Cavalry Division: Generalleutnant Pahlen
Brigade: Generalmajor Delajanov
Grodno Hussar Regiment (6)

Soumy Hussar Regiment (3)
Brigade: Generalmajor Dechterev
Loubny Hussar Regiment (5)
Olviopol Hussar Regiment (2)
Brigade: Generalmajor Lissanewitz
Tchougouiev Uhlan Regiment (6)
Corps Reserve Artillery:
Horse Batteries #11 and #23
Pioneer Company Kanatchikova
Pioneer Company Zetova

Cossacks:
Vlassov II Cossack Regiment
Illowaisky XII Cossack Regiment
Rebrikov III Cossack Regiment
Tschermuschin II Cossack Regiment
Jaroslav Cossack Regiment

Austrian Reserves: Grandduke Prince Hessen-Homburg
Cavalry: FML von Nostitz
1st Division: FML von Klebelsberg
Brigade: Generalmajor von Auersberg
Archduke Francis Cuirassier Regiment #2 (5)
Sommervia Cuirassier Regiment #5 (5)
Brigade: Generalmajor Desfours
Liechtenstein Cuirassier Regiment (5)
Kaiser Cuirassier Regiment (5)
2nd Cuirassier Division: FML von Lederer
Brigade: Generalmajor von Rothkirch
Archduke Albert Cuirassier Regiment #3 (5)
Hohenzollern Cuirassier Regiment #8 (5)
Brigade: Generalmajor von Ruttalek
Lothringen Cuirassier Regiment #7 (5)
Crown Prince Ferdinand Cuirassier Regiment #4 (5)
Division: FML Bianchi
Brigade: Generalmajor von Hirsch
Hiller Infantry Regiment #2 (2)
H. Colloredo Infantry Regiment #33 (2)
Brigade Battery (8-6pdrs) (?)
Brigade: Generalmajor Haugwitz
Hessen-Homburg Infantry Regiment #19 (2)
Simbschen Infantry Regiment #48 (2)
Brigade Battery (8-6pdrs) (?)
Brigade: Generalmajor von Gutemberg
Esterhazy Infantry Regiment #32 (2)
Davidovich Infantry Regiment #34 (2)
Brigade Battery (8-6pdrs) (?)
Division: FML Weissenwolf
Brigade: Generalmajor Fürstenwerther
Grenadier Battalion Czarnozi
Grenadier Battalion Obermayer
Grenadier Battalion Berger
Grenadier Battalion Oklopsia

- Brigade: Generalmajor von Beigel
  - Grenadier Battalion Habinay
  - Grenadier Battalion Portener
  - Grenadier Battalion Fischer
  - Grenadier Battalion Ruber
- Brigade: Generalmajor von Klenau
  - Grenadier Battalion Frisch
  - Grenadier Battalion Mosel
  - Grenadier Battalion Putheany
- Brigade: Generalmajor von Luz
  - Grenadier Battalion Rosmann
  - Grenadier Battalion Lany
  - Grenadier Battalion Hormada
- Artillery: FML von Reisner
  - 5 Foot Batteries (8-6pdrs)
  - 26 Companies Field Artillery
  - 27 Companies Artillery Workers
  - 8 Pioneer Companies
  - 400 Pontooneers

Russo-Prussian Reserves and Guards: Barclay de Tolly

- Cavalry: Generalleutnant Miloradovich (16,000 men)
  - 1st Cuirassier Division: Generalleutnant Depreradovich
    - Brigade: Generalmajor Arsenjeff
      - Chevalier Guard Regiment (6)
      - Horse Guard Regiment (6)
    - Brigade: Generalmajor von Rosen
      - Emperor Cuirassier Regiment (4)
      - Empress Cuirassier Regiment (4)
  - 2nd Cuirassier Division: Generalleutnant Kretov
    - Brigade: Generalmajor Leontiev
      - Gluchov Cuirassier Regiment (5)
      - Pskof Cuirassier Regiment (5)
    - Brigade: Generalmajor Karatheff
      - Ekaterinoslav Cuirassier Regiment (2)
      - Astrakhan Cuirassier Regiment (4)
  - 3rd Cuirassier Division: Generalleutnant Duka
    - Brigade: Generalmajor Protassov
      - Military Order Cuirassier Regiment (5)
      - Little Russia Cuirassier Regiment (4)
    - Brigade: Generalmajor Lewaschoff
      - Novgorod Cuirassier Regiment (4)
      - Starodoub Cuirassier Regiment (5)
  - Guard Light Division: Generalmajor Schevic
    - Guard Hussar Regiment (6)
    - Guard Dragoon Regiment (6)
    - Guard Uhlan Regiment (6)
    - Guard Horse Battery #1 (12-6pdrs)
    - Guard Horse Battery #2 (12-6pdrs)
- Guards Infantry: Generalleutnant Yermolov
  - 1st Guard Division: Generalleutnant Rose
    - Brigade: Generalmajor Potemkin
      - Preobragenski Guard Infantry Regiment (3)

Semenovski Guard Infantry Regiment (3)
Brigade: Generalmajor Chrapowitzky
Ismailov Guard Infantry Regiment (3)
Guard Jager Regiment (3)
Guard Military Equippage Battalion and 2 6pdr guns
2nd Guard Division: Generalmajor Udom I
Brigade: Generalmajor Scheltuchin
Lithuania Guard Infantry Regiment (3)
Leib-Guard Grenadier Regiment (3)
Finland Guard Infantry (2)
Pavlov Guard Grenadiers (2)
Guard Artillery Brigade:
1st and 2nd Guard Position Batteries
1st and 2nd Guard Light Batteries
1 Pioneer Company
Prussian Guard Cavalry Brigade: Generalmajor Laroche von Starkenfels
1/, 2/, 3/, 4/, 5/Garde du Corps Regiment
1/, 2/, 3/, 4/Guard Light Cavalry Regiment
Guard Horse Artillery Battery (8-6pdrs)
Prussian Guard Infantry Brigade: Colonel von Alvensleben
Fus/, Gren/1st Garde Regiment zu Fuss (with 3 Jäger companies)
Fus/, 1/2nd Garde Regiment zu Fuss (with 3 Jäger companies)
Guard Jäger Regiment (1) (with 1 Jäger company)
Guard Foot Artillery Battery (8-6pdrs)
Attached:
Baden Leibgarde Grenadier Battalion (872)
Baden Horse Artillery Battery (7-6prs)

Grenadier Corps: Generalleutnant Lambert
1st Division: Generalmajor Tschoglikov
Brigade: Generalmajor Kniaschnin II
Count Arakcheyev Grenadier Regiment (2)
Ekaterinoslav Grenadier Regiment (2)
Brigade: Colonel Jemilianov
Kexholm Grenadier Regiment (2)
Pernau Grenadier Regiment (2)
Brigade:
1st Jager Regiment
3rd Jager Regiment
2nd Division: Generalmajor Paskevich
Brigade: Generalmajor Pissarev
Kiev Grenadier Regiment (2)
Moscow Grenadier Regiment (2)
Brigade: Colonel Sulima
Tauride Grenadier Regiment (1)
St. Petersburg Grenadier Regiment (2)
Brigade:
8th Jager Regiment
14th Jager Regiment
3rd Grenadier Division:
Brigade: Generalmajor Damas
Astrakhan Grenadier Regiment (1)
Fangoria Grenadier Regiment (1)

Brigade:
- Siberia Grenadier Regiment (2)
- Little Russia Grenadier Regiment (2)
- Grand Duchess Catherine Grenadier Battalion (1)

Brigade:
- 26th Jager Regiment
- 29th Jager Regiment

Artillery:
- Light Battery #2
- Heavy Batteries #1 and #30

Reserve Artillery: Generalmajor Schussnet
- Position Batteries #2, #5, #7, #13, #28, #29 and #34
- Horse Batteries #1, #2, #10 and #18
- 1 Sapper Company
- 1 Pioneer Company

Cossack Corps: Ataman Platoff (probably not present)
- Ataman Don Cossack Regiment
- Grekov V Don Cossack Regiment
- Illowaisky X Don Cossack Regiment
- Kortin IV Cossack Regiment
- Tschernomoren Cossack Regiment
- Scheltonoskin I Cossack Regiment
- Don Light Battery (12-6pdrs)

Appendix LXXI

Capitulation of Paris, 31 March 1814[1]

The four-hour armistice which was convened in order to treat for the occupation of the city of Paris and the withdrawal of the French corps – which is attached – having concluded an arrangement in this regard, the undersigned are authorized by their respective commanders of the opposing forces, do declare and sign the following articles:

Article I
The corps of the Marshals Duc de Trévise and de Raguse shall evacuate the city of Paris on 31 March at 7:00 a.m.

Article II
They shall take away the equipment of their corps.

Article III
The hostilities shall not recommence for two hours after the evacuation – that is to say, until 9:00 a.m. on 31 March.

Article IV
All the arsenals, workshops, establishments and military magazines shall be left in the same state as they find themselves at the signing of this capitulation.

Article V
The National Guard and Urban Guard is totally separated from the line troops. It shall be conserved, disarmed or disbanded according to the wishes of the Allied powers.

Article VI
The municipal gendarmerie shall be treated as part of the National Guard.

Article VII
The wounded and deserters remaining in Paris after 7:00 a.m. shall be prisoners of war.

Article VIII
The city of Paris is recommended to the generosity of the great Allied powers.

Signed in Paris, 31 March 1814 at 2:00 a.m.

Signed by:
Colonel Count Orlof: aide-de-camp to His Majesty the Emperor of all the Russias.

Colonel Count Paer: general aide-de-camp to His Highness the Marshal Prince von Schwarzenberg
Colonel Baron Fabvier: attached to the General Staff of His Excellency, the Marshal Duke de Ragusa
Colonel Denys: first aide-de-camp to His Excellency, the Marshal Duke de Ragusa

1 Rapetti, pp. 107-10.

Appendix LXXII

French forces, Battle of Courtrai, 31 March 1814

I Corps: Général de division Maison[1]

- 4th Young Guard Division: Général de division Barrois
  - Brigade: Général de brigade Darriule
    - 1/, 2/2nd Tirailleur Regiment (949)
    - 1/, 2/3rd Tirailleur Regiment (1,094)
  - Brigade:
    - 1/, 2/4th Tirailleur Regiment (1,062)
    - 1/, 2/12th Voltigeur Regiment (1,864)
- Solignac's division: Général de division Solignac
  - Brigade: Général de brigade Penne
    - Det/27th Légère Regiment (495)
    - Det/17th Line Regiment (619)
    - Det/28th Line Regiment (549)
  - Brigade: Unknown
    - Det/51st Line Regiment (469)
    - Det/55th Line Regiment (469)
    - Det/65th Line Regiment (623)
    - Det/75th Line Regiment (514)
- 6th Young Guard Division: Général de division Roguet[2]
    - 1/, 2/9th Tirailleur Regiment (1,045)
    - 1/, 2/10th Tirailleur Regiment (1,199)
    - 1/, 2/11th Tirailleur Regiment (1,334)
    - 1/, 2/12th Tirailleur Regiment (1,626)
    - 1/, 2/13th Tirailleur Regiment (1,357)
  - Attached:
    - Sapper company
    - Administrative artisans
    - Equipment train
    - Castex's Cavalry Division
    - 2nd Guard Chasseur Regiment (Young Guard) (849 / 762)[3]
    - 1st Gardes d'honneur Regiment (182 / 175)
  - Artillery Park: Colonel Brouet (1,501 men)
    - 3rd Guard Horse Artillery
    - 1st Young Guard Foot Artillery
    - 3rd Young Guard Foot Artillery
    - 7th Young Guard Foot Artillery
    - 13th Young Guard Foot Artillery
    - 9/9th Foot Artillery

1 Strength figures are for 1 April 1814.
2 One regiment was detached to the garrison of Ghent.
3 This formation was called the 2nd Regiment, but actually consisted of the 6th, 7th, 8th and 9th Squadrons of the 1st Guard Chasseurs à cheval Regiment (all Young Guard Squadrons). Numbers are men and horses.

7/1st Horse Artillery
2 12pdrs, 22 6pdrs, 2 4pdrs and 9 5.7" howitzers

Young Guard Train:
7/1st Young Guard Train Regiment
8/1st Young Guard Train Regiment
10/1st Young Guard Train Regiment
12/1st Young Guard Train Regiment
1/2nd Young Guard Train Regiment
7/2nd Young Guard Train Regiment
8/2nd Young Guard Train Regiment
12/2nd Young Guard Train Regiment
Guard Ouvriers Pontooneers
Line Artillery Artisans

Appendix LXXIII

Allied 3rd German Corps, Battle of Courtrai, 30 March 1814[1]

1st Brigade: Generalmajor von Brause
- Staff/, 2/1st (Saxon) Provisional Regiment (14 / 503)
  - (strength figures are as of 25 March 1814)
- 3/1st (Saxon) Provisional Regiment (17 / 624)
- 1/1st (Saxon) Landwehr Regiment (14 / 756)
- 2/1st (Saxon) Landwehr Regiment (13 / 710)
- 3/1st (Saxon) Landwehr Regiment (14 / 750)
- 1/, 2/, 3/ (Saxon) Hussar Regiment (35 / 545 / 525)

2nd Brigade: Generalmajor Prince Paul von Württemberg
- Schwarzberg Landwehr Battalion (12 / 450)
- Bernberg Battalion (Landwehr) (11 / 429)
- 1/3rd (Saxon) Landwehr Regiment (20 / 661)
- 2/3rd (Saxon) Landwehr Regiment (17 / 700)
- 3/3rd (Saxon) Landwehr Regiment (15 / 716)
- 1/, 2/, 3/ (Saxon) Cuirassier Regiment (32 / 547 / 464)
  - (only two squadrons are known to be present)
- 1st Saxon 6pdr Foot Battery (two guns)
- Half Battery (three French 6pdrs)
- Battery (two English 9pdrs)

Other units:
- von Helwig Freikorps

1 Bucher, pp. 178-9; Beilage I.

Appendix LXXIV

French XI Corps, 1 April 1814[1]

XI Corps: Maréchal Macdonald, Duc de Tarente
- Division: Général de division Albert
  - 1st Brigade:
    - 1/139th Line Regiment (124)
    - 1/, 2/1st Regiment de Brest (150)
    - 1/, 2/2nd Regiment de Brest (120)
  - 2nd Brigade:
    - 4/, 140th Line Regiment (221)
    - 1/Regiment de Rochefort (114)
  - Artillery (strength as of 3/15/14):
    - 15/4th Foot Artillery (44)
    - 18/6th Foot Artillery (36)
    - 2/5th Horse Artillery (60)
    - 2/9th Principal Train Battalion (16)
    - 3/6th Principal Train Battalion (64)
    - 2/11th Principal Train Battalion (101)
- Division: Général de division Brayer
  - 1st Brigade:
    - 1/, 2/, 6/19th Légère Regiment (512)
    - 3/5th Line Regiment (108)
    - 3/1lth Line Regiment (164)
  - 2nd Brigade:
    - Grenadiers/3rd Swiss Regiment (29)
    - 1/107th Line Regiment (315)
  - Artillery (strength as of 3/15/14):
    - 6/1st Foot Artillery (25)
    - 19/2nd Foot Artillery (52)
    - 20/5th Foot Artillery (52)
    - 1/8th Principal Train Battalion (79)
    - 2/5th Principal Train Battalion (56)
  - Cavalry:
    - 13th Hussar Regiment (50)
  - Artillery Personnel and Equipment:
    - Artillerists (321)
    - Artillery Train (384)
    - 4 12pdrs
    - 12 6pdrs
    - 8 24pdr howitzers
  - Reserve Artillery (strength as of 3/15/14):
    - 22/1st Foot Artillery (20)
    - 18/4th Foot Artillery (11)
    - 27/1st Foot Artillery (1)

1 French Archives, Carton C^2 556.

Artillery Artisans (1)
4/1st (bis) Train Battalion (2)
1/11th Principal Train Battalion (19)
1/13th Principal Train Battalion (23)
3/14th Principal Train Battalion
4/14th Principal Train Battalion (47)
6/3rd (bis) Train Battalion (33)
3/5th Principal Train Battalion (24)
1/11th Principal Train Battalion

Appendix LXXV

French VI Corps, 1 April 1814[1]

Commanding Officer: Maréchal Marmont

- 8th Division: Colonel Laporte
  - 2nd Légère Regiment (16 / 198)
  - 8th Légère Regiment (8 / 35)
  - 9th Légère Regiment (9 / 37)
  - 16th Légère Regiment (14 / 162)
  - 136th Line Regiment (7 / 40)
  - 138th Line Regiment (19 / 41)
  - 144th Line Regiment (15 / 46)
- 9th Division: Général de brigade Joubert
  - 37th Légère Regiment (19 / 74)
  - 1st Line Regiment (6 / 23)
  - 15th Line Regiment (13 / 30)
  - 16th Line Regiment (1 / 6)
  - 70th Line Regiment (26 / 129)
  - 121st Line Regiment (5 / 13)
  - 1st Marine Regiment (12 / 50)
  - 2nd Marine Regiment (6 / 40)
  - 3rd Marine Regiment (14 / 79)
  - 4th Marine Regiment (9 / 45)
  - 132nd Line Regiment (16 / 61)
  - Reserve of Paris:
    - 65th Line Regiment (10 / 37)
    - 66th Line Regiment (10 / 65)
    - 85th Line Regiment (20 / 38)
    - 43rd Line Regiment (26 / 151)
    - 50th Line Regiment (22 / 630)
    - 72nd Line Regiment (6 / 29)
    - 88th Line Regiment (17 / 70)

1 Rapetti, *La Defection de Marmont en 1814.*

Appendix LXXVI

French VI Cavalry Corps, 2 April 1814[1]

VI Cavalry Corps: Général de division Kellermann
- 4th Light Cavalry Division: Général de division Jacquinot
  - 7th Brigade: Général de brigade Ameil
    - 12th Hussar Regiment (3 / 133)
    - 2nd Hussar Regiment (3 / 10)
    - 21st Chasseurs à cheval Regiment (4 / 15)
    - 22nd Chasseurs à cheval Regiment (3 / 11)
    - 28th Chasseurs à cheval Regiment (3 / 35)
    - 13th Chasseurs à cheval Regiment (13 / 98)
  - 8th Brigade: Général de brigade Wolf
    - 4th Chasseurs à cheval Regiment (6 / 54)
    - 5th Chasseurs à cheval Regiment (10 / 55)
    - 10th Chasseurs à cheval Regiment (11 / 71)
    - 15th Chasseurs à cheval Regiment (6 / 31)
- 5th Heavy Cavalry Division: Général de division Trelliard
  - 9th Brigade: Général de brigade Ismert
    - 4th Dragoon Regiment (20 / 177)
    - 14th Dragoon Regiment (17 / 205)
    - 16th Dragoon Regiment (16 / 135)
  - 10th Brigade: Général de brigade Ormancy
    - 17th Dragoon Regiment (26 / 231)
    - 24th Dragoon Regiment (24 / 198)
  - Artillery:
    - 3/6th Horse Artillery (12 guns) (5 / 97)
    - 6/3rd Principal Train Battalion (3 / 109)

1 French Archives, Carton C^2 557.

Appendix LXXVII

French VI and VII Corps, 4-5 April 1814[1]

VI Corps: (5 April 1814)[2]
- 8th Division: Colonel Laporte
  - 1st Provisional Battalion (28 / 262)
  - 2nd Provisional Battalion (20 / 263)
  - 3rd Provisional Battalion (34 / 240)
  - 4th Provisional Battalion (24 / 233)
- 9th Division: Général de brigade Joubert
  - 37th Légère Regiment (20 / 111)
  - 1st Line Regiment (6 / 31)
  - 15th Line Regiment (12 / 61)
  - 16th Line Regiment (11 / 20)
  - 70th Line Regiment (28 / 154)
  - 121st Line Regiment (7 / 63)
  - 1st Marine Regiment (15 / 65)
  - 2nd Marine Regiment (16 / 134)
  - 3rd Marine Regiment (16 / 104)
  - 4th Marine Regiment (12 / 90)
  - 132nd Line Regiment (13 / 86)
  - Bataillon des Gardes Nationale de la Somme (13 / 320)
- 1st Division, Paris Reserve: Général Lucotte
  - 1st Veteran Battalion (22 / 631)
  - 2nd Veteran Battalion (24 / 680)
  - 2/45th Line Regiment (29 / 162)
  - 2/50th Line Regiment (25 / 80)
  - 1/65th Line Regiment (12 / 38)
  - 1/66th Line Regiment (9 / 73)
  - 1/72nd Line Regiment (11 / 47)
  - 3/85th Line Regiment (25 / 25)
  - 1/88th Line Regiment (15 / 81)
- 2nd Division, Reserve of Paris: Général de division Souham
  - 1st Marine Regiment (2) (10 / 346)
  - 4/3rd Marine Regiment (19 / 266)
  - 1/135th Line Regiment (20 / 286)
  - 1/28th Line Regiment (18 / 295)
  - 1/46th Line Regiment (14 / 339)
  - 4/145th Line Regiment (25 / 817)
  - 1er Bataillon Garde Nationale de Ile-et-Vilaine (25 / 817)
- Division: Général Ledru-des-Essarts
  - 27th Line Regiment (2 / 20)
  - 8th and 24th Line Regiment (1 / 62)

---

1 Source of data on VI Corps – Rapetti, *La Defection de Marmont en 1814*. Source of data on VII Corps – French Archives, Carton C^2 556.

2 Total strength VI Corps: 966 officers and 11,143 men.

4th and 130th Line Regiment (1 / 66)
32nd Line Regiment (11 / 201)
86th Line Regiment (9 / 102)
135th Line Regiment (17 / 119)
Garde Nationale de Oise (4 / 54)
Garde Nationale de Calvados (1 / 38)
Garde Nationale de Eure (2 / 87)
28th Line Regiment (1 / 57)
40th Line Regiment (14 / 138)
62nd Line Regiment (15 / 56)
Garde Nationale de Seine-Inférieur (9 / 138)
Garde Nationale de Deux-Sèvres (12 / 388)
Artillery:
Foot Artillerists (19 / 419)
Horse Artillerists (8 / 147)
Train (14 / 554)
Engineers: Colonel Paris
Polish Sappers (3 / 53)
3rd Sapper Battalion (0 / 21)
1st Light Cavalry Division: Général de division Merlin
1st Brigade: Général de brigade Guyon (32 / 13)
2nd Brigade: Général de brigade Hubert (33 / 360)
3rd Brigade: Général de brigade Latour-Foissac (48 / 238)
2nd Heavy Cavalry Division: Général de division Bordesoulle
1st Brigade: Colonel Dijon (71 / 644)
2nd Brigade: Général de brigade Thiry (53 / 388)
Attached:
Regiment de marche of General Souham (13 / 182)

VII Corps: Maréchal Oudinot, Duc de Reggio (4 April 1814)
5th Young Guard Division: Général de division Rottembourg
1st Brigade: Général de brigade CharriŠre
1/, 2/5th Voltigeur Regiment (21 / 109)
1/, 2/6th Voltigeur Regiment (12 / 80)
2nd Brigade: Général de brigade Bauduin
1/, 2/, 3/7th Voltigeur Regiment (35 / 247)
1/, 2/, 3/8th Voltigeur Regiment (40 / 254)
Artillery:
11th Young Guard Artillery Company (5-6pdrs and 2 howitzers) (2 / 42)
9th Guard Train Company (1 / 42)
7th Division: Général de division Baron Leval
1st Brigade: Général de brigade Pinoteau
1/, 2/, 6/10th Légère Regiment (24 / 450)
1/3rd Line Regiment (8 / 276)
1/15th Line Regiment (12 / 350)
1/, 4/130th Line Regiment (12 / 320)
Artillery:
19/1st Foot Artillery (8-6pdrs and 4 howitzers) (2 / 101)
2/4th Principal Train Battalion (2 / 60)
6/7th (bis) Train Battalion (0 / 13)
5/12th (bis) Train Battalion (1 / 83)
2nd Brigade: Général de brigade Montfort
1/17th Légère Regiment (12 / 279)

1/101st Line Regiment (9 / 293)
1/, 2/105th Line Regiment (18 / 356)
6/118th Line Regiment (12 / 244)

Artillery:

24/6th Foot Artillery (4 12pdrs and 2 howitzers) (3 / 40)
6/7th (bis) Train Battalion (0 / 14)
2/9th (bis) Train Battalion (1 / 42)

3rd Brigade: Général de brigade Chassé

1/16th Légère Regiment (8 / 270)
1/8th Line Regiment (10 / 209)
1/, 3/28th Line Regiment (27 / 439)

Reserve:

22/5th Foot Artillery (2/39) 8-6pdrs and 4 howitzers)
12/8th Foot Artillery (4-6pdrs and 2 howitzers) (8-6pdrs and 4 howitzers) (3 / 40)
8/3rd Horse Artillery (4 6pdrs and 2 howitzers) (2 / 46)
2/12th (bis) Train Battalion (2 / 83)
3/12th (bis) Train Battalion (0 / 35)
6/7th (bis) Train Battalion (1 / 66)
Artillery Artisans (0 / 5)

Appendix LXXVIII

Allied forces commanded by Generalmajor Prinzen von Courland, 3 April 1814

Infantry:

- Imperial Russian Infantry (2) (25 / 78 / 863)[1]
- Ersatz Bataillon von Schirgel (12 / 50 / 545)
- 1st Army Corps, Ersatz Bataillon von Schmeling (7 / 60 / 535)
- 1st Army Corps, Ersatz Bataillon von Klenke (13 / 17 / 720)
- 1st Army Corps, Ersatz Bataillon von Witten (18 / 56 / 652)
- 2nd Army Corps, Ersatz Bataillon von Kurts (4 / 9 / 351)
- 2nd Army Corps, Ersatz Bataillon von Wedelstädt (10 / 28 / 319)
- 2nd Army Corps, Det. Lt.Vietinghoff (2 / 14 / 150)
- 2nd Army Corps, Magdeburg National Jäger Corps (4 / 14 / 188)

Cavalry:

- Det German and Ukrainian Cossacks (100)
- Cuirassier Squadron von Ianson (65 / 10 / 83)
- Dragoon Squadron von Krakow (3 / 8 / 90)
- Uhlan Squadron von Michaells (3 / 13 / 161)
- Uhlan Squadron von Kotzau (4 / 10 / 107)
- Hussar Squadron von Schnuppe (4 / 17 / 74)
- Hussar Squadron von Pritzelwitz (2 / 7 / 73)

1 Numbers are officers, NCOs and men.

Appendix LXXIX

French Army of Lyon, 9 April 1814[1]

Commander-in-Chief: Maréchal Augereau, Duke of Castiglione
Chief of Staff: Général de brigade du Casse
Commander of Artillery: Général de division Desvaux de Saint-Maurice

1st Division: Général de division Musnier
- 2/32nd Légère Regiment (21 / 606)
- 1/, 2/20th Line Regiment (35 / 744)
- 1/, 2/67th Line Regiment (25 / 883)
- 1/, 2/2nd Regiment of Toulon (20 / 397)
- 2/, 6/24th Line Regiment (41 / 420)
- Provisional Regiment (30 / 1,570)
- 16th Line Regiment
- 145th Line Regiment

2nd Division: Général de division Vedel
- 1/, 2/7th Line Regiment (35 / 887)
- 1/, 2/16th Line Regiment (439 / 944)
- 1/, 2/1st Légère Regiment (40 / 1,101)
- 1/, 2/23rd Légère Regiment (36 / 948)

3rd Division: Général de division Bardet
- 6/23rd Légère Regiment (19 / 480)
- 6/60th Line Regiment (21 / 434)
- 6/67th Line Regiment (20 / 407)
- 6/20th Line Regiment (20 / 514)
- 6/115th Line Regiment (20 / 542)

Independent Brigade from Spain: Général de brigade Ordonneau
- 1/, 2/, 3/116th Line Regiment (60 / 1,820)
- 1/32nd Légère Regiment (49 / 742)

Division of Lyon: Général de division Baron Musnier
- 1/, 2/67th Line Regiment (25 / 833)
- 1/, 2/20th Line Regiment (35 / 744)
- 2/32nd Légère Regiment (21 / 606)
- 1/, 2/2nd Line Regiment (20 / 397)
- 2/, 6/24th Line Regiment (38 / 451)

Division of Catalogne: Général de brigade Pannetier
- 1/, 2/7th Line Regiment (41 / 1,149)
- 1/, 2/16th Line Regiment (43 / 1,165)
- 1/, 2/23rd Légère Regiment (44 / 993)
- 1/, 2/1st Légère Regiment (38 / 1,268)

Division of Reserve of Nismes: Général de division Bardet
- 6/23rd Légère Regiment (19 / 480)
- 6/60th Line Regiment (21 / 434)
- 6/67th Line Regiment (20 / 407)

1 Du Chasse, *Les Operations de l'Armée de Lyon* 1814; French Archives, Carton C^2 556.

6/115th Line Regiment (20 / 542)
6/20th Line Regiment (20 / 514)
Brigade: General de brigade Ordonneau (from Spain)
1/, 2/, 3/116th Line Regiment (60 / 1,820)
1/32nd Légère Regiment (19 / 740)
Division Grenoble: Général de division Marchand
3/8th Légère Regiment (14 / 260)
1/18th Légère Regiment (18 / 618)
3/1st Line Regiment (18 / 580)
4/5th Line Regiment (18 / 756)
4/1lth Line Regiment (19 / 705)
3/23rd Line Regiment (16 / 360)
7/60th Line Regiment (4 / 290)
7/79th Line Regiment (14 / 238)
7/81st Line Regiment (13 / 261)
Customs Guards (66 / 140)
4th Chasseurs (5 / 38)
31st Chasseurs (1 / 22)
Foot Artillery (1 / 23)
Division from Army of Italy:
1/, 4/112nd Line Regiment (43 / 1,395)
4/, 8/25th Légère Regiment (25 / 1,200)
29th and 30th Legion of Gendarmes (29 / 504)
4/7th Line Regiment (20 / 700)
7/20th Line Regiment (20 / 500)
7/62nd Line Regiment (20 / 460)
3/156th Line Regiment (20 / 754)
4/4th Foot Artillery (2 / 120)
1/1st Sapper Battalion (3 / 150)
Cavalry: Général de division Digeon
1/, 2/, 3/, 4/13th Cuirassier Regiment (36 / 509)
1/, 2/, 3/, 4/4th Hussar Regiment (30 / 574)
1/, 2/, 3/12th Hussar Regiment (25 / 365)
4th Chasseurs à cheval Regiment (2 / 62)
31st Chasseurs à cheval Regiment (1 / 31)
Artillery: General Devaux
28/3rd Foot Artillery (2 / 94)
28/4th Foot Artillery (1 / 114)
26/7th Foot Artillery (3 / 75)
4 companies of Marine Artillery (16 / 468)
7/2nd Horse Artillery (3 / 89)
9th and 13th Artisan Companies (0 / 47)
3/4th Battalion (bis) Train (1 / 78)
Provisional Train Companies (2 / 297)
9th Bataillon de Train d'Equippage (1 / 112)

Appendix LXXX

French Army, 15 April 1814[1]

1st Old Guard Division: Général de division Friant
  Brigade: Général de brigade
    1st Chasseur à Pied Regiment (33 / 425)
    2nd Chasseur à Pied Regiment (29 / 354)
    9th Chasseur Company (3 / 134)
  Brigade: Général de brigade
    1st Grenadier à Pied Regiment (34 / 1,005)
    2nd Grenadier à Pied Regiment (35 / 417)
    9th Grenadier Company (3 / 37)
  Attached:
    Guard Sappers (16 / 110)
    Guard Marines
    Guard Engineering Train (1 / 7)
    Artillery (4 / 102)
    Artillery Train (2 / 93)
4th Young Guard Division (in Holland under General Maison):
  1st Brigade:
    1/12th Voltigeur Regiment (20 / 363)
    2/12th Voltigeur Regiment (13 / 499)
    1/13th Voltigeur Regiment (20 / 325)
    2/13th Voltigeur Regiment (12 / 395)
    1/2nd Tirailleur Regiment (14 / 278)
    2/2nd Tirailleur Regiment (8 / 266)
  2nd Brigade:
    1/3rd Tirailleur Regiment (15 / 372)
    2/3rd Tirailleur Regiment (12 / 350)
    1/4th Tirailleur Regiment (13 / 297)
    2/4th Tirailleur Regiment (10 / 287)
  Artillery:
    Foot Battery (7 / 92)
    Artillery Train (2 / 135)

Corps: Maréchal Mortier, Duke of Trévise
  2nd Young Guard Division: Général de division Curial
    1st Brigade: Général de brigade Lagrange
      1st Voltigeur Regiment (19 / 92)
      2nd Voltigeur Regiment (12 / 104)
      3rd Voltigeur Regiment (22 / 206)
      4th Voltigeur Regiment (26 / 151)
      5th Voltigeur Regiment (20 / 101)
      7th Voltigeur Regiment (9 / 76)

1 French Archives, Carton C^2 556.

2nd Brigade: Général de brigade Le Capitaine
10th Voltigeur Regiment (24 / 268)
11th Voltigeur Regiment (17 / 100)
Cadre 12th Voltigeur Regiment (8 / 25)
Cadre 13th Voltigeur Regiment (5/24)
14th Voltigeur Regiment (16 / 121)
15th Voltigeur Regiment (20 / 196)
3rd Brigade: Général de brigade Henrion
8th Voltigeur Regiment (42 / 126)
9th Voltigeur Regiment (12 / 285)
7th Young Guard Division: Général de division Charpentier
1st Brigade: Général de brigade Guye
1st Tirailleur Regiment (21 / 78)
3rd Tirailleur Regiment (14 / 53)
9th Tirailleur Regiment (12 / 56)
14th Tirailleur Regiment (12 / 76)
5th Pupilles Bataillon (3 / 201)
2nd Brigade: Général de brigade Bouvard
2nd Tirailleur Regiment (18 / 91)
12nd Tirailleur Regiment (3 / 31)
1st Bataillon de Marche (13 / 196)
2nd Bataillon de Marche (11 / 162)
3rd Bataillon de Marche (16 / 159)
5th Division: Général de division Rottembourg
1st Brigade: Général de brigade Charrière
1/, 2/, 3/5th Tirailleur Regiment (26 / 106)
1/, 2/, 3/6th Tirailleur Regiment (22 / 66)
2nd Brigade: Général de brigade Bauduin
1/, 2/, 3/7th Tirailleur Regiment (37 / 207)
1/, 2/, 3/8th Tirailleur Regiment (42 / 215)
Division: Général de brigade Henrion[2]
Staff/8th Voltigeur Regiment (10 / 7)
1/8th Voltigeur Regiment (10 / 91)
2/8th Voltigeur Regiment (9 / 78)
Staff/9th Voltigeur Regiment (8 / 20)
1/9th Voltigeur Regiment (12 / 255)
2/9th Voltigeur Regiment (12 / 396)
1/Regiment de Marche (17 / 163)
2/Regiment de Marche (16 / 256)
Cavalry:
Gendarmes d'élite (14 / 187)
10th Hussar Regiment (37 / 281)

II Corps:[3]
1st Division: Général de division Duhèsme
1st Brigade: Général de brigade Materre
1/, 2/24th Légère Regiment (19 / 73)
1/, 2/26th Légère Regiment (21 / 164)
1/2nd Line Regiment (18 / 102)

2 Strength figures are as of 20 April 1814.
3 The II Corps return dates from 22 April 1814 and is from the French Archives, Carton C^{2} 555.

1/, 2/19th Line Regiment (28 / 90)
1/37th Line Regiment (15 / 67)
1/, 2/56th Line Regiment (25 / 191)
2nd Brigade: Vacant
1/11th Légère Regiment (28 / 135)
1/, 2/, 4/4th Line Regiment (34 / 209)
1/, 2/, 4/18th Line Regiment (43 / 230)
1/, 2/46th Line Regiment (30 / 154)
1/72nd Line Regiment (18 / 97)
1/93rd Line Regiment (14 / 78)
Artillery:
9/2nd Foot Artillery (2 / 35)
10/6th Foot Artillery (2 / 26) (5 6pdrs and 1 24pdr howitzer)
3/1st Principal Train Bataillon (2 / 56)
4/14th Principal Train Bataillon (0 / 5)
878 canister
105 ball
144 shell
6 howitzer canister
52,290 infantry cartridges
2nd Division: Vacant
1st Brigade: Général de brigade Jarry
2/5th Légère Regiment (11 / 60)
7/12th Légère Regiment (29 / 236)
7/15th Légère Regiment (12 / 32)
6/,7/29th Légère Regiment (23 / 181)
8/32nd Line Regiment (6 / 24)
6/58th Line Regiment (15 / 41)
3/135th and 3/155th Line Regiment (15 / 102)
2nd Brigade: Général de brigade Bellair
4/26th Line Regiment (7 / 36)
4/82nd Line Regiment (14 / 87)
4/86th Line Regiment (13 / 28)
3/122nd Line Regiment (9 / 86)
2/142nd Line Regiment (7 / 55)
Artillery:
17/5th Foot Artillery (4 / 27)
Det/3rd Horse Artillery (3 / 40)
3/8th Principal Train Battalion (2 / 58)
(4 6pdrs and 2 24pdr howitzers)
Reserve:
9/2nd Foot Artillery (2 / 35)
10/6th Foot Artillery (2 / 26)
Det/1st Principal Train Battalion (2 / 56)
17/5th Foot Artillery (4 / 27)
Det/3rd Horse Artillery (3 / 40)
3/8th Principal Train Battalion (2 / 58)
22/8th Foot Artillery (3 / 95)
2/9th Foot Artillery (2 / 42)
24/9th Foot Artillery (3 / 44)
Det/6th (bis) Train Battalion (2/67)
Det/7th Principal Train Battalion (0 / 19)
Det/7th (bis) Train Battalion (2 / 76)

2/14th Principal Train Battalion (1 / 76)
4/14th Principal Train Battalion (1 / 20)
3/6th Sapper Battalion (3 / 20)
4 12pdrs
2 8pdrs
2 4pdrs
3 24pdr howitzers

IV Corps: Général de division Morand (garrison of Mainz)
1st Division: Général de division Damas
1st Brigade: Général de brigade Choisy
Staff/3rd Légère Regiment (12 / 15)
1/3rd Légère Regiment (16 / 264)
2/3rd Légère Regiment (18 / 142)
à la suite (23 / 64)
Staff/23rd Line Regiment (13 / 25)
1/23rd Line Regiment (14 / 267)
2/23rd Line Regiment (16 / 257)
3/23rd Line Regiment (18 / 211)
à la suite (40 / 127)
2nd Brigade: Général de brigade Baron de Bellair
Staff/13th Line Regiment (15/13)
1/13th Line Regiment (14 / 243)
2/13th Line Regiment (13 / 222)
3/13th Line Regiment (15 / 235)
Staff/137th Line Regiment (14 / 21)
1/137th Line Regiment (21 / 181)
2/137th Line Regiment (22 / 267)
3/137th Line Regiment (14 / 202)
à la suite (29 / 123)
Artillery:
5 6pdrs and 3 24pdr howitzers
2nd Division Général de division Guilleminot
1st Brigade: Général de brigade Morio
1/10th Légère Regiment (21 / 269)
2/10th Légère Regiment (38 / 393)
Staff/156th Line Regiment (2 / 7)
1/156th Line Regiment (26 / 218)
2/156th Line Regiment (25 / 217)
2nd Brigade: Général de brigade Aubert
1/104th Line Regiment (27 / 289)
2/104th Line Regiment (26 / 258)
Artillery:
4 6pdrs and 2 24pdr howitzers
3rd Division Général de division Sémélé
1st Brigade: Général de brigade Baron Lagarde
1/21st Légère Regiment (24 / 305)
2/21st Légère Regiment (19 / 141)
1/32nd Line Regiment (39 / 252)
2/32nd Line Regiment (43 / 312)
2nd Brigade: Turreilhac
1/63rd Line Regiment (40 / 266)
2/63rd Line Regiment (42 / 352)

Artillery:
4 6pdrs and 2 24pdr howitzers

IV Corps Artillery: (distribution of units not indicated)
1/2nd Foot Artillery (3 / 12)
3/2nd Foot Artillery (1 / 33)
10/2nd Foot Artillery (2 / 18)
24/2nd Foot Artillery (2 / 19)
28/2nd Foot Artillery (2 / 20)
3/5th Foot Artillery (2 / 32)
12/5th Foot Artillery (2 / 16)
3/5th Horse Artillery (2 / 70)
2/8th Principal Train Battalion (1 / 57)
2/3rd (bis) Train Battalion (2 / 67)
3/3rd (bis) Train Battalion (2 / 65)
4/3rd (bis) Train Battalion (2 / 66)
1/10th (bis) Train Battalion (2 / 43)
2/1st Sapper Battalion (1 / 56)
2/1st Sapper Battalion (2 / 59)
1/4th Sapper Battalion (1 / 62)
4/6th Sapper Battalion (2 / 62)
Reserve Artillery:
6 – 12pdrs
Army of Lyon
Cavalry Division: Général de division Digeon
1/, 2/, 3/, 4/4th Hussar Regiment (30 / 574)
1/, 2, 3/, 12th Hussar Regiment (25 / 365)
1/, 2/, 3/, 4/13th Cuirassier Regiment (36 / 509)
Det/1st Hussar Regiment (4 / 189)
Det/4th Chasseurs à cheval Regiment (2 / 62)
Det/31st Chasseurs à cheval Regiment (1 / 31)
Artillery: Général de division Desvaux de Saint-Maruice
28/3rd Foot Artillery (3 / 94)
28/4th Foot Artillery (1 / 114)
26/7th Foot Artillery (3 / 75)
Marine Artillery (4 companies) (16 / 468)
7/2nd Horse Artillery (3 / 89)
7/5th Horse Artillery (3 / 72)
9th and 13th Artillery Artisan Companies (0 / 47)
Det/3rd Train Battalion (1 / 87)
3/4th (bis) Train Battalion (1 / 78)
Provisonal Train Company (2 / 292)
Det/9th Equipage Train Battalion (1 / 112)

VII Corps: Maréchal Oudinot, Duc de Reggio
7th Division: Général de division Baron Leval
1st Brigade: Général de brigade Pinoteau
Staff/10th Légère Regiment (19 / 11)
1/10th Légère Regiment (13 / 114)
2/10th Légère Regiment (8 / 67)
6/10th Légère Regiment (7 / 74)
1/3rd Line Regiment (17 / 210)
1/15th Line Regiment (17 / 144)

Staff/130th Line Regiment (8 / 15)
1/130th Line Regiment (9 / 89)
4/130th Line Regiment (7 / 101)
Artillery:
24/6th Foot Artillery (68)
5/4th (bis) Train Battalion (83)
2nd Brigade: Général de brigade Montfort
1/17th Légère Regiment (14 / 198)
1/101st Line Regiment (15 / 120)
Staff/105th Line Regiment (9 / 17)
1/105th Line Regiment (10 / 132)
2/105th Line Regiment (8 / 131)
6/118th Line Regiment (14 / 58)
6/122nd Line Regiment (15 / 89)
3rd Brigade: Général de brigade Chassé
1/16th Légère Regiment (13 / 586)
1/8th Line Regiment (18 / 177)
Staff/28th Line Regiment (9 / 11)
1/28th Line Regiment (9 / 149)
3/28th Line Regiment (7 / 166)
3/28th Line Regiment (11 / 70)
Artillery:
24/6th Foot Artillery (4 12pdrs and 2 howitzers) (46)
2/9th (bis) Train Battalion (45)
Division: Général de division Lefol
1st Brigade: Général de brigade Rousseau
1/, 5/2nd Légère Regiment (52 / 475)
24th Légère Regiment (12 / 183)
34th Line Regiment (18 / 111)
2nd Brigade: Général de brigade Jacquemard
4/, 6/12th Line Regiment (33 / 345)
14th Line Regiment (10 / 68)
6/36th Line Regiment (9 / 71)
1/, 4/, 7/122nd Line Regiment (18 / 388)
Division: Général de division Lucotte
1st Brigade:
3/65th Line Regiment (13 / 13)
4/66th Line Regiment (8 / 17)
3/85th Line Regiment (9 / 2)
4/85th Line Regiment (4 / 3)
6/85th Line Regiment (9 / 10)
2nd Brigade:
3/49th Line Regiment (15 / 46)
4/49th Line Regiment (11 / 35)
3/50th Line Regiment (12 / 32)
4/50th Line Regiment (9 / 27)
4/88th Line Regiment (14 / 38)
Artillery:
19/1st Foot Artillery (105)
2/4th Principal Train Battalion (54)
5/12th (bis) Train Battalion (82)
Reserve:
22/5th Foot Artillery (46)

12/8th Foot Artillery (4-6pdrs and 2 howitzers) (44)
8/3rd Horse Artillery (4 6pdrs and 2 howitzers) (58)
2/12th (bis) Train Battalion (107)
5th Artillery Artisans (4)

XI Corps: Maréchal Macdonald
Division: Général de division Brayer
(infantry organization unknown)
Artillery:
6/1st Foot Artillery (42)
19/2nd Foot Artillery (52)
4/6th Horse Artillery (28)
4/1st Principal Train Battalion
1/8th Principal Train Battalion (76)
2/9th Principal Train Battalion
2/5th (bis) Train Battalion (54)
Division: Général de division Albert
(infantry organization unknown)
Artillery:
15/4th Foot Artillery (44)
18/6th Foot Artillery (34)
1/4th Horse Artillery (20)
2/5th Horse Artillery (6)
3/6th (bis) Train Battalion (60)
2/11th (bis) Train Battalion (86)
Reserve:
18/5th Foot Artillery (15)
20/5th Foot Artillery (44)
27/7th Foot Artillery (2)
2/1st Foot Artillery (2)
Artillery Artisans (1)
1/11th Principal Train Battalion (22)
1/13th Principal Train Battalion (18)
4/14th Principal Train Battalion (49)
6/3rd (bis) Train Battalion (36)
1/5th (bis) Train Battalion
3/5th (bis) Train Battalion (24)
2/7th (bis) Train Battalion (23)

Corps: Maréchal Mortier, Duke of Trévise
Only artillery forces are known
Artillery Reserve:
25/3rd Foot Artillery (28)
25/4th Foot Artillery (39)
29/5th Foot Artillery (34)
6 bis/6th Foot Artillery (22)
7/6th Horse Artillery (22)
17th Artillery Artisan Company (6)
2/5th Principal Train Battalion (1)
7/5th Principal Train Battalion (37)
4/7th Principal Train Battalion (4)
2/7th (bis) Train Battalion (7)
3/9th (bis) Train Battalion (22)

4/9th (bis) Train Battalion (19)
4/13th (bis) Train Battalion (3)
4/14th Principal Train Battalion (9)
5/14th Principal Train Battalion (15)
1/15th Military Equipage Battalion (29)
3/15th Military Equipage Battalion (9)

Corps: Maréchal Ney
Infantry organization not known
Artillery:
30/1st Foot Artillery (27)
6/8th Foot Artillery (56)
10/8th Foot Artillery (43)
2/2th Horse Artillery (71)
2/2nd Principal Train Battalion (106)
3/8th (bis) Train Battalion (105)
2/9th (bis) Train Battalion (60)
4/9th (bis) Train Battalion (31)

II Cavalry Corps:
Mounted forces not known
Artillery:
5/5th Horse Artillery (53)
6/6th Horse Artillery (72)
Det. 1st Principal Train Battalion (15)
Det. 10th Principal Train Battalion (63)
Det. 1st (bis) Train Battalion (29)

V Cavalry Corps: Général de division Milhaud
3rd Light Cavalry Division: Général de division Piré[4]
5th Brigade: Général de brigade Subervie
3rd Hussar Regiment
26th Chasseur Cheval Regiment
6th Brigade:
14th Chasseurs à cheval Regiment
27th Chasseurs à cheval Regiment
3rd Heavy Cavalry Division: Général de division Briche
5th Brigade: Général de brigade Montelegier
2nd Dragoon Regiment (24 / 239)
6th Dragoon Regiment (15 / 214)
11th Dragoon Regiment (25 / 283)
6th Brigade: Général de brigade Ludot
13th Dragoon Regiment (20 / 207)
15th Dragoon Regiment (25 / 286)
4th Heavy Cavalry Division: Général de division l'Héritier
7th Brigade: Général de brigade Lamotte
18th Dragoon Regiment (24 / 189)
19th Dragoon Regiment (16 / 132)
20th Dragoon Regiment (12 / 124)
8th Brigade: Général de brigade Collaert

4 May have been detached.

22nd Dragoon Regiment (24 / 271)
25th Dragoon Regiment (22 / 246)
Artillery:
4/2nd Horse Artillery (2 / 46)
2/3rd Horse Artillery (3 / 47)
8/6th Horse Artillery (2 / 39)
1/8th Principal Train Battalion (1 / 43)
1/12th Principal Train Battalion (1 / 46)
2/14th Principal Train Battalion (0 / 21)
4 – 6pdrs
6 – 4pdrs
4 – 24pdr howitzers

VI Cavalry Corps:
Mounted forces unknown
Artillery:
6/2nd Horse Artillery (71)
8/2nd Horse Artillery (29)
2/6th Horse Artillery (38)
1/5th Principal Train Battalion (89)
1/7th Principal Train Battalion (48)
5/12th Principal Train Battalion
Division: Général de division Roussel
Mounted forces unknown
Artillery:
3/2nd Horse Artillery (9)
4th Artillery Artisans (4)
2/5th Principal Train Battalion (95)
1/2nd (bis) Train Battalion (14)
General Park:
30/1st Foot Artillery (81)
1/3rd Foot Artillery (68)
4/3rd Foot Artillery (40)
6/3rd Foot Artillery (49)
11/3rd Foot Artillery (76)
18/3rd Foot Artillery (65)
30/3rd Foot Artillery (61)
8/4th Foot Artillery (38)
11/4th Foot Artillery (99)
13/5th Foot Artillery (95)
26/5th Foot Artillery (42)
30/5th Foot Artillery (10)
1/6th Foot Artillery (66)
7/6th Foot Artillery (90)
29/6th Foot Artillery (43)
30/6th Foot Artillery (108)
31/6th Foot Artillery (52)
1/8th Foot Artillery (27)
13/8th Foot Artillery (45)
5/9th Foot Artillery (72)
18/9th Foot Artillery (67)
20/9th Foot Artillery (89)
1/1st Horse Artillery (23)

6/1st Horse Artillery (56)
8/1st Horse Artillery (60)
3/3rd Horse Artillery (78)
5/3rd Horse Artillery (59)
1/5th Horse Artillery (50)
1/6th Horse Artillery (64)
3/9th Military Equipage Battalion (79)
2/12th Military Equipage Battalion (90)
5th Artillery Artisan Company (45)
6th Artillery Artisan Company (52
17th Artillery Artisan Company (34)
11/1st Pontooneer Battalion (60)
12/1st Pontooneer Battalion (38)
13/1st Pontooneer Battalion (15)
14/1st Pontooneer Battalion (70)
4/3rd (bis) Train Battalion (49)
5/6th (bis) Train Battalion (86)
5/7th (bis) Train Battalion (26)
5/8th (bis) Train Battalion (12)
5/9th (bis) Train Battalion (53)
4/12th (bis) Train Battalion (8?)
3/13th (bis) Train Battalion (117)
3/4th Principal Train Battalion (40)
3/7th Principal Train Battalion (98)
1/12th Principal Train Battalion (18)
3/4th Principal Train Battalion (66)
1/11th Principal Train Battalion (47
2/9th Principal Train Battalion (92)

Appendix LXXXI

French Imperial Guard, VI Corps and I Cavalry Corps, 1 May 1814[1]

1st Old Guard Division: Général de division Count Friant
- 1st Brigade: Général de brigade Petit
  - Staff/1st Grenadier à Pied Regiment (9 / 4)
  - 1/1st Grenadier à Pied Regiment (11 / 422)
  - 2/1st Grenadier à Pied Regiment (11 / 369)
  - Staff/2nd Grenadier à Pied Regiment (5 / 10)
  - 1/2nd Grenadier à Pied Regiment (16 / 191)
  - 2/2nd Grenadier à Pied Regiment (16 / 232)
- 2nd Brigade: Général de brigade Poret de Morvan
  - Staff/1st Chasseur à Pied Regiment (4 / 40)
  - 1/1st Chasseur à Pied Regiment (14 / 341)
  - 2/1st Chasseur à Pied Regiment (9 / 336)
  - Staff/2nd Chasseur à Pied Regiment (6 / 2)
  - 1/2nd Chasseur à Pied Regiment (7 / 171)
  - 2/2nd Chasseur à Pied Regiment (8 / 199)
  - 9th Grenadier à Pied Company (3 / 49)
  - 9th Chasseur à Pied Company (2 / 149)
- Attached:
  - Fusilier Company (2 / 87)
  - Tirailleurs (11 / 128)
  - Student Drummers (0 / 6)

4th Young Guard Division: Général de division Barrois (in Holland under Maison)
- 1st Brigade:
  - 1/12th Voltigeur Regiment (20 / 416)
  - 2/12th Voltigeur Regiment (13 / 437)
  - 1/13th Voltigeur Regiment (20 / 336)
  - 2/13th Voltigeur Regiment (12 / 396)
  - 1/2nd Tirailleur Regiment (16 / 253)
  - 2/2nd Tirailleur Regiment (6 / 261)
- 2nd Brigade:
  - 1/3rd Tirailleur Regiment (15 / 339)
  - 2/3rd Tirailleur Regiment (12 / 292)
  - 1/4th Tirailleur Regiment (15 / 277)
  - 2/4th Tirailleur Regiment (11 / 322)
- Artillery:
  - Foot Battery (6 / 81)
  - Artillery Train (2 / 105)
- Guard Artillery Reserve:
  - 6/, 7/Guard Horse Artillery (24 / 397)
  - 3/, 4/, 5/Guard Foot Artillery (16 / 364)

1 French Archives, Carton C^2 555, C^2 556 and C^2 557.

- Artillery Artisans (2 / 58)
- 2/, 4/, 5/, 6/, 8/, 9/, 10/, 11/, 12/, 14/, 15/ Young Guard Artillery (29 / 415)
- 1/, 2/, 3/, 4/, 5/, 6/, 7/, 8/, 9/, 10/, 11/, 12/, 13/1st Guard Train Battalion (18 / 324)
- 2/, 3/, 4/, 5/, 6/, 9/, 10/, 11/, 12/2nd Guard Train Battalion (26 / 619)
- Compagnie Franche de Seine et Marne (14 / 159)

2nd Old Guard Division: Général de brigade Christiani

- 1st Brigade: Général de brigade Christiani
  - Staff/Fusilier Grenadier Regiment (2 / 14)
  - 1/Fusilier Grenadier Regiment (13 / 88)
  - 2/Fusilier Grenadier Regiment (14 / 103)
  - Staff/Fusilier Chasseur Regiment (7 / 9)
  - 1/Fusilier Chasseur Regiment (10 / 124)
  - 2/Fusilier Chasseur Regiment (12 / 109)
- 2nd Brigade: Général de brigade Gros
  - Vélites of Turin (9 / 25)
  - Vélites of Florence (11 / 12)
  - Staff/Flanqueur Grenadier Regiment (7 / 9)
  - 1/Flanqueur Grenadier Regiment (4 / 30)
  - 2/Flanqueur Grenadier Regiment (4 / 26)
  - 3/Flanqueur Grenadier Regiment (4 / 148)
  - Staff/Flanqueur Chasseur Regiment (6 / 5)
  - 1/Flanqueur Chasseur Regiment (11 / 76)
  - 2/Flanqueur Chasseur Regiment (12 / 77)
- Attached:
  - 4/Guard Sapper Battalion (1 / 13)
  - 5/Guard Sapper Battalion (2 / 6)
- Artillery Park:
  - Staff (4 / 7)
  - 15/1st Foot Artillery (1 / 31)
  - 25/3rd Foot Artillery (1 / 28)
  - 25/4th Foot Artillery (2 / 22)
  - 6/6th Foot Artillery (1 / 20)
  - 6/8th Foot Artillery (1 / 69)
  - 7/6th Horse Artillery (0 / 16)
  - 29/5th Foot Artillery (2 / 27)
    - Guns (4 12pdrs, 8 6pdrs, 2 howitzers)
  - 17th Artillery Artisan Company (0 / 5)
  - 2/, 7/5th Artillery Train Battalion (0 / 36)
  - 6/6th (bis) Artillery Train Battalion (1 / 40)
  - 4/7th (bis) Artillery Train Battalion (0 / 2)
  - 2/7th (bis) Artillery Train Battalion (0 / 7)
  - 4/9th (bis) Artillery Train Battalion (1 / 21)
  - 4/13th Artillery Train Battalion (0 / 3)
  - 4/14th Artillery Train Battalion (0 / 6)
  - 5/14th Artillery Train Battalion (0 / 19)
  - 1/15th Equipage Battalion (1 / 30)
  - 3/15th Equipage Battalion (1 / 9)

VI Corps: Maréchal Marmont, duc de Raguse

- 8th Division: Colonel Laporte
  - 1st Provisional Battalion (28 / 262)
  - 2nd Provisional Battalion (20 / 263)
  - 3rd Provisional Battalion (24 / 240)

4th Provisional Battalion (24 / 223)
20th Division: Général Jobert
37th Légère Regiment (30 / 111)
4/1st Line Regiment (6 / 31)
3/15th Line Regiment (12 / 61)
4/16th Line Regiment (11 / 20)
70th Line Regiment (28 / 154)
3/121st Line Regiment (7 / 63)
1/, 2/1st Marine Regiment (16 / 65)
1/, 2/, 3/, 4/2nd Marine Regiment (16 / 134)
1/, 2/, 3/3rd Marine Regiment (16 / 104)
1/, 2/, 3/4th Marine Regiment (12 / 90)
132nd Line Regiment (13 / 86)
Artillery: Général Digeon
Foot Artillery (19 / 419)
Horse Artillery (8 / 147)
Train (14 / 554)
Engineers: Colonel Parid
Det/3rd Sapper Battalion (0 / 24)
2nd Division, Paris Reserve: Général de division Souham
4/3rd Marine Infantry (10 / 346)
4/135th Line Regiment (19 / 266)
1/28th Légère Regiment (20 / 286)
1/46th Line Regiment (18 / 295)
4/145th Line Regiment (14 / 339)

I Cavalry Corps:
2nd Light Cavalry Division: Général de division Maurin
3rd Brigade: Général de brigade Dommanget
5th Hussar Regiment (9 / 51)
9th Hussar Regiment (3 / 24)
11th Chasseurs à cheval Regiment (23 / 132)
12th Chasseurs à cheval Regiment (31 / 127)
2nd Lancer Regiment (22 / 110)
4th Lancer Regiment (12 / 109)
4th Brigade: Général de brigade Mourier
6th Lancer Regiment (18 / 199)
7th Chasseurs à cheval Regiment (14 / 70)
20th Chasseurs à cheval Regiment (12 / 58)
23rd Chasseurs à cheval Regiment (16 / 135)
24th Chasseurs à cheval Regiment (16 / 161)
Artillery:
Det/5th Horse Artillery (3-6pdrs and 1 howitzer) (2 / 49)
590 canister and 53 ball
Det/1st Principal Train Battalion (1 / 8)
Det/1st (bis) Train Battalion (1 / 23)
2nd Heavy Cavalry Division: Général de division Delort
3rd Brigade: Général de brigade Blancard
1st Carabinier Regiment (16 / 152)
2nd Carabinier Regiment (15 / 142)
1st Cuirassier Regiment (20 / 117)
4th Brigade: Général de brigade Sopransi
5th Cuirassier Regiment (21 / 194)

8th Cuirassier Regiment (16 / 77)
10th Cuirassier Regiment (19 / 125)
13th Cuirassier Regiment (6 / 69)

Artillery Captain Germain:

Det/6th Horse Artillery (3-6pdrs and 1 howitzer) (3 / 53)
590 canister and 52 ball

Det/7th Train Battalion (0 / 11)
Det/10th Train Battalion (1 / 48)

Bibliography

Unlike the 1813 campaign, which was very heavily documented (and, in many cases, by official governmentally-sanctioned accounts prepared by their army general staffs' historical sections), the 1814 campaign lacks the large number of published tomes of official correspondence and analysis. As a result, the preparation of this work became dependent on the limited number of period secondary sources / regimental histories for the bulk of its detail – and a very few more modern works.

Of the various sources used, it is necessary to make some specific comment to a few of them. Koch's *Memoirs pour servier... l'Histoire de la Campagne de 1814* was used heavily. It is a contemporary source which, for this period, is usually not a good thing inasmuch as they are too close to the campaign. The result is that they are often filled with opinion by authors with axes to grind and lacked access to what were classified documents. However, the army states provided by Koch are traceable to the French archives and match precisely with the material found in the various returns. Furthermore, in reading his accounts (though casualty figures are always subjective), his accounts of the various actions appear to be free of any particular bias.

General de Vaudoncourt was a prolific eyewitness and wrote several accounts of Napoleon's campaigns. His *Histoire des Campagnes de 1814 et 1815 en France* has the same lack of bias as Koch and was also heavily used. Vaudoncourt also proved himself a strong proponent of the truth and wrote two of his books to set the record straight on the 1812 and 1815 campaigns when French apologists filled the bookshelves with their distortions of those campaigns.

Von Plotho has many strong biases, but does present a strong picture of the Allied operations in *Der Krieg in Deutschland und Frankreich in den Jahren 1813 und 1814*. His principal problem is that he is a contemporary and had many biases which come through in his work. In addition, in his account of the 1814 campaign, von Plotho's command of details begins to fade. As a result, he was not extensively utilized in the preparation of this work.

In his work *Die Grosse Chronik, Geschichte des Krieges des Verbundeten Europa's gegen Napoleon Bonaparte, in den Jahren 1813, 1814, und 1815* Sporschil makes extensive use of von Plotho, which results in many of his casualty returns and other comments being very, very close to what von Plotho wrote. However, this work is a compilation of several other works and he corrected many of the errors von Plotho made as a result of his use of other sources.

Sporschil's comtemporary, von Damitz, however provides a substantially original perspective in his work *Geschichte des Feldzuges von 1814 in dem östlichen und nördlichen Frankreich bis zur Einnahme von Paris*.

There are the usual collection of memoirs by Langeron, Toll, Marmont, Michailowsky-Danilewsky and others. All of these sources were tempered and enhanced using the various published volumes of official correspondence.

French archives

Archives Nationales, Paris, France
Carton AF^{IV} 1167
Carton AF^{IV} 1168
Carton AF^{IV} 1169A
Carton AF^{IV} 1169B
Carton AF^{IV*} 1347
Carton AF^{IV*} 1348
Carton AF^{IV*} 1349
Carton AF^{IV*} 1350
Carton AF^{IV*} 1351

French army archives, Section Historique de l'armée du terre, Chateau Vincennes, France
Carton $C^2$555
Carton $C^2$556
Carton $C^2$557
Carton $C^2$711
Carton $C^2$712

Publications

Alt, G., *Geschichte der Königl. Preussischen Kürassiere und Dragoner seit 1619 resp 1631-1870*, Krefeld: Heere der Vergagenheit J. Olmes, 1970.

Anonymous, *Die Althannoverschen Ueberlieferungen des Füsilier Regiments Generalfeldmarschall Prinz Albrecht von Preussen (Hannoversches) Nr. 73*, Hanover: Privately published, 1901.

Anonymous, *Die Reorganization der Preussischen Armee noch dem Tilsiter Freiden*, Berlin: E.S. Mittler und Sohn, 1855.

Anonymous, *Geschichte des K. und K. Husaren-Regiments Wilhelm II Deutscher Kaiser und König von Preussen Nr. 7, 1798-1914*, Vienna: L.W. Seidel & Sohn, 1914.

Anonymous, *Geschichte des Magdeburgischen Husaren-Regiments Nr. 10*, Berlin: Verlag von Alexander Duncker, 1863.

Anonymous, *Historique du 2eme Régiment d'artillerie*, Grenoble: Librairie Dauphinoise, 1899.

Anonymous, *Les combats de Mormant, de Villeneuve-le-Comte, et Montereau (17 et 18 Février 1814)*, Paris: L. Baudoin, 1889.

Anonymous, *Victoires, conquêtes, désastres, reverses et guerres civiles des françaises 1792 a 1815*, Paris: C.L. Panckoucke, 1818, Vols 11 & 23.

von Ardenne, Freiherr A., *Bergische Lanziers Westfälische Husaren Nr. 11*, Berlin: E.S. Mittler und Sohn, 1877.

von Ardenne, Freiherr A., *Geschichte des Husaren-Regiments von Zieten (Brandenburgisches) Nr. 3*, Berlin: Ernst Siegfried Mittler und Sohn, 1905.

Arvers, P., *Historique du 82e Régiment d'infanterie de ligne et du 7e Régiment d'infanterie Légère, 1684-1876*, Paris: Typographie Lahure, 1876.

Assollant, A., *La Bataille de Laon*, Paris: E. Plon, 1881.

Atteridge, A.H., *Joachim Murat*, New York: Brentano's, 1911.

Beauchamp, M.A., *Historie de la campagne de 1814 et de la restoration de la monarchie française*, Paris: Le Normant, 1815.

Belhomme, Lt. Col., *Histoire de l'Infanterie en France*, Paris: 1893-1902.

von Bernhardi, T., *Denkwürdigkeiten aus dem Lebel des Kaiserl. Russ. General von der Infanterie Carl Friedrich Grafen von Toll*, Leipzig: Otto Wigand, 1866.

Bienvenu, J. *La Bataille de Montereau, 18 Fevrier* 1814, Montereau: Impererie du Progrès, date unknown.

Bogdanovich, M. *Istoria voini 1814 goda vo Francii i nizlojenia Napoleona I, po dostovernim istochnikam,* Saint Petersburg: 1865.

Bogdanovich, M.I., *Geschichte des Krieges 1814 in Frankreich und des Sturzes Napoleon's I, nach den zuverlässigsten Quellen,* Leipzig: B. Schlicke, 1866.

Bonaparte, N., (Loyd, M.L, editor), *New Letters from Napoleon I Omitted from the Editions Published under the Auspices of Napoleon III,* London: William Heinemann, 1898.

Bonaparte, N., (Vox, M. Editor), *Correspondance de Napoleon, six cents lettres de travaille (1806-1810),* Librairie Galimard, 1943.

Bonaparte, N., *Correspondance de Napoleon ler*, New York: AMS Press, 1974.

Bonaparte, N., *The First Napoleon, Some Unpublished Documents from the Bowood Papers*, New York: Houghton Mifflin Co., 1926.

Bonin, U. von, *Geschichte des Ingenieurkorps und der Pioniere in Preussen,* Weisbaden: LTR Verlag, 1981.

Bory, J.R. *Regiments Suisses au service de France*, Freiburg: Collection "Le Shako", 1975.

Bouchard, S., *Historique du 28e Régiment de Dragons*, Paris: Berger-Levrault et Cie., 1893.

Breton de la Martinière, M., *Campagnes de Bounaparte en 1812,1813, et 1814 jusqu'a son abdication*, Paris: J.G. Dentu, Imprimeur-Librairie, 1814.

Brett-James, A., *Europe Against Napoleon*, New York: Macmillan, 1970.

Brissac, R., *Historique du 7e Régiment de Dragoons 1673-1909,* Paris: Leroy, Editeur, 1908.

Brunswick, Wilhelm, Duke of, *Geschichte des Magdeburgischen Husaren-Regiments, Nr. 10*, Berlin: 1863.

Bucqouy, Cdt., *Gardes d'honneur et troupes étrangers*, Paris: J. Grancher, 1977.

Burghersh, Lord, *Memoir of the Operations of the Allied Operations under Prinz Schwarzenburg and Marshal Blucher During the Latter End of 1813 and the Year 1814*, London: John Murray, 1822.

Calmon-Maison, J.J.R., *Le general Maison et le 1er Corps de la grande armée; campagne de Belgique (decembre 1813- avril 1814)*, Paris: 1870.

von Cammerer, Lt. Gen. Z.D., *Die Befrieungskriege 1813-1815, Ein strategischer Uberblick*, Berlin: E.S. Mittler und Sohn, 1907.

Campana, J., *La Campagne de France 1814*, Paris: Charles-Lavauzelle & Cie, 1922.

Chlapowski, D., *Memoirs of a Polish Lancer*, Chicago, Emperor's Press, 1992.

Chuquet, A., *L'Alsace en 1814*, Paris: Librairie Plon, 1906.

von Ciriacy, F., *Chronologische Übersicht der Geschichte des Preussischen Heeres*, Berlin: E.S. Mittler, 1820.

von Clausewitz, C., *La campagne de 1814*, Paris: Edition Champe Libre, 1972.

Clerc, Cmdt., *Campagne du maréchal Soult dans les Pyrénées occidentales en 18l3-1814*, Paris: L. Baudouin, 1894.

Coldsmith, L., *Supplement du recueil des decrets, manifestos, discours, etc., de Napoleon Bonaparte et des membres de son gouvernment*, London: A.B. Dulau et Cie., 1816.

Corda, H., *Le régiment de la Fère et le 1er Regiment d'artillerie*, Paris: Berger-Levrault & Cie., 1906.

von Czernczitz, G.R.H., *Geschichte des K.u.K. Infanterie-Regiments Graf von Lacy, No. 22*, Zara: Verlag des Regiments, 1902.

von Damitz, K., *Geschichte des Feldzuges von 1814 in dem östlichen und nördlichen Frankreich bis zur Einnahme von Paris*, Berlin: Ernst Siegfrid Mittler, 1842.

Davout, L.N., *Correspondance du maréchal Davout, prince d'Eckmühl, 1801-1815*, Paris: Librairie Plon, 1885.

Davout, L.N., *Le Maréchal Davout, Prince d'Eckmühl, correspondence inédit, 1790-1815*, Paris: Perrin et Cie., 1887.

de Behaine, Cdt L., *La Campagne de France, Napoleon et les Allies sur la Rhin*, Paris: Librairie Academique Perrin et Cie., 1913.

de l'Somme de Courbière, R., *Geschichte der Brandenburg-Preussischen Heeres-Verfassung*, Berlin: Deckernschen Geheimen Ober Hofbuchdruckerei, 1852.

de Saint-Hilaire, E.M., *Geschichte der Kaiser-Garde*, Leipzig: J.J.Weber, 1848 .

de Vaudoncourt, Gen. G., *Histoire des campagnes de 1814 et 1815 en France*, Paris: 1826.

Dechend, z. D., *Geschichte des Fusilier-Regiments von Gersdorff Nr. 80*, Berlin: E.S. Mittler und Sohn, 1901.

Deode, M., 'Bataille de Fère-Champenoise', Extract from the *Encyclopédie des gens du mond*, Vol. X, 2nd Part, pp. 682 and following.

Drexl, Dr. F., *Die Befreiungskriege 1813-1815*, Regensberg: F. Habbel, 1913.

Dupuy, R.E., & Dupuy, T.N., *The Encyclopaedia of Military History from 350 BC to the Present*, New York: Harper & Row, 1986.

Durova, N., *The Cavalry Maiden, Journals of a Female Russian Officer in the Napoleonic Wars*, London: Angle Books, 1988.

von Ebertz, G.W., *Hundertjährige Geschichte des Grenadier-Regiments König Friedrich III, (2. Schlesisches) Nr. 11 (1808-1908)*, Stuttgart: Verlga der Uhland'schen Buchdruckerei, 1909.

Egloffstein, H, *Carl August in Niederlandischen Feldzug 1814*, Weimar: 1927.

Ernst, H., *Die Preussische Armee 1740-1821*, Langenberg: Aug. Forsthoff, 1906.

Esposito, V.J., *A Military History and Atlas of the Napoleonic Wars*, New York: AMS Press, 1978.

Fabry, G., *Journal des campagnes du prince de Wurtemberg, 1812-1814, avec un introduction des notes et des pièces justificatives*, Paris: Librairie Militaire R. Chapelot et Cie., 1907.

Fallou, L., *La Garde Imperiale (1804-1815)*, Krefeld, J. Olmes, Editions Armée du Passe, 1975.

Fortescue, J.W., *A History of the British Army*, London: MacMillian and Co, Ltd., 1920.

von Freytag-Loringhoven, Freiherr, *Kriegslehren nach Clausewitz aus den Feldzügen 1813 und 1814*, Berlin: Ernst Siegfried Mittler und Sohn, 1908.

Friederich, E., *Die Befreiungskriege 1813-1815*, Berlin: E.Siegfried Mittler und Sohn, 1913.

Friedmann W., *Geschichte des k.u.k. Feldjäger-Bataillons Nr. 12 (1813-1913)*, Winterberg, Bohemia, published by the battalion, 1913.

Giraud, P.F.F.J., *Campagne de Paris en 1814*, Paris: Chez A. Eymery, 1814.

Gleich, W., *Die ersten 100 Jahren des Uhlanen-Regiments König Wilhelm (2 Württemberger) Nr. 20*, Stuttgart: Land'schen Buchdruckerei, 1906.

Guerre, J., *Campagnes de Lyon en 1814 et 1815 ou mémoires sur les principaux événmens militaires et politiques qui se sont passés dans cette ville et dans quelques contrées de l'Est et du Midi de la France, à l'occasion de la restauration de la Monarchie française*, Lyon: J.B. Kindelem, 1816.

Gumtau, C.F, *Die Jäger und Schützen des Preussischen Heeres*, Berlin: E.S. Mittler, 1835.

von Hagen, E., *Geschichte des Neumarkischen Dragoner-Regients Nr.3*, Berlin: Ernst Siegfried Mittler und Sohn, 1885.

Haythornthwaite, P.J., *The Napoleonic Source Book*, New York: Facts on File, Inc., 1990.

Henderson, E., *Blucher and the Uprising of Prussia against Napoleon 1806-1815*, New York: AMS Press, 1978.

Henke, C., *Davout und die Festung Hamburg-Harburg, 1813-1814*, Berlin: Ernst Siegfried Mittler und Sohn, 1911.

Hermes, S., Niemeyer, J., *Unter Dem Greifen*, Karlsruhe: Wehrgeschichtlichen Museums Schloss Rastatt, 1984.

Heuman, Lt. Col., *Historique du 148e Regiment d'Infanterie*, Paris: Charles-Lavauzelle, date unknown.

von Hiller, Fritz, *Geschichte des Feldzuges 1814 gegen Frankreich unter besonder Berücksichtigung der Anteilnahme der königlich Württembergischen Truppen*, Stuttgart: W. Kohlhammer, 1893.

Jacomet, Capt, *Campagne de 1814, Le Corps d'observation d'Oudinot et de Victor du 9 au 15 Février*, Paris: Librairie Chapelot, 1919.

James, C., *An Universal Military Dictionary in English and French in which are explained the Terms of the Principal Sciences that are Necessary for the Information of an Officer*, London: T. Edgerton, 1816.

Jany, E., *GeschichtederKöniglichPreussishcenArmee*, Vol. IV, Berlin: Verlag von Karl Siegismund, 1933.
Erzherzog Johann, *Geschichte des K.u.K. Infanterie-Regiment Erzherzog Wilhelm No. 12*, Vienna: L.W. Seidel und Sohn, 1880.

Johnson, D., *Napoleon's Cavalry and its Leaders*, New York: Holmes & Meier Publishers, Inc., 1978.

Jomini, Gen. Baron, *Histoire critique et militaire des campagnes de la Revolution paisant suit au traite des grandes operations militaires*, Paris: Chez Magimel, Anselin et Pouchard, 1816.

Jomini, Gen. Baron, *Traité des grand operations militaires, contenant l'historire critique des campagnes de Frederich II, comparées à celles de l'emperor Napoléon*, Paris: Magimel, 1811.

Kersten, Fritz & Ortenberg, G., *Hessisches Miitar zur Zeit des Deutschen Bundes*, Beckum: Deutschen Gesellschaft für Herreskunde e.V., 1984.

von Knobelsdorff-Brenkenhoff, B., *Briefe aus den Befreiungskriegen. Ein Beitrag zur Situation von Truppe und Heimat in den Jahren 1813/14*, Bonn: Thesis-Verlag, 1981.

Koch, F., *Mémoires pour servier à l'histoire de la campagne de 1814*, Paris: Chez Magimel, 1819.

Kraft, H., *Die Württemberger in den Napoleonischen Kriegen*, Stuttgart: Kohlhammer, 1953.

L.-G. B., *Aus Hannovers Militärischer Vergagenheit*, Hanover: Büchdruckerei von Arnold Weichelt, 1880.

Lachouque, H., *Napoleon en 1814*, Paris: Les Editions Haussman, 1959.

Lachouque, H., *The Anatomy of Glory*, Providence, R.I.: Brown Univ. Press, 1962.

Laffaille, General J.P., *Mémoires (1787-1814)*, Paris: F.Teissedre, 1997.

Lange, G.L., *Geschichte der Preussischen Landwehr seint Entstehung bis auf die Gegenwart*, Berlin: Allgemeine Deutsch Verlag-Anstalt, 1863.

Langeron, A.L.A. de, *Memoires de Langeron, Général d'Infanterie dans l'Armée Russia, Campagnes de 1812, 1813, 1814*, Paris: Alphonse Picard et Fils, 1902.

Lefebvre de Béhaine, F.A.E., *La Campagne de France, La Défense de la Ligne du Rhin, Novembre 1813 à Janvier 1814*, Paris: Librairie Académique Perrin, 1933.

Lemâitre, J.-M., *Combat de Nogent-sur-Seine; episode historique de la guerre de 1814*, Nogent: Petites-Affiches, date unknown.

Lindeberg, L. *De sa det ske Englandskriegen 1801-1814*, Copenhagen: Reden-Guldalder-Statsbankerot, 1974.

Lomier, *Le Bataillon des Marines de la Garde 1803-1815*, Paris: C. Terana, 1991.

von Lüdinghausen-Wolf, Freiherr O., *Geschichte des Königlich Preussischen 2. Garde-Regiments zu Fuss (1813-1882)*, Berlin: Ernst Siegfried Mittler und Sohn, 1882.

Maag, Dr. A., *Geschichte der Schweizer truppen in Franzosischen Dienst vom Ruckzug aus Russland bis zum zweiten Pariser Freiden*, Basel: Ernst Kuhn, 1894.
Maciaga, J., *Geschichte des K.u.K. galizischen Infanterie-Regiments Feldmarschall Friederich Josias Prinz zu Sachsen-Colburg-Saafeld, Nr. 57*, Vienna: Kreisel und Groger, 1898.

Marbot, J.B.A.M. de, *Mémoires du General Baron de Marbot*, Paris: Librarie Plon, 1892.

Martinien, A., *Tableaux par corps et par batailles des Officieres Tués et Blesses pendant les Guerres de l'Empire (1805-1815)*, Paris: Editions Militaires Europeennes, 1984.

Masson, F., *Cavaliers de Napoleon*, Paris: Librairie Ollendorff, 1895.
Maycock, F.W.O, *Invasion of France 1814*, London: George Allen & Unwin, Ltd., 1914.
McQueen, J., *The Campaigns of 1812, 1813, and 1814*, Glasgow: Edward Khull & Co., 1815.
Michailowsky-Danilewsky, A., *Erinnerungen aus den Jahren 1814-1815*, Dorpat: A.C. Kluge, 1831.
Michailowsky-Danilewsky, A., *History of the Campaign in France in the Year 1814*, London: Smith, Elder & Co., 1840.
Mohr, E., *Heeres- und Truppengeschichte des Deutschen Reiches und Seiner Länder 1806- bis 1918*, Osnabrück: Biblo Verlag, 1989.
Munich, F., *Geschichte der Entwicklung der Bayerischen Armee seit zwei Jahrhunderten (1618-1870)*, Meisenheim: Anton Hain KG. 1972.
Niemeyer, J. & G. Ortenberg, *Die Hannoversche Armee*, Beckum: Bernh. Vogel, 1981.
Oechsli, W., *Le Passage des Alliés en Suisse, 1813-1814*, Paris: L. Fournier, 1912.
von Otto, F., *Geschichte des 2. Schlesischen Jäger – Bataillons Nr. 6 und seiner Stammtruppen*, Berlin: Mittler, 1902.
Oyon, J.A., *Campagnes et Souvenirs militaries 1805-1814*, Paris: F.Teissedre, 1997.
Parquin, Cpt, *Souvenirs du Capitaine Parquin 1803-1814*, Paris: Boussod, Valadon, & Cie., 1892.
Paulig, F.R., *Geschichte der Befreiungskriege*, Frankfort: Frederich Paulig, 1891.
von Pflug-Harttung, J., *1813-1815, Illustriert Geschichte der Befreiungskriege*, Germany: Union Deutsche Verlagsgesellschaft, 1913.
Phillippart, J., *Memoires and Campaigns of Charles John, Prince Royal of Sweden*, London: C.J.Barrington, 1814.
Phillippart, J., *Napoleon's Campaign in Germany and France 1813-1814*, London: C.J. Barrington, 1814.
Pichard, E. & L. Tuety, *Unpublished Correspondence of Napoleon I*, New York: Duffield & Co., 1913.
Pitot, Lt., *Historique du 83e Régiment d'infanterie 1684-1891* Toulouse: Privately Published, date unknown.
von Plotho, C., *Der Krieg in Deutschland und Frankreich in den Jahren 1813 und 1814*, Berlin: Carl Friederich Amelang, 1817.
von Poten, B., *Das Preußische Heer vor hundert Jahren*, Berlin: E.S.Mittler und Sohn, 1910.
Prussian General Staff, *Pläne der Schlachten und Treffen Welche von der Preussischen Armee in den Feldzuge der Jahr 1813, 1814, und 1815 geliefert worden*, Berlin: Reimer, 1821.
Rapetti, L.N., *La défection de Marmont en 1814*, Paris: Poulet-Malassis et de Broise, 1858.
Rapp, Count, *Memoires of General Count Rapp*, London: H. Colburn & Co., 1823.
von Ravelsberg, F.S.E., *Geschichte des K.u.K. 12. Dragoner-Regiments*, Vienna: Rudolf Brzezowsky und Sohn, 1890.
Renouard, C., *Die Kurhessen im Feldzuge von 1814*, Gotha: Verlag von Hugh Scheube, 1857.
von Reinhard, C., *Geschichte des Königlich Preussischen Ersten Garde-Regiments zu Fuss, (1740-1857)*, Potsdam: Verlag von Aug. Stein, 1858.
von Reuter, E., 'Erinnerungen eines Preussischen Artillerieoffizieres aus den Jahren 1798 bis 1815', *Beiheft zum Militär-Wochenblatt*, Berlin: Ernst Siegfried Mittler und Sohn, 1890.
Rochefort, R., *Treatise on the Marches and Movements of Armies*, London: James Ridgeway, 1807.
Rössler, *Tagebücher aus den zehen Feldzügen der Württemberger under der Regierung Königs Friderich*, Ludwigsburg: Friedrich Nast, 1820.
Rothwiller, Baron, *Histoire du Deuxième Régiment de Cuirassiers Ancien Royal de Cavalerie, 135-1876*, Paris: E. Plon et Cie., 1877.
Roulin, Lt. Col., *125e Regiment d'Infanterie*, Orleans: Imprimerie de Georges Jacob, 1890.

Savary, M., *Relation de la défense de Hambourg en 1813, et 1814*, Extracted from the *Spectateur Militaire*, Paris: Bourgogne et Martinet, July 1846.

Schlüsser, A., *Geschichte des Lützowischen Freikorps, Ein Beitrag zur Kriegsgeschichte der Jahre 1813 und 1814*, Berlin: E.S. Mittler, 1826.

Schmitt, Lt., *151e Regiment d'Infanterie*, Paris: 1901.

Schubert, F. & H. Vara, *Geschichte des K.B. 13 Infanterie Regiments Kaiser Franz Joseph von Osterreich (1806-1851)*, Munich: J. Lindauersch, 1906.

Schüler, B., *Geschichte des schwarzburg-rudolstädtischen Contingents in den Kriegsjahren 1807 bis 1815*, Rudolstadt: Stroh, 1874.

Schuster, O. & Francke, F.A..*Geschichte der Sächsischen Armee von deren errichtung bis auf die neuste Zeit*, Leipzig, 1855.

Schwarzbach & Wieser, *Geschichte des K.u.K. Siebenten Dragoner-Regiments Herzog Wilhelm von Braunschweig von seiner errichtung 1663 bis Ende Mai 1879*, Vienna: Verlag des Regiments, 1879.

Schwertseger, B., *Geschichte der Königlich Deutsch Legion 1803-1816*, Hanover & Leipzig: Hahnische Buchhandlung, 1907.

Seeliger, E., *Geschichte des K.u.K. Infanterie-Regiments Nr. 32 für immerwährende Zeiten K.u.K. Maria Theresia von seiner Errichtung 1741 bis 1900*, Budapest: Pester Buchdruckerei-Actien-Gesellschaft, 1900.

Sherwig, J.M., *Guineas and Gunpowder, British Foreign Aid in the Wars with France 1793-1815*, Cambridge, MA: Harvard University Press, 1969.

Simond, E., *Le 28e de ligne, Historique du régiment*, Rouen: Megard et Cie., 1889.

Sporschil, J., *Die Grosse Chronik, Geschichte des Krieges des Verbundeten Europa's gegen Napoleon bonaparte, in den Jahren 1813, 1814, und 1815*, Braunschweig: George Westerman, 1841.

St. Cyr, G., *Memoires du Maréchal Gouvion Saint-Cyr 1812-1813*, Paris: Remanences, 1982.

Stiegler, E., *Le Maréchal Oudinot duc de Reggio*, Paris: Librairie Plon, 1894.

Strotha, von, *Die Königlich Preussische Reitende Artillerie von Jahre 1759 bis 1816*, Wiesbaden: LTR Verlag, 1981.

Suremain, de, *Mémoires du Lieutenant General Suremain (1794-1815)*, Paris: Plon-Nourriet et Cie, 1902.

Susane, L., *Histoire de la Cavalerie Francaise*, Paris: C. Terana, 1984.

Ternaux-Compans, M., *Le General Compans (1769-1845)*, Paris: Librairie Plon, 1912.

Thiry, Baron J., *La Campagne de France 1814*, Paris: Editions Berger-Levrault, 1938.

Titze, J., & Hensel, J., *Frankreichs Schweitzerregimenter 1-4 1804-1815*, Leipzig: J. Titze, 1990.

Tondu-Nangis, *La bataille de Montereau*, Montereau: Zanote, 1900.

von Treuenfest, G.A. Ritter, *Geschichte des K.u.K. Infanterie-regimentes Nr. 46*, Vienna: Rudolf Brzezowsky & Sohne, 1890.

Viger, Count, *Davout, maréchal d'Empire*, Paris: H. Bouillant, 1898.

Voigtlander, L., *Das Tagebuch des Johann Heinrich Lang aus Lubeck und die Feldzuge der Hanseaten in den Jahren 1813-1815*, Lubeck: Verlag Schmidt-Romhild, 1980.

Vollmer, U., *Die Bewaffnung der Armeen des Königsreichs Württemberg und des Grossherzogtums Baden*, Schwabisch Hall: Journal Verlag Schwend GmbH., 1981.

von W., C., *Zur Kriegsgeschichte der Jahre 1813 und 1814, Die Feldzüge der schlesischen Armee under dem Feldmarschall Blücher von der Beendigung des Waffenstillstandes bis zur Eroberung von Paris*, Berlin: Ernst Siegfried, Mittler, 1827.

Wagner, A., *Recueil des plans de combat et de batailles livrées par l'armée prussienne pendant les campagnes des annes 1813, 1814, et 1815 avec des,claircissements historiques*, Berlin: G. Reimer, 1821.

Watson, S.J., *Carnot*, London: The Bodley Head, 1954.

Wolter, H.C., *Den Danske Haer i Napoleonstiden 1801-1814*, Compenhagen, Tojhusmusett, 1992.

Wust, G., *Geschichte des K.u.K. 34 Linien-Infanterie-Regiments Prinz Regent von Preussen*, Vienna: K.K. Hof- und Staatsdruckerei, 1860.

Zaluski, General Count J., *Les Chevaulégers polonaise de la Garde (1812-1814), Souvenirs*, Paris: F. Teissedre, 1997.

Index

INDEX OF PEOPLE

INDEX OF PLACES

INDEX OF MISCELLANEOUS TERMS